DATA STRUCTURES WITH JAVA™

William H. Ford
University of the Pacific

William R. Topp
University of the Pacific

PEARSON
Prentice Hall

Upper Saddle River, NJ 07458

Library of Congress Cataloging-in-Publication Data

Ford, William.
   Data structures with Java / William H. Ford, William R. Topp.-- 1st ed.
     p. cm.
   Includes index.
   ISBN 0-13-047724-9
   1. Java (Computer program language) 2. Data structures (Computer science)
I. Topp, William R., 1939- II. Title.
   QA76.73.J38F665 2005
   005.13'3--dc22

                                      2004024783

Editor-in-Chief: *Marcia Horton*
Acquisition Editor: *Kate Hargett*
Supplements Editor: *Sarah Parker*
Editorial Assistant: *Michael Giacobbe*
Vice President and Director of Production and Manufacturing: *David W. Riccardi*
Executive Managing Editor: *Vince O'Brien*
Managing Editor: *Camille Trentacoste*
Production Editor: *Erin Connaughton*
Art Director: *Jayne Conte*
Cover Designer: *Bruce Kenselaar*
Art Editor: *Greg Dulles*
Manufacturing Buyer: *Lynda Castillo*
Cover Image: *Courtesy of Getty Images*
Marketing Manager: *Pamela Hersperger*
Marketing Assistant: *Barrie Reinhold*

© 2005 Pearson Education, Inc.
Pearson Prentice Hall
Pearson Education, Inc.
Upper Saddle River, NJ 07458

Pearson Prentice Hall® is a trademark of Pearson Education, Inc.

Printed in the United States of America

10 9 8 7 6 5 4 3 2 1

ISBN 0-13-047724-9

Pearson Education Ltd., *London*
Pearson Education Australia Pty. Ltd., *Sydney*
Pearson Education Singapore, Pte. Ltd.
Pearson Education North Asia Ltd., *Hong Kong*
Pearson Education Canada, Inc., *Toronto*
Pearson Educación de Mexico, S.A. de C.V.
Pearson Education—Japan, *Tokyo*
Pearson Education Malaysia, Pte. Ltd.

This book is dedicated to very special people who gave us life, loads of love, an opportunity for an education, and an abiding respect for learning.

To Ernestine Ford and Aunt Thelma McLeod
— *William H. Ford*

To Margaret Topp and John Topp
— *William R. Topp*

BRIEF CONTENTS

Preface   xxiii

Chapter 1   Classes and Objects   1

Chapter 2   Class Relationships   38

Chapter 3   Designing Classes   88

Chapter 4   Introduction To Algorithms   114

Chapter 5   Generic Classes and Methods   142

Chapter 6   Recursion   169

Chapter 7   Sorting Algorithms   193

Chapter 8   Collection Types   227

Chapter 9   The Array-Based List Collection   250

Chapter 10   Linked Lists   287

Chapter 11   Implementing the LinkedList Class   321

Chapter 12   Iterators   344

Chapter 13   Implementing Iterators   373

Chapter 14   Stacks   389

Chapter 15   Queues and Priority Queues   422

Chapter 16   Binary Trees   462

Chapter 17   Binary Tree Applications   505

Chapter 18   Binary Search Trees   530

Chapter 19   Sets and Maps   562

Chapter 20   Ordered Set and Map Implementation   604

Chapter 21   Hashing as a Map Implementation   626

Chapter 22   Heaps   662

Chapter 23   Bit Arrays and File Compression   693

Chapter 24   Graphs and Paths   732

Chapter 25   Graph Algorithms   764

Chapter 26   Implementing Graphs   802

Chapter 27   Balanced Search Trees   824

Chapter 28   Number Theory and Encryption   865

Chapter 29   Assorted Algorithms   885

Appendix A   Java Primer   928

Appendix B   Java Keywords   963

Appendix C   ASCII Character Codes   964

Appendix D   Java Operator Precedence   965

Appendix E   The EZJava IDE   967

Index   977

CONTENTS

Preface   xxiii

1   CLASSES AND OBJECTS   1

1.1   WHAT IS THIS BOOK ABOUT?   1

A Dynamic Array   2
Linked Lists   2
An Associative Array   3
A Graph   4
Adapter Structures   4
Data Structures and Object-Oriented Programming   5
Data Structures and Algorithms   6

1.2   OBJECT-ORIENTED PROGRAMMING   6

1.3   UNDERSTANDING A CLASS   7

Designing Class Methods   8

1.4   THE TIME24 CLASS   8

Time24 Class Design   9
Constructors   10
The toString Method   10
Accessor and Mutator Methods   11
Static Methods   12

1.5   DECLARING AND USING OBJECTS   12

Using Object Methods   13
References and Aliases   14

1.6   A TIME24 APPLICATION   15

1.7   REPRESENTING CLASSES   17

UML Diagram of a Class   18

1.8   A CLASS IMPLEMENTATION   18

Time24 Class Declaration   19
Private Utility Methods   20
Accessor and Mutator Methods   21
Constructors   22
Formatted Object Description   22
Incrementing Time   23
Time Interval   23

1.9 ORGANIZING CLASSES 24
The Java Package Hierarchy 25

1.10 THE STRING CLASS 25
String Indexing 26
String Concatenation 26
String Comparison 27

1.11 AN ENUM CLASS 28
An Enum with Additional Class Features 29

2 CLASS RELATIONSHIPS   38

2.1 WRAPPER CLASSES 39
Comparing Integer Objects 40
Static Wrapper Class Members 40
Character Handling 41

2.2 AUTOBOXING AND AUTO-UNBOXING 42

2.3 OBJECT COMPOSITION 44
The TimeCard Class 44
Implementing the TimeCard Class 45
UML for the TimeCard Class 46

2.4 INHERITANCE IN JAVA 47
An Employee Hierarchy 48
Visibility for Members in an Inheritance Hierarchy 48
The Employee Class Declaration 49
The SalaryEmployee Subclass 50
Keyword Super in an Inheritance Hierarchy 51
The HourlyEmployee Subclass 52

2.5 POLYMORPHISM 54
Upcasting and Downcasting 56

2.6 ABSTRACT CLASSES 58

2.7 HANDLING RUNTIME ERRORS 59
The Throw Statement 59
Handling an Exception—Try/Catch Blocks 60
Finally Clause 61
Exception Propagation 61
Java Exception Hierarchy 62
Standard Exceptions 64

2.8 INPUT AND OUTPUT 64
Console I/O 65
File I/O 65

Text Input with Reader Streams   66
Parsing an Input String   67
Text Output with Writer Streams   69
Controlling the Output Stream   70

2.9   THE SCANNER CLASS   **71**
Declaring a Scanner Object   71
Reading from the Input Stream   71
File Input   72
Scanner Class API   73
Application: Using the Scanner   74

3   DESIGNING CLASSES   88

3.1   THE JAVA INTERFACE   **88**
Declaring an Interface   89

3.2   AN INTERFACE AS A TEMPLATE   **90**
Using an Interface Type   92
Interfaces and Inheritance   93

3.3   CREATING AN API WITH JAVADOC   **95**

3.4   DESIGN PATTERNS   **98**
Singleton Design Pattern   98

3.5   GUI APPLICATION DESIGN   **100**
Graphical Components   100
GUI Application Design Pattern   101
Event Listeners and Event Handlers   105
Dice Toss Action Event   105

4   INTRODUCTION TO ALGORITHMS   114

4.1   SELECTION SORT   **114**
Selection Sort Algorithm   116

4.2   SIMPLE SEARCH ALGORITHMS   **118**
Sequential Search   118
Binary Search   120

4.3   ANALYSIS OF ALGORITHMS   **125**
System/Memory Performance Criteria   125
Algorithm Performance: Running Time Analysis   126
Big-O Notation   129
Common Orders of Magnitude   130

4.4   COMPARING SEARCH ALGORITHMS   **132**
The Timing Class   133

5 GENERIC CLASSES AND METHODS   142

5.1 THE OBJECT SUPERCLASS   143
   Object-Array Methods   144
   Generalized Sequential Search   145

5.2 INTRODUCING JAVA GENERICS   146
   Object-Based Store Class   147
   Generic Collections   148
   Generic Store Class   149

5.3 GENERIC INTERFACES   150
   The Comparable Interface   152

5.4 GENERIC METHODS   154
   Basic Generic Methods   154
   Using Bounds for Generic Types   155

5.5 GENERICS AND INHERITANCE   156
   Bounded Generic Types   157
   Generics and Wildcards   159

5.6 GENERIC SEARCH/SORTING ALGORITHMS   160
   Generic Binary Search Method   162

6 RECURSION   169

6.1 THE CONCEPT OF RECURSION   169
   Describing a Recursive Algorithm   171
   Implementing Recursive Methods   171
   How Recursion Works   173
   Multibase Representations   174

6.2 RECURSION APPLICATIONS   177
   Building a Ruler   178
   Towers of Hanoi   180

6.3 EVALUATING RECURSION   183
   Fibonacci Methods   184
   Criteria for Using Recursion   187

7 SORTING ALGORITHMS   193

7.1 INSERTION SORT   193
   Insertion Sort Efficiency   196

7.2 DIVIDE-AND-CONQUER SORT ALGORITHMS   196
   MergeSort   196
   General Sort Methods   199
   The msort Method   200
   Efficiency of MergeSort   204

7.3 QUICKSORT   **205**

Partitioning a List with a Pivot   205

QuickSort Recursive Descent   208

The pivotIndex Method   210

The quicksort() Method   212

Running Time of Quicksort   214

Comparison of Sorting Algorithms   215

7.4 FINDING KTH-LARGEST ELEMENT   **218**

8 COLLECTION TYPES   227

8.1 INTRODUCTION TO COLLECTIONS   **227**

8.2 OVERVIEW OF COLLECTIONS   **229**

List Collection   230

Set Collection   232

Map Collection   233

Adapter Collections   233

Graph Collection   235

Java Collections Framework   236

8.3 THE BAG COLLECTION   **236**

Creating and Using a Bag Collection   237

Application: Sieve of Eratosthenes   239

8.4 IMPLEMENTING THE BAG CLASS   **242**

Private remove() Method   243

Insert and Access Methods   244

Collection toString()   245

9 THE ARRAY-BASED LIST COLLECTION   250

9.1 LIST COLLECTIONS   **250**

UML for the Collection and List Interfaces   253

9.2 THE ARRAYLIST CLASS   **254**

ArrayList Sizing   256

The ArrayList API   258

9.3 ARRAYLIST APPLICATIONS   **258**

Joining ArrayLists   258

The Closest-Pair Problem   261

9.4 IMPLEMENTING THE ARRAYLIST CLASS   **265**

Design of the ArrayList Class   265

Reserving More Capacity   267

Adding and Removing Elements   268

Implementing Index Access   271

9.5 CLONEABLE OBJECTS   **272**
    Cloning Time24 Objects   273
    Cloning Reference Variables   274
    Cloning an ArrayList   276
    Cloning an Array   278
9.6 EVALUATING AN ARRAYLIST COLLECTION   **278**

10   LINKED LISTS   287

10.1 SINGLY LINKED LISTS   **289**
    Creating a Linked List   289
    Scanning a Linked List   291
    Locating a List Position   291
    Updating the Front of the List   292
    General Insert and Delete Operation   292
    Removing a Target Node   294
10.2 DOUBLY LINKED LISTS   **298**
10.3 THE LINKEDLIST COLLECTION   **299**
    The LinkedList Class   300
    LinkedList—Index Methods   301
    Accessing the Ends of a List   302
10.4 LINKEDLIST APPLICATIONS   **304**
    Application: The Draft List   304
    Application: A List Palindrome   307

11   IMPLEMENTING THE LINKEDLIST CLASS   321

11.1 DOUBLY LINKED LISTS   **321**
    DNode Objects   322
    Using DNode Objects   323
11.2 CIRCULAR DOUBLY LINKED LISTS   **325**
    Declaring a Doubly Linked List   326
    Updating a Doubly Linked List   327
    Application: Word Jumble   331
11.3 IMPLEMENTING THE LINKEDLIST CLASS   **333**
    LinkedList Class Private Members   334
    LinkedList Class Constructor   335
    Indexed Access in a List   335
    Searching a List   336
    Modifying a List   337

12 ITERATORS   344

12.1 THE ITERATOR CONCEPT   344

12.2 COLLECTION ITERATORS   345

The Iterator Scan Methods   346

Generic Iterator Methods   349

Iterating with an enhanced for Statement   350

12.3 LIST ITERATORS   351

ListIterator Set Method   353

Backward Scan of a List   353

ListIterator Add Method   355

The Iterator Design Pattern   356

12.4 ITERATOR APPLICATIONS   356

Ordered Lists   357

Removing Duplicates from an Ordered List   359

12.5 ORDEREDLIST COLLECTION   360

OrderedList Class Methods   361

Application—Word Frequencies   362

The Adapter Design Pattern   366

12.6 SELECTING A SEQUENCE COLLECTION   366

13 IMPLEMENTING ITERATORS   373

13.1 ITERATOR IMPLEMENTATION DESIGN   373

Iterator Variables   374

Iterator Interface Methods   375

13.2 THE LINKEDLIST ITERATOR   376

LinkedList Iterator Methods   377

13.3 IMPLEMENTING LIST ITERATOR   379

List Iterator Constructor   379

List Iterator Public Methods   380

13.4 FAIL-FAST ITERATORS   382

14 STACKS   389

14.1 THE STACK COLLECTION   390

Creating a Stack Collection Class   392

14.2 STACK APPLICATIONS   394

Multibase Numbers   395

Balancing Symbol Pairs   398

14.3 RECURSION AND THE RUNTIME STACK   401

14.4 Postfix Expressions   403
Postfix Evaluation   405
The PostfixEval Class   406
The evaluate() Method   408

14.5 Infix Expression Evaluation   410
Infix Expression Attributes   411
Infix-to-Postfix Conversion   411

15 QUEUES AND PRIORITY QUEUES   422

15.1 The Queue Interface   423
Creating a Queue Collection Class   424
Application: Scheduling Queue   425

15.2 The Radix Sort   427
Radix Sort Algorithm   429

15.3 A Bounded Queue   433
The BQueue Class—Implementation Design   435
The BQueue Class—Declaration   437

15.4 Priority Queues   438
A Priority Queue Interface   439
Application: Support Services Pool   440

15.5 Event-Driven Simulation   444
A Bank Simulation   444
Simulation Design Pattern   446
BankSimulation Class   447

16 BINARY TREES   462

16.1 Tree Structures   463
Tree Terminology   464
Binary Trees   465

16.2 Binary Tree Nodes   470
Building a Binary Tree   472

16.3 Binary Tree-Scan Algorithms   475
Recursive Tree Traversals   475
Inorder Scan Algorithm   476
Designing Scanning Methods   478
Iterative Level-Order Scan   480
The Visitor Design Pattern   482
Using the Visitor Pattern   483

16.4 USING TREE-SCAN ALGORITHMS   **487**
Computing the Tree Height   487
Copying a Binary Tree   489
Clearing a Tree   493
Displaying a Binary Tree   493

16.5 A LOWER BOUND FOR SORTING (OPTIONAL)   **495**

17 BINARY TREE APPLICATIONS   505

17.1 EXPRESSION TREES   **505**
Building a Binary Expression Tree   507

17.2 ITERATIVE TREE TRAVERSAL   **511**
Inorder Iterative Traversal   512
Implementing the InorderIterator Class   513

17.3 EULER TOUR TRAVERSAL   **517**

17.4 DRAWING A BINARY TREE   **520**
Building a Shadow Tree   520
Displaying a Shadow Tree   522

18 BINARY SEARCH TREES   530

18.1 BINARY SEARCH TREES   **530**
Building a Binary Search Tree   531
Locating an Object in a Binary Search Tree   532
Removing a Binary Search Tree Node   533

18.2 STREE—A BINARY SEARCH TREE CLASS   **534**
Application: Updating a Search Tree   537

18.3 IMPLEMENTING THE STREE CLASS   **539**
The STree Class Private Members and Constructor   540
Inserting and Locating a Node   541
Deleting a Node   543
Additional Operations   550
Complexity of Binary Search Tree Operations   551

18.4 THE STREE ITERATOR   **551**
The STree Iterator Public Methods   553

19 SETS AND MAPS   562

19.1 SETS   **564**
The TreeSet Collection   564
A Simple Spell Checker   566

19.2 SET OPERATORS   **569**
Implementing Set Operators   570
Application: Updating Computer Accounts   574
Operations with Ordered Sets   576

19.3 MAPS   **579**
The Map Interface   579
The Ordered Map TreeMap   580
Application: A Student-Timecard Map   582
Application: Computer Software Products   585

19.4 MAP COLLECTION VIEW   **587**
The Key Set Collection View   588
The Entry Set Collection View   590
Application: Building a Concordance   592

20 ORDERED SET AND MAP IMPLEMENTATION   604

20.1 IMPLEMENTING THE TREESET CLASS   **604**

20.2 IMPLEMENTING THE TREEMAP CLASS   **606**
The TreeMap Class Design   608
Key Access to an Entry   609
Updating an Entry   611
Removing an Entry   612
Complexity of Insertion and Deletion in TreeSet and TreeMap   612

20.3 IMPLEMENTING A COLLECTION VIEW   **612**
Examining a View   613
Implementing a View   615
The keySet Collection View   616

21 HASHING AS A MAP IMPLEMENTATION   626

21.1 HASHING   **626**
Using a Hash Function   627

21.2 DESIGNING HASH FUNCTIONS   **628**
Java Method hashCode()   628
User-Defined Hash Functions   630

21.3 DESIGNING HASH TABLES   **631**
Linear Probing   632
Chaining with Separate Lists   634
Rehashing   636

21.4 A HASH TABLE AS A COLLECTION   **636**
21.5 HASH CLASS IMPLEMENTATION   **638**
Hash add() and rehash() Methods   639
Hash remove() Method   642
Implementing the Hash Iterator   643
21.6 AN UNORDERED MAP COLLECTION   **646**
Accessing Entries in a HashMap   647
Updating Entries in a HashMap   648
21.7 AN UNORDERED SET COLLECTION   **649**
Implementing HashSet with HashMap Methods   650
21.8 HASH TABLE PERFORMANCE   **651**
Evaluating Ordered and Unordered Sets   652

22   HEAPS   662
22.1 ARRAY-BASED BINARY TREES   **662**
22.2 THE COMPARATOR INTERFACE   **664**
General Comparison Objects   666
Generalized Array Sorts   667
22.3 HEAPS   **668**
Inserting into a Heap   669
Deleting from a Heap   672
Displaying a Heap   675
22.4 SORTING WITH A HEAP   **677**
Making a Heap   678
The Heapsort   680
Summarizing Static Heap Methods   682
22.5 IMPLEMENTING A PRIORITY QUEUE   **683**
Implementing the HeapPQueue Class   683

23   BIT ARRAYS AND FILE COMPRESSION   693
23.1 BIT ARRAYS   **693**
The BitArray Class   696
Implementing the BitArray Class   698
23.2 BINARY FILES   **701**
DataInput and DataOutput Streams   701
23.3 HUFFMAN COMPRESSION   **704**
Building a Huffman Tree   708
Implementing Huffman Compression   710
Implementing Huffman Decompression   715

23.4 SERIALIZATION   718
Serializing an Object   718
Making a Class Serializable   719
Deserializing an Object   719
Application: Serializing Objects   719
Custom Serialization   722

24 GRAPHS AND PATHS   732
24.1 GRAPH TERMINOLOGY   732
Directed Graphs   734
Weighted Graphs   735
24.2 CREATING AND USING GRAPHS   735
The Graph Interface   735
The DiGraph Class   737
24.3 GRAPH-TRAVERSAL ALGORITHMS   741
Breadth-First Search Algorithm   742
Depth-First Visit Algorithm   747
Depth-First Search Algorithm   751
Acyclic Graphs   753

25 GRAPH ALGORITHMS   764
25.1 TOPOLOGICAL SORT   764
Why It Works   765
Implementing the topologicalSort() Method   766
25.2 STRONGLY CONNECTED COMPONENTS   767
Why It Works   769
Implementing the strongComponents() Method   770
25.3 GRAPH OPTIMIZATION ALGORITHMS   772
25.4 SHORTEST-PATH ALGORITHM   773
Implementing the shortestPath() Method   776
25.5 DIJKSTRA'S MINIMUM-PATH ALGORITHM   779
Designing the Dijkstra Algorithm   779
Why It Works   782
Implementing the minimumPath() Method   782
Minimum Path in Acyclic Graphs   785
25.6 MINIMUM SPANNING TREE   789
Prim's Algorithm   789
Implementing the minSpanTree() Method   792

26 IMPLEMENTING GRAPHS   802

26.1 REPRESENTING GRAPHS   802

26.2 DiGRAPH CLASS COMPONENTS   804
   Representing Vertex Information   804
   The Vertex Map and VertexInfo Array List   806

26.3 DiGRAPH CLASS DESIGN   810

26.4 DiGRAPH METHODS   810
   Accessing the ArrayList   811
   Identifying Neighbors   811
   Evaluating In-Degree and Out-Degree   812
   Adding an Edge   813
   Removing a Vertex   813
   Graph Algorithm Support Methods   815
   Graph Collection View   817

27 BALANCED SEARCH TREES   824

27.1 AVL TREES   826
   The AVLTree Class   826

27.2 IMPLEMENTING THE AVLTREE CLASS   828
   The AVLTree add() Method   829
   The Private addNode() Method   835
   The add() Method   836

27.3 2-3-4 TREES   839
   Searching a 2-3-4 Tree   840
   Inserting into a 2-3-4 Tree   840

27.4 RED-BLACK TREES   843
   Representing 2-3-4 Tree Nodes   844
   The Red-Black Tree Representation of a 2-3-4 Tree   845
   Inserting a Node in a Red-Black Tree   847
   Splitting a 4-Node   848
   Insertion at the Bottom of the Tree   852
   Building a Red-Black Tree   853
   Search Running Time   855
   Erasing a Node in a Red-Black Tree   855

27.5 THE RBTREE CLASS   857

28 NUMBER THEORY AND ENCRYPTION   865

28.1 BASIC NUMBER THEORY CONCEPTS   866
Euclid's GCD Algorithms   866
Modular Arithmetic   867
Euler's Totient Function   868

28.2 SECURE MESSAGE PASSING   869
Creating Keys for RSA Encryption   870
Using Keys for RSA Encryption   871
How to Secure RSA Communication   872

28.3 USING BIG INTEGERS   872
BigInteger Prime Numbers   874

28.4 RSA CLIENT AND SERVER   875

28.5 THE RSA ALGORITHM (OPTIONAL)   876
Implementing Euclid's GCD Algorithms   877
The RSA Theorem   880

29 ASSORTED ALGORITHMS   885

29.1 COMBINATORICS   886
Building Combinations   886
Finding All Subsets   887
Listing Permutations   889
The Traveling Salesman Problem   892
Permutations and the TSP   893

29.2 DYNAMIC PROGRAMMING   893
Top-Down Dynamic Programming   895
Combinations with Dynamic Programming   898
Bottom-Up Dynamic Programming   898
Knapsack Problem   900
The Knapsack Class   903

29.3 BACKTRACKING: THE 8-QUEENS PROBLEM   908
Problem Analysis   909
Program Design   911
Displaying a ChessBoard   914

A JAVA PRIMER   928

A.1 STRUCTURE OF A JAVA PROGRAM   928
Comments   930
Keywords and Identifiers   930

Declaring and Using Variables   931
Console Output   931

A.2 THE JAVA PROGRAMMING ENVIRONMENT   **931**
Integrated Development Environment   932

A.3 PRIMITIVE DATA TYPES   **933**
Numeric Types   933
Java char Type   935
Declaring Named Constants   936

A.4 OPERATORS   **936**
Arithmetic Operators   936
Assignment Operator   937
Compound Assignment Operators   937
Increment Operators   938
Operator Precedence   938

A.5 CONVERSIONS BETWEEN TYPES   **940**

A.6 SELECTION STATEMENTS   **941**
The If-Statement   943
Nested If-Statements   944
Multiway If/Else-Statements   945
Conditional Expression Operator   946
The Switch-Statement   946
The boolean Type   948

A.7 LOOP STATEMENTS   **949**
The While-Statement   949
The Do/While-Statement   950
The For-Statement   951
Break Statement   952

A.8 ARRAYS   **952**
Array Initialization   954
Scanning Arrays with Foreach   954
Two-Dimensional Arrays   955

A.9 JAVA METHODS   **956**
Predefined Methods   956
User-Defined Methods   958
Arrays as Method Parameters   960

B   JAVA KEYWORDS   **963**

C   ASCII CHARACTER CODES   **964**

D   JAVA OPERATOR PRECEDENCE   965

E   THE EZJAVA IDE   967

    E.1   INSTALLING EZJAVA   968
    E.2   GETTING STARTED   969
        Creating a New Document   970
        Menu Options   971
    E.3   COMPILING AND RUNNING A PROGRAM   971
        Setting Class Paths   972
    E.4   USING A PROJECT   973

INDEX   977

PREFACE

This book is designed to present the fundamentals of data structures from an object-oriented perspective. Roughly speaking, a data structure is a storage processing machine that handles large sets of data. The structures, called *collections*, have operations that add and remove items and provide access to the elements in the collection. Object-oriented programming provides a means of viewing the data structures as objects with designated operations to handle the data. Class declarations define the underlying storage structures for the data and implement methods that efficiently execute the operations.

Data structures play a critical role in almost every facet of computer science and are a key element in the design and implementation of almost every nontrivial computer application. Not surprisingly, most students look back on the course in data structures as the first step in their understanding and appreciation of computer science as a discipline. This study introduces students to a number of key concepts.

Book Organization

We present a modern view of data structures that combines object-oriented programming principles and concepts of algorithm analysis. We organize our study around interfaces that define categories of collection types. An interface views a data structure as an abstract data type (ADT). It describes how the collection stores elements and defines the key data-handling operations. A collection class is a concrete data structure that implements an interface using a specific approach to storing and accessing the elements.

We have organized our study of data structures using a simple hierarchy of interfaces and classes. The interfaces at the topmost tier describe abstract structures in terms of operations that access and update the objects in a collection. The bottom tier of the hierarchy contains collection classes that use different underlying storage structures to hold the elements and implement the interfaces. The hierarchy of interfaces and collection classes creates an overall organization for data structures, which we refer to as a *collections framework*. In this book, we create a simple framework that is modeled on the Java Collections Framework. Our framework defines interfaces using a limited set of methods that describe the basic features of a collection type.

The Java Collections Framework is a commercial grade software system with a comprehensive assortment of methods to assist applications programmers. The code for the collection classes in the Java Framework relies heavily on abstract classes and a fairly complex inheritance hierarchy. Our collection models the Java Collections Framework by using identical names and method signatures for the interfaces. We also create collection classes with the same names and underlying storage structures. However, we use a straightforward implementation design for the collection classes. In this way, students can read our code and understand the methods and their algorithms. After working with our approach, students will find it easy to transition to the full Java Collections Framework for work in their professional careers.

Figure P.1 displays the interfaces and collection classes in our collections framework. The classes are shaded. The List interface is the model for a data structure that stores elements by position, whereas the Set interface is a model for a collection that stores elements by value without duplicate values. The Map interface is a model for an associative collection that stores elements as key–value pairs. A map stores nonduplicate keys and provides a mechanism to associate each key with a value. In a map collection, the programmer uses a key to access the corresponding value, not an index. Stack, Queue, and PQueue are interfaces for adapter collections. These use another collection as the underlying storage structure but provide only a restricted set of operations from the structure. A graph is a data structure that consists of both vertices and connecting edges. A network is a model for a graph. In this book, we introduce graphs and their classical search and optimization algorithms. The operations are listed in the Graph interface with a directed graph as the concrete data structure.

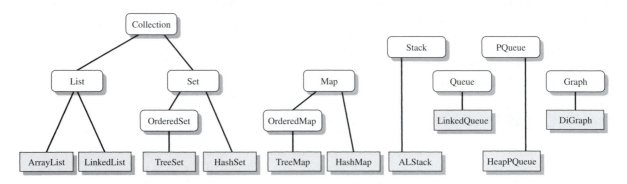

Figure P.1 *Interfaces and classes presented in the book.*

Data Structures and Algorithms

Data structures not only store data but also have operations that manipulate the data. The design and implementation of these operations involve algorithms that consist of a finite sequence of instructions to perform a task. A study of data structures necessarily involves a study of algorithms in order to ensure proper handling of the data. We must also address the issue of large data sets. The choice of a data structure dramatically impacts the efficiency of access and update operations. Consider the problem of maintaining 100,000 credit card accounts. An array-like structure requires on average 50,000 iterations to locate an element. A map can perform the same task in approximately 16 iterations. Both structures have algorithms to look up a value. Their resulting performance, however, is radically different. In our discussion of algorithms, we introduce simple, intuitive but very effective ways to evaluate execution-time performance in a fashion that is independent of a particular machine or programming language.

Data structures need good algorithms. The opposite is also true. You will see this demonstrated in the later chapters when we introduce graphs, data compression and cryptography, and advanced recursive algorithms. We focus on algorithms and algorithm design techniques that depend intimately on structuring data in a specific way for the problem. In this way, we exploit features of data structures that we have learned in the book. The famed computer scientist Niklaus Wirth proclaimed the fundamental importance of both algorithms and data structures for computer programming in his classic text titled *Algorithms + Data Structures = Programs*. In the modern world of object-oriented programming, data structures remain crucially important for both design and analysis of algorithms.

Java and Data Structures

Most of the material discussed in this book applies to any programming language. We emphasize concepts that focus on the design and use of a data structure. However, you must also understand how to implement the data structures and write application programs. This requires that you write code in a particular programming language, and we chose Java. The language has good object-oriented design constructs that support a modern view of data structures. We use the language to present data structures in a hierarchical framework. Java interfaces define categories of data structures (collections), and Java classes define the individual collection types.

Java is portable, allowing a program to be run on any platform without being recompiled. This has many practical advantages. Students may develop programs on Windows, Macintosh, or UNIX systems and then move code from one system to another. A college can provide central computing facilities for labs that allow students to work on projects that are begun or completed on their home systems.

Java is an ideal language for creating interactive GUI (Graphical User Interface) programs. This is the form for most modern applications. In Chapter 3, we present a self-contained introduction to GUI programming using the Java Swing components. Our goal is to promote an understanding of data structures and so most examples, programs, and exercises are console-based with keyboard input and screen output. However, GUI applications are smattered throughout the book and included in the exercises.

The Java language has a number of programming constructs that aid in the use and implementation of data structures. The constructs include:

- Autoboxing and auto-unboxing, which supplies automatic conversion from a primitive type to its associated wrapper type and vice versa. This allows us to store primitive number and character data as objects in a collection.

- Collections use iterators to scan their data. Java introduces an "enhanced for" statement that causes the compiler to take care of the iterator for you. It uses a variation of a for-loop to short-circuit the need to initialize an iterator and use iterator methods to access the elements.

- Java provides an enum facility that allows a program to define a special kind of class whose members are named constants. A programmer can use an enum class to enhance program readability. We illustrate this feature in selected applications and implementations.

- A Scanner object is a simple text scanner for input of data from a file or the keyboard. It partitions characters in the input stream into tokens and uses a variety of methods to convert the tokens into a string or a primitive value.

For data structures, the most significant feature in the Java language is generics. These are extensions to the language that associate a type parameter with an instance of a collection class, an interface, or a method. The compiler can check that code is consistent with the specified type; the code is type safe. Its execution will not result in runtime errors because of improper type checking and type handing that bring into question the quality and reliability of the code.

In Chapter 5, we provide a detailed introduction to Java generics. We begin by showing the motivation that led to the inclusion of generics in the language and then introduce the mechanics that you must employ to create generic classes and methods. Our discussion focuses on the basics that you need to know. As we proceed in this book, we develop the syntax for generics that allow for more sophisticated uses. We proceed on a "need to know" basis. Some features of Java generics lie beyond the scope of this book and are not discussed.

Book Features

This book includes features that enhance student learning and introduces topics that promote deeper understanding of data structures.

- *UML*: The growth of object technology has prompted the creation of notations for program design. One of the most important notations is the Unified Modeling Language (UML). UML uses graphical specifications to assist in object and program design. This book gives students some experience with UML by using its diagrams as an efficient way to list methods in an interface or collection class.

- *Exercise Sets*: Each chapter includes written and programming exercises. The exercises are designed to reinforce basic understanding, to allow students to design and implement methods and complete programs, and to promote more creative knowledge of the material. Each chapter has a programming project that requires more advanced design and programming and substantially more algorithm development.

- *Design Patterns*: Object-oriented solutions to problems are often organized using common design patterns, which facilitate software reuse. We introduce selected design patterns, which enhance our understanding of data structures and their applications. They help us organize the implementation of classes, methods, and objects.

- *Margin Notes*: In the development of topics, we insert key concepts in margin notes. The notes highlight important points and provide students with an easy and effective way to review the material.

Expected Background

This book assumes that the student has completed at least one programming course. For the student who does not have Java programming experience, we provide a tutorial in Appendix A. The "Java Primer" is written in textbook style, with examples and complete programs. It provides the necessary background for someone to read and understand this book. A student should have the mathematical background typically found in a high school's college prep curriculum. Examples of recursion and discussion of runtime efficiency of algorithms use the mathematics in an advanced algebra course.

For the Instructor

This book can be used as part of a two semester introduction to computer science or in a course specifically designed to study data structures. Some schools, like ours, offer a course that combines data structures with an introduction to applied algorithms. We have found that the depth and variety of material as presented in this book works very well, and provides students with the programming tools they need for a later course in the design and analysis of algorithms. This book is designed to allow instructors a great deal of freedom in organizing and presenting the material.

We make extensive use of examples, figures, and margin notes to provide coverage of the material. The first seven chapters in this book introduce the concepts and tools that we employ in our study of data structures.

- Chapters 1 through 3 introduce the object technology features of Java, including use of objects, design and implementation of classes, composition, inheritance, interfaces, and exception handling. Many examples and programs illustrate data structures with Time24 objects.

- Many examples and programs illustrate data structures with Time24 objects.

- Chapter 4 discusses how algorithms can be characterized by their runtime performance independent of any machine or programming language. We develop the Big-O measure of efficiency intuitively and use it throughout the book to motivate the choice of an algorithm or data structure for a specific program application.

- Chapter 5 provides a relatively detailed introduction to Java generics for methods and classes. We use generics throughout the book, and the material in this chapter provides students with critical background.

- Chapters 6 and 7 introduce recursion and its application to the efficient mergesort and quicksort algorithms. An understanding of recursion is critical to the study of binary trees.

Chapters 8 through 19 cover topics typical of a first course in data structures. We use a systematic approach to develop each data structure. The approach recognizes that students need four different areas of understanding for each data structure: the way it stores data, the interface that specifies what a collection class should do, the ability to use the class in applications, and understanding of the class implementation.

- Dynamic arrays, singly linked and doubly linked lists, and binary trees are low-level data structures that provide underlying storage structures for the ArrayList, LinkedList, TreeSet, and TreeMap collection classes, respectively. We introduce these data structures first and develop algorithms to locate, insert, and delete elements.

- The collection type (interface) specifies the majority of the design features for a collection class. A class may include additional methods that exploit characteristics of the underlying storage structure. For instance, the ArrayList class defines the method ensureCapacity(), which updates the size of the underlying dynamic array.

- We provide a range of applications for each data structure. Some simply illustrate how one uses the collection class methods. Others exploit unique characteristics and illustrate the interaction between algorithms and data structures.

- In a course on data structures, students must understand both the abstract design and the implementation design of each collection type. They must know what a data structure does and how it does it. We develop the implementation of each collection class in its own section. The reader is free to study implementation at whatever level of emphasis is desired. The discussion occurs independent of the other areas of understanding.

Chapters 20 through 29 cover topics for an advanced course in data structures and applied algorithms. We recommend that Chapter 19 on Sets and Maps be covered in both introductory and advanced data structures courses. In an introductory course, the chapter introduces students to important collection types that are used in applications and exposes them to elements that are key–value pairs. In an advanced course, the instructor has time to develop a map as an associative array and discuss iterator access methods that distinguish between the key and value field of an element.

An introductory data structures course introduces simple binary search trees with nodes and reference fields. An advanced course extends this concept to include balanced trees and array-based trees that define heaps. It also develops hash tables as an alternative search structure. We discuss these ideas in Chapters 21, 22, and 27, and use them to create efficient implementations for ordered and unordered sets and maps and for priority queues.

Computer Science students typically take a course on the Design and Analysis of Algorithms. There the emphasis is on different algorithm design strategies and more in-depth mathematical analysis of algorithm efficiency. Pseudo-code is used to describe implementation techniques. A course in advanced data structures bridges the gap by illustrating the complex and often ingenious use of data structures to implement algorithms. For this purpose, we include chapters on data and file compression (Chapter 23), graph algorithms (Chapter 25), number theory and cryptography (Chapter 28), and assorted algorithms (Chapter 29). The chapters are independent units, which allows an instructor to pick and choose topics.

Instructor's Guide

An instructor's guide is available to instructors and provides answers to all of the written exercises and solutions for most of the programming exercises and programming projects. Also available are sample chapter tests. In addition, we provide source files for the programs and classes that are developed in the exercises. The instructor's guide is available upon request from your local Prentice Hall sales representative.

Supplements

All of the supplements for this book are available on the Internet at the following locations:

> *http://www.fordtopp.com*
> *http://www.prenhall.com*

Software Supplement

The software supplement resides in the directory *ftjavads*, which consists of the directories *programs*, *packages*, and *docs*. The *programs* directory contains a separate subdirectory for each chapter in this book. Look in the subdirectory to find the source files and data files for programs in the chapter. In some cases, you will also find graphics programs and other listings that are referenced in the chapter. The *packages* directory contains the software that is used throughout the book. Its organization defines a *ds* subdirectory, which branches to directories corresponding to the packages *graphics*, *time*, and *util*. The *util* package contains the interfaces, collection classes, and static method libraries that are introduced in the book.

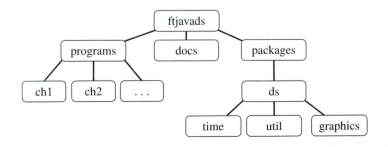

Software API Documentation

The file *docs* includes a complete API specification for the software in the packages directory. This provides students and instructors with easy-to-use and informative online documentation. The Java source files listings in the packages directory include documentation comments. The javadoc tool uses these comments to create a corresponding set of HTML pages. Use the API documentation by having a Web browser open the file *index.html*.

Web Supplements

We have taken every effort to make the book self-contained. In some cases, however, we introduce basic features and algorithms and rely on Web supplements for an expanded discussion. The supplements simply extend the presentation format from the book to provide bonus material.

Modern applications typically use interactive I/O that relies on a GUI (Graphical User Interface) window with components and event-handlers. We introduce GUI application design in Chapter 3 and discuss a basic set of components and the action listener mechanism.

Graphical displays will aid in your understanding of a variety of algorithms such as Towers of Hanoi, 8-Queens, and so forth. We also use graphical displays to illustrate binary trees, insert and delete methods for binary search trees, AVL trees, red–black trees, and heap arrays. The software supplement contains basic drawing software. You can use the Web supplement "Graphics Package" for a detailed discussion of the drawing system. It also provides an excellent example of inheritance.

This book includes a description of algorithms for infix expression evaluation and red–black tree insertion and deletion methods. For the interested reader, we provide the Web supplements "Infix Expression Evaluation" and "RBTree Implementation," which provide a discussion and a listing of the Java implementation code.

The EZJava IDE

EZJava is a flexible Integrated Development Environment (IDE) that allows you to develop and run Java programs on a Windows, Linux, Solaris, or Macintosh OS X system. You can select an appropriate look-and-feel for your system. The IDE allows you to very simply compile and run a main class along with any supporting classes in the same directory. For more advanced software development, you can create a project consisting of many source files within a package structure.

EZJava has features usually found only in more complex programming environments. While you can use it to develop large software systems, EZJava is specifically designed to facilitate the use of Java in academic course work. Individual programs can be created and run outside of a project environment. An application executes in its own runtime window with a command button for multiple runs. EZJava compiles Synchronous Java, which is an extension of Java with concurrent programming tools that are useful in an Operating Systems course.

In Appendix E, we discuss how you obtain and install EZJava and use its key features to create and run a program. A more extensive tutorial is available in the help system integrated into the software.

Acknowledgments

Friends, students, and colleagues have supported us in the preparation of this book. Students have offered valuable criticism of the manuscript by giving us explicit feedback. The University of the Pacific has generously provided resources and support to complete the project.

Our reviewers offered guidance in the writing of the manuscript. They provided detailed comments on both the content and the pedagogical approach. We have taken most of their recommendations into account. Special thanks go to Thomas Sturm—University of St. Thomas, Chris Dovolis—University of Minnesota, Iyad Ajwa—Ashland University, Martin Chetlen—Moorpark College, James Huddleston and Sam Kohn—Thomas Edison State College, Barbara Goldner—North Seattle CC, Phillip Barry—University of Minnesota, Jimmy Chen—Salt Lake CC, and Phil Ventura—University at Buffalo, SUNY. Their insights and support were invaluable to the authors and greatly improved the final contents of the book.

Prentice Hall offered a superb team of dedicated and talented professionals who handled the book design and production. We are especially grateful to Camille Trentacoste, Greg Dulles, and Lynda Castillo, as well as the production teams at nSight and Laserwords. The creativity and dedication to detail by all those involved have produced a book that we hope is attractive, easy to use, and an effective vehicle for learning data structures.

William Ford
William Topp

Chapter 1
CLASSES AND OBJECTS

CONTENTS

1.1 WHAT IS THIS BOOK ABOUT?
A Dynamic Array
Linked Lists
An Associative Array
A Graph
Adapter Structures
Data Structures and Object-Oriented
Programming
Data Structures and Algorithms

1.2 OBJECT-ORIENTED PROGRAMMING

1.3 UNDERSTANDING A CLASS
Designing Class Methods

1.4 THE TIME24 CLASS
Time24 Class Design
Constructors
The toString Method
Accessor and Mutator Methods
Static Methods

1.5 DECLARING AND USING OBJECTS
Using Object Methods
References and Aliases

1.6 A TIME24 APPLICATION

1.7 REPRESENTING CLASSES
UML Diagram of a Class

1.8 A CLASS IMPLEMENTATION
Time24 Class Declaration
Private Utility Methods
Accessor and Mutator Methods
Constructors
Formatted Object Description
Incrementing Time
Time Interval

1.9 ORGANIZING CLASSES
The Java Package Hierarchy

1.10 THE STRING CLASS
String Indexing
String Concatenation
String Comparison

1.11 AN ENUM CLASS
An Enum with Additional Class
Features

1.1 What Is This Book About?

This book deals with data structures. Roughly speaking, these are storage processing machines that handle large sets of data. The structures, called *collections*, have operations that add and remove items and provide access to the elements in the collection.

Why does the study of data structures require a special book? After all, you are already familiar with arrays from a previous course in programming. Arrays are, no doubt, data structures. They store a large collection of data and allow direct access to the elements by using the index operator. They are ideal storage structures for some applications, and we can use them as our starting point. As we will see, however, arrays have serious limitations for many application demands. We need to discover other data structures. Fortunately, professionals before us have addressed this issue. They have evolved a variety of new ways to store, access, and modify data. Let us look at some of the issues that led to this evolution. You will get a feel for some of the challenges we face.

In assessing an array as a storage structure, we are immediately confronted with the fact that it has a fixed length. A programmer must specify the size of an array at the point of its declaration. No remedial action is possible if the runtime demands of the program exceed the capacity of the array. If an array is our only data structure, we would have to know in advance the amount of data to store. For most applications, this information is not available. More fundamentally, applications need storage structures, which are dynamic. The structures need to grow and contract as data is added and removed.

A Dynamic Array

We will discover a data structure, called an *ArrayList*, that has all of the nice indexing features of an array along with the ability to grow dynamically to meet the runtime needs of the program. An ArrayList is a resizable array. It is created with an initial capacity that designates the available space to hold elements. The space is a contiguous block of memory, with elements at the front treated as an array. The back is unused space that is available for new elements. For instance, the ArrayList `alist` has size = 5 in a space with capacity = 8. The elements in the range 0 to size-1 are treated as an array.

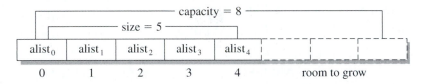

As new elements are added, the available space becomes full. The ArrayList then allocates a new block of memory with more space and copies the existing data to the new memory. In this way, the application can pick up where it left off. If you rent storage space, you understand the process. When you get "too much stuff," you need to rent a bigger space and move things from the old unit to the new unit.

Linked Lists

An ArrayList allows for direct access to its elements through an index. But it is not an efficient storage structure for general insertion and deletion of items at an arbitrary position in the list. Suppose an application wants to store elements in order. If an ArrayList is used, the insert operation requires shifting a block of elements to the right to make room for a new item. Similarly, a deletion requires shifting a block of elements to the left to fill in the gap created by the missing item. Figure 1.1 illustrates the action required to add element 25 into an ordered list and the action required to remove element 20 from the list.

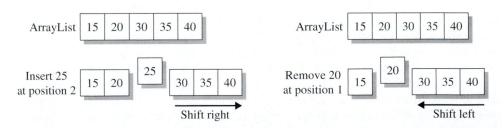

Figure 1.1 *Shifting blocks of elements to insert or remove an ArrayList item.*

If the collection of elements is large and the application calls for frequent insertion and deletion of items, program execution will bog down with the overhead of maintaining the ArrayList. We will discover a new data structure, called a *LinkedList*, that can efficiently add and remove items without involving the entire collection of elements. In the storage structure, each element has references that identify the next and the previous item in the list. Figure 1.2 gives a view of a list where the elements resemble links in a chain. The process of adding a new item involves breaking a link in the chain and then creating two new links to connect the element (Figure 1.2a). The insertion occurs locally in the list and does not require the moving of the other elements to make room for the new element. A similar process removes an element from the list (Figure 1.2b).

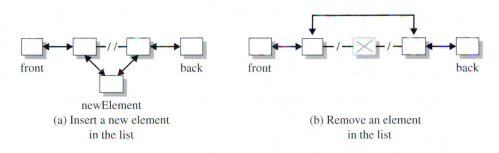

(a) Insert a new element in the list   (b) Remove an element in the list

Figure 1.2 *Adding and removing an item as a link in a chain.*

An Associative Array

An array, an ArrayList, or a LinkedList structure stores elements by position. The first element is at position 0, the second element at position 1, and so forth. To access an element efficiently, we must know its position in the list. Otherwise, we have to revert to an item-by-item search of the list to locate the element. If the list is large, say 100,000 elements, the search requires very time-consuming iterations of a loop to locate the position. The process would render ineffective on-line systems such as express mail tracking or instant credit card checks. These systems do not store data by position but rather by value. For instance, an express mail package has an airbill number consisting of a string of numbers and alphabetic characters. The carrier uses the number to maintain billing and tracking information for the package. We will discover a variety of data structures that store and access elements with a unique identifier called a *key*. One such structure, a *map*, is ideal for applications like express mail and credit checks. It stores data as a key-value pair. The key identifies the element, and the value is associated information. For instance, suppose an express mail package has airbill number "D29Z" with a delivery data and destination "10/6 Dallas Texas." A map allows the program to access a value using the key that acts like an index. For these reasons, maps are referred to as *associative arrays*.

Rather than using a list storage structure, maps can use a tree structure to store the elements. A *tree* is a container whose elements are nodes emanating from a root. We will develop general tree structures that have a variety of applications. We will focus on a special type of tree, called a *search tree*, that allows a program to locate an element by searching down a path from the root. Figure 1.3 is a search tree holding eight airbill numbers. Any search, such as finding airbill "D29Z," requires at most three iterations since that is the length of the longest path from the root to an element. The efficiency of locating an item is even more evident when the tree holds a larger number of elements.

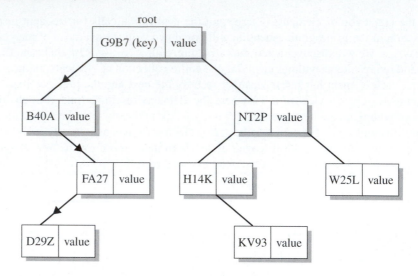

Figure 1.3 *Search path for map pair "D29Z" value in a binary tree.*

A Graph

A graph is a set of vertices connected by links, which are called *edges*. Depending on the application, edges may have a direction from a source vertex to a destination vertex. Illustrations use an arrow from A to B for a directed edge. An edge may also have a *weight* defining a property of the edge. For instance, the weight may specify the distance between two vertices or the amount of network traffic that can flow along the edge. Figure 1.4 is a weighted directed graph, called a *digraph*, containing five vertices and seven edges.

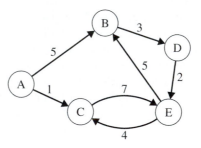

Figure 1.4 *A weighted directed graph (digraph).*

Graphs are involved in many problems of practical interest. For instance, directed graphs are used to represent finite state machines. Optimal routing problems for transportation systems and network messaging are solved using weighted graphs.

Adapter Structures

Most data structures are storage processing machines. They order data, locate and update a value, and so forth. Some applications need a data structure to serve as a simple storage container. The structure acquires data for later release in some organized way. Businesses such as a bank or amusement park create waiting lines so that customers are served on a first-come first-served basis. A waiting line is a *queue*. The data structure is a list with two reference points, the front and the back. Data enters at the back and exits at the front. In Figure 1.5, the queue has the elements A, B, and C, which are added in that order. A new element D enters at position 3, the back, and element A exists from position 0, the front.

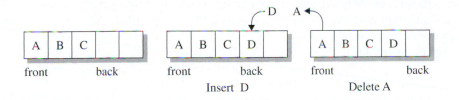

| front | back | front | back | front | back |

Insert D   Delete A

Figure 1.5 *A queue adds element D at the back and releases element A from the front.*

An operating system uses a queue for its print spooler. Print requests are stored in the spooler in the order they are submitted. The print job at the front of the queue is sent to the printer as soon as it becomes available.

A queue is an *adapter structure*, which uses an existing data structure like a LinkedList to store the elements. The queue, however, allows only restricted access to the underlying storage structure at the front and the back of the list. There are two other adapter structures, *stack* and *priority queue*. The former allows access at only one end of the list and models a stack of trays in a cafeteria. The latter assumes that the collection has an ordering. Unlike a queue that removes the first element, a priority queue removes the element with highest rank or priority.

Data Structures and Object-Oriented Programming

The examples in the previous section point out that a data structure is not simply a language construct. It is a data-handling system. From a programming perspective, it is a mini-software system. Modern object-oriented programming is an ideal mechanism for designing and implementing a data structure. A collection is an object and the collection type (class) is the data structure. The object has private members that define the underlying storage structure that holds the data. The public methods provide the data-handling operations.

Most of the material discussed in this book applies to any programming language. We emphasize concepts that focus on the design and use of a data structure. However, you must also understand how to implement the data structures and write application programs. This requires live code for which we chose Java. The language has good object-oriented design constructs that support a modern view of data structures. We will use the Java language and theory to present data structures in an integrated framework. Java interfaces will define categories of data structures (collections), and Java classes will define individual collection types.

You will need some familiarity with basic features of the Java language, including primitive data types, control structures, methods, and one-dimensional arrays. For a reader who is not familiar with Java, we provide a tutorial in Appendix A. The tutorial is written in textbook format with examples and complete programs. It provides the necessary background for you to read and understand this book.

We will begin Chapter 1 with a study of Java classes and objects. We will include a discussion of class design and implementation along with the declaration and use of objects in an application. Some of the material may be a review. All of the material is important because it highlights concepts that are used throughout the book.

Data Structures and Algorithms

Data structures not only store data, they also have operations that manipulate the data. The design and implementation of these operations involve *algorithms* that consist of a finite sequence of instructions to perform a task. A study of data structures necessarily involves a study of algorithms to ensure proper handling of the data. This is particularly true with collections in which the potential number of elements could dramatically impact the efficiency of access and update operations.

Consider the problem of maintaining 100,000 credit card accounts. If we store the data in an array, an instant credit check would take anywhere from 1 to 100,000 iterations to locate the account. On average, the search requires 50,000 iterations. With a structure like a map, accounts can be stored in a tree with nodes packed near the root. A search requires no more than 17 iterations, because this is the longest path from the root to any node. Both an array and a map have algorithms to find elements. Their performance, however, is radically different.

Data structures need good algorithms. The opposite is also true. You will see this demonstrated in the latter chapters when we introduce graphs, data compression and encryption, and advanced recursive algorithms. The renowned teacher and scholar Niklaus Wirth highlighted the interplay between algorithms and data structures when he coined the expression "data structures + algorithms = programming."

1.2   Object-Oriented Programming

An object is an entity with data and operations on the data.

A *computer program* is a sequence of instructions designed to solve a problem. While there is no one way to write a program, we can identify techniques that experienced programmers have found to be useful. One such approach identifies in the problem situation different entities, called *objects*, which feature attributes and behaviors. *Attributes* refer to the properties or characteristics associated with an object, whereas the *behaviors* refer to the set of actions that the object can perform. Program instructions detail interactions among the objects that produce a solution to the problem.

A class is the type of an object. It describes what the object is and can do. Objects are instances of the class.

Creating a computer program using objects as the starting point is called *object-oriented programming*. The design technique describes an object in terms of an abstract model that identifies relevant data and operations. Programs for different university agencies illustrate this idea. They all deal with students who are complex real-world entities with a variety of physical attributes (sex, age, hair color), demographic information (local address, home town), academic records (major, grade point average), and so forth. An agency such as the finance center, registrar's office, or housing office creates its own abstract model of a student with data and operations, which are specific to the function of the agency. For instance, the finance center typically does not care about a student's age, sex, or major. Rather, it is interested in account information such as the student's name, identification number, and current account balance. The major and gpa are important to the registrar, while the housing office needs to take into account a student's sex and age.

A program for the finance center uses StudentAccount objects. The name StudentAccount identifies a *class*, which describes the type of each object. The class defines the data that characterizes an object and operations that access and update the data. Figure 1.6 illustrates the StudentAccount class. The operations allow payment of debt and the posting of charges for tuition, bookstore purchases, and so forth. Other operations allow the finance center to access the current balance and update the student's name to accommodate his or her preference. Objects of StudentAccount type are *instances* of the class. For instance, objects *tdunnAcct* and *mburnsAcct* are instances of the class. A program defines the objects as variables of type StudentAccount. Each object has its own copy of the data, which is referenced when a program associates a class operation with the object. Both the *tdunnAcct* and *mburnsAcct* objects can charge $100 for books. The effect would be to debit the balance of the respective object.

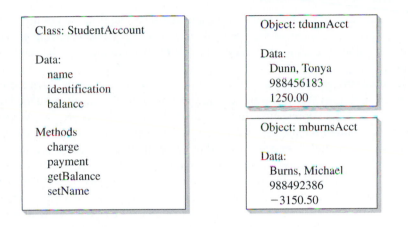

Figure 1.6 *StudentAccount class and objects (instances).*

1.3   Understanding a Class

A key element of object-oriented programming is the design and implementation of classes. The design must specify operations that enable instances of the class (objects) to be used in application programs. The operations, referred to in Java as *methods*, form the *class interface*, which provides an external view that enables a programmer to understand and use the objects.

> A class interface is a specification of the methods that are visible and can be used by instances in an application.

With a class, we distinguish between the behaviors of an object and the mechanism by which the behaviors are achieved. This principle of separation distinguishes the design of methods associated with an object from their implementation using a programming language such as Java. At the design level, we are interested in specifying methods that will allow a programmer to create and use an object in a problem situation. At the implementation level, we are concerned that the class methods are coded so that they execute correctly and efficiently.

The class implementation has its own design. It maps the attributes of an object to a set of data items, called *variables*, and the operations to a set of methods. Typically, the data is characterized as private so that it is accessible only within the class implementation. The interface methods are characterized as public, which makes them accessible in an application. The implementation design may also include private methods that facilitate implementation of public interface methods. Separating private and public members in a class ensures that an application must use public methods to access and modify the data in an object.

> Implementation makes the operations of a class work.

In real life, we have experience with objects at both the interface and implementation levels. For instance, a car has a transmission that a driver controls with a gearshift. The driver has an abstract view of a transmission. He treats it as a "black box" that has operations to place the car in reverse or in a range of forward gears. Other operations allow him to check the transmission fluid level and add new fluid when the level is low. All of these operations are visible to a driver outside of the object. A mechanic has an implementation view of a transmission. He must know how it is constructed from hundreds of individual parts and how they fit together for smooth operation. The driver must know how to use a transmission. The mechanic must know how the transmission works.

Designing Class Methods

Class methods access and update data values in an object and often return information. A method is a process that can accept data values called *arguments*, carry out calculations, and return a value. The arguments serve as input for the method, and the return value is its output.

The description of a method includes an *action statement* that indicates the task that the operation performs and the meaning of any return value. We must view a method in the context of its use in an application. In some cases, the method executes successfully only when certain conditions apply. For instance, a bank will process a customer's check only if the account has a sufficient balance. Part of the description of a method includes a listing of *preconditions* that must apply in order for the operation to execute properly. If a precondition is violated, the method identifies the condition and throws an exception, which allows the calling statement to employ some error handling strategy. The *state* of an object is the current value of its data. A method often alters one or more of the data values. Its description also includes *postconditions* that indicate changes to the object's state caused by executing the method.

Describe a class method using the method signature and an action statement that includes changes to the data. A listing of exceptions describes the preconditions.

Class design uses a format to describe a method. It begins with the *method signature*, which includes the method name, a listing of formal parameters that correspond to arguments, and the object type of the return value. The parameter list is a comma-separated sequence of one or more parameter names and data types.

Method description:
>   ReturnType methodName(Type$_1$ param$_1$, Type$_2$ param$_2$, ...)
>   Action statement that describes the operation and lists changes to the data (postconditions) and exceptions that occur when preconditions are not satisfied.

1.4   The Time24 Class

A Time24 object represents time in a 24-hour clock.

In the next five sections, we will provide a detailed discussion of classes and objects using the Time24 class as an example. You have some familiarity with Time24 objects. Operating systems use them to specify time for the creation date and last-modification date of a file. A programmer might create a file at 9:30 A.M. in the morning and then update it at 4:15 P.M. The system would stamp the creation time as 9:30 and last-modification time as 16:15. The military uses a 24-hour clock with lights out at 22:30 (10:30 P.M.). In these sections, you will see how to design a class and then create and use instances of the class in an application. We will introduce an API (Application Programming Interface) listing of the class and a

UML (Unified Modeling Language) diagram of the class. These are industrywide ways of describing a class. Our discussion concludes with an implementation of the Time24 class.

For some readers, this material is a review, and a quick skim will be sufficient to learn our terminology and approach. Everyone is encouraged to become familiar with the Time24 class. We will use it extensively throughout this book.

Time24 Class Design

Begin the design of a class by describing its data components.

A Time24 object has integer data values – hour and minute – where the hour is in the range 0 to 23 and the minute is in the range 0 to 59. The interface has methods to access and update the data values and create a formatted string that describes the current time. Two main application methods advance the time and determine a time interval.

The Time24 class defines the method addTime() to increment the time of the object. The operation takes an argument *m* specifying the number of minutes to advance the time. The values for hour and minute are adjusted so that they fit into the ranges 0 to 23 and 0 to 59, respectively. We refer to the adjustment as *normalizing* the time. The operation requires that *m* be a positive value since time does not move backwards. The method signature includes a single parameter *m* of type `int` and the return type `void`, which indicates that there is no return value. The following is a description of the method addTime() with an accompanying example. The description format is used for methods in this book.

addTime():

> `void addTime(int m)`
>> Updates the time for this object by the specified number of minutes. The hour and minute values are normalized so that hour is in the range 0 to 23 and minute is in the range 0 to 59. If *m* is negative, the method throws an IllegalArgumentException.

Example: Assume *t* is a Time24 object with time 15:45 (3:45 P.M.). The statement

> `t.addTime(30);`

>> calls addTime() with argument 30 and increments the time for *t* to 16:15.

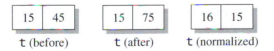

| 15 | 45 | | 15 | 75 | | 16 | 15 |

t (before)   *t* (after)   *t* (normalized)

The method interval() measures the time gap between the current hour and minute of the object and the next 24-hour occurrence of a Time24 argument *t*. The result is a Time24 object that becomes the return value.

interval():

> `Time24 interval(Time24 t)`
>> Returns a Time24 object that specifies length of time from the current hour and minute of this object to the next 24-hour occurrence of time *t*.

Example: Use Time24 objects *tA*, *tB*, and *tC*. Object *tA* has current time 14:45 (2:45 P.M.) and object *tB* has current time 16:15 (4:15 P.M.).

Case 1: tC = tA.interval(tB)   tC is the interval from tA to tB

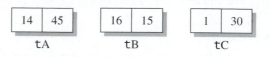

Case 2: tC = tB.interval(tA)   tC is the interval from tB to tA

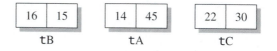

Constructors

An application must create an object before using it. The process involves a method, called a *constructor*, which allocates memory for the object and initializes the data values. The method signature for a constructor uses the class name as the method name and does not have a return type. A class can provide a variety of constructors by using different parameter lists. Of special note is the *default constructor* that has an empty parameter list and assigns default values to the data. The Time24 class has a default constructor that assigns hour and minute to be 0. The object corresponds to midnight (0:00). A second constructor has two integer parameters, hour and minute, which can be any positive integer. The constructor uses the arguments to initialize the data values and then stores the time in normalized form.

Constructors:

```
Time24()
```

> The default constructor initializes the hour and minute to be 0. The time is midnight (0:00)

```
Time24(int hour, int minute)
```

> This object is initialized with the specified hour and minute. The values of the data fields are normalized to their proper range.

Example:

```
Time24()                      // object is 0:00
Time24(4,45)                  // object is 4:45

// 150 minutes is 2:30; hour 23 and minute 150 are normalized
Time24(23,150)                // object is 1:30
```

The toString Method

The design of a class typically provides a method which describes the state of the object. For reasons we will discuss in Chapter 2, Java uses the name *toString* for such a method. The return type is a String containing some formatted representation of the object. The Time24 version of toString() returns the time in the form *hh:mm*. The minute value is always two characters with a leading zero if necessary.

toString():

> `String toString()`
>> Returns a string that describes the time of this object in the form *hh:mm*.

Example: Assume *t* is a Time24 object with hour 14 and minute 45. Use the method toString() and System.out.print() for console output.

> `System.out.print("Time t is " + t.toString());`

Output:
    Time t is 14:45

Using toString()

Note

In building a string expression that includes an object description, you may simply use the variable name for the object. The Java compiler converts the variable to a string by calling the toString() method for the object. For instance, an alternate version of the print() statement in the previous example produces the same output.

> `System.out.print("Time t is " + t);`

Accessor and Mutator Methods

The data associated with an object is part of the internal design of its class. In general, a program may not directly access the data in an object. This must be done with accessor and mutator methods, which are part of the object interface. An *accessor method* returns the current value for an object's data field. The method name typically begins with the word *get*. In the Time24 class, the methods getHour() and getMinute() return the value of the corresponding data field.

> An accessor method retrieves the value of a data field in the object. The name typically begins with get.

getHour():

> `int getHour()`
>> Returns the hour value for this object.

getMinute():

> `int getMinute()`
>> Returns the minute value for this object.

A *mutator method* allows a program to update the value for one or more data fields in the object. The method name typically begins with the word *set*. In the Time24 class, the method setTime (*hour, minute*) uses the integer values hour and minute to assign new values to the corresponding data fields. The method normalizes the time so that hour and minute are in the proper ranges.

> A mutator method changes the value of one or more data fields in the object. The method name typically begins with set.

setTime( ):

> void setTime(int hour, int minute)
>> The arguments update the corresponding data fields in this object. Both arguments must be positive integer values; otherwise, the method throws an IllegalArgumentException.

Example: The methods getHour(), getMinute(), and setTime() combine to move the clock forward one hour. This is equivalent to addTime(60).

> t.setTime(t.getHour() + 1, t.getMinute())

t (before)   t (after)

Static Methods

The methods we have introduced up to this point are associated with a Time24 object. They access and update the data fields of the object. For this reason, these types of operations are called *object methods*. The design of a class can include independent methods that are not bound to any specific object. The methods perform operations that support the class. Their signatures include the modifier *static*. In contrast with object methods, these operations are referred to as *class* or *static methods*. They are called by using the class name to reference the method.

The Time24 class has a static method parseTime(), which takes a string argument *s* representing 24-hour time in the form *hh:mm*. The method returns a Time24 object with the equivalent 24-hour time.

parseTime( ):

> static Time24 parseTime(String s)
>> The method takes a string *s* in the form hh:mm and returns an object with the equivalent Time24 value.

Example: Call the method parseTime() using the class name Time24 as its reference. Assign the return value to the Time24 variable *t*.

> t = Time24.parseTime("13:45"); // t has value 13:45 (1:45 P.M.)

1.5   Declaring and Using Objects

Variables of class type name objects in a different way from variables of primitive type such as *int*, *double*, and *char*. A variable of primitive type is the name of a memory location that stores the actual value. For instance, the declaration

> int count = 64;

allocates memory for an *int* and assigns the name *count* to the location. The declaration places the initial value 64 in the memory location.

A variable of class type is the name of a memory location that holds a reference to an object that is stored in some other place in memory. This is an important distinction, which is not immediately apparent. The declaration of a variable of class type has familiar syntax. It begins with the class name followed by the variable name.

```
Time24 t;
```

In this case, however, the declaration allocates a memory location named *t* that holds the address of a Time24 object but does not create an actual object. For this reason, the variable is called a *reference variable*. Creating the object is the task of the operator new. The operator includes a class constructor. For instance, the following statements create a Time24 object using different versions of the constructor.

You must make a reference variable refer to an actual object. Do this by assigning it a value returned by the new operator that calls a constructor to create an object.

```
t = new Time24();       // creates object with time midnight
                        // (0:00)
t = new Time24(15,30);  // creates object with time 15:30
                        // (3:30 P.M.)
```

For its action, the operator *new* allocates memory for a Time24 object. The memory consists of integer variables *hour* and *minute*. The operator then calls the class constructor, which initializes the variables and returns the address of the newly allocated memory. The address is assigned as the value of the reference variable.

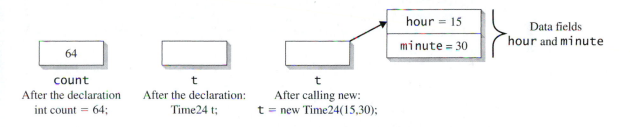

| 64 | t | t | hour = 15 |
| | | | minute = 30 |

Data fields hour and minute

After the declaration int count = 64;

After the declaration: Time24 t;

After calling new: t = new Time24(15,30);

A declaration can define an object reference variable and create the object in one step.

```
Time24 t = new Time24(15,30);
```

Technically, we should say that *t* refers to a Time24 object with a value 15:30. This is a bit awkward, and so we simply say that *t* is the Time24 object 15:30. However, don't lose sight of the fact that the variable *t* and the object referenced by the variable are two separate data items that reside in their own independent area of memory.

Using Object Methods

Once an object is created, a program can call any of its interface methods. The syntax uses the object reference and the method name separated by a "." (dot). The method should include zero or more arguments enclosed in parentheses. For instance, assume *t* is the Time24 object 15:30.

After creating an object, the program can call any of the methods in its interface.

```
// call addTime(45) which advances time for t 45 minutes;
// t becomes 16:15
t.addTime(45);

// access the current hour value for object t; tHour is 16
int tHour = t.getHour();

// interval() returns a Time24 object that is the interval
// from t to supperTime; the return value is assigned to the
```

```
// reference variable freeTime; freeTime is 1:45
Time24 supperTime = new Time24(18:00), freeTime;
freeTime = t.interval(supperTime);
```

In its declaration, an object reference variable can be initially set to *null*. The value is a special constant that can be used to give a value to any variable of class type. It indicates that the variable does not yet reference an actual object. The runtime system identifies any attempt to call an object method when the reference variable has value null as an error and throws a NullPointerException. For instance, the following statements simply declare the Time24 reference variable *wakeUp* and then attempt to advance the time by 30 minutes.

```
Time24 wakeUp = null;    // wakeUp is assigned the value null
wakeUp.addTime(30);      // error! NullPointerException is thrown
```

A program can test whether the variable references an actual object using null and the comparison operators == and !=.

```
// allocates an object only if t is not already referencing one
if (t == null)
    t = new Time24(6,30);
// executes the method addTime() only if t references an object
if (t != null)
    t.addTime(30);
```

References and Aliases

An assignment statement with primitive variables copies the value of the right-side variable to the left-side variable. The result is two variables in separate memory locations but with the same value. For instance, look at the assignment statement with integer variables *m* and *n*.

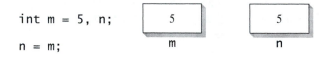

```
int m = 5, n;

n = m;
```

Assignment also applies to reference variables, but you must understand the consequences. Consider two Time24 variables *tA* and *tB*, where *tA* is a reference to object 14:15 (2:15 P.M.).

```
Time24 tA = new Time24(14,15), tB;

tB = tA;
```

Object variables *tA* and *tB* are aliases because they reference the same object. They are two names for the same object.

The assignment is valid and copies the value of *tA* to *tB*. But remember, these are reference variables and the values are addresses. The result is two separate reference variables *tA* and *tB*, both pointing to the same object. We say that *tA* and *tB* are *aliases* because they are two different names for the same object. Using any update method with either variable changes the state of the single object they reference.

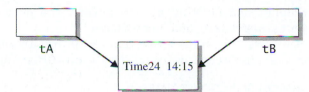

In some applications, we want reference variables to point at separate objects having the same value. Being separate objects, an update to one does not change the value of the other. The task involves creating separate objects for each reference variable and copying the data values from one to the other. The copy can occur when an object is created or later with an update method. The following statements create distinct Time24 objects *bedTime* and *lightsOut* with the same value 22:15 (10:15 P.M.).

```
// declaration creates two Time24 object variables with bedtime
// referencing the object 22:15 (10:15 P.M.); lightsOut is null
Time24 bedTime = new Time24(22,15), lightsOut;
```

Create a copy of an object by allocating a new object having the same data as the original object.

```
// create lightsOut object with the same value as bedtime
lightsOut = new Time24(bedTime.getHour(), bedtime.getMinute());
```

or

```
// create lightsOut object with default values and then update
lightsOut = new Time24();
lightsOut.setTime(bedTime.getHour(), bedtime.getMinute());
```

1.6   A Time24 Application

Let us create a Java application using Time24 objects. The program looks at key times that mark the television network broadcast of a football game. Assume that the game begins at 1:15 P.M. and takes 3 hours and 23 minutes to play. The broadcast concludes with postgame interviews that fill in the time up to 5:00 P.M. when the network switches to its nightly newscast. The program determines when the game ends and the length of time available for postgame interviews.

In designing the application, we need five Time24 reference variables. Times for the start of the game, its length, and the start of the newscast are known and can be used to initialize the three variables, *startGame*, *timeOfGame*, and *startNews*. The static method parseTime() uses a string representation of the news time to return an initial value for *startNews*.

```
// Time24 reference variables
Time24 startGame = new Time24(13,15),          // start game
                                               // at 1:15 P.M.
       timeOfGame = new Time24(3,23),          // game 3 hours,
                                               // 23 minutes
       startNews = Time24.parseTime("17:00");  // news at
                                               // 5:00 P.M.
```

Two other variables, *endGame* and *timeForInterviews*, are simply declared as uninitialized reference variables. During program execution, we will create objects for the variables.

```
Time24 endGame, timeForInterviews;   // uninitialized variables
```

To determine the time when the game ends, use a two-step process. Start by creating an object *endGame*, which is a copy of the value for *startGame*. Update *endGame* using addTime() with an argument that corresponds to the length of the game in minutes.

```
// use getHour() and getMinute() to access the data value
// for objects startGame and timeOfGame;
endGame = new Time24(startGame.getHour(), startGame.getMinute());
endGame.addTime(timeOfGame.getHour()*60 + timeOfGame.getMinute());
```

PROGRAM 1.1 TIME24 BROADCAST TIMES
_____

A complete program implements the television broadcast application. The previous discussion provided both the overall design of the program and instructions to implement key components. The output highlights times when the game begins and ends and the length of the postgame interviews.

```
import ds.time.Time24;

public class Program1_1
{
    public static void main(String[] args)
    {
        // Time24 reference variables
        Time24 startGame = new Time24(13,15),      // game 1:15 P.M.
            timeOfGame = new Time24(3,23),          // length 3:23
            startNews = Time24.parseTime("17:00");  // news 5:00 PM
        Time24 endGame, timeForInterviews;          // uninitialized

        // create object for endGame, with same time as startGame;
        // update it by adding the time for the game in minutes
        endGame =
            new Time24(startGame.getHour(), startGame.getMinute());

        // declare an integer that stores length of game in minutes
        int minutesOfGame = timeOfGame.getHour()*60 +
                                    timeOfGame.getMinute();

        // advance time of endGame using addTime()
        endGame.addTime(minutesOfGame);

        // assign interval() to variable timeForInterviews
        timeForInterviews = endGame.interval(startNews);

        // output
        System.out.println("The game begins at " + startGame);
        System.out.println("The game ends at " + endGame);
        System.out.println("Post game interviews last " +
                                timeForInterviews);
    }
}
```

```
Run:
  The game begins at 13:15
  The game ends at 16:38
  Post game interviews last 0:22
```

1.7   Representing Classes

An application programmer uses a class as an instrument much like a traveler uses a camera. As such, the programmer needs a user's guide that provides documentation on how to use the class. He or she should not have to read the class implementation to understand which methods are available and how they work. In most cases, the source code is not even available.

Java and other object-oriented languages document a class using an *Application Programming Interface (API)*. The API is a summary of the class design and describes each method using the method signature and an action statement. The format for the API begins with a header that includes the class name and the package name, which indicates where you can find the implementation of the class. The rest of the API is a separate listing of class constructors and interface methods. We display constructors in their own section. These methods are used only to create the object. The others methods are operations that control the behavior of the object in a program.

The term *API* is revealing. It provides a view (interface) of the class that allows an application programmer to create a class object and employ its methods in a program. A programmer can use an API to understand a class as a toolkit without reference to its implementation details. As an example, we provide a complete listing of the Time24 class API.

class Time24		*ds.time*
	Constructors	
	Time24()	
	The constructor initializes the hour and minute to be 0. The time is midnight (0:00).	
	Time24(int hour, int minute)	
	The object is initialized with specified hour and minute. The values of the data fields are normalized to their proper range. If hour or minute is negative, it throws an IllegalArgumentException.	
	Methods	
void	**addTime**(int *m*)	
	Advances the time for this object by the specified number of minutes. The resulting hour and minute are normalized to their proper range. If *m* is negative, the method throws an IllegalArgumentException.	
int	**getHour**()	
	Returns the hour value.	
int	**getMinute**()	
	Returns the minute value.	
Time24	**interval**(Time24 t)	
	Returns a Time24 object that specifies the length of time from the current hour and minute to the next 24-hour occurrence of time t.	
static Time24	**parseTime**(String str)	
	The method takes a string s in the form *hh:mm* and returns an object with the equivalent Time24 value.	
void	**setTime**(int hour, int minute)	
	The arguments update the data fields of the object and normalize them to their proper range. Both arguments must be positive integer values; otherwise, the method throws an IllegalArgumentException.	
String	**toString**()	
	Returns a string that describes the state of the object in the form *hh:mm*.	

UML Diagram of a Class

The growth of object technology has prompted the creation of computer-assisted software engineering (*CASE*) tools for program design. One of the powerful features of these tools is visual modeling that uses graphical techniques to assist in object and program design. Software companies use visual modeling extensively to create large application systems.

UML provides a compact view of a class and the relationship of classes to each other.

Modern modeling software uses the *Unified Modeling Language* (UML) to give a graphical representation of classes and their interaction. Figure 1.7 is the UML representation of the Time24 class. The graphical view of a class has three compartments that provide the class name, the instance variables and their types, and the signature for each method. A UML diagram is a compact and efficient view of the class. Each member of the class begins with the symbol "+" or "−" indicating the visibility modifiers public and private, respectively. A static method has its signature underlined. A complete UML representation of a class includes private utility methods, such as normalizeTime(). In this book, we will sometimes limit the representation to the public methods only. In other instances, we will present a complete UML view of the class.

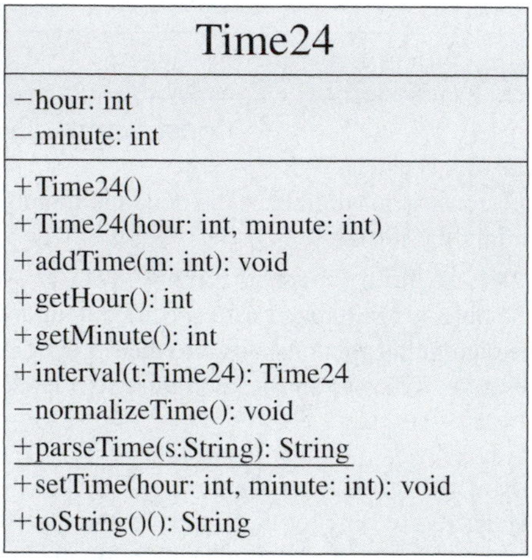

Time24
−hour: int −minute: int
+Time24() +Time24(hour: int, minute: int) +addTime(m: int): void +getHour(): int +getMinute(): int +interval(t:Time24): Time24 −normalizeTime(): void +parseTime(s:String): String +setTime(hour: int, minute: int): void +toString()(): String

Figure 1.7 *UML representation of the Time24 class.*

1.8   A Class Implementation

A class provides an implementation of its abstract design. The implementation, called a *class declaration*, translates the design into Java code. A class declaration begins with a header that includes the reserved word, `class`, and the class name. The rest of the declaration is a block, called the *class body*, which is enclosed in braces. The format of the body includes a declaration of the data and the implementation of the methods.

The use of public and private members promotes information hiding.

Programming language designers have long understood the danger of indiscriminate access to data. For instance, programs used by the registrar at a university should not directly access student data such as grade units, grade points, and gpa. Rather, they should use methods such as addGrade() to modify a student record and postGrades() to create a transcript. The operations provide controls that prevent inappropriate update of an academic record or an unapproved publishing of the record. An object-oriented language like Java protects the integrity of the data using a principle called *information hiding*. The principle relies on two visibility modifiers: private and public. A visibility modifier is included in the declaration of the class header and in the declaration of each class member. The public modifier in the class header indicates that the class and, hence, instances are available to an application class outside of the package. We discuss organization of classes with packages in the next section. For class members, the public modifier specifies that the member is accessible by any instance of the class. The public members represent the class *interface*. The private modifier typically applies to the data in the class and to utility methods that support the class implementation. Only methods of the class can access private members. Figure 1.8 illustrates the different types of access provided to the class methods and to objects in an application program.

A public class member is accessible by any program unit. A private class member is accessible only by class methods.

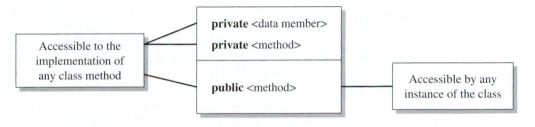

Figure 1.8 *Access rights to public and private members of a class.*

Time24 Class Declaration

Let us look at the Time24 class declaration. We start with a skeletal structure of the class and then fill in the details in subsequent sections. In this way, we can isolate and discuss key features of the declaration and explore implementation design issues. The Time24 class is implemented in the file *Time24.java* and begins with a class header that includes the modifier *public*. The public designation gives application programs access to the class. The data values are two private *instance variables hour* and *minute* of type *int*. The term *instance* implies that the variables are allocated for each instance of the class. The private method normalizeTime() is a utility method that is used whenever arguments or calculations would cause a data value to be out of its designated range. All of the other static and instance methods are public and thus accessible by any application. The private method is used only in the implementation of the public methods.

Time24 class declaration:

The class declaration includes the declaration of instance variables and the declaration instance and static methods.

```
public class Time24
{
    private int hour;       // hour in the range 0 to 23
    private int minute;     // minute in the range 0 to 59

    // utility method sets hour and minute in their proper range
    private void normalizeTime() { . . . }

    // constructors
    public Time24()          { . . . }
    public Time24(int hour, int minute)     {      . . . }
    // methods that increment time and identify time intervals
    public void addTime(int m)      { . . . }
    public Time24 interval(Time24 t) { . . . }
```

```
// accessor and mutator methods for the two data values
public int getHour()    {  . . . }
public int getMinute()      {  . . . }
public void setTime(int hour, int minute)  {  . . . }

// string that describes the object
public String toString()  {  . . . }

// static method converts a string to a Time24 object
public static Time24 parseTime(String s)      {  . . . }
}
```

Private Utility Methods

A private method assists in the implementation of public methods.

Private methods make the implementation of the public methods more efficient and easier to read. The methods are private because they are used only within the class implementation and are not part of the interface. In some cases, an algorithm for a public method is sufficiently complex that a programmer will want to decompose it into subtasks, which are handled by private methods. In other cases, a programmer may use a private method to carry out a task that must be repeated many times during the implementation of class. Such a method promotes *code reuse*.

Private method normalizeTime() converts hour and minute into the ranges
$0 \leq$ hour ≤ 23
$0 \leq$ minute ≤ 59.

The Time24 class provides a good example of a private utility method. An instance always stores its data in normalized form where the hour value is in the range 0 to 23 and the minute value is in the range 0 to 59. The constructor Time24(*hour*, *minute*) and the method setTime(*hour*, *minute*) allow the arguments to have values that are outside of these ranges. In addTime(*m*), the implementation simply adds *m* to the current minute value. This may throw the variable out of range. In each case, an adjustment may be required to store the data values in normalized form. Rather than repeating code, the Time24 class provides a single private utility method, normalizeTime(), to carry out the task.

To understand the algorithm, consider a Time24 object, *t*, that currently holds the value 22 hours and 210 minutes. The normalizing process uses integer division by 60 to adjust the minute value and then integer division by 24 to adjust the hour value. Start with the 210 minutes. The quotient 210/60 identifies the number of hours. We store the value in the variable *extraHours*.

```
int extraHours = minute/60          // extraHours: 3 = 210/60
```

Use the remainder operator "%" to position the minute value within the range 0 to 59.

```
minute = minute % 60;               // minute: 30 = 210 % 60
```

The algorithm concludes by adding the extra hours to the current hour and adjusting the result using the remainder after division by 24. The operation positions the value of hour within the range 0 to 23 and discards all extra full days (24 hours).

```
hour = (hour + extraHours) % 24     // hour: 1 = (22 + 3) % 24
```

normalizeTime():

```
// utility method sets the hour value in the range 0 to 23
// and the minute value in the range 0 to 59
private void normalizeTime()
```

```
{
    int extraHours = minute / 60;

    // set minute in range 0 to 59
    minute %= 60;

    // update hour. set in range 0 to 23
    hour = (hour + extraHours) % 24;
}
```

Accessor and Mutator Methods

The accessor methods getHour() and getMinute() are public methods that an application can use to access the values of the instance variables. An implementation simply uses a return statement for the specified variable.

getHour():

```
// return the current value of the instance variable hour
public int getHour()
{ return hour; }
```

getMinute():

```
// return the current value of the instance variable minute
public int getMinute()
{ return minute; }
```

The mutator method setTime() uses hour and minute as the names for the parameters in the parameter list. This is deliberate because the names identify the variables that will be updated. The implementation uses the keyword *this* to distinguish between a parameter variable and an instance variable with the same name. The keyword is a reference to the object itself and may be used only within the class implementation. One may use the reference with the dot operator to access an instance variable or to call a class method.

> The keyword *this* is a reference to the object that is executing the method.

The implementation of setTime() uses assignment statements that copy the two arguments to the corresponding instance variables. The private method normalizeTime() ensures that the instance variables are in their proper range. The method has preconditions that require that the hour and minute parameters are positive integer values. The implementation of a method with preconditions typically involves testing the conditions and throwing an exception when they are not satisfied. We will discuss exception handling in Chapter 2. The setTime() method throws an IllegalArgumentException if an argument is a negative integer.

setTime():

```
public void setTime(int hour, int minute)
{
    // check that arguments hour and minute are positive
    if (hour < 0 || minute < 0)
        throw  new IllegalArgumentException("Time24 setTime: "
                + "parameters must be positive integers");

    // assign new values and call normalizeTime()
    this.hour = hour;
    this.minute = minute;
    // adjust hour and minute as necessary
    normalizeTime();
}
```

Constructors

A constructor is a public method that uses the class name to identify the method and may not have a return type. A parameter list specifies arguments that initialize the object. The constructor Time24(*hour*, *minute*) initializes an object to the specified values. It behaves like setTime(), except that it is called only when an object is created by the operator *new*. Rather than repeating the setTime() code, the constructor simply calls the method and achieves the same result, including all necessary error handling. This is a variation on code reuse.

constructor Time24(h,m):

```
// constructor creates an instance with values hour and minute
public Time24(int hour, int minute)
{
    setTime(hour,minute);
}
```

The default constructor Time24() creates an object that represents midnight. It is a special form of the general constructor that sets the values for hour and minute to 0. It is possible to implement the default constructor by using the *this* reference with argument list (0,0). The effect is to call the constructor Time24(*hour*, *minute*) with 0 as the arguments.

constructor Time24():

```
// constructor creates an instance set to midnight
public Time24()
{
    this(0,0);
}
```

Formatted Object Description

Most Java classes include a toString() method that returns a formatted string, which describes the current state of the object. In the Time24 class, the method returns time in the form *hh:mm*. The implementation uses the Java predefined class DecimalFormat in *java.text* to create a format object that ensures that the minute value has two decimal places with a leading 0. This produces string representations such as 8:05 and 17:00 when the minute value is in the range 0 to 9.

toString():

```
public String toString()
{
    // create a text format object with two character positions
    // and fill character 0
    DecimalFormat fmt = new DecimalFormat("00");
    return new String(hour + ":" + fmt.format(minute));
}
```

Incrementing Time

The method addTime() takes a positive integer *m* specifying minutes and uses the value to advance the current time. The implementation of addTime() adds *m* to the variable *minute* and then calls normalizeTime() to ensure that the variables *hour* and *minute* are in their specified ranges. The requirement that *m* is positive is a precondition, and the method throws an IllegalArgumentException if the condition is not satisfied.

addTime():

```java
public void addTime(int m)
{
    if (m < 0)
        throw new IllegalArgumentException("Time24.setTime:
                + " argument must be a positive integer");
    minute += m;
    normalizeTime();
}
```

Time Interval

The method interval() takes a Time24 object *t* as an argument and returns the interval of time from this object to *t* as a Time24 object. The implementation converts the values of this object and object *t* to a common unit of measure, minutes. If *t* represents an earlier time, the method adds 24 hours to *t*, which has the effect of designating time in the next cycle (next day). For instance, if the time for this object is 10:15 and *t* is 8:30, update *t* by 24 hours to 32:30. The interval is the difference 22:15.

The return statement creates an *anonymous object* using a Time24 constructor. The term *anonymous* implies that the object does not have a variable name. By using the constructor to create the object, we are assured that time is normalized.

An anonymous object is an object that has not been assigned to a reference variable.

interval():

```java
// return the length of time from current time to time t
public Time24 interval(Time24 t)
{
    // convert current time and time t to minutes
    int currTime = hour * 60 + minute;
    int tTime = t.hour * 60 + t.minute;

    // if t is an earlier time, then add 24 hours so that t
    // represents a time in the "next day"
    if (tTime < currTime)
        tTime += 24 * 60;

    // return a reference to a new Time24 object
    return new Time24(0, tTime-currTime);
}
```

1.9   Organizing Classes

Java organizes software using the package mechanism. A *package* is a group of related classes that are stored in a directory and then made accessible to programs using *import* statements. The use of packages promotes code reuse by allowing a programmer to access preexisting software.

A package is a group of related classes.

Creating a class as part of a package requires adding a package header at the beginning of the source code file and then placing the file in a directory with the same name as the package name. For instance, assume we want to store the declaration for class DemoClass in the package DemoPackage. In the source file *DemoClass.java*, start by adding a package declaration statement that includes the keyword *package* followed by the name DemoPackage.

```
package DemoPackage;

public class DemoClass
{  }
```

Compile the source file and place the *DemoClass.class* file in the folder DemoPackage. The source file may also be included in the folder. However, an import statement accesses only the ".class" file.

Two forms of the import statement are available. A dot (".") separates the package directory from the class names.

An application accesses classes from a package by using the import statement.

```
import DemoPackage.DemoClass;

import DemoPackage.*;
```

The first import statement tells the compiler to search the package DemoPackage and make the class DemoClass available to the program. The second statement uses an asterisk (*), which directs the compiler to make all public classes in the package available to the program.

Classes in a package can have visibility modifiers just like data and methods. The modifiers are included in the class headers. A public class is available to other classes whether they are in the package or not. A class with the private modifier or a class with no modifier at all is available only to classes within the package. In this way, packages allow for encapsulation of related classes when you want to limit access.

In the software supplement, the Time24 class is a member of the *ds.time* package. It is in the *time* subdirectory within a larger directory *ds*. We assume your Java development environment provides a path to the *ds* directory. The set of paths to packages is termed the *classpath* (see Appendix E). The source code file *Time24.java* begins with the headers

```
package ds.time
public class Time24
```

The software supplement resides in *ftjavads*, which consists of the directories named *programs* and *packages*. The *programs* directory contains subdirectories for each chapter in the book. These chapter directories contain the source for each program in the chapter. The *packages* directory defines a *ds* subdirectory, which branches to directories corresponding to the packages *graphics*, *time*, and *util* (Figure 1.9). The util package contains the collection classes and libraries that are introduced throughout this book.

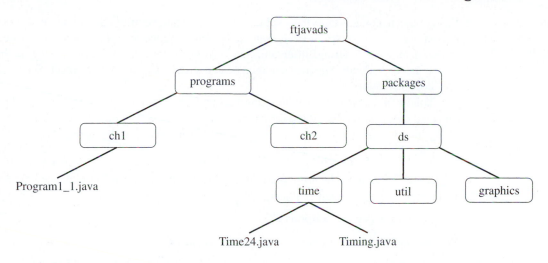

Figure 1.9 *Organization of directories, files, and packages under ftjavads in the software supplement.*

The Java Package Hierarchy

The Java Software Development Kit (SDK) contains hundreds of classes that are organized in a package hierarchy. Java organizes its software by placing the individual package directories under master directories such as "java" and "javax." These directories serve the same purpose as the *ds* directory in the software supplement. In the hierarchy, the package *java.lang* plays a special role. It contains core classes such as Math, String, and wrapper classes such as Integer. They are fundamental classes that are universally accessible by any program. The compiler automatically includes the package without requiring an explicit import statement. Java provides the package *java.util* for all of its predefined collection classes. Our software in the *ds.util* package is modeled on these Java SDK classes. The following list describes some of the more frequently used packages in the Java hierarchy. The *java.awt* and *javax.swing* packages contain classes that define components and events in a GUI application.

The Java Software Development kit organizes its classes within the java and javax master packages.

java.lang	Contains the basic classes needed for developing Java programs. This includes the String class and the System class.
java.util	Provides the Collections Framework classes, the Random class, the StringTokenizer class, and classes dealing with dates and times.
java.io	Classes manage the input and output of data.
java.text	The class DecimalFormat is used for integer and real number format.
java.awt	Contains basic graphical tools for creating windows, dialogs, controls, for performing custom drawing, and for handling images.
javax.swing	Provides second-generation tools for creating graphical user interfaces (GUI).

1.10 The String Class

A string is a sequence of characters that programs use to identify names, words, and sentences. Java provides programmers with a String class in the *java.lang* package. The class has a variety of constructors to create strings. It also has methods to compare strings, to identify an individual character or a character sequence, and to extract a substring.

A String object holds a character string that is immutable (cannot be changed).

String objects are constant; their values cannot be changed after they are created. For this reason, we say that a string is an *immutable* object. When an application needs to edit a string, it may use a StringBuffer object, which has insert, append, and replace methods. The updated character sequence can then be converted back to a String object. See the Java API documentation.

You are already familiar with string literals from examples with the print() and println() methods. A string literal is a sequence of characters enclosed within double quotes. All string literals in Java programs are implemented as instances of the String class.

```
"This is a string literal"
```

A string literal can be used to initialize a String object. For instance, declare the String *city* and assign it the value "Phoenix."

```
String city = "Phoenix";
```

We can also use string literals to create arrays of strings.

```
String[] weekdays = {"Mon", "Tue", "Wed", "Thu", "Fri"};
```

String Indexing

A String object resembles a direct access array. The method charAt() takes an integer argument that serves as an index to an individual character in the string. You must use this method rather than the array index operator *[]* to access a character. Because a string is immutable, there is no corresponding mutator method such as setCharAt(). Determine the number of characters in a string by using its length() method.

Let us look at a typical example that uses the String methods length() and charAt(). A loop scans the characters in a string and outputs only the vowels.

Access individual characters of a String using the method charAt().

```
String str = "this string has vowels";
char ch;

System.out.println("Length is " + str.length());
for (int i=0; i < str.length(); i++)
{
    ch = str.charAt(i);
    if (ch == 'a' || ch == 'e' || ch == 'i' || ch == 'o' ||
            ch == 'u')
        System.out.print(ch + " ");
}
```

```
Output:
  Length is 22
  i i a o e
```

String Concatenation

You can use the concatenation operator + to build a string. The basic form of the operation takes two string operands and appends the second operand to the first. You may also build a string using a character as the operand. Like arithmetic addition, the operator can be used in a compound assignment statement.

```
String strA = "down", strB = "town", strC;
strC = strA + strB;              // strC is "downtown"
strA += " periscope";            // strA is "down periscope"
```

Formatted output in Java is done almost exclusively with string concatenation. The operator assumes one of the operands is a string, whereas the other may be a primitive value or a variable. If an object reference variable is an operand, the compiler appends the string returned by the toString() method for the class.

```
String strA;
Time24 t = new Time24(9,15);
int n = 3;

// concatenated string is "Lunch is 3 hours after 9:15
strA = "Lunch is " + n + " hours  after " + t;
```

String concatenation returns a new string that chains together individual strings or the result of calling toString() for non-String objects.

The + operator is also used for arithmetic addition. The action of + depends on the type of the operands. Just remember that if either or both of the operands are strings, then string concatenation is performed. In the example, + is evaluated from left to right. The fact that the first operand is a string implies that each + operation is a string concatenation. Within parentheses, the two digits are treated as integer constants and + is arithmetic addition.

```
strA = "Total is " + 5 + 9;       // strA is "Total is 59
strA = "Total is " + (5 + 9);     // strA is "Total is 14
```

String Comparison

A programmer may compare two string objects using the methods equals() and compareTo(). The method equals() is an instance method of one string and uses the other string as an argument. The method returns true if the two strings match character by character and false otherwise.

Example: Declare a String object and a *boolean* variable and check for equality.

```
String strA = "goodbye";
boolean b;

b = strA.equals("good"+"bye");    // b is true
b = strA.equals("goodby");        // b is false
```

The method compareTo() takes another string as an argument and compares the strings character by character. It returns an integer value as follows:

$$\text{Return value from compareTo}(\textit{anotherStr}) = \begin{cases} <0 & \textit{thisStr} < \textit{anotherStr} \\ =0 & \textit{thisStr} == \textit{anotherStr} \\ >0 & \textit{thisStr} > \textit{anotherStr} \end{cases}$$

Compare strings by using the compareTo() method.

Example: Let us look at a variety of comparison expressions for the following String objects.

```
String s1 = "John", s2 = "Johnson";
```

Expression:

```
s1.compareTo(s2) < 0            // John < Johnson is true
s2.compareTo("Mike") >= 0       // Johnson >= Mike is false
s1.compareTo("John") == 0       // John == John is true
```

1.11 An Enum Class

Java provides an enum facility that allows a program to define a special kind of class whose members are named constants. The class has a simple declaration that uses the keyword enum followed by the name and a list of identifiers enclosed in braces.

```
public enum Season {fall, winter, spring, summer};
```

An enum type has public members for each of the named enum constants. The members implicitly have the type of the enum class. They are self-typed members. A program can define enum reference variables and literals. An enum constant is denoted by EnumName.<constant>. An enum type has the method toString(), which returns the constant name and the operator == which determines whether two values are the same. The method equals() is also available. Like the String class, the method compareTo() compares two enum values using the order of names in the enum declaration.

Example:

```
// declare two variables of type enum String; initialize
// the variables
Season s = Season.winter, t = Season.spring;

// equals() tests the value of s
if (s == Season.winter || s == Season.spring)
   System.out.println("In " + s + " economy fares apply");

// compareTo() affirms the ordering of the seasons
if (s.compareTo(t) < 0)
   System.out.println(s + " comes before " + t);
```

```
Output:
   In winter economy fares apply
   winter comes before spring
```

Enum variables and constants can be used with slightly extended syntax for a switch statement. The statement evaluates an expression of enum type and then branches to a switch label where the case identifier is an enum constant. Only the constant name is required in the switch label.

An enum defines a self-contained list of constant identifiers. A programmer can use an *enhanced* for statement to scan the list. Each enum defines the static method values() that returns the list of enum constants.

Let us look at an example that uses the Season variable song in an enhanced for statement to scan the list of seasons. A switch statement uses the variable as the selector expression and branches to a case statement with an enum constant as the label. The enhanced for construct is introduced in Appendix A, *The Java Primer*, Section A.8.

Example:

```
for (Season song : Season.values())
{
    switch(song)
    {
        case fall:
            System.out.println("AUTUMN LEAVES");
            break;
        case winter:
            System.out.println("WINTER WONDERLAND");
            break;
        case spring:
            System.out.println("IT MIGHT AS WELL BE SPRING");
            break;
        case summer:
            System.out.println("IN THE GOOD OLD SUMMERTIME");
            break;
    }
}
```

```
Output:
  AUTUMN LEAVES
  WINTER WONDERLAND
  IT MIGHT AS WELL BE SPRING
  IN THE GOOD OLD SUMMERTIME
```

An Enum with Additional Class Features

An enum is a class and so can have instance variables, constructors, and methods. In the declaration of the class, an enum constant may be followed by arguments enclosed in parentheses. The arguments are available to a constructor when the constant is created. The enum class must define a variable that stores the integer value and a constructor that initializes the value. Use an enum in this way for more sophisticated applications. Let us look at one such example.

A city waste collection company has customers separate garbage, recyclable material, and garden clippings. Customers are given three separate containers with different sizes and colors. Program 1.2 introduces the enum class called *TrashContainer* that defines names for the three types of containers with their sizes as arguments. Each enum constant has a private integer variable *containerSize*, which is initialized by the constructor and made accessible by the public method size(). The program defines a second enum class, ContainerColor, with the enum constants brown, yellow, and green. These are the colors that correspond to the waste collection containers.

PROGRAM 1.2 USING ENUM CLASSES FOR WASTE COLLECTION

The program uses the method color() to provide a link between an enum value in the TrashContainer class and the corresponding color value in the ContainerColor class. A container name is an argument, and the color is the return value. The program uses an enhanced for statement to scan the enum constants in the TrashContainer class. For each value, an output statement includes the container name, size in gallons, and color.

```java
public class Program1_2
{
    enum TrashContainer
    {
        // name and size for three types of containers
        garbage(30), recycle(60), garden(90);

        // variable initialized when enum constant is created
        private int containerSize;

        // constructor passed the enum constant integer argument
        private TrashContainer(int size)
        { containerSize = size; }

        // returns value associated with the enum constant
        public int size()
        { return containerSize; }
    }

    public static void main(String[] args)
    {
        // scan values in the TrashContainer enum class
        for (TrashContainer c : TrashContainer.values())
        {
            // display container name, size, and color; the
            // latter value results from a call to color()
            System.out.println(c + ":\t Size " + c.size() +
                                " gal. \tColor " + color(c));
        }
    }

    // private enum class with names for the containers
    private enum ContainerColor {brown, yellow, green}

    // switch statement selects container type and returns color
    private static ContainerColor color(TrashContainer container)
    {
        ContainerColor color = null;

        switch(container)
```

```
        {
            case garbage:
                color = ContainerColor.brown;
                break;
            case recycle:
                color = ContainerColor.yellow;
                break;
            case garden:
                color = ContainerColor.green;
                break;
        }
        return color;

    }
}
```

```
Run:
   garbage:    Size 30 gal.        Color brown
   recycle:    Size 60 gal.        Color yellow
   garden:     Size 90 gal.        Color green
```

Chapter Summary

- This chapter provides an overview of this book's philosophy and intuitively discusses some of the data structures you will study in the book.

- This chapter introduces the concept of an object and the process of object-oriented programming.

- A class is composed of data and operations on the data. The public section of a class constitutes the interface. The private section of a class contains the data and operations that the public members use. An operation is a function and is referred to as a *method*. A method accepts data values (arguments), carries out calculations, and returns a value. Its arguments serve as input, and the return value is its output. In some cases, a method executes successfully only when certain conditions apply. These are known as *preconditions*. If a precondition is violated, the method identifies the condition and throws an exception, which allows the calling statement to employ some error handling strategy. Methods often alter one or more of the data values of the object. A postcondition indicates changes to the object's state caused by executing the method. Each method begins with its method signature, which includes the method name, a listing of formal parameters that correspond to arguments, and the object type of the return value. The parameter list is a comma-separated sequence of one or more parameter names and data types.

- The Time24 class maintains time in 24-hour format. The Time24 class has the static method parseTime(). A static method is associated with a class and not with an instance of the class. One can call parseTime() using the syntax Time24.parseTime(s), where s contains a string whose value is a time in 24-hour notation. In every Java application, the method main() is static. The method is called by the runtime system to begin execution of the program without having an object of the class type.

- There are two types of variables: primitive variables and references. The primitive variables include integers, floating-point numbers, and characters. Reference variables contain the address of an object in computer memory. One can execute a method of an object by following its reference variable by ".", the method name, and its parameters enclosed in parentheses. The assignment of one reference variable to another merely ensures that both references point to the same object in computer memory. The assignment does not make a separate copy of the data. Using any update method with either variable changes the state of the single object they reference. To create a reference to a true copy, the programmer must create a new object composed of the same data as the original object.

- Program 1.1 is an application that uses Time24 objects. The program looks at key times that mark the television network broadcast of a football game. Given initial data, the program determines when the game ends and the length of time available for postgame interviews.

- An Application Programming Interface (API) is a description of the methods and variables in a class. Knowledge of a class API is sufficient for the programmer to effectively use the class in building an object-oriented application. This chapter provides an API for the Time24 class.

- The growth of object technology has prompted the creation of computer-assisted software engineering (CASE) tools for program design. Modern modeling software uses the Unified Modeling Language (UML) to give a graphical representation of a class. The language has visual tools to describe the variables and methods of a class as well as dependencies and interactions when two or more classes are involved.

- The class declaration splits a class into public and private parts. This process is known as information hiding. A class encapsulates information by bundling the data items and operations within an object. As a complete illustration of class implementation, the chapter develops the implementation of the Time24 class.

- In Java, an application accesses classes that are located in packages. The Java Software Development Kit provides hundreds of classes located in a hierarchy of packages, such as *java.lang*, *java.util*, *java.io*, and *javax.swing*. To access a class in a package, use the import statement. Because packages are organized in a directory hierarchy, the import statement must know where to look for packages. The classpath (Appendix E) specifies the directories to search for packages. Many of the classes discussed in the book are located in the packages *ds.util*, *ds.time*, and *ds.graphics*.

- Many applications use strings of characters, and Java provides the String class for such applications. The class provides a large public interface containing many useful operations. This chapter discusses string indexing, concatenation, and comparison. For additional methods that provide pattern-matching capability and that extract substrings, consult the String API.

- The Java enum facility allows a program to define a special kind of class whose members are named constants. A program can define enum reference variables and literals. An enum type has the method toString(), which returns the constant name and the operator == which determines whether two values are the same. The method equals() is also available. Like the String class, the method compareTo() compares two enum values using the order of names in the enum declaration. An enum is often used in a switch statement to select between alternative enum values.

Written Exercises

1. A GradeRecord object has integer attributes that specify the number of units completed, the total grade points, and a real number for the grade point average. A constructor creates an object with default values 0. The operation addGrade() updates the object by entering a grade for a course. Arguments include the number of units and a character that signifies a grade A (4), B (3), C (2), D (1), or F (0). The corresponding grade points are in parentheses. The operation getGPA() returns the grade point average for the grade record. The value is initially 0.0 before any units are recorded.

   (a) Describe the GradeRecord class in API format.
   (b) Display the UML representation of the GradeRecord class.
   (c) Give a declaration of the GradeRecord class.

2. What is the purpose of including a private method in a class?

3. Write a series of statements that create Time24 objects and use them to answer parts (a) to (c). Each answer assumes that you are using all of the information from previous parts.

   ```
   Time24  lunch, startClass, endClass, studyTime;
   ```

   (a) Declare a lunch object having time 12:15. Use the static method parseTime() to assign *startClass* the time 1:30 P.M.
   (b) Assuming the class is 90 minutes, declare an *endClass* object and then update its value to correspond with the end of class.
   (c) Determine how much time you have to study from the end of class until your ride comes at 4:45 P.M. Assign this value to *studyTime* and then output the value as part of the string "Study time is _____."

4. Use the declarations

   ```
   String strA = "john", strB = "son", strC "alexander", strD;
   int index;
   ```

   (a) For each statement, give the resulting string.

   (i) strD = strA + strB;   (ii) strA += strA + strB;

   (b) What is the value of *strC.charAt(6)*?
   (c) The String array, stateList, contains a list of 50 US states, ordered by name.

   ```
   String[] stateList;
   ```

   (i) Give a comparison expression that determines whether the state "New York" is at index 29 in the list.
   (ii) Give a comparison expression that determines whether the state "Montana" occurs in the first half of the list (index 0 to 24).

Programming Exercises

5. The following is a description of the Length class. The data values are two integer instance variables called *foot* and *inch*. An object stores data in normalized form where inch is in the range 0 to 11.

   • A default constructor creates an object with foot = 0 and inch = 0. A second constructor has two integer parameters *ftLen* and *inLen* that initialize the variables in normalized form.

- A Length class has accessor methods getFoot() and getInch() that return the values of the corresponding instance variables. The mutator method setLength() has parameters `ftLen` and `inLen` that update the attributes.
- The methods addLength() and subLength() both have an integer parameter `inLen` specifying a length in inches. The operation addLength() increases the length of the object by the specified amount. The operation subLength() decreases the length of the object. It throws an IllegalArgumentException if the argument represents an amount greater than the current length of the object.
- The method toString() returns a string that describes a Length object in the format

  Length is <foot>' <inch>"   // Example Length is 6' 3"

(a) Provide a declaration of the Length class with the aid of a private method normalizeLength() that updates the instance variables *foot* and *inch* so that the value for *inch* is in the range 0 to 11.

(b) A homeowner wishes to build a parking strip for a car whose length is 12' 3". Write a program that uses Length objects. Declare *parkingStrip* as a Length object measuring 16' 5". Output the length of the unused space when the car is parked on the strip. Give the output as a real number in foot units. Assume the owner also wishes to park an 8' 7" boat behind the car. Output the additional length that must be added to the parking strip to accommodate both the car and the boat.

6. The class Time24m is a miniversion of the Time24 class. It has only three methods.

- A constructor has a real number parameter designating 24-hour time in hour units. For instance, the argument 15.75 initializes a Time24m object with time 15:45.

  ```
  public Time24m(double x)
  ```

- The method isLater() takes a Time24m argument and determines whether the argument is later in the day than the object.

  ```
  public boolean isLater(Time24m t)
  ```

- A static version of toString() takes a Time24m argument and returns a string that represents the corresponding 12-hour time with the suffix A.M. or P.M.

  ```
  public static String toString(Time24m t)
  ```

(a) Provide a declaration of the Time24m class.
(b) Write a program that tests your implementation of the class.

7. A Random class object is a random number generator with methods that return integer and real random numbers falling within a specified range. An integer random number depends on an argument *n* and lies in the range from 0 to $n - 1$. A real random number lies in the interval $0 \leq x < 1$. The Random class has a variety of methods to produce random numbers. For most applications, the method nextDouble() or nextInt(*n*) is sufficient. The following is a listing of key methods. Import statements access the class in the *java.util* package.

class **Random (partial)**		*java.util*

Constructors

Random()
    Creates a new random number generator.

Methods

int | **nextInt**(int *n*)
    Returns a pseudorandom, uniformly distributed *int* value in the range
    from 0 to *n* − 1.

double | **nextDouble**()
    Returns a pseudorandom, uniformly distributed *double* value in the
    interval from *0.0* and *1.0* excluding the value 1.0.

(a) Random integers are uniformly distributed within a range of values. Write a program that uses simulation to see whether random numbers in the range 0 to 9 are uniformly distributed. Declare a 10-element array of integers:

```
int[] digitCount = new int[10];
```

Run the simulation by generating 1 million random integers in the range 0 to 9. Using each number as an index, increment the value of an element in *digitCount*. Conclude by displaying each integer in the range and the corresponding value in *digitCount*.

(b) The sequence of random real numbers can have a long run of successive values that are within a restricted range. Write a program that generates random values of type double. Stop only when the sequence produces a run of 15 successive values that are less than 0.3. Output the length of the sequence required for this run. Produce several different runs of the program.

8. Internet string transmission uses an encoded format that separates the basic tokens in a string with the "+" character. For instance, the encoded form of "walk on water" is "walk+on+water." Write a program that uses command-line argument args[0] as the input string. Use the String class method split(), which returns the array of strings computed by splitting the string object around matches of the given regular expression. A regular expression is a set of symbols and syntactic elements used to match patterns of text.

```
String[] split(String regex)
```

Java predefines a series of regular expressions (see the Pattern class). The expression "\\s" specifies whitespace separator characters. Thus, the following

```
String[] tokenList = "split the string".split("\\s");
for (int i=0;  i < tokenList.length; i++)
   System.out.println(tokenList[i]);
```

has the output

```
split
the
string
```

Using split(), encode the input string and output the result to the terminal.

9. Write a program that uses the method minmax() to identify the minimum and maximum strings in an array of strings.

```
public static String minmax(String[] strArr)
```

The method returns a string in the format minStr-maxStr. For instance, the following call to minmax() returns the string "blue-yellow"

```
String[] colorList = {"red", "blue", "green", "yellow"};
String result = minmax(colorList);
```

10. Declare the enum

```
enum TrafficLight {green, yellow, red};
```

Using an enhanced for loop and a switch statement, sequence through the TrafficLight values and output the color of the light along with a message associated with each color. The messages are as follows:

green   –   "go"
yellow   –   "caution"
red   –   "stop"

Programming Project

11. The String class defines methods that search for a character or a pattern in a string and extract substrings. The following is a brief description of some of the methods.

```
int indexOf(int ch)
```

Returns the index within this string of the first occurrence of the specified character.

```
int lastIndexOf(int ch)
```

Returns the index within this string of the last occurrence of the specified character.

```
String substring(int beginIndex, int endIndex):
```

Returns a new string that is a substring of this string. The substring begins at the specified beginIndex and extends to the character at index endIndex − 1.

```
String substring(int beginIndex):
```

Returns a new string that is a substring of this string. The substring begins with the character at the specified index and extends to the end of this string.

Write a program that analyzes file names. A file can be specified by a *pathname* that contains a collection of names distinguished by the separator "/." The sequence of names prior to the last "/" is called the *path*. The last name is the *filename* and can have an *extension*.

Pathname	/class/programs/testfile.java
Path	/class/programs
Filename	`testfile.java`
Classname	testfile.class

The program should create an array of strings specifying the full pathname of a file. For each string, output the path and the filename. If the filename has the extension *java* create a class file name that replaces the extension with "class." Output the class name. Include in the array the following full path names.

/class/programs/testfile
programs/strings/filedemo.java
/program.java

Chapter 2

CLASS RELATIONSHIPS

CONTENTS

2.1 WRAPPER CLASSES
Comparing Integer Objects
Static Wrapper Class Members
Character Handling

2.2 AUTOBOXING AND
AUTO-UNBOXING

2.3 OBJECT COMPOSITION
The TimeCard Class
Implementing the TimeCard Class
UML for the TimeCard Class

2.4 INHERITANCE IN JAVA
An Employee Hierarchy
Visibility for Members in an
Inheritance Hierarchy
The Employee Class Declaration
The SalaryEmployee Subclass
Keyword Super in an Inheritance
Hierarchy
The HourlyEmployee Subclass

2.5 POLYMORPHISM
Upcasting and Downcasting

2.6 ABSTRACT CLASSES

2.7 HANDLING RUNTIME ERRORS
The Throw Statement
Handling an Exception—Try/Catch
Blocks
Finally Clause
Exception Propagation
Java Exception Hierarchy
Standard Exceptions

2.8 INPUT AND OUTPUT
Console I/O
File I/O
Text Input with Reader Streams
Parsing an Input String
Text Output with Writer Streams
Controlling the Output Stream

2.9 THE SCANNER CLASS
Declaring a Scanner Object
Reading from the Input Stream
File Input
Scanner Class API
Application: Using the Scanner

In Chapter 1, we introduced a class as an object type with data and methods that describe the attributes and behaviors of its objects. In this chapter, we explore object-oriented techniques that relate classes with one another and with primitive types. Our study begins with the design and use of wrapper classes that convert primitive data to objects. The classes are particularly useful since our data structure collections store only objects. Conversion between primitive data values and their corresponding wrapper class objects is burdensome and adds unwanted clutter to a program listing. Java provides automatic conversion. The mechanism involves *autoboxing* that converts a primitive type to the wrapper type and *auto-unboxing* that converts a wrapper type to a corresponding primitive type.

We can create a class from other classes using composition and inheritance. With composition, a class, called the *client*, has an object reference variable. The object type for the variable is called a *supplier class* because it provides methods that can be used to implement the client class methods. With inheritance, the definition of one class is based on another class that already exists. The existing class, called a *superclass*, provides data and methods that are inherited by the new class. Typically, inheritance creates a hierarchy with many derived or *subclasses* that share the resources of the superclass. Inheritance is a fundamental object design construct in Java programming. Both composition and inheritance promote code reuse, which uses existing software to implement new methods and algorithms.

In an inheritance hierarchy, we often define methods in the superclass and then override them in the subclasses. This enables us to use *polymorphism*, which directs the runtime system to select among versions of the methods in the subclasses. An *abstract class* is an inheritance-related concept that defines methods exclusively for polymorphism.

In designing a class, some methods have *preconditions* that must be satisfied in order for the operation to execute successfully. When a program notes that a precondition fails, it should employ some error handling strategy. For this purpose, Java uses a variety of exceptions, which are objects in an inheritance hierarchy.

Java input and output (I/O) uses stream objects to handle the flow of data from a source or to a destination. Streams handle both binary and character data. An input stream carries data from physical devices such as a keyboard, file, or network server. An output stream sends data to a physical device such as a console, file, or printer. In this chapter, we introduce text I/O where the data is characters. In Chapter 23, we will extend our discussion to byte streams that are used, among other things, for data encryption. Java provides the `Scanner` class for character input. The scanner partitions character input into tokens and uses methods to convert the tokens into strings and primitive values. The class is introduced in Section 2.9 and will be used throughout the book for examples, programs, and exercises.

2.1   Wrapper Classes

Java treats primitive types and class types in quite different ways. For instance, a primitive variable is a name for a memory location that stores the value. An object variable is a reference to a separate block of memory that contains the object. These differences affect how arguments are passed to a method or how the assignment operator behaves. Other differences are noteworthy. Primitive data is used in expressions with language-defined arithmetic and logical operators. Objects can be equipped with a variety of user-defined operations that enhance their use in an application.

Java designates classes that enable us to convert a value of primitive type to an object of the corresponding type. The classes, called *wrapper classes*, store a primitive value in an instance variable and supply methods to access and display the value.

> A wrapper class stores a primitive value in an instance variable.

The Java development system defines a wrapper class for each of its primitive types. In the *java.lang* package, you will find the classes `Integer`, `Double`, `boolean`, and so on. Figure 2.1 illustrates the relationship between the primitive type and the corresponding

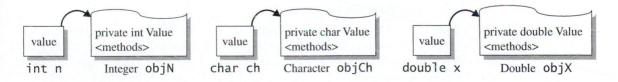

Figure 2.1 *Wrapper classes integer, character, and double whose objects hold a value of primitive type.*

wrapper class. In each case, the wrapper class has an instance variable of primitive type that stores (wraps) the value.

The figure reinforces why these are called "wrapper" classes. For instance, the Integer object *objN* and the primitive *int* variable *n* share the same value. But *objN* is an object with supporting operations to access and display the value.

Let us look at the Integer class. Its design is a model for all wrapper classes. You create an Integer object with a constructor that takes an *int* or string argument. For instance, the two forms of the constructor create objects *intObjA* and *intObjB* that contain integer values 25 and −345 respectively.

```
Integer intObjA = new Integer(25);      // argument is an int
Integer intObjB = new Integer("-345");  // argument is a string
```

Each wrapper class has a method for extracting (unwrapping) the stored value and returning it as a primitive value. For the Integer class, the method is intValue().

```
int n = intObjA.intValue()            // n is 25; the stored value
```

Comparing Integer Objects

Compare Integer objects using the methods equals() and compareTo().

We compare primitive values using the relational operators "<", "==", ">=", and so forth. The instance methods equals() and compareTo() perform the same tasks for wrapper class objects. You are familiar with these methods from the String class.

The Integer class equals() method takes an Integer argument and returns a boolean value that is true when the values of the object and the argument are equal. The more general compareTo() method takes an Integer argument and returns an *int* value that is negative, zero, or positive. These categories indicate a relative ordering among two Integer objects. A negative return value indicates that the object has a value that is less than the value of the argument. Put simply, the object is less than the argument. A positive return value indicates that the object is greater than the argument. A zero is returned when the two objects have the same value.

Example: Compare Integer objects objA and objB.

```
Integer objA = new Integer(35), objB = new Integer(50);
```

Expression:

```
int t = objA.compareTo(objB);              // t < 0 since 35 < 50
boolean b = objB.equals(new Integer("35")); // b is true

// assign to objMax the larger of the two Integer objects

Integer objMin = (objA.compareTo(objB) > 0) ? objA : objB;
```

Static Wrapper Class Members

The Integer class defines the static constants MIN_VALUE and MAX_VALUE, which represent the smallest and largest integer values respectively. The constants define the range of 32-bit integers from −2147483648 to 2147483647. Similar constants are available for values of type double.

```
Integer.MIN_VALUE  and Integer.MAX_VALUE. // extreme int values
```

The numeric wrapper classes Integer and Double have static methods that convert a numeric string to a corresponding primitive value. In the Integer class, the method is parseInt(intStr); in the Double class, the method is parseDouble(doubleStr).

```
int n = Integer.parseInt("356");        // int n has value 356

double x = Double.parseDouble("14.59");  // x has value 14.59
```

In Integer, the static method parseInt() converts a string to an *int*. Double has the static method parseDouble().

Conversion from an *int* to a string is provided by two versions of the static `toString()` method. The simple version takes an integer argument and returns an equivalent decimal string. A second version has an additional argument specifying a number base. The return string represents the number in the specified base. For instance, `toString(n, 2)` is the binary representation of *n*.

Example: For *int n = 45*, we use the static toString() method to output the value as a decimal number and as a binary (base-2) number.

```
// use toString(n) to display 45 as a decimal integer
System.out.println("45 base-10 is " + Integer.toString(n));

// use toString(n,2) to display 45 as a binary (base-2) integer
System.out.println("45 base-2 is " + Integer.toString(n, 2));
```

```
Output:
   45 base-10 is 45
   45 base-2 is 101101
```

Character Handling

`Character` is the wrapper class for the primitive type *char*. It has important static methods, which are used in string parsing algorithms. A series of boolean methods test whether a character has a special classification. For instance, they determine whether a character is a digit ('0'–'9'), a letter ('A'–'Z', 'a'–'z'), whitespace, and so on. Other methods test and convert characters among lowercase and uppercase. The following is a partial listing of the static methods in the Character class.

Classifying a character:

```
public static boolean isLetter(char ch);
public static boolean isDigit(char ch);
public static boolean isWhitespace(char ch);
```

Testing and modifying the case of a character:

```
public static boolean isUpperCase(char ch);
public static boolean isLowerCase(char ch);

public static char toUpperCase(char ch);
public static char toLowerCase(char ch);
```

Example 2.1

1. ```
Character.isUppercase('d')   returns false
Character.toUppercase('d')   returns 'D'
Character.toLowercase('d')   returns 'd'
```

2. The method `cleanString()` strips out all nonletters from a string argument and returns a string with the letters but in uppercase.

   *cleanString():*

   ```
   public static String cleanString(String str)
   {
       String rtnStr = "";
       for (int i = 0; i < str.length(); i++)
           if (Character.isLetter (str.charAt(i)))
               rtnStr += Character.toUpperCase(str.charAt(i));
           return rtnStr;
   }
   ```

   Check:

   ```
   String testStr = "9 atm5 2B!";
   System.out.println("Clean uppercase string is " +
       cleanString(testStr));
   ```

   > Output:
   >   Clean uppercase string is ATMB

2.2   Autoboxing and Auto-Unboxing

The Java wrapper classes associate a primitive value with a corresponding object. As we noted in Section 2.1, conversion between the two types of data is burdensome and adds unwanted clutter to a program listing. Java provides automatic conversion from a primitive type to its associated wrapper type and vice versa. The mechanism involves *autoboxing* that converts a primitive type to the wrapper type and *auto-unboxing* that converts a wrapper type to a corresponding primitive type.

Autoboxing may be used with assignment conversion and with wrapper class method conversion. If *n* is a value of type *int*, then boxing converts *n* to an `Integer` object *objN* such that objN.intValue() is *n*.

Java provides automatic conversion from a primitive type to its associated wrapper type.

Auto-unboxing may be used with assignment conversion, wrapper class methods, and expressions: If objX is an object of type *Double*, then unboxing converts it to the *double* value *x* such that objX.doubleValue() is *x*.

Example:

```
int m = 20, n;
Integer objM = new Integer(10), objN;
```
```

Assignment conversion:

```
objN = m;           // box m to an Integer object; assign to objN
n = objM;           // unbox objM to an int; assign to n
```

Expressions:

```
n = objM + 5;       // unbox objM before using integer addition
objM++;             // unbox objM, increment value, and rebox
objN += 5;          // unbox objN, add 5, and rebox
```

Comparisons: Autoboxing makes necessary conversions that allow a programmer to use the relational operators $<$, $==$, and $>$ as an alternative to the compareTo() method. The boolean expressions objM < 6, = =, objN and objM.compareTo(objN) < 0 are equivalent.

Autoboxing simplifies the initialization of wrapper class arrays and updates for their values. For instance, we create an Integer array with an initialization list consisting of primitive *int* values. A second example creates a Character array and uses autoboxing to load the elements with characters in a string. Do not get confused by the process. The array is a list of Character objects with primitive *char* values.

```
// array of 7 Integer objects with values from the
// initialization list
Integer[] intArr = {8, 3, 14, 7, 2, 12, 10};

// array of Character objects with chars from string "wrapper"
String str = "wrapper";
Character[] chArr = new Character[str.length()];
for (int i = 0; i < str.length(); i++)
   ChArr[i] = str.charAt(i);
```

Example 2.2

The method range() takes an Integer array and returns an *int* that specifies the range of values. The code is a hodgepodge of autoboxing and auto-unboxing conversions and is not good style. A scan of the elements assigns to the Integer object *maxValue* and the primitive variable *minValue* the largest and smallest value in the array respectively. After displaying these values, a return statement computes the range, which is the difference of the values plus 1.

```
Integer[] intArr = {8, 3, 14, 7, 2, 12, 10};
System.out.println("Range for the array is " + range(intArr));

public static int range(Integer[] arr)
{
   Integer maxValue = arr[0];
   int minValue = arr[0];

   for (int i = 1; i < arr.length; i++)
   {
      // use both < and compareTo() for minValue and maxValue
      if (arr[i] < minValue)
         minValue = arr[i];
```

```
                    if (arr[i].compareTo(maxValue) > 0)
                        maxValue = arr[i];
                }

                // output the extreme values
                System.out.println("Max value = " + maxValue +
                                    " Min value = " + minValue);

                return maxValue - minValue + 1;
            }
```

```
Output:
    Max value = 14   Min value = 2
    Range for the array is 13
```

2.3   Object Composition

In a class, instance variables can include a variety of data types. In some cases, the instances are primitive variables; in other cases, they are reference variables. A class whose data include one or more objects makes use of *object composition*. The term *composition* indicates that a class is composed of simpler components in a "part–whole" relationship. A *has-a* relationship is an equivalent way of describing part–whole composition.

In a class design, object composition is an implementation feature that promotes *code reuse*. Rather than building a class with primitive variables, a programmer can use object variables that provide their own methods, which become available to implement class methods. In the language of object composition, a class that is included by composition is called a *supplier class*. The class that includes the object is the *client class*.

The TimeCard Class

The client class has one or more supplier class objects as variables.

Object composition is best understood with an example. Assume a construction company hires temporary workers when it gets behind schedule on a job. The company uses `TimeCard` objects to pay a worker for a day's labor. The data for the `TimeCard` class includes a `String` variable for the Social Security Number and the variable *payrate* of type *double* specifying the hourly pay rate. Two `Time24` variables *punchInTime* and *punchOutTime* are included by composition. They specify when the worker begins and ends work. In the language of object composition, `String` and `Time24` are supplier classes. `TimeCard` is the client class.

```
private String workerID;
private double payrate;
private Time24 punchInTime, punchOutTime;
```

`TimeCard` is a simple class that illustrates all of the key features of object composition. A constructor initializes the instance variables *workerID*, *payrate*, and *punchInTime*. Arguments that specify when a worker quits for the day are passed to the `payWorker()` method. The operation sets the time for the instance variable *punchOutTime* and returns a string with payroll information. The following declaration creates a `TimeCard` object where the *workerID* is "598-81-2936," the *payrate* is $15.00, and work begins at 8:30.

The worker quits at 16:30 (4:30 P.M.). An output statement displays payroll information by calling payWorker() with arguments 16 and 30.

```
TimeCard workerTC = new TimeCard("598-81-2936", 15.00, 8, 30);

System.out.println(workerTC.payWorker(16,30);
```

The figure lists the fields in the *workTC* object. The output illustrates the format for listing worker payroll information.

598-81-2936	15.00	8:30	16:30
workerID	payrate	punchInTime	punchOutTime

```
Output:
    Worker:        598-81-2936
    Start time:   8:30   End time: 16:30
    Total time:   8.00 hours
    At $15.00 per hour, pay is $120.00
```

Implementing the TimeCard Class

A client class constructor initializes its instance variables, including supplier class reference variables. For the reference variables, this involves creating objects using the operator new and supplier class constructors. The client class constructor must provide arguments for each supplier class nondefault constructor. Let us see how this fact applies in the TimeCard class.

The TimeCard class constructor initializes the instance variables *workerID*, *payrate*, *punchInTime*, and *punchOutTime*. The parameter list for the constructor must include a String for *workerID* and a real number for *payrate*. To initialize *punchInTime*, call the Time24 constructor with integer arguments that specify the hour and minute when the worker first begins work. Add the parameters *punchInHour* and *punchInMinute* in the parameter list for the TimeCard constructor. The value for *punchOutTime* is not known when an object is created, and so the TimeCard constructor can use the Time24 default constructor, which creates an object with time 0:00.

> When using object composition, the client class constructor must initialize the supplier class objects.

TimeCard constructor:

```
    public TimeCard(String workerID, double payrate,
                        int punchInHour, int punchInMinute)
    {
        // initialize workerID and payrate
        this.workerID = workerID;
        this.payrate = payrate;

        // create object by calling constructor Time24(hour,minute)
        punchInTime = new Time24(punchInHour, punchInMinute);

        // create object by calling default constructor Time24()
        punchOutTime = new Time24();
    }
```

The method `payWorker()` has two integer arguments that specify the hour and minute when the worker finishes for the day. Its implementation employs code reuse by calling methods `setTime()`, `interval()`, and `toString()` in the `Time24` supplier class. A call to `setTime()` uses the arguments to update punchOutTime. The method `interval()` returns the length of the work day. The wages are computed by converting this length to a fractional number of hours and multiplying by the hourly pay rate. The `payWorker()` method returns a string that summarizes payroll information.

payWorker():

```
public String payWorker(int punchOutHour, int punchOutMinute)
{
    // local variables for time worked and hours worked
    Time24 timeWorked;
    double hoursWorked;           // timeWorked converted to hours

    // numeric format object for hours worked and pay
    DecimalFormat fmt = new DecimalFormat("0.00");

    // update punchOutTime by calling setTime()
    punchOutTime.setTime(punchOutHour, punchOutMinute);

    // evaluate time worked with Time24 interval() method
    timeWorked = punchInTime.interval(punchOutTime);

    // hoursWorked is timeWorked as fractional part of an hour
    hoursWorked = timeWorked.getHour() +
                        timeWorked.getMinute()/60.0;

    // return  formatted string
    return "Worker:        " + workerID + "\n" +
            "Start time:  " + punchInTime + "  End time: " +
                        punchOutTime + "\n" +
            "Total time:  " + fmt.format(hoursWorked) +
                        " hours" + "\n" +
            "At $" + fmt.format(payrate) + " per hour, pay is $"
                        + fmt.format(payrate*hoursWorked);
}
```

UML displays object composition with a diamond-tipped line from the client to the supplier class.

UML for the TimeCard Class

A UML diagram graphically illustrates the relationship of a client class to its supplier classes. Figure 2.2 provides a UML diagram for the `TimeCard` class. An object included by

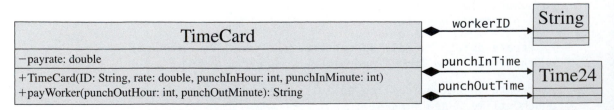

Figure 2.2 *UML for the TimeCard class.*

composition is represented by a line that connects the client class (`TimeCard`) to the supplier classes (`String` and `Time24`). The link is annotated by the name of the corresponding variable in the client class.

2.4   Inheritance in Java

Object composition defines one type of relationship among classes. A client class has one or more instance variables that are supplier class objects. As a result, we call object composition the "has-a" relationship. *Inheritance* is another type of relationship. It involves sharing of attributes and operations among classes. A *superclass* defines a set of common attributes and operations, which it shares with subclasses. A *subclass* extends the resources provided by the superclass by adding its own data and methods. For instance, the class Insurance is a superclass and the classes CarInsurance and LifeInsurance are subclasses. The Insurance superclass has attributes that include the policy number, policyholder, and annual fee. The CarInsurance class has additional attributes that specify liability coverage, medical payments, and accident-related deductibles. In a similar way, the LifeInsurance class includes attributes for the amount of coverage, beneficiaries, and so forth.

Object composition reflects the "has-a" relationship.

A CarInsurance object has access to the attributes and operations in the Insurance superclass. These are resources shared by all subclass objects. It has operations that handle the specific car-related attributes. In effect, the CarInsurance object is a grouping of attributes and operations that include policy number, annual fee, liability coverage, and so forth. The same holds for LifeInsurance objects.

A treelike structure represents inheritance relationships among classes. A superclass exists as a class in the tree with subclasses positioned at a lower level in the hierarchy. A subclass can be a superclass relative to subclasses that reside at yet lower levels in the tree. For instance, WholeLifeInsurance and TermLifeInsurance are subclasses of LifeInsurance with new attributes that specify the length of the policy, changes in benefits, and so on. Figure 2.3 displays the Insurance inheritance hierarchy. An arrow highlights the fact that the subclass has access to the information stored in the superclass. Inheritance is often called the *is-a* relationship. The reason is evident in the fact that a CarInsurance policy is

The insurance hierarchy portrays an "is-a" relationship where a subclass has access to methods and data in a superclass.

A tree structure displays the classes in an inheritance hierarchy.

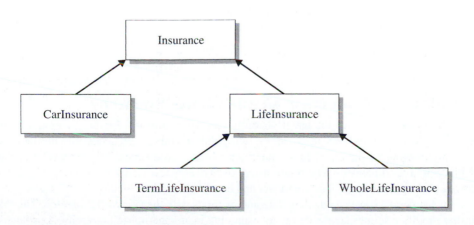

Figure 2.3 *Hierarchy tree describing inheritance relations among insurance policies.*

an Insurance policy and a TermLifeInsurance policy is a LifeInsurance policy. Relationships are valid over multiple levels such as "a WholeLifeInsurance policy is an Insurance policy."

An Employee Hierarchy

The Employee class holds the name and SSN for a worker. SalaryEmployee and Hourly Employee are subclasses that add salary information. An object of one of these classes is *an* Employee.

Describing employees in a company provides a classical example of inheritance. We keep the details simple so as to focus on the syntax used to describe and implement classes in a Java inheritance hierarchy. The example is the basis for our later discussion of polymorphism and abstract classes. The company employs both salaried workers and hourly workers. All of the workers share the fact that they are employees, which involves attributes such as name and Social Security number. These attributes, along with access and update methods, describe the superclass Employee. Company workers differ in their status and in the criteria that define how they are paid. The employee hierarchy defines two subclasses SalaryEmployee and HourlyEmployee that have additional attributes and operations, which the accounting office uses to produce payroll checks. A salaried employee is paid an annual salary broken out into pay periods. An hourly employee is paid on the basis of the number of hours worked and the hourly pay rate. Figure 2.4 illustrates the employee inheritance hierarchy.

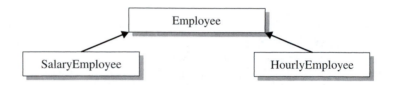

Figure 2.4 *Employee inheritance hierarchy.*

Declare the Employee superclass as a standalone Java class. The declaration of subclasses SalaryEmployee and HourlyEmployee includes the reserved word *extends* in the class header. This indicates that the class is derived from (inherits from) the class Employee.

```
// declaration of the superclass Employee
public class Employee
{ . . . }

// declaration of subclass SalaryEmployee
public class SalaryEmployee extends Employee

// declaration of subclass HourlyEmployee
public class HourlyEmployee extends Employee
```

Visibility for Members in an Inheritance Hierarchy

Superclass members have the usual visibility (scope) conditions. Private members in the class are accessible only by its methods, and public members are accessible by the class and any instance of the class. In an inheritance hierarchy, a superclass has a relationship with each of its subclasses. The relationship gives rise to new visibility criteria, called *protected*, that apply to superclass members and extend to subclass methods.

In a superclass, we can declare data and methods with the keyword *protected*. The visibility modifier defines access that is relevant only in an inheritance hierarchy. A protected member can be accessed by any superclass or a subclass method. Access to a protected member serves as an intermediate level of access between public and private.

Figure 2.5 provides a graphical view of access to members in an inheritance hierarchy. The arrows on the left specify the access of methods in the subclass to members of the superclass. The right side of the diagram illustrates the access provided to a superclass object and to a subclass object. They can access only public methods within their scope of definition. For the subclass object, the public methods in the superclass are within its scope of definition.

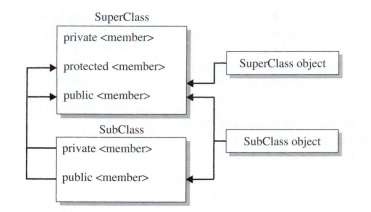

Private members of a superclass are available only to superclass methods. Public members are available to any program component. Protected members are available only to the superclass and subclasses.

Figure 2.5 *Scope rules for public, private, and protected access to superclass and subclass members and objects.*

In the Employee superclass, the variables are the instance variables *empName* and *empSSN*. They are declared as strings with protected access and define the fields used by the personnel office when setting up a new employee record. By using protected access, subclasses such as SalaryEmployee and HourlyEmployee have direct access to the variables.

Employee Instance Variables:

```
protected String empName;
protected String empSSN;
```

The Employee Class Declaration

The Employee class has a constructor with two string parameters to initialize the name and Social Security number. The mutator method setName() allows a program to update the object if the employee changes his or her name. To display employee information, the method toString() returns a string with labels that identify the name and Social Security number. The format of the string is

```
Name:        <empName>
SSN:         <empSSN>
```

The class also contains the public method payrollCheck(), which returns a string. You will, no doubt, question why the Employee class should have a method that more appropriately belongs in a subclass where actual payroll information is available. Having the payrollCheck() method in the superclass will become clear when we introduce the concept of polymorphism. For now, we provide a seemingly meaningless implementation by simply returning an empty string.

Employee class:

```
class Employee
{
    // instance variables are accessible by subclass methods
    protected String empName;
    protected String empSSN;

    // create an object with initial values empName and empSSN
    public Employee(String empName, String empSSN)
    {
        this.empName = empName;
        this.empSSN = empSSN;
    }

    // update the employee name
    public void setName(String empName)
    { this.empName = empName; }

    // returns a string to display employee information
    public String toString()
    { return "Name:     " + empName + '\n' + "SS#:      " +
        empSSN; }

    // method is declared in this class for polymorphism
    public String payrollCheck()
    { return ""; }
}
```

The SalaryEmployee Subclass

The `SalaryEmployee` class extends the `Employee` class by adding salary information. The private instance variable, *salary*, of type *double* specifies an amount for a pay period. A resulting `SalaryEmployee` object consists of three data fields: the name, Social Security number, and salary. You can view the object as having two parts, the superclass portion and the subclass portion. The superclass portion consists of data in the superclass and the subclass portion consists of data in the subclass.

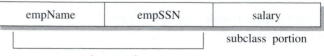

A subclass constructor must include arguments to initialize both the superclass portion and the subclass portion of an object. The SalaryEmployee constructor has `String` arguments for the name and Social Security number attributes in the `Employee` superclass. A third argument provides the salary for a pay period. The class has methods `getSalary()` and `setSalary()` that access and update the salary. The `SalaryEmployee` class defines

The Salary-Employee class extends Employee and adds a salary instance variable along with methods that access the salary.

the method `toString()`, which returns a string with the worker's name and Social Security number along with a status designation "Salaried" and the salary amount. The format for `toString()` is

```
Name:    <empName>
SS#:     <empSSN>
Status: Salaried
Salary: $<salary>
```

We first discovered the method `payrollCheck()` in the `Employee` superclass. In this subclass, the same method is defined but with an implementation that uses the salary value. The superclass method is overridden in the subclass and returns a string that also includes the employee's name and Social Security number. The form of the check is

```
Pay <empName> (<empSSN>) $<salary>
```

The following is an API description of the `SalaryEmployee` class. You can find a listing of the entire employee inheritance hierarchy in Chapter 2 of the software supplement.

class SalaryEmployee extends Employee	
Constructor	
`SalaryEmployee(String empName, String empSSN, double salary)` Creates an object with arguments empName and empSSN initializing the superclass portion of the object.	
Methods	
double	`getSalary()` Returns the salary paid to the employee during each pay period.
String	`payrollCheck()` Returns a string that describes a paycheck. The format includes the employee name, Social Security number, and salary.
void	`setSalary(double salary)` Assigns the specified argument as the new salary.
String	`toString()` Returns a string that describes the object. The format includes the name, Social Security number, status ("salaried"), and the salary.

Keyword Super in an Inheritance Hierarchy

In a Java inheritance hierarchy, a subclass uses the reserved word *super* to access superclass members. This is a key feature in the implementation of a subclass constructor, which reduces to a two-step process. First, take the arguments in the parameter list that are associated with the superclass variables and call the method `super()` to execute a superclass constructor. This must be the first statement in the implementation and is the only way to execute a superclass constructor. The effect is to initialize the superclass portion of the object. Then take the other arguments in the parameter list and initialize the subclass variables. For the `SalaryEmployee` class, the method `super(empName, empSSN)` calls the `Employee` constructor to initialize the superclass variables.

Use super(args) to call the superclass constructor. This must be the first statement. Then initialize subclass variables.

SalaryEmployee constructor:

```
public SalaryEmployee(String empName, String empSSN,
                          double salary)
{
    // call the Employee superclass constructor
    super(empName, empSSN);
    this.salary = salary;
}
```

For methods with the same name in the subclass and superclass, call the superclass method with super.<method>.

Within an inheritance hierarchy, the implementation of a subclass method may access a superclass method with the same signature by using the reserved word *super* followed by the dot (.) operator and the method name. The modifier "super." distinguishes the superclass method from the one which is overridden in the subclass. The `SalaryEmployee` class uses this feature to implement its version of `toString()`. The first two lines of the return string is general employee information, which is provided by the `Employee` method `super.toString()`. The rest of the return string is the employee status "Salaried" and the salary.

SalaryEmployee toString():

```
public String toString()
{
    DecimalFormat fmt = new DecimalFormat("#.00");
    return super.toString() + '\n' +
           "Status:    Salary" + '\n' +
           "Salary:    $" + fmt.format(salary);
}
```

The HourlyEmployee Subclass

HourlyEmployee class extends Employee with information on hourly pay rate and hours worked.

The design of the `HourlyEmployee` class resembles the `SalaryEmployee` class. For salary information, the class declares private instance variables *hourlyPay* and *hoursWorked* of type *double*. The methods `getHourlyPay()` and `setHourlyPay()` together with `getHoursWorked()` and `setHoursWorked()` enable the accounting office to adjust the hourly rate and the work schedule for the employee. The methods `toString()` and `payrollCheck()` play roles similar to those in the `SalaryEmployee` class. The format for `toString()` is

```
Name:       <empName>
SS#:        <empSSN>
Status:     Hourly
Rate:       $<hourlyPay> per hour
Hours:      <hoursWorked>
```

Consult the software supplement for a listing of the class declaration. Figure 2.6 shows a UML diagram for the `Employee` superclass and its subclasses. Note that the symbol "#" before an instance variable in the `Employee` class indicates that it has protected visibility, and that an arrow from the subclass to the superclass indicates the inheritance relation.

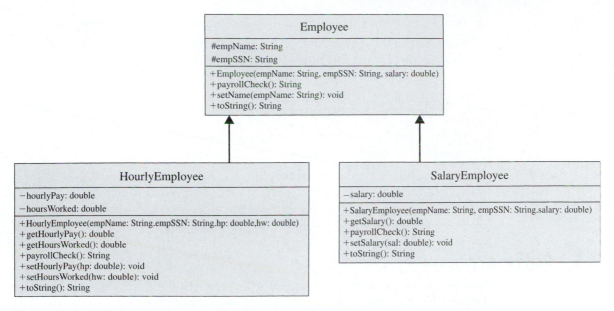

Figure 2.6 *UML for the employee hierarchy.*

Example 2.3

The example illustrates how to create and use both `SalaryEmployee` and `HourlyEmployee` objects.

1. Declare subclass employees and output their information using toString()

```
HourlyEmployee hEmp = new HourlyEmployee("Howard, Steve",
                                "896-54-3217",10.50,40);
SalaryEmployee sEmp = new SalaryEmployee("Dunn, Moira",
                                "456-14-3787",800.0);

System.out.println(hEmp);
System.out.println(sEmp);
```

```
Output:
    Name:       Howard, Steve
    SS#:        896-54-3217
    Status:     Hourly
    Rate:       $10.50
    Hours:      40.00
    Name:       Dunn, Moira
    SS#:        456-14-3787
    Status:     Salary
    Salary:     $800.00
```

2. Provide a paycheck for Steve Howard

```
System.out.println(hEmp.payrollCheck());
```

```
Output:
    Pay Howard, Steve (896-54-3217)  $420.00
```

3. Give Moira Dunn a 10% salary increase and output the new information

```
sEmp.setSalary(sEmp.getSalary() * 1.10);
System.out.println("Moira Dunn's new salary " +
    "information\n" + sEmp);
```

```
Output:
   Moira Dunn's new salary information
   Name:      Dunn, Moira
   SS#:       456-14-3787
   Status:    Salary
   Salary:    $880.00
```

2.5   Polymorphism

In an inheritance hierarchy, a program can assign any subclass object to a superclass reference variable. The assignment sets the superclass reference to point at the subclass object. For instance, the assignment *emp = sEmp* sets the Employee variable to point at the SalaryEmployee object Mike Morris (Figure 2.7).

```
Employee emp;
SalaryEmployee sEmp("Morris, Mike", "569-34-0382", 1250.00);

emp = sEmp;   // assign subclass object a superclass reference
```

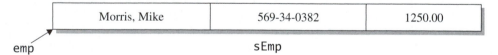

Figure 2.7 *Employee variable emp references the SalaryEmployee object sEmp.*

Assigning a subclass object to a superclass variable influences the scope and action of method calls associated with the superclass reference. The variable may be used to call any public method that is defined only in the superclass. The variable, however, may not be used to call a method that is defined only in the subclass. For instance, the Employee reference variable *emp* may be used with setName() to change the name of the SalaryEmployee *sEmp*. The variable may not be used with setSalary(), which is a method defined only in the SalaryEmployee class. The method is not accessible by *emp*.

```
// invalid! setSalary() not in scope of an Employee reference
emp.setSalary(1500.00);
```

```
// valid!  uses reference emp to call an Employee method which
// changes the employee name from Mike to Michael
emp.setName("Morris, Michael");
```

With static binding, a method call is associated with a particular class at compilation.

When the compiler parses the statements emp.setName() and sEmp.setSalary(), it identifies an association between the reference type of the variable and the method. In each case, the variable calls a public method in its corresponding class. The compiler uses a feature called *static binding* that associates the method with the class type of the reference variable. The term "static" implies that the compiler establishes an association prior to execution.

A different situation occurs when the superclass and a subclass have methods that share identical signatures. We say that the subclass method overrides the superclass method. In the employee hierarchy, the methods `toString()` and `payrollCheck()` are such examples. Calling this type of method with the superclass reference variable invokes polymorphism, and the runtime system executes the method in the subclass object. For instance,

```
// emp = sEmp sets emp to point at sEmp ("Michael Morris")
// the runtime system executes toString() and payrollCheck in the
// SalaryEmployee class
System.out.println(emp.toString());
System.out.println(emp.payrollCheck());
```

```
Output:
   Name:      Morris, Michael
   Social     Security Number:    569-34-0382
   Status:    Salary employee
   Payrate: $1250.00
   Pay Morris, Michael (569-34-0382) $1250.00
```

Polymorphism is a Greek word that means "many forms." In object-oriented programming, polymorphism occurs in an inheritance hierarchy when the superclass and one or more subclasses define methods with the same signature. The runtime system executes the subclass method under the following conditions:

- A subclass object is assigned to a superclass reference variable.
- The method call uses the superclass reference variable.

Rather than using static binding, which would associate the method with the superclass reference variable, the compiler directs the runtime system to determine the subclass type referenced by the variable and then calls the corresponding subclass method. This is called *dynamic binding* because the association between reference variable and method is established at runtime.

In the employee hierarchy, polymorphism occurs when an HourlyEmployee object is assigned to Employee reference variable *emp* and the runtime system executes the statement emp.payrollCheck(). The action is to execute the method in the HourlyEmployee class.

When dynamic binding is used to call a method, the runtime system determines the type of the object that is pointed to by the reference variable and calls the method for that object.

```
// declare a subclass object
HourlyEmployee hEmp = new HourlyEmployee("Holmes, Julie",
                                 "837-68-2198", 12.00, 30);

// assign subclass object hEmp to superclass reference variable
emp = hEmp;

// create a pay check using polymorphism
System.out.println(emp.payrollCheck());
```

```
Output:
   Pay Holmes, Julie (837-68-2198) $360.00
```

Example 2.4

The method `pay()` takes advantage of polymorphism to create payroll checks for all of the different company employees. The parameter list for the method includes a string that describes the range of dates for the pay period and an `Employee` superclass reference variable. A program can use `pay()` with any `SalaryEmployee` or an `HourlyEmployee` argument. The method copies the subclass object to the `Employee` reference parameter and uses polymorphism with `payrollCheck()` to determine the amount of pay. The runtime system executes the version of the `payrollCheck()` corresponding to the subclass type of the argument.

> The Employee argument *emp* actually references a SalaryEmployee or HourlyEmployee object.

pay():

```
public static void pay(String dateRange, Employee emp)
{
    System.out.println("Pay period: " + dateRange);
    System.out.println(emp.payrollCheck());
}
```

Declare a `SalaryEmployee` object and call `pay()` for the period "July 3 to July 9"

```
SalaryEmployee sEmp = new SalaryEmployee("Bonner, Al",
                                "667-21-7128", 1500.00);
pay("July 3 to July 9", sEmp);
```

```
Output:
    Pay period: July 3 to July 9
    Pay Bonner, Al (667-21-7128)   $1500.00
```

Upcasting and Downcasting

> Upcasting occurs when using a superclass variable to reference a subclass object.

A program can use a superclass variable to reference subclass objects. This occurs when a subclass object is assigned to a superclass reference. We refer to this process as *upcasting* because it associates an object at a lower (subclass) level in an inheritance hierarchy with a reference at a higher (superclass) level. The superclass reference variable may call any public method in the superclass and any public method in the subclass where polymorphism applies.

> Let *x* be a super-class reference to a subclass CL with method m() exclusively defined in CL. Downcast and execute m() as follows:
>   ((CL)x).m()

A superclass reference variable may not be used to call a method defined exclusively in a subclass. A programmer must use casting to explicitly change the reference type of the variable to that of the subclass. The syntax is similar to casting a primitive variable. Place the subclass name in parentheses immediately before the reference variable. We refer to the process as *downcasting*. For instance, the `Employee` reference variable *emp* may be used with the method `setSalary()`, provided we cast *emp* to a `SalaryEmployee` reference.

```
((SalaryEmployee)emp).setSalary(2400.00);
```

Casting-Dot Operator Precedence

Note

The casting operator has lower precedence than the "." (dot) operator. Downcasting a reference variable must use double parentheses so that the cast is associated with the variable.

```
// cast emp to be a SalaryEmployee reference variable
((SalaryEmployee)emp).setSalary(2400.00);
```

Without the parentheses, the cast is associated with the method and attempts to change its return type. In the example, the compiler would recognize that setSalary() has a void return type and, thus, flag an error.

The instanceof Operator   A superclass reference variable can be used to call subclass methods once downcasting changes its reference type. In a program, we need to deal with situations in which the subclass type is known only at runtime. The choice of a cast cannot be predefined but must be selected once the subclass type is identified. For instance, suppose an application defines a static method `payIncrease()` that gives an employee a specified percentage pay increase. The method uses an `Employee` reference variable as a parameter which allows the program to pass both `SalaryEmployee` and `HourlyEmployee` objects as arguments.

```
public void payIncrease(Employee emp, double pct)
{ . . . }
```

A problem surfaces in the implementation. The method must use the `Employee` reference *emp* and downcasting to access the appropriate subclass methods which update pay information. For a `SalaryEmployee` object, the appropriate methods are `getSalary()` and `setSalary()`; an `HourEmployee` object uses `getHourlyPay()` and `setHourlyPay()`. The choice depends on the actual subclass object referenced by *emp*. Java provides the operator *instanceof* for such a situation. The operator takes a reference variable as the left-hand operand and a class type as the right-hand operand and returns a boolean value that indicates whether the variable references an object of the class type.

If *x* is a reference and CL is a class, use instanceof to determine if *x* references CL. The programmer can use the operator to avoid illegal casts.

Syntax: `refVariable instanceof ClassType`
Returns true if refVariable references an object of type ClassType and false otherwise.

Example:

```
Time24 t = new Time24(9,30);
if (t instanceof Time24)      // condition is true
    . . .
```

The implementation of `payIncrease()` uses the `instanceof` operator with an if-statement to determine whether the `Employee` reference variable is passed a `SalaryEmployee` or an `HourlyEmployee` object. The choice indicates the cast for the variable *emp* and the choice of methods to update the pay.

payIncrease():

```
public static void payIncrease(Employee emp, double pct)
    {
        // use instanceof to determine the object type for emp
        // if SalaryEmployee, access and update salary
        if (emp instanceof SalaryEmployee)
```

```
                    ((SalaryEmployee)emp).setSalary((1.0 + pct) *
                    ((SalaryEmployee)emp).getSalary());
            else

                    // if HourlyEmployee, access and update hourly pay
                    ((HourlyEmployee)emp).setHourlyPay((1.0 + pct) *
                    ((HourlyEmployee)emp).getHourlyPay());
         }
```

2.6   Abstract Classes

The `Employee` class plays an interesting role in the inheritance hierarchy. Our declaration allows for instances of the class. An application could create an `Employee` object with a name and Social Security number. However, the object would not correspond to a real company employee who is either salaried or an hourly worker. Only subclass objects are real employees. So what is the purpose of the `Employee` class? It does provide data and methods, which are shared by subclass objects. It also declares the `payrollCheck()` method, which can be used with an `Employee` reference and polymorphism to execute the same method in a subclass.

In an abstract class, some methods are specified by signature only. These methods must be implemented in a subclass.

In the `Employee` class, `payrollCheck()` has a meaningless implementation. It returns an empty string. The implementation is given only to satisfy a requirement, namely, a method in a class must have a method body. Up to this point in the book, we have relied on the traditional form of a method body, which consists of a block of code that implements the method. Java allows a method body to be simply a semicolon, indicating the lack of an implementation. This form is used only by *abstract* and *native* methods. The term *native* implies that the method is implemented in another language, typically C. We are interested in abstract methods, which are relevant only in an inheritance hierarchy. The `payrollCheck()` method in the `Employee` class is best defined as an abstract method.

An abstract method is defined in a superclass with the modifier *abstract*. The method body is a semicolon and so the declaration becomes just a method signature terminated by a semicolon. A class containing an abstract method is an *abstract class*, and the modifier must be included in the class header.

Place the keyword abstract in the class header and before each abstract method signature.

```
abstract class ClassName
{
    // abstract class may contain data and concrete methods
    . . .

    // abstract class must contain at least one abstract method
    abstract public returnType methodName(<parameters>);
}
```

The presence of an abstract superclass affects the behavior of the inheritance hierarchy. Each subclass must override all of the abstract methods in the superclass, and a program cannot create an instance of the abstract class. An abstract class provides only resources for a subclass and method declarations that can be used with polymorphism. A subclass provides concrete realizations for methods that are defined abstract in the superclass. A subclass is the type for concrete (real) objects in an application.

Let us introduce an abstract method and class into the employee hierarchy. To avoid confusion, we define a new superclass, called *AbstractEmployee*, that has all of the concrete members in Employee as well as an abstract version of the payrollCheck() method.

If a class is abstract, the programmer cannot create instances of the class.

```
abstract class AbstractEmployee
{
    <concrete members in the Employee class>
    abstract public void payrollCheck();
}
```

New declarations of the SalaryEmployee and HourlyEmployee subclasses extend the abstract superclass AbstractEmployee.

```
class SalaryEmployee extends AbstractEmployee
{
    // class must override payrollCheck()
    public String payrollCheck()
    { . . . }
}
```

2.7   Handling Runtime Errors

A computer program executes instructions under the control of the runtime system. During execution, a serious problem may occur such as dividing by zero, attempting to access an invalid memory location, or linking a stream to a nonexistent file. The problem indicates an abnormal situation, and an alert, indicating an error, should be broadcast to the system. For this error processing, Java uses exceptions and an exception-handling mechanism. The mechanism involves a *throw statement* in the method where the error is identified and "try/catch" blocks that include code for ordinary execution of the method and for processing the exception.

The Throw Statement

An *exception* is an object that is created within a method at a point where an error condition occurs. The object is typically initialized with a string that includes diagnostic information identifying the method and the error. The exception object is created in a *throw statement* that passes the object back through a chain of method calls to a block of code designed to catch the exception. The code, called an *exception handler*, is responsible for displaying an error message with the diagnostic information and for either taking corrective action or terminating the program.

An exception object is thrown when an error occurs and is caught by an exception handler.

```
throw new ClassName_Exception (diagnosticErrorMsg);
```

As an example, consider the method average() that takes an array of real numbers as an argument and returns the average value. The method recognizes that an error condition occurs when the array is empty or null, in which case, it throws a predefined Java Illegal-ArgumentException. We will soon discover other predefined Java exception class names. The *throw clause* is in a simple if-statement that tests the preconditions. If an error is noted, the exception is thrown and an immediate exit from the method occurs.

average():

```
// throws IllegalArgumentException object with message
// "average(): invalid array"
public static double average(double[] arr)
{
    double sum = 0;

    // if array is null or length 0, throw exception and exit
    if (arr == null || arr.length == 0)
        throw new IllegalArgumentException(
            "average(): Invalid array");

    // preconditions satisfied; compute and return the average
    for (int i = 0; i < arr.length; i++)
        sum += arr[i];
    return sum/arr.length;
}
```

Handling an Exception—Try/Catch Blocks

Exception handling is done with try/catch statements. The try statement is a block of code that specifies normal execution of the algorithm. The block includes statements that may generate an exception. A *catch block,* which follows the *try block*, serves as the exception handler. It is defined with an exception parameter, which it uses to perform error handling tasks.

Place code that may cause an exception in a try block and follow with the exception handler in a catch block.

Try/Catch statements:

```
try
{
    <algorithm code>
}
catch (ClassName_Exception e)
{
    <display error message>
    < perform other tasks or exit the program>
}
```

Under normal circumstances, all of the statements in a try block execute successfully and processing continues after the catch block. However, if a statement in the try block results in an exception, an immediate exit from the block occurs and control passes to the catch block specified to handle the exception.

Let us illustrate exception handling with code in the main() method that calls average(). A declaration creates a 4-element array arrA and an array reference variable with value null. The try block includes two output statements that call average(). The first statement executes correctly and displays the result. The second statement passes a null argument which results in an exception. The catch block includes an Illegal-ArgumentException parameter, which passes the exception object as an argument. The catch block displays the error message.

```
public static void main(String[] args)
{
   // declare two array references;
   double[] arrA = {2.5, 5.0, 7.2, 8.1}, arrB = null;

   try
   {
      // arrA is valid and average() returns a value; arrB
      // is not valid (null) and average() throws an exception
      System.out.println("Average is " + average(arrA));
      System.out.println("Average is " + average(arrB));
   }
   catch (IllegalArgumentException e)
   {
      System.out.println(e);
      System.exit(1);                    // exit the program
   }
}
```

```
Output:
   Average is 5.7
   java.lang. IllegalArgumentException: Invalid array
```

Finally Clause

A try statement can have an optional *finally clause*. The finally clause defines a block of code that always executes, no matter whether the algorithm executed successfully or was short-circuited by an exception. Typically, a finally clause is used to manage system resources.

A finally clause is declared with the keyword *finally* and is placed after the try and catch blocks. In this way, instructions in the finally block will execute after any exception processing is complete. In Section 2.8, we use finally clauses to close input and output streams.

```
try
{  . . .   }
catch (ClassName_Exception e)
{ . . . }
finally
{   . . . }
```

Exception Propagation

The exception-handling mechanism involves significant overhead. It should not be used to discover simple logical errors that could be identified with good algorithm testing techniques. Exceptions are used when an error cannot be handled at the location where it occurs but must be handled in a prior method that included a statement that ultimately caused the exception. The exception-handling mechanism may involve a chain of method calls with the exception occurring at some distant point in the chain. For instance, in Figure 2.8, code in `main()` calls method `f()`, which in turn calls method `g()`, which throws an `Exception` object when an error occurs. Any exception that is thrown from `g()` propagates back through the chain of method calls until it locates a catch block that will handle the exception. In the figure, we assume that the try/catch blocks are in `main()`. They could just as well be in `f()`, assuming that the intermediate method is in a position to handle the error.

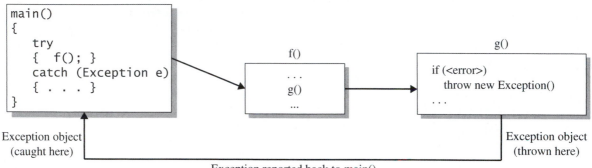

Figure 2.8 *Using a Java exception for an error in a chain of method calls.*

Java Exception Hierarchy

All exceptions are derived from the superclass Throwable.

Java uses an inheritance hierarchy, with *Throwable* as the superclass, to define an assortment of predefined exception classes (Figure 2.9). The subclasses *Error* and *Exception* define two main categories of exceptions. An `Error` is a subclass of Throwable that indicates a serious problem, which an application should not try to handle. An example is a `Virtual-MachineError`, which occurs when the Java Virtual Machine experiences a catastrophic failure. The class `Exception` and its subclasses are a form of `Throwable` that indicate conditions which an application might want to catch. The majority of `Exception` subclasses

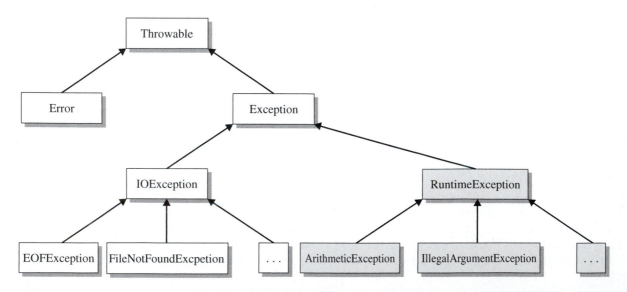

Figure 2.9 *Hierarchy tree for Java exceptions.*

define exceptions indicating permission errors, network connection errors, and so forth. An example is the *IOException* superclass whose subclasses indicate file-handling errors. Of special note is the *RuntimeException* subclass whose subclasses define basic programming exceptions such as divide-by-zero, illegal array index access, and invalid method arguments.

Subclasses of Exception can be caught and corrective action can be taken.

The majority of exceptions indicate that an error condition prevents further execution of the program and some action must be taken. For instance, an exception occurs when a program attempts to open a nonexistent file and further input is meaningless. These types of exceptions must be *checked*, that is, identified and processed. A code segment must handle the exception using a try/catch block or must explicitly pass the exception to a previous method call in the chain using the reserved word *throws*. Runtime exceptions are different. They result from common programming errors and may occur at almost any place in the code. To provide maximum flexibility, Java gives a programmer the option of handling any of the different types of runtime exceptions. A statement that may lead to a runtime exception can be included in a try block with ordinary exception handling. The same statement may be given with no reference to a possible exception, that is, without including it in a try block and without providing a catch block to handle the exception. We say that the exception is *unchecked*. If an error occurs, a runtime exception is thrown but is not caught until it propagates back to the runtime system, at which point the runtime system displays diagnostic information and terminates the program.

Subclasses of RuntimeException do not have to be caught. However, if not caught, they lead to program termination.

As an example, the following code segment includes two statements that use an index to access an array. The operations cause an `IndexOutOfBoundsException`. The first statement checks the exception by including it in try/catch blocks where the catch block simply displays the error message and allows execution to continue. The second statement leaves the exception unchecked. In this case, the runtime system provides very specific diagnostic information.

```java
int[] arr = new int[5];

// checked exception; IndexOutOfBoundsException is handled in
// the catch block
try
{
    arr[10] = 25; //
}
catch (IndexOutOfBoundsException e)
{
    // display message and continue
    System.out.println("In catch: " + e);
}

// the exception occurs outside a try/catch block and thus is
// handled by the runtime system
arr[15] = 30;
```

```
Output:
  In catch: java.lang.ArrayIndexOutOfBoundsException: 10
  Exception in thread "main" java.lang.ArrayIndexOutOfBounds
      Exception: 15
  at RuntimeExcTest.main(RuntimeExcTest.java:19)
```

☞

Note

> ## Throws Clause
>
> Suppose you have a method that can throw an exception, which is not a subclass of RuntimeException. For instance, the method may involve I/O operations that throw exceptions which are subclasses of IOException. The method must explicitly catch and dispose of the exceptions or must declare (acknowledge) that the exceptions can be thrown. The declaration is provided by a *throws* clause in the declaration of the method. Use the syntax
>
> ```
> ReturnType methodName(. . . ) throws IOException
> {
>     // method code may call I/O operation without try/catch blocks
>     . . .
> }
> ```

Standard Exceptions

In this book, our software uses a limited number of runtime exceptions that identify typical programming errors. Programs and examples leave the exceptions unchecked. A list of the key exceptions follows.

ArithmeticException
> Thrown when an exceptional arithmetic condition has occurred. For example, an integer "divide by zero" throws an instance of this class.

IllegalArgumentException
> Thrown to indicate that a method has been passed an illegal or inappropriate argument.

IndexOutOfBoundsException
> Thrown to indicate that an index of some sort (such as an array, a string, or an ArrayList) is out of range.

NullPointerException
> Thrown when an application attempts to use *null* in a case where an object is required.

UnsupportedOperationException
> Thrown to indicate that the requested operation is not supported.

2.8   Input and Output

In Java, files are accessed using streams.

Input and output (I/O) in Java uses stream objects. The term *stream* is chosen deliberately to conjure up the image of water flowing in a river. The I/O streams carry data. *Binary streams* have byte data that may represent a graphic or an executable file. *Text streams* have character data such as an HTML file or a Java source code file.

A stream object carries data from a source such as the keyboard, compact disk, or an Internet server, or carries data to a destination such as the monitor, hard disk, or a printer. If the data flows from a source into the program, the stream is called an *input stream*; if the data flows out of the program to a destination, it is called an *output stream* (Figure 2.10).

Streams throw an IOException when an error occurs.

Java defines the basic stream classes in the package *java.io*. Operations that involve creating and using streams throw a form of IOException, which must be checked. As a result,

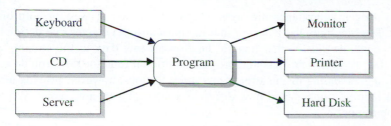

Figure 2.10 *Sources for input streams and destinations for output streams.*

these operations must be included in try block or in a method that defines a throws clause. The IOException superclass and its subclasses are also defined in *java.io*.

In this section, we develop the basic tools that Java uses for text input and output. Input relies on Reader class methods that extract a single character or a sequence of characters from the text stream. A typical approach uses a string tokenizer to partition the sequence into tokens and wrapper class parse methods to convert a token to a primitive value. This is the approach that is dictated by the Java tools in earlier software releases. A recent version of Java defines the Scanner class, which is a simple text scanner that can parse primitive types and strings using regular expressions.

Console I/O

Console I/O involves streams that allow a user to input data from the keyboard and display output in a console window. Three streams are predefined for console I/O: *System.in*, the standard input; *System.out*, the standard output; and *System.err*, the standard error. *System.in* is used to create *Reader* streams that input data from the keyboard. *System.out* and *System.err* are used to create *Writer* streams that output data to the console. We are already familiar with console output that uses these streams with methods print() and println() to display a string.

```
System.out.println("String displayed in the console window");
```

System.err provides a separate console output stream, which is used for immediate posting of an error message. A program may encounter an error or delays in writing to the standard output stream and needs a way to get the message out. The programmer simply uses a print statement with the standard error stream.

```
System.err.println("Posting an error message");
```

File I/O

A *file* is a collection of data that is stored in some medium such as a disk. The data is stored in binary format using sequences of zeros and ones. As such, you can say that every file is a binary file. However, in some cases, the format represents characters and the file can be viewed as a sequence of characters partitioned into lines with newline separators. These files are called *text files*, which can be viewed by an editor and read by a human being. The nontext files are properly called *binary files*. A program that embeds header/format information and uses a compression algorithm to store the data typically creates binary files. They are read by programs that can interpret their internal structures.

Classify files as text files and binary files.

Java uses an inheritance hierarchy to present stream classes for both binary and text I/O. The hierarchy has a design that includes abstract classes that define basic operations, concrete classes that handle the flow of raw data in the stream, and filter streams that transform the data and provide additional functionality. You do not need a detailed understanding of the stream hierarchy. It does, however, provide a backdrop that will help you understand how different stream objects are created and how they share operations.

In this chapter, we introduce console and file I/O for text data. In Chapter 23, we will discuss binary files, which are used for the Huffman compression algorithm. We assume that input files are stored in the same directory as the application program so that we can reference them using just the file name. Similarly, output files are created in the same directory. If you want more flexibility, use full path names for the files.

Text Input with Reader Streams

The FileReader class allows text input from a file.

Text input streams are derived from the abstract *Reader* class, which defines basic character extraction methods. Subclasses of `Reader` create stream objects that are attached to an underlying physical character stream. The *FileReader* subclass is an example. Its stream objects are attached to files on disk. A program that reads text from a file must first create a `FileReader` stream with a constructor that takes the file name as an argument. For instance, the following declaration creates the text input stream *dataIn*, which is attached to the physical file *testdata.dat* on disk.

```
FileReader dataIn = new FileReader("testdata.dat");
```

The predefined standard input stream, *System.in*, provides access to the keyboard. Java defines a converter, called *InputStreamReader*, that reads bytes from an input stream and decodes them into characters. By attaching the converter to standard input, we have a declaration of the keyboard as a `Reader` stream

InputStreamReader converts byte streams to character streams. Use the converter with *System.in* to access the keyboard.

```
Reader keyboard = new InputStreamReader(System.in);
```

Raw input operations with a `FileReader` and an `InputStreamReader` are costly because each read request causes a corresponding read request to the underlying character stream. To remedy the problem, Java defines a *BufferedReader*, which can be wrapped around a `Reader` stream. The `BufferedReader` allocates a block of memory, called a *buffer*, which stores data from the underlying character stream. Input is extracted from the buffer until it is empty, at which point a read request to the underlying character stream extracts a new block of data, which replenishes the buffer.

The declaration of a `BufferedReader` object requires a `Reader` object as an argument where the object is declared as the underlying character stream (Figure 2.11). You cannot simply use the file name. The following are new and preferred declarations for the file stream *dataIn* and the keyboard.

A BufferedReader allows more efficient input from a file by prereading data.

```
// creates a buffered reader attached to file "testdata.dat"
BufferedReader dataIn = new BufferedReader(
        new FileReader("testdata.dat"));

// creates the keyboard as a buffered input stream
BufferedReader keyboard = new BufferedReader(
        new InputStreamReader(System.in));
```

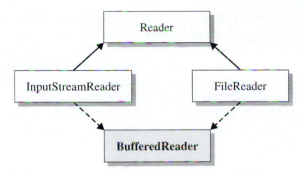

Figure 2.11 *The abstract Reader class with subclasses for buffered input from a file or the keyboard.*

The BufferedReader stream introduces the method readLine(), which reads a single line into a string. The method reads successive characters from the stream until it encounters a newline separator or end of file. The characters that are read are returned as a new String object with the newline separator discarded. The return string is null when the operation attempts to read past the end of file. Treat null as the end-of-file (EOF) flag.

A BufferedReader defines readLine() that inputs an entire line from a file or the keyboard.

After a program finishes reading from a file, it should close the stream that is connected to the file. If fin is the name of the stream variable, execute the statement

```
fin.close();
```

Call close() when you finish with a stream.

The programmer should always explicitly close a file because the operation releases system resources that are associated with the stream. Any streams remaining open at program termination are closed by the runtime system.

Parsing an Input String

We use readLine() to physically extract an entire line of data from a Reader stream. In most applications, we need a way to interpret the line. If it is a single numeric string, the static wrapper class methods parseInt() and parseDouble() convert the string into a primitive data value. Often, the line consists of a series of tokens (substrings), which are separated by a delimiter character. The different tokens may designate two or more items or represent input for a record that consists of different fields. For instance, a line of input for a course grade may include the student ID and fields for the course units and grade.

Methods parseInt(s) and parseDouble(s) convert a numeric string to the corresponding numeric value.

The *StringTokenizer* class in *java.util* has objects that can be used to interpret an input line. Their task is to partition a string into tokens. The declaration of a StringTokenizer object must include the string as an argument. By default, the object uses whitespace characters as delimiters to separate the tokens. An alternative version of the StringTokenizer constructor includes a string that designates the delimiter characters.

StringTokenizer class partitions a string into tokens which are separated by delimiters such as blanks, tabs, and newlines.

```
StringTokenizer stok = new StringTokenizer(str);

// tokenizer that uses a tab character or a hyphen as delimiters
StringTokenizer stok = new StringTokenizer(str, "-\t");
```

Tokenizer methods enable a programmer to sequentially access tokens in the string. The `nextToken()` method returns the next token as a string and advances an internal string pointer to reference the next token. The method throws a `NoSuchElementException` if no additional tokens are available to scan. Access to the state of the scan is provided by methods `countTokens()` and `hasMoreTokens()`. The `countToken()` method provides an updated count of the number of tokens that are available to be scanned. Its value is initially the total number of tokens in the string, but is decremented by each `nextToken()` operation. The boolean `hasMoreTokens()` method is a flag that is true when additional tokens can be scanned and false otherwise.

```
// number of tokens is stored as a separate variable
int numTokens = stok.countTokens();
for (int i = 1; i <= numTokens; i++)
    String str = stok.nextToken();   // access successive tokens

// while loop tests condition hasMoreTokens()
while (stok.hasMoreTokens())
    String str = stok.nextToken();
```

parseTime() converts a string into a Time24 object.

In the `Time24` class, the static method `parseTime()` uses a tokenizer to parse the string argument. This is a good example of a `StringTokenizer` that specifies the string of delimiter characters. The tokenizer uses the delimiters consisting of blank space and colon to split the string into numeric strings for hour and minute. Each string is converted to an *int* using `parseInt()`. The resulting integer values for hour and minute are used to create a `Time24` object, which becomes the return value.

parseTime():

```
public static Time24 parseTime(String s)
{
    // tokens separated by space or colon character
    StringTokenizer stok = new StringTokenizer(s, " :");
    String timePeriod = null;
    int hour, minute;

    // get tokens and convert to hour and minute
    hour = Integer.parseInt(stok.nextToken());
    minute = Integer.parseInt(stok.nextToken());

    // create a Time24 object as the return value
    return new Time24(hour, minute);
}
```

Example 2.5

This example illustrates how we define the keyboard as a BufferedReader and use read-Line() with parsing tools to extract an integer and then a floating-point value from a single input line.

```
BufferedReader keyIn = null;      // stream names the keyboard
String inputStr;                  // string for a line of input
int m;                            // variable for the integer
double x;                         // variable for the real number

try
{
    // declare BufferedReader for the keyboard
    keyIn = new BufferedReader(new InputStreamReader(System.in));

    // read a line from the keyboard
    inputStr = keyIn.readLine();

    // create tokenizer for inputStr with whitespace delimiters
    StringTokenizer stok = new StringTokenizer(inputStr);

    // parse two tokens and assign values to m and x
    m = Integer.parseInt(stok.nextToken());
    x = Double.parseDouble(stok.nextToken());
    System.out.println("m = " + m + " x = " + x);
}
catch (IOException ioe)
{ . . . }
```

```
Input:
    345 78.5

Output:
    m = 345 x = 78.5
```

Text Output with Writer Streams

For text output, Java uses an inheritance hierarchy that resembles the input hierarchy. The abstract *Writer* class defines basic operations for inserting a character or an array of characters in a stream. Concrete subclasses create Writer objects that are attached to an underlying character stream.

A *FileWriter* object is an output stream attached to a file on disk. The declaration uses a string to specify the file name.

```
FileWriter dataOut = new FileWriter("testdata.out");
```

FileWriter is a subclass of Writer class and outputs characters to text files.

If the file does not exist, the declaration creates one with the name *testdata.out*. If the file already exists, this version of the constructor truncates the file by discarding its contents and replacing it with the new output.

Sometimes you may want to add output to the end of the file. This is called *appending to the file* and is done with a second version of the constructor. Add the boolean value *true* as a second argument in the file declaration. If the file already exists, its contents are retained and new output is placed after the old contents.

```
FileWriter dataOut = new FileWriter("testdata.out", true);
```

☞

Note

Console Output

Java requires that a programmer must create a Reader stream for input from the keyboard. The declaration attaches the converter InputStreamReader to *System.in* (standard input). A similar approach could be used for output to the console. Declare a Writer stream with the converter OutputStreamWriter attached to *System.out* (standard output).

```
Writer console = new OutputStreamWriter(System.out);
```

Unlike a Reader input stream, the Java runtime system automatically opens the console window for text output. This allows us to use familiar System.out.print() statements without formally declaring a console stream.

PrintWriter uses print and println statements to output formatted data to a text file.

Output with Print Statements   The methods `print()` and `println()` from the class *PrintWriter* are used to send formatted output to a text file. When used with System.out, these methods write formatted data to the standard output in the console window. Create a `PrintWriter` object by wrapping it around an existing `Writer`, which is connected to an underlying character stream (Figure 2.12).

```
PrintWriter pw = new PrintWriter(
        new FileWriter("testdata.out");
```

In Java, string concatenation is the traditional way of creating formatted output. The operation has great flexibility that enables a programmer to build a string and then use it with a print method.

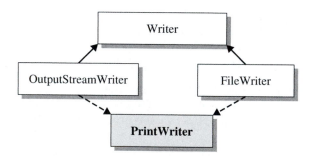

Figure 2.12 *Writer inheritance hierarchy with physical character stream classes and filter class PrintWriter.*

Controlling the Output Stream

Method flush() sends all buffered data to the output stream.

Most output streams buffer data so that it can be sent periodically in larger packets to the destination. This reduces the number of write requests that must be made to the underlying character stream. A programmer can intervene in the buffering process and direct that any pending output be written to the destination. This is accomplished with the method `flush()`. The effect is to direct the I/O system to execute a write request and copy all of the contents of the buffer to the destination.

```
pw.flush();
```

After a program finishes writing to a file, it should close the stream that is connected to the file. This is done with the statement

```
pw.close();
```

Closing a file releases resources that are associated with the stream. It allows the file to be reopened as a source for subsequent input. Good practice has the programmer explicitly close the file. If this is not done, Java will perform the task when the program concludes.

Use close() to shut down an output stream when you are finished.

2.9   The Scanner Class

A *Scanner* object provides a simple text scanner for input of text data from a file or the keyboard. The scanner partitions text from an input stream into tokens. It supplies a variety of "next" methods that extract the next token and convert it to a string or a primitive value. The Scanner class is defined in the *java.util* package.

Declaring a Scanner Object

The constructor uses standard input System.in as an argument to create a Scanner object linked to the keyboard and uses a FileReader with a string argument for the file name to create an object linked to a file.

A Scanner object allows simple input of primitive data and strings from a text file.

```
// create Scanner object sc attached to the keyboard
Scanner sc = new Scanner(System.in);

// create Scanner object fin attached to file "demo.dat"
Scanner fileIn = new Scanner(new FileReader("demo.dat"));
```

When creating a Scanner object attached to a FileReader, an IOException may occur. The constructor statement must be executed in a try block or from a method that includes throws IOException its signature.

Reading from the Input Stream

The Scanner class contains a set of methods that extract and parse tokens from an input stream. View the input stream as a sequence of characters that flow from the keyboard or a file to the computer. A scanner partitions the character sequence into tokens using a delimiter pattern. By default, the delimiter is whitespace that includes one or more space, tab (\t), newline (\n), and return (\r) characters. The resulting tokens may then be converted into values of different types using the various "next" methods.

Assume a user inputs the line of text "17 deposit 450.75 false A" from the keyboard. The Scanner class provides the method nextLine(), which extracts the entire list of tokens as a single string.

The Scanner method nextLine() returns the next line from the input stream.

```
// scan the entire line and return the tokens as a string
String line = sc.nextLine();
```

Alternatively, the input sequence consists of five individual tokens that can be read and converted to a specified type. The method next() returns the next token from the scanner as a string. The methods nextInt(), nextDouble(), and nextBoolean() scan the next token as an *int*, *double*, and *boolean* respectively. Input of a character is a two-step process. First read the character as a string using next() and then extract the *char* value as the first element in the string using the method charAt(0).

The Scanner methods such as nextInt() and nextDouble() return primitive data items from the input stream.

```
int i = sc.nextInt();               // i = 17
String str = sc.next();             // str = "deposit"
double x = sc.nextDouble();         // x = 450.75
boolean b = sc.nextBoolean();       // b = false
char ch = sc.next().charAt(0);      // ch = 'A'
```

Testing for Tokens The Scanner class defines the boolean method hasNext(), which discovers whether an additional token is available in the input stream. The class also provides type-specific boolean methods such as hasNextInt(), hasNextDouble(), and so forth, which return true if a next token exists and can be interpreted as the specified type. In the example, we could use a loop to extract the list of tokens in the input stream.

The Scanner method hasNext() specifies whether there is another token in the input stream.

```
// loop reads tokens in the line
while(sc.hasNext())
{
    token = sc.next();
    System.out.println("In loop next token = " + token);
}
```

```
Output:
    In loop next token = 17
    In loop next token = deposit
    In loop next token = 450.75
    In loop next token = false
    In loop next token = A
```

The various forms of the "next" method will block waiting for further input. In this way, a program may include a series of input requests which the user can supply with tokens on a single line or on separate lines.

File Input

To read from a file, create a Scanner object that inputs from a FileReader with the file name as the string argument. The action has the effect of opening the file by attaching the input stream to the physical file. The operation should be included in try/catch blocks, which provide an error message if the file cannot be opened. This often occurs when the name does not properly denote the file's location in the file system. In the software supplement, we place an input file in the same directory as the application. In this way, the string is simply the relative file name and not an absolute path name. To close the file, the Scanner class provides the method close(). The action detaches the physical file from the input stream. If appropriate, the application can then create a new Scanner object that accesses the same file.

When reading from a file, an application typically inputs data until it reaches the end of the file. Because there is no special character that denotes the last data value, the application must rely on versions of the boolean has-next methods to indicate when an end-of-file condition is true.

Example 2.6

A sports team creates the file *attendance.dat* to store attendance data for home games during the season. The example uses the Scanner object *dataIn* and a loop to read the sequence of attendance values from the file and determine the total attendance. The condition hasNextInt() returns false when all of the data has been read from the file.

```
// create a Scanner object attached to file "attendance.dat"
Scanner dataIn = new Scanner(new FileReader("attendance.dat"));

int gameAtt, totalAtt = 0;

// the loop reads the integer game attendance until end-of-file
while(dataIn.hasNextInt())          // loop iteration condition
{
    gameAtt = dataIn.nextInt();     // input next game attendance
    totalAtt += gameAtt;            // add to the total
}
```

Scanner Class API

The following is a partial listing of the Scanner class API. We include only the key methods, which are used in examples, programs, and exercises. The full Java Scanner API provides a complete listing of methods and a more detailed explanation of the scanner with examples.

class **Scanner**	*java.util*
Constructors	
Scanner((InputStream source) 　　Creates a Scanner object that produces values read from the specified input stream. (Typically standard input *System.in* that denotes the keyboard)	
Scanner(Readable source) 　　Creates a Scanner object that produces values read from the specified input stream. (Typically a FileReader that denotes a file)	
Methods	
Void　　**close**() 　　Close the scanner.	
boolean　　**hasNext**() 　　Returns true if the scanner has another token in the input stream.	

(continued)

class Scanner		*java.util*
boolean	**hasNextBoolean**() Returns true if the next token in the input stream can be interpreted as a boolean value.	
boolean	**hasNextDouble**() Returns true if the next token in the input stream can be interpreted as a double value.	
boolean	**hasNextInt**() Returns true if the next token in the input stream can be interpreted as an int value.	
String	**next**() Finds and returns the next complete token in the input stream as a String.	
boolean	**nextBoolean**() Scans the next token in the input stream into a boolean value and returns that value.	
double	**nextDouble**() Scans the next token in the input stream into a double value and returns that value.	
int	**nextInt**() Scans the next token in the input stream into an int value and returns that value.	

Application: Using the Scanner

Let us look at an application that uses most of the key features in the Scanner class. A file contains a list of items at a grocery store along with pricing and ordering information. Each line in the file includes the name of the item, the quantity requested, the unit price of the item, and a character 'Y' or 'N' indicating whether the item is or is not taxable. A tab separates each field on an input line. The scanner must use a delimiter pattern that recognizes only the tab character and the newline sequence. Depending on the operating system, newline may be a single character (\n or \r) or the two-character sequence "\n\r." The *regular expression* "[\t\n\r]+" defines the delimiter. The notation indicates that the pattern may be one or more characters from the list enclosed in brackets. The Scanner method useDelimiter() assigns the regular expression as the delimiter.

```
fileIn.useDelimiter("[\t\n\r]+");
```

PROGRAM 2.1 USING A SCANNER

The program opens the file *food.dat* and then reads the fields as string, *int*, *double*, and *char* data, respectively. Input terminates at end of file when no more tokens are available. For each product, a line of output lists the product name, quantity requested, price of an item, and the total price of the purchase. The output appends an asterisk (*) to the total cost of items for which tax is included. The output uses the method align() to line up fields in columns.

```java
import java.util.Scanner;
import java.io.*;
import java.text.DecimalFormat;

public class Program2_1
{
    public static void main(String[] args)
    {
        final double SALESTAX = 0.05;

        // input streams for the keyboard and a file
        Scanner fileIn = null;

        // input variables and pricing information
        String product;
        int quantity;
        double unitPrice, quantityPrice, tax, totalPrice;
        char taxStatus;

        // create formatted strings for aligning output
        DecimalFormat fmtA = new DecimalFormat("#"),
                      fmtB = new DecimalFormat("$#.00");

        // open the file; catch exception if file not found
        // use regular expression as delimiter
        try
        {
            fileIn = new Scanner(new FileReader("food.dat"));
            fileIn.useDelimiter("[\t\n\r]+");
        }
        catch (IOException ioe)
        {
            System.err.println("Cannot open file 'food.dat'");
            System.exit(1);
        }

        // header for listing output
        System.out.println("Product" + align("Quantity", 16) +
            align("Price", 10) + align("Total", 12));

        // read to end of file;  break when no more tokens
        while(fileIn.hasNext())
        {
            // input product/purchase input fields
            product = fileIn.next();
            quantity = fileIn.nextInt();
            unitPrice = fileIn.nextDouble();
            taxStatus = fileIn.next().charAt(0);
```

```
                        // calculations and output
                        quantityPrice = unitPrice * quantity;
                        tax = (taxStatus == 'Y') ?
                                quantityPrice * SALESTAX : 0.0;
                        totalPrice = quantityPrice + tax;
                        System.out.println(product +
                            align("", 15-product.length()) +
                            align(fmtA.format(quantity), 6) +
                            align(fmtB.format(unitPrice), 13) +
                            align(fmtB.format(totalPrice),12) +
                            ((taxStatus == 'Y') ? " *" : ""));
                    }
                }

                // aligns string right justified in a field of width n
                public static String align(String str, int n)
                {
                    String alignStr = "";
                    for (int i = 1; i < n - str.length(); i++)
                        alignStr += " ";
                    alignStr += str;
                    return alignStr;
                }
            }
```

```
Input file ('food.dat'):
    Soda       3 2.69 Y
    Eggs       2 2.89 N
    Bread      3 2.49 N
    Grapefruit  8 0.45 N
    Batteries  10 1.15 Y
    Bakery     1 14.75 N

Run:
    Product         Quantity   Price     Total
    Fruit Punch        4       $2.69    $11.30 *
    Eggs               2       $2.89     $5.78
    Rye Bread          3       $2.49     $7.47
    Grapefruit         8       $.45      $3.60
    AA Batteries      10       $1.15    $12.08 *
    Ice Cream          1       $3.75     $3.75
```

Chapter Summary

- A Java collection class assumes that all of its data elements are objects, and methods to add and remove elements use object parameters. Because we want to create collections of integers, doubles, or characters, we need some way to represent a primitive variable as an object. A Java wrapper class is a class in which each object holds a primitive value. The object "wraps" the primitive instance variable and provides supporting methods to access and display the data.

- The Java wrapper classes associate a primitive value with a corresponding object. Conversion between the two types of data using constructs such as

```
Integer n = new Integer(5);
int m = n.intValue();
```

  is burdensome and adds unwanted clutter to a program listing. Java provides automatic conversion from a primitive type to its associated wrapper type and vice versa. The mechanism involves autoboxing that converts a primitive type to the wrapper type and auto-unboxing that converts a wrapper type to a corresponding primitive type. The conversions are automatic. For instance, the declarations can be written as follows using autoboxing.

```
Integer n = 5;
int m = n;
```

- The term *object composition* refers to a condition that exists when a class contains one or more instance variables that are objects of class type. A class that is included by composition is called the supplier class. The class that includes an object by composition is the client class. Object composition is an often-used and very effective way to promote code reuse.

- Object composition is a *has-a* relationship. Inheritance involves sharing of attributes and operations among classes and reflects the *is-a* relationship. A superclass defines a set of common attributes and operations, which it shares with subclasses. A subclass extends the resources provided by the superclass by adding its own data and methods. Inheritance is fundamental to object-oriented programming. The book illustrates the inheritance relationship by developing the superclass Employee and its two subclasses SalaryEmployee and HourlyEmployee. Many other examples of inheritance will be provided throughout the book.

- Polymorphism is a Greek word that means "many forms." In object-oriented programming, polymorphism refers to a situation in which two or more classes in an inheritance hierarchy have methods with the same signature that perform distinct tasks. A program can declare a single superclass reference variable for objects of different subclass types. Any program statement that calls the method using the reference variable will direct the runtime system to execute the method for the specified subclass. The employee hierarchy provides a good example of polymorphism. The Employee superclass and the two subclasses, SalaryEmployee and HourlyEmployee, have methods toString() and payrollCheck(). When an Employee variable references a SalaryEmployee or HourlyEmployee object, the appropriate version of toString() and payrollCheck() is called.

- If we view an inheritance hierarchy tree from the bottom up, successive superclasses become ever more general, more abstract, in terms of their data and methods because they define members that are often common to two or more subclasses. In some cases, a superclass is so general that a program would not create instances of the class. Such a superclass can define a method only to support polymorphism. The method has no meaningful action as a concrete operation in a superclass. Rather than having the superclass give the method a meaningless implementation, Java allows the method to be declared abstract by using the keyword *abstract*. Only a signature specifies such a method. Subclasses must implement the method or they are themselves abstract and cannot generate objects. Indicate the presence of one or more abstract methods by declaring the class abstract.

- Handling errors during method execution is an important aspect of program design. The best alternative is to use the Java exception mechanism. Java exceptions are handled by three keywords, *throw*, *try*, and *catch*. Place one or more method calls that could generate an exception and any code depending on those method calls in a try block. Follow the try block with a catch block that is the exception handler. When a method detects an error, it throws an exception object, which is normally an object of a special class that identifies the exception. The throw bypasses the normal method return mechanism and follows the chain of previous method calls until it locates a catch block that handles the exception. The catch block normally outputs an error message and either takes corrective action or terminates the program.

- Input and output in Java uses stream objects. Binary streams have bytes that may represent a graphic or an executable file. Text streams have character data such as an HTML file or a Java source code file. Character input from text files is done using stream classes derived from the abstract class Reader. Perform text input from a disk file using a BufferedReader stream. Since the keyboard is a character device, input from the keyboard is also done using a BufferedReader stream. After reading a line from a file, the programmer often needs to separate the line into parts called *tokens*. Use the StringTokenizer class from the package *java.util* for that purpose. Character output to files is done using streams derived from the abstract Writer class. Use the class FileWriter to output lines to a text file. If data such as integer and floating-point variables are to be displayed in text form, use the PrintWriter class to format data. There are various methods for controlling an output stream. Any pending output is written to the destination by using the method flush(). In general, an input or output stream can be shut down using the method close().

- A Scanner object provides a simple text scanner for input of text data from a file or the keyboard. The scanner partitions text from an input stream into tokens. It supplies a variety of "next" methods that extract the next token and convert it to a string or a primitive value. The Scanner class is defined in the *java.util* package. Its operations throw IOException if an error occurs. As a result, they must be called in a try block or from a method that includes the clause "throws IOException" in its signature.

Written Exercises

1. Use static `Integer` methods to convert string *str* to an *int* and then display the value in hex (base 16).

```
String str = "109";
int n = _____;
System.out.println(n + " in hex is " + ____);
```

2. Trace the following program and give the output.

```
class ClassA
{
    private int valueA;

    public ClassA(int a)
    { valueA = a + 100; }

    public int getValue()
    { return valueA; }
}
class ClassB                            // superclass ClassB
{
    private ClassA valueB;          // supplier class ClassA

    public ClassB (int b)
    { valueB = new ClassA(2*b); }

    protected ClassA getValue()
    { return valueB; }

    public String toString()
    { return "" + valueB.getValue(); }
}
public class ClassC extends ClassB      // subclass ClassC
{
    public ClassC(int c)
    { super(c); }

    public String toString()
    {
        ClassA objA = getValue();
        return "" + objA.getValue();
    }
    public static void main(String[] args)
    {
        ClassA mainA = new ClassA(200);
        System.out.println(mainA.getValue()); // (a) output:__
```

```
ClassB mainB = new ClassB(400);
System.out.println(mainB);      // (b) output: _____

ClassC mainC = new ClassC(500);
System.out.println(mainC);      // (c) output: _____

mainB = mainC;
System.out.println(mainB);      // (d) output: _____
    }
}
```

3. Distinguish the relationship among classes using composition and those using inheritance.

4. Consider the following inheritance hierarchy and declarations.

```
class SuperClass
{
    private int m;
    protected int n;
    public SuperClass()
    { . . . }
    public void demoMethod();
    { . . . }
}

class SubClass extends SuperClass
{
    private int r;
    public SubClass()
    { . . . }
    public void demoMethod()
    { . . . }
}

// declaring superclass and subclass objects
SuperClass superObj = new SuperClass();
SubClass subObj = new SubClass();
```

(a) Which of the instance variables *m*, *n*, and *r* can be accessed by a method in the subclass?
(b) Which of the instance variables *m*, *n*, and *r* can be accessed by a method in the superclass?
(c) Can *subObj* call demoMethod() in the superclass? Explain.
(d) Can methods in SubClass call demoMethod() in the superclass? Explain.

5. (a) What is an abstract method?
   (b) What type of members can an abstract class contain?
   (c) How does the presence of an abstract superclass class in an inheritance hierarchy affect the declaration of objects and the implementation of derived subclasses?

6. Fill in the statements that illustrate the exception-handling mechanism.

```
public static void testMethod(int n)
{
   if (n == 0)
       // throw an IllegalArgumentException with the message
       // "argument must be positive"

   _____

       . . .
}

public static void callMethod()
{
   try
   { testMethod(intValue); }
   catch _____
   {
       _____        // display the message
       _____        // terminate the program
   }
}
```

7. Describe the conditions that must be present in order for polymorphism to occur with superclass and derived subclass reference variables.

8. An application reads a line of input from the keyboard. The line contains an integer, a double, and a name that may have embedded blanks. A tab character separates the fields. Write a code segment that uses the Scanner object *keyIn* to read values from a line into the variables *n*, *x*, and *name*. Output the variables separated by the character "/."

```
int n;
double x;
String name;
Scanner keyIn = new Scanner(System.in);
```

Example: ($\longrightarrow$ is the tab character)

```
Input:   533 ⟶ 6.02e23 ⟶ Avogadro's number
Output: 533/6.02E23/Avogadro's number
```

Programming Exercises

9. Write a Java program that inputs a string from the keyboard and outputs a converted string to the console. The converted string should have the following features. Use the Character class static methods to make the conversions.

   - Each separate word in the string should begin with an uppercase letter and be followed by lowercase letters.
   - Compress any sequence of whitespace (blank, tab, or newline) characters into a single "+" character.
   - Remove all nonalphanumeric characters (e.g. punctuation marks).

For instance:

Input string: thIS! liNE BeCOmes"

Converted string: This+Line+Becomes

10. Instances of the LawyerBill class provide billing information for a lawyer and client. The class has variables *clientName*, *billingRate*, and *billingTime* for the client name, the lawyer's per-hour billing rate, and the billing time. The latter is a Time24 reference variable. A constructor has parameters for the name, rate, and time specified by its hour and minute values. The method postBill() returns a string with billing information that specifies the client, the rate, the time, and the billing amount. The format for the billing information is

Client: <client>

Rate: $<billingRate>

Time: <billingTime>

Charge: $<amount>

(a) Give a declaration for the LawyerBill class.

(b) Write a program that tests your implementation.

11. The animal hierarchy has Animal as a superclass and Dog and Cat as subclasses. In part (d) you will be adding Terrier as a subclass of Dog.

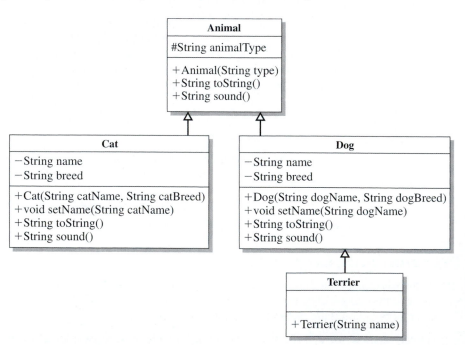

(a) Implement the Animal superclass. The toString() method describes the animal as "A <type>". The sound() method will be used for polymorphism. Give it a dummy implementation.

(b) Implement the Dog and Cat class. In each case, the `toString()` method describes the animal using the format "A <type>, <name> the <breed>". In the implementation of a subclass `toString()` method, call the superclass `toString()` method for the "A <type>" part of the description. The sound for a Dog is "woof woof" and the sound for a Cat is "meow meow."

(c) Write a program that uses the following skeleton code. See the demonstration run.

```java
public class ProgEx2_11
{
    public static void main(String[] args)
    {
        // declare Dog and Cat objects

        // myDog with name Murphy and breed Poodle
        . . .

        // myCat with name Debbie and breed Siamese
        . . .

        // create output statements that describe the objects
        . . . .

        // call announce() with the myDog and myCat
        announce(myDog);
        announce(myCat);

        // change the names for the dog and cat
        changeName(myDog, "Murph");
        changeName(myCat, "DB");

        // create output statements that describe newly
        // named objects
        . . .
    }

    // outputs a description of the animal followed by
    // "Speak!" and the sound the animal makes
    public static void announce(Animal a)
    { . . . }

    // the method changes the name of animal
    public static void changeName(Animal a, String name)
    { . . . }
}
```

(d) Modify the animal hierarchy. Include Terrier as a subclass of Dog. In the Animal class, make sound an abstract method. In the program, add the Terrier object *myPet* with the name "Bruno". Add statements that describe the new object, announce it, and change the name to "Digger".

Run:
```
A dog, Murphy the Poodle
A cat, Debbie the Siamese
A dog, Murphy the Poodle Speak! woof woof
A cat, Debbie the Siamese Speak! meow meow
A dog, Murph the Poodle
A cat, DB the Siamese
```

12. (a) Implement an abstract class `Vector` that maintains a two-dimensional vector $v = (x, y)$ and specifies the signature of a method `magnitude()` that computes the magnitude of the vector. The following UML diagram describes the class.

Vector
#x: double
#y: double
+Vector(x: double, y: double)
+getX(): double
+getY(): double
+magnitude(): double
+setXY(x: double, y: double): void

Note that the # in the declaration of the variables x and y indicate that they have visibility protected.

(b) Implement a subclass `StandardVector` that implements `magnitude()` as the standard vector magnitude.

$$\texttt{magnitude()} = \sqrt{x^2 + y^2}$$

(c) Implement a subclass `OtherVector` that implements `magnitude()` as

$$\texttt{magnitude()} = |x| + |y|$$

where $|x|$ and $|y|$ are the absolute values of the components x and y respectively.

(d) Write a program that defines `Vector` reference variables v and w. The variables are associated with `StandardVector` and `OtherVector` objects respectively. Output the magnitude of each vector.

13. Write a program that uses excepting handling when calling the method `f()`. The method takes a real argument x and returns the value $\sqrt{x^3 - 1}$. Since `sqrt(t)` is not a real number when t is less than 0, `f()` throws an `ArithmeticException` if $x < 1$.

(a) Implement the method. Have the exception message identify the error along value of the argument x.

```
public static double f(double x)
{ ... }
```

(b) Write a program that prompts for *x* and inputs a value from the keyboard. Catch an `ArithmeticException` by displaying the error message and terminating the program.

14. The book hierarchy includes a superclass `Book` and two subclasses `Textbook` and `Manual`. Use the accompanying UML to view the classes.

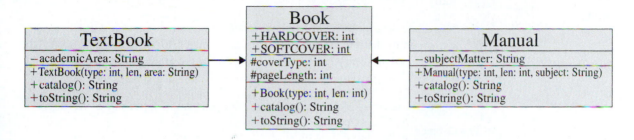

In the `Book` class, `catalog()` is an abstract method. Depending on the type of book, the `Book` class `toString()` method returns a string in the format

        A <pageLength> page hard covered book

or

        A <pageLength> page soft covered book

In the `Textbook` class, the instance variable *academicArea* specifies which discipline would likely use the book. The method `catalog()` returns a string describing the academic area. The method `toString()` gives a description of the object. Use the following formats for the two methods. Assume the `Textbook` object is a HARDCOVER book with page length 200 and `academicArea` Mathematics. The return strings are

    catalog():   A textbook for Mathematics
    toString():   A 200-page hard-covered book for Mathematics

In the `Manual` class, the instance variable *subjectMatter* designates the main topic covered by the manual. The method `catalog()` returns a string describing the subject matter. The method `toString()` gives a description of the object. Use the following formats. Assume the `Manual` object is a SOFTCOVER book with page length 150 and `subjectMatter` "air conditioner repair." The return strings are

    catalog():   A manual for air conditioner repair
    toString():   A 150-page soft-covered book for air conditioner repair

(a) Implement the three classes in an inheritance hierarchy.
(b) Write a program that tests your implementation. Include in the program a static method `topic()` that has a superclass reference parameter. The method outputs a catalog description of the book along with a description of the book provided by `toString()`. Call `topic()` with both `Textbook` and `Manual` objects

        public static void topic(Book b)
        { . . . }

15. The file *grades.dat* in the *ch2ex* directory of the software supplement contains student grade data in the format

    ```
    name→units→gradePoints
    ```

    where ⟶ represents the tab character. For instance, the line

    ```
    Lau, Tuyet→60→230
    ```

    provides grade data for Tuyet Lau, whose grade point average (gpa) is 230/60 = 3.83. Write a program that creates a Scanner object attached to the input file. Read data from the file and produce a grade report. Each line of the grade report should be in the format

    ```
    Name: <name>  GPA: <gpa>   // <name> and <gpa> are values
    ```

    For instance:

    Name: Lau, Tuyet GPA: 3.83.

Programming Project

16. A ZIP archive is a compressed image of one or more files and directories. Java provides the means to read and even create ZIP files. Investigate the classes `ZipFile`, `ZipEntry`, and `Enumeration` in the Java API. Fill in code for an application that prompts the user for the name of a ZIP archive. The program uses an `Enumeration` object to display a listing of files in the archive. It then uncompresses each of the files in the archive. The code skeleton is located in the *ch2ex* directory in the software supplement. The file *graphics.zip* is available for testing your program.

    ```
    ProgPrj2_16
        import java.io.*;
        import java.util.zip.*;
        import java.util.*;

        public class ProgPrj2_16
        {
            public static void main(String[] args) throws Exception
            {
                Scanner keyIn = new Scanner(System.in);
                String filename;
                ZipFile z = null;
                ZipInputStream zipInputStream = null;
                Enumeration e;
                BufferedInputStream zipIn = null;
                BufferedOutputStream unzipOut = null;
                ZipEntry ze = null;
                byte[] buf = null;
                int fileSize, bytesRead;
    ```

```
// Prompt for the archive file name; create a
// ZipFile object and a ZipInputStream
. . .

// use an Enumeration to display files in the archive
System.out.println("Files in the archive " +
                        filename);
. . .

System.out.println("Unzipping files in the archive");
while(true)
{

    // Uncompress files in the archive; each
    // iteration accesses the file as a ZipEntry;
    // use the ZipFile and ZipEntry objects
    // to create an InputStream.  Extract the
    // compressed elements and uses an OutputStream
    // to write the uncompressed
    // data to a file.
    . . .

    }
}
}
```

```
Run:
   Enter name of archive: graphics.zip
   Files in the archive graphics.zip
       DrawTools.java
       LineShape.java
       . . .
   Unzipping files in the archive
       File DrawTools.java  (size 3781)
       File LineShape.java  (size 1220)
       . . .
```

Chapter 3

DESIGNING CLASSES

CONTENTS

3.1   THE JAVA INTERFACE
       Declaring an Interface

3.2   AN INTERFACE AS A TEMPLATE
       Using an Interface Type
       Interfaces and Inheritance

3.3   CREATING AN API WITH JAVADOC

3.4   DESIGN PATTERNS
       Singleton Design Pattern

3.5   GUI APPLICATION DESIGN
       Graphical Components
       GUI Application Design Pattern
       Event Listeners and Event Handlers
       Dice Toss Action Event

In Chapter 2, we introduced the concept of an abstract superclass that includes at least one abstract method in addition to the data and methods that are shared with subclass objects. In this chapter, we introduce a related concept called an *interface*. This classlike structure defines only static data and abstract methods. Corresponding to a superclass are subclasses that extend the resources of the superclass. Corresponding to an interface are implementing classes that override the methods in the interface. Polymorphism is an important feature of classes in an inheritance hierarchy and also applies to an interface and its implementing classes. An interface provides a template that defines categories of classes. The concept of interface is fundamental to our overall design of data structures and classification of collection classes.

In designing an application program, a programmer first looks to identify features that are part of previous problems that have been successfully solved. Over the years, researchers have identified proven design models for creating flexible and maintainable software. The result is a body of design patterns that

programmers may use much as an architect draws on the historical design of columns and arches to build a modern skyscraper or a bridge. We will introduce a variety of design patterns throughout the book. We discuss a pattern only when it reinforces your abstract understanding of a data structure or algorithm.

Most of the examples and programs in this book employ console-based I/O that assumes that input comes from the keyboard and output goes to the console. Modern applications typically use interactive I/O that relies on a GUI (Graphical User Interface) window with components and event handlers. You are accustomed to using text boxes for input, mouse clicks to initiate commands, and text areas to display output. While a study of GUI programming is not a goal for this book, we want to use the technique for some of the examples and exercises in this book. In this chapter, we introduce the basic GUI components and events that comprise most of our examples. A design pattern provides a template for a GUI application. You can simply modify the template to solve selected exercises in each chapter.

3.1 The Java Interface

An abstract method is a method that does not have an implementation. It appears in an abstract class to support polymorphism and to guarantee that the method

is overridden in any subclass. We use abstract methods to describe a new concept called an *interface*. An interface is a pure abstract classlike structure. It consists only of public abstract methods and public static final data. Classes implement the interface rather than extending the interface. A class implements an interface if it provides declarations for all of the methods that are defined in the interface.

The role of an interface is to serve as a template for its implementing classes. The classes share the behaviors described in the interface. An interface describes a category of classes with common operations specified by the interface. Java allows for the declaration of interface reference variables, which can be assigned objects from any implementing class. Calling a method with the interface reference variable invokes polymorphism, and the method in the implementing class is executed. A class can implement more than one interface. It must simply provide declarations for each of the methods specified in the list of interfaces. We use multiple interfaces in the design of a class when we wish to specify diverse behaviors of the class.

An interface is a template for classes that implement the interface. The implementing class must supply declarations for all of the methods that are specified in the interface.

Declaring an Interface

The declaration of an interface begins with a header that includes a visibility modifier, the reserved word *interface* followed by the interface name. Declare the methods using their signatures without modifiers and with a terminating semicolon. The methods are public and abstract by default. Any data must be public static final identifier names with a specified value.

```
public interface InterfaceName
{
    public static final type DATA_NAME = <value>;

    // method declaration using only the signature
    returnType methodName(<parameter list>);
}
```

A class implements an interface by providing method declarations for each method in the interface. The relationship between the class and the interface is established in the class header by appending the reserved word *implements* and the interface name.

An interface does not have instance variables but may have constant declarations.

```
// class - interface declaration
public class ClassName implements InterfaceName
{
    < Define an implementation for each interface method>
}
```

An interface does not have instances. Rather, it ensures that objects for any implementing class must have access to the methods established by the interface. The compiler will flag an error if a class states that it implements an interface but fails to implement one of the methods.

Multiple classes can implement the same interface. The classes provide different declarations for the methods but accomplish the same tasks. We can design general algorithms using interface methods and have them apply to any implementing class. The presence of constants in an interface allows all of the classes that implement the interface to share a set of constants.

Multiple classes may implement the same interface. Each class chooses to code the action of a method in its own way.

Note

> ### An Interface Collection of Constants
>
> In some cases, an interface simply contains constants defined with the modifiers `public static`. The interface mechanism bundles together a set of related constant values, which become available with an import statement. For instance, the Java SDK defines the interface SwingConstants that include constants such as LEFT, SOUTH, and VERTICAL. The constants position and orient components in the frame of a GUI application.

3.2   An Interface as a Template

The Measurement interface is a template for the definition of geometric classes that define the area and perimeter of the shapes.

An interface defines a template that describes the behavior of any class that implements the interface. The interface specifies a category of classes. Let us look at an example. The `Measurement` interface defines a category of geometric classes. The interface includes the operations area() and perimeter() as well as the constant PI which approximates the real number π.

Measurement interface:

```
public interface Measurement
{
    public static final double PI = 3.14159265;

    double area();
    double perimeter();
}
```

The classes `Circle` and `Rectangle` implement the `Measurement` interface. A circle is a geometric figure that is determined by its radius. A rectangle is a geometric figure that is determined by its two dimensions length and width. Both `Circle` and `Rectangle` objects share a common trait: they are measurement tools.

The following is an implementation of the `Circle` class. In the header, `Circle` implements `Measurement`. The class must provide implementations for the methods `area()` and `perimeter()` using the exact method signatures specified in the interface. Other than that requirement, the class may define any other method. In our case, the class has two constructors that initialize the radius with default value 0.0 and with a specified argument, respectively. The class has methods `getRadius()` and `setRadius()` to access and update the radius and `toString()` to return a string describing the object using the format `"Circle with radius <radius>."`

Circle class:

```
public class Circle implements Measurement
{
    private double radius;

    // creates an instance with the specified radius
    public Circle(double radius)
    { this.radius = radius; }

    // interface method area() returns PI * radius (squared)
    public double area()
    { return Math.PI * radius * radius; }
```

```
    // interface method perimeter() returns 2 * PI * radius
    public double perimeter()
    { return 2 * Math.PI * radius; }

    // access and update methods
    public double getRadius()
    { return radius; }

    public void setRadius(double radius)
    { this.radius = radius; }

    // returns a description of the object
    public String toString()
    { return "Circle with radius " + radius; }
}
```

The Rectangle class has a design similar to the Circle class. To accommodate the dimensions length and width, the class has accessor methods getLength() and getWidth() and a single mutator method setSides(length, width). Two constructors initialize an object. The default version sets length and width to 0.0, while the other constructor specifies user-supplied initial values for length and width. The method toString() describes a Rectangle object with the format "Rectangle with length <length> and width <width>".

A UML diagram shows the relationship between an interface and a class that implements the interface. A dotted line with an open arrowhead is drawn from the class to the interface (Figure 3.1). You can find the Measurement interface along with the Rectangle and Circle classes in the directory *program/ch3* of the software supplement.

Rectangle implements area(), perimeter(), and specific methods for length and width.

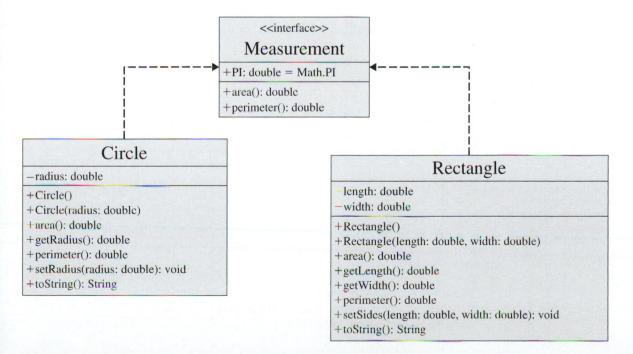

Figure 3.1 *The Measurement interface and two implementing classes.*

Using an Interface Type

While an interface is not a class, it can be a reference type in a variable declaration and then be assigned any object from a class that implements the interface. An interface method that is called with the interface reference uses polymorphism. The runtime system calls the concrete method in the implementing class.

```
InterfaceName ref;
ImplementingClass obj = new ImplementingClass(. . . );

ref = obj;
ref.methodName();      // calls methodName() in ImplementingClass
```

Polymorphism applies to interfaces.

You can see these ideas in the method resize(), which takes a geometric figure and a percentage value as arguments and updates the dimensions of the figure by the percentage amount. For instance, calling resize() with percentage 2.0 doubles the dimensions of the figure. The method uses the `Measurement` interface as a parameter type. The implementation of the method uses the *instanceof* operator to identify the class type of the `Measurement` argument.

resize():

```
public static void resize(Measurement m, double pct)
{
   if (m instanceof Rectangle)
   {
      // cast m as a Rectangle
      Rectangle r = (Rectangle)m;
      // use setSides() to resized the length and width
      r.setSides(r.getLength()*pct, r.getWidth()*pct);
   }
   else if (m instanceof Circle)
   {
      // cast m as a Circle
      Circle c = (Circle)m;

      // use setRadius() to resized the radius
      c.setRadius(c.getRadius()*pct);
   }
}
```

The instance of boolean operator asks if an object is an instance of a specified type.

Example 3.1

Use the following declarations for a `Rectangle` object, a `Circle` object, and a `Measurement` reference variable.

```
Measurement measureRef;
Rectangle rect = new Rectangle(4,6);
Circle circ = new Circle(1);
```

1. Assign an object to the interface reference and call `area()` and `perimeter()`. Execution invokes polymorphism.

```
measureRef = rect;
double x =  measureRef.area();        // area of rect is 24.0

measureRef = circ;
double y = measureRef.perimeter();   // y is 6.28318 (2π)
```

2. For circle *circ*, call resize() with pct = 2.0 to double the radius and then display the updated figure.

```
resize(circ, 2.0);
System.out.println(circ);
```

Output:
```
   Circle with radius 2.0
```

Interfaces and Inheritance

Class hierarchies and interfaces are distinct concepts. You cannot derive an interface from a class or a class from an interface. Nevertheless, there are important relationships between the two concepts.

Interface Inheritance Hierarchy   Interfaces can be part of their own inheritance hierarchy. A parent interface may be used to derive a child interface, which has access to all of the constants and abstract methods in the parent interface. The interface header for the child uses the reserved word *extends* to indicate the inheritance relation. Any class that implements the child interface must implement all of the methods that are declared in both the parent and child interfaces.

One interface can extend another to create an interface hierarchy. A class that implements the child interface must implement all the methods in both the parent and child interfaces.

```
interface ParentInterface
{
    <parent constants>
    <parent methods>
}

interface ChildInterface extends ParentInterface
{
    <child constants>
    <child methods>
}

class ImplementingClass implements ChildInterface
{
    <include declarations of parent and child methods>
    . . .
}
```

Example: The `DiagonalMeasurement` interface extends the `Measurement` interface by adding the method `diagonal()`.

```
public interface DiagonalMeasurement extends Measurement
{
    double diagonal();
}
```

The classes `Circle` and `Rectangle` would naturally implement the `DiagonalMeasurement` interface, while a class such as `Triangle` would not have a well-defined interpretation of the new method. `Triangle` could still implement the `Measurement` interface.

```
public class Circle implements DiagonalMeasurement
{
    < include declarations of area(), perimeter(),
        and diagonal()>
}
```

When a class implements an interface, any subclass of the class also implements the interface.

Extending Interface Implementations   A class that implements an interface can be extended. The derived class automatically implements the interface because the methods are declared in the superclass. For instance, assume class `Square` is derived from `Rectangle`, which implements `Measurement`. The `Square` class automatically implements the `Measurement` interface because it inherits the `area()` and `perimeter()` methods from `Rectangle`. A `Square` class object can be assigned to a `Measurement` reference variable and can participate in polymorphism.

Example: The declaration of `Rectangle` specifies that the class implements `Measurement`.

```
public class Rectangle implements Measurement
{}
```

Declare the `Square` class by simply extending `Rectangle`. The condition *implements Measurement* is automatically associated with the class.

```
public class Square extends Rectangle
{
    <methods area() and perimeter() are inherited from Rectangle>
}
```

Some programming languages allow multiple inheritance. Java does not.

Multiple Interfaces and Inheritance   Java allows only single inheritance; that is, a class may have only one parent. Some languages, such as C++, allow for multiple inheritances, where a subclass may derive attributes and operations from two or more superclasses. This can be useful when a class describes "hyphenated objects" that combine features found in separate objects. For instance, classes TV, DVDPlayer, and VCR describe different electronic devices. Electronic stores carry ComboTV units that combine features from each of the devices.

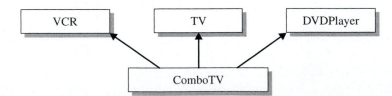

A possible Java design strategy for the ComboTV class begins with TV as the super-class. Operations available to all TV objects are declared in the superclass and ComboTV simply extends TV by adding new attributes and methods. You are familiar with operations that can be performed on modern VCR and DVD equipment. Let the Video interface describe methods associated with the equipment. By having the ComboTV class implement the Video interface, we can ensure that the video-handling operations are available to a ComboTV object.

Java provides some of the features of multiple inheritance by allowing a class to implement multiple interfaces.

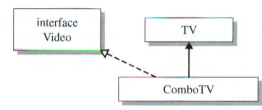

Java provides some of the features of multiple inheritances by allowing a class to implement multiple interfaces. The syntax adds a comma-separated list of interfaces in the class header. The class must then implement all of the methods in the different interfaces.

Example: Assume that the interface AMFM describes the features of an AM/FM radio. The ComboTV class extends the superclass TV and implements the interfaces VCR and AMFM.

```
public class ComboTV extends TV implements VCR, AMFM
{
    . . .
}
```

3.3   Creating an API with Javadoc

Documenting software is important no matter which language you use. The documentation serves to explain the purpose of a class, its access to resources in an inheritance hierarchy, its interface design, and the action, preconditions, and postconditions for its method. Specific comments explain the meaning of program variables and the logic embedded in the coding of an algorithm.

Documentation is needed with any programming language.

Documentation has two goals. When included in the source code, it provides a descriptive trace of the code, which can detail the design of an algorithm or allow a programmer to debug errors and make modifications. A second goal of documentation is to provide a compact summary of the class. Programmers can use the summary to create objects and call methods without having to access the source code.

Java has a mechanism to produce user documentation that is separate from the program code and can be viewed independently of it. Java provides the *javadoc* utility that recognizes comments written in a structured format and produces linked HTML pages. You have seen the result of using javadoc in the Java API documentation.

The javadoc utility produces HTML documentation for classes and interfaces.

Comments recognized by javadoc are referred to as *javadoc comments, documentation comments,* or simply *doc comments.* A javadoc comment begins with the marker /** and ends with the marker */. Within the comment, you may include HTML tags that highlight text by displaying words in bold, computer font, and so forth. The javadoc utility uses javadoc tags to identify elements that will be expanded and formatted in the HTML pages. The tags begin with an ampersand (@) followed immediately by the tag identifer. The following is a list of javadoc tags that we use in documenting the software supplement.

@param   - parameter for a method
@return   - identifies the return type of a method
@throws   - specifies the exception that is thrown when an error occurs

If you search the Web, you will find javadoc tutorials that list additional tags and discuss documentation design. Let us illustrate javadoc documentation for the selected methods in the Circle class. We include the documentation for the class header, the nondefault constructor, and the method area(). These present the key documentation elements.

Circle (selected methods with javadoc comments):

```
/**
 * The <em>Circle</em> class provides measurement
 * operations for objects that are determined by their radius.
 */

public class Circle implements Measurement
{
    /**
     * Creates a circle with the specified radius.
     * @param radius the radius of this object
     * @throws IllegalArgumentException if the argument
     * is negative.
     */

    public Circle(double radius)
    { . . . }

    /**
     * Returns the area of the circle.
     * @return a <code>double</code> having value PI * r
     * (squared).
     */
    public double area()
    { . . . }
}
```

The javadoc utility produces a Web page that describes a class. The Web page documents the package, inheritance hierarchy, and interfaces that are associated with the class. It also gives an API listing of the constructors and methods. Figure 3.2 is a partial listing of the Web page for the Circle class. You recognize the format from the Java API documentation. Note that the "Method Detail" for area() automatically references the fact that the method is specified in the Measurement interface.

Javadoc for the Circle Class

```
java.lang.Object
  | MeasurementFigures.Circle
```

All Implemented Interfaces:
         Measurement

---

public class **Circle**
extends java.lang.Object
implements Measurement

The *Circle* class provides measurement operations for objects that are determined by their radius.

Field Summary
Fields inherited from interface MeasurementFigures.Measurement
`PI`

Constructor Summary
`Circle()`   Creates a circle of radius 0.0.
`Circle(double radius)`   Creates a circle with the specified radius.

Method Summary (Partial Listing)

double	`area()` Returns the area of the circle.
int	`compareTo(java.lang.Object item)` Compares the radius of two objects.
void	`setRadius(double radius)` Updates the radius with the specified value.

Constructor Detail (Partial Listing)

Circle():
```
public Circle(double radius)
```
          Creates a circle of with the specified radius.
     Parameters:
          radius - the radius of this object.
     Throws:
          `IllegalArgumentException` - if the argument is negative.

(continued)

Figure 3.2 *Javadoc Web page for the Circle class.*

Method Detail

area( ):
        `public double` **area**()
                    Returns the area of the circle.
        Specified by:
                area in interface Measurement.
        Returns:
                a *double* having value PI * r (squared).

Figure 3.2 (*continued*)

3.4   Design Patterns

A design pattern documents the solution to a problem in a very general way.

When designing an application, a software engineer first looks to identify features that were part of previous problems that have been successfully solved. Using personal experience and collective industry expertise, the engineer can draw on proven models for creating flexible and maintainable software. This is design reuse that has long been a trademark in the field of architecture. An architect uses well-established designs for columns and arches to build a modern skyscraper, a bridge, or a cathedral.

In the past decade, researchers have sought to identify common software design problems and solutions. The result is the creation of design patterns using abstract object models and object interaction. The patterns document solutions that can be used by others in the software engineering community. Pioneering work by Gamma, Helm, Johnson, and Vlissides (the "gang of four") culminated in the book *Design Patterns: Elements of Reusable Object-Oriented Software* (Addison-Wesley: 1995). The book defines categories of design patterns and a vocabulary for their documentation. In this book, we introduce selective design patterns that are part of our discussion of algorithms and data structures.

Singleton Design Pattern

In some cases, an application should create only one instance of a class. In effect, once the program instantiates an object, it must be prevented from creating additional instances of the class. For instance, a computer system may have many printers but should have only one print spooler. A graphics package provides for different drawing objects that are layered on a single drawing window. The package allows an application to specify when the window is first opened. Any subsequent requests simply return the existing window.

The singleton pattern describes a model for building a class that may only have one instance.

The *singleton design pattern* provides a model for the building of a class that may have only one instance. The idea is relatively simple. In the class, define a static reference variable of the class type. The variable serves as the reference to the single instance of the class. The constructor is a private method. In this way, a user cannot create an instance of the class using the operator new. The single instance is provided by a public static method such as getSingletonObject() that checks the reference variable. If it is null, no object exists, and the method calls the private constructor to create one. If not, the single object has already been created and the method does nothing. In either case, the method returns the reference to the single object.

The Dice class illustrates the singleton design pattern. It allows for a single instance that simulates the random tossing of two dice with methods to identify the individual die and the total. The class defines the static reference variable called dice of type Dice and initializes it to be null. A private constructor establishes an instance of the class by creating the random number generator. The task of creating a Dice object is reserved to the static method getDice(). An initial call to the method instantiates the static variable and returns the object. Any subsequent call returns the same object.

Only getDice() accesses the private constructor. The method assures that only one instance of Dice exists.

The Dice class has a method toss() that throws the two dice and records the value for each die in the instance variables *dice1* and *dice2*. To access the results of the toss, use the methods getOne(), getTwo(), and getTotal(), which returns the total count for the two dice. The singleton pattern assures that a computer-generated casino game like Craps would use a single Dice object and hence a single random sequence of dice tosses.

Dice class (example of a singleton design pattern):

```
class Dice
{
    // static reference that identifies the single instance
    private static Dice dice = null;
    private Random rnd;
    private int dice1, dice2;

    // private constructor is called by the method getDice()
    // to create a single instance of the class
    private Dice()
    {
        rnd = new Random();    // create the random number generator
    }

    // if no object currently exists, call the private
    // constructor to create an instance; in any case, the
    // method returns the static reference variable dice
    public static Dice getDice()
    {
        if (dice == null)
        {
            dice = new Dice();
        }
        return dice;
    }

    // toss the dice and update values for dice1 and dice2
    public void toss()
    {
        dice1 = rnd.nextInt(6) + 1;
        dice2 = rnd.nextInt(6) + 1;
    }

        // access methods getOne(), getTwo(), and getTotal()
    . . .
}
```

3.5   GUI Application Design

Modern applications interact with the user through a graphical interface consisting of windows, dialogs, controls, and so forth.

Up to this point in this book, we have introduced only console-based applications. Input comes from the keyboard or a file and output displays in a console window. The program style is a simple way to illustrate concepts. In reality, most computer programs involve interactive programming using a *graphical user interface* (*GUI*). The programs are designed around graphical components and mouse and keyboard events. We would like you to see some GUI applications and include them in the exercises.

In this book, we use features of graphical programming that are typically covered in a first Java course. We rely almost exclusively on simple design patterns to build the programs with components and event listeners. Examples in this section present the design patterns.

Graphical Components

A frame features a title bar and icons the user clicks to minimize, maximize, or close the frame. The content of a frame consists of panels, labels, buttons, text boxes, and so forth.

GUI programming uses components, which are objects that represent visual elements in a display. From its first release, Java has provided libraries such as the Abstract Windowing Toolkit (AWT) that simplify the creation of GUI applications. Among the components is a high-level container called a *frame*, which is the main application window. The frame holds components such as panels, labels, text boxes, and buttons. A label displays a text string or an image. A text box is a component that allows the input and output of a single line of text (a text field) or multiple lines of text (a text area). A text field is a typical source for input. Events and event handling make a GUI application interactive. Selected components, such as a button, are assigned event listeners that respond to a user-supplied action such as a mouse click or a keyboard entry. An event handler is called to perform specified update tasks (Figure 3.3).

Java uses an inheritance hierarchy to implement components and event handling in GUI applications. The primary packages used are *java.awt* and *javax.swing*.

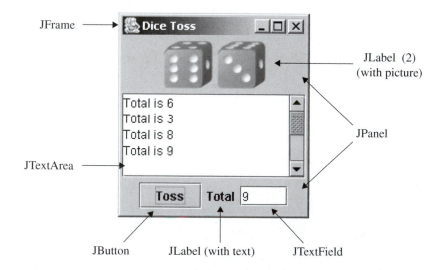

Figure 3.3 *Interactive application Dice Toss featuring key components and a button event.*

Figure 3.3 illustrates a graphical display for the DiceToss application. The frame is a window with a title bar and icons to minimize, maximize, and close the window. The content region below the title bar uses a border layout manager to position the components in the four compass points (north, east, south, or west) or in the center. The components include a panel at the top (NORTH) of the window consisting of two labels that display pictures of the dice faces. A second panel at the bottom (SOUTH) of the window has the command button *Toss*, a label with the text "Total," and a text field that displays the total of the dice toss. In the middle (CENTER) of the window is a text area that displays the outcome from successive tosses. A scroll bar enables the user to look at a full listing of outcomes. The figure is a snapshot of the application after the user has clicked the Toss button four times. The example includes the key elements of GUI programming that we feature in applications and exercises.

Java uses an inheritance hierarchy to present components and event handling in a GUI application. The AWT classes in the *java.awt* package define, among others, Button, Frame, TextField, and TextArea components. Java 2 added Swing classes in the package *javax.swing* to extend the structures and methods in the initial AWT classes. Figure 3.4 gives a partial listing of the component hierarchy. The classes in the shaded boxes are the Swing components, which begin with the letter 'J'. Some knowledge of the hierarchy is useful if you want to look up the AWT and Swing classes in the Java API documentation.

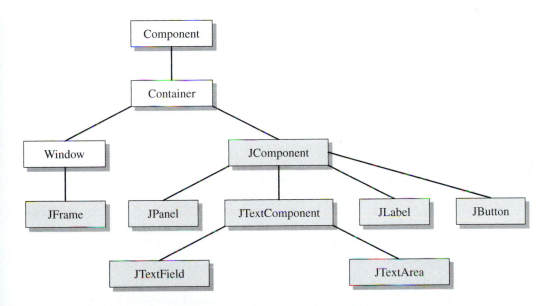

Figure 3.4 *Inheritance hierarchy for Java GUI components.*

GUI Application Design Pattern

Most GUI applications are built with a standard design pattern. The application is a class that extends *JFrame* with a main method that creates an instance of the application. During execution, the runtime system can show or hide a graphical component, including the frame itself. Initially, the frame is invisible and the main method must explicitly show the

The GUI design pattern is a useful starting point when constructing an application that constructs a graphical user interface.

frame by setting its visibility flag to true. The declaration calls a constructor that initializes attributes of the window, creates components, and places them in the content region of the frame. The design pattern consists of five separate program segments that include import statements, a declaration of component and application variables, the main method, a constructor, and inner classes for event handling. The following is the skeletal design structure for the DiceToss application. We will discuss each of the program segments in subsequent sections.

GUI Design Pattern:

```
<import statements>
public class DiceToss extends JFrame
{
    < component and application variables>

    public static void main(String[] args)
    {
        DiceToss app = new DiceToss();
        app.setVisible(true);
    }

    // constructor creates components and adds them to the frame
    public DiceToss()
    {
        <initialize frame attributes, create components>
    }

    // inner class defines an event handler object
    private class EventHandler implements <event interface>
    { }
}
```

Import statements specify the class libraries that the application will use.

Import Statements   The AWT package *java.awt* defines base classes in the GUI inheritance hierarchy with methods that are shared by most of the component classes. The Swing classes, in *javax.swing*, define components and containers, which are alternatives to those defined in the AWT. Event-handling classes and interfaces are defined in the package *java.awt.event*. A GUI application imports these three packages. An application may need to import other problem-specific classes.

```
import java.awt.*;          // original Java AWT
import javax.swing;         // Swing component classes
import java.awt.event.*;    // Java event classes
```

Application Variables   Declare as application variables the components and any data that will be accessed by event handlers and utility methods. In this way, they are accessible to all of the methods and inner classes in the application. In our example, declare reference variables for two *JPanel* containers, the three *JLabel* components, and the *JTextField* and *JTextArea* text boxes. The application uses a Dice object. We use the Dice class from Section 3.4, which ensures that only one instance is created. A JLabel can hold either text or an image, which Java defines as an *ImageIcon* object. The array diePict defines a list of dice pictures for the display. The array has seven elements with the first element, index 0, having value null. The other elements are ImageIcon (picture) objects in the range 1 to 6, which correspond to the six die values.

```
class DiceToss extends JFrame
{
   // application variables
   private JPanel panelA, panelB;
   private JLabel dieLabel1, dieLabel2, totalLabel;
   private JTextField totalField;
   private JTextArea  totalArea;
   private JButton tossButton;
   private Dice d = Dice.getDice();
   private ImageIcon[] diePict = {null,
         new ImageIcon("die1.gif"), new ImageIcon("die2.gif"),
         new ImageIcon("die3.gif"), new ImageIcon("die4.gif"),
         new ImageIcon("die5.gif"), new ImageIcon("die6.gif")};
   . . .
}
```

Application Constructor   The constructor initializes frame properties and loads the components. Start by setting the title using setTitle(titleStr) and then call setBounds(posX, posY, width, height) that specifies the size of the frame and its location on the screen. Dimensions for graphical components are given in pixels, which are units that measure the size of a monitor. Close window is one of the icons in the title bar. An application can determine the action that should occur when a user clicks the icon. Typically, you want to close the window, exit the application, and return to the runtime window. Java does this with a special method, called *setDefaultCloseOperation()*, that specifies the typical window-closing action. We use the method with the static constant JFrame.EXIT_ON_CLOSE as the argument.

> The constructor initializes frame properties and loads components into the frame.

Constructor (initializing the frame):

```
public DiceToss()
{
   setTitle( "Dice Toss" );
   setBounds(100, 100, 175,200);
   setDefaultCloseOperation(JFrame.EXIT_ON_CLOSE);
   . . .
}
```

The components in a frame reside in a region called the *content pane*. The pane is a *Container* object, which you can think of as the region below the title bar. Before beginning to create components for the frame, access its content pane using the method getContentPane() and assign the object to a Container reference variable.

> The components in a frame reside in the frame's content pane.

```
Container content = getContentPane();
```

The next step is to create and organize individual components and add them to the content pane. A component is added as a distinct object or as part of a panel that groups components into a single unit. To place components in a panel, first create a JPanel object and then create the component objects. Add the components to the panel. For the other components, simply create the object. Complete the process by adding all of the panels and individual components to the content pane. When creating a component, you may need arguments that set one or more attributes. For instance, a JLabel takes a string for a text label or an ImageIcon for a picture. A JTextField has an integer argument that determines the width of the box.

Constructor: (creating and adding components to the content pane)

```java
public DiceToss()
{

    . . .

    // establish the content pane for the window
    Container content = getContentPane();
    content.setLayout(new BorderLayout());

    // panel and labels for the two die pictures
    JPanel panelA = new JPanel();
    dieLabel1 = new JLabel();
    dieLabel2 = new JLabel();
    panelA.add(dieLabel1);
    panelA.add(dieLabel2);

    // text area to store results of successive dice tosses
    totalArea = new JTextArea(10, 15);

    // panel with toss button, total label, and total field
    // the toss button has an action listener (see next section)
    JPanel panelB = new JPanel();
    tossButton = new JButton("Toss");
    tossButton.addActionListener(new TossEvent());

    totalLabel = new JLabel("Total");
    totalField = new JTextField(4);
    panelB.add(tossButton);
    panelB.add(totalLabel);
    panelB.add(totalField);

    // add panels and individual components to the content pane
    // using compass point constants from class BorderLayout
    // text area is embedded in a JScrollPane to add scroll bars
    content.add(panelA, BorderLayout.NORTH);
    content.add(new JScrollPane(totalArea),
    BorderLayout.CENTER);
    content.add(panelB, BorderLayout.SOUTH);
}
```

Event Listeners and Event Handlers

In a GUI application, interactive programming is done with events, such as window events, keystroke events, mouse events, and so forth. In the package *java.awt.event*, Java defines event-handling facilities that feature a Listener design pattern. A *listener* is an object that resides in a component waiting for designated user-supplied action. For each listener, there is a method to register the listener on a component and an interface with specified methods that define an event-handler object that responds to the event.

A listener is an object that resides in a component and waits for the occurrence of an event. The listener handles the processing required by the event. Add a listener to a component using the method addTypeListener(), where Type is the type of the event.

Our applications will use only the Java ActionListener. The component method addActionListener() registers the listener on a button or a text field. An event that awakens the listener is called an *action event*. For a button, the listener responds to a mouse click in the component region; for a text field, the listener responds to the user pressing the Enter key.

addActionListener():

```
void addActionListener(ActionListener handlerObj)
```

> Adds an action listener to the component. The parameter is an event handler that responds to an action event on this component.

A private *inner class* defines an event-handler object. An inner class is declared within the application (outer) class and, thus, has access to all of the variables in the outer class. This is important in a GUI program because the event handler typically updates component variables that are defined in the GUI application class. For an action listener, the event-handler class must implement the `ActionListener` interface that includes only one method, `actionPerformed()`.

A private inner class is an often-used method of implementing an event listener.

ActionListener interface:

```
void actionPerformed(ActionEvent ae)
```
> Invoked when an action occurs.

Note the parameter for `actionPerformed()`. An *ActionEvent* object is created by the runtime system when an action event occurs. The object contains information about the component involved in the event. The `ActionEvent` object has methods `getSource()` and `getActionCommand()` that extract the information. Specifically, `getSource()` returns the component and `getActionCommand()` returns the text (string) that identifies the component.

A button generates an Action-Event when it is pressed. The event listener must implement the ActionListener interface.

Dice Toss Action Event

The Toss command in the DiceToss application illustrates key features of Java event handling. An action event (mouse click) in the region of *tossButton* initiates a process that results in dice being tossed and subsequent updates to the label, text field, and text area components. The updates are provided by the method actionPerformed() in the private class TossEvent that implements `ActionListener`.

```
// register the action listener on tossButton with a TossEvent
// object as the argument.
tossButton.addActionListener(new TossEvent());
```

The listener for the Toss button in the Dice application illustrates key features of Java event handling.

An action event involves a dynamic interaction with the user and the runtime system. Figure 3.5 illustrates this interaction for a mouse-click event in the JButton object

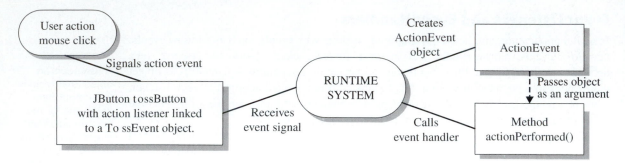

Figure 3.5 *Action event sequence.*

tossButton. The runtime system is alerted to "listen" for a user-supplied mouse click in the component region. When the runtime system receives the event signal, it creates an ActionEvent object with information derived from the component. The runtime system uses the object as an argument for the actionPerformed() method that is associated with the event handler.

The private inner class TossEvent implements the ActionListener interface by defining the method actionPerformed(). The action involves tossing the dice and then using methods setIcon(), append(), and setText() to update the labels, text area, and text field respectively.

Event Handler class:

```java
private class TossEvent implements ActionListener
{
    public void actionPerformed(ActionEvent ae)
    {
        d.toss();
        dieLabel1.setIcon(diePict[d.getOne()]);
        dieLabel2.setIcon(diePict[d.getTwo()]);
        totalArea.append("Total is " + d.getTotal() + "\n");
        totalField.setText("" + d.getTotal());
    }
}
```

You can find a listing of DiceToss in Chapter 3 of the software supplement along with the images for the six different die faces.

Chapter Summary

• An interface contains only method signatures and constant variables. Unlike an abstract class, an interface does not have instance variables or concrete methods. In Java, the reserved *interface* defines the structure and the reserved word *implements* links the interface with a class in an inheritance hierarchy. Any class that implements an interface may access the constant data in the interface and must declare all of the methods defined in the interface or the implementing class is abstract and cannot generate objects. Polymorphism applies to an interface in the same way that it applies to superclasses. As an example, this chapter develops the Measurement interface and the classes Circle and Rectangle that implement the interface. As we will see at the beginning of Chapter 8, the concept of an interface drives the development of the collections framework developed in this book.

- An interface defines a template that describes the behavior of any class that implements the interface. While an interface is not a class, it can be a reference type in a variable declaration and then be assigned any object from a class that implements the interface. An interface method that is called with the interface reference uses polymorphism. Interfaces can be part of their own inheritance hierarchy. A parent interface may be used to derive a child interface, which has access to all of the constants and abstract methods in the parent interface. Any class that implements the child interface must implement all of the methods that are declared in both the parent and child interfaces. A class that implements an interface can be extended. The derived class automatically implements the interface because the methods are declared in the superclass.

- The javadoc utility produces user documentation of a class that includes both the formal and compact specification of its methods. The documentation originates with the class developer who adds javadoc comments to the source code that implements the class. The javadoc utility recognizes comments written in this special format and produces linked HTML pages. These pages produce interactive documentation that a programmer can use when writing a program.

- Design patterns identify common software design problems and solutions using abstract object models and object interaction. The patterns document solutions that can be used by others in the software engineering community. For example, the singleton design pattern provides a model for the building of a class that may have only one instance.

- In console-based applications, input comes from the keyboard or a file and output displays in a console window. The typical modern application is a GUI application that uses windows, dialogs, and controls. We introduce a design pattern for a GUI application and apply it to construct the class DiceToss in some detail. You can use this application as a model for creating your own simple GUI applications. We also reference a more comprehensive tutorial on the Web.

Written Exercises

1. Describe key differences between an abstract class and an interface.

2. Describe the conditions that must be present in order for polymorphism to occur with interface and class reference variables.

3. Describe the actions of the frame methods `setTitle()`, `setBounds()`, and `setDefaultCloseOperation()`.

4. The class `SingletonDemo` demonstrates the singleton design pattern. Complete an implementation that features only the key elements in the design. Use the method `getInstance()` to return a static instance of the class.

```
public class SingletonDemo
{
    <private section>
    <public access method>
}
```

Programming Exercises

5. Declare an interface called Justify that defines only the constants LEFT, CENTER, and RIGHT as integer values. Use the interface in the implementation of a library of static methods fmtString(), fmtInt(), and fmtDouble(). Declare the methods in the class FormatString.

```
// returns a string that positions str in block of w
// characters justified LEFT, CENTER, or RIGHT
public static String fmtString(String str, int w, int justify)

// returns a string that converts n to a string positioned
// in a field of w characters justified LEFT, CENTER,
// or RIGHT
public static String fmtInt(int n, int w, int justify)

// returns a string that converts x to a string positioned
// in a field of w characters with d decimal places,
// justified LEFT, CENTER, or RIGHT
public static String fmtDouble(double x, int w, int d,
                                          int justify)
```

Write a program that tests your implementation of the static FormatString methods.

6. The `Diagonal` interface extends the `Measurement` interface and defines the method `diagonal()`. Modify the classes `Circle and Rectangle` so that they implement `Diagonal`.

Write a program that declares the following objects:

```
Circle c = new Circle(2.5);
Rectangle rA = new Rectangle(2,4),
          rB = new Rectangle(1,5);
Square s = new Square(3);
```

Have the program declare an array with the various figure objects as elements. Use the array to scan the elements and create the following output:

- A listing of information on each figure including description of the figure, its area, perimeter, and diagonal. Do this by creating the method figureInfo().
- The figure with the maximum (longest) diagonal.
- The figure whose difference between the area and perimeter (in absolute value) is the smallest.
- A listing of figures whose area is greater than its perimeter.

7. Design and implement the `RandomGenerator` class using the singleton design pattern. The static method `getGenerator()` returns a reference to a unique `RandomGenerator` object. Include in the class the methods `nextInt(int n)` and `nextDouble()` that correspond to the operations in the `Random` class.

Design and test your implementation of the `RandomGenerator` class. At issue is a strategy to show that the class has only one instance.

8. The following is a definition of the Update interface.

```
public interface Update
{
    void update(int n);
}
```

The class UpdateTime extends Time24 and implements the Update interface. The class has a constructor that takes a Time24 object as the initial value and implements the method update() by adding m minutes to the current time.

The class StoreInt defines value as an integer instance variable. The class implements the Update interface. A constructor takes an integer argument as the initial value. The method getInt() accesses the stored value. A description of the object is provided by toString(), which has the form *Value = <value>*. The update() method adds the argument to the current value.

(a) Give declarations for the UpdateTime class and the StoreInt class.

(b) Write a program that declares an UpdateTime and a StoreInt object, where the initial time is 1:15. The StoreInt object stores the corresponding time in minutes as its value. In this case, the StoreInt object has value 75.

   (i)   Output a description of each object.

   (ii) Prompt the user to input an update value. Use it to update each object by the specified amount and output a description of the object.

   (iii) Implement the method updateObject(), which has parameters that include an update value and a Update reference variable. The method returns an Update object. After identifying the type of Update object (UpdateTime or StoreInt), the method updates the object by the specified argument. It concludes by returning an object of the "other" type with a corresponding value. For instance, if a StoreInt object has value 120 and the update argument is 30, updateObject() updates the StoreInt object to have value 150 and returns an UpdateTime object with time value 2:30. Use updateObject() in your program.

```
public static Update updateObject(Update obj, int n)
{ . . . }
```

9. In Section 3.5, we introduced an action event for a JButton component. A similar event occurs in a JTextField component when the user inputs data and presses the Enter key. Like a button, we must assign an action listener to the text field and then define an event-handler object that implements the actionPerformed() method. Create a GUI application that processes the purchase of volleyball tickets, which are priced at $7.25 per ticket. The user enters an integer *n* in the text field and then presses the Enter key. An event computes the total cost for the *n* tickets.

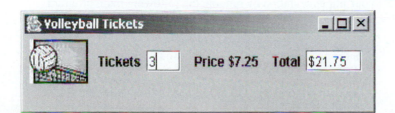

In the application, a `JLabel` contains an `ImageIcon` object, which is a picture of a volleyball from the file *volleyball.jpg* in the directory *ch3ex* in the software supplement. Let the price and amount ("Price $7.25") be a label. Use the following statement to build the icon.

```
ImageIcon teamIcon = new ImageIcon("volleyball.jpg");
```

10. Assume a bank always links a customer's savings and ATM access to one account. Write a program that uses the singleton design pattern to create the class `SingleAccount`. The class has a static method `getAccount()` that returns the one instance, which is initially created with a zero ($0.00) balance. The `SingleAccount` object maintains a balance that is accessed and updated with the methods `getBalance()`, `debit()`, and `credit()`. The latter two change the balance by a specified amount.

     The program should create two other classes called `Savings` and ATM. Each class includes by composition a `SingleAccount` reference variable called account. The constructor in each class initializes the variable. Each class defines the method `getBalance()` that returns the current balance in the `SingleAccount` object. The ATM class has the method `withdraw()` that processes a customer's request for money through an ATM. The method takes an amount and returns a string that serves as a receipt. If the account has sufficient funds, the method debits the account and returns a string that indicates the amount paid out and gives the updated balance; otherwise, no action is taken and the string indicates that the account cannot process the request. The `Savings` class has methods `deposit()` and `withdraw()` providing basic savings account transactions. Both methods provide a receipt for the transaction. The following is a UML representation of the classes.

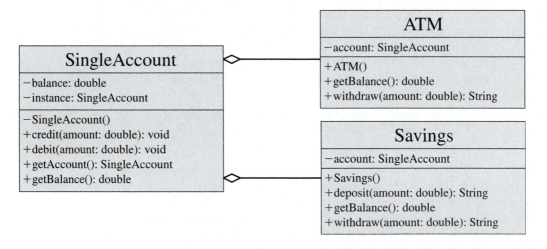

(a) Give a declaration for each class.

(b) Test your implementation by running the following main program.

```
public static void main(String[] args)
{
    Savings svAcct = new Savings();
    ATM atm = new ATM();

    svAcct.deposit(250.00);
```

```
        System.out.println("Initial balance in the account +
                           is $" svAcct.getBalance());
    System.out.println("ATM transactions");
    System.out.println("    Withdraw: " +
        atm.withdraw(200.00));
    System.out.println("    Withdraw: " +
                       atm.withdraw(100.00));

    System.out.println("Saving account transactions");

    System.out.println("    Bank balance is $" +
                       svAcct.getBalance());
    svAcct.deposit(250.00);
    System.out.println("    Deposit $250.00 Bank" +
                       "balance is  $" + svAcct.getBalance());
    svAcct.withdraw(175.00);
    System.out.println("    Withdraw $175.00 Bank" +
                       "balance is $" + svAcct.getBalance());
    }
```

11. Create a GUI application that places two buttons in a panel on the north side of the frame, a label holding pictures in the center, and a label with names on the south side. The subdirectory "icons" in the directory *ch3ex* contains four pictures of U.S. national parks. Create an array of ImageIcon objects for the park images, and an array of String objects for the park names. Add events on the buttons so that pressing the "Next" button cycles the display to the next picture and park and pressing the "Previous" button cycles the display to the previous picture and park. At the last index, the event rotates pictures back to index 0. Figure 3.6 illustrates the display for Mount Rushmore National Park in South Dakota. Hint: insert the picture in the center label using `setIcon()`. Insert the name in the bottom label using `setText()`.

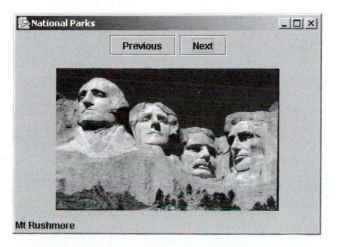

Figure 3.6 *One frame of the GUI application in programming Exercise 3.11.*

Programming Project

12. In the GUI design pattern, we create a `JButton` object or a `JTextField` object with an associated event by allocating the component with a text string (button) or an integer width (text field). In a separate statement, an action listener is added to the component with an event handling, which is an instance of a private class that implements `ActionListener`. For instance,

```
JButton button = new JButton("text");
button.addActionListener(new ButtonHandler());

private class ButtonHandler implements ActionListener
{
    public void actionPerformed(ActionEvent ae)
    { . . . }
}
```

We can use an inheritance hierarchy to create buttons and text fields that enter themselves as an action listener. Let us look at the process for a button component. In the hierarchy, the Java swing class `JButton` is a superclass. The abstract class, call it *JButtonEvent,* extends `JButton` and implements `ActionListener`. The class has a constructor that takes a string argument specifying the text in the button. The constructor registers an action listener and designates that the class serves as the event handler. The method `actionPerformed()` is implemented by calling doAction(), which is declared as an abstract method. An application simply defines a second-level-derived class that overloads doAction(). The object becomes a `JButton` with an action listener and a method to handle an event.

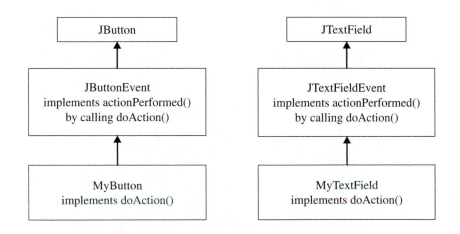

Component Listener Classes

JButtonEvent:

```
public abstract class JButtonEvent extends JButton
                           implements ActionListener
{
   // constructor takes a string as the button text
   public JButtonEvent(String buttonTitle)
   {
      super(buttonTitle);

      // add actionListener;  the reserved this indicates
      // the object itself implements actionPerformed
      addActionListener(this);
   }
      // event handler method calls doAction() in a
      // derived class
      public void actionPerformed(ActionEvent ae)
      {      doAction(); }
      public abstract void doAction();

}
```

To create a button component that enters itself as a listener, define a derived inner class that extends `JButtonEvent`. The class has a constructor that assigns the button text and implements the method `doAction()`. For instance, class `ClearButton` creates the `JButton` "Clear."

```
private class ClearButton extends JButtonEvent
{ . . . }
```

In an application, declare JButton clearButton as a ClearButton object with string "Clear."

```
JButton clearButton = new ClearButton("Clear");
```

(a) Using the JButtonEvent class as a model, give a declaration for the abstract JTextFieldEvent class. The constructor takes an integer argument specifying the width of the field.
(b) Do Programming Exercise 3.9 by declaring a private inner class `TicketField` that extends `JTextFieldEvent`. Use an instance of the class for the Tickets field.
(c) Redo the DiceToss application from Section 3.5 using `JButtonEvent` objects for Toss button.

Chapter 4

INTRODUCTION TO ALGORITHMS

CONTENTS

4.1 SELECTION SORT
Selection Sort Algorithm

4.2 SIMPLE SEARCH ALGORITHMS
Sequential Search
Binary Search

4.3 ANALYSIS OF ALGORITHMS
System/Memory Performance
Criteria

Algorithm Performance: Running
Time Analysis
Big-O Notation
Common Orders of Magnitude

4.4 COMPARING SEARCH ALGORITHMS
The Timing Class

In this chapter, we discuss elements of algorithm design and efficiency. A good starting point is the introduction of array searching and sorting algorithms. The classical selection sort illustrates many of the common features of list-sorting algorithms. Searching an array to locate a target value is a basic problem in computing. The simplest form of searching is the sequential search, which compares the target with every element in the array until it obtains a match or reaches the end of the array. For some applications, we maintain an array in sorted order. In this case, the binary search may be used. The search exploits the structure of an ordered list to produce very fast access times.

This chapter introduces the concept of algorithm efficiency. While the hardware resources of a computer

system may affect runtime efficiency, we focus on a more abstract measure that looks at the number of calculations that must be performed while executing the algorithm. A book on algorithms makes a formal study of algorithm efficiency that results in a variety of measurement approaches. Such a study explores the underlying mathematical justification for the different measures. Our approach is more intuitive. We introduce Big-O notation, which provides estimates of efficiency on the basis of the number of iterations in an algorithm and the number of elements in the array or collection. Big-O measure for an algorithm gives us a tool to effectively compare and contrast different algorithms. We use this measure throughout this book.

4.1 Selection Sort

Array-based sorting algorithms deal with a sequence of elements in a list and use some rearrangement strategy to order the elements. We begin with a very simple example, called the *selection sort*, that proceeds through the list position by position, starting at the beginning of the list. At each position, the algorithm selects the element that is next in order and copies it into the location.

With sorting algorithms, we discover that our understanding is helped when we proceed from the concrete to the abstract. An ideal starting point draws on our everyday experiences with sorting objects. The experiences are many and varied: When a bank returns our monthly checks, we arrange them by check number; we stack lumber vertically in a garage with the longest piece in the back, preceded by the next longest piece, and so forth;

instructors typically sort exams by name to record grades and pass out papers—for a large class, an instructor splits the papers into small piles, sorts each pile, and then merges them back into one ordered set. The problem with our experiences, however, is that we order items almost subconsciously without formally understanding the process as an algorithm. More can be gained if we use a sample list and carry out the sort step by step. This makes explicit the process and thus sets out a design for the algorithm. At the end, we can formulate the sort algorithm as a method with a parameter list. The implementation of the method is a generalization of the example.

Let us illustrate these ideas with a discussion of the selection sort algorithm. A sample problem has us arranging an array of four animals in ascending order of their size.

Step 1:   The ordering begins by locating the smallest animal, the fish, in the first position. The operation occurs by having the owl that currently occupies the first position exchange places with the fish. The effect is to place the smallest animal at the front of the list.

Ordered   Unordered

Step 2:   The tail of the list, starting at the second position, is unordered. The process continues by identifying the smallest animal among the owl, dragon, and dog and arranging it in the second position. The selection is the owl that is already in its proper position, so we can move to the next step.

Ordered   Unordered

Selection sort passes through the list and exchanges the smallest element with the first element. It then passes through the remaining elements and exchanges the second smallest element with the second element, and so forth.

Step 3:   With the fish and owl in position, only the last two animals must be ordered. We identify the dog as the next smallest animal and have it exchange positions with the dragon. After this step, the tail of the list has only one item left, which must be the largest animal. The entire list is ordered.

Selection Sort Algorithm

We develop the *selection sort algorithm* for an array of *n* elements. The resulting list is in ascending order with

$$arr[0] <= arr[1] <= arr[2] <= \ldots <= arr[n\text{-}2] <= arr[n\text{-}1]$$

In selection sort, pass *i* finds the index of the smallest element among arr[i] ... arr[n − 1] and swaps it with arr[i].

The algorithm starts at index 0 and determines the position of the smallest element in the list. An exchange swaps the element at the position with arr[0]. This step places the smallest element in arr[0] and leaves the rest of the list in unsorted order. The process moves to index 1, and a selection determines the position of the smallest element in the sublist arr[1] ... arr[n − 1]. An exchange swaps this smallest element with arr[1], leaving the elements in the first two positions in order. The process repeats for positions 2 through *n* − 2. No selection occurs at position *n* − 1 because all of the previous exchanges have made arr[n − 1] the largest element in the list. The selection sort algorithm involves *n* − 1 iterations, which we refer to as *passes*, because each involves a traversal of elements in a sublist to locate the index of the smallest element.

Assume *arr* is an integer array with *n* = 5 elements having values {50, 20, 40, 75, 35}. Figure 4.1 displays the status of the array after each of the four passes. The passes start at 0 because the first pass stores the smallest element in arr[0].

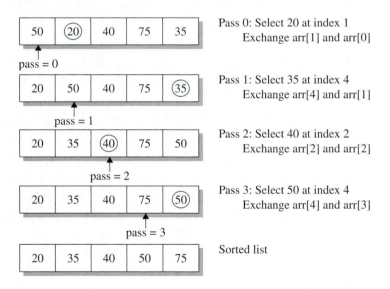

Figure 4.1 *Ordering an integer array with the selection sort.*

Pass 0: Scan the entire list from arr[0] to arr[4] and identify that index 1 is the location of the smallest element 20. Exchange arr[1] = 20 with arr[0] = 50, the first element in the list. After completing pass 0, the first element is correctly positioned.

Pass 1: The sublist from arr[1] to arr[4] is unordered. Scan the elements 50, 40, 75, and 35 and identify that 35 at index 4 is the smallest element in the sublist. Exchange arr[4] = 35 with arr[1] = 50. The front of the list {20, 35} is now ordered.

Pass 2: The sublist from arr[2] to arr[4] remains unordered. The smallest element in the sublist 40, 75, and 50 is 40 at index 2. We want to uniformly handle each pass, which means exchanging arr[2] and arr[2]. This is technically unnecessary since 40 is already in the correct position. However, this saves each iteration from testing whether an exchange is actually necessary.

Pass 3: Two elements remain unordered in the sublist from arr[3] to arr[4]. A final step identifies 50 at index 4 as the smallest element. The exchange of arr[3] = 75 with arr[4] = 50 completes the ordering of the array.

The selectionSort Method   The static method `selectionSort()` in the class `Arrays` implements the algorithm for an integer array. You can find the class in the package *ds.util*. Its signature includes the array *arr* as the parameter. The implementation of the method consists of nested for-loops. The outer loop establishes the $n - 1$ passes over the array where n is the length of the array. The control variable, called *pass*, ranges from 0 to $n - 2$. For each iteration, an inner loop scans the unordered sublist `arr[pass]` to `arr[n - 1]` and assigns to the variable *smallIndex* the position of the smallest element. An exchange between `arr[pass]` and `arr[smallIndex]` completes the iteration and places element `arr[smallIndex]` to its correct position in the final sorted list.

selectionSort (integer array):

The static method
selectionSort()
in Arrays
implements the
selection sort.

```
public static void selectionSort(int[] arr)
{
    int smallIndex;     // index of minimum value in sublist
    int pass, j, n = arr.length;
    int temp;

    // pass has the range 0 to n-2
    for (pass = 0; pass < n-1; pass++)
    {

        // scan the sublist starting at index pass; assume
        // the minimum value is initially arr[pass]
        smallIndex = pass;
        // j traverses the sublist arr[pass+1] to arr[n-1]
        for (j = pass+1; j < n; j++) if smaller element found,
        assign smallIndex to that index if (arr[j]
        < arr[smallIndex])smallIndex = j;

        // swap the next smallest element into arr[pass]

        temp = arr[pass]; arr[pass] = arr[smallIndex];

        arr[smallIndex] = temp;
    }
}
```

Example 4.1

The selection sort orders an array of 10 integers.

```
// declare an integer array
int[] arr = {66, 20, 33, 55, 53, 57, 69, 11, 67, 70};

// call selectionSort() to order the array
Arrays.selectionSort(arr);

System.out.print("Sorted: ");
for (int i=0; i < arr.length; i++)
    System.out.print(arr[i] + "  ");
```

Output:
    Sorted: 11 20 33 53 55 57 66 67 69 70

4.2 Simple Search Algorithms

Array search algorithms start with a target value and employ some indexing strategy to visit the elements looking for a match. If the target is found, the corresponding index of the matching element becomes the return value. Otherwise, the return value indicates that the target is not found. A search frequently wants to cover the entire array. A more general algorithm allows for searches in a sublist of the array. A sublist is a sequence of elements whose range of indices begin at index `first` and continue up to, but not including, index `last`. We denote a sublist by its index range [`first`, `last`). In Figure 4.2, array *arr* contains nine elements. The shaded elements are the sublist [2,6). The array itself is the sublist [0,9). In each case, note that `arr[last]` is not an element in the sublist.

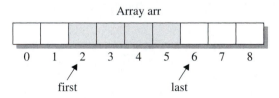

Figure 4.2 *Sublists in an array.*

Sequential Search

The simplest search algorithm for an array is the *sequential search*. The algorithm begins with a target value and indices that define the sublist range. It scans the elements in the sublist item by item, looking for the first occurrence of a match with an item called *target*. If successful, the algorithm returns the index of the match. The search is not successful if the scan reaches the index last before matching the target. In this case, the algorithm returns −1.

The seqSearch() Method We develop the method seqSearch() for an integer array as a static method in the class Arrays. As the book progresses, we will develop additional searching algorithms and add them to this class. For arguments, the method has an array *arr*, the two indices *first* and *last* that specify the index range, and the *target* value. The return value is an index of type *int*.

To illustrate the action of seqSearch(), consider the integer array

```
int[] arr = {6, 4, 2, 9, 5, 3, 10, 7};
```

The figure illustrates a search of the entire array for target 3 and a search of the sublist [2,5) for target 10.

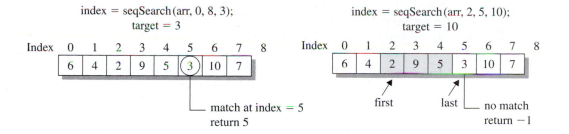

The implementation of seqSearch() uses a for-loop to scan the array elements in the range [first, last). Iterations continue so long as the index is in range and no match is found. The scan terminates on a match and the index becomes the return value. Otherwise, −1 is the return value.

The static method seqSearch() in the class Arrays implements the sequential search.

seqSearch (integer array):

```
public static int seqSearch(int[] arr, int first, int last,
                    int target)
{
    // scan indices in the range first <= i < last; return
    // the index indicating the position if a match occurs;
    // otherwise return -1
    for (int i = first; i < last; i++)
        if (arr[i] == target)
            return i;

    // no return yet if match is not found; return -1
    return -1;
}
```

Sequential search is a "brute force" algorithm that compares the target against each element of the array until it locates a match or reaches the end of the array.

Example 4.2

```
int[] list = {5, 3, 100, 89, 5, 6, 5};
int index;
```

1. Search the entire array list, looking for the first occurrence of 6, and output the return value.

```
index = Arrays.seqSearch(list, 0, list.length, 6);
System.out.println(index);    // output: 5 (search succeeds)
```

2. Search the sublist arrlist[3]...arrlist[4] with index range [3,5), looking for the first occurrence of 100, and output the return value.

```
index = Arrays.seqSearch(list,3,5,100);
System.out.println(index);    // output: -1 (search fails)
```

3. We use the fact that seqSearch() can search a subrange to find all occurrences of 5 in the array. After locating the index of the first 5, continue the search in the tail of the list beginning at the next index. Continue the process until the search fails. Note that a call to seqSearch() is part of an assignment statement within the *while* condition. The assignment statement is enclosed in parentheses and has the value index which is compared with −1 to check whether an additional occurrence of 5 has been found. The parentheses are necessary because the assignment operator = has a lower precedence than *!=*. Programmers frequently combine an assignment statement with a comparison operator in a conditional expression.

```
// initialize index to the start of the array
index = 0;

// search for 5 in the range [index,list.length)
System.out.print("5 occurs at indices ");
while ((index = Arrays.seqSearch(list,index,list.length,5))
    != -1)
{
    System.out.print(index + "  ");
    // increment index to the next position
    index++;
}
```

Output:

5 occurs at indices 0 4 6

The binary search exploits the fact that a list is ordered. This allows large sections of the list to be excluded from the search.

Binary Search

The sequential search is a general search algorithm that applies to any array. It methodically scans the elements one after another until it finds a match or reaches the end of the range. You can employ a more efficient search strategy for an ordered array. You use the strategy when looking up a phone number in a telephone book. Suppose you want to find the number for "Swanson". A phone book maintains names in alphabetical order, so you look for "Swanson" somewhere near the back of the book. If you jump to an approximate location and land in the "P"s, you know to look further back in the book. A second selection may land you in the "U"s, which is too far, so a third choice is made somewhere between the first two locations, and so on. This approach is clearly superior to a sequential search, which would laboriously scan the "A"s, then the "B"s, and subsequent letters in the alphabet. Our problem is to turn the rather haphazard phone number lookup strategy into an algorithm that will work for any ordered array. The solution is the *binary search algorithm*. Given a target value, the algorithm begins the search by selecting the midpoint in the list. If the value at the midpoint matches the target, the search is done. Otherwise, because the list is ordered, the search should continue in the first half of the list (lower sublist) or in the second half of the list (upper sublist). If the target is less than the current midpoint value, look in the lower sublist by selecting its midpoint; otherwise, look in the upper sublist by selecting its midpoint. You can continue the process by looking at midpoints for ever smaller and smaller sublists. Eventually, the process either finds the target value or reduces the size of the sublist to 0, which is the criterion that the target is not in the list.

To get a more formal understanding of the binary search algorithm, we need to specify the meaning of midpoint and lower and upper sublist in terms of array indices. Assume *arr* is an array with n items and that the search looks for the item called *target*. The indices for the full list are in the index range first $= 0 \leq i < n =$ last, or [0,n). Start the search process by computing the middle index for the range [first, last), and then assign the value at the index to the variable *midValue*.

> The midpoint of the array index range [first, last) is at index (first + last)/2.

```
mid = (first + last)/2;  // middle index for [first,last]
midValue = arr[mid];     // save value in midValue
```

Compare midValue with target. Three possible outcomes can occur, which trigger three separate actions.

Case 1.   A match occurs. The search is complete, and *mid* is the index that locates *target*.

> target== arr[mid], we have a match.

target

|————————|————————————————|————————|
first   mid   last−1   last

Case 1: target = midValue
Search is done

```
if (midValue == target)   // found match
    return mid;
```

Case 2.   The value *target* is less than *midValue*, and the search must continue in the lower sublist. The index range for this sublist is [first, mid). Reposition the index *last* to the end of the sublist (last = mid).

> target < arr[mid], search range [first, mid) by assigning last = mid.

```
// search the lower sublist
if (target < midValue)
    <reposition last to mid>
    <search sublist arr[first]…arr[mid-1]
```

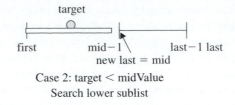

Case 2: target < midValue
Search lower sublist

target > arr[mid], search the range [mid + 1, last) by assigning first = mid + 1.

Case 3. The value *target* is greater than *midValue*, and the search must continue in the upper sublist. The index range for this sublist is [mid+1, last), because the sublist begins immediately to the right of *mid*. Reposition the index *first* to the front of the sublist (first = mid + 1).

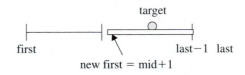

Case 3: target > midValue
Search upper sublist

```
// search upper sublist
if (target > midValue)
    <reposition first to mid+1>
    <search sublist arr[mid+1]...arr[last-1]>
```

The binary search terminates when a match is found or when the sublist to be searched is empty. An empty sublist occurs when first >= last.

Example 4.3

The example gives a few snapshots of the binary search algorithm as it looks for a target in the nine-element integer array, arr.

	0	1	2	3	4	5	6	7	8	9
arr	−7	3	5	8	12	16	23	33	55	

The first case searches for target = 23 and returns the index 6. The second case searches for target = 4 and returns −1 because the item is not in the array.

1. Target = 23

    Step 1: Index range [0, 9)

    Indices first = 0, last = 9, mid = (0 + 9)/2 = 4.

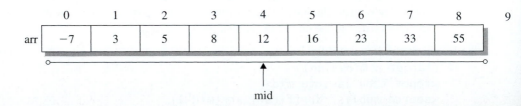

target = 23 > midValue = 12; no match so continue searching in the upper sublist with first = 5 and last = 9.

Step 2: Index range [5, 9)

Indices first = 5, last = 9, mid = (5 + 9)/2 = 7,

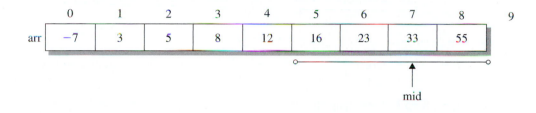

target = 23 < midValue = 33;   continue search in the lower sublist with first = 5 and last = 7.

Step 3: Index range [5, 7)

Indices first = 5, last = 7, mid = (5 + 7)/2 = 6.

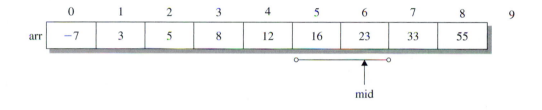

target = midValue = 23;   match is found at index mid = 6, which becomes the return value.

2. Target = 4.

Step 1: Index range [0, 9)

Indices first = 0, last = 9, mid = (0 + 9)/2 = 4.

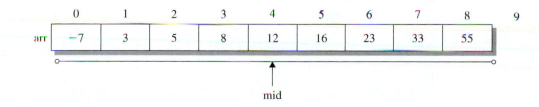

target = 4 < midValue = 12;   continue searching the lower sublist with first = 0 and last = 4.

Step 2: Index range [0, 4)

Indices first = 0, last = 4, mid = (0 + 4)/2 = 2.

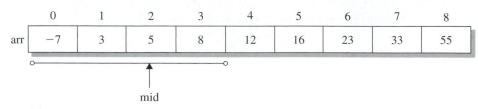

target = 4 < midValue = 5;   search the lower sublist with first = 0 and last 2.

Step 3: Index range [0, 2)

Indices first = 0, last = 2, mid = (0 + 2)/2 = 1.

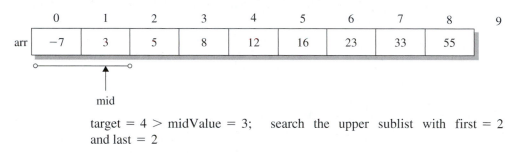

target = 4 > midValue = 3;   search the upper sublist with first = 2 and last = 2

Step 4: Index range [2, 2)

Indices first = 2, last = 2. When first >= last, the search terminate with the target not found. The return value is −1.

The binSearch Method   The static method binSearch() in the Arrays class implements the binary search algorithm for an integer array. The method has four arguments that identify the array, the indices first and last that specify the index range, and the target. The method returns the array index that identifies the first occurrence of a match or −1 if the target is not found. The implementation uses an iterative process on progressively smaller sublists [first, last). Iteration continues so long as the sublist is not empty (first < last) and no match occurs. After determining the middle index of the range and the corresponding array value, multiple selection statements compare the value with the target and treat the three possible outcomes.

The static method binSearch() in the class Arrays implements the binary search.

binSearch (integer array):

```
public static int binSearch(int arr[], int first, int last,
             int target)
{
    int mid;                // index of the midpoint
    int midValue;           // value that is assigned arr[mid]

    while (first < last)    // test for nonempty sublist
    {
```

```
        mid = (first+last)/2;
        midValue = arr[mid];
        if (target == midValue)
            return mid;         // have a match
            // determine which sublist to search
            else if (target < midValue)
              last = mid;       // search lower sublist; reset last
            else
              first = mid+1;  // search upper sublist; reset first
    }
    return -1;                // target not found
}
```

Example 4.4

The example uses the method binSearch() to search for a target in a sorted list of integers.

```
int[] arr = {11, 20, 33, 40, 45, 57, 60, 67, 79};

// search entire list for 60; first = 0, last = arr.length
index = Arrays.binSearch(arr, 0, arr.length, 60); // index = 6

// search the index range [3,7) for 20
index = Arrays.binSearch(arr, 3, 7, 20);          // index = -1
```

4.3   Analysis of Algorithms

A programmer judges code that executes an algorithm by its correctness, its ease of use, and its efficiency; in simple terms, "Does it work?" "Is it friendly?" "Is it fast?" Design and testing of code are the key factors that contribute to its correctness and ease of use. The question of efficiency is more difficult to pin down because the algorithm can be judged by different performance criteria. In this section, we describe system criteria, memory utilization criteria, and the internal complexity of the algorithm as three different ways to judge performance. The first two criteria depend on external resources and are more properly covered in a course on operating systems. We focus on complexity criteria that depend on the design of the algorithm. We are particularly interested in algorithms that apply to an array or a collection of data in which the underlying storage structure might have a large number of elements. For these algorithms, we develop measures of efficiency that depend on n, the number of items in the collection.

System/Memory Performance Criteria

An algorithm ultimately runs on a computer system with a specific instruction set and peripheral devices. If the algorithm is designed to target a particular machine, a programmer can code the method to take full advantage of the system resources. The resulting method will outperform a different implementation that assumes a generic machine. We say that the first algorithm has greater *system efficiency*. This is a relative measure that applies to two or more algorithms that carry out the same task. By running the algorithms on the

System efficiency measures how well an algorithm runs on a particular machine.

same machine with the same data sets, we can determine the relative times by using a system timing mechanism. The ranking of the times becomes the measure of system efficiency for each of the algorithms. For instance, to refresh a window, one algorithm might more effectively use the cache and operations of the video card and thus be more efficient on the particular system.

Space efficiency is a measure of the amount of memory an algorithm uses. If an algorithm uses too much memory, it can be too slow or may not execute at all on a particular system.

Algorithms use memory to store and process data. When comparing two algorithms, we might note that one requires large temporary storage that limits the size of the initial data set or forces the system to use time-consuming disk swapping. On a system with limited memory, the algorithm may not execute at all or may be very inefficient. A second algorithm might be less system efficient but run adequately within the memory constraints. *Space efficiency* is a measure of the relative amount of internal memory used by an algorithm. Depending on the memory resources of the system, the space efficiency of an algorithm dictates what kind of computer is capable of running the algorithm and its impact on overall system efficiency. The issue of space efficiency is becoming less important on modern computers because of the rapid increase in the size of available memory.

Algorithm Performance: Running Time Analysis

Machine-independent measures of efficiency involve counting the number of comparisons, assignment statements, and so on.

For the study of data structures, we want performance criteria for algorithms that are based on their efficiency in accessing large collections of data. Traditionally, computer scientists use criteria that measure the amount of computation involved in executing the algorithm. The criteria often include the number of comparison tests and the number of assignment statements used by the algorithm. These types of measures are independent of any particular computer system and depend solely on the design and implementation of the algorithm. The criteria describe the *computational complexity* of an algorithm. When applied to a data structure, computational complexity measures the computational efficiency of the algorithm relative to n, the number of data items. The computational complexity of an algorithm indicates how fast it performs, so the term *running time* is often used.

To analyze the complexity of an algorithm, identify the dominant operation and measure the number of times it occurs.

To analyze the running time of a data structures algorithm, we need to identify the key operations of the algorithm and determine how frequently they execute relative to the size of the data set. As a by-product of the analysis, we define a function T(n) that counts the frequency of the key operations in terms of n. We use the function to express the running time of the algorithm. In the next section, we develop procedures to estimate T(n) that result in a Big-O measure of the running time for the algorithm. Let us see how we can carry out this analysis for a variety of algorithms that include the finding of the minimum element in an array, the selection sort, and the search algorithms.

Running Time: min() Method   Locating the minimum element in an unordered array is a simple algorithm whose primary operation involves comparing elements. For an array with n elements, the algorithm takes the first element as the implied minimum and performs $n - 1$ comparisons with the other elements in the array. The function T() is a count of the number of comparisons.

To find the minimum requires $n - 1$ comparisons.

$$T(n) = n - 1 \tag{4.1}$$

Running Time: Selection Sort   Trying to find a function T() that measures the running time of the selection sort is more involved because the algorithm requires a series of passes, with comparisons performed on each pass. For an array with n elements, the selection sort executes $n - 1$ passes. Each pass locates the index of the minimum value in the unsorted sublist [pass, n). Let us use our understanding of min() to break out the number of comparisons for each pass.

Pass	Minimum in Range	Number of Comparisons
0	0 to n-1	n-1
1	1 to n-1	n-2
2	2 to n-1	n-3
. . .	. . .	. . .
n-3	n-3 to n-1	2
n-2	n-2 to n-1	1

The total number of comparisons in the selection sort is the sum of the comparisons for passes from 0 to $n - 2$. We record this sum as the value for the function T(n).

$$T(n) = (n - 1) + (n - 2) + \cdots + 3 + 2 + 1 \qquad (4.2)$$

From mathematics, we recognize that T(n) as the arithmetic series for terms from 1 to $n - 1$. The series can be evaluated in terms of n.

Selection sort makes $(n^2 - n)/2$ comparisons.

$$T(n) = \frac{n(n - 1)}{2} = \frac{n^2}{2} - \frac{n}{2}$$

Running Time: Sequential Search   The efficiency of some algorithms depends on the initial ordering of the data. This gives rise to the notion of "best-case," "worst-case," and "average-case" performance of the algorithm. The sequential search exhibits all three cases. The best case occurs when the target is the first element in the sublist. In this situation, the search requires only one comparison, and thus

$$T(n) = 1 \qquad (4.3)$$

The worst case occurs when the algorithm either locates the target as the last element of the sublist or finds no match. In this situation,

$$T(n) = n \qquad (4.4)$$

For the average case, let us look at all possible situations. Finding a match with the first element requires one comparison (iteration); finding a match at the second element requires two comparisons (iterations). Continuing in this way, the total number of comparisons for all of the different possibilities is

On average, a successful search makes $(n + 1)/2$ comparisons.

$$1 + 2 + 3 + \cdots + n - 1 + n = \frac{n*(n + 1)}{2} \qquad (4.5)$$

The value T(n) represents the average or expected number of comparisons for the n possible cases.

$$T(n) = \frac{n*(n + 1)}{n*2} = (n + 1)/2 \qquad (4.6)$$

When the ordering of the data affects the efficiency of the algorithm, the analysis should take this into account and distinguish a *best-case*, *worst-case*, and *average-case* performance for the algorithm. This is certainly true for the sequential search. Algorithms such as the selection sort and minimum value require the same number of comparisons for any ordering of the list. In these cases, a single version of T(n) identifies the runtime efficiency of the algorithm.

Running Time: Binary Search   The binary search is an algorithm that applies to ordered lists. On each iteration, it either finds a match and returns or searches a sublist with approximately one-half of the elements. In effect, it discards one half of the elements on each iteration, which will significantly cut down on the number of comparisons. The binary search is a case of separate "best-case," "worst-case," and "average-case" performance. In the best case, the target is at the midpoint of the list and the search requires only one comparison.

$$T(n) = 1$$

The analysis of the "worst" case requires some intuitive analysis. When an iteration fails to find a match, the length of the sublist is reduced by a factor of 2. The sizes of the sublists are successively n, $n/2$, $n/4$, and so forth. The partition process terminates when the size of the sublist is less than 2. The following sequence depicts reduced sublist sizes.

$$\frac{n}{2^0}, \frac{n}{2^1}, \frac{n}{2^2}, \frac{n}{2^3}, \cdots \frac{n}{2^m} < 2 \tag{4.7}$$

A little mathematical analysis yields a value for m. We use this to define T(n) for the worst case for which the target is not in the list. Start with $m = 1$ and find the first m such that $\frac{n}{2^m} < 2$. It must be the case that $\frac{n}{2^{m-1}} \geq 2$.

Combining these two inequalities, we obtain

$$2^m \leq n < 2^{m+1} \tag{4.8}$$

The logarithm base 2 ($\log_2 x$) is an increasing function of x. If we take the logarithm of the three terms in the inequality, the resulting values must remain in the same relative order

$$m \leq \log_2 n < m + 1 \tag{4.9}$$

The value $\log_2 n$ is a real number that lies in the interval between the integers m and $m + 1$ but cannot equal $m + 1$. For instance, if $n = 25$, $\log_2 n = 4.64385 \ldots$. The value for m is the whole number part 4, denoted by $int(\log_2 25)$. In general,

$$m = int(\log_2 n) \tag{4.10}$$

A binary search that fails to locate a match requires T(n) = $2*(1 + \log_2 n)$ comparisons.

The function T(n) is the number of iterations m.

$$T(n) = int(\log_2 n) \tag{4.11}$$

A sophisticated analysis shows that the average number of comparisons for a successful binary search is only slightly less than the number in the worst case.

Big-O Notation

In analyzing the running time of an algorithm, we define the function $T(n)$ that identifies the activity that most affects overall performance. For instance, performing comparisons is the primary activity in searching and sorting algorithms as well as in locating the minimum value in an array. The function $T(n)$ is a count of the number of times the algorithm performs the primary activity.

In the previous section, we evaluated $T(n)$ for different algorithms in which comparison is the primary activity. The following is a sample of the results.

Algorithm	Function $T(n)$
Minimum value in an array (random list)	$T(n) = n - 1$
Minimum value in an array (ordered list)	$T(n) = 1$
Selection Sort	$T(n) = n^2/2 - n/2$
Sequential Search	
best-case:	$T(n) = 1$
average-case:	$T(n) = (n + 1)/2$
worst-case:	$T(n) = n$
Binary Search (worst-case)	$T(n) = \text{int}(\log_2 n)$

The function $T(n)$ is a measure of algorithm complexity that depends on the size of the list. It seeks to give an exact count or the average count of the number of comparisons for a list with precisely n elements. The function takes on more significance if we observe the change in $T(n)$ for progressively larger values of n. The selection sort illustrates the point. Let us look at $T(n) = n^2/2 - n/2$ for $n = 100, 1000,$ and $10,000$.

$n = 100$: $T(100) = 100^2/2 - 100/2 = 10,000/2 - 100/2$
$$= 5000 - 50 = 4950$$

$n = 1000$: $T(1000) = 1000^2/2 - 1000/2 = 1,000,000/2 - 1000/2$
$$= 500,000 - 500 = 499,500$$

$n = 10,000$: $T(10,000) = 10,000^2/2 - 10,000/2 = 100,000,000/2 - 10,000/2$
$$= 50,000,000 - 5000 = 49,995,000$$

As n gets larger, the value of $T(n)$ is most influenced by the operation of squaring n. We say that n^2 is the *dominant term*. It provides an approximate measure of $T(n)$ and a measure of the change in $T(n)$ relative to n. The 10-fold change in n from 100 to 1000 produces approximately a $10^2 = 100$-fold change in $T(n)$. The same is true for the 10-fold change in n from 1000 to 10,000.

To get an approximate measure of $T(n)$, we define an expression that involves the dominant term. The expression uses the notation O(<term>) and is called the *Big-O* measure for the algorithm. For the selection sort, the dominant term in $T(n)$ is n^2 and the Big-O measure is $O(n^2)$. We say that the measure of computation complexity for the selection sort is $O(n^2)$. Equivalently, the selection sort has running time $O(n^2)$.

In selection sort, the dominant term in $T(n)$ is n^2. The algorithm has Big-O measure $O(n^2)$.

Example 4.5

1. The function $T(n) = n - 1$ computes the number of comparisons required to determine the minimum value in an array with n elements. The dominant term is n, and $O(n)$ is the running time of the algorithm.

2. Finding the minimum value in an ordered array requires only one comparison. $T(n)$ has the constant value 1 independent of n, and $O(1)$ is the running time of the algorithm.

3. In the sequential search, $T(n) = n/2$ is the average number of comparisons required to locate the target. The Big-O measure or running time for the average case of the algorithm is $O(n)$. For the best case, $T(n) = 1$ and the Big-O measure is $O(1)$. With the worst case, $T(n) = n$ and so the Big-O measure is $O(n)$.

4. In the binary search, $T(n) = \text{int}(\log_2 n)$ is the number of iterations to determine the target is not in the list. The Big-O measure or running time for the worst case of the algorithm is $O(\log_2 n)$. For the best case, $T(n) = 1$ and the Big-O measure is $O(1)$. For the average case, the Big-O measure is $O(\log_2 n)$.

5. Assume that analysis of an algorithm results in the following values for $T(n)$:

   a. $T(n) = 6n^3 + 2n^2 - 7n + 8$ (4.12)

   The dominant term is $6n^3$. After discarding $2n^2 - 7n + 8$ and the coefficient 6, we say that the algorithm has running time $O(n^3)$.

   b. $T(n) = \sqrt{n + 1} + n + 5$ (4.13)

   The term n is dominant, and the running time of the algorithm is $O(n)$.

   c. $T(n) = n^{3/2} + n + 5$ (4.14)

   The Big-O measure is $O(n^{3/2})$ since $n^{3/2}$ is the dominant term.

Sequential search running time: best case is $O(1)$; worst and average case is $O(n)$.

When an algorithm has different running times for the best, worst, and average cases, we compute a Big-O estimate for each case. The best case for an algorithm is often not important because the circumstances are exceptional and thus not a useful criterion when deciding on the choice of an algorithm. The worst case can be important despite its rarity. Its efficiency may be so poor that an application could not tolerate the performance. In some cases, a programmer might prefer an algorithm with better "worst-case" behavior even though the average performance is not as good.

Our notion of Big-O measure of efficiency is entirely intuitive. A course in the theory of algorithms develops a mathematical definition of Big-O notation, along with other measures that refine the notion of running time for an algorithm.

Common Orders of Magnitude

In the previous section, we identified algorithms whose Big-O estimates are $O(1)$, $O(n)$, $O(\log_2 n)$ and $O(n^2)$. Each measure describes the effect of increasing the size of a list. For instance, doubling the size of a list with the selection sort creates a fourfold increase in the number of comparisons. The Big-O estimates also define categories that allow a programmer to compare the relative efficiencies of algorithms. Searching an ordered list with the binary search has running time $O(\log_2 n)$, as contrasted with the $O(n)$ running time for the sequential search. A small set of measures defines the running time of most algorithms. The following are categories for the different measures along with sample algorithms.

Constant Time An algorithm is $O(1)$ when its running time is independent of the number of items. The algorithm runs in *constant time*. For instance, the algorithm for finding the minimum value in an ordered array has running time $O(1)$. No matter what the size of the array, just access the value of the first element. Another example involves adding an element at the back of an array, provided you maintain an index that identifies this location. Simply assign a value at index *back*.

A constant time algorithm has running time independent of n.

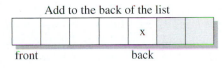

Add to the back of the list

front   back

Linear An algorithm is $O(n)$ when its running time is proportional to the size of the list. Such an algorithm is said to be *linear*. When the number of elements doubles in size, the number of operations double in size. For instance, finding the minimum value in an n element unordered list is $O(n)$. The output of elements in an n-element array is also an example of a linear algorithm.

Linear algorithms have running time proportional to n.

Quadratic and Cubic Algorithms whose running time is $O(n^2)$ are *quadratic*. Most simple sorting algorithms, such as the selection sort, are quadratic. They are practical only for relatively small values of n. An algorithm exhibits *cubic* time if its running time is $O(n^3)$. The efficiency of such algorithms is generally poor because doubling the size of n causes an eightfold increase in the running time. Matrix multiplication involves computing n^3 products and so is an $O(n^3)$ algorithm.

In quadratic algorithms, doubling n increases running time by a factor of 4.

Logarithmic The logarithm of n, base 2, is the exponent for which $2^{\exp} = n$. For instance, $\log_2(2) = 1$, $\log_2(32) = \log_2(2^5) = 5$, $\log_2(75) = 6.2288\ldots$, and so forth. When compared to the methods n and n^2, the function $\log_2 n$ grows very slowly, as depicted in Figure 4.3.

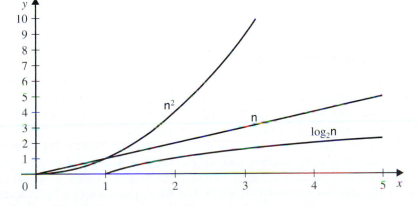

Figure 4.3 *Comparison graphs for the functions n, n^2, and $\log_2 n$.*

Some algorithms have Big-O measures $O(\log_2 n)$ and $O(n \log_2 n)$. They are termed *logarithmic*. The running times occur when the algorithm repeatedly subdivides the data into sublists whose sizes are $1/2, 1/4, 1/8, \ldots$ of the original list size. The binary search has average- and worst-case running time of $O(\log^2 n)$. The famous quicksort algorithm has running time $O(n \log_2 n)$, which is far better than the $O(n^2)$ running time of the selection sort.

Exponential   Some algorithms deal with problems that involve searching through a large number of potential solutions before finding an answer. The algorithms often have running time $O(a^n)$, $a > 1$. This is termed *exponential running time*. Exponential algorithms are useful only for very small values of n. In Chapter 6, we will see that the recursive solution to the problem of generating Fibonacci numbers has exponential running time.

For all but small n, an exponential algorithm is intractable.

Another example is the classical *traveling salesperson problem*. A formulation of the problem has the salesperson planning a trip that will involve visiting n cities. A road connects each city to all of the other cities. To minimize travel time, the salesperson wants to determine a shortest route that starts at the salesperson's home city, visits each of the cities exactly once, and concludes at the home city. All known solutions involve checking the length of a very large number of possible routes. The algorithms have running time at least $O(2^n)$. Running them with $n = 1000$ on a present-day computer is unthinkable.

Table 4.1 gives the linear, quadratic, cubic, exponential, and logarithmic orders of magnitude for selected values of n. Clearly, you should avoid cubic and exponential algorithms unless n is small.

Table 4.1   Various orders of magnitude.

n	$\log_2 n$	$n \log_2 n$	n^2	n^3	2^n
2	1	2	4	8	4
4	2	8	16	64	16
8	3	24	64	512	256
16	4	64	256	4096	65,536
32	5	160	1024	32,768	4,294,967,296
128	7	896	16,384	2,097,152	3.4×10^{38}
1024	10	10,240	1,048,576	1,073,741,824	1.8×10^{308}
65,536	16	1,048,576	4,294,967,296	2.8×10^{14}	Forget it!

4.4   Comparing Search Algorithms

In this section, we run a simulation that allows us to compare experimentally the runtime estimates for the sequential and binary search algorithms. For each algorithm, the program evaluates the total time required to perform 50,000 searches on an array of 100,000 integers. We use a random number generator to initialize two identical 100,000 element integer arrays, *listSeq* and *listBin*, with values in the range from 0 to 999,999. The binary search requires a sorted array, so the selection sort orders *listBin*. To compare the two search algorithms, we create a third array, called *targetList*, which consists of 50,000 random numbers in the same range from 0 to 999,999. Test the sequential search by matching elements in *targetList* with the array *listSeq*. The binary search test matches elements in *targetList* with the ordered array *listBin*. The program must compare the computation time required by the two search algorithms. A Timing class object handles this task.

The Timing Class

The Timing class has methods that simulate using a stopwatch to time a computer process. Declare an instance of the class and call start() to reset the stop watch to 0 and begin timing. Call stop() to halt timing and return the elapsed time for the process in fractional parts of a second.

class Timing		ds.time
	Constructor	
	Timing()	
	Create an instance of the class with all timing variables set to 0.	
	Methods	
void	**start**()	
	Start the timing.	
double	**stop**()	
	Stop the timing and return elapsed time in seconds.	

Example 4.6

Use Timing object *sortTimer* to determine how long a computer takes to sort an array with selectionSort(). Assign the result to the real variable *timeInSec*.

```
Timing sortTimer = new Timing();
double timeInSec;

// flank the process with calls to start() and stop()
sortTimer.start();                    // start timing
Arrays.selectionSort(arr);            // the sorting process
timeInSec = sortTimer.stop();         // get time in seconds
```

PROGRAM 4.1 SEARCH ALGORITHM EFFICIENCY

This program declares integer arrays *listSeq* and *listBin* of size ARRAY_SIZE = 100,000. The two arrays are initialized with the same sequence of random integers in the range from 0 to 999,999. A third array, *targetList*, has TARGET_SIZE = 50,000 elements with random numbers in the same range. A Timing object *t* determines the execution time required to locate each element from *targetList* in array *listSeq* using a sequential search. After sorting array *listBin*, the same Timing object provides the execution time for a binary search of the targets in *listBin*. Output displays the execution time for each search as well as the ratio of the time for the sequential search to the time for the binary search.

Note: The binary search is obviously more efficient but remember that binary search requires an ordered array. If a program needs only a few searches, the sequential search may be preferable. However, if the program has multiple searches, it may be advisable to use a fast sorting algorithm such as quicksort and to apply the binary search.

```java
import java.util.Random;
import java.text.DecimalFormat;
import ds.util.Arrays;
import ds.time.Timing;
public class Program4_1
{
    public static void main(String[] args)
    {
        final int ARRAY_SIZE = 100000, TARGET_SIZE = 50000;

        // arrays for the search
        int[] listSeq = new int[ARRAY_SIZE],
              listBin = new int[ARRAY_SIZE],
              targetList = new int[TARGET_SIZE];

        int i;

        // use Timing object t to compute times for each process
        Timing t = new Timing();
        double seqTime, binTime;

        // random number object
        Random rnd = new Random();

        // format real numbers with three decimal places
        DecimalFormat fmt = new DecimalFormat("#.000");

        // initialize the arrays with random numbers in the
        // range 0 to 999,999
        for (i = 0; i < ARRAY_SIZE; i++)
            listSeq[i] = listBin[i] = rnd.nextInt(1000000);

        // initialize targetList with random numbers in the
        // same range 0 to 999,999
        for (i=0;i < TARGET_SIZE; i++)
            targetList[i] = rnd.nextInt(1000000);

        // time the sequential search with elements from listSeq
        t.start();
        for (i = 0; i < TARGET_SIZE; i++)
            Arrays.seqSearch(listSeq,0,ARRAY_SIZE,targetList[i]);
        seqTime = t.stop();
        System.out.println("Sequential Search takes " +
                    fmt.format(seqTime) + " seconds.");

        // sort listBin
        Arrays.selectionSort(listBin);

        // time the binary search with elements from listBin
        t.start();
```

```
for (i = 0; i < TARGET_SIZE; i++)
    Arrays.binSearch(listBin,0,ARRAY_SIZE,targetList[i]);
binTime = t.stop();
System.out.println("Binary Search takes " +
            fmt.format(binTime) + " seconds.");

System.out.println(
    "Ratio of sequential to binary search time is " +
        fmt.format(seqTime/binTime));
    }
}
```

Run:
  Sequential Search takes 16.094 seconds.
  Binary Search takes .016 seconds.
  Ratio of sequential to binary search time is 1005.875

Chapter Summary

- The design of algorithms is integral to the efficient implementation of data structures.

- The selection sort is an algorithm that illustrates many of the common features of sorting algorithms. The algorithm uses comparisons and exchanges to order a list.

- The simplest form of searching is the sequential search, which compares the target with every element in an array until matching the target or reaching the end of the array. If the array is in sorted order, the binary search algorithm is more efficient. This search exploits the structure of an ordered array to produce very fast search times.

- Big-O notation measures the efficiency of an algorithm by estimating the number of certain operations that the algorithm must perform. For searching and sorting algorithms, the operation is data comparison. Big-O measure is very useful for selecting among competing algorithms.

- The running time of the sequential search is $O(n)$ for the worst and the average cases. However, the worst and average case for the binary search is $O(\log_2 n)$. Timing data obtained from a program provides experimental evidence to support the greater efficiency of the binary search.

Written Exercises

1. Assume an array has values $\{19, 13, 7, 12, 16\}$. Show the order of elements in the array after each pass of the selection sort algorithm.

2. Indicate how to modify the selection sort algorithm so it sorts an integer array in descending order.

3. Use the sequential search to locate the target in the array and give the return value.

   ```
   int[] list = {1, 5, 8, 2, 5, 18, 23, 55, 4, 9}, retValue;
   ```

   (a) `retValue = Arrays.seqSearch(list,0,10,5);`
   (b) `retValue = Arrays.seqSearch(list,2,10,5);`
   (c) `retValue = Arrays.seqSearch(list,1,10,5);`
   (d) `retValue = Arrays.seqSearch(list,4,10,5);`
   (e) `retValue = Arrays.seqSearch(list,6,10,5);`
   (f) `retValue = Arrays.seqSearch(list,7,9,4);`

4. (a) Use the sequential search to find a target value in an array of 10,000 items.

   (i) What is the fewest number of comparisons the search will require?
   (ii) What is the maximum number of comparisons the search will require?
   (iii) What is the expected number of comparisons for the search?

   (b) Use the binary search to find a target value in an array of 10,000 items.

   (i) What is the fewest number of comparisons the search will take?
   (ii) What is the maximum number of comparisons for the search?

5. Consider the integer array

   ```
   int[] arr = {1, 2, 5, 8, 9, 10, 15, 25};
   ```

   List the sequence of steps to execute the binary search algorithm. For each step, give the values of first, last, and mid for the appropriate sublist. Then give the return value.

   (a) `Arrays.binSearch(arr, 0, 8, 2);`
   (b) `Arrays.binSearch(arr, 0, 8, 16);`

6. Each iteration of the binary search compares the target to the value at the midpoint of [first,last]. Indicate the number of iterations required by the binary search algorithm to locate each target in the entire list. The array is

   ```
   int[] arr = {9, 16, 21, 32, 40, 57, 60, 75, 80};
   ```

   (a) target = 75   (b) target = 21   (c) target = 9

7. The following are Big-O estimates for the running times of three sorting algorithms:

   Algorithm 1: $O(n^2)$ Algorithm 2: $O(n \log_2 n)$ Algorithm 3: $O(2^n)$

   Rank the algorithms in order of preference.

8. Perform a Big-O analysis for each algorithm that requires $T(n)$ comparisons. In each case, give the result as $O(g)$, where g is some function of n.

   (a) $T(n) = n + 5$ (c) $T(n) = 6\sqrt[3]{n} + \sqrt{n} + 7$

   (b) $T(n) = n^2 + 6n + 7$ (d) $T(n) = \dfrac{n^3 + n^2 - 1}{n + 1}$

9. (a) For what value of $n > 1$ does 2^n become larger than n^3?

(b) Show that $2^n + n^3$ is $O(2^n)$.

(c) Give a Big-O estimate for $T(n) = \dfrac{n^2 + 5}{n + 3} + 6 \log_2 n$

10. Maintain a list of n integers in random order in an array.

(a) What is the running time to output the last element in the array?

(b) What is the running time to output the entire array?

11. Each method contains a loop as its primary component. Use Big-O notation to express the worst-case running time for each of the following methods in terms of n.

(a)
```java
public static boolean g(int[] arr, int k)
{
    int i;

    for(i=0; i < arr.length; i++)
        if (arr[i] == k)
            return true;
    return false;
}
```

(b)
```java
public static void h(int[] arrA, int[] arrB)
{
    int i, n = arrA.length;

    for (i=0; i < n; i++)
        for (j=0; j < n; j++)
            arrA[i] += arrB[j];
}
```

12. Search an array with n elements and return the maximum value.

(a) What array ordering will always result in running time $O(1)$?

(b) What is the running time of the computation for an unordered array?

Programming Exercises

13. The method `lastIndexOf()` is a variation of the sequential search. The arguments include an array `arr`, the integer `fromIndex`, and a `target` value. The method searches for the last occurrence of the target in the array starting at the specified index and returns its index if found; otherwise, it returns -1.

(a) Implement the method.

```java
public static int lastIndexOf(int[] arr, int fromIndex,
                                          int target)
{ . . . }
```

(b) Check your implementation of `lastIndexOf()` in a program that declares the following array:

```
int[] intArr = {2, 5, 3, 5, 4, 7, 5, 1, 8, 9};
```

Run a series of tests using different starting indices and different targets.

14. The `seqSearch()` method indicates that a target value is in an array range [`first`, `last`) when it returns an index $n \neq -1$ in the range.

(a) The method `isUnique()` returns true if the target value occurs exactly once in the array. Implement the algorithm by using `seqSearch()` with the entire index range [0, `arr.length`) to determine if the target is in the array. If `seqSearch()` returns $n \neq -1$, call `seqSearch()` one more time with index range $n + 1$, arr.length) to determine if there is at least one more occurrence of the target.

```
public static boolean isUnique(int[] arr, int target)
{ . . . }
```

(b) The method `numUnique()` returns an integer that indicates the number of unique values in an array. Implement the method by calling `is Unique()` for the elements in the array.

```
public static int numUnique(int[] arr)
```

(c) Write a program that declares the integer array `intVals`. Output the number of unique elements in the array.

```
int[] intVals = {3, 1, 5, 1, 9, 5, 7, 2, 3, 8, 4};
```

15. Recall that pass i of the selection sort, $0 \leq i < n$, finds the smallest of the elements in the sublist {arr[i], arr[i + 1], ..., arr[n − 1]} and exchanges it with arr[i]. A variation of this algorithm, called the double-ended selection sort, locates both the smallest and largest of the elements in a sublist and positions them at the beginning and the end of the sublist, respectively. Pass 0 locates the smallest and largest elements in {arr[0], arr[1], ..., arr[n − 1]} and places them at indices 0 and n − 1, respectively. Pass 1 locates the smallest and largest elements in {arr[1], ..., arr[n − 2]} and locates them at indices 1 and n − 2, respectively. Continue in this way until the left-most index becomes equal to or greater than the right-most index. The sort makes $n/2$ passes.

(a) Assume an integer array has values {13, 5, 2, 25, 47, 17, 8, 21}. Show the order of elements in the array after each pass of the double-ended selection sort.

(b) Implement the method `deSelectionSort()` that uses the double-ended selection sort algorithm.

```
public static void deSelectionSort(int[] arr)
```

(c) What do you think is the worst-case running time for `deSelectionSort()`? Intuitively explain your answer.

(d) Write a program that creates an array with 20 random integer values in the range 0 to 49. Use `deSelectionSort()` to sort the array and then display the results.

16. The exchange sort is another basic sorting algorithm that repeatedly scans an array and swaps elements until the list is placed in ascending order. The algorithm exchanges a pair of elements when a smaller element is out of order. We illustrate the three-pass process for the 4-element list [8, 3, 6, 2].

Pass 0: Consider the full list {8, 3, 6, 2}. The entry at index 0 is compared with each other entry in the array at index 1, 2, and 3. For each comparison, if the larger element is at index 0, the two entries are exchanged. After all the comparisons, the smallest element is stored at index 0.

Initial List				Action	Resulting List			
8	3	6	2	Exchange	3	8	6	2
3	8	6	2	No Exchange	3	8	6	2
3	8	6	2	Exchange	2	8	6	3

Pass 1: Consider the sublist {8, 6, 3}. With the smallest element already located at index 0, only entries in the array from index 1 to the end are considered. The entry at index 1 is compared with the other entries at index 2 and 3. For each comparison, if the larger element is at index 1, the two entries are exchanged. After all of the comparisons, the smallest element in the sublist is stored at index 1.

Initial List				Action	Resulting List			
2	8	6	3	Exchange	2	6	8	3
2	6	8	3	Exchange	2	3	8	6

Pass 2: Consider the sublist {8, 6}. With the two smallest elements already located at index 0 and 1, only entries in the list from index 2 to the end are considered. The entry at index 2 is compared with the only other element in the array, at index 3. After the comparison, the smallest element in the sublist is stored at index 2. The resulting array is ordered.

Initial List				Action	Resulting List			
2	3	8	6	Exchange	2	3	6	8

(a) Implement the exchange sort algorithm.

```
public static void exchangeSort(int[] arr)

{ . . . }
```

(b) Distinguish the best and worst cases for the exchange sort. Do a Big-O analysis for the number of comparisons in each case.

(c) Do an average-case analysis for the number of comparisons in exchange sort.

(d) Write a program that creates an array with 15 random integer values in the range 0 to 99. Use `exchangeSort()` to sort the array and output the elements.

17. This exercise develops the bubble sort algorithm. During multiple passes through the array, a flag notes whether any local activity occurs. On a pass, compare adjacent elements and exchange their values when the first element is greater than the second element. Set a boolean flag *true* if an exchange occurs. At the end of the pass, the largest element has "bubbled up" to the top of the array. Subsequent passes order the array from back to front. The sort requires at most $n - 1$ passes with the process terminating if the flag notes that no swapping occurs during a pass. The following illustrates two passes of the bubble sort for array arr = {35, 10, 40, 15}. The boxed elements are in their correct location.

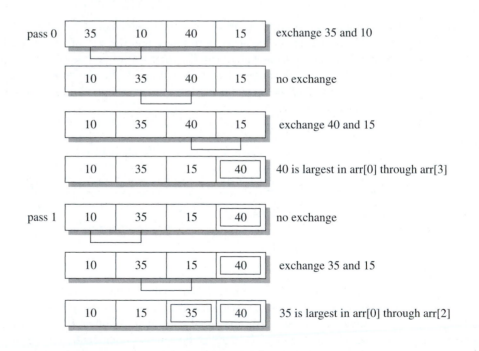

(a) Implement the bubbleSort() method.

```
public static void bubbleSort(int[] arr)

{ . . . }
```

(b) What is the best-case condition for the bubble sort? Give the Big-O measure of running time.

(c) What is the worst-case condition? Give a Big-O measure of running time. How many interchanges are performed in this case?

(d) The average-case analysis for the bubble sort is difficult. What do you think the running time is?

(e) Write a program that illustrates the bubbleSort() algorithm.

Programming Project

18. Write a program that compares the efficiency of bubble sort (ProgEx4-17), exchange sort (ProgEx4-16), and selection sort. Model your program after Program 4.1 that compares the efficiency of the sequential and binary searches. Declare three arrays.

```
int[] arr1 = new int[50000], arr2 = new int[50000],
        arr3 = new int[50000];
```

Fill each array with the same set of random integers in the range 0 to 999,999 and time the separate executions of the algorithms. Then fill each array with the sequence 1, 2, 3, ..., 50,000 and time the algorithms. Finally, fill the arrays with the sequence 50,000, 49,999, ..., 2, 1 and time the algorithms. Do your results correspond to the Big-O analysis?

Chapter 5

GENERIC CLASSES AND METHODS

CONTENTS

5.1 THE OBJECT SUPERCLASS
Object-Array Methods
Generalized Sequential Search

5.2 INTRODUCING JAVA GENERICS
Object-Based Store Class
Generic Collections
Generic Store Class

5.3 GENERIC INTERFACES
The Comparable Interface

5.4 GENERIC METHODS
Basic Generic Methods
Using Bounds for Generic Types

5.5 GENERICS AND INHERITANCE
Bounded Generic Types
Generics and Wildcards

5.6 GENERIC SEARCH/SORTING ALGORITHMS
Generic Binary Search Method

In this chapter, we begin our study of generic programming. The topic includes the design and implementation of classes, interfaces, and methods that can be used to store and process elements of different object types. Generic structures are fundamental to our study of data structures, in which collections can store elements of different types. In a similar way, generic versions of searching and sorting methods apply to arrays with different object types.

Java defines a class called *Object* as the universal superclass of all classes. This fact enables any object to be assigned to an Object reference variable. Object is not an abstract class. It defines and implements a range of methods that can be used with polymorphism to create generalized algorithms. In Section 5.1, we introduce the Object class and use it to build classes and methods that support different types.

Using Object references to generalize algorithms has drawbacks. Applications can assign any object to an Object reference but then must cast the reference back to the original type when the value is accessed. The need for casting clutters the code. More significantly, it can result in a runtime ClassCastException when a specific cast is applied to a reference of the wrong type. The error often signifies a logical design flaw in the code, which should be identified at compile time. To address these problems, Java introduces generics. These are extensions to the language that associate a type parameter with an instance of a collection class, an interface, or a method. The compiler can check that code is consistent with the specified type; the code is type safe. Its execution will not result in runtime errors due to improper type checking and type handling that bring into question the quality and reliability of the code. In Section 5.2, we begin by showing the motivation that led to the inclusion of generics in the language and then introduce the mechanics that you must employ to create generic classes.

In subsequent sections, we will introduce the concepts of generic interfaces and methods. Our discussion focuses on the basics that you need to know. As we proceed in the book, we will develop more sophisticated structures and methods. Corresponding generic syntax and understanding will have to be developed. We proceed on a need-to-know basis. Some features of Java generics lie beyond the scope of this book and are not discussed.

If you have a background in C++ templates, you will recognize a similarity between Java and C++ generic syntax. Use your background to good advantage but keep an open mind. Java generics and C++ templates have different implementations. You will have to understand the Java approach. Do not worry if you have not seen generic programming before. You come to the subject without bias and can learn the material from the very beginning.

5.1   The Object Superclass

In object-oriented programming, inheritance and polymorphism are core concepts. The creator of C++ is quoted as saying "Object-oriented programming is inheritance with polymorphism." This is especially true in Java because every class belongs to a hierarchy. There is a standard class, called *Object*, which is a superclass of every class. Implicitly, all class headers include the directive *extends Object*.

All Java classes extend the universal superclass Object.

```
class Time24 extends Object
{ . . . }

class Employee extends Object
{ . . . }
```

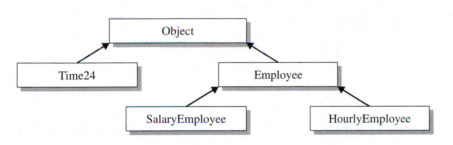

The `Object` class defines a variety of methods, some of which have applications in operating systems and systems programming. In this book, we limit our attention to four methods.

Selected methods in the Object class:

```
// Creates and returns a copy of this object
protected Object clone()
```

```
// Indicates whether some other object is "equal to" this one
public boolean equals(Object obj)
```

```
// Returns a hash code value for the object
public int hashCode()
```

```
// Returns a string representation of the object
public String toString()
```

The `Object` class provides an implementation for each of its methods. The implementations typically access system-related information about an instance and have limited application. For instance, the `Object` version of equals() determines that two reference values x and y are the same if they refer to the same object (x==y).

The Object class and polymorphism is the basis for generic programming.

We will use the four `Object` class methods to support polymorphism. The methods are overriden in the `String` class and the Java primitive wrapper classes. We have designed the Time24 class to also override the methods. Let us look at `equals()`. Typical of most classes that override the `equals()` method, the `Time24` version first checks whether the argument is itself a `Time24` object. If not, it returns false; otherwise the times for the object and the argument are converted to minutes and compared using the integer $==$ operator. In this way, the `equals()` method allows comparison of a `Time24` object with a `String`, `Integer`, or other type object. It returns false. The method returns true when the argument is a `Time24` object and the two time values are identical.

Time24 equals():

```
public boolean equals(Object item)
{
    // check the obj is a Time24 object
    if (item instanceof Time24)
    {
        // convert objects to minutes and compare as integers
        Time24 t = (Time24)item;
        int time, ttime;

        time = hour * 60 + minute;
        ttime = t.hour * 60 + t.minute;

        return time == ttime;   // compare the two times
    }

    return false;              // argument is not a Time24 object
}
```

`Object` is the universal superclass for all Java classes. As a result, any object can be assigned to an `Object` reference variable. This fact provides a mechanism for creating generalized methods and collection classes that apply to different object types. Let us begin by looking at methods with `Object` arrays and then discuss how collection classes could use `Object` references to store the elements.

Object-Array Methods

The Object class defines toString(), which is overridden in many Java classes. We use this fact to define a general static method toString(arr) in the Arrays class. The method takes an Object array and displays the elements as a comma-separated list enclosed in brackets. It can be used by any array whose elements override the Object method toString().

Generalized toString(arr):

```
// returns a string that represents an array of objects
public static String toString(Object[] arr)
{
    if (arr == null)
        return "null";
```

```
      else if (arr.length == 0)
         return "[]";

      // start with the left bracket
      String str = "[" + arr[0];

      // output all but the last element, separating items
      // with a comma
      for (int i = 1; i < arr.length; i++)
         str += ", " + arr[i];

      str += "]";

      return str;
   }
```

The static method toString(arr) lists the array elements as a string in the form [elt_0, elt_1 ,...., elt_{n-1}]

Example 5.1

The example uses the String array *strArr* and the Integer array *intArr*.

```
   String[] strArr = {"hotdog", "pie", "coffee", "salad"};

   Integer[] intArr = {9, 6, 2, 8, 4, 7};
```

1. Display the two arrays using toString(arr).

```
   System.out.println("String array: " + Arrays.toString(strArr));

   System.out.println("Integer array: " + Arrays.toString(intArr));
```

Output:
```
   String array: [hotdog, pie, coffee, salad]
   Integer array: [9, 6, 2, 8, 4, 7]
```

2. Overloaded versions of equals() determine the identity of an object with a specific argument

```
   strArr[0].equals("hot" + "dog");      // true

   intArr[3].equals("eight");            // false
```

Generalized Sequential Search

The sequential search is a scanning algorithm that uses the equality relation to identify an element in an array that matches the target. We provided an integer version of seqSearch() in Section 4.2 that uses the comparison operator "==" for a match.

Sequential search with int:

```
public static int seqSearch( int[] arr, int first, int last,
                             int target)
{
    // scan elements in the range [first, last)
    for (int i = first; i < last; i++)
        if (arr[i] == target)
            return i;

    // match not found
    return -1;
}
```

By specifying an Object array and target and using the method equals(), the sequential search can be made general.

A general version of the sequential search uses an `Object` array and the method `equals()` to test for a match. With polymorphism, the comparison uses the overridden version of `equals()` for the array type. The method is found in the `Arrays` class.

Sequential search with Object:

```
public static int seqSearch(Object[] arr, int first, int last,
                            Object target)
{
    // scan elements in the range [first, last)
    for (int i = first; i < last; i++)
        if (arr[i].equals(target))
            return i;

    // match not found
    return -1;
}
```

Example 5.2

The generic sequential search applies to an array of strings and an array of Integer objects.

```
String[] strArr = {"red", "tan", "green", "blue", "teal"};
Integer[] intArr = {7, 2, 9, 4, 3, 9, 8};

index = Arrays.seqSearch(strArr, 0, 5, "blue");    // index = 3
index = Arrays.seqSearch(intArr, 3, 6, 9);         // index = 5
index = Arrays.seqSearch(intArr, 0, 4, 8);         // index = -1
```

5.2   Introducing Java Generics

In the previous section, we saw how `Object` references can be used to generalize an algorithm such as the sequential search. By using an `Object` reference for the array and the target, a single version of the method `seqSearch()` works for an array of any data type so long as the type implements `equals()`. As we begin a study of collection classes, we need the same kind of generality. The design of these classes is concerned with how data is stored and accessed. Requiring a separate implementation of a class for objects of type `String`, `Integer`, `Time24`, and so forth is impractical. There are other approaches.

One solution has general collection classes store elements of type `Object`. The universal reference type creates collections that can store elements of any object type. In this section, we begin by discussing Object-based collection classes and illustrate them with a very simple example, the `Store` class. This collection holds a single element of type `Object`. In the process, we will show some of the limitations and problems with Object-based collections. This will lead to a second solution for creating general collection classes, namely Java generics. The topic is discussed in the next section.

One approach to the development of generic classes is to store elements of type Object.

Object-Based Store Class

The `Store` class has a single private instance variable called *value* of reference type `Object`. Besides a constructor that initializes the variable, the class has access and update methods `getValue()` and `setValue()` and a `toString()` method that describes an object in the form *value = <value>*.

Object-based Store class:

```
public class Store
{
    private Object value;      // data stored by the collection

    // constructor creates an object with initial value v
    public Store (Object v)
    { value = v; }

    // return the stored value
    public Object getValue()
    { return value; }

    // set v as the new stored value
    public void setValue(Object v)
    { value = v; }


    // a description of the element
    public String toString()
    { return "value = " + value; }
}
```

We can use a `Store` collection to hold any object. For instance, the following declarations create two `Store` objects that hold a `String` and a `Time24` object respectively. In each case, the value is assigned to the reference variable.

```
Store stStr = new Store("good");

Store stTime = new Store(new Time24(9,45));
```

The generality of using an `Object` variable has limitations when we need to access the value. With the method `getValue()`, the compiler can only guarantee that an `Object` is returned. Even though an application presumably knows the type of the element in the collection, it must use casting to reference the actual type. For instance, the element in *stStr* must be cast as a String if the value is going to be updated.

```
String str = (String)stStr.getValue();
str += "bye";
stStr.setValue(str);                    // new value is "goodbye"
```

Frequent casting is part and parcel of any Object-based collection. Casting is required even though it tends to clutter the code.

The use of Object to create generic collection classes requires a cast when a reference is retrieved from the collection. The technique is not type safe. It is possible to add different types to the collection.

More importantly, the universal nature of an `Object` reference prevents the compiler from identifying when a program incorrectly uses an object type with the collection. The problem surfaces as a runtime error that brings into question the quality and reliability of the software. For instance, the `Store` object *stStr* is designed to hold a String object. A program, however, could inadvertently update the value with an Integer object. The error is not detected by the compiler but results in a runtime `ClassCastErrorException` when the element is retrieved.

```
// incorrectly update stStr with an Integer object;
// the compiler does not detect the error
stStr.setValue(new Integer(50));

// error discovered at runtime with a ClassCastException
str = (String)stStr.getValue();
```

```
Run:
   java.lang.ClassCastException: java.lang.Integer
      at Test.main(Test.java:20)
```

Generic Collections

Generic classes allow the compiler to check types. The use of casting is eliminated.

Mindful of the limitations of Object-based collection classes such as Store, we need a new solution to the problem of creating generalized structures. First and foremost, we want them to be *type safe*. This means simply that the compiler should identify any incorrect use of an object type and thus avoid the runtime discovery of the error. In this way, the problem is identified before the software is released, and nasty and embarrassing calls from a client are avoided. Of significance is also the desire to simplify the use of a collection in an application by reducing the need for casting. *Java generics* provide a solution. A collection object is created with a specified type that dictates the kind of elements it stores. The compiler does not allow an element with an invalid type to update the collection, and also recognizes the type of any element that is accessed in the collection.

Before we introduce the syntax for implementing generic classes, let us jump ahead and see what will be accomplished. Assume that Store is redesigned to be a generic class. The declaration of a Store collection must specify an object type.

```
// collections created with String and Time24 arguments; they
// store the string "good" and time 8:45
Store<String> stStr = new Store<String>("good");
Store<Time24> stTime =
       new Store<Time24>(new Time24(8,45));
```

The collection *stStr* can hold only String objects. A compiler error is generated whenever an object of a different type is inserted into the collection.

```
// assign an Integer object in the stStr (String) collection
stStr.setValue(new Integer(45));
```

To create an object of a generic class, include the type in angle brackets "< >" after the class name.

```
Compile time error message:
    C:\Test.java:36: setValue(java.lang.String) in
        Store<java.lang.String> cannot be applied to (java.lang
          Integer)
        stStr.setValue(new Integer(45));
                      ^
```

Because the collection knows the type of data it stores, an element can be extracted without requiring a cast. The method `getValue()` returns a `String` for *stStr* and a `Time24` object for *stTime*.

```
String str = stStr.getValue();         // element is a string
str += "bye";
stStr.setValue(str);

stTime.getValue().addTime(30);         // update time

System.out.println("stStr: " + stStr + " stTime: " + stTime);
```

```
Output:
    stStr: value = goodbye stTime: value = 9:15
```

Generic Store Class

Declaring a generic class is relatively simple. Most of the code remains the same. The main difference is that we define one or more formal type parameters in the class header. Let us use the Store class to illustrate the syntax. A single type parameter specifies the object type for the stored element. It is recommended that one use a simple (one character if possible) identifier that denotes a type. We will use the identifier "T." Add the type parameter in angle brackets to the class name. The type can be used then to declare variables and as method parameters and return types.

Generic Store class:

```
public class Store<T>
{
    private T value;      // data stored by the object

    // constructor creates an object with initial value
    public Store (T v)
    { value = v; }

    // return the stored value as type T
```

Make a class generic by following the class name with the generic type enclosed in angle brackets.

```
public T getValue()
{ return value; }

// update the stored value
public void setValue(T v)
{ value = v; }

public String toString()
{ return "value = " + value; }
}
```

You need to understand how Java implements generic structures. A class like Store is compiled once into a single class file just like an ordinary class such as Rectangle. When an instance is created, the class is passed the type as a formal argument. When a method is called, the type is substituted for the formal generic parameter and then executed.

In the following declarations, the object type Time24 and the object type Integer are passed as arguments to the single Store<T> class file. For object *stTime*, the type Time24 is substituted for T in the declaration of the variable value, in the constructor, and in the methods getValue() and setValue(). A similar substitution occurs for object *stInt*.

```
Store<Time24> stTime;        // Store class with T = Time24
Store<Integer> stInt;        // Store class with T = stint;
```

The UML diagram for a generic class includes a superimposed rectangle area with the parameter type.

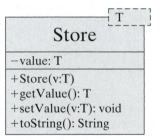

5.3   Generic Interfaces

Interfaces can also be generic structures. Like a generic class, a type parameter is used in the interface header, and the type can be used for method parameters and return types. As an example, we define the Accumulator interface, which has a single method add() that uses the generic type for the parameter *v*.

Accumulator interface:

Interfaces can be generic. Supply the actual type when implementing the interface.

```
public interface Accumulator<T>
{
    public void add(T v);
}
```

Classes implement the interface with a specified object type. For instance, the class
AccumulatorTime has an instance variable total of type Time24. The constructor initializes total with default time 0:00 (midnight). The method add() uses a Time24 argument to increase total by the specified time. Access to the current total is given by the
method getTotal().

AccumulatorTime class:

```
public class AccumulatorTime implements Accumulator<Time24>
{
    private Time24 total;

    // constructor creates an object with initial time 0:00
    public AccumulatorTime ()
    { total = new Time24(); }

    // return the total
    public Time24 getTotal()
    { return total; }

    // update the total time by the specified Time24 amount v
    public void add(Time24 v)
    { total.addTime(v.getHour()*60 + v.getMinute()); }
}
```

A similar class is AccumulatorNumber that has an instance variable, *total*, of type
double. The constructor initializes total as 0.0. The add() method takes a parameter of type
Number. This is an abstract superclass for the numeric wrapper classes Integer and Double. It
defines doubleValue() as an abstract method which ensures that the method is implemented in the wrapper classes. The runtime argument for add() in the AccumulatorNumber
class can be any Integer or Double object. The argument is assigned to a Number reference. The operation increments *total* by the double value of the object.

AccumulatorNumber class:

```
public class AccumulatorNumber implements Accumulator<Number>
{
    private double total;        // accumulation of numeric values

    // constructor initializes total to 0.0
    public AccumulatorNumber ()
    { total = 0.0; }

    // return the total
    public double getTotal()
    { return total; }

    // update the total by the value of v as a double
    public void add(Number v)
    { total = total + v.doubleValue(); }
}
```

PROGRAM 5.1 USING CLASSES THAT IMPLEMENT ACCUMULATOR<T>

The program uses an AccumulatorNumber object to calculate the sum of the elements in an array of type Integer. An AccumulatorTime object computes the total time for Time24 values that are created using parseTime() on elements of the form "hh:mm" in a String array. In each case, the total is output using getTotal().

```java
import ds.time.Time24;

public class Program5_1
{
    public static void main (String[] args)
    {
        Integer[] intArr = {7, 1, 9, 3, 8, 4};
        String[] strArr = {"3:45", "2:30", "5:00"};

        AccumulatorNumber accNumber = new AccumulatorNumber();
        AccumulatorTime accTime = new AccumulatorTime();

        int i;
        for (i = 0; i < intArr.length; i++)
            accNumber.add(intArr[i]);
        System.out.println("Numeric total is " +
                                    accNumber.getTotal());

        for (i = 0; i < strArr.length; i++)
            accTime.add(Time24.parseTime(strArr[i]));
        System.out.println("Time total is " +
                                    accTime.getTotal());
    }
}
```

```
Run:
    Numeric total is 52.4
    Time total is 11:15
```

The Comparable Interface

The Comparable<T> interface defines a standard way to compare objects using the relations less than, equal to, and greater than.

The package *java.lang* defines the generic Comparable interface that consists of a single method, compareTo(), which takes an argument of type T and returns an integer value.

```java
public interface Comparable<T>
{
    int compareTo(T item);
}
```

Classes that implement the Comparable interface define a natural ordering among their objects. The ordering enables us to sort the objects, find the maximum or minimum value, and so forth. The concept of natural ordering is a generalization of linear ordering for integer and real numbers. Using a number line as a model to represent numbers,

we say that "a is less than (<) b" and that "b is greater than (>) a." Two numbers are equal (==) if they have the same value. In a natural ordering, the transitive property holds; that is, if a < b and b < c, then a < c. We can use alphabetic ordering as the natural ordering for strings. Thus, "cat" comes before "dog," and "walk" comes after "crawl." Using comparison operators to describe the ordering, "cat" < "dog," "walk">"crawl," and "hotdog"=="hot" + "dog."

The compareTo() method returns an integer value that is negative, zero, or positive. The actual value is not relevant, only the classifications which correspond to the <, ==, and > relations.

```
obj.compareTo(item) < 0          // obj < item
obj.compareTo(item) == 0         // obj == item
obj.compareTo(item) > 0          // obj > item
```

Time24 objects can be ordered. Beginning with midnight (0:00), different times during the day have a natural ordering; "8:45" is earlier than "9:15" and "16:30" is later than "13:00." Time24 objects can be treated just like String and wrapper class objects. In fact, we do this by having the Time24 class implement the Comparable<Time24> interface. Let us look at the class declaration with its implementation of the compareTo() method. Comparison is done by converting the hour and minute fields for this object and the argument object to minutes and using the natural ordering for integers.

Time24 class with Comparable:

```
public class Time24 implements Comparable<Time24>
{
    . . .

    // the compareTo() method compares times converted to minutes
    public int compareTo(Time24 item)
    {
        int time, ttime;

        time = hour * 60 + minute;
        ttime = item.hour * 60 + item.minute;

        // compare the integer values and return -1, 0, or 1
        if (time < ttime)
            return -1;
        else if (time == ttime)
            return 0;
        else
            return 1;
    }
}
```

5.4   Generic Methods

Methods can be generic. This allows you to create generic algorithms for searching, sorting, and so forth.

Up to this point in the chapter, we have used type parameters to create generic classes and interfaces. The same parameters can be used to create generic methods. We develop the syntax for generic methods using a simple example. The method max() takes two arguments of a specified type and returns the larger element. The example is interesting because it uses compareTo() and thus requires that the generic type implements the Comparable interface. We develop three implementations of max() in stages so that we can explore safe-type checking for generic methods. We begin with a version that introduces the basic syntax for generic methods. We will discover that this version is not type safe. A goal of generic programming is to create type safe methods. In the next section, we introduce the concept of bounds for generic types and use it to implement a new version of max() that does reasonable type checking. In Section 5.5, we extend generics to an inheritance hierarchy. This provides a context to introduce wildcards and a final version of max() which is a robust type-safe form of the algorithm.

Basic Generic Methods

A generic method specifies the generic type <T> as one of the modifiers in the method header. The type must be used by at least one of the method parameters. In our example, the method max() compares two objects of a specified generic type and returns a value of the same type.

```
// tag <T> indicates a generic method; T is the parameter
// and return type
public static <T> T max(T objA, T objB)
```

In the Java handling of a generic method, the type parameter is passed to the method at runtime. The compiler does not verify that the type implements Comparable<T>. As a result, an explicit cast is required in the if-statement to bring compareTo() within the scope of object *objA*.

Generic max():

```
public static <T> T max(T objA, T objB)
{
    if (((Comparable<T>)objA).compareTo(objB) > 0)
        return objA;
    else
        return objB;
}
```

In the first version of max(), a Class-CastException will occur if type T does not implement Comparable<T>.

The fact that the type parameter is passed at runtime has other repercussions. The method max() can be included in a source code statement even when the type does not implement the Comparable interface. The compiler issues an "unchecked cast" warning to indicate that a potential runtime error may occur. A warning does not prevent execution of a program. It is simply an alert to a potential problem that may surface during execution.

```
Compile time error message:
    C:\Test.java:18: warning: [unchecked] unchecked cast to
      type java.lang.Comparable<T>
      if (((Comparable<T>)objA).compareTo(objB) > 0)
                         ^
```

For instance, we can call `max()` with `Rectangle` objects. The fact that Rectangle does not implement `Comparable<Rectangle>` becomes apparent as a runtime error when the method is executed.

```
// Rectangle does not implement Comparable<Rectangle>
Rectangle rectA = new Rectangle(4,5),
          rectB = new Rectangle(6,2), rectC;

// call max() with Rectangle as the type; get compiler warning
rectC = max(rectA, rectB);
```

```
Runtime exception message:
   java.lang.ClassCastException: Rectangle
   at Test.max(Test.java:23)
   at Test.main(Test.java:18)
```

Using `max()` with `String` and `Time24` objects executes correctly because these classes implement `Comparable<String>` and `Comparable<Time24>`, respectively. Consider the following.

```
String strA = "cat", strB = "dog", strC;
Time24 tA = new Time24(16,30), tB = new Time24(13,00), tC;

strC = max(strA, strB);
System.out.println("Larger string is " + strC);

tC = max(tA, tB);
System.out.println("Later time is " + tC);
```

```
Run:
   Larger string is dog
   Later time is 16:30
```

The implementation of `max()` with basic generic syntax is not type safe. The compiler provides a general alert that a problem may occur but does not flag as an error a call to `max()` with a type that does not implement `Comparable`. We will address the problem in the next section.

Using Bounds for Generic Types

A better version of `max()` improves safe type checking. It needs to specify that the compiler must check the type argument to ensure that it implements `Comparable<T>`. This is done by bounding the generic type using the modifier `<T extends Comparable<T>`. The use of the term "extends" is a little confusing. With an interface, you might expect the expression `<T implements Comparable<T>`. In fact, this is precisely what is specified. You will discover later that bounds can be applied to generic superclasses or subclasses in an inheritance hierarchy. Syntax such as "extends T" or "super T" has familiar meaning in that context.

In the second version of max(), type T must implement Comparable<T>. The interface cannot be implemented in a superclass.

Let us look at a declaration of max() in which the interface Comparable<T> bounds the generic type. Because the compiler checks that the type implements the interface, compareTo() is within the scope of each argument, and a cast is not required.

Generic max() with bounded generic type:

```
public static <T extends Comparable<T>> T max(T objA, T objB)
{
    if (objA.compareTo(objB) > 0)
        return objA;
    else
        return objB;
}
```

The compiler flags as an error any statement that calls max() with a type that does not implement Comparable. The error message indicates that the specified type does not conform to the bounds. Look at the following call to max() with Rectangle objects.

```
rectC = max(rectA, rectB);          // creates compiler error
```

```
Compile time error message:
    C:\Test.java:10: <T>max(T,T) in Test cannot be applied to
    (Rectangle,Rectangle); inferred type argument(s) Rectangle
        do not conform to bounds of type variable(s) T
    rectC = max(rectA, rectB);
                    ^
```

The version of max() with bounds for the generic type compiles with no warnings if the method is called with types that implement Comparable. Unfortunately, this is not the end of the story. In the next section, we will look at generics and inheritance. This will raise new problems that will lead us to create a robust declaration of the method max() for types in an inheritance hierarchy.

5.5   Generics and Inheritance

Up to this point, our generics have involved autonomous and independent types. We need to expand our understanding when the type is part of an inheritance hierarchy. First of all, let us develop some context. A good place to start is with the Object class, which is the universal superclass for all Java classes. A Store collection can have Object as the argument type.

```
Store<Object> stObj = new Store<Object>(new Object());
```

The generic type Object allows stObj to be updated with any object value. In the following, a Time24 object updates the value.

```
stObj.setValue(new Time24(8,30));
```

The method getValue() returns an Object reference and so casting is required for operations that are specific to the Time24 class.

```
// updates the stored time in stObj by 45 minutes
((Time24)stObj.getValue()).addTime(45);          // stores 9:15
```

We are familiar with assignment of a subclass object to a superclass reference variable in an inheritance hierarchy. This allows any object to be assigned to an Object reference.

```
String str = "generic";
Object obj = str;          // String assigned to Object reference
```

The usual rules of assignment do not apply to generic collections that use subclass and superclass types. It would seem natural to assume that using Object as the type argument creates a universal generic class or method. The following declarations appear to be legal.

> The compiler is very careful to check that a generic class contains only a specified type.

```
Store<String> stStr = new Store<String>("generic");
Store<Object> stObj = stStr;
```

The declaration of *stStr* is valid and creates a collection that stores only String values. The problem occurs with the declaration of the Store<Object> collection *stObj* as an alias for *stStr* The generic type Object allows stObj to be updated with any object value.

```
// valid for a Store<Object> collection
stObj.setValue(new Time24(8,30));
```

The update would assign a non string value to the alias collection *stStr*, in violation of its type constraints. The Store<String> collection *stStr* would have a Time24 value. The Java compiler prevents this from happening and posts an error message, indicating that the declaration of stObj involves incompatible types. The compiler distinguishes between a generic Store<String> and a generic Store<Object> collection. They are distinct objects.

```
Compile time error message:
    C:\Test.java:8: incompatible types
        found : Store<java.lang.String>
        required: Store<java.lang.Object>
            Store<Object> stObj = stStr;
```

Bounded Generic Types

When a generic class or method is passed a type from an inheritance hierarchy, we must specify how the type relates to others in the hierarchy. This involves bounding the type. We use the example of the employee hierarchy from Chapter 2 with an added feature. The declaration of the Employee class now implements the Comparable interface, in which the ordering among objects compares their Social Security numbers.

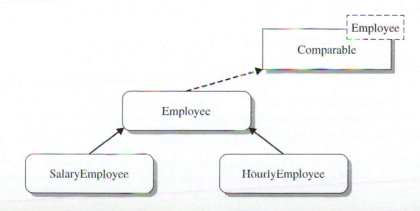

We use the subclass types `SalaryEmployee` and `HourlyEmployee` to declare `Store` collections. Each collection is assigned an initial employee of the corresponding type.

```
// create Employee subclass objects
SalaryEmployee sEmp = new SalaryEmployee("Dunn, Maria",
                        "823-56-7614", 1500.00);
HourlyEmployee hEmp = new HourlyEmployee("Bund, George",
                        "563-18-7629", 35, 20.00);

// use the Employee subclass types with Store collections
Store<SalaryEmployee> stSEmp = new Store<SalaryEmployee>(sEmp);
Store<HourlyEmployee> stHEmp = new Store<HourlyEmployee>(hEmp);
```

In Section 2.4, we introduced the method `pay()` whose parameters were a string and an Employee reference. The method was passed a string designating the dates for the pay period and a subclass object. The method displayed the pay for an employ by calling `payrollCheck()`, which invoked polymorphism. For your convenience, we repeat the declaration of the method `pay()`.

pay() (from Chapter 2; displays a pay check for any subclass object):

```
public static void pay(String dateRange, Employee emp)
{
    System.out.println("Pay period: " + dateRange);
    System.out.println(emp.payrollCheck());
}
```

Use the syntax T extends S to specify that T must be subclass of S.

Now let us introduce the method `payStore()`, which has the same effect as `pay()`. The new method, however, has a `Store` collection parameter instead of an `Employee` parameter. In its implementation, the method uses `getValue()` to extract the `Employee` object and then calls `payrollCheck()` to display a paycheck. The method applies only to an `Employee` object or a subtype object. We specify this in the declaration of the generic method by bounding the type parameter. The modifier `<T extends Employee>` directs the compiler to verify that the method is called with precisely the right kind of generic type, that is, with type Employee or with a subclass type that extends `Employee`.

payStore():

```
public static <T extends Employee> void payStore(String
dateRange, Store<T> st)
{
    System.out.println("Pay period: " + dateRange);
    System.out.println(st.getValue().payrollCheck());
}
```

The generic bound `<T super Sub>` specifies that T must be a super-class of Sub.

Because the method `payrollCheck()` is within the scope of any type that is passed to `payStore()`, no cast is required for `getValue()`. The following calls to `payStore()` use the `Store` collection objects *stSEmp* and *stHEmp*.

```
payStore(stSEmp);  // pay SalaryEmployee value stored in stSEmp
payStore(stHEmp);  // pay HourlyEmployee value stored in stHEmp
```

Output:
```
   Pay Dunn, Maria (823-56-7614) $1500.00
   Pay Bund, George (563-18-7629) $700.00
```

Generic Type Upper Bound

Note

A generic method can define an upper bound for the type by specifying that the type argument must be a superclass of a specified subclass. The declaration uses the modifier <T super SubClass>. The modifier indicates that T must be the superclass of SubClass or a superclass higher up in the inheritance hierarchy.

```
      public static <T super SubClass> void method(Store<T> st)
```

Generics and Wildcards

The Employee class implements the Comparable interface. In the employee hierarchy, the interface extends to the subclasses because they have access to the superclass compareTo() method. For instance, we declare employee subclass objects and use compareTo() to compare Social Security numbers.

```
   // create a SalaryEmployee and an HourlyEmployee object
   SalaryEmployee sEmpA = new SalaryEmployee("Hill, Tom",
                                    "631-45-2789",1000.00),
   HourlyEmployee hEmp = new HourlyEmployee("Herges, Mike",
                                    "761-62-4517",10.50, 40);
   if (hEmp.compareTo(sEmpA) > 0)         // true; pay Mike Herges
       System.out.println(" " + hEmp.payrollCheck());
```

Output:
```
   Pay Herges, Mike (761-62-4517) $420.00
```

The same access to the compareTo() method does not apply to generic methods when a subclass is passed as the argument type. In the previous section, we defined a generic version of max() and specified that the generic type T must extend Comparable<T>. If the method is called with SalaryEmployee objects, the compiler checks whether the type explicitly implements Comparable<SalaryEmployee>. This is not the case, and a compiler error is generated.

```
   // generic type for max() is SalaryEmployee; subclass does
   // not explicitly implement Comparable<SalaryEmployee>
   Employee emp = max(sEmpA, sEmpB);
```

To deal with generic classes and methods that could be passed either a superclass or a subclass as the type argument, Java introduces wildcards. The syntax <?> indicates that the generic structure is handling an unknown type. We use wildcards to create a new version of max() that extends the concept of generic bounds. The generic tag defines a bound on the type that indicates the type itself or some superclass of the type implements the Comparable interface. The syntax is

```
   public static <T extends Comparable<? super T>> T max (T a, T b);
```

The use of the wildcard "?" with bound "super T" directs the compiler to verify that `Comparable` is implemented by type T or by some superclass of T.

In the third version of max(), the interface may be implemented in an unspecified superclass ("?") of T. This is the most general form for max().

max() (supporting Comparable in an inheritance hierarchy):

```
public static <T extends Comparable<? super T>> T max(T a, T b)
{
    if (a.compareTo(b) > 0)
        return a;
    else
        return b;
}
```

This is the most general form for a generic method that bounds `Comparable` to the type. When such a method compiles without a warning message, it is almost assuredly type safe.

5.6 Generic Search/Sorting Algorithms

In Chapter 4, we introduced an integer version of selectionSort(). A generic version is more functional. It can order arrays of different types. For each pass, the integer version of the method uses the operator $<$ to identify the index of the smallest element in the unsorted tail of the list. The generic version specifies that the object type must implement the Comparable interface and uses compareTo() for the ordering relation. With minor adjustment to the code, we can implement a generic version of selectionSort(). Note the generic tag in the headers. You can find a listing of the method in the Arrays class.

Generic selection sort:

The generic selection sort orders any array of type T as long as the Comparable interface is implemented in a superclass of T.

```
public static <T extends Comparable<? super T>>
void selectionSort(T[] arr)
{
    int smallIndex; // index of smallest element in the sublist
    int pass, j, n = arr.length;
    T temp;

    // pass has the range 0 to n-2
    for (pass = 0; pass < n-1; pass++)
    {
        // scan the sublist starting at index pass
        smallIndex = pass;
        // j traverses the sublist arr[pass+1] to arr[n-1]
        for (j = pass+1; j < n; j++)
        // if smaller element found, assign smallIndex
        // to that position
        if (arr[j].compareTo(arr[smallIndex]) < 0)
            smallIndex = j;

        // swap the next smallest element into arr[pass]
        temp = arr[pass];
        arr[pass] = arr[smallIndex];
        arr[smallIndex] = temp;
    }
}
```

PROGRAM 5.2 SORTING DIFFERENT ARRAY TYPES

This program illustrates the generic version of selectionSort() for arrays of Strings, Integers, Time24 objects, and SalaryEmployee objects. In the first three cases, the sort method is called and the resulting array is displayed. With the SalaryEmployee array, the payroll checks for the objects are listed, ordered by Social Security number.

```java
import ds.util.Arrays;
import ds.time.Time24;

public class Program5_2
{
    public static void main (String[] args)
    {
        String[] strArr = {"red", "green", "blue"};
        Integer[] intArr = {40, 70, 50, 30};
        Time24[] timeArr = {new Time24(14,15), new Time24(10, 45),
                            new Time24(22,00), new Time24(3,30)};
        SalaryEmployee[] emp = {
            new SalaryEmployee("Dunn, Moira", "471-23-8092",800),
            new SalaryEmployee("Garcia, Al", "398-67-1298",1200),
            new SalaryEmployee("Ye, Don", "682-76-1298",2000)};

        Arrays.selectionSort(strArr);
        System.out.println("Sorted strings: " +
                           Arrays.toString(strArr));

        Arrays.selectionSort(intArr);
        System.out.println("Sorted integers: " +
                           Arrays.toString(intArr));

        Arrays.selectionSort(timeArr);
        System.out.println("Sorted times: " +
                           Arrays.toString(timeArr));

        Arrays.selectionSort(emp);
        for (int i=0; i < emp.length; i++)
            System.out.println(emp[i].payrollCheck());
    }
}
```

```
Run:
    Sorted strings: [blue, green, red]
    Sorted integers: [30, 40, 50, 70]
    Sorted times: [3:30, 10:45, 14:15, 22:00]
    Pay Garcia, Al (398-67-1298) $1200.00
    Pay Dunn, Moira (471-23-8092) $800.00
    Pay Ye, Don (682-76-1298) $2000.00
```

Generic Binary Search Method

The binary search may be used with any ordered array. Its implementation uses equality to detect a match and either less than (<) or greater than (>) to locate the sublist for the next iteration. A generic version of binSearch() requires that the object type implement the Comparable interface. You can find a listing of the method in the Arrays class.

Generic binSearch():

```
public static <T extends Comparable<? super T>>
int binSearch(T[] arr, int first, int last, T target)
{
    int mid;                    // index of the midpoint
    T midvalue;                 // object that is assigned arr[mid]
    int origLast = last;        // save original value of last

    while (first < last)        // test for nonempty sublist
    {
        mid = (first+last)/2;
        midvalue = arr[mid];
        if (target.compareTo(midvalue) == 0)
            return mid;             // have a match
        // determine which sublist to search
        else if (target.compareTo(midvalue) < 0)
            last = mid;            // search lower sublist. reset last
        else
            first = mid+1;        // search upper sublist. reset first
    }
    return -1;                  // target not found
}
```

The generic binary search searches any array of type T as long as a superclass of T implements the Comparable interface.

Example 5.3

This example uses generic versions of the sequential search and the binary search to find String objects in a list. Before executing a binary search, we order the array by calling selectionSort().

```
String[] strArr = {"red", "green", "blue", "orange", "tan"};
int index;

index = Arrays.seqSearch(strArr,0,strArr.length, "orange"));

// orders strArr: {"blue", "green", "orange", "red", "tan"}
Arrays.selectionSort(strArr);

// search for "blue" in the index range [1, 4)
index = Arrays.binSearch(strArr, 1,4, "blue");
```

Chapter Summary

- There is a standard class, called *Object*, which is a superclass of every class. Implicitly, all class headers include the directive "extends Object." The Object class provides an implementation for each of its methods. Classes usually override the method toString() that returns a string representation of an object and the method equals() that determines if another object is equal to the current one. Object can be used to create generic methods. For instance, a general version of a sequential search uses an Object array and the method equals() to test for a match. With polymorphism, the comparison uses the overridden version of equals() for the array type.

- The design of collection classes is based on how data is stored and accessed. Requiring a separate implementation of a class for objects of type String, Integer, Time24, and so forth is impractical. One solution defines general collection classes that store elements of type Object. The universal reference type creates collections that can store elements of any object type. This approach requires type casting when retrieving data from the collection, and the generality of Object references makes it possible to store data of different types in the collection. Java generics provide strong type checking and eliminate the need for casting.

- To declare a generic class, define one or more formal type parameters in the class header. The Store class illustrates the syntax. Add the type parameter in angle brackets to the class name. The type can be used to declare variables and as method parameters and return types. To declare an object of the generic class, include the object type after the name of the class in angle brackets, for example:

      Store<String> strStore = new Store("Hello World!");

- Interfaces can also be generic structures. Like a generic class, a type parameter is used in the interface header and the type can be used for method parameters and return types. Classes implement the interface with a specified object type. As an example, the classes AccumulatorTime and AccumulatorNumber implement the Accumulator interface.

- Classes that implement the generic Comparable interface define a natural ordering among their objects. The Comparable interface will be used whenever we need to sort objects, find the maximum or minimum value, and so forth.

- The concept of a generic class can be extended to the creation of generic methods. The generic method max() illustrates many of the design features. It takes two arguments of a specified type and returns the larger element. A simple definition of max() with the generic modifier <T> creates a generic method that is not type safe. A more robust definition uses wildcards and a specification that the generic type or a superclass type must implement Comparable. This version of max() does reasonable type checking.

- Additional understanding of generics is necessary when the generic type is part of an inheritance hierarchy. When a generic class or method is passed a type from an inheritance hierarchy, we must specify how the type relates to others in the hierarchy. This involves bounding the type. The bounding action can include the use of wildcards. The Employee hierarchy and the static method max() illustrate the concepts.

- In Chapter 4, we introduced array sorting and searching algorithms using integer arguments. Generic versions can order and search arrays of different types. Generic searching and sorting algorithms specify that the object type must implement the Comparable interface and use compareTo() for the ordering relation.

Written Exercises

1. What are some of the advantages of using generics rather than `Object` references for general-purpose classes and methods?

2. We introduced the `Circle` class in Chapter 3. Provide a new declaration of the class header so that it implements the `Comparable` interface. Implement `compareTo()` as a `Circle` class method by comparing the radius of this instance with another `Circle` object.

3. Section 5.2 has a declaration of the generic `Store` class. Expand the declaration.

   (a) Override the `Object equals()` method in the `Store` class.

   (b) Have the `Store` class implement the `Comparable` interface. Indicate how this would modify the class header and provide an implementation of `compareTo()`.

4. The following is a declaration of the `StorePair` class that stores two integer values.

```
class StorePair
{
    private int first, second;

    public StorePair(int first, int second)
    { this.first = first; this.second = second; }

    public int getFirst()
    {   return first; }

    public int getSecond()
    {   return second; }

    public void setPair(int first, int second)
    { this.first = first; this.second = second; }

    public String toString()
    { return "first = " + first + " second = " + second; }
}
```

   The `equals()` method is used with `StorePair` instance variables *pA* and *pB*. What is the resulting value of the boolean b? Explain.

```
StorePair pA = new StorePair(3,4), pB = new StorePair(3,4);
boolean b = pA.equals(pB);
```

5. What does it mean to say that generic collections are "type safe"?

6. Provide a declaration and implementation of the generic method `minmax()` that takes an array of generic type and returns a string with the following format: `Min = <minvalue> Max = <maxvalue>`. For instance,

```
Integer[] intArr = {5, 3, 7, 1, 4, 9, 8, 2};
String[] strArr = {"red", "blue", "orange", "tan"};

String intStr = minmax(intArr);
    // intStr = "Min = 1 Max = 9"

String str = minmax(strArr);
    // str = "Min = blue Max = tan"
```

7. The StoreMax class is a generic collection class modeled after Store in Section 5.2. Only the method setValue(T v) changes. In StoreMax, the method updates the current value when the argument v is greater than the current value.

```
class StoreMax<T>
{ . . . }
```

The class Rectangle, which does not implement the Comparable interface, is used as a generic argument in the declaration and use of a StoreMax object.

```
Rectangle rectA = new Rectangle(1,2),
          rectB = new Rectangle(5,8);
StoreMax<Rectangle> smRect = new StoreMax<Rectangle>(rectA);
smRect.setValue(rectB);
```

(a) Does the declaration of smRect result in a compile time error? Explain.
(b) Does the call to setValue() result in a compile time or a runtime error? Explain.

Programming Exercises

8. The generic method shuffle() takes an Object array and randomly rearranges (shuffles) the position of the elements.

```
public static void shuffle(Object[] arr)
```

(a) Implement shuffle(). Hint: to position an element at index i, randomly generate a random integer j in the range from 0 to i. Exchange the elements arr[i] and arr[j]. Let us illustrate two steps of the algorithm for an array of integer values. Begin at index i = arr.length − 1. Assume *rndN* is the random value.

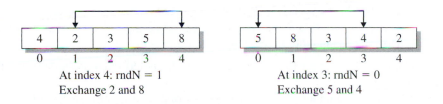

At index 4: rndN = 1   At index 3: rndN = 0
Exchange 2 and 8   Exchange 5 and 4

(b) Write a program that makes a series of calls to shuffle(). After each call, output the reordered elements in the array using the static toString(arr) method in Arrays. Include in the program the arrays

```
String[] strArr = {"red", "blue", "orange", "green",
                   "black"};

Time24[] timeArr = {new Time24(9,30), new Time24(19,15),
                    new Time24(5,45), new Time24(22,0)};
```

9. The generic method lastIndexOf() is a variation of the sequential search. The arguments include an array *arr*, the integer *fromIndex*, and a *target* value. The method

searches for the last occurrence of the target in the array starting at the specified index and returns its location if found; if not found, it returns −1.

(a) Implement the method:

```
public static int lastIndexOf(Object[] arr,
                  int fromIndex, Object target)

{ ... }
```

(b) Check your implementation of lastIndexOf() in a program that declares the following arrays:

```
Integer[] intArr = {2, 5, 3, 5, 4, 7, 5, 1, 8, 9};
String[] strList = {"june", "joe", "glenn", "joe",
                        "glenn"};
```

Run a series of tests using different starting indices and different targets.

10. (a) Create a general version of the StorePair class in Written Exercise 5.4. Use Object references for the variables *first* and *second*. Call the class StorePair0.
    (b) Write a program that creates a StorePair0 object that contains the string "Mike" for one value and the Time24 object 8:45 as the other value. Update the object so that the name is "Michael" and the time advances 30 minutes to become 9:15. Output a description of the object before and after the updates occur.

11. (a) Create a generic version of the StorePair class in Written Exercise 5.4. Call the class StorePairG.

    (b) Write a program that declares the StorePairG object *sp*, which stores Integer objects with initial values 0. Scan the elements in the following integer array and update *sp* so that the first data value (variable *one*) holds the maximum value and the second data value (variable *two*) holds the accumulated sum. For each iteration, use the current values in the object to determine updated values for the maximum and for the accumulated sum. Then, output the current state of object *sp*.

    ```
    Integer[] arr = {7, 12, 6, 10, 14, 2, 5};
    ```

12. The StoreMax class is a generic collection class modeled after Store class in Section 5.2. Only the method setValue() changes. In StoreMax, the method updates the current value when the argument is greater than the current value.

    (a) Create a declaration for StoreMax class. It should compile without warning messages.
    (b) Write a program that declares an array of strings and an array of Time24 objects. Create StoreMax objects of String and Time24 type respectively. The program should scan each array and have the element update the corresponding StoreMax object. For each iteration, output the array value and the current value in the collection object.
    (c) Provide the compiler errors that are created by the following statements.
        (i) Attempt to assign a Time24 object to the StoreMax string collection *smStr*.

        ```
        smStr.setValue(new Time24(6,00));
        ```

        (ii) Declare a StoreMax object *smRect* with Rectangle as the type.

        ```
        Rectangle rect = new Rectangle();
        StoreMax<Rectangle> smRect =
          new StoreMax<Rectangle>(rect);
        ```

13. Modify `StoreMax` from Exercise 12 so that it is a subclass of the generic `Store` class. Call the subclass `StoreMaxI`. You will need to modify `Store` so that the instance variable *value* is protected and not private.

    (a) Give a declaration of the `StoreMaxI` class.
    (b) Write a program that checks your implementation of `StoreMaxI`.

14. An Object array can have elements of different object types. Assume a student has a work schedule that accommodates for classes and study time. The student is paid $7.50 per hour and works each day for a specified number of minutes. Use the Integer array *dailyMinutes*.

    ```
    Integer[] dailyMinutes = {90, 80, 45, 75, 55};
    ```

    Write a program that declares an eight-element `Object` array. The first five elements are `Time24` objects that correspond to entries in the *dailyMinutes* array. The sixth element is the rate stored as an object of type Double, and the seventh element is the total number of minutes worked stored as an `Integer` object. Use only data from the `Object` array to output a summary of the work profile followed by the time worked each day. Your output should be the following:

    ```
    Run:
        Rate per hour $7.50
        Weekly pay $43.12
        Total time 5:45
            Day 1 Time = 1:30
            Day 2 Time = 1:20
            Day 3 Time = 0:45
            Day 4 Time = 1:15
            Day 5 Time = 0:55
    ```

Programming Project

15. The `Entry` class has separate instance variables for a key field and for a value field. Methods allow only access to the key field but both access and update to the value field.

    ```
    class Entry
    {
        private int key, value;

        public Entry(int key, int value)
        { this.key = key; this.value = value; }

        public int getKey()
        {   return key; }

        public int getValue()
        {   return value; }
    ```

```
                    public void setValue(int value)
                    { this.value = value; }

                    public String toString()
                    { return "key = " + key + " value = " + value; }
                }
```

(a) Modify the `Entry` class so that it is generic and stores the variable *key* of type K and the variable *value* of type V. The generic types K and V can be different, for example, K=`String`, V=`Integer`, To include two generic types in a class, place the generic tag <K,V> after the class name. The class implements the method `equals(Object obj)` and the `Comparable` interface in which comparison is made on the key field.

```
        public class Entry<K,V> implements Comparable<Entry<K,V>
        { . . . }
```

(b) Write a program with an array of `Entry<String, Integer>` elements that are created with keys from array *strArr* and values from array *intArr*.

```
        String[] strArr = {"MATH51", "CHEM53", "BIOL147",
                           "PHYS151", "GEOL171"};
        Integer[] intArr = {25, 23, 18, 15, 20};
        Integer[] updates = {5, 3, 1, 2, 2};
```

Note: Java does not allow the allocation of generic arrays. Arrays must have raw type. The following is a declaration of an array of five `Entry` elements.

```
        Entry[] entryArr = new Entry[strArr.length];
```

(i) Assign to the array `Entry` objects whose key-value pairs are ("MATH51", 25), ("CHEM53", 23), and so forth. List the `Entry` elements in the array.

(ii) Scan the array and output the elements whose key begins with a letter less than "L".

(iii) Scan the array and add the corresponding value from the array updates to the value of each object. For instance, the value for "MATH51" becomes $25 + 5 = 30$. Output the updated array.

(iv) Prompt the user to enter a course name (key). Use `seqSearch()` to locate the course in the array. If it is present, output the number of students enrolled in the class, otherwise indicate that the course is not in the list.

(v) Sort the array using `Arrays.sort()` and output the resulting sorted list.

Chapter 6

RECURSION

CONTENTS

6.1 THE CONCEPT OF RECURSION
Describing a Recursive Algorithm
Implementing Recursive Methods
How Recursion Works
Multibase Representations

6.2 RECURSION APPLICATIONS
Building a Ruler
Towers of Hanoi

6.3 EVALUATING RECURSION
Fibonacci Methods
Criteria for Using Recursion

A typical program consists of methods that call other methods to accomplish a task. In this chapter, we will look at methods that call themselves. These are *recursive methods* whose algorithm design requires a new way of thinking. We explore the concept of recursion and aim to foster an ability to think recursively. This ability is essential to using recursion as an algorithm design and programming technique.

Recursion is an important concept. We use it at key points to develop fast sorting methods and to define and scan nonlinear data structures. The use of recursion occurs frequently in operations research models, in game theory, and in the study of graphs. Chapter 29 introduces a variety of advanced algorithms. Many use recursion as the centerpiece. For now, we want to simply understand what recursion is and learn the mechanics of recursive programming. We will spend most of the chapter looking at examples and conclude with a discussion of recursive algorithms that often have iterative solutions, which are far more efficient. You need to know when recursion should and should not be used.

6.1   The Concept of Recursion

You already have some experience with recursion. A computer file system consists of a root directory that holds files and other directories, called *subdirectories*. To make a backup of your hard disk onto a CD-ROM, copy the files from the root directory to the CD-ROM and then proceed to the subdirectories. At each subdirectory, repeat the process again. Copy the files and move to subdirectories, which are actually sub-subdirectories of the root. Eventually, you proceed down the hierarchy of subdirectories until only files exist and the copy is complete. Disk backup is recursive because it involves a process that spawns a like process with the same activities. At each step it performs the simple task of copying files and leaves the more complex task of copying a subdirectory to another (recursive) step, which is just the same process. Eventually the recursive steps lead to a stopping condition in which only files are copied.

Let us look at other processes that are recursive. Our goal is to frame the processes as recursive algorithms and then develop ways to implement the algorithms as methods. Some familiar concepts in mathematics provide a good starting point. Consider the problem of evaluating $n!$ (n-factorial), where n is a nonnegative integer. If asked for a definition of $n!$, most would describe how $n!$ is evaluated; that is, multiply terms from n down to 1.

$$n! = n * n-1 * n-2 * \ldots * 2 * 1$$

Iterative algorithms use a loop.

This is an iterative view of *n*-factorial that involves repeated multiplication. When implemented by the method factorial(), a programmer uses a loop that fills in the missing terms represented by the "...".

Iterative factorial():

```java
// n is a non-negative integer
public static int factorial(int n)
{
    int factValue = 1;

    while (n >= 1)
    {
        factValue *= n;
        n--;
    }

    return factValue;
}
```

We can view the factorial in a different way. Consider the evaluation of 4!, assuming we already know that 3! = 6. The problem of evaluating 4! reduces to a single multiplication step using 4 and the prior understanding of 3!.

$$4! = 4 * 3! = 4 * 6 = 24$$

This is a new strategy that carries out a calculation which involves a previous result. The strategy can be employed to evaluate 7! as long as we are willing to delay each multiplication until we get an intermediate result. The following is an evaluation of 7! assuming that 4! = 24.

7! = 7 * 6!	// multiplication awaits evaluation of 6!
6! = 6 * 5!	// need result for 5!
5! = 5 * 4!	// evaluate assuming 4! = 24
= 5 * 24 = 120	
6! = 6 * 5!	// compute 6! with result for 5!
= 6 * 120	
= 720	
7! = 7 * 6!	// back at 7! with result for 6!
= 7 * 720	
= 5040	

A definition for *n*! describes a recursive process.
$n! = 1$
if $n = 0 = n*n!$
if $n \geq 1$.

You get the idea. Evaluating n! involves multiplying by a term that is itself a factorial, namely (n–1)!. The process repeats with each step laying out a multiplication operation that has a factorial term with the next smaller integer. Ultimately, the process must stop at some n!, which can be evaluated directly. In the example, the process of evaluating 7! stopped at 4! = 24.

In the general case of n!, we choose 0! = 1 as the stopping point. We first set up a series of multiplication statements that evaluate n! for progressively smaller and smaller values of n until we reach the stopping point.

n!	= n * (n-1)!
(n-1)!	= (n-1) * (n-2)!

. . .

2!	= 2 * 1!	
1!	= 1 * 0!	
0!	= 1	// stopping point

The evaluation of n! is done by revisiting the multiplication steps in reverse order. Each step uses the result from the previous step; that is, 1! uses the result 0!, 2! uses the result 1!, and so forth. The recursive process yields a recursive definition for $n!$. The form of the definition distinguishes between the stopping step at $n = 0$ and the recursive multiplication step

$$n! = \begin{cases} 1 & n == 0 \\ n*(n-1)! & n \geq 1 \end{cases}$$

Describing a Recursive Algorithm

The term *recursive* applies when an algorithm solves a problem by partitioning it into sub-problems that are solved by using the same algorithm. For the factorial algorithm, the partitioning process determines the value of $n!$ by first computing $(n-1)!$, and so forth. In executing a recursive algorithm, the partitioning process cannot go on indefinitely. The process must terminate at one or more simple problems that can be solved directly. We refer to these simple problems as *stopping conditions* because they can be solved without any further partitioning. The factorial has a single stopping condition, $n == 0$. When the partitioning process arrives at a stopping condition, a final solution of the problem can be obtained by revisiting the recursive steps in reverse order, using the result from the previous step.

We use a recursive method to implement a recursive algorithm. The design of a recursive method consists of the following elements:

1. One or more *stopping conditions* that can be directly evaluated for certain arguments.
2. One or more *recursive steps*, in which a current value of the method can be computed by repeated calling of the method with arguments that will eventually arrive at a stopping condition.

In a recursive algorithm, there are recursive steps and stopping conditions.

Implementing Recursive Methods

The design of a recursive method must carefully distinguish between the stopping condition and the recursive step. A programmer implements the distinction with an *if-else statement*. The if-portion handles the stopping condition, and the else-portion handles the recursive step. In the case of the factorial() method, the if-portion evaluates the single stopping condition $n == 0$ and returns a result 1. The else-portion first calls factorial() with argument $n-1$ and then returns the result of the expression $n*(n-1)!$.

Use an if-else selection statement to identify the stopping condition (if-portion) and the recursive step (else-portion).

Recursive factorial( ):

```
// n is a non-negative integer
public static double factorial(int n)
{
    if (n == 0)
        return 1;                       // stopping condition
    else
        return n * factorial(n-1);      // recursive step
}
```

Example 6.1

The function S(n) computes the sum of the first n positive integers.

$$S(n) = \sum_{1}^{n} i = 1 + 2 + \cdots + n$$

A recursive definition of the function evaluates S(n) by first computing the sum of the first $n - 1$ terms and then adding n. For instance, S(4) = 1 + 2 + 3 + 4 = 10. The sum of the first five terms is

$$S(5) = S(4) + 5 = 10 + 5 = 15$$

The stopping condition occurs at S(1), which has one term that is the sum.

$$S(n) = \begin{cases} 1, & n = 1 \\ S(n - 1) + n, & n > 1 \end{cases}$$

The method sumToN( ) is an implementation of the mathematical function S(n).

sumToN( ):

```
public static int sumToN(int n)
{
    if (n == 1)
        return 1;
    else
        return sumToN(n-1) + n;
}
```

Infinite Recursion   A recursive algorithm has recursive steps that must lead to stopping conditions. When the steps and the conditions act independently, the process can result in endless recursive calls—a dreaded state of infinite recursion. Consider the following recursive definition for f( ).

$$f(n) = \begin{cases} 0, & n = 0 \\ f(n/4 + 1) + n, & n \geq 1 \end{cases}$$

The form of the recursive definition looks harmless. This is very deceiving as we will quickly discover when we watch what happens with f(5).

```
f(5) = f(5/4 + 1) + 5;    // recursive call to f(5/4 + 1) = f(2)
f(2) = f(2/4 + 1) + 2;    // recursive call to f(2/4 + 1) = f(1)
f(1) = f(1/4 + 1) + 1;    // recursive call f(1/4 + 1) = f(1)
  . . .                   // whoops! infinite recursion
```

The method never reaches the stated stopping condition at n = 0 but rather executes an infinite series of recursive calls to f(1).

How Recursion Works

A recursive algorithm is an alternative form of an iterative process. What makes recursive algorithms difficult to understand is the fact that the method implementation uses only a simple if-else statement that hides the underlying repetitive process. In this section, we illustrate the process for factorial(4) by tracing the recursive steps to the stopping condition and then retracing the steps to the ultimate return value.

Executing the method factorial() sets in motion a whole series of method calls and calculations. Think of factorial(n) as a machine called *n*-Fact that computes *n*! by carrying out the multiplication *n**(*n* − 1)!. In order for the machine to operate, it must be networked with a series of other *n*-Fact machines that pass information back and forth. The 0-Fact machine is the exception. It can work independently and produce the result 1 without assistance from another machine. Figure 6.1 illustrates the networking and interaction of machines, starting with 4-Fact, which computes 4! A calling statement is responsible to create the 4-fact machine. It is this machine that ultimately returns a value to the calling statement which we assume occurred in the main() method.

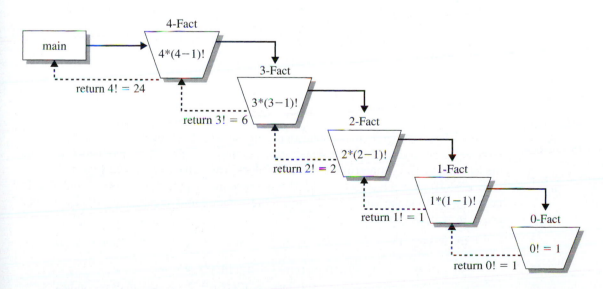

Figure 6.1   *n-Fact Machines for factorial(4).*

4-Fact   Starts up the 3-Fact machine
          Waits for return value (3!) from 3-Fact; computes $4*3! = 24$ and returns to main

3-Fact   Starts up the 2-Fact machine
          Waits for return value (2!) from 2-Fact; computes $3*2! = 6$ and returns to 4-Fact

2-Fact   Starts up the 1-Fact machine
          Waits for return value (1!) from 1-Fact; computes $2*1! = 2$ and returns to 3-Fact

1-Fact   Starts up the 0-Fact machine
          Waits for return value (1!) from 0-Fact; computes $1*0! = 1$ and returns to 2-Fact

0-Fact   Determines that $0! = 1$
          Returns 1 to 1-Fact

Once 0-Fact is activated, it immediately computes $0! = 1$ and returns the value to the 1-Fact machine, which is then capable of completing the operation $1*0! = 1$. The 2-Fact machine uses the return value of 1 from 1-Fact to complete the operation $2*1! = 2$. In turn, 3-Fact uses the result 2 from 2-Fact to evaluate $3*2! = 3*2 = 6$. Obtaining 6 as the return value from 3-Fact enables 4-Fact to compute the final result $4*3! = 24$ and return this value to the calling statement.

Multibase Representations

In most programming languages, computers display numbers in decimal (base-10) format by default. It is sometimes useful to display numbers in other bases. For instance, the number $n = 95$ has the following representations in bases 2, 5, and 8.

$$95 = 1011111_2 \qquad // \; 95 = 1(2^6) + 0(2^5) + 0(2^4) + 0(2^3) + 1(2^2) + 1(2^1) + 0$$
$$= 1(64) + 0(32) + 1(16) + 1(8) + 1(4) + 1(2) + 1$$

$$95 = 340_5 \qquad // \; 95 = 3(5^2) + 4(5^1) + 0$$
$$= 3(25) + 4(5) + 0$$

$$95 = 137_8 \qquad // \; 95 = 1(8^2) + 3(8^1) + 7$$
$$= 1(64) + 3(8) + 7$$

Decimal format is only one representation for numbers. Other bases include 2 (binary), 8 (octal), and 16 (hex).

For systems programming applications, the base-16 (hexadecimal) representation of a number is very useful. The representation has digits consisting of the numbers 0 to 9 and the letters a to f to define 16 different unit values. The letters are the unit values 10 to 15, with $a = 10$, $b = 11, \ldots, f = 15$. The hexadecimal representation of a number uses grouping by 16 in the same way decimal representation uses grouping by 10. The groups are 1, 16, 16^2, and so forth.

$$95 = 5f_{16} \qquad // \; 95 = 5(16^1) + 15 \qquad\qquad // \; 15 \text{ is } f \text{ in hex}$$

$$450 = 1c2_{16} \qquad // \; 450 = 1(16^2) + 12(16^1) + 2$$
$$= 1(256) + 12(16) + 2 \qquad // \; 12 \text{ is } c \text{ in hex}$$
$$= 256 + 192 + 2$$

An integer n > 0 can be represented in different bases by using repeated division. The process generates the digits for the number from right to left by using the "%" and "/" operators. The remainder is the next digit and the quotient identifies the remaining digits. For instance, n = 95 is 137 base 8. See how the repeated division process identifies the digits for the base-8 number in the order "7," "3," and "1." In the representation, the digits appear in the opposite order of their discovery.

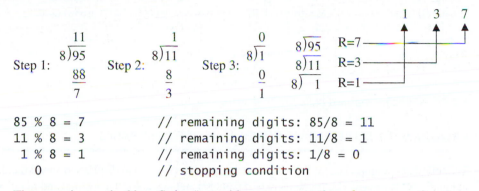

```
85 % 8 = 7          // remaining digits: 85/8 = 11
11 % 8 = 3          // remaining digits: 11/8 = 1
 1 % 8 = 1          // remaining digits: 1/8 = 0
     0              // stopping condition
```

The recursive method baseString() provides a representation of a non-negative number in any base from 2 to 16. The method takes a decimal number n and a base *b*, where $2 \leq b \leq 16$, and returns a string that is the corresponding representation. The method uses repeated division. If n/b is not 0, the recursive step first looks at the quotient (remaining digits) by calling baseString() with n/b as the argument. This recursive call returns a string with the representation of n/b. The step then returns a new string that combines the digits from n/b and the digit n%b. When the quotient is 0, we reach the stopping condition. Just return the empty string "". The revisiting of the recursive steps builds the final representation of n, one digit at a time, from left to right. The following is an implementation of baseString(). To add a digit to the return string, we use the string digitChar that includes the digits 0 to 9 followed by the hex characters a to f. The remainder n%b is an index into the string. The corresponding character is the digit that should be appended to the string.

> Convert *n* to base *b* by converting the smaller number *n/b* to base *b* (recursive step) and adding the digit *n%b*.

baseString():

```java
// returns string representation of n as a base b number
public static String baseString(int n, int b)
{
    String str = "", digitChar = "0123456789abcdef";

    // if n is 0, return empty string
    if (n == 0)
        return "";
    else
    {
        // get string for digits in n/b
        str = baseString(n/b, b);          // recursive step

        // return str with next digit appended
        return str + digitChar.charAt(n % b);
    }
}
```

Figure 6.2 illustrates the series of recursive steps used by baseString() to output $n = 95_{10}$ in base 8 (octal). Solid lines denote the recursive calls, and dotted lines denote the building of the string representation.

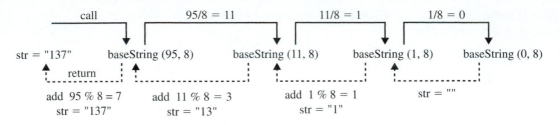

Figure 6.2 *Series of recursive method calls for baseString(95,8).*

PROGRAM 6.1 REPRESENTING NUMBERS IN DIFFERENT BASES

The following program is a GUI application that uses baseString() to display a decimal number in binary, octal, or hex. The frame includes text fields and labels for the decimal and multibase representation of a number. Three buttons create events that allow a user to select the base for the representation. Depending on the choice, the label for the representation field is modified. For instance, selecting button "Octal" creates an event that reads the value from the decimal field, changes the label to "Octal", calls baseString() with base 8, and displays the return string.

A partial listing of the code includes a program outline and the event listener for the buttons.

```
<import statements>

public class Program6_1 extends JFrame
{
    JTextField decimalField, baseField;
    JButton binButton, octButton, hexButton;
    JLabel baseLabel;

    public static void main(String[] args)
    {
        Program6_1 app = new Program6_1();
```

```
        app.setVisible(true);
    }

    public Program6_1()
    {
        <set up text fields and labels>

        // create binButton and add the action listener
        binButton = new JButton("Binary");
        binButton.addActionListener(new ConvertNumber());
        . . .
    }

    private class ConvertNumber implements ActionListener
    {
        public void actionPerformed(ActionEvent ae)
        {
            // getSource() method of ae returns reference to
            // the pressed button
            JButton buttonPressed = (JButton)ae.getSource();
            int n = Integer.parseInt(decimalField.getText());
            String str;

            if (buttonPressed == binButton)
            {   baseLabel.setText(" Binary");
                str = baseString(n, 2);
            }
            else if (buttonPressed == octButton)
            {
                baseLabel.setText(" Octal");
                str = baseString(n, 8);
            }
            else
            {   baseLabel.setText(" Hex");
                str = baseString(n, 16);
            }
            baseField.setText(str);
        }
    }
}
```

6.2   Recursion Applications

Up to this point, our study of recursion has involved algorithms that have alterative iterative solutions that are simple to code. The examples illustrate the design and implementation of recursive algorithms. They do not, however, let you appreciate the true importance of recursion as an algorithm design strategy. One of the most powerful features of recursion is its ability to allow a programmer to solve problems that would be difficult to design and implement as an iterative process. In this section, we illustrate this feature with an algorithm to draw tic marks on a line. A more interesting example is the famous Towers of Hanoi puzzle, which has an elegant recursive solution.

Building a Ruler

A typical ruler is a sequence of inch-long intervals with separator marks. Each inch has a shorter mark at the 1/2-inch point and progressively shorter marks at 1/4-inch intervals, 1/8-inch intervals, and so forth. The problem is to create a program that draws marks at regular intervals on a line. The sizes of the marks differ, depending on the specific interval. The recursive method `drawRuler()` provides the solution. Its algorithm assumes the existence of the method `drawMark()`, which takes a point *x* and an integer value *h* as arguments and draws a vertical line at point *x* with size proportional to *h*.

In `drawRuler()`, a series of recursive steps uses the variable *h* and the endpoints for an interval to draw a mark at the midpoint of the interval. The density of marks on the line depends on an initial value for *h*. Assume *h* = 3. The first recursive step draws a mark at 1/2 inch. The second recursive step draws marks every 1/4 inch. The final recursive step draws marks every $1/2^3$ = 1/8 inch. In general, `drawRuler()` places 2^h-1 marks on the line with a mark each $1/2^h$-inch interval.

Let us trace the sequence of actions for the drawRuler() algorithm, assuming *h* is initially 3 and the interval is 1 inch, with `low` = 0.0 and `high` = 1.0. Each step draws a mark at the midpoint of an interval. Using the midpoint to separate the interval into half-lines, the step makes two recursive calls to drawRuler() to draw smaller marks at the midpoint of each half-line.

Recursive Step (h = 3):

> Interval (0.0, 1.0): Determine the midpoint of the interval and use `drawMark(x,h)` to draw a mark at *x* = 0.5 point with height proportional to *h* = 3 (Figure 6.3a).

Build a ruler in the range (low, high) by drawing a mark at midpt and then recursively draw marks in the ranges (low,midpt) and (midpt, high).

```
midpt = (high + low)/2 = (1.0 + 0.0)/2 = 0.5
drawMark(midpt, 3);
```

> Partition the interval about the midpoint into half-intervals. Make two recursive calls to `drawRuler()` corresponding to the two intervals (0.0, 0.5) and (0.5, 1). Each call passes the argument *h* − 1, which will be used by `drawMark()` to draw shorter marks in the next recursive step.

Recursive Step (h = 2):

> Interval (0.0, 05): The midpoint is 0.25. Draw a mark at *x* = 0.25 with height proportional to *h* = 2 (Figure 6.3b).

```
midpt = (0.5 + 0.0)/2 = 0.25
drawMark(midpt, 2);
```

> Interval (0.5, 1.0): The midpoint is 0.75. Draw a mark at *x* = 0.75 with height proportion to *h* = 2 (Figure 6.3b)

```
midpt = (1.0 + 0.5)/2 = 0.75
drawMark(midpt, 2);
```

> Partition each interval about its midpoint into half-intervals and make two recursive calls to `drawRuler()` corresponding to each half-interval.

Recursive Step (h = 1):

> The algorithm makes four recursive calls to `drawRuler()` with *h* = 1. The marks occur at midpoints 1/8, 3/8, 5/8, and 7/8, with height proportional to 1 (Figure 6.3c).

Stopping Condition (h = 0):

Recursive calls to drawRuler() stop when $h = 0$.

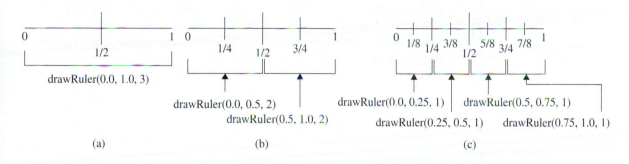

(a)   (b)   (c)

Figure 6.3 *Tracing drawRuler(0.0, 1.0, 3).*

The drawRuler() method takes the endpoints of an interval and the level *h* as arguments. The first action is to draw a mark at the midpoint and then make two recursive calls to draw the marks in the two half-intervals.

drawRuler():

```java
public static void drawRuler(double low, double high, int h)
{
    double midpt;
    if (h >= 1)
    {
        // find the midpoint of interval [low,high)
        midpt = (high + low)/2;
        // draw a mark at the midpoint proportional to h
        drawMark(midpt, h);
        // draw all marks on the left half-interval with h-1
        drawRuler(low, midpt, h - 1);
        // draw all marks on the right half-interval with h-1
        drawRuler(midpt, high, h - 1);
    }
}
```

In Chapter 6 of the software supplement, the program *Ruler.java* illustrates the method drawRuler(). The program draws a ruler for *h* = 1 through *h* = 7, pausing for two seconds between frames. The implementation of drawMark() uses the graphics package in the software supplement. Figure 6.4 shows a snapshot of two frames.

h = 3   h = 5

Figure 6.4 *Run of Ruler.java*

Towers of Hanoi

Move *n* disks from needle A to needle C one disk at a time in such a way that a larger disk is never on top of a smaller disk.

Puzzle fans have long been fascinated with the *Towers of Hanoi* problem, which involves a stack of *n* graduated disks and a set of three needles called A, B, and C. The initial setup places the *n* disks on needle A. The task is to move the disks one at a time from needle to needle until the process rebuilds the original stack, but on needle C. In moving a disk, a larger disk may never be placed on top of a smaller disk.

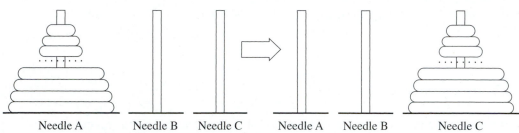

| Needle A | Needle B | Needle C | Needle A | Needle B | Needle C |

Legend has it that the puzzle originated with priests in the Temple of Brahma who were given a brass platform with three diamond needles and 64 golden disks. The mission of the priests was to solve the problem so as to quicken the end of the world. If the legend is true, then we can be assured that the priests are still busy at work, because the solution requires $2^{64} - 1$ moves. At one move per second, the task would require over 584 billion years!

In general, the algorithm that moves *n* disks requires $2^n - 1$ moves.

At first glance, you might think that solving the Towers of Hanoi puzzle would be daunting in terms of both time and strategy. Somewhat surprisingly, perhaps, the Towers of Hanoi has a relatively simple recursive solution. We illustrate the algorithm by looking at the simple three-disk Hanoi puzzle. Watch the steps as we move disks from needle A to C by way of the intermediate needle B. For discussion purposes, we break up the moves into separate stages encompassing several steps. These stages will be used later to develop the recursive method `hanoi()`.

Stage 1: Use three moves to shift the top two disks from needle A to needle B.

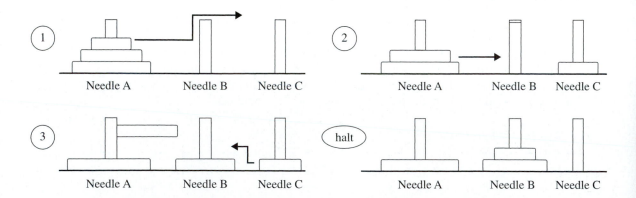

After completing the first stage, only the largest disk remains at needle A.

Stage 2: A simple move shifts the largest disk from needle A to needle C.

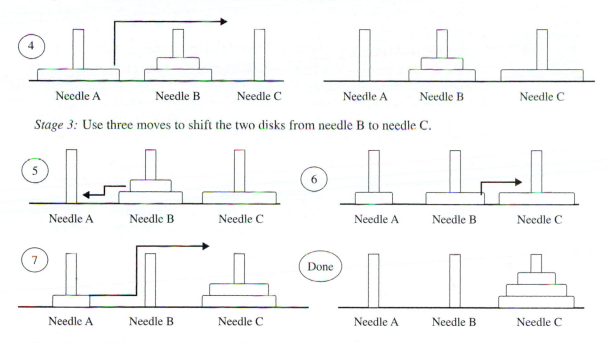

Stage 3: Use three moves to shift the two disks from needle B to needle C.

To understand the recursive nature of the process, note that Stage 1 and Stage 3 both describe separate Towers of Hanoi problems with two disks. In the first stage, two disks move from needle A to needle B, with needle C serving as temporary storage. In the third stage, two disks move from needle B to needle C, with needle A serving as temporary storage. The fact that the Towers of Hanoi algorithm involves a smaller version of the algorithm makes it recursive. The three-disk problem reduces to two two-disk problems.

The Recursive Method hanoi()   The recursive process translates into the method called hanoi(). The arguments include *n*, the number of disks, and three string arguments that denote the name of the starting needle (initNeedle), the destination needle (endNeedle), and the intermediate needle (tempNeedle) that temporarily holds disks during the moves. The following is the method signature.

```
// move n disks from initNeedle to endNeedle using tempNeedle for
// temporary storage
public static void hanoi(int n, String initNeedle,
                         String endNeedle, String tempNeedle)
```

In stage 1, move *n* − 1 disks from initNeedle to tempNeedle (recursive step), using endNeedle for temporary storage.

Stage 1 and Stage 3 correspond to recursive steps. The first stage involves *n*−1 disks that are moved from needle initNeedle to tempNeedle by using endNeedle for temporary storage.

```
// recursive call for stage 1
hanoi(n-1, initNeedle, tempNeedle, endNeedle);
```

Stage 3 moves *n*−1 disks from tempNeedle to endNeedle using initNeedle for temporary storage.

```
// recursive call for stage 3
hanoi(n-1, tempNeedle, endNeedle, initNeedle);
```

In stage 2, move one disk from initNeedle to endNeedle (stopping condition).

In Stage 3, move *n* − 1 disks from tempNeedle to endNeedle (recursive step), using initNeedle for temporary storage.

After completion of Stage 1, the largest disk is left on initNeedle and the other *n*–1 smaller disks are on tempNeedle. The largest disk can be moved directly to endNeedle. An output statement describes this move.

```
System.out.println("Move" + initNeedle + "to" + endNeedle);
```

The recursive steps continue to move shorter and shorter stacks of disks from one needle to another until the stack holds one disk. This is the stopping condition, and the solution to this problem is simply to move the one disk to the correct needle. The following is the code for the hanoi() method. Note that there are two separate calls to hanoi(), corresponding to Stages 1 and 3. In each case, there is a different order of needles in the argument list.

hanoi():

```
// move n disks from initNeedle to endNeedle, using tempNeedle
// for intermediate storage of the disks
public static void hanoi(int n, String initNeedle,
                            String endNeedle, String tempNeedle)
{
    // stopping condition: move one disk
    if (n == 1)
        System.out.println("move " + initNeedle + " to " +
                            endNeedle);
    else
    {

        // move n-1 disks from initNeedle to
        // tempNeedle using endNeedle for temporary storage
        hanoi(n-1,initNeedle,tempNeedle,endNeedle);

        // move largest disk to endNeedle
        System.out.println("move " + initNeedle + " to " +
                            endNeedle);

        // move n-1 disks from tempNeedle to
        // endNeedle using initNeedle for temporary storage
        hanoi(n-1,tempNeedle,endNeedle,initNeedle);
    }
}
```

PROGRAM 6.2 SOLVING THE TOWERS OF HANOI PUZZLE

Let us look at a program that prompts for the number of disks and uses the hanoi() method to solve the Towers of Hanoi puzzle. The run gives a listing of the moves for the case where *n* = 3. Compare the results with the seven moves in the example.

```
import java.util.Scanner;

public class Program6_2
{
    public static void main(String[] args)
    {
        // number of disks and the needle names
        int n;
        String beginNeedle = "A",
```

```
            middleNeedle = "B",
            endNeedle = "C";

    // the keyboard input stream
    Scanner keyIn = new Scanner(System.in);

    // prompt for n and solve the puzzle for n disks
    System.out.print("Enter the number of disks: ");
    n = keyIn.nextInt();

    System.out.println("The solution for n = " + n);
    hanoi(n, beginNeedle, endNeedle, middleNeedle);
  }
  < method hanoi() listed in the program discussion >
}
```

```
Run:
  Enter the number of disks: 3
  The solution for n = 3
  Move A to C
  Move A to B
  Move C to B
  Move A to C
  Move B to A
  Move B to C
  Move A to C
```

Graphical Hanoi Puzzle   In Chapter 6 of the software supplement, the program *HanoiGraphic.java* provides a graphical version of the Towers of Hanoi for 1 to 6 disks. The following are two frames in a run with four disks.

Needle 0   Needle 1   Needle 2   Needle 0   Needle 1   Needle 2

6.3   Evaluating Recursion

The value of using a recursive method depends upon the problem. Sometimes, recursion is not appropriate, because a far more efficient iterative version exists. For some problems, like the Towers of Hanoi, a recursive solution is elegant and easier to code than the corresponding iterative solution. In this section, we use the Fibonacci numbers to compare and contrast iterative and recursive methods. Our discussion will outline some of the advantages and disadvantages of recursion.

Sometimes recursion simplifies algorithm design, but it is sometimes not efficient, and an iterative algorithm is preferable.

Fibonacci numbers are the sequence of integers beginning at position $n = 0$. By definition, the first two terms are 0 and 1. Each subsequent term, beginning at $n = 2$, is the sum of the two previous terms. For instance, $fib(2) = fib(0) + fib(1) = 0 + 1 = 1$.

Fibonacci Sequence: 0, 1, 1, 2, 3, 5, 8, 13, 21, 34, ...
The table lists the terms for n = 2 to n = 6.

n	Value	Sum
2	1	0 + 1
3	2	1 + 1
4	3	1 + 2
5	5	2 + 3
6	8	3 + 5

The term fib(n) in the Fibonacci sequence can be evaluated recursively. The terms fib(0) and fib(1) are 0 and 1, respectively (stopping conditions). From that point on, each term is the sum of the previous two terms (recursive step).

The Fibonacci sequence has a recursive design.

$$\text{fib(n)} = \begin{cases} 0, & n = 0 \\ 1, & n = 1 \\ \text{fib(n} - 1) + \text{fib(n} - 2), & n \geq 2 \end{cases}$$

Fibonacci Methods

In an effort to evaluate recursion, we present recursive and iterative versions of methods that evaluate a Fibonacci number. An analysis of the algorithms provides the Big-O running time of the methods.

The Recursive Method fib()   The recursive method fib() takes a single argument, n, and returns the Fibonacci number fib(n).

```
// compute Fibonacci number n using recursion
public static int fib(int n)
{
    if (n <= 1)    // stopping conditions
        return n;
    else
        return fib(n-1) + fib(n-2);         // recursive step
}
```

The implementation of fib() is a simple and straightforward translation of the recursive definition for terms in the Fibonacci sequence. The execution of the method is far from straightforward. Computing fib(5) requires 15 recursive calls. Figure 6.5 is a hierarchy tree of nodes representing the calls *to* fib() for n = 5, 4, 3, 2, 1, and 0. For the recursive step, a node spawns two other nodes corresponding to the statement fib(n–1) + fib(n–2). Nodes at the bottom of the tree identify stopping conditions.

There are many redundant method calls in fib(n).

The fib() method makes multiple calls to itself with the same argument. This creates enormous redundancy. The evaluation of fib(5) computes fib(3) two times and fib(1) five times. In general, the total number of recursive calls to evaluate the nth Fibonacci number

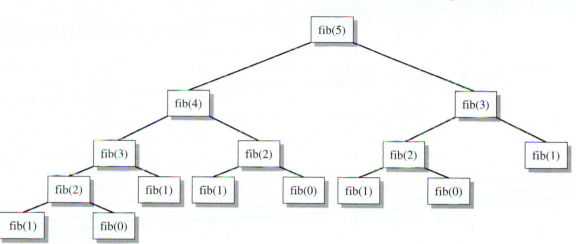

Figure 6.5 *Tree of recursive calls for fib(6).*

is directly related to the value fib(n). Let numCall(n) be the number of method calls required to evaluate fib(n). It can be shown that

```
numCall(n) = 2 * fib(n+1) - 1
```

For instance,

```
For fib(5): numCall(5) = 2*fib(6)-1 = 2*8-1 = 15
For fib(35): numCall(35) = 2*fib(36)-1 = 2*14930352-1 =
                                         29,860,703
```

Because the Fibonacci numbers get large very quickly, it is clear that their recursive evaluation is not efficient. In fact, the recursive computation has exponential running time.

The Iterative Method fibIter()   An iterative version of the method fib() uses a simple loop and two integer variables, oneback and twoback, that maintain a record of the last two Fibonacci numbers. Each iteration of the loop updates these variables. The iterative version has the name fibIter().

Iterative method fibIter():

```
// compute Fibonacci number n iteratively
public static int fibIter(int n)
{
    // integers to store previous two Fibonacci values
    int oneback = 1, twoback = 0, current = 0;
    int i;

    // return is immediate for first two numbers
    if (n <= 1)
        current = n;

    else
        // compute successive terms beginning at 2
```

The iterative method fibIter(*n*) is a linear algorithm.

```
                for (i = 2; i <= n; i++)
                {
                    current = oneback + twoback;
                    twoback = oneback;  // update for next calculation
                    oneback = current;
                }
            return current;
        }
```

For Fibonacci number $n \geq 2$, the iterative form requires $n - 1$ additions and one method call, so the running time is $O(n)$. For $n = 35$, the iterative form requires 34 additions, whereas the recursive method requires 29,860,703 method calls. The Fibonacci example illustrates a cruel irony for recursion. Often, recursion simplifies both the algorithm design and coding, only to fail for lack of runtime efficiency.

PROGRAM 6.3 EVALUATING RECURSION (FIBONACCI EXAMPLE)

The program uses a Timing object to illustrate running times for the iterative and recursive version of the Fibonacci methods. A test run evaluates fib(45) and fibIter(45). The nonrecursive version executes in a fraction of a second, and so the program uses a timer only to display the computation time of the recursive version.

```java
import ds.time.Timing;

public class Program6_3
{
    public static void main(String[] args)
    {
        int fib_45;
        Timing timer = new Timing();
        double fibTime;

        // evaluate fibIter(45) using iterative method
        System.out.println("Value of fibIter 45 by " +
                "iteration is " + fibIter(45));
        // evaluate fib(45) using recursive method
        System.out.print("Value of fib(45) by recursion is ");

        // start/stop timing the recursive method
        timer.start();
        fib_45 = fib(45);
        fibTime = timer.stop();

        // output the value for fib(45) and time of computation
        System.out.println(fib_45);
        System.out.println(
            " Time required by the recursive version is " +
            fibTime + " sec");
    }
    < recursive method fib() defined in the previous discussion >
    < iterative method fibIter() defined in the previous
        discussion >
}
```

```
Run:
   Value of fibIter(45) by iteration is 1134903170
   Value of fib(45) by recursion is 1134903170
      Time required by the recursive version is 34.719 sec
```

Criteria for Using Recursion

The example of Fibonacci numbers should alert you to potential problems with recursion. With the overhead of method calls, a simple recursive method can significantly deteriorate runtime performance. In the case of the Fibonacci numbers, use the O(n) iterative solution in preference to the recursive version.

With the above warnings noted, recursion remains an important design and programming tool. Many algorithms naturally lend themselves to a recursive implementation that distinguishes the stopping conditions and recursive steps. The Towers of Hanoi is a good example. In Chapter 29, we use recursion to solve the 8-Queens problem. This is an elegant algorithm that demonstrates how recursion can solve difficult problems. Equivalent iterative algorithms would be more difficult to devise. In Chapter 7, we use recursion to implement the divide-and-conquer strategy for the famous quicksort, an extremely efficient algorithm for sorting an array.

While recursion is not an object-oriented concept, it has some of the good characteristics of object design. It allows the programmer to manage the key components in the algorithm while hiding some of the complex implementation details. There is no simple rule describing when to use recursion. Use it when it enhances the algorithm design and provides a method implementation that runs with reasonable space and time efficiency.

Chapter Summary

- An algorithm is recursive if it calls itself for smaller problems of its own type. Eventually, these problems must lead to one or more stopping conditions. The solution at a stopping condition leads to the solution of previous problems through a series of method returns. In the implementation of recursion by a Java method, the method calls itself.

- The alternative to recursion is iteration, in which the solution to a problem results from looping rather than recursive method calls. Iteration can be more efficient than recursion.

- Some algorithms are elegantly described using recursion. Drawing tick marks on a ruler is an interesting and simple application of recursion. The Towers of Hanoi puzzle is an example of a complex problem that can be clearly defined and solved by using recursion.

- Use recursion with care and only if it makes the solution to a problem easier to understand and does not create inefficiency. The computation of the Fibonacci numbers is an excellent example of when the recursive solution is simple but extremely inefficient. In fact, the recursive computation has exponential running time.

Written Exercises

1. Give the first six terms in the numerical sequence generated by the recursive method $f()$.

```
public static int f(int n)
{
    if (n == 0)
        return 1;
    else if(n == 1)
        return 2;
    else
        return 2*f(n-2) + f(n-1);
}
```

2. Explain the problem that occurs when executing the recursive method $f()$.

```
public static int f(int n)
{
    if (n == 1)
        return 1;
    else
        return f(n + 1) + n ;
}
```

3. Use the recursive method $rs()$ for parts (a)–(b).

```
public static void rs(String s, int n)
{
    System.out.print(s.charAt(n-1));
    if (n > 1)
        rs(s,n-1);
}
```

   (a) What is the output from the method call $rs("animal", 6)$?
   (b) What is the output from the method call $rs("level", 5)$?

4. Use the recursive method $f()$ for parts (a)–(c).

```
public static void f(int n)
{
    if (n >= 0 && n <= 9)
    {
        System.out.print(n + " ");
        f(n-1);
    }
    else
        System.out.println();
}
```

   (a) Give the output for the specified method calls.

   (i) $f(4)$ (ii) $f(7)$ (iii) $f(0)$

(b) Assume that the output statement and the recursive call are reversed in the method *f( )*.

```
f(n-1);
System.out.print(n + " ");
```

What is the output for each method call?

(i) f(4)   (ii) f(7)   (iii) f(0)

(c) Assume that the recursive call in the method f( ) is f(n + 1) instead of f(n - 1).

```
System.out.print(n + " ");
f(n+1);
```

What is the output for each method call?

(i) f(4)   (ii) f(7)   (iii) f(0)

5. Use the recursive method h( ) for parts (a)–(b).

```
public static void h(char ch, int n)
{
    if (n <= 0)
        System.out.println();
    else
    {
        h((char)(ch-1), n-1);
        System.out.println(ch);
    }
}
```

(a) What is the output for each method call?

(i) h('f',4)   (ii) h('d',3)   (iii) h('x',1)

(b) Assume that the output statement System.out.println(ch) in h( ) occurs before the if-statement. Give the output for the method call h('f',4);

6. Trace the recursive method f() and give the output for the specified method calls.

```
public static int f(int n)
{
    if (n < 2)
        return 0;
    else
        return f(n/2) + 1;
}
```

(a) f(17)   (b) f(8)   (c) f(3)

7. The following is a recursive definition for f(a, b), where *a* and *b* are integer values.

$$f(a, b) = \begin{cases} a - b & a == 0 \text{ or } b == 0 \\ f(a - 1, b) + f(a, b - 1) & \text{otherwise} \end{cases}$$

(a) Write a recursive method that implements f().

(b) Display the "calling tree" that lists the method calls that are required to execute f(3,2). Use Figure 6.5 as an example.

8. Give a declaration for the method fIter(), which is an equivalent nonrecursive version of f().

```
public static int f(int n)
{
    if (n == 1)
        return 1;
    else
        return f(n-1) + n;
}
```

Programming Exercises

9. The method numToNames() converts a positive integer to a string with expanded names for the digits. For instance, if *n* = 372, numToNames() returns the string "three seven two". Implement numToNames() as a recursive method.

```
public static String numToNames(int n)
{ . . . }
```

Write a program that prompts the user to enter a positive integer *n* from the keyboard and uses the method to display the digits using their expanded names.

10. The recursive method ispal() determines whether a string str is a simple palindrome. A simple palindrome is a string consisting entirely of the characters "a"–"z" that reads the same forward and backward. For instance, the following are palindromes:

dad   level   mom   madamimadam

(a) Implement the method ispal().

```
public static boolean isPal(String str, int startIndex,
                            int endIndex)
{ . . . }
```

It returns *true* when the substring of str in the index range [startIndex, endIndex) is a palindrome. The conditions are

Stopping condition:

result is true when startIndex >= endIndex-1

result is false when str[startIndex] != str[endIndex-1]

Recursive step:

Determine whether the substring of str in the index range [startIndex+1, endIndex-1) is a palindrome.

(b) Write a program that inputs five strings and uses `isPal()` to determine if each is a palindrome. Include the strings

amanaplanacanalpanama

gohangasalamiimalasagnahog

abcdecba

11. Section 6.1 develops the recursive method `baseString()` that takes a base-10 integer and returns a string that represents the number in a base between 2 and 16.

(a) Implement a modified version of the method, called `baseString()`, that takes a base-10 number and returns a fixed length string that is the base-2 (binary) representation of the number. Pass the length of the string as a second argument. Assume that the length is sufficient to contain all the significant digits of the number.

```
// return a string that represents the integer n as a
// fixed length base 2 (binary) number
public static String base2String(int n, int length)
{ . . . }
```

For instance, baseString(11, 5) is "01011" and baseString(49, 8) is "00110001".

(b) Write a program that inputs a number n and a length len and calls `baseString()`. Create output that lists the number n, the length len, and the binary string. Include a loop so that you can repeat the process five times. In the run, use input

11 5   97 8   20 6   13 4   65 7

12. The following formula evaluates the sum of the first *n* integers.

```
1 + 2 + 3 + . . . + n = n(n + 1)/2
```

Write a program that gives separate output for the values $n*(n+1)/2$ and sumToN(n), which is the recursive method in Example 6.1 that sums the first *n* integers. Have the program prompt the user to enter a positive integer *n* from the keyboard.

13. Implement the recursive method sumDigits() that sums the digits of a non-negative integer *n*.

$$\text{sumDigits(n)} = \begin{cases} n & n/10 == 0 \\ \text{sumDigits(n/10)} + n\%10 & n/10 \, != 0 \end{cases}$$

Include `sumDigits()` in a program that enters an integer *n* from the keyboard and outputs the sum of its digits. Run the program three times with input 23, 1234, and 90,513.

14. In Chapter 5, we introduced a generic iterative version of the binary search that takes an array `arr`, indices `first` and `last` that describe an index range, and a `target` value, and scans the list looking for a match. The method returns the index of the match or −1 if no match occurs. Implement a recursive version of the binary search algorithm using a divide-and-conquer strategy.

```
public static <T extends Comparable<? super T> int
         binSearchR(T[] arr, int first, int last,T target)
{ ... }
```

Use binSearchR() in a program that uses the following Integer array.

Integer[] a = {13, 18, 22, 30, 37, 42, 50, 57, 68, 81, 88};

Prompt the user to input a target value and search the entire list looking for a match. Use the return index in an output statement that determines whether a match occurs. Run the program with three different target values.

Programming Project

15. Ackermann's function $A(m, n)$ is defined recursively as follows:

$$A(1, j) = 2^j \qquad\qquad\qquad\qquad j \geq 1$$
$$A(i, 1) = A(i - 1, 2) \qquad\qquad\quad i \geq 2$$
$$A(i, j) = A(i - 1, A(i, j - 1)) \qquad i, j \geq 2$$

(a) Compute $A(i, j)$ by hand for the following values of i and j.
    $A(1, 1), A(1, 2), A(2, 1)$, and $A(2, 2)$

(b) Ackermann's function grows very quickly. For instance, show that
    $A(2, j) = 2^{2^{2^{\cdots}}}$, where the number of 2s in the exponent is j.

(c) Implement $A(i, j)$ as a recursive function.

(d) Write a program that computes $A(i, j)$ for the following table.

i	j	A(i, j)
1	1	2
1	2	4
2	1	4
2	2	16
2	3	65,536
3	2	2,147,483,647
4	2	What happens?

Chapter 7

SORTING ALGORITHMS

CONTENTS

7.1   INSERTION SORT
          Insertion Sort Efficiency

7.2   DIVIDE-AND-CONQUER SORT
          ALGORITHMS
          MergeSort
          General Sort Methods
          The msort() Method
          Efficiency of MergeSort

7.3   QUICKSORT
          Partitioning a List with a Pivot
          QuickSort Recursive Descent
          The pivotIndex() Method
          The quicksort() Method
          Running Time of Quicksort
          Comparison of Sorting Algorithms

7.4   FINDING *K*TH-LARGEST ELEMENT

In real life, many things are sorted, such as words in a dictionary, the index for a book, and lists of graduates at a commencement ceremony. We have all seen lists of records sorted by Social Security number or name. As a result, it should not be surprising that sorting is one of the most important operations in computing. Decades of research provide a rich variety of sorting algorithms.

In Chapter 4, we introduced the selection sort for an array. The algorithm requires $n - 1$ passes over the data. Each pass i uses a linear scan of elements in the unordered tail of the array to correctly position the element `arr[i]`. The need for n − 1 passes and the scanning of long sublists contribute to the relative inefficiency ($O(n^2)$) of the algorithm. Section 7.1 presents the insertion sort, which is the best sorting algorithm with quadratic efficiency and is often used when an array is partially sorted.

A recursive technique called *divide and conquer* enables us to sort an array with $O(n \log_2 n)$ running time. The idea is to partition an array into smaller and smaller sublists, which are ordered separately and then combined to form a larger ordered list. Combining the sublists by merging their elements is the basis for the *mergesort* algorithm discussed in Section 7.2. In Section 7.3, we develop a more sophisticated algorithm that partitions the list into two sublists by using a pivot value. The process places the pivot element in the correct location and leaves a sublist of elements that are less than the pivot and a sublist of elements greater than the pivot. This recursive algorithm, called the *quicksort*, provides the fastest known sorting technique, one that works well in all but the most extreme cases. A by-product of the partitioning strategy used by quicksort is a linear algorithm that finds the *k*th-largest number in an unsorted list.

7.1   Insertion Sort

Teachers often have the chore of putting exams in alphabetical order before returning them to students. By looking in on the process, we discover the insertion sort algorithm. Initially, the papers are in random order. Assuming that the first name is correctly positioned, the sort begins with the name on the second paper. If that paper is out of order, it is moved forward to the front of the pile. The third name might be in order ($name_3 > name_2$). If not, it is moved forward in front of the second paper and compared. If it is still out of order, it is forward in front of the first paper. Repeat this process for the fourth, fifth, and subsequent

The insertion sort algorithm inserts a new element into a sorted sublist.

names. For each new name, we know that the papers in the front of the pile (previously sorted papers) are in order. By successive comparison of the name on the new paper with each preceding paper, we find the place to insert the new paper. Let us look at the insertion sort algorithm for the list of five names: Monroe, Chin, Flores, Stein, and Dare.

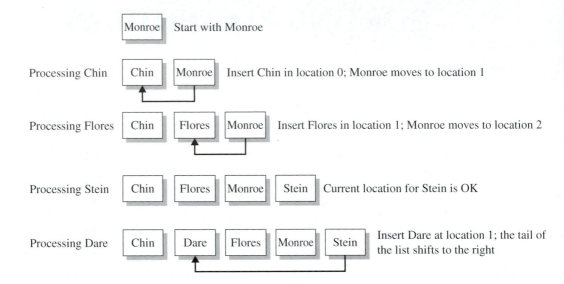

The insertion sort does not perform exchanges. Items larger than the target slide to the right until the algorithm reaches the insertion point.

The method `insertionSort()` takes an array `arr` as an argument and implements the insertion sort algorithm. Assume that n is the length of the array. The ordering assumes that the first element is in its correct position, so the method requires $n - 1$ passes in the range from 1 to n − 1 to order the remaining elements. For a general pass `i`, the elements in the range from 0 to `i-1` are already sorted. The task is to locate the element at position `i` in the proper position within the sublist from 0 to i by scanning the previously sorted sublist. Copy `arr[i]` to a temporary element called `target`. Scan down the list, comparing the target with items `arr[i-1]`, `arr[i-2]`, and so forth. The process stops at the first element `arr[j]` that is less than or equal to the target or at the beginning of the list ($j = 0$). The latter condition is true when `arr[i]` is smaller than any previously sorted element and, thus, will occupy the first position in the newly sorted sublist. During the scan, each element that is greater than the target is moved one position to the right (`arr[j] = arr[j-1]`). As soon as the correct location `j` is determined, the target (original `arr[i]`) is copied to that location. Unlike the selection sort, the insertion sort slides data to the right and does not perform exchanges. You can find the method in the class `Arrays` of the software supplement.

The following is a generic version of `insertionSort()`. The method assumes `arr` is a generic array of elements whose type implements the `Comparable` interface.

insertionSort():

```
// sort an array of elements using insertion sort
public static <T extends Comparable<? super T>>
void insertionSort(T[] arr)
{
    int i, j, n = arr.length;
    T target;

    // place element at index i into the sublist
```

```
    // from index 0 to i-1 where 1 <= i < n,
    // so it is in the correct position
    for (i = 1; i < n; i++)
    {
        // index j scans down list from index i looking for
        // correct position to locate target; assigns it to
        // arr at index j
        j = i;
        target = arr[i];
        // locate insertion point by scanning downward as long
        // as target < arr[j] and we have not encountered the
        // beginning of the array
        while (j > 0 && target.compareTo(arr[j-1]) < 0)
        {
            // shift elements up list to make room for insertion
            arr[j] = arr[j-1];
            j--;
        }
        // the location is found; insert target
        arr[j] = target;
    }
}
```

Example 7.1

The example creates an array of 15 *Integer* objects whose values are random numbers in the range 0 to 99. A call to the insertion sort orders the array. Output uses the Arrays method `toString()` to display the initial array and then the sorted array.

```
Random rnd = new Random();
Integer[] arr = new Integer[15];

// assign random values in the range 0 to 99 to the array
for (int i = 0; i < 15; i++)
    arr[i] = rnd.nextInt(100);

// output the unsorted list
System.out.println("Array(before): " + Arrays.toString(arr));

// call insertionSort() and then output the sorted list
Arrays.insertionSort(arr);
System.out.println("Array(after): " + Arrays.toString(arr));
```

```
Run:
    Array(before): [50, 41, 61, 51, 93, 70, 71, 57, 93, 95, 55,
        67, 94, 69, 49]
    Array(after): [41, 49, 50, 51, 55, 57, 61, 67, 69, 70, 71,
        93, 93, 94, 95]
```

Insertion Sort Efficiency

Assuming that n is the length of the array, the insertion sort requires $n - 1$ passes. For a general pass i, the insertion occurs in the sublist `arr[0]` to `arr[i-1]` and requires on the average i/2 comparisons. The average total number of comparisons is

$$T(n) = 1/2 + 2/2 + 3/2 + \cdots + (n - 2)/2 + (n - 1)/2 = n(n - 1)/4$$

The insertion sort has O(n) best-case running time when the array is already sorted or is "almost sorted." The worst- and average-case running times are O(n^2). The insertion sort is the best of the quadratic sorting algorithms.

From the dominant term in $T(n)$, the average-case running time of the algorithm is O(n^2), which measures the number of comparisons. The best case occurs when the original list is already sorted. In step i, the insertion occurs at `arr[i]` after only one comparison. The total number of comparisons is $n - 1$, with running time O(n). The worst case occurs when the list is in descending order. For each step i, we must scan the entire sorted sublist from i − 1 down to 0 and insert `arr[i]` at the front of the list in `arr[0]`. The scan requires i comparisons. The total number of comparisons is $n(n - 1)/2$ with running time O(n^2).

In general, the insertion sort exhibits the best performance among the quadratic sorting algorithms. The quadratic algorithms are efficient for a list having a small number of elements, say $n \leq 15$. Recall that the insertion sort is linear (O(n)) when the list is already sorted. The insertion sort is still linear when the list is "almost sorted." This condition occurs when many of its elements are already in their correct places. Some more advanced sorting algorithms exploit this fact by partially ordering an array with an O($n \log_2 n$) sorting algorithm such as quicksort and finishing up with the insertion sort (Programming Exercises 7.14 and 7.15, and Programming Project 7.16).

7.2   Divide-and-Conquer Sort Algorithms

Divide and conquer is a problem-solving technique that makes use of recursion. Here is the idea when applied to sorting algorithms.

*   *Divide:* Partition the elements into two groups of roughly equal size.

    Recursively repeat the process by dividing each of the two groups into pairs of groups of smaller size. At some point in the partitioning process, a group is so small (stopping condition) that it can be sorted.
*   *Conquer:* Combine each pair of sorted groups into one large sorted list.

The divide-and-conquer strategy is the basis for the mergesort, which literally partitions the elements in half by splitting them at the midpoint. Recursive steps divide the list into two parts, each holding one-half of the elements, then into four parts, each holding one-fourth of the elements, and so forth. The process continues so long as a sublist has two or more elements. When executing in reverse order, the recursive steps merge the sorted half-lists back into larger and larger ordered lists until the algorithm has rebuilt the original sequence in ascending order.

Algorithms such as selection sort scan long sublists on each pass and have running time O(n^2). The mergesort is an O($n \log_2 n$) sorting algorithm that sorts sublists and merges them.

MergeSort

The idea behind the merge algorithm is familiar to any teacher who has a large class and wants to return student exam papers in alphabetical order. The teacher splits the papers into two piles and sorts them separately. Assume that the piles contain the following ordered list of names.

Pile 1: Bender, Cardona, ..., Johnson, Martinez, and Schwartz
Pile 2: Dolan, ..., Nunez, Stein, Tong, and Walker

The sort merges the two piles. After choosing Bender and Cardona from pile 1, the teacher selects Dolan from pile 2. Eventually, the teacher adds Schwartz to the sorted set of papers, which exhausts the first pile. The merge process concludes by putting the remaining papers from the second pile (Stein, Tong, Walker) on the bottom.

The mergesort algorithm assumes the existence of an original array arr and a temporary array tempArr, both containing *n* elements. The merging process focuses on a sequence of elements in array arr having index range [first, last). The sequence consists of two ordered sublists separated by an intermediate index, called mid. A merge involves copying the elements from the two sublists in array arr to the index range [first, last) in array tempArr so that the new sequence in tempArr is ordered. Consider the following example that describes a sequence of nine integer elements with index range [first, last). The sequence consists of the four-element sorted sublist sublist A and the five-element sublist sublist B, with index ranges [first, mid) and [mid, last), respectively.

> The merge phase of the mergesort algorithm combines two ordered sublists into an ordered list by copying to and from another array.

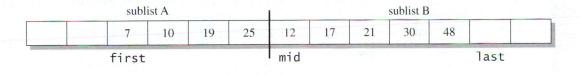

Use indexA and indexB to scan the two sublists in arr and indexC to scan the index range [first, last) in tempArr. Initially, indexA has value first and indexB has value mid corresponding to the beginning location in each sublist. IndexC is initially set to position first in tempArr. The scan compares the elements arr[indexA] and arr[indexB] and copies the smaller value to tempArr[indexC]. The corresponding index is incremented to the next location in the sublist, and indexC moves forward. The process repeats until all of the elements in the array are copied to tempArr. After completing the pairwise scan of the two sublists, the elements in tempArr in the index range [first, last) are an ordered list consisting of a copy of the elements from the two sublists. The algorithm concludes by copying the elements from tempArr back into arr in the index range [first, last). Let us look at the steps for our example.

Step 1: Compare arr[indexA] = 7 and arr[indexB] = 12. Copy the smaller element, 7, to tempArr at indexC. We chose element 7 from sublist A, so increment indexA to the next position in the sublist and increment indexC.

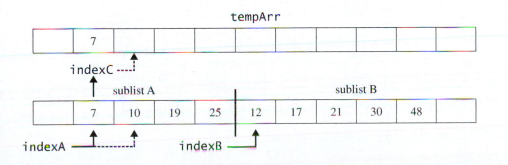

Step 2: Compare `arr[indexA]` = 10 and `arr[indexB]` = 12 Copy the smaller element, 10, to `tempArr`. The smaller element, 10, is again an element in sublist A, and so `indexA` moves to the next position.

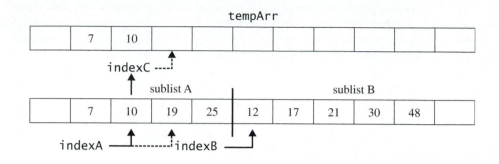

Step 3: The comparison of `arr[indexA]`=19 and `arr[indexB]`=12 provides the first opportunity to copy an element from sublist B to `tempArr`. Since the element is chosen from sublist B, increment `indexB`

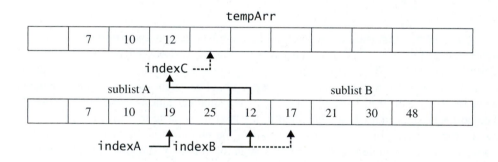

Steps 4–7: The pairwise comparison of elements in the two sublists continues with the copy of elements 17, 19, 21, and 25 to `tempArr`. At this point, `indexA` reaches the end of sublist A (`indexA == mid`), and `indexB` references the value 30.

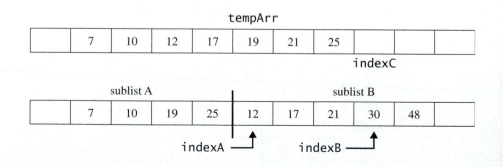

Steps 8–9: The merging process always exhausts one list first, leaving the tail of the second list. In this example, elements 30 and 48 in the tail of sublist B have not been copied to `tempArr`. The algorithm tests to identify the "uncompleted" sublist and copies the remaining elements from that sublist to `tempArr`. Steps 8 and 9 copy the tail of sublist B to `tempArr`, terminating when `indexB` reaches the end of the list (`indexB == last`).

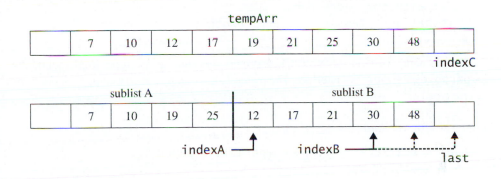

The merge algorithm concludes by copying the elements from `tempArr` back to the original array, starting at index `first`.

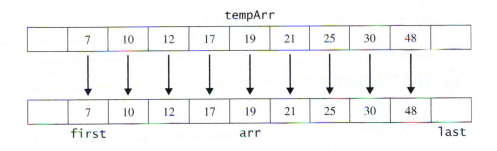

General Sort Methods

In the `Arrays` class, we provide two versions of the static `sort()` method, which implements the mergesort algorithm. One version has the `Object` array `arr` as the lone parameter. The second version is a generic method that specifies `arr` is an array of type T. Both versions of `sort()` are *driver methods*. Their implementations create a temporary array with the same size as array `arr` and then call the private recursive method `msort()` with index range from 0 to `arr.length`. The private method is discussed in the next section and is responsible for implementing the mergesort algorithm. In this book, we use `sort()` as our general sorting algorithm. The nongeneric (`Object`) form of `sort()` will be useful in our study of collection classes, where the method `toArray()` returns the elements in the collection as an `Object` array.

The implementations of sort() uses the method clone() which is discussed in Section 9.5.

sort(): (with Object array)

```
public static void sort(Object[] arr)
{
    // create a temporary array to store partitioned elements
    Object[] tempArr = arr.clone();

    // call msort with arrays arr and tempArr along
    // with the index range
    msort(arr, tempArr, 0, arr.length);
}
```

The sort() methods implement the mergesort for Object arrays and for generic arrays of type T.

The generic version of sort() assumes that the array type implements the Comparable<?super T> interface. *The method creates a temporary array with the same generic type.*

sort(): (generic version)

```
public static <T extends Comparable<? super T>>
void sort(T[] arr)
{
    // create a temporary array to store partitioned elements
    T[] tempArr = (T[])arr.clone();

    // call msort with arrays arr and tempArr along
    // with the index range
    msort(arr, tempArr, 0, arr.length);
}
```

The msort () Method

The msort() method is a recursive algorithm that takes two Object arrays arr and tempArr along with integers first and last that specifies the index range for the sublist which is to be sorted. The method creates two half-lists by computing the index midpt, representing the midpoint of the index range:

```
int midpt = (last + first)/2;
```

Each recursive step makes two calls to msort(). The first one uses indices first and mid to define the index range [first, mid) for the lower half-list of the original sequence. The second call uses indices mid and last to define the index range [mid, last) for the upper half-list. The process sets in motion a chain of recursive calls that partitions the original list into smaller and smaller sublists (half-lists) until their size is 1 (stopping condition). Sublists of size 1 are obviously ordered. When revisiting the chain of recursive calls in reverse order, msort() uses the merge algorithm to build successively larger ordered sublists. The final merging of sublists corresponds to the first recursive step and arranges the original array in sorted order.

Tracing an example is a good way to understand the msort() algorithm. Figure 7.1 illustrates the algorithm for the 11-element Integer array {25, 10, 7, 19, 3, 48, 12, 17, 56, 30, 21}.

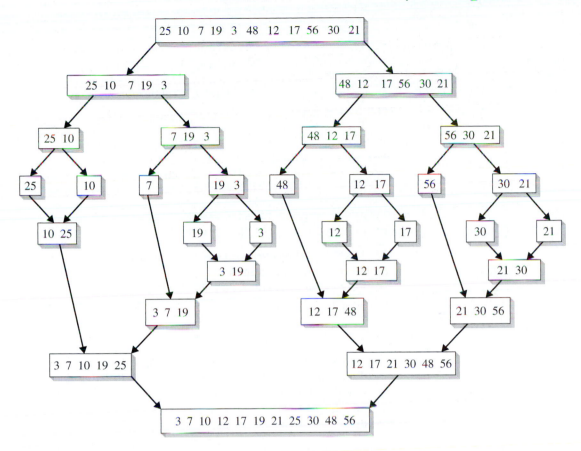

Figure 7.1 *Illustration of the partitioning and merging of sublists in msort().*

The following is the implementation of msort(). The index range for a singleton sublist is [first, first + 1), where first + 1 = last. Thus, the recursive partitioning process continues only as long as first + 1 < last. The concluding merge phase for each recursive step builds an ordered list with range [first, last) from the ordered lower sublist with range [first, mid) and the ordered upper sublist with range [mid, last). The method checks whether the list is already sorted by comparing the last element in the lower sublist (arr[mid-1]) with the first element in the upper sublist (arr[mid]). If arr[mid-1] is less than arr[mid], the list is sorted and no merging of sublists is required. The test would indicate that the following sublist from first to last is already ordered. The test provides optimization that results in faster sorts for nearly ordered lists.

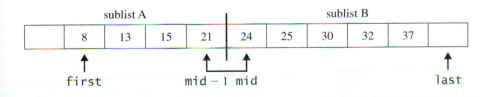

The private
method msort() is
a recursive
algorithm for
mergesort.

msort():

```java
private static void msort(Object[] arr, Object[] tempArr,
                            int first, int last)
{
    // if the sublist has more than 1 element continue
    if (first + 1 < last)
    {
        // for sublists of size 2 or more, call msort()
        // for the left and right sublists and then
        // merge the sorted sublists using merge()
        int midpt = (last + first) / 2;

        msort(arr, tempArr,first, midpt);
        msort(arr, tempArr, midpt, last);

        // if list is already sorted, just copy from src to
        // dest; this is an optimization that results in faster
        // sorts for nearly ordered lists
        if (((Comparable)arr[midpt-1]).compareTo (arr[midpt]) <=
                                        0)
            return;

        // the elements in the ranges [first,mid) and
        // [mid,last) are ordered; merge the ordered sublists
        // into an ordered sequence in the range [first,last)
        // using the temporary array
        int indexA, indexB, indexC;

        // set indexA to scan sublist A with range [first,mid)
        // and indexB to scan sublist B with range [mid, last)
        indexA = first;
        indexB = midpt;
        indexC = first;

        // while both sublists are not exhausted, compare
        // arr[indexA] and arr[indexB]; copy the smaller
        // to tempArr
        while (indexA < midpt && indexB < last)
        {
            if (((Comparable)arr[indexA]).compareTo
                                        (arr[indexB]) < 0)
            {
                tempArr[indexC] = arr[indexA]; // copy to tempArr
                indexA++;                       // increment indexA
            }
            else
            {
                tempArr[indexC] = arr[indexB]; // copy to tempArr
                indexB++;                       // increment indexB
            }
```

```
            // increment indexC
            indexC++;
        }

        // copy the tail of the sublist that is not exhausted
        while (indexA < midpt)
        {
            tempArr[indexC] = arr[indexA];     // copy to tempArr
            indexA++;
            indexC++;
        }
        while (indexB < last)
        {
            tempArr[indexC] = arr[indexB];     // copy to tempArr
            indexB++;
            indexC++;
        }

        // copy elements from temporary array to original array
        for (int i = first; i < last; i++)
            arr[i] = tempArr[i];
    }
}
```

Example 7.2

An example illustrates sort() for an array of integers and an array of strings. In each case, toString(arr) lists the array before and after calling sort().

```
// create an array of integers and of strings for the sort
Integer[] intArr = {25, 10, 7, 19, 3, 48, 12, 17, 56, 30, 21};
String[] strList = {"Dallas","Akron","Wausau","Phoenix",
                                        "Fairbanks"};

// sort integers and output results
Arrays.sort(intArr);
System.out.print("Sorted integers: ");
System.out.println(Arrays.toString(intArr));

// sort strings and output results
Arrays.sort(strList);
System.out.print("Sorted strings: ");
System.out.println(Arrays.toString(strList));
```

Output:
```
  Sorted integers: [3, 7, 10, 12, 17, 19, 21, 25, 30, 48, 56]
  Sorted strings: [Akron, Dallas, Fairbanks, Phoenix, Wausau]
```

Efficiency of MergeSort

An intuitive analysis of the process indicates that the worst-case running time for mSort() is $O(n \log_2 n)$ Assume the array has $n = 2^k$ elements. Figure 7.2 is a tree illustrating the recursive partitioning into progressively smaller and smaller sublists. At each level in the tree, we want to evaluate the amount of work required to merge the half-lists into a single sorted list.

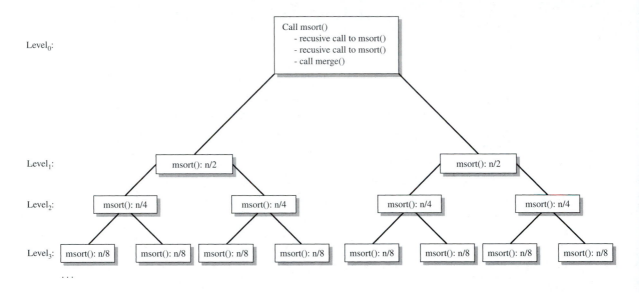

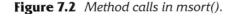

Figure 7.2 *Method calls in msort().*

The mergesort has worst-case and average-case running time $O(n \log_2 n)$.

The first call to msort() at level 0 generates two recursive calls that produce half-lists of size $n/2$, and the merge() method combines the half-lists to create the ordered n-element list. At level 1, there are two calls to msort(); each produces two additional recursive calls with lists of size $n/4$. Each merge joins two sublists of size $n/4$ to create an ordered list of size $n/2$. At level 2, there are $4 = 2^2$ calls to merge(); each creates an ordered sublist of size $n/4$. In general, at level i, there are 2^i calls to merge(), and each call orders $n/2^i$ elements.

Level 0: $1 = 2^0$ call to merge(). The call orders n elements.
Level 1: $2 = 2^1$ calls to merge(). Each call orders n/2 elements.
Level 2: $4 = 2^2$ calls to merge(). Each call orders n/4 = elements.

. . .

Level i: 2^i calls to merge(). Each call orders $n/2^i$ elements.

At each level i in the tree, the merge involves $n/2^i$ elements with linear running time that requires less than $n/2^i$ comparisons. The combined 2^i merge operations at level i require less than $2^i * (n/2^i) = n$ comparisons. Assuming that $n = 2^k$, the partition process terminates at level k with sublists of size $n/2^k = 1$. The total work done on all of the levels is no more than

$$k * n = n \log_2 n$$

and so the worst-case efficiency of msort() is $O(n \log_2 n)$.

7.3 Quicksort

The famous quicksort algorithm uses another form of the divide-and-conquer strategy to order an array. The algorithm, discovered by C. A. R. Hoare, uses a series of recursive calls to partition a list into smaller and smaller sublists about a value called the *pivot*. Each step chooses as the pivot the value at the midpoint of the list. The partitioning algorithm performs exchanges so that the pivot value is placed in its correct final position in the list after the elements are ultimately sorted. Meanwhile, the lower sublist has only elements that are less than or equal to the pivot, and the upper sublist has only elements that are greater than or equal to the pivot.

The quicksort is a divide-and-conquer algorithm like mergesort, but is an in-place algorithm that uses a partitioning strategy.

Mergesort and quicksort use very different approaches to ordering an array. In mergesort, a recursive descent partitions the array into progressively smaller and smaller half-lists. Merging the sublists during the recursive ascent phase of the algorithm creates the order. The original array is ordered only after the final merge, which corresponds to the first recursive step. Quicksort, on the other hand, orders the pivot value in the list and then recursively moves to the resulting lower and upper sublists. The original array is ordered after completing the recursive descent. Note also that the mergesort orders elements by copying them to and from a temporary array. Quicksort is an "in-place" sorting algorithm, because it reorders the sequence by exchanging elements within the list.

Partitioning a List with a Pivot

The best way to understand the overall design of the quicksort algorithm is by working through an example. You understand the key features of the algorithm by viewing in detail a single recursive step. Let `arr` be an array containing 10 integer values:

```
arr: {800, 150, 300, 650, 550, 500, 400, 350, 450, 900}
```

For the first recursive step, the list includes all of the elements in array `arr`. The index range [`first`, `last`) is [0, 10). The partitioning process uses the pivot value at the midpoint of the range.

```
// pivot = arr[mid] where mid = (last + first)/2
mid = (10 + 0)/5 = 5
pivot = arr[5] = 500;
```

The algorithm separates the elements of `arr` into two sublists, S_l and S_h. Sublist S_l is the lower sublist and contains the elements that are less than or equal to the pivot. The higher sublist, S_h, contains the elements that are greater than or equal to the pivot. The pivot 500 is the value that will ultimately lie between the two sublists. We begin by exchanging the pivot with the element 800, which lies at the low end of the index range. The exchange of `arr[first]` and `arr[mid]` has the effect of moving the pivot to the front of the list and setting up a scan of the list with index range [`first + 1`, `last`). The scan uses two indices, `scanUp` and `scanDown`. The index `scanUp` starts at position `first + 1` and moves up the list, identifying the elements in sublist S_l. The index `scanDown` starts at position `last – 1` and moves down the list, identifying elements in sublist S_h.

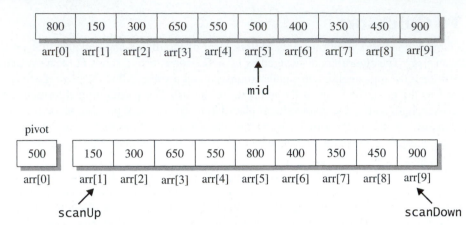

Quicksort partitions elements by locating the pivot in [first,last) so that elements ≤ pivot are to its left and elements ≥ pivot are to its right. This partially orders the range of elements.

The scanning process begins with index `scanUp` and looks for the first element that is greater than or equal to the pivot value. Such an element will ultimately belong in the upper sublist S_h. Once the element is found, the scan halts and attention turns to the upper list. Index `scanDown` moves down the list looking for an element that is less than or equal to the pivot. The element will ultimately belong in the lower sublist S_l. When the element is located, we have the situation where a pair of elements referenced by `scanUp` and `scanDown` are in the wrong sublists; `arr[scanUp]` $\geq$ `pivot` and `arr[scanDown]` $\leq$ `pivot`. A reordering of the list occurs by exchanging the elements at the two positions and then updating the two indices so that the scan with index `scanUp` can resume.

```
// exchange elements and thus place them in the proper sublists
temp = arr[scanUp];
arr[scanUp] = arr[scanDown];
arr[scanDown] = temp;

scanUp++;        // set scanUp at next element up the list
scanDown-;       // set scanDown at next element down the list
```

In the example, `scanUp` stops at index 3 and `scanDown` stops at index 8. The elements 650 and 450 exchange positions, and the indices are moved to positions 4 and 7 respectively.

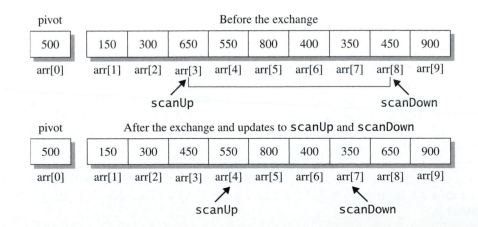

It is critical to understand that the two scans with indices scanUp and scanDown work in tandem. The indices locate the next pair of elements that must be repositioned to form the lower and upper sublists. In the process, the two indices move toward each other until they either land at the same position or pass one another (scanDown ≤ scanUp). When this occurs, we can identify the final position in the array for the pivot value. Index scanUp moves up the list so long as it is less than or equal to scanDown and arr[scanUp] is less than the pivot value. Index scanDown moves down the list so long as the pivot value is less than arr[scanDown].

Let us return to our example. We resume scanning up the list and have index scanUp halt at element arr[4] = 550 ≥ 500. Its partner, scanDown, moves down the list, halting at arr[7] = 350 ≤ 500. Elements arr[4] and arr[7] are the next pair that are in the wrong sublists. We exchange the elements and update the indices to positions 5 and 6 respectively.

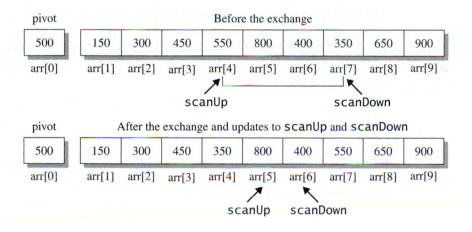

In a final step, scanUp moves up the list, halting at position 5 (arr[5] = 800), and scanDown moves down the list, halting at position 6 (arr[6] = 400). Both positions are their current position. An exchange of elements and updates to the indices leave scanUp at position 6 and scanDown at position 5.

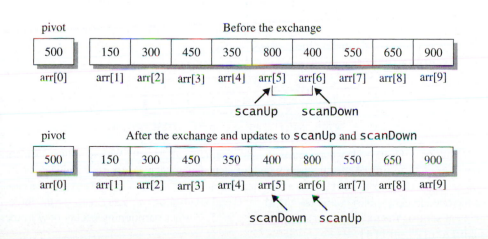

The partition process terminates when scanDown ≤ scanUp. If scanDown = scanUp, arr[scanDown] ≤ *pivot* and arr[scanUp] ≥ pivot. It follows that arr[scanDown] equals pivot. If scanDown < scanUp, then arr[scanDown] ≤ pivot and arr[scanUp] > pivot. In either case, the index scanDown marks the separation point between the two sublists and identifies the final location for the pivot value in the array. The pivot was temporarily stored in arr[0]. Exchanging arr[0] and arr[scanDown] correctly positions the pivot value in the list.

Pivot in its final position

400	150	300	450	350	500	800	550	650	900
arr[0]	arr[1]	arr[2]	arr[3]	arr[4]	arr[5]	arr[6]	arr[7]	arr[8]	arr[9]

QuickSort Recursive Descent

After locating the pivot, the quick-sort algorithm is called for the ranges to the left and right of the pivot.

The quicksort partition process identifies the index for the pivot value and the sublists S_l and S_h. Let the variable pivotLoc denote the index. Recursive steps continue the partitioning process on S_l with index range [first, pivotLoc) and S_h with index range [pivotLoc + 1, last) respectively. Let us continue the example for these two sublists.

Sublist S_1 {400, 150, 300, 450, 350} with index range [0, 5):

```
mid = (0 + 5)/2 = 2
pivot = arr[2] = 300
```

After storing the pivot at the low index in the range, we begin the partitioning process with scanUp = 1 and scanDown = 4. The index scanUp moves up the list, stopping at index 2 (arr[2] = 400 > pivot). The index scanDown then moves down the list, stopping at index 1 (arr[1] = 150 < pivot).

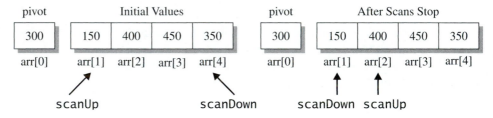

Because scanDown < scanUp, the scans halt, and scanDown is the separation point between two sublists. Complete the process by exchanging arr[scanDown] = 150 and arr[first] = 300.

150	300	400	450	350
arr[0]	arr[1]	arr[2]	arr[3]	arr[4]

With pivotLoc = 1, we are left with a one-element sublist arr[0] and a three-element sublist arr[2] to arr[4] for the next recursive step. The recursive process terminates on an empty sublist (first == last) or on a one-element sublist (first + 1 == last). In the case of the one-element sublist, variables first = 0 and pivotLoc = *last*, and for the three-element sublist, first = pivotLoc and last = 5. Further partitioning occurs only in the sublist arr[2]–arr[4].

Sublist S_h {800, 550, 650, 900} with index range [6, 10):

```
mid = (6 + 10)/2 = 8
pivot = arr[8] = 650
```

After storing the pivot at the low index in the range, we begin the partitioning process with `scanUp` = 7 and `scanDown` = 9. Index `scanUp` moves up the list, stopping at position 8 (arr[8] = 800 > 650), and index `scanDown` moves down the list, stopping at position 7 (arr[7]   = 550 < 650).

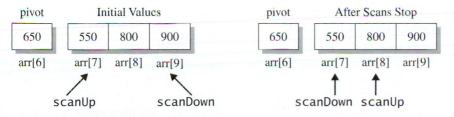

The process terminates because `scanDown` < `scanUp`. Exchanging `arr[scanDown]` and `arr[first]` = 650 locates 650 in the correct location at index 7. The partition leaves a one-element lower sublist and a two-element upper sublist.

Figure 7.3 displays the full set of recursive steps, which partition the list and locate the pivot value. The position of the pivot (`pivotLoc`) is the shaded element. After

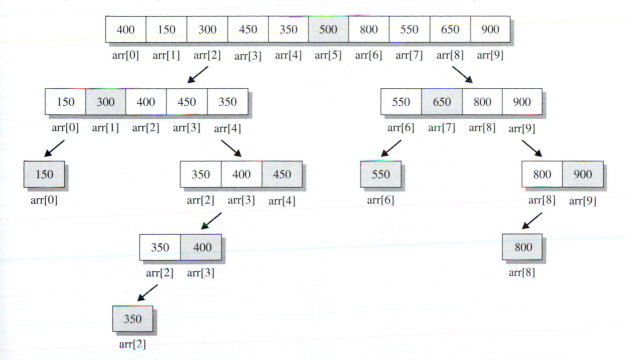

Figure 7.3 *Recursive steps for the quicksort algorithm.*

completing the recursive descent of the progressively smaller sublists, all elements were a pivot at some point or in a 1-element sublist and thus placed in their proper location. The resulting array is ordered.

150	300	350	400	450	500	550	650	800	900
arr[0]	arr[1]	arr[2]	arr[3]	arr[4]	arr[5]	arr[6]	arr[7]	arr[8]	arr[9]

The pivotIndex Method

The method pivotIndex() locates the pivot at index (first + last)/2 in its final place in the range [first,last).

The recursive step in the quicksort algorithm reorders elements in the index range [first, last) about a pivot value. We provide the method pivotIndex() to perform this task. The method takes an array arr of generic type and two indices first and last specifying the index range. The method selects the value of the midpoint of the array as the pivot. The return value is the final location (index) of the pivot value after partitioning the list into two sublists consisting of elements that are less than or equal to the pivot and elements that are greater than or equal to the pivot.

```
// signature for the pivotIndex method
public static <T extends Comparable<? super T>
int pivotIndex(T[] arr, int first, int last)
```

The previous section described the algorithm for pivotIndex(). In the case where the list is empty (first == last), the return value for pivotIndex() is index last. For a one-element list (first + 1 == last), the return value is index first. Otherwise, a partition about the pivot value is executed. After identifying the pivot value, the method exchanges the value with arr[first] and assigns to index scanUp the value first + 1 and to index scanDown the value last – 1. The two indices work in tandem to scan up and down the list. Iterative steps have the indices move toward each other until scanDown ≤ scanUp. Each step begins with index scanUp moving up the list until it halts at an element that belongs in the upper sublist (elements greater than or equal to the pivot).

```
// move up the lower sublist; continue while scanUp is less
// than or equal to scanDown and array value is less than pivot
while (scanUp <= scanDown && arr[scanUp].compareTo(pivot) < 0)
    scanUp++;
```

Index scanDown moves down the list until it halts at an element that belongs in the lower sublist (elements less than or equal to the pivot).

```
// move down the upper sublist while the array value is
// greater than the pivot
while (pivot.compareTo(arr[scanDown]) < 0)
    scanDown--;
```

If scanDown <= scanUp, the iteration process terminates. Otherwise, the two scans halt with scanUp < scanDown and each index points at an element that is in the wrong sublist. The reordering of the list occurs by exchanging the two elements. After the scans conclude, the location of index scanDown separates the list into the two sublists. The method exchanges the pivot in arr[first] with arr[scanDown] and sets scanDown as the return value.

pivotIndex():

```
public static <T extends Comparable<? super T>>
int pivotIndex(T[] arr, int first, int last)
{
   // index for the midpoint of [first,last) and the
   // indices that scan the index range in tandem
   int mid, scanUp, scanDown;
   // pivot value and object used for exchanges
   T pivot, temp;

   if (first == last)
      // empty sublist
      return last;
   else if (first == last-1)
      // 1-element sublist
      return first;
   else
   {
      mid = (last + first)/2;
      pivot = arr[mid];

      // exchange the pivot and the low end of the range
      // and initialize the indices scanUp and scanDown
      arr[mid] = arr[first];
      arr[first] = pivot;

      scanUp = first + 1;
      scanDown = last - 1;

      // manage the indices to locate elements that are in
      // the wrong sublist; stop when scanDown <= scanUp
      for(;;)
      {
         // move up the lower sublist; continue so long as
         // scanUp is less than or equal to scanDown and
         // the array value is less than pivot
         while (scanUp <= scanDown &&
                   arr[scanUp].compareTo(pivot) < 0)
            scanUp++;
```

```
                    // move down the upper sublist so long as the array
                    // value is greater than the pivot
                    while (pivot.compareTo(arr[scanDown]) < 0)
                        scanDown--;

                    // if indices are not in their sublists, partition
                    // complete
                    if (scanUp >= scanDown)
                        break;

                    // indices are still in their sublists and identify
                    // two elements in wrong sublists; exchange
                    temp = arr[scanUp];
                    arr[scanUp] = arr[scanDown];
                    arr[scanDown] = temp;

                    scanUp++;
                    scanDown-;
                }

                // copy pivot to index (scanDown) that partitions sublists
                // and return scanDown
                arr[first] = arr[scanDown];
                arr[scanDown] = pivot;
                return scanDown;
            }
        }
```

The quicksort() Method

The method `quicksort()` provides a user with simple access to the quicksort algorithm. It takes a single array `arr` of generic type as its argument and executes the sort by
calling the private method `qsort()` with the array `arr` and indices 0 and `arr.length`
as arguments.

quicksort():

```
        // sort arr using quicksort
        public static <T extends Comparable<? super T>>
        void quicksort(T[] arr)
        {
            qsort(arr, 0, arr.length);
        }
```

The method
qsort() executes
the partitioning
strategy and
makes the
recursive calls.

The method `qsort()` implements the recursive quicksort algorithm. The method
takes an array `arr` of generic type and two integers `first` and `last`, which specify an
index range. The design for `qsort()` recursively partitions the elements in the index range

into smaller and smaller sublists. The process terminates when the size of a list is 0 or 1. These are stopping conditions because such a list is obviously ordered. For efficiency, we handle a list of size 2 by simply comparing the elements and making an exchange if necessary. For larger lists, the recursive step first calls `pivotIndex()` to reorder the elements and determine the index for the pivot. Assume `pivotLoc` is the return value from `pivotIndex()`. The step makes two calls to `qsort()`. The first call uses the arguments `first` and `pivotLoc` to specify the index range for the lower sublist. The second call uses the arguments `pivotLoc + 1` and `last` to specify the index range for the upper sublist.

qsort():

```
private static <T extends Comparable<? super T>>
void qsort(T[] arr, int first, int last)
{
    // index of the pivot
    int pivotLoc;
    // temp used for an exchange in a 2-element sublist
    T temp;
    // if the range is not at least two elements, return
    if (last - first <= 1)
        return;
    // if sublist has two elements, compare arr[first] and
    // arr[last-1] and exchange if necessary
    else if (last - first == 2)
    {
        if (arr[last-1].compareTo(arr[first]) < 0)
        {
            temp = arr[last-1];
            arr[last-1] = arr[first];
            arr[first] = temp;
        }
        return;
    }
    else
    {
        pivotLoc = pivotIndex(arr, first, last);
        // make the recursive call
        qsort(arr, first, pivotLoc);

        // make the recursive call
        qsort(arr, pivotLoc +1, last);
    }
}
```

We include the implementations for the methods `pivotIndex()`, `qsort()`, and `quicksort()` in the Arrays class.

Example 7.3

The example illustrates use of the `quicksort()` method. Start by declaring an array of strings. Call `quicksort()` with the array as an argument to order the strings in ascending (lexographic) order. Do not question why we use quicksort for a seven-element array. This is only an example.

```
String[] strArr = {"dog", "tiger", "cat", "ant", "snake",
    "pig", "cow"};

Arrays.quicksort(strArr)
System.out.println(Arrays.toString(strArr);
```

Output:
```
[ant, cat, cow, dog, pig, snake, tiger]
```

Running Time of Quicksort

To measure the efficiency of the `quicksort()` algorithm, assume that n is a power of 2: $n = 2^k$ ($k = \log_2 n$). In addition, assume that the pivot lies in the middle of each list, so that quicksort partitions the list into two equal-sized sublists. Under these rather ideal circumstances, we can get a handle on the number of comparisons.

The average-case running time of quicksort is $O(n \log_2 n)$.

For partition level 0, there are approximately n comparisons ($n + 1$, to be exact). The result of the process creates two sublists of approximate size $n/2$. For partition level 1, there are two sublists. Partitioning each sublist requires approximately $n/2$ comparisons. The total comparisons for the two sublists is $2 * (n/2) = n$. For partition level 2, there are four sublists, which require a total $4 * (n/4) = n$ comparisons, and so forth. Eventually, the partition process terminates after k levels with sublists having size 1. The total number of comparisons is approximately

$$n + 2(n/2) + 4(n/4) + \cdots + n(n/n) = n + n + \cdots + n$$
$$= n * k$$
$$= n * \log_2 n$$

The ideal case we have discussed is actually realized when the array is already sorted in ascending order. In this case, the pivot is precisely in the middle of the list.

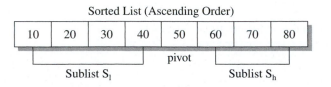

Sorted List (Ascending Order)

| 10 | 20 | 30 | 40 | 50 | 60 | 70 | 80 |

If the array is initially sorted in descending order, partition level 0 locates the pivot in the middle of the list and exchanges each element in both the lower and upper sublists. The resulting list is almost sorted and the algorithm has the same running time, $O(n \log_2 n)$.

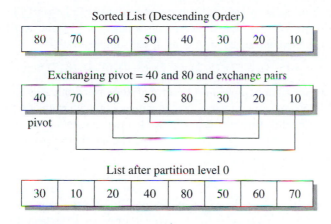

Sorted List (Descending Order)

| 80 | 70 | 60 | 50 | 40 | 30 | 20 | 10 |

Exchanging pivot = 40 and 80 and exchange pairs

| 40 | 70 | 60 | 50 | 80 | 30 | 20 | 10 |

pivot

List after partition level 0

| 30 | 10 | 20 | 40 | 80 | 50 | 60 | 70 |

For an arbitrary array, a mathematical calculation verifies that the average running time, $T(n)$, for quicksort() satisfies the relation

$$T(n) \approx 1.39\, n \log_2 n$$

This shows that the average running time for quicksort() is $O(n \log_2 n)$.

Note

The worst-case scenario for quicksort() occurs when the pivot consistently splits off a one-element sublist and leaves the rest of the elements in the second sublist. This occurs, for example, when the pivot is always the smallest or the largest element in its sublist. For example, the data 5, 3, 1, 2, 9 exhibit this behavior. In partition level 0, there are $n + 1$ comparisons, and the large sublist contains $n - 1$ elements. In partition level 1, there are n comparisons, and the large sublist contains $n - 2$ elements, and so forth. The total number of comparisons is

The worst-case running time of quicksort is $O(n^2)$ and occurs when the pivot is always the smallest or largest element in its sublist.

$$(n + 1) + n + n - 1 + \cdots + 2 + 1 = \frac{n(n + 1)}{2}$$

and the complexity is $O(n^2)$, which is no better than the selection or insertion sort. However, the worst case is unlikely to occur in practice. In general, the overall performance of quicksort is superior to all the other general-purpose sorts we have discussed.

Comparison of Sorting Algorithms

The quadratic sorting algorithms such as insertion sort and selection sort make comparisons within a sequence of adjacent elements and all have worst- and average-case running time $O(n^2)$. The more sophisticated sorting algorithms, such as quicksort and mergesort, also perform comparisons of array elements and have average-case running time of $O(n \log_2 n)$. Why is their performance better than the quadratic algorithms? To answer this question, consider the integer array

Sorting algorithms that make comparisons within a sequence of adjacent elements have running time $O(n^2)$.

```
int[] arr = {5, 3, 8, 2, 4, 7};
```

An *inversion* in an array, arr, is an ordered pair (arr[i], arr[j]), $i < j$, where arr[i] > arr[j]. When sorting in ascending order, arr[i] and arr[j] are out of order. For instance, there are seven inversions in our sample array:

$$(5, 3), (8, 2), (5, 2), (3, 2), (8, 4), (5, 4), (8, 7)$$

The maximum number of inversions in an *n*-element array is $n(n - 1)/2$.

In general, to sort an array, we must remove all the inversions. Algorithms such as insertion sort and selection sort remove at most one inversion with each comparison. Assume that we have an array of distinct elements and we list the elements of the array in descending order: $x_{n-1} > x_{n-2} > \cdots > x_2 > x_1 > x_0$. The number of inversions for this listing of the elements is

$$(n - 1) + (n - 2) + \cdots + 2 + 1 = n(n - 1)/2$$

The O($n \log_2 n$) sorting algorithms compare nonadjacent array elements.

This is the maximum number of inversions possible for the elements of arr. On the average, we expect half this amount for the typical array, so we expect $n(n - 1)/4$ inversions. Each comparison removes at most one inversion, so the average number of comparisons is O(n^2). This result tells us that to sort in better-than-quadratic running time, the algorithm must compare nonadjacent elements.

To sort in better-than-quadratic running time, a sorting algorithm must compare and exchange nonadjacent elements and remove more than one inversion with each comparison.

We discussed the mergesort and quicksort in this chapter. These sorts exhibit O(n $\log_2$ n) performance and execute by making comparisons of nonadjacent array elements. In practice, the quicksort is the algorithm of choice for most sorting tasks. Its O(n^2) worst-case running time has very little likelihood of occurring. Its partition strategy very efficiently moves elements to their final positions in the array. The mergesort is encumbered by having to allocate additional memory, which also slows down its performance.

Can we do any better than the O(n $\log_2$ n) performance of the quicksort? An interesting mathematical result in Chapter 16 shows that any algorithm that performs sorting using comparisons cannot have a worst-case performance better than O(n $\log_2$ n) A similar result also applies to the average-case performance. A sorting algorithm based on comparisons cannot be O(n)! To obtain linear performance, you have to use a sorting algorithm that does not use comparisons, such as the radix sort that we will discuss in Chapter 15. The radix sort applies only to restricted types of data.

PROGRAM 7.1 COMPARING SORTS

The following program compares the performance of the quick, merge, and insertion sorts. Each sorting algorithm is given the same 75,000-element array of random integers in the range from 0 to 999,999. For each type of sort, the main program calls the method timeSort() to execute the sort and evaluate its performance. The method uses a *Timing* object to record the sorting time in seconds. Method timeSort() concludes by outputting results. It calls outputFirst_Last() to list the first and last three elements of the now-sorted array, and then displays the sorting time along with a string identifying the sort. Check the run! The insertion sort, whose efficiency is O(n^2), allows us to vividly contrast a slower sorting algorithm with the faster O(n $\log_2$ n) sorts.

```
import java.util.Random;
import ds.util.Arrays;
import ds.time.Timing;

public class Program7_1
{
```

```java
// types of sorts we will test
enum Sorts {mergesort, quicksort, insertionsort};

public static void main(String[] args)
{
    final int SIZE = 75000;
    Integer[] arr1 = new Integer[SIZE],
              arr2 = new Integer[SIZE],
              arr3 = new Integer[SIZE];
    int rndNum, i;
    Random rnd = new Random();

    // load each array with the same sequence of SIZE
    // random numbers in the range 0 to 999999
    for(i=0; i < SIZE; i++)
    {
        rndNum = rnd.nextInt(1000000);
        arr1[i] = arr2[i] = arr3[i] = rndNum;
    }

    // call timeSort() with each sort type
    timeSort(arr1, Sorts.mergesort, "Mergesort");
    timeSort(arr2, Sorts.quicksort, "Quick sort");
    timeSort(arr3, Sorts.insertionsort, "Insertion sort");
}
// output the first and last 3 elements in a sorted array
public static void outputFirst_Last(Object[] arr)
{
    // capture array size in n
    int i, n = arr.length;

    // output first 3 elements and last 3 elements
    for(i=0;i < 3;i++)
        System.out.print(arr[i] + " ");
    System.out.print(". . . ");
    for(i= n-3; i < n; i++)
        System.out.print(arr[i] + " ");
    System.out.println();
}

// post the time with a description of the sort type
public static <T extends Comparable<? super T>> void
timeSort(T[] arr, Sorts sortType, String sortName)
{

    // create Timing object t and set at start of sort
    Timing t = new Timing();
    double timeRequired;

    t.start();
```

```
            // execute the kind of sort specified by sortType
            switch(sortType)
            {
                case mergesort:         Arrays.sort(arr);
                                        break;
                case quicksort:         Arrays.quicksort(arr);
                                        break;
                case insertionsort:     Arrays.insertionSort(arr);
                                        break;
            }
            // stop timing and capture the elapsed time for the sort
            timeRequired = t.stop();

            // display output with the sort type and time
            outputFirst_Last(arr);
            System.out.print(" " + sortName + " time is " +
                            timeRequired + "\n\n");
        }
    }
```

```
Run:
  26 38 47 ... 999980 999984 999984
    Mergesort time is 0.109

  26 38 47 ... 999980 999984 999984
    Quick sort time is 0.078

  26 38 47 ... 999980 999984 999984
    Insertion sort time is 100.611
```

7.4 Finding *k*th-Largest Element

An application might need to find the median value in an array. The median is a value M such that half the array elements are $<=$ M and the remaining values are $>=$ M. For instance, the Bureau of Labor Statistics reports the median family income as the middle value in a random sample of family incomes. Finding a median is a special case of a more general problem that locates the *k*th-largest element of an array. The SAT Testing Service identifies the quartile scores for students taking the college entrance exam. The quartile scores are the $n/4$th, $n/2$th (median), and $3*n/4$th(-largest) array elements. Our designation "kth largest" implies the value at index k. The 0th largest element is thus the smallest element. We can solve the problem of finding the *k*th-largest element by first sorting the array and then simply accessing the element at position *k*. This is an inefficient algorithm, however, because the sort requires additional work to order all of the elements. We simply need to locate the position of the *k*th-largest value (*k*thLargest) in the list by partitioning the elements into two disjoint sublists. The lower sublist must contain *k* elements that are less than or equal to *k*thLargest, and the upper sublist must contain elements that are greater than or equal to *k*thLargest. Figure 7.4 illustrates the partition. The elements in the lower sublist do not need to be ordered but only have values that are less than or equal to *k*thLargest. The opposite condition applies to the upper sublist.

values • kthLargest	kthLargest	values ≥ kthLargest
0 ... k−1	k	k+1 ... n−1

Figure 7.4 *Partition of a list about the position of the kth-largest element.*

We will apply the "pivoting" technique from the quicksort algorithm to create the partition. The method `findKth()` takes an array `arr`, the indices for the index range `[first, last)`, and the position *k* as arguments. It modifies the array so that the *k*th-largest element is at index *k*. The work is done by calling `pivotIndex()` from within the recursive method `findKth()`. Each call to `findKth()` takes the array and an index range and has `pivotIndex()` rearrange elements about a pivot so that elements smaller than or equal to the pivot are in the lower sublist and elements greater than or equal to the pivot are in the upper sublist. The return value from `pivotIndex()` is the index of the pivot value. If the index is *k*, then the pivot is the *k*th-largest element, and the method `findKth()` returns because it has reached the stopping condition. If the index is greater than *k*, then a recursive call to `findKth()` with index range `[first, index)` continues the search for the *k*th-largest element in the lower sublist. Otherwise, a recursive call to `findKth()` with index range `[index + 1, last)` continues the search in the upper sublist.

findKth():

```
public static <T extends Comparable<? super T>>
void findKth(T[] arr, int first, int last, int k)
{
   int index;
   // partition range [first,last) in arr about the
   // pivot arr[index]
   index = pivotIndex(arr, first, last);

   // if index == k, we are done. kth largest is arr[k]
   if (index == k)
      return;
   else if(k < index)
      // search in lower sublist [first,index)
      findKth(arr, first, index, k);
   else
      // search in upper sublist [index+1,last)
      findKth(arr, index+1, last, k);
}
```

The method findKth() is in the Arrays class.

Example 7.4

The array `scoreList` is a 15-element array. The range of scores is from `lowScore` = 250 to `highScore` = 750. Let us use `findKth()` to list the median score, the range of scores in the top 10%, and the range of scores in the bottom 25%. To aid the example, we list `scoreList` as a sorted array.

```
int lowScore = 250, highScore = 750;
Integer[] scoreList = {250, 300, 350, 400, 400, 450, 500, 500,
    550, 650, 655, 700, 725, 735, 750};
int k, n = scoreList.length;
```

1. Median: located at index $k = n/2$;

   ```
   Arrays.findKth(scoreList, 0, n, k);
   System.out.println("Median: " + scoreList[k]);
   ```

2. Range for top 10%: cut-off index is $k = 9 * n/10$;

   ```
   Arrays.findKth(scoreList, 0, n, k);

   // output the range of scores in the top 10%
   System.out.println("Top 10%: " + scoreList[k] + " - " +
       highScore);
   ```

3. Range for bottom 25%: cut-off index is $k = n/4$;

   ```
   Arrays.findKth(scoreList, 0, n, k);
   // output the range of scores in the bottom 25%
   System.out.println("Bottom 25%: " + lowScore + " - " +
       scoreList[k]);
   ```

```
Output:
   Median: 500
   Top 10%: 735 - 750
   Bottom 25%: 250 - 400
```

Running Time of `findKth()`   This algorithm should have a faster running time than quicksort, because it rejects either the lower or upper sublist at each stage. Let us intuitively develop its running time for an n-element array. Assume, as we did for quicksort, that the pivot always lies at the midpoint of the sublist. Under this assumption, locating the first pivot requires approximately n comparisons, finding the second pivot requires approximately $n/2$ comparisons, finding the third pivot requires approximately $n/4$ comparisons, and so on. The whole process requires no more than

The running time
for findKth() is
O(n).

$$n + \frac{n}{2} + \frac{n}{4} + \frac{n}{8} + \cdots = n\left(1 + \frac{1}{2} + \frac{1}{4} + \frac{1}{8} + \cdots\right) = 2n$$

comparisons when we use the fact that the geometric series $1 + \frac{1}{2} + \frac{1}{4} + \frac{1}{8} + \cdots$ has the sum 2. This intuitive argument indicates that the average running time for `findKth()` is $O(n)$, which is linear.

If the pivot is always the largest or smallest element in its sublist, `findKth()` has the same worst-case running time as quicksort, which is $O(n^2)$.

A mathematical analysis that is similar to that for quicksort, but even more complex, shows that the average running time is approximately

☞

Note

$$2n + 2k \ln\left(\frac{n}{k}\right) + 2(n-k) \ln\left(\frac{n}{n-k}\right)$$

where ln is the natural logarithm function. For any $0 \le k < n$, this algorithm has linear running time. Note that locating the median requires approximately $2n(1 + \ln(2))$ comparisons.

Chapter Summary

- The insertion sort is an $O(n^2)$ algorithm that sorts an array in ascending order without using exchanges. This algorithm is the best of the quadratic ($O(n^2)$) algorithms and is effective for small arrays.

- An excellent example of the divide-and-conquer strategy is the mergesort algorithm. Split the range of elements to be sorted in half, sort each half, and then merge the sorted sublists together. The algorithm has running time $O(n \log_2 n)$ but requires the use of an auxiliary array in order to perform the merge steps.

- The quicksort algorithm uses the divide-and-conquer strategy to perform in-place sorting. It uses a partitioning strategy that finds the final location of a pivot element within an interval [first, last). The pivot splits the interval into two parts, [first, pivotIndex) and [pivotIndex, last). All elements in the lower interval have values $\le$ pivot and all elements in the upper interval have values $\ge$ pivot. The algorithm has average-case running time $O(n \log_2 n)$ and is the choice for most sorting applications. Quicksort does have a worst case of $O(n^2)$, but it is highly unlikely to occur in practice. The partitioning strategy of quicksort very easily provides a linear algorithm that finds the kth-largest element of an array. A primary application of the algorithm is locating the median of n numbers.

- Any sorting algorithm must remove inversions in the data. Sorting algorithms that use comparisons remove the inversions by performing comparisons and exchanges. The quadratic algorithms such as insertion sort make comparisons within a sequence of adjacent elements and remove at most one inversion per comparison. They have running times $O(n^2)$. The more sophisticated algorithms such as quicksort compare nonadjacent elements and remove more than one inversion per comparison.

Written Exercises

1. Show the array after each pass of the insertion sort for the integer values {5, 1, 3, 2, 9, 6}.

2. How many exchanges does the insertion sort perform for the array elements {8, 2, 5, 7, 1, 3}?

3. Implement the generic method max() by using a recursive divide-and-conquer strategy. The method takes an array and two indices defining an index range. Partition the list about the midpoint and then recursively call max() to obtain the maximum value in each sublist. The maximum value for a combined list is the larger of the maximum values (return values) for the two sublists.

```
public static <T extends Comparable<? super T>>
T max (T[] arr, int first, int last)
{ ... }
```

Using the tree of sublists for the mergesort in Section 7.3 as a model, create the tree for max(). Assume the array contains *Integer* objects with values {25, 7, 19, 48, 12, 56, 30, 21, 28}.

4. Draw the tree of recursive calls performed by the mergesort during the process of sorting the following array: {7, 3, 2, 8, 4, 12, 10, 5, 7, 6}.

5. Use the quicksort algorithm to sort array arr. During each recursive step, show all exchanges of a pair of elements in the lower and upper sublists. List the ordering of the elements after each step.

```
Integer[] a = {790, 175, 284, 581, 374, 799, 852, 685, 486,
    333};
```

6. In the quicksort algorithm, assume that the first element in the list, arr[first], is chosen as the pivot instead of the value at the midpoint of the list. What initial ordering of the elements would produce a worst-case running time?

7. Suppose we change the code for pivotIndex() in the quicksort algorithm so the first of the two loops is

```
while (scanUp <= scanDown &&
        arr[scanUp].compareTo(pivot) <= 0)
    scanUp++;
```

What is the running time of the modified quicksort when sorting an array of n equal values? What is the running time for the original version of quicksort?

8. To this point, we have considered the following sorting algorithms in this book:

insertion sort, mergesort, quicksort, selection sort

For each sort, give the average- and worst-case running time, the space requirements, and make some additional comments about its efficiency. The additional comments may indicate the probability that the worst case occurs and special situations that allow the algorithm to run faster.

9. A sorting algorithm is *stable* if two data items having the same value are not rearranged with respect to each other at any stage of the algorithm. For instance, in the five-element array

5_1 55   12 5_2 33

a stable sorting algorithm guarantees that the final ordering is

5_1 5_2 12   33   55

Classify each of the algorithms in Written Exercise 8 as to their stability.

10. A *recurrence relation* is a mathematical formula that describes a recursive algorithm. It is common practice in algorithmic analysis to develop a recurrence relation for the running

time of a recursive algorithm and then solve the recurrence to obtain the running time. For instance, the following is a verbal description of the computation for the worst-case running time for the mergesort:

"Compute the running time for the sort in each 1/2 sublist and add $n - 1$ comparisons for the merge operation."

We translate this description directly into a recurrence relation that describes the running time, $T(n)$, of the mergesort.

$$T(n) = 2\,T(n/2) + (n - 1)$$

The problem of placing marks on a ruler in Section 6.2 involves drawing a single mark and then marking the left and right intervals. It is described by the recurrence relation

$$T(n) = 2\,T(n/2) + 1$$

A discussion of how to solve recurrence relations is outside the scope of the book and belongs to a course on the theory of algorithms. However, sometimes a simple graphical argument is effective in illustrating the relation. Using the recursive tree in Figure 7.2 as a model, illustrate the drawing of tick marks for $n = 4$. The marks partition the line into 1/16th intervals.

Programming Exercises

11. Implement a recursive version of the insertion sort for an array, using the following algorithm description as a guide. The argument n is the number of elements of the array that must be sorted.

    ```
    public static <T extends Comparable<? super T>>
    void insertionSortR(T[] arr, int n)
    ```

    If $n == 0$, then simply return; otherwise, call insertionSortR() with arguments arr and $n - 1$. This will sort the elements in the index range from 0 to $n - 2$. Insert arr[$n - 1$] so that the range from 0 to $n - 1$ is in order. Write a program that tests your implementation of insertionSortR() for arrays of different generic types.

12. This exercise modifies quicksort by implementing a method called qsortNoSwap(). When a partition of the sublist [first, last) results in no swaps, call insertionSortList() to order the sublist. Note that you will have to determine when a partition does not involve a swap and to create a modified version of insertion sort called insertionSortList() that sorts elements in the range [first, last).

    ```
    public static <T extends Comparable<? super T>>
    void insertionSortList(T[] arr, int first, int last)
    { ... }

    public static <T extends Comparable<? super T>>
    void qsortNoSwap(T[] arr, int first, int last)
    { ... }
    ```

In a program, initialize an array with 1000 random integer values in the range from 0 to 4999. Output the first 10 and the last 10 values in the array after applying `qsortNoSwap()` to order the array.

13. Implement a modified version of the quicksort algorithm, called `qsort15()`, that repeatedly partitions an array into smaller sublists until the size of a sublist is less than or equal to 15. Handle the case of a one- or two-element sublist as before; however, if the sublist size is between 3 and 15, call `insertionSortList()` to order the sublist. Note that you will have to create a modified version of insertion sort so it sorts elements in the range [first, last).

```
public static <T extends Comparable<? super T>>
void insertionSortList(T[] arr, int first, int last)
{ ... }

public static <T extends Comparable<? super T>>
void qsort15(T[] arr, int first, int last)
{ ... }
```

In a program, initialize an array with 1000 random integer values in the range from 0 to 4999. Output the first 10 and the last 10 values in the array after applying `qsort15()` to order the array.

14. In the quicksort algorithm, we chose the value at index mid = (first + last)/2 as the pivot. A modified version of the algorithm, called the `qsortMed_3()`, takes the elements at indices `first`, mid, and `last − 1` and reorders (exchanges) them so that they are in order. The quicksort process begins by using `arr[mid]` as the pivot and exchanging the value with `arr[first + 1]`. The scan with index `scanUp` can then begin at index `first + 2`, and `scanDown` begins at index `last − 2`. Implement the method `qsortMed_3()` that uses the median-3 algorithm. Include the following methods in your solution.

```
// define mid = (first + last)/2; put arr[first],
// arr[mid] and arr[last-1] in order
// arr[first] <= arr[mid] <= arr[last-1],
// swap pivot arr[mid] with arr[first+1] and
// return pivot
public static <T extends Comparable<? super T>>
T median3(T[] arr, int first, int last)
{ ... }
// using the value from median3() as the pivot,
// locate the pivot in its final location so all elements
// to its left are <= to its value and all elements to the
// right are >= to its value; return the index of the pivot
public static <T extends Comparable<? super T>>
int pivotIndexMed_3(T[] arr, int first, int last)
{ ... }
```

```
// median-3 quicksort of arr over range [first, last)
public static <T extends Comparable<? super T>>
void qsortMed_3(T[] arr, int first, int last)
{ ... }
```

```
// median-3 quicksort of arr
public static <T extends Comparable<? super T>>
void quicksortMed_3(T[] arr)
{ ... }
```

In a program, initialize an array with 1000 random integer values in the range from 0 to 4999. Output the first 10 and the last 10 values in the array after applying `quicksortMed_3()` to order the array.

15. In this exercise, you will develop a GUI application that uses `findKth()` and sorting method msort() and qsort(). Figure 7.5 shows a snapshot of the running application. The user enters the number of data items for an array in the JTextField with label "N." Pressing the "Generate" button clears the JTextArea and causes the generation of an array of N integer values in the range from 0 to 99. A series of buttons at the bottom of the frame have event handlers that use `findKth()` to create sublists separated by a specified index.

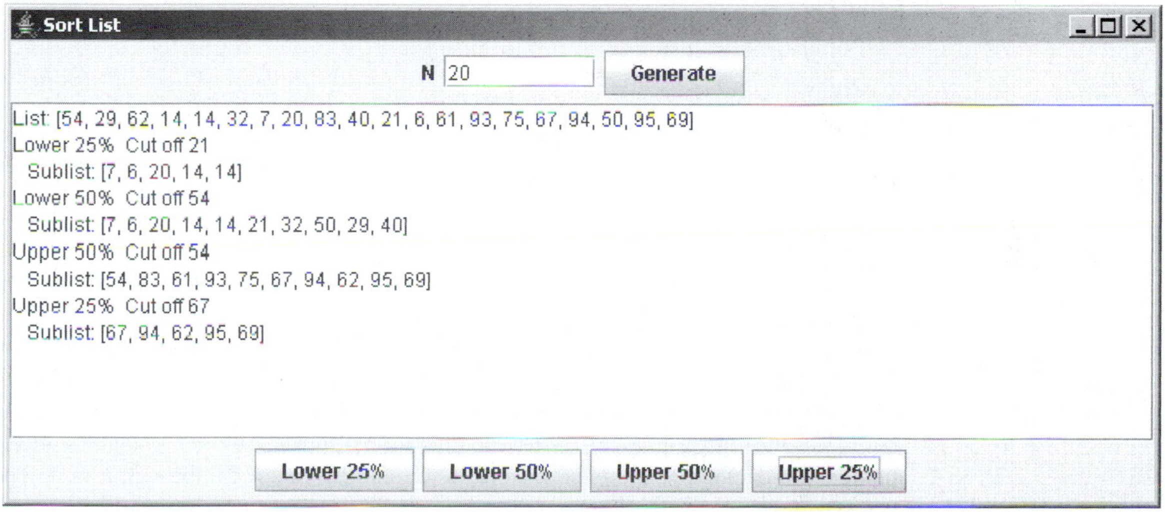

Figure 7.5 *Snapshot of running application for Programming Exercise 15.*

(a) *Lower 25%:* For $k = N/4$, partition an array to create a sublist that contains the bottom 25% of the elements. Use msort() to sort this sublist. Output in the text area should describe the event and display the cutoff value for k. Then, list the elements in the ordered sublist.

(b) *Lower 50%:* Use (a) as a model.

(c) *Upper 50%:* Use (a) as a model, but sort the sublist with qsort().

(d) *Upper 25%:* Use (a) as a model, but sort the sublist with qsort().

Programming Project

16. The Shell sort, named after its inventor Donald Shell, provides a simple and efficient sorting algorithm. The sort begins by subdividing an n-element array, arr, into k sublists, which have members

    ```
    arr[0],      arr[k+0],         arr[2k+0], ...
    arr[1],      arr[k+1],         arr[2k+1], ...
                     . . .
    arr[k-1],    arr[k+(k-1)]],    arr[2k+(k-1)], ...
    ```

    A sublist starts with a first element arr[i] in the range from arr[0] to arr[k - 1] and includes every successive kth element. For instance, with $k = 4$, the following array splits into four sublists:

    7 5 8 6 2 4 9 1 3 0

    Sublist$_0$:   7 2 3

    Sublist$_1$:   5 4 0

    Sublist$_2$:   8 9

    Sublist$_3$:   6 1

    Sort each sublist using the insertion sort algorithm. In our example, we obtain the following sublists:

    Sublist$_0$:   2 3 7

    Sublist$_1$:   0 4 5

    Sublist$_2$:   8 9

    Sublist$_3$:   1 6

    and the partially sorted array

    2 0 8 1 3 4 9 6 7 5

    Repeat the process with successively smaller values of k, and continue through $k = 1$. When $k = 1$, the algorithm corresponds to the ordinary insertion sort that assures the array is in order. The values of k that the algorithm uses are called the *Shell sort increment sequence*. For an effective increment sequence, choose as the starting value of k the largest number from the sequence 1, 4, 13, 40, 121, 364, 1093, 4193, 16577, ... that is less than or equal to $n/9$. After each iteration, replace k by $k/3$ so that the increments move backward in the sequence from the starting value of k through $k = 1$. The data swapping occurs in noncontiguous segments of the array, which moves an element a greater distance toward its final location than a swap of adjacent entries in the ordinary insertion sort. It can be shown through a somewhat complex mathematical argument that the Shell sort does less than $O(n^{3/2})$ comparisons for this increment sequence.

    Implement the Shell sort algorithm in the method shellSort().

    ```
    public static <T extends Comparable<? super T>>
    void shellSort(T[] arr)
    { ... }
    ```

    You may use the following code to find the starting value for k.

    ```
    for(k=1; k <= n/9; k = 3*k+1);
    ```

    In a program, initialize an array with 1000 random integer values in the range from 0 to 4999. Output the first 10 and the last 10 values in the array after applying shellSort() to order the array.

Chapter 8

COLLECTION TYPES

CONTENTS

8.1 INTRODUCTION TO COLLECTIONS

8.2 OVERVIEW OF COLLECTIONS
List Collection
Set Collection
Map Collection
Adapter Collections
Graph Collection
Java Collections Framework

8.3 THE BAG COLLECTION
Creating and Using a Bag Collection
Application: Sieve of Eratosthenes

8.4 IMPLEMENTING THE BAG CLASS
Private remove() Method
Insert and Access Methods
Collection toString()

In this chapter, we begin our study of data structures. In simplest terms, a data structure is a storage container that holds elements. The structure is referred to as a *collection*. We present a modern view of data structures that combine object-oriented programming principles and concepts of algorithm analysis. We organize our study around interfaces that define categories of collection types. A *collection class* is a concrete data structure that implements an interface using a specific approach to storing and accessing the elements. In Section 8.1, we introduce the generic `Collection` interface that defines a common set of operations that are available for most data structures (collection classes). We develop the `Collection` interface in detail.

In Section 8.2, we give an overview of the data structures that are introduced in this book. We will look at different interfaces that define different categories of data structures. For each collection type, we give examples of concrete collection classes that implement the interface. Each class uses an underlying data storage structure and access strategy to handle the elements. The storage structure affects the runtime efficiency of access and update operations. The level of efficiency is a key criterion in selecting a data structure for an application. Section 8.2 provides a roadmap for the study of data structures in the rest of this book.

An abstract model of the `Collection` interface resembles a bag. Section 8.3 creates an implementation of the interface with a class, called, appropriately, `Bag`. This class illustrates how we design a data structure and use it in applications. We use it to introduce important implementation design issues. This class is a simple data structure that later will help us to illustrate concepts such as iterator, cloneable, and serializable.

8.1 Introduction to Collections

A collection is an object that holds other objects. More precisely, it is a storing mechanism with operations that allow for adding and removing elements and for accessing and perhaps updating their values. As we proceed in this book, we will encounter of variety of different collections. For now, we want to start at the very beginning and describe a simple collection that serves as a prototype data structure. In the process, we will define the

The Collection interface represents the core operations in a collection.

generic `Collection` interface, which defines a core set of operations that characterize the behavior of most collection classes. In our integrated development of data structures, the different collection types share this common set of operations.

A bag, say a bag of golf balls, is a model for the most general kind of collection. You toss things into the bag, pull things out of the bag, and reach in to search for an item in the bag. The `Collection` interface provides a template for this basic kind of collection. The interface defines operations `add()` and `remove()` that insert and delete elements from the collection. The operations return true or false, indicating whether any change actually occurred. The design of the operations reinforces the fact that the interface is a very general description of a collection. A collection class that implements the interface may or may not allow duplicates and so an `add()` operation may not actually insert a new element. The method `clear()` removes all elements from the collection and allows it to be reused as a storage structure. At any time, we need to know how many elements are in the collection. The methods `size()` and `isEmpty()` specify the number of elements in the collection and indicate when the collection has no elements.

All collections have common operations such as add(), remove(), clear(), size(), and isEmpty().

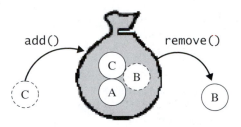

A collection is a dynamic-storage structure. It constantly changes as elements enter and leave. We need some way to find what is in the collection. The method `contains()` indicates whether a specific element is in the collection (true) or is not in the collection (false). At any time, a program must have a way to access the elements in a collection. This function is provided by an iterator object of type *Iterator*, which has methods that allow it to sequentially scan each element and return the value. Responsibility to create an iterator and manage its behaviors belongs to the collection. The `Collection` interface defines the method *iterator()*, which returns an *Iterator* object positioned as a specific element. A collection class that implements the interface defines its own version of *Iterator*. The order in which elements are scanned depends on how the collection stores and accesses its elements. The notion of an iterator is fundamental to an understanding of modern data structures. We will examine the concept in Chapter 12.

We would usually assume that a collection stores objects. In fact, it only holds references to objects. An actual object is created independently and assigned to a reference variable. Adding an object to a collection involves assigning the reference to a new variable in the collection. Removing an element simply deletes the reference variable in the collection without destroying the object. The fact that a collection stores references is critical to your understanding of data structures. The `Collection` interface defines the method `toArray()` that copies the elements in the collection to an `Object` array. The resulting array is a new set of elements (references) that can be used to access the objects associated with the collection.

The array allows access with an index in the range 0 to `size()`-1. The array and the collection are separate entities. Sorting elements in the array does not change the ordering of elements in the collection.

The following is an API for the generic `Collection` interface. Note that the `add()` method requires a generic argument so that the collection contains only elements of the specified type. The methods `contains()` and `remove()` have an `Object` argument. Typically, a collection class implements these methods using `equals()`, which returns false when the comparison involves mixed types. As a result, the methods return false when a program attempts to identify or remove an element that is not of the generic type.

Having collection classes implement an interface forces the collections to share common methods, although each collection may implement a method in its own way.

Interface Collection<T>		*ds.util*
boolean	**add**(T element)	
	Ensures that this collection contains an element; returns true if the operation performs an insertion and false if this collection does not permit duplicates and already contains the specified element.	
void	**clear**()	
	Removes all of the elements from the collection. The collection is empty after the method returns.	
boolean	**contains**(Object element)	
	Returns true if this collection contains an element and false if it does not.	
boolean	**isEmpty**()	
	Returns true if this collection contains no elements and false if the collection has at least one element.	
Iterator<T>	**iterator**()	
	Returns an iterator over the elements in this collection. The order in which elements are returned depends on the implementing class.	
boolean	**remove**(Object element)	
	If an element is present in the collection, removes a single instance of the element from this collection. Returns true if an element was removed and false if it was not.	
int	**size**()	
	Returns the number of elements in this collection.	
Object[]	**toArray**()	
	Returns an array containing all of the elements in this collection.	

8.2 Overview of Collections

The `Collection` interface describes basic collection operations. There is no reference to any ordering that items may have in the collection. These are features that are important in some applications. For instance, we may want to store elements in a natural ordering and create a sorted collection. In other cases, we store items in a linear order by position. This allows for an array-like scan of the items by index or direct access to an item by position.

For some types of applications, the order in which items enter and exit a collection is important. For instance, calls to a computer vendor for technical support are handled on a first-come first-served basis. The collection for storing calls is a familiar waiting line called a *queue*. A variation is a collection that removes the item that most recently entered the collection. This is a stack, which handles items on a last-in first-out basis.

Collections are distinguished by features that are over and above those defined by the Collection interface. The features take into account how elements are stored and accessed. They deal with the ordering of the elements, restrictions on duplicate values, and other conditions. We use the features to organize collections into categories. The organization includes a variety of interfaces that extend the Collection interface and add operations that take advantage of the underlying storage structures.

List Collection

The List collection type describes an object that stores elements by position. The first element is at position 0, the second element at position 1, and so forth. The last element is at position $n = $ size() $- 1$.

The List collection stores elements by position and includes index-based operations.

List Container

The List interface extends the Collection interface by adding index-based operations. The methods allow a program to access and update elements in random order. The index provides sequential access to the elements.

In this book, we develop the ArrayList and the LinkedList collection classes as implementations of the List interface. The data structures offer the same index-based methods but differ significantly in the runtime efficiency of the operations. The efficiency issue often determines which data structure is used.

The ArrayList Collection An ArrayList collection is a generalized array that stores elements in a contiguous block of memory. The underlying storage structure is an array that allows for direct access to the elements. An ArrayList grows dynamically to meet the needs of an application. As elements are added at the back of the list, the array fills up and is then automatically expanded to accept more elements. In Figure 8.1, the ArrayList contains n elements with expansion room at the back of the list.

An ArrayList is a direct-access collection.

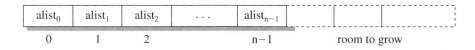

Figure 8.1 *ArrayList collection with n elements and expansion room at the back of the list.*

Assuming there is room to grow, adding an element at the back of the array is an $O(1)$ operation. Using an array to store elements affects the efficiency of an ArrayList to insert and delete elements at intermediate positions in the list. Consider the problem of adding element 5 at position 2 when the list currently contains the elements {9, 12, 3, 8, 6, 14, 22}. Figure 8.2 illustrates a before-and-after view of the sequence.

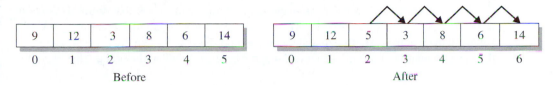

Figure 8.2   *Inserting element 5 at position 2 in an ArrayList.*

The insertion requires shifting the tail of the list to the right to open a gap for the new element. It is an O(n) operation. Deleting an element is also an O(n) operation because it requires shifting the tail of the list to the left one position to fill in the gap left by the exiting element.

Programmers use an `ArrayList` as the data structure of choice when an application needs direct access to list elements and inserts data at the back of a list that can grow dynamically. Addition and removal of data from the back of the list is very efficient. However, the list should require relatively few insertions and deletions in the interior of the list. The `ArrayList` collection is introduced in Chapter 9 along with a series of applications. The chapter also provides an implementation of the `ArrayList` class.

> The ArrayList collection is a generalized array that can grow dynamically at the rear to meet the needs of an application. Insertion or removal at the rear is very efficient, but those operations inside an ArrayList are not.

The LinkedList Collection   A `LinkedList` is a sequence whose elements have a value and links that identify adjacent elements in the sequence. In order to access a specific value in the list, you must start at the first position (front) and follow the links from element to element until you locate the item. Hence, a `LinkedList` is not a direct-access structure but rather a sequential-access structure.

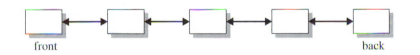

> The LinkedList collection stores elements connected by links. To arrive at a specific element in the list, start at the front and follow links until arriving at the required value. A LinkedList is a sequential-access structure.

The power of a `LinkedList` collection is its ability to add and remove an element efficiently at any position in the sequence. You can think of the list as a chain consisting of a series of connected links. The algorithm to add an element follows the model of inserting a new link in the chain. For instance, Figure 8.3a illustrates how a list adds the value 15 at position 2. The new element enters the list immediately before 6. The insertion involves creating an element with value 15 and setting links to attach it to adjacent elements in the list. A `LinkedList` collection maintains references to the front and back of the list. Adding an element at either end of the list simply updates one of the references and, as such, is an O(1) operation. In Figure 8.3b, value 10 is added at the front of the list and value 7 is added at the back of the list. Deleting an element from a linked list is a similar algorithm that requires updating the references for adjacent elements.

> Inserting or erasing elements in a LinkedList involves altering links in a chain. They are O(1) operations.

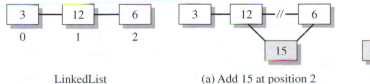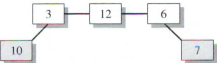

LinkedList   (a) Add 15 at position 2   (b) Add 10 at the front, add 7 at the back

Figure 8.3   *Inserting elements into a LinkedList collection.*

The `LinkedList` class can be extended to create collections that store elements in order. The derived class `OrderedList` overrides the `add()` method. Rather than inserting a new element at the end of the list, the new method searches the existing sorted list to find the location point. For instance, Figure 8.4 adds the string "red" to the ordered list of colors.

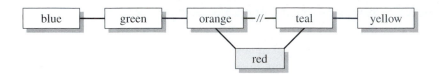

Figure 8.4 *The add() method in the OrderedList class.*

Choose carefully between an ArrayList and a LinkedList. Direct access is efficient for an ArrayList but not for a LinkedList. Insertion or removal inside a list is efficient for a LinkedList but not for an ArrayList.

Features of the `ArrayList` and the `LinkedList` data structures point out an important application design issue. Both classes implement the `List` interface and so share common methods. For some methods, the choice of the data structure significantly affects runtime performance. For instance, an `ArrayList` allows direct access to an element. Executing `get(i)` has O(1) running time. The same method for a linked list has O(n) running time because the algorithm must scan the list from the front in order to locate the element. Adding or removing an element at the first position in the list is an O(1) operation for a linked list collection. The same operation has running time O(n) in an `ArrayList` because the tail of the list must be shifted. In an application design, we may determine that a list collection is appropriate because we want to store elements by position. Once that decision is made, we must evaluate whether an `ArrayList` or a `LinkedList` collection has better runtime performance.

Set Collection

A Set is like a Bag, but no duplicate values are allowed.

Set operations include union, intersection, and difference.

A *Set* is a collection that resembles a `Bag` collection but with the provision that no duplicate values are allowed. The `Set` interface extends the `Collection` interface by stipulating that the `add()` method should add a specified element to the set only if it is not already present.

Applications typically combine a set with another set in a variety of ways. The combination may result in a set union, set intersection, or set difference. You are familiar with the algorithms from mathematics. For instance, `setA` contains the names of U.S. cities that are capitals of their state, while `setB` contains names of cities with a population greater than 700,000. The intersection of the two sets identifies capitals that exceed the specified population level (Figure 8.5).

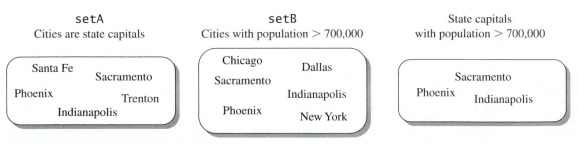

Figure 8.5 *Intersection of set collections for state capitals and cities with a population of over 700,000.*

Map Collection

A *Map* is a collection that stores key-value pairs. The key and the value may be of any object type, although some implementations require that the key type must implement comparison methods. The key field uniquely identifies the element while the value field typically has associated information. Access to an element requires only the key parameter and returns the value component. See how the Map method get() accesses a value.

A Map is a collection of key-value pairs. The key is used to access the associated value.

```
// m is a Map object
value = m.get(key);
```

Arrays and maps have an obvious analogy. An array uses an index to access an element, while a map uses a key to access the associated value of an element. Thus, a map is often referred to as an *associative array*. For instance, the figure below displays a map whose elements represent replacement parts. The part number (string) is the key, and the value is an object that includes the price of the part and its vendor. The method call partMap.get("W91-A83") would correspond to an array expression partArr["W91-A83"].

An array uses an index to access an element, while a Map uses a key to access the associated value. A Map is often termed an associative array.

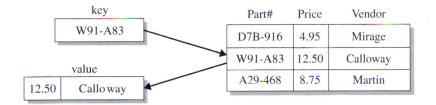

In this book, we will develop tree and hash table implementations for the Set and Map interfaces. The tree classes TreeSet and TreeMap use a binary search tree for the underlying storage structure. As a by-product, an iterator scans the elements in order. This feature allows us to identify the minimum and maximum elements in the collection. We formalize this fact by creating two additional interfaces, OrderedSet and OrderedMap, that extend the corresponding Set and Map interfaces. The new interfaces define the methods first() and last(). The hash table classes HashSet and HashMap maintain unordered collections. Their main feature is a function, called a *hash function*, that converts a key to an integer, which serves as an index into a table. The result can be a very efficient lookup strategy. We introduce trees and hash tables as separate topics so that you gain hands-on experience with the concepts. They are then used to implement collection classes.

The book provides two implementations of a Set and Map. TreeSet and TreeMap maintain ordered data, while a HashSet and HashMap do not.

Adapter Collections

List, Set, and Map interfaces have methods that can add, remove, or update the value of a specified element. They are data-storage and data-handling devices. We introduce other collections called *adapter collections*. An adapter contains another collection as its underlying storage structure; however, the interface for an adapter provides only a restricted set of operations from the structure. Examples are Stack, Queue, and PriorityQueue.

An adapter contains another collection as its underlying storage structure; however, the interface for an adapter provides only a restricted set of operations from the structure.

Stack Collection   A stack is a collection that resembles a rack of serving trays in a cafeteria. It has a single point of reference called the top of the stack. An element is added at the top of the stack. All other items currently on the stack are "pushed lower" to make room. The operation is referred to as *pushing* the item onto the stack. The operation of removing an item from a stack is called *popping* the stack. It deletes the element currently on the top. In Figure 8.6a, objects A, B, and C are pushed onto the stack in that order. A series of pop operations (Figure 8.6b) clear the stack by successively removing the top element.

In a stack adapter, the last item in is the first item out (LIFO).

Note that items come off a stack in the reverse order of their original insertion into the stack. We refer to this as *last-in first-out* (*LIFO*) ordering. A stack collection allows a program to access the value of the element at the top without removing it. We continue our discussion of stacks in Chapter 14 and use them to illustrate the runtime handling of recursive method calls and algorithms to evaluate arithmetic and relational expressions.

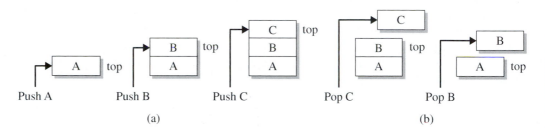

Push A   Push B   Push C   Pop C   Pop B

(a)   (b)

Figure 8.6 *Push and pop operations on a stack.*

In a queue adapter, the first item in is the first item out (FIFO). A waiting line at a grocery store is an example of a queue.

Queue Collection   A *queue* is a collection that allows access only at the front and back. Items enter at the back and exit from the front. This is the model for a waiting line at a grocery store or a bank. Figure 8.7 provides a view of a queue after adding elements A, B, C, and D in that order. An insertion adds E to the back of the queue and a deletion removes the first element A from the queue.

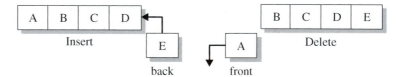

Figure 8.7 *Insert and delete operations on a queue.*

Items leave the queue in the same order as they arrive; hence the collection provides a *first-in first-out* (*FIFO*) ordering. We develop the queue collection in Chapter 15 and illustrate its use with the radix sort algorithm and an event-driven simulation.

Priority Queue Collection   A *priority queue* is a collection that has restricted access operations similar to a stack or queue. Elements can enter the priority queue in any order. Once in the collection, a delete operation removes the maximum (or minimum) value, depending on the specified type of priority. You can visualize a priority queue as a filtering system that takes in elements and then releases them in priority order (Figure 8.8). We develop the priority queue in Chapter 15 and its implementation using a heap in Chapter 22.

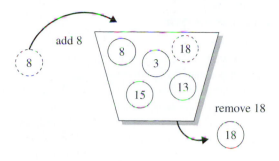

Figure 8.8 *Priority queue.*

Graph Collection

A *graph* is a set of vertices connected by links, called *edges*. Depending on the applica-tions, edges may or may not have a direction. An edge e connecting vertices A and B has a direction when A is identified as the source and B is identified as the destination. Illustra-tions use an arrow from A to B for a directed edge. An edge may also have a weight defin-ing a property of the edge; for instance, the length, the amount of available traffic or signal flow, and so forth. A graph whose edges have direction is called a *directed graph* or *digraph*. If weights are included, the graph is a weighted digraph. Figure 8.9 is a weighted digraph containing five vertices and seven edges.

A graph is a set of vertices and con-necting edges. The edges may or may not have a direction. Also, an edge may have an associated weight.

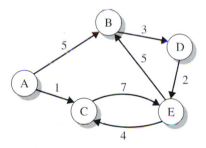

Figure 8.9 *A weighted directed graph (digraph).*

Graphs are involved in many problems of practical interest. For instance, directed graphs are used to represent finite state machines. Optimizing the flow of data in a network is solved using weighted graphs.

The Graph interface defines methods that access and update vertices, edges, and weights for a graph. Access includes global properties such as the number of vertices or edges as well as specific information about individual components. For instance, methods return the number of edges that emanate from a vertex as well as the set of vertices (neigh-bors) that are the destinations for the edges.

The DiGraph class implements the Graph interface. Edges have associated weights, which can all be set to 1 when the graph object represents a simple digraph. We will develop a wide range of graph algorithms and present solutions using DiGraph methods.

A graph is a com-plex data structure with many impor-tant applications.

The Graph inter-face defines meth-ods for a graph, and the DiGraph class provides an implementation for a directed, weighted graph.

Java Collections Framework

The Java Collections Framework is a group of collections defined using interfaces, abstract classes, and inheritance.

The Java software development system presents data structures as a *collections framework* in the package *java.util*. The collections framework is an integrated system for describing and defining collections. It is built on six collection interfaces and a hierarchy of abstract classes and collection classes that implement the different data structures.

We also present data structures using a framework. Our approach designs interfaces to include the key operations that describe the properties and behaviors of a collection type. All of our collection classes are implemented directly without using an inheritance hierarchy with abstract classes. They simply implement an interface and include other methods that take advantage of the underlying storage structure. We developed our framework to promote your understanding of data structures. As professionals, you will probably use the collections in the *Java Collections Framework*. Our framework is similar to the Java framework and will allow you to make a easy transition to the professional software.

The primary interfaces in the framework are Collection, List, Set, and Map.

The following is a summary of the collection interfaces and collection classes that are developed in this book. The unshaded regions are interfaces and the shaded regions are collection classes.

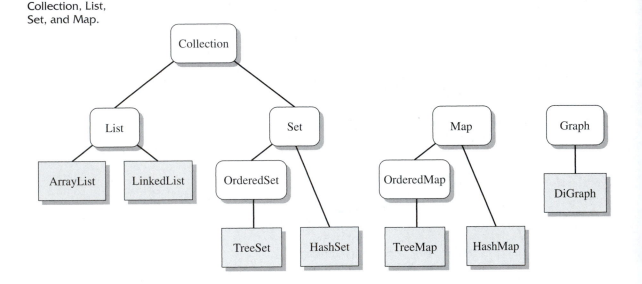

8.3   The Bag Collection

The Bag class is a generic collection that stores elements of type Object. This class implements the Collection interface.

The Collection interface defines methods that describe the most general storage container. One model for the collection is a bag—like a bag of golf balls. In this section, we create a concrete collection class, appropriately called Bag, that implements the interface. The class is a generic collection that stores elements of a specified type. The underlying storage structure is a fixed length array. The length of the array is the maximum number of elements that the bag can hold. We refer to this as its *capacity*. The actual number of elements in a bag at any given time is its size. Figure 8.10 illustrates a Bag collection with capacity 8 and size 5. A constructor uses an integer argument to set the capacity and to initialize the size to 0.

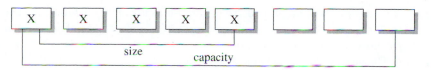

Figure 8.10 *Bag collection with fixed capacity 8 and current size 5.*

The Bag collection implements the Collection interface. This fact identifies the majority of methods in the class. Because the underlying storage structure is a fixed length array, we qualify the action of the add() method. Duplicate values are allowed but a new item is inserted only if the collection has room. If the size is less than the capacity, then add() inserts a new item and returns true; otherwise it simply returns false. Methods in the Collection interface provide only basic data handling operations. In the Bag class, we define the grab() method, which returns a random element in the collection. The method provides access to elements in the collection without having to copy them to an array using toArray(). The class provides a toString() method that returns a comma-separated list of elements enclosed in brackets.

The following is an API for the Bag class. Our listing includes only the constructor, the add() method, and methods not specified in the Collection interface.

class Bag<T> implements Collection<T>	ds.util

	Constructors
	Bag(int capacity)
	Initializes an instance, with capacity setting the maximum size of the collection. The initial size is 0.
	Methods
boolean	**add**(T item)
	Adds the object item to the finite collection (if it is not already full) and returns true. Duplicate values are permitted. When the collection is full, the return value is false.
T	**grab**()
	Returns a random element from the collection; returns null if the collection is empty.
String	**toString**()
	Returns a string with a comma-separated list of elements enclosed in brackets.

Creating and Using a Bag Collection

A Bag collection is not a dynamic structure. It is created with a fixed capacity that cannot be changed. An application would typically use a Bag object only if it has prior information on the potential size of the collection. Let us look at an example that illustrates most of the Bag methods.

We input a string from the keyboard and use two Bag collections to store characters as Character objects. The collection bagA uses add() to store all of the characters in the string. A second collection, bagB, is derived from bagA to contain the distinct characters in the string. We build bagB by repeatedly using grab() to identify an element (character) in bagA and then adding it to bagB. All occurrences of the character are then removed from bagA. The process continues until bagA is empty.

The problem concludes by using the Bag method toArray() to create an array of Object references corresponding to the elements in bagB. Methods applied to the array affect only elements in the list and not the corresponding elements in the bag. We use the static methods sort() and toString(arr) in the Arrays class to order the elements in the array and to display the sorted list of distinct characters from the string.

PROGRAM 8.1 USING BAG COLLECTIONS

The program illustrates the example described above. It uses Bag collections to identify distinct characters in a string and then display them in an ordered list. The string is input from the keyboard and all processing is handled with Bag methods and the static methods sort() and toString(arr) in the class Arrays.

```java
import ds.util.Bag;
import ds.util.Arrays;
import java.util.Scanner;

public class Program8_1
{
    public static void main(String[] args)
    {
        // keyboard input stream and input string
        Scanner keyIn = new Scanner(System.in);
        String str = "";

        // Bag objects hold string characters
        Bag<Character> bagA, bagB;

        // Character object for char value in the input string
        Character ch;

        // flag used to remove duplicates from bagA
        boolean foundDuplicate;

        // prompt for input string
        System.out.print("Enter a string: ");
        str = keyIn.next();

        // create the collections with capacity str.length()
        bagA = new Bag<Character>(str.length());
        bagB = new Bag<Character>(str.length());

        // add characters from the string to bagA
        for (int i = 0; i < str.length(); i++)
            bagA.add(str.charAt(i));

        // use grab() to fetch a character from bagA; add it to
        // bagB and then remove all occurrences of the character
        // from bagA; continue this process until bagA is empty
```

```
while (!bagA.isEmpty())
{
    // remove a random character from bagA and add to bagB
    ch = bagA.grab();
    bagB.add(ch);

    // remove all occurrence of target = chObj from bagA
    do
        foundDuplicate = bagA.remove(ch);
    while (foundDuplicate);
}

// create array of Object references corresponding to
// elements in bagB; sort array and output its values using
// static methods sort() and toString(arr)
Object[] objArr = bagB.toArray();
Arrays.sort(objArr);
System.out.println("Sorted letters: " +
                    Arrays.toString(objArr));
    }
}
```

```
Run:
  Enter a string: mississippi
  Sorted letters: [i, m, p, s]
```

Application: Sieve of Eratosthenes

The Greek mathematician and philosopher Eratosthenes lived in the third century B.C. He discovered an intriguing method of using a bag to find all primes less than or equal to an integer value n. A prime p is an integer greater than 1 that is divisible only by 1 and p (itself). The algorithm begins by creating a bag with capacity n and then inserting into the collection Integer objects corresponding to integer values in the range from 2 to n. As a shortcut, we say that the bag contains all of the integers from 2 to n. A loop makes multiple passes over the elements in the bag using successive integer key values 2, 3, 4, and so forth. Each pass shakes free nonprime numbers and lets them filter through the sieve. At the end, only the prime numbers remain.

The Sieve of Eratosthenes is an ancient algorithm for finding prime numbers that relies on the use of a Bag collection.

The first pass begins with the integer $m = 2$, which is the smallest prime number. The pass removes from the bag all multiples of 2 having the form $2 * k$, where $k \geq 2$. The multiples, $4 = 2*2, 6 = 3*2, 8 = 4*2, \ldots$, cannot be primes because they are divisible by 2. At the end of the first pass, we have removed all of the even numbers except 2, leaving the integers 2, 3, 5, 7, 9, and so on. The second pass uses integer $m = 3$, which is a prime and is responsible for removing all multiples of 3. Formally, the pass removes all multiples of the form $3 * k$, where $k \geq 2$. In reality, the even multiples $6 = 2*3, 12 = 4*3, 18 = 6*3$, and so on have already been removed in the first pass since they are even numbers. This pass deletes only the odd multiples of 3, including $9 = 3*3, 15 = 5*3, 21 = 7*3$, and so on. The third pass uses integer $m = 4$, which is no longer in the bag. No action is taken and the algorithm moves to $m = 5$, which is still in the collection and is a prime. The pass removes the multiples of 5 (25, 35, 55, ...) that remain.

The multiple passes use all values of m in the range $2 \leq m \leq \sqrt{n}$. Using the upper bound $\sqrt{n}$ is an optimization feature of the algorithm. It is sufficient to remove all non-prime numbers from the bag. To verify this fact, assume that some nonprime (composite) number $t = p * q$ remains in the collection. This leads to a contradiction. If both factors p and q are greater than $\sqrt{n}$, then

$$t = p * q > \sqrt{n} * \sqrt{n} > n$$

Hence, at least one factor, say, p, must satisfy the inequality $p \leq \sqrt{n}$. This "small" factor p is the integer m that defines a pass or p is a multiple of m ($p = m * k$) for pass m, where $2 \leq m \leq \sqrt{n}$. For the two cases, $t = m * q$ or $t = m * k * q$ and so t is a multiple of m and has already been removed from the collection, contrary to our assumption.

Example 8.1

The figure illustrates the Sieve of Eratosthenes when finding all prime numbers in the range from 2 through 25. We only need to check m in the range $2 \leq m \leq \sqrt{25} = 5$.

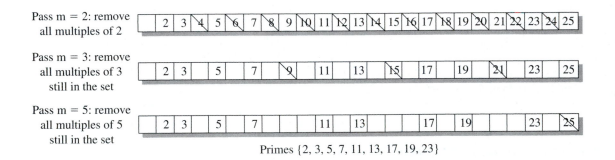

Pass m = 2: remove all multiples of 2

Pass m = 3: remove all multiples of 3 still in the set

Pass m = 5: remove all multiples of 5 still in the set

Primes {2, 3, 5, 7, 11, 13, 17, 19, 23}

The static method `sieve()` takes an integer *n* as an argument and returns a `Bag` that contains `Integer` objects corresponding to the prime numbers in the range from 2 to *n*. The method implements the algorithm for the Sieve of Eratosthenes.

sieve():

```
public static Bag<Integer> sieve(int n)
{
    int m, i;
    Bag<Integer> primeBag = new Bag<Integer>(n);

    // load the set with integers 2, 3, ..., n
    for (m = 2; m <= n; m++)
        primeBag.add(new Integer(m));

    // find the primes using the Sieve of Eratosthenes;
    // look at numbers from m = 2 to m * m > n (m <= sqrt(n))
    for (m = 2; m * m <= n; m++)
        // check is m is still in the set; if so remove all
        // multiples of m starting with 2*m
```

```
            if(primeBag.contains(new Integer(m)))
            {
                // i sequences through successive multiples of m,
                // 2*m, 3*m, ...
                i = 2 * m;
                while (i <= n)
                {
                    primeBag.remove(new Integer(i));
                    // update i to the next multiple of m
                    i += m;
                }
            }
        }
        return primeBag;
    }
}
```

PROGRAM 8.2 SIEVE OF ERATOSTHENES

The following program uses the Sieve of Eratosthenes. The constant PRIMELIMIT =500 sets an upper bound for primes in the range 2 to PRIMELIMIT. A call to sieve() returns a Bag object with primes in the range. The program uses writePrimes() and a StringBuffer object to output each prime number in a field of width 6 with 10 numbers per line.

```
import ds.util.Bag;

public class Program8_2
{
    public static void main(String[] args)
    {
        final int PRIMELIMIT = 500;
        Bag<Integer> bag;

        // call sieve() and return the bag of primes
        bag = sieve(PRIMELIMIT);

        // list elements in the bag as an array
        // output primes in 6 spaces, 10 per line
        writePrimes(bag.toArray());
        System.out.println();
    }

    // output elements in the array in 6 spaces, 10 per line
    public static void writePrimes(Object[] arr)
    {
        String intStr;
        int count = 1, i;
        // initialize sb with 6 blanks
        StringBuffer sb = new StringBuffer("      ");

        for (i = 0; i < arr.length; i++)
        {
```

```
                    // convert integer to a string
                    intStr = arr[i].toString();

                    // use replace() to place intStr in the string buffer.
                    sb.replace(0, intStr.length(), intStr);

                    // output string buffer as a string
                    System.out.print(sb.toString());

                    // every 10 elements output a newline
                    if(count % 10 == 0)
                        System.out.println();
                    count++;
                }
            }

            < sieve() developed in the preliminary discussion >
        }
```

Run:									
2	3	5	7	11	13	17	19	23	29
31	37	41	43	47	53	59	61	67	71
73	79	83	89	97	101	103	107	109	113
127	131	137	139	149	151	157	163	167	173
179	181	191	193	197	199	211	223	227	229
233	239	241	251	257	263	269	271	277	281
283	293	307	311	313	317	331	337	347	349
353	359	367	373	379	383	389	397	401	409
419	421	431	433	439	443	449	457	461	463
467	479	487	491	499					

8.4   Implementing the Bag Class

The Bag class is a simple data structure that affords us the opportunity to discuss implementation design techniques. The ideas extend to more complex collection classes. A concrete collection class implements an interface that characterizes the structure. Its implementation begins with a definition of the underlying storage structure and supporting data that maintain the size of the collection. The main task is to create constructors and implement the methods defined in the interface. Like any class, a collection class may have private methods that facilitate implementation of public methods.

Implement the Bag class by using a fixed-size array. The size of the array is dependent on a constructor argument.

For the Bag class, the storage structure is a fixed length array of elements of generic type called bagArr. The integer variable *bagSize* maintains the current size of the collection. The attribute is updated by the add() and remove() operations. The method grab() returns the value of a random object in the collection. The Bag class provides a private static *Random* object for the implementation of the method. The Bag class has a constructor that takes a capacity argument that fixes the size of the storage array. Its implementation allocates the array and sets bagSize to 0 to specify that the collection is initially empty. The following is a partial listing of the class with its private variables and constructor.

Bag class private data and constructor:

```java
public class Bag<T> implements Collection<T>
{
    private T[] bagArr;         // storage structure
    private int bagSize;        // size of collection

    // used by grab()
    private static Random rnd = new Random();

    // private methods used by the public methods
    . . .

    // constructor creates an empty collection with fixed capacity
    public Bag(int capacity)
    {
        // value of capacity is maximum number of elements
        bagArr = (T[])new Object[capacity];
        bagSize = 0;
    }
    // interface methods and the grab() method
    . . .
}
```

Generic Array Creation

Note

Java does not allow the generic array `bagArr` to be created directly; in other words, the statement

```java
bagArr = new T[capacity];
```

generates a compilation error. To solve the problem, allocate an array whose elements are of type `Object` and cast the result to be an array of type T.

```java
bagArr = (T[])new Object[capacity];
```

In the next two sections, we will implement selected methods of the `Bag` class. You can find a complete listing of the `Bag` class in the software supplement.

Private remove() Method

The `Collection` interface defines a general `remove()` method that deletes an item from the collection. The method returns true if the item is found and false if it is not. As we will discover, an iterator also defines a `remove()` method that deletes the element currently referenced by the iterator. Because elements in the `Bag` class are stored in an array, removing an element requires shifting the tail of the list down one position. This operation is required for both the general `remove()` method and the iterator version. For simplicity and code reuse, we implement the shift in a private `remove(i)` method that deletes an element at index *i*. The private method decrements `bagSize`.

If the item is located, the Bag method remove() shifts the tail of the array bagArr to the left.

Private remove( ) method:

```
// remove the element bagArr[i] by moving the tail of
// the array left one position and decrementing bagSize
private void remove(int i)
{
    // copy bagArr[i+1] ... bagArr[bagSize-1]
    // left one position
    for (int j=i; j < bagSize-1; j++)
        bagArr[j] = bagArr[j+1];

    // decrement bagSize
    bagSize--;
}
```

The public interface method `remove()` scans the array sequentially looking for the target argument of type `Object`. If found, a call is made to the private `remove()` method and the return value is true; otherwise, the return value is false.

General remove( ) method:

```
public boolean remove(Object item)
{
    // scan for item using equals() as the test
    for (int i=0;i < bagSize;i++)
        if (bagArr[i].equals(item))
        {
            // call private remove method to delete bagArr[i]
            remove(i);
            return true;
        }
    return false;
}
```

Insert and Access Methods

The `add()` method inserts a new element in the bag only if space is available. The condition is true when `bagSize` is less than the length of `bagArr` and the element is assigned to `bagArr[bagSize]`. Otherwise, the method simply returns false.

add( ):

```
public boolean add(T item)
{
    boolean returnValue;

    if (bagSize >= bagArr.length)
        return false;
    else
    {
        // append item at index bagSize
```

```
        bagArr[bagSize] = item;

        // increment bagSize and return true
        bagSize++;

        return true;
    }
}
```

The Bag method add() inserts the item at the back of the array bagArr, if space is available.

The `grab()` method uses a random number generator to return an element in the range 0 to `bagSize-1`. If the bag is empty, the return value is null.

grab():

```
    // return value of random object in range [0,bagSize)
    public T grab()
    {
        if (bagSize == 0)
            return null;
        else
            return bagArr[rnd.nextInt(bagSize)];
    }
```

The Bag method grab() generates a random index in the range from 0 to bagSize-1 and returns the value at that index.

Collection toString()

Any collection that implements the `Collection` interface can access the elements using `toArray()`. The method returns an array, which is a copy of the elements in the collection. The array can be converted to a display string using `toString(arr)` in the `Arrays` class. The format is a comma-separated list of elements in brackets. We use this strategy to implement `toString()` for collection classes.

toString():

```
    public String toString()
    {
        Object[] arr = toArray();        // array is copy of elements
        return Arrays.toString(arr);     // listing of elements
    }
```

We will implement toString() for our collection classes by calling toArray() to capture a copy of the elements in an array. We then pass the array as an argument to the method Arrays.toString().

Chapter Summary

- This book presents an integrated study of data structures using collection categories and interfaces. We define the Collection, List, Set, Map, and Graph interfaces.

- The Collection interface defines the core methods for all the collection classes except those that implement a map. Methods include add(), remove(), contains(), isEmpty(), and size().

- The List interface defines the core methods for the sequence collection classes. These classes store and retrieve data by position. Examples include the ArrayList and LinkedList collections. The List interface includes all the methods of the Collection interface and methods specific to sequence collections. Examples include get() and set() at a position as well as add() and remove() at a position.

- The ArrayList collection provides direct access through an index and grows dynamically at the rear as needed. It is an alternative to the use of an array. Insertion and deletion at the rear of the list is very efficient, but these operations inside an ArrayList are not efficient.
- The LinkedList collection stores elements by position. In order to access a specific data value in the list, you must start at the first position (front) and move from element to element until you locate the data value. The power of a list collection is its ability to add and remove items at any position in the sequence efficiently.
- A set is a collection of unique values, called *keys* or *set members*. The Set interface specifies a series of operations that allow a programmer to determine whether an item is a member of the set and to insert and delete items efficiently.
- A map is a storage structure that allows a programmer to use a key as an index to the data. Maps do not store data by position, instead they implement key-access to data, which allows a programmer to treat a map as though it were an ArrayList or array.
- This chapter develops the Bag class that implements the Collection interface. Two programs illustrate use of the Bag collection. One application is the Sieve of Eratosthenes, which determines prime numbers.

Written Exercises

1. For each part, select the collection type (interface) or the collection class that best relates to the descriptive phrase.

   (a) If a larger number is considered more important, the collection's remove operation returns the largest number.

   (i) Queue   (ii) Priority Queue   (iii) Stack   (iv) List

   (b) Access an element in the collection using an index.

   (i) Queue   (ii) Set   (iii) List   (iv) Map

   (c) Input a word from a file and determine it is in a collection of correctly spelled words.

   (i) LinkedList   (ii) TreeSet   (iii) TreeMap   (iv) ArrayList

   (d) The next value out is the last one in.

   (i) Queue   (ii) Stack   (iii) List   (iv) Set

   (e) To get to a value 3/4 of the way through the list, move through the preceding elements.

   (i) Stack   (ii) LinkedList   (iii) HashSet   (iv) ArrayList

   (f) The first data value in is the first data value out.

   (i) Queue   (ii) Map   (iii) Priority Queue   (iv) Stack

   (g) Input a word and look it up in the collection and output its definition.

   (i) Queue   (ii) Set   (iii) Map   (iv) List

2. Distinguish between a collection type and a collection.

3. The generic `Collection` interface defines `remove()` with an `Object` parameter. Would it not be better to use the generic type T as the parameter? Explain.

4. Assume c is a `Collection<T>` reference variable that is assigned a collection object.

   (a) Using methods defined in the `Collection` interface and `sort()` in the `Arrays` class, give a series of instructions that produce an ordered array of the elements in c.

   (b) Use additional instructions to replace the elements in c from the ordered array.

5. Why does the `add()` method in the `Collection` interface return a boolean value? Explain.

6. Stack and Queue are referred to as *adapter collection types*. Explain.

7. If an application needs to store data in a list, what criteria should be used to determine whether an `ArrayList` or a `LinkedList` collection is the better data structure?

Programming Exercises

8. Implement the method `shuffle()` that uses a `Bag` to shuffle the elements in an array into random order. Start with an array and process the elements through a `Bag` using the `grab()` method to extract the elements.

   ```
   public static <T> void shuffle(T[] arr)
   { ... }
   ```

   Write a program that tests your implementation of the method `shuffle()`.

9. `OrderedBag` is a generic collection class that extends the `Bag` class. An instance assumes that the object type for the elements implements the `Comparable` interface. `OrderedBag` overrides the `add()` method by inserting a new item in ascending order. The class also defines the methods `getFirst()` and `getLast()` that take advantage of the ordering. They return the value of the minimum and maximum element in the collection respectively.

   (a) Implement the `OrderedBag` class. You will have to modify the `Bag` class so that the instance variables are protected rather than private. A copy of the `Bag` class is included in the directory ch8ex.

   (b) Write a program that tests your implementation of the `OrderedBag` subclass. After each add operation, use `toString()` to display the elements.

10. `NodupBag` is a generic collection class that extends the `Bag` class. `NodupBag` overrides `add()` so that a new item is inserted in the collection only if no duplicate value exists. In this case, the return value is true. If the underlying storage structure is full or if a duplicate value exists, the method returns false. You will have to modify the `Bag` class so that the instance variables are protected rather than private. A copy of the `Bag` class is included in the ch8ex directory.

    (a) Implement the `NodupBag` class.

    (b) Write a program that tests your implementation of the class.

11. (a) A neighborhood grocery store has a 25-cent vending machine that dispenses toy helmets for the 16 National League baseball teams. A boy wants to acquire the entire collection and expects to pay only $4.00. Unfortunately, he does not realize that the machine randomly dispenses duplicate helmets. Let us create a simulation that reveals a likely cost for the entire set of helmets.

Use a `Bag` to store integers representing the different helmets. Repeatedly generate random numbers in the range 1 to 16 and store nonduplicate values in the `Bag`. Terminate the process when the `Bag` has all 16 helmets. By maintaining a count of the number of iterations, you can output the cost to collect the entire set of helmets.

(Option) A better statistical result occurs when you run the simulation a number of times and compute the average cost to acquire the helmets.

(b) Solve the problem from part (a) by using the `NodupBag` class in Programming Exercise 10.

12. Language arts teachers use Silly Sentences for spelling and grammar lessons. `Bag` collections are a simple way to construct the sentences. Create one file with beginnings of sentences. Each entry includes a noun and an adjective. For instance "My pet rat", "His black hair", and so forth. Create a second file with the endings of sentences. For instance, "loves to dance.", "gets a hug.", and so forth. Read each line in a file as a string and store it in a `Bag`. You have a bag of sentence beginnings and a bag of sentence endings. Grab an element from each bag and join them to form a Silly Sentence. Write a program that creates 20 Silly Sentences. The directory ch3ex contains the files SillyBegins.dat and SillyEnds.dat. Two possible Silly Sentences are

Silly Sentence: His black hair is in a jam.
Silly Sentence: My pet rat gets a hug.

13. Create a window that has a panel with a label and text field on the north end, a text area in the center, and the *Generate* button on the south end. The user specifies an upper limit for primes and then presses the button. In the text area, display in 10 columns all of the primes between 2 and the upper limit.

Programming Project

14. A set in mathematics can be represented as a Bag collection. Assume that a set does not allow for duplicate values. Let us use this representation to develop methods for the operations set union, set intersection, and set difference. You are familiar with the concepts and their representations using Venn diagrams.

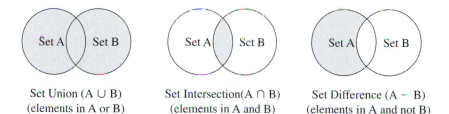

Set Union (A ∪ B)	Set Intersection(A ∩ B)	Set Difference (A − B)
(elements in A or B)	(elements in A and B)	(elements in A and not B)

(a) Implement the method `union()` that returns a Bag containing the set of elements that are in either of the two Bag (set) collections bagA and bagB.

```
public static <T> Bag<T> union(Bag<T> bagA, Bag<T> bagB)
{ ... }
```

(b) Implement the method `intersection()` that returns a Bag containing the set of elements that are in both of the two Bag (set) collection bagA and bagB.

```
public static <T> Bag<T> intersection(Bag<T> bagA,
                                       Bag<T> bagB)

{ ... }
```

(c) Implement the method `difference()` that returns a Bag containing the set of elements that are in bagA but not in bagB.

```
public static <T> Bag<T> difference(Bag<T> bagA,
                                     Bag<T> bagB)

{ ... }
```

(d) Write a program that calls each of the methods `union()`, `intersection()`, and `difference()` for Bag collections of different object types. Output the resulting sets using the Bag `toString()` method.

Chapter 9

THE ARRAY-BASED LIST COLLECTION

CONTENTS

9.1 LIST COLLECTIONS
UML for the Collection and
List Interfaces

9.2 THE ARRAYLIST CLASS
ArrayList Sizing
The ArrayList API

9.3 ARRAYLIST APPLICATIONS
Joining ArrayLists
The Closest-Pair Problem

9.4 IMPLEMENTING THE ARRAYLIST
CLASS
Design of the ArrayList Class

Reserving More Capacity
Adding and Removing Elements
Implementing Index Access

9.5 CLONEABLE OBJECTS
Cloning Time24 Objects
Cloning Reference Variables
Cloning an ArrayList
Cloning an Array

9.6 EVALUATING AN ARRAYLIST
COLLECTION

Chapter 8 presented the Collection interface that defines operations that are shared by most collections. The interface describes a collection with no reference to how elements are stored. The Bag class is a concrete example of a class that implements the Collection interface. In this chapter, we introduce list collections that store elements by position. An index identifies the location of each element in the collection. A new interface, called *List*, extends the Collection interface and introduces a series of index-based methods. The ArrayList collection is an example of a list. As the name implies, an ArrayList is modeled after an array with direct access to the elements. Unlike an array, however, an ArrayList can be resized dynamically to accommodate the resource needs of an application.

9.1 List Collections

A *list* is a collection that stores elements by position. The collection is a dynamic structure that can expand and contract as elements enter and leave the list. At any time, the collection may include duplicate values. Like an array, the elements in a list can be referenced by an index starting at 0, which denotes the first position in the list. For this reason, we often refer to a list as a sequence (Figure 9.1). In our discussions we will use the terms position and index interchangeably.

We use a List interface to describe a category of collections. The interface extends the Collection interface and gives a formal specification of all of the list operations. As a result, it has declarations for all of the Collection methods, including size(), add(), contains(), toArray(), and so forth. A list having positional ordering imposes specific requirements for some of the general collection methods. For instance, the List interface imposes specifications on the add() method which go beyond those given in the Collection interface. Recall how the Collection interface describes the add() operation.

Position 0   Position 1   Position 2   Position 3   · · ·   Position n−1

Figure 9.1 *Illustration of a list as an n-element collection or sequence.*

A list is a se-
quence of ele-
ments stored by
position. If there
are n-elements in
the collection, the
first is at position
0 and the last is at
position *n* − 1.

Collection add( ):

```
// ensures that this collection contains item; returns true if
// item is inserted and false if item is already
// present and no duplicates are allowed
boolean add(T item);
```

In the `List` interface, the specification for `add()` dictates that the element must be inserted at the back of the sequence and allows for duplicate values. The operation always returns true. (Figure 9.2a).

The positional or-
dering in a
list imposes
requirements for
some methods.
For instance,
add(item) inserts
item at the back
of the list.

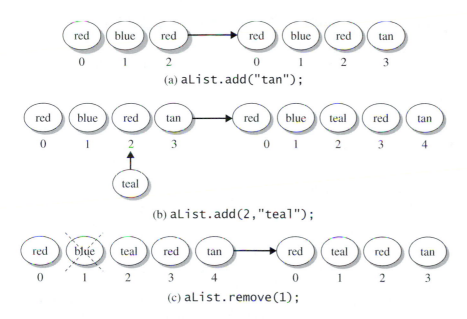

(a) `aList.add("tan");`

(b) `aList.add(2,"teal");`

(c) `aList.remove(1);`

Figure 9.2 *Adding and removing elements in a list.*

List add( ):

```
// appends item to the end of this list and returns true
boolean add(T item);
```

The List `toArray()` method returns an array with elements whose index values correspond to their position in the collection.

The `List` interface defines a series of methods that rely on the positional ordering of the elements. Versions of `add()` and `remove()` take an index argument. With `add(index, item)`, a new element enters the sequence at position `index`, and the elements at the tail move up one position (Figure 9.2b). The `remove(index)` method

The add(),
remove(), and
set() methods
update a list at a
particular position.
The get() method
returns the value
at a specified
position.

deletes the element at position `index`, causing the elements in the tail of the sequence to move down one position (Figure 9.2c). The methods `get(index)` and `set(index, item)` access and update an element at position `index`. Each element in a list is located at a particular index. The method `indexOf(item)` returns the index of the first occurrence of item in the list or -1 if not found. You will recognize that this is essentially the sequential search algorithm. A `List` collection provides `Iterator` objects that scan the elements in the forward direction. `Iterator` objects are available in any collection class. The `List` interface defines a second iterator, called `ListIterator`, that allows for bidirectional scanning of elements in addition to the normal operations that an `Iterator` provides. The `Iterator` and `ListIterator` classes are discussed in Chapter 12.

The following is an API for the generic `List` interface. We include the methods that are not in the `Collection` interface as well as the `Collection` method `add()`, which specifies where the new element is inserted in the sequence.

interface List \<T\>extends Collection\<T\>	*ds.util*
boolean	**add**(T item) Always inserts item as a new element at the end of the sequence and returns true.
void	**add**(int index, T item) Inserts item at position index in this list. If the index is out of the range $0 <= index <= size()$, throws IndexOutOfBoundsException.
T	**get**(int index) Returns the element at the specified position in the list. If the index is out of the range $0 <= index < size()$, throws IndexOutOfBoundsException.
int	**indexOf**(Object item) Returns the index of the first occurrence of item in this list or -1 if item is not in this list.
ListIterator\<T\>	**listIterator**() Returns a list iterator positioned at the first element in the sequence.
ListIterator\<T\>	**listIterator**(int index) Returns a list iterator positioned at the specified index in the list. If the index is out of the range $0 <= index < size()$, throws IndexOutOfBoundsException.
T	**remove**(int index) Removes the element at the specified position in this list. Shifts any subsequent elements to the left (subtracts one from their indices). Returns the element that was removed from the list. If the index is out of the range $0 <= index < size()$, throws IndexOutOfBoundsException.
T	**set**(int index, T item) Replaces the value at the specified position in this list with item and returns the previous value. If the index is out of the range $0 <= index < size()$, throws IndexOutOfBoundsException.

UML for the Collection and List Interfaces

As an extended interface, `List` inherits all of the method signatures from the `Collection` interface. The UML diagram in Figure 9.3 shows that `List` defines other methods such as `get()` and `set()` that are unique to its collection type.

UML can be used to represent interfaces and the extension of one interface by another.

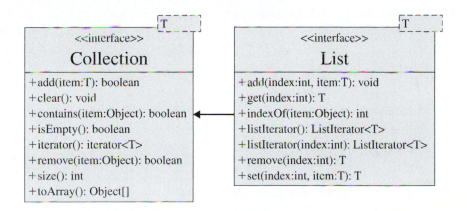

Figure 9.3 *Methods of the Collection and List interfaces.*

Example 9.1

As we proceed, we will develop generic collection classes that implement the `List` interface. For now, assume `aList` is an instance of one of these classes. It stores `Integer` objects. Let us use `aList` to illustrate `List` methods. An abstract view of the collection is a set of discrete elements lined up in a row. Parts 2 through 5 assume results from the previous part.

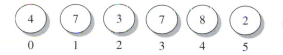

1. Access and update an element at an index using `get(index)` and `set(index, item)`.

   ```
   // get value at index 4; value is 8
   Integer value = aList.get(4);

   // at index 4 assign integer 1
   aList.set(4, 1);                      // list: [4, 7, 3, 7, 1, 2]
   ```

2. Remove an element by value and at an index using `remove(item)` and `remove(index)`. The argument `item` may be given as an `int` value with autoboxing used to convert the value to an `Integer` object. However, if the value is a valid index, the `remove(index)` method is executed.

   ```
   // remove the Integer value 3;  be careful - argument 3
   // would remove value 7 at index 3
   aList.remove(new Integer(3));    // list: [4, 7, 7, 1, 2]

   // remove the element at index 1
   aList.remove(1);                  // list: [4, 7, 1, 2]
   ```

3. Add an element at the back of the list and at an index using `add(item)` and `add(index,item)` respectively.

```
// add the integer 9 at the back
aList.add(9);                          // list: [4, 7, 1, 2, 9]

// add integer 5 at index 2
aList.add(2, 5);                       // list: [4, 7, 5, 1, 2, 9]
```

4. Determine the presence of an element in the list using `contains(item)` and `indexOf(item)`.

```
// search for integer 2
index = aList.indexOf(2);              // index = 4
boolean isPresent = aList.contains(5); // isPresent = true

// search for integer 6
index = aList.indexOf(6);              // index = -1
```

5. Map the elements in the list to an array and output the array.

```
Object[] arr = aList.toArray();
System.out.print(Arrays.toString(arr));
```

```
Output:
   [4, 7, 5, 1, 2, 9]
```

9.2   The ArrayList Class

An ArrayList is a dynamic array. The back of the ArrayList can grow as new elements are added.

An `ArrayList` implements the `List` interface and is modeled after an array. It stores its elements in a contiguous block of memory. Unlike an array, however, an `ArrayList` can grow dynamically by allowing new elements to be added at the back of the sequence. Intuitively, think of an `ArrayList` as an array with indices in the range from 0 to $n - 1$, where n is the current size of the list. The tail of the `ArrayList` has expansion space into which new elements are added (Figure 9.4). An `ArrayList` allows for direct access and update of any element using its index. We thus refer to it as a *direct access* structure.

Figure 9.4 *ArrayList of size n with indices in the range from 0 to n − 1.*

An ArrayList is a generic collection whose elements are Object references.

The `ArrayList` class is a generic collection with elements of a specified type. A default constructor creates an empty list with size = 0.

```
// declare ArrayList for strings; list is initially empty
ArrayList<String> aList = new ArrayList<String>();
```

The List methods get() and set() use an index to access and update an element and serve the same function provided by the index operator [] in an array. The ArrayList methods do *bounds checking* and throw an IndexOutOfBoundsException when an operation attempts to access a position that is outside the range 0 to size()−1.

The ArrayList methods get() and set() allow direct access to elements in the sequence.

Any collection class that implements the Collection interface must provide a toArray() method that copies the elements to an Object array. The method allows a programmer to use array algorithms and, if appropriate, copy the results back to the ArrayList. Consistent with the Java philosophy of creating strings that represent an object, the ArrayList class provides the toString() method that returns a string with a comma-separated listing of the elements, enclosed in brackets.

Example 9.2

Assume aList is an ArrayList<String> object containing four strings.

1. Use an index to scan the elements in aList and convert each string to upper case. The process involves a loop with the get() method to access an element. After creating a new uppercase version of the string, update the element using the method set().

```
String str;

for (int i = 0; i < aList.size(); i++)
{
    str = aList.get(i);
    str = str.toUpperCase();
    aList.set(i, str);
}
```

2. An ArrayList has access to the index-based add() and remove() methods. We will see in Sections 9.4 and 9.6 that they should be used sparingly owing to the overhead of shifting elements on the tail of the list to the right or left. With toString(), we can display the elements as a comma-separated list.

```
aList.remove(1);
System.out.println("Remove string at index 1: " + aList);

aList.add(2, "ARRAYLIST");
System.out.println("Add ARRAYLIST at index 2: " + aList);
```

```
Output:
   Remove string at index 1: [LIST, JAVA, COLLECTION]
   Add ARRAYLIST at index 2: [LIST, JAVA, ARRAYLIST, COLLECTION]
```

The ArrayList method toArray() returns an array containing the elements of the list. The programmer can extract the array, sort it, and then copy the array elements back to the ArrayList.

3. By extracting the elements from aList using toArray(), we can use sort() to order the elements and then copy them back to the collection.

```
Object[] arr = aList.toArray();              // extract elements

Arrays.sort(arr);                            // order array
for (int i = 0; i < arr.length; i++)
    aList.set(i,arr[i]);                     // copy to List

System.out.println("Sorted list: " + aList);
```

Output:
    [ARRAYLIST, COLLECTION, JAVA, LIST]

4. An ArrayList is helpful when an application reads from a file and does not know in advance the number of elements in the file. For instance, the following statements open a text file, *pts.dat*, containing two real numbers per line. The numbers represent the *x*-coordinate and *y*-coordinate of data in the plane. A while loop inputs the coordinates into two ArrayList collections x and y. The implementation works for any number of lines in the file.

```
ArrayList<Double> x = new ArrayList<Double>(),
                  y = new ArrayList<Double>();
double xCoor, yCoor;
Scanner dataIn = new Scanner (new FileReader("pts.dat"));

while (dateIn.hasNextDouble())
{
    xCoor = dataIn.nextDouble();
    yCoor = dataIn.nextDouble();

    x.add(xCoor);
    y.add(yCoor);
}
```

ArrayList Sizing

The capacity of an ArrayList is the number of elements in the block of memory that holds the list. The size is the number of these elements that are in the ArrayList.

You cannot expand or contract an array because it stores elements in a fixed-length block. An ArrayList, on the other hand, is a dynamic structure that has add() and remove() methods that allow the size of the sequence to change.

At any point in a program, an ArrayList occupies a contiguous block of memory that holds the existing elements and has some additional expansion space for new elements. The number of actual elements in the ArrayList is its size, which is the return value from the size() method. The total number of array elements is the *capacity* of the ArrayList (Figure 9.5).

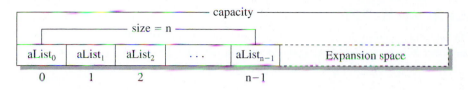

Figure 9.5 *View of an ArrayList of size n and capacity.*

As a program adds new elements, they enter the unused expansion space and the size increases. Eventually, the elements may occupy all of the available capacity. When this occurs (size == capacity), the add() operation creates a new block of memory with larger capacity and copies the elements from the old memory block to the new memory block. The ArrayList then has additional expansion space. The process of allocating more memory for an ArrayList is termed *reallocation*.

When space is available, adding an element to an ArrayList is an O(1) operation. If reallocation is required, however, the operation involves the overhead of expanding the list. The runtime efficiency of a program is improved if reallocation can be kept to a minimum. The ArrayList class has methods that allow the user to control capacity and size. In some cases, the program knows the ultimate size of the ArrayList. The method ensureCapacity(int minCapacity) allocates a block of memory with the specified capacity. The collection will then have sufficient memory to hold all of the elements without requiring any reallocation of memory. If minCapacity is smaller than the current capacity, then no action is taken. In another context, a program may reach a point where all elements have been added to the ArrayList. The process of appending elements may have allocated excess capacity that will never be needed. Rather than tying up unused memory, the program may use the method trimToSize(), which trims the capacity of the ArrayList to its size.

> The method ensureCapacity() can be used to eliminate periodic reallocation when the number of list elements is known in advance.

Example 9.3

Let us look at a series of instructions that manage the capacity of an ArrayList. The default constructor creates an ArrayList with size = 10. We begin by using ensureCapacity() to enlarge the available space to 50 slots. A loop adds 40 random integer values to the collection, increasing the size to 40. The method trimToSize() lops off the excess 10 slots in the list.

```
ArrayList<Integer> aList = new ArrayList<Integer>();
Random rnd = new Random();

// expand the capacity to 50
aList.ensureCapacity(50);

// add 40 random values without requiring reallocation
for (int i = 1; i <= 40; i++)
    aList.add(rnd.nextInt(100));

// trim the excess capacity so that capacity == size
aList.trimToSize();
System.out.println("Size = " + aList.size());
```

```
Output:
Size = 40
```

The ArrayList API

The previous section describes the key operations in the `ArrayList` class and provides examples. The `ArrayList` API provides documentation for the class. We show signatures only for methods not included in the `List` interface.

class ArrayList<T> implements List<T>		*ds.util*
	Constructors	
	`ArrayList()` Creates an empty ArrayList.	
	Methods	
`void`	`ensureCapacity(int minCapacity)` Increases the capacity of this ArrayList, if necessary, to ensure that it can hold at least the number of components specified by the minimum capacity argument.	
`String`	`toString()` Returns a string listing the elements in the ArrayList as comma-separated values enclosed in brackets.	
`void`	`trimToSize()` Trims the capacity of this ArrayList to be the ArrayList's current size.	

9.3 ArrayList Applications

This section includes two applications that demonstrate use of the `ArrayList` class. The method `join()` concatenates one `ArrayList` onto the end of another. We will develop `join()` and use it in a simple program. An `ArrayList` is useful when the amount of storage required is not known in advance. A particularly interesting example of this is the closest-pair problem. Input any number of points in the plane and determine a pair of points that are closest together. We will conclude this section by developing an algorithm that solves the closest-pair problem and using it in an application.

Joining ArrayLists

The concatenation of one string onto the end of another is the model for joining two `ArrayList` objects. The method `join()` takes two lists `listA` and `listB` as arguments. A loop scans the elements of `listB` and copies them onto the end of `listA` by using the `add()` method (Figure 9.6).

The algorithm begins by identifying the size of each `ArrayList`. A call to the method `ensureCapacity()` uses the sum of the two sizes as an argument. If `ArrayList listA` does not have sufficient space to hold the incoming elements from `listB`, the operation makes a single allocation of new memory that contains the current elements in `listA` and space for the elements in `listB`. A simple loop scans the elements in `listB` and appends them to `listA`.

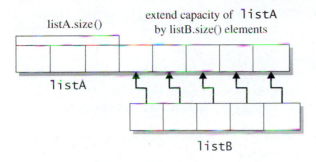

Figure 9.6 *Join ArrayList listB onto the end of ArrayList listA.*

join():

```
// attach listB onto the end of listA
public static <T> void join (ArrayList<T> listA,
                             ArrayList<T> listB)
{

    // capture the size of ArrayLists listA and listB
    int i, sizeA = listA.size(), sizeB = listB.size();

    // insure sufficient capacity for listA
    listA.ensureCapacity(sizeA + sizeB);

    // use index i to access the elements of listB and add()
    // to insert elements from listB at rear of listA
    for (i = 0; i < sizeB; i++)
        listA.add(listB.get(i));
}
```

Note the use of the method ensureCapacity(), which guarantees that no reallocations will be done.

PROGRAM 9.1 JOINING GRADUATION LISTS

The registrar maintains an alphabetical list of graduating seniors along with their degree, BS or BA. At the graduation ceremony, students with a BS degree receive their diplomas first, followed by those with a BA degree. The program reads the registrar's list from the file *gradlist.dat*, which consists of lines of data including the student name and degree separated by a tab character. The application inserts a string consisting of the name and degree into an ArrayList collection. The BS degree graduates enter the ArrayList diplomaList, and the BA degree graduates enter the ArrayList baList. The lists are joined with baList appended on the end of diplomaList and then output.

```
import java.util.Scanner;
import java.io.*;

import ds.util.ArrayList;

public class Program9_1
{
```

```java
public static void main(String[] args) throws IOException
{

    Scanner fileIn =
        new Scanner(new FileReader("gradlist.dat"));
    // input strings from the file
    String inputStr, gradName, gradDegree;

    // string of 20 blank characters for ArrayList names
    String buffer = "                    ";

    // ArrayLists holds diplomaList and baList
    ArrayList<String> diplomaList = new ArrayList<String>(),
                      baList = new ArrayList<String>();
    // the Scanner delimiters are tab, newline, and carriage
    // return
    fileIn.useDelimiter("[\t\n\r]+");

    // read registrar's list to eof and add to array lists
    while(fileIn.hasNext())
    {

        // input tab separated name and degree
        gradName = fileIn.next();

        // input the degree
        gradDegree = fileIn.next();

        // add name and degree as string in specified list
        if (gradDegree.equals("BS"))
            diplomaList.add(gradName + " " + gradDegree);
        else
            baList.add(gradName + " " + gradDegree);
    }

    // join the BA list at end of diploma list
    join(diplomaList, baList);

    // output a header and list of names with degrees
    System.out.println("Diploma List");
    for (int i = 0; i < diplomaList.size(); i++)
        System.out.println("\t" + (String)diplomaList.get(i));
}

< method join() provided in the program discussion >
}
```

```
<File "gradlist.dat">

Bailey, Julie BS
Frazer, Thomas BA
Harkness, Bailey BA
Johnson, Shannon BS
Kilmer, William BA
Miller, Sara BS
Nelson, Harold BS
O'Dell, Jack BA
Wilson, Rebecca BS

Run:
  Diploma List
      Bailey, Julie BS
      Johnson, Shannon BS
      Miller, Sara BS
      Nelson, Harold BS
      Wilson, Rebecca BS
      Frazer, Thomas BA
      Harkness, Bailey BA
      Kilmer, William BA
      O'Dell, Jack BA
```

The Closest-Pair Problem

The closest-pair problem requires finding the two closest points in a set of n points in the plane. Assume that we specify each point using the standard Cartesian coordinate notation (x, y) and that the distance between two points $P_i = (x_i, y_i)$ and $P_j = (x_j, y_j)$ is $d(P_i, P_j) = \sqrt{(x_i - x_j)^2 + (y_i - y_j)^2}$. A simple approach to the problem is to evaluate the distance between every pair of distinct points and determine the pair with the smallest distance. We do not want to determine the distance between the same pair of points twice. For instance, $d(P_2, P_8) = d(P_8, P_2)$. We avoid doing this by only considering pairs (P_i, P_j) where $i < j$.

Our algorithm is similar to the selection sort algorithm that we discussed in Chapter 4. In a nested loop structure, we find the distance between P_0 and the set of points $\{P_1, P_2, \ldots, P_{n-1}\}$, keeping track of the minimum distance. We continue by computing the distances between P_1 and the set of points $\{P_2, P_3, \ldots, P_{n-1}\}$. In general, pass i of the algorithm computes the distances between P_i and the set of points $\{P_i + 1, \ldots, P_{n-1}\}$, $0 \leq i < n - 1$. To optimize our algorithm's performance, we do not compute $d(P_i, P_j)$ but compute $d(P_i, P_j)^2 = (x_i - x_j)^2 + (y_i - y_j)^2$. The square root takes additional time to compute and generally cannot be computed exactly. The question of whether

$d(P_i, P_j) < d(P_k, P_l)$ is equivalent to the question of whether $d(P_i, P_j)^2 < d(P_i, P_l)^2$. This follows because for any nonnegative real numbers a and b, if $a < b$, then $\sqrt{a} < \sqrt{b}$.

The method closestPair() implements the algorithm. Its arguments are ArrayList variables x and y containing the x-coordinate and the y-coordinate of the points. The method returns an array of two integers that contains the indices of the two closest points. The Math class does not contain a function that computes the square of two real numbers, so we include the method sqr().

closestPair():

```java
// return the indices of the two closest points in the set of
// points whose x- and y-coordinates are in ArrayLists x and y
public static int[]
closestPair(ArrayList<Double> x, ArrayList<Double> y)
{
    // capture the number of points in n
    int n = x.size();
    // index1 and index2 will contain the indices of the
    // closest points
    int i,j, index1 = -1, index2 = -1;
    double xi, yi, xj, yj;
    // initialize dmin to the largest possible double value
    double dmin = Double.MAX_VALUE, dsqr;
    // we return this array after determining its values
    int[] closest = new int[2];

    // make n-1 passes through the points
    for (i=0; i < n-1; i++)
        // compute each distance d(Pi, Pj), i+1 <= j < n
        // and record the current minimum distance
        for (j=i+1;j < n;j++)
        {
            // extract the double values from x and y
            xi = x.get(i);
            yi = y.get(i);
            xj = x.get(j);
            yj = y.get(j);
            // compute (xi - xj)^2 + (yi - yj)^2
            dsqr = sqr(xi - xj) + sqr(yi - yj);
            // check for a new minimum distance
            if (dsqr < dmin)
            {

                // new minimum; record it and change indices
                // index1 and index2
                dmin = dsqr;
```

```
            index1 = i;
            index2 = j;
        }
    }

    // initialize the elements of closest[] and return it
    closest[0] = index1;
    closest[1] = index2;

    return closest;
}

// return x squared
public static double sqr(double x)
{

    return x*x;
}
```

PROGRAM 9.2 THE CLOSEST-PAIR PROBLEM

We apply our algorithm to find the closest pair of points. Typically, the coordinates are specified by a textfile. Each line of the file contains an *x*-coordinate followed by a *y*-coordinate. We simplify the example by defining the coordinates as arrays of type double. The application copies the points into ArrayList x and ArrayList y, calls closestPair(), and outputs the pair of points and their distance. Figure 9.7 graphs the data used by the

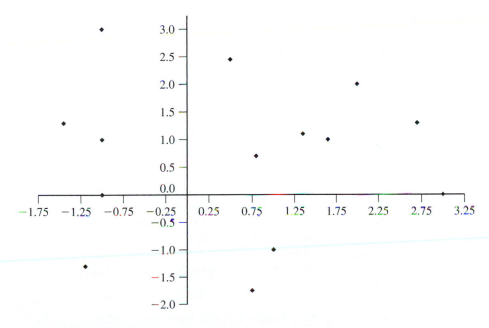

Figure 9.7 *Points used in the run of Program 9.2.*

program. By looking at the graph, you can verify that the algorithm made the correct decision.

```java
import ds.util.ArrayList;

public class Program9_2
{
    public static void main(String[] args)
    {
        // insert coordinates from a file into x and y
        ArrayList<Double> x = new ArrayList<Double>(),
                          y = new ArrayList<Double>();
        double xCoor, yCoor;
        double xclose1, yclose1, xclose2, yclose2;

        // arrays for x-points and y-points and closest points
        double[] xPt = {-1, -1.45, -1, -1, 0.75, 1, 0.8,  1.65,
                         -1.2, 3, 2, 2.7, 1.35, 0.5};
        double[] yPt = {1, 1.3, 0, 3, -1.75, -1, 0.7, 1, -1.3,
                         0, 2, 1.3, 1.1, 2.45};
        int[] closestPoints;

        // add coordinate values at the back of x and y
        for (int i = 0; i < xPt.length; i++)
        {
            x.add(xPt[i]);
            y.add(yPt[i]);
        }

        // execute the closest-pair algorithm
        closestPoints = closestPair(x, y);

        // find the coordinates of the the closest points
        xclose1 = x.get(closestPoints[0]);
        yclose1 = y.get(closestPoints[0]);
        xclose2 = x.get(closestPoints[1]);
        yclose2 = y.get(closestPoints[1]);

        // output the pair of points and their minimum distance
        System.out.println("The closest points are (" +
            xclose1 + "," + yclose1  + ") and (" + xclose2 +
            "," + yclose2 + ")");
        System.out.println("Distance = " +
            Math.sqrt(sqr(xclose1-xclose2) + sqr(yclose1-
            yclose2)));
    }
    < implementation of closestPair() and sqr() given in the
      program discussion
    >
}
```

```
Run:
   The closest points are (1.65,1.0) and (1.35,1.1)
   Distance = 0.31622776601683783
```

Analysis of the Closest-Pair Algorithm   Pass 0 of the algorithm compares $n - 1$ points, and pass 1 compares $n - 2$ points. In general, each pass, i, of the algorithm compares $n - 1 - i$ points. The total number of comparisons is

$$(n - 1) + (n - 2) + \cdots + 1 = \frac{n(n - 1)}{2}$$

The algorithm has running time $O(n^2)$; in other words, it is quadratic.

The technique we used is an example of a *brute force algorithm*. Brute force is a straightforward approach to solving a problem when we have something to search for or when we wish to optimize some property. It is usually based directly on the problem's statement. Normally, the technique enumerates all possible configurations of the input and picks the best of these enumerated configurations. There are important applications of the closest-pair problem. For instance, the algorithm will tell an air traffic controller which pair of n planes is closest during approach to the airport. For this reason, our brute force algorithm is too slow. There is a divide-and-conquer $O(n \log_2 n)$ algorithm for the problem, but it is too involved to discuss here. The book by Sartaj Sahni, *Data Structures, Algorithms, and Applications in Java*, McGraw-Hill, 2000 has a good discussion of this algorithm.

> The solution to the closest-pair problem uses the technique of brute force. It enumerates all possible combinations of pairs and finds the pair of points, the distance between which is minimum.

9.4   Implementing the ArrayList Class

This section shows you how to implement the ArrayList class by using array storage. This is your first major class implementation and yet the implementation is relatively simple. In later chapters, we will implement more complex classes such as the LinkedList and HashMap classes.

We define an ArrayList as an implementation of the List interface. This defines the majority of our task. The term "List" implies that an ArrayList stores elements by position and has a series of index-based methods that access, update, and alter elements in the collection. It also implies that it has methods such as size(), isEmpty(), toArray(), and so forth, that are common to all collection types. We specified a set of common collection methods in the Collection interface and a set of list operations in the List interface. These interfaces provide a template for most of the methods that we must implement. An ArrayList object is a specific type of list collection that is modeled on an array. As such, it has additional operations, over and above the list operations, that take advantage of the way an ArrayList stores elements. The methods ensureCapacity() and trimToSize() are examples of ArrayList-specific operations. Defining these methods and a constructor round out the tasks to implement ArrayList.

Design of the ArrayList Class

An ArrayList object uses an array of specified type to store its elements. The name of the array is listArr, which is declared as a private variable in the class. The size of the array represents the amount of available storage for ArrayList elements. The term *capacity* describes the available space. The number of actual elements in the ArrayList is maintained by the private integer variable listSize. Let us explore this further because it is critical that you understand the difference between the size of the ArrayList and the size of the storage array. When an ArrayList is created, the constructor allocates space for 10 elements in listArr. The ArrayList has no elements (listSize == 0). A program uses an add() method to insert a new element into the ArrayList. The operation grows the collection within the space provided by listArr. The value listSize increases by 1 but the capacity remains the same. Figure 9.8 is a memory view of an ArrayList object aList that stores four elements in listArr. In this case, listSize = 4 and listArr.length = 10 is the capacity.

The ArrayList contains an array of Object references. The capacity of an ArrayList object is the number of elements in the array.

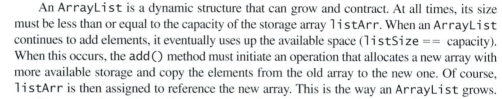

Figure 9.8 *Storage of ArrayList with 4 elements in an array with capacity 10.*

An ArrayList is a dynamic structure that can grow and contract. At all times, its size must be less than or equal to the capacity of the storage array listArr. When an ArrayList continues to add elements, it eventually uses up the available space (listSize == capacity). When this occurs, the add() method must initiate an operation that allocates a new array with more available storage and copy the elements from the old array to the new one. Of course, listArr is then assigned to reference the new array. This is the way an ArrayList grows.

When the size of an ArrayList object equals its capacity, allocate a new larger array and copy the existing values to the new array.

Let us use these ideas to begin a declaration of the ArrayList class that implements the interface List. The following includes a declaration of the private members and an implementation of the constructor. An ArrayList collection is created with size 0 and default capacity 10.

ArrayList class: (instance variables and constructor)

```
public class ArrayList<T> implements List<T>
{
    private T[] listArr;        // stores the elements
    private int listSize;       // number of elements

    // constructs an empty list with initial capacity 10
    public ArrayList()
    {
        listArr = (T[])new Object[10];
        listSize = 0;
    }
    . . .
}
```

Reserving More Capacity

The method ensureCapacity() is the key operation in the implementation of the ArrayList class. It provides the memory management tool that allows for dynamic growth of an ArrayList object. The method takes an integer argument minCapacity that specifies the minimum amount of available space in array listArr. If minCapacity is less than or equal to the current capacity (listArr.length), the method simply returns. In this way, ensureCapacity() can only increase the available space. If minCapacity is greater than the current capacity, the method allocates a new array of size minCapacity and copies the listSize elements into the new space (Figure 9.9).

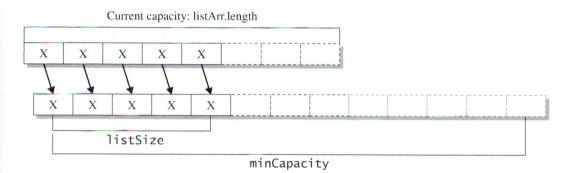

Current capacity: listArr.length

listSize

minCapacity

Figure 9.9 *Illustration of ensureCapacity() that allocates an array of size minCapacity and copies ArrayList elements.*

A program may call ensureCapacity() if it can anticipate the ultimate size requirements for the ArrayList. More typically, the implementation of an add() method calls ensureCapacity() when all of the available space is used up. As part of its design, the add() method specifies how much new capacity should be created.

The following is a declaration of ensureCapacity(). Note that the implementation assigns null to the old array reference. This ensures that there is no reference to the previous array and promotes rapid garbage collection that returns the array to the store of free memory.

> The ArrayList implementation calls ensureCapacity() when the size of an object equals its capacity.

ensureCapacity():

```
public void ensureCapacity (int minCapacity)
{
    // get the current capacity
    int currentCapacity = listArr.length;

    // only take action if the requested capacity
    // is larger than the existing capacity
    if (minCapacity > currentCapacity)
    {
        // capture a reference to the old array
        T[] oldListArr = listArr;

        // create the new array with the new capacity
        listArr = (T[]) new Object[minCapacity];
```

```
            // copy the old data to the new array
            for (int i=0; i < listSize; i++)
                listArr[i] = oldListArr[i];

            // nullify reference to the old array; garbage
            // collection will recover the space
            oldListArr = null;
        }
    }
```

Adding and Removing Elements

The index-versions of add() and remove() as well as the get() and set() methods require an index argument that must be in a certain range for the operation to be valid. These methods call the private method rangeCheck() to verify that the index is in the proper range. The method includes integer arguments for the index and the upper bound. A third argument, msg, is a string which provides a message that is passed along by an IndexOutOfBounds-Exception if the index is outside the range $0 \le$ index $\le$ upperBound.

rangeCheck( ):

```
    // verify that index is in the range 0 <= index <= upperBound;
    // if not throw the IndexOutOfBoundsException exception
    private void rangeCheck(int index, String msg, int upperBound)
    {
        if (index < 0 || index >= upperBound+1)
            throw new IndexOutOfBoundsException(
                "\n" + msg + ": index " + index +
                " out of bounds. Should be in the range 0 to " +
                upperBound);
    }
```

The ArrayList add() methods call ensureCapacity() to double the capacity when the current capacity is exceeded.

The add() Methods   An ArrayList object uses an add() method to insert an element in the list. The operation is not complicated as long as the ArrayList has enough capacity to add a new item. If this is the case, add() merely inserts the element and increments listSize. If the array does not have enough capacity, then additional space must allocated by calling ensureCapacity(). The only problem is determining how much new capacity to allocate. This is an implementation design issue. Having the capacity grow by 1 would be inefficient because each call to add() would immediately fill the available space and require a new call to ensureCapacity() for the next insert. A better design grows the capacity in anticipation of adding more elements. The ArrayList class uses the strategy of doubling the capacity whenever an add() method must allocate a larger array. Double the capacity by calling ensureCapacity() with the argument minCapacity = 2*listArr.length. In this way, the capacity of an ArrayList object grows from 10 to 20, 20 to 40, 40 to 80, and so forth.

Inserting an element is done with the index version of add(). It starts by calling rangeCheck() and then updates the capacity if necessary. The method slides the tail of the list right one position, starting at index, and then inserts the new item at index.

add(index, item):

```
public void add(int index, T item)
{
    // index == listSize is valid; append to the list
    rangeCheck(index, "ArrayList add()", listSize);

    // see if we need to reallocate more memory
    if (listSize == listArr.length)
        ensureCapacity(2*listArr.length);

    // shift elements at positions index through listSize-1 to
    // the right
    for (int j= listSize-1;j >= index;j--)
        listArr[j+1] = listArr[j];

    // insert item at location index and increment the list size
    listArr[index] = item;
    listSize++;
}
```

The general add() method inserts an element at the back of the list. Its implementation calls the index version of add with index == listSize.

add(item) method:

```
// appends item to the end of this list and returns true
public boolean add(Object item)
{
    // call method add() at an index to insert item at the
    // end of the list
    add(listSize, item);

    return true;
}
```

The remove() Methods   An ArrayList object uses remove() to erase an element at a specified position. The remove() method reduces the size of the list by 1 without changing the capacity. The space remains the same; only the number of items filling the space changes. In the implementation of remove(), if the element is the last one in the list, it is only necessary to decrement the list size. Otherwise, it is necessary to slide the tail of the array listArr left one position in order to fill the slot vacated by the removal of the element at `index`. The following figure illustrates the removal of an element at position 1.

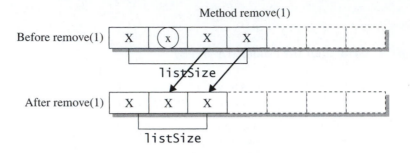

The ArrayList remove() method may have to shift the tail of the list to the left one position.

We let the index version of `remove()` implement the details. Recall that this version returns the element that was deleted. First, call `rangeCheck()` and then shift the tail down one position beginning at `index`;

remove(index):

```
public T remove(int index)
{
    // verify that index is in the proper range
    rangeCheck(index, "ArrayList remove()", listSize-1);

    // save the return value
    T returnElement = listArr[index];

    // shift elements at indices index+1 to listSize-1
    // left one position
    for (int j=index;j < listSize-1;j++)
        listArr[j] = listArr[j+1];

    // make former last entry a null reference and decrement
    // list size
    listArr[listSize-1] = null;
    listSize--;

    // return the value that was removed
    return returnElement;
}
```

The algorithm for `remove(item)` calls `indexOf()` to search for `item` in the list and returns the index of its first occurrence or -1 if not in the list. If `item` is present, the method calls `remove(index)` to erase `item` from the list.

remove(item):

```
// if item is present in the list, removes the first
// instance of it from this list; returns true if
// an element was removed and false otherwise
```

```
public boolean remove(Object item)
{
    int i = 0, j;
    boolean retValue = true;

    // use indexOf() to search for item
    if ((i = indexOf(item)) != -1)
        remove(i);
    else
        retValue = false;

    return retValue;
}
```

The amortized running time for adding at the back of the list is O(1), and the running time for removing the back of the list is O(1). Inside the list, these operations are O(n).

Efficiency of Add and Remove Methods   If the ArrayList has n elements, the complexity of remove(i) is $O(n - i - 1)$ in general, because it must slide the $n - i - 1$ element tail of the list to the left. However, if the index is the location of last element, the algorithm has running time O(1) because all it does is decrement listSize. The efficiency of an add() method is more involved. A reallocation must be done when the list is full.   In this case, the method must expand the capacity, which involves copying elements, and so the operation has running time $O(n)$. In all other cases, a new allocation of space is not required and the operation has running time O(1). When the total effort is averaged (amortized) over the number of insertions, the average running time is constant. Complexity theory designates such operations as having *amortized running time* O(1).

Implementing Index Access

Java defines the index operator [] to access elements in an array. A programmer uses the operator in an expression of the form arr[i] to reference the element at index i. In the ArrayList class, we provide index access by implementing the method get() to retrieve the element at a position and set() to update the element at a position. These methods call rangeCheck() to validate the index argument and then simply access the referenced data at location *index* = i in the array listArr.

get():

```
public T get(int index)
{
    // verify that index is in the proper range
    rangeCheck(index, "ArrayList get()", listSize-1);

    return listArr[index];
}
```

set():

```
// replaces the value at the specified position in this list
// with item and returns the previous value; if the index is
// out of range (index < 0 || index >= size()), throws
// IndexOutOfBoundsException
```

Implement access at index index in an ArrayList object by accessing the internal array element at index index.

```
public T set(int index, T item)
{
    // verify that index is in the proper range
    rangeCheck(index, "ArrayList set()", listSize-1);

    // save the element at listArr[index]
    T previousValue = listArr[index];

    // assign the new element at index index
    listArr[index] = item;

    // return the previous element
    return previousValue;
}
```

The interested reader should consult the source code for the `ArrayList` class to see the implementation of several other methods, including `indexOf()` and `trimToSize()`.

9.5 Cloneable Objects

In designing a class, it is sometimes useful to have an operation that makes a copy, or *clone*, of the object. Ideally, the result should be two separate objects so that an update to one will not affect the other. Some languages such as C++ provide this capability with a copy constructor. The idea is illustrated in the `String` class, which has a constructor that takes a string argument and creates a new string with the same sequence of characters.

```
// copy constructor in the String class
public String(String original)
```

Example:

```
String strA = "A string", strB, strC;

// the String constructor creates a separate string object strB
strB = new String(strA);

// do not confuse a copy with an alias;  strC is an alias that
// references the same string strA
strC = strA.
```

The `String` class, with its constructor, is the exception to the usual way Java creates a copy of an object. The standard approach has a class using a cloning mechanism that relies on the `Object clone()` method. The method performs a field-for-field copy of the object. The following is a declaration of `clone()` in the `Object` class. The keyword *native* means that the implementation of the method is in another programming language, usually C.

Cloning is done by private method clone() that copies each data field.

Object clone():

```
protected native Object clone() throws
CloneNotSupportedException;
```

Because all classes are derived from `Object`, the access modifier `protected` makes `Object clone()` available to any method in a class declaration but prevents it from being called by any instance of a class. For a class to make cloning available for its objects, the class must implement a public version of clone() and implement the Cloneable interface.

Cloneable class declaration:

```
public class ClassName implements Cloneable
{
    . . .
    public Object clone()              // public clone() method
    { ... }
}
```

Cloneable is an interesting interface. It has no methods and only indicates to the Object clone() method that it is legal for that method to make a field-for-field copy of instances of the class. A method throws the CloneNotSupportedException if it calls clone() for an object whose class type does not implement the Cloneable interface.

Cloning Time24 Objects

We illustrate cloning by adding the capability to the Time24 class. The declaration of clone() in the class illustrates how we use the Object method clone() to copy the instance variables hour and minute and thus create a new object. The class header adds Cloneable to the implementation list. The Time24 clone() method calls the Object method clone() using the syntax *super.clone()*.

Make Time24 object cloneable by having class implement Cloneable and a public clone() method.

Cloneable Time24 class:

```
public class Time24implements Comparable<Time24>, Cloneable
{
    ...
    // return clone
    public Object clone()
    {
        // the clone that is returned
        Object copy = null;

        try
        {
            // call the Object method clone(); copy is a reference
            // to a Time24 object
            copy = (Time24)super.clone();
        }
        catch (CloneNotSupportedException cnse)
        {
            // exception indicates a fatal error in the virtual
            // machine throw new InternalError();
        }

        return copy;
    }
}
```

Let us use Time24 clone() to create a new and separate object. The Time24 object tA is 8:30 and the clone is object tB.

```
Time24 tA = new Time24(8,30), tB;
tB = (Time24)tA.clone();
```

The cloning process produces a new object tB with data fields for hour and minute and copies the corresponding fields from tA to tB.

The Time24 class has only primitive data fields. In a clone, all of the data has been duplicated. This is termed a *deep copy*. Updates to the original object or to its clone do not affect the other object. For instance, look what happens when addTime() advances tA by 15 and tB by 45 minutes.

```
tA.addTime(15);          // tA is now 8:45
tB.addTime(45);          // tB is now 9:15
```

Cloning Reference Variables

When a class has a reference variable, cloning still produces a separate object. However, the original object and the copy are not independent in the sense that an update to one may also affect the other. An example illustrates this idea. The class CloneRef has a primitive integer variable n and a Time24 reference variable t as data fields. The cloning algorithm for the Time24 class applies to the CloneRef class.

CloneRef class:

```
class CloneRef implements Cloneable
{
   private int n;
   private Time24 t;
   ...
   public Object clone()
   {
      Object copy = null;

      try
      { copy = super.clone(); }
      catch (CloneNotSupportedException cnse)
      { throw new InternalError(); }

      // return the cloned object
      return copy;
   }
   ...
}
```

To illustrate the relationship between the object and its clone, we add to the `CloneRef` class methods `updateInt(n)` and `updateTime(m)`. The former assigns the argument n as the new primitive value; the latter uses `addTime()` to advance the time of the reference object t by m minutes.

updateInt():

```
public void updateInt(int n)
{ this.n = n; }
```

updateTime():

```
public void updateTime(int m)
{ t.addTime(m); }
```

> Cloning creates copies of primitive and reference data fields. Updates to a reference object affect both the original and the cloned object.

The effect of the update methods on an object and its copy reveal an import property of cloning. Assume `crA` is `CloneRef` object with integer value 20 and time 10:15. Using `clone()`, we create `crB` as a copy of `crA`.

```
// constructor has arguments for n and the hour and minute for t
CloneRef crA = new CloneRef(20,10,15), crB;

crB = (CloneRef)crA.clone();
```

In the cloning process, `crB` has data fields for its primitive and reference variables. Each is assigned the value of the corresponding field in `crA`. Reference variable t is an address and so the field in both `crA` and `crB` point at the same `Time24` object.

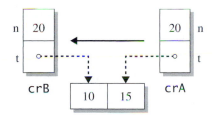

Using method `updateInt(55)` with the original object `crA` changes the value of its primitive variable (Figure (a)). Using `updateTime(30)` with either `crA` or `crB` advances time for the instance variable t. The variable t in each `CloneRef` object points to the same `Time24` object, which is now 10:45 (Figure (b)).

```
crA.updateInt(55);      // crA.n is now 55; crB.n remains 20
crB.updateTime(30);     // crA.t and crB.t reference time 10:45
```

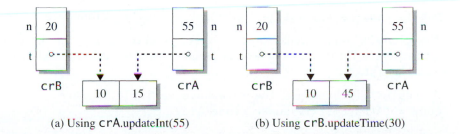

(a) Using `crA.updateInt(55)`   (b) Using `crB.updateTime(30)`

Cloning object with reference data is a shallow copy.

Cloning an object with reference variables creates two separate objects. However, an update of the reference object affects both the original object and the copy. This is termed a *shallow copy*.

☞

Note

Deep Copy with Reference Variables

A class with reference variables that are cloneable can create a deep copy where the references point to distinct objects. The method uses a two-step process. First, create a clone with fields that are a copy of the original object. Then clone the object pointed to by each reference variable and assign the variable to point at the copy. In the CloneRef class, a deep copy is produced by creating a clone of the Time24 object and then having the reference variable t point at the clone.

You will find application programs for `Time24` and `CloneRef` cloning in Chapter 9 of the software supplement. The programs contain the examples we have discussed in this section.

Cloning an ArrayList

The cloning mechanism that we used for the `CloneRef` class applies to collection classes. Additional overhead is involved, however, because we want the clone to have its own underlying storage structure that is a copy of the structure for the original collection. Let us see how the cloning mechanism is implemented in the `ArrayList` class. Recall that an `ArrayList` object has two instance variables, the integer value `listSize` and a reference to an array containing the list elements and additional capacity.

The clone() method for a collection creates a separate storage structure for the clone.

```
// number of elements in the list
private int listSize;

// array holding the elements; the capacity is listArr.length
private T[] listArr;
```

We follow the same pattern for implementing the clone() method in ArrayList and begin by specifying that the class implements the `Cloneable` interface as well as the `List` interface.

```
public class ArrayList<T> implements List<T>, Cloneable
```

The `clone()` method calls `super.clone()` to make a copy of the current `ArrayList` object. The result is a copy of the primitive variable `listSize` and the reference variable `listArr`.

```
// copies listSize and the reference variable listArr
copy = (ArrayList<T>)super.clone();
```

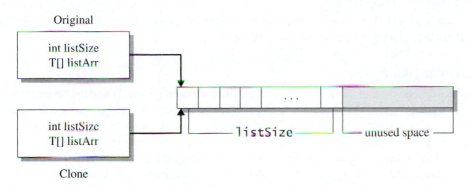

This is not quite what we want because the original and cloned values of listArr reference the same list of elements. We solve that problem by allocating in the clone an array of size listSize referenced by a new value of listArr, and then by copying the elements from the original list to the new list. The copy is not created with excess capacity that may have been available in the original collection.

```
// replace listArr in copy by a new reference to an array
copy.listArr = (T[])new Object[listSize];
// copy the elements from listArr to copy.listArr
for (int i=0;i < listSize;i++)
    copy.listArr[i] = listArr[i];
```

Cloning an ArrayList object creates two separate collections with their own lists. Elements can be added or removed from either collection without affecting the other. Be careful, however, when you update objects in the collection. Remember that elements in a collection are references. The original collection and the cloned collection have separate lists of references that point to a common set of objects (Figure 9.10). For instance, listArr[0] in the original collection references the same object as listArr[0] in the copy. For this reason, we say that the clone of an ArrayList is a *shallow copy*.

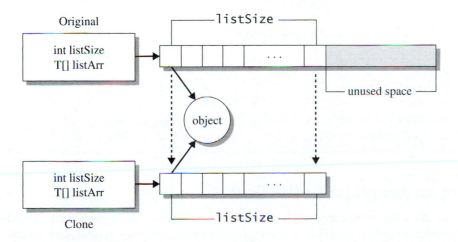

Figure 9.10 *ArrayList collection and its clone with elements that reference the same objects.*

We will add the clone capability to the collection classes in this book. However, we will not add cloning to classes we build in applications.

Cloning an Array

In the implementation of the mergesort algorithm, we used `clone()` and the original array to create a new array that temporarily stores elements during the merge process. The effect is to create a new array of the same size and assign it the elements from the original array. The clone is a shallow copy of the elements (references) from one array to the other.

Let us look at a simple example. A clone array is created for the `Time24` array `timeArr`. An update to the element `timeArr[0]` illustrates that the clone is a shallow copy. We then sort the elements in `cloneTimeArr` to demonstrate that the clone is a separate array.

```
// create a Time24 array and a clone
Time24[] timeArr = {new Time24(7,15), new Time24(14,00),
                    new Time24(3,45), new Time24(12,30)};
Time24[] cloneTimeArr = timeArr.clone();

System.out.println("Original: timeArr[0] = " + timeArr[0] +
            "  cloneTimeArr[0] = " + cloneTimeArr[0]);

// update timeArr[0] by advancing time 30 minutes
timeArr[0].addTime(30);

// display value at index 0 in timeArr and its clone
System.out.println("Updated:  timeArr[0] = " + timeArr[0] +
            "  cloneTimeArr[0] = " + cloneTimeArr[0]);

// sort cloneTimeArr
Arrays.sort(cloneTimeArr);

// display the elements for the two arrays
System.out.println("Unsorted timeArr:    " +
  Arrays.toString(timeArr));
System.out.println("Sorted cloneTimeArr: " +
  Arrays.toString(cloneTimeArr));
```

```
Output:
  Original: timeArr[0] = 7:15  cloneTimeArr[0] = 7:15
  Updated:  timeArr[0] = 7:45  cloneTimeArr[0] = 7:45
  Unsorted timeArr:    [7:45, 14:00, 3:45, 12:30]
  Sorted cloneTimeArr: [3:45, 7:45, 12:30, 14:00]
```

9.6 Evaluating an ArrayList Collection

Arrays are a legacy of early programming language design. An `ArrayList` is a modern data structure that evolved from years of programming experience. It offers distinct advantages over arrays.

- An `ArrayList` is a dynamic structure that can grow to meet the demands of the application; an array has a fixed capacity that cannot change once the structure is created.

- An ArrayList is an object with a built-in set of operations that are designed to facilitate use of the collection. The methods are fully implemented and tested. A programmer must write array-based routines or use independent methods that often require additional parameters.

An ArrayList is very efficient when adding or removing an element at the back of the sequence. This is true even though an ArrayList may require periodic reallocation of memory. Inserting and deleting elements at other positions require shifting of the tail of the sequence. If a large number of elements are involved, the shifting can be an inefficient $O(n)$ operation. For this type of application, the LinkedList is appropriate. We will discuss this structure in the next chapter.

Chapter Summary

- The List interface defines the methods for the sequence collection classes. These classes store and retrieve data by position. Examples include the ArrayList and LinkedList collections. The List interface includes all the methods of the Collection interface and methods specific to sequence collections. Examples include get() and set() at a position as well as add() and remove() at a position.

- The array data structure defines a block of consecutive data values. Because an array allows the use of an index to select any item in the list without referencing any of the other items, it is known as a *direct access structure*. Some sequence containers, such as the LinkedList container, do not allow direct access.

- The ArrayList sequence container extends the functionality of arrays. Arrays have the inherent problem of fixed size. The ArrayList container solves this problem and provides a simple-to-use public interface.

- This chapter contains two programs that use the ArrayList class. Program 9.1 develops the method join() that appends one ArrayList onto the end of another. Program 9.2 develops a brute force algorithm that solves the closest-pair problem.

- This chapter discusses implementation details for the ArrayList class. The implementation allocates an array that stores the list elements. The number of elements in this array is called the capacity of the ArrayList. When the array fills up, the ArrayList class allocates a larger array and allows garbage collection to dispose of the former array. The class allows access to elements by using an index and implements index bounds checking. The versions of remove() and add() that take an index argument generally have linear running time since the tail of the list must be moved to the left or to the right. Adding an element at the back of the sequence has amortized running time $O(1)$, and removing the back of the list has running time $O(1)$.

- A class can be cloned only if it implements the Cloneable interface. The method clone() in the Object class is used for cloning (copying) objects. There are two types of copies, a shallow and a deep copy. Two shallow copies share references to the same data, but deep copies reference distinct but equal data in memory. Most cloning operations produce shallow copies. All the classes in the book's collections framework implement Cloneable.

- Both an array and an ArrayList are direct access structures. If the number of elements is static, an array is the appropriate choice. If the number of elements grows frequently and new elements should be added at the back of the sequence, then an ArrayList is the best choice. The programmer should not use an ArrayList if elements are frequently added or removed inside the sequence.

Written Exercises

1. (a) Implement the method copyList() that takes an ArrayList argument and returns a new ArrayList that is a copy of the argument list.

   ```
   public static <T> ArrayList<T> copyList(ArrayList<T>
      aList)
   { . . . }
   ```

   (b) Implement the method copyListNodup() that returns a copy of the argument list but with no duplicate values.

   ```
   public static <T> ArrayList<T> copyListNodup(ArrayList<T>
      aList)
   { . . . }
   ```

2. What is the main difference between an ArrayList object and an array?

3. What is the problem with using an ArrayList collection if the application needs to perform multiple insertions and deletions at random positions in a sequence?

4. At selected statements, list the elements in the ArrayList.

   ```
   ArrayList<String> aList = new ArrayList<String>();

   aList.add("A");
   aList.add(0,"B");
   aList.add(1,"C");                 // List: _____
   aList.add(3,"D");                 // List: _____
   aList.add(2,"E");                 // List: _____

   aList.remove("B");
   aList.remove(1);                  // List: _____
   aList.remove(aList.size()-1);     // List: _____
   ```

5. Assume the ArrayList aList has size = 65 and capacity = 90. Give the size and capacity after executing each of the following instructions.

   (a) aList.ensureCapcity(75);   // size/capacity = _____
   (b) aList.ensureCapacity(125);   // size/capacity = _____
   (c) aList.trimToSize();   // size/capacity = _____

6. Assume that an ArrayList has n elements. Give the worst- and average-case running times for each operation.

   (a) indexOf()   (b) add(int index, T item)
   (c) add(T item)   (d) remove(int index)

7. Explain why we say that the method add(item) that inserts item at the back of the list has constant amortized running time.

8. Explain why the running time to remove the last element in an ArrayList is O(1).

9. Assume the ArrayList class wishes to add new methods back(), addBack(), and removeBack() to access and update the back (end) of the sequence. Use existing

ArrayList methods to implement these new methods.

```
public T back();
public void addBack(T item);
public T removeBack();
```

Programming Exercises

10. Write a program that declares an ArrayList and inputs strings from the keyboard. Terminate input with the string "done." Add each string to the ArrayList and then output the list.

    (a) Scan the ArrayList and output the longest string; that is, the one with the longest length.

    (b) Scan the ArrayList and output the maximum string; that is, the maximum in lexical order.

11. (a) The method removeFirst() deletes the first element in a collection that implements the List interface and returns its value. Implement the method.

    ```
    public static <T> T removeFirst(List<T> aList)
    { ... }
    ```

    (b) Write a program that creates ArrayLists with elements of different generic types. In a loop, call removeFirst() to output and remove elements from each list until it is empty.

12. The method insertOrder() adds a new item to a list so as to maintain the natural ordering of the elements. Implement the method.

    ```
    public static <T extends Comparable<? super T>> void
    insertOrder(List<T> aList, T item)
    ```

    Write a program that creates an ArrayList with values from an array using insertOrder().

13. (a) Chapter 5 develops the generic selectionSort() method for an array of objects. Create a List version of the method.

    ```
    public static <T extends Comparable<? super T>> void
    selectionSortA(List<T> aList)
    { ... }
    ```

    (b) In a program, create a text file, words.txt, containing a series of words. Read the words from the file and insert them into an ArrayList. Sort the elements using selectionSortA() and output the resulting list.

14. These programming exercises involve the use of a wildcard. The method parameter notation

    ```
    ArrayList<?> arr
    ```

    means that arr is an ArrayList of unknown type. Use a wildcard in this fashion when a method does not need to reference a named generic type in its return value or parameter list. For instance, the method `print()` will output the contents of an `ArrayList`.

```
public static void print(ArrayList<?> arr)
{
    for (int i=0;i < arr.size();i++)
        System.out.print(arr.get(i) + " ");
    System.out.println();
}
```

(a) Implement the method `lastIndexOf()` that returns the index of the last occurrence of element target in an `ArrayList` or -1 if the target is not found.

```
public static int lastIndexOf(ArrayList<?> aList,
                                Object target)
{ ... }
```

(b) Implement method `unique()` that determines whether a specified value occurs exactly once in an `ArrayList`. For instance, in `ArrayList aList`, the element 7 occurs only once and `unique()` returns true; in `ArrayList bList`, the element 3 occurs more than once and `unique()` returns false. Use `lastIndexOf()` and `indexOf()` in the implementation of `unique()`.

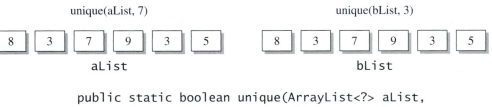

unique(aList, 7)   unique(bList, 3)

aList   bList

```
public static boolean unique(ArrayList<?> aList,
                              Object target)
{ ... }
```

(c) Write a program that creates an `ArrayList` with values from array `arr`. Test your implementation of the method `unique()`.

```
Integer[] arr = {1, 9, 9, 3, 5, 1, 2, 9, 1, 7};
```

15. Implement two different methods that reverse the order of elements in an `ArrayList`.

(a) The first method, `reverseByIndex()`, uses indices to reverse the order of the elements in an `ArrayList`. This is an in-place reordering of the elements. The figure illustrates the algorithm for a seven-element list. Implement `reverseByIndex()`.

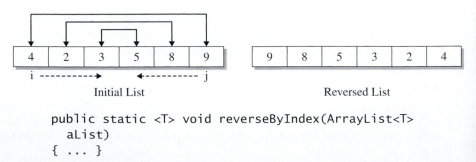

Initial List   Reversed List

```
public static <T> void reverseByIndex(ArrayList<T>
    aList)
{ ... }
```

(b) A second method, `reverseByCopy()`, copies the elements of an `ArrayList` in reverse order to a new `ArrayList`, which then becomes the return value. Implement `reverseByCopy()`.

```
public static <T> ArrayList<T>
reverseByCopy(ArrayList<T> aList)
{ ... }
```

(c) Write a program that creates two `ArrayList` objects `aList` and `bList` with values from array `arr`.

```
Integer[] arr = {9, 12, 6, 24, 16, 8, 3, 19, 11, 4};
```

(i) Use the method `reverseByIndex()` to reverse the order of the elements in `aList`. Output the elements in `aList` using `toString()`.

(ii) Use the method `reverseByCopy()` and the assignment statement

```
bList = reverseByCopy(bList);
```

to reverse the order of the elements in `bList`. Output the elements in `bList` using `toString()`.

16. The method `removeDuplicates()` takes an `ArrayList` as an argument and removes all duplicate elements. For instance, if the `ArrayList` contains `Integer` values $\{1, 7, 2, 7, 9, 1, 2, 8, 9\}$, then the collection after executing `removeDuplicates()` is $\{1, 7, 2, 9, 8\}$.

```
public static <T> void removeDuplicates(ArrayList<T> aList)
{ ... }
```

Implement the method using the following strategy. Scan the `ArrayList` `aList` with an index `i`. Declare a second index `j` that specifies the location in `aList` for assignment of the next nonduplicate entry. Because the first element in `aList` is not a duplicate, initialize `j = 1`. The index `j` is incremented only after it is determined that `aList.get(i)` is not located within the values `aList.get(0)`, `aList,get(1)`, ..., `aList.get(j-1)`. Before returning from the function, delete the elements at indices `aList.size()-1` down to `j`.

Write a program that creates an `ArrayList` with `Character` objects from the string "mississippi". Remove duplicates so that the resulting `ArrayList` is [m, i, s, p].

17. In a program, implement the method `count()`, which counts the number of times a target value occurs a list.

```
public static int count(ArrayList<?> aList, Object target)
{ ... }
```

Create an `ArrayList` and use `add()` to load it with 15 Integer objects with random values in the range from 0 to 4. Output the list. In a loop, call the method `count()`, and display the number of occurrences of each value (0 to 4) in the list.

18. (GUI Application) JComboBox is a GUI component that creates a drop-down list. Entries in the list are an `Object` array. Use the component in an application that has the user select a country from the list and then places the country flag is a label. An action listener on a JComboBox returns the user selection as an index.

In Chapter 9 Exercises, the file *flags.txt* file contains entries that consist of the country name (string) and an image file name (string) separated by tabs. The image files are stored in the *images* subdirectory. For instance, the entry for China is

China → images/china.gif   Note: → represents a tab separator

For the application, store the country name in an `ArrayList<String>` collection and the images in an `ArrayList<Icon>` collection. An `Icon` object is created as an `IconImage` by using the image file name.

```
Icon icon = new IconImage("imageFile");
```

Create a `JComboBox` with an `Object` array derived from the country name array list. Install an action listener on the component and place it on the north end. In the center, place a label that will hold the image. The event handler uses the method `getSelectedIndex()` to identify the index of the country in the list. From the figure, the user selects "China" which become the entry in the combo box text field. The flag appears as a label.

```
int index = comboBox.getSelectedIndex()
```

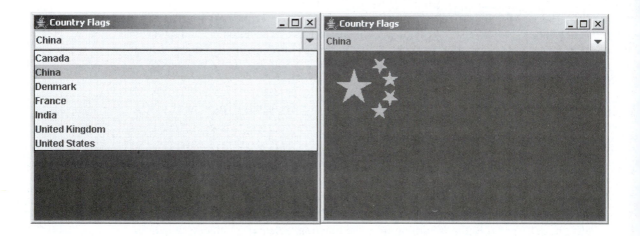

19. This programming exercise adds methods to the `ArrayList` class. Use the copy of the class in Chapter 9 Exercises.

    (a) Add a constructor to the `ArrayList` class that takes an array of objects as an argument.

        ```
        public ArrayList(T[] arr)
        { ... }
        ```

    Hint: The statement `this()` calls the default constructor which initializes the fields and allocates an initial block of memory.

    (b) Add the method `lastIndexOf()` to the `ArrayList` class. It returns the index of the last occurrence of the specified object in the list or −1 if the object is not in the collection.

        ```
        public int lastIndexOf(Object item)
        { ... }
        ```

20. Section 9.5 develops the CloneRef class. Modify the class in Chapter 9 Exercises to implement the method deepClone() that creates a deep copy of a CloneRef object.

```
// returns a deep copy of the CloneRef object; the Time24
// reference variable t of the new object is distinct from
// the current object's reference variable t
public Object deepClone()
{ ... }
```

In a program, declare

```
CloneRef crA = new CloneRef(20,10,15), crB, crC;

crB = (CloneRef)crA.clone();
crC = (CloneRef)crA.deepClone();
```

Add code that proves crB is a shallow copy of crA and crC is a deep copy of crA by showing that the Time24 reference variables for crB and crC point to different objects.

Programming Project

21. The programming project adds methods to the ArrayList class. Use a copy of the class in Chapter 9 Exercises.

(a) Implement the method remove(index, n) in the ArrayList class. The method removes n items from the ArrayList beginning at position index. If there are fewer than n items remaining, remove the tail of the list

```
public void remove(int index, int n)
{ ... }
```

The following code works but is inefficient. Discuss some of the problems and come up with a better solution.

```
public void remove(int index, int n)
{
    int m = listSize-index-n >= 0 ? n : listSize-index;

    for (int j=0;j < m;j++)
        this.remove(index);
}
```

(b) Implement the method insert() in the ArrayList class. The method inserts all of the elements in the array into this list, starting at the specified position.

```
public void insert(int index, T[] arr)
{ ... }
```

Do not use add(i, item) to insert an element because this is very inefficient. It requires shifting the tail of the list for each insertion. After modifying the capacity of the underlying storage array, you can shift the tail only once and then make the insertions.

(c) Test your implementation of the methods by creating an `ArrayList intList` that contains `Integer` values from array `arr1`.

```
Integer[] arr1 = {1, 2, 3, 4, 10, 11, 12, 13},
         arr2 = {5, 6, 7};
```

Prompt the user to enter an index that is used with `insert()` to add the elements from array `arr2` to `intList`. Prompt the user again for an index and a count n. Use these values with `remove()` to delete n elements from `intList` starting at the specified index. After each operation, display the elements in the list.

Chapter 10

LINKED LISTS

CONTENTS

10.1 SINGLY LINKED LISTS
Creating a Linked List
Scanning a Linked List
Locating a List Position
Updating the Front of the List
General Insert and Delete Operation
Removing a Target Node

10.2 DOUBLY LINKED LISTS

10.3 THE LINKEDLIST COLLECTION
The LinkedList Class
LinkedList—Index Methods
Accessing the Ends of a List

10.4 LINKEDLIST APPLICATIONS
Application: The Draft List
Application: A List Palindrome

In Chapter 9, we introduced an `ArrayList` as a concrete realization of a List collection. It is a structure that stores elements in contiguous memory. As a result, an `ArrayList` allows for direct access to its elements. An `ArrayList` is an ideal data structure for applications that need a dynamic array. Its use, however, can introduce significant overhead when adding or removing an element. In Figure 10.1, adding the integer 5 at index 2 requires moving the tail of the `ArrayList` (elements 3, 10, and 8) to the right to accommodate the new element. A similar overhead is required to delete an element. For a large collection, these operations would require excessive computing time to maintain the contiguous storage structure.

We need an alternative structure that stores elements in a sequence but allows for more efficient insertion and deletion of elements at random positions in the list. A linked list provides such an alternative

Insert 5 into the ArrayList {2, 7, 3, 10, 8} at the index 2
Make room by shifting the tail {3, 10, 8}

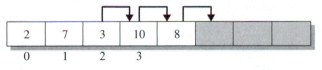

Add 5 at index 2 (Resulting sequence {2, 7, 5, 3, 10, 8})

Figure 10.1 *Insert 5 in an ArrayList by shifting the tail to the right.*

287

To insert or remove an element at an interior location in an ArrayList requires shifting of data and is an O(*n*) operation.

structure. Elements contain links that reference the previous and the successor elements in the list.

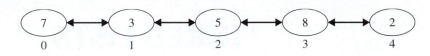

You can think of each element in a linked list as being like an individual piece in a child's pop chain. A piece is a cylinder with a connector on one end and a hole in the back. To form a chain, insert the connector into the back of the next piece (Figure 10.2).

Individual Piece   Pop Chain

Figure 10.2 *Physical model of an element in a LinkedList as pieces in a pop chain.*

Inserting a new piece into the chain involves merely breaking a connection and reconnecting the chain at both ends of the new piece (Figure 10.3).

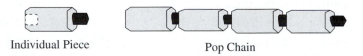

Disconnect   Reconnect

Figure 10.3 *Adding a piece at a position in the pop chain.*

Similarly, the removal of a piece from anywhere in the chain requires breaking its two connections, removing the piece, and then reconnecting the chain (Figure 10.4).

Disconnect   Reconnect

Figure 10.4 *Removing a piece from a pop chain.*

Inserting and deleting an element is a local operation and requires updating only the links adjacent to the element. The other elements in the list are not affected. This is in stark contrast with an ArrayList, which must shift all elements on the tail whenever a new element enters or exits the list.

The goal of this chapter is to introduce the *LinkedList collection*. This is a data structure that implements the `List` interface using a linked list as the underlying storage structure. You will understand the collection better if we first introduce linked lists more formally and do some hands-on manipulations of the elements. Drawing on your experience with arrays simplified our introduction of `ArrayList` collections. Providing you with experience with linked lists will have the same effect when we discuss the `LinkedList` collection.

We start with singly linked lists, which consist of elements with only one link referencing the next element. These lists provide most of the terminology and mechanics to create and update a linked list. In Chapter 11, we extend the concept of a singly linked list to a doubly linked list and use it to implement the `LinkedList` class. We begin with singly linked list so as to provide you with an intuitive understanding of list handling operations. The concepts you learn will ease the transition to doubly linked lists. We rely mostly on pictures and code fragments to tell the story. In a few cases, we implement an operation as a static method in the `Nodes` class of the software supplement.

10.1   Singly Linked Lists

A singly linked list is a linear structure. Each element is a *node* that consists of a value and a reference to the next node in the sequence. A node with its two fields can reside anywhere in memory. We say that a linked structure uses *noncontiguous memory* to store the elements. Figure 10.5 is a view of a singly linked list. An arrow emanating from a node represents a reference to the next (successor) node. The list maintains a reference variable, `front`, that identifies the first element in the sequence. The list ends when the link (reference) is `null`. We use the symbol ⏚ to indicate the null reference.

A singly linked structure uses noncontiguous memory. References provide links to move to the successor of an element.

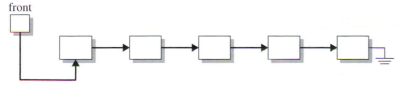

Singly Linked List

Figure 10.5 *Singly linked list where an element is a node.*

A singly linked list is a sequential access structure. Any element at an interior position cannot be directly accessed, as with an `ArrayList`. We must use a sequential scan that begins at the front and moves forward to the element. In this way, an `ArrayList` is like a music CD that allows a listener to immediately jump to any sound track. A linked list is like a music tape that you fast-forward to locate a new song.

A singly linked list is not a direct access structure. It must be accessed sequentially by moving forward one node at a time.

Creating a Linked List

Elements in a linked list are nodes. These are objects that have two instance variables. The first variable, *nodeValue*, is of generic type T. The second variable is a Node reference *next*; it provides a link to the next node.

A singly linked list node has a node value and a reference to the next node in the list.

Let us look at the declaration of the Node class. Be aware that linked lists are implementation structures and so Node objects are rarely visible in the public interface of a data structure. As a result, we declare the instance variables in the Node class public. This greatly simplifies the writing of linked-list methods. The Node class is a *self-referencing* structure, in which the instance variable, *next*, refers to an object of its own type. The class has two constructors that combine with the operator new to create a node. The default constructor initializes each instance variable to be null. The constructor with a type parameter initializes the nodeValue field and sets next to null.

Node class:

```
public class Node<T>
{
    public T nodeValue;            // data held by the node
    public Node<T> next;           // next node in the list

    // default constructor with no initial value
    public Node()
    {
        nodeValue = null;
        next = null;
    }

    // initialize nodeValue to item and set next to null
    public Node(T item)
    {
        nodeValue = item;
        next = null;
    }
}
```

In order to have a linked list, we need to define a reference variable that identifies the first node in the list. Appropriately, we call the Node reference front. The role of front is critical in a linked list. It marks the first node in the list. Once you are at the first node, you can use its reference next to proceed to the second node, then use next in the second node to reference the third node, and so on. In a real sense, front defines the list. If you know front, you can access the first node and then all subsequent nodes. Let us create a two-element linked list in which the nodes have string values "red" and "green." The variable front references the node "red". The process begins by declaring three Node reference variables *front*, *p*, and *q*.

```
Node<String> front, p, q;       // references to nodes
p = new Node<String>("red");    // create two nodes (figure (a))
q = new Node<String>("green");

// create the link from p to q by assigning the next field
// for node p the value q
p.next = q;                     // figure (b)

// set front to point at the first node in the list
front = p;                      // figure (c)
```

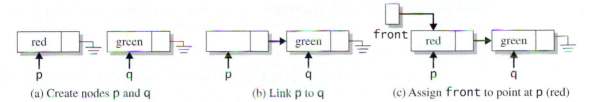

(a) Create nodes p and q   (b) Link p to q   (c) Assign front to point at p (red)

An empty linked list is a list without any nodes. In this case, front does not reference a first node; rather it has the value null. The condition "front == null" tests for an empty list.

Node<T> front = null

Scanning a Linked List

A linked list uses the variable *front* to identify the first element in the sequence. A scan of the list uses a Node reference curr, which is initially set to front. When curr.next is null, the scan is at the last element; when curr == null, the scan is complete. For instance, the static method toString(front) in the Node class returns a string that displays the value of each element. The format is a comma-separated list enclosed in brackets. The argument takes the Node reference for *front* as an argument. This identifies the list.

> Scan a singly linked list by starting at front and using next to proceed down the list.

toString(front):

```
public static <T> String toString(Node<T> front)
{
    if (front == null)
        return "null";

    Node<T> curr = front;
    // start with the left bracket and value of first node
    String str = "[" + curr.nodeValue;

    // append all but last node, separating items with a comma
    // polymorphism calls toString() for the nodeValue type
    while(curr.next != null)
    {
        curr = curr.next;
        str += ", " + curr.nodeValue;
    }
    str += "]";
    return str;
}
```

Locating a List Position

To locate an element at index n, we need to scan the list through a specified number of nodes. This O(n) process uses the scanning principles for the toString() method. Start by declaring a Node reference curr to point at the first element (*front*) of the list. This is

> Access to a linked-list object at an index has running time O(n).

position (index) 0. A for-loop moves `curr` down the sequence until it references the element at index n. The value at index n is `curr.nodeValue`.

```
Node<T> curr = front;

// move curr down the sequence through n successor nodes
for (int i = 0; i < n; i++)
    curr = curr.next;
```

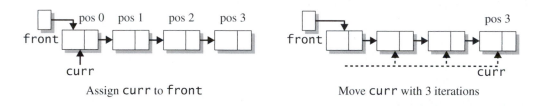

Assign `curr` to `front`   Move `curr` with 3 iterations

Updating the Front of the List

Insert or remove operations at the front of a linked list is an O(1) operation.

Inserting or deleting an element at the front of a list is particularly easy because the sequence maintains a reference that points at the first element. Figure 10.6a illustrates the process of adding a node with value i tem at the front of a list. Start by creating a new node with i tem as its value. Set the new node to point at the current first element. Then update `front` to point at the new first element.

```
Node<T> newNode = new Node<T>(item);
newNode.next = front;
front = newNode;                    // update front to maintain the list
```

Deleting the first element involves setting `front` to point at the second node in the list (`front.next`) (Figure 10.6b).

```
front = front.next;                 // establish a new front
```

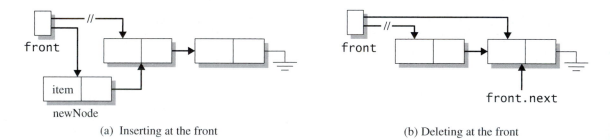

(a) Inserting at the front   (b) Deleting at the front

Figure 10.6 *Adding and removing an element at the front of the list.*

General Insert and Delete Operation

In a list, we are familiar with the concept of inserting a new node at a position or deleting an existing node at a position. The algorithms point out a problem that is inherent in a singly linked list. Because a node can reference only the next (successor) element, updates must occur after a node. Let us look at the algorithm that adds a new node at position `curr`. We want to insert the new element in such a way that it slides the specified node and all subsequent nodes to the right by one position. The effect is to add the new node before the specified node. As the figure illustrates, the algorithm must have access to the predecessor node `prev` because an update occurs with the next field of `prev`.

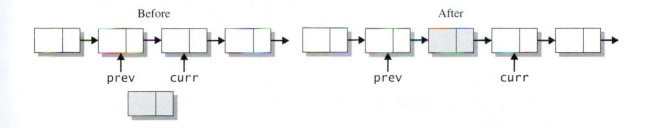

The insertion process begins by creating a new node with `nodeValue` assigned the value `item`. Adding the new node involves updating the links in both the previous node and the new node. Initially, the link field for the node `prev` identifies `curr` as its successor, and `newNode` exists as an isolated node (Figure 10.7a). Connecting `newNode` to the list requires updating the values of `newNode.next` and `prev.next`. The reference field for `newNode` must link to `curr`, and the reference field for `prev` must link to `newNode`. The connections involve two steps (Figure 10.7b).

> Inserting into a list involves creating a new node and assigning two reference values.

```
Node curr, prev, newNode;
// create the node and assign it a value
newNode = new Node(value);

// update links
newNode.next = curr;        // step 1
prev.next = newNode;        // step 2
```

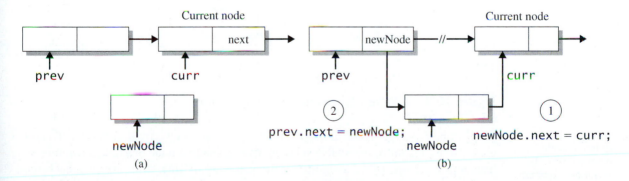

Figure 10.7 *Adding a new node before node curr in the list.*

Deleting the node at position `curr` also requires access to the predecessor node `prev`. The algorithm involves updating the link in the predecessor node. Set the value of `prev` to reference the successor of `curr`. This has the effect of disconnecting `curr` from the list.

To delete a node from a linked list requires changing one reference.

The following statements implement the algorithm. Figure 10.8 illustrates the unlinking process.

```
Node curr, prev;

prev.next = curr.next;        // reconnect prev to curr.next
```

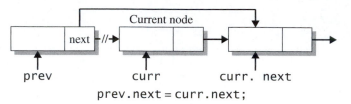

prev.next = curr.next;

Figure 10.8 *Removing a node at position curr in the list.*

Removing a Target Node

A programmer often wants to access or update nodes in a linked list according to their value rather than their position in the list. Let us design an algorithm that removes the first occurrence of a node having a specified value. This provides an opportunity to draw on many of the concepts we developed in the previous sections. We will implement the algorithm with the static method remove(item).

Removing a node with a specified target value begins with a scan of the list to identify the location of the target node. Simply having a reference to the target node is not sufficient because we must also have a reference to the predecessor node. The scan must use a pair of references that move in tandem down the list. One reference identifies the current node in the scan, the other the previous (predecessor) node. Figure 10.9 illustrates the relative location for the tandem references curr and prev. Once curr identifies the node that matches the target, the algorithm uses the reference prev to unlink curr.

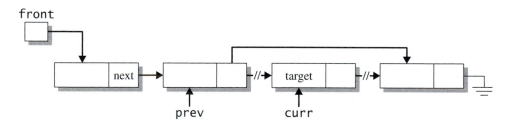

Figure 10.9 *Positions of prev and curr for a deletion.*

To locate and delete a node from a linked list requires maintaining two references, one to the previous node and one to the current node.

To find the target node, initially set reference curr to the front of the list. The reference prev identifies the node just before curr. The first node in a linked list does not have a predecessor, so we assign prev the value null. Using curr, we scan each successive node until its value matches the target or until curr reaches the end of the list (curr == null). During the scan of the list, the two references curr and prev move as a tandem pair. The following statements move the references forward to the next node in the list (Figure 10.10).

```
prev = curr;              // update prev to next position (curr)
curr = curr.next;         // move curr to the next node
```

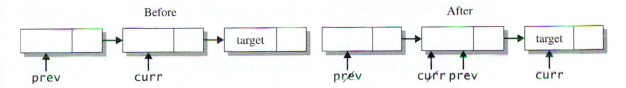

Figure 10.10 *Update of references prev and curr in the scan of nodes in a linked list.*

If the scan of the list identifies a match (`target.equals(curr.nodeValue)`), `curr` points at the node that we must remove and `prev` identifies the predecessor node. There are two possible situations that require different actions. The target node might be the first node in the list, or it might be at some intermediate position in the list. The value of `prev` distinguishes the two cases.

Case 1: Reference `prev` is null, which implies that `curr` is `front`. The search identifies a match at the first node in the list. The action is to delete the front of the list by updating `front` to point at the successor of `curr`.

> When prev is null, delete the first node in the linked list; otherwise, delete the node inside the list referenced by curr.

```
front = curr.next;
```

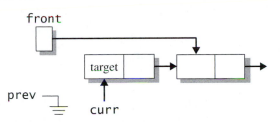

Case 2: The match occurs at some intermediate node in the list. Both `curr` and `prev` have nonnull values. The action is to delete the current node by unlinking it from `prev`.

```
prev.next = curr.next;
```

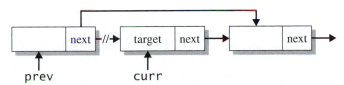

The generic method `remove()` has a parameter list that includes a reference to the front of the list and the target value. The method returns the value of `front`, which may have been updated if the deletion occurs at the first node in the list. We include `remove()` as a static method in the Nodes class.

remove():

```
// delete the first occurrence of the target in the linked
// list referenced by front; returns the value of front
public static <T> Node<T> remove(Node<T> front, T target)
{
    // curr moves through list, trailed by prev
    Node<T>  curr = front, prev = null;
```

```
                    // becomes true if we locate target
                    boolean foundItem = false;

                    // scan until locate item or come to end of list
                    while (curr != null && !foundItem)
                    {
                        // check for a match; if found, check whether deletion
                        // occurs at the front or at an intermediate position
                        // in the list; set boolean foundItem true
                        if (target.equals(curr.nodeValue))
                        {
                            if (prev == null)              // remove the first Node
                                front = front.next;
                            else
                                prev.next = curr.next;     // erase intermediate Node
                            foundItem = true;
                        }
                        else
                        {
                            // advance curr and prev
                            prev = curr;
                            curr = curr.next;
                        }
                    }
                    // return current value of front which is updated when the
                    // deletion occurs at the first element in the list
                    return front;
                }
```

PROGRAM 10.1 ERASING NODES IN DESCENDING ORDER

Let us look at a program that uses most of the singly linked list concepts from this section. A prompt asks the user to enter the number of elements in the list. Building the list involves inserting at the front random values in the range from 0 to 99. A call to `toString(front)` displays the original list. The program then sets in motion an algorithm to output elements in descending order of their value. The key feature is the static method `getMaxNode()`, which scans the list and returns a reference to the node with the maximum value. The value at this node is output and then used with `remove()` to delete the value from the list. Iterations that output and then remove the maximum value continue until the list is empty.

```
import java.util.Random;
import java.util.Scanner;
import ds.util.Node;
import ds.util.Nodes;    // methods toString() and remove()

public class Program10_1
{
    public static void main(String[] args)
    {
        // declare references; by setting front to null,
```

```
    // the initial list is empty
    Node<Integer> front = null, newNode, p;

    // variables to create list and setup keyboard input
    Random rnd = new Random();
    Scanner keyIn = new Scanner(System.in);
    int listCount, i;

    // prompt for the size of the list
    System.out.print("Enter the size of the list: ");
    listCount = keyIn.nextInt();

    // create a list with nodes having random integer values
    // from 0 to 99; insert each element at front of the list
    for (i = 0; i < listCount; i++)
    {
        newNode = new Node<Integer>(rnd.nextInt(100));
        newNode.next = front;
        front = newNode;
    }

    System.out.print("Original list:  ");
    System.out.println(Nodes.toString(front));

    System.out.print("Ordered list:   ");
    // continue finding the maximum node and erasing it
    // until the list is empty
    while (front != null)
    {
        p = getMaxNode(front);
        System.out.print(p.nodeValue + "  ");
        front = Nodes.remove(front, p.nodeValue);
    }
    System.out.println();
}

// return a reference to the node with the maximum value
public static <T extends Comparable<? super T>>
Node<T> getMaxNode(Node<T> front)
{
    // maxNode reference to node containing largest
    // value (maxValue); initially maxNode is front and
    // maxValue is front.nodeValue; scan using reference curr
    // starting with the second node (front.next)
    Node<T> maxNode = front, curr = front.next;
    T maxValue = front.nodeValue;

    while (curr != null)
    {
        // see if maxValue < curr.nodeValue; if so, update
```

```
                         // maxNode and maxValue; continue scan at next node
                         if (maxValue.compareTo(curr.nodeValue)< 0)
                         {
                             maxValue = curr.nodeValue;
                             maxNode = curr;
                         }
                         curr = curr.next;
                    }
                    return maxNode;
               }
          }
```

Run:

```
    Enter the size of the list: 9
    Original list:  [77, 83, 14, 38, 70, 35, 55, 11, 6]
    Ordered list:    83  77  70  55  38  35  14  11  6
```

10.2 Doubly Linked Lists

A more flexible linked structure is the doubly linked list whose nodes contain two references that point to the next (successor) and previous (predecessor) node. Such a list has a
reference, front, that points to (identifies) the first node in the sequence and a reference,
back, that points at the last node in the sequence. You can scan a doubly linked list in both
directions. The forward scan starts at front and ends when the link is a reference to back.
In the backward direction, simply reverse the process and the references.

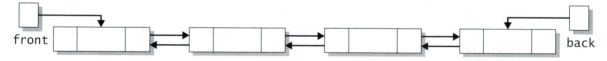

Like a singly linked list, a doubly linked list is a sequential structure. However, you
can reach an element by starting at the front and moving forward using the reference field
next or by starting at back and moving backward using the reference field prev.

To move forward
or backward in a
doubly linked list,
use the node links
next and prev.

A doubly linked list has clear advantages over a singly linked list. Insert and delete operations need to have only the reference to the node in question. For instance, assume you want
to insert a new node at position curr (Figure 10.11). The operation is a little more complex
because you must update both the next and previous references. However, knowing curr,
you can access the predecessor node. It is simply curr.previous. Attaching the new node
takes four statements instead of two for a singly linked list. The running time is still O(1).

```
    prevNode = curr.prev;
    newNode.prev = prevNode;          // statement 1
    prevNode.next = newNode;          // statement 2
    curr.prev = newNode;              // statement 3
    newNode.next = curr;              // statement 4
```

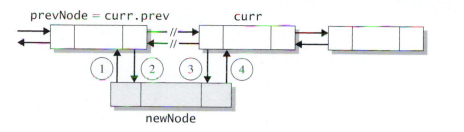

Figure 10.11 *Inserting a new node at position curr in a doubly linked list.*

Deleting the node `curr` is a two-step process. Link the predecessor of `curr` to the successor of `curr`. From `curr`, you can identify its predecessor `prevNode` (`curr.previous`) and its successor `succNode` (`curr.next`) (See Figure 10.12.)

Deleting a node in a doubly linked list requires updating two references.

```
prevNode = curr.prev;
succNode = curr.next;
succNode.prev = prevNode;        // statement 1
prevNode.next = succNode;        // statement 2
```

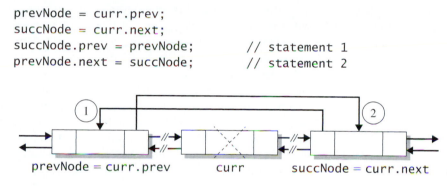

Figure 10.12 *Deleting node curr from a doubly linked list.*

In a singly linked list, adding and removing a node at the front of the list are O(1) operations. They update the reference `front`. With a doubly linked list, you can add and remove a node at the back of the list with same runtime efficiency. Simply update the reference `back`.

We will discuss doubly linked lists in detail in Chapter 11. All you need for now is an intuitive understanding of how the lists work. They provide the storage structure for a new `List` collection called *LinkedList*.

10.3 The LinkedList Collection

A `LinkedList` object is a list collection that provides an alternative to an `ArrayList`. They differ in the way they store elements. An `ArrayList` uses an array in contiguous memory. It is a direct access structure. A `LinkedList` uses a doubly linked list whose elements reside in noncontiguous memory locations. Each element in the list contains links that identify both the next and the previous element in the sequence. The elements are laid out in a row starting at the first element, called `first`, and proceeding in successive order to a final element, called `last`. A LinkedList is a sequential access structure. Figure 10.13 provides views of a `LinkedList` collection as an abstract sequence and as a linked list.

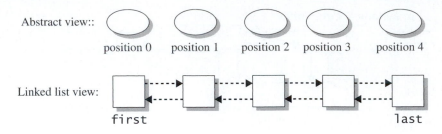

Abstract view::

position 0   position 1   position 2   position 3   position 4

Linked list view:

first   last

Figure 10.13 *Models of a LinkedList object as an abstract sequence and as a linked list.*

The LinkedList Class

The LinkedList class implements the List interface.

The LinkedList class implements the List interface. Thus, you are familiar with most of its methods. ArrayList and LinkedList are alternative data structures that can be used when an application needs to store elements as a sequence. In most cases, programs can use ArrayList and LinkedList objects interchangeably, and they will run correctly. The issue is efficiency. Some applications are best served with a dynamic array structure and some with a linked structure. While we are discussing the LinkedList class, we pay close attention to the runtime efficiency of the methods.

The LinkedList class has a default constructor that creates an empty list. A toString() method returns a string representing the list as a comma-separated sequence of elements enclosed in brackets. By implementing the List interface, the class also implements the Collection interface with its familiar general-purpose collection methods. The methods isEmpty() and size() return information about the number of elements in the list. You can identify whether an element is in the list using contains() and can access the elements in their sequential order using toArray(). The collection add() method takes a reference of generic type and inserts the element at the back of the sequence. A call to remove() with an Object reference deletes the first occurrence of the object in the list. The method returns true or false, depending on whether a match occurs.

Example 10.1

The example creates a LinkedList object aList that stores strings and explores some of its properties.

1. Use the constructor to create an empty-linked list.

```
LinkedList<String> aList = new LinkedList<String>();
```

2. Assume the list contains the strings "Red", "Blue", "Green". Output its size and check whether aList contains the color "White".

```
System.out.println("Size = " +  aList.size());
System.out.println("List contains the string 'White' is " +
                   aList.contains("White"));
```

Output:

```
Size = 3
List contains the string 'White' is false
```

3. Add the color "Black" and a second element with color "Blue". Then delete the first occurrence of "Blue". An output statement uses `toString()` to list the elements in the sequence.

```
aList.add("Black");              // add Black at the end
aList.add("Blue");               // add Blue at the end

aList.remove("Blue");            // delete first "Blue"
System.out.println(aList);       // uses toString()
```

Output:

```
[Red, Green, Black, Blue]
```

LinkedList—Index Methods

The `LinkedList` class implements the index-based methods that characterize the `List` interface. For instance, a collection can access and update an element with the `get()` and `set()` methods and modify the list with the `add(index, element)` and `remove(index)` methods. Because the underlying implementation is a linked list, the index methods have $O(n)$ worst-case running time. A scan is required to locate the node at position `index`. An application should use these methods only for relatively small data sets.

The LinkedList class allows index access; but use these operations sparingly because their running time is linear.

Example 10.2

Let us look at an example that illustrates the `LinkedList` index methods for a collection of `Integer` objects. Assume the collection, `list`, initially contains elements with values [5, 7, 9, 4, 3].

1. Use `get()` to access the object at index 1 and then remove the element. The element at index 1 then has the value 9.

```
Integer intObj = list.get(1);       // intObj has value 7
list.remove(1);
```

2. Use `set()` to update the element at index 2. Give it the value 8. Add a new element with value 6 at index 2. The new element occupies position 2, and its insertion shifts the tail of the list up one position. Thus, the node at index 3 has value 8.

```
list.set(2, 8);
list.add(2, 6);
```

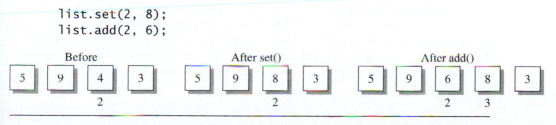

Our warning on the relative inefficiency of index-based `LinkedList` methods is real and significant. You may be tempted to design array-like algorithms for a `LinkedList` collection. For instance, the following statements scan a list of strings and replace each value with its uppercase equivalent.

```
LinkedList<String> list = new LinkedList<String>();
String str;
. . .                                  // add string elements

for (int i = 0; i < list.size(); i++)
{
   str = list.get(i);
   str = str.toUpperCase();
   list.set(i, str);
}
```

The algorithm is clean, and the code looks harmless. The runtime efficiency is horrible. Each access and update requires an O(n) scan to simply locate the element in the list. Clearly, an `ArrayList` would be more appropriate. Well then, what good is a `LinkedList` collection? In the next section, we discuss updates to the ends of a list. These operations play right into the strength of the linked-list storage structure.

We have briefly introduced general collection iterators. These are objects that scan the elements of a collection and extract their values. A `LinkedList` has a second type of iterator, appropriately called a *list iterator*. The object scans the list in both directions and performs update operations that add or remove an element and assign a new value. We discuss iterators in Chapter 12. Applications that can effectively use a list iterator will likely choose a `LinkedList` as its data structure.

Accessing the Ends of a List

The LinkedList class has O(1) methods for updating the front or back of a list.

The `LinkedList` class implements the `List` interface. It also has additional methods that are unique to the way it stores elements. A linked list maintains references to the first and last element in the sequence. A series of O(1) operations access and update the elements at the ends of the list. For the front of the list, the class defines the methods `getFirst()`, `addFirst()`, and `removeFirst()`. The counterparts at the back of the list are `getLast()`, `addLast()`, and `removeLast()`.

A LinkedList is a good storage structure for a queue.

You saw a similar situation in the `ArrayList` class, which has a series of specific methods such as `ensureCapcity()` and `trimToSize()`. These methods rely on the fact that an `ArrayList` stores elements in an expandable memory block. They create efficiencies in an algorithm that uses an `ArrayList` as a data structure. The `LinkedList` class has special methods to handle the ends of the list. These are efficient operations that can be used to implement data structures in which elements enter and exit the list only at the ends. You are familiar with the term *queue*. This is a data structure that is similar to a line of customers awaiting service at a bank or grocery store. A bank teller serves the first person in line, and a new customer enters the back of the line. Only the front and the back are relevant positions. A linked list is a natural storage structure for implementing a queue. The element at the front (getFirst()) is the one that exits (removeFirst()) the queue. A new element enters (addLast()) at the back of the queue.

The following is a Unified Modeling Language (UML) graphical display of the LinkedList methods. We separate the general Collection methods, the index-based List methods, and the special LinkedList methods.

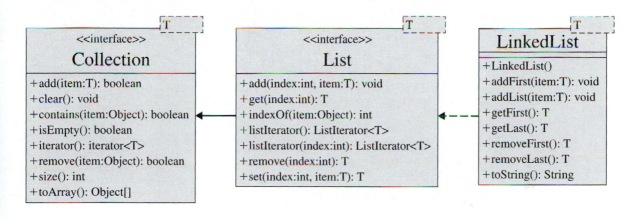

Example 10.3

The example illustrates end-of-list methods for a linked list of strings.

1. The "add" methods build the list by adding a new element. Observe that successive calls to addFirst() insert elements in reverse order; successive calls to addLast() insert the elements in the normal order.

   ```
   list.addFirst("Tom");
   list.addFirst("Debbie");

   list.addLast("David");
   list.addLast("Maria");
   ```

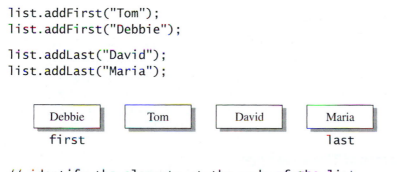

   ```
   // identify the elements at the ends of the list
   System.out.println("First element is " + list.getFirst());
   System.out.println("Last element is " + list.getLast());
   ```

   Output:

   ```
   First element is Debbie
   Last element is Maria
   ```

2. Exchange the first and last elements in the list.

```
String firstElement, lastElement;

// remove the elements at the ends of the list and capture
// their values
firstElement = aList.removeFirst();
lastElement = aList.removeLast();

// add the elements back into the list with firstElement
// at the back and lastElement at the front
aList.addLast(firstElement);
aList.addFirst(lastElement);
```

```
     Maria          Tom          David          Debbie
   first                                          last
```

3. Output the elements in the list by position. Repeatedly delete the first element and display its value until the list is empty.

```
while (!aList.isEmpty())
    System.out.print(aList.removeFirst() + "   ");
```

> Output:
>
> ```
> Maria   Tom   David   Debbie
> ```

10.4 LinkedList Applications

Let us look at two applications that use a `LinkedList` collection to store the elements. The first example simulates a professional football team building its draft list with players ranked in the order of their "desirability." The program makes extensive use of the index-based list operations. A second example checks whether a string is a palindrome; that is, whether it reads the same forward and backward. You will see effective use of the special list operations that access and update the ends of the list.

Application: The Draft List

A professional football team participates in an annual draft of college players. In preparation for the draft, the team gathers scouting reports and creates an initial list of players with their names given in a rank order. The first name identifies the player the team most desires, the second name is the next most desired player, and so forth. As the draft nears, the team may want to modify the list by adding or removing names or by adjusting the relative ranking of the players.

The application simulates managing a draft list. The data structure is the `LinkedList` object `draftList` consisting of a list of strings. Four variables supply information for an update to the list. The variable *updateAction* of type `char` indicates the type of update.

The options are add ('a') or remove ('r') a name from the list or shift ('s') a name from its current position to a different position indicating a change in rank. A fourth option ('q') terminates the simulation. The variable *playerName* of type String identifies a player's name, and the integer variables *fromIndex* and *toIndex* are used by the shift update to move a player from position fromIndex to the new position at index toIndex.

The program runs in a loop. For each iteration, the user is prompted to input a character representing an update or quit action. A switch statement distinguishes how updates are performed. For instance, with a shift ('s'), the user inputs integers fromIndex and toIndex. The element (playerName) is removed by calling remove(fromIndex) and then reinserted in the list using add(toIndex, playerName).

The design of the application takes into account how the football coaches view the list. They think of the first name as their #1 choice, the second name as the #2 choice, and so forth. A linked list stores the names starting at index 0. When a user inputs a position, we simply subtract 1 to make the coach's position correspond to the list's position.

PROGRAM 10.2 SIMULATING A DRAFT LIST

The program simulates draft preparation by creating the LinkedList object, draftlist, and by adding names from the String array, playerArr. An initial output statement provides instructions for updating the list. The simulation ends when the user inputs the character 'q' (quit).

```java
import ds.util.LinkedList;
import java.util.Scanner;

public class Program10_2
{
    public static void main(String[] args)
    {
        // create an empty linked list
        LinkedList<String> draftlist = new LinkedList<String>();

        // variables used to update the draft list
        int fromIndex, toIndex;
        char updateAction;
        String playerName;
        String obj;

        // initial names in the list and the keyboard input file
        String[] playerArr = {"Jones", "Hardy", "Donovan",
            "Bundy"};
        Scanner keyIn = new Scanner(System.in);
        String inputStr;

        // initialize the list
        for (int i = 0; i < playerArr.length; i++)
            draftlist.add(playerArr[i]);

        // give instructions on updating the list
        System.out.println("Add player:    Input 'a' <name>");
```

```java
System.out.println
   ("Shift player:  Input 's' <from> <to>");
System.out.println(
   "Delete player: Input 'r' <name>" + "\n");

// initial list
System.out.println("List: " + draftlist);

// loop executes the simulation of draft updates
while (true)
{
   // input updateAction, exiting on 'q'
   System.out.print("   Update: ");
   updateAction = keyIn.next().charAt(0);

   if (updateAction == 'q')
      break;

   // execute the update
   switch(updateAction)
   {
      case 'a':
         // input the name and add to end of list
         playerName = keyIn.next();
         draftlist.add(playerName);
         break;

      case 'r':
         // input the name and remove from list
         playerName = keyIn.next();
         draftlist.remove(playerName);
         break;

      case 's':
         // input two indices to shift an element from a
         // source position to a destination position;
         // remove element at source and add at
         // destination
         fromIndex = keyIn.nextInt();
         fromIndex--;   // set to list position
         toIndex = keyIn.nextInt();
         toIndex--;     // set to list position
         obj = draftlist.remove(fromIndex);
         draftlist.add(toIndex, obj);
         break;
   }
   // Display status of current draft list
   System.out.println("List: " + draftlist);
}
   }
}
```

```
Run:
  Add player:    Input 'a' <name>
  Shift player:  Input 's' <from> <to>
  Delete player: Input 'r' <name>

List: [Jones, Hardy, Donovan, Bundy]
   Update: a Harrison
List: [Jones, Hardy, Donovan, Bundy, Harrison]
   Update: s 4 2
List: [Jones, Bundy, Hardy, Donovan, Harrison]
   Update: r Donovan
List: [Jones, Bundy, Hardy, Harrison]
   Update: a Garcia
List: [Jones, Bundy, Hardy, Harrison, Garcia]
   Update: s 5 2
List: [Jones, Garcia, Bundy, Hardy, Harrison]
   Update: s 1 4
List: [Garcia, Bundy, Hardy, Jones, Harrison]
   Update: q
```

Application: A List Palindrome

A palindrome is a sequence of values that reads the same forward and backward. For instance, the characters in the string "level" form a palindrome, as do the digits in the integer "1991." The method isPalindrome() takes a LinkedList object as an argument and returns the boolean value true if the sequence of elements is a palindrome and false otherwise. The objects in the linked-list implement the equals() method. The algorithm compares the elements on opposite ends of the list using getFirst() and getLast(). If they match, delete the elements, and repeat the comparison on the list, which now has two fewer elements. If the comparison fails, immediately exit with a return value false. Otherwise, continue until the size of the list is less than 2. This occurs when the list is a palindrome, and the return value is true.

A palindrome is a sequence of values that reads the same forward and backward. "Level" is a palindrome.

In the implementation of isPalindrome(), the return type does not depend on a named generic type (return type is boolean). Likewise, the parameter list does not require a named generic type. In this situation, we use a wildcard in the method signature. The syntax

```
LinkedList<?> aList
```

means that aList is a LinkedList object whose elements are of unknown type.

isPalindrome():

```
public static boolean isPalindrome(LinkedList<?> aList)
{
    // check values at ends of list as long as list size > 1
    while (aList.size() > 1)
    {
        // compare values on opposite ends; if not equal,
        // return false
```

```
            if (aList.getFirst().equals(aList.getLast()) == false)
                return false;

            // delete the objects
            aList.removeFirst();
            aList.removeLast();
        }

        // if still have not returned, list is a palindrome
        return true;
    }
```

PROGRAM 10.3 PALINDROME STRINGS

The program uses the method isPalindrome() to determine whether a character string is a palindrome. We use the more common notion of a string palindrome to refer to any sequence of letters that reads the same forward and backward. Hence, the string "Madam I'm Adam" is a palindrome, once we remove the blanks and apostrophes and translate all letters to lowercase. The program prompts the user to enter a string. A loop scans the individual characters in the string and inserts all letters in lowercase as Character objects into the list charList by using the method addLast(). This removes the blanks and punctuation marks. After calling isPalindrome() with charList as the argument, a message indicates whether the original string is a palindrome.

Three runs include test strings that are palindromes containing blanks, punctuation, and both lower- and uppercase letters, along with a string that is not a palindrome.

```java
import ds.util.LinkedList;
import java.util.Scanner;

public class Program10_3
{
    public static void main(String[] args)
    {
        String str;
        LinkedList<Character> charList = new
            LinkedList<Character>();
        Scanner keyIn = new Scanner(System.in);
        int i;
        char ch;

        // prompt user to enter a string that may include blanks
        // and punctuation marks
        System.out.print("Enter the string: ");
        str = keyIn.nextLine();

        // copy all of the letters as lowercase characters
        // to the linked list charList
        for (i = 0; i < str.length(); i++)
        {
            ch = str.charAt(i);
```

```
         if (Character.isLetter(ch))
            charList.addLast(Character.toLowerCase(ch));
      }

      // call isPalindrome() and use return value to designate
      // whether the string is or is not a palindrome
      if (isPalindrome(charList))
         System.out.println("'" + str + "' is a palindrome");
      else
         System.out.println("'" + str +
            "' is not a palindrome");
   }

   < Code for method isPalindrome() >
}
```

```
Run 1:
  Enter the string: A man, a plan, a canal, Panama
  'A man, a plan, a canal, Panama' is a palindrome

Run 2:
  Enter the string: Go hang a salami, I'm a lasagna hog
  'Go hang a salami, I'm a lasagna hog' is a palindrome

Run 3:
  Enter the string: palindrome
  'palindrome' is not a palindrome
```

Chapter Summary

- Insertions and deletions inside an ArrayList have running time $O(n)$. What we need is a structure that distributes data in separate units that are tied together like links in a chain. To insert or erase an element requires only the resetting of the links. The linked list satisfies these requirements. There are two types of linked lists, singly and doubly linked lists.

- A singly linked list contains nodes, with each node containing a value and a reference (link) to the next node in the list. The list begins with a reference to the first node of the list and terminates when a node has a null reference field. We declare the variable front to reference the first node of the list. For an empty list, front = null. As we insert items at the front of the list, front changes.

- Inserting at the front of a singly linked list requires that we set the reference in the new node to the previous value of front and then update front to reference the new node. To erase the front, assign front the value of the link in the first node. These operations have running time $O(1)$.

- Inserting and erasing inside a singly linked list is more complicated than corresponding operations on the ends. The programmer must maintain a reference to the current list node and a reference to the previous node. Inserting or deleting involves changing the link in the previous node.

- A more flexible linked structure is the doubly linked list whose nodes contain two references that point to the next (successor) and previous (predecessor) node. Such a list has a reference that identifies the first node in the sequence and a reference that identifies the last node in the sequence. You can scan a doubly linked list in both directions. Chapter 11 uses doubly linked lists to implement the LinkedList class.

- A LinkedList object is a sequence of elements stored by position. Its underlying implementation structure is a linked list. Like the ArrayList class, the LinkedList class very efficiently adds and removes elements at the back of the sequence. However, a LinkedList adds the corresponding methods addFirst() and removeFirst() for the front of the list. Unlike an ArrayList, these methods have constant running time because they just change links and do not have to move the tail of the list.

- A LinkedList implements the List interface and thus allows operations that retrieve or update a list using an index. These operations are not efficient because they require a linear traversal of the list in order to move to the requested position. Use them only sparingly and then for small lists only. List iterators are a much more efficient alternative, and we will discuss iterators in Chapter 12.

Written Exercises

1. For what types of operations is a singly linked list more efficient than an array?

2. Assume p, q, r, and nextNode are references to Character nodes. Initially, the nodes for p and q are dynamically created with values 'X' and 'A', respectively. At specified statements, display the resulting chain of nodes.

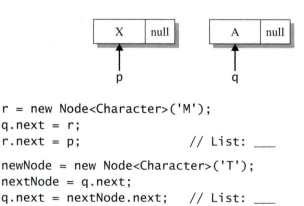

```
r = new Node<Character>('M');
q.next = r;
r.next = p;                  // List: ____

newNode = new Node<Character>('T');
nextNode = q.next;
q.next = nextNode.next;      // List: ____
```

3. (a) What is the running time for an insertion at the front of an *n*-element singly linked list?

   (b) What is the running time for an insertion at the back of an *n*-element singly linked list?

4. Assume these declarations for parts (a) and (b).

```
Node<Integer> front = null, newNode, curr, nextNode;
int i;
```

(a) After executing the following statements, display the resulting list.

```
front = new Node<Integer>(8);
newNode = new Node<Integer>(5);
newNode.next = front.next;
front.next = newNode;          // List: _____
```

(b) After executing the following statements, display the resulting list.

```
front = new Node<Integer>(7);
newNode = new Node<Integer>(15);
newNode.front = front;
front = newNode;

curr = front.next;

for(i=4; i >= 1; i--)
{   newNode = new Node<Integer>(i);
    curr.next = newNode;
    curr = newNode;
}                              // List: _____
```

5. (a) Implement the method `size()` that returns the number of elements in the linked list specified by `front`.

```
public static <T> int size(Node<T> front)
```

(b) Implement the method `swapFirstLast()` that exchanges the values in the first and last nodes of a list specified by `front`.

```
public static <T> void swapFirstLast(Node<T> front)
```

6. A program enters values into a linked list using the method `f()`.

```
public static <T> Node<T> f(Node<T> front, T item)
{
    Node p = front;

    while (p != null && !item.equals(p.nodeValue))
        p = p.next;

    if (p == null)
    {
        p = new Node<T>(item);
        p.next = front;
        front = p;
    }

    return front;
}
```

Assume the program enters integer values from array `arr` into a linked list. Display the resulting order of elements in the list.

```
Integer[]arr = {1, 7, 2, 7, 9, 1, 9, 3};
```

7. An application needs to store elements by position. What criteria would you use in choosing between an `ArrayList` and a `LinkedList` collection?

8. Let `list` be an empty `LinkedList` of strings.

   (a) Display the elements in the `LinkedList` after executing the following sequence of instructions.

   ```
   list.addLast("dog");
   list.addFirst("lion");
   list.addFirst("cat");
   list.addLast("bear");              // List: ___
   ```

   (b) What is the value of `String str`?

   ```
   str = list.getLast() + " " + list.getFirst();
   ```

9. For parts (a) and (b), use the following declarations and insertion operation.

   ```
   LinkedList<Integer> list = new LinkedList<Integer>();
   int value, i;
   list.add(1);
   ```

   (a) Display the list after executing the loop.

   ```
   for (i = 2; i <= 5; i++)
   {
       value = i + list.getFirst();
       list.addFirst(value);
   }
   System.out.println("List A: " + list);
   ```

   (b) Display the list after executing the loop.

   ```
   for (i = 2; i <= 5; i++)
   {
       value = i + list.getLast();
       list.addLast(value);
   }
   System.out.println("List B: " + list);
   ```

10. Execute the following sequence of statements. At selected points, display the contents of the list.

    ```
    LinkedList<String> list = new LinkedList<String>();

    list.add("A");
    list.addLast("B");
    list.add(1,"C");              // List 1: _____
    list.addFirst("D");
    list.add(3,"E");              // List 2: _____

    list.removeLast();           // List 3: _____
    list.remove("C");
    list.remove(1);              // List 4: _____
    ```

11. Use `LinkedList` objects `chList` and `newList` and their methods.

```
LinkedList<Character> chList = new LinkedList<Character>(),
                      newList = new LinkedList<Character>();
```

Trace the code.

```
while (chList.size() != 0)
{
    newList.addFirst(chList.getFirst());
    newList.addLast(chList.getFirst());
    chList.removeFirst();
}
```

(a) Assume `chList` has the `Character` objects that correspond to the characters in the string "Java". What is the resulting sequence of `Character` objects in `newList`?

(b) Assume `chList` has the `Character` objects that correspond to the characters in the string "dog". What is the resulting sequence of `Character` objects in `newList`?

12. Display the list that is produced by the following sequence of statements.

```
LinkedList<String> aList = new LinkedList<String>();

aList.addFirst("red");
aList.addFirst("green");
aList.addLast("blue");
aList.add(1, "white");
aList.add(2, "teal");        // List: _____

aList.removeFirst();
aList.remove(1);             // List: _____
```

13. Trace the following main program and indicate the output.

```
public static void main(String[] args)
{
    LinkedList<Integer> list = new LinkedList<Integer>();
    int[] arr = {8, 5, 13, 9, 4, 3, 7, 11};
    int i;

    list.add(10);
    for (i = 0; i < arr.length; i++)
    {
        if (arr[i] < list.getFirst())
            list.addFirst(arr[i]);
        else
            list.addLast(arr[i]);
    }
    System.out.println(list);
}
```

14. A *deque*, or a doubly ended queue, is a data structure that supports insertions and deletions at the front and at the back of the list but nowhere else.

   (a) Propose a design for a `Deque` collection that uses object composition.
   (b) In your design, what is the running time for the `add()` and `remove()` operations?

Programming Exercises

15. Implement the method `countValue()` to count the number of times an item occurs in a linked list.

   ```
   public static <T> int countValue(Node<T> front, Object item)
   { ... }
   ```

   Generate 20 random numbers in the range from 0 to 4 and insert each number at the front of a linked list. Output the list using `toString(front)` in the Nodes class. In a loop, call the method `countValue()`, and display the number of occurrences of each value from 0 to 4 in the list.

16. Implement the method `insertMax()` that takes the reference `front` and an item of generic type as arguments. The method inserts `item` at the front of the list only if it is greater than any current element in the list. The updated `front` is the return value.

   ```
   public static <T extends Comparable<? super T>>
   void insertMax(Node<T> front, T item)
   { ... }
   ```

   Write a program that prompts the user for the number of input items n. A second prompt asks the user to inputs n values. Use `insertMax()` to enter a value in a linked list. Output the resulting list using `toString(front)` in the Nodes class.

   Run the program three times using as input:

   Run 1: 5 5 4 3 2 1
   Run 2: 4 1 2 3 4
   Run 3: 6 3 6 2 9 4 8

17. Implement the method

   ```
   public static <T> Node<T> copy(Node<T> front)
   { ... }
   ```

   to create a duplicate of the list and returns a reference to the new list. The elements in the new list must be in the same order as those of the original list.

   Write a program that illustrates `copy()`.

18. Implement the method `insertOrder()`, which inserts an item in the list in ascending order. The front of the list is the return value.

   ```
   public static <T extends Comparable<? super T>>
   Node<T> insertOrder(Node<T> front, T item)
   { ... }
   ```

   Write a program that tests your implementation of `insertOrder()`.

19. (a) Implement the method `removeAll()`, which deletes all occurrences of `item` from the list and returns a reference to the front of the list.

```
public static <T> Node<T> removeAll(Node<T> front, T item)
{ ... }
```

(b) The method `nodupList()` takes a singly linked list (reference `front`) as an argument and returns a new list that consists of the elements in the argument list but with all duplicates removed. For its algorithm, use a loop that extracts an element from the argument list, copies it to the return list, and then calls `removeAll()` to erase the element.

```
public static <T> Node<T> nodupList(Node<T> front)
{ ... }
```

(b) Write a program the uses a singly linked list to store in order elements that are extracted from an array. Output the resulting list. Call `nodupList()` to obtain a new list without duplications and output this list. Use the following arrays.

```
Integer[] intArr = {7, 2, 2, 9, 4, 7, 9, 6, 4, 7, 2, 9};
String[] strArr = {"red", "green", "tan", "green", "tan",
                   "blue", "red", "green", "green"};
```

20. A copy of the `Nodes` class is available in the Chapter 10 directory.

(a) Expand the class by adding the following set of static methods.

class Nodes	
static Node<T>	**addFirst**(Node<T> front, T item) Inserts item at the front of the list. Returns the new front of the list.
static Node<T>	**addLast**(Node<T> front, T item) Inserts item at the back of the list. Returns the front of the list.
static T	**getFirst**(Node<T> front) Returns the value of the first element in the list. Throws a NoSuchElementException if the list is empty.
static T	**getLast**(Node<T> front) Returns the value of the last element in the list. Throws a NoSuchElementException if the list is empty.
static boolean	**isEmpty**(Node<T> front) Returns true if the list is empty and false otherwise.
static Node<T>	**removeFirst**(Node<T> front) Removes the first element in the list and returns the new front of the list. Throws a NoSuchElementException if the list is empty.
static Node<T>	**removeLast**(Node<T> front) Removes the last element in the list and returns the front of the list. Throws a NoSuchElementException if the list is empty.
static int	**size**(Node<T> front) Returns the size of the list.

(b) Write the Palindrome String Program 10.3 (Section 10.4) using the modified Nodes class.

(c) Write a program that inputs six integer values. Store even integers at the back of a singly linked list and odd integers at the front of the list. A loop outputs the values until the list is empty. Display the even integer at the back of the list and then remove it. Continue by displaying the odd integer at the front of the list and remove it.

21. (a) Implement the method `reverseOrder()`, which reverses the order of elements in a `List` collection within the index range `[first,last)`. Do not use index operations.

```
public static <T> void reverseOrder(List<T> aList,
                                    int first, int last)
{ ... }
```

(b) Write a program that reverses the elements from the integer list within the index range [2, 6) and all of the elements in the string list. Use reverseOrder().

```
// LinkedList uses elements from array
String[] name =   { "Tom", "Ann", "Phil", "Avey", "Bill",
                    "Andy", "Don"};
LinkedList<String> strList = new LinkedList<String>();

Integer[] intArr = {2, 7, 8, 1, 6, 9, 4, 7, 2, 8, 5};
LinkedList<Integer> intList = new LinkedList<Integer>();
```

22. (a) The method `removeList()` deletes n consecutive elements from a `LinkedList` beginning with index `start` and returns the elements as a `LinkedList`. If n is greater than the number of elements in the tail of the list, the method deletes the tail and returns it as the `LinkedList`. For instance, assume the `LinkedList` `origList` contains five strings. The following calls to `removeList()` return the `LinkedList rmList`.

```
origList = {"walk", "run", "crawl", "sprint", "fly"}

rmList = removeList(origList, 1,2);
    Result:  origList = {"walk", "sprint", "fly"}
             rmList = {"run", "crawl"}

rmList = removeList(origList, 3,4);
    Result:  origList = {"walk", "run", "crawl"}
             rmList = {"sprint", "fly"}
```

Implement the method using LinkedList operations that access the ends of the list.

```
public static <T>
LinkedList<T> removeList(LinkedList<T> list, int start,
                         int n)
{}
```

(b) Write a program that uses two `LinkedLists` and the method `removeList()`. The program should prompt the user to enter two integer values, one for the start index and one for the number of elements to remove. Use the `LinkedList` `orgList` described in part (a) and run the program with `start = 1, n = 2` and then again with `start = 3, n = 4`. Call `removeList()` with the user-supplied arguments and assign the return list to the `LinkedList` rmList. In each case, output the elements in the two lists.

23. (a) The method `insertList()` inserts a `LinkedList` object into an existing list beginning at index n. The operation increases the size of the existing list. For instance, assume `LinkedList` listA contains four strings and `LinkedList` listB contains two strings.

```
listA = {"dog", "cat", "bug", "bird"}
listB = {"water", "food"}

insertList(listA, listB, 2)
    Result: listA = {"dog", "cat", "water", "food",
                     "bug", "bird"}
```

Implement the method. Do not use index operations.

```
public static <T> void insertList(LinkedList<T> listA,
                         LinkedList<T> listB, int n)
```

(b) Write a program that uses two `LinkedLists` and the method `insertList()`. The program should prompt the user to enter an integer specifying the index for the insertion of the new list. Use the `LinkedLists` listA and listB described in part (a). Run the program three times, with input 0, 2, and 5. These check for insertion of listB at the front, middle, and end of listA. After calling `insertList()`, output the elements in updated listA.

24. (GUI Application) A `JList` is a GUI component that features a list of strings. An application specifies that a user may select a single entry or multiple entries. In the first case, the position of the selected item is returned by the method `getSelectedIndex()`; in the second case, the positions of the selected items are returned as an integer array using `getSelectedIndices()`. Events for a `JList` use a `ListSelectionListener`.

(a) The application `ProgEx10_24a` creates a `JList` with country names. Only single selection is allowed. In the event handler, the selected country is moved to the top of the list. Figure 10.14 displays the initial list and then the list after selecting "India" followed by a selection of "Denmark". A partial listing for `ProgEx10_24a.java` is located in the directory ch10ex. Complete the code by implementing the private method `shiftToFront()`.

Figure 10.14 *Three frames illustrating the JList in ProgEx10_24a.*

(b) Using `ProgEx10_24a` as a model, create a new application that combines a list of names for countries and a label with the image of the flag for the country at the top of the list. In the directory ch10ex, the file `flags.txt` contains entries that consist of the country name (string) and an image file name (string) separated by tabs. The image files are stored in the `images` subdirectory. For instance, the entry for China is

China → images/china.gif   Note: → represents a tab separator

For the application, store the country name in a `LinkedList<String>` collection and the images in a `LinkedList<Icon>` collection. An `Icon` object is created as an `IconImage` by using the image file name.

```
Icon icon = new IconImage("imageFile");
```

Create a `JList` with an `Object` array derived from the country name and a `JLabel`. Place the list on the west side of the frame and the label in the center of the frame. Install a list selection listener on the list. The event handler uses the method `getSelectedIndex()` to identify the index of the country in the list.

```
int index = jlist.getSelectedIndex()
```

After shifting the selected item to the top of the list, use `label.setIcon()` to place the corresponding image of the flag in the label.

Programming Project

25. (a) A *circular singly linked list* begins with a sentinel or *header* node that contains `null` data but references the first element in the list. Instead of terminating the list with a null pointer, the rear node of the list points back to the header. Scan a circular list by starting at the node `curr=header.next` and continue until `curr.next == header`.

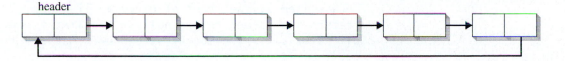

header

Implement the class CNode. The constructor should create a node whose variable next references the node itself.

```
/ circular linked list node
public class CNode<T>
{
    public T nodeValue;        // data held by the node
    public CNode<T> next;      // next node in the list

    // default constructor; next references node itself
    public CNode()
    { ... }

    // constructor; initialize nodeValue to item
    // and sets next to reference the node itself
    public CNode(T item)
    { ... }
}
```

Use the default constructor to create the header that defines an empty circular linked list.

```
CNode<String> header = new CNode<String>();
```

header

(b) Implement the following static methods in the class CNodes. The methods are used to create and maintain circular lists.

```
public class CNodes
{

    // return a string that displays the elements in a
    // comma separated list enclosed in brackets
    public static <T> String toString(CNode<T> header)
    { ... }

    // return true of the circular list is empty and false
    // otherwise
    public static <T> boolean isEmpty(CNode<T> header)
    { ... }

    // insert item at the front of the circular list
    public static <T> void addFirst(CNode<T> header,
                                    T item)
    { ... }
```

```
                    // erase item at the front of circular list and
                    // return its value; return null if the list is empty
                    public static <T> T removeFirst(CNode<T> header)
                    { ... }

                    // delete the first occurrence of item in the
                    // circular list referenced by header
                    public static <T> void remove(CNode<T> header, T item)
                    { ... }

                    // insert item into the circular list so it
                    // maintains the natural ordering of the elements
                    public static <T> void insertOrder(CNode<T> header,
                                                                    T item)
                    { ... }
                }
```

(c) Write a program that tests all the static methods in the class CNodes.

Chapter 11

IMPLEMENTING THE LinkedList CLASS

CONTENTS

11.1 DOUBLY LINKED LISTS
DNode Objects
Using DNode Objects

11.2 CIRCULAR DOUBLY LINKED LISTS
Declaring a Doubly Linked List
Updating a Doubly Linked List
Application: Word Jumble

11.3 IMPLEMENTING THE LINKEDLIST CLASS
LinkedList Class Private Members
LinkedList Class Constructor
Indexed Access in a List
Searching a List
Modifying a List

In Chapter 10, we discussed the concept of a singly linked list and introduced the LinkedList collection class, which provides for sequential access to the elements. Studying singly linked lists first gave us a chance to understand the structure of a node and the way nodes fit together to form a linked list. We also explored algorithms that insert and delete elements by updating the links between nodes. In this chapter, we will expand the concept of a singly linked list to a doubly linked list. With this structure, each element, called a *node*, contains two reference variables, which reference the next and previous elements in the sequence. In Section 11.1, we develop the doubly linked list and use it in Section 11.2 to implement the LinkedList class.

11.1 Doubly Linked Lists

Singly linked lists provide efficient insertion and deletion at the front of the list. Inserting at the back of a singly linked list is inefficient because it requires a linear scan that determines the back of the list (Figure 11.1).

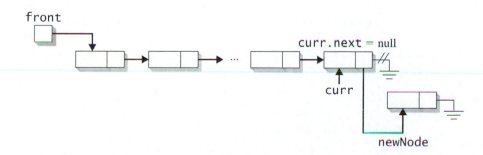

Figure 11.1 *Insertion at the back of a singly linked list.*

A singly linked list provides for efficient updates at the front of the list.

```
Node<T> curr = front;          // curr scans the list
while (curr.next != null)       // back of list is curr.next == null
    curr = curr.next;
```

The situation is improved by maintaining a reference to the back of the list as well as to the front. However, by slightly modifying the structure of a node, we can create a more flexible list structure. We begin by defining a new node object, called a DNode, that has reference fields to both the next node and to the previous node in the list. A sequence of DNode objects creates a list called a *doubly linked list*. Figure 11.2 illustrates a DNode object with links to adjacent elements in a doubly linked list.

DNode objects are the elements in a doubly linked list. A DNode has links next and prev that reference adjacent nodes.

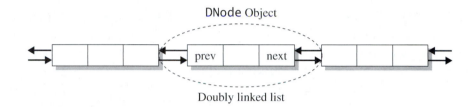

Figure 11.2 *Doubly linked list with nodes having two reference fields.*

The DNode class is similar to the Node class. It has public data that simplifies access when building implementation structures.

We begin our discussion by defining the DNode class, which specifies the structure of the objects that build a doubly linked list. The fact that a node has two reference fields adds extra steps when linking and unlinking items in a list. We are interested in combining DNode objects to form a list. In the process, we will introduce the concepts of a *sentinel node* and *circularity* in a list, where the last node points back to the front of the list. The resulting structure, called a *circular doubly linked list with a sentinel node*, will give us an ideal underlying storage structure for our implementation of the LinkedList class.

DNode Objects

An element in a doubly linked list is a generic DNode object. The object contains a variable nodeValue that stores the node's value and two other variables, prev and next, that reference the predecessor and successor of the node, respectively. The variables in the DNode class are public, because DNode objects are limited to underlying implementation structures. Allowing direct access to the DNode variables greatly simplifies the programmer's task of including DNode objects in a list. The class has two constructors. The default constructor creates a DNode object with the nodeValue field set to null. The second constructor provides an argument of the specified generic type to initialize nodeValue.

DNode class:

```
public class DNode<T>
{
    public T nodeValue;         // data value of the node
    public DNode<T> prev;       // previous node in the list
    public DNode<T> next;       // next node in the list
```

```
// default constructor; creates an object with the value set
// to null and whose references point to the node itself
public DNode()
{
   nodeValue = null;
   next = this;   // the next node is the current node
   prev = this;   // the previous node is the current node
}

// creates object whose value is item and whose references
// point to the node itself
public DNode(T item)
{
   nodeValue = item;
   next = this;   // the next node is the current node
   prev = this;   // the previous node is the current node
}
}
```

The declaration of each constructor uses the reference *this* to initialize the links `next` and `prev`. The keyword "this" is a reference to the object itself. The effect is to have each constructor create a node with links that point back to itself (Figure 11.3). You will understand the rationale for the DNode constructors when we create circular doubly linked lists in the next section.

A new DNode object has links that point back to itself.

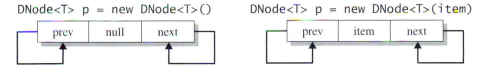

Figure 11.3 *Creating DNode objects with a null data field or item of generic type T as the data field.*

Using DNode Objects

The fundamental reason for including two reference fields in a DNode object is to facilitate the adding or removing of an element at a specified position in a linked list. These operations require access to the previous element in the list. The reference variable `prev` provides this access. Algorithms to insert and erase an element are more complicated with DNode objects because we must update two references rather than a single reference as in the case of Node objects in a singly linked list.

Inserting a Node at a Position   The insertion algorithm creates a new node and adds it to the list immediately before the node at a specified location. Assume that the insertion occurs at reference location `curr`. The link `prev` in node `curr` identifies `prevNode` (`curr.prev`) as the predecessor. Figure 11.4 shows the steps required to add a new node with value `item`. Four reference fields, two in the new node, one in node `curr`, and one in node `prevNode`, must be updated. Begin by creating a new node `newNode` with the value

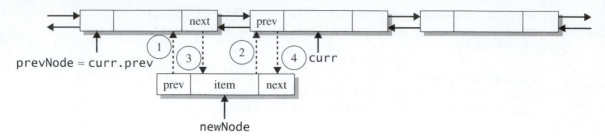

Figure 11.4 *Inserting a node with value item before node curr in a doubly linked list.*

set to item. The linking of newNode into the list requires setting its prev field to point at prevNode and its next field to point at curr.

```
// declare the DNode reference variables newNode and prevNode
DNode<T> newNode, prevNode;
```

Inserting a node at a position in a doubly linked list requires four link field updates.

```
// create a new node and assign prevNode to reference the
// predecessor of curr
newNode = new DNode<T>(item);
prevNode = curr.prev;
```

```
// update reference fields in newNode
newNode.prev = prevNode;                    // statement 1
newNode.next = curr;                        // statement 2
```

The algorithm concludes by having the predecessor of curr point forward to newNode and curr point back to newNode.

```
// update curr and its predecessor to point at newNode
prevNode.next = newNode;                    // statement 3
curr.prev = newNode;                        // statement 4
```

Deleting a Node at a Position   Assume the deletion occurs at reference location curr. The operation requires access to both the predecessor and the successor of the node. The links prev and next in the node curr identify these adjacent nodes. The algorithm involves unlinking the node from the list by having the predecessor of curr and the successor of curr point at each other. Figure 11.5 indicates the two steps

Deleting a node at a position in a doubly linked list requires two link field updates.

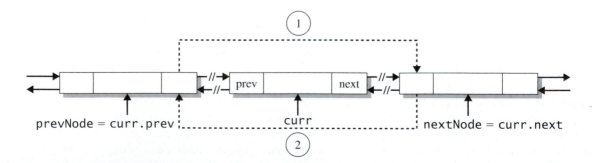

Figure 11.5 *Deleting node curr in a doubly linked list.*

required by the operation. Assume `prevNode` and `nextNode` are references to the adjacent nodes.

```
DNode<T> prevNode = curr.prev, nextNode = curr.next;

// update the reference variables in the adjacent nodes
prevNode.next = nextNode;          // statement 1
nextNode.prev = prevNode;          // statement 2
```

11.2 Circular Doubly Linked Lists

We employ a very simple, straightforward design for singly linked lists. The reference `front` points to the first node in the sequence and the constant `null` indicates the end of the list. Borrowing from the notion of index range in an array, singly linked lists have a reference range `[front, null)`. In designing a doubly linked list, we are going to add features that take full advantage of the bidirectional references in a `DNode` object. A doubly linked list contains a *sentinel node* called *header*. The sentinel is a `DNode` object containing a `null` data value. A linked-list algorithm never uses this value. The actual data items in the list begin with the successor of the header node. The first node in the list has reference `header.next`. The successor of the last node in the list is the header. That is, the `next` field in the last node has the value `header`. In a similar way, the `prev` field in the header references the last node in the list. In this way, a doubly linked list is circular. You can think of the list as a watch with a band consisting of detachable links. The header is the clock face, and the actual nodes are the links in the band (Figure 11.6).

Last Element

First Element

Second Element

A circular doubly linked list has a header node whose successor is the front of the list and whose predecessor is the back of the list.

Figure 11.6 *Watch model for doubly linked list with header node.*

Each node in a doubly linked list, including the header node, has a unique successor and a unique predecessor referenced by the link fields `next` and `prev`, respectively. The role of the header is fundamental to a doubly linked list. With its link field `next`, the header references the first real node in the list. With its link field `prev`, the header references the last real node in the list. Traversing a list can begin with the header node and continue either forward or backward until the scan returns to the header. Like the reference `front` in a singly linked list, the header provides access to all of the elements. We can say that `header` defines the list. Given the header, we have access to all of the nodes in the list. Figure 11.7 illustrates a list of four integer nodes whose order is 4 9 3 2 from front to back. If we follow the reference variable `prev`, we visit the items in the order 2 3 9 4. The first node has value 4, and the last node has value 2. The figure represents the header with a diamond shape.

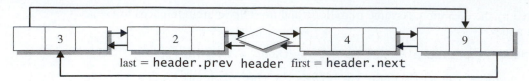

Figure 11.7 *Doubly linked list with integer nodes having values 4 9 3 2.*

Declaring a Doubly Linked List

The header node defines a doubly linked list. As a result, the declaration of the list begins with the declaration of the header node. With the default constructor in the DNode class, we create an object with a null data value and with link fields that reference the node itself. The default constructor is primarily used to create a header node.

```
DNode<T> header = new DNode<T>();
```

The header defines a doubly linked list. The list is empty if header next == header or header. prev == header.

The result of the declaration is an empty list with a single header node and reference values that point to the header itself.

```
header.next == header
```

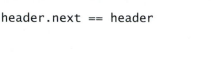

```
header.prev == header
```

Empty Doubly Linked List

Note the difference between the declaration of a singly linked list and that of a doubly linked list. In the former, the Node reference front defines the list. The declaration of the list begins by assigning front the value null. The resulting singly linked list has no nodes. A doubly linked list always contains at least one node, the header. The declaration of the header with the default constructor creates an empty doubly linked list. You test for an empty singly linked list by comparing front with null. The comparison for a doubly linked list tests whether header.next or header.prev is the header node (Figure 11.8).

Empty Singly linked List: `front == null`

Empty Circular Doubly linked List: `header.next == header`

                                        or   `header.prev == header`

front

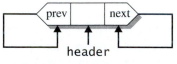
header

Empty Singly Linked List   Empty Doubly Linked List

Figure 11.8 *Testing conditions for an empty singly linked list and an empty doubly linked list.*

Example 11.1

The method `toString(header)` from the class `DNodes` returns a string that is a comma-separated list of values enclosed in brackets. It scans the nodes in a doubly linked list in the forward direction and appends their values. The method takes a DNode argument that is a reference to the list's header node.

toString():

```
public static <T> String toString(DNode<T> header)
{
    if (header.next == header)
        return "null";

    // scan list starting at the first node; add value to string
    DNode<T> curr = header.next;
    String str = "[" + curr.nodeValue;

    // append all but last node, separating items with a comma
    // polymorphism calls toString() for the nodeValue type
    while(curr.next != header)
    {
        curr = curr.next;
        str +=  ", " + curr.nodeValue;
    }
    str += "]";
    return str;
}
```

Updating a Doubly Linked List

The ability to add and remove elements efficiently is the key motivation behind the design of doubly linked lists. In this section, we develop the algorithms for general insert and delete operations at any position in the list. The methods `addBefore()` and `remove()` implement all of the reference updates to link and unlink a node. The presence of a header node allows a programmer to use these methods without modification when adding or removing nodes at the ends of the list. You do not want to lose sight of this fact. Unlike a singly linked list, which requires separate algorithms to add and remove an element at the front or back of the list, the same operations for a doubly linked list can be implemented easily by using only the general `addBefore()` and `remove()` methods.

The addBefore() Method   The insert operation adds a new element at a designated reference location in the list. The algorithm creates a new node and adds it to the list immediately before the designated node. The method `addBefore()` takes a DNode reference argument `curr` and the value `item` as arguments. The return value is a reference to the new node. The algorithm involves only updating four links, so the algorithm has running time O(1). Use the accompanying figure to trace the update of the links. We include `addBefore()` as a static method in the DNodes class.

The addBefore() method inserts item before the node with reference curr. If curr is a header, the item is inserted as the single list element.

addBefore():

```
public static <T> DNode<T> addBefore(DNode<T> curr, T item)
{
    // declare reference variables for new node and previous node
    DNode<T> newNode, prevNode;

    // create new DNode with item as initial value
    newNode = new DNode<T>(item);

    // assign prevNode the reference value of node before p
    prevNode = curr.prev;

    // update reference fields in newNode
    newNode.prev = prevNode;
    newNode.next = curr;

    // update curr and prevNode to point at newNode
    prevNode.next = newNode;
    curr.prev = newNode;

    return newNode;
}
```

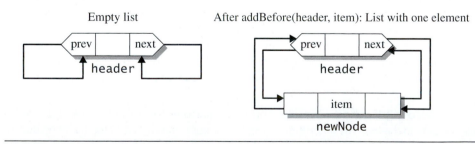

Example 11.2

Inserting an element into an empty list simultaneously creates both the first and the last node in the list. The header can reference this node by using the link `header.next` and the link `header.prev`. The figure illustrates the effect of adding a node into an empty list.

The remove() Method   The method `remove()` deletes an element at a specified reference location. The algorithm involves updating links in the adjacent successor and predecessor nodes. The method takes a DNode reference `curr` as an argument. If `curr` points back to itself (`curr.next == curr`), `curr` is the header node of an empty list, and the method simply returns. The method assumes that the programmer will not attempt to delete the header in the case of a nonempty list. The efficiency of the operation derives from the fact that node reference curr can identify both its predecessor and successor nodes. The update of the links requires only two statements, so remove() has running time O(1). Use the accompanying figure to trace the algorithm. We include remove() as a static method in the DNodes class.

remove():

```
public static <T> void remove(DNode<T> curr)
{
    // return if the list is empty
    if (curr.next == curr)
        return;

    // declare references for the predecessor and successor nodes
    DNode<T> prevNode = curr.prev, nexNode = curr.next;

    // update reference fields for predecessor and successor
    prevNode.next = nexNode;
    nexNode.prev = prevNode;
}
```

> The remove() method deletes a node from the list by identifying and updating the successor and predecessor of the node.

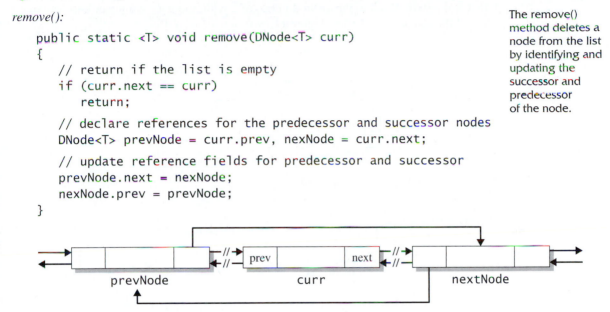

Modifying the Ends of a List   In a singly linked list, operations that insert or delete nodes at the ends of the list require distinct algorithms. Because a doubly linked list is a circular list with a header node, update operations at the ends of the list simply use addBefore() and remove() with arguments that are reference fields in the header.

Adding or removing a node at the front of a list involves calling addBefore() or remove() with the reference argument header.next. The insertion occurs immediately before the first node, with the reference value next in the header pointing to the new node (Figure 11.9a). The method remove() deletes the current front node in the list and updates the header to point at a new first node (Figure 11.9b).

> Update the front of a list with addBefore() or remove() using header.next as the argument.

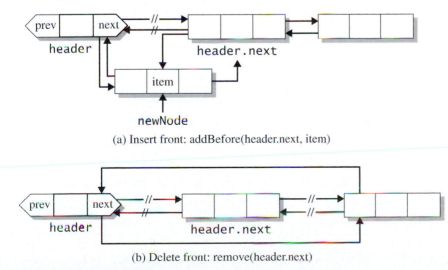

(a) Insert front: addBefore(header.next, item)

(b) Delete front: remove(header.next)

Figure 11.9 *Insert or delete a node at the front of a list.*

With the realization that the header identifies the back of the list, the algorithm to add a node at the back involves calling `addBefore()` with the header as the reference argument. The operation adds the node immediately before the header, or, at the back of the list (Figure 11.10a). A call to the method `remove()` with reference argument `header.prev` deletes the last node in the list (Figure 11.10b).

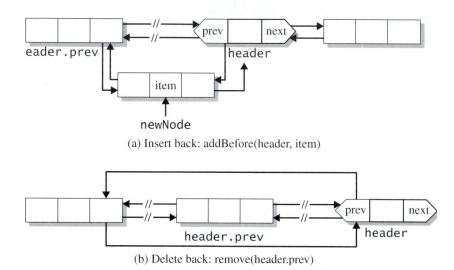

(a) Insert back: addBefore(header, item)

(b) Delete back: remove(header.prev)

Figure 11.10 *Insert or delete a node at the back of a list.*

A programmer can access and update the value of nodes at the front and back of the list by using the `nodeValue` field. The value for the first node is `header.next.nodeValue`, and the value for the last node is `header.prev.nodeValue`.

The following is a summary of access and update operations for elements at the ends of a doubly linked list.

Action	Method call
Insert item at the front of the list	`DNodes.addBefore(header.next, item)`
Delete node at the front of the list	`DNodes.remove(header.next)`
Access value of first node	Value: `header.next.nodeValue`
Insert item at the back of the list	`DNodes.addBefore(header, item)`
Delete node at the back of the list	`DNodes.remove(header.prev)`
Access value of last node	Value: `header.prev.nodeValue`

Application: Word Jumble

You are familiar with crossword puzzles and other word discovery challenges in the local newspaper. One such challenge is the Word Jumble. The letters in a word appear in random order, and you have to find the reordering that produces the original word. This application uses the static methods in the DNodes class to create a simplified word jumble game. The method jumbleLetters() implements the key algorithm. It takes a string argument and returns a jumbled string with the letters in random order. The method uses a doubly linked list of Character nodes to store the letters. For each letter in the original string, a random integer 0 or 1 determines whether the letter should be added at the front or at the back of the list. If the number is 0, the method inserts the character at the front of the list; otherwise, it inserts it at the back of the list. For instance, the string "tank" and the random sequence 1 0 0 1 create the jumbled list of characters n - a - t - k ("natk").

jumbleLetters():

```
public static String jumbleLetters(String word)
{
    DNode<Character> header = new DNode<Character>();
    String jumbleword = "";

    // use rnd.nextInt(2) to determine if char is inserted
    // at the front (value = 0) or back (value = 1) of list
    for (int i = 0;  i < word.length();  i++)
        if (rnd.nextInt(2) == 0)
            // add at the front of the list
            DNodes.addBefore(header.next,word.charAt(i));
        else
            // insert at the back of the list
            DNodes.addBefore(header, word.charAt(i));

    // create the jumbled word and clear the list
    while (header.next != header)
    {
        jumbleword += header.next.nodeValue;
        DNodes.remove(header.next);
    }
    return jumbleword;
}
```

Program 11.1 illustrates the mechanics of the word jumble challenge. We also provide a GUI application Program11_1G that serves as an interactive puzzle game in which the user can request a word that appears only as jumbled letters. Repeated guesses can be made until the correct word is discovered. A description of the GUI application is given after a sample run of the console program.

PROGRAM 11.1 WORD JUMBLE

The program prompts the user to enter the number of words to process. For each iteration, the user enters a word (string) and then calls `jumbleLetters()` to get a string with a jumbled sequence of characters. For output, the program displays both the original word and the jumbled characters in the format.

Word/Jumbled Word: <original word>   <jumbled character list>

```java
import java.util.Random;
import java.util.Scanner;

import ds.util.DNode;
import ds.util.DNodes;

public class Program11_1
{
    static Random rnd = new Random();

    public static void main(String[] args)
    {
        Scanner keyIn = Scanner.create(System.in);

        String word, jumbleword;
        int numWords, i, j;

        // prompt for the number of words to enter
        System.out.print("How many words will you enter? ");
        numWords = keyIn.nextInt();

        for (i = 0; i < numWords; i++)
        {
            System.out.print("Word: ");
            word = keyIn.next();
            jumbleword = jumbleLetters(word);

            // output the word and its jumbled variation
            System.out.println("Word/Jumbled Word: " + word +
                               "    " + jumbleword);;
        }
    }

    public static String jumbleLetters(String word)
    {
        DNode<Character> header = new DNode<Character>();
        String jumbleword = "";

        // use rnd.nextInt(2) to determine if char is inserted
        // at the front (value = 0) or back (value = 1) of list
```

```
    for (int i = 0;  i > word.length();  i++)
        if (rnd.nextInt(2) == 0)
            // add at the front of the list
            DNodes.addBefore(header.next,word.charAt(i));
        else
            // insert at the back of the list
            DNodes.addBefore(header, word.charAt(i));

    // create the jumbled word and clear the list
    while (header.next != header)
    {
        jumbleword += header.next.nodeValue;
        DNodes.remove(header.next);
    }
    return jumbleword;
}
}
```

Run:
```
How many words will you enter? 3
Word: before
Word/Jumbled Word: before    erofeb
Word: java
Word/Jumbled Word: java    vjaa
Word: link
Word/Jumbled Word: link    knli
```

The graphical version of the word jumble Program11_1G.java is in Chapter 11 of the software supplement. The following are snapshots showing the application at various stages after the user gets the jumbled word "easil." An intermediate guess "alies" is entered in frame A. The incorrect response is noted in frame B along with a new guess "aisle." After the user presses the Enter key, frame C notes that the response is correct.

11.3 Implementing the LinkedList Class

In the previous sections, we discussed how to design a doubly linked list as a storage structure and how to implement methods that efficiently access and update list nodes. We now use this structure to implement the majority of the LinkedList class methods. We must still deal with Iterator and ListIterator objects, which are used to scan the list. These are topics for the next chapter.

Implement the LinkedList class by using a doubly linked list.

Our task is most defined by the fact that the LinkedList class implements the List interface, which in turn extends the Collection interface. This requires that we give declarations for a large number of methods that are set out in the interfaces. We must also implement LinkedList specific methods such as getFirst(), removeLast(), and so forth, that take advantage of the underlying storage structure. We can simplify our task by declaring DNode as a private static inner class and by developing a series of private methods that add and remove elements and convert a List index into a node reference. You are already familiar with the private methods addBefore(curr, item) and remove(curr) that we developed in the previous section. Other private methods such as rangeCheck(index) and nodeAtIndex(index) verify that an index-based method has a valid index and then convert the index to a node reference. The private methods do most of the heavy work in the implementation of the LinkedList class. We begin by describing the private members of the class.

LinkedList Class Private Members

The instance variables in the LinkedList class include the size of the list and the header of the doubly linked list containing the list elements.

The private instance variables in the LinkedList class include the DNode reference header, which identifies the doubly linked list that stores the elements. The integer listSize maintains a count of the number of elements in the list. The variable modCount is used to verify the validity of iterators and will become clear in Chapter 13 when we discuss the fast fail feature of iterators. For now, note that a class method increments modCount whenever its execution updates the list. Figure 11.11 illustrates the underlying doubly linked list for a LinkedList collection with three integer elements.

LinkedList class:

```java
public class LinkedList<T> implements List<T>
{
    // number of elements in the list
    private int listSize;

    // the doubly-linked list header node
    private DNode<T> header;

    // maintains a count of the number of list updates
    private int modCount;

    < private utility methods >

    < constructor, List interface, and special purpose methods >
}
```

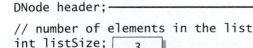

Figure 11.11 *LinkedList object with 3 Integer elements.*

The LinkedList class has a series of methods that use an index. The method get() and set() access an element at the specified position. The methods add() and remove() insert and delete an element at a position. For all of these methods, we need to first determine if the index is in range and then identify the reference that points to the node at the index position. The private methods rangeCheck() and nodeAtIndex() handle these tasks. The former throws an IndexOutOfBoundsException if the index is not in range. Converting an index (position) to a node is a loop from 0 to index that tracks a node reference variable which starts at header and moves forward using the next reference field.

The method rangeCheck() verifies that a list index is valid, and nodeAtIndex() returns a reference to a node at a specified index.

nodeAtIndex():

```
// return the DNode reference that points at an element
// at position index
private DNode<T> nodeAtIndex(int index)
{
    // check if index is in range
    rangeCheck(index);

    // start at the header
    DNode<T> p = header;

    // go to index by moving forward from the front
    // of the list; see Programming Exercise 11.16 for a way
    // to improve the performance of this method
    for (int j = 0; j <= index; j++)
        p = p.next;

    // return reference to node at position p = index
    return p;
}
```

LinkedList Class Constructor

The LinkedList class has a default constructor that creates an empty list. The constructor creates the header node and sets listSize and modCount to 0.

Constructor:

```
// construct an empty list
public LinkedList()
{
    header = new DNode<T>();
    listSize = 0;
    modCount = 0;
}
```

Indexed Access in a List

The indexed access methods get() and set() are implemented by using the private method nodeAtIndex(). We emphasize again that these methods are not efficient if they are used repeatedly in a program because nodeAtIndex() must sequence through the doubly linked list elements until it reaches the node at position index. A LinkedList collection is really designed to be accessed sequentially. With the node in hand, `get()` and `set()` access or update the `nodeValue` field. The following is the implementation of `set()`.

set():

```
// replaces the value at the specified position in this list
// with item and returns the previous value
public T set(int index, T item)
{
    // get the reference that identifies node at position index
    DNode<T> p = nodeAtIndex(index);

    // save the old value
    T previousValue = p.nodeValue;

    // assign item at position index
    p.nodeValue = item;

    // return the previous value
    return previousValue;
}
```

The methods() get() and set() need an O(*n*) scan to locate the node.

Searching a List

The `LinkedList` class has a series of methods that require scanning the list to find a target value. The method `indexOf()` takes an argument of type `Object` and returns the index of the first occurrence of the target in the list, or −1 if it is not found. This is a `List` interface method. It is used by the index-based `add()` and `remove()` methods as well as method `contains()`, which searches the list and returns a boolean value.

The method indexOf() takes an Object parameter and applies equals() as it scans the list sequentially.

The `indexOf()` method is the equivalent of a sequential search of the doubly linked list. A for-loop moves a `DNode` reference, `curr`, through the list until either finding a match using `equals()` or arriving back at the header. The loop maintains a position counter which becomes the return value when a match is found.

indexOf():

```
public int indexOf(Object item)
{
    int index = 0;

    // search for item using equals()
    for (DNode<T> curr = header.next; curr != header; curr =
      curr.next)
    {
        if (item.equals(curr.nodeValue))     // success
            return index;
        index++;
    }

    // item is not in the list; return -1
    return -1;
}
```

The method `contains()` uses the result from a call to `indexOf()` to determine if the item is in the list. The return value is true if `indexOf()` returns an index ≥ 0 and false otherwise.

contains():

```
// returns true if this list contains item and false otherwise
public boolean contains(Object item)
{
    return indexOf(item) >= 0;
}
```

Modifying a List

The `LinkedList` class has various forms of the `add()` and `remove()` methods to insert and delete elements in a list. In each case, the method must position itself at the appropriate node. Once this is done, the insertion or deletion operation is executed by calling the appropriate private method `addBefore(curr, item)` or `remove(curr)`, where `curr` is the node reference. Let us look at the methods `add(T item)` and `remove(int i)`. These illustrate the key features of all list modification methods.

The `add(T item)` method inserts a new node with value `item` at the back of the list. Its implementation uses `addBefore(header, item)` with `header` serving as the reference node. After updating the list size, `add()` returns true. You may question why the method has a return value. Practically, the value serves no purpose in a linked list application. However, the `LinkedList` class implements the `Collection` interface, which defines a very general `add()` method with a boolean return type. Some Java collections that also implement the `Collection` interface do not allow duplicate values. For these collections, the `add()` method returns false if `item` is already in the list.

add():

```
// appends item to the end of this list and returns true
public boolean add(T item)
{
    // insert item at the end of list and increment list size
    DNodes.addBefore(header,item);
    listSize++;

    // the list has changed
    modCount++;

    return true;
}
```

The various add() and remove methods use private methods addBefore() and remove().

The `remove(index)` method deletes the node at position `index` in the list and returns its value. Locating the node is the task of the method call `nodeAtIndex()`, which first uses `rangeCheck()` to validate the index or throw an `IndexOutOfBoundsException`. The actual deletion is handled by the private method `remove(curr)`. The implementation also decrements the list size and updates the integer variable `modCount`.

The method remove(index) deletes the node returned by nodeAtIndex().

remove():

```java
public T remove(int index)
{
    DNode<T> p = nodeAtIndex(index);

    // save the return value
    T returnElement = p.nodeValue;

    // remove element at node p and decrement list size
    remove(p);
    listSize--;

    // we've made a modification
    modCount++;

    // return the value that was removed
    return returnElement;
}
```

The table summarizes the `add()` and `remove()` methods. In each case, the algorithm needs a strategy to locate the position of the update.

Method	Operation	Position strategy
remove(item)	remove(curr)	Scan list for first match with item
remove(index)	remove(curr)	curr = nodeAtIndex(index)
removeFirst()	remove(header.next)	
removeLast(index)	remove(header.prev)	
add(item)	addBefore(header,item)	
add(index,item)	addBefore(curr,item)	curr = nodeAtIndex(index)
addFirst(item)	addBefore(header.next,item)	
addLast(item)	addBefore(header,item)	

Chapter Summary

- A doubly linked list provides the most flexible implementation of a sequential list. Its nodes have references to the next and the previous node, and so a list traversal can take place in either the forward or backward direction. To take full advantage of this structure, implement a circular doubly linked list with a header node. The header node contains a null value, but the program never attempts to access this value. The header's next field references the first node of the linked list, and its prev field references the last node. Traverse a list by starting at the first node and following the sequence of next nodes until you arrive back at the header. To traverse a list in reverse order, start at the last node and follow the sequence of previous nodes until arriving back at the header.

- Insertion before any node in a doubly linked list, including the header, requires four reference assignments. When you have a reference to a node, two assignment statements unlink the node from the list. Do not apply this operation to the header node. To insert a node at the front of the list, insert before the node following the header. To insert at the back of the list, insert before the header node. Remove the front of the list by removing the node following the header, and remove the back of the list by removing the node before the header. These operations are more involved in a singly linked list because they involve handling the special case of an empty list. Removing the back of a singly linked list is an O(n) operation and should be avoided unless the program will perform the operation infrequently.

- We implement the LinkedList class using a doubly linked list. The implementation of LinkedList methods follows directly from the properties of doubly linked lists. For instance, to add an item to the front of the list, build a node containing the item and insert the node after the header. To implement methods that depend on an index, start at the header and move from node to node until arriving at the required position in the list.

Written Exercises

1. At each of the numbered comments, draw the doubly linked list.

```
DNode<Integer> intList = new DNode<Integer>(),
                newNode, curr;
newNode = new DNode<Integer>(5);
newNode.next = intList.next;
intList.next.prev = newNode;
newNode.prev = intList;
intList.next = newNode;                    // #1

newNode = new DNode<Integer>(3);
newNode.prev = intList.prev;
intList.prev.next = newNode;
newNode.next = intList;
intList.prev = newNode;                    // #2

curr = intList.next;
curr = curr.next;
curr.nodeValue = 15;                       // #3

curr = curr.prev;
curr.prev.next = curr.next;
curr.next.prev = curr.prev;                // #4
```

2. Why is inserting at the front or the rear of a doubly linked list an O(1) operation?

3. Fill in the statements that build the doubly linked list.

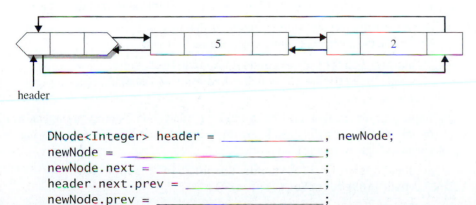

header

```
DNode<Integer> header = _____, newNode;
newNode = _____;
newNode.next = _____;
header.next.prev = _____;
newNode.prev = _____;
header.next = _____;
```

```
newNode = _____ ;
newNode.prev = _____ ;
header.prev.next = _____ ;
newNode.next = _____ ;
header.prev = _____ ;
```

4. Implement the method addAfter(), which inserts item into a doubly linked list after the node pointed to by curr.

   ```
   public static <T> void addAfter(DNode<T> curr, T item)
   { ... }
   ```

5. Implement the method removeAfter(), which deletes the node after curr in a doubly linked list and returns the updated reference curr. Your implementation may assume the node exists.

   ```
   public static <T> DNode<T> removeAfter(DNode<T> curr)
   { ... }
   ```

Programming Exercises

6. (a) Implement the method size(), which returns the number of elements in the doubly linked list.

   ```
   public static <T> int size(DNode<T> header)
   { ... }
   ```

   (b) Write a program that prompts the user to enter an integer value n in the range 1 to 5. Build a doubly linked list by inserting values 1, 2, . . , n at both the front and the rear of the list. Display the list and its size.

7. (a) Implement the method removeMax() that deletes the element with the largest value from a doubly linked list and returns a reference to the value. If the list is empty, removeMax() returns null.

   ```
   public static <T extends Comparable<? super T>>
   T removeMax(DNode<T> header)
   { ... }
   ```

   (b) By repeatedly inserting at the back of the list, build a doubly linked list of Integer objects whose values are $\{6, 5, 1, 9, 8, -19, 1, 25, 13, 3\}$. Output the list. In a loop, call removeMax() and output its return value until the list is empty.

8. (a) Implement the method insertOrder() that inserts item into a doubly linked list so that the elements maintain their natural ordering.

   ```
   public static <T extends Comparable<? super T>>
   void insertOrder(DNode<T> header, T item)
   { ... }
   ```

   (b) Implement the method linkedListSort() that sorts its array argument, arr, by inserting the array elements into an ordered linked list and then copying the elements back to the array.

   ```
   public static <T extends Comparable<? super T>>
   void linkedListSort(T[] arr)
   { ... }
   ```

(c) In a program, initialize an array of 10 randomly generated integer values in the range 10 to 99. Sort the array using `linkedListSort()`, and output the elements.

9. (a) Declare a method `removeRange()` that removes all nodes from a doubly linked list in the reference range `[first, last)`.

```
public static <T> void removeRange(DNode<T> first,
                                   DNode<T> last)

{ ... }
```

(b) Assume that the elements in a doubly linked list are in ascending order. Using `removeRange()`, implement the method `removeOrderedDup()` that removes all duplicate values from the list.

```
public static <T> void removeOrderedDup(DNode<T> header)
{ ... }
```

(c) In a program, construct a doubly linked list containing integer values from the array `arr`.

```
Integer[] arr = {2, 5, 5, 6, 7, 7, 7, 8, 9, 11, 13, 13,
                 13, 13, 15, 15};
```

Call `removeOrderedDup()` to remove all duplicates from the list and then output the list.

10. (a) Implement the method `reverseList()`, which reverses the order of a doubly linked list. Do not use a temporary list for the reversal. Use two variables, `first` and `last`, that reference the ends of the list.

```
public static <T> void reverseList(DNode<T> header)
{ ... }
```

(b) In a program, construct the doubly linked list of `Integer` objects with values {3, 5, 9, 15, 55, 22, 35, 47, 18, 9}. Output the list, call `reverseList()`, and output the new list.

For each of the Programming Exercises 11.11 through 11.14, use a copy of the LinkedList class in the directory ch11ex and make the requested modification to the class.

11. Add a constructor to the `LinkedList` class that takes a generic array of type T as an argument. The method initializes the elements in the list in the same order they appear in the array. Write a program that checks your implementation of this constructor.

```
public LinkedList(T[] arr)
{ . . . }
```

12. Implement the method `removeAll()` that removes all the elements from the `LinkedList` that are also contained in the specified collection. After this call returns, the `LinkedList` will contain no elements in common with the specified collection. The method returns true if an element is removed from the list and false otherwise. Use `toArray()` to gain access to the elements in `Collection c`. Write a program that checks your implementation.

```
// the notation Collection<?> indicates that the type of
// elements in c is unknown
public boolean removeAll(Collection<?> c)
{ ... }
```

13. Implement the method `retainAll()` that retains only the elements in this `LinkedList` that are contained in the specified collection. In other words, it removes from this `LinkedList` all of its elements that are not contained in the specified collection. The method returns true if new elements are added and false otherwise. The method returns true if an element is removed from the list and false otherwise. Use `toArray()` to gain access to the elements in `Collection c`. Write a program that checks your implementation.

```
public boolean retainAll(Collection<?> c)
{ ... }
```

14. (a) Modify the implementation of the private method `nodeAtIndex()` to improve its efficiency. Use the following strategy.

   • If index i < `listSize/2`, move forward from the header to position i.
   • If index i ≥ `listSize/2`, move backward from the header to position i.

   (b) Write a program that empirically compares running times to access elements in a `LinkedList` when the method `nodeAtIndex()` is and is not optimized. Create two list collections using the `LinkedList` class in `ds.util` and your modified version of the class.

```
ds.util.LinkedList<Integer> linkListA =
                          new ds.util.LinkedList<Integer>();
LinkedList<Integer> linkListB = new LinkedList<Integer>();
```

   Fill each list by inserting 50,000 integer values. Using a `Timing` object, display the time to access 25,000 random locations in `linkListA` using `get()`. Repeat the process for `linkListB`.

Programming Project

15. In the world of puzzles, there is a challenge called the Josephus Problem, which resembles the game of musical chairs. A travel agent selects n customers to compete in the finals of a contest for a free world cruise. The agent places the customers in a circle and then draws a number m(1 ≤ m ≤ n) from a hat. The game is played by having the agent walk clockwise around a circle, stopping at every mth contestant. The agent asks the selected person to leave the game and then continues the clockwise walk. Over time, the number of remaining contestants dwindles until only one survivor remains. This is the winner of the world cruise. Figure 11.12 illustrates the Josephus Problem for n = 6 and m = 3.

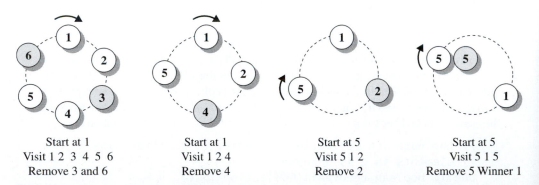

Start at 1	Start at 1	Start at 5	Start at 5
Visit 1 2 3 4 5 6	Visit 1 2 4	Visit 5 1 2	Visit 5 1 5
Remove 3 and 6	Remove 4	Remove 2	Remove 5 Winner 1

Figure 11.12 *Removing contestants in the Josephus Problem with n = 6, m = 3.*

The method `josephus()` assumes that n contestants compete for the cruise and that the deselecting process removes every mth contestant. The values n and m are method arguments. In `josephus()`, the circular doubly linked list, called `dList`, stores the contestants with integer values 1, 2, ..., n. In an iterative process, the algorithm sequences through the ring of remaining nodes and removes the mth node from the list. Because there are n contestants for the cruise, the function uses n − 1 iterations. Because the nodes are stored in a doubly linked list, when moving forward in the list, check for the header so that it is not counted or deleted. Each iteration outputs the deselected contestant. The method terminates by displaying the winner.

```
// for n contestants, remove every mth one until only one
// contestant remains; output each contestant number as he
// or she is removed; then output the winning contestant
public static void josephus(int n, int m)
{ ... }
```

Write a program that begins by prompting the user to enter the number of contestants, numContestants. A random number in the range from 1 to numContestants specifies the value removeM. A call to `josephus()` takes the arguments numContestants and removeM and determines the winner.

Chapter 12

ITERATORS

CONTENTS

12.1 THE ITERATOR CONCEPT

12.2 COLLECTION ITERATORS
The Iterator Scan Methods
Generic Iterator Methods
Iterating with an enhanced for
Statement

12.3 LIST ITERATORS
ListIterator Set Method
Backward Scan of a List
ListIterator Add Method
The Iterator Design Pattern

12.4 ITERATOR APPLICATIONS
Ordered Lists
Removing Duplicates from an
Ordered List

12.5 ORDEREDLIST COLLECTION
OrderedList Class Methods
Application—Word Frequencies
The Adapter Design Pattern

12.6 SELECTING A SEQUENCE
COLLECTION

In any collection, we need a way to scan the elements and at least identify their values. For instance, we may want to display the elements or identify the maximum value in the collection. Modern data structures have evolved the concept of an iterator to address this need. An *iterator* is an object that scans elements in a collection sequentially. In this chapter, we will develop properties of an iterator and introduce the Java iterator design which is part of the `Collection` interface. `List` collections use position to store elements. This creates a natural order for scanning elements in both the forward and backward direction. `List` collections define list iterators which take advantage of this ordering.

Iterators play a central role in data structures. You may understand them best by exploring the issues that led to their creation. Iterators are an ingenious object-oriented solution to a problem that is made difficult by the diverse ways collections store and access elements. We will begin by discussing the issues and then develop iterator terminology that results in the definition of the `Iterator` and `ListIterator` interfaces. Along the way, we will introduce a variety of algorithms that give you a feel for working with iterators. We will leave the implementation of iterators to the next chapter.

12.1 The Iterator Concept

Applications use a collection object to store elements dynamically. At points in the application, there is a need to identify the objects that are currently being stored. The ability to scan the elements in a collection is key to many data structures algorithms. The task is made simple and efficient for an ArrayList collection that can use the `get()` and `set()` methods to access and update an element by index. This allows for an array-like scan of the elements. A LinkedList collection implements List and so has access to the same get() and set() methods. In this case, however, the methods have running time O(n) and so a scan of all of the elements is very inefficient.

The `Bag` class poses a different problem. Our discussion of that class focused on operations to add and remove elements but did not provide tools to scan the collection. We would have to modify the implementation to make the data visible. The Bag class stores the elements in a fixed-length array. By making the array bagArr and the size variable bagSize public, we could use an index to scan the elements in the range 0 to bagSize−1. The strategy works at the price of exposing the underlying storage structure, which violates the principle of information hiding. The problem promises to be even more difficult with set and map collections that store elements by value in a tree or a hash table. Even if the data was public, scanning the elements would require very different algorithms and notation.

> An index can be used to traverse the elements in an ArrayList, but this type of access is not efficient for a LinkedList.

The design of a collection type must address the problem of scanning its elements. We can identify a clear set of guidelines that should apply:

Guideline 1:   A collection must define an efficient scanning mechanism consistent with good object-design principles. Requiring the implementation to make the data public is not a solution. The mechanism should follow a design pattern so that general scanning algorithms apply to all collection types.

Guideline 2:   A collection should provide an object, call it an iterator, that has methods which allow a scan of a collection similar to the scan of an array with an index. The object type of an iterator should implement an iterator pattern that can be uniformly used with all collections. While there can be different designs, methods should allow for a loop to scan the elements sequentially. For instance, a design may view elements in a collection as a sequence over the range from begin() to end() and provide methods to initialize and update an iterator. In this case, the following would be a loop that scans the elements.

> A collection class must provide a method of scanning its elements as part of its basic design.

```
// scan elements in collection c with the iterator iter
for (iter = c.begin(); iter != c.end(); iter.goNext)
    iter.getValue();
```

Guideline 3:   Each collection class is responsible for implementing iterator methods on the basis of its storage strategy. After all, the collection class understands its storage strategy and so should be responsible for scanning the data.

Modern research in data structures evolved the concept of an iterator that meets these three guidelines. Languages such as C++ and Java employ different object-oriented design approaches to implement iterators and a different way to specify the operations. In the next section, we will introduce the Java Collections approach to iterators. The Iterator interface defines methods associated with an iterator.

12.2 Collection Iterators

An iterator is an object that accesses the elements in a collection. You can think of it as a "locator" that scan across the entire range of elements in the collection. At any point in the scan, the iterator can access the value of the corresponding element. The figure illustrates an iterator for a LinkedList object. In (a), the iterator, called *iter*, references the first element in the list with Integer value 8. In (b), iter has moved forward one position and references Integer value 17.

An iterator is an object that access-es the elements in a collection. Every collection pro-vides a method iterator() that returns an iterator for the collection.

The generic `Iterator` interface defines the methods that are available to an iterator. Every data structure that implements the `Collection` interface implements `Iterator` and provides a method that creates an iterator and positions it at an element in the collection. In a program, we typically create an object by using the operator `new` and a class constructor. Creating an iterator is a different process. It must be done by the method iterator() which is specified in the `Collection` interface. The method returns an iterator object that references the first element in the collection. The meaning of "first" depends on the collection type and the way it stores elements. For a List collection, the iterator is initially set to reference the element at position 0.

Obtain an iterator that references the first LinkedList element by using the LinkedList method iterator().

Create an iterator by first declaring an Iterator reference variable. Then call iterator() for the specific collection that you wish to traverse. For instance, the following statements create an iterator that scans a linked list of integers.

```
LinkedList<Integer> aList;      // LinkedList for Integer objects
Iterator<Integer> iter;         // Iterator for Integer objects
iter = aList.iterator();        // create iterator; assign to iter
```

You cannot create an iterator using the operator `new`. The iterator is not an independent object. Rather, it must be associated with a particular collection because it references the elements in the collection. It makes sense that the collection object should assume the responsibility of creating the iterator because the object knows how it stores the elements and can specify a first element.

Note

Factory Method

A factory method is a name for a method that instantiates objects. Like a factory, the job of a factory method is to manufacture objects. The method iterator() for a Collection object is a factory method. You use it to create an iterator.

```
Iterator<String> iter = aStringList.iterator();
```

Note

ArrayList Iterators

Most of our examples define iterator objects for `LinkedList` collections. Being sequential access structures, `LinkedList` collections are a natural motivation for the use of iterators. `ArrayList` collections also have iterators which let them participate in generic algorithms that use `Iterator` parameters. The importance of iterators in an `ArrayList` collection is less significant because the structure can use an index and direct access to efficiently scan its elements.

The Iterator method hasNext() indicates whether more values remain in a collec-tion traversal.

The Iterator Scan Methods

An iterator has a series of methods that allow it to scan a collection from its first to its last element and to access each element during the scan. The method `hasNext()` specifies whether the iterator has additional elements to visit. A programmer normally uses the method in a `while-loop while` statement as follows:

```
// continue while there are remaining elements
while (iter.hasNext())
{
    ...
}
```

The method `hasNext()` has value true whenever the iteration has more elements to scan and the value false when the iteration has completed the scan of all of the elements (Figure 12.1).

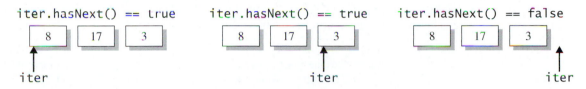

Figure 12.1 *Values for iter.hasNext() at various locations in the list.*

The actual scanning of the list is done by the method `next()`, which returns the value of the next element in the list and moves the iterator forward one position. The method serves a dual purpose. It provides access to the current element referenced by the iterator and then advances the iterator. An attempt to call `next()` when `hasNext()` is false results in a `NoSuchElementException`.

> The Iterator method next() returns the next element in a list traversal.

The following figure illustrates the action that occurs when calling `next()` with an iterator that currently references the second element in the list. The method first extracts the value `Integer` 17 from the list, moves the iterator to the third element, and then returns the value.

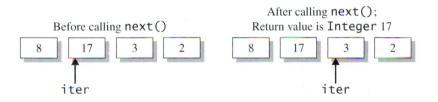

By combining a statement that initializes an iterator with a `while` statement that uses `hasNext()` and `next()`, we have a template for a forward scan of a list.

```
// initialize iter to reference the first element in the list
iter = aList.iterator();

// loop accesses successive elements to the end of the list
while (iter.hasNext())
{
    // obtain the next value and move forward
    value = iter.next();
    <act on value>
}
```

The Iterator method remove() deletes the last element returned by next() from the collection.

An `Iterator` object also has a `remove()` method that deletes an element while traversing the collection. The problem is to understand which element is deleted. Before executing `remove()`, the program must have made a prior call to `next()`. The call accesses the value at the current iterator position and then advances the iterator. It is the accessed value that is deleted by the iterator `remove()` method. In effect, `remove()` deletes the previous element. A second element cannot be removed by the iterator until there has been an intervening call to `next()`. In other words, the iterator `remove()` method must work in tandem with the iterator `next()` method.

The figure below illustrates the `remove()` method. Initially, the iterator references the second element (`Integer 17`). After a call to `next()`, the iterator moves forward, and the original element is the target for the `remove()` operation.

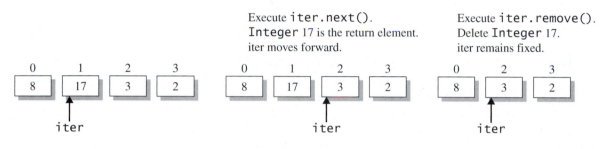

We provide here an API that summarizes the Iterator interface.

interface **Iterator\<T\>**	*ds.util*

	Methods
boolean	**hasNext**() Returns true if the iteration has more elements.
T	**next**() Returns the next element in the list and moves this iterator forward one position.
void	**remove**() Removes from the underlying collection the last element returned by a call to the iterator method next().

`Iterator` provides a uniform interface for traversing elements in different collection structures. It allows us to view every collection as a sequence structure. We will use iterators with nonlinear collections such as binary search trees and hash tables.

Example 12.1

This example creates a LinkedList collection containing string objects. An iterator scans the list and removes all elements that have a string length of less than 5.

```
String[] color = {"green", "red", "yellow", "teal", "black"};
LinkedList<String> list = new LinkedList<String>();
String colorStr;

// load the linked list with colors from the string array
for (int i = 0; i < color.length; i++)
    list.add(color[i]);
```

```
// create an iterator positioned at the first element; use it
// to scan the list; extract each element (string) using
// next() and then delete it if the length is less than 5
Iterator<String> iter = list.iterator();

while (iter.hasNext())
{
    colorStr = iter.next();        // extract element advance iter
    if (colorStr.length() < 5)
        iter.remove();
}

// output the final list
System.out.println(list);
```

In the example, the while statement can be replaced by a for statement that creates the iterator and tests whether the scan has additional elements to visit.

```
// creates an iterator positioned at the first element; the
// method next() extracts a string and moves the iterator to
// the next element so long as additional elements exist
for (Iterator<String> iter = list.iterator(); iter.hasNext(); )
{
    colorStr = iter.next();
    if (colorStr.length() < 5)
      iter.remove();
}
```

Output:
  [green, yellow, black]

Generic Iterator Methods

Iterators provide another mechanism for generic programming. Any collection class that implements the Collection interface must include iterators. The collection object can employ an iterator to scan the elements. An algorithm that relies on traversing elements in a collection and extracting their values can be implemented as a generic method using an iterator.

The method max() is a good example. It returns the value of the largest element in a collection. A generic form of the method includes a parameter of generic type Collection and returns a value of the specified type. Any collection whose elements implement Comparable can call max().

An algorithm that relies on traversing elements in a collection can be implemented as a generic method using an iterator.

max():

```
public static <T extends Comparable<? super T>>
T max (Collection<T> c)
{
    // create an iterator positioned at the first element
    Iterator<T> iter = c.iterator();
```

```
                    // assign maxValue the value of the first element and
                    // advance iter
                    T maxValue = iter.next(), scanObj;

                    // scan the rest of the elements in the collection
                    while (iter.hasNext())
                    {
                        scanObj = iter.next();
                        if (scanObj.compareTo(maxValue) > 0)
                            maxValue = scanObj;
                    }
                    return maxValue;
                }
```

Iterating with an enhanced for Statement

In many applications, you use an iterator to scan a collection solely for the purpose of accessing the elements. The "enhanced for" statement ("foreach" statement) makes the compiler take care of the iterator for you. It short-circuits the need to declare an iterator object and use methods hasNext() and next() to access successive elements in the collection. Here is code with a foreach statement that scans a LinkedList of colors (strings) and outputs the names with length < 5.

The enhanced for (foreach) statement causes the compiler to create an iterator for you and use it to traverse a collection.

```
// list is a collection of names from the array color
String[] color = {"green", "red", "yellow", "teal", "black"};
LinkedList<String> list = new LinkedList<String>();

// the foreach statement uses an implicit iterator; in the
// scan, the next element is extracted and assigned to str
for (String str: list )
{
    if (str.length() < 5)
        System.out.print(str + "  ");
}
```

The foreach statement implicitly allocates an iterator on the list of elements. The statement scans the list by making successive calls to next(), which extracts the element and assigns it to the local variable str.

Example 12.2

The LinkedList collection apptList contains a sequence of appointment times. A foreach statement scans the list and assigns each element to the Time24 variable t. The object associated with t is updated by advancing its time by 1.5 hours (90 minutes).

```
Time24[] apptArr = {new Time24(8,30), new Time24(10,00),
    new Time24(12,30), new Time24(1,45), new Time24(3,15)};

LinkedList<Time24> apptList = new LinkedList<Time24>();

// copy elements from array to LinkedList apptList
for (int i = 0; i < apptArr.length; i++)
    apptList.add(apptArr[i]);
```

```
System.out.println("Original appointments: " + apptList);

// enhanced for creates an iterator scan of apptList
for (Time24 t : apptList)
    t.addTime(90);

System.out.println("Revised appointments:  " + apptList);
```

Output:
    Original appointments: [8:30, 10:00, 12:30, 1:45, 3:15]
    Revised appointments: [10:00, 11:30, 14:00, 3:15, 4:45]

A collection class must implement the generic interface `Iterable` in order to use the enhanced for statement to scan the elements. The interface does not define any methods. It simply allows an object to be the target of the foreach statement. All of the collection classes in this book implement `Iterable`.

12.3   List Iterators

All `List` collections have a second type of iterator, called a *list iterator*, which takes advantage of the linear ordering of elements in the collection. A list iterator can traverse the list in either direction and also modify the list. The methods associated with a list iterator are specified in the generic `ListIterator` interface, which extends the `Iterator` interface. Like an iterator, we must rely on a `List` collection method to create a list iterator. In this case, two choices are available. The `List` method `listIterator()` returns a `ListIterator` object that references the first element.

```
ListIterator<Integer> iter = aList.listIterator();
```

A second version, `listIterator(index)`, takes an `index` position as an argument and returns a `ListIterator` object that references the element at the specified position.

```
ListIterator<Integer> iter = aList.listIterator(index);
```

The LinkedList method listIterator() will accept a parameter. The iterator then begins at the corresponding list position.

If `index == size()`, the iterator points just past the end of the list. This is useful if we intend to scan the list in the reverse direction. The following figure illustrates how `listIterator(index)` creates two iterators that reference the element at position 1 (a) and the position just past the end of the list (b).

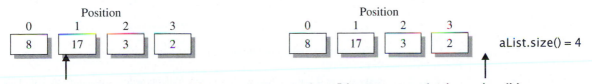

(a) `iter = aList.listIterator(1);`   (b) `iter = aList.listIterator(aList.size());`

The `ListIterator` interface extends the `Iterator` interface, and so it defines the methods `hasNext()`, `next()`, and `remove()`. A list iterator can scan a list in both the forward and backward directions. The methods `hasPrevious()` and `previous()` are available for a backward scan. An `Iterator` object can only remove an element during an iteration.

A `ListIterator` has list update methods `add()` and `set()` that can add a new element and assign an element to have a new value. We use an API to briefly describe the `ListIterator` methods that extend `Iterator` methods. In the next sections, we will explain the methods in detail and give examples. The UML diagram in Figure 12.2 shows the relationship between the `Collection` and `List` and between the `Iterator` and `ListIterator` interfaces.

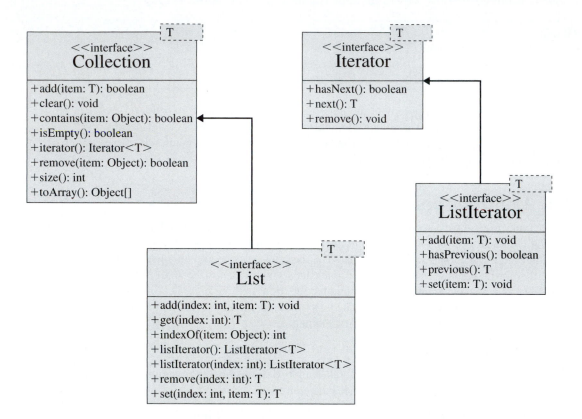

Figure 12.2 *UML comparing collection and list interfaces along with Iterator and ListIterator interfaces.*

interface ListIterator<T> extends Iterator<T>	*ds.util*

	Methods
void	**add**(T item)
	Inserts the specified item into the list at the iterator position.
boolean	**hasPrevious**()
	Returns true if this list iterator has more elements when traversing the list in the reverse (backward) direction.
T	**previous**()
	Returns the previous element in the list and moves this list iterator back one position.
void	**set**(T item)
	Replaces the last element returned by next or previous with the specified item.

ListIterator Set Method

The set() method updates the value of an element during an iteration. This method must be used in tandem with the methods next() (or previous()) because it assigns a new value to the element last returned by one of those extraction methods. In practice, this is how the update process might occur. First, call next() to extract a value, determine what the update should be, and then use set() to assign the new updated value. In the accompanying figure, next() extracts the Integer value 17 from the list and set() updates the value to be 12.

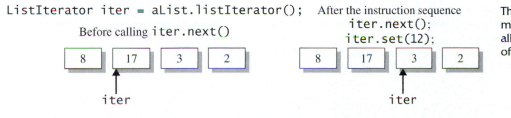

```
ListIterator iter = aList.listIterator();
```

The ListIterator method set() allows an update of a list element.

Example 12.3

A list iterator scans a list of strings. By combining next() and set(), each string is updated to be uppercase. After completing the update, the example displays the list. Assume the list aList is the sequence of strings {"iterator," "next," "scan," "list"}.

```
// declare a list iterator positioned at the first element
ListIterator<String> iter = aList.listIterator();
String scanStr;

// use a loop to scan the list; stop when hasNext() is false
while (iter.hasNext())
{

    // get element referenced by iter and move iter forward
    scanStr = iter.next();

    // convert to uppercase and use set()to update the value
    // of the element in the list
    scanStr = scanStr.toUpperCase();
    iter.set(scanStr);
}

// output the updated list
System.out.println(aList);
```

```
Output:
   [ITERATOR, NEXT, SCAN, LIST]
```

Backward Scan of a List

A list iterator can scan a list in the backward direction. It uses the methods hasPrevious() and previous() to control the scan. The method hasPrevious() returns true if there are list elements remaining when traversing the list in the reverse direction. Put more simply, hasPrevious() is true if the backward scan has not reached the first element. The method previous() returns the value referenced by the iterator and then moves the iterator down one position in the list.

The methods hasPrevious() and previous() are the counterparts of hasNext() and next(). They implement list traversal and access in the reverse direction.

The following figure illustrates the action that occurs when calling previous() with an iterator that currently references the third element in the list. The method extracts the Integer value 17 from the list and moves the iterator to the second element.

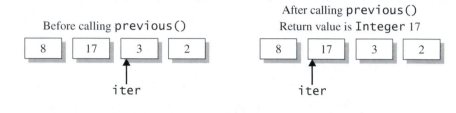

Before calling previous() After calling previous()
Return value is Integer 17

Example 12.4

For each part of the example, use the LinkedList object colorList.

1. The method reverseOutput() takes a linked list as an argument and uses a list iterator to output the list in reverse order. The scan uses the index version of listIterator() and the methods hasPrevious() and previous().

```
public static <T> void reverseOutput(LinkedList<T> aList)
{
    // create iterator that starts just past end of list
    ListIterator<T> revIter =
        aList.listIterator(aList.size());

    // loop outputs value of element accessed by previous()
    while (revIter.hasPrevious())
        System.out.print(revIter.previous() + "  ");
    System.out.println();
}
```

Use reverseOutput() to output colors in the list colorList.

```
reverseOutput(colorList);
```

Output:
  blue   green   black   red

2. Assume a list iterator references the string "black" in colorList. A pair of instructions that use next() and previous() return the same element and leave the iterator referencing the same element.

```
String nextElement, prevElement;

// nextElement is "black", listIter references "green"
nextElement = listIter.next();

// prevElement is "black", listIter references "black"
prevElement = listIter.previous();
```

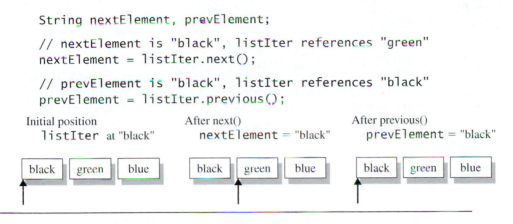

ListIterator Add Method

Up to this point, we have focused on the ability of a list iterator to scan and update a list. The iterator has an additional ability to modify the list by inserting new elements. The list iterator `add()` method inserts a new element at the position currently referenced by the iterator. We need to be more precise. The insertion occurs immediately before the current list value and after the previous list value. For instance, assume that `listIter` is positioned so that calling `next()` will return 2. The following statement inserts 5 between 17 and 2.

> The ListIterator methods add() and remove() allow insertion and deletion during an iterator scan of a LinkedList.

```
listIter.add(5);
```

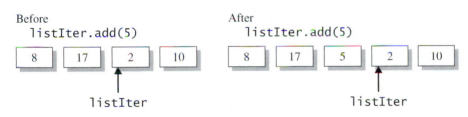

After inserting the element, the iterator still references the same element. However, a call to `previous()` will return the new value 5. Two special cases are worth noting. If the iterator references the first element (`hasPrevious() == false`), then `add()` inserts a new element at the front of the list. Similarly, if the iterator points past the end of the list, then `add()` inserts a new element at the back of the list.

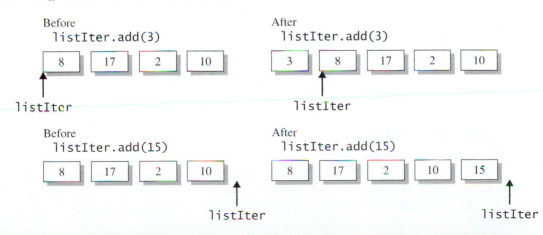

Example 12.5

The method `insertList()` takes two `LinkedList` arguments, `aList` and `bList`, along with an integer argument `pos` specifying a position in `aList`. The method inserts elements from `bList` into `aList` starting at index `pos`. Two list iterators are used. The first uses `listIterator(pos)` to create an iterator in `aList` at the specified index and the second uses `listIterator()` to create an iterator at the first element in `bList`. The method could use a simple iterator to scan elements in `bList`.

insertList():

```
public static <T> void insertList(LinkedList<T> aList,
LinkedList<T> bList, int pos)
{
    // declare iterator and set to start of the list
    ListIterator<T> aIter = aList.listIterator(pos),
                bIter = bList.listIterator();

    // scan bList and insert (add) elements into aList; iterator
    // aList continues to reference the same element
    while (bIter.hasNext())
        aIter.add(bIter.next());
}
```

Assume `stateListA` and `stateListB` are two `LinkedList` collections containing string abbreviations for U.S. states. The statements insert `stateListB` into `stateListA` at position 2 and then display the updated list.

aList: {"NY", "AL", "MT", "MA"}   bList: {"WI", "TN", "NV"}

```
insert(stateListA, stateListB, 2);
System.out.println(stateListA);
```

```
Output:
[NY, AL, WI, TN, NV, MT, MA]
```

The iterator design pattern specifies a means of accessing the elements in a collection in order from first to last without concern for the underlying implementation. Our collection iterators follow this design pattern.

The Iterator Design Pattern

The *iterator design pattern* provides a means of accessing the elements of a collection in order from first to last with no concern for the underlying implementation of the collection. This is precisely what `Iterator` provides in a general collection. For a collection that implements the `List` interface, a `ListIterator` provides additional functionality related to the sequential storage of data. We do not need any understanding of how the iterator is implemented. Put another way, the iterator gives us a way to access the elements of a collection without exposing its internal structure.

12.4 Iterator Applications

List iterators find important applications in algorithms that use a scan to add and remove elements. In this section, we present the method `insertOrder()`, which can be used to build an ordered list. A related algorithm, `removeDuplicates()`, deletes all duplicate elements from an ordered list.

Ordered Lists

In many applications, we wish to maintain an ordered list of elements with its values in ascending or descending order. An algorithm to add a new element must scan the ordered list of existing elements and identify the correct location for the new element. The following discussion illustrates the algorithm for a list in ascending order.

Begin by initializing a list iterator to reference the start of the list. Scan the list, looking for the first element whose value is greater than or equal to the new item. This identifies the insertion location, and we can use the `add()` method to place the new item in the list. The fact that `next()` is used to both access a value and advance the iterator adds complexity to the insertion process. Let us look at an example and explore the different situations in which the new element becomes a minimum value, an intermediate value, or a maximum value in the updated list.

Assume `intList` is a linked list containing the `Integer` values 60, 65, 74, and 82 and `curr` is the list iterator. The following illustrates how one inserts a new value at the front, middle, and back of the 4-element list.

> Many applications require an ordered list. Adding a new element requires scanning existing values and identifying the correct location at which to add the new element.

Insert 50 in the list:

A first call to `next()` extracts the value 60, which is greater than or equal to 50. The scan terminates with `curr` referencing the second element in the list. Value 50 will be the minimum value in the new list and thus should be added at the front of the list immediately before 60; that is, at the element `curr` originally referenced before it advanced to 65. The iterator has moved one position too far and so must be set back to its former position before we can call `add()`. Resetting the iterator is accomplished with a call to the method `previous()`.

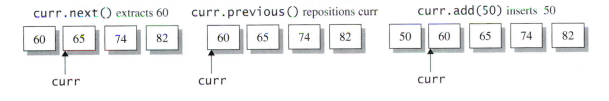

Insert 70 in the list:

The scan terminates when `next()` extracts the value 74, which is the first value that is greater than or equal to 70. As in the first case, the iterator `curr` has advanced to the next position and references 82. Inserting 70 must occur before 74. First, use `previous()` to reset `curr` and then use `add()` to insert the element.

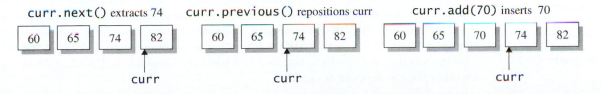

Insert 90 in the list:

The scan of the list fails to find an element which is greater than 90. The iterator curr has reached the end of the list (curr.hasNext() == false). Insert 90 at the back of the list referenced by the current value of curr.

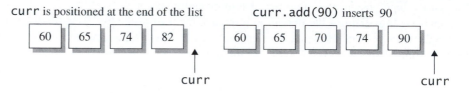

curr is positioned at the end of the list   curr.add(90) inserts 90

The method insertOrder() takes the list and the new value item as arguments and implements the algorithm. As the example illustrates, the new element always enters the list at a position referenced by the iterator curr. In the cases, however, where the new element has a value that is less than or equal to an existing list element, we must take into account the fact that the method next() has moved the iterator forward one position past the insertion point. A call to previous() repositions the iterator prior to using add() to insert the new element.

insertOrder():

```
// insert item into the ordered list
public static <T extends Comparable<? super T>>
void insertOrder(LinkedList<T> orderedList, T item)
{
    // curr starts at first list element
    ListIterator<T> curr = orderedList.listIterator();

    // move forward until encountering the end of the list or
    // locating the insertion point inside the list
    while (curr.hasNext())
        // check if item is <= value extracted by next()
        if(item.compareTo(curr.next()) <= 0)
        {

            // if so, reset curr back one position and exit loop
            curr.previous();
            break;
        }

    // add item before curr; if curr is at the end of the list
    // adds item as the last element of the list
    curr.add(item);
}
```

Inserting an element into an ordered LinkedList has average- and worst-case running time O(*n*).

The efficiency of the insertOrder() algorithm depends on the value of the new item. If the list has n elements, the worst-case performance occurs when the insertion occurs at the end of the list. This case requires n comparisons and has running time O(*n*). On the average, we expect to search half the list to find an insertion point. As a result, the average running time is O(*n*). Of course, the best case is O(1), which occurs when the insertion takes place at the front of the list.

Removing Duplicates from an Ordered List

An algorithm to remove duplicates in an ordered list provides an interesting application of iterators. The process involves scanning the list with an iterator and comparing the current value with a target value. Let us use an example to trace the algorithm. In Figure 12.3a, the iterator `curr` initially references the first element in the list. A call to `next()` extracts the value `Integer` 5 and moves the iterator forward. The initial value becomes the target value. A second call to `next()` extracts a duplicate value, which is removed from the list. Note that `curr` now references `Integer` 7, and the deletion removes the previous element (Figure 12.3b).

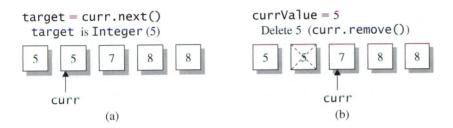

Figure 12.3   *Combining next() and remove() to delete the duplicate value Integer 5.*

Two additional calls to `next()` extract values that are not duplicates. Each value updates the target (Figure 12.4a–b). A final call to `next()` extracts a duplicate value and moves `curr` past the end of the list. The duplicate element is removed, and the scan results in an ordered list without duplicate values (Figure 12.4c).

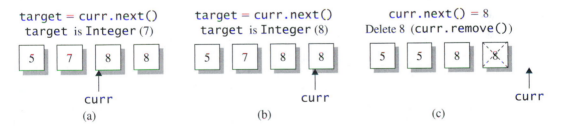

Figure 12.4   *Scanning the list with a deletion of the duplicate value Integer 8 at the end of the list.*

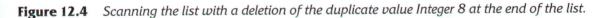

The method `removeDuplicates()` implements the algorithm. It assumes that the object type for the elements in the list implements `equals()`. After verifying that the list is not empty, the method assigns the initial value of `target` as the first list element. A loop scans the list and either removes an element or updates the value for `target`. Note that we only need to use an `Iterator` object. We move through the list in the forward direction.

Duplicate values in an ordered list can be removed in a single pass through the list.

removeDuplicates:

```
// remove duplicate values from the linked list
public static <T> void removeDuplicates(LinkedList<T> aList)
{
    // current value and the target
    T currValue, target;
```

```
    // list iterator that scans the list
    Iterator<T> curr;

    // start at the front of the list
    curr = aList.iterator();

    // assign target the first list element and move to
    // the second element
    target = curr.next();

    // cycle through the list and remove duplicates
    while(curr.hasNext())
    {
        // record the current list value
        currValue = curr.next();

        // if currValue equals target, remove it; otherwise
        // reassign the target to the current value
        if (currValue.equals(target))
            curr.remove();
        else
            target = currValue;
    }
}
```

The class OrderedLists in Chapter 12 of the software supplement contains the two methods insertOrder() and removeDuplicates().

12.5 OrderedList Collection

The LinkedList class describes a general sequential list. For many applications, we need a list structure that stores elements in order. Rather than building an OrderedList collection class from scratch, we can use inheritance to create one by extending the LinkedList class. The subclass can use the basic Collection interface methods in the superclass (LinkedList). It can also use the index-based remove() and get() methods that are defined in LinkedList. All of these methods do not affect the ordering of the elements. However, list update methods such as add() and set() are a different issue. They can destroy the ordering of the list. Iterators pose a separate problem. The OrderedList collection can use iterators and most of the functionality provided by list iterators in the superclass. The exceptions, of course, are the list iterator methods add() and set(), which can likewise destroy the list.

Extend the LinkedList collection to create an ordered list. Override the methods that would destroy the list by having the code throw an exception.

Designing the OrderedList class involves a few simple strategies. Let the LinkedList superclass store the elements and provide methods that give maximal functionality without destroying the integrity of a collection. Override the add(item) method that inserts an element at the back of the list. A new implementation for add(item) uses the insertOrder() algorithm from the previous section that places a new element in its correct location. For all of the other LinkedList methods, you can invalidate their use by overriding them with code that throws an exception. We use this strategy to override the methods add(index, element), addFirst(), addLast(), and set(). For the iterator, the OrderedList class should create a new ListIterator class that invalidates any call to add() or set(). We do not include this feature in our implementation of the OrderedList class.

OrderedList Class Methods

The OrderedList class has a constructor that creates an empty list. Its implementation simply calls the default constructor in the superclass.

```
// constructor creates an empty ordered list
public OrderedList()
{ super(); }
```

All of the LinkedList methods that could destroy the ordering of elements in a collection are overridden with an implementation that throws an UnsupportedOperationException with a message that indicates which form of the method caused the exception. For instance, the following code overrides the indexed-base add() method.

Insert element at an index:

```
public void add(int index, T item)
{
    throw new UnsupportedOperationException
            ("OrderedList add(index, element): Invalid
                operation");
}
```

The main feature of the OrderedList class is its version of add(item). This implementation uses the algorithm for insertOrder() with a final statement that returns the boolean value true, indicating that a new element enters the list.

OrderedList add():

```
public boolean add(T item)
{
    < code from insertOrder() >
    return true;
}
```

> Override
> add(item) so that
> it adds an item at
> its correct position
> in the linked list.

You can find a complete declaration of the OrderedList class in the software supplement.

Example 12.6
_____

This example creates the OrderedList object ordList and uses it to stores strings.

```
// create an empty list and a list iterator reference
OrderedList<String> ordList = new OrderedList<String>();
Iterator<String> iter;
```

1. Create an ordered list, using add().

```
ordList.add("green");      // List: green
ordList.add("blue");       // List: blue green
ordList.add("red");        // List: blue green red
ordList.add("black");      // List: black blue green red
```

2. Illustrate basic list methods.

```
index   = ordList.indexOf("red");    // index = 3
ordList.remove(2);                   // List: black blue red
```

3. Use the iterator.

```
// initialize iter to reference the first element
iter = ordList.iterator();

// output value from next()
System.out.println(iter.next()); // Output: black

// move the iterator, delete element and output list
iter.next();
iter.remove();                           // delete blue
System.out.println(ordList);
```

```
Output:
  [black, red]
```

Application—Word Frequencies

An application that determines the number of occurrences of each word in a document illustrates the use of an `OrderedList` collection. A document is input from a text file, and output displays the distinct words and their frequencies in alphabetical order. The application uses the class `WordFreq`, whose instances store a word and the number of times the word has occurred (the word frequency). The class has a constructor that creates an object with the word and a frequency of 1 as its data values. The `toString()` method outputs an object in the format *word (frequency)*. When a word is first encountered in the document, a `WordFreq` object is created. For each subsequent occurrence of the word, the class supplies the method `increment()`, which increments the frequency field in the corresponding `WordFreq` object. In order that its objects can be stored in an `OrderedList` collection, the `WordFreq` class implements `equals()` and `compareTo()`. These methods use the word field to compare objects. The UML in Figure 12.5 is a graphical representation of the `WordFreq` class.

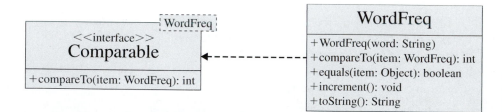

Figure 12.5 *UML representation of the WordFreq class.*

The main application declares the OrderedList collection wordList and a Scanner that is linked to a user-designated text file. The heart of the implementation is a while-loop that processes each word from the file. After reading a word, use the constructor to create a WordFreq object wf with the word as its argument. We need to determine whether the word (actually object wf) is already in the list or must be added to the list. For this purpose, we implement the method search() that looks for a target in an OrderedList and returns an iterator referencing the value or null if the target is not in the list. The method takes advantage of list ordering by returning null if an existing list value is greater than the target. In (Figure 12.6), a search for "pickled" uses the WordFreq object wf = <"pickled", 1>. The return value is an iterator denote by iter. The frequency for the object <"pickled", 3> is incremented to 4.

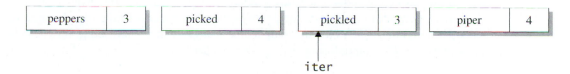

iter

Figure 12.6 *Efficient searching of an ordered list.*

search():

```
public static <T extends Comparable<? super T>>
ListIterator<T> search(OrderedList<T> ordList, T target)
{
    // initialize a list iterator
    ListIterator<T> iter = ordList.listIterator();
    T curr;

    // move through the ordered list
    while (iter.hasNext())
    {
        // get the current list value
        curr = iter.next();
        // see if current value matches target
        if (curr.equals(target))
        {
            // match; move iterator back to the match
            // and return its value
            iter.previous();
            return iter;
        }
        // if the target is less than current value, we won't
        // find the target in the ordered list
        else if (target.compareTo(curr) < 0)
            return null;
    }
    // the target is larger than any value in the list
    return null;
}
```

If the WordFreq object wf is present in the ordered list, we use the iterator value returned by search() to reference the object and call increment() to update its frequency. If the word is not present, the add() method inserts wf in the list, maintaining the lexical ordering of the words.

PROGRAM 12.1   WORD FREQUENCIES

The program implements the word frequency application using an OrderedList to store WordFreq objects. The user uses a command-line argument for the name of a file containing the document. After the file is opened, a loop reads successive words from the file. For each word, the program adds a new WordFreq object or updates the frequency field of the corresponding WordFreq object. After processing all the words in the file, the program calls displayWords(), which that outputs the word and frequency values for each element in the list. The output format is four elements per line.

```java
import ds.util.OrderedList;
import ds.util.ListIterator;
import java.util.Scanner;      // for file input
import java.io.*;

public class Program12_1
{
    public static void main(String[] args) throws IOException
    {
        // words read from file and inserted into wordList
        OrderedList<WordFreq> wordList =
            new OrderedList<WordFreq>();

        //  scanner to parse words in the file
        Scanner fileIn;

        // strings for input line and parse of words on the line
        String word = null;

        // WordFreg object for elements in wordList
        WordFreq wf = null;

        // use to search for the current word in the ordered list
        ListIterator<WordFreq> iter;

        // scanner name is a command-line argument
        fileIn = new Scanner (new FileReader(args[0]));

        // input words to end-of-file
        while (fileIn.hasNext())
        {
            word = fileIn.next();

            // create a wordFreq object with frequency 1
            wf = new WordFreq(word);

            // search to see if object is in the list
            iter = search(wordList, wf);
```

```java
            if (iter != null)
                // yes; increment the word frequency
                iter.next().increment();
            else
                // word is new; insert obj into the list
                wordList.add(wf);
        }
    displayWords(wordList);
}
public static <T extends Comparable<? super T>>
ListIterator<T> search(OrderedList<T> ordList, T target)
{
    // initialize a list iterator
    ListIterator<T> iter = ordList.listIterator();
    T curr;

    // move through the ordered list
    while (iter.hasNext())
    {
        // get the current list value
        curr = iter.next();
        // see if current value matches target
        if (curr.equals(target))
        {
            // match; move iterator back to the match
            // and return its value
            iter.previous();
            return iter;
        }
        // if the target is less than current value, we would
        // not find the target in the ordered list
        else if (target.compareTo(curr) < 0)
            return null;
    }
    // the target is larger than any value in the list
    return null;
}
// output the word and frequency in 15 character positions;
// limit output to 4 elements per line
public static void displayWords(OrderedList aList)
{
    ListIterator iter = aList.listIterator();
    int count = 0, i;
    String blanks;

    while (iter.hasNext())
    {
        String str = iter.next().toString();
        System.out.print(str);
        blanks = "";
```

```
            for (i=0;i < 15-str.length();i++)
                blanks += " ";
            System.out.print(blanks);
            count++;
            if (count % 4 == 0)
                System.out.println();
        }
        System.out.println();
    }
}
```

```
File "wf.dat"
peter piper picked a peck of pickled peppers
a peck of pickled peppers peter piper picked
if peter piper picked a peck of pickled peppers
where is the peck that peter piper picked

Run:

  a (3)             if (1)          is (1)          of (3)
  peck (4)          peppers (3)     peter (4)       picked (4)
  pickled (3)       piper (4)       that (1)        the (1)
  where (1)
```

The Adapter Design Pattern

The OrderedList class is an example of the adapter design pattern.

The *adapter design pattern* converts the public portion (interface) of a class into another interface. You use the adapter pattern when you want to use an existing class whose interface does not match the one you need. The OrderedList class is an application of the adapter pattern. The add() method

```
    public void add(T item)
```

from the LinkedList class inserts item at the back of the linked list. By extending the LinkedList class to create the OrderedList class, we were able to change the behavior of add() so it inserts item into an ordered list. In addition to inheritance, object composition can also be used to realize the adapter pattern. We will see this when we study stacks and queues in Chapters 14 and 15.

12.6 Selecting a Sequence Collection

The completion of this chapter marks the end of our study of sequence structures, including arrays, ArrayLists, and LinkedLists. When designing an application that requires storing data by position, a programmer can choose among these sequence structures. The decision can make a great difference in the performance of the program. Here are some guidelines.

- Use a Java array only for problems in which you know the number of data items in advance. Because an ArrayList also provides direct access using its get() and `set()` methods and has the ability to grow to meet the demands of the application, it is often advisable to use an `ArrayList` instead of an array.

- Use an `ArrayList` if the application needs direct access and the program performs all insertions and deletions at the end of the sequence. The `ArrayList` is the most efficient collection for this type of access. If the application requires infrequent modifications to the sequence at intermediate positions, an `ArrayList` is still acceptable.
- Use a `LinkedList` when the application requires frequent insertions and deletions at arbitrary locations in the list and direct (index) access is not required. For instance, a list is appropriate when creating an ordered list by repeated insertions of new elements into the sequence.

Chapter Summary

- The general Iterator interface has methods hasNext(), next(), and remove(). Every implementation of the Collection interface implements Iterator, thereby providing a uniform mechanism for traversing the values stored in different collection structures. The Collection method iterator() creates an iterator and positions it at the first element in the collection.
- An enhanced for statement can be used with collections that implement Iterable. The statement uses an implicit iterator to scan the elements in a collection and assign their values to a reference variable.
- A ListIterator is a generalized reference tool that scans in the forward or backward direction any collection that implements the List interface. The operations hasNext() and hasPrevious() indicate the presence of list elements in the specified direction, and the methods next() and previous() access the value of a list item and move the iterator forward or backward. The List method listIterator() creates a list iterator and positions it at the first element. The method listIterator(int pos) creates an iterator that initially references the element at position pos.
- The ListIerator methods add() and remove() efficiently modify a list by adding or removing elements. The iterator method set() can be used to change the value of an existing list element.
- The Iterator and ListIterator interfaces are a realization of the iterator design pattern. This pattern provides a means for accessing the elements of a collection in sequential order with no concern for the underlying implementation of the collection.
- As an application of the ListIterator, the method insertOrder() places an item in a list so that the list maintains ascending order. Using an Iterator object and its remove() method, the algorithm removeDuplicates() modifies an ordered list so that it contains only unique values.
- The OrderedList class as a subclass of LinkedList. Its method add(item) overrides the LinkedList version and inserts an item into the list so that the list remains in ascending order. The methods that retrieve or remove items from the list are available in the superclass. However, all the remaining add() methods and the set() method can destroy list order and so they throw an exception when called.
- The adapter design pattern converts the interface of a class into another interface. The OrderedList class is a realization of the adapter pattern. By using inheritance, we change the behavior of the add() method so it inserts the new element in the list in order rather than inserting it at the back of the list.

Written Exercises

1. Trace the method addToList() that inserts a new item into a list.

```
public static <T> void addToList(LinkedList<T> list,
                                          T item)
{
   Iterator<T> iter = list.iterator();

   while (iter.hasNext())
      if (item.equals(iter.next()))
         return;

   list.add(item);
}
```

(a) Consider the empty LinkedList intList and the Integer array arr.

```
LinkedList<Integer> intList = new LinkedList<Integer>();
Integer[] arr = {5, 2, 4, 5, 7, 2};
```

What are the elements in intList after executing the loop?

```
for (int i=0; i < arr.length; i++)
   addToList(intList, arr[i]);
```

(b) Assume LinkedList charList is an empty collection of Character type and string str = "mississippi". What are the elements in charList after executing the loop?

```
for (int i = 0; i < str.length(); i++)
   addToList(charList, str.charAt(i));
```

2. Assume strList is a LinkedList containing the strings {"list", "begin", "insert"} and strIter is a ListIterator.

```
LinkedList<String> strList = new LinkedList<String>();
ListIterator<String> strIter;
```

Use the initial list of elements for each of the following statement sequences. Display the resulting modified list.

(a)
```
strIter = strList.listIterator();
strIter.add("template");                // List (a) ___
```

(b)
```
strIter = strList.listIterator(strList.size());
strIter.add("switch");                  // List (b) ___
```

(c) Assume strIter references "begin".

```
strIter.next();
strIter.remove();                       // List (c) ___
```

(d) Assume strIter references "begin".

```
strIter.previous();
strIter.remove();                       // List (d) ___
```

(e) Assume `strIter` references "begin".

```
striter.next();
striter.set("array");          // List (e) ____
```

(f) Assume `strIter` references "begin".

```
striter.previous();
striter.set("array");          // List (f) ____
```

3. After the execution of the following statements, what is the resulting linked list?

```
LinkedList<String> list = new LinkedList<String>();
ListIterator<String> iter;

list.addFirst("Tom");
list.addFirst("Ann");
iter = list.listIterator();
iter.next();
iter.add("Mike");
iter.next();
iter.add("Vic");
```

4. An array can be sorted by inserting each element into an ordered `LinkedList` and copying the elements from the linked list back to the array.

   (a) Implement the method `listSort()` that uses this technique.

```
public static <T extends Comparable<? super T>>
void listSort(T[] arr)
{ ... }
```

   (b) What is the worst-case running time of the sort as a function of $n = $ `arr.length`? Explain your result.

5. What is the action of the method `f()` on a list of elements?

```
public static <T> void f(LinkedList<T> aList)
{
    ListIterator<T> iter = aList.listIterator();
    int pos = 0;

    while(iter.hasNext())
    {
        aList.addFirst(iter.next());
        pos++;
        iter = aList.listIterator(pos);
        iter.next();
        iter.remove();
    }
}
```

Programming Exercises

6. Implement the method `replace()` that takes a `LinkedList` and two objects `findItem` and `replItem`. The method scans the list looking for all occurrences of `findItem` and replaces them with `replItem`.

```
public static <T>  void replace(LinkedList<T> aList,
                                     T findItem, T replItem)
{ ... }
```

Write a program that builds a `LinkedList` of strings having initial values determined by the array

```
String[] str = {"half", "before", "half", "before",
  "eight"};
```

Replace all occurrences of "before" by "past" and output the new list.

7. (a) Write a program that uses a `LinkedList` `strList` and the string array `strArr`. Store the elements from the array in the linked list. Scan the list and output only those strings whose length is greater than 4. Use an iterator to access the list elements.

```
String[] strArr = {"generic", "Java", "if", "array",
   "LinkedList", "for", "iterator"};
LinkedList<String> strList = new LinkedList<String>();
```

(b) Use the string array and string list from part (a). During an iterator scan of the list, replace any string with length less than 5 by a corresponding string of length 6 that pads with "#". For instance, replace "Java" with "Java##".

8. Write a program that creates a `LinkedList` with `Integer` objects that has values from the array

```
Integer[] arr = {-15, 5, 35, -19, -12, 17, -4};
```

Use the iterator to scan the list and replace each negative value by the corresponding positive number. Output the resulting list.

9. (a) Implement the method `sortListA()` that sorts a `LinkedList` in ascending order. After calling `toArray()` and assigning the return value to an `Object` array, sort the array. Use a list iterator for the `LinkedList` and the iterator methods `next()` and `set()` to scan the `LinkedList` in the forward direction and update the list elements with entries from the sorted array.

```
public static <T extends Comparable<? super T>>
void sortListA(LinkedList<T> list)
```

(b) Implement the method `sortListD()` that sorts a LinkedList in descending order. Use a similar algorithm to that employed by `sortListA()` in part (a). Start the iterator at the back of the list and use the iterator methods `previous()` and `set()` to update the list values.

```
public static <T extends Comparable<? super T>>
void sortListD(LinkedList<T> list)
```

(c) Write a program that tests your implementation of the methods in parts (a) and (b). Use the following array. After sorting the elements, output the resulting list.

```
String[] name = {"Tom", "Ann", "Phil", "Bill", "Andy",
    "David", "Heather", "Bryce", "Richard"};
```

10. Implement the method `maxIter()`, which takes a `list` and an `index` argument and returns a list iterator that references the maximum element in the range `[index, n)`, where `n` is the size of the list.

```
public static <T extends Comparable<? super T>>
ListIterator<T> maxIter(List<T> list, int index)
{ ... }
```

Write a program that tests your implementation of `maxIter()`.

11. Use `maxIter()` from Programming Exercise 12.10 to implement a `LinkedList` version of the selection sort.

```
public static <T extends Comparable<? super T>>
void selectionSortList(LinkedList<T> list)
{ ... }
```

In a loop, let `pass` be an index in the range 0 to n − 1, where `n` is the size of the list. At each iteration, call `maxIter()` to reference the maximum element in the range `[pass, n)`. Remove the element and place it at the front of the list.

Write a program that creates `LinkedList` collections of different object types. Use `selectionSortList()` to order the elements in the list. For each list, display both the unordered and ordered sequence of elements.

12. Implement the method `countByIterator()` by using an `Iterator` to scan the `LinkedList` collection. Return an integer that gives the number of occurrences of the `Object` item in the list.

```
public static int countByIterator(LinkedList<?> aList,
                                  Object item)
{ ... }
```

Write a program that uses `countByIterator()`. Create a `LinkedList` with 20 random numbers in the range from 0 to 4. Insert each number into the list as an Integer object. In a loop, call `countByIterator()` for each value from 0 to 4, and output the number of occurrences of the number in the list.

13. The method `removeList()` takes a `list`, an index `pos`, and a count n and deletes n consecutive elements from the list beginning at the specified position. If n is greater than the size of the tail of the list, delete the tail of the list. Use an iterator for your implementation.

```
public static <T> void removeList(List<T> list, int pos,
                                  int n)
{ ... }
```

Write a program that tests your implementation of `removeList()`.

14. The method insertList() takes two lists, listA and listB, along with an index pos. The method inserts listB into listA beginning at the specified position. Use a ListIterator for your implementation.

```
public static <T> void insertList(List<T> listA,
                                  List<T> listB, int pos)
{ . . . }
```

Write a program that tests your implementation of insertList() using LinkedList and ArrayList collections.

15. Implement a static version of equals() for the LinkedList collection. Two lists are considered equal if they contain the same number of elements in the same order.

```
public static <T> boolean equals(List<T> listA,
                                 List<T> listB)
{ . . . }
```

Write a program that tests your implementation of equals() using two LinkedList collections.

Programming Project

16. Implement a GUI program that generates a random list of integers and then removes duplicate values. The content pane of the JFrame contains a 2 × 2 grid layout. The first row contains the JButton labeled "Generate List" and a read-only text field. The second row contains the JButton labeled "Remove Duplicates" followed by a read-only text field. When the user presses the "Generate List" button, the event handler creates a list containing 15 random integer values in the range from 0 to 9 and displays the list in the text field corresponding to the button. The "Remove Duplicates" button displays the list of unique values in the second text field (Figure 12.7). To implement the "Remove Duplicates" event, create a private method removeDuplicates() that removes duplicate values from a list. The method should use ListIterator objects and not List index operations.

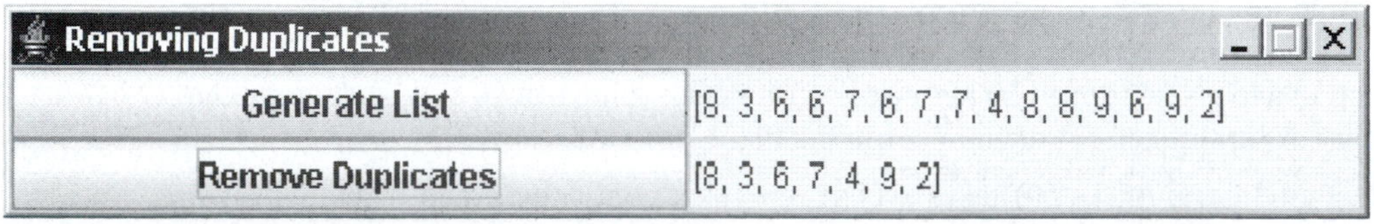

Figure 12.7 *Run of Programming Project 12.16.*

Chapter 13

IMPLEMENTING ITERATORS

CONTENTS

13.1 ITERATOR IMPLEMENTATION
DESIGN
Iterator Variables
Iterator Interface Methods

13.2 THE LINKEDLIST ITERATOR
LinkedList Iterator Methods

13.3 IMPLEMENTING LIST ITERATOR
List Iterator Constructor
List Iterator Public Methods

13.4 FAIL-FAST ITERATORS

Chapter 12 introduced the general concept of an iterator, which allows for the scanning of elements in a collection. We also introduced a special type of iterator, called a *list iterator*, which applies only to List collections. The design of iterators provides a uniform way to create them and to use a relatively small set of methods to scan and update elements of a collection. As a student of data structures, you should have experience with the implementation of iterators. The Bag class and the LinkedList class provide us this opportunity.

In this chapter, we will develop an iterator implementation design. We will see iterators for a variety of collection types that use different data storage strategies. Obviously, the way a collection stores its data affects how the data is scanned and thus the implementation of its iterators. We will begin by discussing the design of an iterator class for the Bag collection. The fact that this collection stores elements in a fixed-length array allows us to effectively highlight an iterator class design and to provide a simple implementation of its methods.

In subsequent sections, we will provide an implementation of an iterator class and a list iterator class for a LinkedList collection. You will already know the design strategy from the Bag class. Implementing LinkedList iterator classes introduces details that involve doubly linked lists, the underlying storage structure for a LinkedList collection.

An iterator is bound to the collection that it traverses. This can cause a potential conflict. An iterator might be actively scanning a collection while intervening collection methods add or remove an element. The methods change the state of the collection, which can temporarily invalidate the iterator. In some cases, the remove() operation deletes the element currently referenced by the iterator. For an iterator to run correctly, it must assume that forces outside of its control do not modify the collection. To prevent this from occurring, Java puts safeguards on the validity of an iterator and its operations. We will discuss these safeguards in Section 13.4.

13.1 Iterator Implementation Design

Two principles must guide the design of any iterator implementation. First, a collection class is responsible for implementing the Iterator interface and second, an iterator must be bound to the collection for which it is created. After all, the iterator will scan those collection elements. A simple technique to satisfy the guidelines is to move the iterator class inside the collection class. The iterator class, called an *inner class*, is a

A collection class is responsible for implementing the Iterator interface, and an iterator must be bound to the collection from which it is created.

member of the collection class just like instance variables and methods. The iterator inner class has access to all of the members of the collection (outer) class.

Let us use this design with the Bag class in which `IteratorImpl` is the name of the iterator class. The `Bag` class has private variables `bagArr` and `bagSize`. The former is an array of generic type that stores the elements and the latter maintains a count of the number of actual elements in the collection. The class `IteratorImpl` implements the `Iterator` interface and is added as a private member. As such, it has access to storage attributes `bagArr` and `bagSize`. However, a program cannot create a `Bag` iterator object using the operator `new`. An iterator object is created by the factory method `iterator()` in the `Bag` class. We add the `Iterable` interface in the header so that we can use an enhanced for-loop to scan a collection.

An inner class is normally used to implement a collection iterator.

Bag class:

```
public class Bag<T> implements Collection<T>, Iterable<T>
{
    private T[] bagArr;              available to IteratorImpl object
    private int bagSize;
    . . .
    private class IteratorImpl implements Iterator<T>
    { . . . }
}
```

With the design structure in place, the implementation of an iterator involves two separate issues. We must implement the `iterator()` method in the collection class to return an iterator object that references a first element in the collection. We must also implement the methods `hasNext()`, `next()`, and `remove()` in the iterator class. The first issue is easy to handle. Simply implement `iterator()` by returning an instance of the iterator class. The following implements `iterator()` in the `Bag` class.

Bag iterator():

```
// return an instance of IteratorImpl which implements Iterator
public Iterator<T> iterator()
{
    return new IteratorImpl();
}
```

Iterator Variables

The design of the iterator class depends on the underlying storage structure of the collection and a scanning strategy for the structure. The `Bag` class uses an array to store elements, and a natural scanning strategy uses an index to traverse elements in order from 0 to `bagSize` -1.

The iterator class needs a variable which identifies the element in the collection that is currently referenced by the iterator. It needs a second variable which identifies the element that was extracted by the most recent call to `next()`. This is the return value for the `next()` method and designates the element, which would be deleted by the iterator `remove()` operation. The type of the variables depends on the way elements are stored in the collection class. In the `Bag` class, elements are in an array, and so the variables are indices of type `int`.

Figure 13.1 is a view of a Bag iterator, called `iter`, which uses `next()` to advance to the next element in the collection. In the underlying storage array, the variable `nextIndex` is the resulting index position of the iterator and the variable `lastIndex` is the position of the element whose value is extracted by the operation.

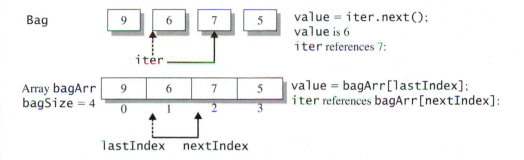

Figure 13.1 *View of a Bag iterator and iterator indices in the underlying storage array.*

The significance of the `lastIndex` requires special notice. Initially, there is no last-extracted element, and after a call to `remove()` the element is deleted. In each case, we need to assign `lastIndex` a value that indicates that it is currently invalid awaiting a subsequent call to `next()`. In the Bag iterator class, `lastIndex` has a value −1 when it is invalid. The following is a declaration of the instance variables. The variable `nextIndex` is set to 0, which is the initial position of the iterator.

IteratorImpl class (Bag inner class):

```
private class IteratorImpl implements Iterator<T>
{
    private nextIndex = 0;
    private lastIndex = -1;         // initially invalid

    . . .
}
```

Iterator Interface Methods

The iterator class must use a scanning algorithm that is consistent with how the collection stores elements. The algorithm determines the starting point and ending point of the scan. The method `hasNext()` verifies whether the iterator has additional elements to scan. The return value is false when the scan algorithm completes and is true otherwise. In the Bag class, we use an array scan in the range [0, `bagSize`) and so `hasNext()` is false when `nextIndex == bagSize`.

hasNext():

```
public boolean hasNext()
{
    return nextIndex != bagSize;
}
```

The method `next()` has two tasks. It must extract the value of the element currently referenced by the iterator and then advance the iterator. The two tasks are accomplished by updating the iterator variables in tandem. In the `Bag` class, update both `lastIndex` and `nextIndex` and use the value `bagArr[lastIndex]` as the return value.

next():

```
public T next()
{
    lastIndex = nextIndex;    // return value at lastIndex
    nextIndex++;              // advance nextIndex
    return bagArr[lastIndex];
}
```

The iterator class implementation of `remove()` uses the collection class version of the operation. An iterator `remove()` operation is valid only if a prior call to `next()` is in effect (`lastIndex` ≠ −1). This precondition must be checked. If the operation is not valid, an exception is thrown; otherwise the private `Bag` class operation `remove()` is employed to delete the array element `bagArr[lastIndex]`. The method concludes by doing some post-deletion housekeeping. In the new iterator state, `lastIndex` is reset to −1 and `nextIndex` is moved back one position (decremented). This reflects the fact that the previous element was deleted and the tail of the array was shifted left one position.

remove():

```
public void remove()
{
    // check for a missing call to next()
    if (lastIndex == -1)
        throw new RuntimeException("Iterator call to next() " +
                "required before calling remove()");

    // use Bag class remove() method
    Bag.this.remove(arr[lastIndex]);

    // we did a deletion; indicate this by setting lastIndex
    // to -1
    // nextIndex is reset to the left one position
    nextIndex--;
    lastIndex = -1;
}
```

13.2 The LinkedList Iterator

A `LinkedList` collection uses a doubly linked list as its storage structure. The elements are DNode objects. A forward scan of the list begins at the first element `header.next` and proceeds from node to node using the reference field `next`. The scan concludes when it reaches the `header` node. The `LinkedList` iterator class uses the DNode reference variable `nextNode` to reflect the position in the doubly linked list that corresponds to an iterator position in the `LinkedList` collection. The DNode reference variable `lastReturned` corresponds to the element that was extracted by the most recent call to `next()`. Figure 13.2

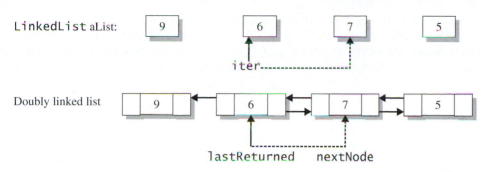

Figure 13.2 *Iterator stepping through a LinkedList collection.*

illustrates the relationship between a LinkedList iterator, iter, and the corresponding DNode references lastReturned and nextNode when the iterator calls next().

A LinkedList iterator uses DNode references to access its storage structure.

   The iterator class, which we call IteratorImpl, is declared as an inner class within the LinkedList class. As a member of the outer class, IteratorImpl has access to the private variables listSize and header. It defines its owns private DNode variables nextNode and lastReturned. The initial value header.next sets nextNode at the start of the list. The value header is used by lastReturned to indicate that a remove() operation is invalid. Initially, lastReturned is assigned the value header. It is reset back to header after each remove() operation because no next() operation has occurred.

LinkedList class and IteratorImpl inner class:

```
public class LinkedList<T> implements List<T>, Iterable<T>
{
    private int listSize;              Available to IteratorImpl object
    private DNode<T> header;
    ...

    private class IteratorImpl implements Iterator<T>
    {
        private DNode<T> nextNode = header.next;
        private DNode<T> lastReturned = header;

        < methods hasNext(), next(), remove() >
    }
}
```

The inner class IteratorImpl implements the Iterator interface by accessing the variables of the enclosing LinkedList object.

LinkedList Iterator Methods

The method hasNext() verifies whether more elements are available to scan. The condition is true if nextNode is not the header; that is, nextNode has not reached the end of the doubly linked list.

hasNext():

```
public boolean hasNext()
{
    // elements remain if nextNode is not the header
    return nextNode != header;
}
```

Elements remain in the list if nextNode is not the header.

The method `next()` first verifies that elements remain in the iteration and throws a `NoSuchElementException` if the condition is false. Advancing the iterator reduces to advancing `nextNode` in the doubly linked list and setting `lastReturned` to reference the previous position. The method concludes by returning the data value in `lastReturned`.

next():

```
// returns the next element in the iteration; throws a
// NoSuchElementException if the iteration has no more elements
public T next()
{

    // check if the iteration has another element
    if (nextNode == header)
            throw new NoSuchElementException(
                    "Iteration has no more elements");

    // save current value of nextNode as lastReturned
    // then advance nextNode
    lastReturned = nextNode;
    nextNode = nextNode.next;

    // return value of lastReturned
    return lastReturned.nodeValue;
}
```

The method `remove()` uses `lastReturned` to verify that the operation is valid. If so, the deletion is done by calling the private `LinkedList  remove(DNode)` method. The method concludes with some housekeeping. The variable `lastReturned` is set to `header`, indicating that a deletion took place and the size is decremented.

remove():

The method
remove() checks
that the operation
is value and
deletes the node
using the private
LinkedList
method remove().

```
public void remove()
{
    // check if operation is value; that is, an intervening
    // call to next() is in effect
    if (lastReturned == header)
        throw new IllegalStateException("Iterator call to " +
            "next() " + "required before calling remove()");

    // use collection class remove()
    LinkedList.this.remove(lastReturned);

    // reset lastReturned to indicate a subsequent remove() is
    // invalid
    lastReturned = header;
    listSize--;
}
```

13.3 Implementing List Iterator

The LinkedList method listIterator() returns an object that implements the ListIterator interface. Using the design we developed for the IteratorImpl class, we implement listIterator() by using an inner class, ListIteratorImpl. The class must implement the methods specified by the Iterator interface and, in addition, must implement the methods hasPrevious(), previous(), add(), and set() that are specific to the ListIterator interface. We implement ListIteratorImpl as a subclass of IteratorImpl. In this way, we can use the already existing implementation of iterator methods in the superclass. The method remove() requires some additional steps in its implementation, so we override it in the subclass.

Implement the ListIterator() methods by using an inner class ListIteratorImpl that extends IteratorImpl.

LinkedList private inner subclass ListIteratorImpl:

```
private class ListItertorImpl extends IteratorImpl
                implements ListIterator<T>
{
    ...
}
```

The ListIteratorImpl inner class has no data of its own. It uses the variables nextNode and lastReturned from the IteratorImpl superclass. This introduces some complexity because nextNode was designed to handle a forward scan of the list. The method previous() advances the iterator in the opposite direction, and so there is a doubling back of the iterator.

List Iterator Constructor

Unlike the IteratorImpl constructor, the private ListIteratorImpl constructor has an initialization task to perform. A programmer has the option of starting a traversal at the first list element by calling the method listIterator() or of starting a traversal at a particular position by calling listIterator(index). As a result, the ListIteratorImpl class must provide a constructor that sets nextNode to reference a specific position. The constructor takes an integer argument index that specifies the starting position. It first verifies that the argument is within the range ($0 \leq$ index $\leq$ listSize) and throws an IndexOutOfBoundsException if it is out of range. It then moves the superclass variable nextNode forward to position index.

ListIteratorImpl constructor:

```
// create the iterator at position index in the list
ListIteratorImpl(int index)
{
    if (index < 0 || index > listSize)
        throw new IndexOutOfBoundsException(
                "Index: "+ index+ ", Size: "+ listSize);

    // go to index by moving forward from the front of the list
    nextNode = header.next;
    for (int i=0; i < index; i++)
        nextNode = nextNode.next;
}
```

The ListIteratorImpl constructor positions nextNode at position index, at which location it begins an iteration.

The two versions of the LinkedList listIterator() methods are simple to implement. The index version returns an iterator at the specified location. The default version uses the index version with the index set to 0.

listIterator() method (index version):

The LinkedList
methods
ListIterator()
simply create
and return an
appropriate
ListIteratorImpl
object.

```
// returns a list iterator beginning at position index
public ListIterator<T> listIterator(int index)
{
    return new ListIteratorImpl(index);
}
```

listIterator() method (default version):

```
// returns a list iterator initially referencing position 0
public ListIterator<T> listIterator()
{
    return new ListIteratorImpl(0);
}
```

List Iterator Public Methods

The method hasPrevious() returns true if there is a list node before the current node referenced by nextNode. All hasPrevious() needs to do is verify that nextNode.prev is not the header node.

hasPrevious():

```
// returns true if the list has more elements when moving
// in the backward direction
public boolean hasPrevious()
{
    return nextNode.prev != header;
}
```

The method previous() advances the iterator one position in the backward direction. Assuming that the iterator has arrived at its current position using next(), the action of previous() is to reset the iterator back to the prior position (Figure 13.3). Note that

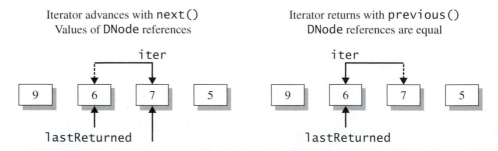

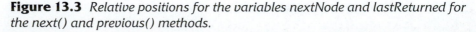

Figure 13.3 *Relative positions for the variables nextNode and lastReturned for the next() and previous() methods.*

the two variables `nextNode` and `lastReturned` reference different elements in the doubly linked list after executing `next()`. With a subsequent call to `previous()`, the two variables reference the same element.

The method first checks that a predecessor node exists. If so, it assigns both `lastReturned` and `nextNode` to reference the predecessor node `nextNode.prev`. The method concludes by returning the value contained in `lastReturned`.

previous():

```
// returns the previous element in the list; throws
// NoSuchElementException if the iteration has no previous
// element
public T previous()
{
    // check that a predecessor node exists
    if (nextNode.prev == header)
        throw new NoSuchElementException(
            "Iteration has no more elements");

    // move backward one position
    lastReturned = nextNode = nextNode.prev;

    return lastReturned.nodeValue;
}
```

> The method previous() validates the iterator, verifies that there is a predecessor to nextNode, moves backward to the predecessor, and returns its value.

The `remove()` method is defined in the `IteratorImpl` superclass. We override this version to account for the presence of the method `previous()`. The `IllegalStateException` message indicates that a call to `next()` or `previous()` is required before calling `remove()`. If in fact, `previous()` was called, then `lastReturned` can equal `nextNode`. When this happens, `remove()` must advance `nextNode` to the successor of the deleted node.

remove():

```
public void remove()
{
    // check for a missing call to next() or previous()
    if (lastReturned == header)
        throw new IllegalStateException(
            "ListIterator call to next() or previous() " +
            "required before calling remove()");

    // use private LinkedList collection class remove() method
    LinkedList.this.remove(lastReturned);
    listSize--;

    // lastReturned can equal nextNode if previous() was called;
    // in this case, move nextNode forward one node
    if (lastReturned == nextNode)
        nextNode = nextNode.next;

    // the list is modified so set lastReturned to header
    lastReturned = header;
}
```

The method add() inserts an item into the list immediately before the node nextNode. This task is accomplished by the LinkedList private method addBefore() with nextNode and the item as arguments. The method inserts item before nextNode.

The method add() uses the LinkedList addBefore() method to insert a new node with a value item into the list before nextNode.

add():

```java
public void add(T item)
{
    checkIteratorState();

    // insert item before nextNode
    LinkedList.this.addBefore(nextNode, item);

    // set lastReturned to header to invalidate a call to set()
    // without an intervening call to next() or previous()
    lastReturned = header;
    listSize++;
}
```

The method set() allows the programmer to change the value of a list element. By comparing lastReturned to header, we verify that a prior call to next() or previous() is in effect since the last add() or remove() operation. The variable lastReturned references the node whose value is to be updated.

set():

```java
public void set(T item)
{
    if (lastReturned == header)
        throw new IllegalStateException(
            "Iterator call to next() or previous() " +
            "required before calling set()");

    lastReturned.nodeValue = item;
}
```

The method set() replaces the data value in the node lastReturned by the argument item.

13.4 Fail-Fast Iterators

An iterator compares its variable expected-ModCount with the list variable modCount to verify its status.

An iterator is bound to the collection that it traverses. Nevertheless, the iterator and the collection are distinct objects with methods that can insert or remove elements. This is a potential problem. An iterator might be actively scanning a collection when intervening collection class methods add or remove an element. The list remove() operation might delete the element currently referenced by the iterator. This action would temporarily invalidate the iterator until the program explicitly resets its location in the list. For an iterator to run correctly, it must assume that forces outside of its control do not modify the collection.

Every change to a LinkedList object increments the variable modCount.

Java uses a strategy that puts some safeguards on the validity of an iterator. The strategy involves defining an integer variable modCount in the collection class. The value of modCount is 0 when the collection object is created and is incremented during the execution of add() and remove() methods, which modify the collection. An iterator has its own instance variable called expectedModCount. When the iterator is created, the constructor assigns to expectedModCount the current value of the list variable modCount.

The iterator is not interested in the actual value of modCount, which simply reflects the past history of changes in the collection. The iterator only wants to know about changes that occur while it exists. Before executing the operations next() and remove(), the iterator first compares expectedModCount and modCount. If they are not the same, then the iterator recognizes that some operation modified the collection and potentially invalidated the iterator. When the iterator modifies the collection with its own add() or remove() method, it increments the variable modCount and assigns the new value to its local variable expectedModCount.

The variables modCount and expectedModCount are used to check the current state of the iterator. The iterator methods next() and remove() along with the list iterator methods previous() and add() begin by calling the utility method checkIteratorState() before performing their action. The method throws ConcurrentModificationException if expectedModCount is not equal to modCount. If the two variables are equal, the iterator is in a consistent state.

Employing a validity check creates a fail-fast iterator.

checkIteratorState():

```
public void checkIteratorState()
{
    if (expectedModCount != modCount)
        throw new ConcurrentModificationException(
            "Inconsistent iterator");
}
```

A complete implementation of the iterator remove() method includes postdeletion housekeeping that updates both modCount and expectedModCount.

remove():

```
public void remove()
{
    // check the state of the iterator
    checkIteratorState();

    // check that the remove() operation is valid and delete the
    // element extracted by the most recent call to next()
    . . .

    // the list is modified
    modCount++;
    expectedModCount = modCount;
}
```

The need to check on the validity of an iterator is particularly evident when an application uses threads. A *thread* is an independently executing series of statements that performs a task. If a system has multiple processors, each thread may run on a separate processor. Threads can share data and can communicate with each other using mechanisms beyond the scope of the book. It is not generally permissible for one thread to modify a collection while another thread iterates through it. In general, the results of the iteration are undefined under these circumstances. In this book, all iterator implementations throw the ConcurrentModificationException if this behavior is detected. Such iterators are known as *fail-fast iterators*, as they fail quickly and cleanly rather than allowing themselves to cause program failure at some later time.

Java documentation warns a programmer about the fail-fast behavior of an iterator. Fail-fast iterators throw `ConcurrentModificationException` on a best-effort basis. Therefore, it would be wrong to write a program that depended on this exception for its correctness: *The fail-fast behavior of iterators should be used only to detect bugs.*

Chapter Summary

- An iterator is defined for any data structure that implements the Collection interface. We illustrate the implementation of the iterator for the Bag class. The iterator() method returns an object implementing the Iterator interface. The method creates an iterator that references a first element in the collection. The object type for the iterator is an inner class, IteratorImpl, that is defined within the collection class and thus has access to the underlying storage structure for the collection.

- The Bag class iterator uses an index to reference elements in the underlying array storage structure. The index nextIndex references the element whose value is returned by a subsequent call to next(). The index lastIndex references the element returned by the most recent call to next(). The element is the one deleted when remove() is called. The method hasNext() simply checks whether nextIndex $\neq -1$. This condition indicates whether the iterator has additional elements to scan. The remove() method verifies that a call to next() has occurred (lastIndex $\neq -1$) and then uses the Bag method remove() to delete the element at lastIndex.

- The chapter applies the principles for constructing the Bag iterator to the implementation of iterators for the LinkedList class. In this case, the iterator references DNode objects in a doubly linked list, which is the underlying storage structure for the collection. The DNode reference nextNode specifies the current location of the iterator. The DNode reference lastReturned identifies that element that was last accessed by next() or previous().

- The listIterator() methods of the LinkedList class return an object implementing the ListIterator interface. Like the implementation of iterator(), these methods create and return an object of an inner class type. The inner class is ListIteratorImpl, which is a subclass of IteratorImpl. This design allows ListIteratorImpl to reuse all but the remove() method of the IteratorImpl class. The hasPrevious() method checks whether a backward scan has additional elements. The method previous() validates the iterator and then moves backward one list position.

- The add() and remove() methods use methods from the LinkedList class to insert or erase a list element. In addition, remove() verifies that a prior call to next() or previous() is pending. If not, it throws an IllegalStateException.

- The method set() assumes a prior call to next() or previous(). It then makes the assignment of item to the last referenced value.

- Collection class iterators are fail-fast. They use a class variable, modCount, to count the number of times a collection has been modified. Methods such as add() and remove() update modCount as part of their operation. When an iterator begins, it copies the value of modCount into its instance variable expectedModCount. At all times, the iterator requires that expectedModCount == modCount. This validity check ensures that the iterator is in a consistent state.

Written Exercises

1. Explain why the use of an inner class is the design technique of choice for implementing iterators.

2. Explain the role of the integer variable modCount in the LinkedList class. Which list methods increment modCount?

3. Explain the role of the node reference variable lastReturned in the IteratorImpl and ListIteratorImpl classes for the LinkedList class. Pay particular attention to how the variable detects errors.

4. Consider the following LinkedList collection whose values are Integer objects and an associated list iterator.

```
Integer[] arr = {8, 1, 3, 5, 7, 2, 9, 4};
LinkedList<Integer> intList = new LinkedList<Integer>();

for (int i=0;i < arr.length;i++)
    intList.add(arr[i]);

ListIterator<Integer> iter = aList.listIterator();
```

   (a) Develop a series of statements that cause a ConcurrentModificationException to be thrown; that is, the statements cause the iterator to become invalid.
   (b) Develop a series of statements that cause an IllegalStateException to be thrown.
   (c) Develop a series of statements that cause a NoSuchElementException to be thrown.

5. Explain how the IteratorImpl class in the LinkedList class checks that its remove() operation can occur only after a prior call to next().

6. Explain how the IteratorImpl class in the LinkedList class checks that two successive calls to its remove() method cannot occur.

7. Explain how the IteratorImpl class in the LinkedList class checks that the iterator is valid. That is, the user has not executed a List operation that would modify the collection.

8. An iterator can be implemented as an external class that takes a reference to the collection it traverses as a constructor argument. Explain why this approach is not as efficient as the approach of using an inner class that implements the Iterator interface.

9. Another approach to iterators is what we term an *internal iterator*. Instead of developing an inner or external class that implements the Iterator interface, the class itself implements the Iterator interface. There are no Iterator objects. For instance, the LinkedList class would implement the public methods hasNext(), next(), and remove(). To do this, the LinkedList class must have instance variables: nextNode, which specifies the current node in a traversal, and lastReturned, which marks the next node subject to removal. The method reset() can initialize nextNode and lastReturned.

```
public void reset()
{
    nextNode = header.next;
    lastReturned = header;
}
```

An internal iterator may be a simpler approach, but does it have disadvantages?

Programming Exercises

10. Use the `LinkedList` class in *ch13ex*. Modify the `ListIteratorImpl` class to improve the efficiency of the `ListIteratorImpl(index)` constructor as follows:

    - If `index` < `listSize`/2, move forward from the `header` to position `index`.
    - If `index` ≥ `listSize`/2, move backward from the `header` to position `index`.

    Write a program that tests your implementation by positioning a list iterator at different positions and displaying the values returned by `next()` and `previous()`.

11. Use the `LinkedList` and `ListIterator` classes in `ch13ex`.

    (a) Add the following two methods to the `ListIterator` interface.

    ```
    public int nextIndex()
    ```

    Returns the index of the element that would be returned by a subsequent call to next(); returns list size if the list iterator is at the end of the list.

    ```
    public int previousIndex()
    ```

    Returns the index of the element that would be returned by a subsequent call to previous(); returns −1 if the list iterator is at the beginning of the list.

    (b) Implement the two methods in the `ListIteratorImpl` inner class for the `LinkedList` class. Hint: In class `IteratorImpl`, define a private integer variable `nextIndex` that identifies the position that corresponds to the reference `nextNode`. Updates to `nextIndex` mirror updates to `nextNode`.

    (c) Write a program that tests your implementation of the methods. Create a list iterator that is positioned at the front of the list. Use a series of calls to `next()` and `previous()` to move the iterator forward and backward in the list. Periodically, identify the values returned by `nextIndex()` and `previousIndex()`.

    (d) To further test your work, write a program that uses the following version of the `reverse()` method, which reverses the order of the elements in a `LinkedList`.

    ```java
    public static <T> void reverse(LinkedList<T> alist)
    {
        ListIterator<T> iter = alist.listIterator();
        int pos = 0;
        T value;

        while(iter.hasNext())
        {
            pos = iter.nextIndex();
            value = iter.next();
            iter.remove();
            alist.addFirst(value);
            iter = alist.listIterator(pos+1);
        }
    }
    ```

12. Use the Bag class in *ch13ex*. Add the instance variable modCount to the class. Add the fail-fast feature to the Bag iterator by introducing the variable expectedModCount in the iterator inner class. Write a program that tests your work.

13. The directory *ch13ex* includes a declaration of the SList class that uses a singly linked list as its underlying storage structure. The following API describes the class.

class SList\<T>	
	Constructor
	SList() Creates an empty SList collection.
	Methods
void	**addFirst**(T item) Inserts item at the front of the list.
void	**addLast**(T item) Inserts item at the back of the list.
T	**getFirst**() Returns the value of the first element in the list. Throws an IllegalArgumentException if the list is empty.
T	**getLast**() Returns the value of the last element in the list. Throws an IllegalArgumentException if the list is empty.
boolean	**isEmpty**() Returns true if the list is empty and false otherwise.
void	**removeFirst**() Removes the first element in the list. Throws an IllegalArgumentException if the list is empty.
void	**removeLast** () Removes the last element in the list. Throws an IllegalArgumentException if the list is empty.
int	**size**() Returns the size of the list.
String	**toString**() Returns a string consisting of a comma-separated list of elements enclosed in brackets.
Iterator\<T>	**iterator**() Returns an iterator over the elements in this list in order first to last.

(a) Create an inner class IteratorImpl that implements the Iterator interface in the SList class. Use the class to implement the method iterator() in the SList class. For remove(), simply throw an UnsupportedOperationException.

(b) Write a program that checks your implementation of the SList iterator.

Programming Project

14. The directory *ch13ex* includes a declaration of the SListR class, which replicates the SList class in Programming Exercise 13.13.

   (a) Create an inner class IteratorImpl that implements the Iterator interface in the SListR class. Include an implementation of remove(). Hint: declare a Node<T> reference variable prevNode that serves as the predecessor of nextNode. The method remove() relies on prevNode to delete the node last referenced by next().

   (b) Add the variable modCount to the class and the variable expectedModCount to the inner class. Then use the variables to make the SList iterator fail-fast.

   (c) Write a program that tests your work. Be sure to check for error conditions that may occur with remove().

Chapter 14

STACKS

CONTENTS

14.1 THE STACK COLLECTION
Creating a Stack Collection Class

14.2 STACK APPLICATIONS
Multibase Numbers
Balancing Symbol Pairs

14.3 RECURSION AND THE RUNTIME STACK

14.4 POSTFIX EXPRESSIONS
Postfix Evaluation
The PostfixEval Class
The evaluate() Method

14.5 INFIX EXPRESSION EVALUATION
Infix Expression Attributes
Infix-to-Postfix Conversion

In Chapters 9 and 10, we introduced the `ArrayList` and `LinkedList` collections, which are basic list storage structures. Each class implements the `List` interface, which allows for the insertion and deletion of an element at any position in the sequence. In this chapter, we will introduce a new storage structure, called a stack, which is a very different type of collection. Unlike a general list collection, a stack supports only a restricted set of access and update methods.

A stack stores elements in a list but allows for access at only one end of the sequence. A pack of papers in the paper tray of a laser printer is a good model of a stack. The tray can hold a large number of sheets; however, the printer feeds only the sheet on the top. If you want to run a letterhead sheet through the printer, you must put it on the top of the pile.

The `Stack` interface specifies the behavior of this data structure. It is an adapter that employs a restricted set of `List` methods with new names that describe operations specific to a stack. In Section 14.1, we use an `ArrayList` collection and composition to create the `ALStack` class, which implements the `Stack` interface. The underlying storage structure enables us to use list methods to implement the corresponding stack methods.

A stack collection is ideal for some applications. We will spend much of this chapter discussing these types of applications. Section 14.2 employs a stack to output integer values in number bases other than base 10. It also describes an algorithm that uses a stack to verify how a compiler can verify the balancing of symbol pairs "()", "[]", and "{}" in expressions, array indexing, and code blocks. Section 14.3 illustrates how the runtime system uses a stack to handle method calls and returns. You will learn how recursion works by observing how the runtime system evaluates the recursive factorial method fact(*n*). A programmer can convert a recursive algorithm to an equivalent iterative version by using a stack to simulate the runtime system.

Compilers use algorithms to evaluate arithmetic expressions. Section 14.4 presents a simple and elegant algorithm that evaluates an expression in postfix (RPN) format. In this format, an operator appears after its two operands. The class `PostfixEval` implements the expression evaluation algorithm, which uses a stack to store operands.

You are probably more familiar with arithmetic expressions in infix format, which puts an operator between its two operands. Evaluating an infix expression is more difficult because the algorithm must account for the order of precedence and the associativity of operators as well as for subexpressions enclosed in parentheses. Section 14.5 provides an overview of this algorithm. We give a detailed implementation of the infix expression evaluation algorithm on the Web.

14.1 The Stack Collection

A *stack* is a list of items that are accessible at only one end of the sequence. Think of a stack as a collection of items that are piled one on top of the other, with access limited to the topmost item. Figure 14.1 provides a model of a stack as a collection of blocks. A child plays with blocks by adding and removing blocks from the top of the pile.

Figure 14.1 *Model of a stack as a pile of blocks.*

A stack performs all insertion and removal operations at the top of the stack.

A stack has operations that add and remove items from the top of the stack. They are defined in a `Stack` interface. A `push()` operation adds an item to the topmost location on the stack. The item that was formerly on the top is pushed down and joins the other elements which are buried in the stack and are not available. A `pop()` operation removes the topmost element from the stack. Consider the problem of putting vegetables onto a skewer prior to placing the skewer on a barbecue. In Figure 14.2, the cook pushes the vegetables

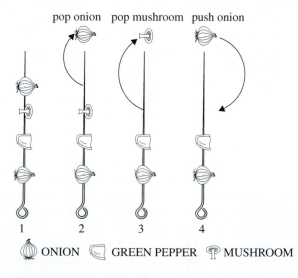

Figure 14.2 *A vegetable stack.*

onto the tip of the skewer (1) in the order onion, green pepper, mushroom, and a second onion. Before putting the skewer onto the grill, a guest indicates that he cannot eat mushrooms and needs to have them removed. To satisfy the request, the cook removes (pops) first the onion from the end of the skewer (2) and then the mushroom (3). The onion can then be pushed back onto the skewer (4).

Figure 14.3 illustrates a sequence of push() and pop() operations for character values. Because pop() removes the item last added to the stack, we say that a stack has *LIFO* (*Last-In/First-Out*) ordering.

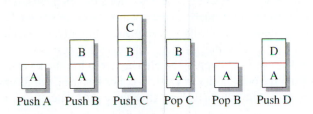

Push A   Push B   Push C   Pop C   Pop B   Push D

Figure 14.3 *Pushing and popping a stack.*

The push() and pop() operations change the stack. In some situations, it is necessary to access the topmost element of the stack without removing it. For this purpose, the Stack interface defines the method peek(). There is no access to elements below the topmost element in the stack.

The abstract concept of a stack allows for an arbitrarily large sequence of data. Hence, the push() operation has no precondition. The same is not true for peek() or pop() because the topmost item cannot be accessed or removed successfully unless the stack has at least one element. A violation of this precondition results in an EmptyStackException being thrown. The method isEmpty() indicates whether the stack has elements, and the method size() returns the number of elements on the stack. The generic Stack interface gives a detailed specification of stack methods.

Method push() inserts, pop() removes, and peek() retrieves the top of the stack. isEmpty() and size() are standard collections methods.

The stack operations pop() and peek() have the precondition that the stack cannot be empty.

The Stack interface specifies all stack operations.

interface Stack<T>		*ds.util*
boolean	**isEmpty**()	
	Returns true if the stack is empty and false otherwise.	
T	**peek**()	
	Returns the element at the top of the stack. If the stack is not empty, throws an EmptyStackException.	
T	**pop**()	
	Removes the element from the top of the stack and returns its value. If the stack is not empty, throws an EmptyStackException.	
void	**push**(T item)	
	Inserts item at the top of the stack.	
int	**size**()	
	Returns the number of elements in the stack.	

Creating a Stack Collection Class

A stack is a collection having methods that allow only restricted access at one location in the sequence. The `Stack` interface is an adapter which defines a restricted set of list methods to depict the behavior of the collection. In designing a stack class, we can use an `ArrayList` or a `LinkedList` collection and composition to define the underlying storage structure. Implementing the `Stack` interface methods then reduces to using related methods in the underlying list collection.

We use this strategy to create the `ALStack` class, which implements the `Stack` interface. This class uses an `ArrayList` object to store the elements. The position at the "back" of the `ArrayList` corresponds to the position "top" in the stack. Think of the elements of the stack as lying horizontally in a sequence. Initially, the stack is empty and the size of the `ArrayList` is 0. Pushing an item onto the stack corresponds to adding an item at the back of the `ArrayList`. Popping an element from the stack corresponds to removing the element from the back of the `ArrayList`. For instance, the following is a stack of characters viewed as a "pile" and as a list. After three push operations, C is on the top of the stack.

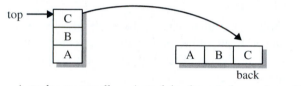

A stack conceptually.   A stack implemented as an Array List.

Implement a stack by including an ArrayList using object composition. Implement stack operations by using operations on the back of the list.

The `ALStack` class includes a private reference variable `stackList` of type `ArrayList`. The constructor creates an empty stack by initializing `stackList` to be an empty `ArrayList` collection.

ALStack class:

```
public class ALStack<T> implements Stack<T>
{
    private ArrayList<T> stackList = null;   // storage structure

    // create an empty stack by creating an empty ArrayList
    public ALStack()
    {
        stackList = new ArrayList<T>();
    }

    . . .

}
```

The implementation of each stack method is trivial. Simply call the corresponding `ArrayList` method to execute the operation. The methods `pop()` and `peek()` require that the stack contain at least one element. If this condition is not satisfied, we have the methods throw an `EmptyStackException`. Our implementation could have the corresponding

ArrayList method test the condition and throw an exception. This, however, would reveal the underlying structure, which is not part of the abstract design of the ALStack class.

Implementing Stack Methods   For the peek() operation, identify the top of the stack by using the ArrayList method get() at the position stackList.size() −1.

peek():

```
public T peek()
{
    // if the stack is empty, throw EmptyStackException
    if (isEmpty())
        throw new EmptyStackException();

    // return the element at the back of the ArrayList
    return stackList.get(stackList.size()-1);
}
```

The push() method inserts an element at the top of the stack by inserting the element at the back of the array list. This is simply the ArrayList add() operation.

push():

```
public void push(T item)
{
    // add item at the end of the ArrayList
    stackList.add(item);
}
```

The pop() method removes and returns the element at the top of the stack by using the ArrayList method remove() with the index of the last element in the list.

pop():

```
public T pop()
{
    // if the stack is empty, throw EmptyStackException
    if (isEmpty())
        throw new EmptyStackException();

    // remove and return the last element in the ArrayList
    return stackList.remove(stackList.size()-1);
}
```

The class also provides the toString() method that returns a string displaying the elements in the stack from top to bottom.

> An ArrayList implements O(1) insertion and removal at the back of the list, so stack operations have running time O(1).

Stack Efficiency   The running time of the ALStack operations depends on the running time of the relevant method in the ArrayList class. The operation add() has constant amortized running time. As a result, the ALStack push() operation has this same running time. The running time of get() and remove() is O(1), so the running time of the ALStack peek() and pop() methods is O(1).

Example 14.1

The `ALStack` collection `stk` contains `Integer` objects. Push the values 1 through 5 onto the stack and then display the contents of the stack by repeatedly calling `pop()` until the stack is empty. On each iteration, we display the element returned by `pop()`. Note that the stack is a LIFO structure, so output of the elements occurs in the reverse order of their storage on the stack.

```java
ALStack<Integer> stk = new ALStack<Integer>();
int i;
int intValue;

// push Integers on the stack with values 1, 2, ..., 5
for (i=1; i <= 5; i++)
    stk.push(i);

// Output the size and display the elements using pop()
System.out.println("Stack size = " + stk.size());
System.out.print("Popping the stack: ");
while (!stk.isEmpty())
{
    intValue = stk.pop();
    System.out.print(intValue + " ");
}
```

```
Output:
    Stack size = 5
    Popping the stack: 5 4 3 2 1
```

Note

Finite Stack

The Stack interface makes no restriction on the number of elements in the stack. In some cases, however, the stack storage space is limited in size. These applications use a bounded (finite) stack and the push operation has a precondition that prevents adding a new item when the stack is full. See Programming Exercise 14.14.

14.2 Stack Applications

A stack is a LIFO storage structure. This makes it ideal for a range of applications. Let us look at two such examples. We use a stack to create a string that represents a decimal number in a base between 2 and 16. In this way, a programmer can view a number base-10 (decimal) or in other bases such as base-2 (binary) or base-16 (hexadecimal). This application is a stack version of the recursive algorithm in Section 6.1.

A second application uses a stack to test whether program source code correctly matches left–right parentheses, brackets, and braces ("() ", " [] ", and "{}"). The technique is used by compilers to verify the balancing of symbol pairs.

Multibase Numbers

Most programming languages display integer values in decimal as the default format. For some applications, particularly systems programming, you may want to display a number in binary, octal (base-8), or hexadecimal. A hexadecimal (hex) number consists of digits chosen from $0, 1, \ldots, 9$, A, B, C, D, E, F, where the letters represent the values 10 to 15. The letters can be upper or lower case. To provide this ability, we design a method `baseString()`, which takes an integer value and a base in the range 2–16 as arguments and returns a string with the digits in the specified base. The implementation uses a stack to store the digits. For instance, the number $n = 75$ has the following representations in bases 2, 8, and 16.

$$75 = 1001011_2 \quad // \ 75 = 1(2^6) + 0(2^5) + 0(2^4) + 1(2^3) + 0(2^2) + 1(2^1) + 1$$
$$75 = 113_8 \qquad // \ 75 = 1(8^2) + 1(8^1) + 3$$
$$75 = 4B_{16} \qquad // \ 75 = 4(16^1) + B$$

An algorithm uses repeated division by the base to describe a nonnegative integer N as a base B number. At each step, the remainder N % B identifies the next digit and the quotient N/B contains the remaining digits that are used for the next step. The process terminates when the quotient is 0. For instance, we identify the digits for 75 base-8 in three steps.

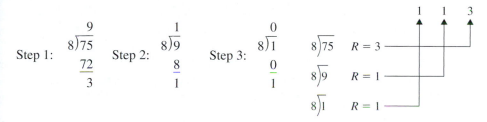

The division process identifies the digits for the return string, but in reverse order. By using a stack, with its LIFO ordering, we store the successive digits as `Character` objects. Emptying the stack builds the return string with the digits in the correct order. During the repeated division process, we convert each remainder to the corresponding digit character by using the remainder as an index to access the character in the string `digitChar`.

> Create a string that describes a number in a specified base by finding its digits from right to left and pushing each digit on a stack. Popping the stack builds the string.

```
String digitChar = "0123456789ABCDE";
```

For instance, if the remainder is 7, `digitChar.charAt(7)` = "7". The conversion to a hexadecimal number could have a remainder 13. The corresponding hex digit is `digitChar.charAt(13)` = "D".

Example 14.2

This example illustrates the conversion of the integer $n = 75$ to the base-8 number string "113" and the integer $n = 431$ to base-16 (hex) number string "1AF". The figures portray the growth of the stack while creating the digit characters for n and the undoing of the stack to build the number strings.

1. The integer $n = 75$ has a base-8 expanded representation $1(8^2) + 1(8^1) + 3$. The value is 113_8.

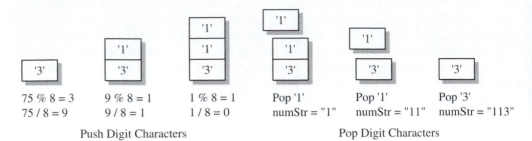

75 % 8 = 3   9 % 8 = 1   1 % 8 = 1   Pop '1'   Pop '1'   Pop '3'
75 / 8 = 9   9 / 8 = 1   1 / 8 = 0   numStr = "1"   numStr = "11"   numStr = "113"

Push Digit Characters   Pop Digit Characters

2. The integer $n = 431$ has a base-16 expanded representation $1(16^2) + 10(16) + 15$. The value is $1AF_{16}$, where the successive remainders upon division by 16 are 15 (hex F), 10 (hex A), and 1 (hex 1).

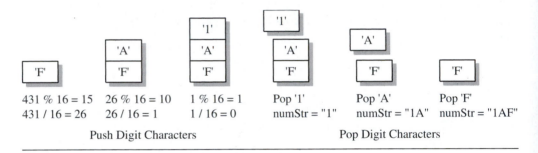

431 % 16 = 15   26 % 16 = 10   1 % 16 = 1   Pop '1'   Pop 'A'   Pop 'F'
431 / 16 = 26   26 / 16 = 1   1 / 16 = 0   numStr = "1"   numStr = "1A"   numStr = "1AF"

Push Digit Characters   Pop Digit Characters

The baseString() Algorithm   The method `baseString()` takes a positive integer num and a integer base b in the range $2 \le b \le 16$. The return value is a string representing the value of num in the specified base b. A stack with `Character` objects stores the digit characters that are created by repeated divisions.

baseString():

```
public static String baseString(int num, int b)
{
    // digitChar.charAt(digit) is the character that represents
    // the digit, 0 <= digit <= 15
    String digitChar = "0123456789ABCDEF", numStr = "";

    // stack holds the base-b digits of num
    ALStack<Character> stk = new ALStack<Character>();

    // extract base b digits right to left and push on stack
    do
    {
        // push right-most digit on the stack
```

```
            stk.push(digitChar.charAt(num % b));
            num /= b;              // remove right-most digit from num
        } while (num != 0);        // continue until all digits found

        while (!stk.isEmpty())  // flush the stack
        {
            // pop stack and add digit on top of stack to numStr
            numStr += stk.pop().charValue();
        }
        return numStr;
    }
}
```

PROGRAM 14.1 MULTIBASE OUTPUT

This program uses the method `baseString()` to output the multibase representation of four nonnegative integer values. In a for-loop, the user is prompted to enter the integer and the base, which must be in the range 2–16.

```java
import java.util.Scanner;
import ds.util.ALStack;

public class Program14_1
{
    public static void main(String[] args)
    {
        int num, b;              // decimal number and base
        int i;                   // loop index

        // create scanner for keyboard input
        Scanner keyIn = new Scanner(System.in);

        for (i = 1; i <= 4; i++)
        {
            // prompt for number and base
            System.out.print("Enter a decimal number: ");
            num = keyIn.nextInt();
            System.out.print("Enter a base (2 to 16): ");
            b = keyIn.nextInt();

            System.out.println(" " + num + " base " + b +
                            " is " + baseString(num, b));
        }
    }
    < listing of baseString() given in the program discussion >
}
```

```
Run:
  Enter a decimal number: 27
  Enter a base (2 to 16): 2
   27 base 2 is 11011
  Enter a decimal number: 300
  Enter a base (2 to 16): 16
   300 base 16 is 12C
  Enter a decimal number: 75
  Enter a base (2 to 16): 8
   75 base 8 is 113
  Enter a decimal number: 10
  Enter a base (2 to 16): 3
   10 base 3 is 101
```

Balancing Symbol Pairs

A syntactically correct Java program must properly match and nest the symbol pairs "()", "[]", and "{}". You have experience with using matching parentheses for type casting and for creating subexpressions within a larger arithmetic expression. Matching brackets and braces are used for array indices and for the designation of a block in a method, a loop, or a conditional statement. For discussion, we use the term left-symbol to describe a character in the set "(", "[", and "{". A right-symbol is a character in the set ")", "]", and "}".

A program properly matches and nests the symbol pairs if each right-symbol matches the last unmatched left-symbol and all of the symbols are part of a matching pair. We use a stack to create an algorithm that checks for valid symbol-pair matching. For simplicity, assume the source code is a string. A scan of the string processes only left-symbol and right-symbol characters. In the case of a left-symbol, we store the character on a stack, awaiting the appearance of its corresponding right-symbol. A test for proper balancing occurs when the scan identifies a right-symbol. Let us look at the different possibilities and illustrate them with an example. Assume scanCh is the value of the character that is currently being scanned and matchCh is the character on the top of the stack.

Case 1: The stack is empty. This occurs when there is no left-symbol to match the current right-symbol and is an error condition. At the current position of scanCh, post a message indicating that the proper left-symbol is missing.

Example: In the assignment statement, the array index brackets match but the ")" has no match. The error message is "at ')', missing matching '('."

$$t = arr[3] + a) - 4;$$

Case 2: The stack is not empty. In this case, the scan has identified left-symbols which are awaiting their corresponding right-symbol. The last unmatched left-symbol is on the top of the stack. Pop the element, assign it to matchCh, and check for a match. If scanCh and matchCh are a symbol-pair, the string is still balanced and the scan should continue. If the characters do not form a symbol-pair, post a message at the current scanCh position indicating that the proper left-symbol is missing.

Example: In the if-statement, the "]" should match with a '['. The error message is "at ']', missing matching '['."

$$\text{if } (arr(3] < 4)$$

After scanning the string, all symbol pairs should be balanced and thus the stack should be empty. If this is not the case, the string has one or more unmatched left-symbol characters. Indicate that the symbol on the top of the stack is missing its matching right-symbol.

Example: At the end of the sting, there is no match for '{'. The error message is "at end of string, missing '}'."

$$\{ b = (int)arr[5];$$

The method `checkForBalance()` implements the algorithm that determines whether an expression properly nests the symbol pairs. The method is passed a string as an argument and returns a string indicating that the expression is balanced or with an error message indicating an offending symbol. The algorithm scans successive characters in the string and builds the corresponding return string, called `msgStr`. If the character at the scan location is valid (maintains balance), a blank space is appended to `msgStr` and the scan continues. If the character is invalid, the algorithm appends the character "^" to msgStr followed by an appropriate error message. In this way, the character is an error flag in `msgStr` which lines up with the offending character in the expression. It pinpoints the error. After scanning an invalid character, we return from the method with `msgStr` as the error message. The process may involve a complete scan of the expression, at which point a final test checks whether the stack is empty and returns with a message indicating a balanced string or an error condition.

In the implementation of `checkForBalance()`, we catch the exception that occurs when attempting to pop an empty stack. In this case, we have identified a missing left-symbol and can create a return error message. Throughout, the method gives only generic error messages such as "Missing left symbol." This allows us to focus on the design of the algorithm. A compiler would generate specific error messages that indicate which type of symbol is missing.

checkForBalance():

```
public String checkForBalance(String expStr)
{
    // holds left-symbols
    ALStack<Character> s = new ALStack<Character>();
    int i = 0;
    char scanCh = ' ', matchCh;
    String msgStr = "";

    while (i < expStr.length())
    {
        // access the character at index i
        scanCh = expStr.charAt(i);

        // check for left-symbol; if so, push on stack
        // otherwise, check for right-symbol and check balancing
        if (scanCh == '(' || scanCh == '[' || scanCh == '{')
            s.push(scanCh);
```

```
            else if(scanCh == ')' || scanCh == ']' || scanCh == '}')
            {
                // get character on top of stack; if stack is empty,
                // catch the exception and return the error message
                try
                {
                    matchCh = s.pop();

                    // check for corresponding matching pair; if match
                    // fails, return an error message
                    if (matchCh == '(' && scanCh != ')'  ||
                        matchCh == '[' && scanCh != ']'  ||
                        matchCh == '{' && scanCh != '}')
                    {
                        msgStr += "^";
                        return "\n" + msgStr + "  Missing left symbol";
                    }
                }
                catch (RuntimeException e)
                {
                    msgStr += "^";
                    return "\n" + msgStr +   "  Missing left symbol";
                }
            }
            i++;
            msgStr += " ";
        }
        // at end of scan, check the stack; if empty,
        // return message that string is balanced; otherwise
        // return an error message
        if (s.isEmpty())
            return  "\n" + msgStr + " Expression is balanced";
        else
        {
            msgStr += "^";
            return "\n" + msgStr +   "  Missing right symbol";
        }
    }
```

PROGRAM 14.2 BALANCING SYMBOL PAIRS

Let us use the method checkForBalance() in a GUI application. The window contains
a text field in the NORTH region and a text area is the CENTER region. A user enters a
string in the text field and presses the Enter key. This creates an action event, similar to a
mouse-click on a button. The event-handler method, actionPerformed(), inputs the
string from the field, calls checkForBalance(), appends the return string in the text
area, and concludes by clearing the text field. In this way, a user may conveniently enter a
series of strings and maintain a history of the output in a scrollable text area. The following
is a run with expressions that demonstrate the different cases.

```
Balancing Symbol-Pairs                          _ □ ✕
t += s[i] + x)

t = arr[3] + a) - 4
              ^   Missing left symbol
if (arr[i] < 0)
         ^   Missing left symbol
System.out.print(str.charAt(3);
                       ^   Missing right symbol
while(i > 100) { sum += i; i++; }
                       Expression is balanced
```

The following is a listing of the event handler. The rest of the problem uses our familiar GUI design pattern.

Event handler actionPerformed():

```java
public void actionPerformed(ActionEvent ae)
{
   // read string from the text field called inputField
   String testStr = inputField.getText();

   // display string in the text area called outputArea
   outputArea.append(testStr);

   // call checkForBalance() and display return message
   outputArea.append(checkForBalance(testStr) + "\n");

   // clear the text field for the next input
   inputField.setText("");
}
```

14.3 Recursion and the Runtime Stack

A program executes with a series of method calls that engage the runtime system. The execution process begins by having the calling statement set up an *activation record*, which includes the list of runtime arguments, space for local variables declared in the method implementation, and a return address. The address is the location of the next instruction to execute after the method returns to the calling statement.

Runtime arguments	Space for local variables and objects	Return address <next instruction>

Activation Record

At the point of a method call, the runtime system pushes the activation record onto a system-supplied stack called the *runtime stack*. Control then transfers to the statements in the method, where the data in the record is available for use in the method body. Upon exiting from the method, the runtime system extracts the return address from the activation record and then pops the record from the stack.

A recursive method makes repeated calls to itself by using a modified argument list for each call. The process pushes a chain of activation records onto the stack until the method identifies a stopping condition. The subsequent popping of the records gives the recursive solution.

We use the factorial method `fact()` to illustrate the use of activation records and the runtime stack. Assume the program makes a call to `fact(3)` from method `main()`. After `fact(3)` completes execution, program control returns to the assignment statement at address `RetAddr1` in `main()`. The statement copies 6 (3!) into `factValue`.

Calling fact() in main:

```
public static void main(String[] args)
{
    int factValue;
    . . .                          ———— RetAddr1

    factValue = fact(3);
    System.out.println("Value fact(3) = " + factValue);
}
```

> Recursion is implemented by creating a stack of activation records. Each activation record contains runtime arguments, space for local variables, and the return address of the method call.

The recursive call with the method `fact()` returns to multiplication operation at address `RetAddr2`. The operation computes the product $n * (n - 1)!$, which becomes the return value for `fact(n)`.

Recursive call to fact():

```
public static int fact(int n)
{
    if (n == 0)
        return 1;              ———— RetAddr2
    else
        return n * fact(n-1);
}
```

Let us view the runtime stack during execution of `fact(3)`. An activation record has a field for the integer argument n and a field for the return address. The method does not define any local variables.

Argument n	Return address <next instruction>

Activation Record for `fact(n)`

The activation record for the call to `fact(3)` from method `main()` has an argument $n = 3$ and the return address `RetAddr1`. Execution initiates a sequence of three recursive method calls with arguments $n = 2, 1,$ and 0 respectively. In each case, the activation record has address `RetAddr2`. The following figure illustrates how the stack grows with activation records for successive method calls. The record for the call from `main()` occupies the bottom of the stack.

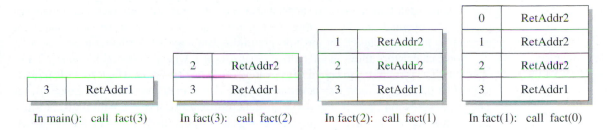

3	RetAddr1

In main(): call fact(3)

2	RetAddr2
3	RetAddr1

In fact(3): call fact(2)

1	RetAddr2
2	RetAddr2
3	RetAddr1

In fact(2): call fact(1)

0	RetAddr2
1	RetAddr2
2	RetAddr2
3	RetAddr1

In fact(1): call fact(0)

The stopping condition occurs in `fact(0)` and begins a sequence of return actions. Each step pops the activation record on the top of the stack and passes program control to the return address, which identifies the next instruction. The figure illustrates the operations that describe the clearing of activation records from the runtime stack.

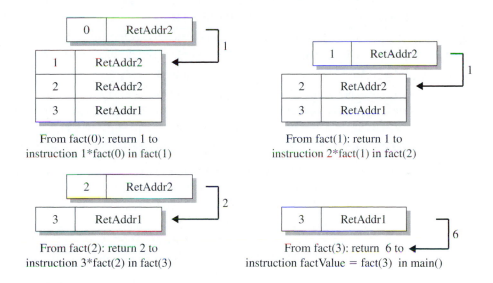

From fact(0): return 1 to
instruction 1*fact(0) in fact(1)

From fact(1): return 1 to
instruction 2*fact(1) in fact(2)

From fact(2): return 2 to
instruction 3*fact(2) in fact(3)

From fact(3): return 6 to
instruction factValue = fact(3) in main()

Upon completion, the stack is empty and the value `fact(3)` = 6 is assigned to `factValue` in method `main()`.

14.4 Postfix Expressions

Electronic calculators illustrate one of the primary applications of a stack. The user enters a mathematical expression by pressing a sequence of numbers (operands) and operators, followed by the "=" key. The calculator computes and displays the result. The process assumes that the user enters the expression in a specific expression format. For instance, an integer expression such as

$$-8 + (4*12 + 5\%2)/3$$

contains *operands* (8, 4, 12, 5, 2, 3), a *unary operator* (−), *binary operators* (+, *, /, %), and *parentheses* that create subexpressions. The operators are termed unary and binary because they require one and two operands respectively. We say the expression is in *infix* format because each binary operator appears between its operands and each unary operator precedes its operand. Infix is the most common format for writing expressions and is the expression format of choice for most programming languages and calculators.

Infix notation places the operator between its operands. Postfix notation places the operator after its operands.

Some calculators allow an alternative *postfix* format, where an operator comes after its operands. The format is also called *RPN* or *Reverse Polish Notation*. The term Polish refers to the fact that the notation was developed by the Polish mathematician Jan Łukasiewicz. The infix expression "a + b" has the equivalent postfix form "a b +". With postfix format, an operator appears in the expression as soon as its two operands are available. To understand how this rule applies, consider the translation of the following infix expressions to postfix.

1. Infix: a + b*c   Postfix: a b c * +

   Because * has higher precedence than +, the evaluation of b*c must come first. The operator + has operands a and b*c. The evaluation of + appears only after we identify the two operands a and b c *.

2. Infix: (a + b)*c   Postfix: a b + c *

   The parentheses create the subexpression "a b +" as the left-hand operand for the operator *. The operator * appears only after we identify the right-hand operand c.

3. Infix: (a*b + c)/d + e   Postfix: a b * c + d/e +

   The subexpression is "a b * c +." Division (/) is the next operator and appears immediately after the operand d. The result after division is the left-hand operand for the operator +, which immediately follows its right-hand operand, e.

We can summarize the conversion from infix to postfix with two simple rules.

Rule 1:   Scan the infix expression from left to right. Immediately record an operand in the postfix expression as soon as it is identified.

Rule 2:   Record an operator as soon as its operands are identified. We will discuss this rule in detail in Section 14.5 when we will develop an algorithm to convert an infix expression to a postfix expression. This algorithm involves interpreting parentheses (subexpressions), operator precedence, and associativity.

Example 14.3

Let us test your understanding of conversion from infix to postfix format. The following is a series of four infix expressions. We also provide four equivalent postfix expressions, but in random order. Match the infix expression with the corresponding postfix expression.

Infix Expressions:

    1. a*b − c/d   2. a*b*c*d*e*f
    3. a + (b*c + d)/e   4. (b*b − 4*a*c)/(2*a)

Postfix Expressions:

    (a) a b*c*d*e*f *   (b) b b*4 a*c* − 2 a*/
    (c) a b*c d/ −   (d) a b c*d + e/ +

Answers: 1(c), 2(a), 3(d), 4(b)

Postfix Evaluation

With an expression in postfix format, we can use a simple algorithm to evaluate the result. The algorithm scans each term of the expression from left to right and uses a stack to hold the operands. If a term is an operand, push it onto the stack. If the term is a binary operator, we can evaluate its result because its two operands already reside on the stack in the top two positions. To carry out the evaluation of the operator, pop the stack twice to retrieve the operands, evaluate the expression, and then push the result back onto the stack. After processing all of the terms in the expression, there will be a single value on the top of the stack, which is the result. Consider the expression "4 3 5 * +". Evaluating it requires five steps.

Upon conclusion, the value of the postfix expression is on the top of the stack.

Steps 1–3: Scan the operands 4, 3, 5, and push each value onto the stack.

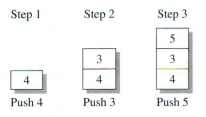

Step 1 — Push 4
Step 2 — Push 3
Step 3 — Push 5

> To evaluate a postfix expression, execute the following steps until the end of the expression.
> 1. If you recognize an operand, push it on the stack.
> 2. If you recognize an operator, pop its operands, apply the operator, and push the value on the stack.

Step 4: Scan the operator *, and evaluate the expression by popping the two operands 5 and 3 from the stack and computing 3 * 5. The value 5 was last pushed onto the stack, so it comes off first and is the right-hand operand for the operator. The operand 3 becomes the left-hand operand. Push the result 15 back onto the stack and make it available as an operand for a subsequent operator.

Step 4

Step 5: Scan the operator +, and evaluate the expression by popping the two operands 15 and 4 from the stack and computing 4 + 15. Push the result 19 back onto the stack.

Step 5

Stack after
evaluating +

After the scan of the postfix expression, the result is the value of the one element that resides on the stack. In our case, the result is 19.

Detecting Errors Errors can occur during the evaluation of a postfix expression. At each step in the algorithm, the state of the stack allows us to identify whether an error occurs and the cause of the error. For instance, the expression

$$3 \ 8 \ + \ *9$$

has too many successive operators. Put another way, the binary operator * is missing a second operand. We identify this error when we input * and note that the stack has only one element 11 (3 8 +). We cannot evaluate the "*" operation because it requires that there be two operands on the stack. We can conclude that "*" has too few operands.

After pushing   After evaluating +
operands 3 and 8

Postfix evaluation errors include "too many operands" or "too many operators." Another error occurs when an expression contains too many operands. We identify this error only after scanning the entire expression. At the conclusion of the process, the stack contains more than one element. It should contain only the result. For instance, consider the postfix expression

$$9 \ 8 \ + \ 7$$

The following figure traces the steps of the algorithm.

After pushing   After evaluating +   After pushing 7
operands 9 and 8

The final stack should contain only the result. Upon noting that the stack size is 2, we can conclude that the expression has too few operators.

The PostfixEval Class

We can design a class, `PostfixEval`, which takes a postfix expression and evaluates it. We assume the operands are single-digit nonnegative integers. This simplifies the process of distinguishing between an operator and an operand. The class handles the standard binary integer operators +, −, *, /, and %. In addition, the class evaluates expressions containing the binary exponentiation operator $^\wedge$, which takes two operands, a and b, and computes

$$a^{\wedge}b = a^b$$

The `PostfixEval` class contains a default constructor that creates an instance without a specified postfix expression to evaluation. The expression is introduced by the method `setPostfixExp()`, which takes a string argument containing the postfix expression. The access method `getPostfixExp()` enables a programmer to retrieve the current expression. The key method, `evaluate()`, attempts to compute the value of the postfix expression. If successful, it returns the value of the expression. If the expression contains an error, the method throws an `ArithmeticException`. If desired, the calling block can catch the exception and output the error message that is created when the evaluation process identifies an error. A series of private methods, `compute()`, `getOperand()`, and `isOperand()`, are used by `evaluate()` to identify operators and operands and to compute the result for an arithmetic operation. The following UML diagram describes the class `PostfixEval`.

PostfixEval
−postfixExpression: String
+PostfixEval() +compute(left: int, right: int, op: chair): int +evaluate(): int −getOperand(): int +getPostfixExp(): String +isOperator(ch: char): boolean +setPostfixExp(postfixExp: String): void

PROGRAM 14.3 EVALUATING A POSTFIX EXPRESSION

The program evaluates a postfix expression. After prompting, the program reads an expression from the keyboard and assigns it to the `PostfixEval` object `postfixExp` using the method `setPostfixExp()`. Enclose the call to `evaluate()` in a try block in case an error occurs. A catch block follows the try block and outputs the message if the expression is invalid and `evaluate()` throws an `ArithmeticException`. The runs display the infix format for each postfix expression that does not contain an error.

```
import java.util.Scanner;

public class Program14_3
{
    public static void main(String[] args)
    {
        // object used to evaluate postfix expressions
        PostfixEval exp = new PostfixEval();
        // postfix expression input
        String rpnExp;
        // for reading an expression
        Scanner keyIn =  new Scanner(System.in);

        System.out.print("Enter the postfix expression: ");
        rpnExp = keyIn.nextLine();

        // assign the expression to exp
        exp.setPostfixExp(rpnExp);

        // call evaluate() in a try block in case an error occurs
        try
```

```
            {
                System.out.println("The value of the expression = " +
                                    exp.evaluate() + "\n");
            }
            // catch block outputs the error
            catch (ArithmeticException ae)
            {
                System.out.println(ae.getMessage() + "\n");
            }
        }
    }
```

```
Run 1:
  (2 + 5)*3 - 8/3
  Enter the postfix expression: 2 5 + 3 * 8 3 / -
  The value of the expression = 19
Run 2:
  2^3 + 1
  Enter the postfix expression: 2 3 ^ 1 +
  The value of the expression = 9
Run 3:
  Enter the postfix expression: 1 9 * /
  PostfixEval: Too many operators
Run 4:
  Enter the postfix expression: 2 3 5 +
  PostfixEval: Too many operands
```

The evaluate() Method

In the PostfixEval class, the task of scanning the postfix expression and computing a result is left to the method evaluate(). It uses an Integer stack, called operandStack, to store the operands. To understand the evaluate() algorithm, we must first look at the private methods. The boolean method isOperand() is called when scanning a non-whitespace character to determine whether it is a valid character ("+", "−", "*", "/","%", "^"). If it is, evaluate() calls getOperand() to retrieve first the right-hand operand and then the left-hand operand. The method checks that the stack is not empty before each pop operation. An empty stack indicates that there are too many operators, and the method throws an ArithmeticException. The operator is processed using the method compute() with integer arguments left and right for the operands and the character op for the operator. The method evaluates the operation "left op right" and pushes the result back onto the stack. A switch statement provides the case selection for the operators and performs the operation corresponding to the selection value op. For the divide (/) and remainder (%) operators, compute() checks the right-hand operand (divisor) to see if it is 0. In this case, the method throws an ArithmeticException with the message "Divide by 0". For the exponential operator ($^\wedge$), compute() checks for (0,0) and throws an ArithmeticException since there is no definition for 0^0.

compute():

```
int compute(int left, int right, char op):
{
  int value = 0;

  // evaluate "left op right"
  switch(op)
  {
     case '+':    value = left + right;
                  break;

     case '-':    value = left - right;
                  break;

     . . .

  }

  return value;
}
```

Rather than simply listing the code for evaluate(), we describe how it implements the algorithm. You can find a complete listing of the method in Chapter 14 of the software supplement. The main loop in evaluate() scans each character of the postfix expression and terminates when all characters have been processed or when an error occurs. Upon completion, the final result resides at the top of the stack and is assigned to the variable expValue, which becomes the return value.

```
int left, right, expValue;
char ch;
int i;

// process characters until the end of the string is reached
// or an error occurs
for (i=0; i < postfixExpression.length(); i++)
{
   // get the current character
   ch = postfixExpression.charAt(i);
   . . .
}
```

The scan uses the static method isDigit() from the Character class to determine whether the current character ch is a digit. The static method returns true if ch >= "0" && ch <= "9." In this case, evaluate() pushes the corresponding Integer value of the operand onto the stack.

```
// look for an operand, which is a single digit nonnegative
// integer if (Character.isDigit(ch))
// value of operand goes on the stack as Integer object
operandStack.push(ch - '0');
```

The method isOperator() determines whether the current character ch in the scan is an operator. If so, evaluate() initiates a process of extracting the operands from the stack and uses compute() to carry out the calculation and return the result. The return value is pushed onto the stack.

```
// look for an operator
else if (isOperator(ch))
{
   // pop the stack to obtain the right operand
   right = getOperand();
   // pop the stack to obtain the left operand
   left = getOperand();
   // evaluate "left op right" and push on stack
   operandStack.push(new Integer(compute(left, right, ch)));
}
```

If the current character ch in the scan is neither an operand nor an operator, evaluate() uses the static method isWhitespace() from the Character class to determine whether ch is a whitespace separator consisting of a blank, newline, or tab. If this is not the case, evaluate() throws an ArithmeticException; otherwise, the loop continues with the next character in the string.

```
// any other character must be whitespace
// whitespace includes blank, tab, and newline
else if (!Character.isWhitespace(ch))
   throw new ArithmeticException("PostfixEval: Improper char");
```

Assuming the scan of the postfix expression terminates without an error, the value of a properly formed expression should be on the top of the stack. The method evaluate() pops the value from the stack. If the stack is then empty, the value is the final result. If the stack still contains elements, evaluate() concludes there are too many operands and throws an ArithmeticException.

```
// the expression value is on the top of the stack; pop it off
expValue = operandStack.pop();
```

```
// if data remains on the stack, there are too many operands
if (!operandStack.isEmpty())
   throw new ArithmeticException(
      "PostfixEval: Too many operands");
```

```
return expValue;
```

14.5 Infix Expression Evaluation

Section 14.4 discusses the use of a stack for postfix expression evaluation. These expressions are relatively easy to evaluate because they do not contain subexpressions and already account for precedence among operators. In addition, the algorithm requires only a single stack that stores operands. Unfortunately, postfix expressions have limited application. Most electronic calculators and programming languages assume expressions are entered with infix notation rather than postfix notation. Evaluation of an infix expression is more difficult. The algorithm must have a strategy to handle subexpressions and must maintain the order of precedence and associativity for operators. For instance, in the expression

```
9 + (2 - 3) * 8
```

we evaluate the subexpression $(2 - 3)$ first and then use the result as the left operand for *. The operator * executes before the + operator because it has higher precedence.

There are two approaches to infix expression evaluation. One approach scans the infix expression and uses separate operator and operand stacks to store the terms. The algorithm produces the result directly (see Programming Project 14.24). A second approach converts the infix expression to its equivalent postfix expression and then calls the postfix expression evaluator from Section 14.4 to compute the result. In this section, we will discuss the second approach.

You can evaluate an infix expression by converting it to postfix and then evaluating the postfix expression.

Infix Expression Attributes

Infix expressions consist of operands, operators, and pairs of parentheses that create subexpressions, which are computed separately. There is an *order of precedence* and *associativity* among operators. The order of precedence dictates that you evaluate the operator with the highest precedence first. Among arithmetic operators, the additive operators $(+, -)$ have the lowest precedence; next are the multiplicative operators $(*, /, \%)$. The exponentiation operator $(^\wedge)$ has the highest precedence. The concept of associativity refers to the order of execution for operators at the same precedence level. If more than one operator has the same precedence, the leftmost operator executes first in the case of left associativity $(+, -, /, \%)$ and the rightmost operator executes first in the case of right associativity $(^\wedge)$. A few examples will clarify the difference between left and right associativity.

The operators * and / have the same order of precedence and are left associative. In the following expression, compute the successive products and then evaluate the quotient.

$$7*2*4/5 \qquad \text{Evaluate:} \qquad ((7*2)*4)/5 = (14*4)/5 = 56/5 = 11$$

The exponentiation operator, $^\wedge$, is right-associative. The following expression involves two successive $^\wedge$ operations. Compute with the rightmost operator $3 ^\wedge 2 = 3^2 = 9$ and use the result as the exponent with the leftmost operator $2 ^\wedge 9 = 2^9 = 512$.

$$2 ^\wedge 3 ^\wedge 2 \qquad \text{Evaluate:} \qquad (2 ^\wedge (3 ^\wedge 2)) = 2^9 = 512$$

An infix expression evaluation algorithm must take operator precedence and associativity into account.

Example 14.4

```
1.  8 + 2*3 = 14          // Precedence: * executes before +
2.  (8 + 2) * 3 = 30      // Evaluate subexpression separately
3.  22 / 4 % 3 = 2        // Associativity: execute / followed by %
```

Infix-to-Postfix Conversion

The infix-to-postfix conversion algorithm takes an infix expression as an input string and returns the corresponding postfix expression as an output (postfix) string. The algorithm has some similarities with the postfix evaluation algorithm. Both scan the expression looking for operands and operators and use a stack to store elements. Postfix evaluation copies operands to a stack and does calculations when an operator is found. The infix-to-postfix conversion algorithm copies operands to the output string and uses a stack to store and process operators and the left-parenthesis symbol. You must understand how the operator stack works to appreciate the algorithm because it manages the order of precedence and associativity of operators as well as handling subexpressions.

A detailed discussion of the infix-to-postfix conversion algorithm is provided on the authors' Web site. You will find the design and implementation of the class `InfixToPostfix`, which defines methods to convert an infix expression containing single-digit integer operands 0–9 and integer operators +, −, *, /, %, and ^ to postfix form. The conversion along with postfix evaluation is used by the GUI application *InfixExpressions.java* to input an expression and evaluate the result. Figure 14.4 is a view of the application, which can be found in Chapter 14 of the software supplement.

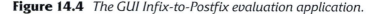

```
Infix Expressions                                    _ □ ×

Infix │

Infix Expression: 2 + 3
    Postfix: 2 3 +    Value = 5
Infix Expression: (3^2 + 2 * 8)/3 - 5
    Postfix: 3 2 ^ 2 8 * + 3 / 5 -    Value = 3
Infix Expression: 3 * (7 - 2 * 4) + 5
    Postfix: 3 7 2 4 * - * 5 +    Value = 2
```

Figure 14.4 *The GUI Infix-to-Postfix evaluation application.*

We will use a series of examples to expose the issues. Each example introduces a new concept that details how the stack handles operators. By tracing the scan of the infix expression, you will see how the stack is involved in the solution.

Example 1: Expression a + b * c.

> Write an operand to the postfix string. Place an operator on the stack, awaiting its right-hand operand.

This example illustrates how the stack temporarily stores operators awaiting their right-hand side operand. Scan the operand a, and immediately write it to the postfix string. The next term is operator +, which cannot be written to the postfix string until the scan identifies its right-hand operand. Push + on an operator stack and proceed (Figure a). Scan the operand b and write it to the postfix string. We next find the operator *, which has higher precedence than +, and hence must appear in the final postfix expression before +. Push * on the stack, which has the effect of driving the + operator with lower precedence further down in the stack (Figure b). Read operand c and write it to the postfix string. After completing the scan of the expression, clear the stack and write the operators to the output string. The operators are released in the order * followed by +, which is the order of their precedence. The result is the postfix expression "abc*+" (Figure c).

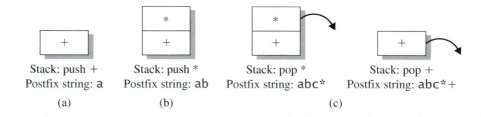

Stack: push +	Stack: push *	Stack: pop *	Stack: pop +
Postfix string: a	Postfix string: ab	Postfix string: abc*	Postfix string: abc*+
(a)	(b)	(c)	

Example 2: Infix expression a * b / c + d.

This example illustrates how to use the stack to handle operators that have the same or lower precedence. Scan the first three terms, writing the operands a and b to the postfix string and pushing operator * on the stack (Figure a). The next item is operator /, which has the same precedence as * but will execute after *. In the postfix string, * must come before /. Accomplish this by ensuring that no operator enters the stack until all of the prior operators with the same or higher precedence have been removed. Pop the operator * and copy it to the postfix string (Figure b). After scanning operand c and writing it to the string, we encounter the operator +, which has lower precedence than / on the stack. Pop the / and then push + on the stack (Figure c). Complete the scan with the operand d and then remove the operator + from the stack (Figure d). The resulting postfix expression is ab*c/d+.

> Push an operator on the stack only after removing all operators of higher or equal precedence.

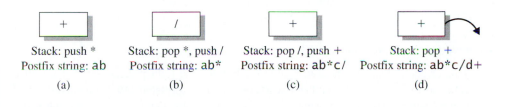

Stack: push *	Stack: pop *, push /	Stack: pop /, push +	Stack: pop +
Postfix string: ab	Postfix string: ab*	Postfix string: ab*c/	Postfix string: ab*c/d+
(a)	(b)	(c)	(d)

Example 3: Infix expression a^b^c.

This example illustrates how to use precedence values to handle the exponential operator ^, which is right associative. This implies we must evaluate the expression b ^ c first and use the result as the right operand of a (a ^ <operand>). Handling the second ^ operator is the problem. After reading the symbols a ^ b, the operands a and b are in the postfix string and the operator ^ is on the stack (Figure a). We must next deal with the second ^ operator. In Example 2, we asserted that an operator goes onto the stack only after we remove all prior operators of equal or greater precedence. If the second ^ operator has the same precedence as the operator ^ on the stack, then we must first pop the operator from the stack and write it to the postfix string producing the expression "ab^". Placing the second ^ operator on the stack and proceeding with the scan results in a final postfix expression "ab^c^" ($(a^b)^c$). This violates right associativity of the ^ operator.

> Making the input and stack precedence of an operator different allows the handling of an operator that is right associative.

To generate a correct solution, we will develop a new strategy. We can associate two precedence values with an operator. One value, called the *scan precedence*, is assigned to an operator when it is scanned. The second value, called the *stack precedence*, is assigned to the operator while it resides on the stack. Table 14.1 gives a listing of the scan precedence and the stack precedence for each of the arithmetic operators. Note that the scan precedence for the right associative ^ operator is greater than its stack precedence and that the two precedences are the same for the left-associative operators. Using the distinction between scan and stack precedence, we can modify the operator insertion policy from Example 2. An operator with its scan precedence goes onto the stack only after we remove all prior operators that have equal or greater stack precedence. In this example, when we scan the second ^ operator, the first ^ operator resides on the stack with stack precedence 3. The second ^ operator has scan precedence 4 and so the second operator is immediately added to the stack. Once there, it assumes a stack precedence 3 so that the top two positions on the stack have the ^ operator when the scan of the expression concludes (Figure b). The figure gives the stack precedence for operators on the stack in square brackets ("[]"). The LIFO ordering assures us that the second $^\wedge$ operator will come off first, thus preserving right associativity (Figure c). The resulting postfix expression is abc$^{\wedge\wedge}$, which is evaluated as a^{b^c}.

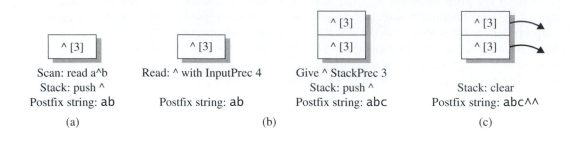

Scan: read a^b
Stack: push ^
Postfix string: ab

(a)

Read: ^ with InputPrec 4

Postfix string: ab

(b)

Give ^ StackPrec 3
Stack: push ^
Postfix string: abc

Stack: clear
Postfix string: abc^^

(c)

Example 4: Infix expression a * (b + c).

Assign "(" an
input precedence
that is greater
than the stack
precedence of any
other operator.
This allows "(" and
the operators in
the subexpression
to remain on
the stack until
the algorithm
encounters ")".

This example illustrates how to handle the left and the right parentheses that set off a subexpression. It must be handled like a separate infix expression with the main difference that the subexpression is converted to a postfix expression when we scan the right parenthesis ")" that corresponds to its left parenthesis "(". We associate both scan and stack precedence with "(" and store it on the stack like any operator until we reach the end of the subexpression. Because the "(" begins a new subexpression, all operators currently on the stack must remain there. We accomplish this by providing "(" with a scan precedence that is greater than the stack precedence of any operator. Once on the stack, no operator in the subexpression may remove the "(" until we identify the corresponding ")". We guarantee that "(" remains fixed by making its stack precedence -1, which is lower than the scan precedence of any operator. See Table 14.1. Once we read the corresponding ")", we have a complete subexpression and can pop all operators on the stack down to the left parenthesis and write them to the postfix string. Complete the handling of the subexpression by removing the "(" from the stack, and continue with the scan of the remaining expression. The following figure assumes the scan has read the symbols a and * and written a to the postfix string while pushing * on the stack. The figure illustrates how we would handle the subexpression (b + c) and then pop * to creating the final postfix expression abc+*.

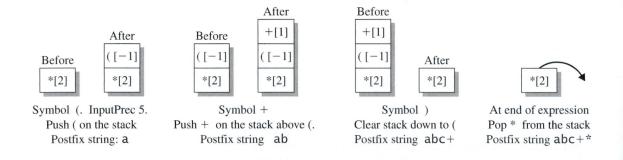

Symbol (. InputPrec 5.
Push (on the stack
Postfix string: a

Symbol +
Push + on the stack above (.
Postfix string ab

Symbol)
Clear stack down to (
Postfix string abc+

At end of expression
Pop * from the stack
Postfix string abc+*

Table 14.1 gives input and stack precedence for the operators +, −, *, /, %, and $^\wedge$, along with the parentheses. Except for the exponential operator $^\wedge$, the other binary operators are left associative and have equal input and stack precedences.

Table 14.1 Input and stack precedence with rank.

Symbol	Input precedence	Stack precedence
+ −	1	1
*/%	2	2
^	4	3
(	5	−1
)	0	0

Chapter Summary

- A stack is a structure whose insert (push) and erase (pop) operations occur at one end of a sequence, called the top of the stack. The last element in is the first element out of the stack, so a stack is a LIFO (Last-In-First-Out) structure. The Stack interface defines the operations push() and pop() that update the stack and the operation peek() that returns a reference to the topmost element of the stack. The Stack interface has the usual collection operations size() and isEmpty(). ALStack implements the interface by using an ArrayList object to contain the stack elements. To implement push(), apply add() to the ArrayList collection; to implement pop(), apply remove() to erase the last element in the ArrayList. Implement peek() using the ArrayList get() operation. ALStack throws an EmptyStackException exception if pop() or peek() is applied to an empty stack. The chapter illustrates the use of a stack by presenting an application that outputs a number in any base b, $2 \leq b \leq 16$. Another application shows the use of stack operations to check the balancing of the symbols "()", "[]", and "{ }" in an arithmetic expression.

- When we introduced recursion in Chapter 6, we gave no indication of how programming languages implement recursion. In fact, its implementation is quite simple and uses a stack. The runtime system maintains a stack of activation records that specify the method arguments, the local variables or objects, and the return address. The system pushes an activation record on the stack when calling a method and pops it off the stack when returning.

- Postfix or RPN expression notation places the operator after its operands. Some calculators use this notation, and it has other applications. A postfix expression is easy to evaluate using a single stack to hold operands. The rules are simple. Immediately push an operand onto the stack. For a binary operator, pop the stack twice to obtain its operands, perform the operation, and push the result onto the stack. At the end of a properly formed postfix expression, a single value remains on the stack. The PostfixEval class performs postfix expression evaluation and throws ArithmeticException if an error occurs.

- Infix notation is the most commonly used expression format. In this notation, a binary operator appears between its operands. Most programming languages and calculators use infix notation. The notation is more complex than postfix because it requires the use of operator precedence and parentheses. In addition, some operators are left associative, and a few are right associative. The chapter outlines the development of an algorithm for converting an infix expression into the equivalent postfix form. The algorithm uses a single stack that holds operators and the left-parenthesis symbols. Consult the authors' Web site for a complete discussion of the algorithm.

Written Exercises

1. Give two applications for stacks in a computer program.

2. What is the output from the following sequence of stack operations?

```
ALStack<Integer> intStack = new ALStack<Integer>();
int x, y = 3;

intStack.push(8);
intStack.push(9);
intStack.push(y);
System.out.println(intStack.peek());    // Output:
intStack.pop();
x = intStack.peek();
intStack.pop();
intStack.push(22 + x);
System.out.println(intStack);           // Output:
```

3. List the elements on the stack from top to bottom after each operation.

```
ALStack<String> s = new ALStack<String>();
String item;
s.push("red");              System.out.println(s);
s.push("blue");             System.out.println(s);
s.push(s.peek());           System.out.println(s);
item = s.pop();             System.out.println(s);
s.pop();
s.push(s.peek());           System.out.println(s);
s.push(item);
```

4. Assume that for each of the following parts, `charStk` is an `ALStack` collection that holds lowercase letters (`Character` objects). Write a code segment that uses only stack operations to:

   (a) search for the first occurrence of character "c". If found, replace it with an upper-case "C". All of the other elements in the stack are unchanged.
   (b) delete all but the bottom two elements in the stack.
   (c) create a new stack `copyStk` that is a copy of the elements in `charStk`. Leave the elements in the original stack unchanged.

5. Over time, the elements 1, 2, and 3 are pushed onto a stack in that order. For each of the following, indicate (yes or no) whether the sequence could be created by popping operations. If yes, list the sequence of `push()` and `pop()` operations that produces the sequence.

   (a) 1-2-3   (b) 2-3-1   (c) 3-2-1   (d) 1-3-2   (e) 3-1-2   (f) 2-1-3

   In general, suppose the element $1, 2, \ldots, n$ are pushed onto a stack in that order. What sequences can be created with pop operations?

6. Trace the method `f()`.

```
public static <T> void f(ALStack<T> s)
{
    ArrayList<T> v = new ArrayList<T>();
    T tmpValue;
    int i;
```

```
    while (!s.isEmpty())
    {
        tmpValue = s.pop();
        if (!v.contains(tmpValue))
            v.add(tmpValue);
    }
    for(i = v.size()-1; i >= 0; i--)
        s.push(v.get(i));
}
```

Assume s has the values {3, 4, 8, 12, 15, 12, 3, 4, 5, 4}, where 4 is on the top of the stack. What is the output from these statements?

```
f(s);
System.out.println(s);
```

7. Convert the following infix expressions to postfix:

(a) a + b*c
(b) (a+b)/(d-e)
(c) (b^2 - 4*a*c)/(2*a)

8. Write the following expressions in infix form:

(a) a b + c *
(b) a b c + *
(c) a b c d e + + * * e f - *

9. Draw the sequence of stack configurations in the evaluation of the postfix expression

    4 5 * 6 3 + / 8 +

Programming Exercises

10. Implement the method get() that returns the value in a stack at position n. The method provides access to any element in a stack from top (position 1) to the bottom (position size()). Throw an IllegalArgumentException if the position n is not in the range 1 to size().

```
    public static <T> T get(Stack<T> stk, int n)
    { . . . }
```

Write a program that tests your implementation of the method.

11. In Chapter 6, we introduced the Fibonacci sequence where the first two values fib(0) and fib(1) are 0 and 1 respectively. Each subsequent value ($n \geq 2$) is the sum of the previous two values; that is, fib(n) = fib(n − 2) + fib(n − 1).

Fibonacci Sequence: 0, 1, 1, 2, 3, 5, 8, 13, 21, 34, ...

Write a program that prompts the user to enter a positive integer n. You are to create a stack using the methods fibStack() and reverseStack(). The resulting stack will contain the values in the Fibonacci sequence from fib(0) to fib(n) from top to bottom. Conclude by displaying the sequence by using the ALStack method toString().

The method fibStack() takes an integer argument n and builds a stack iteratively so that the next value is on the top of the stack. The resulting stack contains successive values in the Fibonacci sequence from bottom to top. At each iterative step starting at fib(2), use stack operations to compute the next value.

```
public static ALStack<Integer> fibStack(int n)
```

The method `reverseStack()` takes a stack as an argument and reverses the elements. The initial top to bottom order is replaced by a bottom to top order.

```
public static <T> void reverseStack(Stack<T> s);
```

12. (a) A music store has a rack in which it periodically puts CDs that it wishes to sell at a discount price. The rack is organized as a stack. The store has a customer who is a great fan of the Boston Pops. One day, this customer decides to buy all of the discounted CDs by this famous orchestra. Very carefully, the customer removes, one by one, each CD from the top of the pile, sets aside those she wants, and then puts back the other CDs in their original order. How would you design an algorithm that uses only stack methods to simulate the action of the customer? Use the algorithm to implement the method `removeAll()` that deletes all elements from a stack that match `item`.

```
public static <T> void removeAll(ALStack<T> s, T item)
{ ... }
```

(b) Write a program that uses two stacks, `stkA` and `stkB`. Assign to `stkA` elements from array `intArr` and the display the stack using `toString()`.

```
Integer[] intArr = {1, 4, 13, 5, 8, 5, 5, 8, 13};
```

In `stkA`, start by accessing 13 at the top of the stack and pushing it onto `stkB`. Using `removeAll()`, delete all duplicates of 13 from the stack. Continue the process with the next element in `stkA` until the stack is empty. Copy elements from `stkB` back to `stkA` and display the contents, which is now the original stack without duplications.

13. A classical implementation of a stack uses an array to hold the elements. Consider the following `BStack` (bounded stack) class outline.

BStack class:

```
public class BStack<T> implements Stack<T>
{
    // array holds the stack elements
    private T[] stackList;

    // topIndex is the index of the stack's top
    private int topIndex;

    // user specified maximum size for the stack
    int maxSize;

    // constructor; create a stack with specified size
    public BStack(int n)
    {
        maxSize = n;
        stackList = (T[])new Object[maxSize];
```

```
        topIndex = -1;
    }
    // push item onto the top of the stack; if stack is full
    // throw IllegalStateException
    public void push(T item)
    { ... }

    // remove and return the item from the top of the stack;
    // if stack is empty, throw EmptyStackException
    public T pop()
    { ... }

    // return the element on the top of the stack; if stack
    // is empty, throw EmptyStackException
    public T peek()
    { ... }

    // determine whether the stack is empty
    public boolean isEmpty()
    { ... }

    // return the number of elements in the stack
    public int size()
    { ... }

    // return true if the stack has maxSize elements
    public boolean full()
    { ... }
}
```

Write a program that uses BStack with strings. Be sure to verify that your implementation of BStack does not insert elements into a full stack.

14. For some applications, we want to use two separate stacks to store a specified number of elements. While the number is known, we cannot predict how many are in each stack. Possibly, all of the elements end up in one stack or they may be split evenly between the two stacks. The task is to create a dual-stack collection type that stores elements in a fixed size array.

Use the BStack class in Programming Exercise 14.13 as a model. Implement the class DoubleStack, which uses an array as the storage structure. The constructor creates an instance with a user-specified maximum size for array that stores the two arrays. Each stack has the usual methods push(), pop(), peek(), size(), and isEmpty() along with isFull() to indicate when the total number of elements in the two stacks exceeds the maximum size for the array. An enum class defines colors red and blue that distinguish the two stacks. Each of the methods includes an enum constant to associate the operation with a specific stack.

DoubleStack class:

```
public class DoubleStack<T>
{
    public enum StackRef {red, blue};

    // array holds the stack elements
```

```
private T[] stackList;
// indices that indicate the top of each stack
. . .;

// user specified maximum size for the two stacks
int maxSize;

// constructor; create dual stacks with specified size
public DoubleStack(int n)
{ . . . }

// push item onto the top of the specified stack;
// if stack is full throw IllegalStateException
public void push(T item, StackRef c)
{ . . . }

< other methods >
}
```

Write a program that tests your implementation of DoubleStack. Create a series of random integers and store the even integers in one stack and the odd integers in the other stack.

15. (a) The ALStack class is a concrete implementation of a stack collection. The class uses an ArrayList object by composition to store the stack elements (Section 14.1). Give a declaration of a second Stack collection class, called EStack, that extends the ArrayList class and implements the Stack interface. The EStack class should provide toString(), which returns a string displaying the elements in the stack from top to bottom enclosed in brackets.

```
class EStack<T> extends ArrayList<T> implements Stack<T>
{ . . . }
```

(b) Are there potential problems with this implementation? In formulating your answer, consider whether it is possible to violate the rules under which a stack operates. Propose a means for solving the problems.

(c) Test the EStack class by running Program 14.1.

16. (a) Implement the method nToTop() that takes a stack stk and an integer n as arguments and moves the nth element in the stack to the top of the stack. All other elements maintain their original order. The first element is at the top of the stack, second element below the top, and so forth.

```
// reorder stack by moving the nth element to the top
// of stack
public static <T> void nToTop(Stack<T> stk, int n)
{ . . . }
```

(b) Write a program that creates the following stack of strings.

In a loop, prompt the user to enter a position in the stack and call nToTop() to move the element from the designated position to the top of the stack. Terminate the program on input 0. At each stage, display the current ordering of strings in the stack from top to bottom.

17. In Chapter 14 Exercises, the class ExtPostfixEval is a copy of PostfixEval that is introduced in Section 14.4. Modify ExtPostfixEval to include the operator unary minus, represented by the symbol ~. For example, the expression "7 ~ 9 +" is the postfix equivalent of "−7 + 9", which evaluates to 2.

Test your modifications to the class by running Program 14.3 with an ExtPostfixEval object. Your run must include the postfix expression "7 ~ 9 + " and the postfix equivalent of the infix expression "−7 + (−4 + 9)*2".

Programming Project

18. The authors' Web supplement includes an extended discussion of infix expression evaluation. The class InfixtoPostfix has methods that enable a user to take an infix expression with single-digit operations and return the postfix equivalent expression. The latter expression can then be evaluated using a PostfixEval object. All of this is illustrated in the GUI application *InfixExpressions.java*.

The infix-to-postfix conversion algorithm uses a stack to hold operators, and the algorithm that evaluates postfix expressions uses a stack to hold operands. Design an algorithm that uses two stacks and directly evaluates an infix expression. One stack holds operators and the other stack contains operands. Implement the algorithm in the class InfixEvaluation and modify the GUI in the Web tutorial so it inputs an infix expression in the text field and outputs its value in the text area. All of the required software components are available in Chapter 14 Exercises.

Chapter 15

QUEUES AND PRIORITY QUEUES

CONTENTS

15.1 THE QUEUE INTERFACE
Creating a Queue Collection Class
Application: Scheduling Queue

15.2 THE RADIX SORT
Radix Sort Algorithm

15.3 A BOUNDED QUEUE
The BQueue Class—Implementation
Design
The BQueue Class—Declaration

15.4 PRIORITY QUEUES
A Priority Queue Interface
Application: Support Services Pool

15.5 EVENT-DRIVEN SIMULATION
A Bank Simulation
Simulation Design Pattern
BankSimulation Class

In Chapter 14, we introduced a stack, which is a storage structure that allows elements to enter and exit at only one end of a list. In this chapter, we will discuss a queue, which is an analogous structure in which elements enter and exit at opposite ends of a list. A real-world example of a queue is the checkout line at a grocery store. Customers enter the checkout (waiting) line at the back, and the clerk serves them one by one from the front of the line (Figure 15.1).

A key element of this chapter is queue applications. An appointment scheduler uses a queue as a waiting line. An interesting example is the sorting algorithm known as the *radix sort*. Rather than comparing elements within a sequence, the algorithm repeatedly uses a set of queues to partition the elements into progressively more ordered sublists.

An abstract view of a queue assumes an unbounded sequence (waiting line). In some applications, a queue models a storage structure that has limited space. We introduce a circular model of a queue to implement this type of structure.

A variation of a queue is a *priority queue*, which removes the item of highest priority from the collection rather than simply the first item in the sequence.

Figure 15.1 *Grocery store checkout line as a model for a queue.*

A priority queue exploits a natural ordering among the elements and makes no reference to how they are stored.

Simulation studies demonstrate important computer applications. They give us an insight into a real-world situation so that we can better understand it. A simulation uses computer objects with methods that model real-world objects and their behaviors. In Section 15.5, we will introduce the design of an event-driven simulation that uses a priority queue to store an account of events that occur over time as the simulation unfolds. The application is a bank simulation that tracks the behavior of customers who are served by a set of tellers. While the study is interesting, the focus is on the overall design of simulations using inheritance and polymorphism.

> A waiting line is a real-world example of a queue and is the classical model. The structure is used for radix sort algorithms.

15.1 The Queue Interface

A *queue* is a sequence of items that allows access only at the two ends of the sequence. We refer to the ends of the sequence as the front and back (Figure 15.2). A queue inserts a new item at the back and removes an element from the front.

> In a queue, data enters at the back and leaves at the front.

front   back

Figure 15.2 *A queue.*

The `Queue` interface describes a queue as a storage structure. It defines the same methods as the `Stack` interface. The operation `push()` adds an item at the back of the queue. The operation `pop()` removes the first element (front) of the queue. To access the value of the first element, use the method `peek()`. Like any collection, a queue uses `size()` and the boolean method `isEmpty()` to reflect the number of elements that are currently stored. Figure 15.3 illustrates the `push()` and `pop()` operations.

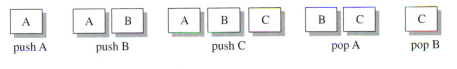

push A   push B   push C   pop A   pop B

Figure 15.3 *Queue push and pop operations.*

> A queue is a FIFO or an FCFS structure.

A queue removes elements in the same order they were stored, and hence it provides *FIFO* (First-In/First-Out) ordering. The abstract concept of a queue allows for an arbitrarily large storage of data. Hence, the `push()` operation has no precondition. The same is not true for the methods `pop()` and `peek()`, which assume that the queue has at least one element. If the queue is empty, the methods throw a `NoSuchElementException`. The following is a listing of the generic `Queue` interface.

The queue interface is similar to that of a stack. Methods pop() and peek() access the first element in the sequence, while push() inserts an element at the back of the queue.

interface Queue<T>		ds.util
boolean	**isEmpty**() Returns true if the queue is empty and false otherwise.	

T	**peek**()
	    Returns the element at the front of the queue; if the queue is empty, the method
	    throws a NoSuchElementException.	

T	**pop**()
	    Erases the element at the front of the queue and returns it. If the queue is empty,
	    the method throws a NoSuchElementException.	

void	**push**(T element) Inserts the element at the back of the queue.	
int	**size**() Returns the number of elements in the queue.	

Creating a Queue Collection Class

Implement a queue by using a LinkedList and object composition. Push() accesses the back of the list and pop() or peek() accesses the front of the list.

In Section 14.1, we developed the ALStack class, which implements the Stack interface by composition. An ArrayList object is the underlying storage structure with methods that correspond to those in the interface. We use the same approach with the LinkedQueue class. In this case, a LinkedList is the storage structure. The collection has methods getFirst() and removeFirst() that efficiently access and delete the front of the sequence. These operations provide a simple implementation of the queue peek() and pop() methods. A linked list also has the method add(), which efficiently inserts an element at the back of the sequence. We will use this to implement the queue push() operation.

The declaration of the LinkedQueue class implements the Queue interface using a private LinkedList reference variable qList and composition. The constructor creates an empty queue by initializing qList as an empty list.

LinkedQueue class:

```
public class LinkedQueue<T> implements Queue<T>
{
    private LinkedList<T> qlist = null;
    public LinkedQueue ()
    {
        qlist = new LinkedList<T>();
    }
    . . .
}
```

Think of a LinkedQueue collection as a sequence of elements organized horizontally in a waiting line. Initially, the queue is empty and the size of the list is 0. Pushing an item on the queue adds the item at the back of the list and increases the size of the list. Popping an item from the queue removes the first element in the list and decreases the size of the list by 1. At all times, we can peek into the queue by extracting the value of the first element in the list. We also know the size of the queue and whether it is empty by extracting this information from the underlying LinkedList object.

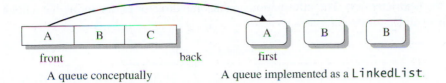

A queue conceptually   A queue implemented as a LinkedList.

Let us look at the relationship between a LinkedQueue collection q and the underlying LinkedList qlist for a series of operations with string objects.

Queue operation	LinkedList operation	Queue
q.push("red")	qlist.add("red")	[red]
q.push("blue")	qlist.add("blue")	[red, blue]
String str = q.peek()	str = qlist.getFirst()	
q.pop	qlist.removeFirst()	[blue]

The implementation of LinkedQueue uses the adapter design pattern.

The implementation of the queue methods is trivial. Call a corresponding LinkedList method to execute the operation. Look at the method pop(). The operation of removing an element at the front of the queue is handled by the LinkedList removeFirst() method. If the queue is empty, the pop() method throws a NoSuchElementException.

pop():

```
public T pop()
{
    // if the queue is empty, throw  NoSuchElementException
    if (isEmpty())
        throw new NoSuchElementException(
            "LinkedQueue pop(): queue empty");

    // remove and return the first element in the list
    return qlist.removeFirst();
}
```

The LinkedList methods add(), getFirst(), and removeFirst() have complexity O(1). It follows that the methods push(), peek(), and pop() in the LinkedQueue class have complexity O(1).

Queue operations all have running time O(1).

Application: Scheduling Queue

Let us look at one of the main applications of a queue, namely, a process or task scheduler. An executive secretary for a personnel director schedules a series of job interviews for applicants seeking a position. The secretary uses a queue to store the starting times for the interviews. The figure illustrates a schedule of eight appointments beginning at 10:00 A.M. The last appointment begins at 16:30 (4:30 P.M.). Because the office closes at 5:00 P.M., the last appointment lasts at most 30 minutes. Throughout the day, the director begins each interview by popping the queue and then calling peek() to identify the time for the next interview. The information enables the director to determine the amount of time available for the interview.

Appointment Schedule

10:00	11:15	13:00	13:45	14:30	15:30	16:30

front   back

PROGRAM 15.1 JOB INTERVIEW SCHEDULING

This program implements the interview scheduler. The appointment calendar is set up in a queue by reading the interview times from the file *appt.dat*. Input is a string designating time in the form *hh:mm*. The string is converted to a Time24 object by calling the method parseTime(), which is then pushed on the queue. A loop creates a listing of appointment times and available interview times. The last appointment can interview the applicant until 17:00 (5:00 P.M.), when the office closes.

```java
import java.io.*;
import java.util.Scanner;
import ds.util.LinkedQueue;
import ds.time.Time24;

public class Program15_1
{
    public static void main(String[] args) throws IOException
    {
        final Time24 END_DAY = new Time24(17,00);
        String apptStr;

        // time interval from current appt to next appt
        Time24 apptTime = null, interviewTime = null;

        // input stream to read times as strings from
        // file "appt.dat"
        Scanner input = new Scanner(new FileReader("appt.dat"));

        // queue to hold appointment time for job applicants
        LinkedQueue<Time24> apptQ = new LinkedQueue<Time24>();

        // construct the queue by appt times as strings from
        // file; use parseTime to convert to Time24 object
        while (input.hasNext())
        {
            apptStr = input.nextLine();
            apptQ.push(Time24.parseTime(apptStr));
        }

        // output the day's appointment schedule
        System.out.println("Appointment    Interview");

        // pop next appt time and determine available time for
        // interview (peek at next appt at front of queue)
```

```
        while (!apptQ.isEmpty())
        {
            // get the next appointment
            apptTime = apptQ.pop();

            // interview time is interval to next appt or to
            // END_DAY
            if (!apptQ.isEmpty())
                interviewTime = apptTime.interval(apptQ.peek());
            else
                interviewTime = apptTime.interval(END_DAY);

            // display appointment time and interview time
            System.out.println("    " + apptTime + "            " +
                interviewTime);
        }
    }
}
```

```
File "appt.dat"
    10:00
    11:15
    13:00
    13:45
    14:30
    15:30
    16:30

Run:
  Appointment  Interview
    10:00         1:15
    11:15         1:45
    13:00         0:45
    13:45         0:45
    14:30         1:00
    15:30         1:00
    16:30         0:30
```

15.2 The Radix Sort

Up to this point, we have discussed a variety of sorting algorithms. The elementary sorting algorithms selection sort and insertion sort are quadratic algorithms that use a brute-force method to order the elements. More advanced sorting algorithms mergesort and quicksort use a divide-and-conquer strategy that results in average runtime efficiency $O(n \log_2 n)$. In this section, we will introduce a new design method for ordering an array of integers. The method, called the *radix sort*, is a linear algorithm that uses successive digits in the elements to partially sort the array. The technique is a two-stage process referred to as *transform-and-conquer*.

At each step, the transform stage passes the elements through a series of queues that correspond to the values at a specified digit. The conquer stage builds a progressively more ordered array by extracting the elements from the queues. The radix sort algorithm works by comparing individual pieces of an element rather than the element in its entirety. In our example, the pieces are digits in an integer. The radix sort algorithm can be used with other types of data in which comparison uses individual bits or sequences of bits.

The radix sort has been used since the early days of computing when data was stored on punched cards. To order the data, an operator ran the cards through a mechanical sorter. For integer data, the machine dropped each card into one of ten bins that represented the digits 0–9. Each bin was a queue in which a card entered at the back and exited at the front. The mechanical sorter implemented the radix sort algorithm. To explain the process, we assume that the cards contain two-digit numbers in the range 00–99. The numbers (cards) pass through the machine twice to separate the data first by the 1's digit and then by the 10's digit. Each pass involves first distributing the cards into the bins and then collecting them back into a sequence.

Initial sequence: {91, 6, 85, 15, 92, 35, 30, 22, 39}

Pass 0: Distribute the cards into bins according to the 1's digit (10^0).

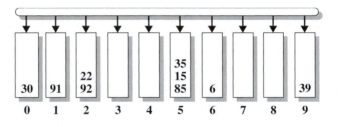

Hence, 30 falls into bin 0, 91 falls into bin 1, 92 and 22 fall into bin 2, and so forth. Collect the numbers from the bins in the order 0 to 9. This determines a sequence that is in order by the 1's digit.

Sequence after pass 0: {30, 91, 92, 22, 85, 15, 35, 6, 39}

Pass 1: Take the new sequence and distribute the cards into bins determined by the 10's digit (10^1).

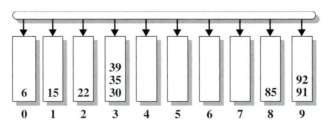

Collect the cards from the bins in the order 0 to 9.

Sequence after pass 1: {6, 15, 22, 30, 35, 39, 85, 91, 92} (Sorted sequence)

In the radix sort for two-digit integers, use queues to sort by the 1's digit and then by the 10's digit.

Some intuitive analysis indicates why the process sorts the numbers after two passes. At the completion of pass 1, the sequence is ordered with elements distributed in groups with the 0's (range from 00 to 09), followed by the 10's (range from 10 to 19), 20's, and so forth. Thus, any two numbers with different 10's digits, such as 35 and 92, will be in the proper relative order because the operator collects numbers from the 3-bin before numbers from the 9-bin. The analysis reduces to considering numbers with the same 10's digit. Pass 0 deals with their ordering. To see this, consider the partially ordered sequence that results from pass 0. This sequence is divided into groups with all numbers ending in 0 located at the start of the sequence, followed by the group of numbers ending in 1, and so forth. In our example, for instance, the original sequence contains three numbers, 30, 35, and 39, in the 30s. Initially pass 0 produces a partially ordered sequence in some manner like

Partially Ordered List After Pass 0

As these numbers move through the sorter on pass 1, they drop into the 3-bin in the order 30, 35, and 39. A similar situation occurs in the other bins. Pass 1 produces an ordered list of two-digit numbers.

Ordered List After Pass 1

6	15	22	30 35 39		85	91 92
0's	10's	20's	30's		80's	90's

Radix Sort Algorithm

We can extend the sorting process for two-digit numbers to d-digit numbers, $d \geq 1$, by performing d passes. Recall that a base-10 number with d digits is a sum of products of its digits with powers of 10. Each digit, x_i, is in the range 0–9.

$$\text{value} = x_{d-1}10^{d-1} + x_{d-2}10^{d-2} + \cdots + x_2 10^2 + x_1 10^1 + x_0 10^0$$

The first pass sorts by the 1's digit (power 10^0), the second by the 10's digit (power 10^1), the third by the 100's digit (power 10^2), and so forth. The static method radixSort() in the class Arrays implements the algorithm. It requires as parameters an integer array, arr, and the maximum number of digits, d, of any integer in the array.

```
// sort arr using the radix sort; each integer has
// d or fewer digits
public static void radixSort(int[] arr, int d)
{ ... }
```

In the implementation, an array of ten queues simulates the sorting bins 0 to 9. Note that Java does not allow arrays of generic type. As a result, generic syntax is not used and digitQueue is declared as a raw LinkedQueue array.

```
// allocate 10 null references to a LinkedQueue
LinkedQueue[] digitQueue = new LinkedQueue[10];

// initialize each element of digitQueue to be
// an empty queue
```

In the radix sort for d-digit integers, use queues to sort by the 1's digit, then by the 10's digit, then by the 100's digit, and so forth.

```
for (i = 0; i < digitQueue.length;i++)
    digitQueue[i] = new LinkedQueue();
```

The `radixSort()` method must execute d iterations, one for each digit. The ith iteration distributes the numbers into the array of queues, `digitQueue`, by using the digit correspon- ding to the power 10^i. For i = 0, distribute the numbers into the queues according to the digit with power 10^0 = 1. For i = 1, distribute the numbers into the queues according to the digit with power 10^1 = 10, and so forth. To determine the value of the digit at any position i, divide a number by `power` = 10^i and take the remainder after division by 10. For instance, suppose the number is 34,758 and the position is 3. This is the 1,000's position with power = 10^3. Dividing the number by 1,000 cuts off the low three digits, leaving the result 34. Obtain the digit in the thousands position by finding the remainder after division by 10.

```
34758/ 1000 = 34, 34 % 10 = 4                        // digit is 4
```

The digit identifies the queue into which the algorithm should push the number.

```
digitQueue[(arr[i] / power) % 10].push(arr[i]);
```

The private method `distribute()` implements the distribution of the numbers into the 10 queues. The parameters include the array of integers, the queue, and the power that designates which digit defines the allocation of a number to a queue.

distribute():

```
// support method for radixSort()
// distribute array elements into one of 10 queues
// using the digit corresponding to power
// power = 1 ==> 1's digit
// power = 10 ==> 10's digit
// power = 100 ==> 100's digit
// ...
private static void distribute(int[] arr, LinkedQueue[]
                                    digitQueue, int power)
{
    int i;

    // loop through the array, inserting each element into
    // the queue (arr[i] / power) % 10
    for (i = 0; i < arr.length; i++)
        digitQueue[(arr[i] / power) % 10].push(arr[i]);
}
```

After the numbers are distributed into the queues, the private method `collect()` scans the array of queues in the order from 0 to 9 and moves all items from the queues back into the array.

collect():

```
// support method for radixSort()
// gather elements from the queues and copy back to the array
```

```
private static void collect(LinkedQueue[] digitQueue, int[] arr)
{
   int i = 0, digit;

   // scan the array of queues using indices 0, 1, 2, etc.
   for (digit = 0; digit < 10; digit++)
      // collect items until queue empty and copy items back
      // to the array
      while (!digitQueue[digit].isEmpty())
      {
         arr[i] = digitQueue[digit].pop());
         i++;
      }
}
```

The method radixSort() is an iterative algorithm that repeatedly calls distribute() followed by collect(), for power = 1, 10, 100, ..., 10^{d-1}.

radixSort():

```
public static void radixSort(int[] arr, int d)
{
   int i;
   // current digit found by dividing by 10^power
   int power = 1;
   // allocate 10 null references to a LinkedQueue
   LinkedQueue[] digitQueue = new LinkedQueue[10];

   // initialize each element of digitQueue to be
   // an empty queue
   for (i = 0;i < digitQueue.length;i++)
         digitQueue[i] = new LinkedQueue();
   for (i = 0; i < d;i++)
   {
         distribute(arr, digitQueue, power);
         collect(digitQueue, arr);
         power *= 10;
   }
}
```

PROGRAM 15.2 RADIX SORT

This program performs a radix sort for an integer array, arr, of five-digit integers. The array consists of 50 random numbers in the range 0–99,999. After calling radixSort() to order the integers, the program calls displayArray() to display the sorted array elements in six columns.

```java
import java.util.Random;
import ds.util.Arrays;

public class Program15_2
{
    public static void main(String[] args)
    {
        // array to hold the data that is sorted
        int[] arr = new int[50];
        Random rnd = new Random();
        int i;

        // initialize array with 50 random numbers in
        // range 0 - 99999
        for (i = 0; i < 50; i++)
            arr[i] = rnd.nextInt(100000);
        // apply the radix sort and output the sorted array
        Arrays.radixSort(arr, 5);
        displayArray(arr);
    }

    private static void displayArray(int[] arr)
    {
        int i, j, strnLength;
        String s, strn;

        for (i=0; i < arr.length; i++)
        {
            // represent value of arr[i] as a string
            strn = String.valueOf(arr[i]);
            // capture the length of strn
            strnLength = strn.length();

            s = "";
            // justify strn in a field of 8 print positions
            for (j=0;j < 8-strnLength;j++)
                s += " ";
            s += strn;

            // output the justified integer value
            System.out.print(s);
            if ((i+1) % 6 == 0)      // newline every 6 numbers
                System.out.println();
        }
        System.out.println();
    }
}
```

Run:

2554	3097	5231	6876	8539	12446
16483	20040	23202	24353	24758	25996
28922	29730	30672	32032	32198	32261
36705	36867	47340	47688	51547	53617
54797	55577	56055	59553	61588	65289
65465	68416	68935	71586	73017	77119
80185	80659	81371	83443	87678	88138
90076	90717	93637	94948	95470	96984
97332	98616				

Efficiency of the Radix Sort   The radix sort orders an array of size n that contains d-digit integers. Each pass inserts the n numbers into the ten queues (bins) and then collects the numbers from the queues. The algorithm performs these 2*n queue operations d times. Section 15.1 discusses the fact that queue push() and pop() operations have running time $O(1)$. It follows that the complexity of the radix sort for d-digit numbers is $0(2 * d * n) = O(n)$. Radix sort appears to be superior to most *in-place sorting* algorithms that reorder the data within the original sequence and do not use temporary storage. The in-place sorts have average-case running times $O(n^2)$ or $O(n \log_2 n)$. The "superior" quality is deceiving because one measure of the efficiency of an algorithm is the amount of memory it requires. The radix sort requires extra space proportional to the size of the array that is being sorted. For very large data sets, the extra storage becomes a real liability.

The radix sort is a linear algorithm. However, it requires additional memory for the queues and is less general than $O(n \log_2 n)$ sorting algorithms such as quicksort.

Another issue is the number of bins (queues) that are required. With integers, 10 queues are sufficient, but the algorithm would require almost 100 separate queues for arbitrary strings. The number of bins does affect the efficiency of the radix sort.

The more general purpose $O(n \log_2 n)$ algorithms, such as quicksort, adapt to a broader variety of applications than the radix sort. They do not assume values in the array can be effectively partitioned into pieces. On a more technical note, the efficiency of the radix sort, as compared to that of an $O(n \log_2 n)$ sort, can depend on features of the computer hardware. For instance, some systems are more efficient with the division operation and the copying of large blocks of data.

15.3 A Bounded Queue

The general description of a queue assumes that the list can grow without bounds. The `LinkedQueue` class in Section 15.1 corresponds to this view. The underlying `LinkedList` storage structure allows a queue to grow as necessary, and so there is no queue-full condition. For some applications, however, entries might have to reside in a memory area of fixed size. For instance, a hardware interface often inserts data from a peripheral device into a buffer that resides inside the interface itself. You are familiar with computer video cards that manage the screen. These cards have internal memory (RAM) that serves as the buffer. The interface must organize all queue elements within the fixed-size buffer. For situations such as this, a programmer might require a specialized queue that stores data in a fixed-size array. When the array fills up, the queue-full condition is true (buffer overrun), and no more elements can be inserted into the queue.

A bounded queue uses an array to hold queue elements. As a result, it has a maximum size. A bounded queue is used for specialized applications.

In this section, we will introduce a bounded-queue class called BQueue. The class uses a finite array as the underlying storage structure. A user may use a default constructor to set the fixed size at 50. A second constructor allows the user to pass the size as an argument.

The BQueue class implements the Queue interface and adds the method full(), which returns a boolean value indicating whether the array is full. If a program attempts to add an element to a full queue, push() throws an IndexOutOfBoundsException. An attempt to access or delete the front of an empty queue results in a NoSuchElementException.

The following is a description of the BQueue class. We include only a listing of the constructors and the method full(). All of the other methods derive from the fact that the class implements the Queue interface.

class BQueue<T> implements Queue<T>	ds.util

	Constructors
	BQueue()
	Creates a queue with fixed size 50.
	BQueue(int size)
	Creates an empty queue with the specified fixed size.
	Methods
boolean	**full**()
	Returns true if the number of elements in the queue equals its fixed size and false otherwise.

Example 15.1

This example illustrates the declaration of a BQueue object and the use of full() to avoid attempting an insertion into a full queue. An exception occurs when we call push() from within a try block and attempt to add an element to a full queue.

```
// declare an empty bounded queue with fixed size 15
BQueue<Integer> q = new BQueue<Integer>(15);
int i;

// fill up the queue
for (i=1; !q.full(); i++)
    q.push(i);

// output element at the front of q and the queue size
System.out.println(q.peek() + " " + q.size());

try
{
    q.push(40);                              // exception occurs
}

catch (IndexOutOfBoundsException iobe)
{
    System.out.println(iobe);
}
```

```
Output:
 1 15
 java.lang.IndexOutOfBoundsException: BQueue push(): queue full
```

The BQueue Class—Implementation Design

The BQueue uses a fixed-length array of generic type to store the elements. The array, called queueArray, uses a set of private integer variables that locate elements in the queue and maintain the size and fixed-length capacity of the queue. The variable qfront is an index that references the front of the queue, and the variable qback is the location at which a new element enters the queue. The variables qcount and qcapacity maintain the current size of the queue and the size of the storage array respectively. The nondefault constructor initializes the variables using the user specified size; the default constructor calls this constructor with size = 50.

BQueue class:

```java
public class BQueue<T> implements Queue<T>
{
    // array holding the queue elements
    private T[] queueArray;
    // index of the front and back of the queue
    private int qfront, qback;
    // the capacity of the queue and the current size
    private int qcapacity, qcount;

    // create an empty bounded queue with specified size
    public BQueue(int size)
    {
        qcapacity = size;
        queueArray = (T[])new Object[qcapacity];
        qfront = 0;
        qback = 0;
        qcount = 0;
    }

    public BQueue()
    {
        // called non-default constructor with capacity = 50
        BQueue(50);
    }

    < method full() and methods in the Queue interface >
}
```

The implementation of the BQueue class involves a circular array model for storing elements in the queue. We illustrate the model by using a queue with qcapacity = 4 elements. Assume that the queue already contains three elements. The index qfront identifies the first element in the queue, and the index qback identifies that location at which the next insertion occurs.

Queue contains
A, B, C

A	B	C	

qfront   qback

As we remove elements A and B from the queue, we could shift the remaining items forward in the array. This would be a happy situation for customers in a grocery checkout line because the movement would get them closer to being served. This is not productive activity for a computer algorithm because the movement takes processor time merely to maintain the array. Suppose the queue contains 1,000 items. When we delete an entry from the front, 999 elements must move toward the front. A better solution leaves the remaining elements at their current location and moves qfront forward in the array.

A problem occurs if we attempt to add elements D and E. The first insertion places D at location qback, which is then positioned past the end of the array. There is no room for E because an element cannot be added beyond the bounds of the fixed-length array. Nevertheless, the array does have room. This room is at the front of the array previously occupied by the deleted elements A and B.

Use a circular buffer to hold elements in a bounded queue.

The situation leads us to a new way of viewing the queue. Think of the queue as a circular sequence with a series of slots that allow elements to enter in a clockwise fashion. The exit point for an element is the slot designated by qfront, and the entry point for a new element occurs at the slot identified by qback. Let us retrace the activity in our four-element queue, assuming the circular storage model (Figure 15.4).

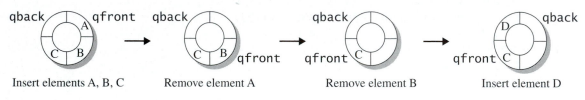

Figure 15.4 *Circular queue model.*

In the circular model, element E can enter the queue at location qback. Note that qback is now the position that was formerly occupied by A. While the circular model is a good abstract view of how items enter and leave a queue, our implementation of the BQueue class must deal with the array, which stores elements sequentially. Treating the array as a circular sequence involves updating qfront and qback to cycle back to the front of the array as soon as they move past the end of the array (index = qcapacity). Figure 15.5 illustrates how E would be added to the queue at the front of the array. Note that qback has

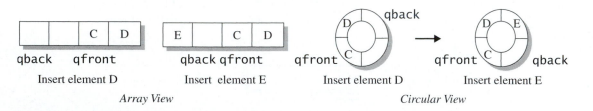

Figure 15.5 *Adding an element to a circular queue.*

a value that is less than qfront. This can be a little disconcerting, even counterintuitive, given our familiar linear view of a queue. Do not let this bother you; the circularity will be handled in the implementation of the class.

To have the indices qfront and qback cycle within the bounds of the array, we use the % operator, which computes the remainder after dividing by qcapacity. On each insertion or deletion from the sequence, increment the appropriate index by 1, and assign it a new value modulo the array size. When the indices move past the end of the array, their values are reset to the start of the array.

> Use the % operator to advance qfront and qback in a circular fashion.

Move qback forward: qback = (qback + 1) % qcapacity;
Move qfront forward: qfront = (qfront + 1) % qcapacity;

With our four-element array, if qfront has value 2, then the new value of qfront after popping an element from the queue is

qfront = (2 + 1) % 4, which has value 3 % 4 = 3

If qback is at the end of the array (index 3), and we push a new element into the queue, update qback to have the new value

qback = (3 + 1) % 4, which is the integer 4 % 4 = 0

The BQueue Class—Declaration

We will now illustrate the actual implementation of the BQueue class for the methods push(), pop(), and full(). The methods access and update all of the private data in the class. The boolean method full() compares the current size of the queue with the size of the fixed-length array. For convenience, we will use the variable qcapacity rather than its equivalent value queueArray.length.

full():

```
public boolean full()
{
   return qcount == qcapacity;
}
```

The push() operation adds an element at the back of the queue. If the queue is full, the method throws the IndexOutOfBoundsException. Otherwise, it adds the element at location qback, increments qcount, and updates qback to the next location in the circular queue.

push():

```
public void push(T item)
{
   // is queue full? if so, throw an IndexOutOfBoundsException
   if (qcount == qcapacity)
      throw new IndexOutOfBoundsException(
         "BQueue push(): queue full");
```

```
                    // insert into the circular queue
                    queueArray[qback] = item;
                    qback = (qback+1) % qcapacity;

                    // increment the queue size
                    qcount++;
                }
```

The pop() operation first checks that the queue is not empty and then accesses the element at index qfront. This becomes the return value. Removing the element is carried out by moving qfront forward to the next location in the circular queue.

pop():

```
            public T pop()
            {
                // if queue is empty, throw a NoSuchElementException
                if (count == 0)
                    throw new NoSuchElementException(
                        "BQueue pop(): empty queue");

                // save the front of the queue
                T queueFront = queueArray[qfront];

                // perform a circular queue deletion
                qfront = (qfront+1) % qcapacity;

                // decrement the queue size
                qcount--;

                // return the front
                return queueFront;
            }
```

Like LinkedQueue, all bounded-queue operations have running time O(1).

In the BQueue class, the operations push() and pop() have complexity O(1), because each method simply accesses the array at one of the indices qfront or qback.i

15.4 Priority Queues

A priority queue acts like a queue collection but with access to the elements determined by their priority or measure of importance.

A queue is a data structure that provides FIFO ordering of elements. Access is limited only to the first or "oldest" element in the queue and a deletion operation removes this element. Applications sometimes require a modified version of a queue in which access is given only to the element with a priority ranking instead of chronological order. This structure, called a *priority queue*, removes the element of highest priority. The ranking of elements in a priority queue is determined by some external criterion. For instance, suppose a business provides a centralized office pool to handle a variety of jobs for the staff. Company policy judges job requests by the president to be of highest priority (priority 3), followed by requests from directors (priority 2), from managers (priority 1), and finally from clerks (priority 0). A person's rank in the company becomes a criterion that measures the relative importance of a job. Instead of handling jobs on a first-come/first-served basis, the office pool uses a priority queue to handle jobs in the order of their assigned importance. For instance, Figure 15.6 shows jobs 1–4 in the priority queue. The office pool processes the jobs in the order #2, #1, #4, and #3 so that the president is handled first and the clerk is handled last.

Figure 15.6 *A priority queue for the secretarial pool.*

The "bucket" display in Figure 15.6 is a good abstract model for a priority queue. There is no assumption on how elements enter the priority queue but only a criterion for their exit. Think of a priority queue as a collection of elements loosely tossed into a bucket. Removing an element involves reaching around in the bucket and pulling out the one with the highest priority.

In a *maximum priority queue*, the highest-priority item has the largest value. The secretarial pool example illustrates a maximum priority queue. In a *minimum priority queue*, the highest-priority item has the smallest value. As an example of a minimum priority queue, an operating system can insert print jobs into a priority queue on the basis of the number of pages. In this situation, the higher-priority jobs are those with the lower page count. It is reasonable to print the 2-, 7- and 10-page jobs before a 100-page job.

> There are two types of priority queues. A maximum priority queue removes the largest value, and a minimum priority queue removes the smallest value.

A Priority Queue Interface

The PQueue interface defines the access methods for a priority queue collection. The interface uses the same method names found in the Stack and Queue interfaces. The operations, however, assume that the generic type of the elements implements the Comparable interface.

interface PQueue<T>	*ds.util*

boolean	isEmpty()
	Returns true if the priority queue is empty and false otherwise.
T	peek()
	Returns the value of the highest-priority item. If priority queue is empty, throws a NoSuchElementException.
T	pop()
	Deletes the highest-priority item and returns it. If priority queue is empty, throws a NoSuchElementException.
void	push(T element)
	Inserts element into the priority queue.
int	size()
	Returns the number of elements in the priority queue.

> The priority queue has the same interface as a stack and a queue. However, the actions of push() and pop() are different.

The collection class `HeapPQueue` implements the `PQueue` interface. We discuss the concept of a heap in Section 22.3. For now, we simply use the class, which, by default, assumes that the element of highest priority is the one with the largest value (a maximum priority queue); that is, if x and y are two elements in a priority queue and $x > y$, then x has higher priority than y.

Example 15.2

This example illustrates how to create and use a `HeapPQueue` object.

```
// create an empty priority queue of generic type String
HeapPQueue<String> pq = new HeapPQueue<String>();
int n;

pq.push("green");
pq.push("red");
pq.push("blue");

// output the size and element with the highest priority
System.out.println(pq.size() + "  " + pq.peek());

// use pop() to clear the collection and list elements in
// priority (descending) order
while (!pq.isEmpty())
    System.out.print(pq.pop() + "  ");
```

```
Output:
 3   red
 red  green  blue
```

Note

Priority Queue Ordering

When one is erasing an item from a priority queue, there could be several elements in the sequence with the same priority level. In this case, we could require that these items be treated like a queue. For instance, the office pool could select jobs for workers at the same rank in their submission order.

Job #1	Job #2	Job #3	Job #4
Clerk	Manager	Manager	Clerk

From this priority queue, select the manager jobs in the order Job #2 and Job #3 and then the clerk jobs in the order Job #1 and Job #4. Programming Exercise 15.16 develops the queue model for a priority queue. The `HeapPQueue` class does not use this model. When deciding between two or more elements that have the same priority, the pop() operation makes no assumption about when the elements first entered the priority queue.

Application: Support Services Pool

Let us look at an application that implements a company's support services. This is the example introduced at the beginning of the section. An office pool provides office services for employees. To control the flow of work within the pool, the company ranks its employees, using the categories president, director, manager, and clerk. The categories create priorities for tasks done by the pool. A job requested by a president has priority over a job requested by a director, and so forth. To use the pool services, an employee must fill out a job request form that specifies the employment category, a job ID, and an estimate of time required to finish the task. These are fields for the JobRequest class.

The application simulates the activities within the office pool. We describe the categories using an enum class, called JobStatus. Each enum value has an associated integer value that is used to compare the status of two JobRequest objects.

```
enum JobStatus
{
    clerk (0), manager (1), director(2), president(3);

    // variable, constructor, and access method that associates
    // an integer value with the enum value
    int jsValue;
    JobStatus(int value) { jsValue = value; }
    public int value() { return jsValue; }
}
```

A support services pool simulation nicely illustrates the concept of a priority queue.

A job request form is an object of type JobRequest. The class has three instance variables, called jobStatus, jobID, and jobTime, along with three corresponding access methods, getStatus(), getJobID, and getJobTime(). For the purpose of comparing two JobRequest objects, the class implements the Comparable interface that compares the status of two objects. For output, the class supplies the toString() method. For input, the class provides a static method readJob() that uses a Scanner to acquire job request information which is returned as a JobRequest object. The following is an API description of the JobRequest class.

class JobRequest implements Comparable<JobRequest>	
	Constructors
	JobRequest (JobStatus status, int ID, int time) Creates an object with the specified arguments.
	Methods
int	**getJobID**() Returns the ID for this object.
int	**getJobStatus**() Returns the status for this object.
int	**getJobTime**() Returns the time for this object in minutes.
static JobRequest	**readJob**(Scanner sc) Reads a job from the scanner assuming the format "<status> <ID> <time>" returns a JobRequest object or null at end of file.
String	**toString**() Returns a string that represents a job in the format "<status> <ID> <time>".
int	**compareTo**(JobRequest item) Compares the current object's jobStatus with the jobStatus of item.

PROGRAM 15.3 MANAGING A SUPPORT SERVICES POOL

The application simulates the support services algorithm. The application uses the static method `readJob()` to input job requests from the file *job.dat*. Each line of the file contains a string identifying the status ("president," "director," etc.), an integer job id, and an integer job time. For instance, an entry for a 35-minute job request (ID = 1002) from a Manager is

```
Manager 1002 35
```

For each request, the application adds a corresponding `JobRequest` object to the priority queue, `jobPool`. The secretary pool provides services by removing the jobs from the queue in the order of their priority and outputting the job description.

At its conclusion, the application outputs the total amount of time spent servicing each of the different types of employees. For this purpose, the program declares the integer array `jobServicesUse`, all of whose elements are initially 0.

```
// time spent working for each category of employee in the
// range 0 to 3
int[] jobServicesUse = {0,0,0,0};
```

As jobs are removed from the priority queue, the application adds the job time to the cumulative time for the corresponding type of employee by using `getStatus()` and `getJobTime()`.

```
// accumulate job time for the category of employee
jobServicesUse[job.getStatus().value()] += job.getJobTime();
```

The program concludes by displaying a summary of the services for each type of employee, using the method `writeJobSummary()`.

```
import java.io.*;
import java.util.Scanner;
import ds.util.HeapPQueue;

public class Program15_3
{
    public static void main(String[] args) throws IOException
    {
        // handle job requests
        HeapPQueue<JobRequest> jobPool =
                                new HeapPQueue<JobRequest>();
        // job requests are read from file "job.dat"
        Scanner sc = new Scanner(new FileReader("job.dat"));

        // time spent working for each category of employee
        // initial time 0 for each category
        int[] jobServicesUse = {0,0,0,0};
        JobRequest job = null;

        // read file; insert each job into priority queue
        while ((job = JobRequest.readJob(sc)) != null)
            jobPool.push(job);
```

```
      // delete jobs from priority queue and output information
      System.out.println("Category     Job ID     Job Time");
      while (!jobPool.isEmpty())
      {
         // remove a job from the priority queue and output it
         job = (JobRequest)jobPool.pop();
         System.out.println(job);

         // accumulate job time for the category of employee
         jobServicesUse[job.getStatus().value()] +=
            job.getJobTime();
      }
      System.out.println();

      writeJobSummary(jobServicesUse);
   }
   private static void writeJobSummary(int[] jobServicesUse)
   {
      System.out.println("Total Pool Usage");
      System.out.println("   President   " +
         jobServicesUse[3]);
      System.out.println("   Director    " +
         jobServicesUse[2]);
      System.out.println("   Manager     " +
         jobServicesUse[1]);
      System.out.println("   Clerk       " +
         jobServicesUse[0]);
   }
}
```

Run:

```
  Category       Job ID      Job Time
  President       303          25
  President       306          50
  Director        300          20
  Director        307          70
  Director        310          60
  Director        302          40
  Manager         311          30
  Manager         304          10
  Manager         305          40
  Clerk           308          20
  Clerk           309          20
  Clerk           301          30

Total Pool Usage
   President    75
   Director     190
   Manager      80
   Clerk        70
```

15.5 Event-Driven Simulation

A simulation creates a model of a real-world situation so that we can better understand it. The simulation uses computer objects with methods that model real-world objects and their behaviors. One very popular type of simulation is an event-driven simulation that uses a minimum priority queue to process events that occur over time. The priority queue consists of different types of event objects that are time-stamped to indicate when they are to occur. The simulation identifies an event, notes its time and circumstances, and adds it to the priority queue. Often, the occurrence of an event triggers other related and subsequent events which are added to the queue. The simulation runs by repeatedly removing and analyzing the next (earliest time) event from the priority queue until the queue is empty or a specified length of time elapses. The simulation provides a progression of discrete events that highlight the key activities in the real-world situation.

An event-driven simulation uses a priority queue to store events that occur over time as the simulation unfolds. Often, an event triggers other events that are added to the priority queue.

In the following sections, we will present design principles for all event-driven simulations and use a bank simulation as the example. Code segments that declare variables and implement key methods will aid our discussion. You can find a complete listing of classes for the bank simulation in Chapter 15 of the software supplement.

A Bank Simulation

In this section, we will describe a bank simulation that looks at the flow of customers through a bank as they are served by a group of tellers. In the process, we will measure the efficiency of service by computing the average waiting time of each customer and the percentage of time each teller is busy. Instead of collecting actual customer data, we introduce probabilistic values that describe different expected arrival rates for customers and different expected service times for a teller to handle a customer. We use a random number generator to mirror the arrival and departure of customers during a bank day. The simulation allows us to introduce new parameters and thus measure the relative effect on service if we change customer or teller behavior. For instance, suppose the bank estimates that a gift promotion would increase customer traffic by 20%. A simulation study would increase the expected arrival rate and measure the effect on waiting times and teller utilization. The results may indicate that customers experience unacceptable wait times, creating dissatisfaction that would diminish the effect of the promotion. The bank could repeat the simulation with additional tellers until reasonable wait times are established.

An event-driven bank simulation looks at the flow of customers through a bank as they are served by tellers. Events include arrival, service, and departure events that are time-stamped.

The bank simulation produces arrival, service, and departure events for each customer. Associated variables maintain an ongoing record of service time that each teller is committed to provide customers that are already in the bank. When a customer enters, the simulation creates an arrival event (A) that marks the time. This event spawns a service event (S) indicating when the customer reaches a teller. The time for the service event depends on prior teller commitments. If a teller is free, service begins immediately. Otherwise, the simulation must evaluate the backlogged service times for each teller and select the minimal value. In effect, the value represents the first time a teller is free. The interval between arrival time and service time denotes waiting time for the customer. The service event spawns a departure event that takes into account the time required by the teller to handle the customer. The service time becomes a further commitment for the teller and is used to update the backlogged service time for the teller, which could affect waiting times for subsequent customers.

Figure 15.7 looks at four customers who enter a bank that employs two tellers. A time-line lays out times for events from the start of the simulation, measured in minutes. The line segments above the timeline detail the events for each customer. The line segments below the timeline track service provided by each teller.

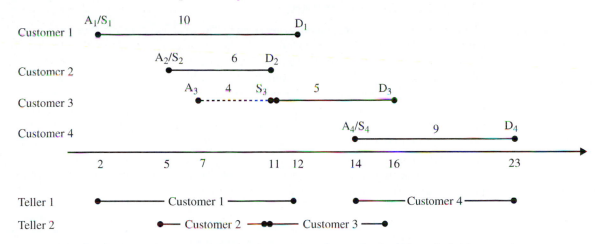

Figure 15.7 *Bank simulation events for four customers and two tellers. Solid lines indicate service; dotted line indicates wait.*

The flow of events in the simulation is dictated by the expected (random) arrival times and service times of customers. Supporting variables monitor the effect of these times on the sequencing of events. Associated with each teller is the variable backService, which monitors the amount of service time that the teller must provide to the customers already in the bank. Whenever a new customer is assigned to a teller, the backService value for that teller is updated. Arrival events are the key points of reference in the simulation. Let us see how events and variables play out during the arrival of the first four customers. The data corresponds to Figure 15.7.

Customer 1: Arrival time = 2
      Tellers 1 and 2 have backService = 0 (both are free); wait time = 0
    Service begins at time = 2 with teller 1 requiring serviceTime = 10
      Teller 1 backService = 10; teller 2 has backService = 0
    Departure occurs at time = 12

Customer 2: Arrival time = 5 Interval from last arrival = 3
      Teller 1 has backService = 7 (10 – 3); teller 2 has backService = 0;
      wait time = 0
    Service begins at time = 5 with teller 2 requiring serviceTime = 6
      Teller 1 has backService = 7; teller 2 backService = 6
    Departure occurs at time = 11

Customer 3: Arrival time = 7 Interval from last arrival = 2
      Teller 1 has backService = 5; teller 2 has backService = 4; wait time = 4
    Service begins at time = 11 with teller 2 requiring serviceTime = 5
      Teller 1 backService = 5; teller 2 backService = 9
    Departure occurs at time = 16

Customer 4: Arrival time = 14 Interval from last arrival = 7
    Teller 1 has backService = 0; teller 2 has backService = 2; wait time = 0

Service begins at time $= 14$ with teller 1 requiring serviceTime $= 9$
Teller 1 backService $= 9$; teller 2 backService $= 2$
Departure occurs at time $= 23$

Simulation Design Pattern

Event is the super-class of all events. It includes the time of an event and the method compareTo(), which compares events by their time of occurrence. It also contains the abstract method doEvent() that each type of event must implement.

The key components of a simulation are events. These objects are instances of different types of activities and behaviors that occur in the simulation. The object type for the different events are part of an inheritance hierarchy that defines Event as a superclass. The Event class includes a single integer variable time, which denotes when the event occurs. An abstract method doEvent() is included for polymorphism. The method is overwritten in each subclass to carry out tasks each time a specific event occurs. The Event superclass implements the Comparable interface by having compareTo() compare the relative times when two events occur. This allows the simulation to store events in a minimum priority queue. The simulation runs by extracting events from the priority queue in order of their times. The simulation is thus like a compressed video recording of a day's activities in which successive frames in the video are the events.

Event class:

```java
public abstract class Event implements Comparable<Event>
{
    protected int time;

    // constructor sets time for the event
    public Event(int t)
    { time = t; }

    abstract void doEvent();    // describes activity

    // used to order the events (elements) in a priority queue
    public int compareTo(Event e)
    {
        if(time < e.time)
            return -1;
        else if (time == e.time)
            return 0;
        else
            return 1;
    }
}
```

In our example, the inheritance hierarchy includes the Event superclass and subclasses for ArrivalEvent, ServiceEvent, and DepartureEvent.

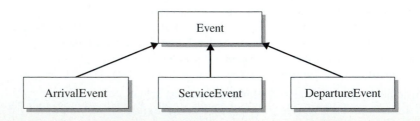

The actual running of the simulation is handled by an `EventDrivenSimulation` class, which provides a priority queue of `Event` references. The class features the method `pushEvent()`, which inserts a new event in the priority queue and the method `run()` which proceeds to empty the queue in a progressive time sequence of events. Each event that is popped from the queue is processed using `doEvent()`.

By default, the `HeapPQueue` class builds a maximum priority queue. The class `EventDrivenSimulation` must create a minimum priority queue. In Chapter 22, you will discover that `HeapPQueue` has a constructor that includes a `Comparator` object of type `Less` or `Greater` to specify the kind of priority queue. The simulation class declares a minimum priority queue by including a `Less` object as the argument.

The superclass EventDriven-Simulation provides a priority queue of events. The method pushEvent() adds an event to the priority queue, and run() runs the simulation by popping the queue and calling doEvent() until the queue is empty.

EventDrivenSimulation class:

```java
import ds.util.HeapPQueue;

public class EventDrivenSimulation
{
    // minimum heap pops event elements in order of their time
    private HeapPQueue<Event> eventQueue =
            new HeapPQueue<Event>(new Less<Event>());

    // adds an Event object to the queue
    public void pushEvent(Event e)
    { eventQueue.push(e); }

    // runs simulation by processing events as they exit the
    // priority queue
    public void run()
    {
        while (!eventQueue.isEmpty())
        {
            // extract event and process it with doEvent()
            Event nextEvent = eventQueue.pop();
            nextEvent.doEvent();
        }
    }
}
```

BankSimulation Class

The `BankSimulation` class drives the bank simulation. By extending `EventDriven-Simulation`, it has access to the priority queue and the method `run()` in the superclass that processes events in a time sequence. `BankSimulation` defines user-supplied parameters that specify the length of the simulation, the number of tellers, and the range (low–high) for expected arrival times and service times. The class defines variables that are updated during execution; for instance, number of customers and total wait time. It also supplies supporting variables such as a random number generator and an array of Teller objects. The method `startSimulation()` inputs parameters for the simulation and creates and stores events in the priority queue. It then calls `run()` to execute the simulation and concludes by displaying a summary of the results. A main program that performs a

BankSimulation drives the simulation by extending EventDriven-Simulation.

simulation creates a BankSimulation object and uses it to start the simulation. The BankSimulation class defines the various event subclasses as inner classes. By using inner classes, the events can access and update the outer class variables. Note that the bank simulation includes the boolean variable verboseRun. This allows the user to specify a "verbose" run, which involves expanded output that displays the time and circumstances of each event.

BankSimulation class:

```java
public class BankSimulation extends EventDrivenSimulation
{
    // parameters used to describe the simulation
    int simulationLength;            // simulation length
    int numTellers;
    int arrivalLow, arrivalHigh;     // next arrival range
    int serviceLow, serviceHigh;     // service range

    // variables used to monitor the simulation
    int numCustomers = 0;
    int totalWaitTime = 0;
    int prevArrTime = 0;             // used for delay between
                                     //    arrivals
    boolean verboseRun = false;      // detail each event?
    Random rnd = new Random();       // use for random times
    Teller[] tList = null;           // list of tellers

    // key method inputs parameters, creates events, runs
    // simulation and outputs results
    public void startSimulation()
    { . . . }
}
```

Launching the Simulation   The method startSimulation() manages the simulation study. It begins by calling inputParameters() to input user-supplied simulation parameters from the keyboard. The following illustrates how the parameters are initialized.

```
Run:
  Use verbose run ('Y' or 'N'): Y
  Enter the simulation time in minutes: 30
  Enter number of available tellers: 2
  Enter range of potential arrival times: 4 8
  Enter range of potential service times: 10 18
```

The inner Teller class with public variables defines teller-specific data. In the simulation, a teller may need to work overtime to serve a customer who arrives near the end of the simulation. At any time, the variable backService is the amount of service time that the teller owes customers who are currently in the bank. With each arrival, we determine the elapsed time from the previous arrival and use this to update backService for each teller currently serving a customer. After all, during the elapsed time, these tellers are working and thus owe that much less service time to existing customers. The startSimulation() method creates the teller array tList for the specified number of tellers.

The method startSimulation() manages the simulation by creating the array of tellers and the arrival events that occur at random intervals. It calls run() in the super-class and outputs the results of the simulation.

```
private static class Teller
{
    public int backService = 0;
    public int totalService = 0;
    public int overtime = 0;
}
```

The key function of startSimulation() is to create arrival events which occur at random intervals during the simulation. Each event is added to the priority queue. Once this is done, a call to run() executes the simulation. At the beginning, the priority queue has only ArrivalEvent objects. As each such event is popped from the queue, it calls its doEvent() method which spawns a corresponding ServiceEvent object that is added to the queue. In a similar way, when a service event is popped from the queue, it calls its doEvent() method, which spawns a DepartureEvent for the queue. During execution of the simulation, the priority queue is dynamically expanding and contracting as events enter and exit. The ability of the queue to identify a next event (minimum time) produces an orderly sequence of event occurrences. Method startSimulation() concludes by displaying the results of the simulation. The following is a sample display of output.

```
Run:
    Simulation Summary
    Number of customers is 4
    Average waiting time is 1.0 minutes
    Service time for tellers
        Teller 1: Busy 82.9% Overtime 11 minutes
        Teller 2: Busy 64.7% Overtime 4 minutes
```

startSimulation():

```
public void startSimulation()
{
    // read simulation parameters from keyboard
    inputParameters();

    // create instances for each teller; for convenience,
    // tellers are referenced with indices beginning at 1
    for (int i = 1; i <= numTellers; i++)
        tList[i] = new Teller();

    // for the length of the simulation, create successive
    // arrival events at random arrival times; push events
    // on the priority queue and update prevArrTime
    int t = 0;
    while (t < simulationLength)
    {
```

```
          // randomTime() returns random integer in the range
          // arrivalLow to arrivalHigh
          t += randomTime(arrivalLow, arrivalHigh);
          if (t >= simulationLength)
             break;
          // create an arrival event and add it to priority queue
          pushEvent(new ArrivalEvent(t, prevArrTime));
          // update prevArrTime for use by next arrival
          prevArrTime = t;
       }

       // with arrival events loaded in the priority queue, begin
       // execution of the simulation; Note: during execution, the
       // queue will dynamically grow since when an arrival event
       // exits the queue, its doEvent() method adds a service
       // event to the queue; when a service event exits the queue,
       // its doEvent() method adds a departure event
       run();

       // display a summary of results
       displayResults();
    }
```

Event SubClasses The bank simulation defines the ArrivalEvent, ServiceEvent, and DepartureEvent as private inner classes. Each class overrides the method doEvent(), which is responsible for updating available information. In ArrivalEvent, the method spawns a corresponding ServiceEvent object that recognizes the first available teller and the time when service can begin. In ServiceEvent, the method spawns a DepartureEvent object that identifies when the customer will leave the bank. In each implementation of doEvent(), we check whether the boolean variable verboseRun is enabled and provide a description of the event including the customer number, the time, and relevant wait time, teller selection, and service time.

Inner classes extend Event and implement the actions required by an arrival, service, and departure event.

Let us look at the ArrivalEvent class in some detail. A simple description of the behavior of the other event classes will be sufficient to understand their design and implementation. An arrival event object is created in the startSimulation() method. The object is passed a time when the event will occur and the time of the previous arrival. The time is recorded in the Event superclass, and the previous arrival time is used to identify elapsedTime, the interval between successive arrivals. In doEvent(), we increment the number of customers and call the method minTellerService() with the teller array tList and elapsedTime as arguments. The private method uses elapsedTime to update backlogged service time owed by each teller who was busy in the interval. The method returns the index of the teller with the smallest backService. The index identifies the next available teller, who will be assigned to serve the customer. The backService value for this teller translates to waiting time for the customer. With the teller identified, the doEvent() method creates a random service time for the customer. The time adds committed backlogged service time to the teller. The method concludes by creating a ServiceEvent object with arguments that specify the time service begins, the number of customers, the teller who will service the customer, and the service time.

ArrivalEvent class:

```java
private class ArrivalEvent extends Event
{
    private int elapsedTime;

    public ArrivalEvent(int time, int prevArrTime)
    {
        super(time);
        elapsedTime = time - prevArrTime;
    }

    public void doEvent()
    {
        int i, minTeller, serviceTime;
        DecimalFormat numberFmt = new DecimalFormat("00");

        // increment number of customers
        numCustomers++;

        // use elapsedTime to update backService for each
        // teller; return teller with minimum backService;
        // this is the next available teller
        minTeller = minTellerService(tList, elapsedTime );

        // backService for teller is wait time for customer
        totalWaitTime += tList[minTeller].backService;
        // generate service time for customer; add to
        // backService for minTeller who will serve customer
        serviceTime = randomTime(serviceLow, serviceHigh);
        tList[minTeller].backService += serviceTime;

        if (verboseRun)
            . . .
        // create ServiceEvent object and add to priority queue
        pushEvent(new ServiceEvent(
                time + tList[minTeller].backService,
                numCustomers,
                minTeller,
                serviceTime));
    }

    private int minTellerService(Teller[] tList,
                                 int elapsedTime)
    {
        int i, minTeller = 1;
        for (i = 1; i <= numTellers; i++)
            tList[i].backService =
                (tList[i].backService - elapsedTime <= 0) ? 0 :
                tList[i].backService - elapsedTime;
```

```
            for (i = 2; i <= numTellers; i++)
                if (tList[i].backService <
                    tList[minTeller].backService)
                    minTeller = i;

            return minTeller;
        }
    }
```

A `ServiceEvent` object occurs when a customer begins service. The object is initialized with arguments for the time service begins, the number of customers, the teller who provides the service, and the service time. The method `doEvent()` increments the total service time for the teller and concludes by creating a `DepartureEvent` object that uses the service time to mark time in the future when the customer exits the bank. The `doEvent()` method for a `DepartureEvent` object is very simple. If the time of the event is after the simulation ends (after bank closing), the difference is assigned to the teller as overtime.

PROGRAM 15.4   RUNNING BANK SIMULATION

The program runs the bank simulation twice. The first run provides a verbose listing of a simulation that runs 40 minutes. The second run uses a simulation of 480 minutes, an 8-hour business day. The nonverbose run looks at a bank with expected arrivals in the range 1–5 minutes and expected service time for three tellers in the range 4–11 minutes.

```
public class Program15_4
{
    public static void main(String[] args)
    {
        // create bank simulation object and start it up
        BankSimulation bank = new BankSimulation();
        bank.startSimulation();
    }
}
```

```
Run 1:
  Use verbose run ('Y' or 'N'): Y
  Enter the simulation time in minutes: 40
  Enter number of available tellers: 2
  Enter range of potential arrival times: 3 7
  Enter range of potential service times: 5 11

  Customer #01 Arrival 6 Wait 6
  Customer #01 Begin service at 12 by teller 1 Service time 6
  Customer #02 Arrival 13 Wait 8
  Customer #01 Departs 18 Served by 1
  Customer #03 Arrival 18 Wait 8
```

```
Customer #02 Begin service at 21 by teller 1 Service time 8
Customer #04 Arrival 22 Wait 11
Customer #03 Begin service at 26 by teller 2 Service time 8
Customer #02 Departs 29 Served by 1
Customer #05 Arrival 29 Wait 9
Customer #04 Begin service at 33 by teller 1 Service time 11
Customer #03 Departs 34 Served by 2
Customer #06 Arrival 36 Wait 6
Customer #05 Begin service at 38 by teller 2 Service time 9
Customer #06 Begin service at 42 by teller 1 Service time 6
Customer #04 Departs 44 Served by 1
Customer #05 Departs 47 Served by 2
Customer #06 Departs 48 Served by 1

Simulation Summary
      Number of customers is 6
      Average waiting time is 0.0 minutes
      Service time for tellers
      Teller 1: Busy 64.6% Overtime 8
      Teller 2: Busy 36.2% Overtime 7


Run 2:
   Use verbose run ('Y' or 'N'): N
   Enter the simulation time in minutes: 480
   Enter number of available tellers: 3
   Enter range of potential arrival times: 1 5
   Enter range of potential service times: 4 11
   Simulation Summary
      Number of customers is 156
      Average waiting time is 1.0 minutes
      Service time for tellers
         Teller 1:  Busy 88.4%  Overtime 12
         Teller 2:  Busy 80.0%  Overtime 10
         Teller 3:  Busy 65.3%  Overtime 19
```

Chapter Summary

- A queue is a first-in-first-out (FIFO) data structure for which insertion operations (push()) occur at the back of the sequence and deletion operations (pop()) occur at the front. The Queue interface describes the structure, and the LinkedQueue class provides an implementation. The LinkedQueue class uses a LinkedList object by composition. The implementation of each queue operation involves calling a corresponding method for the embedded linked list object.

- The radix sort algorithm orders an integer array by using 10 queues (bins). The sorting technique has running time $O(n)$ but has only specialized applications. The more general in-place $O(n \log_2 n)$ sorting algorithms are preferable in most cases.

- For some specialized applications, it is necessary to implement a queue by using a fixed-size array. The class BQueue describes a bounded-queue object that has a method full() and a precondition for push(). In the implementation of BQueue, indices qfront and qback move circularly through the array. The algorithm implements push() and pop() in O(1) running time without wasting any space in the array.

- The PQueue interface does not specify how push() stores a data value, but it requires that pop() must return the highest-priority item in the collection. The highest-priority item in a maximum priority queue is the largest item. The highest-priority item in a minimum priority queue is the smallest item. The PQueue interface specifies the operations of a priority queue. The class HeapPQueue implements the interface and assumes that the objects stored in the priority queue implement the Comparable interface. By default, HeapPQueue assumes that the highest-priority item is the largest item in the collection. To illustrate priority queues, an application schedules jobs in an office pool, in which employees have priority ranging from President to Clerk.

- A simulation creates a model of a real-world situation so that we can better understand it. This chapter develops a bank simulation to illustrate event-driven simulations. An event-driven simulation uses a priority queue to store a sequence of events that occur over time as the simulation unfolds. The priority queue consists of different types of event objects that are time-stamped to indicate when they are to occur. The simulation identifies an event, notes its time and circumstances, and adds it to the priority queue. Often, the occurrence of an event triggers other related and subsequent events which are added to the queue. The simulation runs by repeatedly removing and analyzing the next (earliest time) event from the priority queue until the queue is empty or a specified length of time elapses. The simulation provides a progression of discrete events that highlight the key activities in the real-world situation.

Written Exercises

1. List all that apply. A queue is a structure implementing

   (a) first-in/last-out   (c) first-come/first-served   (e) last-in/last-out
   (b) last-in/first-out   (d) first-in/first-out

2. What is the output from the following sequence of queue operations?

```
LinkedQueue<Integer> q = new LinkedQueue<Integer>();
int x = 5;

q.push(8);
q.push(9);
q.push(x);
System.out.println(q.peek());            // Output: _____
q.pop();
q.push(22);
while (!q.isEmpty())
    System.out.print(q.pop() + " ");   // Output: _____
```

3. What is the action of the method f()?

```
public static <T> void f(LinkedQueue<T> q)
{
    ALStack<T> s = new ALStack<T>();
    T element;
```

```
while (!q.isEmpty())
{
    element = q.pop();
    s.push(element);
}
while (!s.isEmpty())
{
    element = s.pop();
    q.push(element);
}
}
```

4. Use the following code segment to answer parts (a) through (c).

```
LinkedQueue<Integer> q = new LinkedQueue<Integer>();
Scanner keyIn = new Scanner(System.in);

for (int i = 1; i <= 5; i++)
{
    if (keyIn.nextBoolean())
        System.out.print(i + " ");
    else
        q.push(i);
}
while (!q.isEmpty())
    System.out.print(q.pop() + " ");
```

(a) What is the output for the following input sequence?

   true   false   false   true   true

(b) Is it possible to have output: 1 3 5 4 2? If yes, give an input sequence that produces the output; if no, explain.

(c) Give the input sequence(s) that produce the output: 1 2 3 4 5.

5. (a) What are the contents of each bin, 0–9, after pass 0 of the radix sort? What is the order of the list after pass 0?

   Data: 363, 251, 670, 84, 175, 45, 123, 389, 90, 8, 122, 676, 455, 253, 7, 125, 4 91, 593, 528

(b) Show the contents of bins 0–9 after pass 1 of the radix sort. What is the order of the list after pass 1?

(c) Show the contents of bins 0–9 after pass 2 of the radix sort and the final sorted list.

6. (a) Assume a BQueue collection has maximum size of 5. Initially, the queue has the elements 6, 2, 9, 5. Use a circular wheel to display the contents of the array. Be certain to indicate the positions of qfront and qback in your drawing.

(b) Use the same wheel to display the contents of the queue after each operation:

```
q.push(8);
q.pop();
q.pop();
q.push(25);
```

7. Suppose you must implement a queue by using an `ArrayList` and object composition. You will implement `push()` using the `ArrayList` method `add(item)` and `pop()` using the method remove(0). What is the average-case running time for the removal of all elements from the queue having n values?

8. Describe an algorithm that uses a queue to reverse the elements of a stack. If the stack has n-elements, what is the running time of the algorithm?

9. Give the output from the following statements.

```
HeapPQueue<String> pq = new HeapPQueue<String>();
int n;

String[] strArr = {"Tom", "Jane", "Alex", "Phil"};
int i;
String strA, strB;

for(i=0;i < 4;i++)
    pq.push(strArr[i]);

pq.push("Nina");
strA = pq.pop();
pq.push("Dave");
strB = pq.pop();
System.out.println(strA + " " + strB);

while (!pq.isEmpty())
    System.out.print(pq.pop() + " ");
```

10. A queue has the `Integer` elements with values $\{5, 1, 3, 9, 8\}$ from front to back.

    (a) Assume that you pop the elements from the queue and push them into a stack `s`. What is the output?

    ```
    System.out.println(s);
    ```

    (b) Assume that you pop the elements from the queue and push them into a priority queue `pq`. What is the output?

    ```
    System.out.println(pq);
    ```

    (c) Assume that you pop the elements from the queue and push them into a priority queue `pq`. Then pop the elements from the priority queue and push them into a stack `s`. What is the output?

    ```
    System.out.println(s);
    ```

Programming Exercises

11. Write a program that reads a line of text from the keyboard. Place each letter as a lowercase `Character` object into a queue and onto a stack. Disregard all other characters. By repeatedly popping the two collections, verify whether the text is a palindrome. A palindrome is a sequence of letters that reads the same forward and backward. For instance, the letters in the string "Madam I'm Adam" is a palindrome.

12. The `Queue` interface defines the method `size()`, which returns the number of elements in the queue. You are to create a new version of the operation called `queueSize()`, which takes a `Queue` reference parameter. The implementation of the method must not change the order of elements in the queue.

```
public static <T> int queueSize(Queue<T> q)
{ . . . }
```

Write a program that defines two `LinkedQueue` collections qA and qB that store `Integer` objects. Initialize qA with elements from the integer array `intArr`.

```
integer[] intArr = {6, 9, 13, 5, 11, 0, 7, 3, 19, 4, 16};
```

Output the size of qA by calling `queueSize()`. Then split qA so that the back half of the queue is copied to qB and the front half remains in qA. Output the resulting elements in the two queues.

Run:
```
Size of qA is 11
Elements in qA: [6, 9, 13, 5, 11]
Elements in qB: [0, 7, 3, 19, 4, 16]
```

13. (a) Implement the method nToFront():

```
public static <T> void nToFront(LinkedQueue<T> q, int n)
```

that moves the nth element of the queue to the front, leaving the order of all other elements unchanged. In the ordering, the first element is the front of the queue, the second element is the element after the front, and so forth. The figure illustrates the action of nToFront() for a queue of Integer values and n = 4. Use only Queue operations.

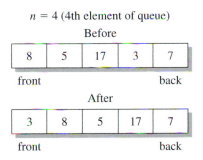

(b) Write a program that uses nToFront() to reverse the order of elements in a queue. Include a second method reverseQueue() that performs the same task with running time O(n). In each case, display the resulting queue using toString().

14. (a) The LinkedQueue class is an implementation of the Queue interface. The class uses a LinkedList object by composition to store the queue elements (Section 15.1). Give a declaration of another implementation of the Queue interface that uses inheritance. The subclass LQueue extends LinkedList and implements the Queue interface.

```
public class LQueue<T> extends LinkedList<T> implements
    Queue<T>
{ ... }
```

(b) Write a program that tests your implementation of LQueue.

15. (a) Write a program that stores the elements from array intArr in a priority queue and then outputs the number of occurrences of 4, 3, 2, 1, and 0. The number of

occurrences should follow the number, using the format n(count). In the case of intArr, the output should be 4(3) 3(2) 2(6) 1(3) 0(1).

```
Integer[] intArr = {2, 3, 0, 1, 2, 4, 4, 2, 1, 2, 4, 1,
    2, 3, 2};
```

    (b) Write a program that stores in a priority queue eight random integer values in the range 0 to 9. First, display the elements in the priority queue; then, using the format from part (a), output the number of occurrences of each value from 9 down to 0, provided there is at least one occurrence of the value in the priority queue.

16. One way to implement a priority queue is to decide on the maximum priority possible, say MAXPRIORITY. Allocate an array, called priority, of MAXPRIORITY+1 queues. To insert an object of priority p into the priority queue, pass the item and its priority p as arguments and add it to the back of the queue priority[p]. Each queue contains only elements of equal priority, in the order of their insertion. When removing an element from the priority queue, find the nonempty queue of largest index and pop the queue.

Use this design strategy to implement the class QPQueue. Check your work by using the class to run Program 15.3. The following outline provides the declaration of the private variables of the class. Note that arrays of generic type are not allowed. In the constructor, declare the array of LinkedQueue objects, priority, as a "raw" type with no generic argument.

```
public class QPQueue<T>
{
    private static int MAXPRIORITY = 10;

    // priority[p] contains all elements with priority p
    // in their order of insertion
    private LinkedQueue<T>[] priority;
    // number of elements in the priority queue
    private int pqsize;

    public QPQueue()
    {
        priority = new LinkedQueue[MAXPRIORITY+1];
        for (int i = 0; i <= MAXPRIORITY; i++)
            priority[i] = new LinkedQueue<T>();
        pqsize =0;
    }

    public void push (T item, int p)
    { . . . }
    <other methods>
};
```

17. An integer value n is either a prime or a composite number. The value n is composite, provided there are factors m and p greater than 1 such that $n = m * p$. For instance, $n = 7$ is a prime; $n = 15$ is a composite because $15 = 3 * 5$. From number theory, we know that every integer > 1 can be written as a product of primes. This is the prime

factorization of the number. Write a program that prompts the user to input an integer
n > 1 and outputs the prime factors. A sample run is

Run:
```
 Enter an integer > 1: 60
 n = 60 prime factors: 2 2 3 5
```

The program uses a queue to store Integer values. Push the input value into the
queue. Iterative steps involve popping the queue. The process terminates when the
queue is empty. When popping an Integer value, use one of the following conditions.

> If the element is a prime, then simply output its value.
> If the element is a composite, determine factors m and p and push each of them
> into the queue.

Hint: Implement a method getSmallestFactor() to facilitate your solution.

```
// return the smallest factor of m > 1
// if return value is m, m is prime
public static int getSmallestFactor(int m)
{ ... }
```

18. This program develops an event-driven simulation for a car wash. Customers bring their
cars to a drive-through car wash. Assume that each car wash takes a fixed amount of time
and that the next customer arrives within an interval of time with uniform probability. For
instance, the next arrival time for a customer may be in the range from 3 to 10 minutes
and a car wash may take 7 minutes. The simulation prompts the user to supply the length
of the simulation, the interval for arrival times, and the fixed time for a car wash and seeks
to identify the number of customers served, the average time each customer must wait,
and the percentage of time the automated car wash equipment is utilized.

Use the BankSimulation as a model. You will need to specify the Arrival,
Service, and Departure events for the car wash. At the end of the run, provide a
summary report of the overall performance of the system in the following format.

```
Simulation Summary
   Total number of cars washed is _____
   Average waiting time is _____ minutes
   Service time for car wash:  Busy ____ %  Overtime ____
```

Programming Project

19. This exercise uses an ArrayList object to implement a priority queue class,
ALPQueue. Assume the name of the ArrayList object included by composition is
pqList. The following is an outline for the implementation of the class methods.

(i) The push() operation inserts a new element at the back of the ArrayList by
using add(). The elements in the ArrayList are not ordered in any way.

pqList
before push(4)

| 3 | 5 | 2 | 1 |

pqList
after push(4)

| 3 | 5 | 2 | 1 | 4 |

(ii) The methods peek() and pop() must identify the largest of the pqList.size() elements. Do this with the private method findMaxIndex(), which assigns to the variable maxIndex the index of the maximum element. If a call to either peek() or pop() follows a call to peek(), there is no need to recompute the maximum, because the location of the highest-priority element has not changed. Declare a boolean variable, recomputeMaxIndex, and initialize it to false. The methods peek() and pop() use recomputeMaxIndex to avoid unnecessary calls to findMaxIndex().

ALPQueue class:

```
public class ALPQueue<T> implements PQueue<T>
{
    private ArrayList<T> pqList;      // storage structure
    private int maxIndex = 0;         // used by peek/pop

    // flag indicates whether a call to findMaxIndex() is
    // required before executing peek() or pop()
    private boolean recomputeMaxIndex = false;

    // return index of maximum element in priority queue
    private int findMaxIndex()

    { . . . }

    < constructor and other methods >
}
```

(iii) The methods peek() and pop() return the maximum value in pqList. They throw a NoSuchElementException if the priority queue is empty.

(iv) If recomputeMaxIndex is true, the method pop() finds the maximum element by calling findMaxIndex(). The method must remove the highest-priority item from the ArrayList, which vacates a position. Sliding the tail of the sequence toward the front of the ArrayList is inefficient. Implement the removal process by taking the last element in the ArrayList and copying its value into the vacated position. Then remove the last element in the ArrayList.

The figures show the sequence of values in pqList as push() and pop() operations execute for the ALPQueue object pq.

```
Integer[] arr = {6, 5, 4};
ALPQueue<Integer> pq = new ALPQueue<Integer>();
int i;

for (i=0;i < arr.length; i++)
    pq.push(arr[i]);

System.out.println(pq.pop());      // output: 6
System.out.println(pq.peek());     // output: 5
```

```
        pq.push(10);

        pq.push(1);
        System.out.println(pq.pop());          // output: 10
```

Implement the class ALPQueue and test the class by running Program 15.3.

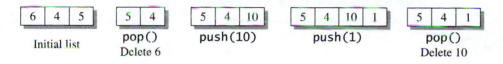

Chapter 16

BINARY TREES

CONTENTS

16.1 TREE STRUCTURES
  Tree Terminology
  Binary Trees
16.2 BINARY TREE NODES
  Building a Binary Tree
16.3 BINARY TREE-SCAN ALGORITHMS
  Recursive Tree Traversals
  Inorder Scan Algorithm
  Designing Scanning Methods
  Iterative Level-Order Scan

The Visitor Design Pattern
Using the Visitor Pattern
16.4 USING TREE-SCAN ALGORITHMS
  Computing the Tree Height
  Copying a Binary Tree
  Clearing a Tree
  Displaying a Binary Tree
16.5 A LOWER BOUND FOR SORTING
  (OPTIONAL)

ArrayLists and LinkedLists are *linear* data structures. Each of the collections has a first and a last element and every element except the last has a unique successor. In many applications, data structures exhibit a *nonlinear* order in which an element may have two or more successors. A tree is the prototype for such a structure. You are already familiar with the term. One of your relatives is, no doubt, building the family tree. Corporations and military commands use an organizational tree to give a top-down delineation of authority and a bottom-up reporting chain (Figure 16.1). A tree consists of elements called *nodes* that emanate from a single source called the *root*. Each node can have multiple links to successor nodes further down in the tree.

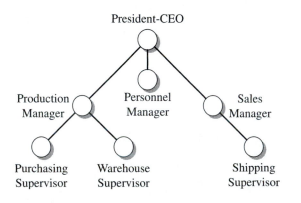

Figure 16.1 *Corporate organizational tree.*

In this chapter, we begin our study of nonlinear data structures with the introduction of trees. We will focus on a special category of trees in which each node can have at most two successors. These are referred to as *binary trees*. They have a recursive structure that we will effectively use to build algorithms. Binary trees have applications in their own right. More importantly, they are very efficient implementation structures for other collection types.

In this chapter, we introduce you to tree terminology and develop basic tree-handling methods. In later chapters, we will explore applications that use these methods and design a new collection type called a *binary search tree*. This tree will be the basis for our implementing ordered sets and maps as well as priority queues.

16.1 Tree Structures

A tree is a *hierarchical* structure that places elements in nodes along branches that originate from a root. Nodes in a tree are subdivided into levels in which the topmost level holds the root node. Any node in a tree can have multiple successors at the next level. Hence, a tree is a nonlinear structure. Operating systems use a general tree to maintain file structures. A node on the tree is a directory. The topmost level is the root directory, and all subsequent levels are subdirectories. Each directory in the tree is recognized by its path name, which is a listing of successive directory names on a path from the root to the node (Figure 16.2a).

> Nodes in a tree can have multiple successors. As such, a tree is a nonlinear data structure.

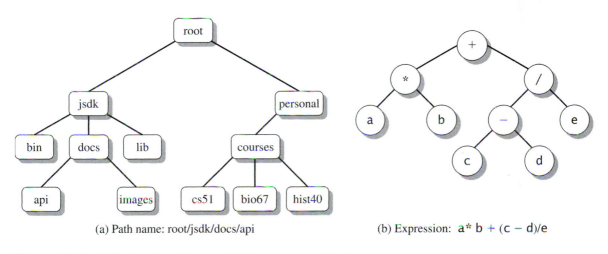

(a) Path name: root/jsdk/docs/api   (b) Expression: **a** * **b** + (**c** − **d**)/**e**

Figure 16.2 *A file structure tree and a binary expression tree.*

Most applications involve a restricted category of trees, called *binary trees*, in which each node has at most two successors. For instance, a compiler builds binary trees while parsing expressions in a program's source code. The resulting trees provide information for the portion of the compiler that must interpret the syntax. To illustrate this fact, consider the following arithmetic expression.

> In a binary tree, each node has at most two successors.

    a * b + (c - d)/e

The compiler parses the expression and creates an *expression tree*, in which the variables or constants (a, b, c, d, and e) occupy nodes at the end of a path (*leaf nodes*). The nonleaf nodes contain an operator. In this case, each operator ($*, +, -, /$) is a binary operator requiring two operands (Figure 16.2b).

Before we develop other examples of trees, let us step back and define some terminology that will allow us to describe the features of trees. We will use the terminology to give a precise definition of a binary tree.

Tree Terminology

A tree structure is characterized as a collection of *nodes* that originate from a unique starting node called the *root*. Each node consists of a value and a set of zero or more links to successor nodes. Using analogies from a family tree, we associate the terms *parent* and *child* to describe the relationship between a node and any of its successor nodes. In Figure 16.3, node A is the root. It is the parent of child nodes B, C, and D. The children are *siblings*. From the perspective of a child, each nonroot node has a unique parent. We classify a node in a tree based on the number of its children. A *leaf node*, such as E, G, H, I, and J, is a node without any children. An *interior node* (nonleaf node) has at least one child. Such a node is sometimes called an *internal node*.

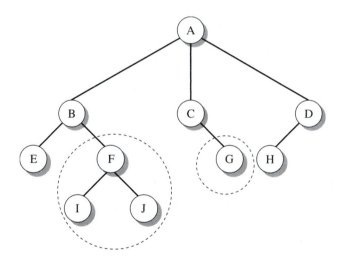

Figure 16.3 *Subtrees F and G.*

A tree has a root, followed by zero or more children. Each child forms a subtree with itself as root.

Each node in a tree is the root of a *subtree*, which consists of the node and all of its descendants. In Figure 16.3, node F is the root of the subtree containing nodes F, I, and J, while G is a one node subtree. Using the family-tree analogy, a subtree describes a node and all of its *descendants*. The definition of a subtree permits us to say that node A is a root of a subtree that happens to be the tree itself.

A path between a parent node P and any node N in its subtree is a sequence of nodes $P = X_0, X_1, \ldots, X_k = N$, where k is the length of the path. Each node X_i in the sequence is the parent of X_{i+1} for $0 \leq i \leq k - 1$. For instance, in Figure 16.4, the path from root A to node F is the sequence $A = X_0, X_1 = C, X_2 = F$, with length 2.

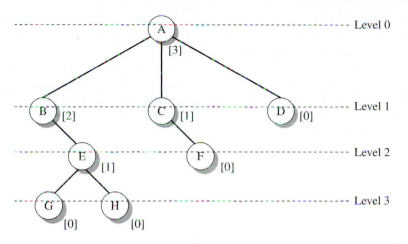

Figure 16.4 *Tree illustrates the level and height of a node.*

In a tree, there is a unique path from the root to any node. The length of the path describes a concept called the *level* of a node. The level of the root node is 0. Each child of the root is a level-1 node, the next generation is level-2 nodes, and so forth. In Figure 16.4, F is a level-2 node. Nodes G and H are level-3 nodes with the longest paths from the root.

The level of a node measures its distance from the root. A related concept is the *height* of a node. Viewing the node as a root of a subtree, the height is the length of the longest path from the node to a leaf node in the subtree. Clearly, a leaf node has height 0. The height of the tree root is the longest path in the tree; that is, the maximum level of the tree. The height of the root is referred to as the *height of the tree*. For the tree in Figure 16.4, we display the height in brackets adjacent to each node. The tree has height 3.

> The level of a node is the length of the path from the root to the node. The height of a node is the length of the longest path in the subtree.

Binary Trees

Although general trees have some important applications, we focus on a restricted category of trees, called *binary trees*, in which each parent has no more than two children (Figure 16.5). A binary tree has a uniform structure that allows us to give a simple description of its node

> In a binary tree, each node has 0, 1, or 2 children.

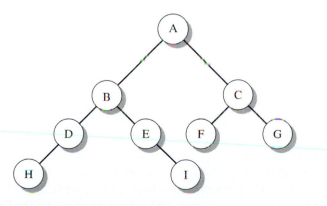

Figure 16.5 *A binary tree.*

structure and to develop a variety of tree-handling algorithms. The limit on the number of possible children for a node is not a serious restriction because most general trees have an equivalent binary tree representation. We develop this fact in the exercises.

Each node in a binary tree has two links that can reference its children. We distinguish the links by the labels `left` and `right`. The left link connects the node to its *left child*, and the right link connects it to its *right child*. Each child is the root of a subtree, so we can also view the left link of each node as a reference to its *left subtree* and the right link as a reference to its *right subtree*. In Figure 16.6, T is the root of the binary tree with left child L_1 and right child R_1. The children are roots of the subtrees T_L and T_R respectively.

> Each node of a binary tree defines a left and a right subtree. Each subtree is itself a tree.

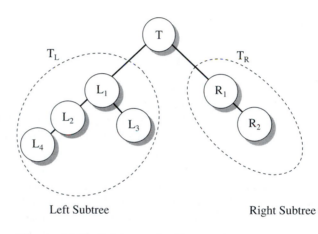

Left Subtree   Right Subtree

Figure 16.6 *Subtrees of a binary tree.*

An alternative recursive definition of a binary tree is useful. T is a binary tree if T

- either has no node (T is an empty tree), or
- has at most two subtrees.

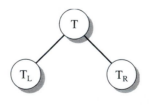

The recursive view of the tree in Figure 16.6 has root T and subtrees L_1 and R_1, which are themselves binary trees. The left subtree, L_1, has the binary trees L_2 and L_3 as its subtrees, and so forth. Note that L_3 is a binary tree with two empty subtrees. The following is a full display of the tree. The graphic ($\equiv$) represents an empty tree.

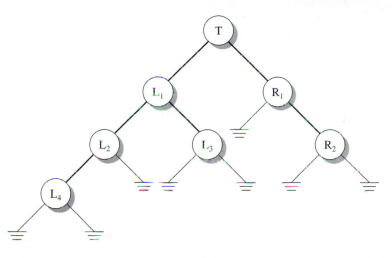

Height of a Binary Tree   The height of a tree is the length of the longest path from the root. In a binary tree, we can use its recursive structure and the concept of tree height to compute the height of a node. If the tree is empty, its height is −1 (stopping condition). The recursive condition applies to a nonempty tree. In this case, the height is defined in terms of the root and its subtrees. The height is one more than the maximum height of its subtrees. View a node N as the root of a subtree T_N; then

The height of a binary tree is the length of the longest path from a root to a leaf node.

$$height(N) = height(T_N) = \begin{cases} -1 & \text{if } T_N \text{ is empty} \\ 1 + \max(height(T_L), height(T_R)) & \text{if } T_N \text{ is nonempty} \end{cases}$$

Any leaf node has height 0 using the recursive condition. Each of its subtrees is empty with height −1 and so the leaf node has height $0 = 1 + \max(-1, -1)$. In Figure 16.7, the tree has height 3, which is one more than the height of its left subtree, namely 2. The height of each node is displayed in brackets.

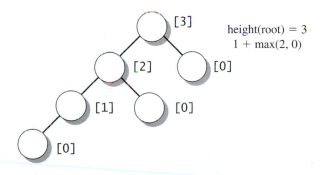

$height(root) = 3$
$1 + \max(2, 0)$

Figure 16.7 *Height of a binary tree in terms of the level of its nodes and its recursive structures.*

The trees in Figure 16.8 contain the same number of nodes but with differing heights 2, 4, and 5 respectively. The last tree (c) is noteworthy. It has a single leaf node, and all interior

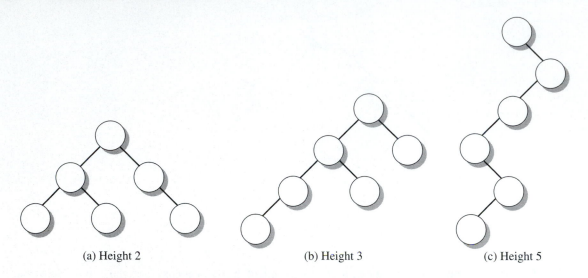

(a) Height 2   (b) Height 3   (c) Height 5

Figure 16.8 *Binary trees with six nodes but different heights.*

nodes have exactly one child. Put another way, each level in the tree contains exactly one node. We use the term *degenerate tree* to describe such a tree and note that it is equivalent to a singly linked list.

A degenerate binary tree has a single leaf node, and all interior nodes have exactly one child.

Density of a Binary Tree In a binary tree, the number of nodes at each level falls within a range of values. At level 0, there is 1 node, the root; at level 1, there can be 1 or 2 nodes. As we process further, the number of nodes at level 2 is in the range 1 to 4. You see the pattern. Each successive level in the tree can have potentially twice as many nodes as the previous level. At any level k, the number of nodes is in the range from 1 to 2^k. The number of nodes per level contributes to the density of the tree. Intuitively, density is a measure of the size of a tree (number of nodes) relative to the height of the tree. In Figure 16.9, tree A contains 9 nodes with a height of 3, while tree B contains 5 nodes with a height of 4.

The density of a binary tree measures the number of nodes relative to the tree height.

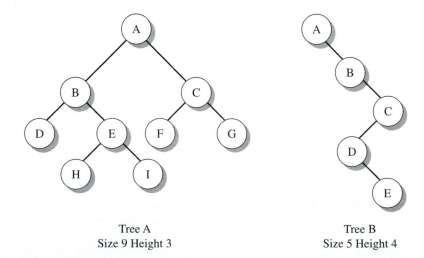

Tree A
Size 9 Height 3

Tree B
Size 5 Height 4

Figure 16.9 *Height of binary trees including a degenerate tree.*

Trees with a higher density are important as data structures because they can "pack" more nodes near the root. A potentially large number of nodes reside on relatively short paths from the root. Let us make this idea more precise. Degenerate trees are one extreme measure of density. At the other extreme, a *complete* binary tree of height h is a tree in which each level from 0 to h−1 has all possible nodes and all leaf nodes at level h are filled in from left to right. The largest possible complete binary tree with height h is one that contains 2^h nodes at level h. Figure 16.10 distinguishes between a complete and noncomplete binary tree. We add shading around the complete tree to highlight its structure.

A complete binary tree of height h has all possible nodes through depth h − 1, and the nodes on depth h exist left to right with no gaps.

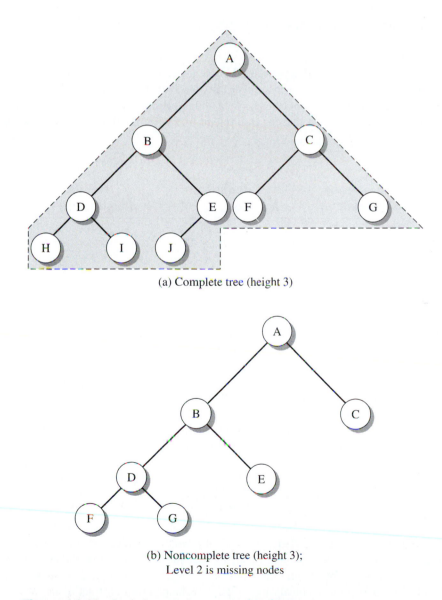

(a) Complete tree (height 3)

(b) Noncomplete tree (height 3);
Level 2 is missing nodes

Figure 16.10 *Complete and noncomplete binary trees.*

Evaluating Tree Density   Complete binary trees are ideal storage structures because of their ability to pack a large number of nodes near the root. A little mathematical analysis determines the minimum height of a complete tree that holds n elements. Through the first $h-1$ levels, the total number of nodes is

$$1 + 2 + 4 + \cdots + 2^{h-1} = 2^h - 1$$

At depth h, the number of additional nodes ranges from a minimum of 1 to a maximum of 2^h (full tree). Hence, the number of nodes n in a complete binary tree of height h ranges between

$$2^h - 1 + 1 = 2^h \le n \le 2^h - 1 + 2^h = 2^{h+1} - 1 < 2^{h+1}$$

After applying the logarithm base 2 to all terms in the inequality, we have

$$h \le \log_2 n < h + 1$$

A complete binary tree with n nodes must have height ($h = \text{int}(\log_2 n)$)

This shows that $\log_2 n$ lies between the integer values h and $h + 1$ but cannot equal $h + 1$. The actual value h is the real number $\log_2 n = h.f_1f_2f_3\ldots$. Since h must be an integer, the height of the tree is $\text{int}(\log_2 n)$. The table illustrates the calculation for three values of n. Appreciate the fact that for a complete tree with one million nodes, the longest path to any node is at most 19.

Number of elements (n)	Calculation ($\log_2 n$)	Height ($h = \text{int}(\log_2 n)$
10	$\log_2 10 = 3.321$	$\text{int}(3.321) = 3$
5,000	$\log_2 5{,}000 = 12.287$	$\text{int}(12.287) = 12$
1,000,000	$\log_2 1{,}000{,}000 = 19.931$	$\text{int}(19.931) = 19$

16.2 Binary Tree Nodes

A binary tree can have different implementations, depending on how you set up the links between a node and its children. An array can be used to store binary trees. Simple index calculations identify the children and the parent of each node. We develop array-based binary trees in Chapter 22. A more flexible implementation defines a node as an instance of the generic TNode class. A node contains three fields. One is the data value, called nodeValue, and the other two are the reference variables, left and right. The references are links that identify the left child and the right child of the node respectively. In the process, the references identify the left and right subtrees of the node.

left	nodeValue	right

TNode Object

A reference field, such as left, has the value null to indicate that the node does not have a left child. This is equivalent to saying that the left subtree of the node is empty. Hence, a leaf node has both a null left and a null right reference field. The root node defines an entry point into the binary tree. Figure 16.11 gives an abstract model of a binary tree, along with the corresponding representation with TNode objects.

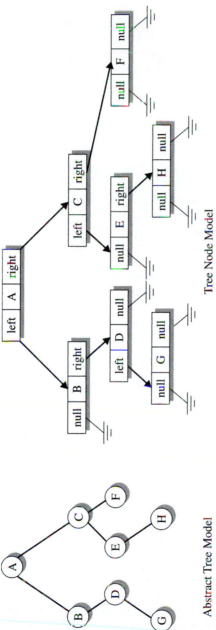

Abstract Tree Model

Tree Node Model

Figure 16.11 *Abstract and tree node model of a binary tree.*

The TNode class allows us to construct a binary tree as a collection of TNode objects.

The generic TNode class has two constructors that create binary tree node objects. The first constructor takes an argument of generic type T, which initializes `nodeValue` field. The reference fields are set to `null`. The resulting object is a node with no children. A second constructor has three arguments that assign initial values to `nodeValue` field and to the two reference fields. We use this constructor to create a parent node with links to its children. The instance variables in the TNode class are public. This simplifies their use when implementing binary tree classes and algorithms and does not violate the object-design principle of information hiding. Programmers use TNode objects as building blocks in a binary tree class. A user relies on the class methods and does not directly access the low-level TNode objects. The following is a declaration of the TNode class.

TNode class:

```
public class TNode<T>
{
    // node's value
    public T nodeValue;
    // subtree references
    public TNode<T> left, right;

    // create instance with a value and null subtrees
    public TNode(T item)
    {
        nodeValue = item;
        left = right = null;
    }

    // initialize the value and the subtrees
    public TNode (T item, TNode<T> left, TNode<T> right)
    {
        nodeValue = item;
        this.left = left;
        this.right = right;
    }
}
```

Building a Binary Tree

A binary tree consists of a collection of TNode objects whose reference values specify links to their children. You build a binary tree one node at a time. The constructor with a single argument of generic type creates a leaf node. The constructor with three arguments creates an interior node. The nonnull reference values in the interior node provide links that attach the node to its children. Let us look at how you create child and parent nodes and link them as part of a larger binary tree. The following statements declare two TNode reference variables, p and q, and create nodes that store Integer values. Node q is created as a parent with a link to node p as its right child. The resulting section of the tree is depicted in Figure 16.12a. The TNode view of the tree in Figure 16.12b includes the null reference pointers that indicate links to an empty tree.

```
TNode<Integer> p, q;              // references to TNode objects
// p is a leaf node with value 8
p = new TNode<Integer>(8);

// q is a node with value 4 and p as a right child
q = new TNode<Integer>(4, null, p);
```

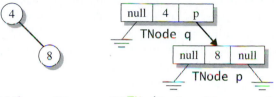

(a) Tree section   (b) **TNode**   view of the tree section

Figure 16.12   *Tree section including a leaf node and a node with a right child.*

Example 16.1

This example uses the TNode class to build the four-node tree of integer values pictured in the accompanying figure. The process begins by creating the two leaf nodes, 20 and 40. The interior node 30 is next with node 40 as its left child. The final statement creates the root node, 10, with nodes 20 and 30 as its left and right children respectively. Note that you build a tree from the "bottom up." Contrary to nature, you create the children first and then the parent.

You can use the TNode class to build a binary tree from the bottom up.

```
// references to Integer tree nodes
TNode<Integer> root, p, q, r;

// create leaf node p with value 20 and leaf node q
// with value 40
p = new TNode<Integer>(20);
q = new TNode<Integer>(40);

// create interior node r with value 30, left child
// q, and a null right child
r = new TNode<Integer>(30, q, null);

// create root node with value 10, left child p,
// and right child r
root = new TNode<Integer>(10, p, r);
```

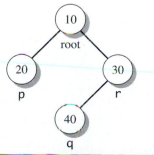

The Method buildTree()   As the previous example illustrates, building a binary tree by hand is a tedious process. Unfortunately, without algorithms to automate the process, we have no alternative. At the same time, we need some examples to illustrate the concepts in this chapter. To address this situation, we provide the static method buildTree() in the class BinaryTree. It builds three trees whose node values contain single Character values 'A', 'B', 'C', and so forth.

The buildTree() method takes an integer argument in the range 0–2. The value determines which of the three trees, Tree 0, Tree 1, or Tree 2, is created. The return value is a TNode reference pointing to the root of the tree. Figure 16.13 displays the three different trees. Look at the implementation of buildTree() in BinaryTree.java. You will see that it is not very glamorous. It builds the tree, node by node, using the technique in Example 16.1.

buildTree():

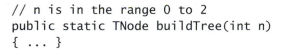

```
// n is in the range 0 to 2
public static TNode buildTree(int n)
{ ... }
```

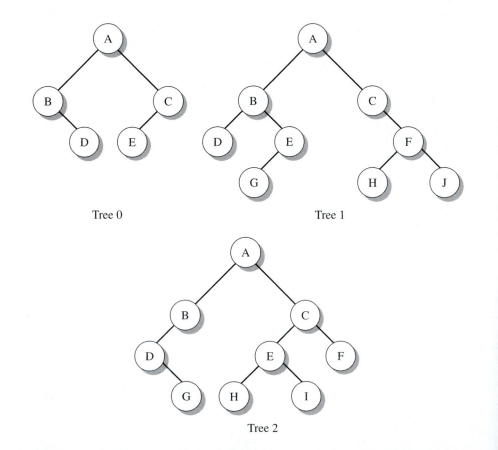

Tree 0

Tree 1

Tree 2

Figure 16.13 *Trees created by buildTree().*

Example 16.2

Using `buildTree()` is very easy. First, declare a `TNode<Character>` reference variable as the root of the tree. Then, call `buildTree()` with an argument *n* in the range from 0 to 2, and assign the return value as the root. For instance, the following statements build Tree 0 and Tree 2 and assign them to the TNode reference variables `root0` and `root2` respectively. The root of a tree is a TNode variable and thus can have any name. In most applications, we suggest you include "root" in the name for obvious reasons.

```
TNode<Character> root0, root2;
root0 = BinaryTree.buildTree(0);    // Tree 0 based at root0
root2 = BinaryTree.buildTree(2);    // Tree 2 based at root2
```

buildTree() gives us access to one of three binary trees.

16.3 Binary Tree-Scan Algorithms

A linear collection, such as a `LinkedList` or `ArrayList`, allows us to scan the elements by using their position in the sequence. Because a binary tree is a nonlinear structure, a sequential scan by position is impossible, because there is no unambiguous meaning for the location of the "next element." At each node, we can select between the left and right child. If the left child is chosen, we proceed to the left subtree of the node. Once there, we have another decision to select the left or right child of this child node. As the process continues, we move further and further from the starting node and have a backlog of unfinished tasks; namely, at each node, we need to visit the other child who was not initially selected. Without some organization, we face the possibility of skipping some of the nodes or accessing them multiple times. Fortunately, the recursive structure of a binary tree offers a variety of techniques that allow us to visit each node exactly once. The tree-scan algorithms identify three tasks that must be carried out at each node in the tree. These tasks include visiting the node to perform some action and selecting each of the children for their own visit. The different scanning strategies depend on the order in which we perform the tasks.

In this section, we discuss the classical tree-scan algorithms. We begin by focusing on strategies that will ensure that the scan visits each node exactly once. A visit to a node simply accesses the value of the node; namely, the value of the `nodeValue` field. In Section 16.4, we use the scanning algorithms to perform more meaningful tasks, such as copying or deleting the node, determining the height of the node, and so forth. For now, the emphasis is on the order in which we visit the nodes. Understanding the variety of ways to scan a tree is fundamental to your understanding of tree algorithms.

Recursive Tree Traversals

A binary tree is a recursive structure in which each node is specified by its value and its left and right subtrees. We use this structure to design a series of scanning algorithms that designate three separate tasks at each node. The tasks include visiting the node and performing some action (N), selecting the left child (L), and selecting the right child (R). Selecting the left child takes us to a node which is the root of a tree. In effect, this is a recursive descent into the left subtree of the node. The same is true for selection of the right child. A chain of recursive descents terminate when we reach an empty tree. This is a stopping condition.

To scan a tree recursively, we must visit the node (N), scan the left subtree (L), and scan the right subtree (R). The order in which we perform the N, L, R tasks determines the scan algorithm.

The recursive step sets into motion a scan of nodes with the repetition of the same three tasks at each node. The order in which we perform the N, L, and R tasks determines the different recursive scan algorithms.

One recursive scan strategy uses an L N R ordering of tasks. At each node, we first select the left child (L) and descend into its left subtree. The result is that all nodes in the left subtree are visited before we return to the node and complete the second task; namely, to visit the node (N). The final task involves selecting the right child (R) and descending into the right subtree. This recursive scan is the *inorder* traversal of the tree. The prefix "in" indicates that the visit (N) occurs between the L and R tasks which select the children. Other traversals are called *preorder (N L R)* and *postorder (L R N)*, reflecting the fact that the visit occurs before or after selecting the children.

Inorder Scan Algorithm

The inorder scan of a binary tree specifies an L N R ordering of tasks at each node in the scan. In following the recursive structure of a tree, the scan contacts a node as the root of a subtree and then immediately departs into its left subtree (L). It returns to make the formal visit (N) and then departs into its right subtree (R).

Let us trace the inorder scan in detail for a simple example, the character tree Tree 0. The visit simply outputs the value of the node. Some notation will help us identify the current node and the various tasks that must be performed. Assuming X is the name of the node, the labels L_X, N_X, and R_X represent the corresponding tasks.

> The inorder scan of a tree visits the left subtree L, visits the node N, then visits the right subtree R.

- L_X: Select the left child and descend into the left subtree
    "Go left to left child of X."
- N_X: Output the value of X
    "Visit X."
- R_X: Select the right child and descend into the right subtree
    "Go right to right child of X."

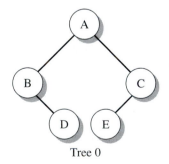

Tree 0

The scan begins at node A, the root of the tree. The following table lists the steps in the order of their execution. The table includes the name of the current node, the task to perform, and a description of the outcome. After completing all of the specified operations at a node, the recursive process returns to the parent node and picks up with the unfinished tasks at that node.

Node	Task	Output	Observation	
A:	L_A: Go left to B			
B:	L_B: Go left		Subtree is empty	L_B is done
	N_B: Action at B	"B"		N_B is done
	R_B: Go right to D			
D:	L_D: Go left		Subtree is empty	L_D is done
	N_D: Action at D	"D"		N_D is done
	R_D: Go right		Subtree is empty	R_D is done
			LNR for D is done	Return to B
B:			LNR for B is done	Return to A
A:	N_A: Action at A	"A"		N_A is done
	R_A: Go right to C			
C:	L_C: Go left to E			L_C is done
E:	L_E: Go left		Subtree is empty	L_E is done
	N_E: Action at E	"E"	N_E is done	
	R_E: Go right		Subtree is empty	R_E is done
			LNR for E is done	Return to C
C:	N_C: Action at C	"C"		N_C is done
	R_C: Go right		Subtree is empty	R_C is done
			LNR for C is done	Return to A
A:			LNR for A is done	Quit scan

The traversal order for the nodes is B, D, A, E, and C. If we step back and get a "tree view" of the scan, we observe that the nodes are visited from left to right. Other scanning algorithms visit the nodes top-down, bottom-up, right to left, and so forth. Understanding the different ways nodes can be visited is often essential to selecting an appropriate scanning method for an application.

An inorder scan visits the nodes from left to right.

Example 16.3

1. For the character tree, Tree 2, the following list describes the order of visits to the nodes for three scanning strategies. In each case, the descent into the left subtree (L) occurs before the descent into the right subtree (R).

   Preorder (N L R):   A   B   D   G   C   E   H   I   F

   Inorder (L N R):   D   G   B   A   H   E   I   C   F

   Postorder (L R N): G   D   B   H   I   E   F   C   A

   Note that the preorder scan visits nodes top-down in the tree while the postorder scan visits nodes bottom-up in the tree. In the latter, visits to the children are completed before the parent is visited.

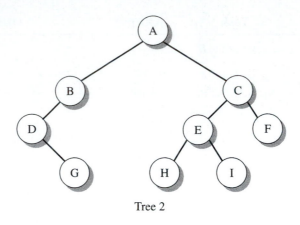

Tree 2

2. The R N L (inorder-right) traversal of Tree 2 visits the nodes in the order F C I E H A B G D. This is a right-to-left view of the nodes in the tree.

Designing Scanning Methods

The recursive tree-scan algorithms have relatively easy implementations as methods. They all follow a pattern. An if-else statement distinguishes the stopping condition and the recursive step. In a scan, the stopping condition occurs when it reaches an empty tree. The recursive step at each node involves the three tasks L, N, and R. The action during a visit is specific to the particular application. The order in which tasks are performed determines the type of scan. A TNode parameter t provides a reference to the current node, which represents the root of a subtree. The return type is void when the visit carries out a self-contained action. A return value is required when the visit acquires information that must be passed back to the parent. In some cases, information is acquired at the stopping condition (empty tree) and must be returned for use by a recursive step.

Recursive scan pattern (assuming an inorder scan (L N R) and a return value)

```
public static <T> ReturnType scanMethod(TNode<T> t)
{
   // check for empty tree (stopping condition)
   if (t == null)
      < return information for an empty tree >
   else
   {
      // descend to left subtree and record return information
      valueLeft = scanMethod(t.left);

      // visit the node
      < action involving t.nodeValue >

      // descend to right subtree and record return information
      valueRight = scanMethod(t.right);
   }
   return <information from valueLeft, valueRight,
      and the visit >
}
```

The pattern for a preorder scan (N L R) or a postorder scan (L R N) adjusts the order for the recursive descent to the children and the visit of the node in the else-block.

Preorder design pattern:

```
<evaluate t.nodeValue>              // visit node first
valueLeft = scanMethod(t.left);     // go left
valueRight = scanMethod(t.right);   // go right
```

Postorder design pattern:

```
valueLeft = scanMethod(t.left);     // go left
valueRight = scanMethod(t.right);   // go right
<evaluate t.nodeValue>              // visit node last
```

Displaying Nodes Inorder   Let us apply the scan pattern to implement two methods, `inorderOuput()` and `inorderDisplay()`, that can be used to display the nodes in a binary tree. In the first method, a visit outputs the value of the node to the console. It is a self-contained operation and so the return type is `void`. The visit is placed between a recursive call with the left child as the argument and a recursive call with the right child as an argument.

Console output for an inorder scan:

```java
// list the nodes of a binary tree using an LNR scan
public static <T> void inorderOutput(TNode<T> t)
{
    // the recursive scan terminates on a empty subtree
    if (t != null)
    {
        inorderOutput(t.left);  // descend left
        System.out.print(t.nodeValue + "  ");
        inorderOutput(t.right); // descend right
    }
}
```

The method `inorderDisplay()` returns a string that provides an inorder listing of the node values. The method illustrates how a recursive scan handles return values. It is also more "Java-like" than the console-specific method `inorderOutput()` because the return string can be used for output to the console, a file, or in a GUI application. You can find the code for the static `inorderDisplay()` method in the `BinaryTree` class as well as the methods `preorderDisplay()` and `postorderDisplay()`.

Some recursive scanning algorithms handle each node by gathering information that is obtained from descents into the subtrees. The information combines with calculations during the visit to provide a return value that is recursively passed back to the parent. Information gained by the root node is passed back to the calling statement. The `inorderDisplay()` method builds a string at each node that includes a listing of the order of visits in the left subtree, the node's own value, and the order of visits in the right subtree. The string becomes the return value.

inorderDisplay():

```java
// list the nodes of a binary tree using an LNR scan
public static <T> String inorderDisplay(TNode<T> t)
{
    // return value
    String s = "";

    // the recursive scan terminates on a empty subtree
    if (t != null)
    {
        s += inorderDisplay(t.left);    // descend left
        s += t.nodeValue + "  ";        // display the node
        s += inorderDisplay(t.right);   // descend right
    }

    return s;
}
```

We have discussed three tree-traversal algorithms that scan the left subtree before scanning the right subtree. We are not left-brain dominant or prejudiced. Three more algorithms choose right before left. They are simple permutations of the order of tasks at a node. A preorder-right scan uses an N R L ordering of tasks. The tree is still scanned top-down except that right subtree nodes are given preference. An inorder-right scan uses an R N L ordering of tasks to visit the nodes from right to left. A bottom-up postorder-right scan uses an R L N ordering of tasks.

Iterative Level-Order Scan

A level-order scan visits the root, then nodes on level 1, then nodes on level 2, and so on.

The recursive tree scans access elements by moving up and down through subtrees. Some applications need to access elements by levels, with the root coming first (level 0), then the children of the root (level 1), followed by the next generation (level 2), and so forth. For obvious reasons, the algorithm is called a *level-order scan*. The character Tree 2 illustrates the order of visits to the nodes.

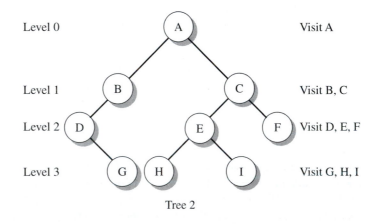

Tree 2

Level-Order Scan Algorithm   A level-order scan is an iterative process that uses a queue as an intermediate storage collection. Initially, the root enters the queue. An iterative step involves popping a node from the queue, performing some action with the node, and then pushing its children into the queue. Because siblings enter the queue during a visit of their parent, the siblings (on the same level) will exit the queue in successive iterations.

The algorithm involves an initialization step and a while-loop that removes the nodes, level by level, from a queue. The loop terminates when the queue is empty. The initialization creates a queue and pushes the root node into the queue.

Let us trace the algorithm, which creates a level-order scan of the nodes in Tree 0. Initially, the root node (A) is pushed into the queue.

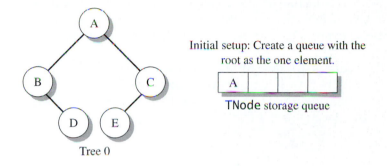

Initial setup: Create a queue with the root as the one element.

TNode storage queue

Tree 0

Step 1:   Pop node A from the queue and visit the node. Then push the two children of A, namely, B and C, into the queue.

Step 2:   Pop node B from the queue. After visiting the node, push D, the nonempty right child of B, into the queue.

Step 3:   Pop node C from the queue. After the visit, push E, the nonempty left child of C, into the queue.

Step 4:   Pop node D from the queue. Since D has no children, the step involves only visiting the node.

Step 5:   Pop node E from the queue. After visiting the node, we observe that E is a leaf node and so no new children enter the queue. The algorithm terminates because the queue is now empty.

levelOrderDisplay() uses a queue to create a string that lists the nodes in level order.

The static method `levelorderDisplay()` in the `BinaryTree` class traverses the nodes of a binary tree in level order and returns a string displaying the value of each node. The method has a TNode reference argument t that designates the starting node (root) of the scan. We use a `LinkedQueue` collection to store the nodes. Each element of the LinkedQueue is an object of type TNode<T>.

levelorderDisplay():

```
// list the value of each node in a binary tree using a
// level order scan of the nodes
public static <T> String levelorderDisplay(TNode<T> t)
{
    // store siblings of each node in a queue so that they are
    // visited in order at the next level of the tree
    LinkedQueue<TNode<T> q = new LinkedQueue<TNode<T>>();
    TNode<T> p;
    // return value
    String s = "";

    // initialize the queue by inserting the root in the queue
    q.push(t);

    // continue the iterative process until the queue is empty
    while(!q.isEmpty())
    {
        // delete a node from queue and output the node value
        p = q.pop();
        s += p.nodeValue + "  ";

        // if a left child exists, insert it in the queue
        if(p.left != null)
           q.push(p.left);
        // if a right child exists, insert next to its sibling
        if(p.right != null)
           q.push(p.right);
    }

    return s;
}
```

The Visitor Design Pattern

The Visitor design pattern applies an action to each element of a collection.

The *Visitor design pattern* represents an operation that applies whenever a program needs to perform an action on each element of a collection. The operation may occur during an iterative or recursive scan of the elements in the collection.

To implement the visitor pattern, we create the `Visitor` interface that defines the method `visit()`. For a specific visitor pattern, create a class that implements the interface. The class overrides `visit()` by specifying the visitor operation. During the traversal of a collection, call the method `visit()` and pass the current value of the element as an argument.

Visitor interface:

```java
public interface Visitor<T>
{
    void visit(T item);
}
```

The Visitor inter-
face defines the
visit() method,
which denotes
what a visitor does.
An actual visitor is
an object that
overrides visit().

Example 16.4

In this example, we provide two implementations of the `Visitor` interface. You will find the `Visitor` interface and the classes `VisitOutput` and `VisitMax` in Chapter 16 of the software supplement.

1. In the class `VisitOutput`, the method `visit()` simply outputs the value of its argument.

```java
public class VisitOutput<T> implements Visitor<T>
{
    public void visit(T item)
    {
        System.out.print(item + "  ");
    }
}
```

2. The class `VisitMax` specifies a generic type that implements the `Comparable` interface itself or in a superclass. The class has an instance variable `max`. At any point in the scan of the collection, the variable holds the maximum value of the elements which have been visited. The method `visit()` compares the argument `obj` with the current value of `max` and updates `max` if it finds a larger value. A program can access the maximum value at any time in the scan by calling the public method `getMax()`.

VisitOutput and
VisitMax objects
carry out specific
visitor tasks.

```java
public class VisitMax<T extends Comparable<? super T>>
    implements Visitor<T>
{
    T max = null;

    public void visit(T item)
    {
        if (max == null)
            max = item;
        else if (item.compareTo(max) > 0)
            max = item;
    }

    public T getMax()
    {
        return max;
    }
}
```

Using the Visitor Pattern

We create a program that illustrates how to combine a `Visitor` objects with a tree scanning algorithm. This program uses the integer tree in Figure 16.14. To illustrate the `Visitor` pattern, we develop the recursive method `scanInorder()`, which takes the root of a binary

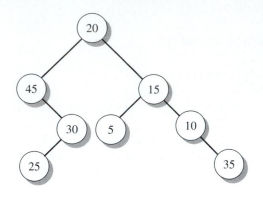

Figure 16.14 *Integer tree to illustrate scanning algorithms and Visitor patterns.*

Method scanInorder() scans a binary tree inorder and calls visit() in the Visitor object v for each node. The actual visit is provided at runtime by the specific Visitor argument.

tree, and an object that implements the `Visitor` interface as parameters. This method provides a generalized inorder traversal of a tree that performs an action specified by the visitor object where the value of the node is the argument.

scanInorder():

```
public static <T> void scanInorder (TNode<T> t, Visitor<T> v)
{
    if (t != null)
    {
        scanInorder(t.left, v);
        v.visit(t.nodeValue);
        scanInorder(t.right, v);
    }
}
```

PROGRAM 16.1 SCANNING METHODS AND THE VISITOR DESIGN PATTERN

This program uses the static method `buildTree16_1()` to create the tree of integers illustrated in Figure 16.14. A series of output statements give the preorder, inorder, postorder, and level-order scan of the tree by calling the corresponding display methods in the class `BinaryTree`. The program illustrate the Visitor pattern using the classes from Example 16.4. A call to `scanInorder()` with a `VisitOutput` object is an alternative to the `inorderDisplay()` method. The same general inorder scan method with a `VisitMax` argument determines the maximum value in the tree. By calling `getMax()`, we output the value.

```
import ds.util.TNode;
import ds.util.BinaryTree;

public class Program16_1
{
    public static void main(String[] args)
```

```java
{
    // root of the tree
    TNode<Integer> root;

    // create the Visitor objects
    VisitOutput<Integer> output = new VisitOutput<Integer>();
    VisitMax<Integer> max = new VisitMax<Integer>();

    // create the tree using buildTree16_1
    root = buildTree16_1();

    // output the recursive scans and the level order scan
    System.out.println("Scans of the tree");
    System.out.println("   Preorder scan:   " +
            BinaryTree.preorderDisplay(root));
    System.out.println("   Inorder scan:    " +
            BinaryTree.inorderDisplay(root));
    System.out.println("   Postorder scan:   " +
            BinaryTree.postorderDisplay(root));
    System.out.println("   Level order scan: " +
            BinaryTree.levelorderDisplay(root) + "\n");

    // use Visitor object and scanInorder() to traverse the
    // tree and determine the maximum value
    System.out.println(
            "Call scanInorder() with VisitOutput: ");
    scanInorder(root, output);
    System.out.println();

    scanInorder(root, max);
    System.out.println(
            "Call scanInorder() with VisitMax: Max value is " +
            max.getMax());
}

public static <T> void scanInorder(TNode<T> t, Visitor<T> v)
{
    if (t != null)
    {
        scanInorder(t.left, v);
        v.visit(t.nodeValue);
        scanInorder(t.right, v);
    }
}

public static TNode<Integer> buildTree16_1()
{
    // TNode references; point to the 8 items in the tree
    TNode<Integer> root20 = null, t45, t15, t30,
                                 t5, t10, t25, t35;
    t35 = new TNode<Integer>(35);
```

```
                        t25 = new TNode<Integer>(25);
                        t10 = new TNode<Integer>(10, null, t35);
                        t5 = new TNode<Integer>(5);
                        t30 = new TNode<Integer>(30, t25, null);
                        t15 = new TNode<Integer>(15, t5, t10);
                        t45 = new TNode<Integer>(45, null, t30);
                        root20 = new TNode<Integer>(20, t45, t15);

                        return root20;
                    }
                }
```

```
Run:
   Scans of the tree
       Preorder scan:     20  45  30  25  15   5  10  35
       Inorder scan:      45  25  30  20   5  15  10  35
       Postorder scan:    25  30  45   5  35  10  15  20
       Level order scan:  20  45  15  30   5  10  25  35

   Call scanInorder() with VisitOutput:
   45  25  30  20   5  15  10  35
   Call scanInorder() with VisitMax: Max value is 45
```

Generalizing Use of the Visitor Pattern   Program 16.1 applies the Visitor pattern only to binary trees. In fact, it is easy to apply the pattern to any object that implements the Collection interface. For instance, consider the following method, traverse(), that has Collection and Visitor parameters. An iterator sequences through the collection and passes the data value to the Visitor object.

The Visitor design pattern can be used during an iterative scan of elements in a Collection.

```java
// traverse c and apply the Visitor pattern to each
// of its values
public static <T> void traverse(Collection<T> c, Visitor<T> v)
{
    Iterator<T> iter = c.iterator();

    while (iter.hasNext())
        v.visit(iter.next());
}
```

Example 16.5

In this example, you will create a LinkedList object containing Integer data. By calling traverse(), output its values and the maximum of its elements.

```java
int[] arr = {5, 7, 15, 3, 21, 2, 6, 8, 9};
LinkedList<Integer> intList = new LinkedList<Integer>();
// create the Visitor objects
```

```
Visitor<Integer> output = new VisitOutput<Integer>(),
                 max = new VisitMax<Integer>();

for (int i=0;i < arr.length;i++)
    intList.add(arr[i]);

traverse(intList, output);
System.out.println();
traverse(intList, max);
System.out.println("The maximum element in intList is " +
                   ((VisitMax)max).getMax());
```

```
Run:
   5   7   15   3   21   2   6   8   9
   The maximum element in intList is 21
```

16.4 Using Tree-Scan Algorithms

The tree-scanning techniques are the basis for most binary tree algorithms.

In the previous section, we developed the classical binary tree-scan algorithms and illustrated them with methods that simply display the values of the node. In this section, we want to apply the tree-scan techniques to develop algorithms where a visit involves some calculation or update action. For starters, we implement an algorithm that computes the height of a tree. Anticipating the construction of the binary search tree class, we develop algorithms that copy and delete nodes in a tree. We implement all of the algorithms as static methods, which you can find in the `BinaryTree` class.

Computing the Tree Height

The height of a node is the length of the longest path in its subtrees. The height of the tree is the height of the root node. In Section 16.2, we showed how the recursive structure of a binary tree is used to compute the height of a node. Recall that the stopping condition is an empty tree, which has height -1. The height of each nonempty node uses the recursive step, where its height is one more than the maximum height of its subtrees. Assigning an empty tree the height -1 ensures that a leaf node has height 0.

height(t) is the max of height(t.left) and height(t.right) + 1.

$$
height(T) = \begin{cases} -1 & \text{if T is empty} \\ 1 + \max\,(height(T_L),\, height(T_R)) & \text{if T is nonempty} \end{cases}
$$

Figure 16.15 illustrates the height for node B in Tree 1. The recursive condition computes the height to be 2, which is one more than the maximum height for the left child D (height 0) and the right child E (height 1). The height of the tree is 3, which is the height of the root node.

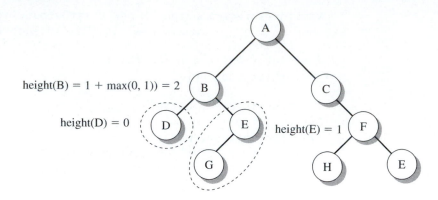

Figure 16.15 *Binary tree of height 3.*

An algorithm uses a recursive scan of the nodes to determine the height of a tree. In the previous section, we identified three types of recursive scan: preorder, inorder, and postorder. These expand to six when you distinguish the order of descent (left or right) into the subtrees. Computing the height of a node requires information about the heights of the subtrees. You must evaluate the children before you evaluate the parent. This involves a postorder, or bottom-up, scan of the nodes. A method that implements the algorithm has a return value that passes the height of a node back to its parent. In a postorder scan, the root is the last node visited. The return value from the root is the height of the tree.

The static method `height()` takes a `TNode` reference `t` and returns the height of the tree with root `t`. The method uses a postorder scan that assigns the heights of the subtree to the variables `leftHeight` and `rightHeight` respectively. A visit to the node involves using the recursive step to compute the height of the node. The stopping condition, an empty tree, must be checked and returns a height −1. We include `height()` as a static method in the `BinaryTree` class.

height():

```
// determine the height of the tree using a postorder scan
public static <T> int height(TNode<T> t)
{
    int heightLeft, heightRight, heightval;

    if (t == null)
        // height of an empty tree is -1
        heightval = -1;
    else
    {
        // find the height of the left subtree of t
        heightLeft = height(t.left);
        // find the height of the right subtree of t
        heightRight = height(t.right);
        // height of the tree with root t is 1 + maximum
        // of the heights of the two subtrees
```

```
        heightval = 1 +
            (heightLeft > heightRight ? heightLeft : heightRight);
    }

    return heightval;
}
```

Example 16.6

The tree in Figure 16.15 is the character Tree 1. After using `buildTree()` to create the tree, output the height by calling the static method `height()`.

```
    // root of the tree
    TNode<Character> root = BinaryTree.buildTree(1);

    System.out.println("The height of the tree is " +
                    BinaryTree.height(root));
```

Output:
    The height of the tree is 3

Copying a Binary Tree

In many applications, a programmer wants to duplicate a tree structure. The duplicate configures nodes with the same parent-to-child relationships although the data might include additional information specific to the application. For instance, the duplicate tree may contain nodes that have an additional field that references the parent. The duplicate allows the programmer to scan up the tree along the path of parents. Figure 16.16

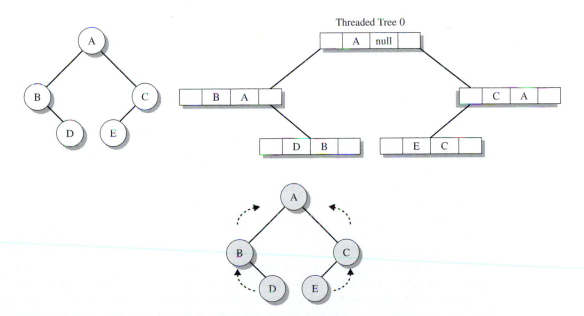

Figure 16.16 *Duplicate of Tree O has references to the parent node.*

illustrates a copy of Tree 0 where a parent field is added to the node. The parent is used to create the path D−B−A that moves from the leaf node D up the tree to the root A.

We will now explore the tree copy algorithm for the simple case, where the copy is an exact duplicate of the original tree. Copying a tree requires a recursive scan of its nodes. At each recursive step, we want to create a duplicate of the node including the value and links to its children. Part of the task is easy. Simply create a new node using the operator `new` and a TNode constructor with the value of the node in the original tree as an argument. The problem lies with the links. The new node must have references "`left`" and "`right`" that point to its children. Each child is a duplicate node that was created at some prior recursive step in the scan. You will quickly understand the issues and the solution by tracing a few recursive steps in the algorithm.

Copy a tree using a postorder scan. This builds the duplicate tree from the bottom up.

Consider the character tree, Tree 0, which has five nodes. Assume that the TNode reference `origRoot` is the root of the tree which is created by calling `buildTree(0)`. The method `copyTree()` builds a duplicate tree. The method takes `origRoot` as the argument, creates a second tree, which is a duplicate of Tree 0, and returns a reference that identifies the root of the new tree. In the example, the new root is the TNode reference `copyRoot` (Figure 16.17).

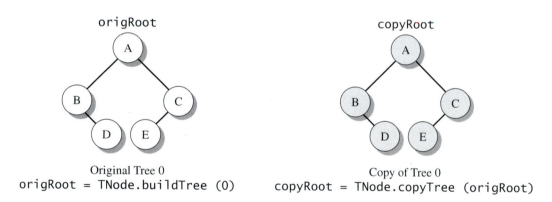

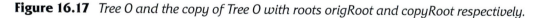

Figure 16.17 *Tree 0 and the copy of Tree 0 with roots origRoot and copyRoot respectively.*

A postorder scan of the original tree visits a node only after it visits both the left and the right subtrees. The postorder visit to the node has access to its children and thus to its two subtrees. In our case, the visit will use knowledge of subtrees and the value of the node to create a duplicate node in the copy tree. Let us illustrate in detail the steps that lead to the creation of duplicate nodes B and D in the copy tree. At each node `t` in the original tree, we use the postorder scan to make a recursive call to `copyTree()` with argument `t.left` and then a recursive call to `copyTree()` with argument `t.right`. The calls create the duplicate left and right subtrees for the node and method returns references to the roots of these subtrees. Assume the reference to the left subtree is `newLeft` and the reference to the right subtree is `newRight`. For the visit to node `t`, allocate a node whose value is `t.nodeValue` but whose subtrees are `newLeft` and `newRight`. The stopping condition for the recursive scan occurs when `t==null`; that is, when the scan in the original tree reaches an empty tree. The return value in this case is `null`, which indicates that a similar empty tree will also be created in the duplicate tree. To assist the tracing of the

algorithm, we include a subscript with the reference variables `newNode`, `newLeft`, and
`newRight` to indicate the association between the new node and the corresponding node
of the original tree.

The postorder recursive scan starts at the root node and then immediately descends to
the left child B. We pick up the trace at this point.

At node B:

   (L) Descend to the left subtree, which is empty. The return value
      is `null`

$$\text{newLeft}_B = \text{null}$$

   (R) Descend to the right subtree with root D

At node D:

   (L) Descend to the left subtree, which is empty. The return value
      is `null`

$$\text{newLeft}_D = \text{null}$$

   (R) Descend to the right subtree, which is empty. The return value
      is `null`

$$\text{newRight}_D = \text{null}$$

   (N) Create a node that is a duplicate of D in the copy tree. The
      children of the node are `newLeft`$_D$ and `newRight`$_D$ respectively.

$$\text{newNode}_D = \text{new TNode(t.nodeValue, newLeft}_D, \text{newRight}_D)$$

      Return the new node reference to the parent B. We have created the
      duplicate node D.

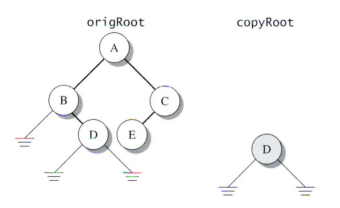

At node B:

   (Recursive calls L and R are complete. Return values are

$$\text{newLeft}_B = \text{null} \text{ and newRight}_B = \text{newNode}_D)$$

   (N) Create a node that is a duplicate of B in the copy tree. The
      children of the node are `newLeft`$_B$ and `newRight`$_B$ respectively.

$$\text{newNodeB} = \text{new TNode(t.nodeValue, newLeft}_B, \text{newRight}_B)$$

      Return the new node reference to the parent A.

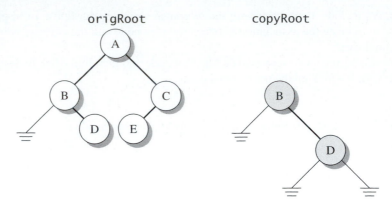

The process continues with the last step creating a duplicate root node with value A. The node reference, newNode$_A$, becomes the return value, which the calling statement uses to initialize the root of the duplicate tree.

copyTree():

```
// create a duplicate of the tree with root t and return
// a reference to its root
public static <T> TNode<T> copyTree(TNode<T> t)
{
    // newNode points at a new node that the algorithm
    // creates; newLptr. and newRptr point to the subtrees
    // of newNode
    TNode<T> newLeft, newRight, newNode;

    // stop the recursive scan when we arrive at empty tree
    if (t == null)
        return null;

    // build the new tree from the bottom up by building the two
    // subtrees and then building the parent. at node t, make
    // a copy of the left subtree and assign its root node
    // reference to newLeft; make a copy of the right subtree
    // and assign its root node reference to newRight
    newLeft = copyTree(t.left);
    newRight = copyTree(t.right);

    // create a new node whose value is the same as the value
    // in t and whose children are the copied subtrees
    newNode = new TNode<T> (t.nodeValue, newLeft, newRight);

    // return a reference to the root of the newly copied tree
    return newNode;
}
```

Clearing a Tree

An application may want to use a tree as a temporary storage structure. When no longer needed, the memory should be released for other purposes. Setting the root to null is not sufficient since this only marks a single node for garbage collection. All of the nodes should be marked. This involves a recursive scan of the tree with the visit operation assigning the value null to the node reference. The effect is to deallocate the tree one node at a time.

A bottom-up scan ensures that the children are deleted before the parent is deleted. The method clearTree() takes a TNode reference t, which represents the root of a sub-tree and uses a postorder scan of the nodes. We include clearTree() as a static method in the BinaryTree class.

Clear a tree with a postorder scan. This removes the left and right sub-trees before removing the node.

clearTree():

```
public static <T> void clearTree(TNode<T> t)
{
    // postorder scan; delete left and right
    // subtrees of t and then node t
    if (t != null)
    {
        clearTree(t.left);
        clearTree(t.right);
        t = null;
    }
}
```

Displaying a Binary Tree

For tree programs and exercises, we need a way to display the tree vertically with nodes at each level on the same line. The design for such a display algorithm involves copying a tree, using inorder and level-order scans and other concepts we developed in this chapter. It is an interesting and informative study, and is a topic in Chapter 17.

In the BinaryTree class, we include the methods displayTree() and drawTree(), which provide a console and a graphical display of a tree respectively. The methods use the same parameters. The method displayTree() returns a string giving a tree layout of the node values. The string includes spaces and newlines so that nodes are properly arranged as subtrees and levels in the tree. The parameters include a TNode reference t specifying the root and an integer maxCharacters, which determines the number of spaces allocated for the node values.

displayTree():

```
// return a string that displays a binary tree; output of
// a node value requires no more than maxCharacters
public static <T> String displayTree(TNode<T> t, int
    maxCharacters)
{ ... }
```

You call the method displayTree() by passing the root of the tree and the maximum number of characters required to output the value of a node. For instance, if the tree

displayTree() is a string that has a layout of the node values in a binary tree. drawTree() is a graphical view of the tree.

has integer values in the range 0–99, pass the length as 2. If `String` is the data type for the node values, pass the length of the longest string.

The static method `drawTree()` displays the tree on a graphical screen. Nodes are displayed as shaded circles with the value in the center and lines representing the edges. The method has the same parameter list as `displayTree()`. A modified form of the method called `drawTrees()` enables you to draw multiple trees in separate frames.

drawTree():

```
// displays a tree in a graphical window
public static <T> void drawTree(TNode<T> t, int maxCharacters)
{ ... }
```

drawTrees():

```
// displays a tree and leaves the window open
public static <T> void drawTrees(TNode<T> t, int maxCharacters)
{ ... }
```

Program 16.2 illustrates the method `copyTree()` and use of the methods `display Tree()` and `drawTree()` to display a tree in the console window or on a graphical screen.

PROGRAM 16.2

This program demonstrates the algorithms for displaying and copying trees. A call to `buildTree()` constructs Tree 2 and `displayTree()` displays the tree on the console. The method `copyTree()` creates a copy of the tree, which is graphically displayed with `drawTree()`. Because the data in each node is a single character, the `maxCharacters` argument is 1.

```java
import ds.util.TNode;
import ds.util.BinaryTree;

public class Program16_2
{
    public static void main(String[] args)
    {
        // roots for two trees
        TNode<Character> root, copyRoot;

        // build the character Tree 2 with root root2
        root = BinaryTree.buildTree(2);

        // display the original tree on the console
        System.out.println(BinaryTree.displayTree(root, 1));

        // make a copy of root1 so its root is root2
        copyRoot = BinaryTree.copyTree(root);

        // graphically display the tree copy
        BinaryTree.drawTree(copyRoot, 1);
    }
}
```

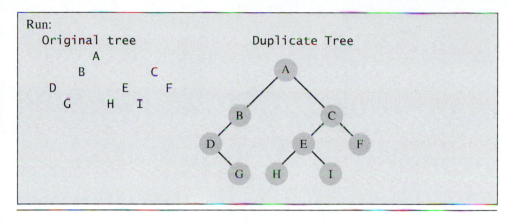

Run:

Original tree   Duplicate Tree

16.5 A Lower Bound for Sorting (Optional)

In previous chapters, we developed a series of sorting algorithms that use comparisons to order the elements. The quadratic sorting algorithms such as insertion sort, bubble sort (Programming Project 4.18), and exchange sort (Programming Exercise 4.16) compare adjacent elements and all have worst- and average-case running time $O(n^2)$. The more sophisticated sorting algorithms, such as quicksort and mergesort, also perform comparisons of array elements and have average-case running time of $O(n \log_2 n)$. To improve on quadratic running time, Section 7.2 discusses the fact that a sorting algorithm must compare nonadjacent elements. Are there as yet undiscovered sorting algorithms that use comparisons and have worst- and average-case running time better than $O(n \log_2 n)$? Since sorting is so important, it would pay to search for such an algorithm.

We answer the question by considering a *decision tree* for a sorting algorithm. Such a tree traces all the possible paths that occur when a sorting algorithm executes. Each interior node has the format "$elt_1 : elt_2$", which means that we perform the test $elt_1 < elt_2$. The two edges from the node represent the results of the comparison, $elt_1 < elt_2$ or $elt_2 < elt_1$. The leaf nodes contain the final sorted sequence.

As an example, we can use the selection sort and construct the decision tree for sorting the 3-element array $\{a, b, c\}$. For simplicity, assume that the array contains no duplicates. The first comparison determines whether $a < b$, so the root node and its edges are

> A decision tree traces all the possible paths that can occur when a sorting algorithm executes.

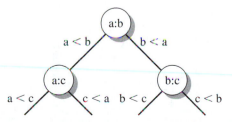

Continuing the first pass, we compare a and c or b and c.

At this point, the first pass concludes and we exchange the smallest element with a. In the second pass, we must compare the elements at positions 1 and 2 of the array. Figure 16.18 shows the final decision tree.

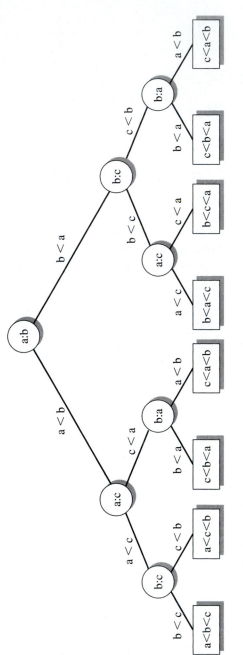

Figure 16.18 *Decision tree for the selection sort of {a, b, c}.*

Assume we sort n elements. Since each leaf node represents a sorted sequence, there must be at least n! leaf nodes in the decision tree for the sorting algorithm. In Figure 16.18, there are eight leaf nodes. Note that the first six (3!) enumerate the possible sorted orders.

We can use the decision tree to obtain a lower bound on the running time for any sorting algorithm that uses comparisons. This is one of the most important results in computer science. To develop the result, we must first note a general fact for a binary tree (see Written Exercise 16.14).

If an array has n elements, there must be at least n! leaf nodes in the decision tree for a sorting algorithm that uses comparisons.

General Fact for a Binary Tree

Note

If a binary tree has L leaf nodes, then

$$L \leq 2^d,$$

where d is the depth of the tree.

Any sorting algorithm that uses comparisons has a decision tree, although it is not practical to construct it. As we have noted, the decision tree has at least n! leaf nodes, each one representing a possible ordering of the elements.

It follows from our general fact that

$$n! \leq 2^d,$$

where d is the depth of the decision tree. Since the $\log_2(x)$ is an increasing function, we can take the logarithm of both sides of the inequality and obtain

$$d \geq \log_2(n!)$$

The worst case for the algorithm is to traverse a path to the deepest point in the decision tree; that is, to execute d comparisons. This tells us that the worst-case running time, T(n), satisfies the inequality

$$T(n) \geq \log_2(n!)$$

It can be shown that for large n, n! is approximately equal to

$$\sqrt{2\pi n}\left(\frac{n}{e}\right)^n$$

where e is the base of the natural logarithms. This is knows as *Stirling's approximation* for n!. It can actually be shown that the following bound holds for all n.

$$n! \geq \sqrt{2\pi n}\left(\frac{n}{e}\right)^n$$

If we omit the square root factor, we conclude that

$$n! > \left(\frac{n}{e}\right)^n$$

This result implies

$$T(n) \geq \log_2(n!) > \log_2\left(\left(\frac{n}{e}\right)^n\right) = n\log_2 n - n\log_2 e$$

Sorting algorithms using comparisons can have a running time of no better than O(n log₂ n).

The term $n\log_2 n - n\log_2 e$ is a lower bound for the running time of any sorting algorithm that uses comparisons. There is a commonly used notation for a result of this type. If the average- or worst-case performance of an algorithm is no better than $g(n)$, we say that the algorithm has running time $\Omega(g(n))$. Ignoring the insignificant term $n\log_2 e$, we have shown that any sorting algorithm that uses comparisons has worst-case running time $\Omega(n\log_2 n)$.

We now know that if a friend tells you that he or she has discovered this fantastic sorting algorithm that uses comparisons and has running time $O(n(\log_2 n)^{1/2})$, your friend has made an error!

Chapter Summary

- A tree is a hierarchical structure that places elements in nodes along branches that originate from a root. Nodes in a tree are subdivided into levels; the topmost level holds only the root node. Any node in a tree can have multiple successors at the next level. Hence, a tree is a nonlinear structure. Most applications involve a restricted category of trees, called binary trees, in which each node has at most two successors. Trees have associated terminology with which you should be familiar. The terms include parent, child, descendant, leaf node, interior node, and subtree. We can measure a tree mathematically by computing its height, which is the maximum depth of any node in the tree. The root is at depth 0.

- A binary tree is most effective as a storage structure if it has high density; that is, if data are located on relatively short paths from the root. A complete binary tree has the highest possible density, and an n-node complete binary tree has height $int(\log_2 n)$. At the other extreme, a degenerate binary tree is equivalent to a linked list and exhibits $O(n)$ access times.

- A programmer implements a binary tree by using a class whose data include the value of the node and references to the left and right children of the node (left and right subtrees). This book implements the TNode class and supplies the method buildTree() in the class BinaryTree to create one of three binary trees for use in algorithm development. The method builds the sample trees from the bottom up.

- A tree is a nonlinear structure, so a fundamental problem involves moving through one in an organized fashion. There are six recursive algorithms for tree traversal. The most commonly used ones are inorder (LNR), postorder (LRN), and preorder (NLR). Many tree algorithms base their method on one of these traversal techniques. Another technique for tree traversal is to move left to right from level to level. This algorithm is iterative, and its implementation involves using a queue. The class BinaryTree contains algorithms that output the nodes of a tree in preorder, inorder, postorder, or level-order.

- The Visitor design pattern represents an operation that applies whenever a program needs to perform an action on every element of a collection. The collection executes a loop or recursive calls and applies the operation at each element. The classes VisitOutput and VisitMax are realizations of the design pattern. Each class is an implementation of the Visitor interface that specifies the action visit() for each value in a collection. These classes are applied in a program that builds a binary tree and outputs its nodes and its maximum node value.

- The chapter discusses algorithms that solve various problems for binary trees, such as computing the height of a tree, copying a tree, and deleting all the nodes in a tree. The chapter also introduces methods that provide a display of a binary tree, using either console or graphical output.

- The quadratic sorting algorithms such as insertion sort compare adjacent elements and have worst- and average-case running time $O(n^2)$. The more sophisticated sorting algorithms, such as quicksort and mergesort, perform comparisons of nonadjacent array elements and have average-case running time of $O(n\log_2 n)$. A mathematical analysis shows that there are no sorting algorithms that both use comparisons and have worst- and average-case running time better than $O(n\log_2 n)$.

Written Exercises

1. Explain why a tree is a nonlinear data structure.

2. What is the minimum height of a binary tree that contains

   (a) 15 nodes   (b) 5 nodes   (c) 91 nodes

3. (a) Draw a binary tree that contains 10 nodes and has height 5.

   (b) Draw a binary tree that contains 14 nodes and has height 5.

4. A binary tree contains the data values 1 3 7 2 12.

   (a) Draw two trees of maximal height containing the data.

   (b) Draw two complete binary trees in which the parent value is greater than either child value.

5. Draw all possible binary trees that contain three nodes.

6. (a) Draw the binary tree that the following allocations create.

```
TNode<Integer> root, a, b, c, d, e;
e = new TNode<Integer>(50);
d = new TNode<Integer>(20, null, e);
c = new TNode<Integer>(30);
b = new TNode<Integer>(45, c, null);
a = new TNode<Integer>(15, b, d);
root = new TNode<Integer>(10,null,a);
```

   (b) List the nodes in the order of their visit for an NLR (preorder) scan.

   (c) List the nodes in the order of their visit for an LRN (postorder) scan.

   (d) List the nodes in the order of their visit for an LNR (inorder) scan.

7. Trace the following tree-traversal method, f(), and describe its action.

```
public static <T> int f(TNode<T> t)
{   int n = 0, leftValue, rightValue;

    if (t != null)
    {
        if (t.left != null || t.right != null)
            n++;
        leftValue = f(t.left);
```

```
                 rightValue = f(t.right);
                 return n + leftValue + rightValue;
          }
          else
                 return 0;
      }
```

8. Assume a binary tree has n nodes. Give the running time for each scan.

   (a) Inorder   (b) Postorder   (c) Preorder

9. Prove that if a binary tree has n nodes, it must have $n-1$ edges.

10. Assume a binary tree with n nodes and height h is complete and has all possible nodes at depth h.

    (a) Show the tree has $n = 2^{h+1} - 1$ nodes.

    (b) Show that the tree has exactly 2^h leaf nodes.

11. Prove that in a complete binary tree with n nodes, the longest path from its root to a leaf node includes $int(\log_2 n) + 1$ nodes.

12. Prove that in a binary tree with n nodes, the longest path from the root to a leaf node must have a length of at least $int(\log_2 n)$ nodes.

13. Some problems, such as implementing a game on a computer, involve general trees. In a general tree, a node may have more than two children. For instance, the following is a tree whose maximum child count is 3.

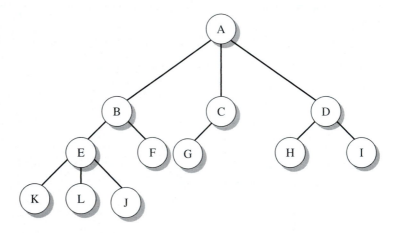

    (a) In a general tree, is an inorder traversal unambiguously defined?

    (b) Give the preorder and postorder traversal of the sample tree.

    (c) A general tree can be converted to a binary tree using the following algorithm:

        (1) The left reference of each node in the binary tree points to the leftmost child of the corresponding node in the general tree.

        (2) The right reference of each node in the binary tree points to a sibling (node with the same parent) of the node in the general tree.

        When drawing the binary tree, place each child directly below a node and place a sibling to the right. Arrange the tree in node columns. For instance, the following is the binary tree corresponding to the sample tree:

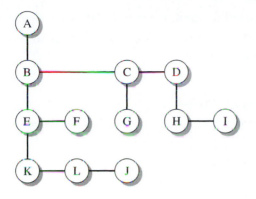

If the tree is turned 45' clockwise, a more familiar binary tree results:

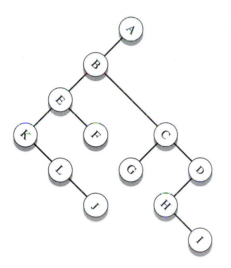

Traverse the binary tree using preorder, inorder, and postorder scans. What similarities do you find among these scans and those for the general tree?

(d) For the following general tree, do the following:

(1) Traverse it using preorder and postorder scans.

(2) Draw the corresponding binary tree.

(3) Traverse the binary tree using preorder, inorder, and postorder scans.

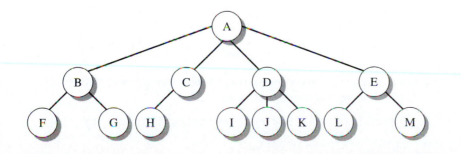

14. Draw the decision tree for the insertion sort of the three distinct values a, b, c.

15. Use mathematical induction to prove the following result for any binary tree. If a binary tree has L leaf nodes, then

$$L \leq 2^h$$

where h is the height of the tree.

16. Show that a binary tree with n nodes has $n + 1$ null subtrees.

Programming Exercises

17. Implement the method

```
public static int treeSize(TNode<?> t)
{ ... }
```

that counts the number of nodes in a binary tree. Test the method in a program that uses `buildTree()` from `BinaryTree` to allocate Tree 0 and Tree 2. Call `treeSize()` for each tree and output the results.

18. Implement the method

```
public static int countOneChild(TNode<?> t)
{ ... }
```

that counts the number of interior nodes in a binary tree having 1 child. Test the method in a program that uses `buildTree()` from `BinaryTree` to allocate Tree 0 and Tree 2. Call `countOneChild()` for each tree and output the results.

19. (a) Using the character `buildTree()` method as a model, implement a method `buildStringTree()` that builds the following binary tree containing `String` values.

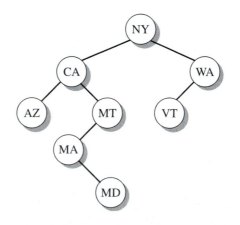

(b) Implement the method `rlnDisplay()` that scans a binary tree in RLN order and returns a string that displays the nodes.

```
public static String rlnDisplay(TNode<?> t)
{ ... }
```

(c) In a program, use `buildStringTree()` to construct a tree and call `rlnDisplay()` to output the nodes of the tree in RLN order. Display the tree using both `displayTree()` and `drawTree()`.

20. (a) This exercise develops the method `displayTreeSideways()` that displays a tree rotated counterclockwise 90°. Figure 16.19 shows Tree 2 output using `displayTree()` and the tree as it is output using `displayTreeSideways()`. Since output is done line by line, the algorithm must use the RNL scan so that nodes in a right subtree are output before nodes in a left subtree. For Tree 2, nodes are output in the order

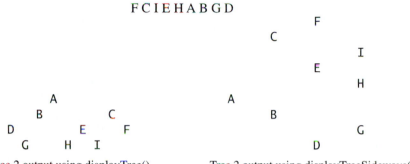

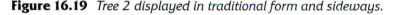

Tree 2 output using displayTree()   Tree 2 output using displayTreeSideways()

Figure 16.19 *Tree 2 displayed in traditional form and sideways.*

Implement the display with the following methods:

```
// spacing between levels
private static final int INDENTBLOCK = 6;

// output num blanks
private static void indentBlanks(int num)
{ ... }

public static <T> String displayTreeSideways(TNode<T> t)
{ ... }

// recursive function that displays a tree sideways
private static <T> String displayNode(TNode<T> t,
    int depth)
{ ... }
```

The function `displayTreeSideways()` calls the recursive function `display Node()` to display each node in the tree. The recursive function uses depth to determine the position of a node on the screen. Initially, the value of depth is 0. For each recursive call to `displayNode()`, the depth of the node is increased by 1. Compute the number of indented spaces as INDENTBLOCK * depth, where INDENTBLOCK is the constant that specifies the number of blank spaces per node depth. Position the node value on a line by calling `indentBlanks()`.

(b) Write a program that builds Tree 2 and outputs the tree using `displayTree Sideways()`.

21. (a) Using `buildTree()` as a model, implement a method `buildIntTree()` that builds the following binary tree.

    (b) Develop a class `VisitSum` that implements the interface `Visitor<Integer>`. The `visitor()` method maintains a running sum of its `Integer` arguments. Use `VisitSum` in a program that builds the tree in part (a) and outputs the sum of its node values.

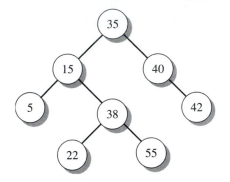

Programming Project

22. (a) Declare the class `ExtTNode` that, in addition to maintaining the node value and references to the left and right subtrees, adds a reference to the parent of the node. This additional reference allows movement up the tree as well as down the tree. For instance, Tree 0 would appear as follows after these modifications.

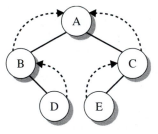

    (b) Implement the method

    ```
    public static String displayPathFrom(ExtTNode<?> t)
    { ... }
    ```

    that returns a string displaying the data for the chain of nodes leading from node `t` to the root.

    (c) Implement the method `extBuildTree()` that builds Tree 2 using `ExtTNode` objects.

    (d) Implement the method

    ```
    public static <T> ExtTNode<T> findNode(ExtTNode<T> t, T
        item)
    { ... }
    ```

    that searches tree `t` and returns a reference to the `ExtTNode` having value `item` or `null` if `item` is not in the tree.

    (e) Write a program that builds Tree 2 by calling `extBuildTree()` and outputs the path of nodes from G, H, and E to the root.

Chapter 17

BINARY TREE APPLICATIONS

CONTENTS

17.1 EXPRESSION TREES
Building a Binary Expression Tree
17.2 ITERATIVE TREE TRAVERSAL
Inorder Iterative Traversal
Implementing the InorderIterator
Class

17.3 EULER TOUR TRAVERSAL
17.4 DRAWING A BINARY TREE
Building a Shadow Tree
Displaying a Shadow Tree

Chapter 16 introduced binary trees. The focus was on designing and implementing tree-handling algorithms. In this chapter, we will use binary trees as a problem-solving tool in a variety of applications. We will wait until Chapter 18 to define a special type of binary tree called a *search tree*. This collection type introduces a whole new category of data structures.

Binary trees have important applications in language parsing. An example is the construction of a binary expression tree. This structure represents an arithmetic expression in the form of a binary tree. Recursive scans of an expression tree return the prefix, infix, and postfix (RPN) form of the expression.

In earlier chapters, we studied iterators for `LinkedList` and `ArrayList` collections. These objects provide sequential access to the elements. The concept of an iterator extends to binary trees. Because a binary tree is a nonlinear structure, the implementation of a tree iterator is more complex than the implementation of an iterator used by structures that implement the `List` interface. We will show how to construct an iterator for a binary tree that implements an iterative inorder scan of the tree nodes.

Section 17.3 develops the Euler tree traversal that generalizes the basic recursive tree scanning algorithms. The traversal defines a Euler tour which is used to solve some interesting problems. In this chapter, we use a Euler tour to fully parenthesize an expression represented by a binary expression tree.

In Chapter 16, we introduced console and graphical tree display methods. They produce an upright (vertical) view of a tree. The algorithm that implements the display methods uses a variety of scanning techniques as well as a modified version of the tree copy algorithm in Chapter 16. It draws on many basic tree handling concepts and is discussed as an application in Section 17.4.

17.1 Expression Trees

A compiler uses a binary tree to represent an arithmetic expression. The nodes of the tree, called an *expression tree*, are binary operators and operands. We will now develop an algorithm that shows you how to take an arithmetic expression in postfix notation and create the expression tree. You can refer back to Chapter 14 in which we introduced infix and postfix notation for an arithmetic expression. These formats specify the position of a binary operator and its operands. In postfix notation, the binary operator comes after its operands, and in infix notation, the operator appears between its operands. A third notation, called *prefix notation*, places a binary operator before its operands. The expressions in Table 17.1 include each of the formats.

An expression tree represents an arithmetic expression.

Table 17.1 Infix, postfix, and prefix notation.

Infix	Postfix	Prefix
a*b	ab*	*ab
a+b*c	abc*+	+a*bc
a+b*c/d−e	abc*d/+e−	−+a/*bcde

In an expression tree, each operator is an interior node whose children are operands or subexpressions. Operands are in leaf nodes.

Assume an arithmetic expression involves the binary operators addition (+), subtraction (−), multiplication (*), and division (/). In the expression tree, each operator has two children that are either operands or subexpressions. A binary expression tree consists of

- leaf nodes which contain a single operand
- nonleaf nodes which contain a binary operator
- the left and the right subtrees of an operator, describing a subexpression, which is evaluated and used as one of the operands for the operator

The trees in Figure 17.1 describe the expressions in Table 17.1.

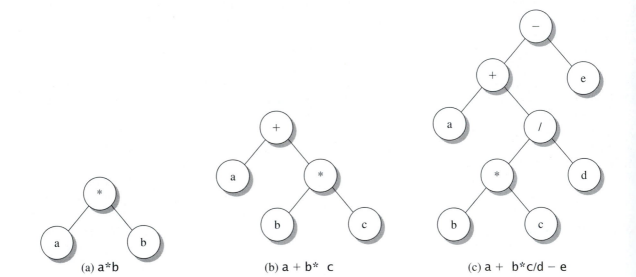

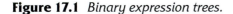

(a) a*b   (b) a + b* c   (c) a + b*c/d − e

Figure 17.1 *Binary expression trees.*

The preorder and postorder traversals of a binary expression tree produce the prefix and postfix notation for the expression. An inorder traversal generates the infix form of the expression, assuming that parentheses are not needed to determine the order of evaluation. For instance, in Figure 17.1c, the following are different traversals of the expression a + b*c/d−e

```
Preorder (Prefix):      − + a / * b c d e     // preorder scan
Inorder (Infix):        a + b * c / d − e     // inorder scan
Postorder (Postfix):    a b c * d / + e −     // postorder scan
```

Building a Binary Expression Tree

To build an expression tree, we need to develop an iterative algorithm that takes a string containing an expression in postfix form. An operand is a single character such as 'a' or 'b'. Our algorithm follows the steps of the postfix evaluation algorithm in Section 14.4. A stack holds the operands, which in this case are trees. More specifically, the stack holds TNode references that are the roots of subtree operands. In the postfix evaluation algorithm, whenever we located an operator, we popped its two operands from the stack and computed the result. In this algorithm, when we locate an operator, we construct a subtree and insert its root reference onto a stack. The following is a description of the action taken when we encounter an operand or an operator in the input string.

- If the token is an operand, we use its value to create a leaf node whose left and right subtrees are null. The leaf node is pushed onto a stack of TNode references.
- If the token is an operator, we create a new node with the operator as its value. Because the operator is binary, it must have two children in the tree. The children hold the operands for the operator. A child may be a single operand (leaf node) or a subexpression represented by a subtree with an operator as the root. The child nodes are on the stack from a previous step. Pop the two child nodes from the stack and attach them to the new node. The first child popped from the stack becomes the right subtree of the new node and the second child popped from the stack becomes the left subtree.

The method `buildExpTree()` implements the algorithm. The following steps illustrate the action of the method for the expression a + b*c in postfix form. We represent the stack horizontally to simplify the view of the elements. Remember, each element is a subtree specified by its root.

a b c * +

Step 1: Recognize 'a' as an operand. Construct a leaf node containing the Character value 'a' and push its reference onto the stack s.

top

Steps 2–3: Recognize 'b' and 'c' as operands, construct leaf nodes, and push their references onto the stack.

top

Step 4:   Recognize '*' as an operator. Create a new node with '*' as its value. Then pop two subtrees (node 'c' and node 'b') from the stack. These are the right and left subtrees of the new node respectively. Attach the subtrees and push the new subtree (root '*') on the stack.

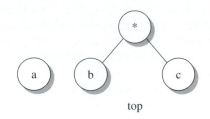

top

Step 5: Recognize '+' as an operator. Create a new node with '+' as its value. Pop its two operands from the stack, attach them to the node, and push the new subtree (root '+') on the stack.

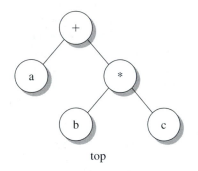

top

Step 6: We have reached the end of the expression. The single item on the stack is the root of the expression tree.

Build an expression tree from the postfix input by modifying the postfix expression evaluation algorithm from Chapter 14.

The method `buildExpTree()` applies this algorithm to construct the expression tree for a correctly formed postfix expression. The method performs no error checking. It assumes that an operand is a single character and that the available operators are $+$, $-$, $*$, and $/$. In addition, the expression can contain the whitespace characters blank or tab.

buildExpTree():

```
public static TNode<Character> buildExpTree(String postfixExp)
{
    // newNode is a reference to the root of subtrees we build,
    // and newLeft/newRight its are its children
    TNode<Character> newNode, newLeft, newRight;
    char token;
    // subtrees go into and off the stack
    ALStack<TNode<Character>> s =
        new ALStack<TNode<Character>>();
    int i = 0, n = postfixExp.length();
```

```
    // loop until i reaches the end of the string
    while(i != n)
    {
        // skip blanks and tabs in the expression
        while (postfixExp.charAt(i) == ' ' ||
                postfixExp.charAt(i) == '\t')
            i++;

        // if the expression has trailing whitespace, we could
        // be at the end of the string
        if (i == n)
            break;

        // extract the current token and increment i
        token = postfixExp.charAt(i);
        i++;

        // see if the token is an operator or an operand
        if (token == '+' || token == '-' ||
            token == '*' || token == '/')
        {
            // current token is an operator; pop two subtrees off
            // the stack
            newRight = s.pop();
            newLeft = s.pop();

            // create a new subtree with token as root and subtrees
            // newLeft and newRight and push it onto the stack
            newNode =
                new TNode<Character>(token,newLeft,newRight);
            s.push(newNode);
        }
        else // must be an operand
        {
            // create a leaf node and push it onto the stack
            newNode = new TNode<Character>(token);
            s.push(newNode);
        }
    }

    // if the expression was not empty, the root of
    // the expression tree is on the top of the stack
    if (!s.isEmpty())
        return s.pop();
    else
        return null;
}
```

PROGRAM 17.1 BUILDING EXPRESSION TREES

This program is a GUI application that illustrates `buildExpTree()`. The window contains a text field, called `expInput`, in the north region and a text area, called `expTree`, at the center. An action event on the text field registers an `ExpressionHandler` object as the listener. The inner class implements `actionPerformed()`. A user enters a correctly formed postfix expression in the text field and presses the Enter key. The event handler displays the expression in the text area and then calls `buildExpTree()` to construct the corresponding binary expression tree. The handler then uses `displayTree()` to view the tree in the text area. It concludes by displaying the preorder, inorder, and postorder scans of the tree.

The application clears the text field so that a user may conveniently enter a series of expressions and maintain a history of the output in a scrollable text area. Figure 17.2 is a snapshot of program execution after the user enters the expression

```
a b c * d-e / +                    // Infix form:  a + (b*c-d)/e
```

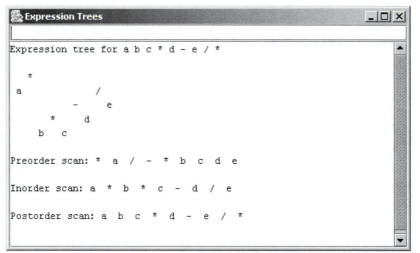

Figure 17.2 *Run of Program 17.1.*

Note that the postorder and preorder scans correspond to the postfix and prefix versions of the expression, but the infix scan does not reflect the parentheses in the original infix expression.

The following is the source code for `actionPerformed()` that handles the event caused when the user presses the Enter key.

```java
public void actionPerformed(ActionEvent ae)
{
    // obtain the expression the user typed
    String expression = expInput.getText();
    // build the expression tree
    TNode<Character> root = BinaryTree.buildExpTree(expression);

    // output the expression and its tree
    textArea.append("Expression tree for " +
                    expression + "\n\n");
    textArea.append(BinaryTree.displayTree(root, 1) + "\n");
    // output the scans
```

```
    textArea.append("Preorder scan: " +
        BinaryTree.preorderDisplay(root) + "\n\n");
    textArea.append("Inorder scan: " +
        BinaryTree.inorderDisplay(root) + "\n\n");
    textArea.append("Postorder scan: " +
        BinaryTree.postorderDisplay(root) + "\n\n");
    // clear the text field
    expInput.setText("");
}
```

17.2 Iterative Tree Traversal

We have observed the power of iterators to scan the elements in a `LinkedList` or `ArrayList` collection. Traversing the nodes in a binary tree is more difficult because a tree is a nonlinear structure and there is no one traversal order. Section 16.3 discusses recursive algorithms for performing a preorder, inorder, and postorder scan in a tree. The problem with each of these traversal algorithms is that there is no escape from the recursive process until it completes. We cannot easily stop the scan, examine the contents of a node, and then continue the scan at another node in the tree. We need an iterative process to implement a binary tree iterator. One choice would be a level-order scan using a queue. As we will discover with binary search trees, an iterative version of a recursive scan is a better choice.

A tree iterator scans the elements as if the tree were linear.

   In this section, we will implement an iterator using an iterative inorder scan. Creating iterators with a preorder and a postorder iterative scan are left for the exercises. You are familiar with iterators and the `Iterator` interface from our discussion of the `LinkedList` class. Our binary tree iterator implements this interface. To provide an iterative scan of the elements, we use a stack to hold the nodes that have been visited. In this way, we can simulate the runtime system, which uses a stack to hold the recursive calls that are made during an inorder recursive scan of the tree. Because it is our stack, we can halt at any time, access a node, and then continue by popping the stack to pick up the scan. Figure 17.3

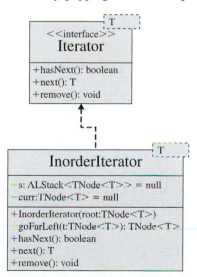

Figure 17.3 `InorderIterator`
implements the `Iterator` *interface.*

gives a UML diagram for the class `InorderIterator`. The diagram includes the instance variables and the private method `goFarLeft()`, which is critical to finding the "next" node.

Inorder Iterative Traversal

Inorder iterative tree traversal is implemented by using a stack to simulate the recursion.

The inorder iterative traversal emulates a recursive scan. Use of a stack is a key feature. Nodes enter the stack when we move down the tree from the current iterator (node) position to the node that references the "next" iterator position. In this way, the iterative algorithm can "remember" each intermediate node on the path so it can come back up the tree and visit the node at a later point. To do this, push on a stack the references to each of the nodes that are discovered on the path to the "next" element.

An iterative scan begins at the leftmost node in the tree. The starting point is found by starting at the root and following the chain of left children until we locate a node with an empty left subtree. An iterator initially references this node. The root and all intermediate nodes on the path of left children are pushed on the stack.

The iterative traversal of the tree is based on the following set of rules.

1. At each node, capture the value of the node.
2. If the right branch of the node is not empty, move to the right child and then traverse the path of left children until we locate a node with a `null` left subtree. The traversal identifies this node as the "next" node. Push on the stack a reference to the right child and each intermediate node on the path.
3. If the right branch of the node is empty, we have completed the scan of the node's left branch, the node itself, and its right branch. The next node to visit is on the stack. If the stack is not empty, pop it to determine the next node in the scan. If the stack is empty, all nodes have been visited and we terminate the scan.

Let us trace the iterative inorder traversal of nodes in the following character tree. The order of visits to the nodes is B F D A E C. We organize the trace around the order in which nodes are scanned. In this way, you can understand how the algorithm uses the stack and the traversal rules to proceed from a "current" scan position to the "next" scan position.

Scan 'B' and then 'F':

The iterator is initially positioned at node B. We arrive there by starting at the root and traversing the path of left children. The one node on this path, namely the root A, is placed on the stack (a). By rule 2, the next element is node F, which is the leftmost node in the right subtree of B. The path to F encounters node D which is pushed on the stack (b).

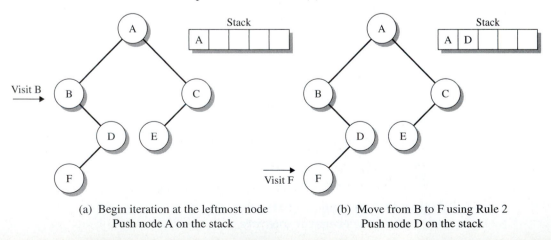

(a) Begin iteration at the leftmost node
    Push node A on the stack

(b) Move from B to F using Rule 2
    Push node D on the stack

Scan 'D' and then 'A':

Node F has no right child. By rule 3, the next node is D, which is popped from the stack (c). The same rule 3 applies to D. The next node is A (d).

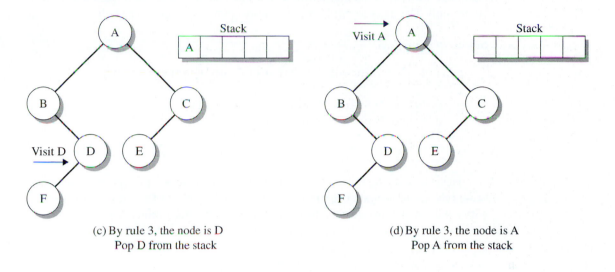

(c) By rule 3, the node is D
Pop D from the stack

(d) By rule 3, the node is A
Pop A from the stack

Scan 'E' then 'C':

From node A, use rule 2 to visit the next node E. Node C is on the path from A to E and thus is pushed on the stack (e). By rule 3, the next node C, which is popped from the stack (f).

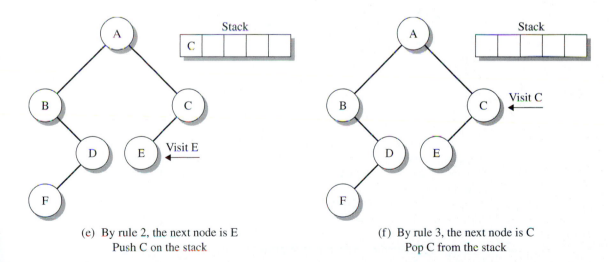

(e) By rule 2, the next node is E
Push C on the stack

(f) By rule 3, the next node is C
Pop C from the stack

At node C, rule 3 applies. The stack is empty, and the scan is complete.

Implementing the InorderIterator Class

The `InorderIterator` class provides instances that execute an iterative inorder scan of a binary tree. The class implements the `Iterator` interface. However, the `remove()` method is defined but does not carry out any operation. Its use throws the

UnsupportedOperationException. In reality, an InorderIterator object is designed to scan a binary tree and simply access the value of the elements. The private data members include a stack of TNode references and the variable curr, which is the next node we visit in the inorder traversal. The end of a traversal occurs when curr becomes null. The method hasNext() simply checks if curr is not null.

InorderIterator class:

```java
public class InorderIterator<T> implements Iterator<T>
{
    private ALStack<TNode<T>> s = null;
    private TNode<T> curr = null;
    . . .
}
```

The class uses the private method goFarLeft() to locate the first element and to execute rule 2. The method begins at node t and stacks all of the nodes until it locates one with a null left subtree. A reference to this node is the return value.

goFarLeft():

```java
// go far left from t, pushing all the nodes with
// left children on stack s
private TNode<T> goFarLeft(TNode<T> t)
{
    if (t == null)
        return null;
    while (t.left != null)
    {
        s.push(t);
        t = t.left;
    }
    return t;
}
```

The constructor allocates the stack and calls goFarLeft() to position curr at the first node inorder. Because InorderIterator is not included in a collection class, the user must create an instance using the operator new and pass the root of the binary tree as an argument.

Constructor:

```java
public InorderIterator(TNode<T> root)
{
    s = new ALStack<TNode<T>>();
    curr = goFarLeft(root);
}
```

The method `next()` implements Steps 1 through 3. In keeping with the requirements of the `Iterator` interface, `next()` throws `NoSuchElementException` if the tree traversal is complete.

next():

```java
public T next()
{
    if (curr == null)
        throw new NoSuchElementException(
            "InorderScan: no elements remaining");
    // capture the value in the node
    T returnValue = curr.nodeValue;

    if (curr.right != null) // have a right subtree
        // stack nodes on left subtree
        curr = goFarLeft(curr.right);
    else if (!s.isEmpty())
        // no right subtree; there are other nodes
        // to visit; pop the stack
        curr = (TNode<T>)s.pop();
    else
        curr = null;          // end of tree; set curr to null

    return returnValue;
}
```

PROGRAM 17.2 ITERATIVE TREE TRAVERSAL

For the purpose of demonstrating `InorderIterator`, we will use the static method `buildTime24Tree()` in the `BinaryTree` class. The method builds the following binary tree of `Time24` objects.

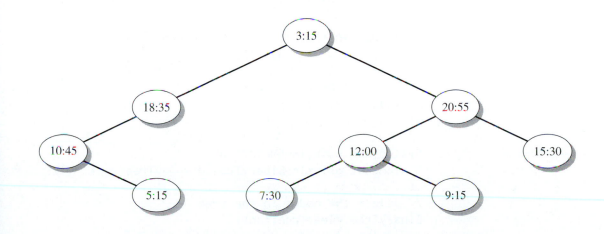

The program calls buildTime24Tree() to create the tree, and then uses an inorder tree iterator to traverse the nodes. After each call to next(), the program updates the time value of the node by adding 60 minutes (1 hour). A call to displayTree() outputs the updated tree.

```java
import ds.util.TNode;
import ds.util.BinaryTree;
import ds.util.InorderIterator;
import ds.time.Time24;

public class Program17_2
{
    public static void main(String[] args)
    {
        // roots for the tree
        TNode<Time24> root;

        // build a tree of Time24 data
        root = BinaryTree.buildTime24Tree();

        // display the tree
        System.out.println("Original tree");
        System.out.println(BinaryTree.displayTree(root, 5) +
            "\n");

        // declare an inorder tree iterator
        InorderIterator<Time24> iter =
            new InorderIterator<Time24>(root);

        // go through the tree and add 1 hour to each time
        while (iter.hasNext())
        {
            // obtain the value in a tree node
            Time24 t = iter.next();

            // add 1 hour to the time
            t.addTime(60);
        }

        System.out.println("Modified tree");
        System.out.println(BinaryTree.displayTree(root, 5));

        // delete the nodes in the tree
        BinaryTree.clearTree(root);
    }
}
```

```
Run:
  Original tree
                              3:15
                    18:35                           20:55
       10:45                           12:00              15:30
            5:15                   7:30        9:15
  Modified tree
                              4:15
                    19:35                           21:55
       11:45                           13:00              16:30
            6:15                   8:30        10:15
```

17.3 Euler Tour Traversal

Up to this point, all of our tree traversal algorithms visit each node exactly once. For instance, the inorder traversal visits the node between visiting the left subtree and the right subtree. We need a more general tree traversal algorithm for some applications, one that will visit each node more than once. The Euler tour traversal provides a solution. We assume that the edges and nodes of a tree T are contained in a walkway with walls on both sides. The Euler tour is a walk around T, touching each node as we encounter it, always keeping the wall on our right. The tour visits each node three times:

- on the left, before the Euler tour of the node's left subtree
- from below, as we finish the tour of the left subtree
- on the right, after we finish the Euler tour of the right subtree

If the node is a leaf, all of the visits are combined into a single visit. The walk in Figure 17.4 traverses an expression tree. The directed edges trace the Euler tour beginning with the root. We encounter nodes in the following order:

Tour visits: + * a * – d – e – * + / b / c / +

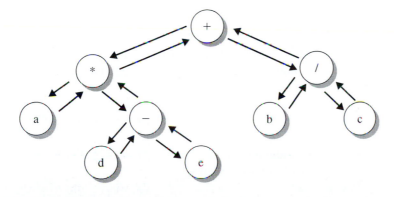

Figure 17.4 *Euler tour of an expression tree.*

The following pseudo-code description of the algorithm summarizes the Euler tour. A single visit to a leaf node and multiple visits to a nonleaf node are simply denoted by "visit" although, in practice, an implementation does not perform the same action.

Algorithm eulerTour(TNode t):

```
if t ≠ null
    if t is a leaf node
        visit t
    else
        visit t                     // on the left
        eulerTour(t.left);
        visit t;                     // from below
        eulerTour(t.right);
        visit t;                     // on the right
```

The Euler tour generalizes the recursive tree traversals by allowing three visits to a node.

The recursive algorithm allows us to pause three times to perform a visit. You should note that the Euler tour generalizes the inorder, postorder, and preorder tree traversals. For instance, if the visit on the left and the visit on the right do nothing, the Euler tour is equivalent to an inorder traversal.

An expression tree provides a good application of a Euler tour. The traversal includes visits that add parentheses and that access the value of a node. The result is a string that represents an equivalent fully parenthesized expression. The algorithm is straightforward. A visit to a leaf node (operand) inserts the operand in the string. For a nonleaf node (operator), insert a '(' as the visit on the left, insert the operator as the visit from below, and insert a ')' as the visit on the right. The static method `fullParen()` in the `BinaryTree` class implements the algorithm.

fullParen():

```
// traverse an expression tree and display the equivalent
// fully parenthesized expression
public static <T> String fullParen(TNode<Character> t)
{
    String s = "";

    if (t != null)
    {
        if (t.left == null && t.right == null)
            s += t.nodeValue;               // visit a leaf node
        else
        {
            s += "(";                       // visit on left
            s += fullParen(t.left);
            s += t.nodeValue;               // visit from below
            s += fullParen(t.right);
            s += ")";                       // visit on right
        }
    }
    return s;
}
```

PROGRAM 17.3 EULER TOUR TRAVERSAL

The program prompts for an RPN expression and constructs an expression tree by calling the method `buildExpTree()` from the `BinaryTree` class. After displaying the tree using `displayTree()`, the program calls `fullParen()` and outputs the equivalent fully parenthesized expression. The run constructs the expression tree in Figure 17.4.

```java
import java.util.Scanner;

import ds.util.TNode;
import ds.util.BinaryTree;

public class Program17_3
{
    public static void main(String[] args)
    {
        // prompt for the RPN expression
        Scanner keyIn = new Scanner(System.in);
        String postfixExp;
        // root of the expression tree
        TNode<Character> root;

        System.out.print("Enter a postfix expression: ");
        postfixExp = keyIn.nextLine();

        // build the expression tree
        root = BinaryTree.buildExpTree(postfixExp);

        // display the tree
        System.out.println("Expression tree");
        System.out.println(BinaryTree.displayTree(root,1));

        // output the full parenthesized expression
        System.out.print("Fully parenthesized expression: ");
        System.out.println(BinaryTree.fullParen(root));
    }
}
```

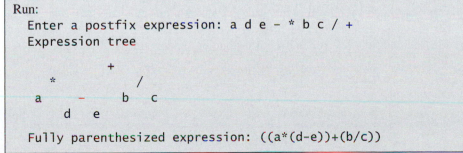

```
Run:
  Enter a postfix expression: a d e - * b c / +
  Expression tree

            +
     *             /
  a       -     b   c
       d     e

  Fully parenthesized expression: ((a*(d-e))+(b/c))
```

17.4 Drawing a Binary Tree

In Chapter 16, we introduced the methods displayTree(), drawTree(), and drawTrees(). These methods implement algorithms that employ many of the basic features of a binary tree. Let us look at the design of the console-based displayTree() method. The graphical methods use the same design. Their implementation differs only when inserting a node. The graphical methods draw a circle, text for the value, and edges to the nonnull children.

The binary tree-drawing algorithm first constructs a shadow tree using an inorder scan.

View the display of the tree as a rectangular grid with a cell denoted by the pair (level, column). The level is a row in the grid corresponding to a level in the tree. The column coordinate designates a region of the display measured left to right. Figure 17.5 is the representation of Tree 0 in the grid. The algorithm to display a tree uses a recursive scan to create a copy of the original tree. The copy is called a *shadow tree*. The nodes of the shadow tree store the value of the node in the original tree formatted as a string and the (level, col) position of the shadow tree node in the grid. A level-order scan of the shadow tree displays the nodes.

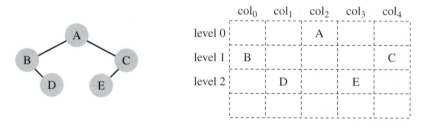

Figure 17.5 *Square grid containing nodes denoted by the pair (level, col).*

Building a Shadow Tree

Each node in the shadow tree defines its column in the grid.

The recursive function buildShadowTree() uses an inorder scan (LNR) of the original tree to build a shadow tree. As the inorder scan progresses, we move from one grid column to another. For instance, with Tree 0, the order of visits is B D A E C. Note in Figure 17.5 that this is the column-order for the nodes in the tree.

A shadow tree maintains the node value as a string and the level (row) and column of the node.

A shadow tree uses an augmented node structure for its elements. The TNodeShadow objects have the basic TNode structure, with additional variables *level* and *column* that specify the coordinates for a cell in the grid. The variable nodeValueStr is a string that describes the value for a node in the original tree. For instance, if a tree node has integer value 135, then nodeValueStr in the corresponding shadow tree is "*135*".

left	nodeValueStr	level	column	right

TNodeShadow object

TNodeShadow class:

```
class TNodeShadow
{
    public static int columnValue;
    public String nodeValueStr;        // formatted node value
    public int level, column;
    public TNodeShadow left, right;

    public TNodeShadow ()
    {}
}
```

The algorithm for buildShadowTree() resembles copyTree() with the exception that it makes an inorder scan of the original tree rather than a postorder scan. Each recursive call allocates a TNodeShadow object and assigns it the string that corresponds to the value of the node in the original tree. It then makes recursive calls that create the left and right subtrees. You will notice that the TNodeShadow class has a static variable columnValue. This variable is key to the algorithm. Because the variable is static, it is global to the recursive process. Each recursive call in the inorder scan creates a node in the column specified by columnValue and then increments the variable for the subsequent recursive call. In this way, columnValue is incremented on each visit to a node. If the tree has *n* nodes, columnValue has values ranging from 0 for the first visit (leftmost node) to *n* − 1 for a visit to the rightmost node. The buildShadowTree() method has two parameters. The TNode reference t provides access to the value of the original tree node. An integer denotes the level in the tree.

buildShadowTree():

```
// build a shadow tree that is used for tree display
private static <T> TNodeShadow buildShadowTree(TNode<T> t,
                                               int level)
{
    // new shadow tree node
    TNodeShadow newNode = null;
    String str;

    if (t != null)
    {
        // create the new shadow tree node
        newNode = new TNodeShadow();

        // allocate node for left child at next level in tree;
        // then attach the node
        TNodeShadow newLeft = buildShadowTree(t.left, level+1);
        newNode.left = newLeft;

        // initialize instance variables in the new node
        str = (t.nodeValue).toString(); // format conversion
        newNode.nodeValueStr = str;
        newNode.level = level;
        newNode.column = TNodeShadow.columnValue;
```

```
                        // update column to next cell in the table
                        TNodeShadow.columnValue++;

                        // allocate node for right child at next level in tree;
                        // then attach the node
                        TNodeShadow newRight = buildShadowTreeD(t.right, level+1);
                        newNode.right = newRight;
                }

                return newNode;
        }
```

Displaying a Shadow Tree

The method displayTree() takes the root, t, of the binary tree as an argument and calls buildShadowTree() to create a shadow tree.

```
        // build the shadow tree
        TNodeShadow shadowRoot = buildShadowTree(t, 0);
```

The algorithm displays the tree using a level-order scan of shadow tree nodes. Each shadow tree node provides the node value as a string and the (level, column) coordinate for an element. The scan uses a queue of TNodeShadow objects to store and access the nodes. As shadow tree nodes emerge from the queue the displayTree() method positions the value at (level, col) in the grid. To determine the location of each node in the grid, we use the argument maxCharacters, which is the number of characters in the longest node value. The variable colWidth, with value maxCharacters + 1, defines the width of each cell in the display (Figure 17.6). The variable currLevel is the current level during the scan and the variable currCol is the current column coordinate in the grid. The string representation of the tree is stored in the variable displayStr.

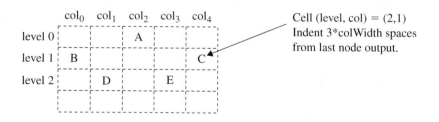

Cell (level, col) = (2,1)
Indent 3*colWidth spaces
from last node output.

Figure 17.6 *Displaying a node value on the current line.*

```
        // use for the level-order scan of the shadow tree
        LinkedQueue<TnodeShadow> q =
                new LinkedQueue<TnodeShadow>();
        String displayStr = "";
        int colWidth = maxCharacters + 1;
        int currLevel = 0, currCol = 0;

        // use during the level-order scan of the shadow tree
        TNodeShadow currNode;
```

As nodes are popped from the queue into the reference variable currNode, display Tree() carries out the task of displaying the node value (currNode.nodeValueStr) at the grid coordinates (currNode.level, currNode.column). The column position combines with the value of colWidth to specify how far we must move to the right before inserting the node. Because the level-order scan visits siblings from left to right, the distance of the move is determined by comparing the column positions for successive siblings. The variable currLevel maintains a record of the current level (line) on which nodes are displayed. The value of currLevel is incremented whenever a node is popped from the queue with a level greater than colLevel. The implementation simply inserts a newline character to move down one level. The string continues to add node values on the same level until another change is required. The private methods formatString() and formatChar() output a string and a character right-justified in a specified number of print positions. They are used to position the tree nodes in their proper columns. The documentation comments in the code listing allow you to understand the remaining details of the method implementation.

Display the tree with a level-order scan of the shadow tree. The scan uses the node data to position and display each node.

displayTree():

```
// return a string that displays a binary tree; output of
// a node value requires no more than maxCharacters
public static <T> String displayTree(TNode<T> t, int
maxCharacters)
{
    // use for the level-order scan of the shadow tree
    LinkedQueue<TNodeShadow> q =
        new LinkedQueue<TNodeShadow>();
    String displayStr = "";
    int colWidth = maxCharacters + 1;
    int currLevel = 0, currCol = 0;

    TNodeShadow.columnValue = 0;
    if (t == null)
        return displayStr;

    // build the shadow tree
    TNodeShadow shadowRoot = buildShadowTree(t, 0);

    // use during the level order scan of the shadow tree
    TNodeShadow currNode;

    // insert the root in the queue and set current level to 0
    q.push(shadowRoot);

    // continue the iterative process until the queue is empty
    while(!q.isEmpty())
    {
        // delete front node from queue and make it the current
        // node
        currNode = q.pop();
```

```
                        // if level changes, output a newline
                        if (currNode.level > currLevel)
                        {
                           currLevel = currNode.level;
                           currCol = 0;
                           displayStr += '\n';
                        }

                        // if a left child exists, insert the child in the queue
                        if(currNode.left != null)
                           q.push(currNode.left);

                        // if a right child exists, insert the child in the queue
                        if(currNode.right != null)
                           q.push(currNode.right);

                        // output formatted node value
                        if (currNode.column > currCol)
                        {
                           displayStr +=
                              formatChar((currNode.column-currCol) * colWidth,
                                 ' ');
                           currCol = currNode.column;
                        }

                        displayStr += formatString(colWidth,
                           currNode.nodeValueStr);
                        currCol++;
                     }
                     displayStr += '\n';

                     // delete the shadow tree
                     shadowRoot = clearShadowTree(shadowRoot);

                     return displayStr;
                  }
```

Chapter Summary

- In a binary expression tree, each operand is located in a leaf node, and each operator is in an interior node. The two children of an operator are either an operand or a subexpression. The method buildExpTree() takes a string argument specifying a postfix expression and builds the corresponding expression tree. The algorithm is very similar to the one that evaluates a postfix expression in Section 14.4; however, in buildExpTree(), the stack maintains subtrees of the final expression tree rather than arithmetic values.

- A recursive tree scan algorithm such as LNR (inorder) does not allow escape from the recursion. The programmer cannot "leave" the method, perform some action, and return later to continue the traversal. Hence, an iterative tree traversal is often useful. We saw an example of iterative traversal when we studied the LinkedList iterator in Chapter 12. The InorderIterator class implements the Iterator interface and uses a stack to implement an iterative traversal of a binary tree. Essentially, the stack simulates the recursion.

- The Euler tour traversal generalizes the recursive tree scanning algorithms and allows the visit of a node three times during a tree traversal. A Euler tour can traverse an expression tree and display the equivalent fully parenthesized expression.

- The displayTree() method of the BinaryTree class first constructs a shadow tree by performing an inorder traversal of the original binary tree. The shadow tree nodes contain the data of the original tree node formatted as a string along with data that specify the position of the node in tree display. A subsequent level-order scan outputs the tree display.

Written Exercises

1. Write the infix expression

$$\frac{a + 2*b}{(c + d)} + 8*e$$

in postfix and prefix form and draw an expression tree for it.

2. Explain why an inorder scan of an expression tree may not be the infix form of the expression. Give an example to illustrate your argument.

3. Why is developing an iterator for a binary tree a more difficult problem than developing an iterator for a linked list?

4. Explain why the Euler tour is more general than any of the preorder, inorder, and postorder scanning algorithms.

5. Explain the role of the shadow tree in the algorithm used by displayTree().

Programming Exercises

6. Implement a method treeSize() that uses an inorder iterator to traverse a binary tree and returns the number of nodes in the tree. In your program, create Tree 0, Tree 1, and Tree 2 using the method buildTree() in the class BinaryTree. Using treeSize(), output the number of nodes in each tree.

```
public static <T> int treeSize(TNode<T> t)
{ ... }
```

7. (a) Implement the method find() that iteratively traverses a binary tree, searches for a specified node value, and returns a reference to a node containing the value or null if the value is not in the tree.

```
public static <T> TNode<T> find(TNode<T> t, T item)
{ ... }
```

(b) In a program, create and display Tree 2 using buildTree() and display Tree() in the class BinaryTree. Prompt the user to input a value in the range 'A' to 'I'. Call find() to locate the node, N, in Tree 2 that matches the input value. Output the left and right children of N.

8. (a) Implement a method `buildCTree()` that takes an `ArrayList` parameter and builds a complete tree from its elements. A level-order scan of the tree returns the original `ArrayList` elements. Implement your algorithm by using a queue to hold `TNode` references in a fashion similar to the level-order scanning algorithm from Chapter 16.

    ```
    public static <T> TNode<T> buildCTree(ArrayList<T> alist)
    { ... }
    ```

    For instance, if alist = {1, 2, 3, 4, 5}, `buildCTree()` should construct the complete tree.

    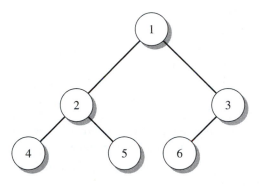

(b) Implement method `buildCIntTree()` that constructs a complete tree containing the values {1, 2, 3, ..., n}.

    ```
    public static TNode<Integer> buildCIntTree(int n)
    { ... }
    ```

(c) Implement method `buildCCharTree()` that constructs a complete tree containing the characters from a specified string.

    ```
    public static TNode<Character> buildCCharTree(String
      str)
    { ... }
    ```

(d) In the program, build complete trees containing the integer values from 1 to 10 and the characters in the string "generics". Using the method `drawTrees()` in the class `BinaryTree`, graphically display the integer tree. Then, using `drawTree()` in the same class, draw the character tree.

9. (a) As we will see in Chapter 18, it is often useful for a tree node to contain a reference to its parent. Using the parent reference, it is possible to begin at a specified node and follow the parent references all the way to the root node. Implement the class `TNodeP` that adds the parent reference.

    ```
    public class TNodeP<T>
    {
        // node's value
        public T nodeValue;
    ```

```
      // subtree references
      public TNodeP<T> left, parent, right;

      // create instance with a value, null subtrees, and
      // null parent
      public TNodeP(T item)
      { ... }

      // initialize the value, the subtrees, and the parent
      public TNodeP (T item, TNodeP<T> parent,
            TNodeP<T> left, TNodeP<T> right)
      { ... }
   }
```

(b) Chapter 16 developed an algorithm that uses a postorder scan of a binary tree in order to produce a copy of the tree. Implement a method `copyTreeP()` that takes the root of a binary tree and creates a copy whose nodes include parent references (TNodeP objects).

```
      // create a TNodeP duplicate of the tree with root t and
      // return a reference to its root
      public static <T> TNodeP<T> copyTreeP(TNode<T> t)
      { ... }
```

(c) In a program, build Tree 1 using the method `buildTree()`. Apply `copyTreeP()` to make a copy that includes parent references. Starting at the root of the new tree, follow the path of right subtrees until encountering node N with a `null` right subtree. Beginning with node N, output the path of nodes from N up to the root.

10. Modify the `buildExpTree()` method so it constructs the binary expression tree from a string containing an expression in prefix format. Modify Program 17.1 so it uses your method.

11. Implement a method `evalExpTree()` that traverses an expression tree whose operands are single-digit integers and evaluates the expression. In your program, input a postfix expression from the keyboard, call `evalExpTree()`, and output the value of the expression.

12. Do Programming Exercise 17.11, but test `evalExpTree()` in a GUI program. The program should output the expression tree and the value of the expression in a text area.

13. (a) Develop a class, `PreorderIterator`, that implements the `Iterator` interface and performs an iterative preorder traversal of a binary tree. The iterator should visit each node, followed by a visit of the left subtree and then the right subtree. Like the class `InorderIterator` of Section 17.2, use a stack to hold node references. Suppose we are at node A of a binary tree and execute the visit. We must next visit the left subtree of A and come back at a later point to visit the right subtree of A. If the right subtree is not empty, use a stack to store the reference to the right subtree. After visiting all of the nodes on the left subtree of A, pop the stack and return to scan the right subtree. We show these two situations in the following figure.

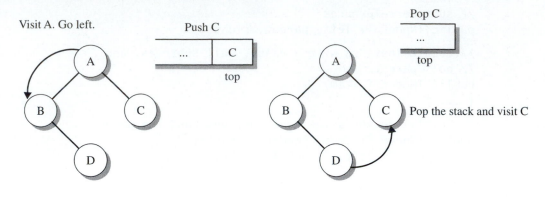

The iterative scan algorithm uses the following steps. Start with the root node. If the root node is `null`, the tree is empty and the iteration is complete.

For each node in the tree,

    (1) capture the value stored in the node.
    (2) if the right subtree is nonnull, save the right child reference in a stack.
    (3) if the left child is nonnull,
          set the current node to be the left child
       else if the stack is not empty,
          pop the stack and assign the return value as the current node
       else
          traversal is complete.

(b) Write a program that creates Tree 0, Tree 1, and Tree 2. Using `PreorderIterator`, output the preorder traversal for each tree.

14. This exercise considers the problem of computing the number of descendants of each node in a binary tree. For instance, in the figure we annotate each node of Tree 1 with its number of descendants.

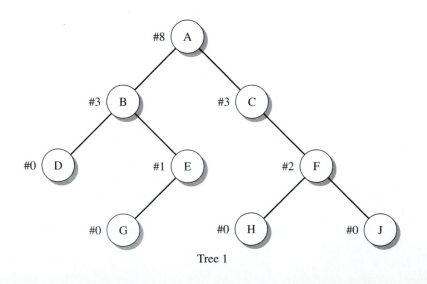

Tree 1

To determine the number of descendants of each node in a binary tree, initialize an integer variable `count` to 0 and execute a Euler tour of a binary tree. When first encountering a node on the left, increment `count` (add the node to the total node count). When returning to the node on the right, the number of descendants is the difference between the current value of the variable and the value when the node was first counted. Implement the strategy in an application that outputs the number of descendants for each node in Tree 1.

Programming Project

15. (a) Develop a class, `PostorderIterator`, that implements the `Iterator` interface and performs an iterative postorder traversal of a binary tree. The problem is more difficult than an inorder or preorder traversal because we must distinguish between moving down the left branch of a node (state 0) or moving up the tree to a node (state 1). When moving up the tree, there are two possible actions: visit the right branch of a node or visit the node. Maintain the integer variable state. If state == 0, motion is down the tree. If state == 1, motion is up. When coming up the tree, the parent of the current node is on top of the stack. To determine if we are coming from the left, compare the node reference to the parent's left child. If they agree and the parent has a right subtree, go down the subtree; otherwise, visit the node and continue up the tree.

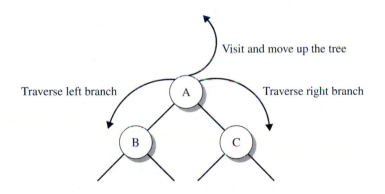

(b) Write a program that creates Tree 0, Tree 1, and Tree 2. Using `PostorderIterator`, output the postorder traversal for each tree.

Chapter 18

BINARY SEARCH TREES

CONTENTS

18.1 BINARY SEARCH TREES
Building a Binary Search Tree
Locating an Object in a Binary
Search Tree
Removing a Binary Search Tree
Node

18.2 STREE—A BINARY SEARCH TREE
CLASS
Application: Updating a Search
Tree

18.3 IMPLEMENTING THE STREE CLASS
The STree Class Private Members
and Constructor
Inserting and Locating a Node
Deleting a Node
Additional Operations
Complexity of Binary Search Tree
Operations

18.4 THE STREE ITERATOR
The STree Iterator Public Methods

ArrayLists and LinkedLists are list collections that store elements by position. They are useful for applications that need to store data in a sequence. Many computer applications store data by value rather than by position. They associate with each element a key that uniquely identifies the element. For instance, a registrar's database stores grade records using the student Social Security number as a key. An instant credit check uses the customer's credit card number as a key to look up account information. For these applications, a list is not an efficient data structure because access to an element requires an O(n) scan of the sequence to locate the value. We need to design a new structure that allows for rapid storage and access of the data by value.

A special form of a binary tree will provide just such a structure. Each element in the tree is associated with a unique path from the root and, in most cases, access and update operations have O($\log_2 n$) running time. The trees are designed as search engines, and hence they are called *binary search trees*. This chapter will give you hands-on experience using binary search trees. We organize the tree operations in an STree class that implements the Collection interface. The design of the class will be a model for our implementation of the ordered set and map classes that we introduce in Chapter 19. A binary search tree is as an implementation structure for TreeSet and TreeMap classes, which are the data structures we include in our framework. In this way, a binary search tree is much like a doubly linked list which provides the underlying storage structure for the LinkedList class.

18.1 Binary Search Trees

A binary search tree is a binary tree in which each element resides on a unique path from the root. The tree can store objects that have a natural order. This means that two objects satisfy a comparison relation < (less than), == (equal to), or > (greater than). The ordering of objects creates an ordering among nodes in the tree.

530

Search Tree Ordering:

For each node in the tree, the values in its left subtree are less than the value of the node and the values in its right subtree are greater than the value of the node.

Figure 18.1 illustrates binary search trees with a variety of object types. Note that the order relation on the subtrees dictates that a binary search tree cannot have duplicate values. The example with Time24 objects is a degenerate tree.

Binary search trees can store large sets of data while providing very efficient access and update operations.

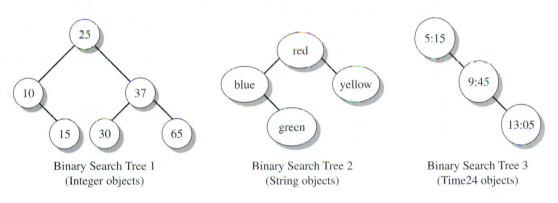

Binary Search Tree 1	Binary Search Tree 2	Binary Search Tree 3
(Integer objects)	(String objects)	(Time24 objects)

Figure 18.1 *Sample binary search trees.*

A binary search tree has algorithms that maintain the ordering when inserting or deleting an element. Assuming the tree already exists, the insert algorithm becomes the basis for locating an element. Let us explore these algorithms using a set of examples.

Binary search trees are an ideal data structure for the implementation of sets and maps.

Building a Binary Search Tree

Elements are inserted into a binary search tree using a strategy that maintains the ordering among the subtrees. The first element becomes the root node. All subsequent elements are added as leaf nodes at the end of a unique path. Identifying the path is an iterative process that begins at the root. Each step involves comparing the value of the new element, called item, with the value in the current node on the path. The following is the insertion strategy.

The nodes in a binary search tree are on unique paths from the root according to an ordering principle.

The left subtree of a node contains smaller values and the right subtree contains larger values.

- If the value of the new element is equal to the value of the current node perform no action, because the insertion strategy does not allow duplicate values.
- If the value of the new element is less than the value of the current node proceed to the left subtree (left child) of the node. If the left subtree is not empty, repeat the insertion strategy by comparing item with the root of the subtree. Otherwise, the left subtree is empty (left child == null), and we have reached the location for the new element at the end of the "insertion" path. Allocate a new node with item as its value, and attach the node to the tree as the left child. This extends the path to the new element.
- If the value of the new element is greater than the value of the current node proceed to the right subtree (right child) of the node. If the right subtree is not empty, repeat the insertion strategy by comparing item with the root of the subtree. Otherwise, the right subtree is empty (right child == null). Allocate a new node with item as its value and attach the node to the tree as the right child.

Example 18.1

The example builds a binary search tree by adding integer values from the sequence {35, 18, 25, 48, 25, 20}. Figure 18.2 illustrates the growth of the tree.

Insert 35: The first element becomes the root of the tree.

Insert 18: Compare 18 with the root 35. Because 18 < 35, go left to an empty tree. This is the insertion location. Insert 18 as the left child of 35.

Insert 25: Compare 25 and 35. With 25 < 35, go left, to node 18. Compare 25 with 18. With 18 < 25, go right to an empty tree. Insert 25 as the right child of 18.

Insert 48: Compare 48 with 35. With 35 < 48, go right to an empty tree. Insert 48 as the right child of 35.

Insert 25: The insertion path includes the nodes 35, 18, and 25. Because the path ends in a match, no insertion occurs. A binary search tree does not have duplicate values.

Insert 20: The insertion path includes the nodes 35, 18, and 25. With the comparison 20 < 25, go left to an empty tree and insert 20 as a left child of 25.

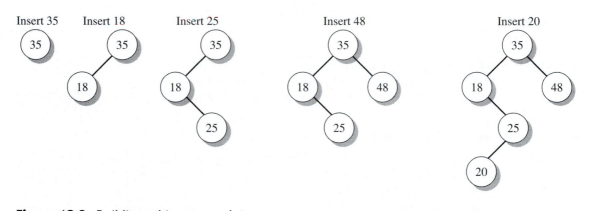

Figure 18.2 *Building a binary search tree.*

Locating an Object in a Binary Search Tree

Search for an element the same way you inserted it.

Each node enters the tree along a specific path. A search for an object uses an iterative process that scans the same path. Compare the value of the root node with the item. If a match occurs, we identify the location of the object in the tree. If the object is less than the node value, the search continues with the left child; otherwise, the search continues with the right child. If the search ends at an empty tree, the object is not in the tree. Let us search for the elements 32, 60, and 12 in the binary search tree in Figure 18.3.

Find 32: Compare 32 and the root value 50. Because 32 < 50, go left to node 30. Compare 32 and 30. Because 30 < 32, go right to node 35. Compare 32 and 35. Because 32 < 35, go left to node 32. A final comparison 32 == 32 identifies a match.

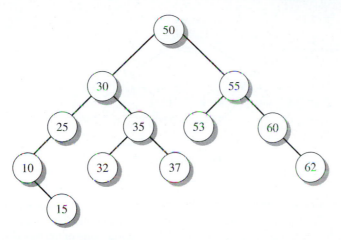

Figure 18.3 *Binary search tree.*

Find 60: Search down the path 50, 55, and 60. After three comparisons, a match is found.

Find 12: Search down the path 50, 30, 25, 10, and 15. Compare 12 and 15 and go left to an empty subtree. The search ends at an empty tree and no match occurs. The search requires six comparisons, including the last one that identifies that the left subtree of 15 is empty.

Inorder Scan of a Binary Search Tree   Because a search tree is a binary tree, we can apply any of the different scan algorithms to visit the nodes. The inorder scan is particularly significant. The order of visit to a node and its children is LNR, where the values are ordered left child < node < right child. The scan initially moves down a path of left children, stopping at the minimum value. In Figure 18.3, the initial path is 50, 30, 25, and 10, which is the minimum value. Next, all elements in the right subtree are visited. These are precisely all of the elements whose value is greater than the value of the node but less than the value of its parent. In the figure, the right subtree contains 15, which lies between 10 and 25. In general, the inorder scan reveals the binary search tree ordering. At the point when a node is visited, the scan has completed visits to all of the nodes in the left subtree (smaller values) and awaits visits to nodes in the right subtree (greater values). The scan visits the elements in ascending order.

The LNR inorder scan visits the nodes in ascending order.

With an RNL (inorder_right) scan, the first node visited is along the path of right children and has the maximum value. The scan visits the nodes in descending order.

Removing a Binary Search Tree Node

In a linked list, removing an element involves unlinking the node and connecting its predecessor to the next node. The process is a little different with a binary search tree. Without detailing the algorithm, let us look at an example that illustrates some of the issues that will concern us as we develop binary search tress as storage collections. In the following search tree, we delete the element 25 in the root node. Note immediately that the root node cannot be removed from the tree because we would be left with two orphaned subtrees.

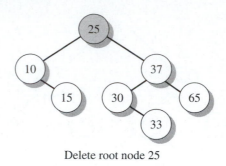

Delete root node 25

To delete a node from a binary search tree, you must find a replacement node, copy its value, and then splice it out of the tree.

We need to find a replacement value for 25. At first glance, we might want to use a child of the node, 10 or 37, as the replacement value. Unfortunately either choice destroys the search ordering of the tree because a subtree would be on the wrong side of the root (Figure 18.4a, b). We need a strategy that locates a replacement value that is "nearest to 25." Because the example is relatively small, we can identify that 15 in the left subtree or 30 in the right subtree would be a good choice. Let us look at 30 in the right subtree. We locate 30 by moving to the right child of 25 namely 37, and then scanning down the path of left children. Assign 30 as the new root value and splice out (delete) node 30 from the tree by connecting its right subtree (33) as the left child of the parent 37 (Figure 18.4c). As the example indicates, developing a general algorithm to delete a node in a search tree is challenging since it must maintain the ordering of the tree.

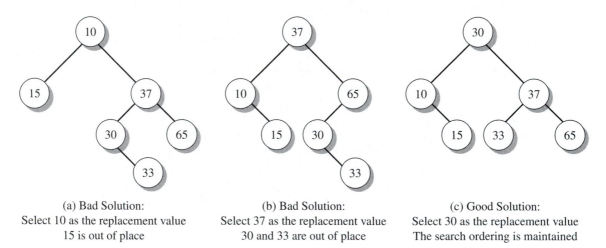

(a) Bad Solution:	(b) Bad Solution:	(c) Good Solution:
Select 10 as the replacement value	Select 37 as the replacement value	Select 30 as the replacement value
15 is out of place	30 and 33 are out of place	The search ordering is maintained

Figure 18.4 *Removing the root from a binary search tree.*

18.2 STree—A Binary Search Tree Class

The STree class implements the Collection interface.

We organize the attributes and operations of a binary search tree in a class, called *STree*, that implements the Collection interface. Using this interface will simplify our use of the class as the implementation structure for the TreeSet and TreeMap data structures. Let us begin by exploring the design of STree class and then using it with several examples.

You are very familiar with the methods in the `Collection` interface. The `STree` class places additional stipulations, beyond those inherited from this interface.

- The `add()` method inserts a new element if a duplicate value is not already present. The `boolean` return value indicates whether the item was added to the tree.
- The class makes use of the fact that an inorder scan visits elements in ascending order. The method `toArray()` returns an `Object` array that mirrors the inorder scan and so the elements are referenced in ascending order. An `Iterator` object scans the elements in ascending order.

The `STree` class has a constructor that creates an empty tree. The method `toString()` returns a string that describes the elements in a comma-separated list enclosed in square brackets. The elements are listed in ascending order. The methods first() and last() return the smallest and largest elements in the tree, respectively. For demonstration purposes, we provide the methods `displayTree()`, `drawTree()`, and `drawTrees()` give a "tree-view" of the elements. The methods take an integer argument that specifies the maximum string length of an element. With `drawTrees()`, you can see tree updates in successive frames. These are just the display methods we introduced in Chapter 16 for a general binary tree.

The method `find()` takes item as an argument and searches the tree looking for an element whose value matches item. The return value is a reference to the value field of the node or `null` if no match occurs. The `find()` method allows an applications programmer to update an element in the tree without having to remove it and reinsert it back in the tree. See Example 18.2 (2).

A UML diagram lists the `STree` methods by including the `Collection` interface and the methods that are specific to the class.

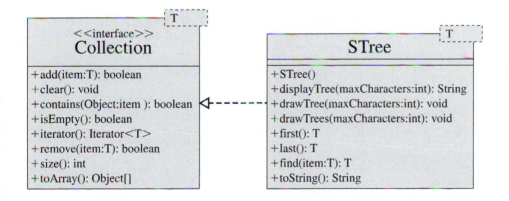

Example 18.2

---

1. The example illustrates the `STree` class constructor and the methods `add()`, `first()`, `last()`, `size()`, and `toString()`. An integer array provides a sequence of data values. The array has duplicate values which we identify by assigning the return value from `add()` to the boolean variable `isNewElement`. Calls to the methods `size()`, `first()`, `last()`, and `toString()` enables us to output the size of the tree, the tree's smallest and largest elements, and the list of elements in ascending

order. We view the tree in a console window and in a drawing window using display-
Tree() and drawTree() respectively.

```
int[] arr = {59, 41, 70, 45, 8, 41, 8, 26, 60};
boolean isNewElement;

// create an STree object
STree<Integer> t = new STree<Integer>();

// add the Integer objects; output
// each value that is a duplicate
for (int i = 0; i < arr.length; i++)
{
    isNewElement = t.add(arr[i]);
    if (!isNewElement)
        System.out.println(arr[i] + " is a duplicate");
}
```

Output:
```
41 is a duplicate
8 is a duplicate
```

```
// output the size and the elements in ascending order
// using toString()
System.out.println("The size is " + t.size());

// output the largest and smallest values in the tree
System.out.println("Minimum/maximum values: " + t.first() +
                   "  " + t.last());

System.out.println("\n" + t); // call toString()

// give a console and a graphical view of the final tree
System.out.println("\n" + t.displayTree(2));
t.drawTree(2);
```

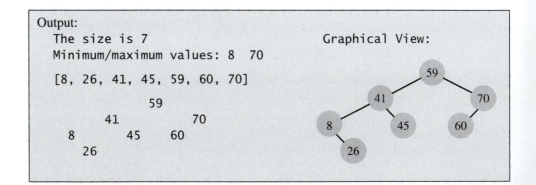

Output:

```
The size is 7                                  Graphical View:
Minimum/maximum values: 8   70

[8, 26, 41, 45, 59, 60, 70]

                59
        41              70
    8        45     60
        26
```

2. In Chapter 2, we introduce the employee hierarchy. The Employee superclass implements Comparable using the Social Security Number field empSSN and as a result, instances of the class can be elements in an STree collection. The example illustrates the use of find() in the search tree, empTree. A search for employee "712-87-3498" returns a reference to the value in the tree or null. In the first case, we call setName() to change the employee name to "Harris, Julie."

```
STree<Employee> empTree;

// create a target employee with social security
// number and no name
Employee targetEmp = new Employee("712-87-3498", "");

// use find() with targetEmp to search for the employee
// in the tree; if present, change the name
Employee emp = empTree.find(targetEmp);
if (emp != null)
    emp.setName("Harris, Julie");
```

Note that find() should be used only if the search tree has elements with key-value components. Updates are restricted to the value component. Changing the key could violate the search ordering of the tree; in effect destroy the tree.

3. For the Integer tree t in Part 1, an STree iterator scans the nodes of the tree and removes each element that has an even integer value. The remaining elements are listed using toString().

```
Iterator<Integer> iter = t.iterator();
int n;

while (iter.hasNext())
{
    n = iter.next().intValue();
    if (n % 2 == 0)
        iter.remove();
}
System.out.println(t);
```

Output:
  [41, 45, 59]

Application: Updating a Search Tree

We provide a GUI application that allows a user to dynamically update a search tree by inserting and deleting elements. The display lets you see how the tree changes. The bottom, or south end, of the window contains a panel with a label, a text field, and two buttons. The user enters a nonnegative two-digit integer in the text field and clicks either the "Add" button or the "Remove" button. The center of the window contains a text area that displays the tree before and after the specified operation is executed. The application does error checking for input. If the user enters an integer n outside the range from 0 to 99, a dialog box pops up and displays an error message.

The application registers the two buttons as action listeners. The constructor loads Integer objects from the array intArr into the STree<Integer> tree.

```
// initial values in the tree
private int[] arr = {12, 3, 15, 8, 9, 5, 18, 25};
private STree<Integer> tree = new STree<Integer>();
                       . . .

// build the initial tree
for (int i=0;i < arr.length;i++)
   tree.add(arr[i]);
```

The following is a display of the window when adding 7 to the original tree, when deleting the root 12, and when using invalid input for an add operation.

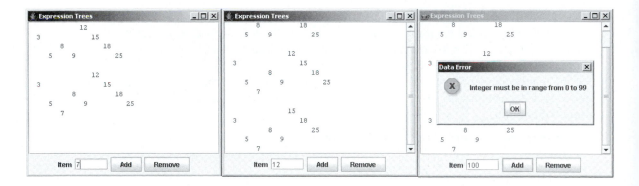

PROGRAM 18.1   DEMONSTRATING BINARY SEARCH TREE UPDATES

You can find a complete listing of the program in Chapter 18 of the software supplement. We include a listing of the method actionPerformed() that is the handler for the ActionEvents generated by the buttons.

actionPerformed():

```
public void actionPerformed(ActionEvent ae)
{
   // ae.getSource() is a reference to the object that caused
   // the ActionEvent
   JButton buttonPressed = (JButton)ae.getSource();
   int n;

   // convert the string in input to an int
   n = Integer.parseInt(itemField.getText());

   if (n < 0 || n > 99)
   {
      JOptionPane.showMessageDialog(
            appFrame, "Integer must be in range from 0 to 99",
```

```
                    "Data Error", JOptionPane.ERROR_MESSAGE);
            return;
    }

    if (buttonPressed == addButton)
        tree.add(n);
    else
        tree.remove(n);

    // display the tree in the text area
    currTreeDisplay += "\n\n" + tree.displayTree(2);
    textArea.setText(currTreeDisplay);
    itemField.setText("");
    itemField.requestFocus(true);
}
```

18.3 Implementing the STree Class

In Chapter 16, we introduce the TNode class to describe the nodes in a binary tree. A tree node object has three instance variables that include the value and references to the left and right children. For the STree class, we extend the structure of a tree node to include a fourth variable, which provides a link to the parent of the node. The STNode class defines the modified tree node object.

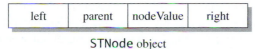

| left | parent | nodeValue | right |

STNode object

In the STree class, we maintain and update the parent field when we add or remove an element from the tree. The implementation of the STree iterator relies on information in the parent field. The iterator scans the tree in ascending order using an iterative version of the inorder traversal. The **parent** link enables us to identify the next element in the scan, which may involve retracing steps along a path of parents from the current node. The following is a UML diagram of the STNode class, which is defined as a private inner class in the STree class. The instance variables of STNode are public. A single constructor takes a value and a parent reference as arguments and creates an instance that assigns the arguments to the corresponding instance variables and sets the left and right pointers to null. We use the constructor to create a new STNode object in the add() method. You will note that in the UML diagram, there is an arrow from the class to itself. This indicates that STNode variables reference other STNodes.

The parent reference in STNode allows the implementation of an inorder tree iterator.

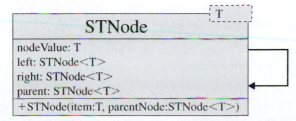

Example 18.3

The example gives a tree view and a node view of an STree object. Dotted lines represent the parent links. Note that the parent of the root node is null.

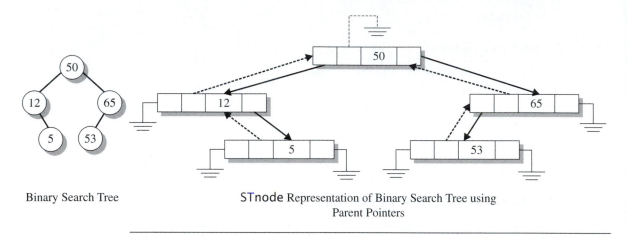

Binary Search Tree   STnode Representation of Binary Search Tree using
                                                        Parent Pointers

The STree Class Private Members and Constructor

The study of the STree class implementation begins with its variables. The instance variable, *root*, is an STNode reference that is the starting point for the binary tree which stores the elements. The integer variable treeSize maintains the number of elements in the tree. The add() and remove() methods are responsible for updating the size. To ensure the integrity of iterator operations, the class maintains an integer value modCount, which is updated each time the tree structure changes.

Private methods
findNode() and
removeNode
promote code
reuse.

Private methods simplify the implementation of the STree class and promote code reuse. The remove() method must use a search algorithm to locate the node to be deleted. This is the same search algorithm used by contains(). Rather than duplicating code, we create a private method findNode() that returns an STNode<T> reference to the node or null if the element is not present. Another private method, removeNode(), is used by the STree remove() and by the STree iterator remove() methods.

The following is a declaration of the instance variables, the private methods constructor in the STree class. The class also has private methods to display the tree. These are available in the code listing in the software supplement and are not developed in this chapter.

STree class (partial declaration):

```
public class STree<T> implements Collection<T>, Iterable<T>
{
    // reference to tree root
    private STNode<T> root;

    // number of elements in the tree
    private int treeSize;

    // increases whenever the tree changes; used by an
    // iterator to verify that it is in a consistent state
    private int modCount;
```

```
// create an instance representing an empty tree;
// the root is null and the variables treeSize and
// modCount are initially 0
public STree()
{
    root = null;
    modCount = 0;
    treeSize = 0;
}

// iteratively traverse a path from the root to the node
// whose value is item; return a reference to the node
// containing item or null if the search fails
private STNode<T> findNode(Object item)
{ . . . }

// private method used by remove() and the iterator
// remove() to delete a node
private void removeNode(STNode<T> dNode)
{ . . . }
}
```

Inserting and Locating a Node

The add() method inserts an element in an STree collection by iterating down a path from the root to an empty subtree. The private method findNode() uses the same algorithm although it looks for a match. Arriving at an empty tree indicates that the item is not found. The method returns a reference to the STNode object in the tree.

Method add() iteratively moves on a path from the root until it locates an empty subtree. It inserts the new node and returns true, If it finds a duplicate, it returns false.

Let us look at the algorithm for the add() method. With item as an argument, it starts at the root and iteratively traverses a path of left and right subtrees until it locates the insertion point or finds a match with an existing value. Because we do not allow duplicates, add() returns false if it encounters a match. For each step in the path, the algorithm maintains a record of the current node (t) and the parent of the current node. The process terminates at an empty subtree (t == null). In this case, the new node replaces the null subtree as a child of the parent. For instance, the following steps insert 32 in the tree depicted by Figure 18.5.

Insert Integer Value item = 32

1. Begin at the root node and compare item = 32 with the root value 25 (Figure 18.5a). Because 25 < 32, we traverse the right subtree and look at node 35.

     t is node 35 and parent is node 25.

2. Compare item = 32 with 35 and traverse the left subtree of 35 (Figure 18.5b).

     t is null and parent is node 35.

3. Create a leaf node with item as its value and parent referencing node 35. Insert the new node as the left child of node 35 (Figure 18.5c).

```
newNode = new STNode(item,parent);
parent.left = newNode;
```

The following is the implementation of the add() method. At each iterative step, a call to compareTo() returns an integer value that indicates the relative order of the new value (item) and the current node value. The value is negative, zero, or positive and is assigned to the variable orderValue.

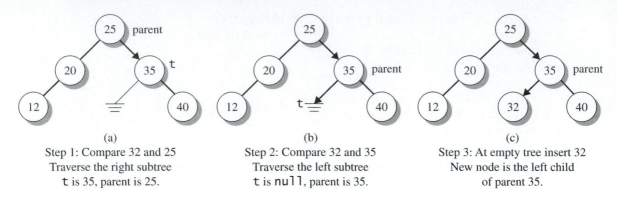

(a)	(b)	(c)
Step 1: Compare 32 and 25	Step 2: Compare 32 and 35	Step 3: At empty tree insert 32
Traverse the right subtree	Traverse the left subtree	New node is the left child
t is 35, parent is 25.	t is null, parent is 35.	of parent 35.

Figure 18.5 *Adding element 32 to the binary search tree. Arrows indicate the path.*

add():

```
// it item is not in the tree, insert it and return true
// if item is a duplicate, do not insert it and return false
public boolean add(T item)
{
   // t is current node in traversal, parent the previous node
   STNode<T> t = root, parent = null, newNode;
   int orderValue = 0;

   // terminate on an empty subtree
   while(t != null)
   {
      // update the parent reference
      parent = t;

      // compare item and the current node value
      orderValue = ((Comparable<T>)item).compareTo(t.nodeValue);

      // if a match occurs, return false; otherwise, go left
      // or go right following search tree order
      if (orderValue == 0)
         return false;                    // exit, item not added
      else if (orderValue < 0)
         t = t.left;
      else
         t = t.right;
   }

   // create the new node
   newNode = new STNode<T>(item,parent);

   if (parent == null)
      // this is the first node added; make it root
      root = newNode;
   else if (orderValue < 0)
      // attach newNode as the left child of parent
      parent.left = newNode;
   else
```

```
        // attach newNode as the right child of parent
        parent.right = newNode;

    // increment the tree size and modCount
    treeSize++;
    modCount++;

    // we added a node to the tree
    return true;
}
```

The private method findNode() provides for low-level access to nodes in the tree. The method is used by find() to locate the node that matches item. Depending on the result, find() returns null or returns a reference only to the value component.

find():

```
    // search for item in the tree and return a reference
    // to its value or null if item is not in the tree
    public T find(T item)
    {
        STNode<T> t = findNode(item);
        T value = null;

        if (t != null)
            value = t.nodeValue;

        return value;
    }
```

Deleting a Node

The private method removeNode() erases a node from the tree by finding a replacement node somewhere else in the tree and using it as a substitute for the deleted node. Issues surrounding the replacement node are critical to understanding the algorithm. First, we must choose the node so that, when it takes the place of the deleted node, its value maintains the search ordering of the tree. Second, subtrees for the deleted node and the replacement node may become orphaned during the process and must be reconnected in such a way that the new tree maintains ordering. Our discussion uses the following notation. The reference dNode identifies the deleted node D. A second reference, pNode, identifies the parent P of the deleted node. Note that when pNode is null, we are deleting the root. The removeNode() method sets out to find a replacement node R with reference rNode. The algorithm for finding a replacement node considers two cases that depend on the number of children attached to node D. We begin with the first case, in which the deleted node has at least one empty subtree; that is, there is one null child. In the next section, we analyze the second case, in which the deleted node has two nonempty subtrees.

Deleted Node Has an Empty Subtree   When the deleted node has a null child, the other child becomes the replacement node R. If the deleted node is a leaf node, it has two null children. In this case, the other node R is null. Figure 18.6 illustrates situations in which the replacement node is nonnull. Part (a) deletes node 35. The parent is node 30 and the replacement node is 33. In part (b), the deleted node is 25 with parent 30 and the replacement node is 26. Remove the node by having P link to the R with the same orientation that the parent had to the deleted node. By updating the parent field for R, we create a link from R to P. The effect is to cut D out of the tree.

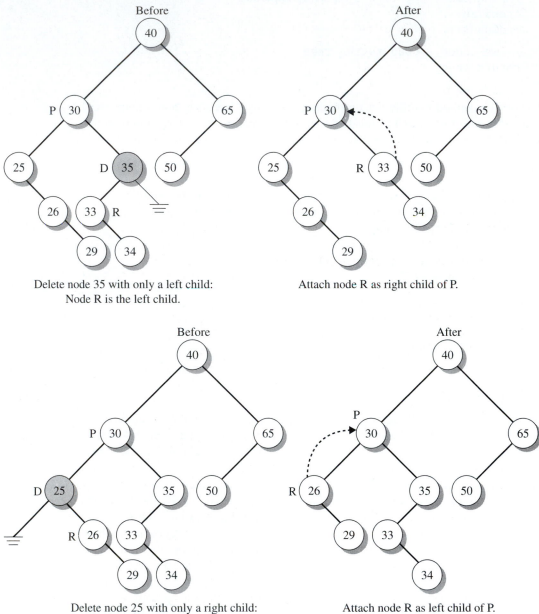

Delete node 35 with only a left child:
Node R is the left child.

Attach node R as right child of P.

Delete node 25 with only a right child:
Node R is the right child.

Attach node R as left child of P.

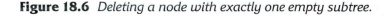

Figure 18.6 *Deleting a node with exactly one empty subtree.*

In Figure 18.6a, node D with value 35 is a right child of parent P = 30 and has a non-null left child 33 which becomes the replacement node R. Attach R to the parent P as a right child and have R point back to P as its parent. In Figure 18.6b, node D with value 25 is a left child of 30 with a right child 26. The right child is the replacement node R and connects to P as a left child. Update the parent field for R to point at P.

If node D has an empty child, the other child is the replacement node R. Link R to the parent of D.

The removeNode() algorithm must address two special cases, one in which the deleted node is a leaf node and the other in which the deleted node is the root. In Figure 18.7a, leaf node 50 is deleted. The replacement node R is null and becomes the right child of the parent. There is no update to the parent field for R.

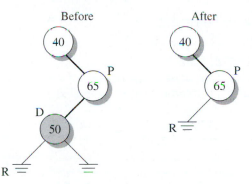

(a) Delete leaf node 50 Replacement node is null

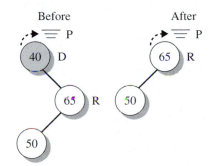

(b) Delete root node 40 Replacement node is the new root

Figure 18.7 *Deleting a leaf node and a root node with a null child.*

When the parent is null, the deletion removes the root node. In this case, the replacement node becomes the new root. In Figure 18.7b, we delete the root 40. The parent field of the replacement node 65 is null.

The examples illustrate the different situations that can occur when the node to be deleted has a null child. The implementation of removeNode() tests for this condition and then uses a series of conditional statements to update the tree. The method uses the variables dNode, pNode, and rNode to reference the deleted node, the parent node, and the replacement node respectively.

removeNode() (deleted node has a null child):

```java
private void removeNode(STNode<T> dNode)
{
    if (dNode == null)
        return;

    // dNode = reference to node D that is deleted
    // pNode = reference to parent P of node D
    // rNode = reference to node R that replaces D
    STNode<T> pNode, rNode;

    // assign pNode as a reference to P
    pNode = dNode.parent;

    // if D has a null child, the
    // replacement node is the other child
    if (dNode.left == null || dNode.right == null)
    {
        if (dNode.right == null)
            rNode = dNode.left;
        else
            rNode = dNode.right;

        if (rNode != null)
            // the parent of R is now the parent of D
            rNode.parent = pNode;

        // complete the link to the parent node

        // deleting the root node; assign new root
        if (pNode == null)
            root = rNode;
        // attach R to the correct branch of P
        else if ((((Comparable<T>)dNode.nodeValue).
                compareTo(pNode.nodeValue) < 0)
            pNode.left = rNode;
        else
            pNode.right = rNode;
    }
    ...
}
```

Deleted Node Has Two Nonnull Children A node with two children has some elements in its subtrees that are less than its value and some elements that are greater than its value. Deleting such a node requires finding a replacement node that maintains the correct ordering among the items. Once the replacement node is found, the algorithm employs a new strategy. Rather than removing the deleted node, it keeps the node in place but updates its value with that of the replacement node. The algorithm then removes (splices out) the replacement node from the tree. Two examples illustrate the different situations which occur. In Figure 18.8, we delete node 25 (part (a)) and node 30 (part (b)).

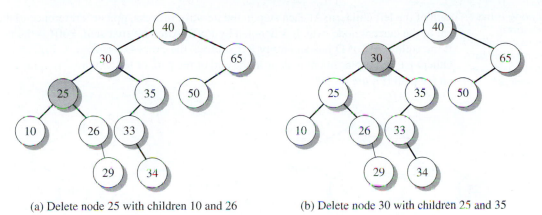

(a) Delete node 25 with children 10 and 26   (b) Delete node 30 with children 25 and 35

Figure 18.8 *Deleting a node with two nonnull children.*

Method `removeNode()` selects as the replacement node R, a value that is "just after" the value of the deleted node. Thus, it selects the node which has the smallest value that is greater than the value of the deleted node. In Figure 18.8a, node 26 is the replacement node. It is the right child of 25. In Figure 18.8b, node 33 is the smallest value that is greater than 30. Locate 33 as the leftmost node in the right subtree of D. Note that in both cases, node R has an empty left subtree. Once we determine R, we copy its value to the deleted node and then splice out (delete) R from the tree. This is done by simply reconnecting the right subtree of R to the parent of R. Both part (a) and part (b) involve the same strategy. For instance, when deleting 30, the replacement node 33 has the right subtree 34. Copy 33 as the new value for the deleted node and attach the right subtree of R to 35, the parent of R. We show the final result in Figure 18.9.

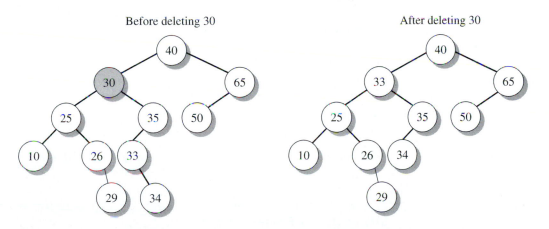

Figure 18.9 *Replacing deleted value 30 with replacement value 33 and attaching right subtree 34.*

The idea is simple, but the devil lies in the details. The problem is to find the replacement node and its parent so that the right subtree can be reconnected to the tree. To find the replacement node, start with the right child of the deleted node and then proceed down the

If the node D has two children, move to its right child and then far left to the replacement node R.

path of the left children. At each step in the iterative process, update a reference to the parent of the current node, which is denoted by PofR. After the first step, PofR is the node D. If the right child of D has an empty left subtree, the process terminates (Figure 18.10a). Otherwise, the replacement node is at the end of the path of left children with PofR a node on the path (Figure 18.10b).

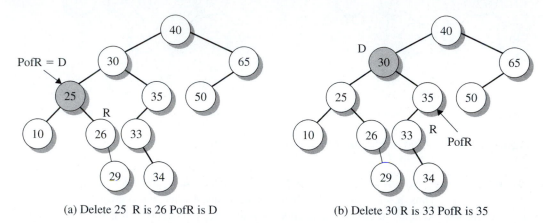

(a) Delete 25 R is 26 PofR is D   (b) Delete 30 R is 33 PofR is 35

Figure 18.10   *Nodes identifying the deleted node D, replacement node R, and its parent PofR.*

Splice out R from the tree, by copying its value in place of the value of D and connect its right subtree to its parent.

Splice out R from the tree by copying its value to D and then connect its right subtree to its parent PofR. The implementation of removeNode() uses a block of code to handle a situation in which the deleted node has two nonempty children. The block uses a loop to identify the replacement node and its parent. The method uses the reference variable pOfRNode for the node POfR.

removeNode() (deleted node has two nonnull children):

```
public void removeNode(STNode<T> dNode)
{
    if (dNode.left == null || dNode.right == null)
    {
        . . .
    }
    // case where deleted node has two nonnull children
    else
    {
        // pOfRNode is reference to parent of replacement node
        STNode<T> pOfRNode = dNode;

        // first possible replacement is right child of D
        // the reference to PofR, pOfRNode, is the deleted node
        rNode = dNode.right;
        pOfRNode = dNode;
```

```
        // descend down path of left children, keeping a record
        // of the current node and its parent;
        // stop at the replacement node
        while(rNode.left != null)
        {
            pOfRNode = rNode;
            rNode = rNode.left;
        }
        . . .
    }
}
```

Complete the process by copying the value of the replacement node to D and then connect the right subtree of R to the tree. If PofR is the deleted node, then connect the right subtree of R as the rightchild of D; otherwise connect the right child of R as the left child of PofR. In either of the two cases, we must assign the parent of the right subtree of R to be pOfRNode, the parent of R.

```
    // copy the value in R to D
    dNode.nodeValue = rNode.nodeValue;

    if (pOfRNode == dNode)
        dNode.right = rNode.right;
    else
        pOfRNode.left = rNode.right;
    // the parent of the right child of R is the parent of R

    if (rNode.right != null)
        rNode.right.parent = pOfRNode;
```

The remove(item) Method   We are now able to show you the implementation of the method remove(). First, use findNode() to locate item in the tree. If item is not in the tree, return false. If item is present, call removeNode() to erase it, decrement the size of the tree, increment modCount, and return true.

remove():

```
    // if item is in the tree, remove it
    // and return true; otherwise, return
    // false
    public boolean remove(Object item)
    {
        // search tree for item
        STNode<T> dNode = findNode(item);

        if (dNode == null)
            return false;
```

```
        removeNode(dNode);

        treeSize--;
        modCount++;

        return true;
    }
```

Additional Operations

In this section, we discuss implementations for the access methods `first()` and `last()` that make use of the structure of a binary search tree to determine its minimum and maximum values. The method `first()` must return the smallest element in the tree. In a binary search tree, this element is in the left-most node from `root`.

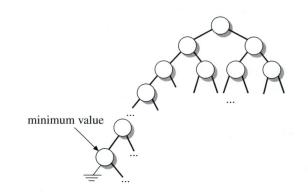

minimum value

The minimum value in a binary search tree is the node farthest left from root.

Initialize an `STNode` variable `nextNode` to have value `root` and keep moving left to node `nextNode.left` until locating a node for which `nextNode.left` is `null`. Return the value in `nextNode`.

first():

```
// returns the first (least) element in this binary search tree
public T first()
{
        STNode<T> nextNode = root;

    // if the set is empty, return null
        if (nextNode == null)
            return null;

        // first node is the furthest node left from root
        while (nextNode.left != null)
            nextNode = nextNode.left;

        return nextNode.nodeValue;
    }
```

The method `last()` must return the largest element in the tree. In a binary search tree, this element is in the right-most node from root. Implement the methods by starting at the root and scan down the path of right children. The value of the last node on the path is the maximum value in the binary search tree.

The maximum value in a binary search tree is the node farthest right from root.

Complexity of Binary Search Tree Operations

The best-case complexity for the `add()` and `remove()` operations occurs when the tree is complete. For a complete tree, the maximum number of comparisons needed to reach a leaf node is $O(\log_2 n)$. It follows that these operations have $O(\log_2 n)$ complexity in their best case. The worst case for these operations occurs when the tree is degenerate. In the degenerate case, the tree reduces to a linked list and the methods have $O(n)$ complexity. An advanced mathematical analysis shows that the average case has complexity $O(\log_2 n)$. In general, the binary search-tree algorithms work well; however, the worst case is linear. In Chapter 27, we eliminate the worst-case condition by extending the search tree concept to balanced AVL trees and red-black trees.

A binary search tree has best-case search time $O(\log_2 n)$, worst-case time $O(n)$, and average time $O(\log_2 n)$.

18.4 The STree Iterator

Iterators have basic operations that allow a program to scan the elements in a collection and access their values. They also allow removal of an element as an update operation. The iterator methods are `hasNext()`, `next()`, and `remove()`. Our task is to implement these methods as well as implement the STree class method `iterator()` that creates an `Iterator` object and gives it an initial value.

In Section 17.2, we introduced an iterative inorder scan of a binary tree. The algorithm used a stack to store node references when we descended down a path to locate the next element. Popping the stack allowed us to reverse steps and move up the path. The design simulated the recursive version of the inorder scan. With the STree iterator, we implement an iterative traversal of the elements using the STNode parent field. Figure 18.11 illustrates

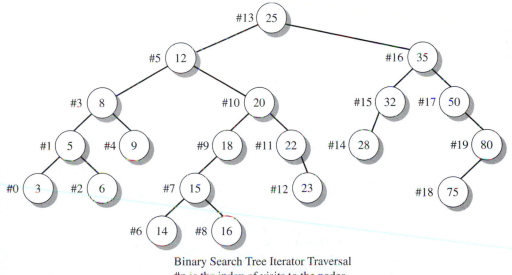

Binary Search Tree Iterator Traversal
#n is the index of visits to the nodes

Figure 18.11 *The order that nodes are visited in an inorder scan of the nodes.*

the order of scan for the 20 elements in the search tree. Look what happens at some of the nodes. If the current iterator position is node 18, the next two elements are found by moving up to the parent 20 and then down the right subtree to node 22 and node 23. From node 23, the next element is the root node 25. We locate the value by scanning four levels up the path of parents.

The Private Variables and Constructor of the STree Iterator Class   Like the LinkedList iterator, we construct the STree iterator using an inner class, IteratorImpl, that implements the Iterator<T> interface. The private portion of IteratorImpl includes the variable nextNode, which references the next node in the inorder traversal of the tree. Its counterpart, lastReturned, references the last node whose value is returned by next(). This variable designates the node that is deleted by the iterator remove() method. The integer expectedModCount is an inner class variable that corresponds to the value of modCount in the STree class. Comparing the two allows the iterator to determine whether an unexpected change occurred in the tree. For instance, the program may insert a new element using the STree class add(). This invalidates an iterator. The only way we can update the tree during an iterator scan is to call the iterator method remove().

IteratorImpl inner class:

```
private class IteratorImpl implements Iterator<T>
{
    // set expectedModCount to the number of list changes
    // at the time of iterator creation
    private int expectedModCount = modCount;
    // node of the last value returned by next() if that
    // value was deleted by the iterator method remove()
    private STNode<T> lastReturned = null;
    // node whose value is returned a subsequent call to next()
    private STNode<T> nextNode = null;
                    . . .
}
```

The first node is the one farthest left from the root. Subsequent nodes are visited in LNR order.

The constructor initializes nextNode to point at the minimum element in the tree. Find the element by starting at the root and traversing the chain of left subtrees. The process stops at a node with a null left subtree. This becomes the first node the iterator visits in the inorder scan.

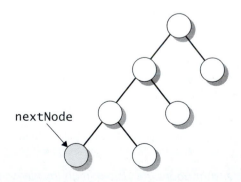

nextNode

IteratorImpl():

```
    // constructor
    IteratorImpl()
    {
        nextNode = root;

        // if the tree is not empty, the first node
        // inorder is the farthest node left from root
        if (nextNode != null)
            while (nextNode.left != null)
                nextNode = nextNode.left;
    }
```

The STree Iterator Public Methods

The STree method `iterator()` simply creates and returns an `IteratorImpl` object. The iterator is positioned at the minimum element whose value is the leftmost node in the tree.

iterator():

```
    // returns an iterator for the elements in the tree
    public Iterator<T> iterator()
    {
        return new IteratorImpl();
    }
```

Implementing next()   To implement the method `next()`, we must execute a series of iterative steps that move us from the current node to the next node in order. We do not look at the left branch of the current tree node, because it contains smaller values that we have already visited. We must either descend down the right subtree or move up the tree. We summarize the possibilities with the following two rules.

- If the right subtree is not empty, obtain the next node in order by moving to the right child and then moving left until we encounter a `null` subtree. For instance, in the tree of Figure 18.11, from the node with value 12, we must move to 20 and then far left to 14.

- If the right subtree is empty, obtain the next node in order by following a chain of parent references until we find a parent, P, for which our current node, `nodePtr`, is a left child. Node P is the next node in order. When this situation occurs, all the nodes on the left subtree of P have been visited, and it is time to visit P. For example, in Figure 18.11, if we are at the node with value 23, we move up the tree until we find that node 12 is the left child of node 25. The root node 25 is the next node in order.

When the right subtree is empty, use the parent reference to move up the tree until we find a left child. The parent is the next node.

The implementation of `next()` follows these two rules even when the method extracts the value of the last node. To see this, look at Figure 18.11. The last node is 80, which is the maximum value in the tree. When we invoke `next()` from this position, the second rule applies because the right subtree is empty. As we move up the tree, we are always in the right

Encountering a null parent means the iteration is complete.

subtree of each parent until we encounter the root node, whose parent is `null`. In this situation, the variable `nextNode` becomes `null`, and we have completed an iteration.

In the following listing, the private method `checkIteratorState()` verifies that the value of `expectedModCount` in the inner class `IteratorImpl` equals the value of `modCount` in the `STree` class. If the values are not equal, an unexpected change has occurred in the tree and an exception is thrown.

next():

```
// returns the next element in the iteration; throws
// NoSuchElementException if iteration has no more elements
public T next()
{
    // check that the iterator is in a consistent state;
    // throws ConcurrentModificationException if it is not
    checkIteratorState();

    // check if the iteration has an another element;
    // if not, throw NoSuchElementException
    if (nextNode == null)
        throw new NoSuchElementException(
                "Iteration has no more elements");
    // save current value of next in lastReturned
    lastReturned = nextNode;

    // set nextNode to the next node in order
    STNode<T> p;

    if (nextNode.right != null)
    {
        // successor is the furthest left node of
        // right subtree
        nextNode = nextNode.right;

        while (nextNode.left != null)
            nextNode = nextNode.left;
    }
    else
    {
        // have already processed the left subtree, and there is
        // no right subtree; move up the tree, looking for a
        // parent for which nextNode is a left child, stopping
        // if the parent becomes null; a non-null parent is the
        // successor; if parent is null, the original node was
        // the last node inorder
        p = nextNode.parent;
```

```
    while (p != null && nextNode == p.right)
    {
        nextNode = p;
        p = p.parent;
    }

    // if we were previously at the right-most node in
    // the tree, nextNode = null
    nextNode = p;
}

return lastReturned.nodeValue;
}
```

The iteration is complete when `nextNode` becomes `null`. The implementation of `hasNext()` simply verifies that `nextNode` is not equal to `null`.

hasNext():

```
// returns true if the tree has more
// unvisited elements
public boolean hasNext()
{
    // elements remain if nextNode is not null
    return nextNode != null;
}
```

The method `remove()` checks for consistency and uses the private `STree` method `removeNode()` to erase the last visited node, `lastReturned`. See the software supplement for a listing of this method.

Chapter Summary

- A binary search tree stores data by value instead of position. Simple rules for descending a path to a null subtree make it easy to build a binary search tree that does not allow duplicate values. The insertion algorithm also defines the path to a data value in the tree. The removal of an item from a binary search tree is more difficult and involves finding a replacement node among the remaining values.
- The class STree implements the Collection interface. A binary search tree stores the data in the collection. In addition to the methods in the Collection interface, the class implements tree drawing algorithms and a method find() that allows the programmer to update data in the search tree.

- The chapter discusses the implementation of various methods of the STree class. The implementation for add() is relatively simple and follows directly from the rules for insertion into a binary search tree. The remove() algorithm is somewhat difficult. In essence, it involves finding a replacement node R for the node D that we wish to remove. If D has less than two children, we link R into the tree in place of D and destroy D. If D has two children, we unlink R from its position in the tree, copy its value in place of the value of D, and destroy R.

- A tree iterator uses an iterative process to move through a binary tree inorder. The STree iterator is implemented using an inner class. The inner class makes use of the parent reference in an STNode object in order to move up the tree when there are no more right subtrees to scan. Without parent references, a stack must be used to store references to tree nodes as the algorithm moves far left.

Written Exercises

1. Consider the following binary search tree. Use this original tree for each part, (a) through (h).

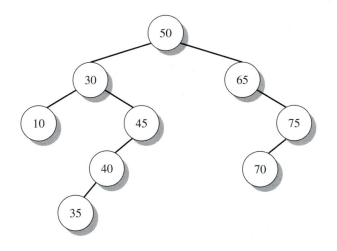

(a) If the value 33 is inserted into the tree, which node is its parent?
(b) If the value 72 is inserted into the tree, which node is its parent?
(c) If the root node 50 is deleted, the erase algorithm selects which node as the replacement node?
(d) If the node 30 is deleted, the erase algorithm selects which node as the replacement node?
(e) Traverse the tree and list the nodes using a preorder scan.
(f) Traverse the tree and list the nodes using an inorder scan.
(g) Traverse the tree and list the nodes using a postorder scan.
(h) Traverse the tree and list the nodes using a level-order scan.

2. For each sequence of characters, draw the binary search tree and then traverse the tree by using inorder, preorder, and postorder scans that begin with the left child.

   (a) M, T, V, F, U, N
   (b) F, L, O, R, I, D, A
   (c) R, O, T, A, R, Y, C, L, U, B

3. (a) Assume that we obtain the following integer sequence by traversing a binary search tree in preorder. Construct a tree that has such an ordering.

      50 45 35 15 40 46 65 75 70

   (b) Construct a binary search tree that would produce the following inorder traversal of its elements:

      40 45 46 50 65 70 75

4. Propose an algorithm for allowing duplicate values in a binary search tree. An inorder scan must traverse the tree values in ascending order.

5. Use the integers from 1 to 9 to build a 9-node binary search tree with no duplicate data values.

   (a) Give the possible root node values if the height of the tree is 4.
   (b) Answer (a) for depths of 5, 6, 7, and 8.

6. Assume the following iterative method is a member of the STree class and determines the height of item in the tree. Implement it.

   ```
   public int nodeLevel(Object item)
   { ... }
   ```

   Return −1 if item is not in the tree, and throw IllegalArgumentException if the tree is empty.

7. To erase a node with two children, we have chosen the replacement node as the node with the smallest value in the right subtree. Propose an alternative node and describe the algorithm for locating it.

8. (a) Why do we not implement tree iterators by using a recursive algorithm?
   (b) Explain why each node in our implementation of a binary search tree has a parent reference.

9. (a) Give a recursive version of the private STree method findNode().

   ```
   // search for item in the binary search tree with root t
   private STNode<T> findNode(STNode<T> t, Object item)
   { ... }
   ```

   (b) The method findNode() is used by the public methods contains(), remove(), and find(). How must you modify those methods so they use the new version of findNode()?

10. Sort an array of n distinct values by inserting them into a binary search tree and then iterating through the tree and copying the values back to the array. What are the best- and worst-case running times for this algorithm?

11. Show that if a node in a binary search tree has two children, then its inorder successor has no left child and its inorder predecessor has no right child.

12. Suppose you insert node A into a binary search tree and then delete node B. In general, do you obtain the same tree if you first delete node B and then insert node A?

13. Let `currNode` reference a node of a binary search tree. Describe an algorithm for finding the inorder predecessor of `currNode`.

Programming Exercises

14. In a program, declare the `STree` object `charTree` with initial values from array `arr`. Display the tree by using the method `displayTree()`.

    ```
    char[] arr = { 'S', 'J', 'K', 'L', 'X', 'F', 'E', 'Z' };
    ```

15. A program prompts the user to enter an integer, n, specifying the number of elements that will be added to an `ArrayList`, `arr`. Use the random-number generator to create n integer values in the range from 0 to 99, adding each value to the `ArrayList`. Output the elements. Insert the elements from the `ArrayList` into the binary search tree `arrListTree`. Output the ordered list and the tree.

16. The `IntegerCount` class maintains an integer value, `intValue`, and a variable `count` that records the number of times `intValue` occurs. The constructor initializes `intValue` and sets `count` to 1. In addition to the "getter" methods `getInt()` and `getCount()`, the class has the method `incCount()` that increases the count by 1. Have toString() describe an object in *the format* <value>(<count>). The `Integer-Count` class implements the `Comparable<IntegerCount>` interface to ensure that its objects can be placed in a binary search tree. Compare two objects by comparing their `intValue` variables. Implement `IntegerCount`, whose UML description follows.

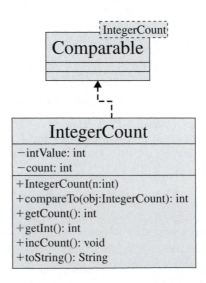

Declare a binary search tree, `integerTree`. Write a program that generates 10,000 random integers in the range from 0 to 6. For each value, construct an `Integer-Count` object and search the tree. If the value is in the tree, increment its count;

otherwise, insert the value, with a count of 1. Using a tree iterator, traverse the tree and output its nodes in order. Picture the tree by calling `displayTree()`.

17. (a) Add the following method to the `STree` class. The generic notation

```
Collection<? extends T>collection
```

means that the elements of collection are of an unspecified type ? that is a subtype of T. In other words, ? "is a" T.

```
// adds all of the elements in the specified collection
// to this collection; returns true if the collection
// was modified and false otherwise
boolean addAll(Collection<? extends T> collection);
{ ... }
```

In the implementation of `addAll()`, if you use an iterator, declare it using the following type:

```
Iterator<? extends T>
```

(b) In a program, create the binary search tree t with values determined by the array `intTreeVals`.

```
int[] intTreeVals = {22, 19, 87, 42, 9, 17, 1, 56,
                     48, 75};
```

Create a `LinkedList` object `list` with values determined by the array `intLnkListVals`.

```
int[] intLnkListVals = {5, 55, 22, 15, 23, 19, 56,
                        25, 35};
```

Using `addAll()`, add the values from `list` to t and output t.

Programming Project

18. A rental store stocks a variety of tools for customers involved in do-it-yourself projects. The store has an online system that maintains a database of the type of tools in the inventory and the number of copies of each tool currently in stock. A second database maintains records of the tools that are currently being rented. The online system handles the rental or the return of a tool by updating the two databases.

Design the online system as a GUI application that has a frame whose content pane uses a `BorderLayout` manager. The top (NORTH) portion of the frame has a label and a text field that accepts user input of a tool that is to be rented or returned. The middle (CENTER) portion has two text areas that list the name and number of tools which are currently available or rented. The bottom (SOUTH) portion is a panel with "Rent" and "Return" buttons and text field displaying a message about the transaction (Figure 18.12).

Maintain the two databases with `STree` objects `inventoryTree` and `rentalTree`. Each of the trees stores `Tool` objects that consist of two private instance variables `toolName` (String) and `toolCount` (int). The `Tool` class implements the

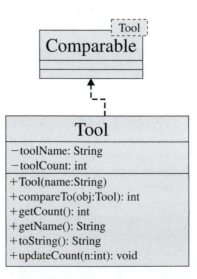

Figure 18.12 *Two views of the online tool rental system. In (a), the customer attempts to rent a Sander which is currently not available. In (b), a customer returns a Ladder, which causes updates to both the Rentals and Tools databases.*

Comparable interface by comparing two objects using their toolName values. This ensures that Tool objects can be placed in a binary search tree. The constructor takes a string argument that is the Tool object name and creates an instance that has a default count of 1. The methods getName() and getCount() provide access to the instance variables. The method updateCount(n) allows the online system to update an inventoryTree and a rentalTree element. Use n = 1 when the tool is added to a database and n = -1 when a tool is removed from the database. For output, provide the method toString() that describes a tool in the form "<toolName> (<tool-Count>)." The following figure is a UML illustration of the Tool class.

Use three methods to handle most of the details. The method setupInventory() is called by the constructor after it creates and positions the graphical components on the frame. The method opens a file and reads a sequence of strings describing tool names. The sequence has duplicate strings which are accounted for by the toolCount field of the corresponding Tool object. The application allows for the rental and return of a tool. In the simulation, the actions involve updating both the inventorySet and the rentalSet. Isolate these two operations in the methods rentalTransaction() and returnTransaction(), respectively.

```
public void setupInventory(STree<Tool> t)
{ ... }
void rentalTransaction(STree<Tool> inventorySet,
  STree<Tool> rentalSet, String toolName)
{ ... }
void returnTransaction(STree<Tool> inventorySet,
  STree<Tool> rentalSet, String toolName)
{ ... }
```

Chapter 19

SETS AND MAPS

CONTENTS

19.1 SETS
The TreeSet Collection
A Simple Spell Checker

19.2 SET OPERATORS
Implementing Set Operators
Application: Updating Computer
Accounts
Operations with Ordered Sets

19.3 MAPS
The Map Interface

The Ordered Map TreeMap
Application: A Student-Timecard
Map
Application: Computer Software
Products

19.4 MAP COLLECTION VIEW
The Key Set Collection View
The Entry Set Collection View
Application: Building a
Concordance

In Chapter 8, we began a study of data structures by introducing the Collection interface, which defines a series of very general collection methods. In the intervening chapters, we focused on data structures that store elements by position. The category specified by the List interface has concrete data structures such as ArrayList and LinkedList. With this chapter, we add to our framework collections that store elements by value.

Modern data structures describe two distinct types of collections that maintain data by value, namely, sets

and maps. A *set* is the simplest type of collection. It has the same basic operations as the Collection interface with the stipulation that each element is unique. The add() method for a set inserts a new element only if it is not already in the collection. The boolean return value from the operation indicates whether an element is actually added to the collection. A physical model of a set is a bag that holds tools, groceries, or other objects. A mathematical concept of a set is a more abstract way of thinking about set collections. Figure19.1 illustrates a set of Integer, String, and Time24 objects.

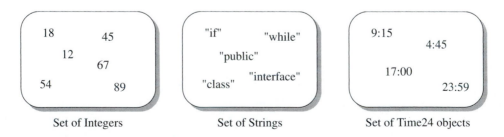

| Set of Integers | Set of Strings | Set of Time24 objects |

Figure 19.1 *Sets with Integer, String, and Time24 elements.*

A *map* stores an element as a *key-value pair*. In a pair, the first field is the key, which is an attribute that uniquely identifies the element. The second field is the value, which is an object associated with the key.

A map is a generic collection with elements referred to as *entries*. The key field is of type K and the value field is of type V. In a database application, the key is typically a string and the value is a record with multiple fields listing data attributes associated with entry. For instance, a textbook is identified by its ISBN number. The book has an author, publisher, price, and so forth, which are all part of the value field of the book entry. Figure 19.2 illustrates a map that might be used for university administration. The map is a collection of `String–Integer` pairs to denote the number of majors in each of its degree programs. The name of the degree program is the key and the number of majors is the value.

A map collection stores key-value pairs.

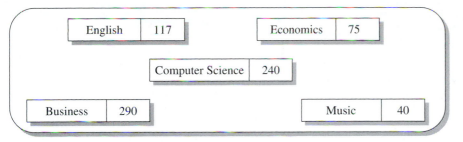

Map of String-Integer pairs

Figure 19.2 *Map of String-Integer pairs with the degree program as the key and the number of majors as the value.*

A map collection uses the key to access the value field of the entry. For instance, assume `degreeMap` is the map collection for departments and major counts. The operation `degreeMap.get("English")` returns the `Integer` component with value 117, which identifies the number of English majors. Notice the similarity between the `get()` method for maps and the `get()` method for an ArrayList. With a map, the argument is a key that returns the value component from the key-value pair; with an ArrayList, the argument is an index that returns the value of the element at the index position. Because the location of data is associated with a key rather than a position, we call a map an *associative collection*.

In a map, each key is associated with a single value. A map is an associative collection.

As part of our framework, we define a `Set` interface and a `Map` interface to specify methods that are available to a concrete set or map collection. A binary search tree is used by the `TreeSet` and `TreeMap` classes to implement the interfaces. Because a search tree orders elements, we can identify the minimum and maximum elements in a collection. We incorporate this fact in new interfaces, `OrderedSet` and `OrderedMap`, which define the methods `first()` and `last()`. In Chapter 21, we will introduce the concept of a hash function and a new type of data structure called a *hash table*. Hashing provides very fast

The Set interface extends the Collection interface, but the Map interface is separate, because it defines methods not relevant to general collections.

access to elements, and the resulting tables are very efficient search engines. We will use hash tables as the storage structure to implement `HashSet` and `HashMap` classes. Unlike search trees, there is no ordering of elements in a hash table.

Figure 19.3 details the interfaces and collection classes that define sets and maps. In this chapter, we focus on the `Set` and `Map` collection types and the tree-based collections. Once you are introduced to hash tables in Chapter 21, we will assume that an application design will determine whether a set or a map is an appropriate data structure and then choose the proper tree or hash collection class. All of this analysis will be clarified in Chapter 21.

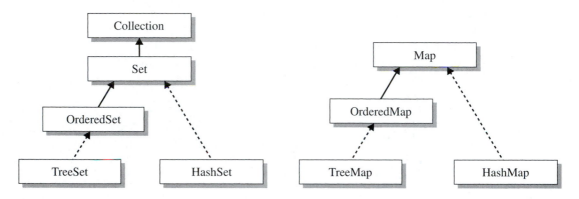

Figure 19.3 *The set and map interfaces.*

19.1 Sets

Set allows access to elements by value. Duplicate values are not allowed.

A *set* is a collection that provides rapid access to an element using its value. This collection uses the model of a mathematical set and serves applications in which a program needs to store and retrieve data or to determine the union or intersection of elements among two or more sets. We will also discover that sets provide access to the keys and entries in a map. The `Set` interface is a carbon copy of the `Collection` interface with the stipulation that the `add()` method inserts an element only if no duplicate value already exists in the set. The `OrderedSet` interface extends the `Set` interface by defining the methods `first()` and `last()`. These return the minimum and maximum values in the collection.

The TreeSet Collection

TreeSet implements the Set interface by using a binary search tree. As a result, it also implements an ordered set.

The `TreeSet` class is a generic collection class that implements the `OrderedSet` interface. This class uses a binary search tree as the underlying storage structure, which guarantees that elements can be accessed in ascending order. As a result, a set must store objects that implement the `Comparable` interface.

The `TreeSet` constructor creates an empty set. Typical of all of our collection classes, `TreeSet` implements `toString()`, which returns a string containing a comma-separated ordered list of elements enclosed in brackets. The following API lists only the methods not listed in the `Set` interface.

class TreeSet<T> implements OrderedSet<T>		ds.util
	Constructor	
	TreeSet()	
	Creates an empty ordered set whose elements have a specified type that must implement the Comparable interface.	
	Methods	
T	**first**()	
	Returns the minimum value of the elements in the set.	
T	**last**()	
	Returns the maximum value of the elements in the set.	
String	**toString**()	
	Returns a string containing a comma-separated ordered list of elements enclosed in brackets.	

Example 19.1

The example illustrates some of the basic set and set iterator operations for a TreeSet collection. Output calls toString().

1. The declaration of colorSet creates an empty set.

   ```
   TreeSet<String> colorSet = new TreeSet<String>();
   ```

2. Initialize the set with elements from the String array strArr. Note that the string "red" appears in the set only once. Use size() and contains() to extract information and toString() to display the elements in order.

   ```
   String[] strArr = {"red", "cyan", "green", "black", "red",
                      "pink"};
   for (int i = 0; i < strArr.length; i++)
      colorSet.add(strArr[i]);

   System.out.println(colorSet.size());
   boolean hasGreen = colorSet.contains("green"); // true
   System.out.println(colorSet);
   ```

   ```
   Output:
      5
      [black, cyan, green, pink, red]
   ```

3. Identify the first and last element in the ordered set collection.

   ```
   System.out.println("First color is " + colorSet.first());
   System.out.println("Last color is " + colorSet.last());
   ```

   ```
   Output:
      First color is black
      Last color is red
   ```

4. Use an iterator to scan the elements in the set. Remove any string that begins with "c" or "p." Output the resulting set.

```
Iterator<String> setIter = colorSet.iterator();
String color;

while (setIter.hasNext())
{
    color = setIter.next();
    if (color.charAt(0) == 'c' || color.charAt(0) == 'p')
        setIter.remove();
}
System.out.println(colorSet);
```

> Output:
>   [black, green, red]

A Simple Spell Checker

Anyone who has used a word processor is familiar with a spell checker. This tool compares a word with a dictionary of correctly spelled words, accounting for plurals, upper and lower case letters, and so forth. Typically, a spell checker displays a word that appears to be misspelled and then does sophisticated pattern matching to identify words in the dictionary that are likely alternative spellings.

A set is an ideal structure for the implementation of a simple spell checker.

A set is an efficient collection for storing the dictionary. We can illustrate this fact with a very simple spell checker for the words in a text file. The method `spellChecker()` takes a string argument that specifies the file name for the document. It interacts with the user to handle words that are initially designated to be "misspelled." The algorithm features the following design.

*   Begin by creating the dictionary as a set of strings containing approximately 25,000 words in lower case. This involves opening the file `dict.dat` and reading each word into the set.
*   Use the file name for the document to open a `Scanner` object.
*   Use the scanner to read each word of the document. For each word, call `contains()` to determine whether the word is in the dictionary set. If not, we assume the word is misspelled and interact with the user for instructions on how to proceed. A prompt lists the word along with three options. For instance, the prompt for the word "contians" is

```
contians
'a'(add) 'i'(ignore) 'm'(misspelled)
```

For the response "a," the checker adds the word to the dictionary. This assumes that the word is actually correct and will be so identified the next time it is input from the document. When the response is "i," the user chooses to ignore the fact that the word is not in the dictionary. This is an appropriate request when the word occurs infrequently and thus there is no need to add it to the dictionary. Respond with "m" when the word is misspelled. The spell checker adds the word to a set of misspelled words.

The `spellChecker()` method concludes by displaying the set of misspelled words.

spellChecker():

```
public static void spellChecker(String filename)
{
    // sets storing the dictionary and the misspelled words
    TreeSet<String> dictionary = new TreeSet<String>(),
                    misspelledWords = new TreeSet<String>();

    Scanner dictFile = null, docFile = null;

    // create Scanner objects to input dictionary and document
    try
    {
        // dictionary and document streams
        dictFile = new Scanner(new FileReader("dict.dat"));
        docFile = new Scanner(new FileReader(filename));
    }

    catch(FileNotFoundException fnfe)
    {
        System.err.println("Cannot open a file");
        System.exit(1);
    }

    // string containing each word from the dictionary and
    // from the document
    String word;
    // user response when a misspelled word is noted
    String response;

    // insert each word from file "dict.dat" into a set
    while(dictFile.hasNext())
    {
        // input next word and add to dictionary
        word = dictFile.next();
        dictionary.add(word);
    }

    // read the document word by word and check spelling
    while(docFile.hasNext())
    {
        // get the next word from the document
        word = docFile.next();

        // look word up in the dictionary; if not present
        // assume word is misspelled; prompt user to add word to
        // the dictionary, ignore it, or flag as misspelled
        if (!dictionary.contains(word))
        {
            System.out.println(word);
```

```
            System.out.print(
                "    'a'(add)  'i'(ignore)  'm'(misspelled) ");
            response = keyIn.next();
            // if response is 'a' add to dictionary;
            // if not ignored, add to set of misspelled words
            if (response.charAt(0) == 'a')
                dictionary.add(word);
            else if (response.charAt(0) == 'm')
                misspelledWords.add(word);
        }
    }

    // display the set of misspelled words
    System.out.println("\nMisspelled words: " +
                            misspelledWords);
}
```

PROGRAM 19.1   A SIMPLE SPELL CHECKER

Let us illustrate the use of the spell checker. The program prompts the user for the document
name and then calls spellChecker(). The dictionary from file *dict.dat* contains words
in lowercase. Only hyphenated words have punctuation marks. To accommodate these facts,
we run the program with a simple document that has only lowercase alphabetic characters
and a hyphen as a punctuation mark.

```
import java.io.FileReader;
import java.io.FileNotFoundException;
import java.util.Scanner;

import ds.util.TreeSet;

public class Program19_1
{
    // keyboard input stream used by main() and spellChecker()
    static Scanner keyIn = new Scanner(System.in);

    public static void main(String[] args)
    {
        String fileName;
        // enter the file name for the document
        System.out.print("Enter the document to spell check: ");
        fileName = keyIn.next();

        // check the spelling
        spellChecker(fileName);
    }

    < method spellchecker() listed in the program discussion >
}
```

```
File "spell.txt"
teh message contians the url for the web-page
and a misspeled url for the email adress
Run:
    Enter the document to spell check: spell.txt
    teh
        'a'(add)   'i'(ignore)   'm'(misspelled) m
    contians
        'a'(add)   'i'(ignore)   'm'(misspelled) m
    url
        'a'(add)   'i'(ignore)   'm'(misspelled) a
    web-page
        'a'(add)   'i'(ignore)   'm'(misspelled) i
    misspeled
        'a'(add)   'i'(ignore)   'm'(misspelled) m
    email
        'a'(add)   'i'(ignore)   'm'(misspelled) i
    adress
        'a'(add)   'i'(ignore)   'm'(misspelled) m
    Misspelled words: [adress, contians, misspeled, teh]
```

19.2 Set Operators

A mathematical set is a good model of a Set collection. For applications, we often need the classical set operations union, intersection, and difference along with the logical operation subset. These enable us to identify how elements are shared between two sets. Let us review these operations using mathematical notation. Venn diagrams describe the results of the operations on two sets, A and B. For example, assume set A $= \{1, 3, 8, 9, 10\}$ and set B $= \{2, 3, 6, 9\}$.

A mathematical set has operations union, intersection, and difference.

Union(A, B)—Operation $A \cup B$:
The set of all elements x such that x is an element in set A or x is an element in set B.

   Example: $A \cup B = \{1, 2, 3, 6, 8, 9, 10\}$

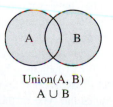

Union(A, B)
$A \cup B$

Intersection(A, B)—Operation A ∩ B:

    The set of all elements *x* such that *x* is an element in set A and *x* is an element in set B.

    Example: $A \cap B = \{3, 9\}$

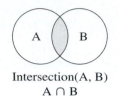

Intersection(A, B)
A ∩ B

Difference(A, B)—Operation A − B:

    The set of all elements *x* such that *x* is an element in set A but *x* is not an element in set B.

    Example: $A - B = \{1, 8, 10\}$

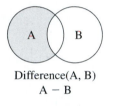

Difference(A, B)
A − B

Subset(A, B)—Operation A ⊆ B:

    A is a subset of B, provided each element *x* in A is also an element in B.

    An equivalent definition is $A \subseteq B$ iff $A \cap B \equiv A$.

    Example: $\{3, 8, 10\} \subseteq A$ (true) $\{2, 5, 6\} \subseteq B$ (false)

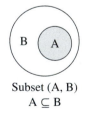

Subset (A, B)
A ⊆ B

Implementing Set Operators

The mathematical set operations of union, intersection, difference, and subset are not part of the `Set` interface or the concrete `TreeSet` and `HashSet` classes. A programmer must provide them as independent methods. They have important applications, however, so we take this opportunity to implement them. We treat them as binary operations and pass the operands `setA` and `setB` as `Set` arguments. In this way, the methods apply to both `TreeSet` and `HashSet` arguments. We assume that both arguments have the same collection type, either `TreeSet` or `HashSet`. The `subset()` method returns a boolean value that indicates whether the first argument is a subset of the second argument. For the other set operations, the `instanceof()` operator determines the type of the arguments and creates a return set collection of that type. The method implementations are given in the *Sets* class and use a standard design.

```java
public static <T> Set<T> setOp(Set<T> setA, Set<T> setB)
{
    Set<T> returnSet;

    // returnSet is a TreeSet or HashSet object depending on
    // argument type
    if (setA instanceof TreeSet<T>)
        returnSet = new TreeSet<T>();
    else
        returnSet = new HashSet<T>();

    . . .
}
```

Set Union   The method union() uses iterators to build the set union. The task is to scan each of the sets and use add() to insert elements in the return set, setUnion. The add() operation does not allow duplicates and so the union does not contain elements common to both sets.

union(setA, setB):

```java
public static <T> Set<T> union (Set<T> setA, Set<T> setB)
{
    Set<T> setUnion;

    // allocate concrete collection object for setUnion
    . . .

    // use iterator to add elements from setA
    Iterator<T> iterA = setA.iterator();
    while (iterA.hasNext())
        setUnion.add(iterA.next());

    // use iterator to add non-duplicate elements from setB
    Iterator<T> iterB = setB.iterator();
    while (iterB.hasNext())
        setUnion.add(iterB.next());

    return setUnion;
}
```

Set Intersection   To find the elements in the intersection of setA and setB, use an iterator to scan the first set. For each element, use contains() to check whether it is also in the second set. If so, the element is added to the setIntersection collection.

intersection(setA, setB):

```java
public static <T> Set<T> intersection (Set<T> setA, Set<T> setB)
{
    Set<T> setIntersection;
    T item;

    // allocate concrete collection object for setIntersection
    . . .
```

```
              // scan elements in setA and check whether they are
              // also elements in setB
              Iterator<T> iterA = setA.iterator();
              while (iterA.hasNext())
              {
                 item = iterA.next();
                 if (setB.contains(item))
                    setIntersection.add(item);
              }

              return setIntersection;
       }
```

Set Difference   The algorithm to find elements in the intersection extends to an algorithm for set difference. Use an iterator to scan the elements in set A. For each element, use
contains() to check whether it is also in the second set. If not, the element is added to
the setDifference collection.

difference(setA, setB):

```
       public static <T> Set<T> difference (Set<T> setA, Set<T> setB)
       {
          Set<T> setDifference;
          T item;

          // allocate concrete collection object for setDifference
          . . .

          // scan elements in setA and check whether they are
          // not in setB
          Iterator<T> iterA = setA.iterator();
          while (iterA.hasNext())
          {
             item = iterA.next();
             if (!setB.contains(item))
                setDifference.add(item);
          }

          return setDifference;
       }
```

Subset Relation   The usual definition of subset $(A \subseteq B)$ determines whether each element in set A is also in set B. For the subset() method, we use the equivalent definition,
$A \subseteq B$ iff $A \cap B \equiv A$. The algorithm returns true when intersection(setA, setB) is
identical with setA. An implementation of subset() verifies the condition by comparing
the size of setA with the size of the intersection.

subset(setA, setB):

```
       public static <T> boolean subset(Set<T> setA, Set<T> setB)
       {
          return intersection(setA, setB).size() == setA.size();
       }
```

Example 19.2

This example illustrates set operations. The TreeSet collections setA and setB have elements from the string arrays strArrA and strArrB respectively. Each tree set is a Set<String> interface reference.

```
String[] strArrA = {"green", "blue", "red", "yellow"},
         strArrB = {"black", "red", "green"};
Set<String> setA = new TreeSet<String>(),
            setB = new TreeSet<String>(), setC = null;
int i;
```

(a) Add the elements from the arrays into the sets.

```
for (i = 0; i < strArrA.length; i++)
    setA.add(strArrA[i]);
for (i = 0; i < strArrB.length; i++)
    setB.add(strArrB[i]);
```

Display the elements.

```
System.out.println("SetA: " + setA);
System.out.println("SetB: " + setB);
```

```
Output:
  SetA: [blue, green, red, yellow]
  SetB: [black, green, red]
```

(b) Use the set operations.

```
setC = Sets.union(setA, setB);
System.out.println("Set Union: " + setC);

setC = Sets.intersection(setA, setB);
System.out.println("Set Intersection: " + setC);

setC = Sets.difference(setA, setB);
System.out.println("Set Difference setA-setB: " + setC);

// setA-setB is a subset of setA
System.out.println("setA-setB is a subset of setB: " +
                        Sets.subset(setC, setA));
```

```
Output:
  Set Union: [black, blue, green, red, yellow]
  Set Intersection: [green, red]
  Set Difference setA-setB: [blue, yellow]
  setA-setB is a subset of setB: true
```

Application: Updating Computer Accounts

Assume the University Computer Center updates student accounts at the beginning of the fall semester. The administrator collects the names of students who want an account for the current year and stores them in the set `currAcct`. A second set, called `oldAcct`, is the collection of accounts that were active during the previous academic year. The update process involves creating new accounts for first-time users of the system, deleting obsolete accounts that will no longer be active in the current year, and copying the carryover accounts for students wishing to maintain access to the system. The operation `setUnion()` identifies the student accounts that must be processed. The operations of `setIntersection()` and `setDifference()` identify the students for each of the update activities.

Update Accounts: All accounts from the previous year and the current year that must be processed by the Computer Center to update the system.

     `updateAcct = Sets.union(currAcct, oldAcct);`

New Accounts: Accounts for the current year that were not active in the previous year.

     `newAcct = Sets.difference(currAcct, oldAcct);`

Obsolete Accounts: Accounts in the previous year that are not active in the current year.

     `obsoleteAcct = Sets.difference(oldAcct, currAcct)`

Carryover Accounts: Accounts that were active in the previous year and will continue to be active in the current year.

     `carryOverAcct = Sets.intersection(oldAcct, currAcct);`

PROGRAM 19.2 UPDATING COMPUTER ACCOUNTS

Let us look at a program that updates computer accounts. Assume the login name identifies each account. The administrator creates five sets containing the login names as string elements.

```
Set<String> oldAcct = new TreeSet<String>(),
            currAcct = new TreeSet<String>(),
            processAcct, newAcct, carryOverAcct, obsoleteAcct;
```

The method `readAccounts()` takes a file name and a set argument and reads names from the file and adds them to the set. This method is responsible for creating the scanner object. In our case, we call `readAccount()` to input account names for the sets `oldAcct` and `currAcct` from the files *oldacct.dat* and *curracct.dat* respectively. The values of the other four sets are the results of set operations. After completing the update, output statements provide a description of each set and its elements.

```
import java.io.*;
import java.util.Scanner;
import ds.util.Sets;
import ds.util.TreeSet;
import ds.util.Set;
```

```java
public class Program19_2
{
    public static void main(String[] args)
    {
        // declare sets for current and new computer accounts
        Set<String> oldAcct = new TreeSet<String>(),
            currAcct = new TreeSet<String>(), processAcct,
            newAcct, carryOverAcct, obsoleteAcct;

        // input names from file into the set
        try
        {
            readAccounts("oldAcct.dat", oldAcct);
            readAccounts("currAcct.dat", currAcct);
        }
        catch(IOException ioe)
        {
            System.err.println("Cannot open account file");
            System.exit(1);
        }

        // use set union to determine all accounts to update
        processAcct = Sets.union(currAcct, oldAcct);

        // use set intersection to determine carryover accounts
        carryOverAcct = Sets.intersection(currAcct, oldAcct);

        // use set difference to determine new
        // and obsolete accounts
        newAcct = Sets.difference(currAcct, oldAcct);
        obsoleteAcct = Sets.difference(oldAcct, currAcct);

        // output statements provide a set description
        // and a list of elements in the set
        System.out.println("Old Accounts:       " +
                            oldAcct);
        System.out.println("Current Accounts:   " +
                            currAcct);
        System.out.println("Process Accounts:   " +
                            processAcct);
        System.out.println("New Accounts:       " +
                            newAcct);
        System.out.println("Carryover Accounts: " +
                            carryOverAcct);
        System.out.println("Obsolete Accounts:  " +
                            obsoleteAcct);
    }

    public static void readAccounts(String filename,
                            Set<String> t) throws IOException
```

```
    {
        Scanner sc = new Scanner(new FileReader(filename));
        String acctName;

        // input the set of current accounts
        while(sc.hasNext())
        {
            acctName = sc.next();
            t.add(acctName);
        }
    }
}
```

```
Run:
   Old Accounts:        [fbrue, gharris, lhung, tmiller]
   Current Accounts:    [ascott, fbrue, wtubbs]
   Process Accounts:    [ascott, fbrue, gharris, lhung, tmiller,
                         wtubbs]
   New Accounts:        [ascott, wtubbs]
   Carryover Accounts:  [fbrue]
   Obsolete Accounts:   [gharris, lhung, tmiller]
```

Operations with Ordered Sets

In the previous section, we implemented the general set methods using "brute-force" algorithms. For instance, with set union, iterators scan each of the two operand sets and use add() to insert all of the elements into the return set. The behavior of the add() method assures us that the union does not have duplicate values.

For TreeSet collections, we can take advantage of the ordering provided by the iterators to more efficiently implement the set operations. Let us look at an algorithm for set intersection. Algorithms for set union, difference, and subset are left as exercises.

The ordered set-intersection algorithm uses iterators to make a pairwise scan of the elements in the two sets. At each step, a comparison is made between elements and if a match occurs, the value belongs to the intersection. An example illustrates how iterators traverse the two sets. Assume that lhsIter and rhsIter are iterators for the two operands and that the corresponding values are lhsValue and rhsValue. Initially, the iterators reference the first element in their respective sets.

If a set is ordered, the intersection of two sets can be computed by using iterators that scan each set.

- If lhsValue < rhsValue, then lhsValue is not an element in the intersection, and we can move the iterator lhsIter forward to the next element in its set. For instance, 3 < 7 and so lhsIter proceeds to element 9.

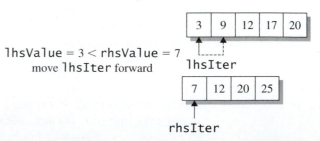

- If rhsValue < lhsValue, then rhsValue is not an element in the intersection. Move the iterator rhsIter forward to the next element in its set. For instance, 7 < 9 and so rhsIter proceeds to element 12.

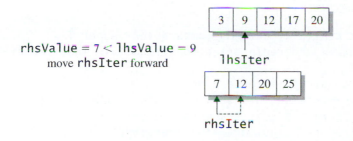

- If lhsValue == rhsValue, the two sets have a common value. After inserting the value into the intersection, move both iterators forward to the next element in their respective sets. For instance, iterators lhsIter and rhsIter find a match at 12. Look at the before and after locations for the iterators.

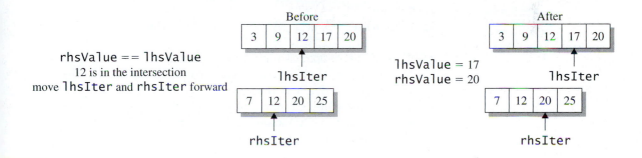

   The algorithm terminates when we exhaust the values in one of the lists. In the example, lhsIter completes the scan first after identifying that 20 is also a value in the intersection.

   The static method orderedIntersection() in the Sets class implements the algorithm. The private method advance() takes an Iterator argument and, if another value exists in the corresponding set collection, moves the iterator forward and returns the next value. The method returns null when no elements remain.

advance():

```
// if more elements remain, return the next value; otherwise,
// return null
private static <T> T advance(Iterator<T> iter)
{
    T value = null;

    if (iter.hasNext())
        value = iter.next();

    return value;
}
```

The method `orderedIntersection()` takes two `TreeSet<T>` arguments and has the compiler determine whether the generic type implements `Comparable`. The method `advance()` handles most of the details.

orderedIntersection():

```
public static <T extends Comparable<? super T>>
TreeSet<T> orderedIntersection(TreeSet<T> lhs,TreeSet<T> rhs)
{
    // construct intersection
    TreeSet<T> setIntersection = new TreeSet<T>();
    // iterators that traverse the sets
    Iterator<T> lhsIter = lhs.iterator(),
                rhsIter = rhs.iterator();
    T lhsValue, rhsValue;

    lhsValue = advance(lhsIter);
    rhsValue = advance(rhsIter);

    // move forward as long as we have not reached the end of
    // either set
    while (lhsValue != null && rhsValue != null)
    {
        if (lhsValue.compareTo(rhsValue) < 0)
            // lhsValue < rhsValue; move to next value in lhs
            lhsValue = advance(lhsIter);
        else if (rhsValue.compareTo(lhsValue) < 0)
            // rhsValue < lhsValue; move to next value in rhs
            rhsValue = advance(rhsIter);
        else
        {
            // lhsValue == rhsValue; add it to intersection and
            // move to next value in both sets
            setIntersection.add(lhsValue);
            lhsValue = advance(lhsIter);
            rhsValue = advance(rhsIter);
        }
    }

    return setIntersection;
}
```

The algorithm for the intersection of two ordered sets has a linear running time.

Complexity of orderedIntersection()   Assume that n_{lhs} and n_{rhs} are the number of elements in lhs and rhs. Each iteration of the loop makes one or two comparisons which we assume occur in O(1) running time. We must make at most $n_{lhs} + n_{lhs}$ comparisons, so the algorithm has worst-case running time O($n_{lhs} + n_{rhs}$). The algorithm is linear with respect to the total number of elements in the two sets.

19.3 Maps

A map is a collection that stores data as a key-value pair, called an *entry*. The key component of an entry is an object that uniquely identifies the element. The value component is an object that has information associated with the key (Figure 19.4).

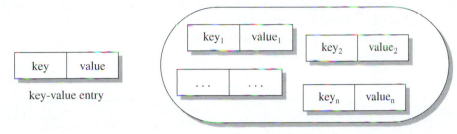

key-value entry

Map as a collection of n entries

Figure 19.4 *A Map entry is a key-value pair. A map is a collection of entities.*

To retrieve an element, the user supplies the key and the map collection returns the associated value. In this way, a map resembles an `ArrayList` structure in which the key is like an index that can be used to identify an element. The analogy goes only so far. In an `ArrayList`, the index is an integer in the range 0 to $n-1$, where n is the size of the sequence. The index is not part of a list element but is an external value that is used to reference the position of the element in the sequence. In a map, the key is stored internally as one of the components of an entry. Because the key provides access to a value associated with the key, a map is sometimes called an *associative array*.

> A map stores data in entries, which are key-value pairs. A key behaves like an array index to locate the corresponding value in the map. As a result, we call a map an *associative array*.

The Map Interface

An entry in a map is a key-value pair in which the key and value may have different object types. In creating a map collection, we use two type arguments for the key and the value types. We have chosen the name K for the key type and V for the value type and parameterized the `Map` interface using the notation `Map<K,V>`. The `Map` interface defines the operations that specify a map collection whose keys are of type K and whose values are of type V. The interface is very different from the `Collection` interface, which describes methods available in all of our previous collection classes. Some similarity remains. The methods `size()` and `isEmpty()` provide information about the number of entries in a map, and `clear()` removes all of the entries from the map. Differences begin to appear when we want to check whether an element is in the map and when we want to delete an element. The `Map` interface methods are `containsKey()` and `remove()`, and they use only the key as an argument.

Two access methods `get()` and `put()` allow an application to use a map as an associative array. The `get()` method takes a key as an argument and returns the value component or `null` if the element is not in the map. The `put()` method has two arguments for the key and the value. If no element matches the key, then the entry (key, value) is added to the map. If a match occurs, then the value argument is assigned as the new value component of

> The Map interface defines methods get() and put(), which access and modify a value using the key.

the entry. The latter case updates the entry. The method `put()` returns the previous value associated with the key, or `null` if there was no entry in the map.

A map does not have an iterator to scan its elements. This feature is provided by a new data structure called a *collection view*. Two methods, `keySet()` and `entrySet()`, return the keys and the entries in a map as a set. These sets are not actual `TreeSet` or `HashSet` collections. Rather, they are abstract objects with all of the `Set` interface operations that act on the map as a *backing collection*. For instance, using `remove()` with a key set element removes the corresponding entry in the map. An iterator with an entry set object scans the actual entries in the map. We provide a detailed discussion of collection views in Section 19.4. The following is a partial API listing of the `Map` interface. The remaining API listings deal with the map collection views.

---

interface Map<K,V> (partial)		*ds.util*

void	`clear()`	
	Removes all mappings from this map.	
boolean	`containsKey(Object key)`	
	Returns `true` if this map contains a mapping for the specified key.	
boolean	`isEmpty()`	
	Returns `true` if this map contains no key-value mappings.	
V	`remove(Object key)`	
	Removes the mapping for this key from this map if present. Returns the previous value associated with specified key or `null` if there was no mapping for key.	
int	`size()`	
	Returns the number of key-value mappings in this map.	
	<div align="center">Access/Update Methods</div>	
K	`get(Object key)`	
	Returns the value to which this map maps the specified key or `null` if the map contains no mapping for this key.	
V	`put(K key, V value)`	
	Associates the specified value with the specified key in this map. Returns the previous value associated with key or `null` if there was no mapping for key.	

The Ordered Map TreeMap

We will define two `Map` collection classes that use a binary search tree and a hash table respectively as the underlying storage structure. There is an obvious parallelism with sets. The tree version, called `TreeMap`, is an ordered collection that accesses elements in the ascending order of its keys. The class implements the `OrderedMap` interface that includes the methods `firstKey()` and `lastKey()`, which return the value corresponding to the minimum and maximum key respectively. We will discuss the unordered map collection `HashMap` in Chapter 21. As with other collection types, maps have a `toString()` method that returns a string representation of the elements. The string is a comma-separated list of entries enclosed in braces ("{ }"). Each entry has the format *key* = *value*.

class TreeMap<K,V> implements OrderedMap<K,V>		ds.util
	Constructor	
	TreeMap() Creates an empty ordered map. The key type K must implement Comparable.	
	Methods	
V	**firstKey**() Returns the value associated with the entry that has the minimum key.	
V	**lastKey**() Returns the value associated with the entry that has the maximum key.	
String	**toString**() Returns a comma-separated list of entries enclosed in braces ("{ }"). Each entry has the format *key = value*.	

Example 19.3

This example looks at a TreeMap collection with entries that have the course name as a key and the course enrollment as the value. A map entry is a <String, Integer> pair.

1. A string array and an integer array have the data that will define entries in the TreeMap object tm. First, declare the collection and then use put() to insert the elements.

```
// arrays for three classes and their enrollment
String[] className = {"ECON 101","CS 173","ENGL 25"};
int[] enrollment = {85,14, 30};

// create a TreeMap object
TreeMap<String, Integer> tm = new TreeMap<String, Integer>();

// the key argument is a string from className
// and the value argument is the corresponding Integer
//object from enrollment
for(int i = 0; i < 3; i++)
    tm.put(className[i], enrollment[i]);
```

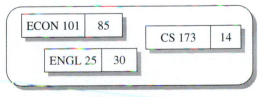

TreeMap tm

2. Display the size of the map and the list of elements using size() and toString().

```
System.out.println("Size of map is " + tm.size());
System.out.println("Initial map: " + tm);
```

Output:
```
Size of map is 3
Initial map: {CS 173=14, ECON 101=85, ENGL 25=30}
```

3. The methods get() and containsKey() use a key to access an element in the map. With get(), we return the value (enrollment) for "ECON 101." We use the argument firstKey() with get() to obtain the enrollment for the minimum key, which is "CS 173."

```
System.out.println("Enrollment in ECON 101 is " +
                   tm.get("ECON 101"));
System.out.println("Map contains MATH 51 " +
                   tm.containsKey("MATH 51"));
System.out.println("First course enrollment is " +
                   tm.get(tm.firstKey()));
```

Output:
```
Enrollment in ECON 101 is 85
Map contains MATH 51 false
First course enrollment is 14
```

4. Update the map by first doubling the enrollment for "CS 173." Then remove the entry with key "ENGL 25" from the map. After each operation, display the elements in the map.

```
// double enrollment in CS 173
int n = tm.get("CS 173");
tm.put("CS 173", n * 2);
System.out.println("Double COMP 173: " + tm);

// remove ENGL 25
tm.remove("ENGL 25");
System.out.println("After removing ENGL 25: " + tm);
```

Output:
```
Double COMP 173: {CS 173=28, ECON 101=85, ENGL 25=30}
After removing ENGL 25: {CS 173=28, ECON 101=85}
```

Application: A Student-Timecard Map

Map applications typically exploit the fact that the collection is an associative array and employ the put() method to insert and update elements. Let us illustrate this fact with an application that maintains information on the total time a student works at a part-time job during a school week. We store the information in the TreeMap object timecardMap in which an entry is a <String, Time24> pair. The key component of an entry is the student name and the value component is the accumulated time worked. The file *studwk.dat* consists of lines containing tab-separated data items that include the student name and the time worked during a specific day. The time is given with separate values for hour and minute.

```
<studentName> <hours worked> <minutes worked>
```

The file includes multiple entries for any student who works two or more days in the week. The program reads each line in the file, placing the name in the string `studName` and the time in the integer variables `workHour` and `workMinute`. With `studName` as the argument, a call to `get()` accesses the value for an entry in the map. If the return value is `null`, no entry is in the map. The method `put()` creates a new entry with the name as the key and a `Time24(workHour, workMinute)` object as the value. Otherwise, an entry already exists in the map and the return value is a `Time24` object indicating the total amount of time the student has worked in previous days. A call to `addTime()` with argument `workHour*60+workMinute` increments the `Time24` object and `put()` uses the updated time as the new value for the entry in the map.

For instance, assume student "Morris" has two entries in the file.

```
Morris  3   45
Morris  2   30
```

For the first file record, `timecardMap.get("Morris")` returns `null`. The `put()` method adds an entry for "Morris".

```
timecardMap.put("Morris", new Time24(3,45));
```

For the second file record, the `get()` method returns the `Time24` object 3:45. The object's value is increased by 150 minutes (2 hours, 30 minutes) to indicate additional time worked during the current day. The `put()` method uses the updated time as its value argument. The result is that the "Morris" entry is updated to have a new value component.

```
Time24 timeValue = timecardMap.get("Morris");      // time 3:45

// increment the time 150 minutes (2 * 60 + 30)
timeValue.addTime(2*60 + 30);                       // time 6:15

// update map entry with new Time24 value
timecardMap.put("Morris", timeValue);
```

PROGRAM 19.3 STUDENT WORK-TIME MAP

The program implements the Student-Timecard application. After reading the data from the file `studwk.dat` and updating entries in the `TreeMap` `timecardMap`, an output statement displays the map entries using `toString()`.

```
import java.util.Scanner;
import java.io.FileReader;
import java.io.FileNotFoundException;

import ds.util.TreeMap;
import ds.time.Time24;
```

```java
public class Program19_3
{
    public static void main(String[] args)
    {
        // a TreeMap object whose entries are a student name
        // and the total hours worked during a week;
        // use a Time24 object for the value component
        // of an entry
        TreeMap<String, Time24> timecardMap =
                new TreeMap<String,Time24>();
        Time24 workTime, timeValue;

        // object used to input the data from file "studwk.dat"
        Scanner fin = null;

        try
        {
            fin = new Scanner(new FileReader("studwk.dat"));
        }
        catch (FileNotFoundException fnfe)
        {
            System.err.println("Cannot open \"studwk.dat\"");
            System.exit(1);
        }

        // variables to store input data
        String studName, endStuff;
        int workhour, workminute;

        // input successive lines in the file consisting of the
        // student name and the scheduled work time
        while (fin.hasNext())
        {
            studName = fin.next();
            // get hours and minutes from the input line
            workhour = fin.nextInt();
            workminute = fin.nextInt();

            workTime = new Time24(workhour, workminute);

            // access the entry corresponding to the student name
            timeValue = timecardMap.get(studName);

            // if timeValue is null, we have a new entry with a
            // Time24 object as the value
            if (timeValue == null)
                timecardMap.put(
                    studName, new Time24(workhour, workminute));
```

```
                else
                // update the current Time24 value and put entry back
                // into the timecardMap
                {
                        timeValue.addTime(workhour*60 + workminute);
                        timecardMap.put(studName, timeValue);
                }
        }

        // display the timecardMap
        System.out.println("Student-Time: " + timecardMap);
    }
}
```

```
File: "studwk.dat"
Tolan  4 15
Dong   3 00
Tolan  3 15
Weber  5 30
Tolan  2 45
Brock  4 20
Dong   4 00
Dong   3 30
Tolan  3 15
Weber  2 30

Run:
   Student-Time: {Brock=4:20, Dong=10:30, Tolan=13:30, Weber=8:00}
```

Application: Computer Software Products

In a map, the value component is often a simple object of type `String`, `Integer`, `Time24`, and so forth. The value, however, can also be a collection object. For instance, a registrar may define a map of `<String, LinkedList<Course>>` entries in which the key is the student ID and the value is a linked list of courses taken by the student during the current semester. A map can have entry elements in which the value component is an `ArrayList`, a `Set` collection, or even another Map collection.

The value in a map that is associated with a key can be another collection, such as a set or a linked list.

We will now develop an application that uses a `TreeMap` collection to store the names of computer software vendors and their products. For instance, the vendor "Microsoft" has products that include "Excel", "Visual Studio.NET", and so forth. The map entries are `<String, TreeSet<String>>` pairs. The vendor name is the key and the value component is an ordered set of associated products. By using tree-based collection classes, we can list the vendors in ascending order and their products in ascending order.

PROGRAM 19.4 COMPUTER SOFTWARE PRODUCTS

This program uses the TreeMap object softwareMap to store the names of software vendors and their products. The value field for an entry in the map is a TreeSet with the product names as its elements. The file *product.dat* contains a series of records that give the vendor name and product name as strings. A tab separates the vendor from the product.

For each record in the file, the method get() with the vendor name as a key attempts to retrieve the set of vendor products. If the return value is null, the program first creates a new TreeSet<String> object as an empty set of products. The action guarantees that a TreeSet object is associated with the vendor. The set may be empty or have products from prior entries. Use add() to insert the new product in the set and then call put() to create a new map entry or to update an existing entry. The program concludes by using toString() to display the contents of the map. In the process, toString() for TreeSet objects is called to list the products in ascending order.

The name of a software product may contain one or more blank characters; for example, "Visual C++". A Scanner object by default uses whitespace as delimiters, and a blank is a whitespace character. The program creates a Scanner object fin that defines only tab, newline, and return to be delimiters using the statement

```
fin = new Scanner(new FileReader("product.dat"));
fin.useDelimiter("[\t\n\r]+");
```

The argument for the method useDelimiter() is a string that defines a pattern called a *regular expression*. In this case, [\t\n\r]+ defines a pattern that consists of one or more tab, carriage return, or newline characters. The '+' symbol denotes "one or more". For instance, a single tab character matches the pattern, as does a string of three consecutive tab characters.

```
import java.io.FileReader;
import java.io.FileNotFoundException;
import java.util.Scanner;
import ds.util.TreeMap;
import ds.util.TreeSet;

public class Program19_4
{
    public static void main(String[] args)
    {
        // softwareMap holds entries that are
        // (String, TreeSet<String>) pairs
        TreeMap<String, TreeSet<String>> softwareMap =
            new TreeMap<String, TreeSet<String>>();
        Scanner fin = null;
        TreeSet<String> prodSet;
        String company, product;

        try
        {
            fin = new Scanner(new FileReader("product.dat"));
            fin.useDelimiter("[\t\n\r]+");
        }
        catch (FileNotFoundException fnfe)
```

```
        {
            System.err.println("Cannot open \"product.dat\"");
            System.exit(1);
        }

        while(fin.hasNext())
        {
            // get company and product names
            company = fin.next();
            product = fin.next();
            // return value (set) corresponding to company name
            prodSet = softwareMap.get(company);

            // if no entry exists, create an empty set
            if (prodSet == null)
                prodSet = new TreeSet<String>();

            // add product name to the set; then add entry with
            // company as key and prodSet as value
            prodSet.add(product);
            softwareMap.put(company, prodSet);
        }
        // display contents of the softwareMap
        System.out.println(softwareMap);
    }
}
```

```
File <product.dat> with tab-separated data
Microsoft    Visual C++
Borland      C++ Builder
Microsoft    Word
Ramsoft      EZJava
Borland      J Builder
Adobe        Photoshop
Microsoft    Excel
Adobe        Illustrator
```

Run:
```
    {Adobe=[Illustrator, Photoshop], Borland=[C++ Builder,
    J Builder], Microsoft=[Excel, Visual C++, Word],
    Ramsoft=[EZJava]}
```

19.4 Map Collection View

A map does not have an iterator for accessing its elements. This task is left to other objects, called *collection views*, which are sets that support the methods in the Set interface but act on the original map as the *backing collection*. Let us first develop an intuitive understanding of a collection view. For example, suppose we have a collection of airports and flights departing from each airport. Each flight is an Integer object denoting the flight number (Figure 19.5).

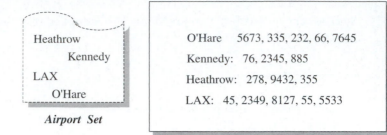

Figure 19.5 *Airport is a collection view of the airport flight map.*

The set of airports is a view of the collection. Think of the set as a list of elements that "look in on" the actual elements in the map collection.

A map collection view is a collection that contains data in the actual map. Operations on elements of the view actually perform operations on the map data. The map is the backing collection.

Set operations access and update the backing collection. For instance, calling `remove()` for the airport set with "LAX" as the argument removes the corresponding airport and flights from the map collection. This interaction goes the other way. Removing an airport and its flights from the map has the effect of removing the airport element from the set.

In the Map interface, the method `keySet()` returns a set of keys in a map. This collection view implements the `Set` interface.

```
Set<String> keys = airports.keySet();
```

Note that you must use the interface name `Set` as the reference type for the key set collection view objects. A collection view is not an independent `TreeSet` or `HashSet` collection, but rather is an object that belongs to a class which is defined within the specific map class. The available methods for a collection view object are defined by the `Set` interface and reference properties and elements in the backing collection.

The Key Set Collection View

A keySet() view is a set of keys in the map. Deleting a key from the set removes the corresponding entry from the map.

A key set views the map and its entries in terms of the keys without regard for the value components. Figure 19.6 illustrates a key set collection view of a map whose entries are `<String, Integer>` pairs. A key set has access to all of the methods in the Set interface. For instance, using a key set with the `contains()` method determines whether the map has an entry with the specified key. The action is the same as the map `containsKey()` method. Using `clear()` with a key set object deletes all of the entries in the map and sets its size to 0. A key set iterator scans the map by sequentially accessing the entry keys. If the backing collection is a `TreeMap`, the iterator scans the entries in ascending order of their keys. The iterator `remove()` method deletes the corresponding map entry.

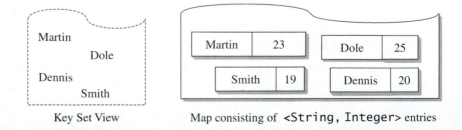

Key Set View · Map consisting of **`<String, Integer>`** entries

Figure 19.6 *A key set views map entries in terms of their keys.*

A key set always maintains an up-to-date view of the map keys. The size of the key set is the current size of the map. If a map operation inserts or deletes an element, the key set view changes.

A key set reference variable must have reference type `Set`. This is important. The variable cannot be used with the operator `new` to create a collection object; rather, the variable must be initialized by the map method `keySet()`. It then has access to a toolbox of operations defined by the `Set` interface. The operations deal directly with the map and its entries.

Example 19.4

This example uses the map and key set in Figure 19.6. The map has `<String, Integer>` entries that are designed to store a person's name and age. The key set comprises strings corresponding to the keys in the map.

1. Start out by declaring the map `tm` as a `TreeMap` collection. The key set is initialized as the return value from the map method `keySet()`. In this way, the map is responsible for the view of itself.

   ```
   TreeMap<String, Integer> tm = new TreeMap<String, Integer>();
       . . .
   Set<String> keys = tm.keySet();
   ```

2. The size of the key set always corresponds to the size of the map. The `Set remove()` method with argument "Dennis" deletes the entry "Dennis = 20" from the map. This adjusts the size of both the key set and the map.

   ```
   System.out.println("Before deleting 'Dennis'," +
                       "size of key set is " + keys.size());
   keys.remove("Dennis");
   System.out.println("After deleting 'Dennis'," +
                       "size of map is " + tm.size());
   System.out.println("After deleting 'Dennis'," +
                       "size of key set is " + keys.size());
   ```

   Output:
   ```
   Before deleting 'Dennis', size of key set is 4
   After deleting 'Dennis', size of map is 3
   After deleting 'Dennis', size of key set is 3
   ```

3. The map uses `put()` to add a new entry `<"Reich", 21>`. The key set views the updated map dynamically. Use `toArray()` to reference the elements in the key set in ascending order before and after adding the new entry.

   ```
   System.out.println("Key set before adding 'Reich': " +
           Arrays.toString(keys.toArray()));
   tm.put("Reich",21);
   System.out.println("Key set after adding 'Reich': " +
           Arrays.toString(keys.toArray()));
   ```

   Output:
   ```
   Key set before adding 'Reich': [Dole, Martin, Smith]
   Key set after adding 'Reich': [Dole, Martin, Reich, Smith]
   ```

4. A key set iterator scans the elements in a collection view and uses the iterator `remove()` method to delete the map entries that have a key with exactly five letters. The resulting map is displayed.

```
Iterator<String> iter = keys.iterator();
while (iter.hasNext())
{
    String name = iter.next();
    if (name.length() == 5)
        iter.remove();
}

System.out.println("After iterator scan, map is " + tm);
```

Output:
  After iterator scan, map is {Dole=25, Martin=23}

Note

Key View add() Method

The Set interface defines an `add()` operation and so a map class must implement the method for its key view. This is a formal requirement even though the operation does not make sense. You do not insert only a key into the map; a key-value pair must be inserted using the map put() method. Faced with implementing a method that should never be called, map classes simply include code that throws an UnsupportedOperationException for the key set add().

The Entry Set Collection View

In the `Map` interface, a second view, called an *entry set*, is the set of key-value entries which is returned by the map method `entrySet()`. You need some details about map notation to effectively use an entry set. Elements in a map implement the `Entry` interface. The identifier "Entry" is defined as an interface within the `Map` interface. Internally, a map class implementation declares a class that implements the `Map.Entry` interface. The elements in the map are instances of this class. The `Map.Entry` interface defines three methods `getKey()`, `getValue()`, and `setValue()`, which access and update components in a map entry. Note that the method `setKey()` is not defined. It would allow a program to update the key and thus destroy the map. The method `entrySet()` returns a set of `Map.Entry` objects.

```
Set<Map.Entry<String, Integer>> entries = tm.entrySet();
```

Entries in a map are objects that implement Map.Entry. It defines methods getKey() getValue() setValue()

interface Map.Entry<K,V>		*ds.util.Map*
K	**getKey**()	
	Returns the key corresponding to this entry.	
V	**getValue**()	
	Returns the value corresponding to this entry.	
V	**setValue**(V value)	
	Replaces the value corresponding to this entry with the specified value. Returns the old value corresponding to the entry.	

An entry set views the elements in a map as a set of key-value pairs. Operations on this set affect the map in the same way that a key view can be used to modify a map. As with a key set view, this set is not an independent TreeSet or HashSet collection but is an object that belongs to a class that is defined within the specific map class. Like the key set view of a map, an entry set does not allow the add() operation. If add() is called, the entry set throws the UnsupportedOperationException. The set can be used to define iterators that scan the elements in the map. Entry set iterators provide us the equivalent of map iterators with the ability to access an entry's key component and both access and update an entry's value component. In particular, the iterator method remove() removes an entry from the map.

> The map entrySet view is a set of Map.Entry objects from the backing map. Operations on the set affect the map.

Entry Set Iterators   You can use the Set methods size(), isEmpty(), clear(), and so forth with an entry set. These operations are typically handled by the corresponding map methods. The primary task of an entry set is to provide iterators that scan the elements in the map. At any point in the iteration, the iterator references a Map.Entry element in the map and the programmer can use the Map.Entry interface methods to access the components. Let us illustrate these ideas with a map that stores <String, Time24> entries. Assume the map confTimeMap represents conference activities and their scheduled times.

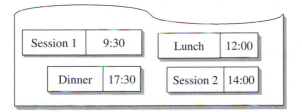

Map with <String, Time24> entries

```
// create map and add entries
TreeMap<String, Time24> confTimeMap =
        new TreeMap<String, Time24>();

confTimeMap.put("Session 1", new Time24(9,30));
confTimeMap.put("Session 2", new Time24(14,00));
confTimeMap.put("Lunch", new Time24(12,0));
confTimeMap.put("Dinner", new Time24(17,30));
```

Creating an iterator to scan the elements in the map is a two-step process. Begin by defining an entry set for the map. Then create an iterator for the entry set.

```
// declare an entry set for map confTimeMap
Set<Map.Entry<String,Time24>> entries = confTimeMap.entrySet();

// declare an iterator for the entry set using Set iterator()

Iterator<Map.Entry<String, Time24>> iter = entries.iterator();
```

Using the iterator to access and update elements in the map involves visiting each entry as a Map.Entry object and employing the methods getValue() and setValue() to first identify the value of the entry and then to change its value. To illustrate the process, assume the conference is delayed so that all of the day's activities must be pushed forward by one half hour. After using the iterator method `next()` to extract an entry, `addTime()` increases the `Time24` value component by 30 minutes.

```java
// use a loop to scan the entries in the map
while (iter.hasNext())
{
    // extract the next element as a Map.Entry object
    Map.Entry<String, Time24> me = iter.next();

    // the value component (me.getValue()) is a Time24 object;
    // add 30 minutes and assign the new value to the entry
    Time24 t = me.getValue();
    t.addTime(30);
    me.setValue(t);
}
```

The iterator can also use the key component when scanning map elements. For instance, suppose we want to list only the sessions and their starting time. We can use the same iteration pattern. Visit each element as a `Map.Entry` object and then use `getKey()` to access the key component which has String type. Below, we illustrate the use of foreach to implicitly iterate through the elements in the entry set.

```java
// use a foreach loop to scan the entries in the map and
// output the starting time of each conference session
for (Map.Entry<String,Time24> i : entries)
{
    // the key component (me.getKey()) is a String object;
    // check if it contains the substring "Session"; if so,
    // output name and time
    String activity = i.getKey();
    if (activity.indexOf("Session") != -1)
        System.out.println("Activity  " + activity +
            "     Starting time " + i.getValue());
}
```

```
Output:
   Activity   Session 1    Starting time 10:00
   Activity   Session 2    Starting time 14:30
```

Application: Building a Concordance

A map is an ideal structure for building a concordance.

A *concordance* is a software tool that reads a text file and extracts all of the words along with the line numbers on which the words appear. Compilers often provide a concordance to evaluate the use of identifiers (including keywords) in a source code file. This application designs and implements such a concordance. It provides an excellent example of maps.

Problem Analysis   A concordance accepts a string parameter that specifies the name of the source file. The tool extracts all of the identifiers and displays them in an alphabetized list that includes the identifier, the number of lines in the file containing the identifier, and the line numbers on which the identifier appears. An identifier is a string that begins with a letter ("A"–"Z", "a"–"z") and is followed by zero or more other characters that are a letter or a digit ("0"–"9"). The concordance outputs the information for an identifier in the following format.

```
identifier        n:  l₁  l₂  l₃  .  .  .  lₙ
```

where n is the number of lines containing the identifier and $l_i(i \geq 1)$ is the list of line numbers on which it appears.

Program Design   A concordance uses a `TreeMap` of `<String, TreeSet<Integer>>` entries. An identifier string is the key component of an entry and the set of line numbers is the value component. By using a `TreeMap`, we can list the identifiers in ascending order. By using a `TreeSet` as the value component of an entry, we are assured that multiple occurrences of an identifier on a line are recorded only once and line numbers will be listed in ascending order.

The concordance algorithm uses a Scanner object to input a line at a time from the source code file. We introduce concepts from the `Pattern` class to extract identifiers from the input line. Each identifier is the key component for an entry in the map. An integer variable, `lineNumber`, maintains the current line number in the source file. Having the scanner input an entire line simplifies the task of maintaining the correct line number. After extracting an identifier, the algorithm must update the map. This involves accessing the map to determine whether the identifier is already included as an entry. If not, the algorithm inserts a new entry with the identifier as the key. In any case, the current line number is added as an `Integer` object in the value (`TreeSet`) component of the entry.

The overall design of a concordance algorithm involves addressing three tasks: recognizing an identifier, updating the map, and displaying the results in the specified format. Let us look at these tasks separately. The implementation of the methods is included in a listing of Program 19.5.

- *Recognizing an Identifier:* We introduce concepts from the Pattern class to extract identifiers from an input line. The Java API for the class gives a rather detailed explanation of how a programmer extracts strings that match a regular expression. We briefly describe the process. A regular expression that defines an identifier is "[a-zA-Z][a-zA-Z0–9]*". The expression says that an identifier begins with a lower-case or an uppercase letter ([a-zA-Z]) followed by zero or more occurrences of a letter or a digit ([a-zA-Z0–9]*). The static `Pattern` class method `compile()` converts a regular expression to a `Pattern` object.

  ```
  Pattern identifierPattern = Pattern.compile(
          "[a-zA-Z] [a-zA-Z0-9]*");
  ```

  The instance method `matcher()` combines with the the Pattern object to take a character sequence (string) as an argument and to create a `Matcher` object that can scan the character sequence and identify subsequences that match the pattern.

  ```
  Matcher matcher = identifierPattern.matcher(inputLine);
  ```

  The `matcher` object is a list of identifiers. It uses the method `find()` to locate the next identifier, that is, the next sub-sequence that matches the regular expression.

The method returns false is no match occurs; if true, the identifier can be extracted as a substring with an index range denoted by `matcher.start()` to `matcher.end()`.

```
while (matcher.find())
{
    identifier = inputLine.substring(matcher.start(),
                                     matcher.end());
}
```

For instance, if inputLine = `"value = 2 * arr[i]"`, then

First find():   start() = 0 end() = 5   "value" = inputLine.substring(0, 5)

Second find(): start() = 12 end() = 15   "arr" = inputLine.substring(12, 15)

Third find():   start() = 16 end() = 17   "i" = inputLine.substring(16, 17)

- *Updating the Map:* We use the identifier as a key with the `get()` method to access the value of an entry in the map. If the return value is `null`, the identifier is not in the map. A new `TreeMap` must be created with the identifier as the key and an empty `TreeSet` object as the value. In either case, add the line number to the set, and use `put()` to update the map. The process of updating the map occurs each time we extract an identifier from the source file.

- *Displaying the Concordance:* The method `writeConcordance()` displays the concordance. The method makes use of the entry set collection view and an iterator to scan the entries. The `Map.Entry` method `getKey()` provides access to the identifier. The method `getValue()` returns the set of line numbers in which the identifier appears. The size of the set is the number of line numbers, and a listing of the elements in the set gives the line numbers in ascending order.

PROGRAM 19.5 SOURCE FILE CONCORDANCE

The program creates a concordance and then outputs the identifiers, number of lines, and line numbers. All of this is done in the method `concordance()`. The main program prompts the user to enter the name of the file and then calls `concordance()` for the results.

```java
import java.io.*;
import java.util.regex.*;
import java.util.StringTokenizer;
import java.util.Scanner;
import ds.util.*;

public class Program19_5
{
    private static Pattern identifierPattern =
                        Pattern.compile("[a-zA-Z][a-zA-Z0-9]*");

    public static void main(String[] args) throws IOException
    {
        String filename;
        Scanner keyIn = new Scanner(System.in);
```

```java
      // get the file name
      System.out.print("Enter the file name: ");
      filename = keyIn.nextLine();
      System.out.println();

      // create the concordance
      concordance(filename);
   }

// builds concordance and calls writeConcordance()
// for output
public static void concordance(String filename)
      throws IOException
{
   // concordance map and set for line numbers
   TreeMap<String, TreeSet<Integer>> concordanceMap =
                  new TreeMap<String, TreeSet<Integer>>();
   TreeSet<Integer> lineNumbers;
   String inputLine, identifier;
   int lineNumber = 0;

   // create scanner to input from document file
   Scanner fin = new Scanner(new FileReader(filename));
   Matcher matcher = null;

   // read the file a line at a time
   while(fin.hasNext())
   {
      // get next line
      inputLine = fin.nextLine();
      lineNumber++;

      // create matcher to find identifiers in inputLine
      matcher = identifierPattern.matcher(inputLine);

      // extract identifiers until end of line
      while (matcher.find())
      {
         identifier = inputLine.substring(matcher.start(),
                                    matcher.end());

         // get value (TreeSet) from entry with
         // identifier as key; if it does not exist (null),
         // create TreeSet object
         lineNumbers = concordanceMap.get(identifier);
         if ( lineNumbers == null )
            lineNumbers = new TreeSet<Integer>();

         // add a new line number to set of line numbers
         lineNumbers.add(lineNumber);
```

```
                              concordanceMap.put(identifier, lineNumbers);
            }
        }

        // output the concordance
        writeConcordance(concordanceMap);
    }

    public static void
    writeConcordance(TreeMap<String,TreeSet<Integer>> map)
    {
        Set<Map.Entry<String,TreeSet<Integer>>> entries =
                map.entrySet();
        TreeSet<Integer> lineNumberSet;
        Iterator<Map.Entry<String,TreeSet<Integer>>> iter =
                entries.iterator();
        Iterator<Integer> setIter;
        int i;

        while (iter.hasNext())
        {
            Map.Entry<String,TreeSet<Integer>> e = iter.next();
            System.out.print(e.getKey());              // output key

            // pad output to 12 characters using blanks
            if (e.getKey().length() < 12)
                for (i=0; i < 12 - (e.getKey().length()); i++)
                    System.out.print(' ');

            // extract the value component as a TreeSet
            lineNumberSet = e.getValue();

            // display number of lines containing the
            // identifier and the actual lines
            System.out.print(formatInt(4, lineNumberSet.size()) +
                            ":     ");
            setIter = lineNumberSet.iterator();
            while (setIter.hasNext())
                System.out.print(setIter.next() + "    ");
            System.out.println();
        }
        System.out.println();
    }

    // private method formatInt() with integer arguments
    // w and n; returns a formatted string with integer n
    // right-justified in a field of w spaces; used to line up
    // output in concordance
    private static String formatInt(int w, int n)
    { . . . }
}
```

```
File "concord.txt"
    int m = 12, n = 14;
    double a = 3, b = 2, hypotenuse

    if (n <= 5)
        n = 2*m;
    else
        n = m * m;
    hypotenuse = sqrt(a*a + b*b);
```

Run:

```
    Enter the file name: concord.txt

    a                 2:    2   8
    b                 2:    2   8
    double            1:    2
    else              1:    6
    hypotenuse        2:    2   8
    if                1:    4
    int               1:    1
    m                 3:    1   5   7
    n                 4:    1   4   5   7
    sqrt              1:    8
```

Recording Each Occurrence of an Identifier

Note

A concordance can record each occurrence of an identifier by including duplicate line numbers in the listing. The implementation simply needs to use an `ArrayList` as the object type for the value component of a map entry. In the output format, n indicates the number of occurrences of the identifier.

Chapter Summary

- The set and map collections store and retrieve data by value rather than by position. A set is a collection of values in which each value is unique. A map is a collection of key-value pairs that associate a key with a value. In a map, there is only one value associated with a key. Both collections implement fast insertion and retrieval of data.

- The TreeSet class implements the OrderedSet interface. Its iterators traverse the set data in sorted order. A simple spell checker illustrates the use of the class.

- The chapter discusses how to implement the set operations of union, intersection, difference, and subset for arbitrary sets and implements an algorithm for ordered set intersection. The algorithm exploits the fact that ordered set iterators traverse a set in order.

- The TreeMap class is a concrete implementation of the OrderedMap interface. A map stores key-value pairs (entries). In each pair, we say the value is associated with the key.

A map is often called an *associative array* because applying the get() method with a key as its argument returns the value associated with the key. The put() method adds data to the map or updates it. If no key-value pair with the specified key is in the map, it inserts one for the key and the value; otherwise, it replaces the value in the map by the specified value. In an ordered map, data is stored internally in order, and the methods firstKey() and lastKey() return the least and greatest keys in the map. Applications that deal with student timecards and the maintenance of computer software products illustrate the concept of a map.

- A map has collection views and does not have an iterator. To sequence through a map, the programmer must extract either a keySet view or an entrySet view. A keySet view is a set containing all the keys in the map, and an entrySet view is a set containing all the entries (key-value pairs) in the map. The map is the backing collection; that is, all operations on an object in a collection view access the actual data in the map. Apply a set iterator to traverse a view. The set method remove() removes the corresponding entry from the map, as does the set iterator method remove(). The add() method cannot be used with a collection view. Because TreeMap is an ordered map, its keySet() and entrySet() methods return an ordered set. An application that builds a word concordance illustrates the collection views of a map.

Written Exercises

1. A TreeSet<Character> collection, strSet, contains the characters from string "bowler". List the resulting output.

        System.out.println(strSet); // [_____]

2. The following Venn diagrams illustrate different set components that result when combining three sets. In each part (a)–(c), describe the shaded regions in terms of union, intersection, and difference for sets A, B, and C.

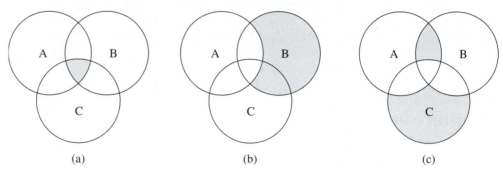

(a)   (b)   (c)

3. Study the following complete program.

```
import ds.util.ArrayList;
import ds.util.TreeMap;

public class Test
{
    public static void main(String[] args)
    {
        int[] intArr = {15, 51, 12, 7, 2379};
        TreeMap<Integer, ArrayList<Integer>> m =
```

```
            new TreeMap<Integer, ArrayList<Integer>>();
        int i, j, n;
        ArrayList<Integer> arr;
        Integer nObj = null;

        for(i = 0; i < intArr.length; i++)
        {
            n = intArr[i];
            j = 2;
            nObj = intArr[i];
            arr = new ArrayList<Integer>();
            do
            {   if (n % j == 0)
                {   arr.add(j);
                    n = n/j;
                }
                else
                    j++;
            }
            while (n > 1);

            m.put(nObj, arr);
        }
        System.out.println(m);
    }
}
```

(a) Determine the output of the program.

(b) If you replace the contents of `intArr` with any set of positive integer values, describe what the output will be.

4. Use the array `strList` of strings along with a `TreeMap<String, Integer>` object `mLength` to write code segments that perform designated tasks. The map contains key-value pairs whose key is the string and whose value is the string length.

```
String[] strList = {"store", "map", "array", "set",
                    "string"};
TreeMap<String,Integer> mLength =
    new TreeMap<String,Integer>();
int i;
```

(a) Write a loop that enters each string from the array into the map as a key-value pair.

(b) Obtain an entrySet view of `mLength` and output all strings whose length is 5.

5. Prove that S = U if and only if S ⊆ U and U ⊆ S.

6. Assume `setA` and `setB` are `Set<Character>` objects consisting of the distinct letters found in strings `strA` and `strB`, respectively. The exercise uses expressions that combine set operations. For instance, consider the expression

```
setC = Sets.intersection(setA, Sets.union(setA, setB));
```

The elements in `setC` are identical to those in `setA`.

(a) Assign to `setC` all of the characters in the two strings that are not found in both strings.

(b) Declare a set called `setVowels` that contains the letters "a", "e", "i", "o", and "u". Assign to `setD` all vowels that are not found in `strA`.

(c) Assign to `setE` all vowels that are in either `setA` or `setB`.

(d) Assign to `setF` the consonants that are in the strings.

7. Prove that a set S is a subset of set U if and only if $S \cup U = U$.

Programming Exercises

8. Write a program that declares three `TreeSet<Integer>` objects `setA`, `setB`, and `setC`. Assign to `setA` all integer values from 0 to 14. Assign to `setB` 10 random `Integer` values in the range 0 to 14.

(a) Display the size and the elements for `setB`.

(b) Using set methods, assign to `setC` the elements in `setA` that are not also in `setB`. Display elements in `setC`.

9. (a) Implement the private method `output()` that outputs a set. For each line, except possibly the last, display five set elements.

```
private static void output(Set<?> s)
{ ... }
```

Access the set elements using an iterator, `iter`, which you should declare as follows:

```
Iterator<?> iter = s.iterator();
```

(b) At a university the athletic program includes

Men's Sports: {football, baseball, basketball, golf, swimming, tennis, volleyball, water polo}

Women's Sports: {softball, basketball, soccer, swimming, water polo, volleyball, cross country, field hockey}

Write a program that creates sets `menSet<String>` and `womenSet<String>` that contain the sports for men and women at the university. Using `output()`, display each set and a list of the sports in which both men and women participate.

10. Write a program that creates a `TreeMap<String, String>` map, containing the following key-value pairs.

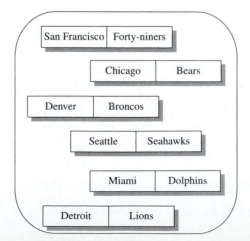

Perform the following actions with the map.

- Output the size of the map and the name of the team in Chicago.
- Change the name of the San Francisco team to "Niners."
- Output whether San Diego has a team in the map.
- Remove Denver from the map.
- Insert the Dallas Cowboys in the map.
- Using an entry set iterator, scan the map and remove all teams in a city beginning with the letters "M"–"Z".
- Output the final map.

11. Using an iterator, implement a static version of the method addAll() that forms the union of a set and elements in a collection and returns the result as a Set.

```
public static <T> Set<T> addAll(Set<T> s,
                  Collection<? extends T> c)
{ . . . }
```

The wildcard notation "? extends T" refers to any type that is a subtype of T. In this situation,

? "is a" T

If you use an iterator to traverse Collection c, declare it as follows:

```
Iterator<? extends T> iter = c.iterator();
```

In a program, create a TreeSet<String> with elements from string array strArrA and an ArrayList with elements from array strArrB. Use addAll() to create a TreeSet that is a union of the set and array list. Output the results.

```
String strArrA[] = {"dog", "cat", "tiger", "pig"},
       strArrB[] = {"frog", "dog", "monkey", "pig", "snake"};
```

12. (a) Assume c is a Collection. Implement the method removeDuplicates() by declaring a set and copying the elements from c into the set. Then clear c and copy the nonduplicate elements from the set back to c.

```
public static <T> void removeDuplicates(Collection<T> c)
{ . . . }
```

(b) Write a program that declares an Integer LinkedList with initial values copied from the array arr{6, 7, 7, 2, 9, 7, 6, 6}. Use the removeDuplicates() to order the list. Output the elements of aList.

13. Modify the concordance algorithm from Program 19.5 to record each occurrence of an identifier. The concordance outputs the information for an identifier in the following format.

```
identifier          n:  l₁  l₂  l₃  l₄  . . .
```

where n is the number of occurrences of the identifier in the source file and l_i ($i \geq 1$) is an ordered list of line numbers on which the identifier occurs. If an identifier occurs $k \geq 1$ times on a line, its line number appears k times in the list.

14. (a) Using the method `orderedIntersection()` for ordered set collections from Section 19.2 as a guide, implement the following methods that have a linear running time.

    ```
    public static <T extends Comparable<? super T>>
    TreeSet<T> orderedUnion(TreeSet<T> lhs,TreeSet<T> rhs)
    { ... }
    ```

    ```
    public static <T extends Comparable<? super T>>
    TreeSet<T> orderedDifference (TreeSet<T> lhs,
                                        TreeSet<T> rhs)

    { ... }
    ```

    ```
    public static <T extends Comparable<? super T>>
    boolean orderedSubset (TreeSet<T> lhs,TreeSet<T> rhs)
    { ... }
    ```

    (b) Write a program that implements the statements in Example 19.2.

15. (a) The symmetric difference of set A and set B is defined as the set of all elements x that are contained in either A or B but not in both. Using set operations, implement the method `symDifference()`, which that takes `setA` and `setB` as arguments and returns the symmetric difference.

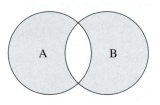

    ```
    public static <T> Set<T>
    symDifference(Set<T> setA, Set<T> setB)
    { ... }
    ```

    (b) Design and execute a program that tests your code for `symDifference()`.

16. Write a program that declares a `TreeMap` whose key-value pairs are a state name and a `LinkedList` of city names. Create a file *statecity.dat* that contains the following listing of states and cities. A tab separates the state and city.

    ```
    Arizona Phoenix
    Illinois Chicago
    Illinois Peoria
    Nevada Reno
    Illinois Evanston
    California Sacramento
    California Arcata
    Mississippi Natchez
    Indiana Gary
    ```

    For each pair, check whether the state is already a key of a map entry. If so, add the city to the linked list value field. Otherwise, create a new entry with the state and city as data. When you have finished, create an entry set and use an iterator to output each state followed by the list of cities from the state.

17. (a) Implement the MyInteger class.

```java
// class that stores an int value
public class MyInteger implements Comparable<MyInteger>
{
    private int value;

    // create an instance with n as the value
    public MyInteger(int n)
    { ... }

    // getter - setter methods access value
    public void setValue(int n)
    { ... }
    public int getValue()
    { ... }

    // add +1 to the data member value
    public void increment()
    { ... }

    public String toString()
    { ... }

    // compares objects by comparing their value
    public int compareTo(MyInteger n)
    { . . . }
}
```

(b) Write a program that declares a TreeMap collection intCount. An entry in the map will be a MyInteger key and a MyInteger value in which the key field represents an int value and the value field represents a count for the number of occurrences of the int value in the key. The program uses a random number generator to produce 10,000 integers in the range 0–9. For each random integer k, create a new map entry if k does not correspond to a map key; otherwise increment the value field for the map entry corresponding to k. Use the map to output the frequency of each integer in the range 0–9.

Programming Project

18. Modify the concordance algorithm in Program 19.5 to record each occurrence of an identifier. The concordance outputs the information for an identifier in the following format.

$$\text{identifier} \qquad n: \quad l_1(m_1) \quad l_2(m_2) \quad l_3(m_3) \quad l_4(m_4) \quad \ldots$$

where n is the number of occurrences of the identifier in the source file and $l_i(m_i)$ ($i \geq 1$) is the list of distinct line numbers (l_i) with m_i indicating the number of occurrences of the identifier on line l_i.

ORDERED SET AND MAP
IMPLEMENTATION

CONTENTS

20.1 IMPLEMENTING
THE TREESET CLASS

20.2 IMPLEMENTING THE
TREEMAP CLASS
The TreeMap Class Design
Key Access to an Entry
Updating an Entry
Removing an Entry

Complexity of Insertion and
Deletion in TreeSet and TreeMap

20.3 IMPLEMENTING A
COLLECTION VIEW
Examining a View
Implementing a View
The keySet Collection View

As the names imply, the `TreeSet` and `TreeMap` collection classes store elements in a binary search tree. Inserting and deleting an item uses the search order of the tree and has $O(\log_2 n)$ efficiency. A binary search tree iterator traverses elements in ascending order. In this chapter, we will develop implementations for these collection classes. Emphasis is on the `TreeMap` class, which uses a search tree of pairs. We will discuss in some detail how a collection view is implemented. The analysis will firm up your abstract understanding of a collection view.

20.1 Implementing the TreeSet Class

In Chapter 18, we developed the `STree` class. Our purpose was to create a collection class that would focus on the design features of a binary search tree and employ many of its algorithms and operations. As you have come to appreciate from our discussion of sets in Chapter 19, the design of the `STree` class very closely resembles the `TreeSet` class. This is intentional. We designed the `STree` class so that it implements the `Set` interface. These facts were never mentioned in Chapter 18 because we had not yet introduced the `Set` and `OrderedSet` interfaces. For all practical purposes, we can simply replace the name "STree" with "TreeSet" and have a collection class in our framework. As a summary we list the interface methods that essentially define the `TreeSet` class. Figure 20.1 displays a UML diagram that details the methods defined by `Set` and `OrderedSet`. The `Set` interface diagram shows only the `add()` method, whose action differs from that of the other `Collection` interface methods. It specifies that the collection contains only one instance of any object.

The implementation of `TreeSet` uses STNode objects to store the elements. The STNode class is defined as a private static inner class within TreeSet. The modifier "static" indicates that the inner class variables

Figure 20.3 illustrates a TreeMap with solid lines connecting a node to its children and a dotted line connecting a node to its parent.

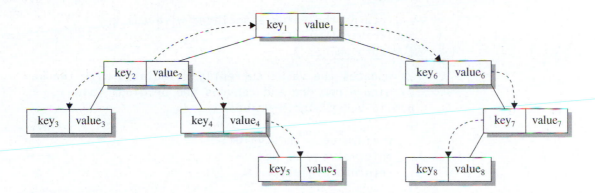

Figure 20.3 *Map as a tree of key-value pairs (Entry objects).*

The class Entry is defined as a static inner class within the TreeMap class. It implements the Map.Entry interface. The class is designated as static because it makes no reference to any variables in the outer class TreeMap. All of the features of the Entry class are shown in the following declaration of the class, including a constructor and the method toString() that returns a representation of an instance in the form *key=value*.

> Entry Is an inner class in the TreeMap class and implements the Map.Entry interface.

Entry as an inner class within TreeMap:

```
public class TreeMap<K,V> implements OrderedMap<K,V>
{
    . . .

    // declares a binary search tree node object
    private static class Entry<K,V> implements Map.Entry<K,V>
    {
        // node data
        K key;
        V value;

        // child links and link to the node's parent
        Entry<K,V> left, right, parent;

        // constructor that initializes the value and parent
        // fields and sets the link fields left and
        // right to null
        public Entry(K key, V value, Entry<K,V> parent)
        {
            this.key = key;
            this.value = value;
            left = null;
            right = null;
            this.parent = parent;
        }
```

```
                    // returns the key
                    public K getKey()
                    { return key; }

                    // returns the value associated with the key
                    public V getValue()
                    { return value; }

                    // updates the value currently associated with the key
                    // with a new one and returns the original value
                    public V setValue(V value)
                    {
                       V oldValue = this.value;
                       this.value = value;
                       return oldValue;
                    }

                    // used by TreeMap toString() to list the pair
                    // as  "key=value"
                    public String toString()
                    { return key + "=" + value; }
                 }
              }
```

The TreeMap Class Design

The TreeMap class builds a binary search tree of Entry objects. The private instance variable root is a reference to an Entry node that defines the search tree. Two integer variables mapSize and modCount maintain the size of the collection and the number of tree modifications (insertions and deletions). The class constructor creates an empty map and toString() displays the entries as a comma-separated list of elements enclosed in braces ("{", "}"). Each element has the form *key=value* The other methods implement OrderedMap interface operations. Figure 20.4 shows a UML diagram that illustrates the design of the TreeMap class. The

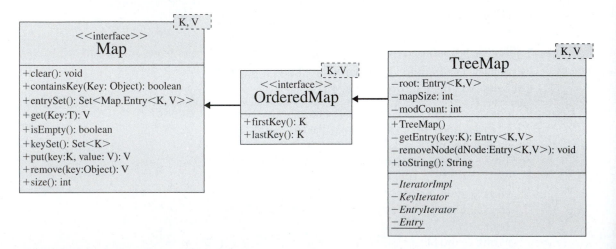

Figure 20.4 *Design of the TreeMap class.*

inner classes `IteratorImpl`, `KeyIterator`, and `EntryIterator` are discussed in Section 20.3 in conjunction with the collection views of a map.

The following is a skeletal declaration of the `TreeMap` class that includes an implementation of the constructor.

TreeMap class—basic design structure:

```
public class TreeMap<K,V> implements OrderedMap<K,V>
{
    // root defines the search tree of Entry nodes
    private Entry<K,V> root;

    // size of the map
    private int mapSize;

    // modCount maintains a record of changes to the
    // map for iterators
    private int modCount;

    // constructor creates an empty map
    public TreeMap()
    {
        root = null;
        mapSize = 0;
        modCount = 0;
    }

    < Methods defined by the OrderedMap interface >
    . . .

    // declares a binary search tree node object
    private static class Entry<K,V> implements Map.Entry<K,V>
    { . . . }
}
```

Key Access to an Entry

Map methods such as `get()`, `containsKey()`, and `remove()` use a key argument to access an entry in the map. We provide access with the private method `getEntry()`, which takes a key and searches the tree for a pair with the specified key. It returns a reference to the key-value pair in the tree or `null` of it failed to locate an entry with the key. The `getEntry()` method is the search engine that provides low-level access to the entry nodes based only on the key.

Private method `getEntry()` takes a key and returns the Entry object or null if the map does not contain the key.

getEntry():

```
    // iteratively traverse a path from the root to the entry
    // key; return a reference to the node containing key or null
    // if the search fails
    private Entry<K,V> getEntry(K key)
    {
        // scan variable entry references the current node
        // in the traversal
```

```
Entry<K,V> entry = root;
int orderValue;

// terminate on an empty subtree
while(entry != null)
{
    // compare item and the current node value based on
    // the key
    orderValue = ((Comparable<K>)key).compareTo(entry.key);

    // if a match occurs, return true; otherwise, go left
    // or go right following search tree order
    if (orderValue == 0)
        return entry;
    else if (orderValue < 0)
        entry = entry.left;
    else
        entry = entry.right;
}
return null;
}
```

The method containsKey() indicates whether an entry with the specified key is in the map. Its implementation is a direct application of getEntry(). It simply returns true if the return reference is nonnull and false otherwise.

containsKey():

Use getEntry() to implement the methods get() and containsKey().

```
// returns true if this map contains an entry with the
// specified key
public boolean containsKey(Object key)
{
    return getEntry((K)key) != null;
}
```

Access to the value component of a key-value pair is provided by the method get(). After calling getEntry() to locate the entry, the method returns null or the contents of the value field depending on whether the entry is in the map. The contents are accessed using the method getValue().

get():

```
// returns the value corresponding to key
public V get(K key)
{
    Entry<K,V> p = getEntry(key);

    if (p == null)
        return null;
    else
        return p.getValue();
}
```

Updating an Entry

For a map, the put() operation with arguments for the key and the value serves a dual purpose. It adds a new entry or it updates the value field for an existing entry. The algorithm is the binary search tree insertion algorithm. Start at the root and search down a path using search tree ordering. If a match occurs, then an entry with the specified key is already in the map. Simply use setValue() with the value argument to update the value field in the matching entry. Otherwise, the scan ends in an empty tree, which becomes the insertion location. Create an Entry object with the specified key and value arguments and add the new node.

put():

```java
// associates the specified value with the specified key in
// this map; returns the previous value associated with the
// key, or null if there was no mapping for key
public V put(K key, V value)
{
    // entry is current node in traversal, parent the
    // previous node
    Entry<K,V> entry = root, parent = null, newNode;
    int orderValue = 0;

    // terminate on an empty subtree
    while(entry != null)
    {
        // update the parent reference
        parent = entry;
        // compare key to the current node key
        orderValue = ((Comparable<K>)key).compareTo(entry.key);

        // if a match occurs, replace the value in entry
        // and return the previous value; otherwise, go left
        // or go right following search tree order
        if (orderValue == 0)
            return entry.setValue(value);    // return; put() is
                                             // an update
        else if (orderValue < 0)
            entry = entry.left;
        else
            entry = entry.right;
    }

    // create the new node
    newNode = new Entry<K,V>(key, value, parent);

    if (parent == null)
        // this is the first node added; make it root
        root = newNode;
    else if (orderValue < 0)
        // attach newNode as the left child of parent
        parent.left = newNode;
```

```
else
    // attach newNode as the right child of parent
    parent.right = newNode;

// increment the tree size and modCount
mapSize++;
modCount++;

// the return is the value of a matching entry; returning
// null indicates we added a new pair to the tree
return null;
}
```

Removing an Entry

The implementation of remove() uses getEntry() to determine if there is a key-value pair in the map with the specified key. If there is, the private method removeNode() takes a reference to the node and deletes it from the tree. The method removeNode() uses the deletion algorithm for binary search trees discussed in Section 18.3. With remove(), we have some housekeeping to do. The size of the map is decremented, modCount is incremented, an the value of the deleted node is the return value.

remove():

```
// removes the entry containing key from this map
// if present
public V remove(Object key)
{
    // search tree for key
    Entry<K,V> dNode  = getEntry((K)key);

    if (dNode == null)
        return null;

    V returnObj = dNode.getValue();
    removeNode(dNode);

    mapSize--;
    modCount++;

    return returnObj;
}
```

Methods add() and remove() for a TreeSet and a TreeMap have average-case running time $O(\log_2 n)$.

Complexity of Insertion and Deletion in TreeSet and TreeMap

Because the TreeSet and TreeMap classes implement insertion and deletion using a binary search tree, the average running time for these operations is $O(\log_2 n)$. However, a binary search tree can be degenerate, so the worst-case running time for these operations is $O(n)$. We can guarantee uniform $O(\log_2 n)$ performance by using balanced trees such as a red-black tree or an AVL tree instead of a normal binary search tree. We will discuss balanced trees in Chapter 27.

20.3 Implementing a Collection View

In this section, we focus on the design and implementation of the keySet collection view for a map. The entrySet collection view will be discussed in Chapter 21 when we implement the HashMap collection. Understanding the difference between a collection and a collection view is critical. A collection is an object consisting of data and operations that specify elements and methods to access and update their values. A collection-view object does not have its own data. It uses the data in the *backing collection*. The view object does have operations, however, but these are tied to operations in the backing collection. They have the effect of accessing and updating elements in the backing collection. A keySet view for a map has operations that reference the key fields among the key-value elements in the collection. The keySet methods implement the Set interface but with the add() operation disallowed by having the method throw an exception.

Examining a View

The concept of a view is relatively straightforward. The implementation is more difficult since it involves specialized concepts and techniques. A very simple example illustrates the techniques. Extending them to the keySet collection view becomes a matter of details.

The class StoreOneTwo has data members one and two that hold integer values. A constructor initializes the values and toString() provides a representation of the object in the form *one=two*. The class defines the method setOneTwo() that allows the programmer to update the instance variables. Associated with the class we create an interface called *View*. The interface defines methods get() and set(), which may be used by a view object to access and update a field in the backing object.

View interface:

```
// an object that implements View has methods to access and
// update a data item in a backing object
public interface View
{
    int get();
    void set(int value);
}
```

> A view is an object that implements an interface and acts on the data in a backing collection.

The StoreOneTwo class defines the method viewOne(), which returns a View object that is associated with field one in a StoreOneTwo object. The method is responsible for creating an object of type View and for implementing the interface methods as they pertain to the variable one in StoreOneTwo, the backing collection. The following is an implementation of the StoreOneTwo class. Only the method header for viewOne() is included. Its implementation will be the focus of this section.

StoreOneTwo class:

```
public class StoreOneTwo
{
    // object has two integer fields
    private int one, two;

    // constructor; initialize data fields
    public StoreOneTwo(int one, int two)
    {
        this.one = one;
        this.two = two;
    }
```

```
// return a representation of the object
public String toString()
{ return one + "=" + two; }

// update the data fields
public void setOneTwo(int one, int two)
{
    this.one = one;
    this.two = two;
}

// object that is returned by viewOne()
private View viewObj = null;

// method returns a View object associated with field one
public View viewOne()
{ . . . }
}
```

Example 20.1

Before we look at an implementation of the method viewOne(), let us use it in an example. The StoreOneTwo object st has initial values 5 and 35. A call to viewOne() creates a View object that has access to the first field, variable one, in object st. The data values for st are displayed by using toString() and the value of its first field by using the view method get(). To illustrate how a view can modify data in the back object, we call set() and then display the updated values.

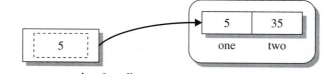

View v = st.viewOne()   st = new StoreOneTwo(5,35)

```
// create object and display its current values
StoreOneTwo st = new StoreOneTwo(5, 35);
System.out.println("Initial object st: " + st);

// use the View object v to access the first field in st
View v = st.viewOne();
System.out.println("Value viewed from st = " + v.get());

// use View object v to update the first field in st
v.set(25);
System.out.println("Update object st with View :  " + st);

// use setOneTwo() to update the object directly, then
// display the view of the object using v.get()
st.setOneTwo(3, 7);
System.out.println("Value viewed from updated st: " + v.get());
```

Output:
```
   Initial object st: 5=35
   Value viewed from st = 5
   Update object st with View:   25=35
   Value viewed from updated st: 3
```

Implementing a View

In the StoreOneTwo class, the method viewOne() returns an object that implements the
View interface. The object does not have its own data; rather, it relies on access to the variable one in a StoreOneTwo object. To create the View object returned by viewOne(), we
use an *anonymous inner class*; that is, an inner class that does not have a name. An anonymous inner class combines the declaration of an inner class with the creation of an instance
of the class in one step. In our example, the anonymous inner-class declaration creates a
variable that is an instance of a class that implements the View interface.

Prior to its implementation of the method viewOne(), the StoreOneTwo class declares
the instance variable viewObj of type View and assigns it the value null. The variable is instantiated in the method viewOne() as an object of anonymous class type that implements
the View interface. The body for the anonymous class is provided in a block that accompanies the declaration of viewObj. The anonymous class implements, View and so must implement the methods get() and set(), which access the variable one in the outer class.

In the implementation of viewOne(), the instance variable viewObj is instantiated
with the operation new View(). This looks strange since a variable cannot be instantiated
as an interface object. In fact, viewObj is not an interface object but rather an object of
anonymous class type that implements View.

```
// object that is returned by viewOne()
private View viewObj = null;

// method returns a View object that accesses the
// StoreOneTwo field one
public View viewOne()
{
    // we only generate one instance of the anonymous inner
    // class object
    if (viewObj == null)
        viewObj = new View()
            {
                // methods in the View interface
                public int get()
                { return one; }

                public void set(int value)
                { one = value; }
            };
    // return the object created by the method viewOne()
    return viewObj;
}
```

A collection view
is implemented
using an anony-
mous inner class.

☞

Note

Anonymous Inner Class

An anonymous inner class cannot have a constructor. The Java compiler creates one automatically. Also, an anonymous inner class can be built and immediately passed as a method parameter rather than assigning the anonymous object to a variable.

```
public ViewType viewCreate()
(   new ViewType()
    {
        <method declaration₁>
        <method declaration₂>
                ...
    }
);
```

Many Java development tools use anonymous inner classes to generate event listeners.

The keySet Collection View

The TreeMap class implements its keySet and entrySet views by returning an anonymous inner-class object that implements the Set interface and uses the map data.

In the TreeMap class, the method keySet() returns a collection view that implements the Set interface. Using the approach discussed in the previous section, we implement the method keySet() by creating an anonymous inner-class object and making it the return value.

```
private Set<K> keySet = null;

public Set<K> keySet()
{
    if (keySet == null)
    {
        keySet = new Set<K>()
        {
            public Iterator<K> iterator()
            {... }

            public int size()
            {... }

            public boolean contains(Object item)
            {... }

            public boolean remove(Object item)
            {... }

            public void clear()
            {... }
```

```
        public boolean isEmpty()
        {...}

        public boolean add(K key)
        {
            throw new UnsupportedOperationException();
        }

    };
}

    return keySet;

}
```

We must implement the methods defined in the interface. Remember that all of the methods work on the backing map collection. The `Set` methods `size()`, `isEmpty()`, and `clear()` have implementations that use the corresponding `TreeMap` methods. Note that when you use "this" in an inner class, it references the inner-class object. To reference "this" for the enclosing class, preface it by the name of the enclosing class followed by the "." operator. For instance, `TreeMap.this.size()` refers to the method `size()` in the `TreeMap` class. Here is the implementation for `size()` in the collection view.

keySet collection view size():

```
// access size in the backing map
public int size()
{ return TreeMap.this.size(); }
```

The methods `contains()` and `remove()` have a single `Object` argument. In the keySet view, the argument represents a key in a key-value entry in the map. Their implementations use corresponding `TreeMap` methods that require the key for their argument. For instance,

keySet collection view contains():

```
// use containsKey() to check if the entry with item
// as its key is in the map
public boolean contains(Object item)
{ return containsKey(item); }
```

The `Set` method `add()` requires special attention. Since it is in the interface, the method must be implemented. However, the `Set` `add()` operation makes no sense in the collection view. Inserting an object in `KeySet` should correspond to adding a key-value entry in the map. The object would become a key without any associated value. The implementation of `add()` in `KeySet` throws an `UnsupportedOperationException`, which has the effect of making the operation invalid.

The keySet and the entrySet collection view provide an iterator that scans the keys in the map. In the implementation of `keySet()`, the method `iterator()` returns an `Iterator` object of type `KeyIterator`. In the implementation of `entrySet()`, the return `Iterator` object is of type `EntryIterator`. Both of these `Iterator` classes must implement `next()`, `hasNext()`, and `remove()`. We simplify the task by creating a single generic iterator class `IteratorImpl<T>` that sequences through the key-value pairs in the map and implements all of the iterator methods except `next()`. The inner class `KeyIterator` is a subclass of the inner class `IteratorImpl` with generic type K. The class `KeyIterator` adds an implementation for `next()` that returns the next key in the map.

```
private class KeyIterator extends IteratorImpl<K>
{
    public K next()
    {...}
}
```

The inner class `EntryIterator` is a subclass of the inner class `IteratorImpl` with generic type `Map.Entry<K,V>`. This class adds an implementation for `next()` that returns the next key-value pair (Entry) in the map.

```
private class EntryIterator extends
IteratorImpl<Map.Entry<K,V>>
{
    public K next()
    {...}
}
```

You can find a complete implementation of the `TreeMap` class in the software supplement. The source code gives you a chance to explore in more detail the `EntrySet` collection view and the iterators for each view.

Chapter Summary

- The TreeSet class implements the OrderedSet interface by creating and maintaining a binary search tree.

- We implement an ordered map class, TreeMap, by using a binary search tree of key-value pairs. The method get() searches for an entry in the binary search tree having the specified key and returns the associated value. The method put() takes a key and a value as an argument and searches the tree for an entry containing the key. If it locates one, it updates its value to that of the argument and returns the original value; otherwise, it inserts the key and value as a new entry in the map and returns null.

- Implementing a map collection view involves using an anonymous inner class to create an object that implements the Set interface. All operations of this object occur with the actual data in the map, the backing collection.

Written Exercises

1. An `OrderedSet` can be realized by any class that implements the `Collection` interface and whose iterators traverse the data in order. The running times vary with the underlying collection. For each of the following collections, give the average-case running times for the following set operations.

	contains()	add()	remove()	first()	last()
OrderedList					
Sorted ArrayList					
Binary search tree					

2. A *multiset* is a set that allows duplicate elements. If you want to use a binary search tree to implement a multiset, what problems will you face?

3. Can you think of a way to use a TreeMap to implement a TreeSet?

4. Is it possible for the TreeMap class get() method to have worst-case behavior O(n)? Explain.

5. (a) What is an anonymous inner class?
   (b) Explain how an anonymous inner class is used to implement a collection view of a map.

Programming Exercises

For Programming Exercises 20.6 through 20.11, the TreeSet and TreeMap classes that you should modify are in the directory "ch20ex". For Programming Exercises 20.6, 20.7, and 20.11, the type of elements in a collection must be a subtype of a generic type T. We indicate this with the wildcard notation

```
<? extends T>
```

6. Implement a constructor for the TreeSet class that takes a Collection object, such as an ArrayList or LinkedList, and initializes the TreeSet with its elements.

```
// constructs a new set containing the elements in the
// specified collection
public TreeSet(Collection<? extends T> c)
{ ... }
```

Test the class by initializing a TreeSet from the elements of an ArrayList containing the Integer values $\{1, 7, 3, 5, 8, 15, 37, 19, 55\}$. Output the smallest and largest values in the set.

7. (a) Implement the following method of the TreeSet class.

```
// adds all of the elements in the specified collection
// to the set and returns true if the set changed as a
// result of the operation
public boolean addAll(Collection<? extends T> c)
{ ... }
```

   (b) If c is a mathematical set, what operation is implemented by addAll()?
   (c) Create a TreeSet s of Integer objects with values $\{7, 12, 15, 19, 53, 68, 3, 33,$ $57, 45, 25\}$ and a TreeSet t of Integer objects $\{22, 9, 15, 42, 53, 79, 3, 33, 97,$ $45, 25\}$. Using the method addAll(), insert all the members of t into s and output s.

8. (a) Implement the following method of the TreeSet class.

```
// retains only the elements in this set that are
// contained in the specified collection; in other words,
// removes from this set all of its elements that are not
// contained in the specified collection; returns true
// if the set changes as a result of the operation
public boolean retainAll(Collection<?> c)
{ ... }
```

(b) Which mathematical set, operation, union, intersection, or difference, corresponds to the collection set method `retainAll()`?

(c) Create a `TreeSet` s of `Integer` objects with values {7, 12, 15, 19, 53, 68, 3, 33, 57, 45, 25} and a `TreeSet` t of `Integer` objects {22, 9, 15, 42, 53, 79, 3, 33, 97, 45, 25}. Using the method `retainAll()`, find all the values common to both s and t.

9. (a) Implement the following method of the `TreeSet` class.

```
// removes all this set's elements that are also
// contained in the specified collection; after this
// call returns, this set will contain no elements in
// common with the specified collection; returns true
// if the set changes as a result of the operation
public boolean removeAll(Collection<?> c)
```

(b) Which mathematical set, operation, union, intersection, or difference, corresponds to the collection set method `removeAll()`?

(c) Create a TreeSet s of `Integer` objects with values {7, 12, 15, 19, 53, 68, 3, 33, 57, 745, 25} and a TreeSet t of `integer` objects {22, 9, 15, 42, 53, 79, 3, 33, 97, 45, 25}. Using the method `removeAll()`, find all the members of s that are not in t.

10. (a) The `TreeSet` inner class `IteratorImpl` initializes an iterator to begin at the smallest value in the binary search tree. If item is a value of type T, a more interesting problem is to initialize the iterator to begin at the smallest value in the tree $\geq$ item. Such a value is called a *lower bound*. For instance, the figure shows a binary search tree and indicates the position of an iterator marking the smallest value in the tree $\geq$ 25. Implement the required constructor using the following outline.

```
IteratorImpl(T item)
{
    // parent will reference the lower bound
    STNode<T> parent = null, curr = root;

    // cycle until we find an empty subtree
    while (curr != null)
        if (((Comparable<T>)item).compareTo(curr.nodeValue)
                            <= 0)
        {
            < item <= curr.nodeValue. record curr as a
              possible lower bound (curr = parent) and move
              to the left to look for an even smaller one >
        }
        else
            < keep the current parent and move right >
    nextNode = parent;
}
```

(b) Using the new `IteratorImpl` constructor in part (a), implement the following method of the `TreeSet` class.

```
// return an OrderedSet whose elements range from first,
// inclusive, to last, exclusive; that is, the elements
// lie in the range first <= element < last
public OrderedSet<T> subset(T first, T last)
{ ... }
```

For instance, if the set s contains values [5, 7, 9, 12, 15, 23, 35, 50, 55, 75, 100], then s.subset(14, 70) contains [15, 23, 35, 50, 55].

(c) Create a `TreeSet s` of `Integer` objects with values {7, 12, 15, 19, 53, 68, 3, 99, 33, 127, 57, 45, 25}. Using the method `subSet()`, obtain a `TreeSet` containing all members of `s` in the range from 53 to 120 and output the set.

(d) What is the average running time of `subSet()`? If we did not implement the new `IteratorImpl` constructor, what would be the running time of the algorithm?

11. (a) Implement the following method of the `TreeMap` class.

```
// constructs a new map containing the same mappings as
// the given map; the method runs in n*log(n) time
public TreeMap(Map<? extends K,? extends V> m)
```

Hint: Declare an iterator over the entry set for m and a `Map.Entry` object as follows.

```
Iterator<? extends ds.util.Map.Entry<? extends K,
    ? extends V>> iter = m.entrySet().iterator();
Map.Entry<? extends K,? extends V> entry;
```

(b) Create a map m1 containing the following key-value pairs:
{"California", "Sacramento"}, {"Nevada", "Carson City"},
{"Washington", "Olympia"}, {"Massachusetts", "Boston"},
{"Illinois", "Springfield"}, {"Arizona", "Phoenix"}, {"Texas", "Austin"},
{"New Mexico", "Santa Fe"}, {"New York", "Albany"},{"Oregon", "Salem"}
Create a second map m2 by using the constructor. Output the two maps.

12. (a) Implement the class `StateCities` that stores a state and a `LinkedList` of city names.

```
// object stores the state name and city in the state
public class StateCities
{
    private String state;
    private LinkedList<String> cities;

    public StateCities(String state,
        LinkedList<String> cities)
    { ... }

    // output the state and the cities in the format
    //    stateName: city1 city2 ... cityn
    public String toString()
    { ... }
}
```

(b) Add the method `getView()` to the class `StateCities` that returns a collection view of a `StateCities` object. The collection view should implement the following interface.

```
public interface StateCitiesView
{
    // obtain the state
    String getKey();
    // insert a new city if it is not already in
    // the object
    boolean add(String city);
    // is the city contained in the object?
    boolean contains(String city);
    // return the number cities in the object
    int size();
    // remove city from the object if it is present
    boolean remove(String city);
    // return an iterator over the cities in the object
    Iterator<String> iterator();
}
```

(c) Write a program that creates a `StateCities` object `arizona` containing the following data.

State: Arizona
Cities: Phoenix, Tucson, Flagstaff, Globe

Output the object `arizona` using `toString()`, and then add the following cities to `arizona`.

Ajo, Kingman, Tempe

Remove "Globe" from `arizona`. Output the number of cities in `arizona` and iterate through the object, displaying the names of the cities.

13. (a) In the `StoreOneTwo` class, implement `viewTwo()` that returns a `View` object, which accesses the data field `two`.

(b) The `ViewPair` interface defines operations on an object that contains two instance variables.

```
public interface ViewPair
{
    int getK();
    int getV();
    void setV(int value);
}
```

In the `StoreOneTwo` class, implement `viewPair()` that returns a `ViewPair` object, which accesses the two data fields.

(c) Write a program that tests your implementation of the two views `viewTwo()` and `viewPair()`.

Programming Projects

14. (a) A *multiset* is a set that allows duplicate values. Create the class `MultiSet` that uses the `LinkedList` class as the implementation structure for a multiset. The list does not have to be ordered, but make sure that duplicate values occur in consecutive list elements.

```
public class MultiSet<T> implements Collection<T>
{
    // multiset implemented using a linked list
    private LinkedList<T> multisetList;

    public MultiSet()
    { ... }

    public boolean isEmpty()
    { ... }

    public int size()
    { ... }

    // return the number of duplicate occurrences of item
    // in the multiset
    public int count (Object item)
    { ... }

    // search for item in the multiset
    public boolean contains(Object item)
    { ... }

    // add item to the multiset and return true
    public boolean add(T item)
    { ... }

    // removes all of the items from the collection
    public void clear()
    { ... }

    // attempt to remove a single instance of item and
    // return true if the item was erased
    public boolean remove(Object item)
    { ...}

    // erase all occurrences of item from the multiset
    // and return the number of items erased
    public int removeAll(Object item)
    { ... }

    public Iterator<T> iterator()
    { ... }
```

```
                    public Object[] toArray()
                    { ... }

                    // return a string in the format
                    //    value1 value1 ... value1
                    //    value2 value2 ... value2
                    //            ...
                    //    valuen valuen ... valuen
                    public String toString()
                    { ... }
                }
```

(b) A university computer lab maintains CDs that contain applications used by students. In a program, create a multiset containing the following software titles:

Visual C++	3 copies
Photoshop	2 copies
Excel	2 copies
Illustrator	2 copies
X-Win32	2 copies
EZJava	5 copies

Perform the following tasks:

- Output the multiset.
- Output the number of copies of "EZJava".
- Add the following title to the inventory.

Paint Shop Pro   3 copies

- The main computer center has decided to handle all spreadsheet applications. Remove "Excel" from the inventory.
- Iterate through the inventory and output the name of each CD.

15. The class `TreeSet2` duplicates the functionality of the `TreeSet` class. Implement the class `TreeSet2` by using a `TreeMap` variable and object composition.

```
        // set implemented using a TreeMap
        private TreeMap<T, Object> map;
```

A `TreeMap` is a collection of key-value pairs. To implement a set using a map, we are interested in the set of keys, but we must account for a value that corresponds to each key. Place an Object reference, PRESENT, as the value for each key in the map.

```
        // value for each key in the map
        private static final Object PRESENT = new Object();
```

Implement each method of TreeSet2 by calling a corresponding method for the embedded object, map. For instance, here is the implementation for the set add() method.

add():

```
public boolean add(T item)
{
   return map.put(item, PRESENT) == null;
}
```

Call the map put() method with item as the key and PRESENT as the value. A return value of null indicates that the map did not contain the key obj.

Test your class by running Program 19.2.

Chapter 21

HASHING AS A MAP IMPLEMENTATION

CONTENTS

21.1 HASHING
Using a Hash Function

21.2 DESIGNING HASH FUNCTIONS
Java Method hashCode()
User-Defined Hash Functions

21.3 DESIGNING HASH TABLES
Linear Probing
Chaining with Separate Lists
Rehashing

21.4 A HASH TABLE AS A COLLECTION

21.5 HASH CLASS IMPLEMENTATION
Hash add() and rehash() Methods

Hash remove() Method
Implementing the Hash Iterator

21.6 AN UNORDERED MAP COLLECTION
Accessing Entries in a HashMap
Updating Entries in a HashMap

21.7 AN UNORDERED SET COLLECTION
Implementing HashSet with
HashMap Methods

21.8 HASH TABLE PERFORMANCE
Evaluating Ordered and Unordered
Sets

An ArrayList collection allows direct access to an element, provided you know its position. Access is given by a mapping from the index position to the element. In this chapter, we present a new data structure called a *hash table* that stores elements by value (key) with a mapping that allows for "almost" direct access to an element from its key. The hash table distributes elements in a series of linked lists, referred to as *buckets*. A hash function maps a key to an index in the table. The function provides access to an element much like an index provides access to an array element. Like a binary search tree, a hash table provides an implementation of the Set and Map interfaces. We begin by discussing hash table concepts and algorithms, which we incorporated into the Hash class. The class and its implementation will consolidate your understanding of hash tables as very fast search and store collection. We use the design of the Hash class to implement the unordered HashMap and HashSet collections and conclude by discussing hash table performance. This will give you insights on when to use an ordered versus an unordered set or map in an application.

21.1 Hashing

A binary search tree can access data stored by value with $O(\log_2 n)$ average search time. Ideally, we would like to design a storage structure that approximates $O(1)$ average retrieval time. In this way, access to an item is independent of the number of other items in the collection. A hash table is such a structure. The table is an array of references. Associated with the table is a hash function that takes a key as an argument and returns an integer value that leads to a table index. To gain some understanding of a hash function, you can view a hash table as a storage array. Later, we will describe a more general table consisting of an array of references to linked lists.

A hash function returns an integer value, referred to as a *hash value*. By using the remainder after dividing the hash value by the table size, we have a mapping of the key to an index in the table. In the figure, the table size is *n*. A two-step process uses the hash function hf() to convert the key to an integer value and the "%" operator to telescope the value to an index in the range [0, n).

Search tree access to an element has $O(\log_2 n)$ running time. Access in a hash table is near $O(1)$.

Hash Value: $hf(key) = hashValue$
HashTable index: $hashValue \% n$

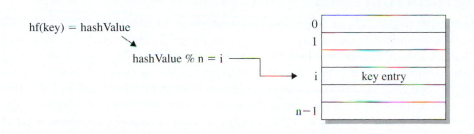

Using a Hash Function

Let us look at the behavior of a simple hash function in which the key is a nonnegative integer. The hash function $hf(x) = x$ is the *identity function*. The remainder after dividing *x* by *n* is the hash table index. Assume the table is the array tableEntry with $n = 7$ elements. The hash function takes key = 4 and maps it to tableEntry[4]. Key = 22 is mapped to tableEntry[1].

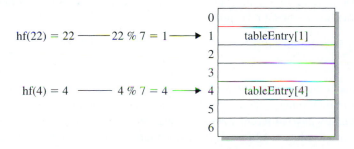

The need to divide the hash value by the table size can create a many-to-one association between items and a table entry. If two items have keys that differ by a multiple of 7, the hash process maps the items to the same table location. For instance, items with keys 22 and 36 map to index 1 in the table, and a *collision* occurs. Similarly, keys 5 and 33 map to the same index 5.

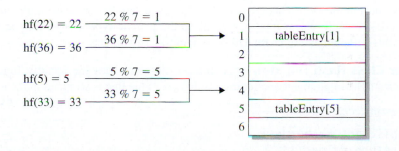

With hash function hf() and table size *n*, the table index for a key is $i = hf(key) \% n$. Collisions may occur.

A perfect hash function produces no collisions.

The presence of collisions does not indicate an error in the hash function. Treat it as a fact of life. Collisions will occur, and attempting to avoid them is often unrealistic. The problem is to design the hashing process so it efficiently handles collisions. We discuss this issue in the next two sections, where we design hash functions and the corresponding hash table.

21.2 Designing Hash Functions

A good hash function should uniformly map keys to table indices.

The identity function for an integer key is an example of a hash function. We need other functions for different types of keys. Some general design principles guide the creation of all hash functions. Evaluating a hash function should be efficient. The goal of the hashing process is efficient access to the corresponding table entry. A hash function's ability to compute the hash value efficiently is an important factor in attaining this goal. A hash function can produce collisions when the value is telescoped into the table range by using the % operator. Ideally, we would create a *perfect hash function* that produces no collisions. Short of this ideal situation, a hash function should produce *uniformly distributed hash values*. This spreads the hash table indices around the table, which helps minimize collisions.

Java Method hashCode()

Hash table applications involve elements that typically use strings or numeric values as the key. A design strategy must include hash functions that deal with integer, real, and string types. The field of algorithms provides extensive research on this topic. We limit our discussion to a small set of hash functions that meet our design criteria.

The Java programming language provides a general hashing function with the hashCode() method in the Object superclass.

Create a hash function by overriding hashCode() in the superclass Object.

```
public int hashCode()
{ . . . }
```

The implementation of this general hashCode() method converts the internal address of the object into an integer value. This has limited application because two different objects will normally have different values for hashCode(), even if they store the same data. For instance, hashCode() would produce distinct values for the following strings

```
// strings one and two are the same; not so for integer values
// one.hashCode() and two.hashCode()
String one = "java", two = "java";
```

Key Java classes such as String, Integer, and Double override hashCode() in the Object class with implementations that are based on the data in the object. As a result, we have access to predefined hash functions for most hash table applications. The presence of hashCode() in the Object superclass allows us to declare generic hash-table–based collection classes where the method is specific to the generic type. Let us look at the Java hashCode() implementations for Integer and String objects.

Integer Class Hash Function   The Integer class provides the identity function for hashCode(). The implementation returns the integer value that is wrapped in the object.

Integer hashCode:

```
public int hashCode()
{ return value; }
```

With an integer key, the identify function can serve as a good hash function, provided all or a portion of the number is random. Assume a television manufacturer marks its products with seven-digit serial numbers, in which the low-order five digits are random. Using a table with size $n \leq 10^k$ ($k \leq 5$), the identify hash function maps the serial number to a random table index.

The Integer class provides the identity hash function.

```
Integer tv = 682401;

// index for a serial number in a 10000-element table
tv.hashCode() % 100000 = 6824015 % 100000 = 24015
```

String Class Hash Function   In the majority of hash-table applications, the key is a string, such as a Social Security number, a license number, or a policy number. For instance, compilers often keep track of identifiers in a program by using a hash table. To create an efficient hash function, we must combine the sequence of characters in the string to form an integer. This task is carried out by the String class hashCode() method. The algorithm assumes that the class internally stores the n characters of the string in a character array. The following is the definition of the hash value for string str. Let s be the corresponding array with characters from the string and size $n =$ str.length(). The calculations include both multiplication and addition.

$$\text{hash} = s[0]*31^{n-1} + s[1]*31^{n-2} + \ldots + s[n-1]$$

The String class hashCode() method is implemented with a loop having n (string size) iterations. Note that the hash value of the empty string is zero.

String hashCode:

The hash function for a string combines the characters in some numeric calculations.

```
public int hashCode()
{
    int hash = 0;

    for (int i = 0; i < n; i++)
        hash = 31*hash + s[i];

    return hash;
}
```

Example 21.1

1. Let us trace the evaluation of hashCode() for the string key $=$ "and". The iterations deal with the characters "a," "n," and "d" in that order. Each iteration updates the integer value hash, which is initially 0. The ASCII value for 'a' is 97, for 'n' is 110, and for 'd' is 100.

```
'a':    hash = (0 * 31) + 97 = 97
'n':    hash = (97 * 31) + 110 = 3117
'd':    hash = (3117* 31) + 100 = 96727
```

2. The following are hash code values for three different strings. The value for string strB is a negative number due to integer overflow.

```
String strA = "and", strB = "uncharacteristically",
strC = "algorithm";

hashValue = strA.hashCode();    // hashValue = 96727
hashValue = strB.hashCode();    // hashValue = -2112884372
hashValue = strC.hashCode();    // hashValue = 225490031
```

☞

Note

Mapping a Hash Value to a Table Index

Calculations in a hash function may result in integer overflow and return a negative number. When we divide the hash value by the table size to determine a table index, the remainder cannot be negative. With a simple machine-level operation, we can ensure that the table index is nonnegative.

Computers store a signed integer using a storage scheme called *twos-complement*. In the format, the left-most bit determines the sign and is called the *sign bit*. When the sign bit is 0, the number is nonnegative, and when it is 1, the number is negative. If hashValue is the return value of the hash function, the expression

hashValue & Integer.MAX_VALUE

uses the bitwise "AND" operator "&" to retain all of the bits of the original hash value and set the sign bit to 0. Dividing this value by the table size produces a nonnegative table index.

tableIndex = (hashValue & Integer.MAX_VALUE) % tableSize

User-Defined Hash Functions

A class would override the method hashCode() only if instances of the class could serve as a key. We do this for the Time24 class. The hash value for an object is its time converted to minutes. Because hour and minute are normalized to fall within the ranges 0–23 and 0–59 respectively, each time is a unique positive value.

Time24 hashCode():

```
public int hashCode()
{
    // hash value is time in minutes; as normalized time,
    // value is positive
    return hour*60 + minute;
}
```

The hash function in the String class uses multiplication to create random values that limit collision. A function that simply added the ASCII values of the characters would result in the same hash value for the strings "dog" and "god". Similar calculations may be needed for integer keys. The integer identity function is a good hash function if low-order digits in the integer keys are random. When this is not true, too many collisions may occur. For instance, suppose a television manufacturer stamps each item with a serial number that uses the last four digits to record the year in which the item is made. If the hash table size is 10,000, the identity hash function maps all of the products for a given year to the same index. Only TV sets manufactured in different years would avoid a collision. If the television serial number will be a key, we need to design a custom hash function that "mixes up" the bits and produces more uniformly distributed values.

Algorithm:

> Assume serialNum is a 32-bit integer value specifying a product's serial number. Its value is in the range from 0 to $2^{31} - 1$ (between 0 and Integer.MAX_VALUE). Assign the integer value into the 64-bit long variable, hashValue. Nonnegative long values have a range from 0 to $2^{63} - 1$. With the relative bit-sizes for int and long variables, the square of hashValue must be a nonnegative 64-bit number, because

> $$(\text{Integer.MAX\_VALUE})^2 = (2^{31}-1)^2 = 2^{62} -2^{32} + 1 < 2^{63} - 1$$

> Return the remainder after dividing the square by Integer.MAX_VALUE. This is a nonnegative 32-bit integer that contains "jumbled up" bits from the original value.

The custom hash function for Product objects mixes the bits for the serial number to create a random value.

Television sets are instances of the Product class, which defines the instance variable serialNum. We use the custom algorithm to override the method hashCode() in the class.

Product class with hashCode():

```
public class Product
{
    private int serialNum;
        ...
    public int hashCode()
    {

        // assign serialNum to a long variable
        long hashValue = serialNum;

        // square to obtain a nonnegative long integer
        hashValue *= hashValue;

        // return the remainder after dividing by the largest
        // int value; its bits are "jumbled up"
        return (int)(hashValue % Integer.MAX_VALUE);

    }
}
```

21.3 Designing Hash Tables

In the previous section, we focused on the concept of a hash function. To understand its action, we used an array to introduce a hash table and had the hash function map a key to an index position in the array. In this section, we turn our attention to the design of a hash table. In the process, we define different storage models that work with a hash function to resolve collisions. We assume the table does not contain duplicate values and so collisions result from the hashing process. The issue is clear. When two or more data items hash to the same table index, they cannot occupy the same position in the table. We are left with the option of locating one

When resolving collisions with linear probing, one item enters a table slot (bucket). The number of elements cannot exceed the table size.

of the items at another position in the table or of redesigning the table to store a sequence of colliding keys at each index. In the latter case, a list holds all of the elements that hash to that location. These options represent two classical strategies for collision resolution called *linear probing* and *chaining with separate lists*. The strategies result in two models for a hash table collection. We illustrate the linear probing model with an example, but we focus our attention on chaining with separate lists because it represents the most commonly used design for a hash table.

Linear Probing

This technique assumes that the hash table is an array of elements with an associated hash function. Initially, we tag each entry in the table as "empty." To add an item to the table, apply the hash function to the key and divide the value by the table size. The resulting index is a location in the table. If the entry is empty, the algorithm inserts the item at the index position. Otherwise, it "probes" the table looking for the first open slot, hence its name. The probe starts at the next hash index and begins a sequential search at successive indices. The search wraps around to the start of the table after it probes the last table entry. An insertion occurs at the first open location. The search could cycle through all of the indices and return to the original hash location without finding an open slot. In this case, the table is full, and the algorithm throws an exception.

Example 21.2

A hash table of size 11 combines with the identity hash function to store eight distinct integer data items. The table lists the items and the corresponding hash index, whose value is item % 11.

Data item	54	77	94	89	14	45	35	76
Hash index	10	0	6	1	3	1	2	10

Inserts 54, 77, 94, 89, 14:
> The first five items hash to different indices. In each case, the table location is empty and the item is inserted at the hash index. Figure 21.1a displays the table with the annotation "1" next to the occupied cells, indicating that only one probe (test for empty) was necessary to insert the item.

Insert 45:
> The hash index for 45 is 1, which provides the first collision. The location is occupied by 89 from a previous insertion. The linear probe picks up at index 2 and continues until the table has an open slot. This occurs immediately because no item occupies the position at index 2. Inserting 45 requires only two probes (Figure 21.1b).

Insert 35:
> As the table begins to fill, the likelihood of collisions increases along with the number of probes required to insert an item. With data value 35, which hashes to index 2, there is no collision with any previous value. However, we require additional probes because the value 45 took slot 2 in response to a collision with 89. Value 35 requires three probes before landing at index 4 (Figure 21.1c).

Insert 76:

Adding 76 to the list dramatically illustrates a potential problem with linear probing. The value hashes to index 10 but finds an open slot only after seven probes
(Figure 21.1d).

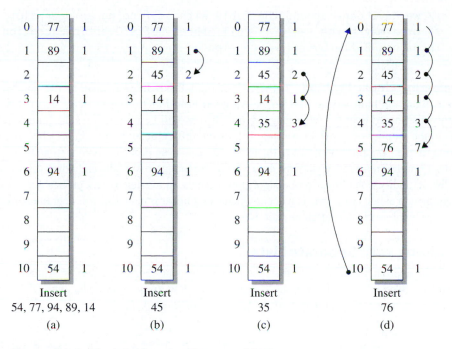

Insert
54, 77, 94, 89, 14

(a)

Insert
45

(b)

Insert
35

(c)

Insert
76

(d)

Figure 21.1 *Hash table using linear probing.*

The following code outline describes the linear probe insertion algorithm, assuming no duplicate values.

```
int index, origIndex;

// compute the hash index of item for a table of size n
index = (item.hashCode() &
Integer.MAX_VALUE) % n;

// save the original hash index
origIndex = index;

// cycle through the table looking for an empty slot, a
// match, or a table full condition (origindex == index)
do
{
    // test whether the table slot is empty or the key matches
    // the data field of the table entry
    if table[index] is empty
        insert item in table at table[index] and return
    else if table[index] matches item
        return
```

The efficiency of linear probing is high when the ratio of the number of entries in the table is small.

```
        // we are not yet successful; begin a probe starting at
        // the next table location
        index = (index+1) % n;
    } while (index != origIndex);

    // we have gone around the table without finding an open slot
    // or a match the table is full! throw BufferOverflowException
    throw new BufferOverflowException();
```

Evaluating Linear Probing   If the size of the table is large relative to the number of items, linear probing works well because a good hash function generates indices that are evenly distributed over the table range, and collisions will be minimal. As the ratio of table size to the number of items approaches 1, inherent difficulties with the process become apparent. In the example, adding 76 to the table requires seven probes, which is more than 40% of the 17 probes required to store the entire list. Even though five of the eight data values hash to distinct indices, the linear probe algorithm requires an average of 2.1 probes per item. A phenomenon called *clustering* can occur when using linear probes and will degrade performance. We explore clustering in the exercises.

Chaining with Separate Lists

When resolving collisions using chaining with separate lists, a bucket is a linked list of items that hash to the same table index.

A second approach to hashing defines the hash table as an indexed sequence of linked lists. Each list, called a *bucket*, holds a set of items that hash to the same table location. This collision resolution strategy is referred to as *chaining with separate lists*.

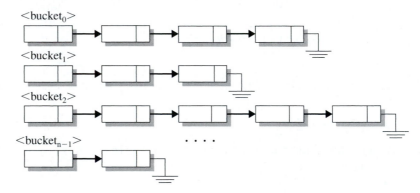

A bucket is a singly linked list. Each entry of the table is a reference to the first node in a sequence of items that hash to the table index. A node has the familiar structure with two fields for the value and for the reference to the next node.

To add object item, begin with the key and use the hash function to identify the index, i, for the appropriate bucket (linked list) in the table. Assume the array of node references is called `table`. If `table[i]` is `null`, add `item` as the first entry in the list; otherwise, a scan of the list compares `item` with the value of each node. If the scan ends with no match, then `item` is not in the list. Add it to the front of the list.

To illustrate a hash table that uses chaining with separate lists, consider the sequence of eight elements in Example 21.2. The table is an array consisting of 11 LinkedList collections. For reference, we repeat the list of elements and their hash values.

Data item	54	77	94	89	14	45	35	76
Hash index	10	0	6	1	3	1	2	10

Figure 21.2 displays the lists corresponding to the table indices. Each entry in a table includes the number of probes to add the element.

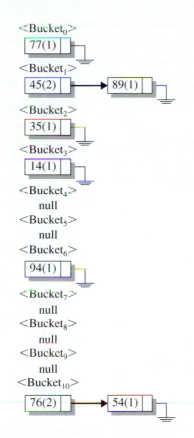

Figure 21.2 *Hash table using chaining with separate lists.*

Evaluating Chaining with Separate Lists   Chaining with separate lists is generally faster than linear probing because chaining only searches items that hash to the same table location. In the example, note that the total number of probes to insert the 8 items is 10, an average of 1.25 probes per item. This compares favorably with the 2.1 probes required to insert an element when the table uses linear probing. Furthermore, with linear probing, the number of table entries is limited to the table size, whereas the collections used in chaining grow as necessary and hence the number of elements in the table is limited only by the amount of memory. In addition, deleting an element from the hash table is simple. Just erase it from the associated list. Deleting an element from a hash table that uses linear probing is more diffi-cult. See Written Exercise 21.6 for further discussion of this.

Rehashing

As the number of entries in the hash table increases, search perform-ance deteriorates. The technique known as *rehash-ing* increases the hash table size when the number of entries in the table is a specified percentage of its size.

When using chaining with separate lists, the number of elements is not limited by the size of the hash table. However, the individual linked lists increase in length, which increases the search time for elements in a list. We can solve these problems by using a strategy known as *rehashing*. The idea is relatively simple. When the number of elements in the current hash table is a specified percentage of the table size, create a larger hash table. Elements from the old table must be hashed into the new table. Divide the value of the hash function by the new table size and relocate each element in the new hash table. The new hash table will provide better performance until it begins to fill up, at which time apply rehashing again. We use this strategy in building the Hash and HashMap classes. Figure 21.3 shows the result of rehash-ing when the original table size is 7 and the new table size is 15.

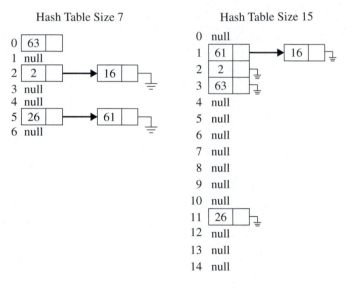

Figure 21.3 *Rehashing.*

21.4 A Hash Table as a Collection

The Hash class implements hash-ing using chaining with separate lists. It implements the Collection inter-face and is used to implement unordered maps and sets.

The goal of this chapter is to create set and map collections that use a hash table as the stor-age structure. The collections take advantage of hash code access to the elements. To achieve this goal, we must develop hash table algorithms to insert, access, and delete an element and design an iterator to scan the elements. These are the same tasks we faced when using a bi-nary search tree to implement the TreeSet and TreeMap collection classes. Recall that we implemented the TreeSet class in Chapter 20 by directly building a binary search tree using the algorithms we developed for the class STree in Chapter 18. In a similar fashion, we will create a Hash class that stores elements in a hash table using chaining with separate lists. The design of the class and the implementation algorithms will be the basis for our implementing HashSet and HashMap collection classes.

The generic Hash class implements the familiar Collection interface. All of the methods that need a hash value use hashCode(), which must be provided by the specified generic type. The constructor creates a hash table with initial size 17. The table grows as rehashing occurs. The method `toString()` returns a comma-separated list of elements enclosed in square brackets. The list is not ordered because hash tables store elements on the basis of their hash value and not their natural ordering. Figure 21.4 is a UML diagram for the `Hash` class and the `Collection` interface.

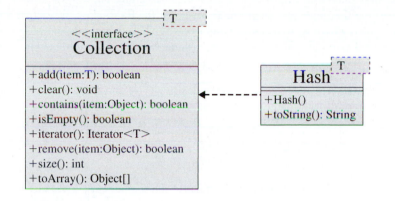

Figure 21.4 *UML for the Hash class that implements the Collection interface.*

Example 21.3

The example illustrates how we might use a `Hash` collection in a program. The elements are of type `Integer` and of type `String`, which override the `hashCode()` method.

1. Declare a `Hash<Integer>` object that stores elements in a hash table. The elements are random integers in the range 0 to 99. Access to the hash table is provided by the identity hash function in the `Integer` class.

```
Hash<Integer> hInt = new Hash<Integer>();
Random rnd = new Random();

// add 10 elements to the collection
for (int i = 1; i <= 10; i++)
    hInt.add(rnd.nextInt(100));
```

2. A `Hash<String>` object stores the `String` elements from array `strArr`. The method `toString()` displays the elements as an unordered list.

```
String[] strArr = {"a", "more", "bucket", "hash", "table",
                   "class"};
Hash<String> hStr = new Hash<String>();

for (int i=0;i < strArr.length;i++)
    hStr.add(strArr[i]);

System.out.println("String hash table: " + hStr);
```

```
Output:
  String hash table: [class, hash, table, more, bucket, a]
```

21.5 Hash Class Implementation

We provide a detailed implementation of the Hash class. You will see how chaining with separate lists works. By understanding the Hash class, we can focus on design principles for the implementation of the HashMap class.

The Hash class uses a hash table as its storage structure. The table is an array whose elements are the first node in a singly linked list. For the Hash class, we define a new node structure called *Entry* with an integer field hashValue that stores the hash code value. Adding the field simplifies the process of rehashing the table. We avoid having to recompute

```
item.hashCode() & Integer.MAX_VALUE
```

during the rehash. The other fields in the node are value and next.

value	hashValue	next

Entry node

The following is a declaration of the generic static inner class Entry<T>. A constructor creates an Entry object with specified value, next node, and hashValue parameters.

Entry inner class:

```
private static class Entry<T>
{
   // value in the hash table
   T value;

   // save value.hashCode() & Integer.MAX_VALUE
   int hashValue;

   // next entry in the linked list of colliding values
   Entry<T> next;

   // entry with given data and node value
   Entry(T value, int hashValue, Entry<T> next)
   {
      this.value = value;
      this.hashValue = hashValue;
      this.next = next;
   }
}
```

The Hash class private variables describe the hash table. The Entry array, called table, defines the singly linked lists (buckets) that store the elements. The integer variable hashTableSize specifies the number of entries in the table. The variable tableThreshold has the value

```
(int)(table.length * MAX_LOAD_FACTOR)
```

The constant MAX_LOAD_FACTOR is a value that specifies the maximum allowed ratio of the elements in the table and the table size. The value of 0.75 (number of hash table entries is 75% of the table size) is generally a good value. When the number of elements in the table equals tableThreshold, a rehash occurs. The variable modCount is used by iterators to determine whether external updates may have invalidated an iterator scan of the elements. Note that table is an array of the raw type Entry, not the generic type Entry<T>. It is necessary to declare table in this fashion, because arrays of generic types are not allowed.

The Hash class constructor creates the 17-element array table, whose elements default to null. This has the effect of creating 17 empty lists. A rehash will first occur when the hash collection size equals 12.

Hash class:

```java
public class Hash<T> implements Collection<T>
{
    // the hash table
    private Entry[] table;
    private int hashTableSize;
    private final double MAX_LOAD_FACTOR = .75;
    private int tableThreshold;

    // for iterator consistency checks
    private int modCount = 0;

    // construct an empty hash table with 17 buckets
    public Hash()
    {
        table = new Entry[17];
        hashTableSize = 0;
        tableThreshold = (int)(table.length * MAX_LOAD_FACTOR);
    }
    . . .
}
```

The figure illustrates a Hash collection with table size n. Each table index is the first Entry node in a linked list containing elements that hash to the same index.

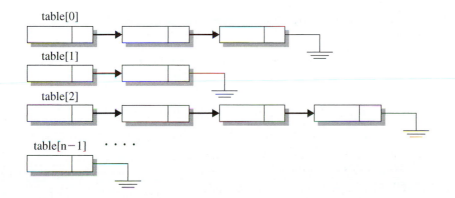

Hash add() and rehash() Methods

The algorithm for add() computes the hash index for the parameter item. The index identifies the linked list (bucket) whose first node is at table[index]. A reference variable scans the list to see if item is currently in the hash table. If so, the scan terminates and the method returns the boolean value `false`. Otherwise, a new `Entry` object is created with value `item` and inserted at the front of the list. Note that `hashValue` is assigned to the entry so it will not have to be computed when rehashing occurs. The variables `hashTableSize` and `modCount` are incremented. If the size of the hash table has reached the table threshold (at least 75% full), the private method `rehash()` locates the table items in a larger hash table. The size of the new table is

```
2*table.length + 1
```

Table sizes are always odd, being one more than twice the previous size. Using this approach, table sizes follow the sequence $17, 35, 71, 143, 287, 575, \ldots$.

add():

```java
// add item to the hash table if it is not already present and
// return true; otherwise, return false
public boolean add(T item)
{
    // compute the hash table index
    int hashValue = item.hashCode() & Integer.MAX_VALUE,
        index = hashValue % table.length;
    Entry<T> entry;

    // entry references the front of a linked list of colliding
    // values
    entry = table[index];

    // scan the linked list and return false if item is in list
    while (entry != null)
    {
        if (entry.value.equals(item))
            return false;

        entry = entry.next;
    }

    // we will add item, so increment modCount
    modCount++;

    // create the new table entry so its successor
    // is the current head of the list
    entry =
        new Entry<T>(item, hashValue, (Entry<T>)table[index]);

    // add it at the front of the linked list and increment
    // the size of the hash table
    table[index] = entry;
    hashTableSize++;

    if (hashTableSize >= tableThreshold)
        rehash(2*table.length + 1);

    // a new entry is added
    return true;
}
```

Method add() hashes to table index *i* and searches list for item. If a match occurs, it returns false, otherwise it adds a new node at the front of the list.

Rehashing the Table The method rehash() takes the size of the new hash table as an argument and performs rehashing. After creating a new table with the specified size, it uses a nested for-loop to cycle through the nodes in the original table. For each node, use the hashValue field modulo the new table size to hash to the new index. Simply insert the node at the front of the linked list. Saving the hashValue optimizes the rehashing process.

rehash():

```
private void rehash(int newTableSize)
{
   // allocate the new hash table and record a reference
   // to the current one in oldTable
   Entry[] newTable = new Entry[newTableSize],
           oldTable = table;
   Entry<T> entry, nextEntry;
   int index;

   // cycle through the current hash table
   for (int i=0; i < table.length;i++)
   {
      // record the current entry
      entry = table[i];
      // see if there is a linked list present
      if (entry != null)
      {
         // have at least one element in a linked list
         do
         {
            // record the next entry in the original
            // linked list
            nextEntry = entry.next;

            // compute the new table index
            index = entry.hashValue % newTableSize;

            // insert entry the front of the new table's
            // linked list at location index
            entry.next = newTable[index];
            newTable[index] = entry;

            // assign the next entry in the original linked
            // list to entry
            entry = nextEntry;
         } while (entry != null);
      }
   }

   // the table is now newTable
```

```
            table = newTable;
            // update the table threshold
            tableThreshold = (int)(table.length * MAX_LOAD_FACTOR);

            // let garbage collection get rid of oldTable
            oldTable = null;
    }
```

Hash remove() Method

The algorithm for remove() computes the hash index for the parameter item. This provides the table index for the linked list which may contain item. Removing an element from a singly linked list requires two reference variables, curr and prev. Initially, curr is the front of the list and prev is null. The variables move in tandem down the list until they find a match or reach the end of the list. In the latter case, item is not found and remove() simply returns with a value false. Otherwise, the prev reference next is updated to point at the successor of curr. If a match occurs at the first element, the front of the list, table[index] must also be updated. The remove() method decrements hashTableSize, increments modCount, and returns true.

remove():

```
    public boolean remove(Object item)
    {
        // compute the hash table index
        int index = (item.hashCode() & Integer.MAX_VALUE) %
        table.length;
        Entry<T> curr, prev;

        // curr references the front of a linked list of colliding
        // values; initialize prev to null
        curr = table[index];
        prev = null;
        // scan the linked list for item
        while (curr != null)
            if (curr.value.equals(item))
            {
                // we have located item and will remove
                // it; increment modCount
                modCount++;
                // if prev is not null, curr is not the front
                // of the list; just skip over curr
                if (prev != null)
                    prev.next = curr.next;
                else
                    // curr is front of the list; the new front
                    // of the list is curr.next
                    table[index] = curr.next;

                // decrement hash table size and return true
                hashTableSize--;
```

```
        return true;
    }
    else
    {
        // move prev and curr forward
        prev = curr;
        curr = curr.next;
    }

    return false;
}
```

To remove an item from a hash table, locate its bucket and search for the item. If not found, return false; otherwise, delete the element from the linked list, update variables, and return true.

Implementing the Hash Iterator

The design of an iterator class focuses on a strategy to scan the elements in the corresponding collection. For the Hash class, the strategy involves searching the hash table for the first nonempty bucket in the array of linked lists. Once the bucket is located, the iterator traverses all of the elements in the corresponding linked list and then continues the process by looking for the next nonempty bucket. The iterator reaches the end of the table when it reaches the end of the list for the last nonempty bucket.

Iterator objects are instances of the inner class IteratorImpl. The instance variables in the inner class maintain information on the current state of the iterator relative to the elements in the outer class collection. These variables include the integer index that identifies the current bucket (table[index]) scanned by the iterator. The Entry reference next points to the current node in this bucket. The variable lastReturned is the value that was returned by the most recent call to next(). A program can update a Hash collection by calling the outer class add() and remove() methods. These operations place the iterator in an inconsistent state. The iterator variable expectedModCount and the collection variable modCount are used to check consistency.

Implement a hash table iterator using an inner class.

Inner class IteratorImpl:

```
    // inner class that implements hash table iterators
    private class IteratorImpl implements Iterator<T>
    {
        Entry<T> next;              // next entry to return
        int expectedModCount;       // to check iterator consistency
        int index;                  // index of current bucket
        T lastReturned;             // reference to the last value
                                    // returned by next()

        . . .

    }
```

Figure 21.5 displays a Hash collection with five buckets and four elements. The elements enter the collection in the order (19, 32, 11, 27) using the identify hash function. An Iterator object, hIter, scans the collection. The initial position is provided by the Hash method iterator() and points to element 11. This is the first element in the linked list table[1]. The figure includes the initial iterator variables and the updated variables after hIter.next() returns 32. In the figure, the dotted lines indicate traversal from one bucket to another. The iterator visits the elements in the order (11, 32, 27, 19).

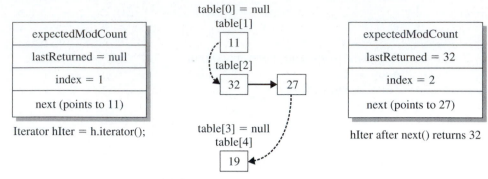

Hash table with tableSize = 5

Figure 21.5 *Hash iterators.*

Hash Iterator Constructor   The constructor positions the `Entry` reference `next` at the front of the first nonempty linked list (bucket). A loop iterates up the list of buckets until it locates this first nonempty bucket. The loop variable `i` becomes the initial value for `index` and `table[i]` references the front of the list. This is the initial value for `next`.

Constructor:

```
IteratorImpl()
{
    int i = 0;
    Entry<T> n = null;

    // the expected modCount starts at modCount
    expectedModCount = modCount;

    // find the first nonempty bucket
    if (hashTableSize != 0)
        while (i < table.length && ((n = table[i]) == null))
            i++;

    next = n;
    index = i;
    lastReturned = null;
}
```

Implementing next()   The iterator is currently positioned at some node in a linked list. The method `next()` first determines that the operation is valid by checking that `modCount` and `expectedModCount` are equal and that we are not at the end of the hash table. If the iterator is in a consistent state, `next()` uses a loop index `i` and an `Entry` reference called `entry` to perform the iterator scan. Initialize `i` and `entry` with the instance variables index and next, respectively. The method extracts the value at entry as the object lastReturned and then moves entry to the next position in the linked list. In case the position is at the end of the current list, we must search up the list of buckets beginning at index i + 1 to locate the next nonempty bucket. The front of this list becomes the value for the instance variable next, and the bucket index is the new value for index.

next():

```
public T next()
{
    // check for iterator consistency
    if (modCount != expectedModCount)
        throw new ConcurrentModificationException();

    // we will return the value in Entry object next
    Entry<T> entry = next;

    // if entry is null, we are at the end of the table
    if (entry == null)
        throw new NoSuchElementException();

    // capture the value we will return
    lastReturned = entry.value;
    // move to the next entry in the current linked list
    Entry<T> n = entry.next;
    // record the current bucket index
    int i = index;

    if (n == null)
    {
        // we are at the end of a bucket; search for the
        // next nonempty bucket
        i++;
        while (i < table.length && (n = table[i]) == null)
            i++;
    }

    index = i;
    next = n;

    return lastReturned;
}
```

Implementing remove()   The remove() method first determines that the operation is valid by checking that lastReturned is not null and that modCount and expectedModCount are equal. If all is well, the iterator remove() method calls the Hash class remove() method with lastReturned as the argument. By assigning to expectedModCount the current value of modCount, the iterator remains consistent.

remove():

```
public void remove()
{
    // check for a missing call to next() or previous()
    if (lastReturned == null)
        throw new IllegalStateException(
            "Iterator call to next() " +
            "required before calling remove()");
    if (modCount != expectedModCount)
        throw new ConcurrentModificationException();

    // remove lastReturned by calling remove() in Hash;
    // this call will increment modCount
    Hash.this.remove(lastReturned);
    expectedModCount = modCount;
    lastReturned = null;
}
```

21.6 An Unordered Map Collection

In the previous section, we used a hash table as the underlying storage structure for the Hash class. We extend this notion to create an implementation of an unordered map, called HashMap. A HashMap is not ordered because the position of elements depends on hashing the keys. This affects the method toString(), which returns a listing of the elements based on the iterator order.

Implement an unordered map with a hash table of key-value pairs (entries).

The HashMap class stores elements, which are key-value pairs. The storage structure for a HashMap object is a hash table of Entry objects that reference nodes in a linked list. The objects (nodes) are instances of the inner class Entry, which declares variables for the key and value components. It also defines the variable next to reference the subsequent pair in the current list. A hash value is computed once when a new entry enters the map. The integer value is stored as a field in the node.

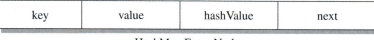

HashMap Entry Node

The inner class Entry implements the Map.Entry interface, which defines the method getKey() to access the key field and the methods getValue() and setValue() to access and update the value component. A toString() method in the Entry class returns a representation of an entry in the format *key=value*. The constructor has arguments for each field in the node.

Entry class (partial listing):

```
static class Entry<K,V> implements Map.Entry<K,V>
{
    K key;
    V value;
```

```
    Entry<K,V> next;
    int hashValue;

    // make a new entry with given key, value
    Entry(K key, V value, int hashValue, Entry<K,V> next)
    {
        this.key = key;
        this.value = value;
        this.hashValue = hashValue;
        this.next = next;
    }
    ...
}
```

Accessing Entries in a HashMap

The methods get() and containsKey() take a key reference argument and must locate a corresponding entry in the map. This task is performed by the private method getEntry(), which searches for an element in the hash table. The implementation of getEntry() takes a key as an argument, applies the hash function to the key, and searches the resulting list for a key-value pair with the same key.

getEntry():

```
    // return a reference to the entry with the specified key
    // if there is one in the hash map; otherwise, return null
    public Entry<K,V> getEntry(K key)
    {
        int index = (key.hashCode() & Integer.MAX_VALUE) %
                table.length;
        Entry<K,V> entry;

        entry = table[index];

        while (entry != null)
        {
            if (entry.key.equals(key))
                return entry;
            entry = entry.next;
        }

        return null;
    }
```

Private method getEntry() uses a key argument to locate an entry in the hash table or returns null if not found.

The public method get() takes a key as the argument and uses getEntry() to obtain low-level access to an Entry node. The return value is the value component of the node or null if an entry matching the key is not found.

get():

```
    // returns the value that corresponds to the specified key
    public V get(K key)
    {
```

```
        Entry<K,V> p = getEntry(key);

    if (p == null)
        return null;
    else
        return p.value;
}
```

Updating Entries in a HashMap

The method put() first searches the collection by applying the hash function for the key to obtain the table index and then scans the corresponding linked list for a match with the key. If a match occurs, the method calls setValue() to update the entry and returns the original value. If the key does not occur in the list, put() inserts a new Entry object at the front of the linked list. Note that we record the hash value as we did in the Hash class. If the hash map size has reached the table threshold, we apply rehashing so the new table size is 2*table.length + 1 and conclude by returning null.

put():

```
// assigns value as the value associated with key
// in this map and returns the previous value associated
// with the key, or null if there was no mapping for the key
public V put(K key, V value)
{
    // compute the hash table index
    int hashValue = key.hashCode() & Integer.MAX_VALUE,
            index = hashValue % table.length;
    Entry<K,V> entry;

    // entry references the front of a linked list of colliding
    // values
    entry = table[index];

    // scan the linked list and return false if item is in list
    while (entry != null)
    {
        if (entry.key.equals(key))
            return entry.setValue(value);

        entry = entry.next;
    }

    // we will add item, so increment modCount
    modCount++;

    // create the new table entry so its successor
    // is the current head of the list
    entry = new Entry<K,V>(key, value, hashValue,
            (Entry<K,V>)table[index]);
    // add it at the front of the linked list
    // and increment the size of the hash map
```

```
        table[index] = entry;
        hashMapSize++;

        if (hashMapSize >= tableThreshold)
            rehash(2*table.length + 1);

        return null;        // a new entry is inserted
}
```

Summary of the HashMap Design   The following UML diagram illustrates the design of the `HashMap` class, including the `Map` interface and the `Map.Entry` interfaces. The class `KeyIterator` is a subclass of the inner class `IteratorImpl` which implements all the iterator methods except `next()`. The class `KeyIterator` provides an implementation for `next()` by returning the next key in the map. In a similar fashion, the class `EntryIterator` extends `IteratorImpl` by adding an implementation for `next()` that returns the next entry in the map. The implementation of `IteratorImpl` in the `HashMap` class is very similar to the implementation of `IteratorImpl` in the `Hash` class.

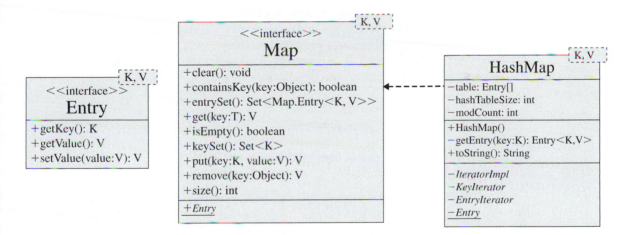

21.7 An Unordered Set Collection

`HashSet` completes our discussion of set and map classes. We introduce a new design strategy that implements `HashSet` using a `HashMap` object and composition. Using a map to implement a set makes sense. Each collection type stores elements by value. In the case of a map, elements are entry pairs identified by their key. You can view elements in a set as being only keys without an associated value component. A set of elements in the `HashSet` collection corresponds to a set of keys in the map. The value component of a map entry is not used but we must account for its presence in the entry.

We implement a set by using a map. A set element corresponds to a map element in which the key is the element.

The `HashSet` class uses a `HashMap` by composition. The class defines a static `Object` reference called PRESENT. This becomes the value component for each entry in the map. The constant reference serves as a dummy placeholder in an entry pair. Declare a private instance variable `map` of type `HashMap` having T as the type of the set elements and `Object` as the value type. The constructor instantiates the map collection. This has the effect of creating an empty set.

HashSet class:

```
public class HashSet<T> implements Set<T>
{
    // value for each key in the map
    private static final Object PRESENT = new Object();

    // set implemented using a hash map
    private HashMap<T, Object> map;

    // create an empty set object
    public HashSet()
    { map = new HashMap<T,Object>(); }
      . . .
}
```

Implementing HashSet with HashMap Methods

The static Object
PRESENT is the
value component
in each map
entry.

HashSet access and update methods take a single reference argument item. The set methods are implemented with map methods that use the entry< item, PRESENT >as the argument. For instance, here is the implementation for the HashSet add() method. The corresponding map method put() inserts a new element in the map or updates the value component if the element is already present. In HashSet, we are interested in using put() to insert a new element if a duplicate is not already present.

add():

```
public boolean add(T item)
{
    return map.put(item, PRESENT) == null;
}
```

The HashSet iterator must traverse the keys in the map. Implement the method iterator() by returning an iterator for the key set collection view of the map.

iterator():

```
// returns an iterator for the elements in the set
public Iterator<T> iterator()
{
    return map.keySet().iterator();
}
```

As a final example, the HashSet remove() method calls the remove() method for the map. Recall that the map remove() method returns the value field in the key-value pair that was erased from the map or null if the key is not in the map. To determine whether an element was removed from the set, verify that the return value from the map remove() call is the reference PRESENT.

remove():

```
public boolean remove(Object obj)
{
    return map.remove(obj) == PRESENT;
}
```

21.8 Hash Table Performance

The hashing process includes both the hash function and the hash table. The design of the process has the goal of providing very efficient search operations. In this section, we discuss the performance of hashing using linear probing and chaining with separate lists. As with any performance analysis, we look at the search algorithm under both worst-case and average-case conditions.

The analysis of hashing performance depends upon the quality of the hash function and the size of the hash table. A poor hash function maps all of the keys to a single table index; a good hash function provides a uniform distribution of hash values. A concept called *load factor* provides a measure of table size. If a hash table has m entries, and n is the number of elements currently in the table, the load factor λ for the table is

$$\lambda = n/m$$

In the case of linear probe, m is the size of the array (table range); for chaining with separate lists, m is the number of buckets. When the table is empty, λ is 0. As we add more items to the table, λ increases. For linear probe, λ attains the maximum value of 1 when the table is full ($m = n$). When the table uses chaining with separate lists, the individual buckets can grow as large as needed, and λ can become greater than 1.0.

The worst-case linear probe or chaining with separate lists occurs when all data items hash to the same table location. If the table contains n elements, the search time is O(n), no better than that for the sequential search. To analyze the average case for a search, we assume that the hash function uniformly distributes indices around the hash table. That is, any item is equally likely to hash into any of the m slots, independent of where any other element falls in the table. To attain a uniform distribution, it is best for m to be a prime number. Any discussion of the average case for linear probe is beyond the scope of this book. Consider the case in which the table uses chaining with separate lists. For the target named `item`, the time to compute the hash value `hf(item)` is O(1), so the number of comparisons it takes to locate `item` depends on the length of the list at array location `bucket[hf(item)]`. The assumption of a uniform hash distribution implies that we can expect $\lambda = n/m$ elements in each bucket (list). There are two cases. Either item is in the list and the search is successful, or item is not in the list and the search fails. On average, an unsuccessful search makes λ comparisons before arriving at the end of a list and returning failure. Computing the average running time for a successful search is more difficult. A mathematical analysis shows that the average number of probes for a successful search is approximately $1 + \lambda/2$. For instance, when the table is half full ($\lambda = 1/2$), a successful search requires no more than 1.25 probes. When the table is 2/3 full ($\lambda = 2/3$), chaining requires no more than 1.33 probes.

Fine-Tuning Hashing   The performance of chaining is a function of the load factor λ. In theory, $\lambda = n/m$ can increase without bounds when the table stores elements in a fixed number of buckets. As λ grows, the search performance deteriorates. For this reason, a programmer does not use a hash table if there is no upper bound on the total number of elements. We can assume the number of elements n in the hash table is bounded by some amount, say, $R * m$. In this case, $\lambda = n/m \leq (R * m)/m = R$. The running time for a successful and an unsuccessful search satisfies the relationships

$$S \approx 1 + \frac{\lambda}{2} \leq 1 + \frac{R}{2} \quad \text{(Successful Search)}$$

$$U = \lambda \leq R \quad \text{(Unsuccessful Search)}$$

Load factor λ is the ratio of the number of items in the hash table to the number of table entries. The running time of hash algorithms depends on λ.

The worst case for hashing is O(n); the average case for a successful and an unsuccessful search is O(1) if a bound is placed on n.

The terms on the right-hand side of the inequalities are constants, so the average search has running time O(1)! That is, the running time is independent of the number of data items. The challenge is to make the constant time reasonably small, which is equivalent to saying that λ is reasonably small. The programmer can fine-tune the hashing process by adjusting the number of buckets. The choice of m must take into account system resources and the need to have the hash function uniformly distribute its values in the index range from 0 to $m - 1$. Note that difficult mathematical analysis indicates that the average performance of linear probing is also O(1).

Evaluating Ordered and Unordered Sets

Use an ordered set or map if an iteration should return elements in order. Use an unordered set or map when fast access and updates are needed without any concern for the ordering of elements.

An unordered set or map class uses a hash table, so it provides average constant-time performance for the insertion, removal, and retrieval operations. An ordered set or map stores elements in a binary search tree. Access and update operations have runtime efficiency $O(\log_2 n)$. The application will dictate which type is more appropriate. If the programmer needs very efficient access and updates without any concern for the ordering of the elements, the unordered set or map is appropriate. When order is important, an ordered collection is more appropriate.

Example 21.4

This example presents the results of the program *SearchComp.java* in Chapter 21 of the software supplement. The program uses the file `dict.dat`, which contains 25,025 randomly ordered words. It reads the file and inserts each word into a `TreeSet` and into a `HashSet`. The program uses a `Timing` object to determine the amount of time required to build both of the data structures. The program then shuffles the words from the dictionary and times a search of the `TreeSet` for each word in the shuffled list. The same action is applied to the hash table. A message displays the time required for each search technique. A run of the program follows.

```
Run:
    Number of words is 25025
    Built TreeSet in 0.078 seconds
    Built HashSet in 0.047 seconds
    TreeSet search time is 0.078 seconds
    HashSet search time is 0.016 seconds
```

Note that the `HashSet` search time is considerably better than that for a `TreeSet`.

Chapter Summary

- The fastest searching technique is to know the index of the required value in an array and apply the index to access the value. This is an O(1) algorithm. A hash table simulates this process by applying a hash function that converts the data to an integer. After obtaining an index by dividing the value from the hash function by the table size and taking the remainder, access the table. Normally, the number of elements in the table is much smaller than the number of distinct data values, so collisions occur. To handle collisions, we must place a value that collides with an existing table element into the table in such a way that we can efficiently access it later. The two most commonly used algorithms for collision resolution are *linear probing* and *chaining with separate lists*.

- The hash function for a class overrides the method hashCode() of the Object class. It is critical to the performance of hashing that we compute the hash function efficiently. In addition, the hash function should uniformly distribute data over the table index range. The chapter develops hash functions for Integer and String data.

- With linear probing, the table is an array of objects. After using the hash function to compute a table index, look up the entry in the table. If the values match, perform an update if necessary. If the table entry is empty, insert the value in the table. Otherwise, probe forward circularly, looking for a match or an empty table slot. If the probe returns to the original starting point, the table is full. For this algorithm, you may search table items that hashed to different table locations.

- For chaining with separate lists, a hash table entry is a reference to the first node in a linked list of objects. Each list is a sequence of colliding items. After applying the hash function to compute the table index, search the list for the data value. If it is found, update its value; otherwise, insert the value at the front of the list. With this algorithm, you search only items that collided at the same table location. In addition, there is no limitation on the number of values in the table, and deleting an item from the table involves only erasing it from its corresponding list. Deleting an item from a linear probe table is more difficult.

- The performance of hashing can be improved using the technique known as *rehashing*. When the number of elements in the current hash table is a specified percentage of the table size, create a larger hash table. Divide the value of the hash function by the new table size and relocate each element in the new hash table. The new hash table will provide better performance until it begins to fill up, at which time apply rehashing again. We use this strategy in building the Hash and HashMap classes.

- The chapter discusses design and implementation details for the collection class Hash that implements hashing using chaining with separate lists. The iterators for the class do not traverse the data in sorted order.

- A hash table is used to construct the unordered map class HashMap, which in turn is used to implement the unordered set class HashSet.

- The worst-case performance of a hash table is linear (O(n)). However, the average-case performance of hashing is constant time (O(1)).

- A program illustrates the performance of ordered sets implemented with binary search trees and unordered sets implemented with hash tables. If order is not required, a hash set exhibits better average search capability.

Written Exercises

1. Show that the identity hash function $hf(x) = x$ is unacceptable if the table size m is even. Is the situation changed if m is odd?

2. Assume that a hash function has the following characteristics:

   (i) Keys 257 and 567 hash to 3.   (iii) Keys 987 and 313 hash to 6.
   (ii) Keys 734, 189, and 575 hash to 5. (iv) Keys 122 and 391 hash to 8.

Assume that we perform insertions in the order 257, 987, 122, 575, 189, 734, 567, 313, 391.

(a) Indicate the position of the data if we use linear probing to resolve collisions.

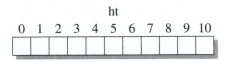

(b) Repeat part (a) if we reverse the order of the insertions.

3. Use the hash function `hf(x) = x % 11` to map an integer value to a hash table index. Insert the data 1, 13, 12, 53, 77, 29, 31, 22 into the hash table.

(a) Construct the hash table by using linear probing.
(b) Construct the hash table by using chaining with separate lists.
(c) For both techniques, determine the load factor, the average number of probes needed to locate a value in the table, and the average number of probes needed to determine that a value is not in the table. For linear probing, when counting the number of probes needed to locate a value that is not in the table, count the discovery of an empty slot as a probe. For chaining with separate lists, record encountering the end of a list as a probe.

4. Assume that the character array s contains n characters. Consider the following hash function. Evaluate the design of the hash function.

```java
public int hashCode()
{
    int i;
    int hashval = 0;

    for(i=0;i < n;i++)
        hashval += s[i];

    return hashval;
}
```

5. A problem with linear probe is that it produces table *clustering*. Entries tend to "bunch together" in areas of the table as collisions occur. Suppose there are m table entries. If the hash function uniformly distributes indices, what is the probability of hashing to location p? Once data occupies table location p, location p + 1 can be occupied by data hashing to location p or location p + 1. What is the probability of filling location p + 1? What is the probability of filling slot p + 2? In general, explain why clustering occurs.

6. Hash tables are suited to applications in which the primary operation is retrieval: Insert a data value and then "look it up" many times. The linear probe hashing method is poorly suited to an application that requires that data elements be deleted from the hash table.

    Consider the following hash table of 101 entries with hash function hf(key) = key % 101.

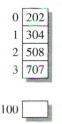

  (a) Delete 304 by placing -1 (Empty) in table location 1. What happens when we search for 707? Explain in general why just marking a slot as empty is not a correct solution to the problem of deletions.

  (b) A solution to the problem involves placing a special value, deletedData, in the location of the deletion. When searching for a key, we skip table locations marked with deletedData. Use the key value -2 in the table to indicate that a deletion occurred at the particular table location. Show that this approach to deleting 304 allows a correct search for 707.

The insertion and retrieval operations in the linear probe algorithm must be modified to accommodate deletions.

  (c) Describe an algorithm to delete a table element.

  (d) Describe an algorithm to locate an element in the table.

  (e) Describe an algorithm to insert an element in the table.

7. Given a set of keys k_0, k_1, ... k_{n-1}, a *perfect hash function* hf() is a hash function that produces no collisions. It is not practical to find a perfect hash function unless the set of keys is static. A situation for which a perfect hash function is desirable is a table of reserved words (such as "while", "interface", "class") that a compiler searches. When an identifier is read, only one probe is necessary to determine whether the identifier is a reserved word.

    It is very difficult to find a perfect hash function for a particular set of keys, and a general discussion of the subject is beyond the scope of this book. Furthermore, if a new set of keys is added to the set, the hash function normally is no longer perfect.

  (a) Consider the set of integer keys 81, 129, 301, 38, 434, 216, 412, 487, 234 and the hash function

$$hf(x) = (x + 18)/63$$

    Is hf() a perfect hash function?

  (b) Consider the set of keys consisting of the strings

        Bret, Jane, Shirley, Bryce, Michelle, Heather

    Devise a perfect hash function for a table containing seven elements.

8. The Hash class initially creates 17 buckets and then rehashes as necessary.

```
Hash<String> ht = new Hash<String>();
```

Insert the strings "saxophone", "dog", "walrus", "tea", "networking", "key", "icon", "course" into the hash table. The following table gives the hash table index for each string.

String	hashIndex
Saxophone	17
Dog	8
Walrus	18
Tea	1
Networking	8
Key	2
Icon	13
Course	4

Give the order in which an iterator visits the strings.

Programming Exercises

9. (a) Implement the LinearProbingHash class using a hash table with linear probing as the hashing algorithm. You need not implement the iterator() or remove() methods.

```
public class LinearProbingHash<T> implements
    Collection<T>
{
        ... // private section

    public LinearProbingHash(int tableSize)
    { ... }

    public boolean add(T item)
    { ... }

    public boolean contains(Object item)
    { ... }

    void clear()
    { ... }

    public int size()
    { ... }

    boolean isEmpty()
    { ... }

    Iterator<T> iterator()
    { return null; }
```

```
        boolean remove(Object item)
        { return false; }

        Object[] toArray()
        { ... }

        public String toString()
        { ... }
    }
```

(b) Write a program which creates a LinearProbingHash collection of Integer objects with values {7, 12, 15, 19, 53, 68, 3, 33, 57, 45, 25}. Output the hash table and its size. Add instructions that test your implementation.

10. (a) Using our model for implementing HashSet using HashMap, implement the collection MyTreeSet using TreeMap. MyTreeSet must implement the interface OrderedSet.

(b) Run Program 21.1 using your class.

11. (a) Implement the collection MyHashSet by using a Hash object by composition.

(b) Write a program that uses string objects to test your implementation.

For Programming Exercises 21.12 and 21.13, when the type of elements in a collection must be a subtype of a generic type T, indicate this with the wildcard notation

```
    <? extends T>
```

When the type of elements in a collection can be of any unspecified type, indicate this with the wildcard notation

```
    <?>
```

12. (a) Implement the class ExtHashSet, which extends the HashSet class and includes the following methods.

```
    // adds all of the elements in the specified collection
    // to the set
    public boolean addAll(Collection<? extends T> c)
    { ... }

    // retains only the elements in this set that are
    // contained in the specified collection; in other words,
    // removes from this set all of its elements that are not
    // contained in the specified collection
    public boolean retainAll(Collection<?> c)
    { ... }

    // removes all this set's elements that are also
    // contained in the specified collection; after this call
    // returns, this set will contain no elements in common
    // with the specified collection
    public boolean removeAll(Collection<?> c)
    { ... }
```

(b) Write a program that creates a set s1 of Integer objects with values {7, 12, 15, 19, 53, 68, 3, 33, 57, 45, 25} and an ArrayList arr of Integer objects {22, 9, 15, 42, 53, 79, 3, 33, 97, 45, 25}. Clone s1 to create additional sets s2 and s3.

(1) Using the method addAll(), output s + t (set union).
(2) Using the method retainAll(), output u = s * t (set intersection).
(3) Using the method removeAll(), output u = s − t (set difference).

13. (a) Implement the class ExtHashMap, which extends the HashMap class and adds the following methods.

```
// returns true if this map maps one or more keys for
// the specified value
public boolean containsValue(Object value)
{ ... }

// copies all of the mappings from the specified map
// to this map; these mappings will replace any mappings
// that this map had for any of the keys currently in
// the specified map
public void putAll(Map<? extends K, ? extends V> m)
{ ... }
```

(b) Create an ExtHashMap m1 containing the following key-value pairs: {"California", "San Francisco"}, {"Nevada", "Reno"}, {"Massachusetts", "Springfield"}, {"Arizona", "Phoenix"}, {"Texas", "Austin"}

Determine whether the values "Phoenix" and "Chicago" correspond to keys in the map. Create a second map m2 by using putAll(). Output the two maps.

Programming Project

14. (a) Develop the class LinearProbe, which maintains a hash table by using linear probing using the following as a suggested class declaration. Use Written Exercise 21.6 as a guide for implementing the remove() method. You do not need to implement rehashing.

```
public class LinearProbe<T> implements Collection<T>,
    Iterable<T>
{
    // the hash table is an array of TableRecord objects
    private TableRecord[] table;
    // number of elements in the hash table
    private int hashtableSize;

    // increases whenever hash table changes; used by an
    // iterator to verify that it is in a consistent state
    private int modCount = 0;

    // constructor specifying number of buckets in
    // the hash table
```

```
public LinearProbe(int nbuckets)
{ ... }

// adds the specified element to the hash table if
// it is not already present
// Precondition: there must be an available table slot
// for item; if the table is full, throw
// the BufferOverflowException exception defined in
// the package java.io
public boolean add(T item)
{ ... }

< remainder of public interface same as Hash >

private static class TableRecord<T>
{
   // entry available (true or false)
   boolean available;
   // data was previously deleted (true or false)
   boolean deletedData;

   // the data itself
   T data;

   public TableRecord()
   {
      available = true;
      deletedData = false;
   }
}

private class IteratorImpl implements Iterator<T>
{ ... }
}
```

(b) Using your LinearProbe class, run the following program.

```
// The program declares a hash table with integer data.
// It inserts the elements from the array intArr into
// the hash table, noting which values
// are duplicates that do not go into the table. After
// displaying the size of the hash table, a loop prompts
// the user for 2 values. If a value is
// in the table, the remove() method deletes it.
// The program terminates by using an iterator to
// traverse and output the elements of the hash table.

import java.util.Scanner;
import ds.util.Iterator;
public class ProgPrj21_14
{
```

```java
public static void main(String[] args)
{
   // array that holds 10 integers with some
   // duplicates
   Integer[] intArr = {20, 16, 9, 14, 8, 17, 3, 9, 16,
                       12, 35, 18, 55};

   // hash table with 7 buckets and iterator
   LinearProbe<Integer> ht = new
   LinearProbe<Integer>(17);
   Iterator<Integer> iter;
   Scanner keyIn = new Scanner(System.in);
   int item, i;
   boolean itemAdded;

   // insert elements from intArr, noting duplicates
   for (i = 0; i < intArr.length; i++)
   {
      itemAdded = ht.add(intArr[i]);
      if (itemAdded == false)
        System.out.println("Duplicate value " +
                                intArr[i]);
   }

   // output the hash size which reflects duplicates
   System.out.println("Hash table size " + ht.size());

   // prompt for item to erase and indicate if
   // not found
   for (i = 1; i <= 2; i++)
   {
      System.out.print("Enter a number to delete: ");
      item = keyIn.nextInt();

      if (!ht.contains(item))
        System.out.println(item +
             " not found in the hash table");
      else
      {
        System.out.println("Erasing " + item);
        ht.remove(item);
      }
   }

   System.out.println("Modified hash table:");
   System.out.println(ht);
   // using an iterator scan, output each odd value
   // and delete each one
   System.out.print("After removing even values, " +
        "hash table has values ");
```

```
            iter = ht.iterator();
            while (iter.hasNext())
            {
                Integer n = iter.next();

                if (n % 2 == 1)
                    System.out.print(n + "   ");
                else
                    iter.remove();
            }
            System.out.println("\nThe final hash table size " +
                "is " + ht.size());
        }
    }
```

```
Run:
  Duplicate value 9
  Duplicate value 16
  Hash table size 11
  Enter a number to delete: 10
  10 not found in the hash table
  Enter a number to delete: 17
  Erasing 17
  Modified hash table:
  [35, 18, 20, 3, 55, 8, 9, 12, 14, 16]
  After removing even values, the hash table has values
  35  3  55  9
  The final hash table size is 4
```

(c) Run the program SearchComp.java in Chapter 21 of the software supplement using LinearProbe instead of HashSet.

Chapter 22

HEAPS

CONTENTS

22.1 ARRAY-BASED BINARY TREES

22.2 THE COMPARATOR INTERFACE
General Comparison Objects
Generalized Array Sorts

22.3 HEAPS
Inserting into a Heap
Deleting from a Heap
Displaying a Heap

22.4 SORTING WITH A HEAP
Making a Heap
The Heapsort
Summarizing Static Heap Methods

22.5 IMPLEMENTING A PRIORITY QUEUE
Implementing the HeapPQueue
Class

In Chapter 16, we developed a linked implementation of binary trees in which each node is an object consisting of a data field and two reference fields that point to the children of the node. An array can also be used to store a binary tree. The root node is the element at index 0, and simple index calculations identify the children and parent of any node.

An array-based implementation of a binary tree forms the basis for a new collection type, called a *heap*, whose insertion and deletion algorithms have $O(\log_2 n)$ running time. A heap stores elements with a heap ordering principle that compares elements by using either the $<$ or the $>$ relation. The storage technique locates the maximum element ($>$ order) or the minimum element ($<$ order) in the collection in the root node. In a maximum heap, a deletion removes the largest element from the collection; a deletion from a minimum heap removes the smallest element. The operation then efficiently reorders the elements so that the next deletion can immediately access the appropriate element. Because heap operations have logarithmic performance and deletions return the largest or the smallest value, the structure provides a famous and very efficient sorting algorithm, appropriately called the *heapsort*. The sort has no worst case and is an $O(n \log_2 n)$ algorithm in all situations.

We will use the heap collection as the underlying storage structure in the implementation of the HeapPQueue class. We introduced the PriorityQueue interface in Chapter 15 and used the class in of several applications include event simulation.

Comparator objects provide flexibility so that a heap collection can be a minimum or a maximum heap. The objects have their own comparison operator which orders elements in ascending or descending order. A Comparator object can also be passed as an argument in generalized array sorting methods to direct the final ordering of the elements. We will discuss the Comparator interface in Section 22.2 and present the generalized selectionSort() method.

22.1 Array-Based Binary Trees

In Chapter 16, we built binary trees by using tree nodes. Each node has a data value and left and right references that identify the left and right subtrees of the node. Insertions and deletions involve allocating nodes and assigning the references to the subtrees. This representation handles trees ranging from degenerate to complete trees. In this section, we introduce a tree that uses an array to store the data and indices to identify the nodes. We use the term *array-based tree* to describe the data structure. We can derive a very powerful relationship between the array and a complete binary tree.

An array has a representation as a complete binary tree, termed an *array-based tree*.

Recall from Chapter 16 that a complete binary tree of depth d contains all possible nodes through level d −1 and that nodes at level d occupy the leftmost positions in the tree. We can view an array `arr`, with its indexed structure, as a complete binary tree. The root is `arr[0]`, the first-level children are `arr[1]` and `arr[2]`, the second-level children are `arr[3]`, `arr[4]`, `arr[5]`, `arr[6]`, and so forth. Figure 22.1 illustrates a 10-element array viewed as a complete tree.

```
Integer[] arr = {5, 1, 3, 9, 6, 2, 4, 7, 0, 8};
```

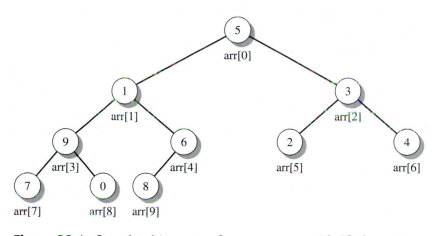

Figure 22.1 *Complete binary tree for an array arr with 10 elements.*

The power of array-based trees becomes evident when an application requires access to node data. There are simple index calculations that identify the children and the parent of nodes. For each node `arr[i]` in an *n*-element array, the following formulas compute the indices of the child nodes.

| Item arr[i] | Left child index is | $2 * i + 1$ |
| | | undefined if $2 * i + 1 \geq n$ |

| Item arr[i] | Right child index is | $2 * i + 2$ |
| | | undefined if $2 * i + 2 \geq n$ |

For element arr[i] in an array-based tree, the left and right children are at indices $2i + 1$ and $2i + 2$ respectively; parent of *i* is at Index $(i − 1)/2$.

A similar calculation allows us to identify the parent of any node `arr[i]`. The index for the parent node is given by

| Item arr[i] | Parent index is | $(i − 1)/2$ |
| | | undefined if $i = 0$ |

Note that we can start at any node and move up the tree along the path of parents until we arrive at the root. This feature was not available with the TNode implementation of a binary tree. An STree collection with its STNode objects could scan the path of parents by using the parent reference field.

Example 22.1

Let us see how these index calculations apply to the array-based tree in Figure 22.1.

1. The root is arr[0] with value 5. Its left child has index $2*0 + 1 = 1$ and its right child has index $2*0 + 2 = 2$. The values for the children are arr[1] $= 1$ and arr[2] $= 3$.

2. Start at the root and select the path of left children.

    root index $= 0$
    left child of arr[0] has index $= 2*0 + 1 = 1$
    left child of arr[1] has index $= 2*1 + 1 = 3$
    left child of arr[3] has index $= 2*3 + 1 = 7$
    left child of arr[7] is undefined $(2*7 + 1 = 15 \geq 10)$

    The path of left children is: arr[0] $= 5$, arr[1] $= 1$, arr[3] $= 9$, arr[7] $= 7$.

3. To identify the path of parents from any node arr[i], evaluate successive parent indices as $(i - 1)/2$. Assume we start at arr[8] $= 0$. Successive parent indices are $(8 - 1)/2 = 3, (3 - 1)/2 = 1, (1 - 1)/2 = 0$, which is the root. The path of parents starting at arr[8] is arr[8] $= 0$, arr[3] $= 9$, arr[1] $= 1$, arr[0] $= 5$.

We can associate with any array a binary tree representation. In general, the representation is not useful because the values that happen to be stored in the array may not match the tree structure in a meaningful way. In Section 22.3, we will organize an array by placing an ordering on its elements. The resulting array, called a *heap*, is best illustrated as a binary tree. A heap has very efficient insertion and deletion operations. We will use the array as the underlying storage structure for an implementation of the priority queue. The heap ordering will be exploited to create a fast sort algorithm called the *heapsort*.

22.2 The Comparator Interface

Up to this point, we have been able to order an array of objects by using the compareTo() method when the objects in the array implement the Comparable interface. This ordering is referred to as the class's *natural ordering*, and the class's compareTo() method is referred to as its *natural comparison method*. The Comparator interface defines objects containing a comparison method which imposes a total ordering on some collection of objects. Comparators can be passed to a sort method (such as the selection sort) to allow precise control over the sort order. Comparators can also be used to control the order of certain data structures such as a heap.

The Comparator interface specifies two comparison methods, compare() and equals(). A class that implements the interface defines an ordering between objects. The following is the API for the Comparator interface in the package *java.util*.

interface Comparator<T>	*java.util*
	Methods

`int`	`compare`(T x, T y) Compares its two arguments for order. Returns a negative integer, zero, or a positive integer to specify that *x* is less than, equal to, or greater than *y*.
`boolean`	`equals`(Object obj) Returns true if the specified object is also a comparator and imposes the same ordering as this comparator.

The method `compare()` is similar to the `Comparable` method `compareTo()`, except that it takes two arguments. As an example, we create a class `CircleLess` that we can use to determine if one Circle object is less than another based on the relative size of their radius. Note that the `Circle` class does not implement the `Comparable` interface and so there is no predefined ordering among instances of the class. Our `CircleLess` class and the `compare()` method create an ordering.

```
public class CircleLess implements Comparator<Circle>
{
    public int compare(Circle x, Circle y)
    {
        double radX = x.getRadius(), radY = y.getRadius();

        // returns < 0 if radX < radY, 0 if radX == radY,
        // and > 0 if radX > radY
        return (int)(radX - radY);
    }
    <
        The method equals(Object obj) is
        inherited from the Object superclass
    >
}
```

> A Comparator object implements the `compare()` method and acts like a function that compares two objects.

`CircleLess` is external to the `Circle` class and so does not have access to the private instance variable `radius`. The `compare()` method must access the radius using the public method `getRadius()`. That said, we can compare two Circle objects by using an instance of the `CircleLess` class.

```
Circle circA = new Circle(5), circB = new Circle(7.5);
CircleLess circComp = new CircleLess();      // comparing object

if (circComp.compare(circA, circB) < 0)
    System.out.println("Circle A is less than circle B");
```

```
Output:
  Circle A is less than circle B
```

General Comparison Objects

If we assume that objects implement the Comparable interface, we can develop generic Comparator classes that compare two objects for either the < or the > relation. The classes implement compare() by using the compareTo() ordering between objects.

We will define and then extensively use the generic Comparator classes Less and Greater. Their implementation of compare() casts one of the arguments to a Comparable object and makes the comparison using compareTo(). The class Less compares two objects for "less than."

```
import java.util.Comparator;

// constructs the < Comparator
public class Less<T>implements Comparator<T>
{
    public int compare(T x, T y)
    {
        return ((Comparable<T>)x).compareTo(y);
    }
}
```

For object types that implement Comparable, we can construct generic classes Less and Greater that compare two objects.

A Less object can be used to determine if one object has a lesser value than another. The underlying assumption is that the objects implement the Comparable interface. For instance, consider two Integer objects intObjA and intObjB. Define a Less object and use it with the compare() method to determine if the value of intObjA is less than intObjB.

```
Comparator<Integer> less = new Less<Integer>();
Integer intObjA = 3, intObjB = 5;

if (less.compare(intObjA,intObjB) < 0)
    System.out.println(intObjA + " < " + intObjB);    // 3 < 5
```

In general, for any Comparator object comp, the expression *comp.compare(x,y) < 0* is used to evaluate success for the comparison. This is an important fact that we exploit in the design of the Comparator class Greater. We want compare() to be negative (<0) when the first object is greater than the second object.

```
// constructs the > Comparator
public class Greater<T> implements Comparator<T>
{
    public int compare(T x, T y)
    {
        return -((Comparable<T>)x).compareTo(y);
    }
}
```

Let us use the same Integer objects intObjA and intObjB with a Greater comparison object. The same "< 0" relation implies success.

```
Comparator<Integer> greater = new Greater<Integer>();

if (greater.compare(intObjB,intObjA) < 0)
    System.out.println(intObjB + " > " + intObjA);    // 5 > 3
```

Generalized Array Sorts

We have developed methods for a variety of array sorting algorithms. In each case, the method uses compareTo() for comparisons and the array is sorted in ascending order. This approach has a serious limitation. If we want to use a method to sort the array in descending order, we would need an alternate version that simply changes the order of comparison to "greater than."

We can cut through this needless duplication by defining sorting methods that include a Comparator parameter. Using a Less or Greater object as argument that calls compare(), the same sorting method can be used to order an array in ascending or descending order. Let us illustrate the idea with a new version of selectionSort(). You will find the static method in the Arrays class.

The following code is essentially a copy of the selectionSort() method in Chapter 5. The expression *Comparator<? super T>* indicates that comp is an object that implements the Comparator interface in T itself or in some superclass of T. We continue to use the identifier smallIndex. The term "small" means "comes first" with the comparison expression "< 0". With the Greater comparator, "comes first" means that the first element is greater than the second element.

Selection Sort with Comparator:

```
// new version adds a Comparator parameter
public static <T> void selectionSort(
    T[] arr, Comparator<? super T> comp)
{
    int smallIndex; // index of smallest element in the sublist
    int pass, j, n = arr.length;
    T temp;

    // pass has the range 0 to n-2
    for (pass = 0; pass < n-1; pass++)
    {
        // scan the sublist starting at index pass
        smallIndex = pass;

        // j traverses the sublist arr[pass+1] to arr[n-1]
        for (j = pass+1; j < n; j++)
            // if smaller element found, assign smallIndex
            // to that position
            if (comp.compare(arr[j], arr[smallIndex]) < 0)
                smallIndex = j;

        // swap the next smallest element into arr[pass]
        temp = arr[pass];
        arr[pass] = arr[smallIndex];
        arr[smallIndex] = temp;
    }
}
```

Example 22.2

This example uses a `Less` comparator and `selectionSort()` to sort an array of strings in ascending order. A second call to `selectionSort()` with a `Greater` comparator orders the array in descending order. In each case, the resulting sorted list is output.

```
String[] arr = {"red", "green", "blue", "yellow", "teal",
                "orange"};
Less<String> less = new Less<String>();
Greater<String> greater = new Greater<String>();

Arrays.selectionSort(arr,less);
System.out.println("Sort with less: " + Arrays.toString(arr));

Arrays.selectionSort(arr,greater);
System.out.println("Sort with greater: " +
        Arrays.toString(arr));
```

```
Output:
  Sort with less: [blue, green, orange, red, teal, yellow]
  Sort with greater: [yellow, teal, red, orange, green, blue]
```

22.3 Heaps

A *heap* is an array-based binary tree. That is, the data structure is an array, which we view and handle as though it were a binary tree. Index calculations identify the children and parent of each node. Associated with the array is a `Less` or `Greater` comparator that defines a less than or a greater than relation between any pair of elements.

A maximum heap is an array-based tree in which the value of a parent is ≥ the value of its children. A minimum heap uses the relation ≤.

A heap has an order relationship between a parent and its children that is based on the type of comparator. For a *maximum heap*, the value of a parent is greater than or equal to the value of each of its children. For a *minimum heap*, the value of the parent is less than or equal to the value of each of its children. A maximum heap uses a `Greater` comparator and a minimum heap uses a `Less` comparator. These situations are depicted in Figure 22.2, which illustrates these two types of heaps. In a maximum heap, the root contains the largest element; in a minimum heap, the root contains the smallest element.

A heap is an array with an ordering among the elements that locates the largest (maximum) or smallest (minimum) element at index 0. A heap is not an independent data structure but rather an array ordering. Heaps have very efficient operations for inserting and deleting elements. The algorithms update the array to maintain heap ordering between parents and children. The ordering of elements and the associated insert and delete operations make a heap an ideal storage structure to implement a priority queue. The algorithms can be used to convert a general array to a heap. By exploiting the heap ordering on the array, we develop a fast array sort algorithm, called the *heapsort*. In this section, we focus on key heap algorithms, which we implement as static generic methods in the class `Heaps`. The methods include a `Comparator` argument so that they apply to both a maximum and a minimum heap. Our discussion assumes we are working with a maximum heap and that the generic type for the array elements implements the `Comparable` interface.

We start with algorithms to insert and delete an element in a heap. We will use these operations in the implementation of the `HeapPQueue` class, which allocates a heap as the

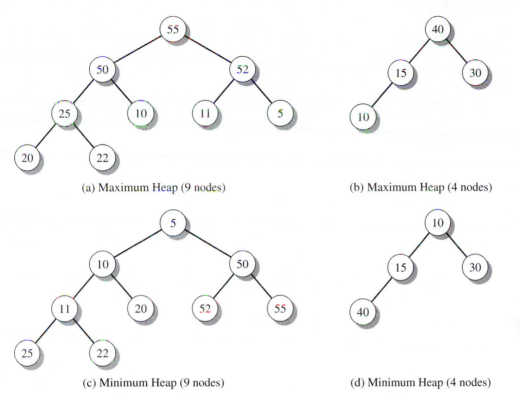

(a) Maximum Heap (9 nodes)   (b) Maximum Heap (4 nodes)

(c) Minimum Heap (9 nodes)   (d) Minimum Heap (4 nodes)

Figure 22.2 *Maximum and minimum heaps.*

storage structure. For obvious reasons, we call the insert method `pushHeap()` and the delete method `popHeap()`. Each of these methods must ensure that heap ordering is maintained between parents and children. To this end, we will define a utility method called `adjustHeap()` that reassigns values along a path of nodes to reestablish the heap order.

Inserting into a Heap

Inserting into a heap involves assigning a value to an element in the *n*-element array. The context assumes that the heap is an initial sublist of the array. That is, for some index, called `last`, the elements in the index range [0, `last`) are a heap and the elements in the index range [`last`, n) are not currently part of the heap. The new element will enter the array at index `last` with the heap expanding by one element. In the figure, the shaded boxes in the array correspond to the current nodes in the heap. An insertion occurs at index `last` = 5.

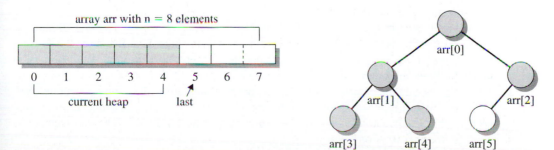

The heap update algorithms have a Comparator argument so they can build either a maximum or a minimum heap.

An insertion expands the heap to include index `last`. The new value initially enters the heap at index `last`. It must then be positioned somewhere on the path of parents, which begins at index `last` and proceeds up the tree to the root at index 0. We must add the value in such a way that heap order is maintained. Let us look at an example to appreciate the problem. Figure 22.3a displays a heap with `last= 10`. A new value 50 enters the heap at `arr[10]` and then is positioned along the path of parents `arr[10]`, `arr[4]`, `arr[1]`, and `arr[0]` (Figure 22.3b).

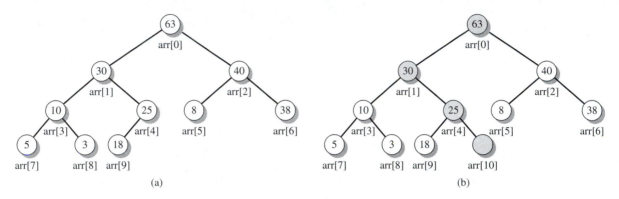

(a)   (b)

Figure 22.3 *Heap before and after insertion of 50.*

Insert item into a heap by moving nodes on the path of parents down one level until the item is assigned as the parent that has heap ordering.

The insert algorithm involves local repositioning of elements in the tree so that the heap order is maintained. The example illustrates what we mean by "local." If value 50 enters the heap at index 10, it would be out of order relative to its parent 25 and grandparent 30. The problem occurs along the path of parents and does not affect the other elements.

The static method `pushHeap()` inserts a new value in the heap. The parameter list includes the array `arr`, the index `last`, the new value `item`, and a `Comparator` object of type `Greater` or `Less` indicating whether the heap is a maximum or minimum heap. Our example assumes a maximum heap.

pushHeap():

```
public static <T> void pushHeap(T[] arr, int last, T item,
                                Comparator<? super T> comp)
```

The algorithm uses an iterative scan with variable `currPos` initially set to `last`. At each step, compare the value `item` with the value of the parent and if `item` is larger, copy the parent value to the element at index `currPos` and assign the parent index as the new value for `currPos`. The effect is to move the parent down one level. Stop when the parent is larger and assign `item` to the position `currPos`.

Let us look at the algorithm for the example in Figure 22.4. We are inserting 50 into the heap and `currPos` is 10. The first step compares 50 with the parent 25. Because 50 is greater than 25, move the parent down one level and update `currPos to index` 4. We illustrate the operation by circling only the affected nodes (see Figure 22.4). The process continues by comparing 50 with the parent of `currPos`, namely 30, and moves the parent down one level with `currPos` set to index 1. The next iteration compares 50 with the parent (root), which has value 63. The parent has a greater value and the process terminates. The new element is assigned to `arr[currPos] = arr[1]`.

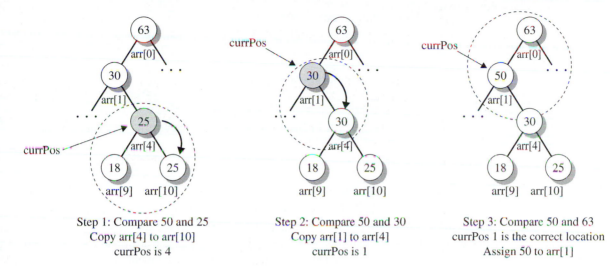

Step 1: Compare 50 and 25
Copy arr[4] to arr[10]
currPos is 4

Step 2: Compare 50 and 30
Copy arr[1] to arr[4]
currPos is 1

Step 3: Compare 50 and 63
currPos 1 is the correct location
Assign 50 to arr[1]

Figure 22.4 *Reorder the tree in pushHeap().*

The method `pushHeap()` sets out along the path of parents to insert `item`. The indices `currPos` and `parentPos` move in tandem up the parent path, beginning with `currPos = last`.

pushHeap():

```
// the array elements in the range [0, last) are a heap;
// insert item into the heap so that the range [0, last+1) is
// a heap; use the Comparator comp to perform comparisons
public static <T> void pushHeap(T[] arr, int last, T item,
        Comparator<? super T> comp)
{
    // assume the new item is at location arr[last] and that
    // the elements arr[0] to arr[last-1] are in heap order
    int currPos, parentPos;

    // currPos is an index that traverses path of parents;
    // item is assigned in the path
    currPos = last;
    parentPos = (currPos-1)/2;

    // traverse path of parents up to the root
    while (currPos != 0)
    {
        // compare target and parent value
        if (comp.compare(item,arr[parentPos]) < 0)
        {
            // move data from parent position to current
            // position; update current position to parent
            // position; compute next parent
            arr[currPos] = arr[parentPos];
```

pushHeap()
assumes elements
in the range
[0, last) form a
heap and inserts
item into the heap
so the range
[0, last+1) forms
a heap.

```
                    currPos = parentPos;
                    parentPos = (currPos-1)/2;
                }
                else
                    // heap condition is ok; break
                    break;
            }
            // the correct location has been discovered; assign target
            arr[currPos] = item;
        }
```

Deleting from a Heap

Deletion from a heap is normally restricted to the root only. Hence, the operation removes the maximum (or minimum) element. The static method popHeap() implements the algorithm and then returns the deleted value. The parameter list includes the array and a Comparator object. The integer parameter last specifies that only the elements in the index range [0, last) comprise the heap.

popHeap():

```
// delete the maximum (minimum) element in the heap and
// return its value
public static <T> T popHeap(T[] arr, int last,
                                Comparator<? super T> comp)
```

> To erase the root of an n-element heap, exchange the element at index n − 1 and the root and filter the root down into its correct position in the tree.

The algorithm begins by exchanging the root with the last element in the heap. The effect is to tuck the root away in a safe position. Unfortunately, the exchange can destroy the heap order: the new root might not be greater than or equal to its children. The algorithm then reestablishes heap order in the tree, minus its last value, by moving the new root down a path of children until it finds a proper location.

Let us look at an example that illustrates the initial steps in the popHeap() algorithm. Figure 22.5 displays a heap before beginning a deletion and then immediately after we exchange the root with the last element in the tree. The exchange of 18 and 68 destroys the heap, because the new root 18 is not greater than or equal to its children 30 and 40. Note that we consider only the unshaded elements as part of the remaining heap. To complete the deletion, we need to adjust the heap.

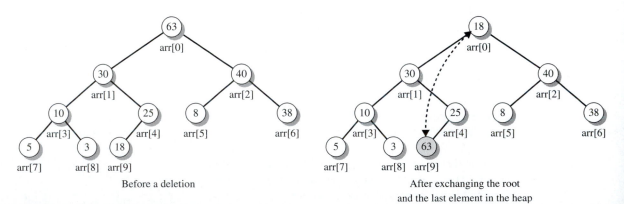

Before a deletion

After exchanging the root
and the last element in the heap

Figure 22.5 *Exchanging elements in popHeap().*

Adjusting the Heap   The algorithm to delete the root node may need to reestablish heap order. This involves moving (filtering) the root down the tree along a path of children until it locates a valid position. For the heap in Figure 22.5, we will move the target (root) value 18 down the path of large children 40 and 38, moving each node up one level. As a result, 40 becomes the new root and 18 will be positioned at a leaf node. The filtering process has application beyond the deletion algorithm and so we promote code reuse by declaring a method, called `adjustHeap()`, that performs the task. The method has parameters that include the array, the integers `first` and `last`, and a Comparator object. The parameter `first` is the index of the element that must filter down the tree and parameter `last` indicates that we will only check a child index that is less than `Last`.

adjustHeap():

```
// filter the array element arr[first] down the heap with index
// range [first, last)
public static <T> void adjustHeap(T[] arr, int first, int last,
                        Comparator<? super T> comp)
```

We illustrate the iterative `adjustHeap()` algorithm when index `first = 0`. This is the situation with `popHeap()`, where the root must move down the tree until we reestablish heap order. Start by comparing the root value (target) with the values of its two children. If the root is not greater than or equal to both children, heap order is violated. We select the larger child and move it up one level. The child then becomes the root. Shift the focus to the child position. The process continues until the target value is greater than or equal to both children or the current position is a leaf node. The target is assigned to this position and heap order is restored.

We illustrate the algorithm for the example in Figure 22.5. The steps are displayed in Figure 22.6. The root 18 is the target. Because 18 is less than its children 30 and 40, the larger child 40 is moved up one level and the child position, index 2, is the focus for the next step. At level 1, 18 is greater than 8 but not 38 and so child 38 moves up one level. At level 2, the element `arr[6]` is a leaf node. Any value in a leaf node satisfies heap order because the node has no children. We have identified a valid position, which is then assigned the target value.

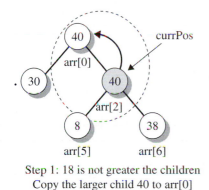   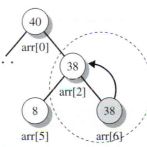   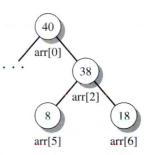

Step 1: 18 is not greater the children   Step 2: 18 is not greater children 8 and 38   Step 3 Assign 18 to a leaf node
Copy the larger child 40 to arr[0]   Copy the larger child 38 to arr[2]
Update currPos to 2   Update currPos to 6

Figure 22.6 *Adjusting the heap for popHeap().*

The implementation of adjustHeap() uses the integer variables currPos and childPos a target value to scan the path of children. Initially, currPos is first and the target is arr[first]. The iterative scan proceeds until we reach a leaf node or target is greater than or equal to the values of the children at the current position. If the latter condition is not true, we must identify the value of the larger child. At index currPos, the child indices are 2 * currPos + 1 (left child) and 2 * currPos + 2 (right child). Initially, set childPos to be the index of the left child. If the value of the right child is greater, update childPos to this index. Both currPos and childPos move down the path of children in tandem. When one of the stopping conditions is true, terminate the iterative process and assign target to arr[currPos].

adjustHeap():

```
// filter the array element arr[first] down the heap with index
// range [first, last)
private static <T> void adjustHeap(T[] arr, int first, int last,
                                        Comparator<? super T> comp)
{
    int currentPos, childPos;
    T target;

    // start at first and filter target down the heap
    currentPos = first;
    target = arr[first];

    // compute the left child index and begin a scan down
    // path of children, stopping at end of list (last)
    // or when we find a place for target
    childPos = 2 * currentPos + 1;
    while (childPos < last)
    {
        // index of right child is childPos+1; compare the
        // two children; change childPos if
        // comp.compare(arr[childPos+1], arr[childPos]) < 0
        if ((childPos+1 < last) &&
            comp.compare(arr[childPos+1], arr[childPos]) < 0)
            childPos = childPos + 1;

        // compare selected child to target
        if (comp.compare(arr[childPos],target) < 0)
        {
            // comp.compare(selected child, target) < 0;
            // move selected child to the parent;
            // position of selected child is now vacated
            arr[currentPos] = arr[childPos];

            // update indices to continue the scan
            currentPos = childPos;
            childPos = 2 * currentPos + 1;
        }
```

```
        else
            // target belongs at currentPos
            break;
    }
    arr[currentPos] = target;
}
```

Implementing popHeap()   No matter whether the operation occurs in a maximum heap or a minimum heap, the root (`arr[0]`) holds the optimal value. The implementation first captures the optimal value and then exchanges it with the last value in the heap (`arr[last-1]`). A call to `adjustHeap()` reestablishes heap order in a heap which now has index range [0, last−1). Method `popHeap()` concludes by returning the optimal value.

popHeap():

```
// the array elements in the range [0, last) are a heap;
// swap the first and last elements of the heap and then
// make the elements in the index range [0, last-1) a heap;
// use the Comparator comp to perform comparisons
public static <T> T popHeap(T[] arr, int last,
                    Comparator<? super T> comp)
{
    // element that is popped from the heap
    T temp = arr[0];

    // exchange last element in the heap with the deleted
    // (root) element
    arr[0] = arr[last-1];
    arr[last-1] = temp;

    // filter down the root over the range [0, last-1)
    adjustHeap(arr, 0, last-1, comp);
    return temp;
}
```

popHeap() deletes the root from a heap with index range [0, last).

Displaying a Heap

For a search tree, the method `displayTree()` returns a string that describes the hierarchical order of nodes in the tree. The methods `drawTree()` and `drawTrees()` provide a graphical display of the tree. The latter allows for multiple frames, which illustrate changes in the tree. We have similar methods for a heap. In the `Heaps` class, you can find `displayHeap()`, `drawHeap()`, and `drawHeaps()`. In each case, the parameter list includes an array `arr` of type `Object`, an index n, and the integer `maxCharacters` that specifies the maximum length for a string representation of the values.

```
// used for console and GUI output
public static String displayHeap(Object[] arr, int n,
                        int maxCharacters);
```

```
// provides graphical display of the heap;  drawHeaps() keeps
// the window open for new frames that illustrate changes
// in the heap
public static void drawHeap(Object[] arr, int n,
                             int maxCharacters);
public static void drawHeaps(Object[] arr, int n,
                             int maxCharacters);
```

Methods such as pushHeap() and popHeap() assume that only the array elements in the index range [0, n) form a heap. The range is expanded and contracted as elements are added or removed from the heap. The heap display methods use the integer parameter n to specify the upper bound for the index range of elements in the heap.

PROGRAM 22.1 HEAP OPERATIONS

Let us look at a simple program that illustrates the heap methods. Array intArr is initialized with seven Integer values. The program creates uninitialized Integer arrays heapArrA and heapArrB with the same number of elements as intArr. In a loop, calls to pushHeap() transform heapArrA into a maximum heap and heapArrB into a minimum heap. A call to displayHeap() outputs heapArrA on the console. After graphically displaying heapArrB using drawHeaps(), a call to popHeap() removes the minimum value from heapArrB. After outputting the minimum value, a call to drawHeap() graphically displays the modified heap.

```
import ds.util.Heaps;
import ds.util.Greater;
import ds.util.Less;

public class Program22_1
{
    public static void main(String[] args)
    {
        // integer array used to create heaps arrA and arrB
        Integer[] intArr = {15, 29, 52, 17, 21, 39, 8},
                  heapArrA = new Integer[intArr.length],
                  heapArrB = new Integer[intArr.length];
        int i;

        // comparators to specify maximum or minimum heap
        Greater<Integer> greater = new Greater<Integer>();
        Less<Integer> less = new Less<Integer>();

        // load elements from intArr into heapArrA to form
        // a maximum heap and into heapArrB to form a
        // minimum heap
        for (i = 0; i < intArr.length; i++)
        {
            Heaps.pushHeap(heapArrA, i, intArr[i], greater);
            Heaps.pushHeap(heapArrB, i, intArr[i], less);
        }
```

```
        // display the heapArrA
        System.out.println("Display maximum heap:");
        System.out.println(Heaps.displayHeap(heapArrA,
                        heapArrA.length, 2));

        // graphically display heapArrB before and after
        // popHeap()
        Heaps.drawHeaps(heapArrB, heapArrB.length, 2);

        Integer minObj =
            Heaps.popHeap(heapArrB, heapArrB.length, less);
        System.out.println("\nMinimum value is " + minObj);

        // the index range is 0 to heapArrB.length-1
        Heaps.drawHeap(heapArrB, heapArrB.length-1, 2);
    }
}
```

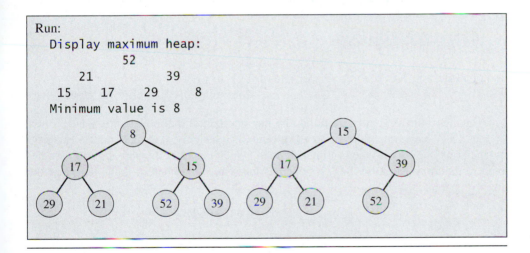

```
Run:
  Display maximum heap:
              52
        21          39
     15    17    29     8
  Minimum value is 8
```

Complexity of Heap Operations   A heap stores elements in an array-based tree that is a complete tree. The pushHeap() and adjustHeap() operations reorder elements in the tree by moving up the path of parents or down the path of largest (smallest) children. Assuming the heap has n elements, the maximum length for a path between a leaf node and the root is $\log_2 n$, so the runtime efficiency of the algorithms is $O(\log_2 n)$.

A heap is a binary tree. Operations have running time $O(\log_2 n)$.

22.4 Sorting with a Heap

Recall the selection sort algorithm that orders elements in array arr of size n in ascending order. A traditional approach describes the algorithm as a series of iterative steps that place the correct element at index 0, then index 1, index 2, and so forth. A modification of the algorithm works in the opposite direction. An iteration at index n − 1 searches the sublist from arr[0] to arr[n-1] looking for the largest element and exchanges it with arr[n-1]. The next iteration, at index n − 2 searches for the largest element in the sublist from arr[0] to arr[n-2] and exchanges it with arr[n-2]. The process concludes at index 0. The selection sort is a brute-force $O(n^2)$ algorithm because each iteration involves an $O(n)$ scan to locate the largest element.

If the original array is a heap, a simpler and more efficient form of the selection sort can be used. For each iteration i, the largest element in the sublist from `arr[0]` to `arr[i]` is `arr[0]`. Simply exchange this largest element with `arr[i]` and then reorder the array so that elements in the index range [0, i) are a heap. You should recognize that the exchange and reordering is precisely the `popHeap()` algorithm. The efficiency that is gained when the array is a heap is obvious. At each iteration, the largest (maximum) element is at a specified location and no search is required. The only overhead involves reestablishing the sublist as a heap. In this section, we develop this "sorting with a heap" algorithm, which is appropriately called the *heapsort*.

Making a Heap

Some applications, like the heapsort, start with an array and need to reorder the elements so that the corresponding array-based tree is a heap. The process is called "heapifying" the array. We use the reordering algorithm to implement the static method `makeHeap()` in the Heaps class. The parameter list includes the array and a `Comparator`.

makeHeap():

```
public static <T> void makeHeap(T[] arr,
                        Comparator<? super T> comp)
```

Turn an *n*-element array into a heap by filtering down each parent in the tree beginning with the last parent at index $(n - 2)/2$ and ending with the root node at index 0.

The algorithm is greatly simplified by the fact that all leaf nodes satisfy heap order (because they have no children). So `makeHeap()` looks only at nonleaf nodes. Heapifying the array begins with the last interior node, which is in fact the parent of the last element in the array. Because the last node has index n − 1, where n is the length of the array, its parent is at index

$$curr Pos = \frac{(n - 1) - 1}{2} = \frac{n - 2}{2}$$

Processing the interior nodes begins with the last interior node and then continues sequentially back to the root node at index 0. Each interior node is handled the same way. We first check to see if the value of the node is greater than or equal to its children. If the condition is true, the node satisfies heap order and we proceed to the next smaller index. If the condition is not true, however, the node must be positioned somewhere in the path of largest children. The reordering operation is precisely the task performed by `adjustHeap()`.

As an example, consider the following `Integer` array shown in the figure. The unshaded nodes are leaf nodes with indices $5, 6, \ldots, 9$. The last interior node appears at index

$$curr Pos = \frac{10 - 2}{2} = 4$$

Method makeHeap() will apply adjustHeap() to successive nodes at indices 4, 3, ..., 0.

```
Integer[] arr = {9, 12, 17, 30, 50, 20, 60, 65, 4, 19};
```

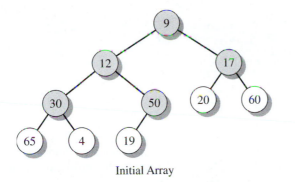

Initial Array

We illustrate the process of "heapifying" the array into a maximum heap. Each picture highlights the subtree that is accessed by the method adjustHeap().

Locate element at index 4: The value arr[4] = 50 is greater than its child arr[9] = 19, and the heap condition for the subtree is satisfied. No exchanges occur (Figure a).

Locate element at index 3: The value arr[3] = 30 is less than its child arr[7] = 65 and must exchange with its child (Figure b).

Locate element at index 2: The value arr[2] = 17 is less than its child arr[6] = 60 and must exchange with the child (Figure c).

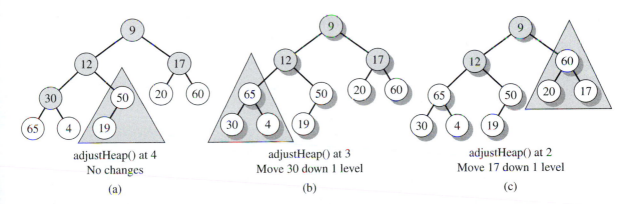

adjustHeap() at 4
No changes

(a)

adjustHeap() at 3
Move 30 down 1 level

(b)

adjustHeap() at 2
Move 17 down 1 level

(c)

Locate element at index 1: The value arr[1] = 12 is less than its child arr[3] = 65 and must exchange with the child. The value 12 must subsequently exchange with 30 so that the heap condition is satisfied for the subtree (Figure d).

Locate element at index 0: The process terminates at the root node. The value arr[0] = 9 must exchange positions with its child arr[1] = 65 and then continue down two more levels. The resulting tree is a maximum heap (Figure e).

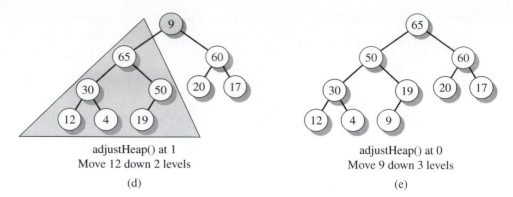

adjustHeap() at 1
Move 12 down 2 levels

(d)

adjustHeap() at 0
Move 9 down 3 levels

(e)

The implementation of `makeHeap()` takes an array and a `Comparator` object as arguments. The comparator indicates whether the heapification creates a maximum or a minimum heap. Use a comparator `Greater` to create a maximum heap and `Less` to create a minimum heap. The code makes repeated calls to `adjustHeap()`, starting at the index of the first nonleaf node. Decrement the index down to 0 (root).

makeHeap():

```
// arrange the array elements into a heap; use the Comparator
// comp to perform comparisons
public static <T>
void makeHeap(T[] arr, Comparator<? super T> comp)
{
    int heapPos, lastPos;

    // compute the size of the heap and the index
    // of the last parent
    lastPos = arr.length;
    heapPos = (lastPos - 2)/2;

    // filter down every parent in order from last parent
    // down to root
    while (heapPos >= 0)
    {
        adjustHeap(arr, heapPos, lastPos, comp);
        heapPos--;
    }
}
```

The Heapsort

A maximum heap sorts the array in ascending order, a minimum heap in descending order.

The heapsort is a modified version of the selection sort for an array `arr` that is a heap. Iterations handle indices in order from $n - 1$ down to 1. For each index `i`, the iteration exchanges the element of highest priority, which is `arr[0]`, with `arr[i]` and then reheapifies the array in the index range [0, i). The task at each iteration is precisely the algorithm `popHeap()`, which pops the highest priority from the heap and assigns it at the rear of the array. With a maximum heap, the first call to `popHeap()`, with `last = n`, copies the largest element in the list to `arr[n-1]`. The next call copies the second largest element to `arr[n-2]`, and so forth. The array is sorted in ascending order. A minimum heap sorts the array in descending order.

The following is an implementation of the heapsort algorithm. The first instruction calls makeHeap() to build the array as a heap. You can find the method heapSort() in the Heaps class of the software supplement.

heapSort():

```
public static <T>
void heapSort(T[] arr, Comparator<? super T> comp)
{
    // "heapify" the array  arr
    Heaps.makeHeap(arr, comp);

    int i, n =  arr.length;

    // iteration that determines elements arr[n-1] ... arr[1]
    for(i = n; i > 1; i--)
    {
        // call popHeap() to move next largest to  arr[n-1]
        Heaps.popHeap(arr, i, comp);
    }
}
```

Example 22.3

This example illustrates the heapsort for an array with integer values in the range 0–9. By calling heapSort() with a Greater comparator object, the array is sorted in ascending order. A second call, with the comparator Less, sorts the list in descending order. After each sort, the list is output.

```
Integer[] arr = {7, 1, 9, 0, 8, 2, 4, 3, 6, 5};

// call heapSort() with comparator Greater
Arrays.heapSort(arr,new Greater<Integer>());
System.out.println("Sort (ascending): " +
                    Arrays.toString(arr));

// call heapSort() with comparator Less
Arrays.heapSort(arr,new Less<Integer>());
System.out.println("Sort (descending): " +
                    Arrays.toString(arr));
```

```
Output:
  Sort (ascending):   [0, 1, 2, 3, 4, 5, 6, 7, 8, 9]
  Sort (descending):  [9, 8, 7, 6, 5, 4, 3, 2, 1, 0]
```

Computational Efficiency of makeHeap() and Heapsort It would appear that the running time of makeHeap() is $O(n \log_2 n)$ because it performs n/2 filter-down operations, each with worst-case running time $O(\log_2 n)$. However, a mathematical analysis actually shows that the worst-case running time of makeHeap() is $O(n)$.

The heapsort is a fast O(n log₂ n) in-place algorithm.

An n-element array corresponds to a complete binary tree of depth $k = int(\log_2 n)$. During the second phase of the heapsort, popHeap() executes $n - 1$ times. Each operation has efficiency $O(\log_2 n)$. Because makeHeap() is an $O(n)$ operation, the worst-case complexity of the heapsort is $O(n) + O(n \log_2 n) = O(n \log_2 n)$.

The heapsort does not require any additional storage, so it is an in-place sort. Some $O(n \log_2 n)$ sorts have a worst-case behavior of $O(n^2)$. The quicksort that we discussed in Chapter 7 is an example. In contrast, the heapsort has worst-case complexity $O(n \log_2 n)$, regardless of the initial distribution of the data.

Summarizing Static Heap Methods

In the previous sections, we introduced a series of static methods that create and maintain a heap. The following is an API listing of the methods.

class Heaps	*ds.util*
	Static methods
static \<T> void	**adjustHeap**(T [] arr, int first, int last, Comparator\<? super T> comp) Filters the array element arr[first] down the heap. Called by make Heap() to convert an array to a heap.
static String	**displayHeap**(Object [] arr, int n, int maxCharacters) Returns a string that presents the array elements in the index range [0, n) as a complete binary tree.
static void	**drawHeap**(Object [] arr, int n, int maxCharacters) Provides a graphical display of a heap as a complete binary tree.
static void	**drawHeaps** (Object [] arr, int n, int maxCharacters) Provides a graphical display of a heap as a complete binary tree. Keeps the window open for new frames created by subsequent calls to drawHeap() or drawHeaps().
static \<T> void	**heapSort**(T [] arr, Comparator\<? super T> comp) Sorts the array in the ordered specified by the Comparator; if comp is Greater, the array is sorted in ascending order; if comp is Less, the array is sorted in descending order.
static \<T> void	**makeHeap**(T [] arr, Comparator\<? super T> comp) The method that is responsible for converting an array to a heap. At each element that may not satisfy the heap property, the algorithm reorders elements in the subtree by calling adjustHeap().
static \<T> T	**popHeap**(T [] arr, int last, Comparator\<? super T> comp) The index range [0, last) is a heap. Deletes the optimum element from the heap, stores the deleted value at index last – 1, and returns the value. The index range [0, last−1) is a heap with one less element.
static \<T> void	**pushHeap**(T [] arr, int last, T item, Comparator\<? super T> comp) Inserts item into a heap that consists of the array elements in the index range [0, last). The elements in the index range [0, last+1) become a heap.

22.5 Implementing a Priority Queue

In Chapter 15, we defined a priority queue and presented an application. The PQueue interface defines the operations. Elements are added with a push() operation and are removed with a pop() operation. Elements in a priority queue have a priority status that dictates the order in which they exit the collection.

The HeapPQueue class implements the interface PQueue. As the name implies, the class uses a heap as the underlying storage structure. The user is free to specify either a Less or Greater object, which dictates whether a deletion removes the minimum or the maximum element from the collection. By default, a HeapPQueue collection is a "maximum queue" and the element of highest priority is deleted by the pop() operation. The following is a UML diagram for the PQueue interface and the class (Figure 22.7).

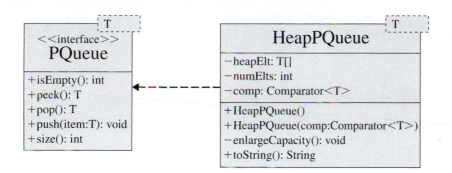

Figure 22.7 *UML diagram for the PQueue interface and the HeapPQueue class.*

Implementing the HeapPQueue Class

The HeapPQueue class uses a heap as the underlying storage structure. The private instance variable, heapElt, is the array that contains the heap. A second instance variable, comp, is the Comparator object that indicates whether heapElt contains a maximum or minimum heap, and the integer variable numElts specifies the number of elements in the heap.

Two constructors create an empty HeapPQueue collection. One version takes a Comparator argument that dictates the type of heap. The default constructor uses the Greater comparator with a resulting maximum heap. In each case, the initial array has 10 elements. The following is a skeletal listing of the HeapPQueue class including an implementation of the default constructor.

HeapPQueue class:

```
public class HeapPQueue<T> implements PQueue<T>
{
    // heapElt holds the priority queue elements
    private T[] heapElt;

    // number of elements in the priority queue
    private int numElts;
```

Implementing a priority queue with a heap ensures $O(\log_2 n)$ running time for push() and pop() operations.

```
// Comparator used for comparisons
private Comparator<T> comp;

// create an empty maximum priority queue
public HeapPQueue()
{
    comp = new Less<T>();
    numElts = 0;
    heapElt = (T[]) new Object[10];
}
. . .
}
```

The HeapPQueue method peek() returns the element of highest priority. This is just the element in the array heapElt at index 0 (the root). If the priority queue is empty, the method throws NoSuchElementException.

peek():

```
// return the highest priority item
// Precondition: the priority queue is not empty;
// if it is empty, throws NoSuchElementException
public T peek()
{
    // check for an empty heap
    if (numElts == 0)
        throw new NoSuchElementException(
            "HeapPQueue peek(): empty queue");
    // return the root of the heap
    return heapElt[0];
}
```

The push() and pop() methods check preconditions and then use the corresponding static methods in the Heaps class to maintain the heap. In the case of pop(), the implementation first checks for an empty priority queue and throws NoSuchElementException. Otherwise, it calls popHeap() with heapElt and numElts as arguments. The heap has index range [0, numElts) in the array. After decrementing numElts, it returns the value obtained from popHeap().

pop():

```
// erase the highest priority item and return it
// Precondition: the priority queue is not empty;
// if it is empty, throws NoSuchElementException
public T pop()
{
    // check for an empty priority queue
    if (numElts == 0)
```

```
        throw new NoSuchElementException(
            "HeapPQueue pop(): empty queue");
    // pop the heap and save the return value in top
    T top = Heaps.popHeap(heapElt, numElts, comp);

    // heap has one less element
    numElts--;

    return top;
}
```

The push() method calls pushHeap() to add an element. The method assumes that there are elements available at the tail of the array in which to grow the heap. This condition is not true when the size of the heap is the same as the size of the array. In this case, we must first increase the size of the array. The ArrayList class deals with this problem by increasing the capacity of the collection. The same algorithm is implemented by the private HeapPQueue method enlargeCapacity(), which doubles the current size of the array. A call to pushHeap() with arguments for the array, the size of the heap, and the new item carries out the insert operation.

push():

```
// insert item into the priority queue
public void push(T item)
{
    // if the current capacity is used up, reallocate
    // with double the capacity
    if (numElts == heapElt.length)
        enlargeCapacity();

    // insert item into the heap
    Heaps.pushHeap(heapElt, numElts, item, comp);
    numElts++;
}
```

Chapter Summary

- There is a natural mapping from an array, arr, to a complete binary tree, called an *array-based tree*. The root is at index 0, the level 1 nodes from left to right are at indices 1 and 2 the level 2 nodes are at indices 3 through 6 and so forth. Index calculations identify the children and the parent of a node. By using these relations, it is possible to follow a path of children from the root to a leaf node and to follow the path of parents from a leaf node to the root.

- An object that implements the Comparator interface implements the compare() method and acts like a function that compares two objects. The classes Less and Greater implement Comparator for any generic type that defines compareTo(). Instances of these classes are used in a generalized selection sort that orders an array in ascending (Less) or descending (Greater) order.

- A heap is an array-based tree that has heap order. In a maximum heap, a parent is greater than or equal to each of its children; in a minimum heap, the parent is less than or equal to each of its children. It follows that in a maximum heap, the root is the maximum value in the array, and in a minimum heap the root is the minimum value.

- Insert into a heap by placing the new value at the back of the heap and filtering it up the tree. Delete the root of the heap by exchanging its value with the back of the heap and then filtering the new root down the tree, which now has one less element. Both of these operations have running time $O(\log_2 n)$. The well-known $O(n \log_2 n)$ heapsort algorithm converts an array to a heap and then uses heap algorithms to order the elements in-place. To convert an array to a heap, apply the filter-down operation to the interior nodes, from the last interior node in the tree down to the root. This operation is termed "heapifying" the array and has running time $O(n)$.

- A priority queue class is easily implemented by using heap operations. Implement push() using the heap operation pushHeap(), and implement pop() using the operation popHeap(). The peek() method simply returns the element at index 0, which is the root of the array-based tree that contains the heap.

Written Exercises

1. Give the output of the following statements.

```
HeapPQueue<String> pq = new HeapPQueue<String>();
int n;

String[] strArr = {"Joyce", "Dion", "Frank", "Warren"};
int i;
String strA, strB;

for(i=0;i < 4;i++)
    pq.push(strArr[i]);

pq.push("Mona");
strA = pq.pop();
pq.push("David");
strB = pq.pop();
System.out.println(strA + " " + strB);

while (!pq.isEmpty())
    System.out.print(pq.pop() + " ");
```

2. (a) Starting with an array, copy the elements into a minimum heap and then use repeated deletions to copy them to a stack. A final step deletes successive elements from the stack and copies them back to the array beginning at index 0. What is the resulting order of elements in the array?

   (b) What would be the resulting order of elements in the array if the first copy went to a maximum heap and the second copy went to a queue?

3. Draw the complete tree corresponding to each of the following arrays.

   (a) `Integer[] arr = {15, 9, 3, 6, 2, 1, 4, 7};`

   (b) `String b = "array-based tree";`
       `Character[] arr = new Character[b.length()];`

       `for (int i=0;i < b.length();i++)`
           `arr[i] = b.charAt(i);`

4. (a) For each node `arr[i]` in an n-element array, prove that the following formulas compute the indices of the child nodes.

   | Item `arr[i]` | Left child index is | $2 * i + 1$ |
   | | | undefined if $2 * i + 1 \geq n$ |

   | Item `arr[i]` | Right child index is | $2 * i + 2$ |
   | | | undefined if $2 * i + 2 \geq n$ |

   (b) Prove that the parent of any node `arr[i]` is at index $(i - 1)/2$, $i \neq 0$.

5. (a) Implement a `CollectionLess` class that implements the `Comparator` interface. The `compare()` method should compare the relative size of two collection operands.

   (b) Write a code segment that creates two collection objects and a `CollectionLess` object and outputs the size of the larger collection.

6. Assume `arr` is an array-based tree with 70 members.

   (a) Is `arr[45]` a leaf node?

   (b) What is the index of the first leaf node?

   (c) Who is the parent of `arr[50]`?

   (d) Who are the children of `arr[10]`?

   (e) Does any element have exactly one child?

   (f) What is the depth of the tree?

   (g) How many leaf nodes does the tree have?

7. In a complete binary tree, show that the number of leaf nodes is greater than or equal to the number of nonleaf nodes. If the depth of the tree is d and there are 2^d nodes on level d, show that there are more leaf nodes than nonleaf nodes.

8. For each tree, indicate whether it is a heap (maximum or minimum).

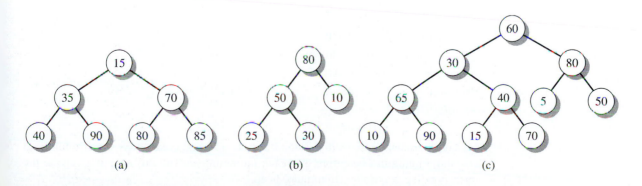

(a)   (b)   (c)

9. For the following heap, list the value of the nodes along the designated path:

   (a) the path of parents beginning with node 47;
   (b) the path of parents beginning with node 71;
   (c) the path of minimal children beginning with node 35;
   (d) the path of minimal children beginning with node 10;
   (e) the path of minimal children beginning with node 40 (level 1).

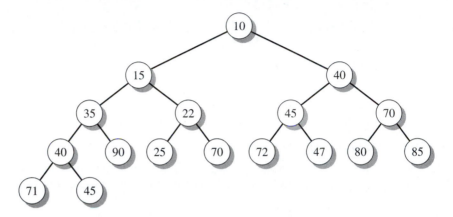

10. This exercise inserts and deletes elements in heaps (a) and (b). An insert corresponds to pushHeap() and a delete corresponds to popHeap(). Corresponding to each heap, there is a sequence of operations that are to be executed sequentially. Use the result of the previous operation as you execute each part of the exercise. Draw the modified heaps at the conclusion of the operations.

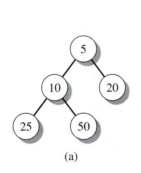

(a)

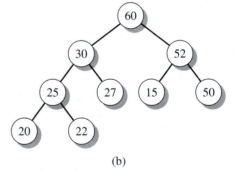

(b)

Heap (a)	Heap (b)
(a) insert 15	(a) delete
(b) insert 35	(b) insert 35
(c) delete	(c) insert 65
(d) insert 40	(d) delete
(e) insert 10	(e) delete
	(f) insert 5

11. Take each nonheap tree from Written Exercise 22.8 and create both a maximum heap tree and a minimum heap tree. For each minimum (maximum) heap tree, create the corresponding maximum (minimum) heap.

12. "Heapify" the following tree to create a maximum heap.

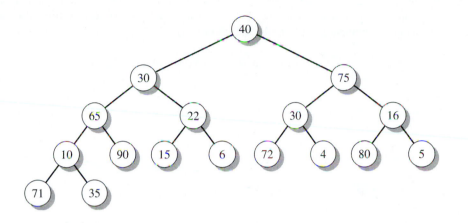

13. Begin with the array and build the corresponding maximum heap. List the new ordering for the array.

(a) `Integer[] arr = {40, 20, 70, 30, 90, 10, 50, 100, 60, 80};`

(b) `Integer[] arr = {3, 90, 45, 6, 16, 45, 33, 88};`

(c) `String str = "heapify";`

```
Character[] arr = new Character[str.length()];
for (int i=0;i < str.length();i++)
    arr[i] = str.charAt(i);
```

(d) `String str = "minimal-heap";`
```
Character[] arr = new Character[str.length()];

for (int i=0;i < str.length();i++)
    arr[i] = str.charAt(i);
```

14. (a) What is the largest number of nodes that can exist in a tree that is both a minimum heap tree and a binary search tree? Do not allow duplicate values.
   (b) What is the largest number of nodes that can exist in a tree that is both a maximum heap tree and a binary search tree? Do not allow duplicate values.

15. Implement the method `isHeap()`, which determines whether the elements of an array in the index range [0, `last`) form a heap.

```
// determine whether arr[0] ... arr[last-1] is a heap
public static <T> boolean
isHeap(T[] arr, int last, Comparator<? super T> comp)
{ ... }
```

16. Trace the heapsort for an array with elements {7, 12, 5, 2, 15, 25, 1}. Draw the initial heap and show the status of the heap after every `pop()` operation. Also show the contents of the array at each step.

Programming Exercises

17. (a) The `ListPQueue` class is an implementation of the `PQueue` interface as a maximum priority queue. The class uses an `OrderedList` object to store the elements. Implement the `ListPQueue` class.

    ```
    public class ListPQueue<T> implements PQueue<T>
    { ... }
    ```

    (b) Test your implementation of the `ListPQueue` class by executing the following code.

    ```
    public class ProgEx22_17
    {
        public static void main(String[] args)
        {
            ListPQueue<String> pq = new ListPQueue<String>();
            String[] strArr = {"run", "walk", "crawl",
                                "sprint"};

            for (int i = 0; i < strArr.length; i++)
                pq.push(strArr[i]);
            System.out.println("Size = " + pq.size());
            System.out.println("First string is " +
                                pq.peek());

            while (!pq.isEmpty())
                System.out.print(pq.pop() + " ");
            System.out.println();
        }
    }
    ```

18. Implement `adjustHeapRec()` as a recursive version of `adjustHeap()`. Use the new method to implement `makeHeapRec()`, which is a modified version of `makeHeap()`, and `popHeapRec()`, which is a modified version of `popHeap()`. Test your work by creating an array with 10 random integers in the range 0–99, and output the resulting values. Call `makeHeapRec()` to heapify the array. Again, output the array. Use `popHeapRec()` to remove elements from the heap until it is empty. Output the final values in the array.

19. A computer system runs programs (processes) by assigning a priority to each process. Priority 0 is the highest priority, 39 the lowest. Assume that when a user requests that a program be run, the operating system inserts a process request record into a priority queue. When the CPU is available, the operating system deletes the highest priority process request record and runs the corresponding process. The process request record has the following UML description.

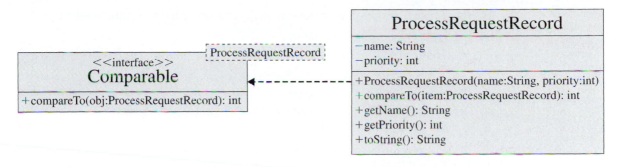

The name *attribute* identifies the process. Implement the `ProcessRequestRecord` class. Method toString() returns a string in the format *<name>=<priority>*. Declare a `HeapPQueue` object `mpq` and assign to it process request records, whose names are "Process A", "Process B", ..., "Process J" and whose priority values are random integers in the range 0–39. Output and delete records from the priority queue until it is empty.

20. Consider the UML description for the class `PriorityData` that contains a data value and a priority level.

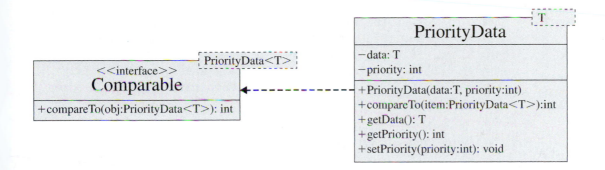

Use the class and a `HeapPQueue` object by composition to declare the class `PDataQueue`, which implements the Queue interface. HINT: Declare a priority queue containing `PriorityData` objects ordered by the priority level of each record. In the `PDataQueue` class, define the integer variable `priorityLevel`, which the method `push()` uses as the priority level of a record. The method increments `priorityLevel` after inserting an item into the priority queue.

Test your queue by reading five integers. Let `push()` store each item in the queue. Then delete the items and output their values until the queue is empty.

21. Use the model from Programming Exercise 22.20 to implement the class `PDataStack`, which maintains a stack of objects by using a priority queue. Test the new stack class by reading five integers. Let `push()` store the values in a stack. Delete the items by using `pop()` until the stack is empty, and output their values.

22. Implement Comparator versions of the insertionSort and mergeSort methods.

```
public static <T> void
insertionSort(T[] arr, Comparator<? super T> comp)
{ ... }

public static <T> void
mergeSort(T[] arr, Comparator<? super T> comp)
{ ... }
```

Write a program that tests the methods on arrays of different object types. Use Less and Greater objects as comparators to sort the arrays in ascending and descending order.

Programming Project

23. (a) Implement the method erase(), which removes the item at index i from the heap by first exchanging its value with the element at the end of the heap and adjusting the heap. The operation should run in $O(\log_2 n)$ time for an n-element heap.

```
// the array elements in the range [0, last) are a heap;
// i is the index of an element in the heap;
// swap the element at index i and the last element
// and then make the elements in the index range
// [0, last-1) a heap
public static <T> void erase(T[] arr, int i, int last,
                             Comparator<? super T> comp)
{ ... }
```

(b) Prove that your algorithm has running time $O(\log_2 n)$.

(c) Write a program that tests your implementation of erase().

Chapter 23

BIT ARRAYS AND FILE COMPRESSION

CONTENTS

23.1 BIT ARRAYS
The BitArray Class
Implementing the BitArray Class

23.2 BINARY FILES
DataInput and DataOutput Streams

23.3 HUFFMAN COMPRESSION
Building a Huffman Tree
Implementing Huffman
Compression

Implementing Huffman
Decompression

23.4 SERIALIZATION
Serializing an Object
Making a Class Serializable
Deserializing an Object
Application: Serializing Objects
Custom Serialization

Some applications, such as compilers, require bit-level access. In Section 23.1, we present the BitArray class that creates a sequence of bits that grows as needed. The bits of a BitArray are referenced using indices, and individual bits can be examined, set, or cleared. Essentially, this class allows the programmer to treat a stream of bits as if each bit were an element of an array. The BitArray class is implemented using the Java bit-handling operators.

Up to this point in this book, all applications have used text files, which contain character data. Many files used in practice are binary files, which are not printable and contain arbitrary sequences of binary data. For instance, a file saved by a word processor is

a binary file, as is output from compression software. Section 23.2 provides a very basic discussion of binary files.

A compression algorithm reads data in a file, encodes it, and writes it to a new file whose size is appreciably smaller than the original. A decompression algorithm reads the compressed file and decodes it to restore the original file. One of the oldest and most easily understood compression schemes is the Huffman compression algorithm, named after its inventor David Huffman. The algorithm finds many uses today. Section 23.3 develops the Huffman compression and decompression algorithm that uses bit arrays, binary files, and a priority queue.

23.1 Bit Arrays

Applications such as compiler code generation and compression algorithms create data that includes specific sequences of bits. For instance, the machine code for an addition instruction is often a specific sequence of 16 bits. Certain bits have fixed values, but others belong to bit fields that indicate the size of the data, the source and

the destination of the data for the operation. For instance, assume the bit pattern for the add instruction include an "X" field for the size (8, 16, 32 bits), a "Y" field for the register number, and a "Z" field for the type of operation; for instance add register to memory, add register to register, add memory to register, and so forth.

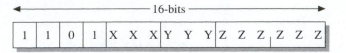

One add instruction might have the following bit sequence that denotes the 8-bit instruction "add reg1, memory".

| 1 | 1 | 0 | 1 | 0 0 0 | 0 0 1 | 1 1 1 , 0 0 1 |

Many applications, such as compilers, generate specific sequences of bits.

Another might have the following bit sequence to denotes the 8-bit instruction "add reg5, memory".

| 1 | 1 | 0 | 1 | 0 0 0 | 1 0 1 | 1 1 1 , 0 0 1 |

Java allows manipulation of individual bits with the operators OR ("|"), AND ("&"), NOT ("~"), and XOR ("^"). The operators take operands of type int, $long$, $short$, $byte$, and $char$. A $short$ is a 16-bit integer in the range from -32768 to 32767, and a $byte$ is an 8-bit integer value in the range from -128 to 127. Table 23.1 defines the operators. The operator XOR ("^" *exclusive OR*) may not be familiar. It produces a 1 only if the two bits differ. Java applies the binary bit operations for n-bit integer operands by executing the operation on each bit. Assume that

$$x = x_0\ x_1\ x_2\ \ldots\ x_{n-2}\ x_{n-1}, \qquad y = y_0\ y_1\ y_2\ \ldots\ y_{n-2}\ y_{n-1},$$

The result $z = x\ op\ y$ where $z = z_0\ z_1\ z_2\ \ldots\ z_{n-2}\ z_{n-1}$

$$
\begin{array}{l}
\ x_0\ x_1\ x_2\ \ldots\ x_{n-2}\ x_{n-1} \\
op\ \ y_0\ y_1\ y_2\ \ldots\ y_{n-2}\ y_{n-1} \\
\hline
\ z_0\ z_1\ z_2\ \ldots\ z_{n-2}\ z_{n-1}
\end{array}
$$

where

Binary bit-handling operators |, &, and ^ act on pairs of bits and return the new value. The unary operator ~ inverts the bits of its operand.

$$z_i = x_i\ op\ y_i\ ,\ \ 0 \le i \le n - 1 \text{ and } op = |, \&, ^$$

The unary operator ~ inverts the bits of its operand; that is a 0 becomes a 1 and a 1 becomes a 0

Table 23.1 Bit operations.

x	y	~x	x | y	x & y	x^y
0	0	1	0	0	0
0	1	1	1	0	1
1	0	0	1	0	1
1	1	0	1	1	0

Example 23.1

In this example, we will declare three byte (8-bit) integers and apply each bitwise operator we have discussed. For each operation, we list the decimal value of the result in parentheses.

> Promoting a result for bit operations to an int requires a type cast when assigning the value to a byte variable.

```
byte x = 0111 0011 (115), y = 0011 0111 (55), z;
```

The operations are

(a) z = x | y   (b) z = x & y   (c) z = x ^ y   (d) z = ~x

```
(a)    x 0111 0011        (b)    x 0111 0011        (c)    x 0111 0011
      |y 0011 0111              & y 0011 0111              ^y 0011 0111
       z 0111 0111 (119)         z 0011 0011 (51)          z 0100 0100  (68)
```

```
(d)  ~x 0111 0011
      z 1000 1100 (-116)
```

Note that the result in part (d) is a negative value. The left-most bit is called the *sign bit*, and is 0 for a non-negative value and 1 for a negative value.

Java also provides bit-shifting operators that shift the bits of an integer or character value left ("<<") or right (">>" and ">>>") by n-bits. Shifting a value to the left n-bits fills the vacated bits on the right with 0 and multiplies the value by 2^n. Assume that x and y are 32-bit integers.

> The operator << shifts integer or char values to the left. Operators >> and >>> shift values to the right using signed or unsigned arithmetic, respectively.

$$x = 0\ldots10110110 \qquad x << 2 = 0\ldots1011011000$$

The operator ">>" shifts the bits right. The original left-most bit (sign bit) fills the vacated bits. For this reason, it is called the *signed right shift*. It performs a signed division by 2^n.

$$x = 101\ldots11011100 \qquad x >> 3 = 111101\ldots11011$$

$$x = 101\ldots11011100 \qquad x >>> 3 = 000101\ldots11011$$

The operator ">>>" shifts the bits right and fills the vacated bits on the left with 0 bits. It is termed the *unsigned right shift* and does an unsigned division by 2^n.

$$x = 101\ldots11011100 \qquad x >>> 3 = 000101\ldots11011$$

Binary Numeric Promotion

Note

Before performing the bitwise operator |, &, or ^, Java performs *binary numeric promotion* on the operands. The type of the bitwise operator expression is the promoted type of the operands. The rules of promotion are as follows:

- If either operand is of type long, the other is converted to long.
- If either operand is not of type long, both operands are converted to type int.

In the case of the unary operator ~, Java converts a byte, char, or a short to int before applying the operator, and the resulting value is an int.

The BitArray Class

The BitArray class lets programmers use bit operations at a higher level than the "down and dirty" use of the Java bit operators.

Rather than requiring a programmer to use low-level bit operations, we develop the BitArray class as an alternative. A BitArray object treats a sequence of n bits as an array, with bit 0 the first bit on the left, bit 1 the second bit, and bit n − 1 the last bit on the right. For instance, if we use a bit array to represent the 5-bit stream 1 0 1 1 1, bit 0 is 1, bit 1 is 0, and bit 2 through bit 4 are 1. To be effective, a bit array must supply operations that return the value of a particular bit in the bit stream and that set and clear individual bits. In addition, the class should provide methods that implement a set of bit-handling operators.

The first constructor creates a bit array all of whose bits are 0. The second constructor simplifies the creation of short bit vectors by using a Java integer array containing the values 0 and 1 to initialize the individual bits. Three methods, assignInt(), assignChar(), and assignByte(), allow a convenient conversion between an integer, a character, or a byte, and the corresponding bit array. The methods read() and write() implement I/O for a binary stream. We discuss binary streams in Section 23.2. The class has the toString() method, which returns a binary string representation of the bits in the bit array. The following is a skeletal listing of the class that includes private data members and constructions. The other methods are grouped into categories and displayed after the class listing.

BitArray class:

```java
public class BitArray
{
    // number of bits in the bit array
    private int numberOfBits;

    // number of byte values used for the bit array
    private int byteArraySize;

    // the array itself
    private byte[] member;

    // constructor; create bit array of numBits bits having
    // value 0
    public BitArray(int numBits)
    { ... }

    // constructor; let n = b.length; creates a bit array
    // whose bits are
    // initialized as follows:
    //    bit 0:    b[0]
    //    bit 1:    b[1]
    //         ...
    //    bit n-1: b[n-1]
    public BitArray(int[] b)
    { ... }


    . . .
}
```

BitArray class methods:

Conversion from a primitive type:

```
public void assignChar(char c);
public void assignInt(int n)
```

Bit access and update:

```
public int bit(int i);
public void set(int i);
```

Bit operators:

```
public BitArray and(BitArray x);
public BitArray or(BitArray x);
public BitArray xor(BitArray x);
public BitArray not();
public BitArray shiftLeft(int n);
public BitArray shiftRight(int n);
public BitArray shiftUnsigned(int n);
```

Input/Output:

```
public void read(DataInputStream istr, int numBits);
public void write(DataOutputStream ostr);
public String toString();
```

Miscellaneous:

```
public void clear();
public void clear(int i);
public void equals(Object x);
public int size();
```

Example 23.2

In this example, let us declare `BitArray` objects and use them in a sequence of operations.

1. Declaration

```
int[] a = {1, 0, 1, 1, 0, 0}, b = {1, 0, 0, 0, 1, 0};
BitArray x = new BitArray(a), y = new BitArray(b),
        z = new BitArray(a.length);
```

2. Operations

```
y.set(0);
y.set(4);              // y = 100010

x.clear(2);            // x = 100100

z = x.or(y);           // 100110
z = x.and(y);          // 100000
z = x.xor(y);          // 000110
```

```
z = x.not();                    // 011011

z = x.shiftLeft(2);             // 010000

z = x.shiftSignedRight(2);      // 111001

z = x.shiftUnsignedRight(2);    // 001001

z.assignInt(31);
System.out.println(z);          // 00000000000000000000000000000
                                // 11111

z.assignChar('a');
System.out.println(z);          // 0000000001100001
```

Implementing the BitArray Class

The BitArray class stores the bits in a byte array. Methods map bit numbers into the correct bit in the array.

The `BitArray` class uses Java bit operators on individual bits in a byte to efficiently implement a `BitArray` object. An array of byte type stores the range of individual bits with numbers 0 to `numberOfBits-1`. The implementation views the array, called `member`, as a stream of bits. The element `member[0]` provides 8 bits, `member[1]` provides 8 more bits, and so forth. There is a mapping from a bit in `member` to a bit number in the range $0 \ldots$ `numberOfBits-1`. The left-most bit of `member[0]` represents bit 0, and the right-most bit of `member[0]` represents bit 7. We continue with the left-most bit of `member[1]` representing bit 8, and so forth. The following figure illustrates the storage scheme.

The private methods `arrayIndex()` and `bitMask()` implement the storage scheme. The method `arrayIndex()` determines the array element to which bit i belongs. Simply divide i by 8. In this way, i = 0 through i = 7 belongs to `member[0]`, i = 8 through i = 15 belongs to `member[1]`, and so forth.

arrayIndex():

```
// determine the index of the array element
// containing bit i
private int arrayIndex(int i)
{
    return i/8;
}
```

After locating the correct array index, apply the method `bitMask()` that returns a byte value containing a 1 in the bit position representing i. This value, called a *mask*, can be used to set or clear the bit.

bitMask():

```
// bit i is represented by a bit in member[arrayIndex(i)]
// return a byte value with a 1 in the
// position that represents bit i
private byte bitMask(int i)
```

```
{
    // use & to find the remainder after dividing by
    // 8; remainder 0 puts a 1 in the left-most bit
    // and 7 puts a 1 in the right-most bit
    return (byte)(1 << (7 - (i & 7)));
}
```

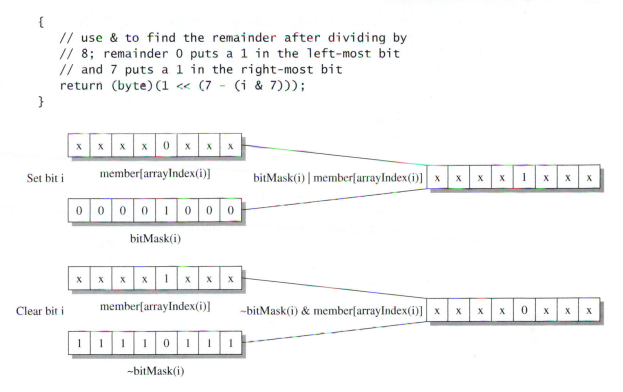

The BitArray Constructors   There are two constructors that create a `BitArray` object. One creates an empty bit array of a specified size; the second constructor initializes the bit array by using a Java integer array of 0 and 1 values. Build an empty bit array by determining the number of byte array elements needed to represent the range of bit numbers, allocate the array member to have that number of elements, and fill the array with 0 values.

Constructor (creates empty bit array):

```
// constructor; create bit array of numBits bits
// each having value 0
public BitArray(int numBits)
{
    numberOfBits = numBits;

    // number of bytes needed to hold
    // numberOfBits elements
    byteArraySize = (numberOfBits+7)/8;

    // initialize the array with all bytes 0
    member = new byte[byteArraySize];
    for (int i=0;i < member.length;i++)
        member[i] = 0;
}
```

BitArray Operators   The class implements the bitwise operators `or()`, `and()`, `xor()` and `not()`, as well as the left and right shift operators. For instance, to implement the bitwise `or()` method, construct a `BitArray` object, tmp, of the same size as the number of bits in the current object and x. Assign its elements to be the bitwise OR of the array elements representing the current object and x. Return this new bit array as the value of the method. Note that the method throws the `IllegalArgumentException` if the current object and x do not have the same size.

or():

```
// bitwise OR
public BitArray or(BitArray x)
{
    int i;

    // the bit arrays must have the same size
    if (numberOfBits != x.numberOfBits)
        throw new IllegalArgumentException(
            "BitArray |: bit arrays are not the same size");

    // form the bitwise OR in tmp
    BitArray tmp = new BitArray(numberOfBits);

        // each member element of tmp is the bitwise
        // OR of the current object and x
        for (i = 0; i < byteArraySize; i++)
            tmp.member[i] = (byte)(member[i] | x.member[i]);

        // return the bitwise OR
        return tmp;
}
```

Implement a BitArray operator by creating an object tmp and set its byte array by doing the bitwise operation on the operands, and returning the object as the value of the operator.

Bit Access and Modification Methods   Methods such as `bit()` and `clear()` access individual bits by applying the private methods `arrayIndex()` and `bitMask()`. The method `bit()` returns 1 if it finds a 1 in the bit corresponding to i, 0 if it does not.

bit():

```
// return value of bit i
public int bit(int i)
{
    // is i in range 0 to numberOfBits-1 ?
    if (i < 0 || i >= numberOfBits)
        throw new IndexOutOfBoundsException(
                        "BitArray bit(): bit out of range");

    // return the bit corresponding to i
    if ((member[arrayIndex(i)] & bitMask(i)) != 0)
        return 1;
    else
        return 0;
}
```

Use arrayIndex() and bitMask() to access and modify an individual bit in a BitVector.

The method `clear()` turns off the bit corresponding to i. The process uses the AND operator and a mask that contains all 1s except for the specific i bit. Create the mask by using the bitwise NOT operator ~.

clear():

```
// clear bit i
public void clear(int i)
{
    // is i in range 0 to numberOfBits-1 ?
    if (i < 0 || i >= numberOfBits)
        throw new IndexOutOfBoundsException(
            "BitArray clear(): bit out of range");

    // clear the bit corresponding to i; note
    // that ~bitMask(i) has a 0 in the bit;
    // we are interested in a 1 in all others
    member[arrayIndex(i)] &= ~bitMask(i);
}
```

23.2 Binary Files

Recall that a *text file* contains characters with a newline sequence separating lines. A *binary file* consists of data objects that vary from a single byte to more complex structures that include integers, floating-point values, programmer-generated class objects, and arrays. In this section, we give an overview of binary file I/O and use it in the implementation of Huffman compression in Section 23.3.

File types are text files and binary files. Java deals with files by creating a byte stream that connects the file and the application.

Binary files can be handled with DataInputStream and DataOutputStream classes.

DataInput and DataOutput Streams

In Chapter 2, we introduced the Java stream hierarchy for text input and output. The design of the hierarchy begins with abstract `Reader` and `Writer` classes that define basic text I/O operations. The `FileReader` and `FileWriter` classes have objects that are attached to a physical file on disk as the underlying character stream. Most applications use a `BufferedReader` and a `PrintWriter` stream for text I/O. A `BufferedReader` serves as a filter on the underlying input stream and provides the method `readLine()` to extract a line of characters. A `PrintWriter` object has versions of `print()` and `println()` that prints formatted representations of primitive data and objects to a text-output stream.

Java handles I/O for binary streams in a similar way. The abstract classes `InputStream` and `OutputStream` define basic byte stream operations. `FileInputStream` and `FileOutputStream` are concrete classes that extend the respective abstract classes. Their objects are attached to physical files on disk that provide an underlying byte stream. For instance,

```
FileInputStream fin = new FileInputStream("dataIn.dat");
FileOutputStream fout = new FileOutputStream("dataOut.dat");
```

are binary input and output streams that are attached to the files *dataIn.dat* and *dataOut.dat* respectively. These file streams process only a single byte or an array of bytes. Often, an application needs formatted I/O to read and write primitive data types. For binary files, the filter streams `DataInputStream` and `DataOutputStream` provide these operations. A data input stream lets an application read primitive Java data types from an underlying input stream in a machine-independent way. A data output stream lets an application write primitive Java data types to an output stream in a portable way. An application can then use a data input stream to read the data back in.

These classes, DataInputStream and DataOutputStream, have a number of methods that cover all of the primitive types along with array and string handling. We need only a few of the methods for our implementation of Huffman compression. We list these methods in a combined API description of the two classes. A program will illustrate the concepts.

classes **DataInputStream** and **DataOutputStream**	*java.io*

	Constructors
	DataInputStream(InputStream in)
	Creates a DataInputStream that uses the specified underlying InputStream.
	DataOutputStream(OutputStream out)
	Creates a new data output stream to write data to the specified underlying output stream.
	Methods
void	**close**() throws IOException
	Closes a stream and releases any system resources associated with the stream.
int	**read**(byte[] b) throws IOException
	Reads some number of bytes from the input stream and stores them into the byte array b. The return value is the number of bytes actually read or -1 if there is no more data because the end of the stream has been reached.
void	**write**(byte[] b, int off, int len) throws IOException
	Writes len bytes from the specified byte array starting at array index off to the underlying output stream.
int	**readInt**() throws IOException
	Reads four input bytes and returns an int value in a machine-independent fashion. This method is suitable for reading bytes written by the writeInt() method. Throws EOFException if this file reaches the end before reading four bytes.
void	**writeInt**(int v) throws IOException
	Writes an int to the underlying output stream as four bytes.
long	**readLong**() throws IOException
	Reads eight input bytes and returns a long value in a machine-independent fashion. This method is suitable for reading bytes written by the writeLong() method. Throws EOFException if this file reaches the end before reading eight bytes.
void	**writeLong**(long v) throws IOException
	Writes a long to the underlying output stream as eight bytes.
short	**readShort**() throws IOException
	Reads two input bytes and returns a short value in a machine-independent fashion. This method is suitable for reading bytes written by the writeShort() method. Throws EOFException if this file reaches the end before reading two bytes.
void	**writeShort**(int v) throws IOException
	Writes a short to the underlying output stream as two bytes.
int	**available**() throws IOException
	Returns the number of bytes that can be read from this input stream without blocking.

PROGRAM 23.1 DEMONSTRATING BINARY FILES

This program simply illustrates methods in the DataInputStream and DataOutput-Stream classes. After writing an int value, a short value, and a long value to the binary file *data.out* using a DataOutputStream, the program writes an array of bytes to the file. After closing the file, the program opens a DataInputStream and reads the int, short, and long values and outputs them. At this point, only the byte array remains unread. Using the method available() to determine the number of bytes remaining in the file, the application inputs the array and outputs its values.

```java
import java.io.*;
public class Program23_1
{
    public static void main(String[] args) throws IOException
    {
        int intVal = 100;
        short shortVal = 1500;
        long longVal = 4294967295L;
        byte[] buf = {3, 5, 2, 7, 15, 100, 127, 55};

        // create a DataOutputStream that writes to
        // the file "data.dat" in the local directory
        DataOutputStream  fout = null;
        // use to input data from "data.dat"
        DataInputStream fin = null;

        try
        {
            fout = new DataOutputStream(
                new FileOutputStream("data.dat"));
        }
        catch (FileNotFoundException fnfe)
        {
            System.err.println("Cannot create \"data.dat\"");
            System.exit(1);
        }

        // write each variable and the array to f
        fout.writeInt(intVal);
        fout.writeShort(shortVal);
        fout.writeLong(longVal);
        fout.write(buf, 0, buf.length);

        // close the stream and open it as a DataInputStream
        fout.close();
        try
        {
            fin = new DataInputStream(
                    new FileInputStream("data.dat"));
        }
```

```
                              catch (FileNotFoundException fnfe)
                              {
                                 System.err.println("Failure to open \"data.dat\"");
                                 System.exit(1);
                              }

                              // input the int, short, and long from the file
                              System.out.println("int:    " + fin.readInt());
                              System.out.println("short:  " + fin.readShort());
                              System.out.println("long:   " + fin.readLong());

                              // input the byte array that was written to the file;
                              // the number of bytes in the array is the number of
                              // bytes remaining unread in the file
                              byte[] b = new byte[fin.available()];

                              System.out.print("byte array: ");
                              // input the array
                              fin.read(b);
                              // output the bytes
                              for (int i=0;i < b.length;i++)
                                 System.out.print(b[i] + "  ");
                              System.out.println();

                              // close the stream
                              fin.close();
                           }
                        }
```

```
Run:
   int:    100
   short:  1500
   long:   4294967295
   byte array: 3  5  2  7  15  100  127  55
```

23.3 Huffman Compression

Lossless compression loses no data and is used for data backup. Lossy compression is used for applications such as sound and video compression and causes minor loss of data.

Data compression is a software technology that takes information and represents it in compact form. Compression algorithms create these compact representations by detecting patterns in the data and then representing them by using less information. The data can consist of a simple textfile or a binary word processing file. More complex examples include sound and audio files. Most computer users have applied a compression program to save disk space.

There are two basic types of data compression. With *lossless compression*, the data compression loses no information. The original data can be recovered exactly from the compressed data. We normally apply this type of compression to "discrete" data, such as text, word processing files, computer applications, and so forth (Figure 23.1). A *lossy compression* technique loses some information during compression and the data cannot be recovered exactly (Figure 23.2). However, this type of compression tends to shrink the data further than lossless compression techniques. Sound files often use this type of compression because they can omit in the compressed image certain frequencies that cannot be detected by the human ear.

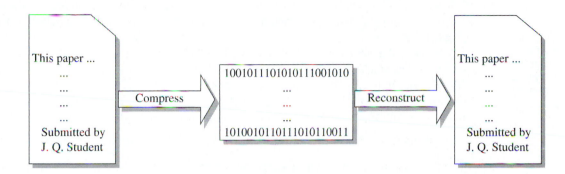

Figure 23.1 *Lossless compression.*

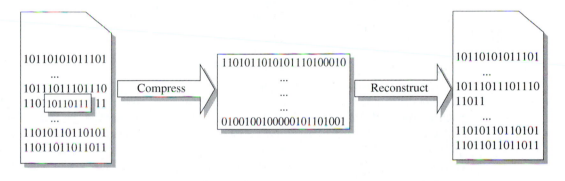

Figure 23.2 *Lossy compression.*

Evaluation of a compression algorithm can include a mathematical complexity analysis that determines its computing requirements. Other criteria assess how much compression the algorithm produces. When evaluating a lossy compression technique, another criterion is how closely the decompressed image resembles the original. Often, a mathematical analysis is very difficult to perform, so we use the latter criteria. The *compression ratio* is the ratio of the number of bits in the original data to the number of bits in the compressed image. For instance, if a data file contains 500,000 bytes and the compressed data contains 100,000 bytes, the compression ratio is 5:1.

The compression ratio measures the effectiveness of a compression algorithm.

In this section, we will consider a compression technique, known as *Huffman compression*, that relies on counting the number of occurrences of each 8-bit byte in the data and generating a sequence of optimal binary codes called *prefix codes*. Algorithms that perform optimization normally execute a series of steps requiring choices. At each step, a *greedy algorithm* always looks at the data on hand and makes the choice that looks best on the basis of the local data. It hopes that the locally optimal choices will lead to an optimal solution to the whole problem. The Huffman algorithm is an example of a greedy algorithm.

A greedy algorithm makes an optimal choice at each local step in the hope of creating an optimal solution to the entire problem.

Huffman compression is a popular and effective technique for data compression. The technique tends to be very effective for textfiles, in which compression ratios of at least 1.8

(at least 45% reduction) are common. The technique is successful for binary files, but the savings are generally not as good. The algorithm generates a table that contains the frequency of occurrence of each byte in the file. Using these frequencies, the algorithm assigns each byte a string of bits known as its *bit code* and writes the bit code to the compressed image in place of the original byte. It is hoped that the sum total of the bit codes is smaller than the original file.

> Compression occurs if each 8-bit char in a file is replaced by a shorter bit sequence.

Suppose that a file contains only the ACSII (8-bit) characters 'a' through 'f' and that the characters have the frequencies specified in Table 23.2. For example, the character 'e' occurs 20,000 times in the file. If we assign each character a fixed-length bit code, we will need 3 bits for each character ('a' = 000, 'b' = 001, ..., 'f' = 101), as shown in Table 23.2. If we replace each character by its bit code, the resulting compressed image uses a total of

$$(16(3) + 4(3) + 8(3) + 6(3) + 20(3) + 3(3)) \times 1000 = 171{,}000 \text{ bits}$$

Computers store data in 8-bit bytes, so the image will have a size of 21,375 bytes. The original file has a size of 57,000 bytes, so the compression ratio is 2.67 (savings of 62.5%).

Table 23.2   Bit codes.

	a	b	c	d	e	f
Frequency (in thousands)	16	4	8	6	20	3
Fixed-length code word	000	001	010	011	100	101

The goal of the Huffman algorithm is to create an "optimal" binary tree that represents the bit codes. We will explain the meaning of optimal when we develop the algorithm. For now, let us explore a tree that illustrates the issues. In the example, each leaf node contains a byte and its frequency of occurrence. Each internal node contains the sum of the frequencies of its children. Starting at the root, a left child designates a bit of 0 and a right child designates a bit of 1. The tree grows until the branches create all bit codes as leaf nodes. The tree structure for the bit codes in Table 23.2 is as follows.

> Use a binary tree to represent bit codes. A left edge is a 0 and a right edge is a 1. Each interior node specifies a frequency count, and each leaf node holds a character and its frequency.

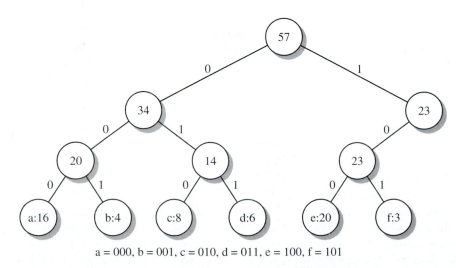

a = 000, b = 001, c = 010, d = 011, e = 100, f = 101

Note that, in the tree, no bit code is also a prefix for another bit code. This is guaranteed, because a byte occurs only in a leaf node. Such codes are called *prefix codes*.

In the tree, each nonleaf node contains a frequency count. This becomes part of our strategy to create an optimal tree. Another issue of optimality involves the right subtree of the root. There are two codes beginning with 10 but no codes beginning with 11. The reason is that the tree is not a full binary tree. A *full binary tree* is one in which each interior node has two children. By converting the tree to a full tree, we can generate better bit codes for 'a'–'f'. If we replace the 23 on level 1 by its subtree, the following full tree results (Figure 23.3).

An optimal binary tree that represents bit codes should be a full tree. If each character occurs only in a leaf node, the bit codes are termed *prefix codes*.

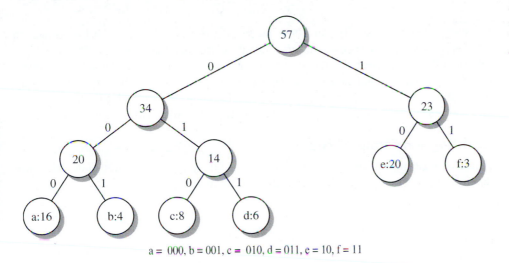

Figure 23.3 *Prefix codes for data in Table 23.2.*

The bit codes for 'e' and 'f' are both 1 bit shorter, so the compressed file will now have

$$(16(3) + 4(3) + 8(3) + 6(3) + 20(2) + 3(2)) \times 1000 = 148{,}000 \text{ bits,}$$

which corresponds to a compression ratio of 3:1.

Now that we have seen a tree of bit codes, we can begin to understand the design of a file-compression algorithm. Begin by reading the file and determining the frequencies of the bytes in the file. Then use the frequencies to build a tree of prefix codes that determines unique bit codes for each byte. Write the tree to the compressed file and then reread the source file. For each byte in the second pass, write its corresponding bit code to the compressed file. For instance, using the tree in Figure 23.3, the bit codes for the 8-bit ASCII characters in the string "ead" are 10 000 011.

To decompress a file, decode the stream of bits by using the prefix codes. To determine the first byte of the original file, start at the root of the tree and read a bit from the compressed file. If the bit is 0, move to the left child; if the bit is 1, move to the right. Read the next bit, and move again. Continue until you encounter a leaf node, which is a byte that corresponds to the bit code. No bit code is a prefix of any other bit code, so there is no ambiguity. Continue in this fashion until reaching the end of the compressed file. For instance, for our sample file and the tree of Figure 23.3, the bit sequence 1100001010 separates into the individual bit codes 11 000 010 10, which decodes to "face."

To compress a file, replace each char by its prefix code. To uncompress, follow the bit code bit by bit from the root of the tree to the corresponding character. Write the character to the uncompressed file.

The overriding issue in using bit codes for compression is to choose an optimal tree. It can be shown that the optimal bit codes for a file are always represented by a full tree. Any full tree with n leaf nodes has exactly n – 1 internal nodes, and so it has a total of n + (n – 1) = 2n – 1 nodes. Thus, if a file contains n unique bytes, and we compress it by replacing its bytes by bit codes, the corresponding tree will have 2n – 1 nodes. There is a simple formula for the number of bits in the compressed image. For each byte b in the original file, let f(b) be the frequency of the byte and d(b) be the depth of the leaf node containing b. The depth of the node is also the number of bits in the bit code for b. We refer to the number of bits necessary to compress the file as the *cost* of the tree, which we specify by the following relation:

$$\text{Cost} = \sum_{\substack{\text{all unique} \\ \text{ch in file}}} f(b)\, d(b)$$

A Huffman tree generates the minimum number of bits in the compressed image.

It can be shown that a Huffman tree generates *optimal prefix codes*. That is, among all trees representing prefix codes, a Huffman tree gives the minimum cost. The Huffman algorithm constructs the tree so that the most frequently occurring bytes correspond to leaf nodes near the top of the tree, and the least frequently occurring bytes occur at the bottom. In this way, frequently occurring bytes have short bit codes and less frequently occurring bytes have longer bit codes. As we describe the algorithm, we illustrate each step with the data in Table 23.2.

Building a Huffman Tree

Huffman uses a minimum priority queue.

For each of the n bytes in a file, assign the byte and its frequency to a tree node, and insert the node into a minimum priority queue ordered by frequency.

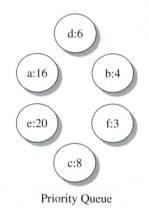

Priority Queue

Remove two elements, x and y, from the priority queue, and attach them as children of a node whose frequency is the sum of the frequencies of its children. It does not matter which node is the left child and which node is the right child. The byte value in an interior node is not used. Insert the resulting node into the priority queue.

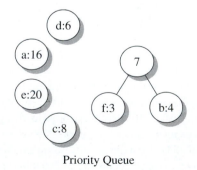

Priority Queue

In a loop, perform this action n − 1 times. Each loop iteration creates one of the n − 1 interior nodes of the tree. Because each interior node has two children, the resulting tree is full. Figure 23.4 shows each step in the construction of a Huffman tree for the sample file.

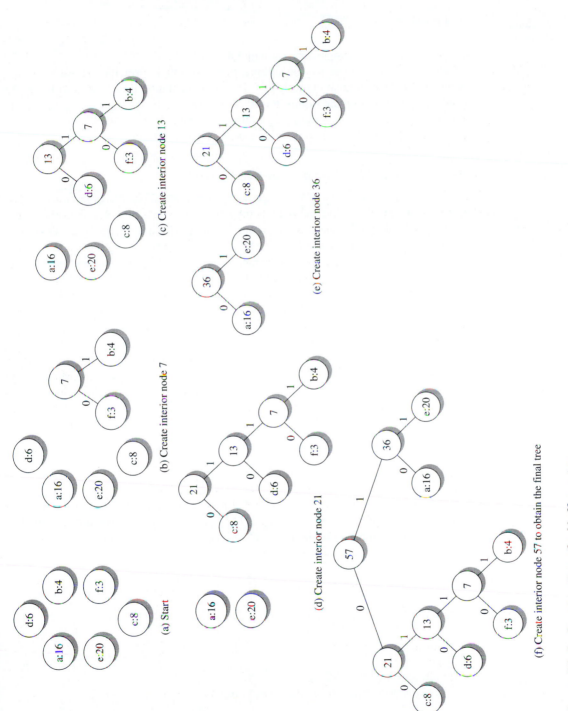

(a) Start

(b) Create interior node 7

(c) Create interior node 13

(d) Create interior node 21

(e) Create interior node 36

(f) Create interior node 57 to obtain the final tree

Figure 23.4 Construction of a Huffman tree.

With a minimum priority queue, the least frequently occurring characters have longer bit codes, and the more frequently occurring chars have shorter bit codes.

Implementing Huffman compression uses a priority queue, bit arrays, inheritance, and binary files.

The class HCompress implements Huffman file compression and writes progress messages to a text area.

For the Huffman tree, the compressed file contains

$$(16(2) + 4(4) + 8(2) + 6(3) + 20(2) + 3(4)) \times 1000 = 134,000 \text{ bits},$$

which corresponds to a compression ratio of 3.4.

Building a Huffman tree for file compression is simple in principle. However, its implementation involves a great many details. The implementation uses a variety of tools we have developed, including the HeapPQueue class based on the heap, the bit array, and inheritance. Because the compression algorithm writes binary data to disk and the decompression algorithm reads binary data from disk, we use binary files.

Implementing Huffman Compression

The HCompress class is designed for use in a GUI application. An object of the class HCompress compresses a file and outputs progress reports to a text area. The class has a constructor that takes a file name as an argument, along with a reference to a JTextArea object. It opens the source file and creates a binary output file by adding the extension .huf to the name. The compression process includes accompanying progress messages that are output to the text area. To use the same HCompress object for additional files, call setFile() with a new source file name. The public method compress() executes the compression steps. To understand some of the internal parameters of the compression process, we provide the methods compressionRatio() and size(). The latter gives the number of nodes in the Huffman tree. For instructional purposes, we include the method displayTree(), which displays the resulting Huffman tree. The class is very simple to use. After creating an HCompress object, call the method compress() that writes a compressed image to an output file whose name is the name of the source file with the extension .huf. If the source file has an extension, .huf replaces the extension. Messages output to the text area trace the progress of the compression. The method displayTree() outputs the Huffman tree in vertical format. Use it only for small trees.

Example 23.3

This example shows the results of applying Huffman compression to a file *demo.dat* that contains the ASCII characters 'a' through 'f' in precisely the frequencies specified in Table 23.2. After compressing the file, the statements output the compression ratio and call displayTree() to output the tree.

```
JTextArea textArea = new JTextArea(30, 80);
                    . . .
HCompress hc = new HCompress("demo.dat", textArea);

hc.compress();

if (hc.size() <= 11)
    textArea.append(hc.displayTree());

// output the compression ratio
textArea.append("The compression ratio = " +
        hc.compressionRatio() +    "\n\n");
```

Output:

```
Frequency analysis ...
   File size: 57000 characters
   Number of unique characters: 6

Building the Huffman tree ...
   Number of nodes in Huffman tree: 11

Generating the Huffman codes ...

Tree has 11 entries.   Root index = 10
```

Index	Sym	Freq	Parent	Left	Right	NBits	Bits
0	a	16000	9	-1	-1	2	10
1	b	4000	6	-1	-1	4	0111
2	c	8000	8	-1	-1	2	00
3	d	6000	7	-1	-1	3	010
4	e	20000	9	-1	-1	2	11
5	f	3000	6	-1	-1	4	0110
6	Int	7000	7	5	1		
7	Int	13000	8	3	6		
8	Int	21000	10	2	7		
9	Int	36000	10	0	4		
10	Int	57000	0	8	9		

```
Generating the compressed file

The compression ratio is 3.389830508474576

Huffman tree
                                          57000
         21000                                        36000
   c:8000              13000               a:16000        e:20000
            d:6000               7000
                        f:3000        b:4000
```

Summary of compress()   The method compress() directs the file compression. We present an outline of its steps and then discuss the implementation of selected private methods. For the full implementation of compress() and the private methods, see the class HCompress. The charFreq array contains 256 elements. Our example involves only six elements, for characters 'a' through 'f' that correspond to the index range 97–102.

1. *Call freqAnalysis()*   Read the file and tabulate the number of occurrences of each byte. The first time a byte is input, increment a count of the number of leaf nodes. The algorithm uses the leaf node count to allocate the Huffman tree. Also, compute the size of the file to support the computation of the compression ratio.

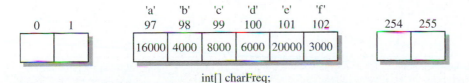

int[] charFreq;

2. *Call buildTree()* Construct a Huffman tree for the file. Build it in an array because pointers must be integer index values and not dynamically generated variables that reference memory only during a specific run of the program.

3. *Call generateCodes()* For each leaf node, follow the path to the root and determine the bit code for the byte. In the process, determine the cost of the tree, which is the total number of code bits generated.

4. This completes all data gathering. Write the 16-bit size of the Huffman tree to the compressed file.

5. Write the Huffman tree to the compressed file.

6. Write the total number of bits in the bit codes to the compressed file.

7. *Call writeCompressedData()* Read the source file again. For each byte, write its bit code to the compressed file.

From the actions of `compress()`, we see that the format of the compressed file is as follows.

Tree Size	Huffman Tree	Size of Bit Codes	Bit Codes

Building a Huffman Tree The decompression algorithm requires tree nodes that contain child locations and, in the case of a leaf node, the byte value. However, the compression algorithm requires that a node contain more data, such as the byte frequency, the parent location, and the bit code for a byte. A simple inheritance hierarchy implements these two different requirements. The super class `DiskHuffNode` specifies the byte data used by a node and the locations of the children. Use inheritance to add the remaining attributes by extending `DiskHuffNode` to create the class `HuffNode`.

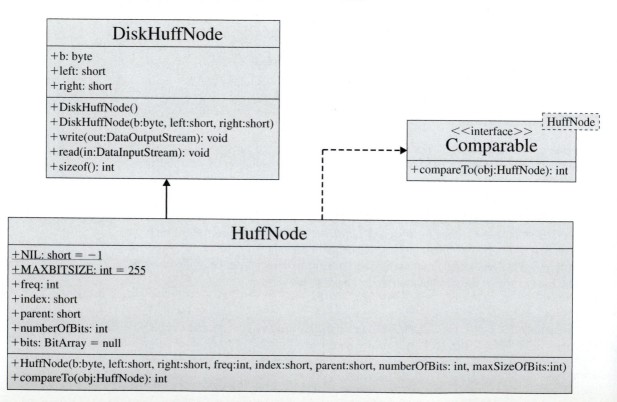

The need for the instance variables will be explained as we continue our discussion of the implementation for the class HCompress. The minimum priority queue uses the compareTo() method as the algorithm builds the Huffman tree from the bottom up. It is theoretically possible for a bit code to have a size of 255 bits (Written Exercise 23.9). Only leaf nodes have a bits attribute with nonzero size.

The method buildTree() executes the priority queue-based algorithm that constructs the tree in the array tree. It requires some attention to detail, including the special case in which the tree contains only one unique byte. In this situation, in order to create a full tree with three nodes, the method creates a dummy leaf node that contains a byte not in the source file. The method creates leaf nodes in the index range 0 to numberLeaves-1 that contain each byte, its frequency, and the index of the node itself. It then executes a loop numberLeaves-1 times and builds the interior nodes. The fact that each node coming out of the queue contains a record of its own index allows the assignment of that index to the appropriate left or right location in the parent. It also allows the children's parent attribute to be set. The following figure shows the structure of the Huffman tree built for the demonstration file. The notation INT means that the node is internal.

> The DiskHuffNode class contains the data and the location of children. Its subclass HuffNode contains the remaining attributes required by the Huffman compression implementation.

> The HCompress method buildTree() executes the Huffman algorithm to build the tree.

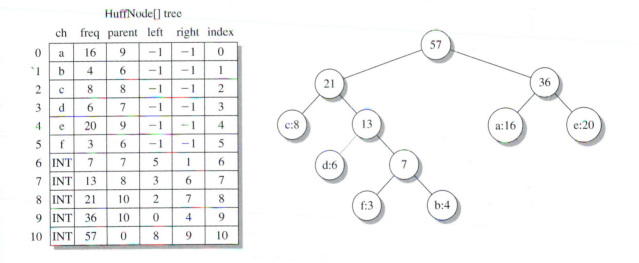

HuffNode[] tree

	ch	freq	parent	left	right	index
0	a	16	9	-1	-1	0
1	b	4	6	-1	-1	1
2	c	8	8	-1	-1	2
3	d	6	7	-1	-1	3
4	e	20	9	-1	-1	4
5	f	3	6	-1	-1	5
6	INT	7	7	5	1	6
7	INT	13	8	3	6	7
8	INT	21	10	2	7	8
9	INT	36	10	0	4	9
10	INT	57	0	8	9	10

Generating the Bit Codes The method generateCodes() determines the bit codes by starting at each leaf node and following the path of parents until it finds the root node (parent = 0). As it makes each transition upward, it records a 0 bit if the node is a left child of its parent, 1 otherwise. This process finds the bit codes in the reverse order, so the method reverses the bits when it assigns them to the bits instance variable of the leaf node.

Writing the Bit Codes To output the bit codes, the method writeCompressedData() declares a BitArray object, compressedData, whose bit size is the cost of the Huffman tree. It sets the file pointer to the beginning of the file using seek() and inputs the bytes again. The bit codes for each byte were determined by generateCodes() and reside in the corresponding leaf node. For each bit in the bit codes for a byte, set or clear the next bit in compressedData. For instance, if the first five ASCII characters of the sample file are "befac", initialize compressedData as follows.

Byte	Bit Code	compressedData
b	0111	0111
e	11	011111
f	0110	0111110110
a	10	011111011010
e	11	01111101101011

Upon the conclusion of input, writeCompressedData() calls the write() method of the BitArray class to output the bits to the compressed file.

writeCompressedData():

```java
// reread the source file and write the Huffman codes specified
// by the Huffman tree to the stream dest
private void writeCompressedData() throws IOException
{
    // vector that will contain the Huffman codes for
    // the compressed file
    BitArray compressedData = new BitArray(totalBits);
    int bitPos, i, j;
    int b;

    // close the source file and reopen it
    source.close();
    source = new DataInputStream(new FileInputStream(fname));

    // bitPos is used to put bits into compressedData
    bitPos = 0;

    // re-read the source file and generate the Huffman codes in
    // compressedData
    while (true)
    {
        try
        {
            // try to input a byte
            b = source.readUnsignedByte();
        }
        catch (EOFException eofex)
        {
            // we are at end-of-file
            break;
        }
        // index of the tree node containing ch
        i = charLoc[b];

        // put the bit code for tree[i].b into the bit vector
        for (j=0;j < tree[i].numberOfBits; j++)
        {
            // only need to call set() if tree[i].bits.bit(j) is 1
```

```
        if (tree[i].bits.bit(j) == 1)
            compressedData.set(bitPos);
        // always advance bitPos
        bitPos++;
    }
}

// write the bit codes to the output file
compressedData.write(dest);
}
```

Chapter 23 of the software supplement contains a textfile, `webster.dict`, that has 234,946 words comprising 2,721,849 bytes. Application of the Huffman algorithm gives a compression ratio of 1.8. The supplement also contains the file `mspaint.exe`, which is a large binary file. In this case, all 255 bytes occur, and the compression ratio is only 1.36.

Implementing Huffman Decompression

The class `HDecompress` performs Huffman decompression. The public method `decompress()` decodes the file.

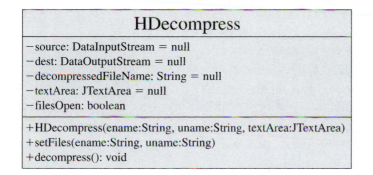

HDecompress
−source: DataInputStream = null −dest: DataOutputStream = null −decompressedFileName: String = null −textArea: JTextArea = null −filesOpen: boolean
+HDecompress(ename:String, uname:String, textArea:JTextArea) +setFiles(ename:String, uname:String) +decompress(): void

Example 23.4

The example creates an `HDecompress` object that takes the name of the compressed file and the name of the restored file as arguments. A call to `decompress()` restores the original file.

```
String compFile, ucompFile;
JTextArea textArea = new JTextArea(30, 80);
    ...
HDecompress ucomp = new HDecompress(compFile, ucompFile,
                                        textArea);
// decompress the file
ucomp.decompress();
```

The method `decompress()` is straightforward. From the header data in the compressed file, input the size of the Huffman tree (`treeSize`), and then input the tree into the array tree of `DiskHuffNode` objects. Read the number of code bits (`totalBits`) and use the `BitArray` method `read()` to place the bits in the `BitArray` object bits. Sequence through the bits, tracing paths from the root to leaf nodes and writing the corresponding byte to the destination file.

decompress():

The HDecompress method decompress() sequences through the bits of the compressed image, tracing paths from the root node to leaf nodes, and writes the corresponding byte to the uncompressed file.

```java
// decompress the file
public void decompress() throws IOException
{
    int i, bitPos;

    // treeSize and totalBits are read from the compressed file
    short treeSize;
    int totalBits;
    int decompressedFileSize = 0;

    textArea.append("Decompressing ... \n");

    // input the Huffman tree size
    treeSize = source.readShort();

    // treeSize DiskHuffNode nodes are read from the
    // compressed file
    // into the tree
    DiskHuffNode[] tree = new DiskHuffNode[treeSize];

    // input the tree
    for (i=0;i < treeSize;i++)
    {
        tree[i] = new DiskHuffNode();
        tree[i].read(source);
    }

    // input the number of bits of Huffman code
    totalBits = source.readInt();

    // allocate a 1-bit bit array, whose contents we
    // immediately replace by the bits in the compressed
    // file
    BitArray bits = new BitArray(1);
    // read totalBits number of binary bits from the compressed
    // file into bits
    bits.read(source, totalBits);

    // restore the original file by using the Huffman codes to
    // traverse the tree and write out the corresponding
    // characters
    bitPos = 0;
    while (bitPos < totalBits)
    {
        // root of the tree is at index treeSize-1
        i = treeSize-1;
        // follow the bits until we arrive at a leaf node
        while (tree[i].left != HuffNode.NIL)
        {
            // if bit is 0, go left; otherwise, go right
            if (bits.bit(bitPos) == 0)
                i = tree[i].left;
            else
```

```
            i = tree[i].right;
         // we have used the current bit; move to the
         // next one
         bitPos++;
      }
      // we are at a leaf node; output the character
      // to the file
      dest.writeByte(tree[i].b);
      decompressedFileSize++;
   }

   textArea.append("Decompressed file " + decompressedFileName
      +  " (" + decompressedFileSize + ") characters\n");

   // close the two streams
   source.close();
   dest.close();

   filesOpen = false;
}
```

PROGRAM 23.2 HUFFMAN COMPRESSION

The source files HCompress.java and HDecompress.java implement the Huffman compression and decompression algorithms. The application *Program23_2.java* in Chapter 23 of the software supplement is a GUI application that uses the Huffman algorithms. Figure 23.5

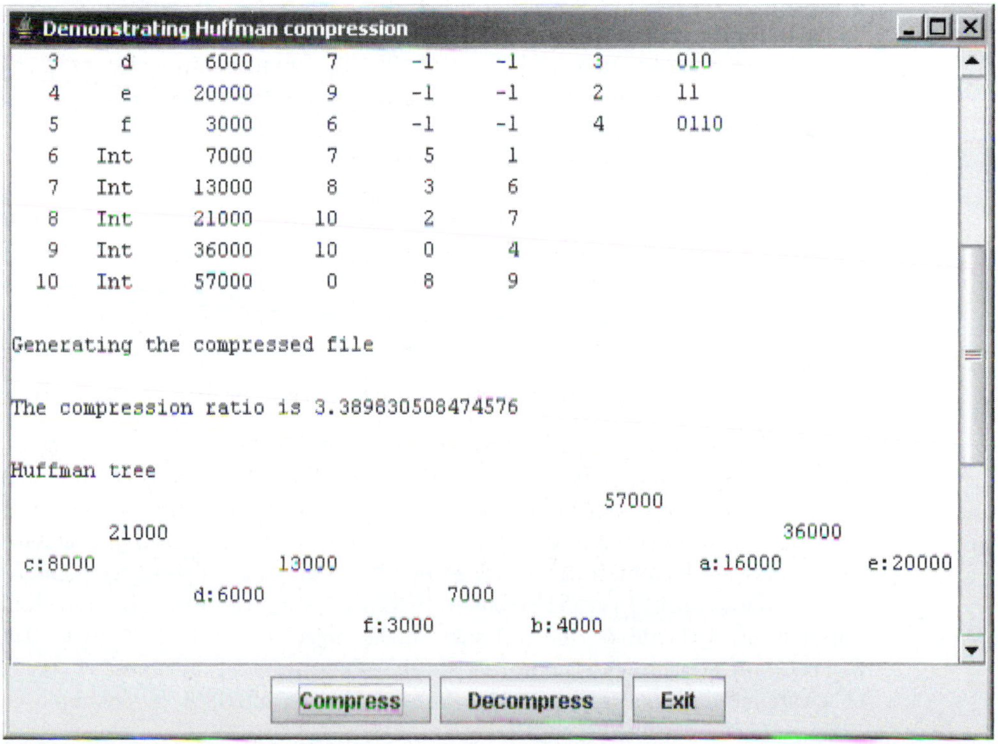

Figure 23.5 *Snapshot of Program23_2.java.*

provides a snapshot of the running application. The accompanying data files `demo.dat`, `webster.dict`, and `mspaint.exe` allow the reader to experiment with the software.

23.4 Serialization

A persistent object can exist apart from the executing program and can be stored in a file.

An object is *persistent* if it can exist apart from the executing program that loaded it into memory. There are good reasons why persistent objects are useful. They can be saved to an external file and then later retrieved. In Internet applications, they can be input and output between a client and a server. We will now illustrate examples that use an external file.

Serialization involves storing and retrieving objects from an external file.

The process of storing and retrieving objects in an external file is called *serialization*. Writing an object to a file is called *serializing* the object, and reading the object back from a file is called *deserializing* an object. In Java, serialization occurs, for the most part, automatically. You can read and write objects of almost any class type, even when the classes are part of an inheritance hierarchy that shares common data. The process will involve saving not only variables of primitive type such as `int` and `double` but also saving objects, arrays, arrays of objects, and other more complex data.

In the *java.io* package, the classes `ObjectOutputStream` and `ObjectInputStream` are used for serialization. The class `ObjectOutputStream` implements the same interface as `DataOutputStream` and so can process basic types of data. The same is true of `Object-InputStream`, which implements the same interface as `DataInputStream`.

Serializing an Object

The classes ObjectOutput-Stream and ObjectInputStream are used for serialization.

The `ObjectOutputStream` class is used to write an object to a file. The stream is created with a `FileOutputStream` argument that becomes the underlying byte stream linked to a file that will store the object. For instance,

```
// the stream oos uses a FileOutputStream that is attached to
// file "storeFile" for storage of an object
ObjectOutputStream oos = new ObjectOutputStream(
            new FileOutputStream("storeFile"));
```

The `ObjectOutputStream` class defines the method `writeObject()` with an `Object` parameter. You can use the operation to write any object to a file so long as its class type implements the `Serializable` interface. We will look at this criterion in a moment. If `anObject` is an instance of a class that implements `Serializable`, then write it to file *storeFile* using the stream `oos` and `writeObject()` with `anObject` as the argument.

```
oos.writeObject(anObject);    // write anObject to "storeFile"
```

The operation writes to the file all the necessary information about the object so that it can be reconstructed later. Reconstructing the file will involve a read operation that deserializes the object. The information that is output does not include just the data in the object. There is information on the class and any superclasses as well as the name and data type of each variable. If the object has reference variables which may themselves point to reference data, `writeObject()` is called recursively for each variable. If the class type for each data object is `Serializable`, the full state of the object is copied to the file. The method `writeObject()` throws a `NotSerializableException` if the object's class or the class of a variable does not implement the `Serializable` interface. An example is found in Chapter 23 of the software supplement.

Making a Class Serializable

Like Cloneable, the Serializable interface defines no methods. It simply signals to the Java compiler that objects of the class may be serialized. Making a class Serializable is often very simple. Just include in the class header the directive implements *java.io.-Serializable*. No additional code is necessary. For instance,

For a class to be Serializable, it must implement the Serializable interface.

Serializable Time24 class:

```
public class Time24 implements Comparable, Cloneable,
    java.io.Serializable
{
    < code for the class>
}
```

In the case of collection classes, the serialization process must be customized. We will discuss customizing serialization later in this section. In some cases, a class has variables which are not Serializable or variables which should not be copied to the file. For instance, the object may maintain the current time and date, which becomes irrelevant when stored in the file. This is data that can be updated after the object is deserialized. To specify that a variable should not be saved, declare it to be *transient*. The method writeObject() will not write data declared transient to the stream.

Deserializing an Object

Reading an object back from a file reverses the serializing process. Start with an ObjectInputStream that uses a FileInputStream to create an underlying byte stream connected to the file. Use the method readObject(), which completely restores the object and returns reference type Object. Finish the process by casting the return object back to its original class type.

```
// the stream ois uses a FileInputStream that is attached to
// file "storeFile" to retrieve an object
ObjectInputStream ois = new ObjectInputStream(
            new FileInputStream("storeFile"));

ClassName recallObj;
recallObj = (ClassName)ois.readObject(); // retrieve object
```

Method readObject() throws a ClassNotFoundException if the definition of the class for the object read from the stream is not in the current program.

Application: Serializing Objects

An application illustrates default serialization of objects. The class SerializableClass simply implements the Serializable interface. Its instance variables include a primitive integer type and an array of Integer objects. These variables are Serializable by default. The objects in the array are copied to a file because their class type, Integer, is Serializable. Two other instance variables, str and t, have class type String and Time24, which implement Serializable. The class has a transient reference variable, currentTime, of type Time24.

For demonstration purposes, we make all of the variables public and include a constructor with initial values for the integer, the string, and the two time objects. The array is created with four `Integer` elements having values 1 to 4.

Class SerializableClass:

```
import ds.time.Time24;

public class SerializableClass implements java.io.Serializable
{
   public int n;
   public String str;
   public Time24 t;
   public Integer[] list = new Integer[4];
   transient public Time24 currentTime;

   public SerializableClass(int n, String str, Time24 t,
                            Time24 currentTime)
   {
      this.n = n;
      this.str = str;
      this.t = t;
      for (int i = 0; i < list.length; i++)
         list[i] = new Integer(i + 1);
      this.currentTime = currentTime;
   }
}
```

PROGRAM 23.3 SERIALIZING AND DESERIALIZING AN OBJECT

This program creates a `Serializable` class object `obj` with initial integer and string value 45 and "Shooting star" respectively. The instance variable `t` is set at *9:30* and the transient variable at *7:10*. A runtime change advances time `t` by 45 minutes to *10:15*, a which point a call to `writeObject()` uses the `ObjectOutputStream oos` to copy the object to file *storeFile.dat*.

The method `readObject()` uses `ObjectInputStream ios` to retrieve the object from the file and assign it to `recallObj`. The value of `recallObj.currentTime` is `null`. The program allocates a new `Time24` object that simulates `currentTime` for `recallObj`. Output displays all of the fields of the object before it is serialized and after it is deserialized.

```
import ds.time.Time24;
import ds.util.Arrays;
import java.io.*;

public class Program23_3
{
   public static void main(String[] args) throws Exception
   {
      // objects used for serialization
      SerializableClass obj, recallObj;
```

```
// object stream connected to file "storeFile"
// for output
ObjectOutputStream oos = new ObjectOutputStream(
        new FileOutputStream("storeFile.dat"));

// initial object with runtime update of 45 minutes
obj = new SerializableClass(45, "Shooting star",
        new Time24(9,30), new Time24(7, 10));
obj.t.addTime(45);

// output object info before copy to the file
System.out.println("Serialized object:");
System.out.println("    Integer: " + obj.n + " String: "+
    obj.str + " Time: " + obj.t + "\n    Current time:" +
    obj.currentTime + " List: " +
    Arrays.toString(obj.list));
// send object and close down the output stream
oos.writeObject(obj);
oos.flush();
oos.close();

// object stream connected to file "storeFile"
// for output
ObjectInputStream ois = new ObjectInputStream(
        new FileInputStream("storeFile.dat"));

// reconstruct object and allocate new currentTime
recallObj = (SerializableClass)ois.readObject();
recallObj.currentTime = new Time24(15, 45);
// output object after recall from the file
System.out.println("Deserialized object:");
System.out.println("    Integer: " + recallObj.n +
    " String: " + recallObj.str + " Time: " +
    recallObj.t + '\n' + "    Current time: " +
    recallObj.currentTime + " List: " +
    Arrays.toString(obj.list));
    }
}
```

```
Run:
  Serialized object:
      Integer: 45 String: Shooting star Time: 10:15
      Current time: 7:10 List: [1, 2, 3, 4]
  Deserialized object:
      Integer: 45 String: Shooting star Time: 10:15
      Current time: 15:45 List: [1, 2, 3, 4]
```

Custom Serialization

For many classes, the default serialization of its objects works fine. In some cases, however, a programmer wants to customize the write/read process. This is true when the object's data does not effectively move back and forth from a file. With collection objects, elements are generated dynamically and stored with some kind of ordering. The deserialization process must retrieve the elements and then rebuild the underlying storage structure for the collection. The ArrayList class is a good example.

In an ArrayList collection, elements are stored in the array listArr of type T, which has capacity listArr.length. The actual elements in the collection, with count listSize, are stored in the front of the array. The tail represents unused capacity (Figure 23.6).

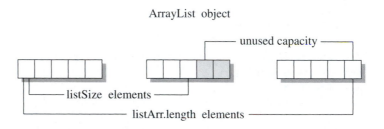

Figure 23.6 *Instance of an ArrayList object.*

Default serialization of an ArrayList object would copy all of the array elements to a file, even those in the unused capacity. This is inefficient in terms of both time and disk storage. A better serialization algorithm copies only the current collection elements to a file. When the object is deserialized, memory for the array is allocated and the elements are copied back. The process rebuilds the collection dynamically.

To customize serialization for the ArrayList class, we must implement two special methods with these exact signatures.

Serializable ArrayList class:

```
public class ArrayList<T> implements List<T>, Cloneable,
Serializable
{
   . . .
   private void writeObject(java.io.ObjectOutputStream out)
     throws IOException
   { ... }

   private void readObject(java.io.ObjectInputStream in)
       throws IOException, ClassNotFoundException
   { ... }
}
```

The first step in the implementation of writeObject() is to call out.default-WriteObject() which writes the instance variables to the stream. In particular, it will write listSize and the reference listArr to the ObjectOutputStream. The output of the reference listArr is not used when we deserialize an ArrayList object. We next use the method writeInt() to output the size of the array (the capacity) and follow this by writing the first listSize number of elements from listArr to the stream.

Custom serialization is necessary for classes with dynamic data. For such classes, the programmer must implement private methods writeObject() and readObject().

writeObject():

```
private void writeObject(ObjectOutputStream out)
    throws java.io.IOException
{
    // write out element count
    out.defaultWriteObject();

    // write out the ArrayList capacity
    out.writeInt(listArr.length);

    // write the first listSize elements of listArr
    for (int i=0; i<listSize; i++)
        out.writeObject(listArr[i]);
}
```

The implementation of readObject() simply reverses the effects of writeObject(). First, call in.defaultReadObject() to restore instance values. Then read the capacity from the stream using readInt() and allocate an array listArr of type T with that number of elements. Finally use readObject() to read back listSize number of objects from the stream. The objects are copied in order into the newly allocated array.

readObject():

```
private void readObject(ObjectInputStream in)
    throws IOException, ClassNotFoundException
{
    // read in list size
    in.defaultReadObject();

    // read in array length and allocate the array
    int listCapacity = in.readInt();

    listArr = (T[]) new Object[listCapacity];

    // read listSize elements into listArr
    for (int i=0; i<listSize; i++)
        listArr[i] = (T)in.readObject();
}
```

Serializing Collections

Note

In this book, we also include serialization for the collection classes LinkedList, ALStack, STree, and HashMap. These collections illustrate key differences in serialization algorithms. Comments describe the serialize/deserialize strategies.

Chapter Summary

- Java supplies a series of bit manipulation operators: A programmer can use these operators to perform operations on specific bits within a character or integer value. Rather than using these low-level operators, it is convenient to build a class that automates bit handling. The class BitArray supplies a high-level implementation for these operators. It allows the programmer to treat a sequence of bits as an array, with bit 0 the left-most bit of the sequence. Operations allow access to specific bits. In addition, the class has I/O operations for binary files.

- A binary file is a sequence of 8-bit bytes with no concern for a newline sequence that terminates lines. The programmer often uses a binary file for both input and output, and the Java classes DataInputStream and DataOutputStream contain methods to support these types of files. DataInputStream allows input of primitive types from a binary file. Output primitive types to a binary file by using DataOutputStream methods.

- A file-compression algorithm encodes a file as a sequence of bytes that consume less disk space than the original file. There are two types of compression algorithms: lossless compression and lossy compression. With lossless compression, the decompression algorithm restores the original file. A lossy compression algorithm loses some information during compression and the data cannot be recovered exactly. Lossy compression algorithms are normally used with sound and video files. One approach to lossless compression is to count the frequency of occurrence of each byte in the file and assign a prefix bit code to each byte. With a prefix code, no bit code is the prefix of any other code. Generate the compressed image by replacing each byte with its bit code. The size of the compressed file is the sum of the products of each bit-code length and the frequency of occurrence of the corresponding byte. There is a natural tree representation for prefix codes. Each interior node contains the sum of the frequencies of its children. Begin at the root and move left for a 0 and right for a 1. Continue until reaching a leaf node that contains a byte. The Huffman compression algorithm builds optimal prefix codes by constructing a full tree with the most frequently occurring bytes near the top of the tree. These bytes have shorter bit codes. The less frequently occurring bytes occur near the bottom of the tree and have longer bit codes. At each step of a loop, the algorithm uses a minimum heap to select the two nodes with smallest frequencies. It joins these two nodes to a parent and inserts the parent into the heap. If the file contains n distinct bytes, the loop concludes after n – 1 iterations, having built the Huffman tree. The bit sequences it defines are optimal prefix codes. Although the algorithm is easy to understand, it is not easy to implement. The implementation requires the use of a heap, bit operations, and binary files. The use of the BitArray class simplifies the construction of the classes HCompress and HDecompress, which perform Huffman compression and decompression. The technique works better with textfiles—they tend to have fewer unique bytes than binary files.

- When a Java application terminates, the data it used is destroyed unless there is a means of saving its binary data in an external medium such as a file. At that point, we say the object persists. Java specifies a mechanism called *object serialization* for creating persistent objects. To serialize an object, we must transform it into a sequence of bytes and transfer the bytes to an external medium. Later, we must be able to input the binary data and reconstruct the object. To serialize an object requires the implementation of the Serializable interface and the use of the two stream classes ObjectOutputStream and ObjectInputStream. To serialize a simple object, create an instance of the class ObjectOutputStream and call its method writeObject() with the object you wish to serialize as its parameter. To deserialize the object, use the method readObject() from the class ObjectInputStream. When a class is more complex, it requires the implementation of the methods writeObject() and readObject() in the class with specific signatures. These methods are generally required when a class generates dynamic memory, such as the ArrayList or LinkedList classes.

Written Exercises

1. Assume that the objects x, y, and z are defined as follows:

```
short x = 14, y = 11, z;
```

What value is assigned to z as a result of each of the following statements?

(a) z = (short)(x | y);

(b) z = (short)(x & y);

(c) z = (short)((~0 << 4) & (~0 >>> 25));

(d) z = (short)(~x & (y >> 1));

(e) z = (short)((1 << 3) & x);

2. This exercise presents four methods that perform bit-handling operations. Match each method with one of the following descriptive phrases:

(a) Determine the number of bits in an int.
(b) Return the numerical value of the n bits of an integer beginning at bit position p. Bit p = 0 is the least significant bit of the integer value.
(c) Return the result of inverting n bits of an integer beginning at bit position p. Bit position 0 is the most significant bit of the integer value.
(d) Return the result of rotating the bits of an integer clockwise.

Method one():

```
public static int one(int x, int b)
{
    int rightbit;
    int lshift = three() - 1;

    while (b != 0)
    {
        rightbit = x & 1;
        x = x >>> 1;
        rightbit = rightbit << lshift;
        x = x | rightbit;
        b--;
    }

    return x;
}
```

Method two():

```java
public static int two(int x, int p, int n)
{
    int mask = ~(~0 << n);

    return (x >>> (p-n+1)) & mask;
}
```

Method three():

```java
public static int three()
{
    int i = 0;
    int u = ~0;

    while (u != 0)
    {
        i++;

        u = u >>> 1;
    }

    return i;
}
```

Method four():

```java
public static int four(int x, int p, int n)
{
    int mask;

    mask = ~0;
    return x ^ (~(mask >>> n) >>> p);
}
```

3. Consider the following bit arrays:

```java
int[] xarr = {1, 0, 1, 1, 0, 1, 0, 0},
      yarr = {0, 1, 1, 0, 1, 1, 0, 1};

BitArray x = new BitArray(xarr), y = new BitArray(yarr),
         mask = new BitArray(8);
```

Specify the output of the following statements. Each statement assumes the initial values for x, y, and mask.

(a) `System.out.println(x.and(y));`
(b) `System.out.println(x.or(y));`
(c) `System.out.println(x.xor(y));`
(d) `System.out.println(x.not());`
(e) `x.assignByte((byte)0);`
    `System.out.println(x.not());`
(f) `System.out.println(x.xor(y) + " " +`
    `(x.not().and(y)).or(x.and(y.not())));`

(g)
```
mask.assignByte((byte)7);
System.out.print(x.and(mask) + "  ");
mask = mask.shiftLeft(3);
System.out.println(x.and(mask));
```

(h)
```
mask.set(0);
mask.set(1);
mask.shiftUnsignedRight(4);
System.out.print(mask.and(y) + "  ";
x = mask.or(x);
x.clear(2);
System.out.println(x);
```

4. This multipart question involves the use of `DataInputStream` and `DataOutputStream` objects and the `Employee` class. The following is a partial declaration of the class. You will be asked to complete the code for selected methods.

Employee class:

```
class Employee
{
    private int id;
    private double salary;

    // constructor; initialize id and salary
    public Employee(int id, double salary)
    {
        this.id = id;
        this.salary = salary;
    }

    // default constructor; id and salary set to 0
    public Employee()
    {
        this.id = 0;
        this.salary = 0.0;
    }

    // return a string representation of an Employee
    public String toString()
    {
        return id + "/" + salary;
    }

    // read the object from f
    public void read(DataInputStream f) throws IOException
    {
        _____;
        _____;
    }

    // write the object to f
```

```
public void write(DataOutputStream f) throws IOException
{
    _____;
    _____;
}

// return the number of bytes in an Employee object
public int sizeof()
{ _____; }
}
```

(a) Complete the implementation for the `Employee` methods `read()`, `write()`, and `sizeof()`.

For parts b–f, use the following declarations.

```
Employee[] arr = {
        new Employee(1,35000), new Employee(2,65000),
        new Employee(5,55000), new Employee(8,28500),
        new Employee(15,75000), new Employee(25, 23000)};

Employee emp = new Employee();
DataInputStream fin = null;
DataOutputStream fout = null;
```

(b) Create a `DataOutputStream` object for `fout` that is attached to the physical file `rec.dat`. Do error checking.

(c) Using the stream `fout`, write the records in `arr` to the file.

(d) Close the stream `fout` and create a `DataInputStream` object for `fin` that is attached to the same physical file `rec.dat`.

(e) Declare an integer variable `size` and assign to it the number of employee records in the file.

(f) Using the value of the variable `size` from part (e), write a loop that inputs each record from the file and then outputs a description of the record to the screen.

5. Consider the following set of frequencies:

   a:8   b:6   c:8   d:3   e:12   f:2   g:15

   (a) Construct a binary tree for the fixed-length codes

   a ->000,   b ->001,   c ->010,   d ->011,   e ->100,   f ->101,   g ->110

   (b) Answer the following questions about the codes and tree in part (a).
   (i) Are the codes prefix codes?
   (ii) Is the tree full?
   (iii) What is the cost of the tree?
   (iv) If your answer to part (ii) is no, modify the tree so it is full and compute the cost of the modified tree.

   (c) Construct a Huffman tree. What is the cost of the tree?

   (d) What are the optimal prefix codes?

6. For a given file F, is the Huffman tree unique? If your answer is no, specify a file and show at least two Huffman trees that give the optimal prefix code.

7. Why is the Huffman algorithm classified as a greedy algorithm?

8. Is there a relationship between the cost of a Huffman tree and the sum of the frequencies in the internal nodes? If you find a relationship, show that you are correct.

9. Recall that Fibonacci numbers are defined as follows:

$$f_0 = 0, \ f_1 = 1,$$
$$f_n = f_{n-1} + f_{n-2}, \ n \geq 2$$

They form the sequence 0, 1, 1, 2, 3, 5, 8, 13, 21, 34, 55, ... Suppose that the frequencies of the ASCII characters in a file F are based on Fibonacci numbers f_1 through f_8.

a:1	b:1	c:2	d:3	e:5	f:8	g:13	h:21

(a) Determine a Huffman tree and give the bit codes for the bytes.

(b) If the frequencies of the bytes correspond to Fibonacci numbers f_1 through f_n, what are the bit codes?

(c) What is the maximum depth of a full binary tree with n leaf nodes?

(d) Is it possible to construct a file whose longest optimal prefix code has 255 bits? If so, what would be the approximate size of the file in bytes? Is it practical to construct such a file?

10. Prove that any full tree with n leaf nodes has n − 1 internal nodes.

11. (a) What is object serialization?

(b) Is serialization useful with the Internet?

(c) Show how you would make the class `Circle` from Chapter 3 serializable. Explain why you do not need to implement the special methods `writeObject()` and `readObject()` for `Circle`.

(d) Why are the implementations of the special methods `writeObject()` and `readObject()` required when serializing the `ArrayList` class?

Programming Exercises

12. Use the `BitArray` class to develop a program that inputs a 32-bit integer value and outputs it as a base-4 (quaternary) number. Obtain the quaternary representation for an integer by replacing each pair of bits in the binary representation by its value, from 0 to 3. For instance, the binary value

    0 0 0 0 0 0 0 0 0 0 0 0 0 0 0 1 0 0 1 1 0 1 1 1 0 1 1 0 1 0 0

has the quaternary representation

    0 0 0 0 0 0 0 0 2 1 2 3 2 3 1 0

(HINT: Make the declaration

```
final int INTSIZE = 32;
BitArray b = new BitArray(1),
          lastTwoBits = new BitArray(INTSIZE),
          mask = BitArray(INTSIZE);
```

and give `mask` the value 1 1 0 0 . . . 0. Input the integer, and assign its value to b. In a loop, use the mask to isolate the two left-most bits of b in `lastTwoBits`. Using the `bit()` method, convert the two bits into an integer value and output it.)

13. Write a program that generates 10 random integers and 10 floating-point values, stores them in a data file, retrieves the data from the file, and then displays the data on the console.

14. The `LinkedData` class maintains a linked list of objects by inserting an object at the front of the list. The method `toString()` returns a string that displays the contents of the list.

```
public class LinkedData<T>
{
    private Node<T> front = null;

    public LinkedData()
    {}

    public void add(T item)
    {
        Node<T> newNode = new Node<T>(item);
        newNode.next = front;
        front = newNode;
    }

    public String toString()
    {
        return Nodes.toString(front);
    }
}
```

Modify the declaration of the `LinkedData` class so that it is `Serializable`.

Test your implementation by developing a program that creates a `LinkedData` object and then uses `ObjectInputStream` and `ObjectOutputStreams` to serialize and then deserialize the object. Display the elements in the object before and after the stream transfers.

15. Create a textfile `huf.dat` containing the following ASCII characters and frequencies:

a:17   b:8   c:16   d:18   e:36   f:8

Using a pencil and paper, construct the Huffman tree and the corresponding bit codes. Use Program 23.2 to compress the file. Compare the program results with your hand calculations. Remove the original file, and use the program to restore the original file from the compressed image. Verify that the decompression worked correctly.

Programming Projects

16. (a) Section 8.3 discusses a method of finding prime numbers known as the *Sieve of Eratosthenes*. The implementation uses a set of Integer objects. Implement the algorithm so it uses a BitArray instead of a set, prompt for an integer value n, and output all prime numbers p in the range $2 \leq p \leq n$.

    (b) Consult the Java API and read the documentation for the class BitSet in the package java.util. Do part (a) by using BitSet instead of BitArray.

17. Add the following methods to the BitArray class.

```
// rotate the bits to the right n times; for each
// rotation, the least significant bit becomes the
// most significant bit
public BitArray ror(int n)
{ ... }

// rotate the bits to the left n times; for each
// rotation, the most significant bit becomes the
// least significant bit
public BitArray rol(int n)
{ ... }
```

Using Example 23.2 as a model, write a program that tests your work.

Chapter 24

GRAPHS AND PATHS

CONTENTS

24.1 GRAPH TERMINOLOGY
Directed Graphs
Weighted Graphs

24.2 CREATING AND USING GRAPHS
The Graph Interface
The DiGraph Class

24.3 GRAPH-TRAVERSAL ALGORITHMS
Breadth-First Search Algorithm
Depth-First Visit Algorithm
Depth-First Search Algorithm
Acyclic Graphs

This chapter continues our study of data structures by introducing graphs, which are structures consisting of vertices and edges that connect the vertices. Graphs are an important topic in finite mathematics, with applications in computer science and other areas of study. A graph is the most general collection in the book, because it allows arbitrary relationships among the vertices. With structures like `ArrayLists` and `LinkedLists`, there is a linear relationship among the objects, defined by their positions in the collection. Trees are hierarchical structures in which the relationships flow from parent to child. In a graph, any vertex is potentially connected to any other vertex. We begin a study of graphs with terminology that describes the relationship between vertices and edges.

You will see that there are two types of graphs, *undirected graphs* and *directed graphs,* which are more commonly referred to as digraphs. As with other data structures, we define a `Graph` interface that lists basic graph operations. The interface applies to both directed and undirected graphs. We provide the `DiGraph` class, which is a directed graph implementation of the interface.

A graph algorithm typically requires a traversal of vertices, just like binary tree algorithms require a traversal strategy to visit the nodes. In Section 24.3, we develop the two fundamental graph-traversal algorithms, namely, *breadth-first search* (bfs) and *depth-first search* (dfs). These algorithms bear marked similarity with the level-order and postorder scans of a binary tree.

24.1 Graph Terminology

A graph consists of a set of *vertices* V, along with a set of *edges* E that connect pairs of vertices. An edge $(e = v_i, v_j)$ connects vertices v_i and v_j. A *self-loop* is an edge that connects a vertex to itself. We assume that none of our graphs have self-loops.

$$\text{Vertices} = \{v_1, v_2, v_3, \ldots, v_m\}$$

$$\text{Edges} = \{e_1, e_2, e_3, \ldots, e_n\}$$

In Figure 24.1, the buildings and the connecting walkways in a civic center form a graph. The vertices consist of three government facilities, an opera, and a library.

The *degree* of a vertex is the number of edges originating at the vertex. Two vertices in a graph are *adjacent* (neighbors) if there is an edge connecting the vertices. The term *path* describes a more general notion of connection. Two vertices v_s and v_e lie on a path, provided that there is a sequence of vertices beginning with v_s and ending with v_e such that each successive pair are adjacent vertices. The *length of the path* is the number of edges connecting the vertices.

> A graph is a set of vertices along with a set of edges that connect pairs of vertices.

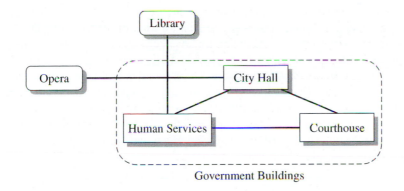

Figure 24.1   *Civic center graph.*

$$P(v_s, v_e): v_s = v_0\, v_1\, v_2 \cdots v_{(n-1)}\, v_n = v_e \qquad (v_i, v_{i+1}) \text{ are adjacent } 0 \le i \le n - 1$$

$$\text{Length } P(v_s, v_e) = n$$

For instance, in Figure 24.1, the Library and the Human Services building are adjacent vertices. The Library and the Opera are not adjacent, but they do lie on a path of length 3.

$$P(\text{Library}, \text{Opera}) = \text{Library-Human Services-City Hall-Opera}$$

> A path between vertices v and w is a series of edges leading from v to w. The path length is the number of edges in the path.

A graph exhibits different kinds of paths. A *simple path* has distinct edges. For instance, Opera-City Hall-Human Services is a simple path, but Human Services-Courthouse-Human Services is not. A *cycle* is a simple path of positive length that starts and ends at the same vertex. Among the government buildings, a path from City Hall back to City Hall by way of Human Services and the Courthouse is a cycle. A graph with no cycles is said to be *acyclic*.

> A path is simple if all its edges are distinct. A cycle is a simple path that starts and ends on the same vertex.

The existence of a path indicates that two vertices are connected. In terms of access, we say one vertex is *reachable* from the other. The terminology can be extended to the entire graph. A graph is *connected* if each pair of distinct vertices has a path between them. The Civic Center is an example. A *complete graph* is a connected graph in which each pair of vertices is linked by an edge. Figure 24.2 displays examples of connected, disconnected, and complete graphs.

> A graph is connected if there is a path between any pair of distinct vertices.

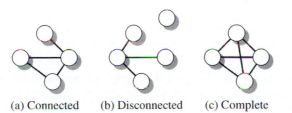

(a) Connected   (b) Disconnected   (c) Complete

Figure 24.2   *Graph categories.*

Directed Graphs

In a digraph, edges have a direction. There might be an edge from v to w but no edge from w to v.

Up to this point, we have described an edge as a pair that connects two vertices. Movement between vertices can occur in either direction. Edges of this type are called *undirected edges* and the corresponding graph is called an *undirected graph*. For many applications, such as a city map that includes one-way streets, we want the edges of the graph to have a direction representing flow. For these graphs, an edge is an ordered pair $E = (v_i, v_j)$ connecting vertex v_i to v_j. The graph must provide a second edge, $E = (v_j, v_i)$, if flow between the vertices occurs in both directions. Graphs with ordered edges are called *directed graphs* or *digraphs*. Figure 24.3 is an example of a digraph with five vertices and seven edges. In this chapter, we present a `Graph` interface that applies to both undirected graphs and digraphs, and we discuss an implementation, called `DiGraph`, that represents a digraph. For applications that need an undirected graph, we use a `DiGraph` object and provide pairs of directed edges to connect the vertices.

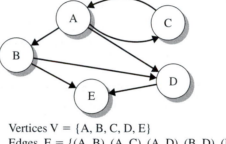

Vertices V = {A, B, C, D, E}
Edges E = {(A, B), (A, C), (A, D), (B, D), (B, E), (C, A),
               (D, E)}

Figure 24.3 *Sample digraph with five vertices and seven edges.*

Much of the terminology for undirected graphs carries over to digraphs. For instance, vertex v_i is adjacent to vertex v_j if there is a directed edge (v_i, v_j) between the vertices. The notation $E = (v_i, v_j)$ highlights the fact that the edge emanates from the source vertex v_i and terminates in the destination (ending) vertex v_j. A *directed path* (path) connecting vertices v_s and v_e is a sequence of directed edges that begin at v_s and end at v_e. The number of the edges that emanate from a vertex v is called the *out-degree* of the vertex. The number of the edges that terminate in vertex v is the *in-degree* of the vertex. In Figure 24.3, vertex A has out-degree 3 and in-degree 1. The out-degree of vertex E is 0, while its in-degree is 2.

A digraph can be strongly connected, weakly connected, or neither.

The concept of connectivity in a digraph distinguishes between a strongly connected and a weakly connected digraph. A digraph is *strongly connected* if there is a path from any vertex to any other vertex. The digraph is *weakly connected* if, for each pair of vertices v_i and v_j, there is either a path $P(v_i, v_j)$ or a path $P(v_j, v_i)$. Figure 24.4 illustrates different types of connectedness for a digraph.

An acyclic graph has no cycles.

A *cycle* in a digraph is a path of length 2 or more that connects a vertex to itself. In the directed graph of Figure 24.4c, the vertices {A, B, C} are in a cycle. In the digraph of Figure 24.4b, the path A-B-A is considered a cycle. A digraph that contains no cycles is called an *acyclic* digraph.

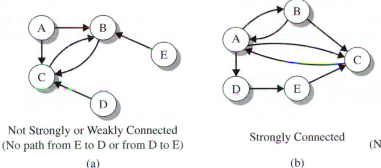

Not Strongly or Weakly Connected
(No path from E to D or from D to E)

(a)

Strongly Connected

(b)

Weakly Connected
(No path from D to any other vertex)

(c)

Figure 24.4 *Types of connectedness for a digraph.*

Weighted Graphs

Edges in a graph describe links between vertices. The edges may also have an associated value, called a *weight*, that represents an attribute such as length, flow potential, and so forth. Graphs with weighted edges are called *weighted graphs*. The wiring diagram of a house is an undirected graph. If each edge of the graph is labeled with the distance between outlets, the diagram is a weighted graph. Transportation managers use a weighted digraph to describe potential traffic flow on city streets. All of our graphs are weighted graphs. When the weight component is not relevant, we simply assign a weight of 1 to each edge in the graph. Figure 24.5 illustrates a weighted job-scheduling digraph. The value of an edge defines the length of time to finish a task.

> Each edge in a weighted digraph has a cost associated with traversing the edge.

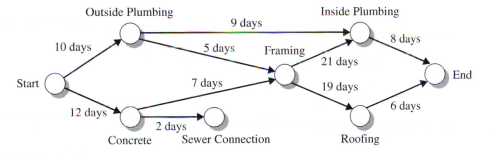

Figure 24.5 *Home construction schedule.*

24.2 Creating and Using Graphs

Our ultimate goal is to develop graph algorithms and use them in applications. We need tools to create a graph and operations to access and update its properties. We do this in two steps. The `Graph` interface defines methods that describe graph operations. The `DiGraph` class implements the interface and enables us to input the vertices and edges and display the key graph attributes.

The Graph Interface

The `Graph` interface defines all of the methods you need to build a graph. The interface applies to both undirected and directed graphs. The sheer number of methods in the interface is deceiving. With a closer look, you will see similarities with the interfaces we developed for the list, set, and map structures. Just remember, we must deal with vertices, edges, and weights. Rather than a simple add() method, the Graph interface has addVertex() and addEdge(). The same is true for remove(), contains(), and size(). The following is an API listing of the interface.

The Graph interface specifies all basic graph operations including inserting and erasing vertices and edges.

interface Graph<T>		*ds.util*
	Methods	
boolean	**addEdge**(T v1, T v2, int w) If the edge (v1, v2) is not in the graph, adds the edge with weight w and returns true. Returns false if the edge is already in the graph. If v1 or v2 is not a vertex in the graph, throws IllegalArgumentException.	
boolean	**addVertex**(T v) If v is not in the graph, adds it to the graph and returns true; otherwise, returns false.	
void	**clear**() Removes all of the vertices and edges from the graph.	
boolean	**containsEdge**(T v1, T v2) Returns true if there is an edge from v1 to v2 and returns false otherwise. If v1 or v2 is not a vertex in the graph, throws IllegalArgumentException.	
boolean	**containsVertex**(Object v) Returns true if v is a vertex in the graph and false otherwise.	
Set<T>	**getNeighbors**(T v) Returns the vertices that are adjacent to vertex v in a Set object. If v is not a graph vertex, throws IllegalArgumentException.	
int	**getWeight**(T v1, T v2) Returns the weight of the edge connecting vertex v1 to v2. If the edge (v1,v2) does not exist, return −1. If v1 or v2 is not a vertex in the graph, throws IllegalArgumentException.	
boolean	**isEmpty**() Returns true if the graph has no vertices or edges and false otherwise.	
int	**numberOfEdges**() Returns the number of edges in the graph.	
int	**numberOfVertices**() Returns the number of vertices in the graph.	
boolean	**removeEdge**(T v1, T v2) If (v1,v2) is an edge, removes the edge and returns true; otherwise, returns false. If v1 or v2 is not a vertex in the graph, throws IllegalArgumentException.	
boolean	**removeVertex**(Object v) If v is a vertex in the graph, removes it from the graph and returns true; otherwise, returns false.	
int	**setWeight**(T v1, T v2, int w) If edge (v1, v2) is in the graph, updates the weight of the edge and returns the previous weight; otherwise, returns −1. If v1 or v2 is not a vertex in the graph, throws IllegalArgumentException.	
Set<T>	**vertexSet**() Returns a set view of the vertices in the graph.	

Two methods need to be highlighted. Graph-scanning algorithms require that we proceed from a vertex along a variable number of edges to a designated vertex. The method `getNeighbors()` returns all of the adjacent vertices as a `Set`. An iterator on the set provides access to adjacent vertices. A class that implements the `Graph` interface does not have an iterator. We use the collection view concept from maps. The method `vertexSet()` returns a `Set` reference with methods that allow us to access and update the backing graph collection.

The methods in the `Graph` interface are a template for implementing directed or undirected graphs. However, there will be differences in implementation. For instance, `addEdge(v1, v2, w)` in an undirected graph makes `v2` a neighbor of `v1` and `v1` a neighbor of `v2` (Figure 24.6a). In a digraph, the method only makes `v2` a neighbor of `v1` (Figure 24.6b). The same type of difference occurs with the method `removeEdge()`.

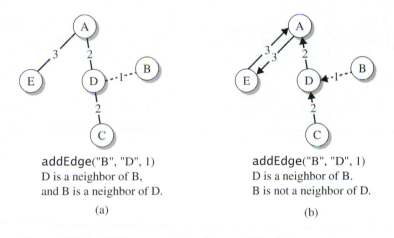

addEdge("B", "D", 1)
D is a neighbor of B,
and B is a neighbor of D.

(a)

addEdge("B", "D", 1)
D is a neighbor of B.
B is not a neighbor of D.

(b)

Figure 24.6 *Differences in implementation between a digraph and an undirected graph.*

The DiGraph Class

The `DiGraph` class implements the `Graph` interface and adds other methods that are useful in applications. A constructor creates an empty graph. The methods `inDegree()` and `outDegree()` are special methods that access properties that are unique to a digraph.

Building the graph vertex by vertex with `addVertex()` and edge by edge with `addEdge()` would be a tedious task. The class provides the static method `readGraph()`, which builds a graph whose vertices are strings. The method inputs the vertices, edges, and weights for the graph from a textfile whose name is passed as an argument.

```
public static DiGraph<String> readGraph(String filename)
    throws FileNotFoundException
```

The format treats the vertices and edges separately. Input begins with the number of vertices, followed by a list of the vertex names. Each vertex name is a string.

(Number of Vertices m)
Vertex$_1$ Vertex$_2$ ... Vertex$_m$

DiGraph method
readGraph()
inputs the vertex
values and the
edges from a
textfile.

For the edges, begin with their number, followed by a sequence of triples where the first two entries are the source and destination vertices of an edge and the third entry is the weight of that edge. For nonweighted graphs, assign the weight of an edge as 1.

(Number of Vertices m)
Source$_1$ Destination$_1$ Weight$_1$
Source$_2$ Destination$_2$ Weight$_2$
. . .
Source$_n$ Destination$_n$ Weight$_n$

The method `toString()` provides a representation of a graph. For each vertex, the method gives the list of adjacent vertices along with the weight of the corresponding edge. The information for each vertex also includes its in-degree and out-degree. Output is in sorted order of vertices.

Output format:

```
vertex name: in-degree <value>    out-degree <value>
    Edges: (list of adjacent vertices and edge weights)
```

Example 24.1

The example creates an empty graph and uses `readGraph()` with the file *samplegraph*
.dat to load the vertices, edges, and weights. An output statement uses `toString()` to display the graph. The following is a listing of the file with an accompanying picture of the graph.

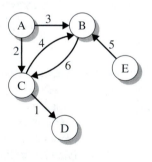

File samplegraph.dat:

```
5                   // data for the vertices
A B C D E
6                   // data for the edges
A B 3
A C 2
B C 6
C B 4
C D 1
E B 5
```

```
// input vertices, edges, and weights from samplegraph.dat
DiGraph g = DiGraph.readGraph("samplegraph.dat");

// display the graph
System.out.println(g);
```

```
Output:
    A:   in-degree 0   out-degree 2
         Edges: B(3)   C(2)
    B:   in-degree 3   out-degree 1
         Edges: C(6)
    C:   in-degree 2   out-degree 2
         Edges: B(4)   D(1)
    D:   in-degree 1   out-degree 0
         Edges:
    E:   in-degree 0   out-degree 1
         Edges: B(5)
```

Note that you will find all the graph input files used in this chapter in Chapter 24 of the software supplement.

PROGRAM 24.1   USING GRAPH METHODS

The program illustrates most of the `DiGraph` methods. The graph uses `readGraph()` to input graph data from the file `"graphIO.dat"`. Statements output the in-degree and out-degree of vertex A and the weight of the edge e(A, B). Update methods change the weight for edge e(A, B) to 8 and delete both the edge e(B, A) and vertex E. These are replaced by a new vertex F and a new edge e(F, D) with weight 3. The figure gives you a view of the graph before and after the updates occur. An output statement gives a detailed listing of the graph.

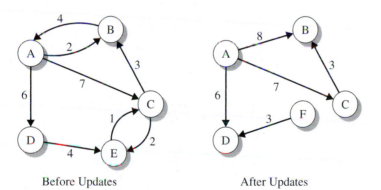

Before Updates   After Updates

The program illustrates how we might use `vertexSet()` to get a collection view of the graph. An iterator scans each vertex and uses its value with `getNeighbors()` to output a list of the adjacent vertices.

```java
import java.io.FileNotFoundException;

import ds.util.Set;
import ds.util.Iterator;
import ds.util.DiGraph;

public class Program24_1
{
    public static void main(String[] args)
```

```
                      throws FileNotFoundException
      {
         // construct graph with vertices of type String by
         // reading from the file "graphIO.dat"
         DiGraph<String> g = DiGraph.readGraph("graphIO.dat");
         String vtxName;
         // sets for vertexSet() and adjacent vertices
         // (neighbors)
         Set<String> vtxSet, neighborSet;

         // output number of vertices and edges
         System.out.println("Number of vertices: " +
                            g.numberOfVertices());
         System.out.println("Number of edges: " +
                            g.numberOfEdges());

         // properties relative to vertex A
         System.out.println("inDegree for A: " + g.inDegree("A"));
         System.out.println("outDegree for A: " +
                            g.outDegree("A"));
         System.out.println("Weight e(A,B): " +
                            g.getWeight("A","B"));

         // delete edge with weight 2
         g.removeEdge("B", "A");

         // delete vertex "E" and edges (E,C), (C,E) and (D,E)
         g.removeVertex("E");

         // add and update attributes of the graph
         g.setWeight("A","B",8);    // increase weight from 4 to 8
         g.addVertex("F");          // add vertex F
         g.addEdge("F","D",3);      // add edge (F,D) with weight 3

         // after all updates, output the graph and its properties
         System.out.println("After all the graph updates");
         System.out.println(g);

         // get the vertices as a Set and create set iterator
         vtxSet = g.vertexSet();
         Iterator vtxIter = vtxSet.iterator();

         // scan the vertices and display the set of neighbors
         while(vtxIter.hasNext())
         {
            vtxName = (String)vtxIter.next();
            neighborSet = g.getNeighbors(vtxName);
            System.out.println("   Neighbor set for vertex " +
                              vtxName + " is " + neighborSet);
         }
      }
   }
```

```
Run:
   Number of vertices: 5
   Number of edges: 8
   inDegree for A: 1
   outDegree for A: 3
   Weight e(A,B): 4
   After all the graph updates
   A:  in-degree 0   out-degree 3
       Edges: B(8)   C(7)   D(6)
   B:  in-degree 2   out-degree 0
       Edges:
   C:  in-degree 1   out-degree 1
       Edges: B(3)
   D:  in-degree 2   out-degree 0
       Edges:
   F:  in-degree 0   out-degree 1
       Edges: D(3)

     Neighbor set for vertex D is []
     Neighbor set for vertex F is [D]
     Neighbor set for vertex A is [D, B, C]
     Neighbor set for vertex B is []
     Neighbor set for vertex C is [B]
```

24.3 Graph-Traversal Algorithms

In Chapter 16, we developed a series of scanning algorithms for binary trees. The algorithms described an iterative level-order scan and recursive preorder, inorder, and postorder scans of the tree. By beginning at the root, the algorithms visit each node of the tree exactly once. Traversing a graph is more involved. Graphs do not have a vertex, like a root, that initiates unique paths to each of the vertices. From any starting vertex in a graph, it might not be possible to search all of the vertices. In addition, a graph could have a cycle that results in multiple visits to a vertex. To avoid this from happening, the search algorithms need a strategy to mark a vertex once it has been visited. As you will see, we color the vertices WHITE, GRAY, or BLACK to implement the strategy.

Traditionally, graph-traversal algorithms are termed *search* algorithms. In some cases, the scan has the traditional purpose of looking for a target value. In other cases, the search determines relationships between vertices and their edges. In this book, we will use the terms *graph-search* algorithms and *graph-traversal* algorithms interchangeably. The algorithms reduce to two standard methods, the breadth-first search and depth-first search. The breadth-first search visits vertices in the order of their path length from a starting vertex. The search involves only the vertices that are path connected (reachable) from the starting vertex. In some cases, this list is a subset of the full set of vertices. The depth-first search traverses all the vertices of a graph by making a series of recursive calls that follow paths through the graph. The fact that the latter search visits all of the vertices is notable. It does this by executing a series of depth-first visits, which carry out the recursive process assuming a starting vertex. The depth-first visit may include only a subset of the graph vertices. The depth-first

Graph algorithms discern the state of a vertex during the algorithm by using the colors WHITE, GRAY, and BLACK.

search simply repeats depth-first visits with starting vertices chosen from the list of unvisited vertices. A chain of depth-first visits eventually includes all of the graph vertices. All of these details will make sense when we look at graph applications.

Breadth-First Search Algorithm

The breadth-first search is modeled after the level-order scan in a binary tree with a notable difference. The tree scan always begins at the root. A graph scan is relative to a specified starting vertex and visits occur only with vertices that are path connected (reachable) from the starting vertex. Let us illustrate the process with the graph in Figure 24.7. We assume the search originates with vertex A. The first vertex visited is A, which has a path length 0 from itself. We then visit each of its neighbors B, C, and G, which have path length 1 from A. There is no specific ordering among the neighbors and so the ordering of the visits may vary. Assume the order of visits for the first four vertices is

A, B, C, G   // A has path length 0 from A, B, C, and G have path length 1

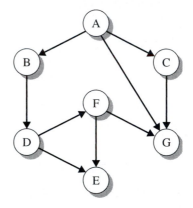

Figure 24.7 *Demonstration graph for the breadth-first search.*

Breadth-first search visits vertices in the order of their path length from the starting vertex.

From vertex B, we visit its neighbor D with path length 2. The search concludes by visiting vertices E and F, which are the neighbors of D with path length 3 from A. In all cases, the breadth-first search visits vertices in the order of their path length from A. Since the search does not specify an order of visits to vertices at the same path length, there is no unique breadth-first search protocol. Given our assumptions for this example, the breadth-first search visits the vertices in the order

A, B, C, G, D, E, F

The breadth-first search of the graph starting at vertex A allows us to visit all of the vertices in the graph. If we had started at vertex D, the breadth-first search would have included only vertices D, E, F, and G. A search from vertex E would visit only the one vertex because E does not have any adjacent vertices.

As in the level-order scan of a binary tree, we design the breadth-first search as a process that uses a queue to store temporarily the vertices awaiting a visit. At each iterative step, the algorithm pops a vertex from the queue, marks it as visited, and then inserts it into a list of visited vertices. The step concludes by placing all unvisited neighbors of the vertex in the queue. In order to maintain information on the "visit" status of each vertex, we associate a color (WHITE, GRAY, BLACK) with each vertex in the graph. Initially, all vertices have color WHITE (unvisited). When a vertex enters the queue, its color is set to GRAY to indicate that it is discovered. Upon removal from the queue, the color is set to BLACK, indicating that the vertex has been visited. Using the color attribute assures that we do not visit a vertex more than once during the traversal.

The following are the iterative steps for the graph in Figure 24.7, assuming A is the starting vertex. The initial action pushes A into visitQueue, which is the queue that temporarily stores the vertices.

Step 1: Pop A from the queue, color it BLACK, and insert it into visitList, which is the list of visited vertices. The neighbors of A are vertices B, C, and G, which are still colored WHITE. Push the vertices into the queue and color them GRAY. Figure (a) displays the elements in visitList and visitQueue after the completion of the first iteration of the search.

Step 2: Pop B from the queue and place it in visitList with color BLACK. The only adjacent vertex for B is D, which is still colored WHITE. Color D GRAY and add it to the queue (Figure [b]).

Step 3: Pop C and place it in visitList (Figure [c]). C has an adjacent vertex G, but the color of this neighbor is nonwhite, indicating that it is either visited or in the queue awaiting a visit. In fact, G is in the queue with color GRAY. No new vertices enter the queue, and we are ready for the next step.

The breadth-first search uses a queue. All vertices are initially colored WHITE. They are colored GRAY while in the queue and then BLACK when they exit the queue. BLACK denotes a visited vertex.

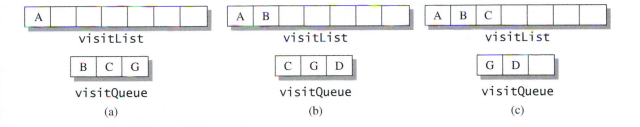

visitList	visitList	visitList	
(a)	(b)	(c)	

Steps 4–5: Continue the process by popping vertex G from the queue and placing it in visitList (Figure [d]). G has no adjacent vertices, so continue to Step 5, which pops D from the queue. The neighbors, E and F, enter the queue (Figure [e]).

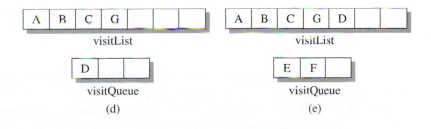

Steps 6–7: The previous steps identify the key features of the algorithm. In Step 6, pop E from the queue and add it to visitList (Figure (f)). E has no neighbors, so proceed to Step 7, which removes F from the queue. The adjacent vertices E and G are already visited (colored BLACK), so the algorithm concludes since the queue is empty (Figure (g)).

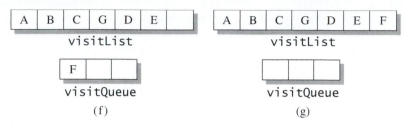

Implementing the Breadth-First Search   To implement the breadth-first search, we need a mechanism for assigning colors to vertices. Vertex colors for the breadth-first search and other graph algorithms are found in the class `VertexColor`. This class defines the color of a vertex as an `enum`.

```
public enum VertexColor
{
    WHITE, GRAY, BLACK
}
```

The `DiGraph` class declares three methods that access and update the color attribute of a vertex.

class DiGraph<T> (color methods)		*ds.util*
void	**colorWhite**()	
	Set the color in each vertex to WHITE.	
VertexColor	**getColor**(T v)	
	Returns the color of vertex v. If v is not a graph vertex, throws IllegalArgumentException.	
VertexColor	**setColor**(T v, VertexColor c)	
	Sets the color of vertex v and returns the previous color. If v is not a graph vertex, throws IllegalArgumentException.	

The algorithm for the breadth-first search is relatively easy to understand, and we implement it with the static method `bfs()` in the class `DiGraphs`. The method visits only the subset of vertices reachable from the starting vertex. We include a complete listing of the method, along with extensive comments to illustrate the design of the algorithm. The method takes a graph and a starting vertex and returns a `LinkedList` object containing the vertices reachable from the starting vertex in the order in which they were discovered by the algorithm.

bfs():

```
// perform the breadth-first traversal from sVertex and
// return the list of visited vertices
public static <T> LinkedList<T> bfs(DiGraph<T> g, T sVertex)
{
```

```
// queue stores adjacent vertices; list stores visited
// vertices
LinkedQueue<T> visitQueue = new LinkedQueue<T>();
LinkedList<T> visitList = new LinkedList<T>();

// set and iterator retrieve and scan neighbors of a vertex
Set<T> edgeSet;
Iterator<T> edgeIter;

T currVertex = null, neighborVertex = null;

// check that starting vertex is valid
if (!g.containsVertex(sVertex))
      throw new IllegalArgumentException(
          "bfs(): starting vertex not in the graph");

// color all vertices WHITE
g.colorWhite();

// initialize queue with starting vertex
visitQueue.push(sVertex);

while (!visitQueue.isEmpty())
{
   // remove a vertex from the queue, color it black, and
   // add to the list of visited vertices
   currVertex = visitQueue.pop();
   g.setColor(currVertex,VertexColor.BLACK);
   visitList.add(currVertex);

   // obtain the set of neighbors for current vertex
   edgeSet = g.getNeighbors(currVertex);
   // sequence through the neighbors and look for vertices
   // that have not been visited
   edgeIter = edgeSet.iterator();
   while (edgeIter.hasNext())
   {
      neighborVertex = edgeIter.next();

      if (g.getColor(neighborVertex) == VertexColor.WHITE)
      {
         // color unvisited vertex GRAY and
         // push it onto queue
         g.setColor(neighborVertex,VertexColor.GRAY);
         visitQueue.push(neighborVertex);
      }
   }
}

return visitList;
}
```

The method bfs() returns a list of vertices visited during the breadth-first search from a starting vertex.

Running Time for Breadth-First Search In the breadth-first search algorithm, the method `colorWhite()` visits each vertex once and assigns the color WHITE to it. This is an O(V) operation, where V denotes the number of vertices. Each vertex enters the queue once, at the most, and hence is popped from the queue at most once. Each queue operation has efficiency O(1), so the total running time for queue handling is O(V). When a vertex enters the queue, the algorithm searches its adjacency list. The total number of elements in all of the adjacency lists is E, the number of edges in the graph; the running time to search the lists is at most O(E). The combination of the activities that initialize the graph, process the vertices in the queue, and search the edges determines the running time for the breadth-first search, which is O(V + E).

The breadth-first search has running time O(V + E).

Example 24.2

The example illustrates a code segment that calls `bfs()` with a specified starting vertex and outputs the list of reachable vertices. The example uses the demonstration graph for the breadth-first algorithm, which we repeat for your convenience. The graph file is *bfsgraph.dat*. We assume the code is run with starting vertices "A", "D", and "E".

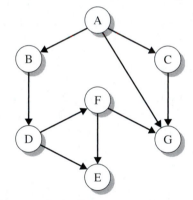

```
// create a graph g and declare startVertex and visitList
DiGraph<String> g = DiGraph.readGraph("bfsgraph.dat");
String startVertex;
List<String> visitList;

        ...
// call bfs() with arguments g and startVertx
visitList = DiGraphs.bfs(g, startVertex);

// output the visitList
System.out.println("BFS visitList from " + startVertex +
                   ":    " + visitList);
```

```
Output:
    Run 1: (startVertex = "A")
           BFS visitList from A:    [A, G, B, C, D, E, F]
    Run 2: (startVertex = "D")
            BFS visitList from D:    [D, E, F, G]
    Run 3: (startVertex = "E")
            BFS visitList from E:    [E]
```

Depth-First Visit Algorithm

The concept of depth-first search begins with the notion of a depth-first visit from a starting vertex. The depth-first visit algorithm is modeled after the recursive postorder scan of a binary tree. In the tree, a node is visited only after visits are made to all of the nodes in its subtree. In the graph, a vertex is visited only after visiting all of the vertices in paths that emanate from the vertex.

As with the breadth-first search, we use colors to indicate the status of vertices. Initially, all vertices are WHITE. A vertex is colored GRAY when it is first contacted in a recursive descent. Only when the vertex is actually visited does it become BLACK. A depth-first visit begins at a starting vertex and searches down paths of neighbors until it reaches a vertex that has no neighbors or only neighbors that have already been visited. At this point, a visit occurs at the "terminal" vertex. We then backtrack to the previous recursive step and look for another adjacent vertex to launch a scan down its paths. There is no ordering among vertices in an adjacency list, so the paths and hence the order of visits to vertices can vary.

An example illustrates the process. Consider the graph in Figure 24.8 where a depth-first visit starts at vertex A. We follow the process by noting each vertex when it is first discovered in a recursive descent, when it is recontacted through backtracking, and when it is actually visited. In the figure, the notation d/f describes two integer values d and f that denote the order in which a vertex is discovered (colored GRAY) and visited (colored BLACK) during the search. Graph applications sometimes refer to these values as the "*discovery time*" and "*finishing time*" for a vertex. The values for d and f will become clear as we trace the depth-first visit.

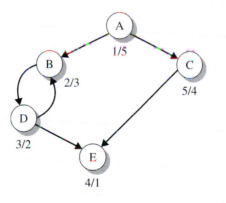

Figure 24.8 *Graph illustrating depth-first visit.*

Discover A: The recursive process first discovers A and colors it GRAY. Continue the scan with one of the neighbors of A, namely B or C. Assume B is chosen.

Discover B: Vertex B is discovered and colored GRAY. Move to D, the only neighbor of B.

Discover D: Like vertex B, color it GRAY. The two neighbors of D are B and E. However, B is GRAY and so it has been discovered even though it is not visited. We know B is accounted for somewhere in a recursive descent from the starting vertex A. Select E, which is still a WHITE vertex.

Discover E: Initially, the vertex is colored GRAY. However, it does not have any neighbors, and so we have reached a stopping condition. Visit E by coloring it BLACK and then backtrack to the previous vertex.

Backtrack D: We are again at a stopping condition. The two neighbors of D are either discovered (vertex B) or visited (vertex E). So we visit D and color it BLACK.

Backtrack B: Like vertex D, we are at a stopping condition and so we visit B by coloring it BLACK.

Backtrack A: Choose vertex C, which is the other (undiscovered) neighbor of A.

Discover C: Once we are at C, we note that its only neighbor E has already been visited and so C becomes the next vertex visited (BLACK).

Backtrack A: This vertex has been involved in the recursive process three times. It was the first vertex to be discovered and the last vertex to be visited. Color it BLACK. The recursive process concludes when the starting vertex is visited.

> The depth-first visit is a recursive algorithm that distinguishes the discovery and finishing time of a vertex.

A depth-first visit returns a list of vertices in the reverse order of their visits or finishing times. In our example, the list is [A, C, B, D, E]. The vertex at the front of the list is the last vertex visited. This is, of course, the starting vertex. The vertex at the back of the list is the first vertex visited. The list is the collection of vertices that are reachable from the starting vertex. We need to appreciate the significance of the ordering of vertices in the list. A vertex in the list is visited only after all of the vertices in the tail of the list are visited. For instance, a visit to C occurs only after visits to vertices reachable from C, and these vertices are found in the tail of the list (vertices B, D, and E) and not vertex A. The list indicates that a visit to B results from searching activity involving only vertices D and E, which form the tail of the list.

> The depth-first visit returns a list of the vertices found in the reverse order of their finishing times.

Discovering a Cycle

Graph algorithms often make use of a depth-first visit. For instance, we can use it to discover the presence of a cycle within the set of reachable vertices. Recall that a cycle is a directed path of length 2 or more that connects a vertex to itself.

$$P(v, v): v = v_1, v_2, \ldots, v_{m-1}, v_m = v \quad m > 1$$

> A depth-first visit has a cycle if and only if it has a back edge.

We use the coloring of vertices in the recursive depth-first visit and look for an edge that connects a vertex to a neighbor that has color GRAY. The edge, called a *back edge*, links a vertex back to a neighbor that has already been discovered in a previous recursive step. A back edge indicates the presence of a cycle. More explicitly, a depth-first visit has a cycle if and only if it has a back edge.

To understand why a back edge in a depth-first visit indicates the presence of a cycle, assume the recursive scan identifies the back edge (w, v). Since v is GRAY, we know that at some point in the scan, we discovered v and then proceeded down a path from v that includes w. The length of the path depends on the number of recursive calls from the point when v was first discovered to the current vertex w, which identifies v as a neighbor. If we add the edge (w, v) to the path from v to w, the length of the new path is at least two and is a cycle (Figure 24.9).

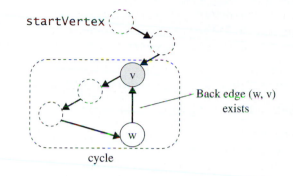

Figure 24.9 *Discovering a cycle assuming w is a GRAY neighbor of v (Edge (v, w) is a back edge).*

Conversely, if a depth-first visit has a cycle within its path, it will find a back edge. To see this, assume that v is the first vertex in the cycle and that the cycle path is v, ..., w, v. The depth-first visit first discovers v and colors it GRAY. The scan will continue around the cycle and eventually discover w. At this time, the vertex v is GRAY and so (w, v) is a back edge.

Implementing the Depth-First Visit   The static method dfsVisit() in the class DiGraphs implements the depth-first visit algorithm. The method includes a graph and a WHITE starting vertex sVertex as its first two parameters. A third parameter is the LinkedList dfsList that stores the list of visited vertices in reverse order of their finishing times. A fourth parameter is the boolean variable checkForCycle. We use this argument only for applications that require an acyclic graph. The method dfsVisit() routinely checks for a cycle. When the method detects one, it checks the boolean flag and, if true, throws a runtime exception. A program that uses dfsVisit() can test for a cycle by setting the argument to true and including the method call within a try/catch block. The method descends through the graph, discovering and processing all of the WHITE vertices it finds.

dfsVisit():

```
// depth-first visit assuming a WHITE starting vertex;
// dfsList contains the visited vertices in reverse order
// of finishing time; when checkForCycle is true, throws
// IllegalPathStateException if it detects a cycle
public static <T> void dfsVisit(DiGraph<T> g, T sVertex,
          LinkedList<T> dfsList, boolean checkForCycle)
{
    T neighborVertex;
    Set<T> edgeSet;
    // iterator to scan the adjacency set of a vertex
    Iterator<T> edgeIter;
    VertexColor color;
```

Method dfsVisit() returns a list of the discovered vertices in reverse order of the finishing time and optionally checks for a cycle.

```
        if (!g.containsVertex(sVertex))
            throw new IllegalArgumentException(
                    "dfsVisit(): vertex not in the graph");

        // color vertex GRAY to note its discovery
        g.setColor(sVertex, VertexColor.GRAY);

        edgeSet = g.getNeighbors(sVertex);

        // sequence through the adjacency set and look for vertices
        // that are not yet discovered (colored WHITE);
        // recursively call dfsVisit() for each such vertex; if a
        // vertex in the adjacency list is GRAY, the
        // vertex was discovered during a previous call and there
        // is a cycle that begins and ends at the vertex; if
        // checkForCycle is true, throw an exception
        edgeIter = edgeSet.iterator();
        while (edgeIter.hasNext())
        {
            neighborVertex = edgeIter.next();
            color = g.getColor(neighborVertex);
            if (color == VertexColor.WHITE)
                dfsVisit(g,neighborVertex, dfsList, checkForCycle);
            else if (color == VertexColor.GRAY && checkForCycle)
                throw new IllegalPathStateException(
                    "dfsVisit(): graph has a cycle");
        }

        // finished with vertex sVertex; make it BLACK
        // and add it to the front of dfsList
        g.setColor(sVertex, VertexColor.BLACK);
        dfsList.addFirst(sVertex);
    }
```

Example 24.3

The example illustrates `dfsVisit()` and uses it to check for a cycle. Assume the following graph in which all of the vertices are initially WHITE.

1. The call to `dfsVisit()` has starting vertex B. The output uses the `LinkedList finish-Order` to display the vertices in the reverse order of their visits (finishing times).

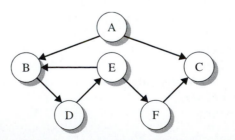

```
LinkedList<String> finishOrder = new LinkedList<String>();
g.colorWhite();
DiGraphs.dfsVisit(g, "B", finishOrder, false);
System.out.println("finishOrder: " + finishOrder);
```

Output:
```
   finishOrder: [B, D, E, F, C]
```

2. Check for a cycle among the reachable vertices emanating from vertex E. The set of vertices are B, C, D, E, and F. Include a call to dfsVisit() within try/catch blocks and make argument checkForCycle true. Since the path B-D-E-B is a cycle, the method will throw an exception that identifies the presence of a cycle.

```
finishOrder = new LinkedList<String>();
g.colorWhite();

try
{
    DiGraphs.dfsVisit(g, "E", finishOrder, true);
    System.out.println("finishOrder: " + finishOrder);
}
catch (IllegalPathStateException ipse)
{
    System.out.println(ipse.getMessage());
}
```

Output:
```
   dfsVisit(): cycle involving vertices D and E
```

Depth-First Search Algorithm

The method dfsVisit() searches only vertices that are reachable from the starting vertex. Some algorithms require a visit to all of the graph vertices with a list of the visits in the order of decreasing finishing times. We provide a depth-first search algorithm for all of the vertices in a graph. The design of the algorithm is simple. We select a vertex and use it as the starting vertex for dfsVisit() to create a list of visited vertices. The list includes only vertices that are reachable from the starting vertex and so may be a subset of the graph vertices. If that is the case, we repeat the process by using one of the unvisited vertices as a starting vertex for a second call to dfsVisit(). The call adds to the front of the list the newly visited vertices in the reverse order of their finishing times. The front of the list has visits from the second call to dfsVisit() and so they occur after visits at the tail of the list, which were part of the first call to dfsVisit(). We continue the process until all vertices are visited.

The depth-first search begins with all WHITE vertices and performs depth-first visits until all vertices of the graph are BLACK.

Figure 24.10 is a complete depth-first search that requires m calls to dfsVisit() and yields m sublists. The vertices in $dfsList_m$ have later finishing times than the vertices in $dfsList_{m-1}$. The vertices in $dfsList_{m-1}$ have later finishing times than the vertices in $dfsList_{m-2}$, and so forth. The vertices in $dfsList_1$ have the earliest finishing times.

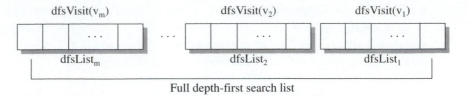

Full depth-first search list

Figure 24.10 *Combined list of visits for the depth-first search.*

The static method `dfs()` in `DiGraphs` implements the algorithm. The method takes the graph and a `LinkedList`, `dfsList`, as parameters. Initially, all of the vertices are colored `WHITE` to indicate that they are undiscovered. To identify starting vertices for calls to `dfsVisit()`, use the `DiGraph` method `vertexSet()` to obtain a set view of the vertices and use an iterator to traverse the vertices. Each call to `dfsVisit()` for a `WHITE` starting vertex accumulates vertices in `dfsList` in the reverse order of their finishing times. Each call to `dfsVisit()` colors more vertices `BLACK`. Using the iterator, find the next `WHITE` vertex and repeat the call to `dfsVisit()`. The process terminates when we visit all vertices (every vertex is colored `BLACK`). Note that the parameter `checkForCycle` in calls to `dfsVisit()` is set to `false`. This algorithm is interested in visiting all the vertices of the graph and not in determining the presence of cycles.

Upon return from `dfs()`, `dfsList` consists of all graph vertices in the reverse order of their finishing times.

dfs():

The depth-first
visit returns a list
of all the graph
vertices in reverse
order of their
finishing time.

```
// depth-first search; dfsList contains all the graph vertices
// in the reverse order of their finishing times
public static <T> void dfs(DiGraph<T> g,
                 LinkedList<T> dfsList)
{
   Iterator<T> graphIter;
   T vertex = null;

   // clear dfsList
   dfsList.clear();

   // initialize all vertices to WHITE
   g.colorWhite();

   // call dfsVisit() for each WHITE vertex
   graphIter = g.vertexSet().iterator();
   while (graphIter.hasNext())
   {
      vertex = graphIter.next();
      if (g.getColor(vertex) == VertexColor.WHITE)
         dfsVisit(g,vertex, dfsList, false);
   }
}
```

Running Time for Depth-First Search An argument similar to that of the breadth-first search shows that the running time for dfs() is $O(V + E)$, where V is the number of vertices in the graph and E is the number of edges.

Example 24.4

The example traces execution of dfs() for the graph in Figure 24.11. Assume the graph iterator traverses the vertex set view, beginning with vertex E. In this case, dfsVisit() initially has "E" as the starting vertex. The first call to dfsVisit() finishes with vertices D, G, F, and E in that order. In reverse order of finishing time, dfsList has four elements:

>   dfsList: [E, F, G, D]

The next WHITE vertex is A. The call to dfsVisit() starting at A finishes with vertices in the order C, B, and A. Adding these vertices in reverse order of finishing time gives the final list:

>   dfsList: [A, B, C, E, F, G, D]

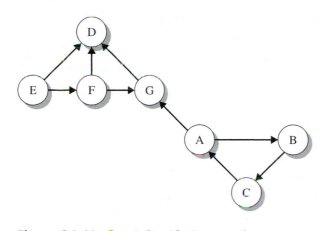

Figure 24.11 *Graph for dfs() example.*

Acyclic Graphs

A graph is acyclic if it contains no cycles. This is a global property of the graph. The method dfsVisit() can identify a cycle, but only within the set of vertices that are reachable from a starting vertex. To check for a cycle anywhere in the graph, we traverse all of the vertices by using multiple calls to dfsVisit(). This is essentially the dfs() algorithm, where the focus is on identifying cycles and not on obtaining a list of visited vertices. This approach relies on the fact that any cycle must be included within one of the calls to dfsVisit(). The method, with checkForCycle set to true, identifies the cycle.

To verify this fact, assume that a graph has a cycle that begins and ends at vertex v. The condition implies the existence of a path P(v, v) of length at least 2,

> $P(v,v) : v = v_0, v_1, \ldots, v_{m-1}, v_m = v, m \geq 2$

where vertex v_{i+1} is a neighbor of v_i. Let v_s be the starting vertex for a call to dfsVisit() that reaches v. The depth-first traversal ensures that there is a path $P(v_s, v)$ that connects v_s to v. By combining the paths $P(v_s, v)$ and $P(v,v)$, we note that all of the vertices in the cycle are reachable from v_s and, thus, are visited by dfsVisit() when v_s is the starting vertex.

The static method `acyclic()` in the class `DiGraphs` takes a graph as an argument and returns a `boolean` value indicating whether a cycle is present. The implementation uses the strategy for `dfs()`. A loop searches the vertices of the graph and makes a call to `dfsVisit()` for each unvisited (`WHITE`) vertex with the argument `checkForCycle` set to true. By placing the `dfsVisit()` call within a try block, `acyclic()` can catch the exception thrown by `dfsVisit()` if it finds a cycle and returns `false`. Otherwise, `acyclic()` returns `true`.

acyclic():

```java
// determine if the graph is acyclic
public static <T> boolean acyclic(DiGraph<T> g)
{
   // use for calls to dfsVisit()
   LinkedList<T> dfsList = new LinkedList<T>();
   Iterator<T> graphIter;
   T vertex = null;

   // initialize all vertices to WHITE
   g.colorWhite();
   // call dfsVisit() for each WHITE vertex
   // catch an IllegalPathStateException in a call to
   // dfsVisit()
   try
   {
      // call dfsVisit() for each WHITE vertex
      graphIter = g.vertexSet().iterator();
      while (graphIter.hasNext())
      {
         vertex = graphIter.next();
         if (g.getColor(vertex) == VertexColor.WHITE)
            dfsVisit(g,vertex, dfsList, true);
      }
   }

   catch (IllegalPathStateException iae)
   {
      return false;
   }

   return true;
}
```

The method acyclic() checks for a cycle while executing a depth-first search of the graph.

PROGRAM 24.2 TESTING FOR CYCLES

Let us see how we might use the method `acyclic()` in an application. We start with the accompanying graph where the solid arrows indicate edges. Input for the graph comes from file *cycle.dat*. A first call to the method determines that the graph is acyclic. By adding edge (E, B), we create a cycle E-B-D-E. A second call to `acyclic()` identifies the presence of a cycle. The output simply displays these facts.

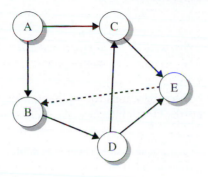

```java
import java.io.FileNotFoundException;

import ds.util.DiGraph;
import ds.util.DiGraphs;

public class Program24_2
{
    public static void main(String[] args)
        throws FileNotFoundException
    {
        DiGraph<String> g =
                    DiGraph.readGraph("cycle.dat");

        // determine if the graph is acyclic
        if (DiGraphs.acyclic(g))
            System.out.println("Graph is acyclic");
        else
            System.out.println("Graph is not acyclic");

        // add edge (E,B) to create a cycle
        System.out.print("   Adding edge (E,B): ");
        g.addEdge("E", "B", 1);

        // retest the graph to see if it is acyclic
        if (DiGraphs.acyclic(g))
            System.out.println("New graph is acyclic");
        else
            System.out.println(
                    "New graph is not acyclic");
    }
}
```

```
Run:
  Graph is acyclic
    Adding edge (E,B): New graph is not acyclic
```

Chapter Summary

- There are two types of graphs, an *undirected graph* and a *directed graph (digraph)*. Both types of graphs can be either *weighted* or *nonweighted*. Each type of graph has its own set of applications.

- The Graph interface specifies operations for undirected and directed graphs, and the DiGraph class implements the Graph interface. An API shows you how to use the primary class methods.

- The *breadth-first search*, bfs(), locates all vertices reachable from a starting vertex. The *depth-first search*, dfs(), produces a list of all graph vertices in the reverse order of their finishing times. The depth-first search is supported by a recursive depth-first visit method, dfsVisit() that does most of the work.

- By applying the depth-first search strategy, an algorithm can check to see whether a graph is *acyclic* (has no cycles). The depth-first search has other applications, and we discuss some of these in Chapter 25.

Written Exercises

For exercises 24.1 through 24.4, use the following figure for the references to graph A and graph B.

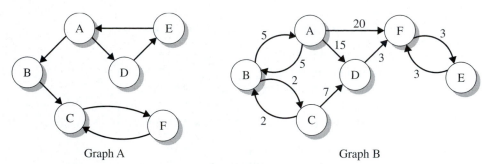

Graph A   Graph B

1. Use graph B to answer the following questions on paths. If a path does not exist, respond "No path."

   (a) Find two distinct directed paths from vertex C to vertex E.
   (b) Find a directed path from vertex F to vertex B.
   (c) List all of the vertices that have out-degree 1.
   (d) List all of the vertices that have the same in-degree and out-degree.
   (e) Find a vertex that has maximum out-degree.

2. In graph A, find all distinct cycles.

3. (a) List the vertices in graph A in the reverse order of their finishing time for a depth-first search that starts at vertex A. Repeat the process, and produce a different list by assuming that the scan accesses neighbors in a different order.
   (b) List the vertices in graph B in the reverse order of their finishing time from a depth-first search starting at vertex C and first accessing neighbor D.
   (c) For both graph A and graph B, identify the starting vertices that would produce a breadth-first scan that visits all of the nodes in the graph.
   (d) In graph B, list a possible order of visits to vertices in a breadth-first scan that begins at vertex C.

(e) List the elements in dfsList that result from a depth-first scan (dfs()) of graph A. Assume that the first scan (dfsVisit()) begins at vertex B and that, upon completing those recursive calls, dfsVisit() resumes at vertex A.

4. (a) Is graph A or graph B strongly connected? Weakly connected?
   (b) List all of the strong components for each graph.
   (c) If we add an edge in graph A from vertex C to vertex A, is the new graph strongly or weakly connected?

5. The following program builds the graph shown below and then executes DiGraph class methods. Give the output of the program and draw the final graph.

```java
import java.io.FileNotFoundException;

import ds.util.*;

public class Test
{
    public static void main(String[] args)
        throws FileNotFoundException
    {
        DiGraph<String> g = DiGraph.readGraph("wex24-5.dat");

        System.out.println(g.numberOfVertices() + "  " +
                            g.numberOfEdges());
        System.out.println(g.inDegree("A") + "  " +
                            g.outDegree("D"));
        System.out.println(g.getWeight("D","C"));
        g.addVertex("G");

        g.addEdgFe("F","G",1);
        g.addEdge("G","D",2);
        g.addEdge("G","E",1);

        g.setWeight("E","D", 5);

        g.removeEdge("D","E");

        g.removeVertex("C");
        System.out.println(g);
    }
}
```

6. During a recursive depth-first search of a digraph, what is a back edge? What is the relation between a back edge and an acyclic graph?

7. (a) If a digraph has n vertices, show that it can have a maximum of $n(n - 1)$ edges.
   (b) If a graph algorithm is $O(V^2 + E)$, explain why we can equivalently write that the algorithm is $O(V^2)$.

8. A DAG (Directed Acyclic Graph) has n vertices. Give the minimum and the maximum number of strong components that exist in the graph.

9. (a) Note that a tree is a connected, acyclic, undirected graph. The depth-first search applies to an undirected graph. During dfsVisit(), the set of edges that connect a vertex with a WHITE neighbor form a tree. If the graph is connected, the depth-first search generates a single tree called the *DFS tree*. When a graph is not connected,

each `dfsVisit()` generates a series of trees called the *DFS forest*. Since a depth-first search can proceed in many ways, the DFS forest is not unique. For example, the graph

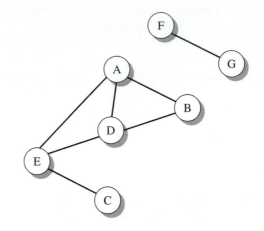

produces the following DFS forest.

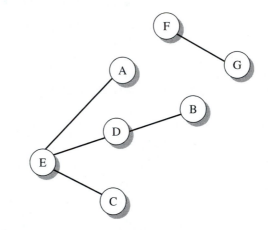

For the following undirected graph, give the DFS forest.

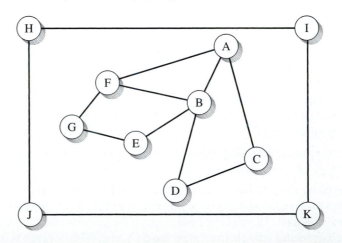

(b) A back edge must be defined differently for an undirected graph than it is for a digraph. Give a definition for a back edge during the depth-first search of an undirected graph.

Programming Exercises

In order to simplify your writing of programs, we use the following three graphs for most of the problems. In Programming Exercise 24.10, you will create the data file *graphA.dat* for graph A. The files for graph B and graph C are in the ch24ex directory of the software supplement with file names *graphB.dat* and *graphC.dat*, respectively.

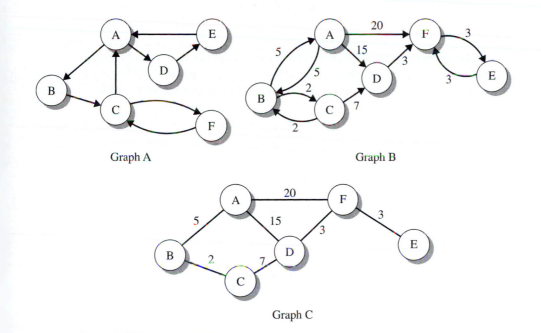

Graph A

Graph B

Graph C

10. Create the data file for graph A. In a program, input the file, and then include statements that carry out the following tasks.

  Insert an edge from F to D with weight 1.

  Delete vertex B.

  Erase the edge (A, D).

  Prompt the user to input a vertex, and list all of the neighbors of the vertex.

  Insert the new vertex G.

  Add the following edges with weight 1: (G, C), (G, F), (D, G).

  Output the graph using the toString() method.

11. Using graph B, write a program that prompts the user to input a vertex. With the input value, carry out a breadth-first search and display the set of reachable vertices. Perform a depth-first search of the entire graph and display the list of vertices in the reverse order of their finishing times.

12. Consider the following graph.

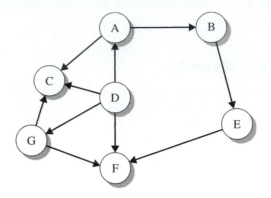

Write a program that determines whether the graph has a cycle and change the orientation of two edges to make the graph strongly connected. Verify that the graph is strongly connected by showing that `dfsVisit()` from each vertex visits all vertices of the graph.

13. (a) An Euler Tour of a strongly connected digraph is a cycle that visits each edge exactly once (but a vertex may be visited more than once). A mathematical argument shows that a directed graph has an Euler Tour if and only if `inDegree(v)` = `outDegree(v)` for each vertex v. Implement the method `eulerTour()` that takes a strongly connected graph g as the argument and returns `true` if the graph has an Euler tour; otherwise, it returns `false`.

```
public static <T> boolean eulerTour(DiGraph<T> g)
{ ... }
```

Example: Graph 1 has an Euler Tour and graph 2 does not.

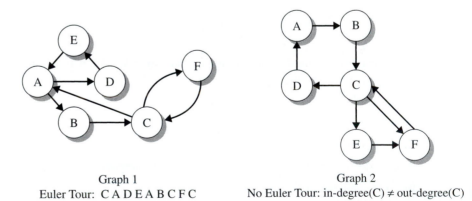

Graph 1
Euler Tour: C A D E A B C F C

Graph 2
No Euler Tour: in-degree(C) ≠ out-degree(C)

(b) In a program, check your implementation of `eulerTour()` by using graph 1 and graph 2. Output whether the graph has an Euler Tour.

14. (a) For each pair of vertices in a graph, we say that v_j is reachable from v_i if and only if there is a directed path from v_i to v_j. This defines the reachability relation $R(v_i R v_j)$. For each vertex v_i, the breadth-first scan identifies the set of all vertices

that are reachable from v_i. If we use the scan for each vertex of the graph, we get a series of reachability sets that defines the relation R.

v_0:   <reachability set for v_0>
v_1:   <reachability set for v_1>
....
v_{n-1}: <reachability list for v_{n-1}>

The same relation can also be described with an n by n reachability matrix (two-dimensional array) that has a 1 in location (i,j) if and only if v_i R v_j. The following are a possible reachability set and a corresponding reachability matrix for a graph.

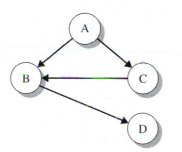

Reachability Sets   Reachability Matrix

A: {A, B, C, D}
B: {B, D}
C: {B, C, D}
D: {D}

Implement the method `reachMat()` that takes a graph as its argument and returns the reachability matrix.

```
public static <T> int[][] reachMat(DiGraph<T> g)
{ ... }
```

HINT: Use the method `vertexSet()` and an iterator to scan the vertices in the graph. For each vertex, call `bfs()` to obtain the reachability set. This set determines a row of the reachability matrix. To get column entries, use a second iterator to scan the vertices in the graph. Determine whether the vertex in the graph is also in the reachability set (current row) and, if yes, insert a 1 in the column of the current row; otherwise, insert a 0. The rows and columns of the matrix have indices 0, 1, ..., n − 1. Index 0 corresponds to the first vertex scanned by a `vertexSet()` iterator, index 1 corresponds to the second vertex, and so forth.

(b) Write a program that inputs the name of a graph file, inputs the graph, and then calls `reachMat()` to create the reachability matrix. Output the result as a series of rows and columns. Optional: Enhance the output by including the names of the vertices as labels for the rows and columns. Run the program twice. In the first case, create an input file for the graph in part (a); then use graph B.

15. (a) A *rooted tree* can be described as an undirected, connected, acyclic graph, where one node is distinguished as the root. If each vertex is the source for at most two edges, the tree is termed a *binary tree*. Assume gTree is a graph that corresponds

to a rooted binary tree. Implement the method `leafNodes()`, which returns an `ArrayList` of all vertices (nodes) that are leaf nodes. For instance, the following graph represents a binary tree where A is the root.

```
public static <T> ArrayList<T> leafNodes(DiGraph<T> gTree)
{ ... }
```

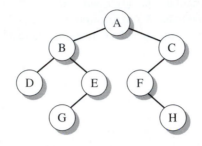

(b) Write a program that inputs the graph in part (a) and outputs the leaf nodes.

16. (a) The method `dfsVisit()` uses a recursive algorithm for the depth-first visit. Implement an iterative form, `dfsIterVisit()`, that uses a stack to hold the vertices of the scan in much the same way as `bfs()` uses a queue. The method visits the vertices reachable from the starting vertex in preorder; that is, the method places the current vertex `v` at the back of the visit list, and then visits its neighbors. The method does not include a test for a cycle.

```
public static <T> void dfsIterVisit(DiGraph<T> g,
                    T sVertex, LinkedList<T> dfsList)
{ ... }
```

(b) Write a program that uses your implementation of `dfsIterVisit()`. The program should input graph B and call `dfsIterVisit()` for each vertex in the graph. After each call, output the list.

Programming Project

17. (a) Implement the method `pathConnected(g,s,e)` that returns `true` if there is a path from vertex `s` to vertex `e` in graph `g` and false otherwise.

```
public static <T> boolean
pathConnected(DiGraph<T> g, T sVertex, T eVertex)
{ ... }
```

(b) The efficient computation of the strong components of a digraph is not an easy problem. We discuss an efficient algorithm for this problem in Chapter 25. For now, we suggest a simple but inefficient way to compute the strong components by developing the method `strongComponents()`.

```
// find the strong components of the digraph g; component
// is an ArrayList of Set objects, each of which contains
// the vertices in a strong component
public static <T> void
strongComponents(DiGraph<T> g, ArrayList<T> component)
{ ... }
```

Color all the vertices of the graph WHITE. Using an iterator, visit each vertex v of the graph. For each vertex, see if it is WHITE. If so, a new strong component containing v must be built. Clear a set scSet that will contain the vertices of the new strong component and use the depth-first visit to determine the list dfsList of all vertices reachable from v. For each WHITE vertex in dfsList, use pathConnected() to determine if there is a path back to v. Whenever such a path exists, add the vertex to scSet and color it BLACK. Since there is a path from v to each vertex in scSet and a path from each vertex in scSet back to v, it follows that there is a path between any two vertices in scList. The vertices in scList are the next strong components. Since each vertex in scList is BLACK, it will not be considered again.

(c) Using graph B, create a program that determines the strong components and outputs their vertices. Remove from the graph all vertices that belong to a one-element strong component. After deleting the vertices, recompute and display the strong components for the updated graph.

Chapter 25

GRAPH ALGORITHMS

CONTENTS

25.1 TOPOLOGICAL SORT
Why It Works
Implementing the topologicalSort()
Method

25.2 STRONGLY CONNECTED
COMPONENTS
Why It Works
Implementing the
strongComponents() Method

25.3 GRAPH OPTIMIZATION
ALGORITHMS

25.4 SHORTEST-PATH ALGORITHM
Implementing the shortestPath()
Method

25.5 DIJKSTRA'S MINIMUM-PATH
ALGORITHM
Designing the Dijkstra Algorithm
Why It Works
Implementing the minimumPath()
Method
Minimum Path in Acyclic Graphs

25.6 MINIMUM SPANNING TREE
Prim's Algorithm
Implementing the minSpanTree()
Method

In Chapter 24, we introduced basic graph traversal techniques. Now we use them to develop a series of classical graph algorithms. The depth-first search returns a list of vertices that identifies visits to vertices in the order of their finishing times. We draw on the ordering in Section 25.1 to produce a topological sort of vertices in an acyclic graph. The sort identifies a precedence relation among the vertices. In a *strongly connected graph*, we can find a path between any two vertices. In a general graph, the property applies locally to strongly connected components which are strongly connected subgraphs. In Section 25.2, we develop an algorithm that partitions the vertices of a graph into a collection of strongly connected components.

In Sections 25.3 through 25.6, we introduce graph optimization algorithms. These include a *shortest-path algorithm* that determines the minimum number of edges that must be traversed in moving from a starting to an ending vertex. In contrast, when we associate a cost to the edges, *Dijkstra's minimum-path algorithm* determines a least-cost path from a starting to an ending vertex. This chapter concludes by presenting *Prim's minimal-spanning-tree algorithm*, which identifies a subset of edges of minimum weight that can maintain the structure of the graph. The algorithm has important networking applications.

All of the graph algorithms in this chapter are implemented as static methods in the class DiGraphs.

25.1 Topological Sort

In Section 24.3, we developed the depth-first method dfs(), which searches all of the vertices in a graph by using a series of calls to dfsVisit(). Method

dfs() returns a list, called dfsList, that sequences the vertices in the reverse order of their finishing times. The order of vertices in dfsList depends on the selection of starting vertices for the calls to `dfsVisit()`. When the graph is acyclic, we will show that `dfsList` has a *topological order* implying that if P(v, w) is a path from v to w, then v must occur before w in the list. We say that `dfs()` produces a *topological sort* of the vertices.

A topological sort has important applications for graphs that define a precedence order in the scheduling of activities. For instance, a department at a university uses a graph to lay out the courses for its major. Edges in the graph define course prerequisites. Figure 25.1 is a graph of courses for a religious studies major. A student can elect courses R51 and R37 in any order, but R63 can be taken only after the student completes these two courses because they are prerequisites. Another example: Large construction projects can use a graph with precedence order to establish starting conditions for the subcontractors. Framers can begin to work only after the foundation is poured. Once the walls are raised, the roof, electrical, and heating subcontractors are free to start.

> Topological sort is the list (in reverse order) of vertices returned by the depth-first search of an acyclic graph.

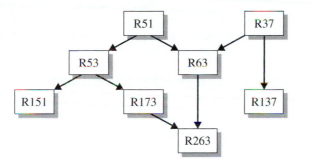

Figure 25.1 *Major program graph listing courses and their prerequisites.*

The previous examples are clearly acyclic graphs. A topological sort of the vertices (activities) provides the student a possible four-year schedule of courses or the contractor a schedule for the subcontractors.

Why It Works

Assume a depth-first search returns a list that describes an order of visits to all of the vertices in an acyclic graph. We must show that for any pair of vertices v and w in the graph that are connected by a path P(v, w), v must appear before w in the list. We do this in two stages. We first establish that both v and w are visited by one of the `dfsVisit()` calls that were used by `dfs()` to create the list. Then we establish that within the sublist created by `dfsVisit()`, v must occur before w.

The `dfs()` algorithm builds the list of visits to the vertices by making repeated calls to `dfsVisit()`. For some starting vertex v_s, `dfsVisit($v_s$)` recursively scans down a path of neighbors and discovers v; that is, v is reachable from v_s. Because there is a path P(v, w), we know that w is reachable from v_s and thus is in the sublist of vertices returns by `dfsVisit($v_s$)` (Figure 25.2a). Establishing that v must occur before w in the sublist relies on the fact that the graph is acyclic. Assume that v occurs after w in the list. This implies that `dfsVisit($v_s$)` discovers w before it discovers v. Equivalently, there is a path P(w, v) connecting w to v. By appending the path P(v, w), we have a cycle of length 2 or more connecting vertex w to itself, contrary to the fact that the graph is acyclic (Figure 25.2b).

> The topological-Sort() method returns a list of vertices. If P(v, w) is a path from v to w, then v occurs before w in the list.

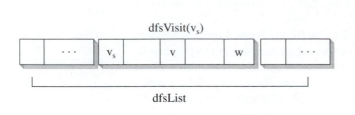

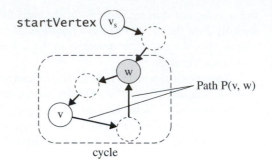

(a) Vertices v and w are on a path
     path from starting vertex v_s and
     in the list determined by dfsVisit(v_s)

(b) Since vertex w occurs before v in the list
     for dfsVisit(v_s), there is a path P(w, v). Assuming
     a path P(v, w), we have a cycle of length 2 or more
     connecting w to w.

Figure 25.2 *Illustration to verify that with a path P(v, w) in an acyclic graph, v comes before w in dfs().*

Implementing the topologicalSort() Method

The static method topologicalSort() implements the topological sort algorithm. The output is dfsList from the depth-first search algorithm discussed in Chapter 24, so we use the code structure of that algorithm, with one modification: A topological sort requires an acyclic graph, so topologicalSort() checks for a cycle when calling dfsVisit(). This simply means setting the argument checkForCycle to true and including the call in a try block. The catch block in topologicalSort() catches an exception from dfsVisit() and throws a second IllegalPathStateException.

topologicalSort():

```
// find a topological sort of an acyclic graph
public static <T> void topologicalSort(DiGraph<T> g,
                LinkedList<T> tlist)
{
    Iterator<T> graphIter;
    T vertex = null;

    // clear the list that will contain the sort
    tlist.clear();

    g.colorWhite();

    // cycle through the vertices, calling dfsVisit() for each
    // WHITE vertex; check for a cycle
    try
    {
        // call dfsVisit() for each WHITE vertex
        graphIter = g.vertexSet().iterator();
        while (graphIter.hasNext())
        {
            vertex = graphIter.next();
```

```
              if (g.getColor(vertex) == VertexColor.WHITE)
                 dfsVisit(g,vertex, tlist, true);
          }
      }
      catch (IllegalPathStateException ipse)
      {
          throw new
             IllegalPathStateException (
                "topologicalSort(): graph has a cycle");
      }
   }
```

Running Time for the Topological Sort   The topological sort uses the algorithm for dfs(), so its running time is also $O(V + E)$, where V is the number of vertices in the graph and E is the number of edges.

Example 25.1

_____

Let us create a schedule for a religious studies student. The graph of courses, with their prerequisites, is in Figure 25.1, and the graph input is from the file *courses.dat*. After calling topologicalSort() to create a precedence list, we output the list as a "possible schedule of courses."

```
// graph specifying the courses and prerequisite edges
DiGraph<String> g = DiGraph.readGraph("courses.dat");

// a list holding the topological order of courses
LinkedList tlist = new LinkedList();

// execute a topological sort; store results in list
DiGraphs.topologicalSort(g,tlist);

// output the list of possible courses
System.out.println("Possible schedule of courses");
System.out.println("    " + tlist);
```

```
Run:
   Possible schedule of courses
      [R51, R37, R137, R63, R53, R151, R173, R263]
```

Note that you will find all the graph input files used in this chapter in Chapter 25 of the software supplement.

_____

25.2 Strongly Connected Components

A graph is strongly connected if for any pair of two distinct vertices v and w, there exists a path P(v, w) and a path P(w, v). In general, the vertices of a graph can be decomposed into disjoint maximal subsets of vertices that are mutually accessible; these subsets are called *strongly connected (strong) components*. Each component is a strongly connected subgraph and

Any graph can be partitioned into a unique set of strong components.

the set of components is unique. Many graph algorithms begin with this decomposition; the approach often allows the original problem to be divided into subprograms, one for each strongly connected component. For instance, the graph in Figure 25.3 has three strong components.

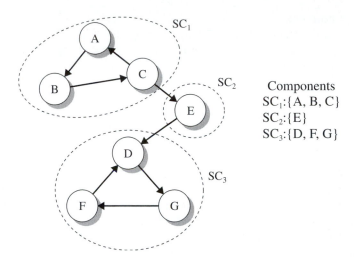

Components
SC_1:{A, B, C}
SC_2:{E}
SC_3:{D, F, G}

Figure 25.3 *Strongly connected components in a directed graph.*

Graph theory provides an assortment of algorithms for identifying strongly connected components. A simple but very inefficient $O(V^2)$ algorithm uses repeated breadth-first searches to identify all vertices w that are reachable from a starting vertex v. The subset of such vertices w that have a path back to v is a strongly connected component. In this section, we will discuss a more efficient algorithm, which makes use of two depth-first searches. The algorithm introduces the *transpose graph* G^T for a graph G. The transpose has the same set of vertices V as graph G but a new edge set E^T consisting of the edges of G but with the opposite direction. More precisely, $e^T = (v, w)$ is in E^T if and only if $e = (w, v)$ is in E. Extending this fact to paths, it is clear that $P^T(v, w)$ is a path in G^T if and only if $P(w, v)$ is a path in G.

The algorithm follows a series of steps.

- Execute the depth-first search dfs() for the graph G, which creates the list dfsList consisting of the vertices in G in the reverse order of their finishing times.
- Generate the transpose graph G^T, the algorithm.
- Using the order of vertices in dfsList, make repeated calls to dfsVisit() for vertices in G^T. The list returned by each call is a strongly connected component of G.

Let us carry out the steps for our demonstration graph and later show why the algorithm works. Figure 25.4 includes the graph and its transpose.

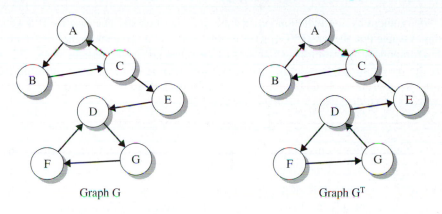

Graph G   Graph G^T

Figure 25.4 *Graph G and its transpose G^T.*

Begin by calling dfs() for graph G. The method returns a list of vertices ordered by visit times.

$$\text{dfsList: } [A, B, C, E, D, G, F]$$

Using the order of vertices in dfsList, make successive calls to dfsVisit() for graph G^T.

Vertex A: dfsVisit(A) returns the list [A, C, B] of vertices reachable from A in G^T. The set of vertices is strongly connected component SC_1.

$$SC_1 = \{A, B, C\}$$

Vertex E: The vertices A, B, and C have been visited. The next unvisited vertex in dfsList is E. Calling dfsVisit(E) returns the list [E]. The singleton vertex creates the strongly connected component SC_2.

$$SC_2 = \{E\}$$

Vertex D: The next unvisited vertex in dfsList is D; dfsVisit(D) returns the list [D, F, G] whose elements form the last strongly connected component set SC_3.

$$SC_3 = \{D, F, G\}$$

Why It Works

Assume SC is the set of vertices visited by a call to dfsVisit() in G^T, in which the method uses v_s as the starting vertex. Remember that vertex v_s is selected as the first re-maining nonvisited vertex in dfsList. We must show that SC is strongly connected; that is, for vertices v and w in SC, there exist paths $P^G(v, w)$ and $P^G(w, v)$ consisting of ver-tices in SC. We must also show that if x is a vertex in a strong component that includes v_s, then x is in SC. We deal with each of these issues separately.

Set SC Is Strongly Connected   Assume v and w are vertices in SC. They are visited by the recursive scan dfsVisit(v_s), so there are paths $P^T(v_s, v)$ and $P^T(v_s, w)$ in G^T and hence paths $P^G(v, v_s)$ and $P^G(w, v_s)$. We will establish the existence of paths $P^G(v_s, v)$ and $P^G(v_s, w)$ in G. The joining of paths $P^G(v, v_s)$ and $P^G(v_s, w)$ is a path $P^G(v, w)$ through v_s. Similarly, the joining of paths $P^G(w, v_s)$ and $P^G(v_s, w)$ is the path $P^G(w, v)$ through v_s.

An argument by contradiction verifies that $P^G(v_s, v)$ exists. The case for $P^G(v_s, w)$ is similar. Assume that the path $P^G(v_s, v)$ does not exist. Let us go back to the first step in the strong-component algorithm in which dfs() searches all of the vertices in G. This produces the list dfsList that defines vertices in the reverse order of their finishing times. We use the ordering to obtain the starting vertex for each dfsVisit() call in G^T. At some point, dfs() first discovers v having color WHITE.

$$\text{dfsList: } [\cdots, \text{ v, } \cdots]$$

The contradiction stems from the fact that when v is first discovered, vertex v_s has no valid color. Look at the different possible colors for v_s.

BLACK: Vertex v_s is BLACK only if v_s has already been visited by dfs() and thus v_s is already in dfsList and v would have a later finishing time.

$$\text{dfsList: } [\cdots, \text{ v, } \cdots, \text{ } v_s, \cdots]$$

The dfsVisit() in G^T that created SC would not have chosen v_s as its starting vertex. Vertex v or some previous vertex in dfsList would have been chosen. Hence, the vertex v_s cannot be BLACK.

GRAY: Some dfsVisit() in the depth-first search dfs() discovers v. If v_s is GRAY, then the dfsVisit() recursively scans down a path that first discovers v_s. This implies a path $P^G(v_s, v)$, contrary to our assumption. Hence, the vertex v_s cannot be GRAY.

WHITE: Because there is a path $P(v, v_s)$, a dfsVisit() in the depth-first search will discover and subsequently visit v_s before visiting v. Thus, v_s will have an earlier finishing time and will occur after v in dfsList, contradicting our assumption that v_s is WHITE.

Under our assumption, vertex v_s would not have a valid color and so the path $P^G(v_s, v)$ exists. The conclusion follows that $P^G(v, w)$ is a path in SC. The same argument shows that $P^G(w, v)$ is a path in SC and so SC is a strongly connected component.

SC Is a Maximal Set   To complete the algorithm, we show that if x is any vertex in a strong component that includes v_s, it must be in SC. This is obvious when you recall that SC is the set of all elements visited by dfsVisit(v_s) in G^T in which v_s is the starting vertex. The assumption that x is in a strong component that contains v_s implies that $P^G(x, v_s)$ exists, so $P^T(v_s, x)$ exists. Thus x would be visited by dfsVisit(v_s) and hence be in SC.

Implementing the strongComponents() Method

The static method strongComponents() takes a graph g and an ArrayList as arguments and implements the three steps of the strongly connected component algorithm. Initially, a call to dfs() creates dfsList. The method transpose() takes the graph as an argument and returns the transpose graph. The implementation of strongComponents then uses elements in dfsList as starting vertices for repeated calls to dfsVisit() in the transpose graph. Each call to dfsVisit() for the transpose graph creates a LinkedList object which is added as an element in the ArrayList. In the end, the ArrayList, called component, is a collection of lists that represent strongly connected components in the graph. See the class DiGraphs for a listing of the method transpose() that takes a graph g and returns g^T.

strongComponents():

```
// find the strong components of the graph; each element of
// component is a LinkedList of the elements in a strong
// component
public static <T> void
strongComponents(DiGraph<T> g,
                 ArrayList<LinkedList<T>> component)
{
    T currVertex = null;
    // list of vertices visited by dfs() for graph g
    LinkedList<T> dfsList = new LinkedList<T>();
    // list of vertices visited by dfsVisit() for g transpose
    LinkedList<T> dfsGTList = null;
    // used to scan dfsList
    Iterator<T> gIter;
    // transpose of the graph
    DiGraph<T> gt = null;

    // clear the return vector
    component.clear();
    // execute depth-first traversal of g
    dfs(g, dfsList);

    // compute gt
    gt = transpose(g);

    // initialize all vertices in gt to WHITE
    // (unvisited)
    gt.colorWhite();

    // call dfsVisit() for gt from vertices in dfsList
    gIter = dfsList.iterator();
    while(gIter.hasNext())
    {
        currVertex = gIter.next();
        // call dfsVisit() only if vertex has not been visited
        if (gt.getColor(currVertex) == VertexColor.WHITE)
        {
            // create a new LinkedList to hold next strong
            // component
            dfsGTList = new LinkedList<T>();
            // do dfsVisit() in gt for starting vertex currVertex
            dfsVisit(gt, currVertex, dfsGTList, false);
            // add strong component to the ArrayList
            component.add(dfsGTList);
        }
    }
}
```

Running Time for the strongComponents()   Recall that the depth-first search has running time O($V + E$), and the computation for G^T is also O($V + E$). It follows that the running time for this algorithm to compute the strong components is O($V + E$).

Example 25.2

The example outputs the strong components for the graph in Figure 25.4. Assume that g is the graph and `componentList` is the `ArrayList` of strong component lists returned by the method `strongComponents()`.

```
// graph and list of strong components
DiGraph<String> g = DiGraph.readGraph("sc.dat");
ArrayList<LinkedList<String>> componentList =
        new ArrayList<LinkedList<String>>();

// count the strong components
int scCount = 0;

// call strongComponents()
DiGraphs.strongComponents(g, componentList);

// sequence through componentList to output individual
// strong components with a label
for(LinkedList<String> component : componentList)
{
    scCount++;
    System.out.println("Component " + scCount + ": " +
                            component);
}
```

```
Run:
   Component 1: [A, C, B]
   Component 2: [E]
   Component 3: [D, F, G]
```

25.3 Graph Optimization Algorithms

Graph algorithms often involve optimizing paths in the graph.

An airline uses a weighted graph to list the cities it serves. Each edge indicates a connecting flight and the weight specifies the distance between two cities. We want to use the graph to solve a variety of different problems. A customer wishes to book a flight from San Diego, California, to Charlotte, North Carolina, on the shortest possible route. Another customer wishes to fly between the two cities with the fewest number of intermediate stops to prevent time-consuming airport layovers. A customer service supervisor makes an annual visit to each of the cities to check out airline operations. The supervisor needs to schedule the stops so as to minimize the total distance traveled.

Graph optimization is a common thread in all of these examples. We need a solution that identifies vertices (cities) and edges (connecting flights) to optimize some condition.

In each case, we could identify all possible routes, lay out the distances or number of intermediate stops and select the optimal solution. This brute force approach is inefficient because it would involve routes that crisscross the country with no chance of providing a solution. In this chapter, we will look at a series of efficient graph optimization algorithms.

Finding the shortest route between two cities is an example of the *minimum-path* problem. We are given a weighted digraph with a weight function w(E) ->R that associates with each edge E(u, v) a positive real number. For any path $P = v_0, v_1, \ldots, v_n$, the total weight of the path is

$$w(P) = \sum_{1}^{n} w * (v_{i-1}, v_i)$$

The minimum-path weight from vertex u to vertex v is the minimum of the total weight over all paths that connect u and v. If no path exists, the minimum-path weight is infinity (∞). In Section 25.5, we develop the classical Dijkstra's algorithm, which provides a very efficient solution to the minimum-path problem. It computes the minimum-path weight from a specified vertex v to all of the other vertices in the graph.

Booking a customer flight that has the fewest number of intermediate stops is a *shortest-path* problem. We are interested in finding the minimum-path length without regard to the path weight. Dijkstra's algorithm provides a solution when each of the edges in the graph is considered to have unit weight. In Section 25.4, we develop a more efficient algorithm that uses the breadth-first search. From some starting vertex v, we visit all vertices reachable from v. Each visit identifies the shortest-path length from v to the specified vertex. In case a vertex is not reachable from v, we assign ∞ as the shortest-path length.

Our minimum-path and shortest-path algorithms are examples of *single-source shortest-path* problems. From a single source, we find the shortest path to every vertex in the graph. There are variations to these algorithms. A *single-destination shortest-path* problem looks to find the shortest path from each vertex to a single-destination vertex. This is just the single-source problem using the transpose of the graph. For some applications, we are interested in finding the shortest path from a specified source vertex to a specified destination vertex. This *single-pair shortest-path* problem is the one posed by a customer wishing to book a flight of minimum distance between two cities.

If there are flights in both directions between cities, we can view the airline graph as an undirected graph. Helping the supervisor schedule visits to all of the airline cities is a global graph optimization problem. We want to find an acyclic set of edges that connect all of the vertices in the graph with the smallest total weight. Such a subgraph is called a *minimum spanning tree*. In Section 25.6 we develop *Prim's algorithm* for building a minimum spanning tree.

Dijkstra's algorithm computes minimum-path weight from a specified vertex to all other vertices in the graph.

The breadth-first search can be used to find the shortest path from a specific vertex to all the other vertices in the graph.

A minimum spanning tree for a connected, undirected graph is the set of edges that connect all vertices in the graph with the smallest total weight.

25.4 Shortest-Path Algorithm

Transportation companies and communication networks use graphs to describe links between hubs in their systems. To optimize customer service and the flow of cargo or data, these systems often need to determine the shortest-path length between two points (vertices). An algorithm, called the *shortest-path algorithm*, takes a specified v_s. For each vertex v in the graph that is reachable from v_s, the algorithm determines the length of a shortest path connecting v_s to v. Vertices that are not reachable from v_s have path length infinity (∞). For each reachable vertex, the algorithm provides both the length of the path and parent references so that the path of vertices can be constructed.

We can use the design of the breadth-first search to find shortest paths. The algorithm begins at a starting vertex sVertex and then proceeds to visit its neighbors (path length 1 from sVertex) followed by vertices with successively larger path lengths. It fans out from sVertex along paths of adjacent vertices until it visits all vertices reachable from sVertex. In order to determine the path length from sVertex to a vertex v, we need to modify bfs() so each vertex maintains a record of its parent and its path length from sVertex. The DiGraph class provides methods that allow the programmer to associate two fields of information with a vertex. One field identifies the parent of a vertex and the other field is an integer dataValue associated with the vertex. The method initData() prepares a graph for the application of an optimization algorithm by assigning a representation for ∞ to each dataValue field of the graph vertices.

class DiGraph<T> (dataValue and parent methods)		*ds.util*
int	**getData**(T v)	
	Returns the integer data value associated with vertex v. If v is not a graph vertex, throws IllegalArgumentException.	
T	**getParent**(T v)	
	Returns the parent of vertex v. If v is not a graph vertex, throws IllegalArgumentException.	
int	**setData**(T v, int value)	
	Sets the integer data value associated with vertex v and returns the previous value. If v is not a graph vertex, throws IllegalArgumentException.	
T	**setParent**(T v, T p)	
	Assigns the parent of vertex v to be p and returns the previous parent. If v or p is not a graph vertex, throws IllegalArgumentException.	
void	**initData**()	
	Assigns the dataValue field of each vertex to ∞.	

A breadth-first search visit to a vertex defines a path of shortest length from the starting vertex.

The shortest-path algorithm is an iterative process that uses a queue to store the vertices. At each step, the algorithm pops an element from the queue. This becomes the current vertex and provides access to an adjacency list that may include unvisited neighbors. Before pushing an unvisited adjacent vertex on the queue, the algorithm assigns values to the parent and dataValue fields of the adjacent vertex. The current vertex is the parent and the dataValue is the path length from the starting vertex to the adjacent vertex. This is simply one more than the path length to the current vertex. The iterative process terminates when the queue is empty. The dataValue field of each vertex is the shortest-path length and its parent field allows us to backtrack along a path of parents to list the vertices in the shortest path. A proof that this algorithm does yield the shortest path is difficult and beyond the scope of the book. The interested reader should consult a book on the theory of algorithms.

Let us see how all of this plays out for the graph in Figure 25.5. We will find the shortest path from vertex C to each of the reachable vertices in the graph.

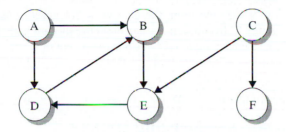

Figure 25.5 *Shortest-path graph.*

Start the algorithm with sVertex = C. In the vertex, set the dataValue (path length) to 0 and make sVertex its own parent. Initialize the queue by adding C as the first element. In the figure, we represent a queue element with the name of the vertex and use subscripts for the pathLength and parent. Columns in the table identify the order in which vertices are visited and the current path length from vertex C.

Step 1: Pop C from the queue. Identify the two neighbors, E and F, and set their colors to GRAY (discovered). Their path lengths are 1 = 0 + 1, and C is their parent. Add the neighbors to the queue (Figure [a]).

Step 2: Pop E from the queue. Its neighbor, vertex D, is not discovered and so we add it to the queue with path length 2 from C and with E as its parent (Figure [b]).

Step 3: Pop F from the queue. F has no undiscovered neighbors, so simply proceed to Step 4 (Figure [c]).

Step 4: Pop D from the queue. Add the undiscovered neighbor B to the queue with path length 3 and parent D (Figure [d]).

Step 5: Pop B from the queue. The neighbor E has been discovered. In fact, it was visited in Step 2. No new element is added to the queue. The algorithm terminates because the queue is empty (Figure [e]).

> The parent field of the vertex sets out the order of vertices from the starting vertex.

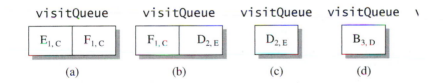

	visitQueue	visitQueue	visitQueue	visitQueue
	$E_{1,C}$ $F_{1,C}$	$F_{1,C}$ $D_{2,E}$	$D_{2,E}$	$B_{3,D}$
	(a)	(b)	(c)	(d)

	Pop C **Path [empty]**	**Pop E** **Path C - E**	**Pop F** **Path C - F**	**Pop D** **Path C - E - D**	**Pop B** **Path C - E - D - B**
A	∞	∞	∞	∞	∞
B	∞	∞	∞	∞	3
C	0	0	0	0	0
D	∞	∞	∞	2	2
E	∞	1	1	1	1
F	∞	∞	1	1	1

At the conclusion of the algorithm, the data value for a vertex is the shortest-path length from starting vertex C. In addition, we can build the shortest path. For instance, look at vertex B. The parent reference field indicates that the parent of B is D. We can backtrack to the starting vertex using the fact that P(B) = D, P(D) = E, and P(E) = C. The shortest path from C to B is [C, E, D, B].

Backtrack: B ---> D ---> E ---> C   Path: [C, E, D, B]

Implementing the shortestPath() Method

shortestPath() finds the shortest-path length from v_s to all of the vertices in the graph. The value is ∞ if the vertex is not reachable from v_s.

The implementation of the static method `shortestPath()` includes arguments for the graph and the starting vertex. A queue holds the vertices that the algorithm discovers. After the pushing the starting vertex onto the queue, a loop continues until the algorithm finds the shortest-path length to all vertices that are reachable from the starting vertex. This occurs when the queue is empty. The path length can be accessed using the `getData()` method.

shortestPath():

```
// use the breadth-first traversal algorithm to determine the
// minimum number of edges in any path from sVertex to all
// vertices in the graph reachable from sVertex; upon return,
// the dataValue field of each vertex in g is either the
// shortest path length to the vertex or is INFINITY if the
// vertex was not reachable from sVertex; call
// path(g, sVertex, v) to find the shortest path from sVertex
// to v
public static <T> void shortestPath(DiGraph<T> g,
                                     T sVertex)
{
    // BFS uses a queue to store adjacent vertices
    LinkedQueue<T> visitQueue = new LinkedQueue<T>();
    Set<T> edgeSet;
    Iterator<T> edgeIter;
    T currVertex = null, neighborVertex = null;
    int currentPathLength;

    if (!g.containsVertex(sVertex))
        throw new IllegalArgumentException(
            "shortestPath(): starting vertex not in the graph");

    // set each vertex data value to INFINITY
    g.initData();
    // sVertex is its own parent and the shortest path
    // to itself has length 0
    g.setParent(sVertex, sVertex);
    g.setData(sVertex, 0);

    // insert starting vertex into the queue
    visitQueue.push(sVertex);

    // process vertices until the queue is empty
    while (!visitQueue.isEmpty())
    {
```

```
    // delete a queue entry
    currVertex = visitQueue.pop();

    edgeSet = g.getNeighbors(currVertex);
    // sequence through the edge set and look for vertices
    // that have not been visited; assign each such vertex
    // a dataValue of currentPathLength + 1
    currentPathLength = g.getData(currVertex);
    edgeIter = edgeSet.iterator();
    while (edgeIter.hasNext())
    {
        neighborVertex = edgeIter.next();
        if (g.getData(neighborVertex) == INFINITY)
        {
            g.setData(neighborVertex, currentPathLength + 1);
            g.setParent(neighborVertex, currVertex);
            visitQueue.push(neighborVertex);
        }
    }
  }
 }
}
```

The shortest-path algorithm stores parent references that identify the parent of each vertex on a path of shortest length. The method `path()` builds the path. The arguments include the graph and two vertices specifying the starting and ending vertices. The method assumes that an optimum path method has been called and that appropriate parent references are defined. The return value is a linked list of vertices designating the path from the starting vertex to the ending vertex.

path():

```
// returns the path computed by a graph algorithm from sVertex
// to eVertex
public static <T> LinkedList<T> path(DiGraph<T> g,
                    T sVertex, T eVertex)
{
   T currVertex = eVertex;
   LinkedList<T> path = new LinkedList<T>();

   if (g.getData(eVertex) == DiGraphs.INFINITY)
      return path;

   while (!currVertex.equals(sVertex))
   {
      path.addFirst(currVertex);
      currVertex = g.getParent(currVertex);
   }

   path.addFirst(sVertex);

   return path;
}
```

Running-Time Analysis The shortest-path algorithm simply uses the breadth-first search. There is additional O(V) overhead to initialize the dataValue for each vertex. With the breadth-first search having running time O(V + E), the total running time for the shortest path is O(V + E).

Example 25.3

The example uses the method shortestPath() to find the length of the shortest path from vertex C to each vertex in the graph in Figure 25.5. By using an iterator on a vertexSet() collection view, we scan the vertices in the graph and output the shortest-path length from vertex C. Nonreachable vertices are noted. A call to path() displays the path from C to the current vertex. The graph is read from the file *shpath.dat*. We repeat the graph for your convenience.

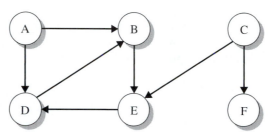

```
DiGraph<String> g = DiGraph.readGraph("shpath.dat");
String sVertex = "C";
int dataValue;

// compute shortest path lengths
DiGraphs.shortestPath(g,sVertex);

// sequence through the vertices
for (String vertex : g.vertexSet())
{
    dataValue = g.getData(vertex);

    if (dataValue != DiGraphs.INFINITY)
        System.out.println("Distance from " + sVertex +
            " to " + vertex + " is " + dataValue +
            " and the path is " +
            DiGraphs.path(g,sVertex, vertex));
    else
        System.out.println(vertex + " is unreachable from " +
                                sVertex);
}
```

```
Output:
    Distance from C to D is 2 and the path is [C, E, D]
    Distance from C to E is 1 and the path is [C, E]
    Distance from C to F is 1 and the path is [C, F]
    A is unreachable from C
    Distance from C to B is 3 and the path is [C, E, D, B]
    Distance from C to C is 0 and the path is [C]
```

25.5 Dijkstra's Minimum-Path Algorithm

The shortest-path problem finds the path of shortest length connecting a starting vertex to each of the reachable vertices in the graph. The algorithm uses a breadth-first search of the vertices. Minimum path is a similar problem for weighted graphs. The problem determines a path of minimum weight from a starting vertex to each reachable vertex in the graph. As the graph in Figure 25.6 illustrates, a shortest path may not be the minimum path. Assume A is the starting vertex and E is the reachable vertex. Three paths, A-B-E, A-C-E, and A-D-E, have path length 2, with weights 15, 17, and 13 respectively. The minimum path is A-C-D-E, with weight 11 but path length 3.

> The minimum-path problem is to find a path with minimum total weight from v_s to v_e. The path may contain more vertices than the shortest path from v_s to v_e.

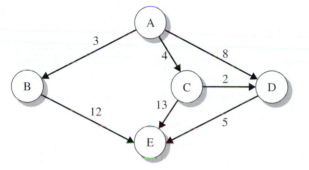

Figure 25.6 *Weighted graph comparing shortest path and minimum path connecting A to E.*

The Dijkstra algorithm solves the minimum-path problem. It uses a *greedy strategy* that solves the problem in stages. At each stage, we select the adjacent vertex x that defines a minimum path from the starting vertex. The term "greedy" indicates that the strategy attempts to maximize short-term gains, even though the decision might need to be reversed as we discover new vertices. In the sample graph in Figure 25.6, we start at A and discover neighbors B, C, and D. Vertices C and D define path A-C and path A-E having path weights 4 and 8, respectively. However, the path A-B has minimum weight among all of the neighbors of A. From vertex B, we discover its neighbor E using edge e(B, E) with weight 12. The total weight of path A-B-E is 15. We record our findings for vertex E that include the value 15 for the path weight and B as the parent. Later, we discover that using C as an intermediate vertex yields a path A-C-E that connects A to E with a smaller path weight 14. Properties for E are updated to have a new path weight 14 and parent C. As new vertices are discovered, we continually make updates. In the end, we discover that the path A-C-D-E with weight 11 is the minimum path.

> Dijkstra's algorithm makes an optimal choice at each point en route to finding the solution to the complete problem. It is an example of a greedy algorithm.

Designing the Dijkstra Algorithm

The Dijkstra minimum-path algorithm uses the iterative strategy that we employed for the shortest-path problem, with one major difference. The search uses a minimum-priority queue rather than a queue to store the vertices. To define objects in the priority queue, we declare the static inner class `MinInfo`. A `MinInfo` object contains a vertex reference and the path weight as data members. The vertex is the ending vertex on a path from the starting vertex and `pathWeight` is sum of the weights for the edges of the path. The class implements the `Comparable` interface by defining `compareTo()` using the `pathWeight` attribute. This allows us to use the objects in a priority queue.

> Dijkstra's algorithm has a priority queue with elements that store the minimum-path weight from the starting vertex.

MinInfo class:

```
// priority queue data used by minimumPath() and
// minSpanningTree() algorithms
private static class MinInfo<T>
    implements Comparable<MinInfo<T>>
{
    public T endV;
    public int pathWeight;

    public int compareTo(MinInfo<T> item)
    { ... }
}
```

Each step in the algorithm removes a `MinInfo` object from the priority queue and identifies the vertex. Because no subsequent step could find a new path to the vertex with a smaller weight, we have the minimum-path weight and can color the vertex BLACK (visited). The next action is to look at each of the neighbors of the vertex. For each neighbor that is not BLACK, check whether adding the edge to the minimum path from the starting vertex to the current vertex will create a path from the starting vertex to the neighbor that is "better" than any which have been determined previously. The data value for the neighbor vertex stores the minimum-path weight for any of the prior paths or is infinity when the neighbor is initially discovered. If the new path is better, create a `MinInfo` object with the neighbor and the total path weight as arguments and insert it into the priority queue. At the same time, update the data value and parent reference for the neighbor. The algorithm terminates whenever the priority queue becomes empty or when the number of visited vertices matches the vertex size of the graph. The priority queue could become empty when a relatively small number of vertices are reachable from the starting vertex.

Let us illustrate the algorithm by using the graph in Figure 25.6, which is repeated by your convenience. Vertex A is the starting vertex. To simplify notation, let MI(v, w) designate a `MinInfo` object with v as the ending vertex for path P(A, v) and with total path weight w. The algorithm begins with vertex A.

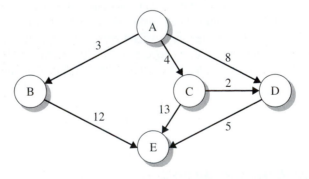

Setup: Assign ∞ as the data value for each vertex. For starting vertex A, assign its data value to be 0 and let A be the parent reference. Create the `MinInfo` object MI(A, 0) that represents a path from A to itself with initial weight 0. The object is the first entry in the priority queue. See Figure (a).

Each iterative step pops a `MinInfo` object from the priority queue and identifies its vertex. If the edge from the vertex to a nonvisited neighbor creates a better path, updates occur to both the data field and parent reference field of the neighbor. Each column in the table lists the data value and current parent reference for each vertex after any updates occur.

Step 1:   Pop MI(A, 0) from the priority queue. Color A BLACK to indicate that it is visited with the minimum path from A to A having weight 0. The vertices B, C, and D are neighbors of A with data values ∞. Create MinInfo objects MI(B, 3), MI(C, 4), and MI(D, 8) indicating that paths from A to the vertices have weights 3, 4, and 8, respectively. Use the weights to update the data fields in the three vertices and assign A as their parent references. Push the objects into the priority queue. See Figure (b).

Step 2:   Pop the element with minimum weight. In this case, pop MI(B, 3) from the priority queue and color the vertex B BLACK. The only neighbor of B is vertex E. Using the minimum path from A to B with weight 3 and adding the weight of the edge (B, E) creates a "better" path A-B-E from A to E with weight 12. Clearly, this path is better because currently E has never been discovered and its data value is ∞. Let 12 be the new data value for E and assign B as its parent reference. Create the object MI(E, 12) and push it into the priority queue (Figure [c]).

MI(A, 0)

(a) Setup: Push MI(A, 0)   (b) Pop MI(A, 0). Push MI(B, 3), MI(C, 4),   (c) Pop MI(B, 3). Push MI(E, 15)
    into the priority queue.   and MI(D, 8) into the priority queue.   into the priority queue.

Step 3:   Pop MI(C, 4) from the priority queue and color the vertex C BLACK. The vertex has two nonvisited neighbors, D and E. The data value and parent reference for D indicates a path exists from A to D with weight 8 containing A as the parent of D. Using the minimum path from A to C with weight 4 and adding edge (C, D) with weight 2 creates a path with total weight 6, which is better than the current path to D.

$$\text{New weight for path A-C-D} = \text{weight to C} + \text{weight (C, D)}$$
$$= 4 + 2 = 6$$

Update the fields for D so that the data is 6 and the parent reference is C. Push the object MI(D, 6) into the priority queue. Note that the priority queue now has two MinInfo objects that reference vertex D (Figure [d]). The one with weight 6 will come out of the priority queue first. The data field for vertex E indicates a path from A of weight 15. A second path from A to C followed by the edge (C, E) with weight 13 has total weight 17 and is not a better path.

Step 4:   Pop MI(D, 6) from the priority queue and color the vertex D BLACK. The neighbor, E, has a path from A with weight 15. A new path that uses the minimum path to D and the edge (D, E) with weight 5 creates a better path.

$$\text{New weight for path A-C-D-E} = \text{weight to D} + \text{weight (D, E)}$$
$$= 6 + 5 = 11$$

Assign 11 as the new data value for E and let D be the parent reference. Push the object MI(E, 11) into the priority queue (Figure [e]).

Steps 5–6: Pop MI(D, 8) from the priority queue. The vertex is already BLACK from Step 4, so proceed to the next step (Figure [f]). Pop MI(E, 6) from the priority queue and color it BLACK. The algorithm terminates because all five vertices have been visited.

| MI(E, 15) | MI(D, 6) | MI(D, 8) | | MI(E, 15) | MI(E, 11) | MI(D, 8) | | MI(E, 15) | MI(E, 11) |

(d) Pop MI(C, 4). Push MI(D, 6) into the priority queue.   (e) Pop MI(D, 6). Push MI(E, 11) into the priority queue.   (f) Pop MI(D, 8).

	Pop MI(A, 0)	Pop MI(B, 3)	Pop MI(C, 4)	Pop MI(D, 6)	Pop MI(E, 11)
A	d = 0 p = A	d = 0 p = A	d = 0 p = A	d = 0 p = A	d = 0 p = A
B	d = 3 p = A	d = 3 p = A	d = 3 p = A	d = 3 p = A	d = 3 p = A
C	d = 4 p = A	d = 4 p = A	d = 4 p = A	d = 4 p = A	d = 4 p = A
D	d = 8 p = A	d = 8 p = A	d = 6 p = C	d = 6 p = C	d = 6 p = C
E	∞	d = 15 p = B	d = 15 p = B	d = 11 p = D	d = 11 p = D

Why It Works

To verify the Dijkstra algorithm results in a minimum path, assume that the algorithm finds a path from starting vertex v_s to the ending vertex v_e, which is not optimal. That is, a second path connects the vertices with a smaller weight. Assume this second path and the Dijkstra path are the same up to vertex u and that the weight of the path $P(v_s, v_e)$ found by Dijkstra's algorithm is W. The better (second) path has an intermediate vertex x that is in the priority queue but is not marked. The weight to x is

```
w = weight for P (vs, x) = weight of P(vs, u) + weight(u, x)
```

The weight w must be less than W, so the `MinInfo(x, w)` object will come out of the priority queue before the path found by the algorithm. Continuing in this way, all the vertices on the better path will come out of the priority queue, and the algorithm will find the optimal path, contradicting our assumption that the algorithm does not find the minimum path.

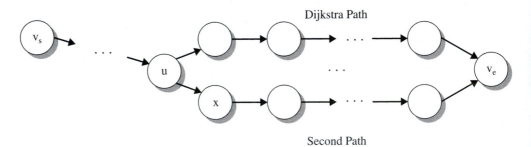

Dijkstra Path

Second Path

Implementing the minimumPath() Method

The method `minimumPath()` implements the Dijkstra algorithm. The method has the same signature as `shortestPath()`. The arguments are a graph and the starting vertex. The storage collection for `MinInfo` objects is the minimum-priority queue `minPathPQ`. The design of the algorithm is also modeled on the shortest-path algorithm. The `boolean` variable `foundMinPath` indicates when the minimum path is found. The search is an iterative process that uses a minimum-priority queue to store `MinInfo` objects.

minimumPath():

```
// find the path with minimum total weight from sVertex to
// each vertex in the graph reachable from sVertex; upon
// return, the dataValue field of each vertex in g is either
// the minimum path weight to the vertex or is INFINITY if the
// vertex was not reachable from sVertex; call
// path(g, sVertex, v) to find the minimum path from sVertex
// to v
public static <T> void minimumPath(DiGraph<T> g, T sVertex)
{
    T currVertex = null, neighborVertex = null;
    // heap (priority queue) that stores MinInfo objects
    HeapPQueue<MinInfo<T>> minPathPQ =
        new HeapPQueue<MinInfo<T>>(new Less<MinInfo<T>>());
    // used when inserting MinInfo entries
    // into the priority queue or erasing entries
    MinInfo<T> vertexData = null;
    // edgeSet is edge set of vertex we are visiting;
    // edgeIter is used to traverse edgeSet
    Set<T> edgeSet;
    Iterator<T> edgeIter;
    // computed minimum weight
    int newMinWeight, numVisited = 0, numVertices;

            . . .
}
```

The key element of the implementation is a loop that processes a vertex after deleting a corresponding MinInfo object from the priority queue.

```
// terminate on an empty priority queue or when
// the number of vertices visited is numVertices
while (numVisited < numVertices && !minPathPQ.isEmpty())
{
    // delete a priority queue entry and record its vertex;
    vertexData = minPathPQ.pop();
    currVertex = vertexData.endV;

    // if currVertex is BLACK, we have already
    // found the optimal path from sVertex to currVertex
    if (g.getColor(currVertex) != VertexColor.BLACK)
    {
        // mark the vertex so we don't look at it again and
        // increment numVisited
        g.setColor(currVertex, VertexColor.BLACK);
        numVisited++;

        // find all neighbors of the current vertex; for each
        // neighbor that has not been visited, generate a
        // MinInfo object and insert it into the priority
```

```
                        // queue provided the total weight to get to the
                        // neighbor is better than the current dataValue of
                        // neighborVertex
                        edgeSet = g.getNeighbors(currVertex);
                        edgeIter = edgeSet.iterator();
                        while (edgeIter.hasNext())
                        {
                            neighborVertex = edgeIter.next();

                            if (g.getColor(neighborVertex) ==
                                VertexColor.WHITE)
                            {
                                newMinWeight = g.getData(currVertex) +
                                        g.getWeight(currVertex, neighborVertex);

                                // if we have found a better path to
                                // neighborVertex, create a new MinInfo object
                                // for neighborVertex and push it onto the
                                // priority queue; update the dataValue and
                                // parent of neighborVertex; NOTE: if
                                // neighborVertex is WHITE, its
                                // data value is INFINITY and a new MinInfo
                                // object will enter the priority queue
                                if (newMinWeight < g.getData(neighborVertex))
                                {
                                    vertexData = new MinInfo<T>();
                                    vertexData.endV = neighborVertex;
                                    vertexData.pathWeight = newMinWeight;
                                    minPathPQ.push(vertexData);
                                    g.setData(neighborVertex, newMinWeight);
                                    g.setParent(neighborVertex, currVertex);
                                }
                            }
                        }
                    }
                }
            }
        }
```

> Push a vertex on the priority queue only if the current path has a better total weight than any other path found earlier.

Running-Time Analysis   Coloring the vertices WHITE and initializing the dataValue field is an $O(V)$ operation. The actions in the loop "while (!minPathPQ.empty())" dominate the running time. In the worst case, the algorithm pushes all edges into the priority queue and pops all edges. Each push() and pop() operation is $O(\log_2 E)$, so the running time for all these priority-queue operations is $O(E \log_2 E)$. Because

> Dijkstra's algorithm has running time $O(V + E \log_2 V)$.

$$E \le V(V - 1) = V^2 - V,$$

it follows that $\log_2 E \le 2 \log_2 V = O(\log_2 V)$. The running time for Dijkstra's algorithm is thus $O(V + E \log_2 V)$.

Example 25.4

Let us look at the minimum-path algorithm for the sample graph in Figure 25.6. The string argument "A" defines the starting vertex. After calling `minimumPath()`, we output the minimum-path weight and the path for all vertices reachable from A. The graph is read from the file *minpath.dat*.

```
DiGraph<String> g = DiGraph.readGraph("minpath.dat");
String sVertex = "A";
int dataValue;

DiGraphs.minimumPath(g, sVertex);

for (String vertex : g.vertexSet())
{
    dataValue = g.getData(vertex);
    if (dataValue != DiGraphs.INFINITY)
        System.out.println("Minimum weight from " +
            sVertex + " to " + vertex + " is " + dataValue +
            " and the path is " +
            DiGraphs.path(g, sVertex, vertex));
    else
        System.out.println(vertex + " is unreachable from " +
                            sVertex);
}
```

```
Output:
  Minimum weight from A to D is 6 and the path is [A, C, D]
  Minimum weight from A to E is 11 and the path is [A, C, D, E]
  Minimum weight from A to A is 0 and the path is [A]
  Minimum weight from A to B is 3 and the path is [A, B]
  Minimum weight from A to C is 4 and the path is [A, C]
```

Minimum Path in Acyclic Graphs

When the weighted digraph is acyclic, the problem of finding minimum paths is greatly simplified. The depth-first search creates a list of vertices in topological order.

$$\text{dfsList}: [v_0, v_1, \ldots, v_i, \ldots, v_{n-1}]$$

Assume v_i is the starting vertex for the minimum-path problem. Vertices in the list v_0 to v_{i-1} are not reachable from v_i because a path from v_i would indicate that the vertex has an earlier finishing time and so would come after v_i in `dfsList`.

The algorithm begins at v_i. After initializing the data value for all of the vertices to ∞, set the data value for v_i to 0 and its parent reference to v_i. This establishes a minimum path from v_i to v_i with weight 0. Iteratively scan the tail of the list. For each vertex v in the index range $[i, n)$, its data value is the minimum-path weight for any path from v_i to v. If the value is ∞, then no path exists, and you proceed to the next vertex in the list. Otherwise, look at each neighbor w of v. We have found a path from v_i to w that goes through v. The weight of this path is $P(v_i, v) + \text{weight}(v, w)$. Compare this weight with the weight of a previously discovered path from v_i to w. The notation data(v) is the value of the data field for vertex v, which corresponds to the weight of a path from v_i to v. Perform the comparison

```
weight(P(v_i, v) + (v, w)) = data(v) + weight (v, w) < data(w)
```

If the new path to w through v is better, update the data and parent reference fields for w. When the sequential scan concludes, the data field for each vertex has the minimum-path weight. For all reachable vertices, the parent reference field can be used to reconstruct the actual minimum path.

The method dagMinimumPath() implements the minimum-path algorithm for an acyclic graph. The method has parameters for the graph and the starting vertex.

dagMinimumPath( ):

```
// in the directed acyclic graph, find the path with minimum
// total weight from sVertex to each vertex reachable from
// sVertex; upon return, the dataValue field of each vertex in
// g is either the minimum path weight to the vertex or is
// INFINITY if the vertex was not reachable from sVertex;
// call path(g, sVertex, v) to find the minimum path from
// sVertex to v
public static <T> void dagMinimumPath(DiGraph<T> g, T sVertex)
{
    LinkedList<T> tlist = new LinkedList<T>();
    Iterator<T> topSortIter, setIter;
    T currVertex, neighborVertex;
    int w, dataValue;

    // perform a topological sort of g
    topologicalSort(g, tlist);

    // set all dataValues to INFINITY
    g.initData();
    // set dataValue and parent for sVertex
    g.setData(sVertex, 0);
    g.setParent(sVertex, sVertex);

    topSortIter = tlist.iterator();
    // sequence through the topological sort and update the
    // distance to each neighbor
    while (topSortIter.hasNext())
    {
        // get the next vertex in the topological sort
        currVertex = topSortIter.next();

        // get the dataValue of currVertex; if it is
        // INFINITY, the vertex is not reachable from sVertex
        if ((dataValue = g.getData(currVertex)) != INFINITY)
        {
            // obtain an iterator for the neighbors of currVertex
            setIter = g.getNeighbors(currVertex).iterator();
```

```
while (setIter.hasNext())
{
    // get the next neighbor of currVertex
    neighborVertex = setIter.next();

    // reset dataValue and parent if adding the
    // edge (currVertex, neighborVertex) to the
    // path sVertex --> currVertex provides a
    // better path to neighborVertex
    w = dataValue +
            g.getWeight(currVertex, neighborVertex);
    if (w < g.getData(neighborVertex))
    {
        g.setData(neighborVertex, w);
        g.setParent(neighborVertex, currVertex);
    }
}
        }
    }
}
```

A simple intuitive argument indicates why the algorithm works. At a vertex v in the sequential scan of dfsList, we use its current data value as the minimum-path weight from v_i to v. This value, data(v), is the weight of the minimum path from v_i to v. For there to be a better path, there must be an unvisited vertex, v', reachable from v_i, that has an edge to v.

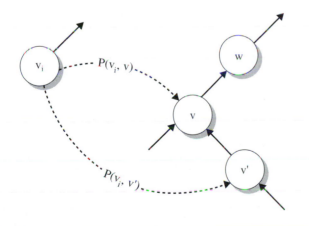

This is not possible, because topological order guarantees that v' will come earlier in dfsList.

Running-Time Analysis   The algorithm first creates a topological sort of the vertices with running time $O(V + E)$. A loop visits all of the vertices in the graph once and examines edges that emanate from each vertex only once. Access to all of the vertices and edges has running time $O(V + E)$ and so the total running time for the algorithm is $O(V + E)$.

Example 25.5

The example uses dagMinimumPath() to determine minimum-path weights for the following acyclic graph. The graph is read from the file *dagminpath.dat*.

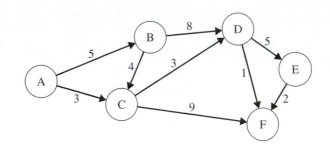

The topological sort creates the dfsList [A, B, C, D, E, F]. Vertex B is the starting vertex for the minimum-path problem. Output includes a listing of minimum weights and the actual path from B to a reachable vertex.

```
DiGraph<String> g = DiGraph.readGraph("dagminpath.dat");
String sVertex = "B";
int dataValue;

DiGraphs.dagMinimumPath(g, sVertex);

for (String vertex : g.vertexSet())
{
    dataValue = g.getData(vertex);
    if (dataValue != DiGraphs.INFINITY)
        System.out.println("Minimum weight from " + sVertex +
            " to " + vertex + " is " + dataValue +
            " and path is " +
            DiGraphs.path(g, sVertex, vertex));
    else
        System.out.println(vertex + " is unreachable from " +
                           sVertex);
}
```

Output:
```
    Minimum weight from B to D is 7 and path is [B, C, D]
    Minimum weight from B to E is 12 and path is [B, C, D, E]
    Minimum weight from B to F is 8 and path is [B, C, D, F]
    A is unreachable from B
    Minimum weight from B to B is 0 and path is [B]
    Minimum weight from B to C is 4 and path is [B, C]
```

25.6 Minimum Spanning Tree

The minimum-path algorithm finds an optimal path connecting a starting vertex with each vertex in a directed graph. A more general problem deals with a connected undirected graph. We want to find an acyclic set of edges that connect all of the vertices in the graph with the smallest total weight. Let E be the set of edges in the graph and T be the acyclic subset of E. Because T is acyclic and connects (spans) all the vertices, it forms a tree called the *minimum spanning tree*. The concept has important applications. A network connects hubs in a system. The minimum spanning tree links all of the nodes in the system with the least amount of cable (Figure 25.7). There are a variety of minimum-spanning-tree algorithms. One is Prim's algorithm, which builds the tree vertex by vertex. At each stage, the algorithm adds a new vertex and an edge that connects the new vertex with the ones already in the tree.

> A minimum spanning tree for an undirected graph is an acyclic set of edges that connect all the vertices of the graph having the smallest total weight.

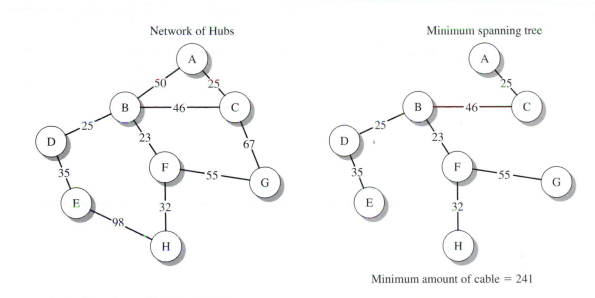

Figure 25.7 *A minimum spanning tree.*

Prim's Algorithm

Prim's algorithm creates a minimum spanning tree for a weighted undirected graph that is connected. The mechanics are very similar to the Dijkstra minimum-path algorithm. The iterative process begins with any starting vertex and maintains two variables `minSpanTreeSize` and `minSpanTreeWeight`, which have initial values 0. Each step adds a new vertex to the spanning tree. The process terminates when all of the vertices are added to the tree. Adding a vertex also involves adding the edge of minimal weight that connects the vertex to those already in the minimal spanning tree. The weight of the edge updates the variable `minSpanTreeWeight`.

Let us look at the algorithm for the graph in Figure 25.8 with A selected as the first vertex in the spanning tree.

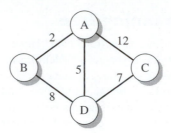

Figure 25.8 *Connected undirected graph to illustrate Prim's algorithm.*

Prim's algorithm uses a priority queue in which elements store a vertex and the weight of an edge that can connect it to the tree.

We implement Prim's algorithm by using a priority queue of MinInfo objects, much as we do in the Dijkstra minimum-path algorithm. An iterative step inserts an element into the priority queue when there is an edge e = (v, w), v is a vertex already in the minimum spanning tree, w is a vertex not in the tree, and adding the edge provides a smaller weight than the weight from any previously discovered edge that will connect a vertex to the spanning tree. The endV field of a MinInfo object is w, and the pathWeight field is the weight of the edge. We also use the vertex color, data, and parent reference properties.

color: Initially, all vertices are colored WHITE, to indicate that they are not in the spanning tree. When a vertex enters the tree, the color is set to BLACK. The colors BLACK and WHITE distinguish whether vertices are in the spanning tree.

data: This is the minimum weight of an edge that would connect the vertex to an existing vertex that is already in the spanning tree. As the tree grows, the data value is updated, because there are more and more available edges to connect the vertex to the tree. Initially, the data value is ∞.

When an object comes out of the priority queue, it defines a new edge that connects a vertex to the spanning tree.

parent: This is the source vertex for the minimum edge associated with the data value. The parent reference is a vertex in the spanning tree. Each update to the data value has a corresponding update for the parent reference field.

The following details the setup for the algorithm and the iterative steps. We include a display of MinInfo objects in the priority queue and the status of the color, data, and parent fields for each vertex.

Setup: Create the object MI(A, 0) and push it into the priority queue. The object creates an implied edge e = (A, A) with weight 0. At the same time, set the data value to 0 and the parent reference to A.

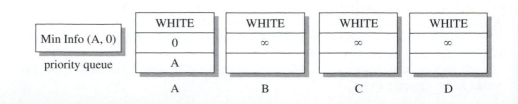

Step 1:   Pop MI(A, 0) from the priority queue and color A BLACK. This has the effect of placing A in the spanning tree. With each deletion, we increment the variable `minSpanTreeSize` and add the data value to `minSpanTreeWeight`. The resulting variables have values 1 and 0. We search the adjacency list for A to locate the edges that could connect an adjacent vertex not in the spanning tree to the single vertex already in the tree and improve on the existing weight for connection to the spanning tree. The vertices B, C, and D are neighbors of A with edges having weights 2, 12, and 5, respectively. For each neighbor v, create the `MinInfo` object with v as the ending vertex and the weight of the edge e = (A, v) as the `pathWeight`. Also, update `dataValue` to the edge weight and set A as the parent (Figure 25.9a).

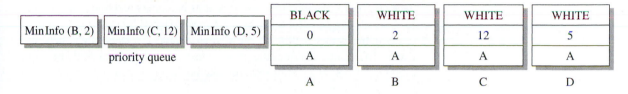

			BLACK	WHITE	WHITE	WHITE
Min Info (B, 2)	Min Info (C, 12)	Min Info (D, 5)	0	2	12	5
	priority queue		A	A	A	A
			A	B	C	D

Step 2:   Remove `minInfo(B,2)` from the priority queue. Because vertex B is WHITE (not visited), color it BLACK. The importance of checking whether the vertex is already in the spanning tree will become clear in the comment following Step 4. Increment `minSpanTreeSize` to 2, and update `minSpanTreeWeight` by adding the `dataValue` 2. The spanning tree now has two vertices, A and B. We have already taken care of vertex A, so we need only look for nonvisited (WHITE) neighbors of B to find additional edges that would connect a vertex to the spanning tree. In the example, D is such a neighbor, with edge (B, D) having weight 8. This is a key point in the minimization algorithm. The `dataValue` of D is 5. This implies that an edge already exists which would connect D to the existing spanning tree. In fact, it is edge (A, D) from Step 1. This is a better (lower-weight) connection than the new edge (B, D), and so we take no action (Figure 25.9b).

		BLACK	BLACK	WHITE	WHITE
Min Info (C, 12)	Min Info (D, 5)	0	2	12	5
	priority queue	A	A	A	A
		A	B	C	D

Step 3:   Pop `MinInfo(D,5)` from the priority queue. D is WHITE; color it BLACK. The number of vertices in the spanning tree (`minSpanTreeSize`) is 3, and `minSpanTreeWeight` becomes 7 (5 + 2). The vertex has only one WHITE neighbor, C. The edge (D, C) has weight 7, which is less than the current "best" edge weight of 12 for C. The new edge is a better choice, and so we create `MinInfo(C, 7)` and update the C so its `dataValue` is 7 and its parent is D. Push the `MinInfo` object onto the priority queue (Figure 25.9c).

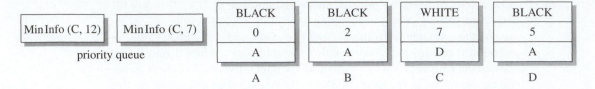

	BLACK	BLACK	WHITE	BLACK
Min Info (C, 12) Min Info (C, 7)	0	2	7	5
priority queue	A	A	D	A
	A	B	C	D

Step 4: Pop MinInfo(C,7). The value for minSpanTreeWeight becomes 14 (7 + 7). Because minSpanTreeSize now equals the vertex size of the graph, the process terminates. The weight for the minimum spanning tree is 14 (Figure 25.9d).

Note that, in Step 3, vertex C appears twice in the priority queue. Initially, it enters the queue as a neighbor of A, in which edge (A, C) has weight 12. Once D is in the spanning tree, we look at its neighbors and find a better edge, (D, C), with weight 7. In this step, we pop minInfo(C, 7) and put C into the spanning tree (color it BLACK). In a larger example, a subsequent step may delete minInfo(C, 12) from the priority queue, but C would already be in the spanning tree (BLACK), so we would take no action, because we cannot connect C a second time with weight 12.

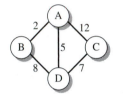

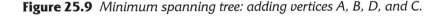

Original Graph	Vertex A minSpanTreeSize = 1 minTreeWeight = 0	Vertices A, B minSpanTreeSize = 2 minTreeWeight = 2	Vertices A, B, D minSpanTreeSize = 3 minTreeWeight = 7	Vertices A, B, D, C minSpanTreeSize = 4 minTreeWeight = 14
	(a)	(b)	(c)	(d)

Figure 25.9 *Minimum spanning tree: adding vertices A, B, D, and C.*

Implementing the minSpanTree() Method

In the minSpanTree() method, we are interested in taking a graph as an argument and deriving both a minimum spanning tree and its total weight. We do this by using a signature with two graph references as arguments and an integer return value. The first argument is the original graph and the second argument is the minimum spanning tree that is created by the method. The return value is the total weight. The following is a list of the key variables that are used in the method.

minSpanTree():

```
// find the minimum spanning tree for the connected graph g;
// g is represented as a digraph with bidirectional edges
// of equal weight
public static <T> int minSpanTree(DiGraph<T> g,
                                   DiGraph<T> MST)
{
```

```
    // priority queue that stores MinInfo objects
    HeapPQueue<MinInfo<T>> minTreePQ =
        new HeapPQueue<MinInfo<T>>(new Less<MinInfo<T>>());
    // used when inserting MinInfo entries
    // into the priority queue or erasing entries
    MinInfo<T> vertexData = null;
    // edgeSet is adjacency set of vertex we are visiting;
    // edgeIter is an iterator that scans the list; vertexSet
    // used to traverse graph vertices
    Set<T> edgeSet, vertexSet;
    Iterator<T> edgeIter;
    T sVertex = null, currVertex = null, neighborVertex = null;
    Iterator<T> graphIter;
    int edgeWeight;
    // size of the minimum spanning tree
    int minSpanTreeSize = 0;
    // current minimum total weight for spanning tree
    int minSpanTreeWeight = 0;
            ...
}
```

The code design for `minSpanTree()` is almost identical to the Dijkstra `minimumPath()` method. A minimum-priority queue holds the `MinInfo` objects that identify potential edges for the spanning tree. The iterative process takes the first vertex in the vertex set of the graph and uses the vertex as the starting point for the addition of vertices and edges to the tree. The process terminates when all of the vertices are added to the tree (`minSpanTreeSize == g.numberOfVertices()`).

```
    // add vertices until we span the entire graph
    for (;;)
    {
        if (minTreePQ.isEmpty())
            throw new IllegalArgumentException(
                "minSpanTree(): graph is not connected");

        // delete a priority queue entry
        vertexData = minTreePQ.pop();
        currVertex = vertexData.endV;

        // if vertex is not part of the new graph (unvisited)
        // add the weight of the edge to the total tree weight
        // and increment the number of vertices in the tree
        if (g.getColor(currVertex) == VertexColor.WHITE)
        {
            minSpanTreeWeight += vertexData.pathWeight;
            minSpanTreeSize++;

            // if we spanned all vertices, break
            if (minSpanTreeSize == g.numberOfVertices())
                break;
```

```
                    // mark the vertex BLACK so we don't look
                    // at it again
                    g.setColor(currVertex, VertexColor.BLACK);

                    // find all unmarked neighbors of the vertex
                    edgeSet = g.getNeighbors(currVertex);
                    edgeIter = edgeSet.iterator();
                    while (edgeIter.hasNext())
                    {
                        neighborVertex = edgeIter.next();
                        // if neighbor is unmarked, check whether adding
                        // the new edge to the tree is better than using
                        // the current edge
                        if (g.getColor(neighborVertex) == VertexColor.WHITE)
                        {
                            edgeWeight =
                                g.getWeight(currVertex,neighborVertex);
                            if (edgeWeight < g.getData(neighborVertex))
                            {
                                // if new edge is a better connection,
                                // create MinInfo object for new vertex;
                                // update dataValue and parent variables
                                vertexData = new MinInfo<T>();
                                vertexData.endV = neighborVertex;
                                vertexData.pathWeight = edgeWeight;
                                g.setData(neighborVertex, edgeWeight);
                                g.setParent(neighborVertex, currVertex);
                                minTreePQ.push(vertexData);
                            }
                        }
                    }
                }
            }
        }
    }
```

The loop identifies all of the vertices in the original graph and the set of minimal edges that should be part of the spanning tree. It also computes the value for minSpanTreeWeight. The minSpanTree() method concludes by taking this information and building the graph MST, which is the minimal spanning tree. Search the vertices in the original graph and insert them into MST. For each vertex v, obtain

```
parentVertex = g.getParent(v)
```

and

```
edgeWeight = g.getWeight(parent, v)
```

Insert the edges e1 = (parentVertex, v) and e2 = (v, parentVertex) with weight edgeWeight into MST. The return value is minSpanTreeWeight.

```
    // add all of the vertices
    graphIter = vertexSet.iterator();
    while (graphIter.hasNext())
        MST.addVertex(graphIter.next());
```

```
// add the edges to the minimum spanning tree
graphIter = vertexSet.iterator();

T parentVertex = null;

graphIter.next();
while (graphIter.hasNext())
{
   currVertex = graphIter.next();
   parentVertex = g.getParent(currVertex);
   edgeWeight = g.getWeight(parentVertex, currVertex);
   MST.addEdge(parentVertex, currVertex, edgeWeight);
   MST.addEdge(currVertex, parentVertex, edgeWeight);
}

return minSpanTreeWeight;
```

Running Time Analysis Prim's algorithm is just a variation of Dijkstra's algorithm, so its running time is $O(V + E \log_2 V)$.

Example 25.6

After prompting the user for the name of the graph input file, construct the graph and use the algorithm `minSpanTree()` to compute the minimum spanning tree. Display the total weight for the resulting minimum spanning tree along with its vertices and edges. We apply Prim's minimum-spanning-tree algorithm for two graphs. The first run uses the graph in Figure 25.9 ("minspan.dat"), and the second run computes the tree for the graph in Figure 25.7 (*network.dat*).

Like Dijkstra's algorithm, Prim's algorithm has running time $O(V + E \log_2 V)$.

```
int weight;
// graph file name
String fileName;
BufferedReader keyIn =
   new BufferedReader(new InputStreamReader(System.in));

System.out.print("Graph input file: ");
fileName = keyIn.readLine();
System.out.println();

DiGraph<String> g = DiGraph.readGraph(fileName),
            minSpan = new DiGraph<String>();

// get minimum spanning tree and its weight
weight = DiGraphs.minSpanTree(g, minSpan);
System.out.println("MST has weight "+ weight);

// display minimum spanning tree
System.out.println(" --- MST Graph ---\n" + minSpan);
```

```
Run 1:
  Graph input file: minspan.dat

  MST has weight 14
   --- MST Graph ---
```

```
A:   in-degree 2   out-degree 2
     Edges: D(5)  B(2)
B:   in-degree 1   out-degree 1
     Edges: A(2)
C:   in-degree 1   out-degree 1
     Edges: D(7)
D:   in-degree 2   out-degree 2
     Edges: A(5)  C(7)
```

Run 2:

```
Graph input file: network.dat

MST has weight 241
 --- MST Graph ---
A:   in-degree 1   out-degree 1
     Edges: C(25)
B:   in-degree 3   out-degree 3
     Edges: F(23)  D(25)  C(46)
C:   in-degree 2   out-degree 2
     Edges: A(25)  B(46)
D:   in-degree 2   out-degree 2
     Edges: E(35)  B(25)
E:   in-degree 1   out-degree 1
     Edges: D(35)
F:   in-degree 3   out-degree 3
     Edges: B(23)  G(55)  H(32)
G:   in-degree 1   out-degree 1
     Edges: F(55)
H:   in-degree 1   out-degree 1
     Edges: F(32)
```

Chapter Summary

- By application of the depth-first search strategy, an algorithm can perform a topological sort of a *directed acyclic graph* (*DAG*). The depth-first search also forms the basis for an efficient algorithm that finds the strong components of a graph.

- Many very important graph applications find minimum values in a graph. In particular, the breadth-first search can be used to find the minimum distance from a starting vertex in a graph to any vertex of the graph reachable from the starting vertex.

- For a weighted graph, *Dijkstra's algorithm* uses a priority queue to determine a path from a starting vertex to each reachable vertex, with minimum weight. If a digraph is acyclic, the minimum path from a starting vertex can be computed very efficiently by visiting vertices in the order determined by the topological sort.

- Dijkstra's algorithm can be extended to *Prim's algorithm*, which computes the minimum spanning tree in an undirected, connected graph. Instead of the priority queue containing path weights from a starting vertex, it contains the weights of edges that have not yet connected a vertex to the spanning tree.

Written Exercises

1. Give a topological sort for the following graph.

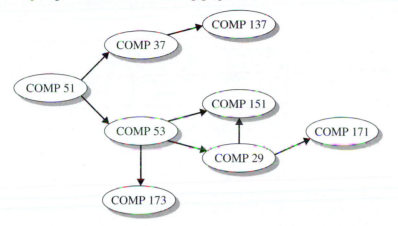

2. (a) A DAG has n vertices. Give the minimum and the maximum number of strong components that exist in the graph.
   (b) Prove that the topological sorting problem has a solution for a digraph if and only if it is a DAG.
   (c) For a digraph with n vertices, what is the largest number of distinct solutions the topological sorting problem can have?

3. Can we use the discovery time of vertices to solve the topological sorting problem?

4. Apply the algorithm for finding the strong components of a digraph to the graph in Figure 25.10. Give dfsList for the depth-first search of the graph and draw the transpose graph. Show how the depth-first search of the transpose in the order specified by dfsList produces the strong components.

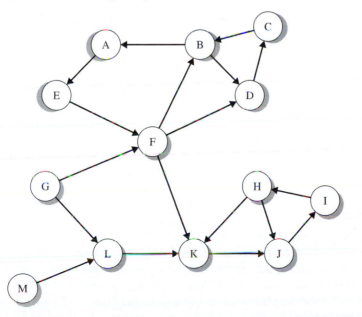

Figure 25.10 *Graph illustrating strong components.*

5. Use the accompanying graph to determine minimum and shortest paths. For the minimum path, give the total weight. For the shortest path, give the total path length. In each case, list a path providing the minimum value.

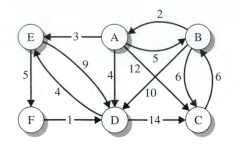

(a) Shortest-path distance from C to D
(b) Shortest-path distance from E to B
(c) Shortest-path distance from C to F
(d) Minimum path from C to D
(e) Minimum path from E to B
(f) Minimum path from C to F

6. For the graph in Figure 25.11a, replicate the trace of Dijkstra's algorithm to find the minimum path from vertex A to F. For each step, create the list of MinInfo elements in the priority queue and indicate which element is removed from the queue.

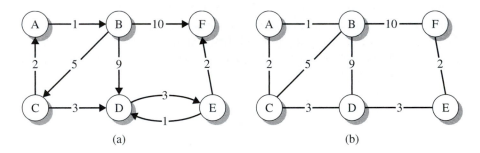

(a)   (b)

Figure 25.11 *Graphs for Written Exercises 25.6 and 25.7.*

7. For the graph in Figure 25.11b, replicate the trace of Prim's algorithm to create a minimum spanning tree. For each step, create the list of MinInfo elements in the priority queue and indicate which vertices and edges are in the current spanning tree, along with the accumulated total weight.

Programming Exercises

8. Using the graph in Figure 25.10 (*graph25-8.dat* in ch25ex), create a program that determines the strong components. The components are returned as a LinkedList of objects, which are the vertices in a strong component. Output the strong components. Remove from the graph all vertices that belong to a one-element strong component. After deleting the vertices, recompute and display the strong components for the updated graph.

9. Have the user input one of the vertices from the following graph (*graph25-9.dat* in ch25ex). For each of the other vertices v in the graph, determine the weight of the minimum path from the user supplied vertex to v. Output the vertex that has the largest minimum-path weight, the weight of the minimum path, and the path itself.

10. Find the minimum spanning tree for the following graph (*graph25-10.dat* in ch25ex). Output the graph and the sum of its edge weights.

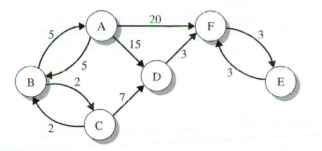

11. The method minimumPath() implements Dijkstra's algorithm, which is a single-source shortest-path algorithm. The method minimumPathPair() is a single-pair shortest path version of the algorithm. The parameter list includes both a source vertex and a destination vertex and returns the minimum-path weight that connects the source to the destination. A return value −1 indicates the destination is not reachable from the source.

```
public static <T> int
minimumPathPair(DiGraph<T> g, T v, T w)
{ ... }
```

Implement the new method and write a test program that inputs the following graph (*graph25-11.dat* in ch25ex) and requests the user to enter both a source and a destination vertex.

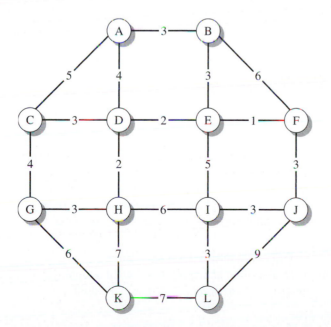

12. The method `minimumPathDest()` is a single-destination shortest-path version of the Dijkstra's algorithm. The parameter list includes a single vertex that designates a destination. The algorithm finds the shortest path connecting each vertex in the graph to the destination vertex.

    ```
    public static <T> void minimumPathDest(DiGraph<T> g, T w)
    { ... }
    ```

    Implement the new method and write a test program that inputs the graph in Programming Exercise 25.12 (*graph25-12.dat* in ch25ex) and requests the user to enter the destination vertex. (HINT: use the transpose of the graph).

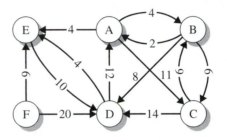

13. Write a program that creates a topological sort of the following digraph (*graph25-13.dat* in ch25ex) and uses the `dagMinimumPath()` method to find the path of minimum total weight from vertices A, B, and G to all of the vertices in the graph.

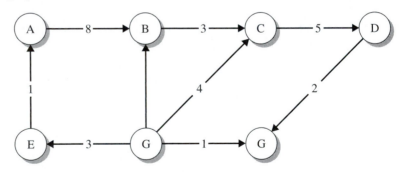

Programming Project

14. Consider another algorithm for performing a topological sort. Repeatedly identify in a digraph a source which is a vertex with no incoming edges, and delete it along with all the edges outgoing from it. (If there are several sources, choose one arbitrarily.) If there is none, there is no topological sort (see part (a)). The order in which the vertices are deleted gives a solution to the topological sorting problem. Figure 25.12 shows the algorithm in action.

    (a) Prove that a DAG must have at least one source.
    (b) Implement the algorithm and apply it to obtain a topological sort of the graph in Written Exercise 25.1 (*graph25-14.dat* in ch25ex).

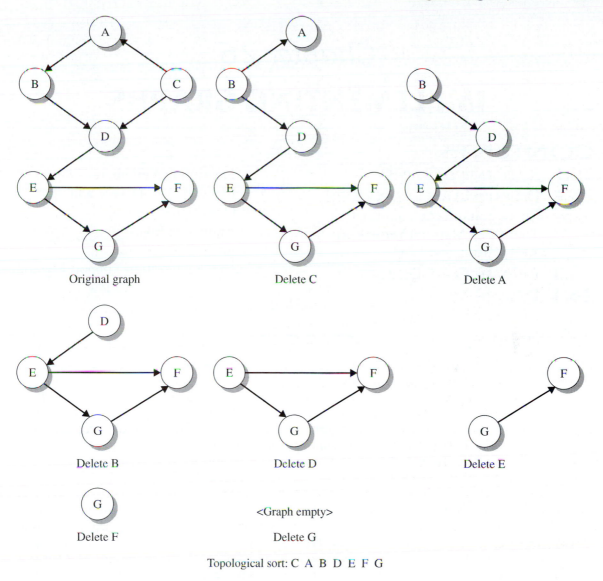

Topological sort: C A B D E F G

Figure 25.12 *An alternative algorithm for producing a topological sort.*

Chapter 26

IMPLEMENTING GRAPHS

CONTENTS

26.1 REPRESENTING GRAPHS

26.2 DiGRAPH CLASS COMPONENTS
Representing Vertex Information
The Vertex Map and VertexInfo
Array List

26.3 DiGRAPH CLASS DESIGN

26.4 DiGRAPH METHODS
Accessing the ArrayList

Identifying Neighbors
Evaluating In-Degree and
Out-Degree
Adding an Edge
Removing a Vertex
Graph Algorithm Support Methods
Graph Collection View

Chapters 24 and 25 used the DiGraph class for search algorithms and applications. You are familiar with the Graph interface methods that define access and update operations for vertices, edges, and weights. The DiGraph class extends the interface to include methods that handle the color, data value, and parent attributes of a vertex, which are key to implementing many of the algorithms.

The DiGraph class is the most sophisticated data structure in this book. The complexity derives from the fact that we need map, set, and two list collections to store and access all of the different vertex attributes. Take time to understand the class design. Once you see the relationships among the different collection types, implementing the DiGraph methods will be relatively simple.

In Section 26.1, we will describe both an adjacency matrix and an adjacency-list representation of a graph.

In this book, we use an adjacency list, which becomes a field within a vertex information record that also includes the color, data value, parent, and so forth. In Section 26.2, we will develop all of the object and collection types that are part of the information record. Vertices are stored in a map collection and associated vertex information is stored in an array list.

In Sections 26.3 and 26.4, we will give the overall design of the DiGraph class and implement selected methods. The design of the methods illustrates the relationship between a vertex in the map collection and its attributes in an array list objects. A graph does not have an iterator. Scanning the vertices is left to a set view of the vertices with operations that access and update the backing graph collection. We will conclude the section by defining the iterator inner class and the remove() method.

26.1 Representing Graphs

In order to implement a graph, we need some way to represent the set of vertices and their edges. Assume the vertices are v_0, v_1, v_2, ..., v_{m-1}. An m by m matrix, called an *adjacency matrix*, identifies the edges. An entry in row i and column j corresponds to the edge

$e = (v, v_j)$. Its value is the weight of the edge, or 0 if the edge does not exist. For instance, Figure 26.1 shows a nonweighted and a weighted graph, with the corresponding adjacency matrices.

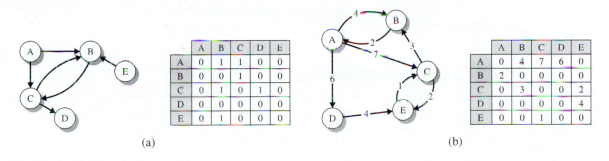

Figure 26.1 *Graph representation by means of an adjacency matrix.*

The adjacency matrix representation has the disadvantage that, regardless of the number of edges, it always requires $V \times V = V^2$ entries, where V is the number of vertices. Another representation of a graph associates with each vertex a list of its adjacent vertices (neighbors). This model is often more efficient because it stores information for precisely the edges that actually belong to the graph. For each vertex, an element in the adjacency list is a pair consisting of the destination vertex and the weight of the edge. For the graphs from Figure 26.1, we give the *adjacency-list* representation (Figure 26.2).

Adjacency matrix representation of a graph uses a matrix whose entries give the weight of an edge (v_i, v_j) or 0 if there is no edge from v_i to v_j.

An Adjacency list representation of a graph includes the vertex with the list of its neighbors.

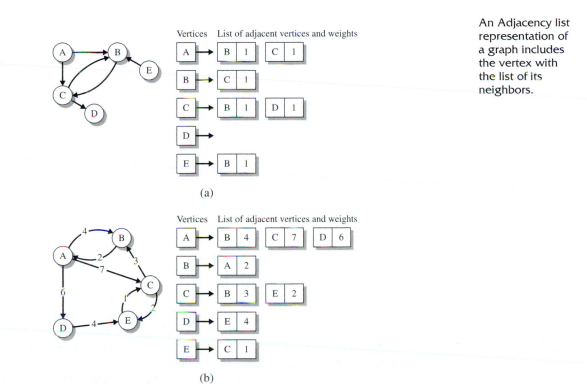

Figure 26.2 *Graph representation by means of an adjacency list.*

The DiGraph class uses the adjacency-list representation for a graph. Programming Project 26.15 develops the DiGraph class via an adjacency matrix.

26.2 DiGraph Class Components

The Edge class holds data that references the destination of an edge and the weight of the edge.

In the DiGraph class, each vertex has an associated adjacency list that contains all of its adjacent vertices and the weight of each connecting edge. We define the Edge class to provide a data type for each element in an adjacency list. The variables in the class are public integer variables dest and weight. The data identifies the adjacent (destination) vertex and the weight of the edge. As we will see soon, dest is an integer index into the ArrayList vInfo that contains vertex properties. The Edge class contains a constructor that initializes the variables and the method equals() that enables comparison of edges. Two edges are considered equal if they terminate at the same vertex. Note that the class is not declared public because it is a class that supports the public class DiGraph.

Edge class:

```
class Edge
{
    // index of the destination vertex in the ArrayList
    // vInfo of vertex properties
    public int dest;
    // weight of this edge
    public int weight;

    public Edge(int dest, int weight)
    {
        this.dest = dest;
        this.weight = weight;
    }
    public boolean equals(Object obj)
    {
        return ((Edge)obj).dest == this.dest;
    }
}
```

Representing Vertex Information

The VertexInfo class has a reference to the vertex value, the in-degree of the vertex, a list of edges originating at the vertex, and other information used by graph algorithms.

The DiGraph class stores the vertices in a map collection. Each element in the map is a key-value pair, in which the key is the vertex and the value component is an Integer object specifying an index into the ArrayList of VertexInfo elements. A VertexInfo object has fields that identify properties of a vertex and other information that is used by graph algorithms. We introduce the ArrayList in the next section. For now, let us focus on the structure of a single VertexInfo object, which is associated with a vertex.

A VertexInfo object consists of seven public variables. The first two variables, called vertex and edgeList, identify the vertex in the map and its adjacency list. The adjacency list, edgeList, is a LinkedList of Edge objects that contain both the destination vertex and the weight of the connecting edge. A third variable, called inDegree, indicates the number of edges that terminate in the vertex. The boolean field, called occupied, specifies whether the position in the ArrayList contains valid vertex data. When we remove a vertex from the map collection, we set the occupied field in the corresponding VertexInfo object to false. In this way, we avoid the overhead of deleting an element from the ArrayList. An unoccupied VertexInfo object can be used when we insert a new vertex in the map. The idea is to promote object reuse. The other three variables in the VertexInfo object contain color, data value, and parent information that is used by graph algorithms (Figure 26.3).

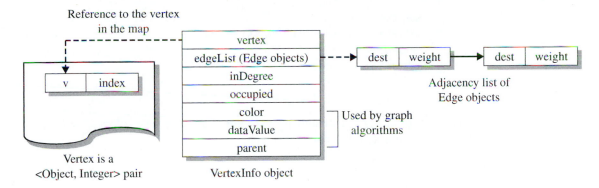

Figure 26.3 *VertexInfo object with a vertex field for the vertex name and a list of the adjacent vertices.*

The VertexInfo class is used only in the implementation of the DiGraph class. The variables are declared public for easy access. The constructor takes a vertex as an argument and uses it to initialize the vertex field of the object. The constructor also initializes the edgeList, inDegree, and occupied fields.

VertexInfo class:

```
// maintains vertex properties, including its set of Edges
class VertexInfo<T>
{
    // vertex reference back to the vertex in the map
    public T vertex;

    // list of Edge objects (adjacent vertices) for the
    // current vertex
    public LinkedList<Edge> edgeList;

    // maintains the in-degree of the vertex
    public int inDegree;

    // indicates whether the object currently represents a vertex
    public boolean occupied;

    // indicates vertex color for use in algorithms
    // that traverse the vertices of a Graph
    public VertexColor color;

    // available to algorithms for storing relevant
    // data values
    public int dataValue;

    // available to Graph algorithms; holds parent which is
    // a vertex that has an edge terminating in the current
```

```
    // vertex
    public T parent;

    // constructor creates an object with initial values for
    // the vertex, edgeList, inDegree, and occupied fields
    public VertexInfo(T v)
    {
        vertex = v;
        edgeList = new LinkedList<Edge>();
        inDegree = 0;
        occupied = true;
    }
}
```

The VertexColor class maintains the color of a vertex. The colors of WHITE, GRAY, and BLACK are values of the enumerated type.

VertexColor class:

```
public enum VertexColor
{
    WHITE, GRAY, BLACK
}
```

The Vertex Map and VertexInfo Array List

To store the vertices in a graph, we use the HashMap collection, vtxMap, in which an entry is a <T, Integer> pair. Type T specifies the vertex and the Integer object specifies an index in an ArrayList collection of VertexInfo objects, called vInfo.

```
private ArrayList<VertexInfo<T>> vInfo;
```

There is a 1 to 1 correspondence between an entry in the map and a vertexInfo element in the ArrayList (Figure 26.4).

The vertex map contains key-value pairs in which the key is a reference to the vertex and the value is an index into an ArrayList of VertexInfo objects.

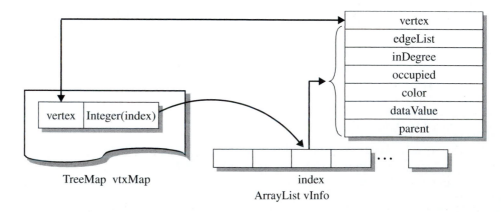

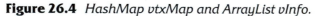

Figure 26.4 *HashMap vtxMap and ArrayList vInfo.*

Let us look at code fragments that relate a vertex in the HashMap collection with a VertexInfo element in the ArrayList vInfo. A vertex v in the HashMap vtxMap is a key-value entry <v, Integer(index)> where v is the a String specifying the vertex name. The index is the position of the corresponding VertexInfo object in the ArrayList vInfo. Access the position using the map get() method.

```
// index of VertexInfo object in vInfo that corresponds to
// vertex v in vtxMap; extract value field and convert to int
int index = vtxMap.get(v);
```

Use the ArrayList get() method to access the VertexInfo object. The following code fragments access properties in a VertexInfo object.

```
// use the index to extract the VertexInfo object from the
// ArrayList
VertexInfo<T> vtxInfo = vInfo.get(index);

// the vertex field is a String which is a copy of the key
// in the map
String vertexName = vtxInfo.vertex;
// the adjacency list contains the neighbors of v and
// the weight of the edges emanating from v
LinkedList edges = vtxInfo.edgeList;

// the in-degree of v is the number of edges terminating at v
int indegreeV = vtxInfo.inDegree;
```

Example 26.1

This example describes the map vtxMap and the ArrayList vInfo for vertices in the accompanying weighted digraph (see next page). The figure includes the vertex map and a listing of the first three VertexInfo fields for each vertex. We assume that vertex A in the map vtxMap corresponds to index 0 in the ArrayList, vertex B corresponds to index 1, and so forth.

Let's look at vertex A in the map. The vertex is the key component in a map entry whose value component is an Integer representing index 0. The corresponding VertexInfo object is the first element (index 0) in the ArrayList vInfo. The first field in the object is the vertex A. The third field, inDegree, is the in-degree of vertex A. The edgeList field is a LinkedList of Edge objects that defines the adjacency list for vertex A. The first field in an Edge object is an integer designating the destination vertex. The index is the element in vInfo that corresponds to the vertex. For instance, vertex B is a neighbor of A with corresponding VertexInfo element at index 1 in vInfo. The weight of edge (A, B) is 7. For your convenience, the figure uses the vertex name rather than the vertex index to display the dest field in an Edge object.

```
// VertexInfo object at index 0 corresponding to vertex A
VertexInfo<T> vtxInfo = vInfo.get(0);

vtxInfo.vertex = "A"        // vertex name
vtxInfo.edgeList            // two element adjacency list
vtxInfo.inDegree = 1        // edge (C,A) terminates at A
```

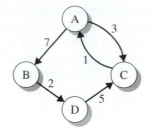

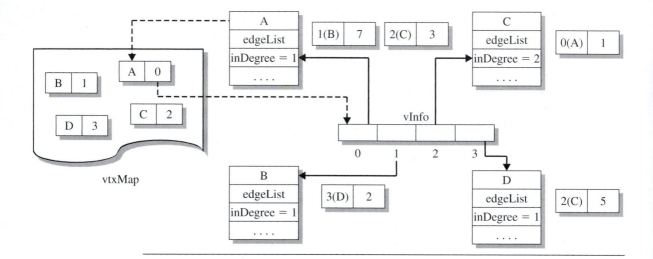

Exploring the Adjacency List of a Vertex　A LinkedList of Edge objects is the adjacency list for a vertex. To access the neighbors of the vertex, declare an iterator and use the next() method to scan the list.

```
VertexInfo<T> vtxInfo = vInfo.get(i);
// declare an iterator for edgeList and position it at the
// first element in the adjacency list
Iterator<Edge> iter = vtxInfo.edgeList.iterator();

// extract the first element and output its weight
Edge e = iter.next();
System.out.println(e.weight);

// use the dest field to access the vInfo element that
// corresponds to the adjacent vertex; the index of the element
// is e.dest; output the name of the vertex
VertexInfo<T> edgeVtxInfo = vInfo.get(e.dest);
System.out.println(edgeVtxInfo.vertex);
```

A VertexInfo object allows access to all the neighbors of the vertex.

Let us look at a code segment that scans the adjacency list looking for the edge of minimum weight. In order to output the edge, we must maintain the vInfo index of the destination vertex.

```
// declare variables for the minimum dest index and minimum
// weight
int minDest, minWeight = Integer.MAX_VALUE;

// VertexInfo objects for elements in ArrayList vInfo; current
// vertex element in vInfo is vtxInfo; vInfo element for
// a neighbor is edgeVtxInfo
VertexInfo<T> vtxInfo = null, edgeVtxInfo = null;
               ...
// iterator to scan adjacency list for current vertex
Iterator<Edge> iter = vtxInfo.edgeList.iterator();
while (iter.hasNext)
{
    // extract next element (Edge object) from adjacency list
    Edge e = iter.next();

    // update if new minimum weight is discovered
    if (e.weight < minWeight)
    {
        minWeight = e.weight;
        minDest = e.dest;
    }
}

// output the edge that has minimum weight;  first get the
// corresponding vInfo element and then access the vertex field
edgeVtxInfo = vInfo.get(minDest);
System.out.println("Edge (" + vtxInfo.vertex + ", " +
        edgeVtxInfo.vertex + ") has weight + 
        edgeVtxInfo.weight);
```

The "occupied" Field   The DiGraph class maintains a 1 to 1 correspondence between entries in the vertex map and elements in the ArrayList vInfo. Initially, the class builds the ArrayList by adding an element for each vertex that is inserted in the map, and the occupied field for the element is set to true. The class and the collection view iterator have remove() methods that delete an entry in the map. The methods do not erase the corresponding element in the ArrayList but rather set its occupied field to false.

The implementation of many DiGraph methods requires us to search the elements in ArrayList vInfo. During the search, we should check the occupied field to determine whether the element corresponds to an actual vertex.

The occupied field of a VertexInfo object indicates If the object corresponds to an existing vertex entry in the map.

```
for (i = 0; i < vInfo.size(); i++)
{
    VertexInfo<T> vtxInfo = vInfo.get(i);
    if (vtxInfo.occupied)
        < vInfo element corresponds to an actual vertex>
}
```

26.3 `DiGraph` **Class Design**

With the background from the previous section, the overall design of the `DiGraph` class is straightforward. The private variables `vtxMap` of type `HashMap` and `vInfo` of type `ArrayList` store the vertices and the vertex information. The variable `numberOfEdges` maintains a count on the edges. To facilitate adding and removing vertices, the class provides an *availability stack* to store indices for the `ArrayList`. Whenever a vertex is deleted from the map, we push the index for the corresponding `vInfo` element onto the stack. When adding a new vertex, we first check to see whether an index is available on the stack. If so, we pop it and reuse the corresponding `vInfo` element to store vertex properties, thus ensuring more efficient memory management.

Private method getVInfoIndex() looks up a vertex in the map and returns the vInfo index of the vertex.

The `DiGraph` class includes a private method that is called frequently. The method `getVInfoIndex(Object v)` takes a vertex argument, locates the map entry, and returns the value component as an integer designating the index of the corresponding element in the `ArrayList vInfo`. A return value -1 indicates the vertex is not in the graph.

The `Edge` and `VertexInfo` classes define objects for the graph edges and for the `ArrayList` that stores vertex properties. The `DiGraph` class implements the `Graph` interface. In addition, it has I/O methods `readGraph()` and `toString()` along with access and update methods for vertex properties such as in-degree and out-degree, color, data, and parent references. The following is a UML diagram that displays the `DiGraph` class design.

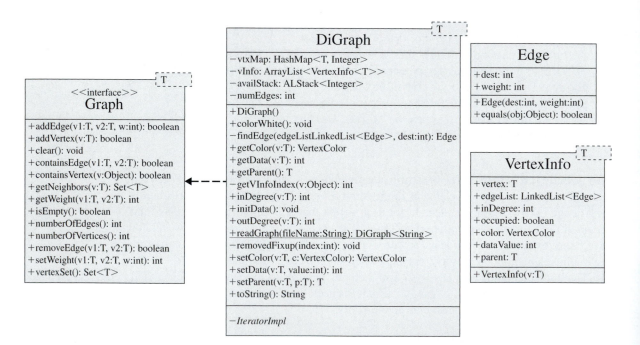

26.4 `DiGraph` **Methods**

With a few examples, you can understand how we design and implement `DiGraph` class methods. Most of the details center on the interaction between the vertex map and the corresponding `ArrayList` of `VertexInfo` objects. In the next several sections, we will look at a representative set of methods. In some cases, we will include the complete implementation and for others, we will describe the steps in the algorithm and list small code segments that perform the tasks. The `removeVertex()` algorithm is the most interesting because it draws on many of the design features of the `DiGraph` class.

Accessing the ArrayList

The method `getVInfoIndex()` takes a vertex as an argument and returns the index of the corresponding element in the `ArrayList`. The index is in the value field of the `vtxMap` entry. A return value −1 indicates that the vertex is not in the graph.

getVInfoIndex():

```
// takes vertex v in the map and returns the index of the
// corresponding vInfo element or -1 if v is not a vertex
private int getVInfoIndex(Object v)
{
    // get the Integer value field of the vtxMap entry
    Integer indexObj = vtxMap.get(v);

    // if value is null, there is no entry in the map; return
    // -1; otherwise, convert object to an int
    if (indexObj == null)
        return -1;
    else
        return indexObj;
}
```

Identifying Neighbors

The method `getNeighbors()` takes a vertex v as an argument and returns the adjacent vertices (neighbors) in a set. In the `VertexInfo` object that corresponds to the neighbors that are stored in a linked list of `Edge` objects in which the integer `dest` field identifies the neighbor. The `dest` field is not the adjacent vertex name but rather the index of the `ArrayList` element corresponding to the adjacent vertex. The element is a `VertexInfo` object whose vertex field is the vertex name.

Begin by calling the private method `getVInfoIndex()`, which returns the index of the corresponding element in `vInfo`. If the vertex is not in the set, throw an `IllegalArgumentException`. This is the usual way by which we can test whether a vertex argument is in the graph (in the map).

```
// find the VertexInfo object for index v
int index = getVInfoIndex(v);

// check for an error and throw exception if vertices not
// in graph
if (index == -1)
    throw new IllegalArgumentException(
            "DiGraph getNeighbors(): vertex not in graph");
```

The getNeighbors() method scans the adjacency list of a vertex and returns a set containing its neighbors.

To return the adjacent vertices as a Set collection, create a HashSet<T> object that contains the vertices. Use an iterator to scans the adjacency list. For each Edge element in the list, use the dest field as the index of the vInfo object corresponding to the adjacent vertex. Add the vertex field of the object to the set.

getNeighbors():

```
// returns the vertices that are adjacent to vertex v in a
// Set object; if v is not a graph vertex,
// throws IllegalArgumentException
public Set<T> getNeighbors(T v)
{
    // find the VertexInfo object for index v
    int index = getVInfoIndex(v);

    // check for an error and throw exception if vertices
    // not in graph
    if (index == -1)
        throw new IllegalArgumentException(
                "DiGraph getNeighbors(): vertex not in graph");

    // create HashSet object to hold vertices, obtain
    // the VertexInfo object, and initialize an iterator
    // to scan the adjacency list of the VertexInfo object
    HashSet<T> edgeSet = new HashSet<T>();
    VertexInfo<T> vtxInfo = vInfo.get(index);
    Iterator<Edge> iter = vtxInfo.edgeList.iterator();
    Edge e = null;

    while (iter.hasNext())
    {
        e = iter.next();
        edgeSet.add(vInfo.get(e.dest).vertex);
    }

    return edgeSet;
}
```

Evaluating In-Degree and Out-Degree

A VertexInfo object that corresponds to the vertex contains all of the information needed to return the in-degree and out-degree of the vertex. Assume vtxInfo is the VertexInfo object corresponding to the vertex. The in-degree is a field in vtxInfo.

```
// in-degree of vertex v
vtxInfo.inDegree
```

The out-degree of the vertex is the number of its adjacent vertices. This value is simply the size of the adjacency list, which is the size of the collection edgeList.

```
// out-degree is the number of elements in adjacency list
vtxInfo.edgeList.size();
```

Adding an Edge

To insert an edge e(v1,v2, w), we must add an Edge object in the adjacency list for v1. The object includes the ArrayList index for v2 and the weight w. The operation includes incrementing the in-degree for v2 and updating the private variable numEdges. Start by finding the indices for the two VertexInfo objects in vInfo corresponding to v1 and v2.

```
pos1=getVInfoIndex(v1);
pos2=getVInfoIndex(v2);
```

If pos1 or pos2 is −1, one of the vertex arguments is not valid. If pos1 == pos2, the edge would create a self-loop, which we do not allow. If either error condition occurs, the method throws an IllegalArgumentException. Adding vertex v2 as a neighbor of v1 involves updating edgeList for vertex v1. Using pos2 and w as arguments, the operation creates an Edge object and adds it to edgeList. Because the out-degree for vertex v1 is the size of its adjacency list, adding the object to edgeList updates out-degree. To increase the in-degree for vertex v2, use pos2 to locate the VertexInfo object for v2 and increment its inDegree field. Conclude the algorithm by incrementing the variable numEdges and returning true. Note that if the edge is already in the graph, the method returns false.

> To add an edge to a graph, obtain the vInfo index of the source vertex and insert an Edge object for the destination vertex in the adjacency list. Update the in-degree of the destination vertex.

```
// get VertexInfo objects for vertices v1 and v2
VertexInfo<T> vtxInfo1 = vInfo.get(pos1),
               vtxInfo2 = vInfo.get(pos2);

Edge e = new Edge(pos2, w);

boolean returnValue = true;

// try to add an Edge reference v1-v2;
// if it already exists, just return
if (!vtxInfo1.edgeList.contains(e))
{
   vtxInfo1.edgeList.add(e);
   // increment inDegree for vertex v2 and number of edges
   vtxInfo2.inDegree++;
   numEdges++;
}
else
   returnValue = false;

return returnValue;
```

Removing a Vertex

Deleting a vertex is the most interesting method and uses operations on the graph map collection and the ArrayList of VertexInfo objects. We will describe the algorithm by outlining the order of operations and by including code fragments. The algorithm begins by finding the index of the VertexInfo object in vInfo that corresponds to the vertex. If the vertex is not in the graph, the method throws an IllegalArgumentException. Delete the vertex by calling the map remove() method with the vertex as the key.

```
// find the index for the VertexInfo object in vInfo
int index = getVInfoIndex(v);
```

```
            if (index == -1)
                return false;
        vtxMap.remove(v);
```

The remaining actions are performed by the private method removeFixup() that takes as a parameter the index for the VertexInfo object in vInfo. We will outline its tasks.

```
        private void removeFixup(int index)
        { ... }
```

Task 1: Get the VertexInfo object in vInfo that corresponds to the index. Set the occupied field to false and then push the index onto an availability stack for use by a vertex that might be added later.

To erase a vertex, remove all of the edges to and from the vertex prior to erasing the vertex itself.

```
    // iterator used to scan Edge objects in adjacency lists
    Iterator<Edge> iter = null;
    Edge e = null;
    VertexInfo<T> vtxInfo = vInfo.get(index), edgeVtxInfo;

    vtxInfo.occupied = false;
    availStack.push(index);
```

Task 2: Delete all edges that terminate in v. These edges have the form (v_i, v) and are found by scanning all of the elements in vInfo. Consider only the elements with the occupied field set to true. These correspond to a vertex $v_i \neq v$ in the graph. Remember, the ArrayList element corresponding to v has the occupied field false from task 1. Extract the adjacency list for each vertex and use an iterator to scan the element, removing the Edge object that indicates v is an adjacent vertex. The action of removing an edge from an adjacency list must be accompanied by a decrement of the variable numEdges.

```
    // remove all the edges that terminate at the vertex being
    // removed; use a loop to check all of the VertexInfo
    // elements in vInfo for which occupied is true; these
    // correspond to actual vertices in the map
    for (int i = 0; i < vInfo.size(); i++)
    {
        // get the VertexInfo object for index i
        edgeVtxInfo = vInfo.get(i);
        // check if vertex is valid
        if (edgeVtxInfo.occupied)
        {
            // obtain an iterator to scan the adjacency list
            iter = edgeVtxInfo.edgeList.iterator();

            while (iter.hasNext())
            {
                // get the Edge object and check if the dest field
                // has value index which identifies vertex v;
                // if so, remove it and decrement numEdges
                e = iter.next();
                if (e.dest == index)
                {
```

```
            iter.remove();
            numEdges--;
            break;
         }
      }
   }
}
```

Task 3:   Delete all edges that emanate from v. These edges constitute the adjacency list for
the vertex. First, determine the number of edges and decrement numEdges. Then,
search the list of Edge objects and decrement the in-degree for each adjacent vertex. Delete each edge during the scan.

```
// reduce numEdges by number of elements in adjacency list
numEdges -= vtxInfo.edgeList.size();

// scan the adjacency list for vertex v and decrement
// the in-degree for each adjacent vertex
iter = vtxInfo.edgeList.iterator();
while (iter.hasNext())
{
   e = iter.next();
   edgeVtxInfo = vInfo.get(e.dest);
   iter.remove();
   edgeVtxInfo.inDegree--;
}
```

Efficiency of the addEdge() and removeVertex() Methods   The addEdge() method
involves adding an element to the adjacency list for the source vertex. The first action is to obtain the vInfo index for the starting and ending vertex. Because the DiGraph class stores the
vertices in a HashMap, each of these operations has average case running time O(1). The
LinkedList add() operation has constant running time; however, an initial scan of the
source vertex adjacency list with running time O(E) must check whether the edge is already in
the graph. If we put these estimates together, the running time for addEdge() is O(E).

The Big-O analysis for the removeVertex() method is more complicated because
the operation involves a number of tasks. The average case running time for deleting the
vertex from the map is O(1). The rest of the algorithm involves updating information in
the adjacency lists for the V entries of vInfo. To update the in-degree of each adjacent
vertex, the elements in the list must be searched. This is an O(E) operation. The most
process-intensive task is removing all edges that terminate in the vertex and updating the
edge count for the graph. This involves searching all of the entries in vInfo and then
searching the adjacency list for each entry. There are V entries in vInfo and the total
number of edges is E, so the task has efficiency O(V + E). By combining the efficiencies of each task, we see that the total efficiency is O(V + E).

*Running time of
graph methods is
generally a
function of the
number of edges
E and vertices V.*

Graph Algorithm Support Methods

The DiGraph class includes access and update methods for the color, data, and parent
reference properties of a vertex. The properties are found in the VertexInfo object corresponding to the vertex. The implementations are relatively simple. Identify the object
and access the appropriate field. Let us look at a few examples.

The method `getColor()` returns the current color of a vertex.

getColor():

```
// returns the color of vertex v; if v is not a graph vertex,
// throws IllegalArgumentException; for use by graph
// algorithms
public VertexColor getColor(T v)
{
    // find the vInfo index for v
    int pos = getVInfoIndex(v);

    if (pos != -1)
        return vInfo.get(pos).color;
    else
        // throw an exception
        throw new IllegalArgumentException(
            "DiGraph getColor(): vertex not in graph");
}
```

The method `setParent()` updates the parent reference for the vertex. Include in the argument list the vertex object v and the vertex object p, which is assigned to the parent field of the `ArrayList` elements associated with v.

setParent():

```
// assigns the parent of vertex v to be p and returns the
// previous parent; if v or p is not a graph vertex, throws
// IllegalArgumentException; for use by graph algorithms
public T setParent(T v, T p)
{
    // find the vInfo index for v
    int pos1 = getVInfoIndex(v), pos2 = getVInfoIndex(p);
    VertexInfo<T> vtxInfo;
    T oldParent = null;

    if (pos1 != -1 && pos2 != -1)
    {
        vtxInfo = vInfo.get(pos1);
        oldParent = vtxInfo.parent;
        vtxInfo.parent = p;
    }
    else
        // throw an exception
        throw new IllegalArgumentException(
            "DiGraph setParent(): vertex not in graph");

    return oldParent;
}
```

The method `colorWhite()` cycles through `vInfo` and changes the color of each vertex to `WHITE`. As with any scan of the `ArrayList`, check the `occupied` field to ensure that the element corresponds to a vertex in the graph.

colorWhite():

```
// sets the color of each vertex to VertexColor.WHITE;
// for use by graph algorithms
public void colorWhite()
{
    VertexInfo<T> vtxInfo;

    for (int i = 0; i < vInfo.size(); i++)
    {
        vtxInfo = vInfo.get(i);

        if (vtxInfo.occupied)
                vtxInfo.color = VertexColor.WHITE;
    }
}
```

Graph Collection View

The method `vertexSet()` returns a set view of the graph vertices. The implementation of `vertexSet()` is similar to the implementation for a set view of map keys or entries (see Sections 19.4 and 20.3). We list the implementation for the `remove()` method of the set view.

Set view remove():

```
public boolean remove(Object item)
{
    boolean retValue = false;

    if (vtxMap.containsKey(item))
    {
        removeVertex(item);
        retValue = true;
    }

    return retValue;
}
```

The implementation of the graph set view iterator uses an inner class `IteratorImpl` similar to iterator implementations we have discussed for the `LinkedList` and other collections. The class includes a variable that is an iterator for the `keySet` collection view associated with the vertex map.

DiGraph inner class IteratorImpl:

```
// implements graph iterators
private class IteratorImpl implements Iterator<T>
{
    Iterator<T> iter;
    T lastValue = null;
```

```
                public IteratorImpl()
                {
                    // iter traverses the map vertices
                    iter = vtxMap.keySet().iterator();
                }

                public boolean hasNext()
                {
                    return iter.hasNext();
                }

                public T next()
                {
                    lastValue = iter.next();
                    return lastValue;
                }

                public void remove()
                {
                    if (lastValue == null)
                        throw new IllegalStateException(
                                "Graph vertex set iterator call to next() " +
                                "required before calling remove()");

                    // find the index of lastValue in vInfo
                    int index = getVInfoIndex(lastValue);

                    // remove the current vertex from the map
                    iter.remove();

                    // remove all edges that terminate at lastValue, and
                    // update the in-degree of each neighbor of lastValue
                    removeFixup(index);
                }
            }
```

Chapter Summary

- The two primary approaches for representing a graph are the use of adjacency lists or an adjacency matrix.
- The primary components of the DiGraph class are the vertex map and the ArrayList, vInfo, of vertex properties. These properties include the list of adjacent vertices (edges).
- This chapter discusses the overall design of the DiGraph class and the implementation of selected methods.

Written Exercises

1. (a) Give the adjacency list and adjacency matrix representation for graph A in Figure 26.5.
    (b) Give the adjacency list and adjacency matrix representation for graph B in Figure 26.5.

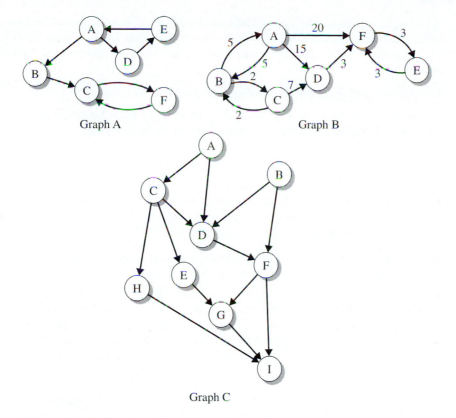

Graph A   Graph B

Graph C

Figure 26.5 *Graphs for use in exercises.*

2. (a) Draw the graph that corresponds to the adjacency list representation.

A: Edges: B (2)   C (3)
B: Edges: A (8)   D (3)
C: Edges: A (2)   B (7)
D: Edges   C (5)   B (8)
E: Edges: A (2)   C (1)

(b) Draw the graph that corresponds to the adjacency matrix representation.

$$
\begin{array}{c c c c c c}
 & A & B & C & D & E \\
A & 0 & 1 & 5 & 2 & 0 \\
B & 1 & 0 & 0 & 3 & 2 \\
C & 1 & 0 & 0 & 2 & 6 \\
D & 1 & 2 & 5 & 0 & 0 \\
E & 0 & 0 & 9 & 1 & 0 \\
\end{array}
$$

3. Assume that a graph uses an adjacency matrix to represent the edges. Describe how
   you would update the matrix for the following algorithms.

   (a) Insert an edge.   (c) Delete an edge.
   (b) Insert a new vertex.   (d) Delete a vertex.

4. A binary tree can be viewed as an undirected, connected, acyclic graph. Give an adjacency-list representation for a complete binary tree with seven vertices. Also give the adjacency matrix representation. Assume the vertices have values from 'A' through 'G'.

Use the following definition for Written Exercises 26.5 and 26.6.

The *transpose* A^T of an $n \times n$ matrix A is obtained by interchanging the rows and columns of A. Equivalently, the elements a_{ij}^T satisfy the relationship

$$a_{ij}^T = a_{ji}, \quad 0 \le i, j \le n - 1$$

5. The transpose of a digraph g is the digraph g^T whose edges are those of g reversed. If the digraph g uses the adjacency matrix representation with matrix A, show that the adjacency matrix of g^T is A^T.

6. (a) A matrix is *symmetric* if $A = A^T$. Assume that an undirected graph has an adjacency matrix representation. Show that the adjacency matrix A is symmetric.

(b) An *upper-triangular matrix* is an $n \times n$ matrix all of whose elements below the main diagonal are 0. Propose an algorithm that uses a one-dimensional array to store only the elements on and above the main diagonal of an upper-triangular matrix. How can you use this algorithm for minimizing the storage used for the adjacency matrix of an undirected graph? The full adjacency matrix has n^2 entries. How many elements must we store using the algorithm?

7. Assume that a digraph uses the adjacency matrix representation. Using just the matrix, describe algorithms for finding the in-and out-degree of a vertex.

8. (a) If A is the adjacency matrix for an undirected graph g, the number of different paths of length $k > 0$ from vertex v_i to vertex v_j is the element in row i, column j of the matrix A^k; that is, the number of paths is

$A^k[i]\,[j]$

Apply this algorithm to the following digraph and compute the number of paths of length 2 and 3 between any two vertices.

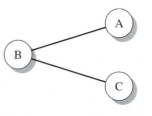

Verify that your results are correct by enumerating the paths by hand. For instance, a path of length 3 from A to B is $P(A, B) = $ A-B-C-B.

(b) Use mathematical induction to prove that the algorithm is correct.

Programming Exercises

Programming Exercises 26.9 through 26.13 ask you to add a new method to the DiGraph class. You will find a copy of the DiGraph class in the directory ch26ex.

9. Add the method totalWeight() to the DiGraph class. Apply the method to Graph B of Figure 26.5 and output the sum of its weights.

   ```
   // return the sum of the weights of the graph edges
   public int totalWeight()
   { ... }
   ```

10. Add the method maxInDegree() to the DiGraph class. Apply the method to Graph B of Figure 26.5 and output the vertex with maximum in-degree and the value of its in-degree.

    ```
    // return the vertex with maximum in-degree
    public T maxInDegree()
    { ... }
    ```

11. In a digraph, a *source* is a vertex that has an in-degree of 0. Add the method findSources() to the DiGraph class. Apply the method to Graph C of Figure 26.5 and output all its sources and the out-degree of each source.

    ```
    // return a list containing all the sources in the graph
    public LinkedList<T> findSources()
    { ... }
    ```

12. A *sink* in a directed graph is a vertex with out-degree 0. Add the method findSinks() to the DiGraph class. Apply the method to Graph C of Figure 26.5 and output all its sinks and the in-degree of each sink.

    ```
    // return a list containing all the sinks in the graph
    public LinkedList<T> findSinks()
    { ... }
    ```

13. (a) For some applications, it is necessary to build a new graph that is a duplicate of an existing graph. The new graph has the same set of vertices and edges as the existing graph. It also has its own ArrayList vInfo with VertexInfo objects that have the same color, dataValue, and parent fields as their counterparts in the vInfo ArrayList for the existing graph. You are to implement a DiGraph class method buildGraph() that copies an existing graph.

    ```
    // builds a new graph which is a copy of g
    public static <T> DiGraph<T> buildGraph(DiGraph<T> g)
    { ... }
    ```

    Assume that g and newG are references to the existing graph and the new graph respectively. The algorithm begins by assigning newG an empty DiGraph object and then carries out a sequence of tasks that build the vertex map and the

ArrayList vInfo for newG. The tasks use the set of vertices in g and the methods addVertex() and addEdge(). Access to the vertices is provided by an iterator that scans the elements returned by the method vertexSet().

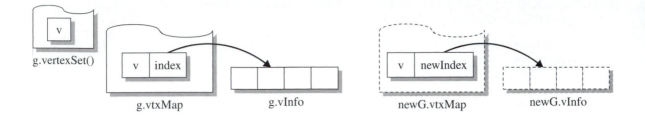

g.vertexSet()   g.vtxMap   g.vInfo   newG.vtxMap   newG.vInfo

Task 1:   For each vertex in g, use addVertex() to insert an equivalent vertex in newG.

Task 2:   Use addEdge() to insert edges into the new graph.

Task 3:   As a by-product of the first two tasks, each element in the vInfo ArrayList for the new graph properly defines its vertex, edgeList, and inDegree fields. The last task scans the vertex set of g and ensures that the vertices of newG have the same color, dataValue, and parent fields as g.

(b) In a program, create a copy of Graph B of Figure 26.5. Using the copy, find all the strong components of the graph and erase all vertices in a strong component with less than three vertices. Output the original and the modified graphs.

14. (a) Modify the DiGraph class to create the class UGraph that represents an undirected, weighted graph. You will only need to modify a few methods. For instance, when inserting an edge from vertex v to vertex w, you will need to add the edge e(w,v) to the adjacency list of vertex w. In an undirected graph, there is no separate in-degree and out-degree. Each vertex has a degree, which is the number of edges originating at v.

(b) Modify the class DiGraphs to create the class UGraphs, which implements the methods bfs(), dfsVisit(), dfs(), and acyclic().

(c) Test the classes by reading a graph, displaying it using toString(), inserting and removing a series of vertices and edges, and finally doing a depth-first search of the whole graph and a breadth-first search from a vertex.

Programming Project

15. Modify the DiGraph class to use an adjacency matrix rather than an adjacency list to store the neighbors of a vertex. Name the class AdjDiGraph. Modify the class DiGraphs so it uses the new class. Name the class AdjDiGraphs.

Assume that the graph will contain no more than MAXGRAPHSIZE vertices. Use the map structure to store the vertices and their index into the vInfo ArrayList. The VertexInfo object corresponding to a vertex does not store the adjacency set. Rather, the adjacency matrix is a variable in the AdjDiGraph class. The index from the map serves as a row or column index into the adjacency matrix as well as the index of the vertex in vInfo. When deleting a vertex, assign weight 0 to the entries in the corresponding row and column of the adjacency matrix, and use an availability stack to indicate that the index is available for reuse. A call to addVertex() when the graph has MAXGRAPHSIZE vertices should throw IndexOutOfBoundsException.

Test the class by writing a program that inputs the graph in Figure 26.6a and outputs the result of a breadth-first search from vertex A. Delete vertex C and edge (B, E). Output the graph. Next, add vertex F and edges (F, A) with weight 3, (E, F) with weight 2, and (B, F) with weight 5. Output the final graph (Figure 26.6b).

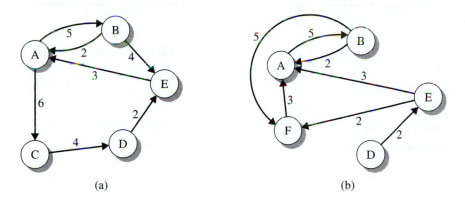

(a)   (b)

Figure 26.6 *Graphs for Programming Project 26.15.*

Chapter 27

BALANCED SEARCH TREES

CONTENTS

27.1 AVL TREES
The AVLTree Class

27.2 IMPLEMENTING THE AVLTREE CLASS
The AVLTree add() Method
The Private addNode() Method
The add() Method

27.3 2-3-4 TREES
Searching a 2-3-4 Tree
Inserting into a 2-3-4 Tree

27.4 RED-BLACK TREES
Representing 2-3-4 Tree Nodes

The Red-Black Tree Representation of a 2-3-4 Tree
Inserting a Node in a Red-Black Tree
Splitting a 4-node
Insertion at the Bottom of the Tree
Building a Red-Black Tree
Search Running Time
Erasing a Node in a Red-Black Tree

27.5 THE RBTREE CLASS

Binary search trees are designed for efficient access to data. They are built to be search engines that locate an element along a path from the root. In an application, the actual efficiency depends on the shape of the tree. The order in which data enters the tree may cause a subtree to be heavily weighted to one side or the other. In the worst case, the tree is "degenerate" or "almost degenerate," where most of the n elements are stored as a lone child of a parent. The shape resembles a linked list (Figure 27.1a) and has search efficiency $O(n)$. The other extreme is a complete binary tree that stores the n elements in a tree of minimum height by uniformly distributing the nodes in the left and right subtrees. Access to any element requires no more than $\text{int}(\log_2 n) + 1$ comparisons and the search efficiency is $O(\log_2 n)$. A complete tree represents an ideal shape for a search tree.

The STree class described in Chapter 18 uses search tree ordering to insert an element. The add() method follows a rigid set of rules that locates an element as a leaf node without regard for the overall shape of the tree. We need search trees that have an associated insert algorithm that rearranges elements whenever a subtree gets out of balance. The goal is to have a search tree with a measure of balance among the subtrees, similar to a complete tree. Over the years, researchers have developed such search trees. In this chapter, we will discuss *AVL search trees* and *red-black search trees*. AVL trees were discovered in 1962 by two Russian scientists, G. M. Adelson-Velsky and E. M. Landis, after whom the trees are named. The recursive add-and-remove algorithms maintain height-balance at each node. By this we mean that for each node, the difference in height of its two subtrees is in the range -1 to 1. Figure 27.1b is an AVL tree. For node 70, the height of its left subtree is 2 and the height of its right subtree is 3. The difference $\text{height}_L - \text{height}_R = -1$, and the tree is slightly tilted to the right. In contrast to a simple binary search tree, an AVL tree can never become heavily weighted to one side or the other. A red-black search tree provides a different kind of a structure and balance criteria. The design of a red-black tree has its origins in a balanced search tree called a *2-3-4 tree*. The description comes from the fact that each node has 2, 3, or 4 links (children). A 2-3-4 tree is perfectly balanced in the sense that no interior node has a null child and all leaf nodes are at the same level in the tree (Figure 27.1c). A red-black tree provides a representation of 2-3-4 trees. The tree features nodes that have the color attribute BLACK or RED. The tree maintains a measure of balance called the *BLACK-height*. Figure 27.1d is a representation of the 2-3-4 tree with RED nodes displayed with shading. It is BLACK-height balanced because the path from the root to any empty subtree contains two black nodes. This concept will become clear when we introduce red-black trees in Section 27.4. Modern data structures use red-black trees to implement ordered sets and maps such as the TreeSet and TreeMap collection classes. The class RBTree implements the red-black tree algorithms, including deletion. We present implementation details in Section 27.5, which is in the Web supplement.

A binary search tree is designed for efficient access to an element.

Red-black or AVL trees balance a binary search tree so that it more nearly resembles a complete tree.

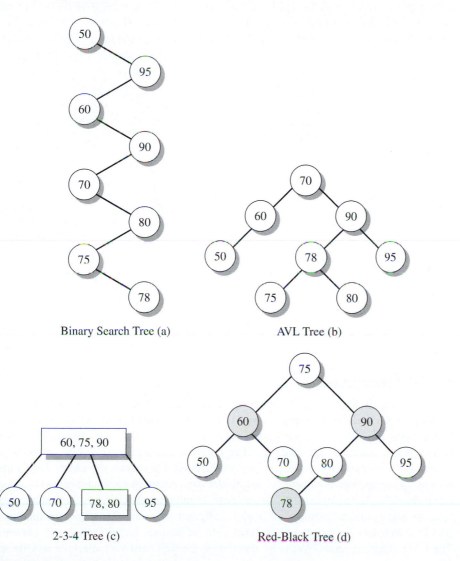

Binary Search Tree (a)

AVL Tree (b)

2-3-4 Tree (c)

Red-Black Tree (d)

Figure 27.1 *Different search tree structures for the list* {50, 95, 60, 90, 70, 80, 75, 78}.

27.1 AVL Trees

For each AVL tree node, the difference between the heights of its left and right subtrees is either −1, 0, or +1.

AVL trees are modeled after binary search trees but with new algorithms to insert and delete an element. These operations must preserve the balance feature of the tree. Associated with each AVL tree node is its `balanceFactor`, which is the difference between the heights of its left and right subtrees.

$$\text{balanceFactor} = \text{height(left subtree)} - \text{height(right subtree)}$$

An AVL tree is *height-balanced* when the `balanceFactor` for each node is in the range −1 to 1. If `balanceFactor` is positive, the node is "heavy on the left" since the height of the left subtree is greater than the height of the right subtree. With a negative `balanceFactor`, the node is "heavy on the right." A balanced node has `balanceFactor` = 0. Figure 27.2 describes three AVL trees with tags −1, 0, or 1 on each node to indicate its `balanceFactor`.

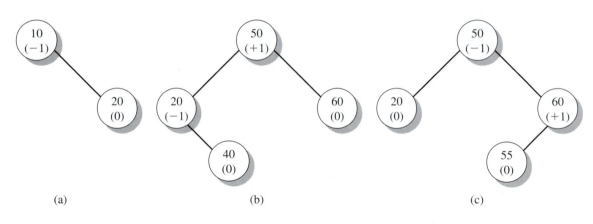

Figure 27.2 *AVL trees with height-balance factor.*

The AVLTree Class

The AVLTree class implements the Collection interface and builds an AVL tree. It has the same public methods as the STree class.

The AVLTree class has the same public methods as the STree class. Removing a node from an AVL tree is a difficult operation and is not implemented in the class. The `remove()` method performs no action and simply returns false. The AVLTree class implements the Collection interface and adds familiar methods that make it a good implementation structure. The constructor creates an empty collection. For output, the `toString()` method returns a comma-separated ordered list of elements enclosed in square brackets. Modified versions of the `displayTree()`, `drawTree()`, and `drawMultiTree()` methods provide console and graphical displays of a tree. Different from the `BinaryTree` methods, the AVLTree versions display the node label with its balance factor included in parentheses. The UML diagram details AVLTree methods in the Collection interface and the special class methods.

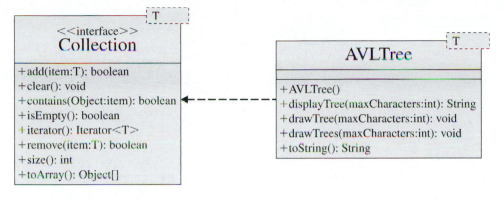

Example 27.1

This example illustrates AVLTree specific operations.

1. Declare AVLTree objects avltreeA and avlTreeB, which are initially empty collections. A loop inserts String objects into avlTreeA from the array stateList that contains two-letter abbreviations for U.S. states. A second loop inserts objects into avlTreeB from the integer array intArr.

```
String[] stateList = {"NV", "NY", "MA", "CA", "GA"};
int[] arr = {50, 95, 60, 90, 70, 80, 75, 78};
int i;

// avlTreeA and avlTreeB are empty collections
AVLTree<String> avltreeA = new AVLTree<String>();
AVLTree<Integer> avltreeB = new AVLTree<Integer>();

for (i = 0; i < stateList.length; i++)
    avltreeB.add(stateList[i]);
for (i = 0; i < arr.length; i++)
    avltreeB.add(arr[i]);
```

2. The method toString() returns a comma-separated ordered list of elements in avlTreeA. Methods displayTree() and drawTree() provide a tree display for elements in avlTreeB.

```
// output list of elements
System.out.println("States: " + avltreeA);

// display the tree
System.out.println(avltreeB.displayTree(2));
avltreeB.drawTree(2);
```

```
Run:
   States: [CA, GA, MA, NV, NY]
               70(-1)
         60(1)                      90(1)
     50(0)              78(0)                    95(0)
                75(0)           80(0)
```

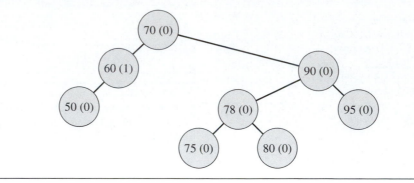

27.2 Implementing the AVLTree Class

The building blocks of an AVL tree are AVLNode objects. Like an STNode for the STree class, an AVLTreeNode includes a nodeValue field and references left and right that reference the two children. The node also contains a height field that defines the height of the node as the root of a subtree.

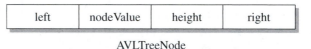

AVLTreeNode

The height of the node is defined in terms of the heights for the left and right subtrees.

        height(node) = max (height(node.left), height(node.right)) + 1;

An AVLNode contains the node value, references to the node's children, and the height of the subtree.

The following is a declaration of the AVLTreeNode class. It is defined as a private inner class within the AVLTree class. Because a node object is used only as an implementation structure, we define the instance variables to be public. This allows us to reference the fields directly when accessing and updating their values. The constructor takes an argument that initializes the nodeValue field. The height field is set to 0 and the subtree references are set to null. We also declare AVLNode to be a static class. This means that AVLNode has no access to instance variables of AVLTree; in other words, it is not associated with any objects of AVLTree. It is nested in AVLTree purely as a packaging scheme.

AVLNode class:

```
// declares a binary search tree node object
private static class AVLNode<T>
{
    // node data
    public T nodeValue;
```

```
    // child links and link to the node's parent
    public AVLNode<T> left, right;

    // public int height;
    public int height;

    // constructor that initializes the value, balance factor,
    // and parent fields and sets the link fields left and
    // right to null
    public AVLNode (T item)
    {
        nodeValue = item;
        left = null;
        right = null;
        height = 0;
    }
}
```

The AVLTree add() Method

The implementation of `add()` uses the private recursive method `addNode()` to insert a new element. The algorithm provides for the reordering of elements when a node falls out of balance; that is, when the balance factor of a node is −2 or +2. As we will discover, the algorithm introduces single and double rotations that restore height-balance at a node.

The `addNode()` algorithm traverses down a path of nodes from the root using the usual search tree criteria. It proceeds to the left subtree if the new element is less than the value of the current node and to the right subtree if the new element is greater than the value of the current node. The scan terminates at an empty subtree, which becomes the new location for the element in the tree.

The recursive addNode() algorithm moves to the insertion point, using the usual rules for a binary search tree.

Adding an element to the tree may change the balance factor associated with one or more nodes in the search path. As a result, the tree may fall out of balance and require reordering of nodes to reestablish the height-balance criteria. Because the insertion process is recursive, we have access to the nodes in the search path in reverse order. This allows the method to visit each successive parent back to the root and check its balance factor. In some cases, the factor is changed but remains within the valid range −1 to 1. In other cases, the parent has a balance factor of −2 or 2, indicating that the subtree is out of balance. The algorithm then employs rebalancing operations.

The addition of an element may cause the tree to be out of balance. The recursive addNode() algorithm reorders nodes as it returns from function calls.

Let us look at examples in which an insertion maintains the height-balance of the AVL tree. Figure 27.3 displays the effect of inserting element 55 and then 65 into an AVL tree that initially contains six elements. For the element 55, the search path includes the nodes 40-50-60, which have balance factor 0. After the insertion, the balance factor for each node on the path changes but still remains in range. The same search path is used for element 65 and only the balance factor for 60 is changed.

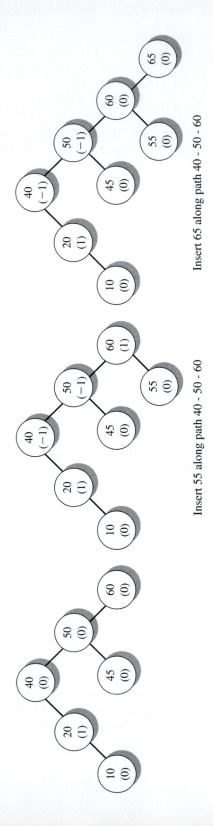

Insert 65 along path 40 - 50 - 60

Insert 55 along path 40 - 50 - 60

Figure 27.3 *Inserting 55 and 65 maintains AVL height-balance.*

Imbalanced Subtrees The insertion of a new element in an AVL tree may cause a parent node to become imbalanced when the element is added as a leaf node in a subtree of one of the parent's children. Let us look at the different situations. A parent node has balance factor 2 when a new element X is inserted as a leaf node in a subtree of the parent's left child. The new element is in the left (outside) grandchild subtree when its value is less than the value of the left child (LC) (Figure 27.4a). The new element is in the right (inside) grandchild subtree when its value is greater than the value of the left child (Figure 27.4b).

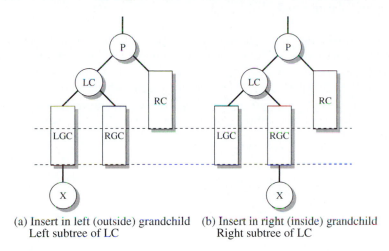

Inserting a node on the left subtree of P may cause P to be "heavy on the left" (balance factor +2). The new node is either in the outside or inside grandchild subtree.

(a) Insert in left (outside) grandchild   (b) Insert in right (inside) grandchild
    Left subtree of LC   Right subtree of LC

Figure 27.4 *Inserting X imbalances the parent node P with balance factor 2.*

A parent node has balance factor −2 when a new element X is inserted as a leaf node in a subtree of the parent's right child. The new element is in the right (outside) grandchild subtree when its value is greater than the value of the right child (RC) (Figure 27.5a). The new element is the left (inside) grandchild subtree when its value is less than the value of the right child (Figure 27.5b).

Inserting a node on the right subtree of P may cause P to be "heavy on the right" (balance factor −2). The new node is either in the outside or inside grandchild subtree.

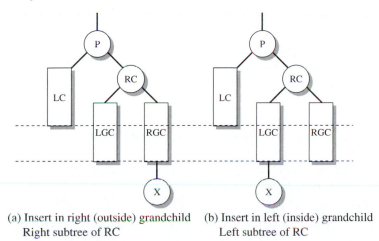

(a) Insert in right (outside) grandchild   (b) Insert in left (inside) grandchild
    Right subtree of RC   Left subtree of RC

Figure 27.5 *Inserting X imbalances the parent node P with balance factor −2.*

When correcting an imbalance for a parent node, addNode() uses either a single or a double rotation.

When a parent node becomes imbalanced, the addNode() method uses a single or a double rotation to reorder the subtree and reestablish AVL height-balance in the parent node. Single rotations occur when the new element is inserted in an outside grandchild subtree and double rotations occur when the element is inserted in an inside grandchild subtree. We will look at single rotations first and then discuss double rotations. As you will discover, an AVL tree uses right rotations to handle imbalances that occur in the left subtree of the parent node and symmetric left rotations if the imbalance occurs in the right subtree of the parent node.

Single Rotations   When the new element enters the subtree of an outside grandchild, a single rotation exchanges the parent and child node. The figure illustrates the case where element X enters the subtree of the left grandchild of P. A *single right rotation* rotates the nodes so that the left child (LC) replaces the parent, which becomes a right child. In the process, the nodes in the right subtree of LC (RGC) are attached as a left child of P. This maintains the search tree ordering since nodes in the right subtree are greater than LC but less than P.

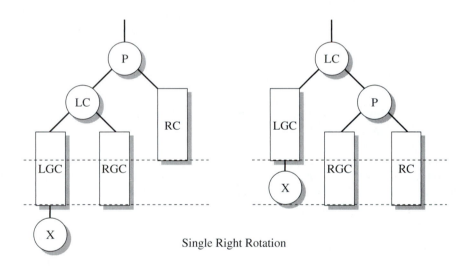

Single Right Rotation

The rotation methods need to determine the height of left and right subtrees of a node. The private method height() returns the height of a nonempty subtree and −1 if the subtree is empty (null).

height():

```
private static <T> int height(AVLNode<T> t)
{
    if (t == null)
        return -1;
    else
        return t.height;
}
```

The private method singleRotationRight() reorders the nodes and updates the height field for both the parent and child. The new subtree with the left child LC as the root is the return value.

singleRotateRight():

When a new item enters the subtree of an outside grandchild, a single rotation exchanges the parent and the child node. A left or right rotation is done.

```
// perform a single right rotation for parent p
private static <T> AVLNode<T> singleRotateRight(AVLNode<T> p)
{
    AVLNode<T> lc = p.left;

    p.left = lc.right;
    lc.right = p;
    p.height = max( height( p.left ), height( p.right ) ) + 1;
    lc.height = max( height( lc.left ), lc.height ) + 1;

    return lc;
}
```

A symmetric single left rotation occurs when the new element enters the subtree of the right outside grandchild. The rotation exchanges the parent and right child nodes, and attaches the subtree LGC as a right subtree of the parent node.

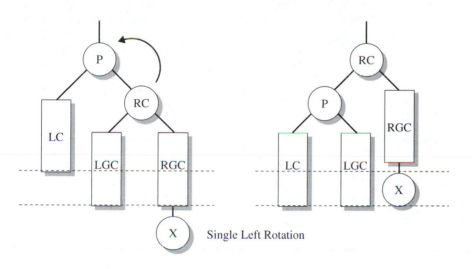

Single Left Rotation

The private method `singleRotateLeft()` updates the `height` field for both the parent and its right child. The child is the root of the reordered subtree and is the return value.

singleRotateLeft():

```
// perform a single left rotation for parent p
private static <T> AVLNode<T> singleRotateLeft(AVLNode<T> p)
{
    AVLNode<T> rc = p.right;

    p.right = rc.left;
    rc.left = p;
    p.height = max(height(p.left), height(p.right)) + 1;
    rc.height = max(height(rc.right), rc.height) + 1;

    return rc;
}
```

When a new item enters the subtree for an inside grandchild, the imbalance is fixed with a double rotation, which consists of two single rotations.

Double Rotations A different rebalancing algorithm occurs when the new element is added to the subtree of an inside grandchild. Let us look at the case where the balance factor of the parent is 2 and thus the imbalance occurs in the left subtree (Figure 27.6). The new element X is less than the value of the parent and greater than the value of the left child. To rebalance the parent subtree, use a double right rotation, which is a series of two single rotations. Start with a single left rotation about the left child (LC) and follow that with a single right rotation about the parent (P). The two single rotations update the height field for the affected nodes.

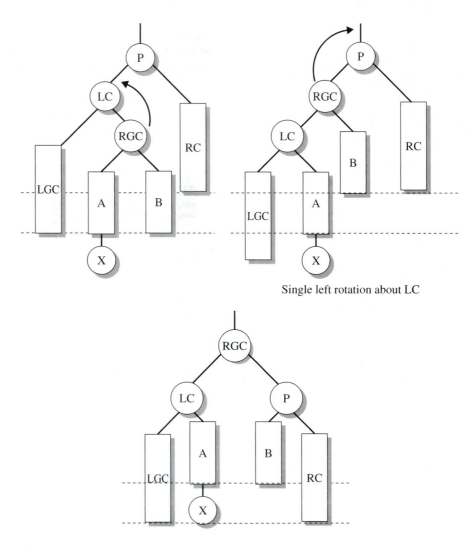

Single left rotation about LC

Single right rotation about P

Figure 27.6 *Double right rotation implemented by two single rotations.*

The private method `doubleRotateRight()` calls the single rotate methods. The right child of LC is the return value.

doubleRotateRight():

```
// perform a double right rotation for parent p
private static <T> AVLNode<T> doubleRotateRight(AVLNode<T> p)
{
    p.left = singleRotateLeft(p.left);
    return singleRotateRight(p);
}
```

A symmetric double left rotation rebalances a parent node which has balance factor -2 after a new element is added to the subtree of an inside grandchild. The double rotation involves a single rotation about the right child followed by a single left rotation about the parent node.

doubleRotateLeft():

```
// perform a single left rotation for parent p
private static <T> AVLNode<T> doubleRotateLeft(AVLNode<T> p)
{
    p.right = singleRotateRight(p.right);
    return singleRotateLeft(p);
}
```

The Private addNode() Method

The private `addNode()` method is a recursive form of the familiar binary search tree insert algorithm. It takes an argument of type T named `item` and descends down a path from the root, moving to a left or right child by comparing `item` with the value of the current node. When the scan lands on an empty tree, it inserts a new node with `item` as the value. The recursive descent down a path ensures that upon return each node is revisited in the reverse order. During a revisit to a node, the balance factor is checked to determine whether rebalancing should occur. In each case, the height of the node is recomputed.

If the recursive descent was from a parent to a left child, then during backtracking, the parent is out of balance if its balance factor is 2. The choice of a single rotation or a double rotation depends on which subtree of the left child holds the new element. If the element is in the left subtree, it is an outside grandchild of the parent and a single rotation rebalances the parent; otherwise, a double rotation is required.

```
// recursive descent to the left child
t.left = addNode(t.left, item);

// when backtracking to the parent, check for balance
if( height(t.left) - height(t.right) == 2 )
    // if out of balance, determine whether item is in the left
    // or the right subtree of the left child
    if( ((Comparable<T>)item).compareTo(t.left.nodeValue) < 0 )
        t = singleRotateRight(t);
    else
        t = doubleRotateRight(t);
```

Recursive `addNode()` descends to the insertion point and inserts the node. As it returns, it visits the nodes in reverse order, fixing any imbalances using rotations.

The implementation of addNode() uses symmetric code if the original descent is into the right subtree and the parent has a balance factor −2 when backtracking.

addNode():

```
private AVLNode<T> addNode(AVLNode<T> t, T item)
{
    if( t == null )
      t = new AVLNode<T>(item);
    else if (((Comparable<T>)item).compareTo(t.nodeValue) < 0)
    {
      t.left = addNode( t.left, item);

      if (height(t.left) - height(t.right) == 2 )
        if (((Comparable<T>)item).compareTo
                (t.left.nodeValue) < 0)
          t = singleRotateRight(t);
        else
          t = doubleRotateRight(t);

    }
    else if (((Comparable<T>)item).compareTo
                    (t.nodeValue) > 0 )
    {
      t.right = addNode(t.right, item );

      if (height(t.left) - height(t.right) == -2)
        if (((Comparable<T>)item).compareTo
                  (t.right.nodeValue) > 0)
          t = singleRotateLeft(t);
        else
          t = doubleRotateLeft(t);
    }
    else
      // duplicate; throw IllegalStateException
      throw new IllegalStateException();

    t.height = max( height(t.left), height(t.right) ) + 1;

    return t;
}
```

The add() Method

Method add() assures that item is not in the tree, calls addNode() to insert it, and then increments treeSize and modCount.

The details of inserting a new element in a tree are handled primarily by the addNode() method. Overseeing the operation is the responsibility of the add() method. Note that addNode() throws an exception if a duplicate element is already in the tree. This allows an immediate exit from the recursive process. The method add() simply catches the exception and returns the value false to indicate that no new element is added to the tree. Otherwise, addNode() does the insertion and returns the root, which may have changed owing to rebalancing. The method concludes by incrementing the tree size and the variable modCount and then returns true.

add():

```
// it item is not in the tree, insert it and return true
// if item is a duplicate, do not insert it and return false
public boolean add(T item)
{
    try
    {
        root = addNode(root, item);
    }
    catch (IllegalStateException ise)
    { return false; }

    // increment the tree size and modCount
    treeSize++;
    modCount++;

    // we added a node to the tree
    return true;
}
```

Example 27.2

This example illustrates each of the four AVL tree rotations. We build a tree with elements from the integer array {24, 12, 5, 30, 20, 45, 11, 13, 9, 16}. Rotations occur when inserting elements 5, 45, 9, and 16. The figure displays the tree after adding each of these key elements. You first see the tree after the familiar binary search tree insert algorithm appends the element as a leaf node. The imbalanced parent node is shaded. The next view is the tree after a rotation has reestablished height-balance for the parent.

Part 1: Insert the first three elements 24, 12, and 5. At 5, node 24 has balance factor 2. Viewing 24 as a parent, the new element 5 enters as an outside grandchild in the left subtree 12. The parent is rebalanced with a single right rotation.

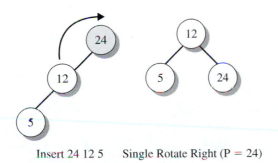

Insert 24 12 5   Single Rotate Right (P = 24)

Part 2: Insert the next three elements 30, 20, and 45. At 45, node 12 has balance factor −2. Since 45 entered as an outside grandchild in the right subtree 24, rebalance the parent with a single left rotation.

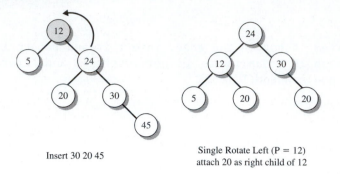

Insert 30 20 45

Single Rotate Left (P = 12)
attach 20 as right child of 12

Part 3: Insert the three elements 11, 13, and 9. At 9, node 5 has balance factor −2. The new element 9 enters as an inside grandchild relative to the right child 11. The parent, 5, is rebalanced with a double left rotation that involves a single right rotation about 11 followed by a single left rotation about 5.

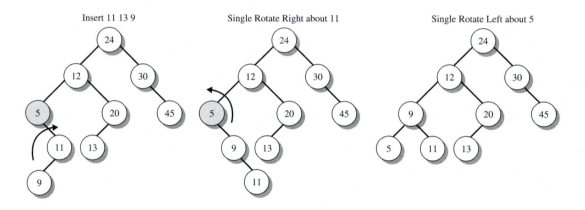

Insert 11 13 9

Single Rotate Right about 11

Single Rotate Left about 5

Part 4: Insert the last element 16. Node 20 has balance factor +2. The new element enters as an inside grandchild relative to the left child 13. Node 20 is rebalanced with a double right rotation that involves a single left rotation about 13 followed by a single right rotation about 20.

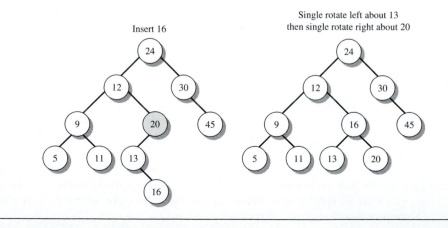

Insert 16

Single rotate left about 13
then single rotate right about 20

Efficiency of AVL Tree Insertion A mathematical analysis shows that the height of an AVL tree is bounded both above and below by logarithmic functions. In particular,

$$\text{int}(\log_2 n) \leq \text{height} < 1.4405 \log_2(n + 2) - 1.3277$$

The strange-looking numbers are rounded values related to Fibonacci numbers and the golden ratio (see Section 6.3). The inequalities imply that the worst-case number of comparisons for searching and insertion are $O(\log_2 n)$. The average case is not known, but extensive experiments indicate that it is approximately $1.01 \log_2 n + 0.1$ except when n is small. This indicates that the number of comparisons on average is about the same as those required by the binary search of an ordered list. The deletion algorithm is difficult and we will not present it in the book. However, its worst-case running time is also $O(\log_2 n)$. The interested reader should consult Wirth and Niklaus, *Algorithms + Data Structures = Programs* (Prentice-Hall, 1976) for a thorough discussion of this algorithm.

27.3 2-3-4 Trees

An AVL binary search tree uses height-balance to ensure that nodes are uniformly distributed in the left and right subtrees of a node. As a result, the tree always has efficient $O(\log_2 n)$. search operations. This is a distinct advantage over simple binary search trees that exhibit worst-case $O(n)$ running time for the operations. The algorithms to insert and delete an element in an AVL tree have a disadvantage, however. They are recursive and use the bottom-up revisiting of nodes to identify when rebalancing should occur. What we would like is a new structure that maintains a measure of balance while employing iterative `add()` and `remove()` algorithms. To this end, we develop a new type of binary search tree, called a *red-black tree*. The color RED or BLACK is associated with each node and any path from the root to an empty subtree has the same number of black nodes. The count of black nodes on a path provides an effective measure of balance that makes the trees efficient to create, access, and modify.

We develop red-black trees in a two-stage process. We begin by extending the node structure for a binary search tree to a more general tree whose nodes can have more than one data value and more than two children. In particular, we design a *2-3-4 search tree*, consisting of a collection of nodes that have 2, 3, or 4 children. The resulting structure is *perfectly balanced* in the sense that the depths of the left and right subtree for each node are equal. While 2-3-4 trees provide a very high degree of balance, they are difficult to implement. We can, however, map features of a 2-3-4 tree into an equivalent red-black tree. The process involves converting each of the different types of 2-3-4 nodes into red-black tree node. In the end, we will identify properties that characterize a red-black tree. The properties become the basis for an implementation of the `RBTree` class.

Let us look at a 2-3-4 tree. We begin by defining a 2-node as a node containing a data value and references for two subtrees (hence the name 2-node). If A is the data value and the left subtree is not empty, the value of the root of the left subtree is less than A. Similarly, the value of the root of the right subtree is greater than A. A 2-node is simply a normal binary search tree node. A 3-node is a node containing two ordered data values, A and B, such that A < B, and three references to subtrees. The values A and B must be distinct because a 2-3-4 tree cannot have duplicate values. Assuming the subtrees are not empty, the value of the root for the left subtree is less than A, the value of the root for the middle subtree lies between A and B, and the value of the root for the right subtree is greater than B.

In a 2-3-4 tree, a 2-node has two children and one value, a 3-node has 3 children and 2 values, and a 4-node has 4 children and 3 values.

The final node structure in a 2-3-4 tree is the 4-node. It contains three ordered data values, $A < B < C$, along with four references to subtrees. The value of the root of the left subtree is less than A; the value for the root for the second subtree lies between A and B; the value of the root for the third subtree lies between B and C; and the value for the fourth (rightmost) subtree is greater than C.

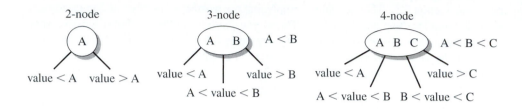

Searching a 2-3-4 Tree

Search a 2-3-4 tree much like searching a binary search tree.

A 2-3-4 tree is a search tree, and the process of locating a value is similar to the algorithm for a binary search tree. To find a value called item, start at the root and compare item with the values in the existing node. If no match occurs, move to the appropriate subtree. Repeat the process until you find a match or encounter an empty subtree. Figure 27.7 is a 2-3-4 tree that contains integer data. To locate 7, begin at the root and compare 7 with the value 12. Because 7 is less than 12, move to the 4-node (4, 8, 10), which is the left child of the root. The value 7 is not in the node but rather lies between 4 and 8. Proceed to the second subtree from the left, landing in the 3-node (5, 7). The search concludes with a match at this node. When looking for 30, follow the path from the root to the right subtree since 30 is greater than 12. In the 2-node, compare 30 and 25 and proceed to the 3-node (35, 55), because 30 is greater than 25. The next comparison has 30 less than 35, and the search continues to the left subtree of the node, which is empty, indicating that 30 is not in the tree.

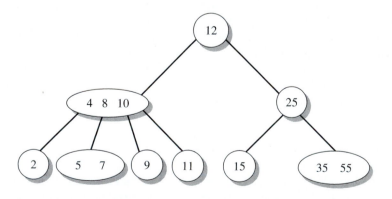

Figure 27.7 *2-3-4 tree.*

Inserting into a 2-3-4 Tree

Place values in a node until it is a 4-node.

Building a 2-3-4 tree uses an insertion algorithm similar to that for a binary search tree. The process begins by inserting the first element in a 2-node, which becomes the root. Each subsequent element enters a leaf node along the search path from the root. If the leaf node into which you must insert the new element is a 2-node or a 3-node, add the new element in the proper order. If the node is a 4-node, it already has three elements and is "full." In this case, the algorithm splits the 4-node. The median value moves up one level in the tree and the other two values enter 2-nodes as its left and right children. For instance, if the root is a 4-node, we split the node as follows.

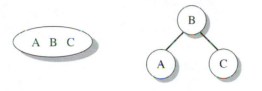

Split a 4-node by moving the middle value up one level with the left and right values as its children.

Building a 2-3-4 Tree   Let us use the insertion strategy to build a 2-3-4 tree. The elements are integer values in the sequence {2, 15, 12, 4, 8, 10, 25, 35, 55, 11}. Note particularly how 4-nodes are created and then split as the tree grows.

Part 1:   Insert 2, 15, and 12: Create a 2-node with value 2 as the root. Combine 15 with 2 to form a 3-node at the root and then conclude by adding 12. The root is then a 4-node with values in the order 2 < 12 < 15.

Part 2:   Insert 4: There is no room in the root node. It is already a 4-node and so we perform the first split. The middle value 12 becomes the parent, and values 2 and 15 become the left and right child respectively. The depth of the tree increases by 1 but the tree remains perfectly balanced. The element 4 then enters the tree. Remember, all insertions occur at a leaf node. Because 4 < 12, insert 4 into the left child of the root, creating the 3-node (2, 4).

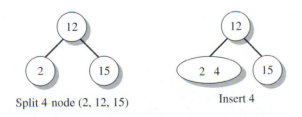

Part 3:   Insert 8, 10: The value 8 is less than the root value 12, and thus is inserted into the left child of the root. The resulting leaf node becomes the 4-node (2, 4, 8). The value 10 is also less than the root value 12 and should enter the left child of the root. However, this child node is full, and a split must occur. The middle value 4 moves up to the parent (the root) and creates a 3-node with 4 < 12. The value 2 becomes the left child of the root and the value 8 becomes the middle child of the root. This frees up room in the leaf nodes to add 10. The

insertion rule compares 10 with values in the root node and determines that 10 lies between 4 and 12. The new value enters the middle child of the root, creating the 3-node (8, 10).

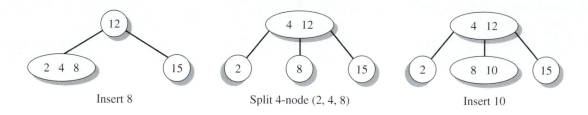

Insert 8   Split 4-node (2, 4, 8)   Insert 10

Part 4: Insert 25, 35, 55: Using the insertion rule, place 25 in the right child of the root, because 25 > 12. Similarly, place 35 in the same right child, creating a 4-node (15, 25, 35). The rule next indicates that 55 should enter the right child of the root. However, this node is now full and requires splitting. The middle value 25 moves up to the root, creating the 4-node (4, 12, 25). The other two values, 15 and 35, then become children on the right side of the tree. Complete the insertion by adding 55 to node 35.

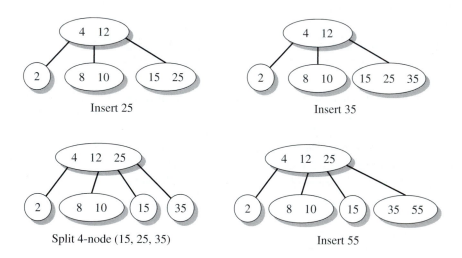

Insert 25   Insert 35

Split 4-node (15, 25, 35)   Insert 55

Split all 4-nodes on the descent to the insertion point. The point is a 2- or a 3-node. This avoids a pass back up the tree splitting nodes.

Part 5: Insert 11: We could apply the simple insertion rule. Because 11 lies between 4 and 12 in the root node, place 11 in the 3-node (8, 10), which creates a 4-node (8, 10, 11) at level 1. A problem would occur if we then attempt to add a value say 7. The insertion path for 7 proceeds from the 4-node root to the 4-node we just created when adding 11. We must proceed by splitting the 4-node at level 1, which would move the value 10 up to the root. This triggers a second split in the parent (root) node, which is also a 4-node. This bottom-up approach to splitting 4-nodes is inefficient, particularly when the tree gets bigger. An insertion at the bottom of the tree could begin a long chain of splits back up the path of parent nodes. A modification of the algorithm optimizes insertions.

Top-Down Insertion   A top–down 2-3-4 tree insertion algorithm splits 4-nodes as they are encountered during the scan down the tree. The approach guarantees that whenever we come to the bottom of the tree we are inserting into a 2- or 3-node. The insertion transforms either a 2-node to a 3-node or a 3-node to a 4-node.

Let us use this approach to insert 11 into our sample 2-3-4 tree. The root is a 4-node, so split it. The first two levels of the tree become 2-nodes. With search tree ordering, scan down the path from the root 12, to the left subtree 4, and then to the 3-node (8, 10). Insert 11 in this node.

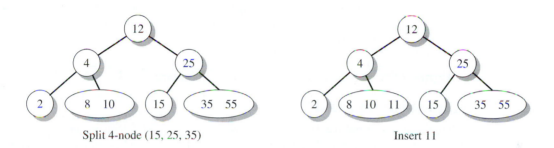

Split 4-node (15, 25, 35)   Insert 11

Efficiency of 2-3-4 Trees   You should expect that searching a 2-3-4 tree is a logarithmic operation. We develop the following facts about 2-3-4 trees in the exercises.

Fact 1: In a 2-3-4 tree with n elements, the maximum number of nodes visited during the search for an element is int $(\log_2 n) + 1$.

Fact 2: Inserting an element into a 2-3-4 tree with n elements requires splitting no more than int$(\log_2 n) + 1$ 4-nodes, and normally requires far fewer splits.

27.4 Red-Black Trees

Implementing a 2-3-4 tree poses problems. Because any node can have up to three values and four children, a node object would need to provide seven variables; yet, most nodes are not 4-nodes, so, many of the values are unused. A program might need to allocate a large amount of wasted space. Besides the space consideration, handling the more complex structures is likely to make the program using 2-3-4 trees run more slowly than if the program used standard binary search trees. Fortunately, there is a way to create a new binary tree, called a *red-black tree*, that is derived from a 2-3-4 tree and retains the good balance and insertion features of a 2-3-4 tree. A red-black tree has operations that require little more computation than those used by standard binary search trees.

A red-black tree is a binary search tree in which each node has the color attribute BLACK or RED. It was designed as a representation of a 2-3-4 tree, using different color combinations to describe 3-nodes and 4-nodes. The link between these two types of trees is critical to your understanding of the structure of a red-black tree and its operations. We will motivate every red-black tree operation by looking at the corresponding 2-3-4 tree structure. Much of our presentation consists of pictures that illustrate how red-black tree algorithms must identify color patterns among the nodes and perform color changes and rotations to restructure the tree.

A red-black tree is a binary tree representation of a 2-3-4 tree.

Figure 27.8 is an example of a red-black tree. In our discussion, a shaded node represents a RED node. If you do not consider color, the tree is simply a binary search tree. You will discover that the tree corresponds to the accompanying 2-3-4 tree.

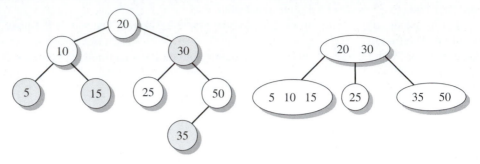

Figure 27.8 *Red–black search tree and the equivalent 2-3-4 tree.*

Representing 2-3-4 Tree Nodes

A 2-node is a red-black tree node. Represent a 4-node with a BLACK parent and 2 RED children.

To indicate how a red-black tree is a representation of a 2-3-4 tree, we need a way to use binary nodes and colors to describe the 2-3-4 tree nodes. The task is simple for a 2-node and a 4-node. A 2-node is always BLACK. A 4-node has the middle value as a BLACK parent and the other values as RED children. Assume a 4-node has values A, B, and C. In the red-black tree, the center node B is BLACK and values A and C are RED children.

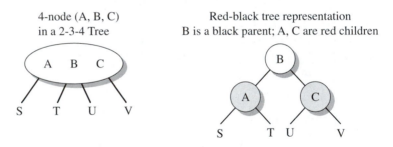

Represent a 3-node with a BLACK parent and a smaller RED left child, or with a BLACK parent and a larger RED right child.

A 3-node is more complex, because it has two possible red-black tree representations. Assume the 3-node has values A and B. Two representations using red-black tree nodes are possible. Designate A as a BLACK node and B as its right RED child or designate B as a BLACK node and A as its left RED child. With two choices for a 3-node, a red-black tree representation of a 2-3-4 tree is not unique (Figure 27.9). In the equivalent red-black tree structure, there are three child references available for the subtrees corresponding to values less than A, for values in the range between A and B, and for values greater than B.

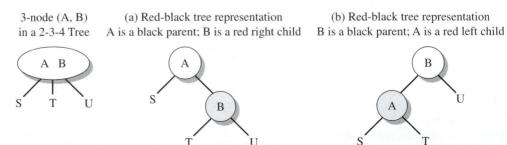

Figure 27.9 *Representing a 3-node in a red-black tree (two options).*

In a red-black tree, look for the color grouping of nodes to indicate the configuration of 2-, 3-, and 4-nodes in the corresponding 2-3-4 tree. For instance, a grouping that includes a BLACK parent and two RED children corresponds to a 4-node; a collection that includes a BLACK parent and exactly one RED child corresponds to a 3-node.

The Red-Black Tree Representation of a 2-3-4 Tree

With the ability to represent each node in a 2-3-4 tree as a color-coordinated collection of nodes in a red-black tree, we can build a red–black tree representation of a 2-3-4 tree. The top–down technique starts at the root and then proceeds to the nodes at level 1, level 2, and so forth. For each node in the 2-3-4 tree, use a red-black tree representation. Because 3-nodes have two possible representations, the conversion is not unique.

Let us go through an example in detail. The process will reveal important properties of red-black trees that we will use when we design algorithms to build the trees. Use the 2-3-4 tree in Figure 27.10, which consists of 11 values on two levels.

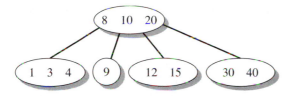

Figure 27.10 *2-3-4 tree with 11 values and two levels.*

Step 1:   Convert the root node: The root node is a 4-node which translates to three red-black nodes where the middle value 10 is a BLACK node and the values 8 and 20 are RED children.

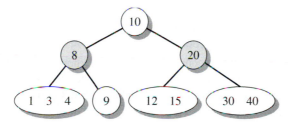

Step 2:   Convert the children of 8: The left child of 8 is a 4-node that converts to a BLACK parent and two RED children. The right child, node 9, is a simple 2-node that converts to a BLACK node.

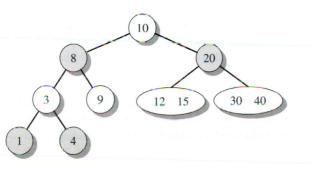

Splitting a 4-Node

During the scan down a path in a red-black tree, we encounter a 4-node when the subtree has a BLACK parent and two RED children. The algorithm requires an immediate splitting of the node. From our understanding of the 2-3-4 tree representation of a red-black tree, the split requires moving the BLACK parent up one level. We know that the node at the higher level could not be a 4-node, because it would have been split previously during the scan down the tree. Hence, moving the BLACK parent up one level will create a new 3-node or a new 4-node at the higher level.

For discussion purposes, assume that X is the name of the BLACK node in the 4-node. There are four situations that can occur when we discover a 4-node. The situations distinguish the color of the parent of X, called P, and the orientation (left or right) of X as a child of P. Figure 27.11 illustrates the different possibilities.

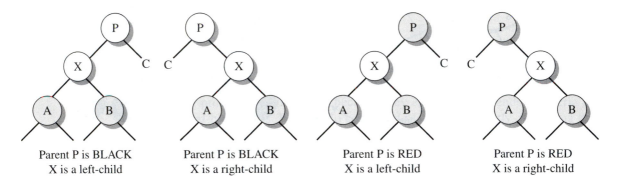

| Parent P is BLACK | Parent P is BLACK | Parent P is RED | Parent P is RED |
| X is a left-child | X is a right-child | X is a left-child | X is a right-child |

Figure 27.11 *Four situations in the splitting of a 4-node.*

Split a 4-node by coloring the subtree root RED and its children BLACK (color flip). The subtree root moves up one level in the corresponding 2-3-4 tree.

In each case, the splitting of a 4-node begins with a *color flip* that reverses the color of each of the nodes. Node X become RED, and its two children become BLACK. Making X RED has the effect of moving the node up one level. The algorithm must assess the effect of the color flip on the status of the tree. The focus is on the parent node P.

Parent P is BLACK.   The color flip splits the 4-node and the resulting tree remains correct, no matter whether X is a left or right child of P. In Figure 27.12, the 4-node is a left child of P. The figure includes the 2-3-4-tree view of the red-black tree, before and after the color flip.

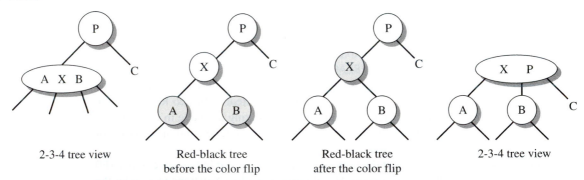

| 2-3-4 tree view | Red-black tree before the color flip | Red-black tree after the color flip | 2-3-4 tree view |

Figure 27.12 *Splitting a 4-node that is the left child of a BLACK parent P.*

Example 27.4

This example illustrates the splitting of a 4-node prior when inserting element 55 in a red-black tree. In scanning down a path from the root, we encounter a 4-node in the right subtree of 30. The BLACK node 50 has two RED children 40 and 60. The parent of the 4-node is the BLACK root. The color flip maintains the black-height balance of the tree. The new element then enters the tree as a RED node and the left child of 60. You can view the equivalent process in a 2-3-4 tree.

If the parent is BLACK, a color flip does not cause a rotation.

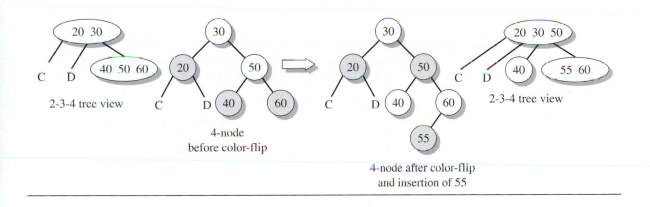

Parent P is RED When the parent of the 4-node is RED, a color flip leaves two successive red nodes in a path. Figure 27.13 illustrates two situations that may occur. In (a), the 4-node is an outside child of P and in (b), the 4-node is an inside child of P. Rebalancing of the tree involves rotations with nodes G, P, and X. We will develop a single rotation for an outside child and a double rotation for an inside child. The rotations are termed left or right, depending on whether P is a left or right child of G. Left and right rotations are symmetric, and so the main focus must be on the distinction between single and double rotations.

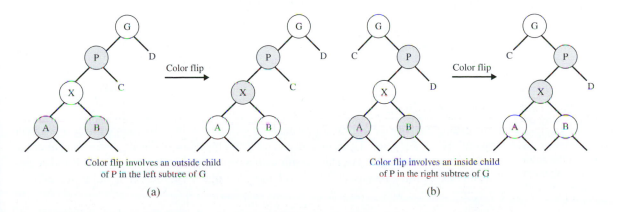

Figure 27.13 *A color flip of a 4-node with a RED parent leaves successive red nodes.*

If the parent is RED, two successive RED nodes result and a rotation must be done to fix the conflict.

Rebalancing with a Single Rotation   When a 4-node is an outside child of its parent P and the color flip imbalances the tree, use a single rotation about node P. The rotation involves G and X and a repositioning of the inside child of P. Figure 27.14a is the case where P is a left child of G and the 4-node is a left child of P. A single right rotation with P as the pivot makes G a child of P and attaches the right child of P as the left child of G. In the process, change the color for nodes P and G. Figure 27.14b is the symmetric single left rotation when P is a right child of G and the 4-node is a right child of P.

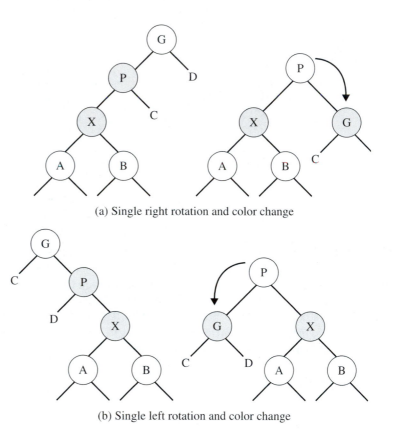

(a) Single right rotation and color change

(b) Single left rotation and color change

Figure 27.14 *Single left and right rotations with color changes.*

A left–left or right–right ordering of G, P, and X requires a single rotation to remove the color conflict and maintain balance. The pivot is P.

Example 27.5

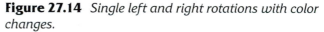

The example relates the splitting of a 4-node followed by a single rotation with the equivalent operation in a 2-3-4 tree. The figure includes a 2-3-4 tree view of the tree before and after the split and rotation occurs. The steps begin with a color flip. The resulting nodes P and X create a color conflict, because they are both RED. A single right rotation about P makes node

G a right child of P and moves the right subtree C of P across as the new left subtree of G. Node P changes color to BLACK, and the grandparent node G becomes RED. The changes in color maintain the black-height of the tree. The before-and-after views of the 2-3-4 tree correspond to the splitting of the 4-node (A, X, B).

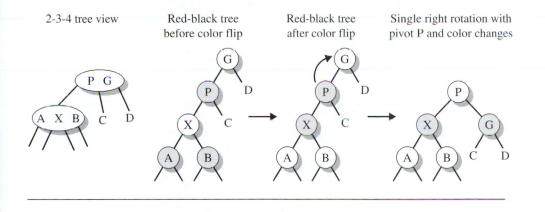

Rebalancing with a Double Rotation   A double rotation is used when the 4-node is an inside child of the parent and the color flip creates a color conflict. As with single rotations, double rotations are symmetric, depending on whether the parent P is a left or a right child of G. Let us look at the case where P is a left child of G. The figure initially displays the tree before and after a color flip occurs. A double right rotation consists of a single left rotation about X followed by a single right rotation about X. Hence the term "double." The rotations and the coloring of the nodes are treated as separate operations. After the second rotation, color X BLACK and make the grandparent G RED. The nodes P X G are a new 4-node, because the parent node X is BLACK and its children P and G are RED. This new 4-node will not be split until a subsequent insertion causes a new scan down the tree.

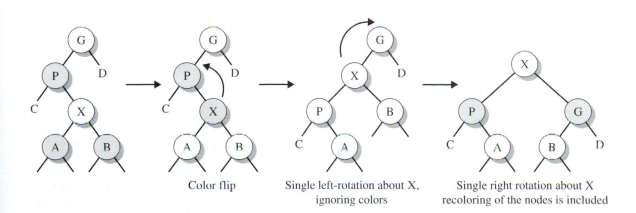

Example 27.6

This example relates the splitting of a 4-node followed by a double rotation with the equivalent operations in a 2-3-4 tree. The figure displays a red-black tree before the splitting of a 4-node, after a color flip, and then after the double rotation. The before-and-after views of the 2-3-4 tree correspond to the splitting of the 4-node (A, X, B).

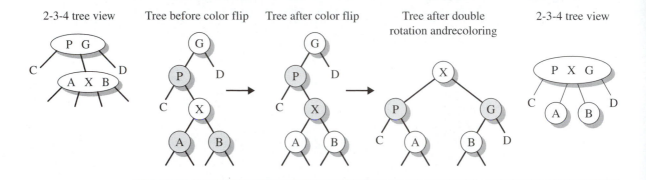

| 2-3-4 tree view | Tree before color flip | Tree after color flip | Tree after double rotation andrecoloring | 2-3-4 tree view |

Insertion at the Bottom of the Tree

Inserting a node into the tree with color RED may require a rotation.

An item enters the bottom of a red-black tree as a RED node. If the parent node is already RED, there is a color conflict and some additional action is required. The process involves a single or a double rotation, depending on whether the new node enters as an inside or outside child. You are familiar with these rotations and can readily apply them to situations that may occur.

Let us look at two different examples that occur when we add a new node to a red-black tree with elements 5 and 12. Node 5 is the BLACK root and node 12 is a RED child. Inserting 14 into the tree places a RED node as the child of the existing RED node 12. Two RED nodes occur as successive right children. Use a single left rotation about 12 to rebalance the tree. Node 12 becomes the new root. The resulting tree is a 4-node (BLACK parent 12, RED children 5 and 14).

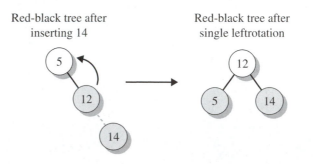

Red-black tree after inserting 14   Red-black tree after single leftrotation

Suppose 10 is the new item rather than 14. The element enters as a RED node and as an inside child of the RED node 12. This situation requires a double left rotation to rebalance the tree. The rotation moves node 10 up two levels to become the new BLACK root. The grandparent, node 5, becomes a RED left child of node 10 and RED node 12 becomes the right child of node 10.

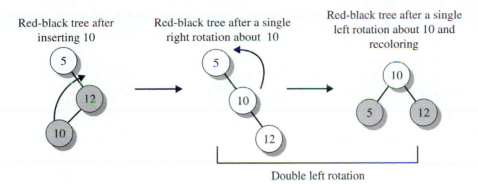

Red-black tree after inserting 10

Red-black tree after a single right rotation about 10

Red-black tree after a single left rotation about 10 and recoloring

Double left rotation

Building a Red-Black Tree

In the previous section, we provided guidelines for inserting an element in a red-black tree. Let us use these guidelines to build a red-black tree with elements from the array {40, 20, 10, 35, 50, 25, 30}. We will focus on the steps that involve splitting a 4-node and rebalancing a tree with a rotation.

Part 1:   Insert 40: All items enter the tree as a RED node. Since 40 becomes the root node, it is colored BLACK. Red-black trees always maintain the root as BLACK. After coloring the root BLACK, the tree is still a red-black tree (see Written Exercise 27.13).

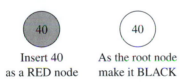

Insert 40 as a RED node

As the root node make it BLACK

Part 2:   Insert 20, 10: Add 20 as a RED left child of 40. Then, add 10 as a RED left child of 20. The tree has two successive RED nodes with 10 being an outside child of the parent node 20. A single right rotation about 20 rebalances the tree. Color changes in the rotation create 20 as the BLACK root.

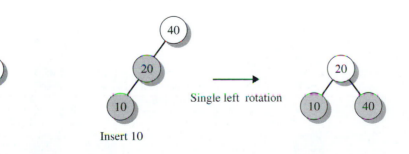

Insert 20

Insert 10

Single left rotation

Part 3:   Insert 35: In the scan down the tree, we encounter a 4-node (BLACK root 20, RED children 10, 40) at the root. Split the 4-node with a color flip, which makes the children BLACK. Add 35 as a RED node and the left child of 40. Color the root BLACK. Node 20, which is RED from the color flip, is colored BLACK.

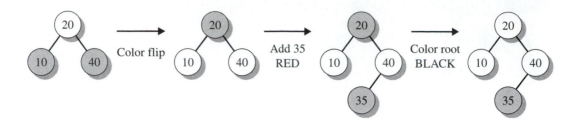

Part 4: Insert 50, 25: Add 50 as the right RED child of 40. The tree remains balanced. In the search down a path to add 25, we discover the 4-node (BLACK 40, RED children 35, 50). The color flip produces no conflicts. Add 25 as a RED left child of 35, which is now BLACK from the color flip.

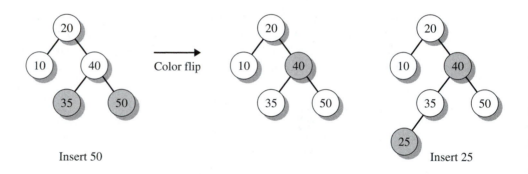

Insert 50   Insert 25

Part 5: Insert 30: Add 30 as a RED right child of 25. This creates a color conflict with successive RED nodes. Since 30 enters as an inside child, use a double right rotation to rebalance the tree. The double right rotation moves 30 up two levels and recolors nodes 30 and 35.

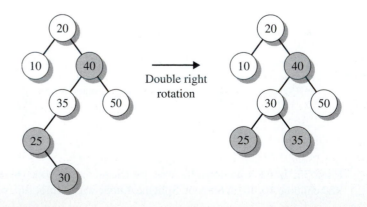

Search Running Time

The purpose for building red-black trees is to guarantee that the running time for a search is $O(\log_2 n)$. We should intuitively expect that this is true, because 2-3-4 trees have a worst-case search time of $O(\log_2 n)$. and we build red-black trees by modeling the 2-3-4 tree operations.

We apply some simple mathematics to verify the running time. The analysis relies on the following fact, which the interested reader can prove using mathematical induction.

Let B be the black-height of a red-black tree with n nodes and let blackNum be the number of BLACK nodes. Then,

$$2^B - 1 \leq \text{blackNum} \leq n \qquad \text{or equivalently} \qquad 2^B \leq \text{blackNum} + 1 \leq n + 1$$

Computing the $\log_2()$ for each term, we have

$$B \leq \log_2(n + 1).$$

The maximum length of a path in a red-black tree with black-height B is $2*B - 1$. This would occur when the tree has a path to an empty subtree that alternates between BLACK and RED nodes. Such a path contains $2*B$ nodes.

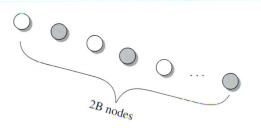

2B nodes

The worst-case running time to search a red-black tree or insert an item is $O(\log_2 n)$.

If the tree has height h, the following inequality relates h, B, and $\log_2(n + 1)$.

$$h \leq 2*B - 1 < 2*B \leq 2*\log_2(n + 1)$$

Thus, the height of the tree is $O(\log_2 n)$, and a search makes at most $O(\log_2 n)$ comparisons. An insertion involves scanning a path that may involve splitting 4-nodes. There are at most $O(\log_2 n)$ comparisons on the way down the insertion path and no more than $O(\log_2 n)$ 4-node splits that require only color changes and updates to subtree references. Hence, the insertion has running time $O(\log_2 n)$.

Erasing a Node in a Red-Black Tree

Erasing a node from an ordinary binary search tree is more difficult than inserting a node. The same is true for a red-black tree. We will not develop the algorithm but will simply discuss some of the issues that must be addressed. The algorithm to remove a node D from a binary search tree first locates a node R containing the replacement value. The deletion is handled by removing R from the tree, reattaching its children, and assigning its value into node D. In a red-black tree, the color of R becomes critical. If it is RED, the black-height of the tree is not changed and no other action is necessary. The situation is illustrated in Figure 27.15, when the root is the deleted node. The replacement node is RED with value 78. The node is deleted from the tree and its value is assigned to the root node.

No further action is necessary when the replacement node is RED.

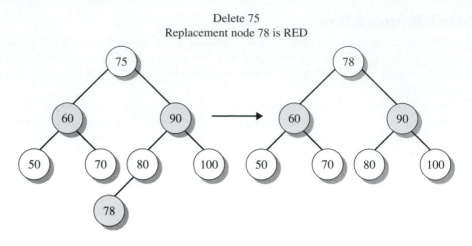

Figure 27.15 *RED replacement node in a deletion.*

When the replacement node is BLACK, we must make adjustments to the tree from the bottom up in order to maintain black-height balance. Look at the tree in Figure 27.16, where 90

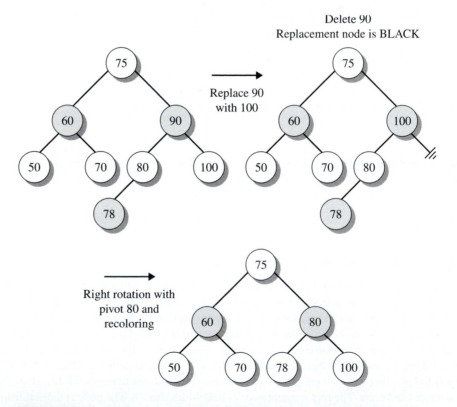

Figure 27.16 *Replacement node is BLACK during red-black tree node deletion.*

is the deleted node. The replacement is the BLACK node 100. We replace the value 90 by 100 and delete the BLACK node containing 100 from the tree. The "deleted" node now has value 100 but remains RED. The path 75–100 has only one BLACK node, whereas the other paths have two BLACK nodes. The tree is out of balance. We regain balance by performing a single right rotation and a recoloring of nodes. In general, the bottom-up algorithm that balances the tree when the replacement node is BLACK requires a series of color flips and at most 3 rotations as it moves up the tree. Thus, the algorithm to delete a node from a red-black tree has running time $O(\log_2 n)$. The interested reader should consult Cormen, Leiserson, and Rivest, *Introduction to Algorithms* (McGraw-Hill, 2002) for a full discussion of the somewhat complex algorithm.

Erasing a node from a red-black tree requires recoloring and rotations when the replacement node is BLACK.

27.5 The RBTree Class

In Chapter 18, we developed the binary search tree class STree using STNode objects. STree is a generic class that implements the Collection interface. RBTree is a similar class that uses RBNode objects to create a red-black tree that implements the Collection interface. An RBNode extends STNode by including a fifth instance variable for the node color. Enum constants define the colors RED and BLACK.

An RBNode must store the color as well as the value, subtree references, and the parent.

| left | nodeValue | parent | color | right |

RBNode

The implementation of the class is somewhat complex and will not be presented in the text. The Web supplement contains the document *RBTree Class.pdf*, which provides an expanded explanation of the RBTree class implementation. The document includes a discussion of the private section of the class and the algorithms for splitting a 4-node and performing a top-down insertion. The file *RBTree.java* provides a listing of the source code. Extended comments detail the algorithms for the class methods including the red-black tree deletion algorithm.

The following is a listing of RBTree class methods that are not included in the Collection interface. Draw methods provide a graphical display of the tree with coloration of the nodes.

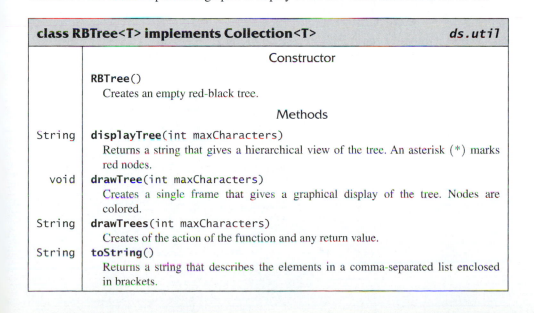

class RBTree<T> implements Collection<T>	*ds.util*

Constructor

RBTree()
   Creates an empty red-black tree.

Methods

String **displayTree**(int maxCharacters)
   Returns a string that gives a hierarchical view of the tree. An asterisk (*) marks red nodes.

void **drawTree**(int maxCharacters)
   Creates a single frame that gives a graphical display of the tree. Nodes are colored.

String **drawTrees**(int maxCharacters)
   Creates of the action of the function and any return value.

String **toString**()
   Returns a string that describes the elements in a comma-separated list enclosed in brackets.

PROGRAM 27.1 ILLUSTRATING THE RBTree

The following program illustrates uses of the RBTree class. An instance of the class is created to store Integer objects. A loop adds elements to the tree from the array intArr. After each insertion, drawTrees() shows the current state of the tree in a graphical window. The completed tree is displayed in a console window using displayTree(). The program concludes by deleting a red node 25 and the black root node 45 and updating the graphical display. A run displays two frames of the window after five elements are added and after all 10 elements are added.

```java
import ds.util.RBTree;

public class Program27_1
{
    public static void main (String[] args)
    {
        // list of elements for the red-black tree
        int[] intArr = {10, 25, 40, 15, 50, 45, 30, 65, 70, 55};
        RBTree<Integer> rbtree = new RBTree<Integer>();
        int i;

        // load the tree with values from intArr; display
        // available after each insert
        for(i = 0; i < intArr.length; i++)
        {
            rbtree.add(intArr[i]);
            rbtree.drawTrees(4);
        }

        // display the final tree in the console windows
        System.out.println(rbtree.displayTree(2));

        // remove red-node 25
        rbtree.remove(25);
        rbtree.drawTrees(4);

        // remove black-node root
        rbtree.remove(45);
        rbtree.drawTree(3);
    }
}
```

Run:
   Display with drawTrees(): adding elements:

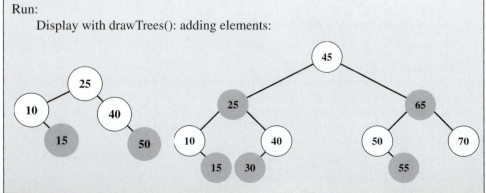

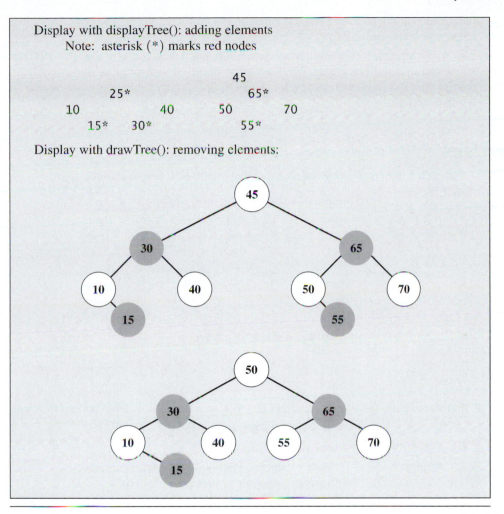

Display with displayTree(): adding elements
    Note: asterisk (*) marks red nodes

Display with drawTree(): removing elements:

Chapter Summary

- An AVL tree is a balanced binary tree structure. Associated with each AVL tree node is its balanceFactor, which is the difference between the heights of the left and right subtrees. In an AVL tree, the balanceFactor for each node is in the range from -1 to 1.

- The AVLTree collection class implements the Collection interface. Insertions are performed using a recursive algorithm. Elements are inserted in a leaf node and rebalancing of the tree occurs during the backtracking stages of the algorithm. Rebalancing involves single and double rotations which update the balance factor of the parent node.

- In a 2-3-4 tree, a node has either 1 value and 2 children, 2 values and 3 children, or 3 values and 4 children. This chapter develops an algorithm for building a perfectly balanced 2-3-4 tree. The actual construction of 2-3-4 trees is complex, so we build an equivalent binary tree known as a red-black tree. We develop all operations on red-black trees by looking at the corresponding 2-3-4 tree.

- A red-black tree is another balanced tree structure. Using pictures primarily, we show how to insert into a red-black tree by modeling the operations with the corresponding 2-3-4 tree. The algorithms involve single and double rotations that are similar to those for AVL trees. Deleting a node from a red-black tree is rather difficult. We present only a basic idea of the problems involved.

- The Web supplement contains a discussion of the implementation for the class RBTree, which builds a red-black tree. We discuss the insertion algorithm in some detail. Although the class implements the erase() operation, the supplement does not discuss its implementation.

Written Exercises

1. For each search tree, carry out rotations that create AVL height-balance.

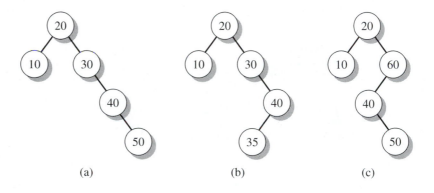

(a)   (b)   (c)

2. For each of the following, construct the AVL tree that results from adding the items

   (a) Integers: {30, 50, 25, 70, 60, 40, 55, 45, 20}
   (b) Characters: Letters in the string "hyperbola"
   (c) Strings: {"class", "object", "public", "private", "subclass", "abstract", "border", "method", "inherit"}

3. Does the red-black tree represent a valid 2-3-4 tree? If not, modify the tree so that it is a valid 2-3-4 tree.

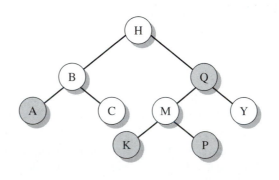

4. Draw a 2-3-4 tree that contains the characters in the string
   SEARCHTWO

5. Draw the red-black tree that results from inserting `Integer` objects that correspond to the array `arr`.

    ```
    int[] arr = {15, 55, 28, 45, 32, 40, 35, 38, 36, 37}
    ```

6. Create the red-black tree for each of the following 2-3-4 trees.

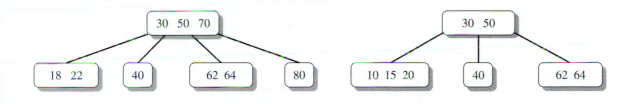

7. (a) If `arr` has `Integer` values {3, 8, 12, 35, 2, 8, 12, 55}, what are the values in `arr` after a call to the method `f()`?

```
public static <T> void f(LinkedList<T> llist)
{
    RBTree<T> t = new RBTree<T>();
    Iterator<T> i;

    i = llist.iterator();
    while (i.hasNext())
        t.add(i.next());

    i = t.iterator();
    llist.clear();

    while (i.hasNext())
        llist.add(i.next());
}
```

   (b) In general, what is the action of `f()`? Determine the average- and worst-case running time for `f()` as a function of n = `llist.size()`.

8. In parts (a)–(c), assume the binary tree has n elements.

   (a) What is the worst-case running time for searching an AVL tree?
   (b) What is the worst-case complexity for insertion into a red-black tree? O (_____)
   (c) The `erase()` algorithm used by `RBTree` moves up the tree, performing at most three rotations, until the tree is in balance. What is the worst-case complexity for the algorithm? O (_____)

9. (a) Draw the AVL tree that is built when you insert the keys E A S Y Q U T I O N (in that order) into an initially empty tree.
   (b) Draw the 2-3-4 tree built when you insert the keys from part (a) into an initially empty tree.
   (c) Draw a red-black representation of the tree in (b).

10. For the case of a double rotation with an inside right grandchild, draw the corresponding 2-3-4 tree configuration before and after the recoloration and rotation.

Double Rotation - X is inside left grandchild

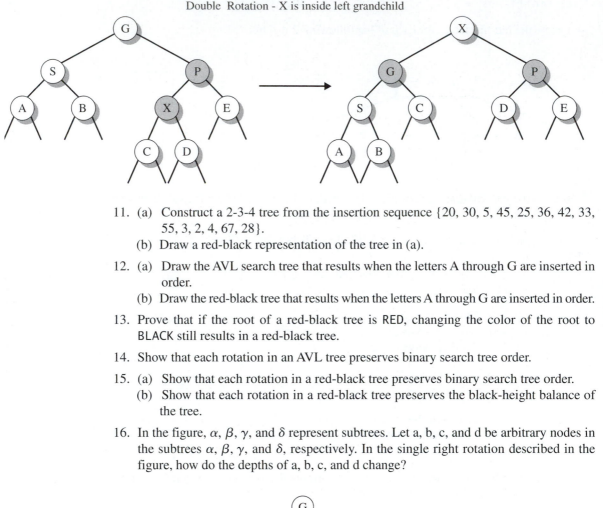

11. (a) Construct a 2-3-4 tree from the insertion sequence {20, 30, 5, 45, 25, 36, 42, 33, 55, 3, 2, 4, 67, 28}.
    (b) Draw a red-black representation of the tree in (a).

12. (a) Draw the AVL search tree that results when the letters A through G are inserted in order.
    (b) Draw the red-black tree that results when the letters A through G are inserted in order.

13. Prove that if the root of a red-black tree is RED, changing the color of the root to BLACK still results in a red-black tree.

14. Show that each rotation in an AVL tree preserves binary search tree order.

15. (a) Show that each rotation in a red-black tree preserves binary search tree order.
    (b) Show that each rotation in a red-black tree preserves the black-height balance of the tree.

16. In the figure, α, β, γ, and δ represent subtrees. Let a, b, c, and d be arbitrary nodes in the subtrees α, β, γ, and δ, respectively. In the single right rotation described in the figure, how do the depths of a, b, c, and d change?

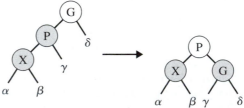

17. In the *tree sort*, the elements of an array are inserted into a binary search tree, the tree is traversed in order, and the elements are copied back to the array.

    (a) Assume the binary search tree is an ordinary one; in other words, it is not balanced. What is the worst-case running time for the algorithm? The average-case running time is difficult to determine mathematically. What do you think it is?

    (b) Assume the binary search tree is an AVL or red-black tree. What is the worst-case running time for the algorithm?

18. Prove the following facts about 2-3-4 trees.
    (a) In a 2-3-4 tree with n elements, the maximum number of nodes visited during the search for an element is int $(\log_2 n) + 1$. HINT: Assume that all nodes are 2-nodes.
    (b) Inserting an element into a 2-3-4 tree with n elements requires splitting no more than int$(\log_2 n) + 1$ 4-nodes and normally requires far fewer splits. HINT: Assume that all nodes are 4-nodes.

19. We asserted at the beginning of Section 27.4 that if a 2-3-4 node contains 4 references and 3 data values, a program might need to allocate a large amount of wasted space. Assume that a 2-3-4 tree contains n nodes.
    (a) What is the number of subtree references present in the tree?
    (b) How many edges are present in the tree?
    (c) Compute the number of unused subtree references.

Programming Exercises

The directory ch27ex contains a copy of the AVLTree and RBTree classes that are not in the package ds.util. For Programming Exercises 27.21 and 27.22, make your modifications to these classes.

20. In a program, declare the STree object charSTree, the AVLTree object charAVLTree, and the RBTree object charRBTree. Load values into the trees from array arr. Display each tree using the method displayTree().

    ```
    char[] arr = { 'S', 'J', 'K', 'L', 'X', 'F', 'E', 'Z'};
    ```

21. Add to the AVLTree class the recursive method heightEqual() that returns the number of nodes that have the same height for the left and right subtrees.

    ```
    public int heightEqual()
    ```

    Write a program that creates an AVLTree with letters from the string "problematic". Display the tree and then output the result of calling heightEqual().

22. (a) Add to the RBTree class the recursive method count4Nodes(), which returns the number of nodes that correspond to a 2-3-4 tree 4-node. Add a second method display4Nodes(), which returns a string containing the values of all 4-nodes in the tree using the format

    $$\text{"} <value_A> \; <value_B> \; <value_C> \text{"}$$

    for each 4-node.

    ```
    // return the number of 4-nodes in the red-black tree
    public int count4Nodes()
    { ... }

    // display the 4-nodes in the red-black tree
    public String display4Nodes()
    { ... }
    ```

    Write a program that creates an RBTree with letters from the string "exclusionary". Display the tree and then output separate results from the methods count4Nodes() and display4Nodes() respectively.

(b) Using part(a) as a model, implement methods `count3Nodes()` and `display3Nodes()`.

```
public int count3Nodes()
{ ... }

public String display3Nodes()
{ ... }
```

Write a test program that creates an `RBTree` with letters from the string "centrifugal". Display the tree and then output separate results from the methods `count3Nodes()` and `display3Nodes()` respectively.

The directory ch27ex contains a copy of the `STree`, `AVLTree`, and `RBTree` classes that are not in the package `ds.util`. For Programming Project 27.23, make your modifications to these classes.

Programming Project

23. (a) Using mathematical induction, prove the following result:
Let B be the black-height of a red-black tree with n nodes and let `blackNum` be the number of BLACK nodes. Then,

$$2^B \leq blackNum+1 \leq n+1$$

(b) Add a method pathDepth() to the STree, AVLTree, and RBTree classes. In each case, the method returns the depth from the root of the node containing item. If item is not in the tree, the method returns -1.

```
// returns the depth of the node containing item from
// the tree root or -1 if item is not in the tree
public int pathHeight(T item)
{ ... }
```

(c) In this exercise, compare the performance of binary search, red-black, and AVL trees. Create an array intArr with 500,000 integers in the range from 0 to 9,999,999. Insert the elements in each type of tree. Scan the array and search for each item in each tree, maintaining a count of the accumulated depth of the items from the root. For output, compute the average depth of an element in the three trees.

Chapter 28

NUMBER THEORY AND ENCRYPTION

CONTENTS

28.1 BASIC NUMBER THEORY
CONCEPTS
Euclid's GCD Algorithms
Modular Arithmetic
Euler's Totient Function

28.2 SECURE MESSAGE PASSING
Creating Keys for RSA Encryption
Using Keys for RSA Encryption
How to Secure RSA
Communication

28.3 USING BIG INTEGERS
BigInteger Prime Numbers

28.4 RSA CLIENT AND SERVER

28.5 THE RSA ALGORITHM
(OPTIONAL)
Implementing Euclid's GCD
Algorithms
The RSA Theorem

In this chapter, we will develop the RSA encryption algorithm, which allows secure Internet communication for such activities as online banking. RSA encryption relies on concepts and algorithms from number theory. These include the computation of the greatest common divisor (gcd), prime numbers, and modulo arithmetic. We begin by setting out the number theory terminology and theorems that enable RSA encryption. Section 28.5 provides the reader with a detailed analysis of key theorems.

The concept of encrypted data transmission is relatively simple. View transmission in terms of interacting client and server processes. To send data or a message, the client process encrypts the information into some obscure form that is transmitted across the Internet. At the other end is a server process, which receives the message and then decrypts it back to its original form. The techniques of encryption and decryption are called *cryptography*. Secure data transmission uses public and private (secret) keys that are created by the server. The *public key* is available to the client who uses it to create a numeric encryption of a message. The server uses the *secret key* to decrypt the transmission back to the original message. We use the mathematical facts from the first two sections to create the keys and demonstrate how they work.

Public and secret keys are number pairs. Secure transmission is provided when we use numbers of enormous size consisting of hundreds of digits. Creating arithmetic operations for large integers has long been a favorite topic in the study of data structures. Java provides the `BigInteger` class that supplies the operations and produces instances with specified random number attributes. We include a GUI application that builds a socket connection between a client and a server to illustrate RSA data transmission. We use the `BigInteger` class to create the transmission keys.

28.1 Basic Number Theory Concepts

a divides b if b = a*h for some integer h.

Let us start by developing some basic number theory concepts and definitions. Assume a and b are integers. Then a divides b if b is a multiple of a; that is, b = a * h for some integer h. Equivalently, a divides b if b/a = h for some integer h. For instance, 6 divides 72 since $72 = 6*12$; but 5 does not divide 36. The notion of divisor splits integers into two types, prime numbers and composite numbers. An integer p is a *prime number* if p ≥ 2 and the only divisors of p are 1 and p. An integer n is a *composite number* if n is the product of two integers ≥ 2 called *factors*. The integer p = 7 is a prime number and integer n = 15 is a composite number since $15 = 3*5$.

An integer p is a prime if p ≥ 2 and p has only two divisors 1 and p. A composite number is the product of two integers ≥ 2 called factors.

Euclid's GCD Algorithms

The concept of *greatest common divisor* relates the notion of divisor to a pair of integers. We assume that a and b are two nonnegative integers neither of which are 0. The greatest common divisor of a and b (gcd(a, b)) is the largest integer that divides both a and b. As a special case when b = 0, gcd(a, 0) = a.

Integers a and b are relatively prime if gcd(a, b) is 1.

Examples: $\gcd(10, 4) = 2$ $\gcd(9, 32) = 1$ $\gcd(54, 30) = 6$
$\gcd(30, 45) = 15$ $\gcd(67, 0) = 67$

Among the examples, note that $\gcd(9, 32) = 1$. In this case, a and b have no common divisors except 1, and we say that a and b are *relatively prime*. This is an important number theory concept.

Euclid's Algorithm is based on the equality gcd(a, b) = gcd(b, a%b).

The Greek mathematician Euclid provided an elegant recursive algorithm for computing gcd(a, b), The algorithm, appropriately called the *Euclid's*, computes gcd(a, b) by using a recursive process that relies on the fact that gcd(a, b) = gcd(b, a%b). This is the basis for the recursive step. The stopping condition occurs when b = 0 and gcd(a, 0) = a.

EuclidGCD(a, b):

Assume a and b are nonnegative integers.

```
if (b == 0)
    gcd(a,b) = a;                   // stopping condition
else
    gcd(a,b) = g(b, a % b)          // recursive step
```

Examples:

1. Let a = 54, b = 30

```
gcd(54,30) = gcd(30,54 % 30)   = gcd(30,24)
gcd(30,24) = gcd(24,30 % 24)   = gcd(24,6)
gcd(24,6)  = gcd(6,24 % 6)     = gcd(6,0)
gcd(6,0)   = 6                 // stop: gcd(54,30) = 6
```

2. Let a = 45, b = 16

```
gcd(45,16) = gcd(16,45 % 16)   = gcd(16,13)
gcd(16,13) = gcd(13,16 % 13)   = gcd(13,3)
gcd(13,3)  = gcd(3,13 % 3)     = gcd(3,1)
gcd(3,1)   = gcd(1,3 % 1)      = gcd(1,0)
gcd(1,0)   = 1                 // stop: gcd(45,16) = 1
```

A *linear combination* of integers a and b is an expression of the form a*i + b*j, where i and j are integer values. For instance, the expression 4*3 + 7*5 is a linear expression involving a = 4 and b = 7. The integers i and j in the expression are 3 and 5 respectively. An extension of Euclid's Algorithm carries out a different task. Rather than using a chain of recursive calls to evaluate gcd(a, b), the extension uses the same chain to represent gcd(a, b) as a linear combination of a and b; that is, the algorithm determines integers i and j such that

> Expression b*i + c*j is a linear combination of b and c.

$$\gcd(a, b) = a * i + b * j \quad \text{for some integers } i \text{ and } j$$

ExtendedEuclidGCD(a, b):

Let a and b be two positive integers. The extended Euclid's Algorithm returns a triple (d, i, j) such that

$$d = \gcd(a, b) = a * i + b * j$$

> The extended Euclid's Algorithm computes gcd(a, b) as a linear combination of a and b.

Examples:

1. Let a = 54, b = 30; the extended Euclid's Algorithm determines that gcd(54, 30) = 6 and finds integers i = −1 and j = 2 such that 6 is a linear combination of 54 and 30.

```
6 = gcd(54, 30) = 54 * -1 + 30 * 2   // i = -1, j = 2
                = -54 + 60
```

2. Let a = 45, b = 16; the extended Euclid's Algorithm determines that gcd(45, 16) = 1 and finds integers i = 5 and j = −14 such that 1 is a linear combination of 45 and 16.

```
1 = gcd(45, 16) = 45 * 5 + 16 * -14  // i = 5, j = -14
                = 225 + -224
```

The importance of the extended Euclid's Algorithm will become clear in the next two sections when we look at modular arithmetic and apply it to RSA encryption.

Modular Arithmetic

A traditional view for the set of integers is a line that marks discrete values centered about 0. The integers are an unbounded linear collection of numbers.

By taking the remainder after division by a positive number n, we can map the integers into a finite set of integers in the range [0, n). The mapping uses the % operator, which is often referred to as the *mod* operator. For an integer a, the mapping is a -> a % n.

Example: Assume n = 15

18 -> 18 % 15 = 3	25 -> 25 % 15 = 10	50 -> 50 % 15 = 5
3 -> 3 % 15 = 3		

For a description of the mapping, we say that 18 is *congruent* to 3 *modulo* 15. This is written 18 = 3 (mod 15). In the example, 25 = 10 (mod 15), 50 = 5 (mod 15), and 3 = 3 (mod 15). A formal definition of the mod operator describes the mapping in terms of divisors.

> If a = b (mod n), then b − a = n*k for some integer k.

Mod operator: a = b (mod n) if and only if b − a = n * k for some integer k

Example: Assume n = 15

18 = 3 (mod 15)	18 - 3 = 15 = 15 * 1	// k = 1
50 = 10 (mod 15)	50 - 10 = 45 = 15 * 3	// k = 3

Z(n) = (0, 1, 2 . . .
n−1} with
operators +, *,
and ^ (exponent).
Results are computed modulo n.

When dividing a positive integer by n, the remainder is in the range from 0 to n − 1. The possible values constitute a finite set $Z(n) = \{0, 1, 2, \ldots, n - 1\}$. The elements in Z(n) define a number system that implements the arithmetic operations of addition, multiplication, and exponentiation. We summarize the operations in terms of the mod operator. Assume a and b are values in Z(n).

Arithmetic operations in Z(n):

Add (+):	a + b = (a + b) (mod n)	
Multiply (*):	a * b = (a*b) (mod n)	
Exponent(^):	$(a)^e = (a^e)$ (mod n)	// exponent is e

Example 28.1

This example illustrates arithmetic operations in Z(15). Let a = 7 and b = 11 be elements in Z(15).

Add(+):	7 + 11 = 18 (mod 15) = 3
Multiply(*):	7 * 11 = 77 (mod 15) = 2
Exponent(^):	7^2 = 49 (mod 15) = 4

Inverse in Z(n) For multiplication, a number a in Z(n) has a inverse i provided a * i = 1 (mod n). Integer i is called the *multiplicative inverse* of a. A classical result in number theory states

> Theorem (Inverse in Z(n)): Let a be a number in Z(n); then a has a multiplicative inverse if and only if a and n are relatively prime (gcd(a, n) = 1).

If *a* is in Z(n) and
gcd(a,n) = 1,
then *a* has an
inverse in Z(n);
there exists an i
in Z(n) such that
a*i = 1 (mod n).

In fact, if we know that gcd(a, n) = 1, we can use extended Euclid's Algorithm to determine the inverse. Recall that for integer a such that gcd(a, n) = 1 there exist integers i and j such that 1 = a * i + n * j. Using the mod operator, 1 = a * i (mod n).

Examples: Assume n = 15

1. 1 = gcd(7, 15) = 7 * 13 + 15 * −6   Thus: 1 = 7 * 13 (mod 15)
2. 1 = gcd(2, 15) = 2 * 8 + 15 * −1   Thus: 1 = 2 * 8 (mod 15)

Euler's Totient Function

The mathematician Euler did groundbreaking work in many fields including number theory. He defined a function, called the *totient function*, which applies to elements in Z(n).

Euler Totient Function: $\phi(n)$ is the number of integers in Z(n) that are relatively prime to *n*.

Euler totient
function ϕ(n) is
the number of
integers in
Z(n) relatively
prime to *n*.

Examples:

1. $\phi(5) = 4$ (numbers 1, 2, 3, and 4 are relatively prime to 5)
2. $\phi(6) = 2$ (numbers 1 and 5 are relatively prime to 6)
3. $\phi(7) = 6$ (numbers 1, 2, 3, 4, 5, and 6 are relatively prime to 7)
4. $\phi(15) = 8$ (numbers 1, 2, 4, 7, 8, 11, 13, and 14 are relatively prime to 15)

In the example, note that for n = 5 and n = 7, $\phi(n)$ is n − 1 (Why?). For RSA encryption, we use the fact that when n is the product of two primes, we can evaluate the totient function directly.

Theorem (Euler totient function for a product of primes):

    If p and q are prime numbers, then $\phi(p * q) = (p − 1) * (q − 1)$.

Example: 15 = 3*5 where both 3 and 5 are prime numbers; $\phi(15) = \phi(3*5)$
          = (3 − 1)*(5 − 1) = 8

> If *p* and *q* are prime, $\phi(pq)$ = $\phi(p)*\phi(q)$ = $(p − 1)(q − 1)$.

An important application of the Euler totient function is Euler's Theorem, which involves using $\phi(n)$ as an exponent with modular arithmetic. The theorem is critical to the understanding of RSA encryption.

Euler's Theorem:

    Let n be a positive integer and let a be an integer such that gcd(a, n) = 1. Then $a^{\phi(n)} = 1 \pmod{n}$.

Example 28.2

Let us check Euler's Theorem for values $\phi(n)$ that have already been computed. For n = 5, 6, 7, and 15, we select a number a such that gcd(a, n) = 1. The "Power" column computes $a^{\phi(n)} \pmod{n}$.

Euler $\phi(n)$	Number a	gcd (a, n) = 1	Power $a^{\phi(n)}$ (mod n)
$\phi(5) = 4$	a = 3:	gcd(3, 5) = 1	$3^4 = 81 = 1 \pmod 5$
$\phi(6) = 2$	a = 5:	gcd(5, 6) = 1	$5^2 = 25 = 1 \pmod 6$
$\phi(7) = 6$	a = 2:	gcd(2, 7) = 1	$2^6 = 64 = 1 \pmod 7$
$\phi(15) = 8$	a = 4:	gcd(4, 15) = 1	$4^8 = 65536 = 1 \pmod{15}$

28.2 Secure Message Passing

Today, the Internet is an increasing popular vehicle for e-commerce. Its effectiveness relies on secure data transmission between the customer and the bank or retailer. The concept is relatively simple. View the customer as a client process and the retailer as a server process. To send a message, the client encrypts the information into numeric data and transmits it across the Internet. The retailer decrypts the data back to the original message. The techniques for encryption and decryption are called *cryptography*.

One of the most important cryptography techniques is RSA, associated with a scheme proposed by Rivest, Shamir, and Adleman in 1977. RSA data transmission uses a public key and a private (secret) key for encryption and decryption. These keys are used in an algorithm to modify the binary representation of data. When secure transmission is requested, the server generates separate public and private (secret) keys. The server retains the secret key but sends the public key to the client who uses it to encrypt a message. The term "public" is meaningful. The server makes no attempt to hide the value from an eavesdropper when sending the key. The client uses the public key even though it may be compromised.

> RSA data encryption uses a public key and a private key to encrypt and decrypt a message.

Transmission from the client begins with a message M. Assume that $E_{pk}(M)$ is a function that takes a message M and uses the public key pk to encrypt it to a numeric value C.

The result is a value represented by a stream of binary data. The server has a function D_{sk} (C) that uses the secret key sk to decrypt the binary value C. When combined, we have $D_{sk}(E_{pk}(M)) = M$ (Figure 28.1). The security in the transmission comes from the fact that the secret key is retained by the server. An eavesdropper would have to derive the secret key, only knowing the public key. As we will see, this is technically possible assuming that the values for the keys are small. In reality, the server uses enormous integers with several hundred digits. This makes the task of discovery of the secret key by "brute force" unrealistic both in terms of time and computing resources.

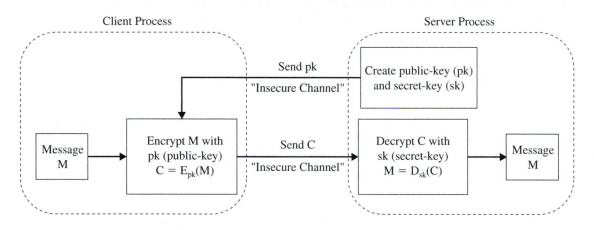

Figure 28.1 *Obtaining secure data transmission between client and server across an "insecure channel."*

Creating Keys for RSA Encryption

The server uses a series of steps to create both a public key and a private or secret key. At two stages, random integer values are used. We will illustrate the steps with a simple example and supply the number theory justification for each calculation.

Step 1: Begin by selecting (at random) two prime numbers p and q and form the product n = p * q.

Example: Let p = 5 and q = 11; the product n = 55.

Step 2: Let t be the value of the Euler totient function for a product of primes.

$$t = \phi(n) = (p - 1) * (q - 1).$$

Example: $t = \phi(55) = \phi(5*11) = (5 - 1)*(11 - 1) = 4*10 = 40$

Step 3: Select at random an encryption key e subject to the conditions e < t and gcd(e, t) = 1. Do this by looking at random integers e < t until one is relatively prime to t; that is gcd(e, t) = 1. The public key pk is the pair (e, n). It is the encrypting key for the client.

Example: Find e such that e < 55 and gcd(e, 40) = 1. A random choice is e = 3. The public key is pk = (3, 55).

Step 4: Compute the decryption key d, which is the inverse of e modulo t. Since gcd$(3, 40) = 1$, e $= 3$ has an inverse (mod t). Apply the extended Euclid's GCD Algorithm to express gcd(e,t) as a linear combination of e and t.

$$1 = gcd(e,t) = e * d + t * j \qquad \text{for some integers d and j}$$

The integer d is the inverse of e modulo t; that is, $1 = e * d$ (mod t). The secret key sk is the pair (d, n). It is the decrypting key for the server.

Example: With e $= 3$, the inverse of e (mod 40) is 27. Check: $1 = 3 * 27 = 81(\text{mod } 40) = 1$ (mod 40). The secret key is sk $= (27, 55)$.

Using Keys for RSA Encryption

The selection of keys starts with n $= p * q$ where p and q are prime numbers. While the actual keys are derived from the Euler totient function, they apply to all integers a in Z(n). This important fact is the conclusion of the RSA theory.

Theorem (RSA): Let n $= p * q$ where p and q are prime numbers and let e and d be encryption and decryption keys that is, $1 = e * d$ (mod t) where t $= (p - 1) * (q - 1)$. Then for any integer a in Z(n),

$$a = a^{e*d} \text{ (mod } n)$$

From the process that creates e and d, it is clear that the equality is true (mod t). The force of the RSA theorem is that exponentiation using e $*$ d modulo n is an identity operation for any integer a in Z(n).

Encrypting and decrypting a message occurs when exponentiation is split into two operations. Assume M in Z(n) is a numeric representation of a message.

$$M = M^{e*d} \text{ (mod } n) = (M^e \text{ (mod } n))^d \text{ (mod } n)$$

Starting with M, encryption uses the exponent e in the public key (e, n). The resulting value is

$$C = M^e \text{ (mod } n)$$

$C = M^e$ (nod n)

Decryption uses the exponent d in the secret key (d, n) with the value C. The result is the initial integer value M.

$$C^d \text{ (mod } n) = (M^e \text{ (mod } n))^d \text{ (mod } n) = M^{e*d} \text{ (mod } n) = M$$

C^d (mod n) = M

Let us illustrate the process for Z(55) with public key (3, 55) and secret key (27, 55). The client has a message, which is the one-character string "1". The message converts to an integer M using the numeric value for the character: M $= 49$ in Z(55). Encrypt M using the public key pk $= (3, 55)$. The resulting value is C $= M^3$ (mod 55) $= 49^3$ (mod 55).

$$C = 49^3 \text{ (mod } 55) = 117649 \text{ (mod } 55) = 4$$

Decrypt C with the secret key (27, 55). The resulting value is M $= 4^{27}$ (mod 55) $= 49$.

$$M = 4^{27} \text{ (mod } 55) = 18014398509481984 \text{ (mod } 55) = 49$$

How to Secure RSA Communication

Using the RSA algorithm securely requires using large primes p and q for n = p*q.

In the previous section, RSA encryption uses the prime numbers 5 and 11 with n = 5 * 11 = 55. This does not provide secure communications. We must assume that an eavesdropper has access to n and e in the public key. With even pencil and paper calculations, the eavesdropper could check various primes and obtain the factors p and q for n and thus the value t. Knowing e from the public key, he could derive d, making the private key no longer secret. What we need is larger prime numbers. Suppose we choose p = 1063 and q = 23899. The value for n = p * q is 25404637, which allows us to send longer messages with values from Z(25404637). It also increases the time required for an eavesdropper to discover the factors of n. Pencil and paper is out of the question. But, modern computers would require only few seconds to execute a brute-force check of factors and thus break the code for a message.

RSA encryption relies on a server choosing huge random integer values (hundreds of digits) for p and q and the product n = p * q. Determining the prime factors of large integers is very difficult. The best algorithms for factoring large integers have exponential running time based on the number of digits in n. To guarantee security, RSA encryption uses large enough integers so that discovering the secret key would take over 1000 years on a system that executes a million instructions per second.

28.3 Using Big Integers

The class BigInteger in the package *java.math* allows for the creation and manipulation of integers with an arbitrarily large number of digits. The class has methods such as add(), subtract(), and multiply() that carry out operations similar to the Java primitive integer operations. In addition, there are methods that implement modular arithmetic, evaluate the GCD, and generate prime numbers. The static constant ONE defines the BigInteger value 1. The class provides the tools for RSA encryption. In fact, encryption algorithms have motivated the design of the class. We describe some of the relevant BigInteger methods and constants.

BigInteger class:

```
static BigInteger ONE     //  The BigInteger constant one

// returns a BigInteger whose value is (this + val)
BigInteger add(BigInteger val)

// returns a BigInteger value which is the inverse of
// this (mod n)
BigInteger modInverse(BigInteger n)

// returns a BigInteger value this^exp (mod n)
BigInteger modPow(BigInteger exp, BigInteger n)

// returns a BigInteger whose value is (this * val)
BigInteger multiply(BigInteger val)

// returns a BigInteger whose value is (this - val)
BigInteger subtract(BigInteger val)
```

String and BigInteger Objects The String class and BigInteger class have methods that convert objects to and from byte arrays. The methods are critical to RSA encryption.

The String method getBytes() encodes a string into a sequence of bytes consisting of the numeric values for each character. A BigInteger constructor creates a large integer that chains together the bits from the array. The client uses the integer as the numeric representation of the message (string).

```
// convert a String to a BigInteger representation
String message;
BigInteger bigInt = new BigInteger(message.getBytes());
```

Going from a BigInteger to a String, we begin with the BigInteger method toByteArray() that returns a byte array containing the representation of the BigInteger. A String constructor creates a string whose characters correspond to the bytes in the array.

```
// convert a BigInteger to a String
BigInteger bigInt;
String message = new String(bigInt.toByteArray());
```

PROGRAM 28.1 BUILDING RSA KEYS

In the previous section, we manually developed the public and secret keys for RSA encryption using primes p = 5 and q = 11. An example encrypted and then decrypted the single character string "1" with numeric value 49 in Z(55). This program repeats the process using the BigInteger class. You will get a feel for how the methods work to create the keys.

Since this is a demonstration program, we will create BigInteger objects p and q with values 5 and 11 respectively. A constructor uses string arguments for the values.

```
import java.math.BigInteger;

public class Program28_1
{
    public static void main(String[] args)
    {
        BigInteger p, q, n;      // define Z(n)
        BigInteger t, e, d;      // used for keys

        // sent and received messages
        String clientMsg, serverMsg;

        // BigInteger variables for data encryption
        BigInteger strData, encryptedData, decryptedData;

        // create BigInteger objects p = 5, q = 11
        p = new BigInteger("5");
        q = new BigInteger("11");

        // compute n = p * q
        n = p.multiply(q);

        // use BigInteger operations to compute t = (p-1)*(q-1)
        t = p.subtract(BigInteger.ONE).multiply(
                        q.subtract(BigInteger.ONE));

        // create BigInteger e = 3 which is relatively prime to
```

```
                    // t; that is, (e,t)=1
                    e = new BigInteger("3");

                    // modInverse() returns d, the inverse of e (mod t);
                    // that is, e*d = 1 (mod t)
                    d = e.modInverse(t);

                    // convert the single character string "1" to a
                    // BigInteger
                    clientMsg = "1";
                    strData = new BigInteger(clientMsg.getBytes());
                    System.out.println("Client message: \"" + clientMsg +
                        "\"  Data value: " + strData);

                    // use modPow() to encrypt strData by raising it to
                    // power e mod n
                    encryptedData = strData.modPow(e,n);
                    System.out.println("Encrypted data: " + encryptedData);

                    // decrypt the encrypted data by raising it to
                    // power d mod n
                    decryptedData = encryptedData.modPow(d,n);
                    System.out.println("Decrypted data: " + decryptedData);

                    // convert BigInteger back to a string
                    serverMsg = new String(decryptedData.toByteArray());
                    System.out.println("Server message: \"" + serverMsg +
                        "\"");
            }
        }
```

```
Run:
   Client message: "1"  Data value: 49
   Encrypted data: 4
   Decrypted data: 49
   Server message: "1"
```

BigInteger Prime Numbers

The BigInteger class has methods that produce random prime numbers of arbitrary size. The static method probablePrime() returns positive BigInteger that is probably prime, with a specified bit length. The probability that a BigInteger returned by this method is prime is greater than or equal to $1-2^{-100}$ (approximately 0.99999999999999999999999999999921).

```
public static BigInteger probablePrime(int bitLength,
                                       Random rnd)
```

For instance, if the RSA communication uses 255 bit integers, then create large prime numbers p and q so their product will generate 255 bits.

```
BigInteger p = BigInteger.probablePrime(128, rnd),
           q = BigInteger.probablePrime(127, rnd);
```

After determining $n = p * q$ and $t = (p - 1) * (q - 1)$, it is necessary to get a prime number e such that $\gcd(e, t) = 1$. The method `randomModValue()` discovers such a prime number using a second `BigInteger` constructor that creates a randomly generated `BigInteger` prime number, which is uniformly distributed over the range 0 to $(2^{numBits} - 1)$, inclusive.

```
// returns a number relatively prime to t
public static BigInteger randomModValue(BigInteger t)
{
    BigInteger k = null;
    Random rnd = new Random();

    // generate a sequence of random numbers and exit
    // the loop when the number is relatively prime to t
    do
    {
        // random number k is in the range 0 to 2^64 -1
        k = new BigInteger(64,rnd);
    } while(!t.gcd(k).equals(BigInteger.ONE));
    return k;
}
```

28.4 RSA Client and Server

We illustrate the sending and receiving of secure messages using the client–server pattern. Imagine that the server is a bank transaction program and the client is a customer running an on-line GUI application. We present the steps that start with the customer requesting secure transmission and end with the server decrypting a message. The steps are illustrated in Figure 28.2. The customer (client) first requests that the server launch a process that will use RSA secure transmission (1). The server generates public and secret keys and sends the public key to the client (2). The client inputs a message and sends it as an encrypted `BigInteger` using the public key (3). The server receives the transmission and decrypts the `BigInteger` value back to the original message (4).

In the software supplement, you can find RSAServer and RSAClient programs that use encryption for client–server message handling.

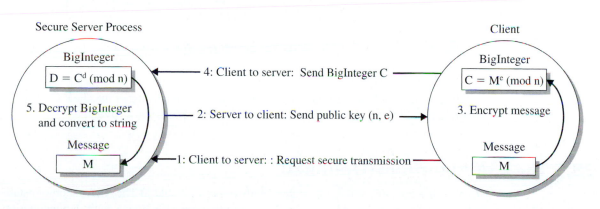

Figure 28.2 *RSA client-server pattern.*

For our application, the client program and the server program share an Internet connection using a Java socket. The client application is a frame with a "Request Secure Connection" button on the south end and a panel with a label and a text field for the message in the center. The button event simply requests a connection with the server and sets in motion a handshaking protocol between the server and the client. Each party opens input and output streams, which connect through the socket.

The remainder of the example implements the series of steps outlined in Figure 28.2. The client enters a message in the text field and presses the Enter key, which launches a message-passing event. On the server side, we see the output of the `BigInteger` values for the secret key (e, n) and the public key (d, n). You can see the encrypted data value from the client and the resulting decrypted message. Figure 28.3 is a snapshot of the client–server interaction.

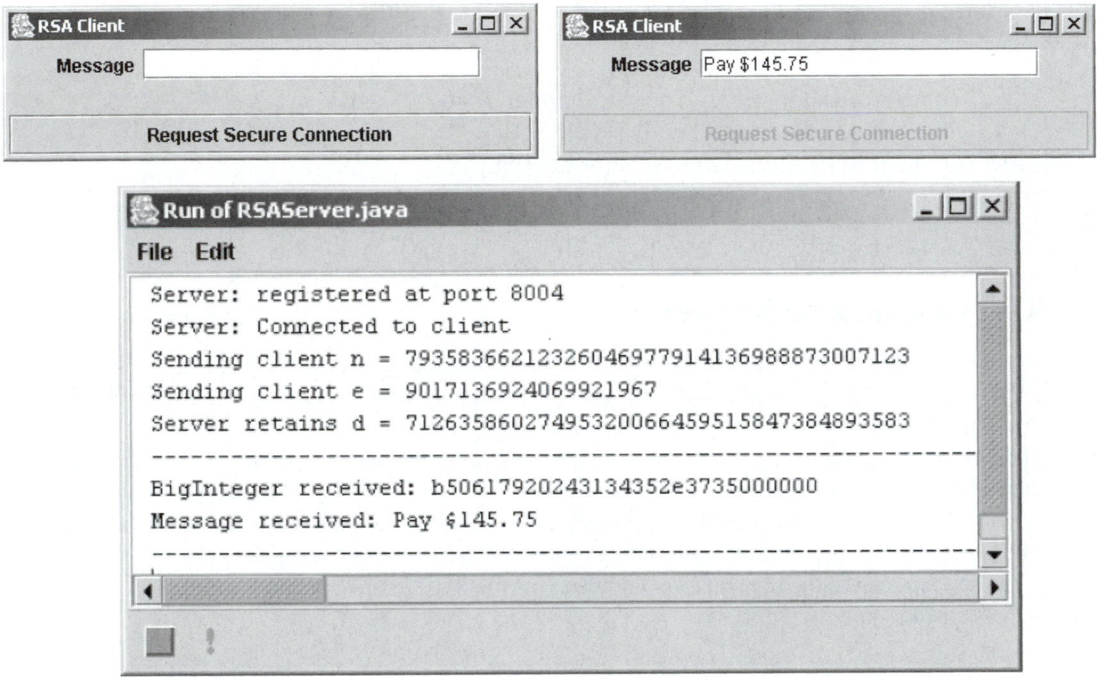

Figure 28.3 *Snapshot of the running applications RSAServer and RSAClient.*

In Chapter 28 of the software supplement, you can find a listing of the client GUI application in *RSAClient.java* and the server program in *RSAServer.java*.

28.5 The RSA Algorithm (Optional)

RSA secure transmission relies on keys with values e, d, and n. The RSA theorem establishes that the encrypting key e and the decrypting key d combine with exponentiation modulo n as an identity operator for integers in Z(n). In this section, we look at implementations for Euclid's GCD Algorithms that determine e and d. An explanation of why Euclid's Algorithm works is also included. The section concludes by providing a proof for the RSA theorem.

Implementing Euclid's GCD Algorithms

Euclid's GCD Algorithm computes gcd(a, b) for nonnegative integers a and b where both are not 0. The algorithm is a recursive process that relies on the fact that gcd(a, b)= gcd(b, a%b). This is the basis for the recursive step. The stopping condition occurs when b = 0 and gcd(a, 0) = a.

The recursive method gcd() implements Euclid's Algorithm. By using the % operator, the method descends recursively to a stopping condition that evaluates gcd(a, 0) with return value a.

Greatest common divisor gcd():

```
// compute the greatest common divisor of the nonnegative
// integers a and b where both a and b cannot be 0
int gcd(int a, int b)
   {
      if (b == 0)
         return a;                 // a divides a and 0
      else
         return gcd(b, a%b);    // recursive step
   }
```

Why gcd() Works   The basis of Euclid's Algorithm is the fact that gcd(a, b) = *gcd* (b, a%b). To see why this is true, verify that the two forms of the gcd function have the same value. Assume s = gcd(a, b) and t = gcd(b, a%b). The task is to show that s = t. We do this in two steps by showing that s ≤ t and that t ≤ s. Recall that % is an operator that combines with the operator "/" for integer division. When dividing a by b, the value a%b is the remainder r and a/b is the quotient q. The values q and r enable us to define a in terms of b.

a = b*q + r

Step 1 (s ≤ t):

By definition s divides both a and b and so there are integers i and j such that

$$\frac{a}{s} = i \qquad \frac{b}{s} = j$$

Since s divides b, we only need to show that s divides a%b. We can then conclude that s <= t because s divides both b and a%b and t is the largest integer that satisfies this condition.

With integer division, a = b*q + r where q = a/b and r = a % b. Hence, a % b = r = a − b*q. Divide each term by s and substitute the values for i and j.

$$\frac{a - b*q}{s} = \frac{a}{s} - \frac{b*q}{s} = i - j*q \qquad // \text{ s divides a \% b}$$

Step 2 (t ≤ s):

By definition, t divides both b and a%b = r and so there are integers k and l such that

$$\frac{b}{t} = k \qquad \frac{r}{t} = l$$

Similar to step 1, we will show that t divides a. Since t is then a divisor of both a and b, $t <= s$ because s is the largest divisor of both a and b.

$$\frac{a}{t} = \frac{b*q + r}{t} = \frac{b*q}{t} + \frac{r}{t} = k*q + l \qquad \text{// t divides a}$$

Extended Euclid's Algorithm An extension of Euclid's GCD Algorithm carries out a different task. Rather than using a chain of recursive calls to evaluate gcd(a, b), the extension uses the same chain to represent gcd(a, b) as a linear combination of a and b; that is, the algorithm determines integers i and j such that

gcd(a, b) = a * i + b * j   for some integers i and j

For instance, Euclid's Algorithm determines that $gcd(54, 30) = 6$. The extended version of the algorithm finds integers i and j such that 6 is a linear combination of 54 and 30. One such combination uses $i = -1$ and $j = 2$.

6 = 54 * -1 + 30 * 2

The extended Euclid's Algorithm defines two static integer variables i and j. At the stopping condition gcd(a, 0), the extended algorithm initializes the variables. In retracing each recursive step, the variables are updated to create a linear combination for gcd(b, a%b) in terms of b and a%b. The recursive step updates values for i and j in terms of a and b using the fact that $gcd(a, b) = gcd(b, a\%b)$.

At the stopping condition $gcd(a, 0) = a$. Let the initial values for i and j be 1 and 0 respectively. The linear combination is

gcd(a,0) = a = a*1 + b*0   // assign i = 1 and j = 0

For the update process in the recursive step, assume that $i = x$ and $j = y$ are values that define gcd(b, a%b) as a linear combination involving b and a%b.

gcd(b, a%b) = b*x + a%b * y
           = b*x + r*y   // let r = a%b

The task is to find new values for i and j in terms of the old values x and y that define gcd(a,b) as a linear combination using a and b.

gcd(a,b) = gcd(b, a%b)
       = b*x + r*y
       = b*x + (a - b*q)*y   // substitute r = a - b*q
       = b*x + a*y - b*q*y
       = a*y + b*(x - q*y)   // gather terms; factor out b

The equation defines gcd(a,b) as a linear combination of a and b with $i = y$ and $j = x - q*y$. These are assigned as new values for i and j before returning from each recursive call. The final return provides values i and j in terms of the initial arguments a and b,

gcd(a,b) = a*i + b*j

Let us trace the algorithm for $a = 54$ and $b = 30$. The figure identifies updates for integers i and j beginning with the stopping condition and proceeding through the series of return calls in the recursive step.

Compute gcd(a, b) (Recursive descent)
   (with recursive descent)
gcd(a, b) -> gcd(b, a%b) -> gcd(a, 0)

Step 1:   gcd(54, 30) = gcd(30,54%30)
                   = gcd(30,24)

Step 2:   gcd(30, 24) = gcd(24,30%24)
                   = gcd(24,6)

Step 3:   gcd(24, 6) = gcd(6,24%6)
                   = gcd(6,0)

Step 4:   gcd(6, 0)   = 6

Determine $gcd(a, b) = a*i + b*j$
   (with recursive backtracking)
gcd(a, 0) -> gcd(b, a%b) -> gcd(a, b)

x = 1, y = -1
i = -1, j = 1-54/30*-1 = 2
gcd(54, 30) = 54*(-1) + 30(2)

x = 0, y = 1
i = 1, j = 0-30/24*1 = -1
gcd(30, 24) = 30*1 + 24*(-1)

x = 1, y = 0
i = 0, j = 1-24/6*0 = 1
gcd(24, 6) = 24*0 + 6*1

i = 1, j = 0
gcd(6, 0) = 6 = 6*1 + 0*0

Using both the classical and extended Euclid's method, we have the $gcd(54, 30) = 6$ as an integer and the $gcd(54, 30) = 54*(-1) + 30*2$ as a linear combination.

extGCD():

```
// variables defined outside the scope of extGCD()
static int i;
static int j;
        ...
// computes values i, j such that gcd(a,b) = a * i + b * j
public static void extGCD(int a, int b)
{
    int x, y;

    // stopping condition corresponds to gcd(a,0) = a
    // the linear combination is gcd(a,b) = a * 1 + b * 0
    // assign i = 1 and j = 0
    if (b == 0)
    {
        i = 1;
        j = 0;
    }
    else
    {
        extGCD(b,a%b);
```

```
// gcd(b, a%b) = b*i + (a%b)*j; recompute i and j
// so gcd(a, b) = a*i + b*j

// save i and j in x and y
x = i;
y = j;

// update i and j in terms of x, y, and a/b
i = y;
j = x - (a/b) * y;
    }
}
```

The RSA Theorem

The RSA theorem is the basis for RSA encryption.

Theorem (RSA): Let n = p*q where p and q are prime numbers. Let e be relatively prime modulo $\phi(n)$ and let d be the multiplicative inverse of e modulo $\phi(n)$. Then for any integer a such that $0 < a < n$,

$a = a^{e*d} \pmod{n}$

As background, recall that if t = $\phi(n)$, the Euler theorem states that for any integer k that is relatively prime to n, $k^{\phi(n)} = k^t = 1 \pmod{n}$. Since e is an integer that is relatively prime to t, gcd(e, t) = 1 can be written as a linear combination with integers d and i; in other words,

$$1 = \gcd(e, t) = e * d + t * i \text{ for some integer } i$$

or

$$e * d = t * k + 1, \text{ where } k = -i$$

It follows that the value d is the inverse of e modulo t. In other words, e*d = 1 (mod t).

Proof: The problem $a^{ed} \pmod{n} = a$ breaks up into two cases depending on whether a is divisible by one of the primes p or q.

Case 1: a in Z(n) is not divisible by either p or q.

Since the integers p and q are prime, gcd(a, n) = 1, and Euler's Theorem applies.

$$a^{\phi(n)} = a^t = 1 \pmod{n}$$

Raise both sides of the equation to the power i and derive the fact that $a^{t*k} = 1 \pmod{n}$.

$$a^{t*k} \pmod{n} = (a^t \pmod{n})^k \pmod{n} = 1^k \pmod{n} = 1 \pmod{n}$$

The result follows from a series of computations.

$$a^{e*d} = a^{t*k+1} \pmod{n}$$
$$= a * a^{t*k} \pmod{n}$$
$$= a * (a^{t*k} \pmod{n}) \pmod{n}$$
$$= a * 1 \pmod{n}$$
$$= a$$

Case 2: a in Z(n) is divisible by either p or q.

Note that a cannot be divisible by both p and q because in that case a $\geq$ p*q = n. Therefore, we may assume a is divisible by p and a is not divisible by q. Thus, a = p * h for some h and gcd(a, q) = 1. Recall that the task is to show that

$$a^{e*d} = a^{k*t+1} \ (mod \ n) = a \ (mod \ n)$$

Begin by applying the Euler's theorem to a (mod q). Since gcd(a, q) = 1,

$$a^{\phi(q)} = 1 \ (mod \ q)$$

Recall that e*d = t*k + 1. Carry out a series of operations that begin with raising both sides of the equality to the power k*ϕ (p).

$(a^{\phi(q)})^{k*\phi(p)} = 1^{k*\phi(p)} \ (mod \ q)$

$a^{k*\phi(p)*\phi(q)} = 1 \ (mod \ q)$ // rearrange terms and evaluate
                               // $1^{k*\phi(p)}$

a^{t*k} = 1 (mod q)   // $\phi(p)*\phi(q) = \phi(n) = t$

a^{t*k} = 1 + q*i for some integer i   // remainder after dividing a^{t*k} by
                                            // q is 1

Multiply both sides of the equation by a and use the fact that a = h * p.

$a *a^{t*k} = a *(1 + q*i)$

$a^{t*k+1} = a * 1 + a * q * i$ // rearrange terms

$a^{t*k+1} = a + h * p * q * i$ // substitute a = h * p

$a^{t*k+1} = a + n * (h * i)$ // n = p * q

$a^{t*k+1} = a \ (mod \ n)$ // a is the remainder when dividing a^{t*k+1} by n

We conclude that $a^{t*k+1} = a^{e*d} = a \ (mod \ n)$.

Chapter Summary

- Number theory has many uses in computing. In particular, number theory is the basis for the RSA encryption algorithm that secures Internet communication. The first two sections of the chapter discuss basic results from number theory and show how to apply them to encryption. Section 28.1 develops recursive algorithms for the computation of the greatest common divisor (GCD) and the extended GCD. The section also develops modular arithmetic in the set Z(n), including a discussion of the Euler totient function, $\phi(n)$. The totient function is a critical component of the RSA encryption algorithm that is presented in Section 28.2.

- For secure transmission, the algorithm must be applied to very large integers; in Section 28.3, we discuss the BigInteger class. This class implements modular operations for very large integers and contains methods for generation of the large prime numbers required by the RSA algorithm.

- Section 28.4 discusses the client–server pattern. The implementation of the RSA algorithm is an excellent example of this pattern. The section then develops the RSA algorithm.

The number theoretic tools discussed in Sections 28.1 and 28.2 led to the development of the public and private keys that are used to encrypt and decrypt messages.

- Section 28.5 looks at implementations for Euclid's GCD Algorithms that are involved in determining the public and private keys for RSA encryption. An explanation of why Euclid's Algorithm works is also included. The section concludes by providing a proof for the RSA theorem.

Written Exercises

1. Assume $a = b$ (mod n) and c is any integer. Prove each of the following properties of modular arithmetic.

   $a + c = b + c$ (mod n)
   $a * c = b * c$ (mod n)
   $a^c = b^c$ (mod n)

2. Prove each of the following properties of modular arithmetic.

   a(mod n) $+ b$(mod n) $= (a + b)$ (mod n)
   a(mod n) $* b$(mod n) $= (a*b)$ (mod n)
   $(a$(mod n)$)^e = (a^e)$ (mod n)

3. Trace the execution of the recursive Euclid's Algorithm gcd() for

   (a) gcd(136, 2415)   (b) gcd(36, 462)

4. Determine RSA public and secret key parameters n, e, and d for the two primes $p = 19$ and $q = 23$. Encrypt the message containing the ASCII character 'A' with integer value 65, decrypt the result, and verify that the RSA algorithm works for this data.

5. Prove Fermat's Little Theorem.

   Fermat's Little Theorem:

   Let p be a prime and x be an integer such that x (mod p) $\neq$ 0. Then,

   $x^{p-1} = 1$ (mod p)

6. (a) Assume $n = 5$. Find all the numbers in the range 1 through 4 that are relatively prime to 4. For each number, verify Euler's Theorem.

   (b) Repeat part (a) with $n = 12$.

7. Propose an algorithm computing a^e (mod n) that keeps the calculations working with smaller numbers and thus reduces the time of the computation at each step.

8. (a) Assume d and n are relatively prime. Show that application of the computation

   $i = (i + d)$ (mod n)

   for $i = 0, 1, 2, \ldots, n-1$ generates all the numbers in Z(n).

   (b) The integers $d = 3$ and $n = 93$ are not relatively prime. Show that application of the computation

   $i = (i+3)$ (mod 93)

   generates only one-third of the values in Z(93).

9. What do you think is the running time of Euclid's Algorithm? You do not have to perform a mathematical analysis.

10. Verify using the extended Euclid's Algorithm that a number k in Z(n) has a multiplicative inverse if and only if k and n are relatively prime $(\gcd(k, n) = 1)$; that is, there exists an integer m in Z(n) such that k*m = 1 (mod n).

Programming Exercises

11. Implement the methods `square()` and `power()` that return `BigInteger` objects. Check your work by running the accompanying program.

```java
import java.math.*;

public class BigIntegerTest
{
    // Calculate the square of a number
    public static BigInteger square ( int number )
    { . . . }

    // Calculate the power of a number
    public static BigInteger power (int num1, int num2)
    { . . . }

    public static void main (String[] args)
    {
        int n = Integer.MAX_VALUE;
        System.out.println("n is " + n + "  Square is " +
        square(n));
        System.out.println("Power(" + n + ", " + 2 + ") is "
            + power(n, 2));

        n = 10;
        System.out.println("n is " + n + "  Square is " +
            square(n));

        int m = 6;
        System.out.println("Power(" + n + ", " + m + ") is "
            + power(n, m));
    }
}
```

12. Implement `extGCD_I()` as an iterative version of the extended Euclid's Algorithm. Assume integers i and j are declared as static variables.

```java
static int i, j;
    . . .
public static extGCD_I(int a, int b)
{ . . . }
```

Write a program that calls extGCD_I() for a series of four pairs (a, b) where one pair is the example (54, 30) in Section 28.1 and another pair is (189, 55).

13. You will use the BigInteger class for this exercise. Read in three integers, a, b, and n and output gcd(a, b). If a and n are relatively prime, output the inverse of a (mod n), and conclude by displaying a^{15} (mod n). Run the program for each of the following data sets.

$$a = 7, \ b = 3, \ n = 12 \qquad a = 4, \ b = 18, \ n = 7$$
$$a = 5, \ b = 6, \ n = 17$$

Programming Project

14. A number is called *perfect* if it is equal to the sum of all of its proper divisors, that is, all divisors other than the number itself. For instance, 6 and 28 are perfect numbers.

$$6 = 1 + 2 + 3$$
$$28 = 1 + 2 + 4 + 7 + 14$$

Over 2300 years ago, Euclid proved that if $2^k - 1$ is a prime number, then $2^{k-1}*(2^k - 1)$ is an even perfect number. A few hundred years ago, Euler proved that every even perfect number has this form. It is still unknown if there are any odd perfect numbers (but if there are, they are large and have many prime factors).

Write a program that displays the first 10 perfect numbers. Use BigInteger objects to store values 2^{k-1} for k = 2, 3, 4, and so forth. For each value $m = 2^{k-1}$, use the BigInteger method isProbablePrime(int certainty) to check whether $2*m - 1$ is a prime. If so, apply Euclid's result and display

```
m*(2*m - 1)
```

as the next perfect number.

Implement the method getDivisors() that takes a BigInteger argument and returns an ArrayList with the divisors of the number.

```
public static ArrayList<Integer> getDivisors(BigInteger b)
{ ... }
```

For the first three perfect numbers, call the method getDivisors() and output the elements in the ArrayList.

The output of your program should be

```
# 1 is 6   Divisors = [1, 2, 3]
# 2 is 28   Divisors = [1, 2, 3, 7, 14]
# 3 is 496   Divisors = [1, 2, 4, 8, 16, 31, 62, 124, 248]
# 4 is 8128   Divisors = [1, 2, 4, 8, 16, 32, 64, 127, 254, 508,
                          1016, 2032, 4064]
# 5 is 33550336
# 6 is 8589869056
# 7 is 137438691328
# 8 is 2305843008139952128
# 9 is 2658455991569831744654692615953842176
# 10 is 191561942608236107294793378084303638130997321548169216
```

Chapter 29

ASSORTED ALGORITHMS

CONTENTS

29.1 COMBINATORICS
Building Combinations
Finding All Subsets
Listing Permutations
The Traveling Salesman Problem
Permutations and the TSP
29.2 DYNAMIC PROGRAMMING
Top-Down Dynamic Programming
Combinations with Dynamic
Programming

Bottom-Up Dynamic Programming
Knapsack Problem
The Knapsack Class
29.3 BACKTRACKING: THE 8-QUEENS
PROBLEM
Problem Analysis
Program Design
Displaying a ChessBoard

In this book, we have used recursion for sorting arrays and traversing trees. Now in the last chapter, we look at a variety of design strategies for recursive algorithms. We choose applications that exploit different collection types.

Recursion finds many interesting applications in *combinatorics*, which is the branch of mathematics concerned with the enumeration of various sets of objects. Section 29.1 will introduce four such problems. A recursive computation evaluates C(n, k), which is the number of different combinations of n items taken k at a time. The same strategy can be used to list all 2^n subsets of a set having n elements. The set of subsets is called the *power set*. Combinations look at the different grouping of element from a collection. Permutations distinguish the different ordering of the elements. We explore techniques that develop a listing of all n! permutations of the numbers 1 ... n. As an example, if n = 3, the 3! = 6 permutations are 123, 132, 213, 231, 312, and 321. The section concludes with an introduction to the Traveling Salesman Problem, which is one of the most famous problems in computer science.

In Chapter 6, we discussed the Fibonacci numbers, which can be generated by a recursive method. In Section 29.2, we show that, although the recursive

solution has the structure of a divide-and-conquer algorithm, it fails to partition the problem into independent subproblems and results in exponential running time. A technique called *top-down dynamic programming* can often improve the performance of a recursive method by eliminating redundant calculations. We illustrate the technique with the Fibonacci numbers and with the problem of generating the combination of n items taken k at a time. An alternative strategy, called *bottom-up dynamic programming*, performs a computation starting at the lowest level and using previously computed values at each step to compute the current value. We illustrate this technique with the statistical problem of determining combinations and by solving the famous 0/1 knapsack problem.

A number of very interesting algorithms use a recursive technique called *backtracking*. The algorithm uses progressive steps that move forward toward a final solution. At each step, the algorithm attempts to create a partial solution that appears to be consistent with the requirements of the final solution. If no such solution is available at the step, the algorithm backtracks one or more steps to the last consistent partial solution. At times, backtracking entails one step forward and n steps backward. The approach occurs frequently in operations research models, game theory, and the study of graphs. In Section 29.3, we illustrate back-tracking by solving the famous 8-Queens problem.

For this chapter, you can find the methods that implement the algorithms in Chapter 29 of the software supplement.

29.1 Combinatorics

Recursion finds many interesting applications in combinatorics, which is the branch of mathematics concerned with the enumeration of various sets of objects. In this section, we discuss algorithms for two such applications. The first algorithm provides a recursive computation of C(n, k), which is the number of different combinations of n items taken k at a time. The second algorithm lists all 2^n subsets of a set having n elements. The set of subsets is called the *power set*. For instance, if set $S = \{A, B\}$, the power set has $2^2 = 4$ elements, namely, the subsets $\{\}, \{A\}, \{B\}$, and $\{A, B\}$. A third algorithm develops a listing of all n! permutations of the numbers 1 ... n. As an example, if n = 3, the 3! = 6 permutations are 123, 132, 213, 231, 312, and 321. We conclude the section by using permutations to develop a brute-force solution to the famous Traveling Salesman Problem. The static methods that implement the algorithms are found in the Combinatorics class.

Building Combinations

The function C(n, k) evaluates the number of different combinations of n items taken k at a time. Mathematics provides a definition of the function in terms of factorials.

Recursive algorithms are used in the study of combinatorics.

$$C(n, k) = \frac{n!}{(n - k)!k!} \qquad n, k \geq 0 \text{ and } n \geq k$$

Computing C(n, k) directly from the equation can run into overflow problems because factorials grow quickly as n gets large. With a 32-bit integer, 13! is greater than 2^{32}. A recursive definition for C(n, k) allows for larger values of n.

C(n, k) can be computed in a recursive function.

To explore the design of a recursive definition, consider a sample case with n = 5 and k = 3. The numbers are small, so we can anticipate the solution by organizing a grid to display an exhaustive list of the C(5, 3) = 10 different combinations. Assume the items are A, B, C, D, and E. The combinations are as follows.

$$\{A, B, C\} \quad \{A, B, D\} \quad \{A, B, E\} \quad \{A, C, D\} \quad \{A, C, E\}$$
$$\{A, D, E\} \quad \{B, C, D\} \quad \{B, C, E\} \quad \{B, D, E\} \quad \{C, D, E\}$$

A recursive approach uses a divide-and-conquer strategy that splits the problem into two simpler subproblems. The design begins by removing an item, say item A, from the collection. This leaves a smaller collection with n − 1 items. In the example, there are four items B, C, D, and E.

Subproblem 1: Form all possible combinations from the four items {B, C, D, E} taken three at a time. While these combinations do not include item A, they are, nevertheless, part of the C(5, 3) combinations.

List 1:   (B, C, D)   (B, C, E)   (B, D, E)   (C, D, E)

Subproblem 2: Form all possible combinations from the four items {B, C, D, E} taken
two at a time.

List 2:   (B, C)   (B, D)   (B, E)   (C, D)   (C, E)   (D, E)

Adding item A to each of the distinct two-element combinations in List
2 creates a new list of distinct three-element combinations.

List 2 (with A):   (A, B, C)   (A, B, D)   (A, B, E)   (A, C, D)   (A, C, E)   (A, D, E)

The number of combinations in List 1 is $C(4, 3) = 4$, and the number of combinations in
List 2 (with A) is $C(4, 2) = 6$. The total for the two lists is 10 and represents all of the different $C(5, 3)$ combinations. The fact that the two lists define all of the combinations is an exercise.

In general, we can evaluate C(n, k) by adding the total number in List 1 $(C(n - 1, k))$
and the total number in List 2 $(C(n - 1, k - 1))$. This defines the recursive step for C(n, k).

```
C(n,k) = C(n-1,k) + C(n-1,k-1);                   // recursive step
```

The stopping conditions consist of several cases that can be directly evaluated. If $k = n$,
there is only one possible combination, namely the one with all n items. Having $k = 1$ is
the other extreme, and each of the n singleton collections consisting of one of the n items is
a valid combination. We allow $k = 0$ and define C(n, 0) to be 1. By combining the stopping
conditions and the recursive step, we can give a recursive definition for C(n, k).

$$
C(n, k) = \begin{cases}
1 & k = 0 \text{ or } k = n \\
n, & k = 1 \\
C(n - 1, k) + C(n - 1, k - 1), & \text{recursive step}
\end{cases}
$$

The method comm(n,k) implements the function C(n, k). You are familiar with the
process of translating a recursive definition to code. Use if-else statements that identify stopping conditions and the recursive step. In this case, the statements must test three separate
stopping conditions.

comm():

```
public static int comm(int n, int k)
{
    if (n == k || k == 0)                      // stopping condition
        return 1;
    else if (k == 1)
        return n;                              // stopping condition
    else
        return comm(n-1,k) + comm(n-1,k-1);    // recursive step
}
```

Finding All Subsets

For a set S, we say that A is a subset of S if all of the elements of A are also elements of S.
The empty set is a subset of S. The set of all subsets of a set S is called the *power set* of S. By

> The power set of
> an n-element set
> S is the set of all
> subsets of S. The
> size of the power
> set is 2^n.

mathematical induction, it can be shown that if S has n elements, then the number of elements in its power set is 2^n. For instance, assume S = $\{1, 2, 3\}$. The power set has $2^3 = 8$ subsets

$$\{\}\{1\}\{2\}\{3\}\{1, 2\}\{1, 3\}\{2, 3\}\{1, 2, 3\}$$

where the notation "$\{\}$" represents the empty set.

To create the power set, we develop a recursive algorithm that builds the subsets from the bottom up. It uses a chain of recursive calls to isolate, one by one, the individual elements in a set. A return from a recursive call uses the isolated element to add clusters of subsets to the power set. The last return value is the power set. Start with set S of size n. Remove one of the elements, x, from the set to create a new set S′ with n – 1 elements. The new set, S′, has the form S′ = S – $\{x\}$. The power set of S′ contains 2^{n-1} subsets. Adding the element x back into each of these subsets creates a second collection of 2^{n-1} subsets. The power set of S is the union of the power set for S′ and the elements in the second collection. The "recursive" part of the algorithm involves creating the power set of S′. Just repeat the process by removing an element from S′ to form (S′)′, which is a set with n – 2 elements. The stopping condition occurs when removing an element leaves the empty set $\{\}$. The power set of the empty set is the one-element set whose only member is $\{\}$.

$$\{A, B, C\} \xrightarrow{} \{B, C\} \xrightarrow{} \{C\} \xrightarrow{} \{ \} \quad \text{stop!}$$

remove A	remove B	remove C
(step 1)	(step 2)	(step 3)

Let us trace the recursive process for set S = $\{1, 2, 3\}$. A series of recursive calls removes successive elements from set S.

Move back through the recursive chain, in reverse order. At each step, build a new power set by taking the union of the existing power set and the sets created by adding the removed element.

Stopping Condition: Begin to create the power set by adding the empty set $\{\}$.

```
Set S = {}
Power Set: { {} }
```

Step 3:   C is the removed element. Create a new subset by adding C to the empty set. The power set now contains the empty set and the singleton set with element C.

```
Set S = {C}
Power Set: { {}, {C} }
```

Step 2:   B is the removed element. Using the existing power set, create a cluster of two more subsets that include B.

```
Set S = {B,C}
Power Set: { {}, {C}, {B}, {B, C} }
```

Step 1:   A is the removed element. Using the existing power set, create a cluster of four more subsets that include A.

```
Set S = {A,B,C}
Power Set: { { }, {C}, {B}, {B, C}, {A}, {A, C},
             {A, B}, {A, B, C} }
```

In the exercises, you are asked to implement the recursive method `powerSet()` that returns a set representing the power set for any set S.

```
public static Set powerSet(Set s)
{ ... }
```

Listing Permutations

A *permutation* on n items (1, 2, . . . , n) is an ordered arrangement of the items. For n = 3, the ordering (1, 3, 2) is a permutation that is different from the orderings (3, 2, 1), (1, 2, 3), and so forth. A classical combinatorics result determines that the number of permutations is n!, a fact that is intuitively clear by looking at the individual positions in a permutation. For position 1, there are n choices from the list of n items. For position 2, there are n − 1 choices, because one item already occupies position 1. The number of choices decreases by one as we move down the position list. The total number of permutations is the product of the number of choices in each position.

```
numPermutations(n) = n * n − 1 * n − 2 * ... * 2 * 1 = n!
```

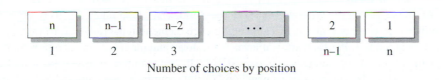

Number of choices by position

An interesting recursive algorithm derives an actual listing of the n! permutations assuming n ≥ 1. For demonstration purposes, we derive a hierarchy tree that displays the 6 (3!) permutations on three items. Level 0 in the tree is the list of items. Level 1 has three separate lists that derive from the list at level 0 by exchanging each element with the one in the first position. The first list is simply a copy. The other two lists represent the permutation that exchanges the elements in positions 1 and 2 with the element in position 0. Each list in level 1 produces a pair of lists at level 2 representing the permutation of elements in positions 1 and 2. The lists at level 2 are the distinct permutations.

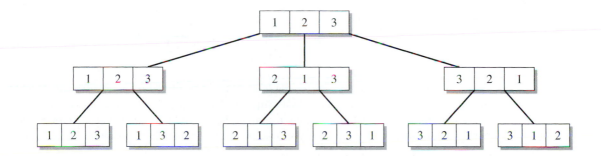

An algorithm for listing all of the permutations follows the building of levels in the tree. Each permutation is an n-element array. Start with the original array, which serves as the root of the hierarchy tree. Subsequent levels in the tree correspond to the permutation of elements at index 0, index 1, and so forth. The last level corresponds to the permutation of the elements at index n − 2. The process combines both iterative and recursive steps.

The recursive algorithm for *n*! traverses a recursion tree. Permutations are leaf nodes at the bottom level.

Index 0:

Starting with the initial array, the permute() algorithm uses a loop to create n − 1 copies of the array by exchanging each element in the index range [1, n) with the element at index 0. The initial array and the copies define all of the arrays that have distinct values at index 0 and correspond to the elements at level 1 in the tree.

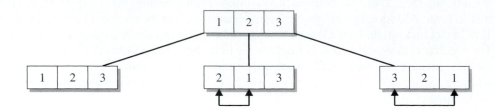

Index 1:

For each of the n arrays with distinct elements at index 0, a recursive call is made to permute() with the array and index 1 (next index). A loop takes the array argument and creates n − 2 new arrays by exchanging each element in the range [2, n) with the element at index 1. For each array at level 1, the array and the n − 2 copies represent n − 1 distinct ordering of elements at indices 0 to 1. In our example, consider the array [2, 1, 3] at level 1. This step creates a new copy of the array by exchanging the only element in the range [2, 3), namely 3 with 1, which is the element at index 1. The process identifies two arrays at level 2. For each array, a recursive call with index 2 reaches a stopping condition (index == n − 1) and the elements in the array are displayed as a permutation.

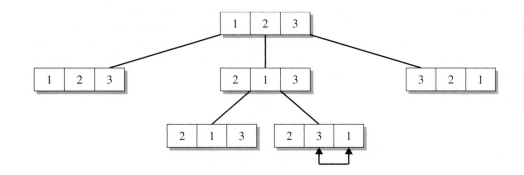

A recursive call is made for the each array and for all of the copies that are created during the loop (iterative process). As a result, permutations are created and then displayed by following the different paths in the tree from left to right. The array at the end of each path is a permutation. The following shows the order in which each permutation is created.

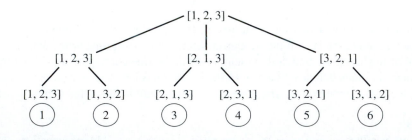

The permute() Method   The recursive permutation algorithm is implemented in the permute() method. The parameter list includes an n-element array of Object elements and an index that will be used in exchanges to create new arrays. The method produces all possible orderings of the elements in the array. The stopping condition occurs when the index is n - 1 and defines a permutation. The recursive step creates a new copy of the array and employs a loop to create additional copies by exchanging each element in the index range [index+1, n) with the element at index. After each copy, the recursive step passes the array and index+1 to permute(). In the following code, the stopping condition displays the permutation. When the permutation algorithm is used in applications, the stopping condition performs a task specific to the application. Simply replace the output statement with code for the task.

The method permutation() is a simple driver that takes only the array of n items as an argument. The driver launches the recursive process by calling permute() with index 0.

permutation():

```
public static void permutation(Object[] permList)
{
    permute(permList, 0);
}
```

permute():

```
private static void permute(Object[] permList, int index)
{
    int i, j, arrSize = permList.length;
    Object temp;

    if (index == arrSize-1)
        // display the permutation
        System.out.println(Arrays.toString(permList));
    else
    {
        Object[] newPermList = new Object[arrSize];
        for (i = 0; i < arrSize; i++)
            newPermList[i] = permList[i];

        // find all permutations over the range [index, arrSize)
        permute(newPermList, index+1);
        // exchange permList[index] with permList[i]
        // for i=index+1 to the end of the array and
        // find all permutations
        for (i=index+1; i < arrSize; i++)
        {
            temp = permList[i];
            permList[i] = permList[index];
            permList[index] = temp;
```

```
            newPermList = new Object[arrSize];
            for (j = 0; j < arrSize; j++)
                newPermList[j] = permList[j];

            permute(newPermList, index+1);
        }
    }
}
```

Example 29.1

Let us illustrate the method permutation() for the Integer items [1, 2, 3].

```
// create an array of 3 Integer objects
Integer[] itemArr = {1, 2, 3};

Combinatorics.permutation(itemArr);
```

> Output:
>   [1,2,3]   [1,3,2]   [2,1,3]   [2,3,1]   [3,2,1]   [3,1,2]

The Traveling Salesman Problem

The Traveling Salesman Problem (TSP) describes an interesting and challenging combinatorics problem that can be stated very simply. A salesman is responsible for n cities in a territory that has paths that connect any two cities. The problem is to identify a tour (a simple cycle) that has the salesman visit each city just once and finish up where he started. The order of visits should minimize the total distance traveled. In Figure 29.1, we use a complete undirected graph to represent a salesman responsible for five cities.

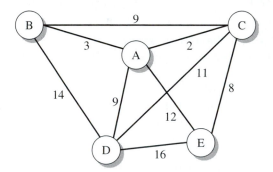

Figure 29.1 *Complete undirected graph for the Traveling Salesman Problem.*

Assuming the salesman starts at vertex (city) A, there are three possible tours with weights 51, 43, and 45, respectively. The TSP solution is Tour 2 that includes edges with distances 3 (A to B), 14 (B to D), 16 (D to E), 8 (E to C), and 2 (C back to A).

```
Tour 1: [A, B, C, D, E]     Weight 51
Tour 2: [A, B, D, E, C]     Weight 43
Tour 3: [A, B, C, E, D]     Weight 45
```

The Traveling Salesman Problem has a variety of applications. For example, a school district must arrange bus routes to pick up students at a variety of stops and deliver them to the school, or a robot arm must be programmed to move efficiently over a circuit board to drill holes and solder connections.

The problem is also significant in the study of computational complexity. Since there is an edge connecting any two cities, given a starting point, the salesman has n – 1 choices for the first visit, n – 2 choices for the second visit, and so forth.

Possible Tours: (n-1) * (n-2) * ... * 2 * 1 = (n-1)!

The Traveling Salesman Problem is NP-complete. There is likely no solution with polynomial running time.

For large n, the number of possible tours is so large that an exhaustive search of all possible paths is unrealistic. No one has found an algorithm to solve the general problem with polynomial runtime efficiency. In fact, the Traveling Salesman Problem belongs to a large class of algorithms called *NP* or *nondeterministic polynomial* problems. For this class of problems, a general $O(n^a)$ solution may not exist, but any specific solution can be verified in polynomial running time. In a more advanced study of complexity theory, you will discover that the Traveling Salesman Problem is also *NP-complete*. This is a category of NP problems with the property that if any particular problem can be solved by an algorithm with polynomial running time, the same is true for all NP-problems; in other words, P = NP. The issue remains open because no one has found a polynomial running time solution for any NP-complete problem nor has anybody been able to prove that such an algorithm cannot exist.

Permutations and the TSP

We can use permutations to solve the Traveling Salesman Problem for relatively small n. Assume that a complete undirected graph G uses vertices and edges to define the cities and links. We can create an array with the starting city in position 0 and the other cities occupying the other positions. The collection of permutations represents different possible routes for the salesman. A check can verify whether the ordering of elements (cities) is a tour and maintain a record of the minimum distance. This algorithm is developed in the exercises and applies to small n where n $\leq$ 12.

29.2 Dynamic Programming

In Chapter 6, we introduced the Fibonacci sequence. A simple recursive definition describes the sequence. The first two terms are 0 and 1. All subsequent terms are the sum of the two previous values.

Fibonacci sequence: 0, 1, 1, 2, 3, 5, 8, 13, 21, 34, 55, ...

Recursive definition:

$$\text{fib}(n) = \begin{cases} 0, & n = 0 \\ 1, & n = 1 \\ \text{fib}(n-1) + \text{fib}(n-2), & n \geq 2 \end{cases}$$

The method `fib()` uses a straightforward translation of the definition for its implementation.

Recursive fib( ):

```
// recursive computation of Fibonacci number n
public static int fib(int n)
{
    if (n <= 1)                          // stopping conditions
        return n;
    else
        return fib(n-1) + fib(n-2);      // recursive step
}
```

Running time for the recursive method fib(n) is exponential owing to the redundant function calls.

The execution of the method is far from straightforward. In Section 6.3, we show that the number of method calls required to evaluate `fib(n)` increases exponentially. This means that the recursive computation of `fib(n)` is an exponential algorithm and is so inefficient as to be impractical for even small values of n. The problem stems from all of the redundant recursive calls. For instance, the hierarchy tree in Figure 29.2 illustrates the method calls required to compute fib(5) = 5. The redundancy is evident when you see that the execution makes multiple calls to fib(0) ... fib(3) including five calls to fib(1).

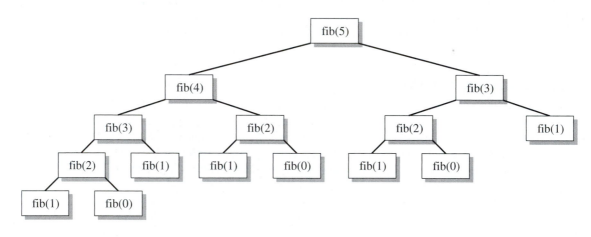

Figure 29.2 *Tree of recursive calls for fib(5).*

The recursive solution for fib(n) fails to partition the problem into nonoverlapping subproblems.

The format for `fib()` has the structure of a divide-and-conquer algorithm. It lacks, however, the efficiency ordinarily associated with this technique because it fails to partition the problem into independent subproblems. Recall the design of the merge sort and quicksort algorithms that partition a list into separate (nonoverlapping) sublists. In general, when a divide-and-conquer strategy results in nonindependent subproblems, a straightforward recursive implementation often produces very poor running time because the overlap can require a prohibitively large number of redundant calculations and method calls. In this section, we develop a new technique, called *dynamic programming*, which can often address the problem. This technique defines an array to store intermediate results and then directly accesses values in the array rather than recomputing results.

We begin by developing a dynamic programming solution to the Fibonacci sequence problem. This introduces you to the key concepts. Many important applications involve polynomials of the form $(1 + x)^n$. These mathematical expressions are the sum of terms consisting of binomial coefficients and powers of x. Computing binomial coefficients is an excellent example of dynamic programming and allows us to discover both a top-down and bottom-up implementation of the technique. We conclude the section by looking at the famous knapsack problem from the field of operations research.

Top-Down Dynamic Programming

A slight change in the algorithm for `fib()` allows us to reduce redundancy and produce a method with running time $O(n)$. The approach includes, as an argument, an array that stores the return values from intermediate method calls. The recursive step first checks the array to see whether the result has already been computed. If so, it directly accesses the value without requiring redundant calculations. If not, the recursive step executes, then adds, the result to the array for later access. The top-down strategy stores values as they are computed in the recursive descent to a stopping condition. Top-down dynamic programming is also referred to as *memorization*.

> Top-down dynamic programming gains efficiency by storing previously computed values during a recursive process.

Let us see how dynamic programming would affect the calculation of fib(5). In Figure 29.3, the unshaded nodes with numbers below the box represent values that are stored in the array. The actual numbers indicate the order they are added to the array. The circled nodes have values that are already in the array because they involve calculations that were previously obtained. These values can be extracted from the array and thus save redundant calculations represented by the shaded nodes.

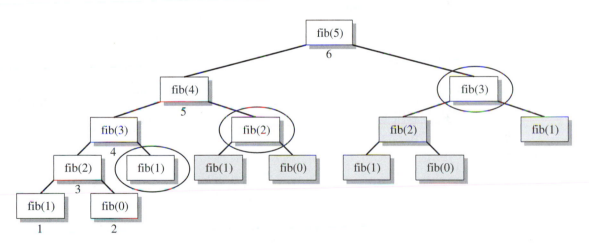

Figure 29.3 *Improvement in Fibonacci number computation using dynamic programming.*

The method `fibDyn()` is the top-down dynamic programming version for the `fib()` algorithm. The method `fibDyn()` includes an integer array argument with at least $n + 1$ elements, whose initial values are -1. The array stores intermediate Fibonacci numbers in the index range 0 to n. The recursive step identifies a nonnegative value in the array as a previously computed result.

> With top-down dynamic programming, we can compute fib(n) with running time $O(n)$.

fibDyn():

```
// computation of the nth Fibonacci number using top down
// dynamic programming to avoid redundant recursive
// method calls
```

```java
public static int fibDyn(int n, int[] fibList)
{
    int fibValue;

    // check for a previously computed result and return
    if (fibList[n] >= 0)
        return fibList[n];

    // otherwise execute the recursive algorithm to obtain
    // the result

    // stopping conditions
    if (n <= 1)
        fibValue = n;
    else
        // recursive step
        fibValue = fibDyn(n-1, fibList) + fibDyn(n-2, fibList);

    // store the result and return its value
    fibList[n] = fibValue;

    return fibValue;
}
```

Example 29.2

1. We get a dramatic realization of how dynamic programming can improve efficiency by looking at the two Fibonacci methods `fib()` and `fibDyn()` for large values of n. The example shows the number of method calls required to execute `fib()` and `fibDyn()` for n = 20 and n = 40.

   n = 20:
   ```
       fib(20) is 6765
           Number of method calls is 21891
       fibDyn(20) is 6765
           Number of method calls is 39
   ```

   n = 40:
   ```
       fib(40) is 102334155
           Number of method calls is 331160281
       fibDyn(40) is 102334155
           Number of method calls is 79

       Compute fib(40) = 102334155 in 11.407 seconds
       Compute fibDyn(4000) = 1489622139 in 0.01 seconds
   ```

2. If a program makes two or more calls to `fibDyn()`, the programmer must reset each array element to −1 before making the next call. The class `Arrays` in *java.util* defines the static method `fill()`, which is convenient for this purpose. The method takes an array and a value as arguments and assigns the value to each element in the

array. The following statements create an array `fibList` with 16 elements and use it to compute `fibDyn(8)` and `fibDyn(15)`.

```
// create array with 16 elements set to -1
int fibList[] = new int[16];
Arrays.fill(fibList, -1);

// output value of fibDyn(15)
System.out.println("Fib(15) = " +
        Combinatorics.fibDyn(15,fibList));

// reset value in fibList to -1 and display fibDyn(8)
Arrays.fill(fibList, -1);
System.out.println("Fib(8) = " +
        Combinatorics.fibDyn(8,fibList));
```

```
Output:
    Fib(15) = 610
    Fib(8) = 21
```

Running Time of fibDyn()   Figure 29.4 shows that $n + 1$ method calls reach the bottom of the tree. On the way back up, $fibDyn(1), fibDyn(2), \ldots, fibDyn(n - 2)$ return without performing any more recursive calls. The number of method calls to compute $fibDyn(n)$ is $n + 1 + (n - 2) = 2n - 1$, so this algorithm for the computation of the Fibonacci numbers is linear.

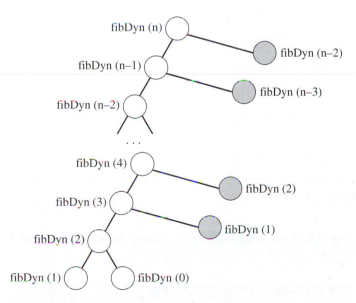

Figure 29.4 *Tree of method class for fibDyn(n) using top-down dynamic programming.*

Combinations with Dynamic Programming

In Section 29.1, we developed the recursive method comm(), which returns the number of different combinations of n items taken k at a time. Like the recursive method fib(), evaluation of comm() involves redundant calculations. For instance, computing comm(50, 6) = 158, 90, 700 requires 3,813,767 method calls.

Top-down dynamic programming can be used to improve the recursive algorithm for C(n, k).

$$C(n, k) = \begin{cases} 1, & k = 0 \text{ or } k = n \\ n, & k = 1 \\ C(n-1, k) + C(n-1, k-1) & \text{recursive step} \end{cases}$$

A top-down dynamic programming implementation of comm() stores intermediate results in the matrix (2-dimensional array) commMat, which has n + 1 rows and k + 1 columns, where commMat[i][j] is the solution for C(i, j). Initially, all of the values in the matrix are set to −1. Each recursive call to commDyn(n,k) first checks whether the value commMat[n][k] is nonzero. If so, it uses the matrix element as its return value.

commDyn():

```
// computation of C(n,k) using top down dynamic programming
// to avoid redundant recursive method calls
public static int commDyn(int n, int k, int[][] commMat)
{
    int returnValue;

    // check if value is already computed
    if (commMat[n][k] >= 0)
        return commMat[n][k];
    if (n == k || k == 0)
        returnValue = 1;
    else if (k == 1)
        returnValue = n;
    else
        // carry out the recursive step
        returnValue =
               commDyn(n-1,k,commMat) + commDyn(n-1,k-1,commMat);

    // before returning, assign value to the matrix
    commMat[n][k] = returnValue;

    return returnValue;
}
```

Computing C(50, 6) by using commDyn() requires only 441 method calls, a little better than the almost four million calls required by comm().

Bottom-Up Dynamic Programming

Top-down dynamic programming is a design strategy for a recursive progress. A method implements the design by supplying a container that stores intermediate results that are derived from chains of method calls. This allows a method call to return without performing additional recursive calls. An alternative strategy, called *bottom-up dynamic programming*, replaces a recursive algorithm by one using a storage container and iteration. Rather than storing results as they occur in a recursive chain, bottom-up dynamic programming builds the storage container in order, starting at the lowest level. An iterative process uses previously computed values at each step to compute the next value.

Bottom-up dynamic programming builds the solution in order, starting at the lowest level and moving upward, using values from the previous level.

Let us apply the bottom-up strategy in a new algorithm for the function C(n, k). The key is creation of a matrix that contains values C(i, j), where $0 \le i \le n$ and $0 \le j \le k$. This involves computing a series of sequences.

i = 0:	C(0, 0)				
i = 1:	C(1, 0)	C(1, 1)			
i = 2:	C(2, 0)	C(2, 1)	C(2, 2)		
i = 3:	C(3, 0)	C(3, 1)	C(3, 2)	C(3, 3)	

. . .

i = k:	C(k, 0)	C(k, 1)	C(k, 2)	C(k, 3)	. . . C(k, k)
i = k+1	C(k+1, 0)	C(k+1, 1)	C(k+1, 2)	C(k+1, 3)	. . . C(k+1, k)
i = k + 2:	C(k + 2, 0)	C(k + 2, 1)	C(k + 2, 2)	C(k + 2, 3)	. . . C(k + 2, k)

. . .

i = n−1:	C(n−1, 0)	C(n−1, 1)	C(n−1, 2)	C(n−1, 3)	. . . C(n−1, k)
i = n:	C(n, 0)	C(n, 1)	C(n, 2)	C(n, 3)	. . . C(n, k)

The formula $C(n, k) = C(n - 1, k) + C(n - 1, k - 1)$ indicates that we can compute intermediate values for entries in row i by using results from row i − 1. Table 29.1 displays the matrix for n = 6, k = 6. When n = k, the table of entries is often called *Pascal's Triangle*.

Table 29.1 Pascal's Triangle for n = 6.

i	C(i, 0)	C(i, 1)	C(i, 2)	C(i, 3)	C(i, 4)	C(i, 5)	C(i, 6)
0	1						
1	1	1					
2	1	2	1				
3	1	3	3	1			
4	1	4	6	4	1		
5	1	5	10	10	5	1	
6	1	6	15	20	15	6	1

In the table, note that the first entry (C(i, 0)) and last entry (C(i, i)) in each row i is 1. The intermediate entries C(i, j) for $1 \le j \le i - 1$ are the sum of entries from the previous row. We apply this fact to the building of a matrix that is at the core of the dynamic bottom-up design of an algorithm for function C(n, k).

The implementation of the method commDynB( ) that computes C(n, k) begins with the allocation of an n + 1 square matrix commMat. The algorithm builds the matrix row by row starting at row 0 until it finds the value C(n, k) in row n, column k of the matrix. Note that once we have computed Pascal triangle through row k, column k, it is only necessary to compute rows k + 1, k + 2, . . . , n through column k (Figure 29.5). Note that commMat[i][j] = 1 when j == 0 or j == i.

Bottom-up dynamic programming very efficiently computes C(n, k) by building the Pascal triangle.

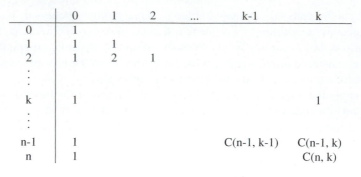

Figure 29.5 *Bottom-up computation of C(n, k).*

commDynB():

```
// computation of C(n,k) using bottom-up dynamic programming
public static int commDynB(int n, int k)
{
   // create an n+1 by k+1 matrix
   int[][] commMat = new int[n+1][k+1];
   int i, j;

   // rows range from 0 through n
   for (i=0; i <= n; i++)
      // only generate columns 0 through k
      for (j = 0; j <= Math.min(i,k); j++)
         // commMat[i][j] = 1 when j == 0 or j == i
         if (j == 0 || i == j)
            commMat[i][j] = 1;
         else
            commMat[i][j] = commMat[i-1][j-1] + commMat[i-1][j];

   // return the entry commMat(n,k)
   return commMat[n][k];
}
```

Knapsack Problem

Operations research is a branch of mathematics that solves, among other things, optimization problems. One such example is the knapsack problem, which has a dynamic programming solution. We are given a knapsack to hold a set of items that have specified sizes and values. The knapsack has a limited capacity, measured in volume. The problem is to find a subset of objects that will fit into the knapsack and provide the maximum value. The problem is a prototype for many important applications. For example, it will help transport companies that want to load cargo on a truck, freight car, or ship in such a way that the cargo returns a maximum profit or a contestant who has won a shopping spree and wants to load the cart with items that represent the maximum value.

There are several versions of the knapsack problem. One version allows us to split items into fractional parts to fill up all of the space in the knapsack. For instance, a camper could cut a slab of bacon into small pieces or take only part of the bag of rice if necessary. The 0/1 version of the knapsack problem is more interesting. In this case, we are given a choice of rejecting (0) or accepting (1) an item from the collection. We explore this version.

A brute-force solution of the knapsack problem checks all subsets of items, which is an exponential algorithm.

A simple but impractical solution to the knapsack problem involves an exhaustive evaluation of every possible subset of items. Since the power set has 2^n items, the algorithm has exponential running time $O(2^n)$. There is a dynamic programming solution that applies the *principle of optimality* to each item in the collection. The principle of optimality states that no matter what the first decision, the remaining decisions must be optimal with respect to any state in the algorithm that results from the first decision.

Assume we want to fill the knapsack from among a list of n items. Using bottom-up dynamic programming, we compute the values for an integer matrix maxValueMat. The row and column dimensions for the matrix are n + 1 and capacity + 1 respectively. The entry maxValueMat[i][cap] is the maximum value of a subset of items chosen from {item$_1$, item$_2$, ..., item$_i$}, where the total size of the elements in the subset is ≤ cap. Assume each item is a record with a value field and a size field. The mathematical definition of maxValueMat[i][cap] is

Solve the knapsack problem by using the principle of optimality in the generation of the knapsack matrix.

$$\max \sum_{j=1}^{i} a_j \, (item_j.value) \quad \text{subject to the constraint that} \quad \sum_{j=1}^{i} a_j \, (item_j.size) \leq cap$$

where a_j = 1 if item$_j$ is in the subset and a_j = 0 if item$_j$ is not in the subset. After we build the matrix, matValueMat[n][capacity] is the solution to the problem.

An example will give you a clearer understanding of the knapsack problem. Suppose we can select from five items to fill a knapsack that has capacity 12. In the algorithm, we build the 6 by 13 matrix maxValueMat row by row starting with row 1. For demonstration purposes, we will build three rows, which are sufficient to develop the key features of the algorithm.

Item	Size	Value
1	2	1
2	3	4
3	4	3
4	5	6
5	6	8

Row 1 in the matrix looks at the set {item$_1$}, which is a subset of all of the available items, and includes the element having size 2 and value 1. The task is to assign values to maxValueMat[1][cap], where $0 \leq cap \leq capacity$. This is easy. Only when cap ≥ 2 do we have enough space for item$_1$. Placing it in the knapsack produces value 1. The first row of the matrix becomes

	0	1	2	3	4	5	6	7	8	9	10	11	12
row 1	0	0	1	1	1	1	1	1	1	1	1	1	1

$$\text{Contents of row 1} \quad \begin{cases} 0 & cap < 2 \\ item_1.value & cap \geq 2 \end{cases}$$

Row 2 in the matrix looks at the set $\{\texttt{item}_1, \texttt{item}_2\}$, where $\texttt{item}_2$ has size 3 and value 4. Again, `cap` < 2 is too small to hold any item. With `cap` $= 2$, there is room for only $\texttt{item}_1$ with value 1. We begin to understand the algorithm when `cap` $= 3$. Because $\texttt{item}_2.\texttt{size} = 3 \le \texttt{cap}$, we can place $\texttt{item}_2$ in the knapsack. The effect is to create a value of 4 and leave no additional space in the knapsack ($\texttt{cap} - \texttt{item}_2.\texttt{size} = 0$). The new value 4 is an improvement over value 1 from `maxValueMat[1][3]`. A similar analysis applies to `cap` $= 4$, except that placing $\texttt{item}_2$ in the knapsack leaves 1 unit of unused space. For `cap` ≥ 5, the knapsack has room for both items, with a total value of 5.

	0	1	2	3	4	5	6	7	8	9	10	11	12
row 1	0	0	1	1	1	1	1	1	1	1	1	1	1
row 2	0	0	1	4	4	5	5	5	5	5	5	5	5

$$\text{Contents row 2} \quad \begin{cases} 0 & \text{cap} < 2 \\ \text{item}_1.\text{value} & \text{cap} = 2 \\ \text{item}_2.\text{value} & 3 \le \text{cap} \le 4 \\ \text{item}_1.\text{value} + \text{item}_2.\text{value} & \text{cap} \ge 5 \end{cases}$$

For entries in row 3, we look at values created by filling the knapsack with any subset of the first three items. Row 2 contains the maximum value for each capacity when only the first two items are used. We need to determine whether adding the third item with size 4 and value 3 will improve the situation. When `cap` $= 4$, there is sufficient space to use the item. The effect is to produce a value 3 and leave no additional space for any other item ($\texttt{cap} - \texttt{item}_3.\texttt{size} = 0$). From row 2, we already have a value 4 by using only the first two items (`maxValueMat[2][4]` = 4). Adding $\texttt{item}_3$ does not improve the maximum value for the capacity, and so we retain the existing value.

```
maxValueMat[3][4] = maxValueMat[2][4] = 4
```

With `cap` $= 6$, adding $\texttt{item}_3$ contributes value 3 and leaves 2 units of space, sufficient to add $\texttt{item}_1$. The total

```
item₃.value + maxValueMat[2][2] = 4
```

is not an improvement on the existing maximum value of 5 (`maxValueMat[2][6]`), which we derived in row 2 by using only the first two items, and so we again retain the value from row 2.

```
maxValueMat[3][6] = maxValueMat[2][6] = 5
```

When `cap` $= 7$, adding $\texttt{item}_3$ leaves 3 units of additional space. Using the maximum value for capacity 3 (`maxValueMat[2][3]` = 4) from row 2, we have a new value, 7, which is greater than the value, 5, derived from using only the first two items.

```
maxValueMat[3][7] = item₃.value + maxValueMat[2][7 - item₃.size]
                  = item₃.value + maxValueMat[2][3]
                  = 3 + 4
                  = 7
```

After completing all of the entries in row 3, we have

	0	1	2	3	4	5	6	7	8	9	10	11	12
row 1	0	0	1	1	1	1	1	1	1	1	1	1	1
row 2	0	0	1	4	4	5	5	5	5	5	5	5	5
row 3	0	0	1	4	4	5	5	7	7	8	8	8	8

$$
\text{Contents of row 3} \begin{cases} 0 & \text{cap} < 2 \\ \text{item}_1.\text{value} & \text{cap} = 2 \\ \text{item}_2.\text{value} & 3 \le \text{cap} \le 4 \\ \text{item}_1.\text{value} + \text{item}_2.\text{value} & 5 \le \text{cap} \le 6 \\ \text{item}_2.\text{value} + \text{item}_3.\text{value} & 7 \le \text{cap} \le 8 \\ \text{item}_1.\text{value} + \text{item}_2.\text{value} + \text{item}_3.\text{value} & \text{cap} \ge 9 \end{cases}
$$

You have now seen all of the elements of the algorithm. In general, for row i, computing maxValueMat[i][cap] involves determining whether $item_i$ should be part of the subset of items from set $\{item_1, item_2, ..., item_i\}$ that produces the maximum value for the specified capacity. First, test whether the new item fits in the space.

```
if (cap - item₃.space >= 0)
    <see if we can increase the value for the capacity cap>
```

Adding $item_i$ provides value but reduces the space available to store items from the list $\{item_1, ..., item_{i-1}\}$. If we use $item_i$, the remaining capacity is (cap − $item_i$.size), and the maximum value for that capacity is the matrix entry maxValueMat[i−1][cap−$item_i$.size]. The sum of this value and $item_i$.value is the best we can do for this capacity by adding $item_i$. On the other hand, the entry maxValueMat[i−1][cap] is the maximum value from using only the elements $\{item_1, ..., item_{i-1}\}$. A test compares the effect of adding $item_i$ with the value that does not use $item_i$. The matrix entry is the larger value.

Optimal value for the knapsack problem is the value at row n, column cap of the knapsack matrix.

```
testMax = itemᵢ.value + maxValueMat[i-1][cap - itemᵢ.size];

// if new item increases value, use new value for matrix entry
if (testMax > maxValueMat[i-1][cap])
    maxValueMat[i][cap] = testMax;
else
    // retain maximum value provided by previous items
    maxValueMat[i][cap] = maxValueMat[i-1][cap];
```

In the next section, we discuss the knapsack class that includes the private method build-MaxValueMat(), which builds the matrix by using the dynamic programming algorithm.

The Knapsack Class

The class Item describes the items in the knapsack. Two integer variables define the size and value of an object. To simplify access, we declare the members public. A constructor creates an instance of the class using two arguments for the size and value.

Item class:

```
// specifies the size and value of an item
public class Item
{
    public int size, value;

    public Item(int size, int value)
    {
        this.size = size;
        this.value = value;
    }
}
```

The Knapsack class includes an Item array called itemList and the integer matrix (2-dimensional array) maxValueMat as instance variables, along with integer variables for the capacity and the number of items. The constructor takes a list of Item objects and a capacity as arguments and initializes the corresponding instance variables. The constructor also allocates space for the knapsack matrix. The private method buildMaxValueMat() implements the dynamic programming version of the knapsack algorithm. For output, the method displayKnapsack() displays the maximum value and the list of the items that fit into the knapsack to produce the value. The display also notes the amount of unused space.

Knapsack class:

```
public class Knapsack
{
    private int capacity;            // capacity of the knapsack
    private Item[] itemList;         // the list of items
    private int numItems;            // the number of items
                                     // (itemList.length)
    private int[][] maxValueMat;     // the knapsack matrix

    // initialize variables and build the knapsack matrix
    public Knapsack(Item[] list, int cap)
    { ... }

    // builds maxValueMat for specified capacity
    private void buildMaxValueMat()
    { ... }

    // displays capacity, items in knapsack, max value,
    // and unused capacity
    public void displayKnapsack()
    { ... }
}
```

Building the Knapsack Matrix   We build the [row][column] entries in maxValueMat one element at a time. To simplify the calculations, all of the entries in row 0 have value 0. The outer loop uses the control variable i to scan the items in the row range 1 ... numItems. An inner loop uses the control variable cap to compute the column values in the range 0 ... `capacity`. For each entry `maxValueMat[i][cap]`, we use the value from the previous row as its initial value.

```
// initially assume the max value for capacity
// cap is produced by using items from 1 to i-1
maxValueMat[i][cap] = maxValueMat[i-1][cap];
```

The effect is to assume that `itemList[i]` will not be added to the knapsack. We override this assumption only after successfully completing a series of tests. The first test checks whether `itemList[i]` fits in the knapsack (`cap – itemList[i].size >= 0`). A second test determines whether adding `itemList[i]` and sacrificing the space it occupies would produce a greater value. If so, the algorithm assigns the new value to the matrix entry.

buildMaxValueMat():

```
// builds maxValueMat for specified capacity
private void buildMaxValueMat()
{
   int i, cap, testMax;
   // compute entries in the matrix
   for (i = 1; i <= numItems; i++)
      for (cap = 1; cap <= capacity; cap++)
      {
         // initially assume the max value for capacity
         // cap is produced by using items from 1 to i-1
         maxValueMat[i][cap] = maxValueMat[i-1][cap];

         // test if itemList[i] fits into the knapsack
         if (cap-itemList[i].size >= 0)
         {
            // test if maximum value increases
            testMax = maxValueMat[i-1][cap-itemList[i].size] +
                          itemList[i].value;
            // if yes, assign new max
            if (testMax > maxValueMat[i-1][cap])
               maxValueMat[i][cap] = testMax;
         }
      }
}
```

Identifying the Items The matrix `maxValueMat` not only determines the maximum value for the specified capacity, it also provides information that will allow us to determine the items that fill the knapsack. The maximum value is `maxValueMat[numItems][capacity]`, which is an entry in the last row of the matrix. Starting with this entry, we can work back through the matrix to discover the items in the knapsack. To understand the algorithm, recall how we built the matrix. In row i, `maxValueMat[i][cap]` is not equal to `maxValue-Mat[i-1][cap]` only if adding `itemList[i]` increases the value. This becomes the criterion to determine whether `itemList[i]` is in the knapsack.

Let us return to the our example and look at `maxValueMat` for capacity 12. The solution to the problem is `maxValueMat[5][12] = 14`.

Identify items in the knapsack solution by going backward from the item in the knapsack matrix, row n, column cap.

	1	2	3	4	5	6	7	8	9	10	11	12
1	0	1	1	1	1	1	1	1	1	1	1	1
2	0	1	4	4	5	5	5	5	5	5	5	5
3	0	1	4	4	5	5	7	7	8	8	8	8
4	0	1	4	4	6	6	7	10	10	11	11	13
5	0	1	4	4	6	8	8	10	12	12	14	14

Maximum value matrix for capacity 12

Because maxValueMat[4][12] = 13, itemList[5] with size 6 and value 8 is in the knapsack. There are 6 units of unused space (cap – itemList[5].size) remaining, which can be filled from the sublist itemList[1] ... itemList[4]. Working backwards, maxValueMat[4][6] indicates that the sublist produces value 6. Now maxValue-Mat[3][6] = 5, so the test criterion indicates that itemList[4] with size 5 and value 6 is in the knapsack. Only 1 unit of additional space remains. Because the values maxValueMat[i][1] are identically 0 for rows 3, 2, and 1, we conclude that none of the corresponding items is in the knapsack. This fact is obvious; no item would fit into 1 unit of space. We conclude that the knapsack holds itemList[5] and itemList[4] and has 1 unit of unused space.

The method displayKnapsack() implements this algorithm. A loop scans the list of items in descending order and identifies an item in the knapsack when its presence adds value. The listing of the items in the knapsack includes their size and value.

displayKnapsack():

```
// displays capacity, items, max value, unused capacity
public void displayKnapsack()
{
    int i = numItems, cap = capacity;

    // create label with capacity and maximum value
    System.out.println("Capacity: " + capacity + "  Value: " +
            maxValueMat[numItems][capacity]);

    // list items in the knapsack by reading from maxValueMat
    System.out.println("Contents: ");
    while (i > 0)
    {
        // if values in successive rows are not equal,
        // itemList[i] is part of the solution
        if (maxValueMat[i][cap] != maxValueMat[i-1][cap])
        {
            System.out.println("   item" + i + '(' +
                itemList[i].size + ',' +
                itemList[i].value + ')');
            // look for maximum value remaining space
            cap -= itemList[i].size;
        }
        i--;
    }
    System.out.println("   Unused capacity: " + cap);
}
```

PROGRAM 29.1 FILLING THE KNAPSACK

We have provided the Knapsack class, whose methods implement the knapsack algorithm. Let us put it all together in a program that defines an array with the five Item objects used in our examples. A prompt asks the user to enter a capacity. After using the value to create the Knapsack object, ks, the program calls displayKnapsack() to display the solution.

```java
import java.util.Scanner;

public class Program29_1
{
    public static void main(String[] args)
    {
        // array of Item objects for the knapsack
        Item[] itemList = {new Item(2,1), new Item(3,4),
                new Item(4,3), new Item(5,6), new Item(6,8)};
        // use for keyboard input
        Scanner keyIn = new Scanner(System.in);

        int capacity;

        System.out.print("Enter the capacity: ");
        capacity = keyIn.nextInt();

        // create a knapsack object
        Knapsack ks = new Knapsack(itemList,capacity);

        // display the solution
        ks.displayKnapsack();
        System.out.println();
    }
}
```

```
Run 1:
  Enter the capacity: 12
  Capacity: 12   Value: 14
  Contents:
     item5(6,8)
     item4(5,6)
     Unused capacity: 1

Run 2:
  Enter the capacity: 19
  Capacity: 19   Value: 21
  Contents:
     item5(6,8)
     item4(5,6)
     item3(4,3)
     item2(3,4)
     Unused capacity: 1
```

Running time for the knapsack problem is O(nC), where n is the number of items and C the capacity.

Evaluating the Knapsack Problem Solution   The running time of our bottom-up dynamic programming solution to the knapsack problem is $O(nC)$, where n is the number of items and C is the capacity. This follows directly from the fact that the algorithm builds a matrix of size $(n + 1) \times (C + 1)$ that has $O(nC)$ elements. The amount of computation depends critically on C. For instance, if $C = n$ the algorithm is $O(n^2)$, but if $C = 2^n$, the algorithm has running time $O(n2^n)$.

29.3 Backtracking: The 8-Queens Problem

With recursive backtracking, we move forward and possibly several steps backward until reaching a solution.

Some recursive algorithms use the principle of *backtracking*. The principle applies when we are faced with a problem that requires a number of steps, with decisions at each step. In an effort to obtain a final solution, we move step by step and make decisions that create a partial solution that appears to be consistent with the requirements of the final solution. If, at any step, we discover that decisions made in previous steps will not allow us to proceed to a final solution, we backtrack to a previous step, change our decision, and then proceed forward looking for a final solution. At times, backtracking entails one step forward and then several steps backward. The 8-Queens problem provides a classic example.

The 8-Queens problem has an elegant solution implemented by using backtracking.

On a chessboard, the queen is the most mobile piece; it can move any number of spaces horizontally in its row, vertically in its column, and along both diagonals. The 8-Queens problem attempts to position eight queens on a chessboard in such a way that no two queens can attack each other. To understand what "attack" means, think of a chessboard as an 8-by-8 grid with cells labeled as a (row, col) pair. One queen can attack another queen by moving along a row (horizontally), along a column (vertically), or along a diagonal (slope-up or slope-down) and intersecting the second queen. In Figure 29.6, the queen in cell (4, 2) is vulnerable to a row attack by the queen in cell (4, 6), to a column attack by the queen in cell (7, 2), and to diagonal attacks by the queens in cells (2, 0) and (1, 5), respectively.

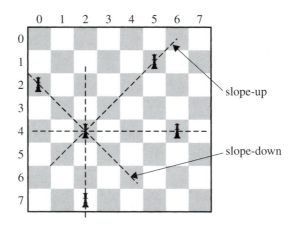

Figure 29.6 *Attacking queens for the queen in cell (4, 2).*

A queen can be attacked by a queen in the same row or column and by a queen on one of the two diagonals.

For a queen at cell (row_i, col_j), a second queen can launch a fatal attack from the following positions.

By row:	cells (row_i, j)	where $0 \le j \le 7$
By column:	cells (i, col_j)	where $0 \le i \le 7$

By "slope-up":   all cells (row, col) that satisfy the equation
$$\text{col} + \text{row} = \text{col}_j + \text{row}_i, 0 \le \text{row} \le 7, 0 \le \text{col} \le 7$$
By "slope-down":   all cells (row, col) that satisfy the equation
$$\text{col} - \text{row} = \text{col}_j - \text{row}_i, 0 \le \text{row} \le 7, 0 \le \text{col} \le 7$$

Example 29.3

Use Figure 29.6 with the queen in cell (4, 2), with row = 4, col = 2. The locations for an attacking queen are as follows:

Row:	positions (4, j), $0 \le j \le 7$	Cells: (4, 0) (4, 1) (4, 3) (4, 4) (4, 5) (4, 6) (4, 7)
Column:	positions (i, 2), $0 \le i \le 7$	Cells: (0, 2) (1, 2) (2, 2) (3, 2) (5, 2) (6, 2) (7, 2)
Slope-up:	positions (row, col), col + row = 6	Cells: (6, 0) (5, 1) (3, 3) (2, 4) (1, 5) (0, 6)
Slope-down:	positions (row, col), col − row = −2	Cells: (2, 0) (3, 1) (5, 3) (6, 4) (7, 5)

Problem Analysis

One could solve the 8-Queens problem by a pure guess method, which looks at all possible arrangements of 8 queens on the 64-cell board. The total number of such arrangements is the combination of 64 cells taken 8 at a time.

$$C(64, 8) = 4, 426, 165, 368$$

A more structured approach uses a backtracking strategy that does not require our positioning all of the queens on the board at one time. We build a solution column by column, starting with column 0. In each succeeding column, we move from row 0 to row 1, then to row 2, and so forth, until we find a "safe" cell in which the queen can be positioned without being vulnerable to attack by any of the other queens already positioned on the board. Using this strategy, we observe the board after placing five queens in "safe" cells in columns 0 through 4 (Figure 29.7).

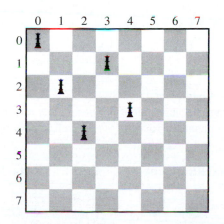

Figure 29.7 *Location of queens in columns 0–4.*

No safe cell may exist in column col.

The approach fails in column 5 because placing a queen in any of the eight rows leaves it vulnerable to attack by one of the five queens on the board. Table 29.2 identifies an attacking queen for each of the rows in column 5. In case two or more queens can attack, we select the queen from the smallest column.

Table 29.2 Attacking queens for column 5.

Row	Cell in column 5	Attacking queen	Row	Cell in column 5	Attacking queen
0	(0, 5)	(0, 0)	4	(4, 5)	(4, 2)
1	(1, 5)	(4, 2)	5	(5, 5)	(0, 0)
2	(2, 5)	(2, 1)	6	(6, 5)	(2, 1)
3	(3, 5)	(1, 3)	7	(7, 5)	(4, 2)

Move forward to another row in column col if a queen at (row, col) does not lead to a solution.

In Figure 29.7, the decisions that led us to place the first five queens in the designated cells create conditions that preclude our reaching a final solution. We are at a dead end and must backtrack to a previous step where our decision can be modified. In our example, the backtracking algorithm undoes the successful step in column 4, which placed a queen in cell (3, 4). At this point, we continue our strategy in column 4 by looking at positions (4, 4), (5, 4), and so forth, until we locate the next safe cell. Figure 29.8 illustrates that cells (4, 4), (5, 4), and (6, 4) are open to attack. A safe position first occurs at cell (7, 4).

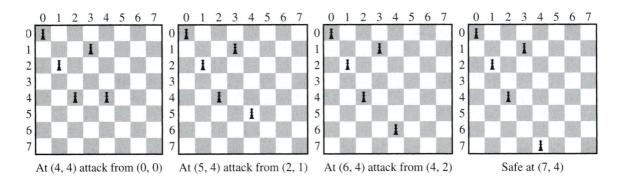

At (4, 4) attack from (0, 0)   At (5, 4) attack from (2, 1)   At (6, 4) attack from (4, 2)   Safe at (7, 4)

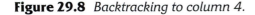

Figure 29.8 *Backtracking to column 4.*

Backtrack to a previous column when all rows of current column do not lead to a solution.

We move forward to column 5 and continue the algorithm. Placing the queen in cell (7, 4) is a short-lived success because it does not permit any queen to be safely positioned in column 5. We provide an attacking queen for each cell in column 5.

Cell	Attacking queen	Cell	Attacking queen
(0, 5)	(0, 0)	(1, 5)	(1, 3)
(2, 5)	(2, 1)	(3, 5)	(1, 3)
(4, 5)	(4, 2)	(5, 5)	(0, 0)
(6, 5)	(7, 4)	(7, 5)	(7, 4)

Faced with another dead end in column 5, we backtrack to column 4 and discover that this is also a dead end; there are no more rows in which to position a queen. The algorithm returns to column 3 and looks to reposition the queen that currently occupies cell (1, 3). The strategy picks up by looking at row 2, then row 3, and so forth. You get the idea. Lest you think column 5 will always be a dead end, Figure 29.9 gives a partial solution that locates nonattacking queens in the first six columns.

> Backtracking may involve going back more than one column to find a solution.

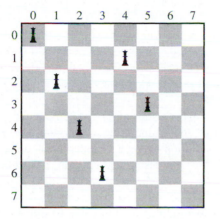

Figure 29.9 *An 8-Queens solution through column 5.*

With the previous discussion as background, let us leave the problem-analysis phase of the 8-Queens problem and move to program design.

Program Design

A solution to the 8-Queens problem involves finding a row for each of the columns from 0 to 7 so that a queen in cell (row, col) is safe from attack. Let us create an 8-element integer array, queenList, to store the rows. An array index corresponds to a column. Hence, queenList[col] = row indicates that a queen occupies cell (row, col) = (queenList[col], col).

```
// queen located in cell (queenList[col],col) for 0 <= col < 8
int[] queenList = new int[8];
```

For the six queens in Figure 29.9, the values in the array are as follows.

queenList[0] = 0	queenList[1] = 2
queenList[2] = 4	queenList[3] = 6
queenList[4] = 1	queenList[5] = 3

The 8-Queens Algorithm The 8-Queens algorithm begins at index col = 0 and assigns a value (row) to queenList[0]. For each successive index col > 0, the algorithm looks for a row so that a queen in cell (row, col) is not vulnerable to attack by any queen in cell (queenList[i], i) where 0 ≤ i < col. We call the cell (row, col) a *safe location*. The problem, however, is that a "safe cell" may not be a "good cell" in the sense that placing a queen at that location may lead to a dead end at some subsequent step in the algorithm. This is the key idea you must understand. At any step i, we can determine whether a location (row, col_i) is safe by checking the positions of queens that were placed in columns col_0 to col_{i-1} during previous steps. The question of whether the location is good requires a chain of recursive steps that place queens in columns col_{i+1}, col_{i+2}, and so forth, ending at column 7. A success occurs when the recursive steps are able to complete the board by finding a safe location in the last column. When this occurs, the recursive steps reach a stopping condition and return true. At any step, if no safe location is found, the recursive process terminates and returns false. We now have a technique for determining whether the safe location (row, col_i) is good. Place a queen in the cell by assigning a row to queenList[col_i] and launch recursive calls to complete the board. If the return value is `true`, we know cell (row, col_i) is good because our strategy will ultimately be successful. We tested it. If the return value is `false`, then cell (row, col_i) is not good even though it is safe and we must look for another row in col_i for the queen.

The method placeQueens() implements the backtracking strategy.

The recursive method `placeQueens()` implements the 8-Queens algorithm. It takes the array `queenList` and an index `col` as arguments. The method assumes the array represents a partial solution to the 8-Queens problem, with nonattacking queens in columns 0 to col − 1. For the designated column, `placeQueens()` uses a loop to scan rows 0, 1, ..., 7 and search for the first row that identifies cell (row, col) as a safe location for the next queen. If no row is found, the method returns `false`. On the other hand, if a row exists, the method assigns the value to `queenList[col]` and makes a recursive call to `placeQueens()` with argument col + 1, which puts in motion a process of placing a nonattacking queen in each of the subsequent columns. The stopping condition for `placeQueens()` occurs when the `index = 8`. This is the column past the end of the board and the call would be made only if nonattacking queens already occupy columns 0 to 7, that is, we have a solution. In this case, `placeQueens()` returns `true`. Otherwise, it returns `false`, which is recursively passed back to the current version of `placeQueens()` with index col, and execution continues in the loop with the next row.

SafeLocation() checks if a queen at (row, col) is safe from attack by queens in columns 0 through col − 1.

As part of its implementation, `placeQueen()` calls the `boolean` method `safeLocation()` that takes row and column indices and the array `queenList` as arguments. The method returns `true` if a queen in the cell (row, col) is free from attack by the queens in the columns from 0 to col − 1 identified by the array; otherwise it returns `false`. The method defines a cell (qRow, qCol) = (queenList[qCol], qCol) for each element in `queenList` and compares it with (row, col) to see whether the two cells lie on the same row, same column, or diagonals (slope-up or slope-down).

safeLocation():

```
// determine if cell (row,col) is safe from attack by queens in
// cells (queenList[0],0), ..., (queenList[col-1],col-1)
public static boolean safeLocation(int row, int col,
int[] queenList)
{
    int qRow, qCol;

    // check previous columns only
    for (qCol = 0; qCol < col; qCol++)
    {
        qRow = queenList[qCol];
```

```
        if (qRow == row)              // same row
            return false;
        else if (qCol == col)         // same col
            return false;
        // can they attack on a diagonal?
        else if(qCol-qRow == col-row || qCol+qRow == col+row)
            return false;
    }
    return true;
}
```

The static method `placeQueens()` returns a `boolean` value that indicates when a current partial solution will lead to a complete solution of the problem, that is, when it is possible to take the current arrangement of queens in columns 0 to `col – 1` (defined by `queenList`) and locate safe cells for the queens in the remaining columns.

placeQueens():

```
// cells (queenList[0],0), ..., (queenList[col-1],col-1) are
// safe positions; determine if the solution can be extended
// to columns col, col+1, ..., 7
public static boolean placeQueens(int[] queenList, int col)
{
    int row;
    boolean foundLocation;

    if (col == 8) // stopping condition
        foundLocation = true;
    else
    {
        foundLocation = false; // start with row 0
        row = 0;
        while (row < 8 && !foundLocation)
        {
            // check whether cell (row, col) is safe; if so,
            // assign row to queenList and call placeQueens()
            // for next column; otherwise, go to the next row
            if (safeLocation(row,col,queenList) == true)
            {
                // found good location
                queenList[col] = row;

                // recursive step; try to place queens in columns
                // col+1 through 7
                foundLocation = placeQueens(queenList,col+1);
                if (!foundLocation)
                    // use next row since current one does not lead
                    // to a solution
                    row++;
            }
```

```
                        else
                            // current row fails; go to the next row
                            row++;
                    }  // end while
                }

                // pass success or failure back to previous col
                return foundLocation;
            }
```

The method
queens() facilitates
calling the recur-
sive method
placeQueens().

We use a driver method queens() to call the recursive method placeQueens(). The driver takes the 8-element array queenList as an argument along with a row value that positions the first queen in column 0. After assigning the row value as the first element in queenList, the method calls placeQueens() in an attempt to extend the current 1-column solution to a solution for the 8-Queens problem. By using queens() we can generate eight different solutions to the 8-Queens problem by using a different row as the position of the first queen.

queens():

```
    // place a queen in (row, 0) and try to find a solution
    // to the 8-Queens problem for columns 1, 2, ..., 7
    public static boolean queens(int[] queenList, int row)
    {
        // place first queen at (row,0)
        queenList[0] = row;

        // locate remaining queens in columns 1 through 7
        if (placeQueens(queenList, 1))
            return true;
        else
            return false;
    }
```

Displaying a ChessBoard

Class ChessBoard
simulates a chess-
board for the
8-Queens
problem.

In order to display a solution to the 8-Queens problem, we create a class called ChessBoard that draws an 8×8 grid of characters corresponding to the 64 cells on the board. A 'Q' designates the presence of a queen and a '−' designates an empty cell. The ChessBoard class has a private instance variable board, which is an 8 by 8 two-dimension array of boolean values. A private utility method clearBoard() sets all of the elements in the array to false. The constructor creates the board object and calls clearBoard() to initialize its values. The method setQueens() has the array argument queenList, which identifies the location of queens on the board as (row,col) pairs. The method creates a representation of a chessboard by assigning the [row][col] entry a value true if a queen is present and the value false to indicate a free cell. The actual drawing of a grid to represent an 8×8 chessboard is left to the method drawBoard(). Depending on the boolean value of an entry in the two-dimension array, the corresponding cell on the chessboard has the letter 'Q' or the symbol '−'. Figure 29.10 illustrates the relationship between the matrix and corresponding chessboard.

	0	1	2	3	4	5	6	7
0	Q	−	−	−	−	−	−	−
1	−	−	−	Q	−	−	−	−
2	−	Q	−	−	−	−	−	−
3	−	−	−	−	Q	−	−	−
4	−	−	Q	−	−	−	−	−
5	−	−	−	−	−	−	−	−
6	−	−	−	−	−	−	−	−
7	−	−	−	−	−	−	−	−

T	F	F	F	F	F	F	F
F	F	F	T	F	F	F	F
F	T	F	F	F	F	F	F
F	F	F	F	T	F	F	F
F	F	T	F	F	F	F	F
F	F	F	F	F	F	F	F
F	F	F	F	F	F	F	F
F	F	F	F	F	F	F	F

Figure 29.10 *ChessBoard and boolean matrix board.*

We are now in a position to illustrate the 8-Queens problem. The recursive method `placeQueens()` carries out the backtracking algorithm by creating an 8-element array, `queenList`. Each index in the array corresponds to a column on the chessboard. The value `queenslist[col]` is the row containing the nonattacking queen. The program declares a `ChessBoard` object, `board`, and passes the location of the queens on the board by using the method `setQueens()`. A call to `drawBoard()` displays the solution.

PROGRAM 29.2 ILLUSTRATING THE 8-QUEENS ALGORITHM

Let us find different solutions for the 8-Queens problem. The following program asks the user to enter a row that positions the queen in column 0. With that input value, the program solves the 8-Queens problem and outputs the solution.

```java
import java.util.Scanner;

public class Program29_2
{
    public static void main (String[] args)
    {
        int row;
        // the array needed by the 8-Queens algorithm
        int[] queenList = new int[8];
        // board will display the solution
        ChessBoard board = new ChessBoard();
        Scanner keyIn = new Scanner(System.in);

        // enter a starting row for queen in column 0
        System.out.print("Enter row for queen in column 0: ");
```

```
                    row = keyIn.nextInt();
                    System.out.println();

                    // see if there is a solution
                    if (Queens.queens(queenList, row))
                    {
                        // insert the solution into the chessboard
                        board.setQueens(queenList);
                        // display the solution
                        board.drawBoard();
                    }
                    else
                        System.out.println("No solution");
                }
            }
```

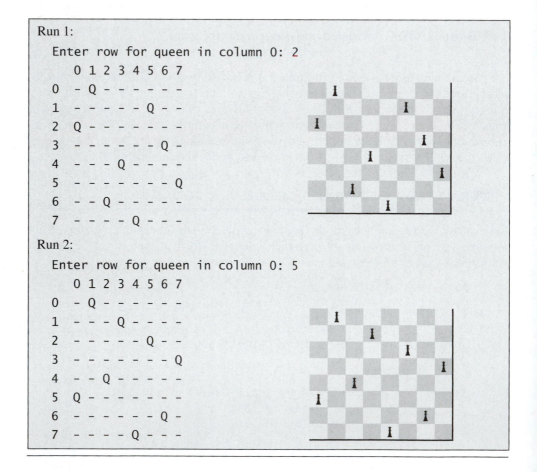

```
Run 1:
    Enter row for queen in column 0: 2
        0 1 2 3 4 5 6 7
    0   - Q - - - - - -
    1   - - - - - Q - -
    2   Q - - - - - - -
    3   - - - - - - Q -
    4   - - - Q - - - -
    5   - - - - - - - Q
    6   - - Q - - - - -
    7   - - - - Q - - -

Run 2:
    Enter row for queen in column 0: 5
        0 1 2 3 4 5 6 7
    0   - Q - - - - - -
    1   - - - Q - - - -
    2   - - - - - Q - -
    3   - - - - - - - Q
    4   - - Q - - - - -
    5   Q - - - - - - -
    6   - - - - - - Q -
    7   - - - - Q - - -
```

Chapter 29 of the software supplement contains classes `ChessBoardGUI` and `QueensGUI`, which implement a graphical solution to the 8-Queens problem. The interested reader should run the application `QueensGUI` and take a look at the source code for the classes. Figure 29.11 contains two snapshots of the running application.

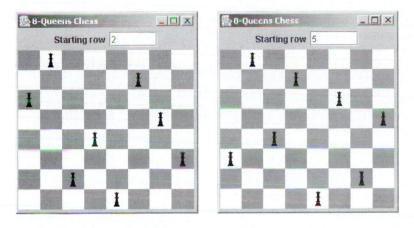

Figure 29.11 *GUI solution to the 8-Queens problem.*

Chapter Summary

- Section 29.1 discusses some recursive problems that occur in combinatorics. Finding the combinations of n items taken k at a time has an interesting, but inefficient, recursive solution. A set of n elements has 2^n subsets, and the set of those subsets is called the *power set*. Using a divide-and-conquer strategy, we compute the power set by removing an element from the set and then adding the element back into each subset. The section also develops a recursive algorithm to list all the n! permutations of n items and concludes by providing an overview of the famous Traveling Salesman Problem that is a member of a set of problems termed *NP-complete*.

- Section 29.2 provides an overview of *dynamic programming.* We illustrate top-down dynamic programming by using an array to store Fibonacci numbers as a recursive method computes them. This avoids costly redundant recursive calls and leads to an $O(n)$ algorithm that computes the Fibonacci number n. The recursive method that does not apply dynamic programming has exponential running time. The section also applies top-down dynamic programming to improve the recursive computation for C(n, k), the combinations of n things taken k at a time. Another dynamic programming strategy is *bottom-up dynamic programming*. It evaluates a method by computing all the method values in order, starting at the lowest level and using previously computed values at each step to compute the current value. We illustrate this technique by again visiting the problem of computing combinations. Dynamic programming often finds uses in optimization problems in operations research and other fields. Such problems are very well illustrated by the 0/1 knapsack problem. The section develops the Knapsack class, which solves the problem by using bottom-up dynamic programming.

- A *backtracking algorithm* finds a consistent partial solution to a problem and then tries to extend the partial solution to a complete solution by executing a recursive step. If the recursive step fails to find a solution, it returns to the previous state and the algorithm tries again from a new consistent partial solution. A backtracking algorithm takes "1 step forward and n steps backward." Such algorithms have application for solving advanced problems in graph theory and operations research. The 8-Queens problem provides a very interesting and relatively simple example of a backtracking algorithm. Section 29.3 solves this problem by developing the Queens and ChessBoard classes.

Written Exercises

1. Trace the method f() and give the list of elements in the LinkedList alist after calling f(alist, 0). Assume that we initialize alist with Integer objects.

```
Integer[] arr = {6, 2, 9, 4, 7, 3, 8};

public static void f(LinkedList alist, int index)
{
    if(index < alist.size())
    {
        alist.addFirst(alist.get(index));
        alist.remove(index+1);
        f(alist,index+1);
    }
}
```

2. Trace the recursive method f().

```
public static int f(int n)
{
    if (n == 1 || n == 2)
        return 1;
    else
        return 2*f(n-1) + 3*f(n-2);
}
```

(a) Give the results for

   (i) f(4)   (ii) f(6)   (iii) f(1)

(b) Using the model for the method fib() in Section 29.2, draw the "calling tree" (binary tree) that lists the recursive calls made during execution of f(7).

(c) Assume we use dynamic programming to store intermediate results and that in the recursive step, the method call f(n – 1) is made before the method call f(n – 2). From part (b), circle all of the recursive calls (nodes) having values that are already in the array. Shade nodes that represent redundant calculations that are saved by dynamic programming.

(d) Implement fDyn() as an alternative version for f(), using an array and dynamic programming to store and access intermediate calculations.

```
public static int fDyn(int n, int[] arr)
{ ... }
```

3. Trace the program and give the output for each input.

```
public static int h(int b, int n)
{
    if (n == 0)
        return 1;
    else
        return b * h(b,n-1);
}
```

(a) What are values for h(), assuming inputs as follows?
    (i) Input: 5 3   (ii) Input: 3 5   (iii) Input: 2 2

(b) Describe the action of the method. What is the method in the Math class that performs a similar calculation?

4. The following is a recursive definition for f(a, b), where a and b are nonnegative integer values, a $\geq$ b.

$$f(a, b) = \begin{cases} a - b & \text{if } a==0 \text{ or } b==0 \\ f(a - 1, b) + f(a, b - 1) \end{cases}$$

(a) Write a recursive method that implements f().
(b) Display the "calling tree" that lists the method calls required to execute f(3,2).

5. For the knapsack problem, assume the following statements.

```
Item[] itemList = {new Item(3,1), new Item(2,1),
                   new Item(5,8), new Item(3, 5)};
Knapsack ks = new Knapsack(itemList,12);
```

Build and display the matrix maxValueMat that determines the solution. What are the contents of the knapsack?

6. If a set S has n items, prove that the number of items in the power set of S is 2^n.

Programming Exercises

7. (a) In Section 5.6, we introduced a generic iterative version of the binary search that takes an array, an index range first $\leq$ index $<$ last, and a target and scans the list looking for a match. The method returns the index of the match or -1 if no match occurs. Implement a recursive version of the binary search algorithm.

```
public static <T extends Comparable<? super T>>
int binSearch(T[] arr, int first, int last, T target)
{ ... }
```

(b) Code a facilitator method that allows a user to provide only the array and the target and search the entire array.

```
public static <T extends Comparable<? super T>>
int binSearch(T[] arr, T target)
{ ... }
```

(c) Use the binSearch() method from part (b) in a program that initializes an array of Integer objects.

```
Integer[] arr[] = {13, 18, 22, 30, 37, 42, 50, 57, 68,
                   81, 88};
```

Prompt the user to input a target value and search the entire list looking for a match. Use the return index in an output statement that determines whether a match occurs. Run the program with three different target values, exactly two of which are in the array.

8. The following is a recursive definition for f(a, b), where a and b are nonnegative integer values, a ≥ b.

$$f(a, b) = \begin{cases} a - b & \text{if } a == 0 \text{ or } b == 0 \\ f(a - 1, b) + f(a, b - 1) \end{cases}$$

Implement a method fDyn() that uses dynamic programming and a matrix (2-dimensional array) mat to store intermediate values. If a ≥ b, then f(a, b) ≥ 0. Use the value mat[a][b] = -1 to indicate that f(a, b) has not been computed. The dimension of mat must be at least (a + 1) 3 (b + 1). Prompt for a and b and compute f(a,b). Run the program three times and compute the following values.

f(8,5), f(7,7), f(15,8)

9. The *generalized Fibonacci numbers* of order k ≥ 2 are given by

$$F_n^k = \begin{cases} 0, & 0 \le n < k - 1 \\ 1, & n = k - 1 \\ \sum_{i=1}^{k} F_{n-i}^k, & n \ge k \end{cases}$$

For instance, the generalized Fibonacci numbers of order 2 are {0, 1, 1, 2, 3, 5, 8, 13, 21, 34, ... } and those of order 3 are {0, 0, 1, 1, 2, 4, 7, 13, 24, 44, ... }.

(a) Implement a method, fibg(), that computes the generalized Fibonacci numbers of order k.

```
public static int fibg(int n, int k)
{ ... }
```

(b) Implement an iterative method, fibgDyn(), that finds the generalized Fibonacci numbers of order k by using bottom-up dynamic programming.

(c) Write a program that prompts for integer values n and k and outputs the generalized Fibonacci numbers of order k for i = 0, 1, 2, ... n by using the recursive method fibg(). Output the same sequence by using the iterative method fibgDyn().

(d) What do you think is the running time for each algorithm? HINT: The running time for fibgDyn() depends on n and k.

10. (a) For two sequences of objects {$s_0, s_1, s_2, \ldots, s_{n-1}$} and {$t_0, t_1, t_2, \ldots, t_{m-1}$}, with n and m elements, respectively, an *interleaving* is a permutation of n + m objects such that within the permutation, each original set retains the same relative ordering. That is, s_0, comes before s_1, s_1 before s_2, t_3 before t_4, and so forth. For instance, assume s = {ab} and t = {12}. The set of all interleavings of s and t contain six elements:

ab12   a1b2   a12b   1ab2   1a2b   12ab

The permutations that appear in the set of interleavings have the relative order restriction, so the set of all interleavings is a subset of the set of all permutations.

There are $(m + n)!$ permutations of $m + n$ objects, and there are $(m + n)!/m!n!$ interleavings. For instance, the number of interleavings in the example is

$$(2 + 2)!/2!2! = 4!/2*2 = 24/4 = 6$$

A recursive method, `interleavings()`, outputs all the interleavings for the characters contained in two strings s and t. Assume that

$$s = \text{``}s_0s_1s_2\ldots s_{n-1}\text{''} \text{ and } t = \text{``}t_0t_1t_2\ldots t_{m-1}\text{''}$$

The design of the method uses the following recursive steps and stopping conditions. During execution, i is the index of the current character we are looking at in s, and j is the index of the current character in t. As we apply the recursive step, the remaining characters that we must examine in the strings become smaller, so eventually we reach a stopping condition.

Recursive steps:

Generate all interleavings of the remaining characters that begin with s_i:
  ... earlier characters ... s_i interleavings
$(s_{i+1}s_{i+2}\ldots s_{n-1}\text{''}, \text{``}t_jt_{j+1}t_{j+2}\ldots t_{m-1}\text{''})$

Generate all interleavings of the remaining characters that begin with t_j:
  ... earlier characters ... t_j interleavings
$(\text{``}s_is_{i+1}s_{i+2}\ldots s_{n-1}\text{``}, \text{''}t_{j+1}t_{j+2}\ldots t_{m-1}\text{''})$

Stopping conditions:
 If string s is empty, add all remaining characters of t onto the end of the interleaving.
 If string t is empty, add all remaining characters of s onto the end of the interleaving.

Implement the method `interleavings()`.

```
// output all interleavings of the characters in s and t;
// i is the current position in s, and j is the current
// position in t; ci is the interleaving
public static String interleavings(String s, int i,
                        String t, int j, StringBuffer ci)
{ ... }
```

(b) Write a program that prompts for two strings, s and t, and outputs the set of all interleavings of the characters in s with those in t.

11. (a) The implementation for the method `commDynB()` in Section 29.2 returns an integer that is the number of combinations of n things taken k at a time (C(n, k)) by building a portion of Pascal's triangle. Modify the method so it computes the entire $(n + 1) \times (n + 1)$ triangle and returns row n as its value. Element k of this array is C(n, k).

```
// return row n of Pascal's triangle
public static int[] commDynBArr(int n)
{ ... }
```

(b) The expression $(x + 1)^n$ has the expansion

$$(x + 1)^n = C_{n,n}x^n + C_{n,n-1}x^{n-1} + C_{n,n-2}x^{n-2} + \cdots + C_{n,2}x^2 + C_{n,1}x^1 + C_{n,0}x^0$$

where $C_{n,k}$ is the combination of n items taken k at a time. Using the method commDynBArr() from part (a), write a program that inputs n and outputs the terms of $(1 + x)^n$. Represent x^k by using the notation x^k. In your output, omit coefficients that are 1, do not include x^0, and output x instead of x^1. For instance, your output for $n = 2$ should be

```
(x + 1)^2 = x^2 + 2x + 1
```

12. (a) Create a version of the permute() method that displays all of the strings created by permuting the characters of a string.

```
public static void permute(String str, int index)
{ ... }
```

(b) Write a program that prompts the user to enter a string and then calls permute() to display the permutations.

13. In a *complete graph*, an edge connects every pair of vertices. Assume that a complete undirected graph G with n vertices defines the cities and paths for the Traveling Salesman Problem. Prompt for an initial city to launch the travel and create an array with the starting city at index 0 and the remaining cities occupying the other positions. The collection of permutations of the cities at indices 1, 2, . . . , n – 1 represents different possible routes for the salesman. Sequence through the permutations and maintain a record of the tour with the minimum distance. Output the corresponding tour. Run the program with the graphs in Figure 29.12 (*graph29-13a.dat* and *graph29-13b.dat* in ch29ex).

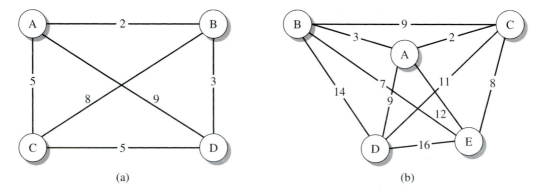

(a)   (b)

Figure 29.12 *Graphs for Programming Exercise 29.13.*

14. For the knapsack problem, assume the following capacities and values.

Item	Capacity	Value
1	2	1
2	3	4
3	4	3
4	5	6
5	6	8
6	3	2
7	1	6
8	9	8
9	7	1
10	3	6
11	4	2
12	10	5

Write a program that solves the knapsack problem. Run the program for each of the following capacities and output the optimal value and the items in the knapsack.

$$\text{Capacity} = 28, 19, 18, 50, 42$$

15. Generalize the solution to the 8-Queens problem to the n-Queens problem, in which the board is of size $n \times n$. Position a queen in column 0, and attempt to place the other $n - 1$ queens so that all n queens are nonattacking. Write a program that inputs n and a starting row in column 0 and determines whether there is a solution to the n-Queens problem. If a solution exists, output the board that shows the placement of the queens.

16. Let S be a set of positive integers $\{x_0, x_1, x_2, \ldots, x_{n-1}\}$ and total be a positive integer. The *subset-sum* problem asks whether there exists a subset of S that adds up exactly to the target value total. Here is an example.

$S = \{1, 4, 16, 64, 256, 1040, 1041, 1093, 1284, 1344\}$, total $= 3754$

One solution: $\{1, 4, 16, 64, 1041, 1284, 1344\}$

Another solution: $\{1, 16, 64, 256, 1040, 1093, 1284\}$

The following is a description of a backtracking solution.

subsetsum():

```
// find a subset of the positive integers arr[index],
// arr[index+1], ..., arr[arr.length-1] that sums
// to total > 0; if subset[i] == true, arr[i] is in
// the sum, 0 <= i < arr.length
public static boolean subsetsum(int[] arr, boolean[] subset,
                                int total, int index)
{ ... }
```

Example:

Input:

$$arr = \{6, 26, 3, 15, 12, 8, 5, 18, 6, 25\}$$

$$total = 28, index = 0$$

$$subset = \{false, false, false, false, false, false, false, false, false, false\}$$

Output:

Return value true.

$$subset = \{true, false, true, false, false, true, true, false, true, false\}$$

$$28 = 6 + 3 + 8 + 5 + 6$$

Code outline:

```
public static boolean subsetsum(int[] arr, boolean[] subset,
                int total, int index)
{
   boolean result;

   if (total == 0)
      result = true;            // success
   else if (index >= arr.length || total < 0)
      return false;             // failure

   else
   {
      subset[index] = true;

      < try using arr[index] and moving forward; if this
        fails, do not use subset[index] and move forward>
   }

   return result;
}
```

(a) When no solution exists that contains `arr[index]`, why can we move forward and try `arr[index+1]` without considering the values `arr[0]` to `arr[index - 1]`? Why is this a backtracking algorithm?

(b) Implement `subsetsum()`.

(c) Write a program that constructs the following objects:

```
int[] arr = {6,26,3,15,12,8,5,18,6,25};
boolean subset = new boolean [arr.length];
```

Using `subsetsum()`, determine whether there is a subset of arr that adds to i for all numbers $1 \le i \le 50$. For each success, output one such subset.

17. Section 29.1 discusses an algorithm for determining the power set of a set. Write a program that implements the method `powerSet()`.

```
// return the power set of s
public static Set powerSet(Set s)
{ ... }
```

Run the program with four sets of different sizes where the n elements are the first n strings in

```
String[] setElt = {"A", "B", "C", "D", "E", "F", "G", "H"}
```

Programming Project

18. This problem is known as the Knight's Tour. You are given an n × n board on which a knight (allowed to move according to the rules of chess only) is placed on the board with specified initial coordinates. The problem is to compute a tour of $n^2 - 1$ moves (if there is one) such that the knight visits every square on the board once and only once . Write a program that solves the problem by using a backtracking approach.

(a) Represent the board by a two-dimensional n × n matrix, all of whose initial values are 0.

```
int[][] board = new int[n][n];
```

Keep track of the order in which the knight reaches the squares by using the following convention:

```
board[i][j] = 0:   square (i, j) has not been visited.
board[i][j] = k:   square (i, j) is the kth square visited in the tour, where
                   1 <= k <= n².
```

(b) We must find a way to represent the list of possible moves from the current position. Given a particular position (i, j), there are eight (8) potential candidates for the knight's next move. Starting on the right and going counterclockwise, these are as follows:

```
(i+2, j+1), (i+1, j+2), (i-1, j+2), (i-2, j+1),
(i-2, j-1), (i-1, j-2), (i+1, j-2), (i+2, j-1)
```

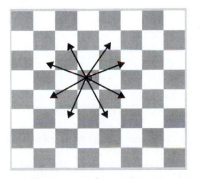

We can conveniently represent these eight moves by using two arrays:

```
int[]  dx = {2,1,-1,-2,-2,-1,1,2},
       dy = {1,2,2,1,-1,-2,-2,-1};
```

The knight at position (i, j) can move to position (u, v), where

```
u = i + dx[m], v = j + dy[m], for 0 ≤ m ≤ 7.
```

Here is an outline of a method, `knight()`, that solves the problem.

```
// A matrix, board, represents a chessboard with
// n = board.length rows and columns. knight()
// computes a tour of (n*n)-1 moves (if there is one) such
// that the knight visits every square on the board once
// and once only. The values of (i,j) when the method is
// first called are the starting square for the knight,
// and k = 1. As the search for a solution progresses,
// the current position of the knight is (i,j). If (i,j)
// is in the tour, it will be the kth square visited by
// the knight. We record this information by assigning
// board[i][j] = k. If the square (i,j) is not on
// the tour, board[i][j] = 0. The search for a solution is
// successful if k reaches n*n, and knight() returns true;
// otherwise, knight() returns false to indicate that
// a tour does not exist.
bool knight(int[][] board, int k, int i, int j)
{
    bool result;
    int n = board.length, u, v, m;
    const int n = board.rows();
    int dx[] = {2,1,-1,-2,-2,-1,1,2},
        dy[] = {1,2,2,1,-1,-2,-2,-1};

    <assume this square will be move k>

    f (k == n*n)
        // success! return true
        result = true;
    else
    {
        // assume result is false
        result = false;
        m = 0;

        // look at all 8 possible moves and see if one
        // leads to a solution
        while ( <no solution yet and there are moves to check>)
        {
            <use dx, dy to determine (u,v)>

            <if board[u][v] is on the board and has not been
            visited, try to find a solution by moving there>

            m++;
        }
```

```
        <if this position (i,j) did not work out, assign
        0 to board[i][j] and return false; we'll come
        back here later>
    }

    return result;
}
```

Write a program that prompts for the board size and the starting position for the knight and determines whether there is a tour. If a tour exists, output the board, showing the sequence of moves.

NOTE: This algorithm performs an exhaustive search. For some positions, particularly near the edge of the board, the number of method calls the algorithm makes is very large. Here are some data concerning the amount of work the algorithm does.

n	Starting point	Number of method calls	Starting point	Number of method calls
5	(0, 0)	8840	(0, 3)	1,829,421 (no solution)
6	(0, 0)	248,169	(0, 3)	1,129,763,556

Appendix A

JAVA PRIMER

CONTENTS

A.1 STRUCTURE OF A JAVA PROGRAM
Comments
Keywords and Identifiers
Declaring and Using Variables
Console Output

A.2 THE JAVA PROGRAMMING
ENVIRONMENT
Integrated Development
Environment

A.3 PRIMITIVE DATA TYPES
Numeric Types
Java char Type
Declaring Named Constants

A.4 OPERATORS
Arithmetic Operators
Assignment Operator
Compound Assignment Operators
Increment Operators
Operator Precedence

A.5 CONVERSIONS BETWEEN TYPES

A.6 SELECTION STATEMENTS
The If-Statement
Nested If-Statements
Multiway If/Else-Statements
Conditional Expression Operator
The Switch-Statement
The boolean Type

A.7 LOOP STATEMENTS
The While-Statement
The Do/While-Statement
The For-Statement
Break Statement

A.8 ARRAYS
Array Initialization
Scanning Arrays with Foreach
Two-Dimensional Arrays

A.9 JAVA METHODS
Predefined Methods
User-Defined Methods
Arrays as Method Parameters

This tutorial introduces the basic syntax and semantics of the Java programming language. We assume that you are familiar with a high-level programming language. You should have a basic understanding of primitive data types, control structures, functions, and one-dimensional arrays. This tutorial provides a guide to Java for readers with a variety of backgrounds.

The main text discusses objects, object design, and object-oriented programming techniques as they pertain to a development of data structures and algorithms. In this tutorial, we will introduce objects and classes for a reader who does not have background in object-oriented programming.

A.1 Structure of a Java Program

Let us start by creating a simple Java program. The example below illustrates the overall design of a Java program and introduces syntax for comments, identifiers, variables, and console output. This program converts height in inches into English and metric units and then outputs the results.

Problem statement: A person has a height of 74 inches. The program converts the height into feet and inches and into centimeters. The conversion factor "1 inch = 2.54 cm" is used for the metric measure. Output to the console displays the conversion in the form `Height of <foot> foot <inch> in metric is <centimeter> cm` in which the bracketed symbol <value> is the actual value of the corresponding unit.

Use an editor to type program source code into a file. On a Windows system, Notepad can serve as an editor. Java requires that data and operations be defined within a program unit called a *class*. The operations are referred to as *methods*. Begin the program with a class declaration that includes a header with the modifiers *public class* and an identifier that specifies the main application class. The class name with the extension `.java` becomes the file name. By convention, all class names in Java begin with a capital letter. In our example, the class name is DemoProgram and the file name is *DemoProgram.java*. The body of the class is enclosed in a pair of braces and includes a special method called *main()*. This method designates where the runtime system will begin execution of the program. The following is the structure of our Java program including the main application class and the main method.

```
// main class for source code in file "DemoProgram.java"
public class DemoProgram
{
    public static void main(String[] args)
    {
        <code to implement main()>
    }
}
```

You can think of the declaration of the main class and the main method as a template that says that the program is "DemoProgram" in file *DemoProgram.java* and execution should begin here in method `main()`.

The program listing includes line numbers in square brackets at the beginning of each line. They are not part of the source code and are given only as references for our discussion of program features in the next section. A sample run displays the following output.

Run:
```
    Height of 6 foot 2 in metric is 187.96 cm
```

Program listing:

```
[1]     /* DemoProgram: Converts height in inches into units of
            feet and inches as well as metric units and then
[2]         outputs the results.
[3]     */
[4]
[5]     // application class that contains the main method
[6]     public class DemoProgram
```

```
[7]   {
[8]       public static void main(String[] args)
[9]       {
[10]          // the constant conversion factor inches to
              // centimeters
[11]          final double IN2CM = 2.54;
[12]
[13]          // variables for height, feet, inches, and
              // centimeters
[14]          int height = 74, foot, inch;
[15]          double centimeter;
[16]
[17]          // convert height to feet and inches
[18]          foot = height / 12;
[19]          inch = height % 12;
[20]          centimeter = height * IN2CM;
[21]
[22]          // display the output
[23]          System.out.println("Height of " + foot + " foot " +
[24]               inch + "in metric is" + centimeter + "cm");
[25]      }
[26]  }
```

Comments

A *comment* contains documentation that describes the meaning of critical variables and instructions. It helps a person read and understand the program and is not part of the run-time code. Java allows three types of program comments. A *single-line* comment starts with the character sequence "//" and continues to the end of the line. For instance, [5] and [10] are single-line comments. A *multi-line* comment includes all of the text that is enclosed within the pair of delimiters /* and */ This form is useful for writing long documentation notes (e.g., [1]–[3]). A third form is a Javadoc comment that we introduced in Chapter 3 to create documentation in linked HTML pages.

Keywords and Identifiers

A Java program begins with a main class declaration (line [6]). The format for the declaration includes the modifier *public*, the word *class*, and the class name DemoProgram. The words public and class are called *reserved words* or *keywords*. These are words that have special predefined meaning in the Java language. They may be used only with their intended meaning and not as programmer-defined names for a class or other components in the program. Appendix B contains a list of Java keywords.

The name of a class, a method, or a variable is called an *identifier*. An identifier is a series of characters consisting of letters (a . . . z, A . . . Z), digits (0 . . . 9), underscores (_), and dollar signs ($). An identifier may not begin with a digit. Java is *case-sensitive*, meaning that it distinguishes between equivalent upper-and lowercase letters. Some valid identifiers are count, salesTax, and sales_tax. The name 2over is not a valid identifier because it begins with a digit. A sample of identifiers in the program is the class name `DemoProgram` and the parameter `args` in the declaration of the method `main()`([8]).

Declaring and Using Variables

A variable is the program's name for a memory location that holds data. In a Java program, a variable must have an associated type that indicates whether the data is an integer, a real number, a character, or another kind of value. Java has two kinds of types, primitive and reference. A reference type, called a *class type*, is associated with an object. The type of an object is a user-defined class. We discuss classes and object in Chapter 1. Primitive types are predefined in the Java language and designate variables that have simple integer or real number values, character values, or logical values (true or false). We discuss Java primitive types such as `int` and `double` in Section A.3.

A variable declaration allocates memory for data of the specified type and allows a program to use the variable name to access the memory location. By convention, variable names begin with a lowercase letter. The declaration begins with the data type followed by a list of variable names separated by a comma and ending with a semicolon. Lines [14] and [15] are declarations of integer variables `height`, `foot`, and `inch`. The declaration assigns `height` an initial value 74. The variable `centimeters` of type `double` holds real numbers which include a whole and a fractional part.

```
[14]     int height = 74, foot, inch;
[15]     double centimeter;
```

The identifier `IN2CM` ([11}) is the name for a constant value. The modifier *final* indicates that the value cannot be changed.

```
[11]     final double IN2CM = 2.54;
```

Console Output

Java provides the predefined stream `System.out` for console output. Use the stream with methods `print()` and `println()` (read "print line") to display strings and other information in a console window. The form of the output is provided by a string that is built with elements separated by the "+ " character. The elements may include quoted strings (string literals), variables, and constants. For instance, line [22] uses `println()` with a string argument that is the concatenation of seven elements. The string extends to line [23] and consists of string literals such as "Height of "and" in metric is" as well as strings representing the value of variables such as `foot` and `centimeter`.

```
[23]   System.out.println("Height of " + foot + " foot " + inch +
[24]        "in metric is " + centimeter + " cm");
```

A.2   The Java Programming Environment

Java programs are initially written as a sequence of statements which are then translated by a compiler into *bytecode*. Bytecode is a language that contains machine instructions for a hypothetical computer. To execute the bytecode, Java provides an interpreter, called a *Java Virtual Machine* (JVM), that translates each bytecode instruction into native machine code and executes it on the local computer. This two-step process creates platform-independent programs, a distinctive feature of Java. What does this mean? The compiler produces bytecode, which is common to all computer operating systems running Java. Each system, however, has its own JVM that uses the computer's native instruction set. For instance, computers running a Windows Operating System, a version of UNIX, or the Macintosh Operating System have distinct virtual machines.

Compiling and running a Java program occurs within an environment. The most basic one is a *command-line environment* that uses a separate application from the *Java Software Development Kit (SDK)* for each task. To compile the program, use the command "javac" with a file name that includes the extension `.java`. The command calls the Java compiler, which converts the source code into intermediate bytecode instructions. The resulting file has the extension `.class`.

```
// javac compiles "DemoProgram.java" to bytecode
// "DemoProgram.class"
javac DemoProgram.java
```

To execute the program, use the command "java" with the name of the `.class` file. The extension is not included. The application loads the JVM for the system and executes the bytecode instructions.

```
// execute the bytecode in file "DemoProgram.class"
java DemoProgram
```

Figure A.1 shows the commands to compile and run our demonstration program on a Windows system. The output appears in the same console window.

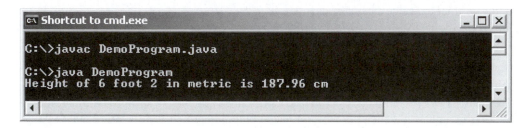

Figure A.1 *The action of compiling and running our demonstration program in a Windows command-line environment.*

Integrated Development Environment

A command-line environment has the programmer use separate applications to compile and run a program. An alternative is an *Integrated Development Environment (IDE)* that provides tools to support the entire program development and execution process. The tools include an editor for writing programs, debuggers to locate errors, a window to display compiler messages, and a runtime window to execute the program. Examples are JBuilder from Borland and CodeWarrior from Metrowerks. These products provide an IDE for Windows, UNIX, and Macintosh systems. The authors of this book provide an alternative IDE, EZJava, which also runs on multiple environments. It has many of the features of a commercial environment in addition to a variety of instructional tools. A tutorial in Appendix E describes how to use EZJava. Figure A.2 illustrates the development environment for our demonstration program. Figure A.2 shows the editor window for the source code, a dialog box that posts the status of the compilation, and a runtime window, which displays the output.

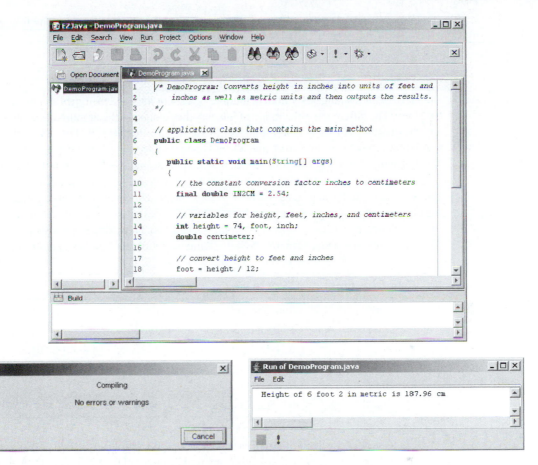

Figure A.2 *Using the EZJava editor and commands to compile and run DemoProgram.java with a display window.*

A.3 Primitive Data Types

This section will introduce primitive data types. These include types for integers, real numbers, and characters. In the process, we provide a brief discussion of how computers use memory to store data.

Numeric Types

Integers are positive and negative whole numbers that consist of a sign and a sequence of digits. Integers are referred to as *signed numbers*. An integer is a *discrete number* type that represents data values that can be counted, for example, -2, -1, 0, 1, 2, 3, and so forth. For instance, the following are integer values called *integer literals*.

19   +3568   -289716

Many applications require numbers that have fractional values. These numbers, called *real numbers*, consist of a whole and a fractional part using either a *fixed-point* or a *floating-point* representation. A fixed-point number is a pure decimal number A floating-point number uses scientific notation with a mantissa and an exponent. The representation uses the letter "e" to identify the base-10 exponent, which must be an integer. The following are equivalent fixed- and floating-point representations of a real number.

```
400000.0            4e5
-781.675            -7.81675e2
```

Java defines a range of primitive number types. For integers, the types are, byte, short, int, and long. The difference is the range of integers they store and the amount of computer memory they require. A *byte* is an 8-bit integer in the range −128 to 127. The other integer types use 16-bit (`short`), 32-bit (`int`), and 64-bit (`long`) storage. The type *int* is the most common form of integer. It is a good compromise between range and storage requirements. Typically, an application uses a byte or a *short* integer only when calculations will fall within a limited range of values and storage size is critical. A *long* integer allows for very large values but at the cost of 8 bytes of storage. Java has two real number types, *float* and *double*, which are 32-bit and 64-bit numbers respectively. A program typically uses type `double` for its real variables. One of the reasons is that Java uses 64-bit arithmetic for all real-number operations.

Primitive type	Size in bits	Range
byte	8-bit integer	−128 to 127
short	16-bit integer	−32,768 to 32,767
int	32-bit integer	−2,147,483,648 to 2,147,483,647
long	64-bit integer	(approx) -9×10^{18} to 9×10^{18}
float	32-bit real number	(approx) -3.4×10^{38} to 3.4×10^{38}
double	64-bit real number	(approx) -1.7×10^{308} to 1.7×10^{308}

Let us look at the declaration of primitive numeric variables. The declaration may simply allocate memory without assigning an initial value. The variable is then said to be *uninitialized*. You can initialize a variable with a value. Simply follow the variable name with an "=" sign and the initial value.

```
byte b;                 // uninitialized variable of type byte
int m, n = 15500;       // declaration of two int variables;
                        // n is initialized
```

A declaration can have an initial value so long as it is in range. Violating this condition causes a compiler error because assigning the value may result in a loss of precision.

```
byte badByte = 1000;    // compiler error; range is -128 to 127
```

The declaration of a real number uses type `float` or `double`. In practice, most applications use type `double`. A declaration can have an initial value using fixed or floating-point notation. Special care must be used when initializing a variable of type `float`, no matter which notation is used. By default, a real number literal is a 64-bit `double`. To specify that the literal is a `float`, append the letter F or f. Failure to do so results in a compiler error that indicates a possible loss of precision.

```
double slope;           // uninitialized variable
double x = 14.89;       // use fixed-point notation
double y = 2.3e-5;      // use floating-point notation
float t = 0.0775f;      // the literal is a 32-bit float
```

Java char Type

Character data includes uppercase and lowercase letters, digits, punctuation marks, and special symbols. The computer industry uses different representations of characters. Historically, the 128-element ASCII character codes had the widest acceptance. The code uses 7-bit binary numbers to represent 95 printable characters and 33 control characters that are used in data communications and console input and output. Appendix C includes a discussion of the ASCII character set. In recent times, languages such as Java use an expanded 16-bit *Unicode character set* to reflect other language alphabets. For our purposes, this is not a big issue. The ASCII character set is a subset of the Unicode set and defines the characters we will use.

The Java primitive type *char* specifies a single character. A character literal is a character enclosed in single quotation marks. We can combine these ideas in the declaration of character variables.

```
// declare the variables ch and letter; assign letter
// the character 'A'
char ch, letter = 'A';
```

Escape Sequences   The double quotation character (") denotes the start and end of a string. In some cases, we want a double-quote character as part of the string. Just including the character will not work. For instance, suppose we want to output the string *Source file is "DemoProgram.java"*; the following print statement results in a compile-time error because the double-quote character is used to delimit the string.

```
System.out.println("Source file is "DemoProgram.java"");
```

To address this problem, Java defines a set of *escape sequences* to represent special characters. The format begins with a backslash character (\), which indicates that the next character should be interpreted in a special way. For instance, the escape sequence \" in a string denotes the double quotation character. Escape sequences allow us to recognize control characters such as newline, tab, and carriage return from an input stream or to send control characters to an output stream. We list the most important escape codes in Table A.1.

Table A.1   Common escape codes.

Character	Escape code
backslash	\\
carriage return	\r
double quote	\"
newline	\n
tab	\t

Let us look at some examples using println() statements. The first statement correctly outputs the string with the quoted file name "*DemoProgram.java*". The escape code \n is the newline character. This is particularly significant because it enables us to create a single string that displays in multiple lines. For instance, we insert the newline character in a string literal to display file names on two lines. The string uses the escape code \\ to designate the backslash character in a Windows-like filename.

```java
System.out.println("Source file is \"DemoProgram.java\"");

System.out.println("Input c:\\dataIn.dat\n" + "Output c:\\dataOut.dat");
```

```
Output:
    Source file is "DemoProgram.java"
    Input c:\dataIn.dat
    Output c:\dataOut.dat
```

Declaring Named Constants

A program often uses a number or string to define a value that should not be changed. For instance, circle calculations use the value 3.14159265 for π, and point-of-sales transactions calculate a tax on the basis of the local sales-tax rate. Good programming practice creates an identifier name as a substitute for the actual value and references the name in an expression. The identifier is termed a *named constant*. In Java, create a named constant using the keyword *final* followed by the declaration format for an initialized primitive variable.

```java
final type VARIABLE = constant;
```

By convention, named constants consist of only uppercase letters. For instance,

```java
final int LIMIT = 50;
final double PI = 3.14159265;
final char DELIMITER = ':';
```

A.4   Operators

A key part of many programming statements are expressions which consist of operands and operators that evaluate to some value. The operands may be constants or variables. The operators act on the operands and are of two types. A binary operator takes two operands and a unary operator takes only one operand. This section will present the Java arithmetic and assignment operators.

Arithmetic Operators

An arithmetic expression combines numeric values and operators. The familiar binary operators addition ($+$), subtraction ($-$), and multiplication ($*$) apply to both integers and real numbers. The unary operator negation ($-$) changes the sign of the operand; for instance, $-3 * 4 + 15 = -12 + 15 = 3$.

The division operation is different for integer and real number operands. With real numbers, division ($/$) is fractional division that evaluates to a single real number. With integers, division is in fact long (integer) division that evaluates to a quotient and a remainder. The operator $/$ returns the quotient. The $\%$ operator gives the remainder; that is, the amount left over after doing the division. The % operator is called the *modulo* or *mod operator*. The sign of the result of a remainder operation is the sign of the numerator. Thus 11 % 4 is 3 and −17 % 5 is −2. Examples of division are

```
17 / 5 = 3           // integer division quotient
17 % 5 = 2           // integer division remainder
17.0 / 5.0 = 3.4     // fractional division
6.0 % 4              // Error: % must have integer operands
```

Assignment Operator

Java uses the *assignment operator* = to copy the value of an expression on the right-hand side (rhs) into a variable on the left-hand side (lhs). An assignment statement is terminated by a semicolon.

```
lhs = rhs;
```

The following examples illustrate use of the assignment operator with integer variables. The integer literal 8 is assigned to the variable m. The expression m * 2 is first evaluated and the result is assigned to the variable n.

```
int m, n;

m = 8;          // rhs is the integer literal 8
n = m * 2;      // rhs is an expression which evaluates to 16
```

Java extends the use of the assignment operator to include multiple assignments. The operator chains together assignment operations in order from right to left. We say that assignment is *right associative*.

```
n = m = 25;     // assigns 25 as value of m and then the
                // value of m to n
```

Compound Assignment Operators

The assignment operator combines with an arithmetic operator such as + to produce an operator that updates a variable. For instance, the following increases the value of the variable m by 25.

```
m += 25;
```

The operator += is one form of compound assignment and is really a shortcut for

$$m = m + 25;$$

There is a compound assignment operator for each of the binary operators +, −, *, /, and %. In each case, the format uses a binary operator symbol followed immediately by the assignment symbol "=". The action of a compound assignment operator takes the current value of the variable on the left-hand side (lhs) as one operand and the value of the expression on the right-hand side (rhs) as a second operand. Using the binary operator to combine the operands, the resulting value is assigned as the new value of the variable. The action is equivalent to a simple assignment statement.

Compound assignment: lhs <op>= rhs   Simple assignment: lhs = lhs <op> rhs

Example: Assume m = 14 and n = 3.

```
m += 5;          // m = m + 5;              m is 19
n += m - 2;      // n = n + (m - 2);        n is 15
n *= 2;          // n = n * 2;              n is 6
m /= 5;          // m = m / 5;              m is 2
m %= 5;          // m = m % 5;              m is 4
```

Increment Operators

Algorithms frequently use variables as a counter in a loop or as an index to scan a list of elements. The operations need to increment (add 1) or decrement (subtract 1) the value of the variables. As a convenience, Java provides unary operators ++ and −− for the *increment* and *decrement* operations respectively. For instance, the following is a Java statement that increases the value of the variable count by one.

```
count++;                // increment operator
```

If the value of count is 8 before the statement is executed, the resulting value is 9. A similar statement decreases the value of count by one. From an initial value 8, the result becomes 7.

```
count--;                // decrement operator
```

Note

Prefix Increment and Decrement

Java has *prefix* and *postfix* forms of the increment and decrement operators. In the prefix form, the operator occurs before the variable name; for instance, ++*x* or−−*x*. In an expression, the increment (decrement) operation occurs first and the resulting value is used in a calculation. For instance, assume *X* = 5.

```
y = ++x * 10;          // the ++x operation occurs first and x = 6
                       // the value for y is 6 * 10
```

Operator Precedence

An arithmetic expression can include two or more operators. For instance, the expression 2 + 4*3 involves both addition and multiplication. Evaluating such an expression requires an understanding of the order in which operations are performed. In this case, the multiplication operation 4*3 is done first, followed by the addition operation 2 + 12, which gives the final result 14.

```
2 + 4 * 3    // evaluate 4 * 3 = 12 first, result is 2 + 12 = 14
```

In Java, each operator has a *precedence level* and the compiler generates code to execute operators in the order of their precedence. In our example, we use the fact that multiplication has a higher precedence level than addition and so the order of execution is * followed by +. When an expression has two or more operators at the same precedence, the compiler imposes an ordering on their execution. The ordering is called the *associativity* of the operators. The arithmetic operators at the same precedence level are executed from left to right, an ordering we call *left-associative*. In the previous section, we had an example that used multiple assignment operators. The evaluation was from right to left, indicating that the = operator is *right-associative*.

Precedence can be forced in an expression by using parentheses. Any expression in parentheses is evaluated first.

```
(2 + 4) * 3    // evaluate 2 + 4 = 6 first, result is 6 * 3 = 18
```

The expression Table A.2 gives a listing of the operator precedence and associativity for the basic arithmetic and assignment operators. Appendix C includes a table for all of the Java operators that we use in this book.

Table A.2 Operator precedence and associativity for arithmetic and assignment operators.

Level	Operator	Operation	Associativity
0	=	Assignment	R to L
1	+	Addition	L to R
	−	Subtraction	L to R
	*	Multiplication	L to R
2	/	Division	L to R
	%	Remainder	L to R
3	+	Unary plus	R to L
	−	Unary minus	R to L

Let us look at examples that illustrate the order of operations in a complex expression. The first example involves simply the precedence of operators. Note that assignment has the lowest level priority so that the operation is executed last.

```
int m = 40, n;
n = -m + 14 % 4;
```

First execute negation:	n = -40 + 14 % 4	
Second execute remainder:	= -40 + 2	// 14 % 4 = 2
Third execute addition:	= -38	// -40 + 2 = -38

A multiple assignment statement introduces associativity. In the example, the expression on the right-hand side is evaluated and then assignments copy the value of the expression to first q and then p.

```
int m = 9, n = 5, p, q;
p = q = 4 * m / n;
```

First execute multiplication:	p = q = 36 / n	// 4 * m = 4 * 9 = 36
Second execute division:	p = q = 7	// 36 / n = 36 / 5 = 7
Third execute assignment	q = 7	// assign 7 to q
Fourth execute assignment	p = q	// assign q = 7 to p

A.5 Conversions between Types

Java is a strong typed language; that is, it associates a type with each data value. Applications often need to convert data from one type to another so that important information is not lost. For instance, converting a real number to an integer retains only the whole number part of the real number and discards the fractional part. Conversions between one primitive type and another are classified as *widening conversions* or *narrowing conversions*. Widening conversions among numeric values go from one data type to another that uses the same or more memory space to store the values. Narrowing conversions go from one type to another that uses a smaller space to store values. The result is often a loss of both the magnitude and precision of the value and should be used only when necessary. The ordering of the widening conversions for numeric types is

byte -> short -> int -> long -> float -> double

For instance, a `byte` is an 8-bit integer in the range from -128 to 127. Converting it to a 16-bit `short` is widening conversion and will preserve all of the information. Widening conversion from an `int` or `long` to a floating-point number maintains the magnitude of the number although some precision may be lost because of round-off.

In Java, data conversions can occur in three ways: *arithmetic promotion*, *explicit casting*, and *assignment conversion*. Let us look at each in turn.

Arithmetic Promotion   Arithmetic promotion occurs automatically. A computer can only perform operations on values of the same type. For instance, when adding two `int` values, the result is an `int`, which is the type of the operands. Similarly, division of two operands of type `double` yields a quotient of type `double`. The types involved in each expression are called the *mode* of the expression. An expression may involve operands of different types. You can add an `int` and a `double`. Execution of the expression, called a *mixed-mode expression*, involves promotion (widening conversion) of operands to the largest type. In the following example, the integer operand is automatically promoted to a `double` and the result has type `double`.

```
4 + 6.5   is evaluated as 4.0 + 6.5 = 10.5
```

Explicit Casting   Casting is the most general form of data conversion. A cast is an explicit directive to the compiler, indicating that a conversion should occur. The format for a cast places the desired type in parentheses in front of the operand, which may be variable, literal, or complex expression.

```
(type)operand
```

Casting frequently occurs when you want to change the default mode of an expression. For example, assume the integer variable `total` has value 22 and represents the sum of four numbers. The statement

```
double avg = total/4;
```

assigns the value 5 as the average because integer division is used to evaluate the expression on the right-hand side. If you want fractional division with a value 5.5, change the mode of the expression by casting the operand total to have type `double`.

```
double avg = (double)total/4;
```

The operand is converted to `double` and the mixed expression is evaluated as 22.0/4.0. Changing the mode of the integer constant 4 has the same effect and yields the result avg = 5.5.

```
double avg = total/4.0;
```

Assignment Conversion   Assignment conversion occurs when the expression on the right side of an assignment statement has a different type than the left-hand side. Assignment accomplishes only widening conversion from the right-hand side to the left-hand side. Otherwise, the right-hand side must be explicitly cast.

```
int m = 15, n = 65;
double x;
char ch;

x = m;                      // with widening conversion, x is 15.0
ch = (char)n;               // explicit casting, ch is 'A'
```

A.6   Selection Statements

A computer program consists of a series of statements that dictate the order in which actions are performed. The ordering is the program's *flow of control*. Without some control construct, instructions are executed sequentially in the order in which they are written. We want to explore ways of designing programs with more complicated flow of control. Programming languages, such as Java, use two different types of control techniques. A *selection statement* tests a condition and then chooses from one or more possible actions (options) based on the condition. A *loop statement* repeats an action over and over again until some stopping condition is met.

Control statements involve testing a `boolean` expression which is either `true` or `false`. The name `boolean` is linked to George Boole, an English mathematician who did pioneering research on logical expressions. Simple boolean expressions use relational operators that compare numbers, variables, and other expressions. Table A.3 lists the Java comparison operators. You are be familiar with them from mathematics, although with different notation.

Table A.3   Java comparison operators with equivalent mathematics notation.

Mathematics notation	Java notation	Meaning	Java example
$=$	$==$	Equal to	$n \% 2 == 0$
$\neq$	$!=$	Not equal to	response $!=$ "Y"
$<$	$<$	Less than	$4 < 6$
$\leq$	$<=$	Less than or equal to	age $<= 21$
$>$	$>$	Greater than	balance >0
$\geq$	$>=$	Greater than or equal to	ch $=$ "A"

Boolean expressions combine with the operators AND, OR, and NOT to create new expressions. Java defines the logical operators using a compact notation.

Logical operator	Java operator
AND	&&
OR	||
NOT	!

If P and Q are `boolean` expressions, then

- P && Q is true provided both P and Q are true; it is false in all other cases.

  Example: `'a' <= ch && ch <= 'z'`   `// true if ch is a`
  `// lowercase letter`

- P ‖ Q is true if P is true or if Q is true; it is false only when both P and Q are false.

  Example: `n % 2 == 0 || n == 5`   `// true if n is even`
  `// or n is 5`

- !P is the logical opposite of P. It is true when P is false and false when P is true.

  Example: `!(n % 5 == 0)`   `// true if n is not`
  `// divisible by 5`

Short-Circuit boolean Expression Evaluation   Java uses a method of partial evaluation to determine the value of a logical expression. To understand this method, let's look at some examples.

(a) `a == b || a > 30`   (b) `a < 5 && b % 2 == 0`

With expression (a), the "‖" operator applies to the values of the relational expressions "a == b" and "a > 30". The result is true if either operand is true. With *short-circuit evaluation*, the computer evaluates the operands from left to right and stops as soon as the logical value of the entire expression is known. If the left-hand operand "a == b" is `true`, the ‖ expression is `true` and the right-hand operand "a > 30" is not evaluated. In (b), the "&&" operator is `false` if either of the operands is `false`. Using shortcut evaluation, the computer evaluates the left-hand operand "a < 5" and stops if its result is `false`. In this case, the && expression is `false` and the right-hand operand "b % 2 == 0" is not evaluated.

Example:
  In the following expression, the division is not done if x is 0.0.
  `x!= 0.0 && 20/x < 1`

Note

Other boolean Operators

There are `boolean` operators that do not perform short-circuit evaluation. The operator ‖ takes two `boolean` operands and evaluates the `boolean` OR relation without using short-circuit evaluation. Similarly, the operator & does not perform short-circuit evaluation for a `boolean` AND expression.

Example:
  A divide by 0 error will occur if x == 0.0.
  `x!= 0.0 & 20/x < 1`

The operators ‖ and | evaluate the logical or *inclusive OR* relation. If either operand is true, then the expression is true. The `boolean` operator $^\wedge$ evaluates the *exclusive OR* relation without using short-circuit evaluation. P $^\wedge$ Q is true if one but not both of P and Q are true; it is false when both P and Q are true or both are false.

Example:
  `(n % 3 == 0) ^ (n >= 5)`   `// true if n is 17 and false`
  `// if n = 18`

The If-Statement

In the logic of a program, there are often decision points where the program needs to test a condition and then select from one or more possible actions (options) on the basis of the condition. Like other programming languages, Java provides an *if-statement* that uses a boolean expression as a condition and code blocks to designate the options. An if-statement executes by testing the condition and then branching to an appropriate code block.

A *code block* is a group of one or more statements that are combined to carry out a single task. Instructions within the block are set off by braces and may contain declarations. In the case of a single statement, the braces may be omitted. A variable declared in a block can only be used in the block. We say that the block defines the *scope* of the variable in the sense that the variable can only be referenced by statements within the block and is not visible outside of the block.

Block syntax:

```
{
    Declarations   // declaration of variables
    Statement₁     // sequence of statements
    . . .
    Statementₙ
}
```

The simplest form of an if-statement uses a logical expression as a condition and executes code block Code_T if the expression evaluates to true. The subscript T indicates that the code will execute only when the condition is true.

Syntax:

```
if (condition)
    Code_T
```

> *Example:* Order the values for integer variables m and n so that m has the larger value. An if-statement checks whether m < n; if so, it exchanges (swaps) the values in the two integers. The code block declares the variable `temp` as temporary storage for the value in m. The variable has scope only within the block and thus cannot be accessed outside of the block.
>
> ```
> if (m < n)
> {
>     int temp;          // the exchange needs temporary storage
>
>     temp = m;          // hold m in temporary storage
>     m = n;             // copy n to m
>     n = temp;          // copy original value of m to n
> }
> ```

The most common form of an if-statement has the program choose from among two options. In other words, the program makes an "either-or" choice. The form of the if-statement uses the reserved word *else* to designate the second option. The statement, called an *ifelse statement*, tests the condition and executes Code_T if the condition is true and Code_F if it is false.

Syntax:

```
if (condition)
    Code_T                          // if true, execute this code
else
    Code_F                          // if false, execute this code
```

Example: A course grade is "P" or "F", indicating pass or failure. The instructor passes a student when the average score is 70 or above.

```
if (avgScore >= 70)
    grade = 'P';
else
    grade = 'F';
```

Nested If-Statements

An if/else-statement can contain any sort of statements within its code blocks. In particular, it can constitute a nested if-statement by placing if/else-statements within the blocks. The following example illustrates the situation.

Example 1: A lumber company prices sheets of plywood based on their grade: F (finished) or U (utility). In addition, the company offers customers a reduced price on a sheet if they buy in quantity. The following table lists the price of a sheet of plywood based on grade and quantity.

Plywood price (per sheet)		
	Utility	**Finished**
Quantity 1–9	12.50	18.75
Quantity 10+	11.25	17.25

A nested if-statement computes the total cost of purchasing n sheets of plywood for a designated grade ('U' or 'F').

```
// first test for the grade; nested if/else-statements for each
// grade test the quantity
if (grade == 'U')
    if (quantity < 10)
        totalCost = n * 12.50;   // option: U grade, quantity 1-9
    else
        totalCost = n * 11.25;   // option: U grade, quantity 10+
else
    if (quantity < 10)
        totalCost = n * 18.75;   // option: F grade, quantity 1-9
    else
        totalCost = n * 17.25;   // option: F grade, quantity 10+
```

Example 2: In Example 1, both Code$_T$ and Code$_F$ contain an if/else-statement and so the nested if-statement distinguishes four options. Nesting can also occur when only one of the code blocks has a selection statement. A bank charges customers a fee to handle a check. All customers are charged $20.00 for a bad check (`balance < checkAmt`). Otherwise, the fee is $1.00 for a regular customer and $0.50 for a senior citizen (`age >= 60`).

```
// check for sufficient funds
if (balance < checkAmt)        // Option: bad check
   fee = 20.00;
else
   if (age >= 60)              // Option: senior citizen
      fee = 0.50;
   else
      fee = 1.00;              // Option: regular customer
```

Multiway If/Else-Statements

The nested selection statements in the previous examples start with an if/else-statement that allows us to branch in two ways and then have each of the choices create branches to two other choices. In the lumber store example, the main if/else-statement uses the grade of plywood to specify two categories of purchase and then splits each category into two options on the basis of the quantity. The nested if/else-statement allows selection among four options. The format carefully indents the nested if/else-statements to highlight categories and options.

In many applications, we want a selection statement to specify branches into a number of different options. This is done with nested if-statements but without indenting to list the choices. The format creates a *multiway if/else-statement* that better describes how we view the options. Let us look at examples.

Example 1: An instructor uses multiway selection to assign traditional letter grades 'A' through 'D' and 'F' based on average score. The format combines "else if" on a single line to represent options in a multiple selection process. The compiler treats the code as a series of nested if/else-statements.

```
if (avgScore >= 90)
   grade = 'A';
else if (avgScore >= 80)
   grade = 'B';
else if (avgScore >= 70)
   grade = 'C';
else if (avgScore >= 60)
   grade = 'D';
else if (avgScore < 60)        // could be a simple else
   grade = 'F';
```

Example 2: Use multiway selection to output whether integer n is positive, negative, or zero. A simple else-statement terminates the sequence because an integer that is not negative or zero must be positive.

```
if (n < 0)
   System.out.println("Integer n is negative ");
else if (n == 0)
   System.out.println("Integer n is zero");
else
   System.out.println("Integer n is positive");
```

Conditional Expression Operator

Java provides an alternative to the if/else-statement using the *conditional expression operator* (?:). The syntax for the operator requires three operands. The first is a condition (boolean expression) and the other two are expressions (choices) that are set off with separators "?" and ":" respectively.

Syntax: condition ? expression$_T$: expression$_F$

The runtime system executes the operator by first testing the condition. If it is true, the value of expression$_T$ is returned; if it is not true, the value of expression$_F$ is returned. Programmers typically use a conditional expression to assign a variable one of two values depending on some condition. For instance, the following conditional expression assigns the larger of two values x and y to the variable max.

```
max = (x >= y) ? x : y;
```

The conditional expression is shorthand for assigning to max within an if/else-statement.

```
if (x >= y)
   max = x;
else
   max = y;
```

A conditional expression can be part of a more complex expression or part of an output statement.

```
System.out.println("Grade is " +
   ((score >= 70) ? "Pass" : "Fail"));
```

The Switch-Statement

The *switch-statement* is a special form of multiway selection that transfers control to one of several statements, depending on the value of an expression. The Java syntax for the statement begins with the reserved word *switch* and a selector expression enclosed in parentheses. The body of the statement is a block, which contains one or more *switch* labels consisting of the reserved word *case*, a constant, the delimiter colon, and a list of statements that are the action for the specific case.

Syntax:

```
switch (selector expression)
{
    case constant₁:        Statement for constant₁
                           break;

                . . . . . .
    case constantₙ:        Statement for constantₙ
                           break;

    default:               Statement if no case matches selector
                           break;

}
```

The selector expression must have a discrete (integer or character) value. The switch-statement executes by taking the selector value and comparing it with each case constant. If a match occurs, the corresponding statement sequence is executed. If no match occurs, then control passes to the *default* label if it exists, or to the first statement following the switch block. When a statement sequence concludes, there is not an automatic transfer to the statement following the switch block. Instead, control continues with the next statement sequence. This situation is not normally desired and so Java provides a *break* statement, which forces a branch out of the switch-statement.

Example: Describe types of coins for different values of the integer selector `coinValue`. This example allows two or more case options to be included with a single statement.

```
switch(coinValue)
{
    case 1:
    case 5:
    case 10:
    case 25:   System.out.println(coinValue +
                        "cents is a standard coin");
               break;
    case 50:   System.out.println(coinValue +
                        "cents is a special coin");
               break;
    default:   System.out.println("No coin for " + coin +
                        "cents");
               break;
}
```

```
Run:
  For coinValue = 25, the output is "25 cents is a standard coin"
  For coinValue = 50, the output is "50 cents is a special coin"
  For coinValue = 15, the output is "No coin for 15 cents"
```

☞

Note

Missing Break Statement

If a break statement is not placed at the end of a case-option, the runtime system will execute instructions in the next case-option. For instance, assume the example includes no break statements and `coinValue` is 25. A run would produce output that includes the case 50 option and the default option.

Output:

```
25 cents is a standard coin
25 cents is a special coin
No coin for 25 cents
```

The boolean Type

The `boolean` type is a primitive type like `int`, `double`, and `char`. The type has values `true` and `false` that can be used in program statements. Like the other primitive types, you can have constants and variables of `boolean` type. A variable is typically used as a flag to indicate the status of a condition in an algorithm or as a name for a `boolean` expression.

```
final boolean VALID_ID = true;

// isEnrolled is a flag that indicates the registration status
// of a student in a course; The flag is set to false if the
// student drops the course
boolean isEnrolled = true;

// variables are names for a boolean expression; the value
// of the variable is the value of the boolean expression
boolean isLowercase = 'a' <= ch && ch <= 'z';
boolean onProbation = gpa < 2.0;
```

Using `boolean` variables improves program readability. Look at an alternative version of the nested if/else-statement that a bank uses to set fees for processing a check. Recall that the fee is $20.00 for a bad check and either $0.50 or $1.00 for a good check, depending on whether the customer is or is not a senior citizen.

```
boolean haveIsufficientFunds = balance < checkAmt;
boolean isSenior = age >= 60;

if (haveInsufficientFunds)
   fee = 20.00;
else
   if (isSenior)
      fee = 0.50;
   else
      fee = 1.00;
```

Example A.1

The `boolean` expression that determines whether a year is a leap year is complex. We are taught that a leap year is a year that is divisible by 4. That is true most of the time except when the year is a turn-of-the-century like 2100. In fact, a year is a leap year when it is divisible by 4 but not divisible by 100, or is divisible by 400. Years such as 1992 and 2004 are leap years, and 2007 is not a leap year. A turn-of-the century year is divisible by 100 and thus is a leap year only when it is divisible by 400. The year 2000 was a leap year, but 2100, 2200, and 2300 will not be leap years. The Java form of the `boolean` expression that tests whether a year is a leap year uses both the AND (&&) and OR (‖) operators. A program should use a `boolean` variable as a substitute for the expression.

```
boolean isLeapYear = (year % 4 == 0 && year % 100 != 0) ||
                     (year % 400 == 0);
```

A.7 Loop Statements

A program often has an action that must be repeated time and time again until some stopping condition is met. The portion of the program that repeats the action is called a *loop* and the statements that carry out the action are called the *loop body*. Each repetition of the body is an *iteration* of the loop. For instance, a professor has a grading program that assigns each student a letter grade. The program uses a loop to repeat code that gives an individual student a grade based on test and homework scores.

Java provides a variety of looping statements. Each form of the statement includes a controlling condition that determines whether another iteration of the loop should execute. The controlling condition is a `boolean` expression which is part of the loop *test*.

The While-Statement

A *while-loop* is the most general form of loop statement. The while-statement repeats its action until the controlling condition (loop test) becomes `false`. Put another way, the statement repeatedly executes "while" the condition is true; hence the name. The while-statement begins with the keyword *while* followed by a `boolean` expression in parentheses. The expression is part of the loop test that is carried out before beginning another iteration. If the test is true, program control passes to the loop body; if `false`, control passes to the statement after the body.

Syntax: `while (logical expression)`
                  `body`

> *Example 1:* A while-statement computes the sum of the first 10 integers, $1 + 2 + \cdots + 10$. The integer variable i is a counter in the range 1 to 10. Its initial value is 1 and the loop test checks whether i is in range (i <= 10). The loop body adds the current value of i to the variable `sum` and then increments the value of i. This is an example of a counter-controlled loop in which a count on the number of iterations is maintained and is used as part of the loop control test.

```
int i, sum = 0;
i = 1;                  // initialize the counter i
while (i <= 10)         // loop test; exit when i > 10
{
    sum += i;           // add current value of i to sum
    i++;                // increment i
}
```

Example 2: A while-statement sums successive even integers $2 + 4 + 6 + \cdots$ until the total is greater than 250. The loop is like Example 1 except that the loop test checks the sum rather than the counter i. An update statement increments i by 2 so that it becomes the next even integer. This is an event-controlled loop because iterations continue until some non-count–related condition (event) stops the process.

```
int i, sum = 0;
i = 2;                  // initial even integer for the sum
while (sum <= 250)      // loop test; check current value of sum
{
    sum += i;           // add integer to sum
    i += 2;             // update i to next even integer
}
```

The Do/While-Statement

The *do/while*-loop is similar to a while-loop except that it places the loop test at the end of the loop body. A do/while-loop executes at least one iteration and then continues execution so long as the test condition remains true.

Syntax:
```
do
{
    body
} while (logical expression);
```

Example: During a rocket launch, scientists count down the last 10 seconds before blast off. A do/while-statement simulates the countdown.

```
int count = 10;
do
{
    System.out.print(count + "  ");
    count--;                          // decrement count
}
while (count > 0);                    // repeat until count is 0

System.out.println("Blast Off!!!");
```

Output:
```
    10  9  8  7  6  5  4  3  2  1  Blast Off!!!
```

The For-Statement

The *for-statement* is an alternative loop structure for a while-statement. It is typically used for counter-controlled loops. The format of the for-loop has three separate fields, separated by semicolons. The fields enable a programmer to initialize variables, specify a loop test, and update values for control variables.

Syntax: `for (initialize statement; loop test; update statement)`
          `body`

Initialize statement:

> The *initialize statement* consists of assignment statements separated by commas. Typically, there is one assignment statement that initializes a counter-control variable. A for-statement executes the initialization only once before making the loop test and any iterations of the loop body.

Test condition (loop test):

> The test condition is a `boolean` expression which serves as the loop test. The expression is evaluated prior to any iteration of the loop. If the condition is `true`, control passes to the loop body; if `false`, control passes to the first statement after the loop body.

Update statement:

> Update statements assign new values to the loop control variables. The statements typically use the increment ($++$) or decrement ($--$) operator to update the control variable if it changes by 1 or a compound assignment statement if it changes by some other amount. An update statement is executed with each iteration after completing the loop body and before the next check of the test condition.

> *Example 1:* The syntax in a for-loop is best understood by contrasting the statement with a while-statement. Look at the problem of computing the sum of the first 10 integers, $1 + 2 + \cdots + 10$. The variable i is the counter. For each loop, use the following declaration.

> `int i, sum = 0;`

	while-LOOP	for-LOOP
init:	`i = 1;`	`for (i = 1; i <= 10; i++)`
test:	`while (i <= 10)`	`    sum += i;`
	`{`	
	`    sum += i;`	
update:	`    i++;`	
	`}`	

Example 2:   A for-statement simulates countdown to blast off. The integer control variable is declared within the initialize statement and so has scope only within the for-loop.

```
for (int count = 10; count > 0; count--)
    System.out.print(count + " ");       // loop body
System.out.println("Blast Off!!!");   // after loop body
```

Break Statement

Within a loop body, a *break* statement causes an immediate exit from the loop to the first statement after the loop body. The break allows for an exit at any intermediate statement in the loop.

Syntax: `break;`

Using a break statement to exit a loop has limited but important applications. Let us describe one of these situations. A program may use a loop to input data from a file. The number of iterations depends on the amount of data in the file. The task of reading from the file is part of the loop body, which thus becomes the place where the program discovers that data is exhausted. When the end-of-file condition becomes true, a break statement exits the loop. In selecting a loop construct to read data from a file, we recognize that the test for end-of-file occurs within the loop body. The loop statement has the form of an infinite loop; that is, one that runs forever. The assumption is that we do not know how much data is in the file.

Versions of the for-loop and the while-loop permit a programmer to create an infinite loop. In the for-loop, each field of the loop is empty. There are no control variables and no loop test. The equivalent while-loop uses the constant `true` as the logical expression.

```
for(;;)              while (true)
    loop block           loop block
```

Let us look at a code structure that reads data from a file. An infinite while-loop ensures that the input process repeats. The loop terminates when the loop body recognizes that an input request was not carried out because the process reached the end of the file. The condition end-of-file (eof) is true.

```
while (true)
{
    <read data from the file)
    if (eof)
        break;
    <process data from this input>
}
```

A.8   Arrays

An *array* is a fixed-size collection of elements of the same data type that occupies a block of contiguous memory locations. The array name specifies the collection of elements. Like any other variable, an array declaration includes the name of the array and the data type for the elements in the sequence. To specify that the variable is an array, add a pair of square brackets immediately after the data type. For instance, the declaration of `intArr` for our example is

```
int[] intArr;
```

Up to now, we have declared a variable of primitive type only. The variable is the name of a memory location that stores its value. An array is a different kind of entity called a *reference variable*. It contains a value which is a reference (address) to the first location in the associated block of memory. A simple declaration of an array assigns it the value *null*. As such the array does not point to any actual memory locations. To allocate a block of memory for the array and assign the address of the block to the array variable, the *operator new* is used. The syntax for the operator includes the data type and the number of elements in the array enclosed in square brackets. For instance, the following statement allocates four integer elements.

```
intArr = new int[4];
```

The variable `intArr` is the reference (address) of the block of memory that stores integer elements. The figure distinguishes the array reference variable from the memory that holds the array elements.

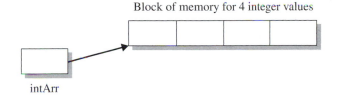

Block of memory for 4 integer values

intArr

The declaration of an array reference variable and the allocation of memory can be done in a single step.

```
int[] intArr = new int[4];        // array of 4 integers
char[] charArr = new char[80];    // array of 80 characters
double[] dblArr = new double[12]; // array of 12 real numbers
```

Assume n is the size of the array. Access to an individual element in the array is provided by an index in the range 0 to n−1. The index denotes the position of the element in the sequence. The element at index i is denoted by `arr[i]`. The sequence of elements in the array is

```
arr[0], arr[1], arr[2],..., arr[n-2], arr[n-1]
```

For instance, let `intArr` be an array of four integers 21, 7, 30, and 15. The figure below displays the sequence as a contiguous block of memory with an index listed below each cell.

intArr

The array name and the index can be used to access the value of an element in an array directly. On the left side of an assignment statement, they provide a reference to the array element.

```
item = arr[i];      // arr[i] is element at index i
arr[i] = item;      // item assigned to element at index i
```

The range of valid indices is 0 to $n - 1$ where n is the size of the array. An attempt to access an element outside of the valid index range results in a runtime error. Once an array is created, a program may access its size using the expression `arr.length`. Java defines `length` as a variable associated with the array. Hence, with any array, the valid index range is 0 to `arr.length` $- 1$.

A loop provides efficient sequential access to the elements in an array. Let the loop control variable serve as an index. For instance, the following statements declare an array `arr` of 100 integer elements and uses a for-loop to initialize the sequence with values 1, 2, ..., 100.

```
int[] arr = new int[100];    // declare array and allocate space
for (i=0; i < arr.length; i++)
    arr[i] = i+1;
```

Array Initialization

A primitive variable can be initialized in a declaration statement. The same feature applies to an array. After declaring the array, use "=" followed by an array initializer list, which is a comma-separated sequence of values enclosed in braces. There is no need to use the operator `new` because the compiler uses the size of the initializer list to allocate memory. For instance, the following declares the array `intArr` in our example and initializes its values.

```
int[] intArr = {21, 7, 30, 15};
```

Additional examples create an array of characters that identifies the arithmetic operators and an array of strings for the days in the week.

```
char[] operator = {'+', '-', '*', '/', '%'};
String[] day = {"Sun", "Mon", "Tue", "Wed", "Thu", "Fri",
                "Sat"};
```

Scanning Arrays with Foreach

Java provides an enhanced for-statement that allows for a read-only scan of an array without using indices. The syntax includes a declaration of a variable of the array type and the array name separated by a colon(:).

Syntax: `for (Type varName : arrayName)`
            . . .

For instance, let `intArr` be an array of integer elements. The enhanced for-statement scans the sequence and computes the sum.

```
int [] intArr = {6, 1, 8, 4, 9};
int sum;
```

```
// variable eltValue must be declared within the enhanced
// for statement
for (int eltValue : intArr)
    sum += eltValue;
```

The enhanced for-statement makes the compiler take care of the scan of the array and access to elements using an index. The scan is "read-only" because the value of each array element is copied to the local variable `eltValue`. The enhanced for-statement is more commonly referred to as the "foreach" statement. When you read it out loud, the colon is pronounced "in."

Two-Dimensional Arrays

A two-dimensional array is a table with access specified by row and column indices. The concept can be extended to cover general multidimensional arrays, in which elements are accessed by three or more indices. The declaration of a two-dimensional array is a straightforward extension of a one-dimensional array, including the use of the operator `new`. Rather than using one pair of square brackets to denote an array, the two-dimensional array uses two pairs of brackets. We often refer to a two-dimensional array of numbers as a *matrix*.

The declaration defines `mat` as a two-dimensional array of integers. The operator `new` allocates memory for the matrix with 2 rows and 4 columns and assigns to `mat` the address of a block of eight integers that store the matrix.

```
int[][] mat;             // declare two-dimensional reference
                         // variable
mat = new int[2][4];     // allocate 8 integer locations
                         // partitioned as 2 rows, 4 columns
```

Elements of `mat` are accessed using double-bracket notation

```
mat[i][j] where 0 <= i < 2, 0 <= j < 4
```

For instance, assume the following table displays the elements in `mat`. Nested for-loops scan the elements and compute the sum of the elements.

	0	1	2	3
0	20	5	30	0
1	−40	15	100	80

```
int row, col, sum = 0;

for (row = 0; row < 2; row++)
    for (col = 0; col < 4; col++)
        sum += mat[row][col];
```

A program may access an entire row of the matrix using a row index in brackets. The resulting structure is a one-dimensional array.

```
// mat[0] is the first row in the matrix; as a 1-dimensional
// array, it has an associated length variable
columnSize = mat[0].length;                 // value 4
```

Like a one-dimensional array, you can use an initializer list to allocate a matrix with initial values. The initializer list for `mat` includes two comma-separated blocks of four values. Each block defines initial values for the columns corresponding to a row in the matrix. The following declaration creates the matrix `mat` in our example.

```
int[][] mat = {{20, 5, 30, 0}, {-40, 15, 100, 80}};
```

A.9   Java Methods

A method is a collection of statements that perform a task. It provides specialized services, much like a subcontractor handles a phase of construction that is under the control of the head contractor. A method can accept data values, carry out calculations, and return a value. The data values serve as input for the method and the return value is its output.

The declaration of a method begins with its header, which consists of modifiers, a return type, a method name, and a parameter list. The list is a comma-separated sequence of variable declarations that include the variable name and data type. The list defines the *formal parameters* of the method. We refer to the format of the header as the *method signature*. The code that implements the method is a block called the *method body*.

```
modifiers returnType methodName(Type₁ var₁, Type₂ var₂,
                                Type₃ var₃, . . .)
{
    // method body
}
```

Methods are always declared within a class. In Chapter 1, we introduced objects and their object types, which are classes. Methods in these classes are typically associated with an object which must be included in the method call. Other methods are associated with the class. These methods begin with the modifiers `public static`. A method may return a value. The `returnType` specifies the data type for the return value. If the method does not return a value, use the keyword *void* as the return type.

We are already familiar with the method `main()`. Note its signature. The method name is `main` and the return type is `void` because it does not return a value. The parameter list is a single variable specifying an array of strings. The method has the modifier `public static`, which indicates that it is associated with the main application class.

```
public static void main(String[] args)
{
    // body is the main program
}
```

Predefined Methods

Java provides a collection of methods that implement familiar mathematical functions for scientific, engineering, or statistical calculations. The methods are defined in the `Math` class. We give a partial listing that includes the power function, the square root function, and the standard trigonometric functions. In most cases, the parameter types and the return type for the methods are of type `double`.

Power function:

```
public static double pow(double x, double y);     // x^y
```

Square root function:

```
public static double sqrt(double x);
```

Trigonometric functions:

```
public static double cos(double x);    // trigonometric cosine
public static double sin(double x);    // trigonometric sine
public static double tan(double x);    // trigonometric tangent
```

To access a Java method defined in the Math class, a calling statement must access the method by using both the class name Math and the method name separated by a "." (dot). Follow the method name by a list of *arguments* enclosed in parentheses. The arguments, which are also referred to as *actual parameters*, correspond to the formal parameters in the method header. They must be constants or variables of the same type as the corresponding formal parameters or the compiler must provide automatic type conversion to the same type. If available, the return value may be used in an assignment statement or as part of an expression.

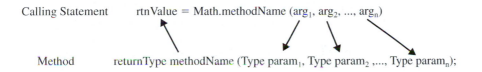

Calling Statement   rtnValue = Math.methodName (arg$_1$, arg$_2$, ..., arg$_n$)

Method   returnType methodName (Type param$_1$, Type param$_2$,..., Type param$_n$);

As an example, let us look at the pow() method, which implements the power function x^y. The two formal parameters for pow() are of type double. A call to pow() must provide arguments of type double or arguments that can be promoted to type double by the compiler.

```
// variables for one argument and the return value
double a = 4.0, powValue;
```

```
// call pow() from the Math class; integer 3 is promoted
// to a double; then assign powValue the return value 64.0
powValue = Math.pow(a,3);
```

A method executes as part of a call-return mechanism. The calling statement uses the method name followed by a list of arguments in parentheses. If no arguments are specified, the call must still include the parentheses. Execution begins by having the runtime system first allocate memory for the variables (parameters). The actual arguments are then copied to the new variables. After executing code in the method block, program control returns to the calling statement with any specified return value.

Figure A.3 illustrates the call-return mechanism for the calling statement powValue = Math.pow(a,3). The process involves allocating variables x and y in the parameter list and then copying the value of argument a to x and the constant 3 (promoted to 3.0) to y. After exiting the method block, program control passes back to the calling statement and carries out assignment of the return value, 64.0, to powValue.

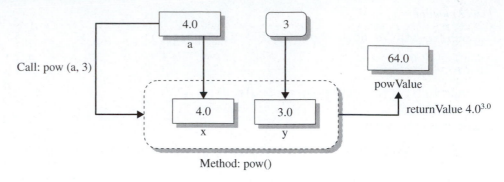

Call: pow (a, 3)

Method: pow()

Figure A.3 *Function call and return mechanism.*

Example A.2

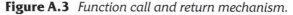

1. The Math class defines the constant π. The named constant is Math.PI. A trigonometric function takes an angle in radians. If you want to compute a trigonometric value for an angle in degrees, convert the argument to radians (angle * $(\pi/180)$).

```java
double theta = 0.0, angle = 30;
System.out.println("cosine of 0 radians is " +
                    Math.cos(theta));
System.out.println("sine of 30 degrees is " +
                    Math.sin(angle*(Math.PI/180)));
```

```
Output:
    cosine of 0 radians is 1.0
    sine of 30 degrees is 0.5
```

2. We illustrate the Math class methods pow() and sqrt() for a variety of arguments.

```java
double value;
value = Math.pow(3.0,4);     // value = 3.0^4 = 243.0
value = Math.pow(2,8);       // value = 2^8 = 256
value = Math.pow(9,0.5);     // value = 9^0.5 = √9.0 = 3.0
value = Math.sqrt(5.0);      // value = 2.23606798
```

User-Defined Methods

An annuity is a popular investment tool for retirement. An amount of money (principal) is invested at a fixed interest rate (rate) and allowed to grow over a period of time (nyears). The value of the annuity after nyears is given by the formula

$$\text{annuity} = \text{principal} * (1 + \text{rate})^{\text{nyears}}$$

Let us create a method that returns the value of an annuity. We include the method in a main application class and call it from the method main(). The declaration of the method begins with its signature. The method name is annuity and the modifiers are public static. The parameter list has two variables, principal and rate, of type double and a third parameter nyears of type int. The return type is a double.

```java
public static annuity(double principal, double rate, int nyears)
```

The implementation of the method uses the power function to evaluate the formula. The result becomes the return value. In a method, we provide the return value with a statement that uses the reserved word *return* and the value. The data type of the return value must be compatible with the return type in the method header. The general form of the statement is

```
return expression;
```

The following is an implementation of the method annuity().

annuity():

```
public static double annuity(double principal, double rate,
                             int nyears)
{
   return principal * Math.pow(1+rate,nyears);
}
```

A return statement can be used anywhere in the body of the method. It causes an immediate exit from the method with the return value passed back to the calling statement. When a method has a `returnType` other than `void`, a return statement with a return value is required. When the method has a void `returnType`, a return from the method body either may be provided by a simple return statement with no argument or occurs after execution of the last statement in the body.

```
return;    // may be used if returnType is void
```

For instance, the method `printLabel()` takes a string argument for a label along with string and integer arguments for the month and year. Output includes the label and the month and year separated by a comma (","). The method has a `void` return type.

printLabel():

```
public static void printLabel(String label, String month,
                              int year)
{
   System.out.println(label + " " month + ", " + year);

   // a return statement provides explicit exit from
   // the method;   typically we use an implicit return that
   // occurs after executing the last statement in
   // the method body
   return;
}
```

Example A.3

This example illustrates calls to both `printLabel()` and `annuity()`. A $10,000 annuity with interest rate 8% was purchased in December 1991. We determine the value of the annuity after 30 years.

```
// month and year for purchase
String month = "December";
int year = 1991;

// principal invested and interest earned per year
double principal = 10000.0, interestRate = 0.08, annuityValue;
```

```
// number of years for the annuity
int nyears = 30;

// call the method and store the return value
annuityValue = annuity(principal, interestRate, nyears);

// output label and a summary description of the annuity
printLabel("Annuity purchased:", month, year);
System.out.println("After " + nyears + " years, $" +
        principal + " at " +interestRate*100 +
        "% grows to $" + annuityValue);
```

Output:
```
    Annuity purchased: December, 1991
    After 30 years, $10000.0 at 8.0% grows to $100626.57
```

Arrays as Method Parameters

A method can include an array among its formal parameters. The format includes the type of the elements followed by the characters "[]" and the array name.

```
returnType methodName (Type[] arr, ...)
```

For instance, let us define a method max() that returns the largest element in an array of real numbers. The method signature includes an array of type double as a parameter and a return type double. For the implementation, assume the first element is the largest and assign it to the variable maxValue. Then carry out a scan of the array with an index in the range 1 to the length of the array. As the scan proceeds, update maxValue whenever a new and larger value is encountered. After completing the scan, maxValue is the return value.

```
public static double max(double[] arr)
{
    double maxValue = arr[0];      // assume arr[0] is largest

    // scan rest of array and update maxValue if necessary
    for (int i = 1; i < arr.length; i++)
        if (arr[i] > maxValue)
            maxValue = arr[i];

    // return largest value which is maxValue
    return maxValue;
}
```

In a declaration of an array, the name is a reference that designates the address of the block of memory that holds the array elements. When a method has an array parameter, call the method by passing the name of an existing array argument. This has the effect of passing a reference to the method identifying the sequence of elements. For instance, let arrList be an array of five integer elements.

```
int[] arrList = new int[5];
```

To determine the largest element in the array, call max() with arrList as the argument. The runtime system copies the constant reference arrList to the corresponding method parameter reference arr. The parameter reference points to the memory block of elements for arrList.

```
maxValue = max(arrList);
```

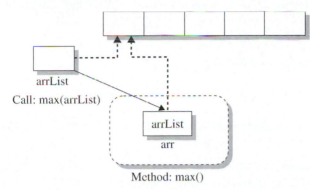

Call: max(arrList)

arrList

arrList
arr

Method: max()

Array Update   The algorithm for max() simply performs a read-only scan of the elements in the array to determine the maximum value. The issue is quite different if the method updates array elements. Because the parameter is pointing at the array allocated in the calling program, the update modifies this array and the change remains in effect after returning from the method. For instance, the method maxFirst() finds the largest element in the tail of an array beginning at index start and exchanges it with the element at the index start. The method has no return value.

maxFirst():

```java
public static void maxFirst(int[] arr, int start)
{
   // maxValue and maxIndex are the value and location of the
   // largest element that is identified during a scan of
   // the array
   int maxValue = arr[start], maxIndex = start, temp;

   // scan the tail of the list beginning at index start+1
   // and update both maxValue and maxIndex so that we know
   // the value and location of the largest element
   for (int i = start+1; i < arr.length; i++)
      if (arr[i] > maxValue)
      {
         maxValue = arr[i];
         maxIndex = i;
      }

   // exchange arr[start] and arr[maxIndex]
   temp = arr[start];
   arr[start] = arr[maxIndex];
   arr[maxIndex] = temp;
}
```

PROGRAM A.1   SORTING AN ARRAY

This program sorts an array in descending order. At the same time, it illustrates features of arrays. An integer array intArr is declared with initial values. A loop scans the first n − 1 elements in an n-element array. At each index i, a call to maxFirst() places the largest element from the unsorted tail of the array at location i. A second scan of the list displays the sorted array.

```java
// main application class
public class ProgramA_1
{
    public static void main(String[] args)
    {
        int[] intArr = {35, 20, 50, 5, 40, 20, 15, 45};
        int i;

        // scan first n-1 positions in the array where n =
        // intArr.length; call maxFirst() to place largest
        // element from the unsorted tail of the list into
        // position i
        for (i = 0; i < intArr.length-1; i++)
            maxFirst(intArr, i);

        // display the sorted array
        for (i = 0; i < intArr.length; i++)
            System.out.print(intArr[i] + "  ");
        System.out.println();
    }

    // <include code for maxFirst()>
}
```

Run:
       50   45   40   35   20   20   15   5

Appendix B

JAVA KEYWORDS

The following is a list of Java keywords. All of them are reserved so you cannot use them as names in a Java program.

abstract	assert	boolean	break
byte	case	catch	char
class	continue	default	do
double	else	enum	extends
final	finally	float	for
if	implements	import	instanceof
int	interface	long	native
new	package	private	protected
public	return	short	static
strictfp	super	switch	synchronize
this	throw	throws	transient
try	void	volatile	while

Figure B.1 *Java keyword chart.*
Note: The literals true, false, and null are reserved words but are not keywords. They also cannot be used as names in a program.

Appendix C
ASCII CHARACTER CODES

Computers store all data as binary numbers. Numeric codes must be used to represent characters such as 'A', '5', and '?'. In this book, we are interested in the American Standard Code for Information Interchange (ASCII) character set. The ASCII code for a character uses 7 bits that are stored in an 8-bit number. The $2^7 = 128$ different codes are divided into 95 printable characters and 33 control characters that are used in data communications.

With global communication and commerce, software developers needed an encoding scheme for a larger set of world characters and symbols. In response to the problem, a new coding system, called the *Unicode Standard*, was designed to support the worldwide interchange, processing, and display of the written texts of the diverse languages and technical disciplines of the modern world. The Unicode Standard is maintained by the Unicode Consortium, with members from leading computer software companies. Java has adopted the Unicode Standard for encoding characters. The ASCII character set is a subset of the Unicode character set.

Figure C.1 is a listing of the ASCII character set with decimal values in the range 0–127. The digits in the left column are the left digit of the character code and the digits in the top row are the right digit of the character code. For instance, the character 'T' has ASCII value 84 and the character 'k' has ASCII value 107.

	0	1	2	3	4	5	6	7	8	9
0	nul	soh	stx	etx	eot	enq	ack	bel	bs	ht
1	lf	vt	ff	cr	so	si	dle	dc1	dc2	dc3
2	dc4	nak	syn	etb	can	em	sub	est	fs	gs
3	rs	us	space	!	"	#	$	%	&	'
4	(	)	*	+	,	-	.	/	0	1
5	2	3	4	5	6	7	8	9	:	;
6	<	=	<	?	@	A	B	C	D	E
7	F	G	H	I	J	K	L	M	N	O
8	P	Q	R	S	T	U	V	W	X	Y
9	Z	[	\	]	^	_	`	a	b	c
10	d	e	f	g	h	i	j	k	l	m
11	n	o	p	q	r	s	t	u	v	w
12	x	y	z	{	|	}	~	del		

Figure C.1 *ASCII character set.*

Appendix D

JAVA OPERATOR PRECEDENCE

Operator	Meaning	Associativity	Usage
.	member access	left to right	object.member
[]	array index	left to right	arr [index]
()	method call	left to right	(argument_list)
++	post-increment	right to left	value++
++	pre-increment	right to left	++value
--	post-decrement	right to left	value--
--	pre-decrement	right to left	--value
~	bitwise complement	right to left	~expr
!	boolean NOT	right to left	!expr
-	unary minus	right to left	-expr
+	unary plus	right to left	+expr
new	object creation	right to left	new type()
(type)	type cast	right to left	(type)expr
*	multiplication	left to right	expr * expr
/	division	left to right	expr / expr
%	remainder	left to right	expr % expr
+	addition	left to right	expr + expr
-	subtraction	left to right	expr - expr
+	string concatenation	left to right	str + str
<<	signed bit shift left	left to right	expr << expr
>>	signed bit shift right	left to right	expr >> expr
>>>	unsigned bit shift right	left to right	expr >>> expr
<	less than	left to right	expr < expr
<=	less than or equal to	left to right	expr <= expr
>	greater than	left to right	expr > expr
>=	greater than or equal to	left to right	expr >= expr
instanceof	type comparison	left to right	obj instanceof type
==	equal to	left to right	expr == expr
!=	not equal to	left to right	expr != expr
&	bitwise AND	left to right	expr & expr
&	boolean AND	left to right	expr & expr
^	bitwise exclusive or (XOR)	left to right	expr ^ expr
^	boolean XOR	left to right	expr ^ expr
|	bitwise OR	left to right	expr | expr
|	boolean OR	left to right	expr| expr
&&	boolean AND (short-circuit)	left to right	expr && expr
||	boolean OR (short-circuit)	left to right	expr || expr

Operator	Meaning	Associativity	Usage
? :	conditional	left to right	expr ? expr : expr
=	assignment	right to left	value = expr
*=	multiplication assignment	right to left	value *= expr
/=	division assignment	right to left	value /= expr
%=	remainder assignment	right to left	value %= expr
+=	addition assignment	right to left	value += expr
-=	subtraction assignment	right to left	value -= expr
<<=	bitwise left shift assignment	right to left	value <<= expr
>>=	bitwise unsigned right shift assignment	right to left	value >>= expr
>>>=	bitwise right shift assignment	right to left	value >>>= expr
&=	bitwise AND assignment	right to left	value &= expr
|=	bitwise inclusive OR assignment	right to left	value |= expr
^=	bitwise exclusive OR assignment	right to left	value ^= expr

Appendix E

THE EZJava IDE

CONTENTS

E.1   INSTALLING EZJAVA

E.2   GETTING STARTED
    Creating a New Document
    Menu Options

E.3   COMPILING AND RUNNING
    A PROGRAM
    Setting Class Paths

E.4   USING A PROJECT

EZJava is a flexible Integrated Development Environment (IDE) that allows you to develop and run Java programs on a Windows, Linux, Solaris, or Macintosh OS X system. In general, it will run on any Unix system for which there is Java Virtual Machine (JVM), version 1.4.2 or later. You can select an appropriate look-and-feel for your system. The IDE allows you to compile and run a main class along with any supporting classes in the same directory. For software development, you can work with multiple main-class source files or can create a project consisting of many source files within a package structure. With individual source files, you simply select the active main class. With a project, the software compiles only the modified files. If the project contains a main class, you can run the application.

EZJava has features usually found only in more complex programming environments. You can open multiple editing windows in tabbed panes and search a file hierarchy for a pattern that can include the use of regular expressions. Editing and printer options allow you to set fonts and tabs, execute find/replace commands, and reformat text by replacing tabs with blanks and changing

cases. EZJava provides options for automatically creating program documentation and for setting paths to the class and jar files required by applications.

While EZJava can be used to develop large software systems, it was designed to facilitate the use of Java in academic course work. Individual programs can be created and run outside of a project environment. New documents can be created using templates for console and GUI applications as well as applet programs and their associated HTML files. An application executes in its own runtime window with a command button for multiple runs. EZJava compiles Synchronous Java, which is an extension of Java with concurrent programming tools that are useful in an Operating Systems course. For further information, see *http://ltiwww.epfl.ch/sJava/*.

In this appendix, we will discuss how you obtain and install EZJava and use its key features to create and run a program. EZJava development is ongoing. New releases reflect feedback from students and faculty.

E.1 Installing EZJava

EZJava can be downloaded from *http://www.EZJava.org*. Before running the application, you must have already installed the Java software development kit.

If you are running Windows, download the installation files *EZJavaInstall.bat* and *EZJavaInstaller.jar*. Run the batch file *EZJavaInstall.bat* that starts the application in the JAR file. This brings up a self-explanatory GUI application that guides you through the installation.

If you are running Linux, Solaris, or Macintosh OS X, you need to download only the file *EZJavaInstaller.jar*. To begin the installation, execute the command

```
java -jar EZJavaInstaller.jar
```

that runs the installer.

E.2 Getting Started

On a Windows system, you can start up EZJava by selecting its icon on the desktop or the menu item in the *Start Menu*. The application is also available from the "EZJava IDE" group in the *All Programs* menu. On a Unix system or Macintosh OS X, run the shell script named *ezjava* in the installation directory. The application opens a window with menu items and a toolbar of icons that represent key commands in the building, compiling, and running of Java applications or Java applets. The window is partitioned into three regions (views) that include Source Window, Open Files, and the Build (Compiler) Window. The source window holds text files that correspond to class, applet, HTML, and data files. The Open Files section is a listing of files that are currently active. The Build Window holds messages that are created when you compile a program.

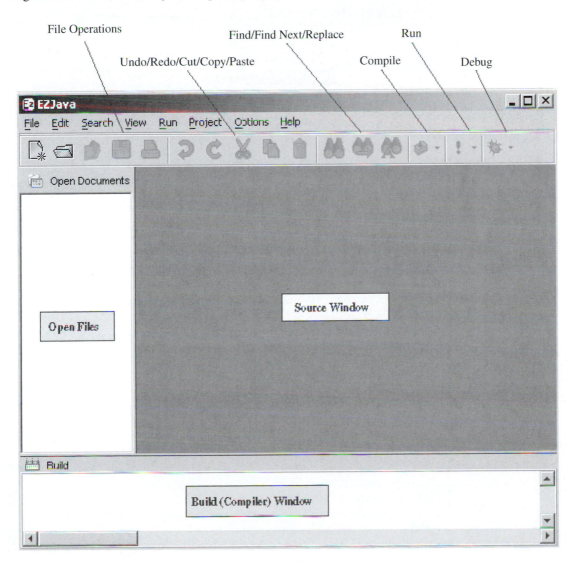

Creating a New Document

Use the *New* command to create a document. In a dialog box, you can select from five options. The option "Empty Document" simply creates an empty document that you can use for a data file or to create a Java source code file from scratch. The other options create template classes for Java console, GUI, and applet programs or an HTML document to be used with an applet. In each case, you will get a dialog box to enter the class name. Figure E.1 illustrates a user selecting a new Console Application document with the main class named *DemoApplication*.

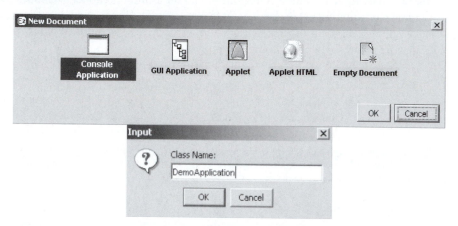

Figure E.1 *Dialog boxes for selecting an application type and the main class name.*

A source window is created in a tab pane. The document includes the public main application class *DemoApplication* and the `main()` method. The class name with the extension *.java* is the default file name when you save the new document.

```
// the "DemoApplication" class

public class DemoApplication
{
    public static void main (String[] args)
    {
        // your code here

    }
}
```

Template support for a GUI application imports the AWT, Swing, and Event classes and builds the `main()` method and constructor. Similar resources are provided for applet programs and their corresponding HTML files.

Menu Options

The menu bar includes familiar *File*, *Edit*, *Search*, *Options*, and *Window* items. The *Run*, *Debug*, and *Project* items have commands that organize and run the Java program. These items are discussed separately. Besides the usual editing commands, EZJava has special options that support the writing of Java source code. Let us briefly note these options.

File   The menu item presents the standard file-handling operations. In addition, a *Rename* command enables you to change the name of an existing file. This comes in handy with Java's insistence that the class or interface name must match the source file name.

Edit   The *Text Utilities* submenu has an option to uppercase, lowercase, or sentence case selected text. Traditionally, constant identifiers are uppercase and class and interface names begin with an uppercase letter (sentence case). You can use this for named constants as well as class and method names. A second option allows you to convert between tabs and blanks to align text in a source code file.

Search   The standard Find/Replace operations are available. In addition, a *Find in Files* command allows you to search recursively within a directory and its subdirectories for a word or phrase. The search can include regular expressions and designate only those files with a specified extension. The command *Go To* <line number> is useful when a runtime error message identifies the statement (with line number) that is the source of the problem.

Options   You can set the font and point size for text in the source window and specify the tab size. An option allows you to specify a margin width for text in the source window. A line appears in the window that will indicate when you have overrun the margin. *Editor Options* set parameters for the smart editor. *Look and Feel* is a submenu that allows you to determine the appearance of the program components. The user can select the Metal or Motif look and feel as well as any look and feel unique to the system, such as *Windows*.

E.3   Compiling and Running a Program

After creating the source file, you must first compile it to intermediate bytecode. The resulting file has the extension `.class`. The *Compile* operation is a command in the *Run* menu. You may also select an icon in the toolbar or use the keystroke command Ctrl+1. A dialog box indicates whether any errors occur. If so, the errors are listed in the Compiler window. When you place the cursor over the file name in an error message, it becomes the hand cursor. A single click causes the offending line to be selected.

```
2 errors 0 warnings

C:\HelloWorld.java:5: unclosed string literal
           System.println("Hello World!);
                                         ^
C:\HelloWorld.java:6: ')' expected
       }
         ^
```

A system-dependent JVM executes the program. The JVM application is called by the *Run* command in the *Run* menu. You can also use an icon in the toolbar or the keystroke command Ctrl+2. Execution brings up a runtime window with a *File* menu allowing you to print the text of the run and an *Edit* menu to copy and paste selected text. The paste feature is useful when you have captured text in the clipboard. Instead of typing the text when prompted for input, paste it in. The window has the title *Run of ClassName.java*. For instance, suppose the application *DemoApplication* outputs the string "Running DemoApplication".

```
// the "DemoApplication" class

public class DemoApplication
{
    public static void main (String[] args)
    {
        System.out.println("Running DemoApplication");
    }
}
```

The runtime window is

A *Run* icon appears at the bottom of the window. Click the icon to rerun the program.

Note that if the source file is modified and not recompiled, the *Run* command will call the compiler to create a new bytecode file and then execute the program.

Setting Class Paths

When converting a Java file to bytecode, the compiler must locate all of the external .*class* files that are referenced. To this end, the compiler uses a *class loader*. The loader automatically searches the standard Java classes in the Java software development kit. If the class is not a standard one, the loader searches the *classpath*, which defines a list of locations in which class files are stored. A programmer can include the *"-classpath"* option when compiling and running programs or can set the *CLASSPATH* environment variable to define the list. EZJava will automate this for you. In the *Run* menu, select the *Class Paths* option, which shows a dialog that lets you add, remove, or edit a list of directories which should be searched by the class loader.

E.4   Using a Project

In EZJava, a project is a mechanism for compiling and running a collection of class and interface files in a package structure, to create a Jar-archive of the files, and to create javadoc HTML documentation of the files. The *Project* menu provides the necessary tools.

Begin by using the command *New Project* to create a new project in a directory. In the example, *ProjectName.prj* is created in the directory *ProjectDirectory*.

In Java, a package is identified with a directory. Use the *New Package* command to create a directory within the project directory. You can build the package with new or existing Java source code files for classes and interfaces. Choose the *Main Class* menu item to associate a main application with the project. At each stage in the process, all of the `.java` files and subdirectories (packages) are listed in a hierarchy in the Open File view. The figure illustrates a project with a main class `MainApplication.java` in the project directory and a package called `PackageName` containing classes and interfaces. Note that the main class can also be within a package.

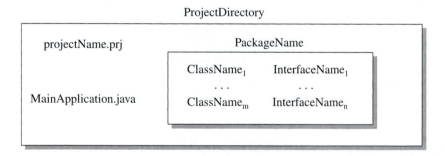

The *Make Project* command compiles all of the Java files in the project directory and in all subdirectories. This is a "smart compile" in that only files which have been modified since the last compile are affected. The *Rebuild Project* command compiles all of the files in the project.

When the *Main Class* command is used to select a main class, the *Run Project* command is operative. Like run for a single program, the command creates a runtime window, which can be used for input and output.

The *Utilities* submenu enables you to create HTML documentation for the project. This assumes, of course, that you used javadoc comments to document source files in the package. The resulting HTML files are created in the *docs* subdirectory of the project directory. The option also allows you create a *jar* file for the project class files.

Example E.1

This example illustrates a project called *MeasurementProject.prj*. The file *Measurement.java* specifies an interface. That file, along with the class files *Rectangle.java*, *Circle.java*, and *Square.java*, are in the measurement subdirectory of the project. The interface and classes are in the package *measurement*. The Java file *MeasurementDemo.java* is in project directory. It is designated as the main class, which becomes the starting point for the run of the project. The figure is the Open Files view of the project.

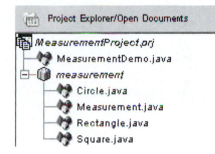

Measurement.java:

```java
package measurement;

// the interface defines the static double PI and the prototypes
// for measurement operations
public interface Measurement
{
    // the constant PI uses the value from the Math class
    public static final double PI = Math.PI;

    // return the area of the figure
    public double area();

    // return the perimeter of the figure
    public double perimeter();
}
```

MeasurementDemo.java:

```java
import measurement.*;

public class MeasurementDemo
{
    public static void main(String[] args)
    {
        Measurement[] figure = {
            new Circle(5), new Rectangle(3,5), new Square(2) };
        for (int i = 0; i < figure.length; i++)
```

```
                    System.out.println("Area = " + figure[i].area() +
                              "  Perimeter = " + figure[i].perimeter());
         }
      }
```

```
Run:
   Area = 78.53981633974483   Perimeter = 31.41592653589793
   Area = 15.0   Perimeter = 16.0
   Area = 4.0   Perimeter = 8.0
```

INDEX

2

2-3-4 trees, 839
    building, 841, 842
    inserting into, 840
    perfectly balanced, 839
    red-black tree representation, 845
    runtime analysis, 843
    searching, 840
    top-down insertion, 843

8

8-Queens problem, 908

A

Abstract
    class, 58
    effect on inheritance, 58
    method, 58
Accessor method, 11
Accumulator interface, 150
AccumulatorNumber class, 151
AccumulatorTime class, 151
Ackermann's function, 192
ActionEvent class, 105
ActionListener interface, 105
    actionPerformed method, 105
Activation record, 401
Acyclic, 733, 734
Adapter, 5
    design pattern, 366
    priority queue, 438
    queue, 423
    stack, 390
Adelson-Velsky, G.M., 824
Adjacency
    list, 803
    matrix, 802
Adleman, Leonard, 869
Algorithm analysis, 6, 114
    backtracking, 885
    brute force, 119
    computational complexity, 126
    greedy, 705, 779
    iterative, 169
    recursive, 169
    running time. *See* Runtime analysis

    space efficiency, 126
    system efficiency, 125
Algorithms
    See Compression algorithms
    See Cryptograph algorithms
    See Dynamic programming algorithms
    See Graph algorithms
    See Hash algorithms
    See Heap algorithms
    See List algorithms
    See Map algorithms
    See Number theory algorithms
    See Recursive algorithms
    See Search algorithms
    See Set algorithms
    See Sorting algorithms
    See Tree algorithms
Aliases, 14
ALStack class, 392
    implementation, 392
Anonymous
    inner class, 615
    object, 23
API, 17
    ArrayList class, 258
    Bag class, 237
    BQueue class, 434
    Collection interface, 229
    Comparator interface, 665
    DataInputStream class, 702
    DataOutputStream class, 702
    DiGraph class, 744, 774
    Graph interface, 736
    Heaps class, 682
    Iterator interface, 348
    javadoc, 97
    JobRequest class, 441
    List interface, 252
    ListIterator interface, 352
    Map interface, 580
    Map.Entry interface, 590
    Nodes class, 315
    PQueue interface, 439
    Queue interface, 424
    Random class, 34, 35
    RBTree class, 857
    SalaryEmployee class, 51
    Scanner class, 73

API (*continued*)
    SList class, 387
    Stack interface, 391
    Time24 class, 17
    Timing class, 133
    TreeMap class, 581
    TreeSet class, 565
Application
    list
        closest-pair problem, 261
        handling a draft list, 304
        ordered, 357
        palindrome, 307
        removing duplicates, 359
        word frequency, 362
        word jumble, 331
    map
        software products, 585
        student time card, 582
    priority queue
        bank simulation, 444
        support services, 440
    queue
        appointment scheduler, 425
    recursion
        building a ruler, 178
        Euler tour, 519
        multibase numbers, 174
        Towers of Hanoi, 179
    running time
        comparing search algorithms, 132
        comparing sorting methods, 216
        evaluating recursion, 186
    Scanner
        food checkout, 74
    set
        computer accounts, 574
        Sieve of Eratosthenes, 239
        spell checker, 565
    stack
        balancing symbol pairs, 398
        multibase numbers, 395
        postfix expressions, 407
    tree
        building an expression tree, 507
        displaying a binary tree, 493
        fully-parenthesized expressions, 518
        iterative binary tree traversal, 515
        visitor design pattern, 483
Application programming interface. *See* API
Array-based structures
    binary tree, 662
        finding children/parent, 663
    bounded queue, 433
    bounded stack, 418
ArrayList class, 254
    API, 258
    application, 258, 261

    bounds-checking, 255
    cloning, 276
    design, 254
    implementation, 265
        ensuring capacity, 267
    iterators, 346
    runtime analysis, 271
    serializing, 722
    sizing, 256
Arrays class, 117
    binSearch method, 124
    binSearch method (generic), 162
    fill method (in java.util.Arrays), 896
    findKth method, 219
    insertionSort method, 194
    quicksort method, 212
    radixSort method, 431
    selectionSort method, 117
    selectionSort method (generic), 160
    seqSearch method, 119
    sort method (generic), 199
    sort method (Object), 199
    toString(arr) method, 144
ASCII codes, 964
Assignment
    of reference variables, 14
    subclass object to superclass object, 54
Associative
    array. *See* Map
    collection, 563
Autoboxing, 38, 42
Auto-unboxing, 38, 42
AVL tree, 824
    balance factor, 826
    height balance, 826
    imbalance, 831
    rotations
        double, 834, 835
        single, 832, 833
AVLTree class, 826
    add method, 837
    AVLNode class, 828
    displaying a tree, 826
    drawing a tree, 826
    implementation, 828, 836, 837
        add method, 829
        addNode method, 835
        double rotations, 835
        single rotation, 833
    running time analysis, 839
    UML, 827

B

Back edge, 748
Backtracking, 885
    8-Queens problem, 908
    Knight's tour, 925
    subset-sum problem, 923

Bag class, 236
    API, 237
    application, 239
    capacity, 236
    creating and using, 237
    implementation, 242
        general toString method, 245
        generic arrays, 243
        grab method, 245
Bank simulation, 447
    See Event-driven simulation
BankSimulation class, 447
Big integers, 872
    BigInteger class, 872
Big-O, 129
Binary file, 65, 701
Binary numeric promotion, 694
Binary search, 120
    binSearch method, 124
    demonstrating the process, 120
    generic, 162
    recursive implementation, 919
Binary search tree, 530
    building, 531
    class. *See* STree
    deleting, 533
    inorder scan, 533
    searching, 532
Binary tree, 465
    array-based, 662
    building, 472, 474
    clearing nodes, 493
    complete, 469
    copying nodes, 489
    degenerate, 468
    density, 468
    display a tree, 493, 523
    draw, 494
    draw a tree, 520
    Euler tour, 517
    expression tree, 505
    finding height, 488
    full, 707
    height, 467, 487
    left subtree, 466
    recursive definition, 466
    representing bit codes, 706
    right subtree, 466
    scan algorithms, 475
        inorder, 476, 479
        level order, 480
        scan pattern, 478
    shadow tree, 520
BinaryTree class
    buildExpTree method, 508
    buildShadowTree method, 521
    buildTime24 method, 515
    buildTree, 474

clearTree method, 493
copyTree method, 492
displayTree method, 493, 523
drawTree method, 494
drawTrees method, 494
fullParen method, 518
height method, 488
inorderDisplay method, 479
levelOrderDisplay method, 482
postorderDisplay method, 479
preorderDisplay method, 479
Binding
    dynamic, 55
    static, 55
Bit code, 706
Bit operations
    and, 694
    exclusive or, 694
    not, 694
    or, 694
    shifting
        signed left, 695
        signed right, 695
        unsigned right, 695
BitArray class
    implementation, 698
    methods, 696
Boolean class, 39
Bottom-up dynamic programming, 885
Bounded queue. *See* BQueue class
Bounded stack. *See* BStack class
BQueue class, 433
    API, 434
    design, 435
    implementation, 437
Breadth-first search, 742
    running time, 746
BStack class
    bounded, 418
Bubble sort, 140
Bucket, 634
Buffer, 66
BufferedFileReader class, 66

C

CASE tool, 18
Casting
    dot operator precedence, 57
    downcasting, 56
    upcasting, 56
Catch block, 60
Chaining with separate lists, 634
    bucket, 634
    demonstrating the process, 635
    evaluating, 635

Character class, 41
    classify a character, 41
    test a character, 41
    update a character, 41
Circle class, 90
    implements Measurement, 90
    UML, 91
Class, 7
    abstract, 58
    autoboxing, 38, 42
    auto-unboxing, 38, 42
    client, 44
    constructor, 10
    declaration. *See* Class implementation
    default constructor, 10
    downcasting, 56
    header, 18
    implementation, 18
    inheritance, 47
    instance, 7
    instance variable, 19
    interface, 7, 19
    member scope, 48
    method, 8, 12
    polymorphism, 54
    private data, 7
    private visibility modifier, 19
    protected data, 48
    public method, 7
    public visibility modifier, 19
    subclass, 47
    superclass, 47
    supplier, 44
    toString method, 10
    upcasting, 56
    utility method, 19
    variable, 7
    wrapper class, 39
Classes in the book
    AccumulatorNumber, 151
    AccumulatorTime, 151
    Arrays, 117
    AVLNode, 828
    AVLTree, 826
    Bag, 236
    BankSimulation, 447
    BigInteger, 872
    BitArray, 696
    BQueue, 433
    Circle, 90
    Dice, 99
    DiGraph, 737
    DiGraphs, 744
    DNode, 322
    Edge, 804
    Employee, 48
    Event, 446
    EventDrivenSimulation, 447

    Greater, 666
    Hash, 638
    HashSet, 650
    HCompress, 710
    HeapPQueue, 683
    Heaps, 671
    HourlyEmployee, 52
    InorderIterator, 511
    Knapsack, 903
    Less, 666
    LinkedList, 300
    LinkedQueue, 424
    MinInfo, 780
    Node, 290
    Object class, 143
    OrderedList, 360
    PostfixEval, 406
    RBTree, 857
    SalaryEmployee, 50
    STNode, 539
    Store, 147, 149
    STree, 535
    Time24, 8
    TimeCard, 44
    Timing, 133
    TNode, 470
    TreeMap, 606, 609
    TreeSet, 604
    VertexInfo, 804
Client class, 44
Client-server pattern, 875
Clone method, 272
Cloneable, 272
    interface, 273
Cloning, 273
    array, 278
    ArrayList, 276
    clone method, 273
    deep copy, 276
    reference variables, 273
    shallow copy, 277
    Time24, 273
Closest-Pair problem, 261
Clustering, 634, 654
Code reuse, 20
Collection, 1, 227
    categories
        adapter structures, 233
        graph, 235
        list, 230
        map, 233
        set, 232
    class, 227
    data structure, as a, 228
    framework, 236
    generic, 148
    interface, 229
    modeled as a bag, 228
    overview

array list, 230
linked list, 231
map as an associative array, 233
priority queue, 234
queue, 234
set, 232
stack, 233
weighted directed graph, 235
view. *See* Collection view
Collection interface, 229
API, 229
iterator. *See* Iterator
methods, 228
UML, 253
Collection view, 587
demonstrating a view, 613
implementing a view, 615
map. *See* Map
Combinations, 886
Combinatorics, 885, 886
building combinations, 886
finding powerset, 887
listing permutations, 889
traveling salesman problem, 892
Comparable interface, 152
compareTo method, 153
Integer, 40
String, 27
Time24, 153
Comparator interface, 664
API, 665
Greater implementation, 666
Less implementation, 666
Comparison
Comparator, with, 664
compareTo method, 27
natural comparison, 664
natural order, 664
Complete
graph, 733, 922
tree, 469
Composite number, 866
Compression
bit code, 706
lossless, 704
lossy, 704
prefix codes, 705, 706
ratio, 705
Compression algorithms
Huffman compression, 706
Computational complexity, 126
Concordance, 592
Congruent modulo, 867
Connected graph, 733
Constructor, 10, 22
Copying a tree, 489
Cryptography, 865, 869
private key, 869

public key, 865, 869
secret key, 865
Cryptography algorithms
RSA, 876
secure message passing, 869
Cycle, 733, 734
back edge, and a, 748
discovering, 748

D
DAG, 757
Data structures, 6
DataInputStream class, 701
API, 702
DataOutputStream class, 701
API, 702
Decompression, 707
Deep copy, 274, 276
Default constructor, 10
Degenerate tree, 468
Depth-first search, 751
forest, 758
running time, 753
tree, 757
Depth-first visit, 747, 748
Deserialization, 718
Design pattern, 98
adapter, 366
GUI, 101
iterator, 356
simulation, 446
singleton, 98
Dice class, 99
visitor, 482
Dice class, 99
Digraph, 4, 734
acyclic, 734
cycle, 734
directed path, 734
sink, 821
source, 821
strongly connected, 734, 767
weakly connected, 734
weighted, 735
DiGraph class, 737
API, 774
color methods, 744
dataValue methods, 774
design, 810
Edge class component, 804
implementation, 810
vInfo ArrayList, 806
vtxMap, 806, 807
parent methods, 774
UML, 810
using, 737
VertexInfo class component, 804

DiGraphs class
  acyclic method, 754
  bfs method, 744, 745
  dagMinimumPath method, 786
  dfs method, 752
  dfsVisit method, 749
  minimumPath method, 782
  minSpanTree method, 792
  path method, 777
  shortestPath method, 776
  strongComponents method, 771
  topologicalSort method, 766
  transpose method, 770
Dijkstra, Edsger, 773
Dijkstra's algorithm, 779
  running time, 784
DiskHuffNode class
  UML, 712
Displaying a binary tree, 493
Divide and conquer, 196
DNode class, 322
DNodes class
  addBefore method, 327
  remove method, 328
  toString method, 327
Documentation
  goals, 95
  with javadoc, 95
Double class, 39
  autoboxing, 42
  auto-unboxing, 42
Doubly linked list, 298, 321
  deleting, 328
  empty, 326
  header, 325
  inserting into, 327
Downcasting, 56
Drawing a binary tree, 494, 520
Driver method, 199
Dynamic array, 2
  direct access, 254
  evaluating when to use, 278
Dynamic binding, 55
Dynamic programming, 893
  bottom-up, 885, 898
  top-down, 885, 895
Dynamic programming algorithms
  computing combinations, 898
  generating Fibonacci numbers, 893, 895
  knapsack problem, 900

E

Edge class, 804
Eight-Queens problem, 908
Employee class
  design, 48
  implementation, 49
  UML, 53

Employee hierarchy, 48
  UML, 53
Encryption. *See* Cryptography
Enhanced for statement, 28
  enum methods, 28
Entry set, 590
  iterator, 591
Enum, 28, 29
  constant, 28
  constructor, 29
  enhanced for, 28
  methods, 28
  switch statement, 28
  variables, 28
Euclid, 866
Euclid's algorithm
  extended gcd, 867
    implementation, 878
    why it works, 878
  gcd, 866
    implementation, 877
    why it works, 877
Euler totient funtion, 868
Euler tour, 517, 760
  expression tree, 517
  method, 518
  parenthesizing expressions, 518
Euler's theorem, 869
Event, 105
  ActionEvent class, 105
  ActionListener interface, 105
  actionPerformed method, 105
    dice toss, 106
  adding a listener, 105
  event listener, 105
  inner class event handler, 105
Event-driven simulation, 444
  BankSimulation class, 447
    application, 452
    arrival event, 450
    departure event, 452
    design, 447
    service event, 452
  demonstrating the process, 445
  design pattern, 446
  Event class, 446
  EventDrivenSimulation class, 447
Exception, 59
  catch block, 60
  checked, 63
  finally clause, 61
  handler, 59
  handling mechanism, 60
  Java exception hierarchy, 62
  propogation, 61
  throw statement, 59
  try block, 60
  unchecked, 63

Exceptions in the book
ArithmeticException, 64
ArrayIndexOutOfBounds, 63
BufferOverflowException, 634
ClassCastException, 142
ClassNotFoundException, 719
CloneNotSupportedException, 272
ConcurrentModificationException, 383
EmptyStackException, 391
Error, 62
Exception, 62
IllegalArgumentException, 64
IllegalStateException, 378
IndexOutOfBoundsException, 64
IOException, 63
NonSerializableException, 718
NoSuchElementException, 68
NullPointerException, 64
RuntimeException, 63
Throwable, 62
UnsupportedOperationException, 64
VirtualMachineError, 62
Exchange sort, 139
Exclusive or, 694
ExpectedModCount, 382
Expression tree, 463, 505
building, 507
Extended Euclid's algorithm, 867
implementation, 879
Extends. *See* Inheritance
EZJava, 967
compile and running programs, 971
creating a new document, 970
getting started, 969
installing, 968
menu options, 971
setting class paths, 972
using projects, 973

F

Factor, 866
Factory method, 346
Fail-fast iterator, 382
Fermat's little theorem, 882
Fibonacci sequence, 183, 893
generalized, 920
File, 65
binary, 65, 701
text, 65, 701
File compression
bit code, 706
lossless, 704
lossy, 704
prefix codes, 705, 706
ratio, 705
File decompression, 707
FileReader class, 66

FileWriter class, 69
Finally clause, 61
Finite queue. *See* BQueue class
Finite stack. *See* BStack class
First-in/first-out (FIFO), 423
Full binary tree, 707

G

Generalized Fibonacci numbers, 920
Generic
arrays, 243
bounded types, 155, 157
collection, 148
interface, 150
methods, 154
Store class, 149
type-safe, 148
Generics
bounds, with, 156
inheritance, and, 156
wildcards, with, 159
Graph, 732
acyclic, 733, 753
adjacency
list, 803
matrix, 802
back edge, 748
breadth-first search, 742
class. *See* DiGraph class
complete, 733, 922
connected, 733
cycle, 733
depth-first search, 751
directed. *See* Digraph
edges, 732
minimum spanning tree, 789
optimization problems, 772
minimum-path, 773
shortest-path, 773
path, 732
path length, 733
search (traversal) algorithms, 741
self-loop, 732
simple path, 733
topological sort, 764
transpose, 768
vertex, 732
degree, 732
neighbors, 732
weighted, 735
Graph algorithms
adding a graph edge, 813
breadth-first search, 742
checking for an acyclic graph, 753
depth-first search, 751
depth-first visit, 747

Graph algorithms *(continued)*
   Dijkstra's algorithm, 779
   minimum path (DAG), 785
   Prim's algorithm, 789
   removing a graph vertex, 813
   shortest-path, 773
   strongly connected components, 767
   topological sort, 764
Graph interface, 736
   API, 736
   methods, 739
Graphical User Interface. *See* GUI
Greater comparator class, 666
Greatest common divisor, 866
Greedy algorithm, 705, 779
GUI, 100
   application design pattern, 101
   AWT classes, 100
   components, 101
   Container class, 103
   content pane, 103
   design, 100
      constructor, 103
      import statements, 102
      variables, 102
   event, 100. *See also* Event
   frame, 100
   JComboBox class, 283
   JFrame class, 101
   JLabel class, 102
   JList class, 317
   JTextArea class, 102
   JTextField class, 102
   layout manager, 100
   Swing classes, 100
GUI applications
   8-Queens problem, 915
   balancing symbol pairs, 401
   dice toss, 104
   displaying an expression tree, 510
   drawing a ruler, 179
   Huffman compression, 717
   infix expression evaluation, 411
   multibase numbers, 176
   RSA client-server, 875
   Towers of Hanoi, 183
   updating a search tree, 538
GUI design pattern, 101

H

Has-a relationship, 44
Hash algorithms
   chaining with separate lists, 634
   customizing hash functions, 631
   inserting into a hash table, 639
   linear probe hashing, 632
   rehashing, 639

   removing from a hash table, 642
   string hash function, 629
Hash class, 636
   design, 636
   implementation, 638
   iterator implementation, 643
   load factor, 638
   rehashing, 641
   UML, 637
Hash function
   collision, 627
   designing, 628
   hash value, 626
   hashCode method, 628
   identity, 627
   integer, 628
   perfect, 628, 655
   string, 629
   uniformly distributed, 628
   user-defined, 630
Hash table
   bucket, 626
   chaining with separate lists, 632
   designing, 631
   linear probing, 632
   load factor, 651
   performance, 651
   rehashing, 636
Hashing, 626
   fine-tuning, 651
HashMap class, 646
   implementation, 646
   UML, 649
HashSet class, 649
   implementation, 650
HCompress
   methods, 710
Header, 325
Heap
   building, 678
   deletion, 672
   insertion, 669
   maximum, 668
   minimum, 668
   operation complexity, 677
Heap algorithms
   heap deletion, 672
   heap insertion, 669
   heapsort, 680
   making a heap, 678
Heapifying, 678
HeapPQueue class, 683
   implementation, 683
   UML, 683
Heaps class
   API, 682
   adjustHeap method, 673, 674
   displayHeap method, 675

drawHeap method, 676
drawHeaps method, 676
heapSort method, 680
makeHeap method, 678, 680
popHeap method, 675
pushHeap method, 671
Heapsort, 678
Height of a tree, 465
Height-balanced binary tree, 826
HourlyEmployee class, 52
   design, 48
   UML, 53
Huffman
   compression, 704
   decompression, 707
   tree, 708, 712
Huffman, David, 693
HuffNode class, 712

I

Immutable object, 25
In-degree, 734
Infix
   expression, 410
   notation, 505
   to postfix, 411
Information hiding, 19
Inheritance, 47
   abstract class, 58
   abstract method, 58
   casting, 56
   Employee hierarchy, 48
   extending an interface, 94
   instanceof operator, 57
   multiple, 94
   polymorphism, 54
   scope rules, 49
   super, 51
      constructor, 52
      method call, 52
Inner class, 105, 607
   anonymous, 615
Inorder tree scan, 476
InorderIterator class, 511
   implementation, 513
   UML, 511
In-place sort, 205
Input/Output (I/O). *See* Stream
InputStream class, 701
InputStreamReader class, 66
Insertion sort, 193
Instance variable, 19
Integer class, 39
   autoboxing, 42
   auto-unboxing, 42
   comparison method, 40
   constructors, 40

   equals method, 40
   MAX_VALUE, 40
   MIN_VALUE, 40
   toString methods, 41
Interface, 88
   constant data, 89
   declaring, 89
   declaring an implementing class, 89
   inheritance, and, 93
   multiple inheritance, and, 94
   template, as a, 90
Interfaces in the book
   Accumulator, 150
   ActionListener, 105, 106
   Cloneable, 273
   Collection, 227, 228
   Comparable, 152
   Comparator, 664
   DiagonalMeasurement, 94
   Graph, 735
   Iterator, 348
   List, 252
   ListIterator, 352
   Map.Entry, 590
   Measurement, 90
   OrderedMap, 580
   Queue, 423
   Serializable, 718
   Set, 564
   Stack, 391
   View, 613
   Visitor, 483
Interleaving, 920
Inversion, 216
Iterative algorithm, 169
Iterator, 228, 344
   enhanced for, 350
   fail-fast, 382
      expectedModCount, 382
      modCount, 382
   guidelines, 345
   interface, 348
   scan methods, 346
   use with generic methods, 349
   variables, 374
Iterator design pattern, 356
Iterator interface
   API, 348
   Bag iterators, 374
   hash table iterators, 643
   iterative tree traversal, 511
   LinkedList iterator, 376
   search tree iterator, 551

J

Java Collections Framework, 236
Java review
   arrays, 952
   boolean type, 948

Java review (*continued*)
  comments, 930
  console output, 931
  conversions, 940, 941
  escape sequences, 935
  identifiers, 930
  integrated development environment, 932
  Java programming environments, 931
  keywords, 930, 963
  loop statements, 949
  methods, 956
  named constants, 936
  operators, 936
  primitive data types, 933
  program structure, 928
  selection statements, 941
  variables, 931
Java software development kit. *See* SDK
Javadoc, 95
  API documentation, 95
  comments, 95
  tags, 96
JComboBox class, 283
JFrame class, 101
JLabel class, 102
JList class, 317
JobRequest class, 441
JTextArea class, 102
JTextField class, 102

K
Key set, 588
Keyword
  abstract, 58
  catch, 60
  class, 18
  enum, 28
  extends, 48
  finally, 61
  implements, 89
  import, 24
  instanceof, 57
  interface, 89
  native, 272
  null, 14
  package, 24
  protected, 48
  static, 12
  super, 51
  this, 21
  throw, 59
  throws, 64
  transient, 719
  try, 60
Knapsack class, 903
Knapsack problem, 900
Knight's tour, 925
*k*th largest, 218

L
Landis, E.M., 824
Less comparator class, 666
Level in a tree, 465
Level order tree scan, 480
Linear combination, 867
Linear probing, 632
  clustering, 634, 654
Linked list
  doubly linked list, 298
  singly linked list, 289
LinkedList class, 300
  accessing ends of list, 302
  application, 304, 307
  design, 300
  implementation, 333
  index methods, 301
  Iterator implementation, 376
  list iterator, 376
  ListIterator implementation, 379
  UML, 303
LinkedQueue class, 424
List
  definition, 250
  dynamic array list, 254
  linked list, 300
List algorithms
  balancing symbol pairs, 398
  cloning an ArrayList, 278
  closest-pair, 261
  doubly-linked list operations, 323
  joining ArrayLists, 258
  Josephus problem, 342
  ordered list, 357
  removing duplicates, 359
  serializing an ArrayList, 722
  singly-linked list deletion, 294
  singly-linked list insertion, 293
List interface, 250
  add method, 251
  API, 252
  list iterator, 252
  UML, 253
List iterator, 351
ListIterator interface, 352
Load factor, 651

M
Map, 3
  backing collection, 587
  collection view, 587
    entry set, 590
    key set, 588
  entry, 579
  entry set, 590
    iterator, 591
  key set, 588
  key-value pair, 563
  unordered, 646

Map algorithms, 611
Map interface, 563, 564
   API, 580
   backing collection, 580
   collection view, 580
      entrySet method, 590
      keySet method, 588
   methods, 579
   UML, 606
Map.Entry interface
   API, 590
   getKey method, 590
   getValue method, 590
   setValue method, 590
Matcher class, 593
Matrix
   symmetric, 820
   upper-triangular, 820
Measurement interface, 90
   UML, 91
Memorization, 895
Merge sort, 196
   demonstrating the process, 197
   msort method, 200
   running time, 204
Method, 7
   abstract, 58
   accessor, 11
   action statement, 8
   mutator, 11
   parameters, 8
   postconditions, 8
   preconditions, 8
   signature, 8
   static, 12
Minimum spanning tree, 789
Minimum-path algorithm, 779
   acyclic graph, 785
MinInfo class, 780
ModCount, 382
Modular arithmetic, 867
Multiset, 623
Mutator method, 11

N

New operator, 13
Node, 289
Node class, 290
   self-referencing, 289
Nodes class, 315
   API, 315
   remove method, 295
   toString method, 291
Null, 14
NullPointerException, 14
Number theory
   composite number, 866
   congruent modulo, 867

Euclid's extended gcd algorithm, 867
Euclid's gcd algorithm, 866
Euler totient function, 868
Euler's theorem, 869
factors, 866
Fermat's little theorem, 882
greatest common divisor, 866
linear combination, 867
modular arithmetic, 867
perfect number, 884
prime number, 866
relatively prime numbers, 866
Z(n), 868
Number theory algorithms
   Euclid's extended gcd algorithm, 867
   Euclid's gcd, 866

O

Object, 6
   anonymous, 23
   attributes, 6
   behaviors, 6
   composition, 44
   deserialization, 718
   method, 12
   persistent, 718
   serialization, 718
   state, 8
Object class, 143
   clone method, 143
   equals method, 143
   hashCode method, 143
   toString method, 143
ObjectInputStream class, 719
Object-oriented programming, 6
ObjectOutputStream class, 718
Optimal prefix codes, 708
Optimality principle, 901
Ordered lists, 357
OrderedList class, 360
   design, 360
   implementation, 361
OrderedMap interface
   methods
      firstKey(), 580
      lastKey(), 580
   UML, 606
OrderedSet interface, 605
Out-degree, 734
OutputStream class, 701
OutputStreamWriter class, 70

P

Package, 24
   accessibility rules, 24
   ds.graphics, 24
   ds.time, 24
   ds.util, 24

Package (*continued*)
  header, 24
  java.io, 25
  java.lang, 25
  java.util, 25
Pascal's triangle, 921
Path length, 733
Pattern class, 593
Perfect
  hash function, 628, 655
  number, 884
Permutations, 889
Polymorphism, 54
  guidelines, 55
Postconditions, 8
Postfix expression, 403
  evaluation, 405
  RPN, 404
PostfixEval class, 406
Postorder iterator, 529
Power set, 885, 887
PQueue interface, 439
  API, 439
  HeapPQueue class, 683
Preconditions, 8
Prefix codes, 705, 708
Preorder iterator, 528
Prime number, 866
Prim's algorithm, 789
Principle of optimality, 901
PrintWriter class, 70
Priority queue, 438
  application, 440
  HeapPQueue class, 683
Private, 7
  data, 7
  method, 19
Private key, 869
Protected, 48
Public, 7
  method, 7, 19
Public key, 869

Q

Quaternary number, 729
Queue, 423
  application, 425, 427
  bounded, 433
  circular, 436
  first-in/first-out (FIFO), 423
  interface, 423
Queue algorithms
  circular queue, 436
Queue interface, 423
  API, 424
  LinkedQueue class, 424

Quicksort, 205
  demonstrating the process, 205
  median-3, 224
  pivot, 205
  pivotIndex method, 210
  quicksort method, 212
  recursive descent, 208
  running time, 214

R

Radix sort, 427
  demonstrating the process, 427
  running time, 433
Random class, 34
RBTree class
  API, 857
Reachability relation, 760
Reachable vertex, 733
Reader class, 65, 66
Rectangle class, 91
  implements Measurement, 91
  UML, 91
Recurrence relation, 222
Recursion, 169
  Ackermann's function, 192
  backtracking, 908
  criteria for using, 187
  divide and conquer, 196
  evaluating, 183
  implementing recursive methods, 171
  infinite, 172
  introduced with factorial, 169
  recurrence relation, 222
  runtime stack, 401
  tracing method execution, 173
Recursive
  algorithm, 169
  methods, 169
  steps, 171
  stopping conditions, 171
Recursive algorithms
  8-Queens, 908
  building combinations, 886
  building a ruler, 178
  combinations (dynamic programming), 898
  finding subsets, 888
  knight's tour, 925
  listing permutations, 889
  multibase numbers, 174
  subset-sum, 923
  Towers of Hanoi, 180
Red-black tree, 824, 843
  2-3-4 node representation, 844
  black-height, 846
  building, 853, 854
  color, 825

clashes, 849
flip, 848
deletion, 855
insertion, 847
at the bottom, 852
properties, 846
relationship to 2-3-4 tree, 845
rotation
double, 851
single, 850
running time, 855
splitting 4-node, 848
Reference variable, 13
Regular expression, 74
Rehashing, 636
Relatively prime numbers, 866
Reserved word. *See* Keyword
Rivest, Ronald, 869
Rooted tree, 761
RPN expressions, 404
RSA algorithm, 869
client-server pattern, 875
creating keys, 870
providing secure communications, 872
RSA theorem, 880, 881
Running time
2-3-4 tree operations, 843
ALStack methods, 393
ArrayList methods, 271
AVL tree insertion, 839
binary search, 129
breadth-first search, 746
closest-pair problem, 265
DAG minimum path algorithm, 787
depth-first search, 753
DiGraph class methods, 815
Dijkstra's algorithm, 784
doubly-linked list methdos, 327
empirical test of searches, 133
findKth method, 220
graph add edge, 815
graph remove vertex, 815
graph shortest-path, 778
hash table search, 651
heapsort, 681
insertion sort, 196
knapsack problem, 908
LinkedList index methods, 301
lower bound for sorting, 497
making a heap, 681
merge sort, 204
minimum path DAG, 787
ordered set intersection, 578
Prim's algorithm, 795
quicksort method, 214
radix sort, 433
RBTree search, 855
red-black tree deletion, 857

red-black tree search, 855
selection sort, 129
sequential search, 129
shortest-path algorithm, 778
strong components, 772
topological sort, 767
TreeMap insert/remove, 612
TreeSet insert/remove, 612
updating a heap, 677
Runtime analysis, 126
average case, 127
best case, 127
Big-O measure, 129
binary search, 128
constant, 131
dominant term, 129
exponential, 132
iterative vs. recursive methods, 183
linear, 131
logarithmic, 131
operation count, 126
quadratic, 131
worst case, 127
RuntimeException, 63

S
SalaryEmployee class, 50
API, 51
design, 48
UML, 53
Scanner class, 65, 71
API, 73, 74
application, 74
creating a file scanner, 71
creating a keyboard scanner, 71
file input example, 73
input primitive data, 72
string input, 72
testing for tokens, 72
Scope, 48
SDK, 24
Search algorithms
binary search, 120
binary search (generic), 162
finding the *k*th largest, 218
generalized sequential search, 146
sequential search, 118
Secure message passing, 869
Selection sort, 114
demonstrating the process, 116
generic, 160
selectionSort method, 117
Sentinel node, 325
Sequential search, 118
seqSearch method, 119
seqSearch method (Object), 146

Serializable interface, 718
Serialization, 718
    application, 719
    custom, 722
    transient variable, 719
Set algorithms
    difference, 572
    intersection, 571
    ordered set intersection, 576
    Sieve of Eratosthenes, 239
    subset, 572
    union, 571
Set interface, 564
    UML, 605
Set operations
    implementing for ordered set, 576
Set operators
    difference, 570
    intersection, 570
    subset, 570
    union, 569
Sets class
    difference method, 572
    intersection method, 571
    orderedIntersection method, 578
    subset method, 572
    union method, 571
Shadow tree, 520
    building, 521
Shallow copy, 277
Shamir, Adi, 869
Shell sort, 226
Shortest path
    algorithm, 773
    single-pair, 773
    single-source, 773
Sieve of Eratosthenes, 239, 731
Signature of a method, 8
Simple path, 733
Simulation design pattern, 446
    Event class, 446
    EventDrivenSimulation class, 447
Singly linked list, 289
    creating a list, 289
    front, 290
    general insert, 293
    removing a target node, 294
    scanning a list, 291
    updating the front, 292
SList class, 387
Sorting
    in-place, 205
    lower bound for, 495
    removing inversions, 216
    stable, 222
Sorting algorithms
    bubble sort, 140
    comparison of, 215

exchange sort, 139
heapsort, 678, 680
insertion sort, 193
merge sort, 196
quicksort, 205
radix sort, 427
selection sort, 114
selection sort (Comparator), 667
selection sort (generic), 160
shell sort, 226
sort method (generic), 199
sort method (Object), 199
tree sort, 862
Space efficiency, 126
Spell checker, 566
Stack, 390
    application, 394, 395, 398
    bounded, 418
    finite, 394
    interface, 391
    last-in/first-out (LIFO), 391
    recursion, and, 401
Stack algorithms
    infix expression evaluation, 410
    multibase numbers, 395
    postfix expression evaluation, 405
Stack interface, 391
    ALStack class, 392
    API, 391
Static
    binding, 55
    keyword, 12
    method, 12
STNode class, 539
Store class
    implementing using Object, 147
    implementing with generics, 149
    UML, 150
Stream, 64
    appending to a file, 69
    binary, 64
    input, 64
    output, 64
    System.err, 65
    System.in, 65
    System.out, 65
    text, 64
Stream classes
    BufferedReader, 66
    DataInputStream, 701
    DataOutputStream, 701
    FileReader, 66
    FileWriter, 69
    InputStream, 701
    InputStreamReader, 66
    ObjectInputStream, 719
    ObjectOutputStream, 718
    OutputStream, 701

OutputStreamWriter class, 70
PrintWriter class, 70
Reader, 65
Scanner, 65, 71
Writer, 65, 69
STree class, 535
    application, 537
    deleting a value, 543
    finding a value, 541
    finding maximum in, 550
    finding minimum in, 550
    implementation, 539
    inserting a value, 541
    iterator, 551
    runtime analysis, 551
    STNode, 539
    UML, 535
String
    hash function, 629
    literals, 26
String class, 25
    comparison, 27
    concatenation, 26
    immutable property of objects, 25
    indexing, 26
    parsing with StringTokenizer, 67
StringTokenizer class, 67, 68
Strongly connected components, 767
Strongly connected digraph, 734
Subclass, 47
Subset-sum problem, 923, 924
Super. *See* Inheritance
Superclass, 47
Supplier class, 44
Symmetric matrix, 820
System efficiency, 125

T

Text
    file, 65, 701
    stream, 64
This keyword, 21
Throw statement. *See* Exception
Time24 class, 8
    API, 17
    application, 15
    constructors, 22
    design, 9
    implementation, 19
        compareTo method, 153
        equals method, 144
        interval method, 23
        normalizeTime method, 20
    UML, 18
TimeCard class, 44
    constructor, 45
    implementation, 45

payWorker method, 46
    UML, 46
Timing class
    API, 133
TNode class, 470, 472
Top-down dynamic programming, 885
Topological sort, 764
ToString method, 10
Towers of Hanoi, 179
Transient, 719
Transpose
    of a graph, 768
    of a matrix, 820
Traveling salesman problem, 132, 892, 922
Traversal operations
    breadth-first search, 742
    depth-first search, 751
    depth-first visit, 747
    inorder tree scan, 476
    level-order scan, 480
    postorder tree scan, 476
    preorder tree scan, 476
Tree, 463
    height, 465
    interior node, 464
    internal node, 464
    leaf node, 464
    level, 465
    path, 464
    root, 464
    subtree, 464
Tree algorithms
    2-3-4 tree operations, 840
    AVL tree insertion, 829
    binary tree height, 487
    building an expression tree, 507
    copying a tree, 490
    display a binary tree, 493
    drawing a tree, 520
    Euler tour, 517
    fully-parenthesized expressions, 518
    inorder iterative tree traversal, 512
    inorder scan, 476
    level-order scan, 480
    red-black tree deletion, 855
    red-black tree insertion, 847
    search tree deletion, 543
    search tree find, 541
    search tree insertion, 541
Tree scan algorithms. *See* Binary tree
Tree sort, 862
TreeMap class, 580
    API, 581
    application, 582, 585, 592
    design, 608
    implementation, 606, 609
    key set view, 616
    UML, 608

TreeSet class, 564
  API, 565
  application, 566
  implementation, 604
  ordered set operations, 565
Try block, 60
Type safe, 148

U

UML, 18
  CASE tools, 18
  diagram, 18
UML in the book
  Animal hierarchy, 82
  AVLTree class, 827
  Circle class, 91
  Collection-List interfaces, 253
  DiGraph class, 810
  Employee hierarchy, 53
  Hash class, 637
  HashMap class, 649
  HDecompress class, 715
  HeapPQueue class, 683
  HuffNode class, 712
  InorderIterator class, 511
  IntegerCount class, 558
  LinkedList class, 303
  List-ListIterator interface, 352
  Map-OrderedMap interfaces, 606
  Measurement interface, 91
  PostfixEval class, 407
  PriorityData class, 691
  ProcessRequestRecord class, 691
  Rectangle class, 91
  Set-OrderedSet interfaces, 605
  SingleAccount interface, 110
  STNode class, 539
  Store class, 150
  STree class, 535
  Time24, 18
  TimeCard class, 46
  Tool class, 560
  TreeMap class, 608

Vector class, 84
  WordFreq class, 362
Undirected graph, 734
Unicode, 964
Unified modeling language. *See* UML
Unordered map, 646
Unordered set, 649, 652
Upcasting, 56
Utility method, 19

V

Vertex, 732
  color, 741
  degree, 732
  finding adjacency list, 808
  in-degree, 734
  neighbors, 732
  out-degree, 734
  reachable, 733
VertexInfo class, 804, 805
  occupied field, 809
VirtualMachineError, 62
Visitor design pattern, 482
  implementations, 483
  inorder scan, 484
  iterator scan, 486
Visitor·interface, 483

W

Weakly connected digraph, 734
Weighted graph, 735
WordFreq class, 262
Wrapper class, 39
  Boolean, 39
  Double, 39
  Integer, 39
Writer class, 65, 69

Z

Z(n), 868
ZIP archive, 86